ENCYCLOPEDIA OF WORLD BIOGRAPHY

13

ENCYCLOPEDIA OF
WORLD BIOGRAPHY

SECOND EDITION

$$\frac{\text{Raffles}}{\text{Schelling}} \quad \textbf{13}$$

GALE

DETROIT · NEW YORK · TORONTO · LONDON

Staff

Senior Editor: Paula K. Byers
Project Editor: Suzanne M. Bourgoin
Managing Editor: Neil E. Walker

Editorial Staff: Luann Brennan, Frank V. Castronova, Laura S. Hightower, Karen E. Lemerand, Stacy A. McConnell, Jennifer Mossman, Maria L. Munoz, Katherine H. Nemeh, Terrie M. Rooney, Geri Speace

Permissions Manager: Susan M. Tosky
Permissions Specialist: Maria L. Franklin
Permissions Associate: Michele M. Lonoconus
Image Cataloger: Mary K. Grimes

Production Director: Mary Beth Trimper
Production Manager: Evi Seoud
Production Associate: Shanna Heilveil
Product Design Manager: Cynthia Baldwin
Senior Art Director: Mary Claire Krzewinski

Research Manager: Victoria B. Cariappa
Research Specialists: Michele P. LaMeau, Andrew Guy Malonis, Barbara McNeil, Gary J. Oudersluys
Research Associates: Julia C. Daniel, Tamara C. Nott, Norma Sawaya, Cheryl L. Warnock
Research Assistant: Talitha A. Jean

Graphic Services Supervisor: Barbara Yarrow
Image Database Supervisor: Randy Bassett
Imaging Specialist: Mike Lugosz

Manager of Data Entry Services: Eleanor M. Allison
Data Entry Coordinator: Kenneth D. Benson

Manager of Technology Support Services: Theresa A. Rocklin
Programmers/Analysts: Mira Bossowska, Jeffrey Muhr, Christopher Ward

Copyright © 1998
Gale Research
835 Penobscot Bldg.
Detroit, MI 48226-4094

ISBN 0-7876-2221-4 (Set)
ISBN 0-7876-2553-1 (Volume 13)

Library of Congress Cataloging-in-Publication Data

Encyclopedia of world biography / [edited by Suzanne Michele Bourgoin and Paula Kay Byers].
     p. cm.
     Includes bibliographical references and index.
     Summary: Presents brief biographical sketches which provide vital statistics as well as information on the importance of the person listed.
     ISBN 0-7876-2221-4 (set : alk. paper)
     1. Biography—Dictionaries—Juvenile literature. [1. Biography.]
I. Bourgoin, Suzanne Michele, 1968- . II. Byers, Paula K. (Paula Kay), 1954- .
CT 103.E56 1997
920'.003—dc21
                        97-42327
                        CIP
                        AC

Printed in the United States of America
10 9 8 7 6 5 4 3

ENCYCLOPEDIA OF WORLD BIOGRAPHY

13

Sir Thomas Stamford Raffles

Sir Thomas Stamford Raffles (1781-1826) was an English colonial administrator, historian, and founder of Singapore. A man of vision, industry, and feeling, he made incalculable contributions to the knowledge of the Malay Archipelago and to the British overseas empire.

Born on July 6, 1781, off the coast of Jamaica on board a ship under the command of his father, Benjamin Raffles, Stamford Raffles became a clerk in the office of the East India Company in London at the age of 14. In 1805 he was sent to Penang to serve as assistant secretary. Prior to his departure he married a widow, Mrs. Olivia Fancourt, who died in 1814.

On the trip out, Raffles studied the Malay language intensively, and his proficiency in this then little-known language was remarked upon by those who came in contact with him. Three years after his arrival his health broke, and he was sent to Malacca to recuperate. The East India Company was on the point of abandoning this port, but a report which Raffles prepared and in which he argued the superiority of Malacca over Penang as a potential port persuaded the company to rescind its order.

Java Annexation

Lord Minto, the governor general of India, was so impressed with the report that he called Raffles on 2 months' leave to Calcutta. During his visit Raffles convinced Lord Minto of the necessity of annexing Java, then in French hands, and the governor general appointed him agent to the governor general of the Malay States. Raffles then returned to Malacca and participated in preparations for the attack on Java.

In August 1811 a British fleet of some 100 ships with an expeditionary force of about 12,000 men arrived off Batavia, and the city fell without a struggle. Gen. Janssens retreated to Semarang on the north-central coast of Java; in September he capitulated to the British. Lord Minto thereupon appointed Raffles lieutenant general of Java and admonished him, "While we are in Java, let us do all the good we can."

Raffles introduced numerous reforms, among which were the division of Java into 16 residencies, the introduction of a land tax, and improvements in the legal and judicial system; he also attempted to abolish slavery. He himself regarded his new land-tenure system, which prevented the native rulers from exacting feudal services, as the most solid accomplishment of his administration. The lands which were withdrawn from the control of feudal rulers were leased on a short-term basis at a moderate rental and were assessed at the value of two-fifths of the rice crop, with the remainder of the yield free of assessment and the growers exempt from personal taxes.

In spite of his excellent intentions and superb knowledge of the people, their language, and their customs, Raffles was not able to make Java a profitable enterprise. His hope of turning Batavia into the hub of a new British insular empire was dashed, and when the Netherlands regained its independence, Lord Castlereagh vigorously opposed British retention of the Dutch holdings in the East.

Raffles sent in a report explaining the great importance of Java to Britain, but his failure to make Java financially viable, together with Britain's desire to conciliate the Dutch, militated against a reversal of Lord Castlereagh's decision,

and in March 1816 Raffles was removed from office and recalled. The following year he married Sophia Hull in London. His lasting contributions in Java can be seen in the fact that when the Dutch received this island back they adopted many of his reforms.

Founding of Singapore

In November 1817 Raffles, now Sir Stamford, departed England for Ft. Marlborough (or Benkoelen), in southern Sumatra, where he assumed the residentship of this town. He and Col. R. J. Farquhar, former British resident at Amboina, were on the lookout for a strategically situated way station in the Malay Archipelago which would play in the East the role Malta was playing in the West.

On Jan. 28, 1819, they landed on the Island of Singapore and immediately recognized it as ideal for their purpose. They arrived at an agreement with the Sultan of Johore, and on February 6 a treaty was signed marking the establishment of Singapore as a British settlement. Farquhar was installed as its first governor under the supervision of Raffles at Benkoelen. As Charles E. Wurtzburg (1954) wrote, "It would be difficult to imagine that, had there been no Raffles, there would have been any Singapore."

During the next 4 years four of Raffles's children died in Benkoelen; his health and that of his wife deteriorated; and in 1823 he submitted his resignation. Before leaving for England, however, he decided to pay a final visit to Singapore, where he remained 9 months. He planned the city,

prepared laws, and laid the foundation of the Singapore Institution, a Malay school.

In 1824 Raffles returned to England to face a charge brought against him by the East India Company, which required him to repay to it a substantial sum for salaries and expenses that had been disbursed to him and only years later disallowed by the court of directors. Raffles was endeavoring to arrange payment when he became seriously ill again. On July 5, 1826, less than 3 months after receiving the court's letter demanding repayment, Raffles died of an apoplectic stroke.

In his short span of life Raffles had suffered numerous crushing blows which would have felled a lesser man. That he survived them in spite of a less than robust constitution can be explained, in part at least, by his tremendous interest in, and enthusiasm for, every aspect of life in the East. He was, at once, amateur natural scientist, archeologist, Oriental philologist, and reviver and active president of the Batavian Society of Arts and Sciences. An enduring monument to his knowledge and indefatigable industry is his famed *History of Java* (2 vols., 1817), which was the first comprehensive work on this subject and, although outdated, is still regarded as a classic in its field.

Further Reading

An intimate and contemporary account of Raffles is in Lady Sophia H. Raffles, *Memoir of the Life and Public Services of Sir Thomas Stamford Raffles* (1830; new ed., 2 vols., 1835), which contains many private letters and public dispatches. Although there is no adequate biography of Raffles, the most extensive study is Charles E. Wurtzburg, *Raffles of the Eastern Isles,* edited by Clifford Witting (1954). A very readable account, with interesting plates, is Maurice Collis, *Raffles* (1966).

The following are less valuable because they make little use of the records in the India Office Library: Demetrius C. Boulger, *The Life of Sir Stamford Raffles* (1897); Hugh Edward Egerton, *Sir Stamford Raffles: England in the Far East* (1900); J. A. Bethune Cook, *Sir Thomas Stamford Raffles* (1918); Reginald Coupland, *Raffles: 1781-1826* (1926); Emily Hahn, *Raffles of Singapore: A Biography* (1946); and Colin Clair, *Sir Stamford Raffles: Founder of Singapore* (1963). Two important studies by John Bastin deal with Raffles's policies: *Raffles' Ideas on the Land Rent System in Java and the Mackenzie Land Tenure Commission* (1954) and *The Native Policies of Sir Stamford Raffles in Java and Sumatra* (1957).

Additional Sources

Raffles, Sophia, Lady, *Memoir of the life and public services of Sir Thomas Stamford Raffles,* Singapore; New York: Oxford University Press, 1991.

Raffles, Thomas Stamford, Sir, *Statement of the services of Sir Stamford Raffles,* Kuala Lumpur; New York: Oxford University Press, 1978.

Wurtzburg, C. E. (Charles Edward), *Raffles of the Eastern Isles,* Singapore; New York: Oxford University Press, 1984. □

Akbar Hashemi Rafsanjani

Raised on a pistachio farm, Akbar Hashemi Rafsanjani (born 1934) rose to become the most important political leader in revolutionary Iran. Known as a shrewd survivor, Iran's "smiling powerbroker" worked towards building a "kinder, gentler" Iran.

Akbar Hashemi was born in 1934 as the second of nine children of Ali Hashemi, a modest farmer and local clergyman in the remote Kermanian town of Rafsanjan—thus the family name, Rafsanjani. At age 14, Akbar Rafsanjani traveled to Qom to pursue advanced Islamic studies. He soon was involved in the "Devotees of Islam" agitation for nationalization of Iran's oil industry. After the demise of Premier Mussadiq's nationalist movement, Ayatollah Borujerdi, one of Rafsanjani's eminent mentors, prevailed upon clergy not to criticize politicians. During this period of quietism Ayatollah Rohollah Khomeini had the greatest impact upon Rafsanjani's formal education, which resulted in his clerical recognition as hojatolislam, a rank just below an ayatollah.

With Borujerdi's death in 1961, Ayatollah Khomeini organized mass protests against the westernizing "White Revolution" of Mohammad Reza Shah Pahlavi. After the Shah's agents stormed the Qom Seminary and forced Khomeini into exile, Rafsanjani became a key operative link in Khomeini's underground resistance. Along the way, Rafsanjani's writings included two significant books that presaged subsequent thinking. *The Story of Palestine* angrily chronicles a "Black Record of Colonialism." His 1967 biography of Amir Kabir admires the 19th-century Iranian prime minister's early conception of foreign policy non-alignment.

The Shah's agents suspiciously watched Rafsanjani and meted out periodic imprisonments, tortures, and even an illegal forced stint in military service. According to an official biography, his 1975 imprisonment resulted from his efforts to "correct the ideological thinking" of the Mujahedin-e-Khalq guerrilla organization, an organization Khomeini later condemned as hypocritically melding Marxism and Islam.

Disciplinarian of the Revolution

As a prominent revolutionary player, some observers perceived Rafsanjani as a mere opportunist who aligned himself with whichever directions the revolutionary winds blew. Others denounced his moderate appearances as sheepskin covering for a hard-line "wolf." However, Rafsanjani is best understood as a principled pragmatist whose coalition and consensus building efforts help explain the continuing survival of the Islamic revolution.

In early revolutionary phases Rafsanjani was Khomeini's clerical liaison to diverse dissident groups, including secular nationalists and communists. Rafsanjani later rationalized his collaboration with the Mujahedin as part of a strategy which "considered any form of struggle against SAVAK [the Shah's secret police] a blessing." Rafsanjani's revolutionary credits include: organizer of local revolutionary *Komitehs,* crisis foreman of Abadan oil production, member of the secret Islamic Revolutionary Council, co-founder of the Islamic Republican Party, and deputy interior minister. In May 1979 he was nearly assassinated by the Furqun (Distinction), a shadowy group claiming pious opposition to clerics in government. Rafsanjani arguably sought to slow the momentum towards extremism. When the nationalists sought elections for a constitutional review assembly, Rafsanjani warned that they would regret the resulting "fistful of ignorant and fanatic fundamentalists" who will "do such damage."

Rafsanjani subsequently was elected to the new Majlis (Islamic Consultative Assembly), which he presided over as parliamentary speaker for nearly a decade. In September 1980 Iraq's invasion of Iran energized hawkish sentiment, Rafsanjani included. As a populist Friday prayer leader in Tehran and as a Khomeini representative to the powerful Supreme Defense Council, Rafsanjani helped undermine remaining nationalist "doves" by advocating harsh retribution as Iran's war aim. Rafsanjani also backed a severe 1982 crackdown on the Mujahedin. Given Mujahedin assassinations of over 1,200 regime leaders, Rafsanjani later explained that without the "imperative" execution of over 4,000 Mujahedin guerrillas, "Iran would have become Lebanon." Grave circumstances demanded "determined" means.

With militant opposition crushed and Iraq on the defensive, Speaker Rafsanjani deftly maneuvered amidst years of raucous Majlis bickering over the precise social, economic, and international implications of Islamic governance. Often enigmatically seeming to be all things to all sides, his calls for just wealth redistribution did not square neatly with his reassurances to business interests about the sanctity of private property. Yet Rafsanjani could also resourcefully break impasses, as with his 1986 theatrical use of television to intimidate "conservative" recalcitrants from "standing up" to vote against an emotion laden, yet long blocked, land reform bill. (Rafsanjani's educated [University of California] brother directed Iranian television.)

Rafsanjani's most dangerous innovation was in foreign policy. Recognizing the severe costs of Iran's international pariah status, Rafsanjani sought to break Iran's isolation through openings to both eastern and western countries. Outraged purists leaked the arms dealings with the United States and Israel in what became known to the West as the "Iran-contra" affair. Yet Khomeini squelched recriminations with the admonition that "the path to hell is paved with discord."

As the warfront deteriorated in 1988, Khomeini turned over personal command of all Iranian armed forces to Rafsanjani. Still the coalition builder, Rafsanjani ended the destructive rivalries among regular, ideological, and paramilitary forces by integrating them under one command. Following American pummeling of Iranian naval units and the shooting down of an Iranian civilian airliner, Iran's radicals called for a river of American blood. But

Rafsanjani and President Ali Khamenei quietly convinced Khomeini that the time had come to accept a "poisonous chalice" cease-fire. Rafsanjani's nationally broadcast sermon simply asserted that "the main issue is that we can stop making enemies without reason."

A Powerful, Pragmatic President

After Khomeini's death in June 1989, Rafsanjani soon emerged as Iran's most powerful leader. He was a key architect of Ali Khamenei's swift selection to Khomeini's post as supreme spiritual guide. Policy differences between Khamenei and Rafsanjani were real, yet common bonds were much stronger. Khamenei supported Rafsanjani's presidential election, along with the simultaneous constitutional reforms that vastly strengthened the presidency's authority. Despite howls from the Majlis, Rafsanjani's cabinet excluded all prominent radicals.

As president, Rafsanjani continued the momentum towards pragmatic policies. In social policy Rafsanjani candidly advocated such reforms as liberalized laws on women's privileges. In defending pursuit of Western loans and private investments, Rafsanjani castigated "statists" and fanatics with "religious pretensions" for being "frozen in their beliefs . . . and unable to adjust themselves to the circumstances of the day. Dams cannot be built by slogans."

Events will reveal Rafsanjani's popularity with the masses. His relatively easygoing, often witty, Friday "prayer sermons" genuinely seemed to delight Tehran crowds, though grandiloquence at times undercut his pragmatic efforts. In May 1989, during services commemorating Jerusalem day, Rafsanjani opined that Palestinians could end Israeli repression if they killed five Americans for every martyred Palestinian. Official Iranian news sources quickly toned down such remarks as simply emphasizing that Israel's depredations would be impossible without American financing.

Overall, Rafsanjani's presidency was marked by increasingly candid and pragmatic rationales for recasting revolutionary principles in light of necessity. In November 1989 Rafsanjani delighted geographic neighbors with an unprecedented renunciation of Iran's historical policeman role for the Persian Gulf in favor of cooperative strategies. Soon thereafter Rafsanjani characterized Ayatollah Khomeini's death decree against author Salman Rushdie for blasphemy as a mere "expert" religious opinion. (However, many Shiites vowed to carry out the sentence.) Such rationalization continued after Iraq's August 1990 invasion of Kuwait. Rafsanjani supported full compliance with international sanctions against Iraq, despite massive U.S. military involvement in the Gulf.

Rafsanjani was reelected to a second four-year term in June 1993, but only received 63.2 percent of the vote with his opponent, Ahmad Tavakkoli, receiving 27 percent. Analysts said that the failure of Rafsanjani to win a landslide victory indicated that Iranians had lost confidence in the Islamic regime—particularly in regard to its handling of economic conditions.

Further Reading

Within the growing literature on Iran's revolution and its regional and world impact, several well written and widely circulated English studies stand out: Shaul Bakhash, *The Reign of the Ayatollahs: Iran and the Islamic Revolution* (1984); R. K. Ramazani, *Revolutionary Iran: Challenge and Response in the Middle East* (1988); Robin Wright, *In the Name of God: The Khomeini Decade* (1989); and R.K. Ramazani, editor, *Iran's Revolution: The Search for Consensus* (1990). English translations of key Iranian speeches can be found in the Foreign Broadcast Information Service, available at most U.S. Government depository libraries. □

Karl Rahner

The German theologian Karl Rahner (1904-1984) was a major influence on 20th-century Roman Catholic thought. His work is characterized by the attempt to reinterpret traditional Roman Catholic theology in the light of modern philosophical thought.

Karl Rahner was born on March 5, 1904, in Freiburg im Breisgau in what is now the German Federal Republic. He followed his older brother Hugo into the Society of Jesus in 1922 and pursued the Jesuits' traditional course of studies in philosophy and theology in Germany, Austria, and Holland. He was ordained a priest in 1932 and continued his studies at the University of Freiburg. After receiving his doctorate in philosophy in 1936, he taught at the universities of Innsbruck and Munich. In 1967 he was appointed professor of dogmatic theology at the University of Münster. He was a *peritus* (official theologian) at the Second Vatican Council (1962-1965), and in 1969 he was one of 30 appointed by Pope Paul VI to evaluate theological developments since the Council.

Thomism, Kantianism, and contemporary phenomenology and existentialism are the three sources of Rahner's thought. During his early years of seminary training, he studied the works of Immanuel Kant and Joseph Maréchal, along with the works of the great medieval theologian St. Thomas Aquinas. While at the University of Freiburg he came under the influence of Martin Heidegger. The overriding concern of all his work was the need to bring the best thought of the past into contact with the best thought of the present.

Rahner's Theology

Often linked with Bernard Lonergan as a "transcendental Thomist," Rahner employed a method characterized by an attempt to discover the general principles underlying the various doctrines of the Roman Catholic faith. In his first work, *Geist in Welt* (1936; *Spirit in the World*), he presented his interpretation of Aquinas's doctrine of knowledge, indicating that man's capacity to know, although rooted in the data of the senses, is nonetheless a capacity open to the infinite or to being as such. This ability

to transcend particular being allows man to think metaphysically—to analyze the general structure of being necessary for the actual condition of the world known through the senses. *Spirit in the World,* in conjunction with Rahner's second major work, *Hörer des Wortes* (1941; *Hearers of the Word*), established the epistemological and speculative foundation of his later thought.

Rahner's thought is best described as a theological anthropology. Beginning with the nature of man as a being open to the infinite, Rahner's thought sees a person's quest for fulfillment satisfied only in union with the God of Christian revelation, the God who became man in Jesus Christ. A proper understanding of humans cannot be divorced from an understanding of God and the context of relationships uniting humans and God. The fundamental fact underlying the existence of the world is that it stands in relation to God. Rahner calls this situation the supernatural existential and sees in this fundamental fact the root of all further explanations of sin, grace, and salvation. Rahner's vision of theology can also be understood through his work *Foundations of Christian Faith: An Introduction to the Idea of Christianity* (1976). While most religious scholars see Rahner as one of the most influential theologians of the 20th century, he also encountered critics along the way. Some within the Catholic Church found his writings too radical—in the early 1960's, Rahner's writings could only be published after approval from the Jesuits in Rome.

In March of 1984, after a birthday celebration that also honored his scholarship, Rahner fell ill from exhaustion in Innsbruck, Austria. He did not recover and died on March

30. Rahner was buried at the Jesuit church of the Trinity in Innsbruck.

Further Reading

Rahner's own writings are difficult. His *The Dynamic Element in the Church* (trans. 1964) and *Nature and Grace: Dilemmas in the Modern Church* (trans. 1964) provide good starting points for the reader interested in sampling his work. Patrick Granfield, *Theologians at Work* (1967), has an interesting interview with Rahner. The best study of Rahner in English is Louis Roberts, *The Achievement of Karl Rahner* (1967). Rahner's ideas are presented in a simplified form in Donald Gelpi, *Life and Light: A Guide to the Theology of Karl Rahner* (1966). Jakob Laubach's chapter on Rahner in Leonard Reinisch, ed., *Theologians of Our Time: Karl Barth and Others* (trans. 1964), provides a brief introduction to his thought. Sylvester Paul Schilling, *Contemporary Continental Theologians* (1966), has a critique of Rahner's work.
(Dych, William)*Karl Rahner* Liturgical Press, 1992.
(Kelly, Geffrey, ed.)*Karl Rahner: Theologian of the Graced Search for Meaning* Fortress Press, 1992.
The Christian Century (April 11, 1984).
Commonweal (April 20, 1984). □

Lala Lajpat Rai

Lala Lajpat Rai (1865-1928) was an Indian nationalist leader and was well known for his many publications regarding national problems.

Lala Lajpat Rai was born in the Ferozepore district of the Punjab to a respectable Hindu family. He studied law in Lahore and in 2 years passed the first examination, which qualified him to practice. While a student, he became active in the nationalist and revivalist Arya Samaj Society of Swami Dayananda. Rai joined the Samaj in 1882 and soon emerged as a prominent leader in its "Progressive," or "College," wing. He also taught at the Anglo-Vedic College, run by the Samaj; his fiery nationalism was largely the product of this involvement.

In 1886 Rai moved to Hissar, where he practiced law, led the Arya movement, and was elected to the Municipal Committee (of the local government). In 1888 and 1889 he was a delegate to the annual sessions of the National Congress. He moved to Lahore to practice before the High Court in 1892.

In 1895 Rai helped found the Punjab National Bank, demonstrating his practical concern for self-help and enterprise among Hindus. Between 1896 and 1898 he published popular biographies of Mazzini, Garibaldi, Shivajee, and Swami Dayananda. In 1897 he founded the Hindu Orphan Relief Movement to keep the Christian missions from securing custody of these children. In the National Congress in 1900 he stressed the importance of constructive, nation-building activity and programs for self-reliance.

In 1905 Rai went as a Congress delegate to London, where he fell under the influence of the Hindu revolutionary Shyamji Krishna Varma. Later, in the 1905 Congress session, Rai joined Bal Tilak and Bipin Chandra Pal in support of a militant program around boycott, *swadeshi* (homemade goods), and *swaraj* (self-rule for India). In 1906 he tried to play the role of mediator between the moderates and the extremists in the Congress. The following year the Punjab government arrested and transported him without trial to Burma; he was released in time for the 1907 meetings of the National Congress, when Tilak backed him for the presidency. Rai refused to accept the office for fear of a split in the ranks of that body.

Rai lived in the United States from 1914 until 1920. He founded the Indian Home Rule League in New York City and published several important volumes on the Indian problem. Soon after his return to India he was elected president of the Calcutta session of the Congress. In 1925 he entered the Imperial Legislature as a member of the "Swarajist" group. In 1926 he broke with the leaders of the Swarajist group and formed his own "Nationalist party" within the legislature.

In 1928 Rai led the demonstrations against the Simon Commission on Indian constitutional reforms. He was injured by the police in a mass demonstration and died a few weeks later, mourned as a nationalist martyr.

Further Reading

Among Rai's many books see especially *Young India: An Interpretation* (1917) and *Unhappy India* (1928). Extensive selections from his writings are in the works edited by Vijaya C. Joshi: *Lal Lajpat Rai: Writings and Speeches* (2 vols., 1965-1966), which also contains information on Rai's life, and *Autobiographical Writings* (1965). N. N. Kailas, ed., *Laj Patrai: His Relevance for Our Times* (1966), contains articles on and by Rai. Works on his life and influence include P. D. Saggi, ed., *Life and Work of Lal, Bal, and Pal: A Nation's Homage* (1962), and Naeem Gul Rathore, *Indian Nationalist Agitation in the United States: A Study of Lala Lajpat Rai and the India Home Rule League of America, 1914-1920* (1966). □

Chakravarti Rajagopalachari

Chakravarti Rajagopalachari (1879-1972) was a prominent Indian nationalist leader, first Indian governor general of his country, and founder of the Swatantra party. He also wrote a popular version of the "Mahabharata."

Chakravarti Rajagopalachari was born in a village in Madras and graduated from the Central Hindu College of Bangalore. He then took a law degree from the Madras Law College. In 1921 Rajagopalachari was chosen general secretary of the Indian National Congress under Mohandas Gandhi's leadership. Soon thereafter his daughter married into Gandhi's family. In subsequent years he was intermittently a member of the all-powerful Congress Working Committee, the top executive arm of the National Congress, and worked very closely with Gandhi.

Government Loyalist

In 1937, when the Congress won the provincial elections in several Indian provinces, Rajagopalachari became chief minister of Madras. He held this position until the outbreak of World War II caused all of the Congress provincial ministries to resign.

In 1942, at the time of the Cripps mission from the British Parliament to India, Rajagopalachari was among the minority of top Congress leaders who favored acceptance of the offer made by Cripps in an effort to end the political deadlock. In 1946 Rajagopalachari maintained his posture as a moderator when he advised acceptance of the Pakistan demand as the price which had to be paid for independence. Also in 1946, he became minister in the interim government which guided India in the final months up to partition and independence.

Parting Ways

Rajagopalachari was the first Indian governor of West Bengal after independence in 1947. In 1948 he was named the first Indian governor general of India, succeeding Lord Mountbatten, the last English governor general. In 1950 Rajagopalachari was named home minister in the Jawaharlal Nehru Cabinet, and in 1952 he returned to Madras as chief minister. He, however, disagreed with the Nehru government's socialist leanings. Soon thereafter Rajagopalachari parted company with the Nehru Congress, and in 1959 he was instrumental in the creation of the anti-Congress Swatantra party, which became the chief propo-

nent of the free-enterprise philosophy in the Republic of India. In 1971, Rajagopalachari organized a right-wing coalition against Indira Gandhi, but it was soundly defeated.

Rajagopalachari played a prominent role in the international Ban-the-Bomb movement. Among other causes not popular with the Congress government was his campaign for religious instruction in the public schools. He also published a highly regarded, abridged edition of the Hindu epic *Mahabharata* . Rajagopalachari repeatedly denounced the government of India for alleged corruption, bureaucracy, inefficiency, and lack of impartiality. He died on December 26, 1972 in Madras. The Indian government proclaimed seven days of mourning for his death.

Further Reading

An interesting but not comprehensive biography of Rajagopalachari is Monica Felton, *I Meet Rajaji* (1962). See also Nikan Perumal, *Rajaji,* edited by Duncan Greenless (1953). Interesting material on Rajagopalachari is in the official history by B. Pattabhi Sitaramayya, *History of the Indian National Congress,* vol. 2 (1947; repr. 1969).

Additional Sources

(Ahluwalia, B. K.) *Rajiji and Gandhi Allora,* 1978.
(Copley, Antony) *C. Rajagopalachari: Gandhi's Southern Commander* Indo-British Historical Society, 1986.
New York Times (December 26, 1972). ☐

Rajaraja I

Rajaraja I (reigned 985-1014) was possibly the greatest of the Cola kings of southern India. He made the Colas the paramount power in southern India, Sri Lanka, and the southern seas. A political and organizational genius, he was also a grand patron of religion and the arts.

Traditional Cola territories center on the fertile lands around Tanjore in southern India (about 220 miles south of Madras city). Representatives of the family seem to have been agents of the Pallavas during the period of that dynasty's great achievements and subsequently to have broken away. When Rajaraja (meaning "king of kings") took the throne, the Colas were still suffering the consequences of invasions from the Deccan earlier in the century.

Rajaraja first reduced traditional Cera rivals in the southwest (present-day Kerala) and then subdued the Pandya contenders in the extreme south. Thereafter he invaded and took control of the island kingdom of Ceylon, now Sri Lanka. Next, Rajaraja's armies conquered the territories in what is present-day Mysore State. In less than a decade Rajaraja had become master of southern India.

Accompanying Rajaraja's undoubted military genius was a talent for political and economic administration. He elaborated a network of subordinate administrators and per-

fected a set of procedures which assured a reliable and efficient cohesion in his "empire" while allowing great autonomy to the local units. Most famous of the deeds of Rajaraja is the building of the "Great Temple," the Rajarajesvara, at Tanjore. The mighty tower (*vimana*) that surmounts the central shrine rises 216 feet to dominate the city and the adjacent land. The stone sculpture on the tower and its base is Cola art at its most vigorous. The many inscriptions at the temple provide vital information concerning the dynasty.

Rajaraja's son Rajendra I (reigned 1012-1044, initially with his father) extended the Cola sway. One military expedition reached the Ganges. The Cola navy was strengthened, and profitable campaigns were waged in Southeast Asia. Rajendra built a new capital city, Gangaikondacolapuram ("city of the Cola who brought the Ganges"), and, emulating his father, he crowned it with an exquisite "sister" temple to the Tanjore shrine.

Under Rajendra, the Cola dynasty flourished, as did art and literature. Though he surpassed his father's achievement, Rajendra owed to Rajaraja the conditions and the examples without which his own achievement would have been inconceivable.

Further Reading

The authoritative study of the dynasty remains K. A. Nilakanta Sastri, *The Colas* (1935). Several chapters in Ghulam Yazdani, ed., *The Early History of the Deccan* (2 vols., 1960), are useful. For the general reader, K. A. Nilakanta Sastri, *A History of South India* (1955), places the Colas in the context of southern Indian history from the earliest times to the middle of the 16th century. A helpful monograph on the Rajarajesvara Temple is J. M. Somasundaram Pillai, *The Great Temple at Tanjore* (1935). ☐

Bhagwan Shree Rajneesh

Bhagwan Shree Rajneesh (1931-1990) was a religious leader who developed a following which included many Americans at Poona, India. In 1981 he and many followers moved to a large ranch in central Oregon in the United States and there began to build a small city as a home for his devotees. His unusual form of Indian spirituality, especially known for its encouragement of free sexual activity, attracted many followers as well as considerable controversy.

Bhagwan Shree Rajneesh was born at Kuchwada, India, on December 11, 1931, and received the name Rajneesh Chandra Mohan at about six months of age. He graduated from high school in Gadarwara in 1951 and went to Jabalpur, where he enrolled at Hitkarini College. He received a B.A. degree from Jabalpur University in 1955 and an M.A. in philosophy from Saugar University in 1957.

Filled with doubts which were spurred in part by his college philosophy courses, Rajneesh spent a year engaged in meditation and personal struggle. During this time he also suffered severe headaches. All of that came to a peak on March 21, 1953, when, he said, he was enlightened. Seven days earlier he had decided that his effort to achieve enlightenment was futile, and in a feeling of helplessness he had abandoned the search. As he described what then happened, "Those seven days were of tremendous transformation, total transformation. And the last day the presence of a totally new energy, a new light and new delight, became so intense that it was almost unbearable, as if I was exploding, as if I was going mad with blissfulness."

Following his enlightenment Rajneesh went on to finish his studies. In 1957 he received a teaching position at Raipur Sanskrit College. The next year he became a professor of philosophy at Jabalpur University. Frenetic activity, including far-flung travels around India and controversies surrounding his unconventional ideas, marked his years there. In 1964 he began to hold organized meditation camps. In 1966 he resigned from the university. He then became more outspoken, challenging prevailing ideas about such issuesas sex, Hinduism, socialism, and the teachings of Mahatma Gandhi. In 1968 he jolted Indian traditionalists by giving a lecture in which he advised his listeners that "sex is divine," that through sex one could achieve the first step toward "superconsciousness."

In 1970, at Bombay, Rajneesh introduced what has come to be called "Dynamic Meditation," which Rajneesh synthesized from Yoga, Sufism, Tibetan Buddhism, and

contemporary psychological thought. Rajneesh taught that meditation properly began with the body, not the mind; thus Dynamic Meditation involved such activities as screaming, shouting, and the removal of clothing. Rajneesh's disciples became extremely devoted to him, feeling deeply moved simply by being in his presence, and later in 1970 he founded a *sannyas* (discipleship) movement for those wanting to commit themselves to him and his work. Many who joined the *sannyas* movement were Western, not Indian. They adopted new Indian names, wore *malas* (beaded necklaces with lockets containing Rajneesh's picture), and orange and red clothing, representing the many who became *sannyasin* (members of the *sannyas*).

Rajneesh had until then been using the title "Acharya," which means "teacher." In 1971 he felt that he had outgrown that role, so he assumed the title "Bhagwan," which means "God." The change, he said, was symbolic rather than literal, indicating that his work would now not be intellectual, but a matter of direct heart-to-heart communication.

Rajneesh and the *sannyasin* outgrew their quarters in Bombay, and Rajneesh, suffering from diabetes and asthma, believed that Bombay's climate was a part of the reason for his bad health. Thus in 1974 they moved to a six-acre compound in Poona, 80 miles away. There at the Ashram Rajneesh welcomed ever-increasing numbers of followers, especially from Europe and the United States. Daily life there involved Dynamic Meditation, listening to discourses by Rajneesh, and working at an assigned job for six hours a day. Various psychological therapeutic practices were part of the program, and many trained psychologists were among those who joined the movement. Arts and crafts flowered, especially pottery and weaving. There were cultural activities, including a theatrical troupe. By the late 1970s, the six acres of the Ashram could not hold the growing numbers of *sannyasin*, and new land was secured 20 miles away. In 1979 the new commune at Jadhavwadi was opened.

But opposition mounted as well. Dynamic Meditation, with its overt sexuality, had never been fully accepted by conservative Indians, and the movement had become one largely composed of Westerners. Criticism from outside was constant and came to a peak in 1980 when an Indian opponent tried to kill Rajneesh during a morning discourse.

In 1981 Rajneesh took a vow of silence, following the example of certain other Eastern religious leaders. Now communication between Bhagwan and his followers would be purely heart to heart. That phase lasted until 1984, when Rajneesh began to give limited spoken presentations again.

Continuing opposition, some of it violent, to the movement in India led to a decision to relocate in the United States. After some searching the leaders found a venerable cattle ranch for sale in an isolated spot in central Oregon, comprising an area of 100 square miles—surely a vast enough expanse to encompass any foreseeable future growth. His followers—and soon Rajneesh himself—began moving to the ranch in 1981 and started building a city which they called Rajneeshpuram. Heated disapproval from neighbors arose at once, and both public officials and private organizations acted to restrict or remove Rajneeshpuram on the grounds that it violated the state's land-use planning laws. The prosperous commune, however, fought back in court and continued to expand its presence in Oregon, amid enormous controversy.

Finally, in November 1985, the United States charged Rajneesh with immigration fraud. He pled guilty with the understanding that he would be allowed to leave the country. After a time Rajneesh returned to a commune in Poona. Meanwhile, the community's assets—including 93 custom-built Rolls Royces—were auctioned off. Thirteen of his lieutenants were convicted of crimes ranging from attempted murder to wiretapping.

After returning to India in 1986, Rajneesh directed his followers to stop using the term "Bhagwan." After a time failing health caused him to stop giving discourses, and word came to his followers that the name Rajneesh was also being dropped. He began to be called "Osho," which he said was derived from an expression of the American psychologist of religion William James, "oceanic experience." The commune in India was thereafter called the Osho Institute and Osho Meditation Centers could be found in major cities around the world.

Rajneesh died of heart disease at Poona, India, January 19, 1990.

Further Reading

Rajneesh's discourses have been tape recorded for many years, and the tapes have often been transcribed into books; hundreds of those books of his teachings have been published by the Osho (formerly Rajneesh) Foundation International, and hundreds of tapes of his discourses are available. Several of his books have been published by commercial publishers; probably the most important is *My Way: The Way of the White Cloud* (1978). A three- volume digest of Rajneesh's teachings on many subjects is *The Book* (1982).

A biography of Rajneesh by a disciple, published by a major commercial press, is Vasant Joshi's *The Awakened One: The Life and Work of Bhagwan Shree Rajneesh* (1982). □

Sir Walter Raleigh

The English statesman Sir Walter Raleigh (ca. 1552-1618) was also a soldier, courtier, explorer and exponent of overseas expansion, man of letters, and victim of Stuart mistrust and Spanish hatred.

Born into a prominent Protestant Devonshire family, Walter Raleigh (or Ralegh) spent time at Oriel College, Oxford, before leaving to join the Huguenot army in the French religious war in 1569. Five years in France saw him safely through two major battles and the massacre of St. Bartholomew's Day. By 1576 he was in London as a lodger (not a law student) at the Middle Temple and saw his verses, prefixed to George Gascoigne's *Steele Glas,* in print. His favorite poetic theme, the impermanence of all earthly things, was popular with other Renaissance

poets. However, Raleigh's verse differs from theirs: for their richly decorated quality and smoothly musical rhythms, he substituted a colloquial diction and a simplicity and directness of statement that prefigured the work of John Donne and the other metaphysical poets.

After 2 years in obscurity Raleigh accompanied his half brother, Sir Humphrey Gilbert, on a voyage ostensibly in search of a Northwest Passage to the Orient but which quickly degenerated into a privateering foray against the Spanish. On their return in 1579, Raleigh and Gilbert faced the displeasure of the Privy Council. Raleigh's subsequent conduct did little to placate the Council: he engaged in several altercations and was imprisoned twice in 6 months for disturbing the peace. Once out of jail, and at the head of a company of infantry, he sailed to serve in the Irish wars.

In Ireland, Raleigh spent less than 2 years on campaign. He helped condemn one of the leaders of the rebellion, bombed a Spanish-Italian garrison into surrender, and then oversaw their massacre. After some minor but well-fought engagements, he was appointed a temporary administrator of Munster. Not satisfied, he criticized his superiors and by the end of 1581 had been sent back to London with dispatches for the Council, £20 for his expenses, and a reputation as an expert on Irish affairs.

Progress at Court

Extravagant in dress and in conduct (whether or not he spread his costly cloak over a puddle for Elizabeth to step on, his contemporaries believed him capable of the ges-

ture), handsome, and superbly self-confident, Raleigh at first rose rapidly at court. His opinion on Ireland was sought and apparently taken by Elizabeth; when he obtained a new commission for service there, the Queen kept him home as an adviser. He received more concrete tokens of royal favor as well: a house in London, two estates in Oxford, and, most lucrative, the monopolies for the sale of wine licenses and the export of broadcloth all came from Elizabeth in 1583-1584.

Raleigh was knighted in 1584 and the next year became warden of the stannaries (or mines) in Devon and Cornwall, lord lieutenant of Cornwall, and vice admiral of the West (Devon and Cornwall). Although he was hated for his arrogance at Westminster, in Devon and Cornwall his reforms of the mining codes and his association with local privateering ventures made him very popular; he sat for Devonshire in the Parliaments of 1584 and 1586.

In 1586 Raleigh succeeded Sir Christopher Hatton (newly made lord chancellor) as captain of the Queen's Guard—his highest office at court.

Overseas Ventures

The patent under which Gilbert had led his expedition of 1578 had authorized him not merely to explore but to claim unknown lands (in the Queen's name, of course) and to exploit them as he saw fit. By 1582 Gilbert had organized a company to settle English Catholics in the Americas. Although forbidden by Elizabeth to accompany his half brother, Raleigh invested money and a ship of his own design in the venture. After Gilbert's death on the return from Newfoundland, Raleigh was given a charter to "occupy and enjoy" new lands. A preliminary expedition sailed as soon as Raleigh had his charter, reached the Carolina shore of America, and claimed the land for the court-bound empire builder.

At the same time, Raleigh sought to entice Elizabeth into a more active role in his proposed colonizing venture: not only did he name the new territory Virginia (after the Virgin Queen) but he sponsored Richard Hakluyt's *Discourse of Western Planting* and brought this great imperialistic treatise to Elizabeth's attention. Although unconvinced, she gave a ship and some funds; Raleigh remained at court and devoted his energies to financing the scheme. The first settlers were conveyed by Raleigh's cousin Sir Richard Grenville. Quarrels, lack of discipline, and hostile Indians led the colonists to return to England aboard Francis Drake's 1586 squadron, bringing with them potatoes and tobacco, both hitherto unknown in Europe.

John White led a second expedition the next year. The coming of the Armada delayed sending supplies for more than 2 years. When the relief ships reached the colony in 1591, it had vanished. Raleigh sent other expeditions to the Virginia coast but failed to establish a permanent settlement there; his charter was revoked by James I in 1603.

Retirement from Court

Raleigh played a minor role in the defeat of the Spanish Armada in 1588. He organized the Devon militia and was a member of Elizabeth's War Council but did not participate in the naval battle. When he returned to court, he clashed with Elizabeth's new favorite, Robert Devereux, Earl of Essex. After the Privy Council halted an incipient duel between them, Raleigh left for Ireland, where he cultivated his estates and the friendship of his neighbor, the poet Edmund Spenser, whom he introduced to Elizabeth in 1590.

The next year Raleigh was to have gone to sea in search of the Spanish plate fleet, but again Elizabeth refused permission. Grenville, who went in his stead, was trapped by Spanish galleons, and Raleigh raised a new fleet to avenge his cousin. At sea finally, he was immediately summoned back by Elizabeth. Upon his tardy return he was imprisoned in the Tower, for the Queen had discovered his alliance with Elizabeth Throgmorton, one of her own maids of honor. (Raleigh later married Elizabeth Throgmorton.) After the return of an enormously wealthy prize taken by Raleigh's sailors, and after Elizabeth took an inordinate share of the profits, she permitted the Raleighs to go to their estate of Sherborne in Dorset.

Forbidden access to the court, Raleigh devoted time to study and speculation about the nature of matter and the universe. During this time he sat in Parliament, joined the Society of Antiquaries, assisted Hakluyt in preparing his *Voyages,* and joined Ben Jonson and Shakespeare at the Mermaid Tavern in London.

By the end of 1594 Raleigh had regained enough of Elizabeth's favor to obtain her consent for a prospecting expedition to Guiana (Venezuela). From this he brought back many samples of gold ore and a belief in the existence of a rich gold mine.

In 1596 Raleigh and his rival Essex led a brilliantly successful raid on Cadiz, and he seemed to have finally placated Elizabeth. He was readmitted to court, continued to serve in Parliament, was given a monopoly over playing cards, held more naval commands, and became governor of the island of Jersey, where he proved again to be an excellent administrator. With Essex's execution for treason, Raleigh's place as favorite seemed secure. But the Queen herself was near death, and Raleigh's enemies lost no time in poisoning the mind of James Stuart, her heir apparent and successor, against him.

His Imprisonment

Upon James I's accession, Raleigh was dismissed as captain of the guard, warden of the stanneries, and governor of Jersey. His monopolies were suspended, and he was evicted from his London house. Soon after, he was implicated (falsely) in a plot against James and, upon being committed to the Tower, tried to commit suicide. A farcical trial before a special commission at Winchester at the end of 1603 resulted in a death sentence, followed by a reprieve and imprisonment in the Tower for 13 years.

James stripped Raleigh of all his offices and even took Sherborne on a technicality to give to his own favorite, Robert Carr. The remainder of his property was restored, and Raleigh was well treated: his family joined him in a large apartment in the Bloody Tower; his books were brought as well. Raleigh attracted the sympathy and friendship of James's eldest son, Henry, who sought his advice on matters of shipbuilding and naval defense. Raleigh dedicated his monumental *History of the World,* written during this period of imprisonment, to the prince. Henry protested Raleigh's continued incarceration but died before he could effect his release.

Last Voyage

From 1610 on, Raleigh, aware of James's need for money, sought permission to lead another search for the gold mine of his earlier Guiana voyage and at last got his way. Freed early in 1616, he invested most of his remaining funds in the projected voyage. The expedition, which sailed in June of the following year, was a disastrous failure. No treasure and no mine were found, and Raleigh's men violated James's strict instructions to avoid fighting with Spanish colonists in the area. Still worse, during the battle with the Spaniards, Raleigh's older son, Walter, was killed.

Upon his empty-handed return Raleigh was rearrested; James and Sarmiento, the Spanish ambassador, wished him tried on a charge of piracy, but as he was already under a sentence of death, a new trial was not possible. His execution would have to proceed from the charge of treason of 1603. James agreed to this course, and Raleigh was beheaded on Oct. 29, 1618.

Further Reading

Raleigh's *History of the World,* first published in 1614, has been reissued many times. *A Report of the Truth of the Fight about the Isles of Acores* (1591) and *The Discovery of . . . the Empire of Guiana* (1596) are published in *Works of Sir Walter Ralegh* (8 vols., 1829), which also contains works published posthumously. The standard edition of Raleigh's poetry is *The Poems of Sir Walter Ralegh,* edited by Agnes M. C. Latham (1929). There is no completely satisfactory biography of Raleigh. Edward Edwards, *The Life of Sir Walter Ralegh Based on Contemporary Documents . . . Together with His Letters* (2 vols., 1868), lacks much material that is now available. Among the most useful works are Edward Thompson, *Sir Walter Ralegh: The Last of the Elizabethans* (1935), and Willard M. Wallace, *Sir Walter Raleigh* (1959). Raleigh's role in natural philosophy and his connection with Thomas Hariot are treated in Robert Kargon, *Atomism in England* (1966). His contact with Christopher Marlowe is explored at length in M. C. Bradbrook, *The School of Night: A Study in the Literary Relationships of Sir Walter Relegh* (1936), and in Ernest Albert Strathmann, *Sir Walter Raleigh: A Study in Elizabethan Skepticism* (1951). A. L. Rowse's *The England of Elizabeth: The Structure of Society* (1950) and *The Expansion of Elizabethan England* (1955) provide a valuable general view of the period. □

Rama Khamhaeng

Rama Khamhaeng (ca. 1239-ca. 1299) was king of Sukhothai in Thailand and the founder of Thai political power in central Indochina. He remains the Thai model of the patriarchal ruler.

Rama Khamhaeng was the third son of King Sri Indraditya, who had seized power in Sukhothai from the Cambodian empire of Angkor between 1219 and 1245. When Rama's brother, King Ban Müang, died, he inherited a small kingdom in the foothills of north-central Siam. By a combination of shrewd alliances, careful diplomacy which ensured the neutrality of rivals, and forceful military campaigns, especially in the 1290s, he extended his kingdom to Luangprabang and the Vientiane region in Laos to the north, westward to the Indian Ocean coast of Burma, and south to Nakhon Si Thammarat on the Malay Peninsula.

Apart from colorful but unreliable myth, almost all that is known of Rama Khamhaeng comes from his great inscription of 1292, the oldest known inscription in the Thai language and script. That lengthy document portrays the King as a father to his subjects, available day and night to petitioners for justice, liberal in his gifts and in his treatment of his vassals, merciful in warfare, and pious in his devotion to Buddhism. His state is depicted as happy and prosperous: "This state of Sukhothai is good. In the waters there are fish; in the fields there is rice." Implicit in this account are policies strongly in contrast to the bureaucratic complexity, impersonality, and economic rigidity of Angkor. Sukhothai under Rama Khamhaeng was a simple state with no pretensions, where justice was to be had, trade could flourish, and peace would reign. These policies, and the strong leadership of the King, were responsible for the kingdom's phenomenal success in detaching so much territory from mighty Angkor. Still experimenting with political institutions, however, Rama Khamhaeng's son and successor, Lö Thai (reigned ca. 1299-1346), was unable to hold the state together in the face of challenges from other Thai princes to the south, and the kingdom of Ayudhya (1350-1767) ultimately reduced Sukhothai to a province (1438).

The 1292 inscription, lost for many centuries, was rediscovered by King Mongkut, then a Buddhist monk, in 1834, and the image of Rama Khamhaeng, resurrected, became a powerful ideal for subsequent rulers.

Further Reading

The kingdom of Sukhothai, still relatively neglected by scholars, may be studied in George Coedès, *The Making of South East Asia,* translated by H. M. Wright (1966), and in Alexander B. Griswold's marvellous *Towards a History of Sukhodaya Art* (1967). □

Sri Ramakrishna

Sri Ramakrishna (1833-1886) was an Indian mystic, reformer, and saint who, in his own lifetime, came to be revered by people of all classes as a spiritual incarnation of God.

Born in a rural Bengal village, Ramakrishna was the fourth of five children. His parents were simple but orthodox Brahmins deeply committed to the maintenance of traditional religious piety. As a child, he did not like routine schoolwork and never learned to read or write. Instead, he began to exhibit precocious spiritual qualities, which included ecstatic experiences, long periods of contemplation, and mystical absorption in the sacred plays of the Indian epic tradition, especially with the roles of the gods Shiva and Krishna. During his formal initiation ceremony into the Brahmin caste, he shocked his highcaste relatives by openly accepting a ritual meal cooked by a woman of low caste.

Though Ramakrishna resisted orthodox priestly studies, at the age of 16 he went to Calcutta to assist his brother, who was serving as a priest for a number of local families. He was disturbed by the gross commercialism, spiritual drabness, and inhumanity of the urban environment. However, when his brother was asked to become a priest at a large temple complex at Dakshineswar near the Ganges outside Calcutta, Ramakrishna found a new and ultimately permanent environment for his spiritual maturation and teaching.

Spiritual Struggles

That temple complex—one of the most impressive in the area—had been built by a wealthy widow of low caste whose spiritual ideal was the mother goddess Kali. This great deity traditionally combines the terror of death and destruction with universal motherly reassurance and is often

embodied in a statue of ferocious appearance. She represents an immense spectrum of religious and human emotions, from the most primitive to the most exalted, and consequently has a symbolic universality not easily contained within conventional religious forms.

Ramakrishna was selected to serve as priest in the Kali temple, and it was in this context that he had a series of crucial religious experiences in which he felt that Kali was calling him to a universal spiritual mission for India and all mankind. His ecstatic, unorthodox, and often bizarre behavior during this period of spiritual transformation was interpreted by many as a sign of madness; but it clearly represents an aspect of his struggles to free himself from routine religious patterns and achieve a new and more profound spirituality: he imitated the actions of the god-monkey Hanuman (a sign of humility and service); he fed animals from the same food prepared for Kali (a blasphemy to the orthodox); he cleaned an outcaste's hovel with his hair (a terrible defilement for a Brahmin); he sang and danced wildly when the spirit moved; he rejected his Brahminical status, asserting that caste superiority was spiritually debasing—all of this symbolizing his inward spiritual transformation.

Spiritual Maturity

When Ramakrishna was 28, his emotional confusion subsided, and he began studying a wide variety of traditional religious teachings. His teachers were astounded at his powers of assimilation, prodigious memory, and innate spiritual skill. He was openly proclaimed a supreme sage. At the age of 33 he began to study Moslem tradition, and after a short period of instruction he had a vision of a "radiant figure"—interpreted as Mohammed himself, which confirmed his universal religious calling.

In 1868 Ramakrishna undertook an extensive pilgrimage; but despite the honors accorded him he was saddened by the poverty of the masses and took up residence with outcaste groups to dramatize their plight, insisting that his rich patrons make formal efforts to alleviate their condition. He was always a man of the people, simple, full of affective warmth, and without artificial intellectualism or religious dogma.

World Mission

By now Ramakrishna had a wide following from all classes and groups. He was not merely a great teacher; he was regarded as an embodiment of the sacred source of Indian religious tradition and of the universal ideals toward which all men strive. His spiritual vitality and magnetism were combined with a sharp sense of humor—often aimed at himself or his disciples when the hazards of pride and self-satisfaction seemed imminent.

During the last decade of his life, one of the most important events was the conversion of his disciple Vivekananda, who was destined to organize and promote Ramakrishna's teachings throughout India, Europe, and the United States. In 1886, when Ramakrishna was near death, he formally designated Vivekananda his spiritual heir.

Ramakrishna's teachings do not appear in systematic form. He wrote nothing. His disciples recorded his words only in the context of the spiritual force of his personality, and consequently in collected form these sayings have the character of a gospel—a message of salvation centered in the spiritual paradigm of his own life. He rejected all efforts to worship him personally; rather, he suggested that his presentation of man's spiritual potentialities serve as a guide and inspiration to others. Above all, Ramakrishna had a ''grass-roots'' appeal equaled by few others in any religious tradition, marked by his love of all men and his enthusiasm for all forms of spirituality.

Further Reading

The sayings of Ramakrishna are available in several editions, such as *The Gospel of Ramakrishna* (1907) and *The Gospel of Sri Ramakrishna,* translated and introduced by Swami Nikhilananda (1942). Among the many works devoted to Ramakrishna's life and influence are Friedrich Max Mueller, *Ramakrishna: His Life and Sayings* (1898); Romain Rolland, *The Life of Ramakrishna* (trans. 1931); Christopher Isherwood, *Ramakrishna and His Disciples* (1965); and Nalini Devdas, *Sri Ramakrishna* (1966). □

Sir Chandrasekhar Venkata Raman

The Indian physicist Sir Chandrasekhar Venkata Raman (1888-1970) was awarded the Nobel Prize in 1930 for his work on the scattering of light and the discovery of the Raman effect, which has to do with changes in the wavelength of light scattered by molecules.

On Nov. 7, 1888, C. V. Raman was born at Trichinopoly, Madras, where his father taught physics in a church college. A few years later the family moved to Vizagapatam, when the father was appointed as lecturer in the local college. Raman received his early education there until he entered Presidency College in Madras in 1902. He graduated with a bachelor's degree in 1904, standing first in his class and winning the Gold Medal in physics. By the time he completed his master's degree in physics in 1907, he had already done original work in optics and acoustics, but since at that time there was little scope for scientific research in India, he took the competitive examination for a post in the Finance Department of the government of India. Again he won first place and as a result was appointed assistant accountant general in the central government offices in Calcutta.

During the next 10 years, while working in the Finance Department, Raman continued his scientific researches on his own in the laboratory of the Indian Association for the Cultivation of Science. The importance of his work was recognized by his appointment in 1917 to the first endowed

chair in physics at Calcutta University. He kept this post until 1933.

Raman's years at Calcutta University were marked by great creativity and intellectual excitement, although by Western standards his laboratory facilities were meager. Many honors came to him as the significance of his work was acknowledged in India and abroad, as in 1929, when he was invited to do research at the California Institute of Technology. The most tangible evidence of this recognition came in 1927, when the British government conferred a knighthood on him, and in 1930, when he was awarded the Nobel Prize.

Raman Effect

Raman's early scientific interests were centered on phenomena associated with the scattering of light, the most familiar example of which is the effect created when light enters a darkened room through a small hole. The beam of light is then clearly seen because the light is scattered by the particles of dust in the air. That scattered light contained wavelengths in different proportions from the wavelengths of the main beam of light had been known since Tyndall's experiments in 1868, but a fully satisfactory analysis of the phenomenon had not been made.

It was this and related problems that Raman was studying at Calcutta when he discovered that when an intense light was passed through a liquid and was scattered by the molecules in the liquid, the spectrum of the scattered light showed lines not in the spectrum of the incident light. This discovery was the Raman effect, which had such great influence on later work on molecular structure and radiation that Raman was recognized as one of the truly seminal minds in the history of modern physics.

After Raman retired from Calcutta University, he became director of the Indian Institute of Science in Bangalore, where he remained until 1948, when he became head of the new Raman Research Institute in the same city. Here he continued to guide research and to inspire his students and coworkers. They spoke of his intense enthusiasm and volcanic energy and of his great generosity in acknowledging the contribution of others. According to one former student, he would "give away whole lines of research which lesser men would be tempted to keep for themselves."

Raman's attractiveness as a person was rooted in his esthetic approach to science, with his choice of subjects for investigation reflecting his love of music, color, harmony, and pattern. He told how his great discovery of the Raman effect was stimulated during a voyage to Europe in 1921, when he saw for the first time "the wonderful blue opalescence of the Mediterranean Sea" and began to think that the phenomenon was due to the scattering of sunlight by the molecules of water.

Raman influenced Indian scientific development through the *Indian Journal of Physics,* which he helped found and which he edited. He was also a gifted popularizer of modern scientific ideas, and he lectured widely to lay audiences. He died in Bangalore on Nov. 21, 1970.

Further Reading

Raman sets forth his own views on modern science in an attractive way in his *The New Physics* (1951). Some biographical details and a brief account of his scientific work are in Niels H. de V. Heathcote, *Nobel Prize Winners in Physics, 1901-1950* (1953). A more technical discussion is S. Bhagavantam, *Scattering of Light and the Raman Effect* (1940). A consideration of Raman's many-sided contribution to science is made by his students and colleagues in *Proceedings of the Indian Academy of Sciences,* vol. 28 (1949). □

Srinivasa Ramanujan Aiyangar

The Indian mathematician Srinivasa Ramanujan Aiyangar (1887-1920) is best known for his work on hypergeometric series and continued fractions.

Srinivasa Ramanujan, born into a poor Brahmin family at Erode on Dec. 22, 1887, attended school in nearby Kumbakonam. By the time he was 13, he could solve unaided every problem in Loney's *Trigonometry,* and at 14 he obtained the theorems for the sine and the cosine that had been anticipated by L. Euler. In 1903 he came upon George Shoobridge Carr's *Synopsis of Elementary Results in Pure and Applied Mathematics.* The book, its coverage

reaching 1860, opened a whole new world to him, and he set out to establish the 6,165 theorems in it for himself. Having no contact with good books, he had to do original research for each solution. Trying to devise his own methods, he made some astounding discoveries, among them several new algebraic series.

Ramanujan became so absorbed in mathematics that when he entered the local government college in 1904 with a merit scholarship, he neglected his other subjects and lost the scholarship. Despite two later attempts, he never qualified for the first degree in arts. Ramanujan married in 1909, and while working as a clerk he continued his mathematical investigations; in 1911 he started to publish some of his results.

In January 1913 Ramanujan sent some of his work to G. H. Hardy, Cayley lecturer in mathematics at Cambridge. Hardy noticed that whereas Ramanujan had rediscovered, and gone far beyond, some of the latest conclusions of Western mathematicians, he was completely ignorant of some of the most fundamental areas. In May the University of Madras gave Ramanujan a scholarship.

In 1914 Ramanujan went to Cambridge. The university experience gave him considerable sophistication, but his mind, by this time somewhat hardened, generally continued to work according to the old pattern, in which intuition played a more important role than argument. In Hardy's opinion, if Ramanujan's gift had been recognized early, he could have become one of the greatest mathematicians of all time. In hypergeometric series and continued fractions, "he was unquestionably one of the great masters." His patience, memory, power of calculation, and intuition made him the greatest formalist of his day. But his passionate, prolific, and in some ways profound work in the theory of numbers and his work in analysis were seriously marred by misdevelopment.

In 1918 Ramanujan was elected a fellow of the Royal Society and a Fellow of Trinity College, Cambridge. He died on April 26, 1920.

Further Reading

Godfrey Harold Hardy and others, eds., *Collected Papers of Srinivasa Ramanujan* (1927), and Hardy's *Ramanujan: Twelve Lectures on Subjects Suggested by His Life and Work* (1940) include biographical material. Shiyali Ramamrita Ranganathan, *Ramanujan: The Man and the Mathematician* (Bombay, 1967), is a disappointing biography. Scientific American, *Lives in Science* (1957), and James Roy Newman, *Science and Sensibility* (2 vols., 1961), have useful accounts of Ramanujan's life.

Additional Sources

Abdi, W. H. (Wazir Hasan). *Toils and triumphs of Srinivasa Ramanujan, the man and the mathematician,* Jaipur: National, 1992.

Kanigel, Robert. *The man who knew infinity: a life of the genius Ramanujan,* New York: Washington Square Press, 1992, 1991.

Nandy, Ashis. *Alternative sciences: creativity and authenticity in two Indian scientists,* New Delhi: Allied, 1980.

Rajagopalan, K. R. *Srinivasa Ramanujan,* Madras: Sri Aravinda-
    Bharati, 1988.
Srinivasa Ramanujan (1887-1920): a tribute, Madras: Macmillian
    India, 1988, 1987. □

Matemela Cyril Ramaphosa

**Matemela Cyril Ramaphosa (born 1952) became
general secretary of the powerful National Union of
Mineworkers (NUM) in South Africa beginning in
1982. A prominent figure in extra-parliamentary
politics in the 1980s through his work in NUM and
the Congress of South African Trade Unions
(COSATU), he was elected secretary general of the
African National Congress in 1991.**

Cyril Ramaphosa was born in Johannesburg, South
Africa, on November 17, 1952, to Erdmuth and
Samuel Ramaphosa. His father was a policeman.
He grew up in the sprawling black township of Soweto and,
in his late teens, moved (like many urban young people) to
complete his schooling at a rural boarding school. He finished his high school in Sibasa in the northern Transvaal in
1971 and enrolled in law at the local Bantustan university,
the University of the North (Turfloop), the scene in later
years of particularly violent clashes between black African
students and the South African state. At the university he
was heavily involved in student politics, becoming in 1974
chairman of the local branch of two black consciousness
organizations, the South African Student's Organisation and
the Student Christian Movement. He knew, and like a large
number of his peers, was greatly influenced by Steve Biko.
In 1974 he served on various committees of the Black
People's Convention while serving with a firm of attorneys
in Johannesburg.

In the mid 1970s, along with many other student activists, Ramaphosa spent time in detention. On the first occasion, in 1974, he was detained for eleven months in Pretoria
Central Prison. In 1976, following the outbreak of the
Soweto uprising, he spent six months in the infamous John
Vorster Square detention center in Johannesburg. Only his
high political profile and position of leadership in the National Union of Mineworkers prevented further periods of
harassment and detention in the 1980s.

Ramaphosa completed his law degree by correspondence in 1981 through the University of South Africa and,
disillusioned with private legal practice, joined the independent trade union movement as a legal adviser to the
black consciousness-oriented Council of Unions of South
Africa (CUSA). In mid 1982, in a momentous decision that
was to transform labor relations in the wealthy South African mining industry, the Chamber of Mines and the South
African Government announced that they would allow
black African mineworkers to join unions. Union rights had
always been denied to black African mineworkers, who
were cruelly exploited, low-paid migrant workers living in

single-sex, regimented barracks known as compounds or
hostels. Access to the compounds was denied to families,
union organizers, and other outsiders. The change of policy
prompted a number of unions to try and organize the country's 700,000 black mineworkers. CUSA detailed Ramaphosa to undertake the task, and in mid-1982 the National
Union of Mineworkers was born.

As first general secretary of the NUM Ramaphosa embarked on an exhausting round of union organizing, collective bargaining, and public activities that showed few signs
of abating even in the 1990s. Under his skillful direction the
NUM grew rapidly, learning from its mistakes and concentrating its organizing efforts on those mines where management was most receptive. Within five years the NUM had a
membership of over 300,000 workers, making it the fastest
growing union in the world and one of South Africa's largest
and most powerful unions. The NUM focused its campaigns
on wages and working conditions and on the color bar that
for years had reserved skilled mining jobs for whites only.
The NUM won some significant victories in the courts and
at the bargaining table. Mineworkers, denied a voice for
many decades, became far more assertive and militant. In
"Comrade Cyril" they had an articulate and confident
spokesman who, though he had never been a mineworker
himself, enjoyed enormous personal credibility and popularity with mineworkers.

In 1987, after the breakdown of wage talks between the
NUM and the Chamber of Mines, Ramaphosa and NUM
president James Motlatsi led the union out on a three-week
work stoppage that turned out to be the longest and costliest

strike in the history of the mining industry. The strike was also costly for the NUM. In breaking the strike, the mining companies fired over 40,000 workers. Afterwards, they made life much more difficult for union organizers and officials. The union began the slow and painful task of rebuilding morale and worker support.

Ramaphosa, meanwhile, was increasingly drawn into the national political arena. In 1985 the NUM broke with CUSA and threw its weight behind the giant Congress of South African Trade Unions (COSATU). COSATU espoused a "charterist" approach to national politics and forged links with the exiled political movement, the African National Congress (ANC). In 1986 Ramaphosa was part of a COSATU delegation to meet the ANC leadership in Lusaka, Zambia. In 1987 the NUM membership elected the imprisoned ANC leader, Nelson Mandela, as its honorary life president and endorsed the political platform outlined in the ANC's "Freedom Charter." When Nelson Mandela was released from prison in early 1990 and made his first public speech in 30 years from the steps of City Hall in Cape Town, Ramaphosa was at his side and introduced the veteran politician to the crowd.

Mandela's confidence in Ramaphosa was evident when he chose Ramaphosa as secretary general for the ANC on July 5, 1991. This position was second only to that of President Mandela. During the next few years Ramaphosa played a crucial role in negotiations with the former South African regime to bring about a peaceful end to apartheid and to set the stage for the country's first democratic elections held in April 1994. He was re-elected to the general secretary post that same year and at the insistence of Mandela, also took the job of co-chairing the Constitutional Assembly. His negotiating talents and skill in building and leading effective teams made a significant difference.

When pressured by ANC party politics not to seek the Minister of Fiance post, a position to which he aspired, Ramaphosa announced that he would enter private business in early 1996. Within six months he had been appointed as Deputy Chairman of New Africa Investments Limited (NAIL) and chairman of the National Empowerment Consortium (NEC). The one time activist and union founder quickly adopted to the business world. By November 1996, he was described by a reporter for the *Weekly Mail & Guardian* as one of South Africa's newest millionaires with "immaculate pin-stripe suit, sober ties and gun-metal grey BMW."

Further Reading

Interviews with Ramaphosa on labor and political issues have appeared in *Leadership S. A.* (1989) and in *South African Labour Bulletin* (1987). Consistent with the antielitism of many union leaders, he declined to be interviewed on personal matters. The history of the gold mining industry is considered in F. Wilson, *Labour to the South African Goldmines* (1972) and in A. Jeeves, *Migrant Labour in South Africa's Mining Economy* (1985). The best overview of the Black union movement in South Africa is S. Friedman, *Building Tomorrow Today: African Workers in Trade Unions* (1987), which contains a chapter on the rise of the NUM. Later studies of the NUM include J. Crush, "Migrancy and

Militance: The Case of the National Union of Mineworkers of South Africa," in *African Affairs* (1989) and J. Leger, "From Fatalism to Mass Action: The South African National Union of Mineworkers' Struggle for Safety and Health," in *Labour, Capital and Society* (1988).Information on Ramaphosa can also be found in South African newspapers such as the *Weekly Mail & Guardian.* □

Ram Camul Sen

Ram Camul Sen (1783-1844) was a Bengali intellectual and entrepreneur. Part of a group that inaugurated the Bengal renaissance, he proved less a prolific writer and scholar and more a gifted organizer and administrator.

A Kashatriya by caste and, according to his own account, a descendant of the medieval Bengali king Ballal Sena, Ram Camul Sen left a Hooghly village for Calcutta in 1790, at the age of 7. His father was proficient in Persian and secured clerical positions, and Ram Camul himself learned English, Sanskrit, and Persian in the manner of the sons of the Calcutta elite.

Ram Camul found his first job in 1803, as a subordinate clerk's assistant in the Calcutta chief magistrate's office. The chief magistrate was evidently impressed with Ram Camul's industrious work habits. In 1804 two scholars associated with the Asiatic Society of Bengal invited Sen to work for the Hindoostanee Press as a compositor.

Despite a very low salary of 8 rupees a month, Ram Camul always performed far more than was expected of him, profited from his knowledge of English, and extended his range of contacts. In 1810, after he met the eminent Orientalist Horace H. Wilson at the Press, Ram Camul's fortunes took a rapid upward swing. The two men developed a warm friendship that lasted until Sen's death. Under Wilson's sponsorship, and utilizing the skills and techniques acquired during his employment at the Hindoostanee Press, Ram Camul began his extraordinary rise as an intellectual entrepreneur. By 1814 he had been appointed the "native" manager of the Hindoostanee Press.

In 1829 Wilson, then secretary of the Asiatic Society, proposed that members of the Bengali intelligentsia, including Ram Camul Sen, be admitted to membership in that association. In December 1833, shortly before Wilson's departure for England to be Oxford University's first Sanskritist, Sen reviewed his "29 years with the Society" in a letter accepting the post of native secretary.

A year later Ram Camul completed a project by publishing the second volume of his *Dictionary of the English and Bengalee Languages,* one of the best efforts of its kind in the 19th century and the earliest accurate and comprehensive dictionary of the Bengali language compiled by a Bengali. The introduction to the second volume is important not only for a linguistic analysis of Bengali but for its history of modern Bengali prose from 1800, when the missionary

William Carey was hired to teach that language to civil service trainees at the College of Fort William.

Ram Camul, however, was best known during his own time as an efficient, activist intellectual whom the British frequently employed to help manage their newly introduced institutions, especially educational facilities. During the last 20 years of his life, he became the most influential Asian in associations as diverse as the Hindu College and the Calcutta Mint. Largely as a result of such administrative endeavors, when Sen died in August 1844, he left an estate estimated at 1 million rupees.

Further Reading

There is only one full-length biography of Ram Camul Sen in English, Peary Chand Mitra, *Life of Dewan Ram Camul Sen* (1880). As with most figures of the 19th-century Bengali intelligentsia, aspects of Sen's life and career are continually referred to in numerous books on modern Indian history, but he has not been the subject of a serious scholarly monograph. Some attempt to update Sen's role in the light of modern scholarship is made in David Kopf, *British Orientalism and the Bengal Renaissance* (1969). ☐

Jean Philippe Rameau

Jean Philippe Rameau (1683-1764) was a French theoretician of music and a composer. His theoretical works provided the scientific basis for the development of traditional, functional harmony in the 18th century. His operas were the first national creations to rival those of Lully.

Jean Philippe Rameau was born in Dijon on Sept. 25, 1683, the son of a provincial organist. It is presumed that he studied with his father, no other formal training being known. He was in Italy in 1701 and then served as organist for a time at Clermont-Ferrand. In 1706 he was in Paris, where his first collection of harpsichord pieces was published. Rameau dropped out of sight for nearly a decade, returning sometime about 1715 to his former position at Clermont-Ferrand. Here he wrote his famous *Treatise on Harmony Reduced to Its Natural Principles* (1722).

In 1731 Rameau came under the patronage of one of the wealthiest, most remarkable 18th-century French aristocrats, La Pouplinière. Rameau was active as a teacher, harpsichordist, conductor, and composer in his establishment until 1753. His patron provided the necessary arrangements for Rameau to attempt his hand at opera composition.

In 1733 *Hippolyte et Aricie,* to a libretto by the Abbé Pellegrin, was presented in Paris; it was Rameau's first major public success. *Les Indes galantes* followed in 1735, and *Castor et Pollux,* generally considered to be his crowning triumph in the music theater, in 1737. These works challenged the then-prevailing taste for simpler, more tuneful diversions and entertainments, as well as the belief that Jean Baptiste Lully was the only significant composer of French operas. The ensuing quarrels in French intellectual circles over the respective merits of Lully and Rameau and later over the merits of Italian versus French music assured Rameau of lasting fame. In 1745 the King awarded Rameau a lifetime pension on the basis of his pleasure with *La Princesse de Navarre,* a *comédie-ballet* (a unification of stage play and ballet) composed for the marriage of the Dauphin to Maria Theresa of Spain.

In his keyboard music Rameau followed in the steps of François Couperin. Nearly 20 years elapsed between Rameau's first publications in 1706 and a second collection of orderly, elegant pieces for the harpsichord, *Pièces de clavecin avec une méthode pour la mécanique des doigts* (1726). The *Pièces de clavecin en concert avec un violon ou une flûte et une viole ou un deuxième violon* (1741) is generally acknowledged as his masterpiece of chamber music. He died in Paris on Sept. 12, 1764.

Rameau's keyboard music is of exceptionally high quality, but he is even more widely acclaimed as a theorist. He was the only major composer who gained a reputation as a theorist before being acclaimed for composition. All his life he fought against the widely held erroneous notion that to be "scientific" in music is to be mechanical and lifeless.

Rameau's *Treatise on Harmony* established the primacy of triadic harmony as the central "law" of music. He claimed that melody must be subordinated to harmony and that harmonic considerations alone should dictate composition. He established the significant theoretical concept that the inversions of chords did not create new chords but were further manifestations of a single harmony. While Rameau's ideas were much debated and attacked, their importance for the future of theory and practice cannot be overestimated. His codification of functional harmony provided much of the theoretical basis for traditional composition well into the 19th century.

Further Reading

The standard biography and study of Rameau's music is Cuthbert Girdlestone, *Jean-Philippe Rameau: His Life and Work* (1957; rev. ed. 1970). See also Donald J. Grout, *A Short History of Opera* (1947; rev. ed. 1965) and *A History of Western Music* (1960). □

Ram Mohun Roy

Ram Mohun Roy (1772-1833) was a Bengali social and religious reformer thoroughly identified with the cultural self-image of the people. He has been called the father of modern India.

Ram Mohun Roy was born to a Kulin Brahmin family at Radhanagar, Hooghly District, West Bengal. According to early biographers, as a result of wanderings over Asia in search for religious truth, he became a gifted linguist in Persian, Arabic, Sanskrit, Hebrew, and Greek before he was 22. New evidence suggests that his father, a *zamindar* (landowner) of the traditional ruling class of Bengal, lost his property in 1800, went to jail, and died a ruined man in 1803.

It appears that between 1799 and 1802 Ram Mohun lent money to British civil servants in Calcutta as a livelihood. In 1804 he joined the East India Company as a subordinate official and was evidently employed in that fashion until 1814, when he retired from government service with a lucrative income from landed property.

After settling in Calcutta in 1815, Ram Mohun challenged the orthodox defenders of the contemporary religious and social systems. In the *Abridgement of the Vedanta* (1815), *Translation of the Cena Upanishad* (1816), and the *Defense of the Monotheistical System of the Vedas* (1817) he condemned such common practices as caste distinction, idolatry, Kulin polygamy, and sati (or suttee; burning widows on the funeral pyres of their husbands) as excrescences upon the authentic Hindu tradition. Scripturally, that authentic tradition consisted of the *Vedas,* the *Upanishads,* and the *Vedanta Shastras.* Historiographically, his differentiation between a pure Hinduism of a remote past and the aberrational form in existence during his own time contributed to a new historical outlook among the intelligentsia, who increasingly divided the Indian past into a golden age and a subsequent dark age.

In the 1820s Ram Mohun's aim was to provide the means for awakening India and to guide it back again into the mainstreams of world progress. He sought an ideology of religious modernism which would be compatible with India's authentic tradition and equally in line with the dynamic and progressive forces shaping contemporary western Europe and America. He chose Christian Unitarianism for its rationalism and liberalism. With the assistance of a former Baptist named William Adam, Ram Mohun actually formed a Calcutta Unitarian Committee. In 1828 he and his followers founded the Brahmo Sabha, precursor of the Brahma Samaj (Society of God), which for most of the century was India's most effective indigenous agency for social and religious reform.

From 1830 Ram Mohun lived in England. In 1833 in Bristol a meeting was arranged of Unitarian leaders representing three continents: Ram Mohun of Asia, Joseph Tuckerman of the United States, and Lant Carpenter of Great Britain were the delegates. Ram Mohun died before the conference took place.

Further Reading

Perhaps the best book on Ram Mohun Roy is the 1962 Sadharan Brahma Samaj edition of Sophia Dobson Collet's *The Life and Letters of Raja Rammohun Roy* (1962), originally published in 1900. Dilip Kumar Biswas and Prabhat Chandra Ganguli coedited the volume, updating it with extensive supplementary notes. The most useful collection of Ram Mohun's writings in English is *The English Works of Raja Rammohun Roy* (6 vols., 1945-1951), edited by Kalidas Nag and Debajyoti Burman. See also U. N. Ball, *Rammohun Roy: A Study of His Life* (1933), and Igbal Singh, *Rammohun Roy* (1958). □

Fidel Valdez Ramos

Fidel Valdez Ramos (born 1928) was inaugurated president of the Philippines in June 1992. He had the mandate to continue the democratic reforms gained by the country during Corazon Aquino's peaceful people-power revolution of 1986.

The eighth president of the postwar Philippine Republic, Fidel Valdez Ramos was known as a hero of the 1986 people-power revolution, the bloodless coup that ousted dictator Ferdinand Marcos. Corazon Aquino, the widow of Marcos' assassinated archenemy, was installed in the presidency at that time.

People power was Ramos' idea of how to fight the weapons of the Marcos regime when the dictator, losing confidence in Constabulary Chief Fidel Ramos and his defense minister, Juan Ponce Enrile, set out to destroy them. Ramos asked Jaime Cardinal Sin to send people to protect their fortress, the Constabulary Camp at EDSA (Epifanio de los Santos Avenue). Cardinal Sin appealed to the people by radio, and millions of people surrounded the camp to protect Ramos, Enrile, and the soldiers who joined them. The people at EDSA thwarted tanks and armored vehicles, and in four days in 1986 caused the flight to Hawaii of Marcos and his family. Corazon C. Aquino, who may have won a controversial election against Marcos weeks before, became president, and democracy was restored after 20 years of autocratic rule.

After the EDSA victory, "Eddie" Ramos, who had been a soldier all his adult life, served President Aquino as chief of staff of the armed forces of the Philippines and later as secretary of national defense. During the six years of Aquino's administration Ramos defeated seven coup attempts, two of them serious. His successful maneuvers against the coups earned for him the trust and confidence of President Aquino, who, towards the end of her term, openly supported him to be her successor to the presidency.

Ramos won in the May 1992 elections over six other candidates, garnering only 24 percent of the votes but winning 800,000 votes more than his closest rival. Within his first year in office he was able to win over to his side a majority of the people, who developed confidence in his government. He gained their support through a strategy of reconciliation and a strong hands-on leadership. The restoration of democracy was a long, difficult task, while at the same time Ramos had to attend to major economic and social problems that had grown during the Marcos years.

Under Ramos' presidential leadership, the Phillipines became known as the "Asian Tiger." He was widely credited for reviving the country's economy, and it grew at a brisk pace of seven percent annually through the mid-1990s. Admirers of his businesslike approach called him "Steady Eddie," and many foreign investors poured money into the country. He also ended crippling regulation of the telecommunications, banking, insurance, shipping and oil

industries. Meanwhile, Ramos quieted long-standing troubles with Communist guerrillas, right-wing military offices and Muslim separatists, making life in the Phillippines more stable than it had been in decades.

Ramos grew up with a sense of government. His father served the Philippine Republic in the 1960s as secretary of national defense. He also came to the job of president educationally prepared, with a degree from the United States Military Academy at West Point and an engineering degree from the University of Illinois at Champaign-Urbana. In a country where law is the typical training for the presidency, Ramos came with atypical qualifications. He had only a short stint as a member of a political party, the ruling LDP (*Lakas ng Demokratikong Pilipino* or Fight of Democratic Filipinos), which then spurned him as their nominee for the presidency. However, Ramos ascended to the highest post in the land via a new party, the *Lakas ng EDSA* (Strength of EDSA) or NUCD (National Union of Christian Democrats). Lastly, in a country that was 85 percent Catholic, Ramos was the first Protestant president. He was married and the father of five daughters.

The unusual people-power revolution at EDSA enabled an unusual person like Ramos to lead the Philippines. In December 1996, Ramos had surgery to remove a life-threatening blockage in the artery to his brain, but he recovered. Near the end of his term, supporters advocated changing the country's young Constitution to allow him to run for a second six-year term in 1998. They wanted to continue his steady leadership and the Phillippine economic rennaissance, arguing that no other candidate could fill his shoes as president. However, many others, including former president Aquino and the nation's 100 Roman Catholic bishops, strongly objected. They urged respect for the Constitution, warning any such change could plunge the country back to a Marcos-like dictatorship. Ramos, ever low-key, did not reveal his plans, but told reporters "I would not want the policies, the momentum, the tremendous progress we have achieved wasted."

Further Reading

For a biography of Ramos before his election see Jose Apolinario L. Lozada, *Who's Afraid of Eddie Ramos?* (Manila, 1991). The president's own writing may be found in Fidel V. Ramos, *To Win the Future: People Empowerment for National Development* (Manila, 1993). See also *The First 365 Days* (Manila, Office of the Press Secretary, 1993). Accounts of Ramos' years as president can be found in *The New York Times* (Dec. 26, 1996 and April 4, 1997); *The Economist* (April 12, 1997); *Business Week* (Oct. 28, 1996); and *Newsweek* (Dec. 2, 1996). □

Shridath Surendranath Ramphal

Shridath Surendranath Ramphal (born 1928), a Guyanese barrister, politician, and international civil servant, was the secretary-general of the Com-

monwealth of Guyana. An architect of regional integration in the Caribbean, he helped to increase the role of Guyana in world affairs.

Shridath S. Ramphal—"Sonny," as he was widely known—was born on October 3, 1928, in New Amsterdam, British Guiana. His ancestors were Indians who arrived there in the 1880s. The eldest of five children, his father, James I. Ramphal, was a Presbyterian schoolteacher and a pioneer of secondary education in Guiana. He later became the first Guyanese to be appointed to a senior government post when he was made a commissioner in the Department of Labour soon after the outbreak of World War II.

Ramphal attended a private school founded by his father in the capital city, Georgetown. He was also educated at the Modern Educational Institute, which also was run by his father. During those early years his father had a profound influence on his life, and Ramphal wrote that his father's "passionate belief in the basic goodness within all men" made a deep impression on him. He completed his secondary education at Queen's College, a government school in Georgetown.

In 1947 he began his legal training at King's College, London, and was called to the bar from Gray's Inn in 1951. As a pupil in chambers, he worked with a distinguished barrister and politician, Dingle Foot, who at the time was chairman of the Liberal Party. He continued his studies for a Master's degree in law and did part-time work in the Legal Section of the Colonial Office to support himself.

He returned to British Guiana in 1953 and served as crown counsel in the Attorney General's Office. It was during this period that he became interested in constitutional law and started his enthusiastic support for the creation of a West Indian federation. However, the next five years were unhappy ones, primarily because of serious ideological differences between him and the Marxist People's Progressive Party leader, Cheddi Jagan. In 1958 he joined the federal government of the West Indies as legal draftsman. The following year he was appointed solicitor-general, and in 1961 he became assistant attorney-general. However, the federation was short-lived, and after a referendum in Jamaica it broke up.

Ramphal then went to Harvard Law School for a year as a Guggenheim Fellow. He returned to Kingston, Jamaica, in 1962 and entered private practice. In 1965, while he was still in Kingston, he was invited by Forbes Burnham, the prime minister of British Guiana, to return home and become the country's attorney-general and to begin drafting Guyana's independence constitution. This was the beginning of his ten years in national politics.

In 1967, the year after Guyana's independence, Ramphal was appointed minister of state for foreign affairs. In 1972 he became minister of foreign affairs, and a year later he took on the portfolio of justice minister as well. He was instrumental in shaping Guyana's foreign policy—which is based on the principle of non-alignment—and in establishing its foreign service. He was actively involved in Caribbean politics and in the major international organizations of which Guyana is a member—the United Nations, the Commonwealth, the Group of 77, and the Non-Aligned Movement. He also strengthened relations between the countries of the Caribbean and those of Latin America. He was a key spokesman for the developing countries of Africa, the Caribbean, and the Pacific in the negotiations with the European Community which resulted in the Lomé Convention of 1975.

At the Commonwealth heads of government meeting in Kingston, Jamaica, in 1975, Ramphal was unanimously appointed the Commonwealth's second secretary-general, the first from the Third World. Articulate, dynamic, and self-confident, he was a strong advocate of the interests of the Third World, the need for a new international economic order, and the need to end apartheid in South Africa. Soon after his appointment he challenged a statement by Henry Kissinger that the international economic system had worked well and argued that the developing countries had not been well served by it. He stressed the importance of increased North-South cooperation, and he played an important role as a member of the Independent Commission on International Development Issues, the Brandt Commission. He had a deep commitment to human rights and served as a member of the International Commission of Jurists beginning in 1970. After the end of his term as secretary-general of the Commonwealth in 1989, he served as head of the World Conservation Union and played an important role in the Earth Summit in 1992. His book *Our Country, the Planet* (1992), published just in advance of the Summit, expresses his commitment to the causes of international economic reform and environmental protection. In all he served on five international commissions on global development and the environment.

Ramphal joined many leading international legal, political, economic, and humanitarian organizations. He received honorary degrees from universities all over the world and awards from various national governments. Although he received a knighthood in 1970, he preferred the simple title of "Mr." He married Lois Winifred Ramphal (née King) in 1951, a nurse whom he met while he was a student in London. They had four children, two sons and two daughters.

Further Reading

There is as yet no biography of Ramphal nor any detailed account of his work as secretary-general of the Commonwealth. However, *One World to Share* (1979), which is a selection of his speeches as secretary-general from 1975 to 1979, and *Inseparable Humanity* (1989), a selection of speeches and essays from 1971 to 1987, have much relevant material on his views on major international issues. In addition to these and *Our Country, the Planet* (1992), he had two other publications: *Nkrumah and the Eighties* (1980) and *Sovereignty or Solidarity* (1981), in which he argued that national sovereignty should yield to international solidarity. □

David Ramsay

David Ramsay (1749-1815) was a second-line political figure of the American Revolution but a first-rate and most important contemporary historian of that epoch.

David Ramsay was born in Pennsylvania on April 2, 1749, of substantial landowning parents. He graduated from the College of New Jersey (now Princeton University) and, after teaching for a while, took a medical degree from the University of Pennsylvania in 1772.

Ramsay settled in Charleston, S.C., and made it his home for the remainder of his life. The beginning of his political career coincided with the outbreak of the American Revolution. Much of that career was spent in the legislature of his adopted state, but he also served for 2 years in the 1780s in the Continental Congress, where he emerged as an early supporter of a strong federal government. After the ratification of the Constitution, Ramsay served in the upper house of South Carolina and on three occasions was named president of that body.

In these years Ramsay earned his way rather precariously by practicing medicine. He also used his ample talent as a writer to turn out occasional first-rate essays on the history of medicine. These did not pay anything, though, and Ramsay was in chronic financial need. Despite his talents, he proved a poor businessman. He speculated in land with such disastrous consequences that even a steady medical practice could not recoup his losses. He went bankrupt in 1798, having opposed leniency to debtors throughout his political career. He died in Charleston on May 8, 1815.

Ramsay is best remembered as the author of the most objective and sophisticated contemporary account of the Revolution. His *History of the American Revolution* (1789) forms the basis today for most of the multicausation theories of that epoch. Like many historians writing at this time, he relied heavily for information on the *Annual Register,* a British publication that summarized events each year; like contemporary historians, too, Ramsay was not always careful with the truth. But his interpretations were his own, and he was the first—and for a century the only—historian to suggest that a variety of motives had induced men and governments to support independence first and the Constitution later.

Ramsay emphasized the key role of "independent men" in motivating American nationalism, creating changes in the social structure, and capitalizing on expanding economic opportunity in the young republic. In approaching his assessment of the era in this sophisticated way, Ramsay, as one historian has suggested, may have "penetrated further into the essential meaning of the Revolution than the more arduous researches of twentieth-century historians have done."

Further Reading

There is no book-length biography of Ramsay. For a brief biographical sketch and an excerpt from Ramsay's writings see Edmund S. Morgan, *The American Revolution: Two Centuries of Interpretation* (1965).

Additional Sources

Shaffer, Arthur H. *To be an American: David Ramsay and the making of the American consciousness,* Columbia, S.C.: University of South Carolina Press, 1991. □

Sir William Ramsay

The British chemist and educator Sir William Ramsay (1852-1916) discovered the rare gases and did important work in thermodynamics.

William Ramsay was born at Queen's Crescent, Glasgow, on Oct. 2, 1852. Both his father, a civil engineer, William Ramsay, and his mother, Catharine Robertson Ramsay, came from families noted for scientific attainment. Ramsay studied the classics, mathematics, and literature at the University of Glasgow (1866-1869) and then entered Robert Tatlock's laboratory while attending scientific lectures at the university. In 1870 he joined Robert Bunsen at Heidelberg, but he left there in 1871 to work with Rudolf Fittig at Tübingen, where he received the doctorate in 1872. On his return to Glasgow he became an assistant at Anderson's College and later an assistant in the department of chemistry at the University of Glasgow. University College, Bristol, appointed him professor of chemistry in 1880 and principal in 1881. In 1887 he succeeded Alexander W. Williamson to the chair of general chemistry at University College, London. He retired in 1912 to Hazelwood, in Buckinghamshire, where he also built a small laboratory. He had been made a fellow of the Royal Society in 1888; in 1902 he was knighted; and in 1904 he received the Nobel Prize. He died on July 23, 1916.

While Ramsay was at Glasgow, he worked as an organic chemist, synthesizing pyridine in 1877, and showing how close the relationship was between this compound and the alkaloids quinine and cinchonine. At Bristol he worked primarily as a physical chemist and, with his assistant, demonstrated the complexity of the molecular structure of pure liquids by studying the variation in their molecular surface energy with temperature. In London, Ramsay gradually shifted his attention to making very accurate determinations of the density of gases. He noted the small difference between the density of atmospheric nitrogen and that of "chemically pure" nitrogen. Together with Lord Rayleigh he discovered in 1894 a new element, christened "argon" because of its apparent chemical inertness; they announced their discovery in early 1895. Subsequently Ramsay was able to show that the gas given off when the mineral clevite was heated had a spectrum identical with that of helium.

Ramsay, now convinced that there was an entire group of elements missing from the periodic table, embarked upon a diligent search for them. In 1898, with the assistance of M. W. Travers, by careful fractional distillation of liquid air, Ramsay found three other elements: neon, krypton, and xenon. In 1903 he and Frederick Soddy announced the isolation of the final member of the series, radon, which they called "radium emanation." Ramsay also showed that the disintegration of radium proceeds with the emission of charged helium nuclei—alpha particles. For a while he believed that he had produced transmutations of copper to lithium and of thorium to carbon by exposing those materials to the products of radium disintegration. These claims were shown to be mistaken but were, nonetheless, important, for they suggested that the energy and particles from natural nuclear disintegrations might possibly be used to effect changes in more stable nuclei.

Further Reading

The chief sources of biographical information on Ramsay are Sir William A. Tilden, *Sir William Ramsay . . . Memorials of His Life and Work* (1918); and Morris William Travers, *William Ramsay and University College London, 1852-1952* (1952) and *A Life of Sir William Ramsay* (1956). □

Ramses II

Ramses II (reigned 1304-1237 B.C.) was the third ruler of the Nineteenth Dynasty of Egypt. A great warrior, he was also the builder of some of Egypt's most famous monuments.

Ramses, or Ramesses, was the son of Seti I. Prior to his accession as sole ruler in 1304 B.C., Ramses had been coregent with his father. During the last years of Seti I the reins of government had slackened, and the first 3 years of Ramses' reign seem to have been occupied with setting in order the internal affairs of Egypt. Early in his reign he undertook the task of securing an adequate water supply for the gold-mining expeditions to and from the Wadi el-Allaqi in Lower Nubia.

Ramses' royal residence, known as Per-Ramesse, the "House of Ramses," was situated in the Delta. Its site is still a matter of debate; various scholars have identified it with the cities of Tanis and Qantir in the eastern half of the Delta. The situation of the residence in this area was convenient for a pharaoh so concerned with events in Palestine and Syria.

Hittite Campaigns

The outstanding feature of Ramses II's reign was his protracted struggle with the Hittites. An inscription of year 4 of his reign, at the Nahr el-Kalb near Beirut, records his first Asiatic campaign. In year 5 he launched a major attack on the Hittite Empire from his base in northern Palestine and Phoenicia. During the course of this offensive, Ramses at Qadesh fought the greatest battle of his career. Although neither side could claim victory, Ramses never ceased to boast on his monuments of his own part in the battle. Strategically, however, the result was a defeat for the Egyp-

tians, who were obliged to retire homeward. The sight of the Pharaoh's army retreating encouraged many of the petty states of Palestine to revolt, and in year 6 or 7 and in year 8 Ramses was obliged to suppress uprisings in the area.

By year 10 Ramses was again on the Nahr el-Kalb, and the next year he broke the Hittite defenses and invaded Syria. Although he penetrated deep into Hittite territory, he found it impossible to hold indefinitely against Hittite pressure territories so far away from base, and in year 21 a treaty was concluded which terminated 16 years of hostilities between Egypt and the Hittites. After the restoration of peace, relations between the two powers became friendly, and a regular exchange of diplomatic correspondence ensued. In year 34 Ramses married the eldest daughter of the Hittite king. In addition to his wars in Palestine and Syria, Ramses vigorously combated Libyan incursions into the Delta.

No pharaoh ever surpassed the building achievements of Ramses II. Among the most famous of his constructions are his temple at Abydos, his funerary temple, known as the Ramesseum, at Thebes, and the great rockcut temple at Abu Simbel in Nubia.

Further Reading

An excellent account of Ramses II's reign is given by R. O. Faulkner in volume 2 of *The Cambridge Ancient History* (12 vols., 1924; 2d rev. ed. 1966). See also A. H. Gardiner, *Egypt of the Pharaohs* (1961). □

Arthur Michael Ramsey

The Right Reverend and Right Honorable Arthur Michael Ramsey (1904-1988) was the 100th archbishop of Canterbury. He also served as archbishop of York and bishop of Durham and was a leading ecumenical churchman and a president of the World Council of Churches. Ramsey was Regius Professor of Divinity at Cambridge University and an influential Anglican theologian.

Arthur Michael Ramsey was born November 14, 1904, in Cambridge, England. His father was a nonconformist and a mathematics don (and later president) at Magdelene College. Michael spent his childhood in the late Victorian academic environment of Cambridge and attended the famous Choir School of King's College and then Sandroyd in Surrey. He won a scholarship to Repton, one of the most respected English public schools. The young headmaster was Geoffrey Fisher, later to be Ramsey's immediate predecessor as primate of all England.

On leaving Repton in 1922 Ramsey won a scholarship to Cambridge and the next autumn entered Magdelene College. He established himself as one of the most skilled speakers in the student union and served as president of the Cambridge Union in 1926. His reading of William Temple and the lectures of the New Testament scholar Edwyn Hoskyns especially impressed Ramsey. He received a second class in the classical tripos or examinations in 1925. By then he had decided to study for the Anglican priesthood. After a year of graduate study he received a first class in the theological tripos.

Ramsey entered Cuddesdon College near Oxford in July 1927 to commence his seminary training. That year his mother died in an automobile accident and shortly after that tragic event his brother Frank, a brilliant economist at Trinity College, also died suddenly. Ramsey underwent a period of acute depression and did not return to Cuddesdon for a term. In September 1928 he was ordained a deacon at the Church of Our Lady and St. Nicholas near the Liverpool docks, a parish he served for two years. This was a sharp break with his previous sheltered academic life. Ramsey was ordained a priest on September 22, 1929.

In 1930 he accepted the call to be sub-warden of Lincoln Theological College, an Anglican seminary in the cathedral town. It was at Lincoln that Ramsey published his first book, *The Gospel and the Catholic Church,* in 1936. The book was widely acclaimed and gave him a position of some prominence in the Church of England. In the fall of 1936 he moved to Boston Parish Church, England's largest parish church, to serve as lecturer—that is, preacher.

Two years later, in December 1938, he left Boston to become vicar of St. Benedict's Church, Cambridge, where he remained only one year before moving to Durham to be canon of Durham Cathedral and professor of divinity at Durham University. In April 1942 Ramsey married Joan Hamilton. His second book, *The Resurrection of Christ,* was

published in 1944. It was during his ten years at Durham (1940-1950) that Ramsey's interest in the Eastern Orthodox Church became widely known, as did his support of Anglo-Catholicism in the English Church.

In 1950 Ramsey was appointed Regius Professor of Divinity at Cambridge and a Fellow of Magdelene College. Expecting to settle in the academic life in Cambridge for life, he was, nevertheless, soon asked by Prime Minister Winston Churchill to permit his name to be submitted to the queen for nomination as bishop of Durham. He was consecrated bishop in York Minster on September 29, 1952. A seat in the House of Lords came as a prerogative of the See of Durham. In 1954 Ramsey took an active, if critical, role in the deliberations of the World Council of Churches at its meetings in Evanston, Illinois.

On April 25, 1956, Ramsey was enthroned as primate of England and 92nd archbishop of York, the second highest position in the Church of England. His rapid rise was a remarkable accomplishment for a man just past 50. During his five years as archbishop he travelled extensively—to the Soviet Union, the United States, and Africa—on behalf of the church. He also had major responsibilities for the Anglican Lambeth Conference in 1958.

In 1960 his sixth book appeared, entitled *From Gore to Temple*. It is an interpretation of a half century of Anglican theology from the 1880s to World War II. The essay reveals Ramsey's own Catholic predilections and his disapproval of the Modernist theology which had gained a following in the English Church in the early years of the 20th century.

Ramsey's cordiality toward Catholicism and his ecumenical concerns were further demonstrated in 1960 when he appeared on television with J. C. Heenan, the Roman Catholic archbishop of Liverpool, to discuss the recent meeting between the archbishop of Canterbury and Pope John XXIII in Rome. Later, at Lambeth, Ramsey was to meet with Augustin Cardinal Bea, who headed the Vatican Secretariat for Promoting Christian Unity, and with Patriarch Benedictos of Jerusalem.

Ramsey was enthroned as the 100th Archbishop of Canterbury on June 27, 1961, about three weeks after his formal election by the Greater Chapter (the canons) of Canterbury Cathedral. Like previous primates of all England, Ramsey and his wife took up residence at Lambeth Palace in London. A few months after his enthronement, Ramsey attended the third assembly of the World Council of Churches in New Delhi, India, where he again played an important role. He served as president of the World Council of Churches from 1961 to 1968.

Ramsey presented an especially imposing figure in his regalia as archbishop. A large, rugged, yet gentle and jovial man, he looked far older than his years. He was almost a caricature of a great ecclesiastical figure. A writer commented that in the presence of Ramsey "you feel that all the power and authority of Christendom is concentrated in his stooping presence. The wisdom of the ages seems entombed in his craggy head." The slow, sonorous cadences of his speech had a musical, even mystical effect, fitting High Church ritual and a man of his ecclesiastical position.

While stressing the Catholic tradition of the church, Ramsey was essentially a theological liberal, certainly no reactionary. He said he could only be happy in Anglicanism because "in Anglicanism there exists Catholic religion and intellectual liberty." His liberal theological views were reflected in his comments about the virgin birth and hell. On the virgin birth: "It is possible to believe that Jesus is divine without believing in the virgin birth, though if you do believe him divine then the virgin birth becomes congruous." On hell: "It is certainly not a physical place. It is a state of those who make hell for themselves by denying God a place in their lives." He thoroughly disliked and opposed evangelistic emotionalism and fundamentalism in the church.

Ramsey resigned as archbishop of Canterbury in 1974 at the age of 70. He retired to Durham. However, he remained active, a fact reflected in his writing of four books and numerous additional undertakings. Ramsey was a Life Peer and received innumerable honors. He was an honorary fellow of Magdelene College and Selwyn College, Cambridge, and of Merton College, Keble College, and St. Cross College, Oxford. He was honorary master of the bench, Inner Temple (1962); trustee of the British Museum (1963-1969); and honorary Fellow of the British Academy (1983). He held honorary degrees from Durham, Leeds, Edinburgh, Cambridge, Hull, Manchester, London, Oxford, Kent, and Keele and from a number of overseas universities.

Further Reading

In addition to Ramsey's works mentioned above, the following books will be of interest: *The Glory of God and the Transfiguration of Christ* (1949); *F. D. Maurice and the Conflicts of Modern Theology* (1951); *Durham Essays and Addresses* (1956); *Canterbury Essays and Addresses* (1964); *Sacred and Secular* (1965); *God, Christ and the World* (1969); with Cardinal Suenans, *The Future of the Christian Church* (1971); *The Christian Priest Today* (1972); *Canterbury Pilgram; Holy Spirit* (1977); *Jesus and the Living Past* (1980); and *Be Still and Know* (1982). No critical biography of Ramsey has been written to date. James B. Simpson's *The Hundredth Archbishop of Canterbury* (1962) deals with his life to 1962; it does not cover the period as archbishop of Canterbury, nor is it an adequate treatment of his theology. ☐

Frank Plumpton Ramsey

The English mathematician and philosopher Frank Plumpton Ramsey (1903-1930) was recognized as an authority in mathematical logic.

Frank Ramsey was born on Feb. 22, 1903. His father, Arthur Ramsey, was president of Magdalen College. Ramsey's excellent work at Winchester College won him a scholarship to Trinity College, Cambridge. He was Allen University scholar in 1924 and in the same year was elected a fellow of King's College and appointed lecturer in mathematics at the university.

Ramsey's precocious talents were legendary at Cambridge. From about his sixteenth year he was consulted by theorists in mathematics and other subjects in which mathematics is largely used. The economist John Maynard Keynes reported, "Economists living in Cambridge have been accustomed from his undergraduate days to try their theories on the keen edge of his critical and logical faculties." And indeed in his brief life Ramsey made two important contributions to economic theory: "A Mathematical Theory of Saving" and "A Contribution to the Theory of Taxation." Of the first of these, Keynes wrote that it is "one of the most remarkable contributions to mathematical economics ever made."

But Ramsey's contributions to the subject that taxed the best abstract theorists of the day, the foundations of mathematics, were even more impressive. At the age of 22 he presented a brilliant defense of the mathematical theories of Bertrand Russell and Alfred North Whitehead against Continental critics. Using the *Tractatus* of Ludwig Wittgenstein, which he was among the first to appreciate, Ramsay succeeded in removing some of the most serious objections to the logicist theory. He showed how the ad hoc axiom of reducibility, one of the most vulnerable parts of *Principia Mathematica*, by Russell and Whitehead, could be eliminated, and he offered ways of improving the concept of identity used in that work.

Ramsey also made important contributions to the philosophy of science. In an effort to clarify the role played by

theory in science, he introduced the important idea that scientific laws could be regarded as "inference licenses," a theme that was developed further by Gilbert Ryle and S. E. Toulmin. Taking up the work of the American philosopher C. S. Peirce on inductive logic, Ramsey sought to provide sharper criteria for the acceptability of beliefs.

On the question of whether there are important truths inaccessible to language, Ramsey went still further than his friend and colleague Wittgenstein. He gave an answer that was repeated by a generation of Cambridge students: "What we can't say, we can't say and we can't whistle it either."

Ramsey was widely regarded as having no equal in his generation for sheer power and quality of mind and in the originality and promise of his work. A man of large, "Johnsonian" build, he was straightforward and blunt in conversation and modest about his exceptional gifts. He died after an operation at the age of 26 on Jan. 19, 1930, survived by his wife and two daughters.

Further Reading

Ramsey's most important essays were published posthumously by R. B. Braithwaite, *The Foundations of Mathematics and Other Logical Essays* (1931), which also contains a eulogy by G. E. Moore and a bibliography of the remaining works. Further background is in John Maynard Keynes, *Essays in Biography* (1933; rev. ed. 1951). ☐

Norman Foster Ramsey Jr.

American physicist Norman Foster Ramsey, Jr. (born 1915) was both an experimentalist and theoretician, who was awarded the Nobel Prize in Physics for his invention of the separated-oscillatory-field method and its use in the hydrogen maser.

Norman Foster Ramsey, Jr., was born in Washington, D.C., on August 27, 1915. His father, a West Point graduate, was an officer in the Army Ordnance Corps, and, as is characteristic of life in the military, the Ramsey family moved frequently from place to place. Norman, a gifted student, benefited from these moves as he was twice advanced a grade when he enrolled in a new school. As a high school student in Fort Leavenworth, Kansas, Ramsey became interested in science and won a scholarship to the University of Kansas; however, his father was transferred to Governor's Island, New York, so Ramsey entered Columbia University at age 16 and graduated in 1935 with a Bachelor of Arts in mathematics.

Ramsey majored in mathematics, but by the time he graduated from Columbia it was physics that aroused his curiosity. Thus, with a Kellett fellowship provided by Columbia University, Ramsey entered Cambridge University, England, as an undergraduate in physics. At that time the Cavendish Laboratory at Cambridge was a leading center of physics, and in this active environment it was an essay Ramsey wrote for his tutor that first stimulated his interest in molecular beams. When he obtained his second bachelor's degree, he returned to New York City in 1937 and joined I.I. Rabi's molecular beam group at Columbia University.

It was an auspicious time to join Rabi's research group. In 1937 Rabi's molecular beam research had evolved to the point where the magnetic resonance method was about to break on the scene and Ramsey, the first graduate student to work with the new method, shared in the discovery of the quadrupole moment of the deuteron. In 1940 Ramsey received his Ph.D. from Columbia University for his studies of the rotational magnetic moments of molecules. Ramsey's Ph.D. came during the early years of World War II, and for the duration of the war he was involved in the war effort: first with the development of radar at the MIT Radiation Laboratory (1940-1943) and later at Los Alamos with the Manhattan Project (1943-1945). When the war ended Ramsey returned to Columbia (1945-1947) and to molecular beam research. In 1947 he accepted a position at Harvard University where he founded an active research program in molecular beam physics, particle physics, and neutron-beam physics. By the time he retired as Higgins Professor of Physics in 1986, Ramsey had guided 84 graduate students through their theses research.

At Harvard, Ramsey began his own laboratory with the objective of carrying out accurate molecular beam magnetic resonance experiments. Plagued by difficulties in obtaining magnetic fields with sufficient homogeneity to achieve the desired accuracy, Ramsey created his separated-oscillatory-field method. In this method, the effective path length of the region in which quantum transitions of the

beam particles are induced can be increased without maintaining a homogeneous magnetic field over the entire path length. This increase in path length means that beam particles spend more time in the resonance region, which results in a dramatic decrease in the width of the observed resonance peaks and, consequently, in increased precision. With the separated-oscillatory-field method, Ramsey and his students measured nuclear spins, nuclear magnetic dipole and electric quadrupole moments, rotational magnetic moments of molecules, spin-rotational interactions, spin-spin interactions, and electron distributions in molecules.

In Ramsey's molecular beam experiments, the time spent in the resonance region was determined by the spatial separation of the first and second oscillating fields. Ramsey's desire to increase still further this time factor and thereby to increase the precision of his magnetic resonance measurements led to the invention of the hydrogen maser in 1960. In this device, atoms of hydrogen were sent into an enclosure where they resided for approximately 10 seconds, which is 1,000 times longer than the time spent in a typical molecular beam apparatus; thus the line widths were reduced by a factor of 1,000. The hydrogen maser was used for extremely accurate measurements of the hyperfine separations of atomic hydrogen, deuterium, and tritium. Since its invention, the hydrogen maser has become one of the most accurate atomic clocks, and it has been used in applications ranging from sensitive tests of the theory of general relativity to the tracking of Voyager II in its encounter with Neptune.

Ramsey was primarily an experimental physicist; however, he was one of those rare physicists who was adept as both an experimentalist and a theoretician. In addition to developing theories of nuclear interactions in molecules that were directly related to his experimental work, Ramsey was the first to develop a successful theory of chemical shifts that has been central to the analysis of nuclear magnetic resonance spectra. He also published a paper providing the theory of thermodynamics and statistical mechanics at negative absolute temperatures.

In addition to his scientific work, Ramsey was an active leader in the world of physics. Together with Rabi, Ramsey initiated the discussions that led to the formation of the Brookhaven National Laboratory on Long Island, and he served as Brookhaven's first head of the Physics Department. On the 50th anniversary of the lab in 1995 he delivered the keynote speech. He held many administrative positions, including director of the Harvard Cyclotron; chairman of the MIT-Harvard committee in charge of the construction of the Cambridge electron accelerator; president of Universities Research Association, the governing body of Fermilab in Illinois; president of the American Physical Society; and chairman of the board of governors of the American Institute of Physics. Ramsey was also the first assistant secretary general for science in the North Atlantic Treaty Organization (NATO), where he initiated the NATO programs for advanced study institutes, fellowships, and research grants.

As might be expected, Ramsey was the recipient of many honors. In 1989 he won the Nobel physics prize for "the invention of the separated-oscillatory-field method and its use in the hydrogen maser and other atomic clocks." He has also received the Presidential Certificate of Merit, the E.O. Lawrence Award, the Davisson-Germer prize, the IEEE Centennial Medal, the IEEE Medal of Honor, the Rabi prize, the Rumford premium, the Compton medal, the Oersted Medal, and the National Medal of Science.

After his retirement from Harvard, Ramsey continued to receive recognition and honors for his contributions to physics and science. In 1995 he was selected by the National Science Board to receive the Vannevar Bush Award. That same year the country of Guyana issued a stamp in his honor. Ramsey actively supported the advancement of scientific research. He was one of sixty Nobel Prize winners signing a letter sent to President Clinton and Congress, on June 19, 1996, asking for increased federal funding to support university-based research.

Further Reading

Information on his work can be found in Norman F. Ramsey, "The Method of Successive Oscillatory Fields," *Physics Today* (July 1980). There is a biography of Ramsey in Volume I of the *McGraw-Hill Modern Men of Science and Engineering* (1980). Additional information on his work can be found in John S. Rigden, *Rabi: Scientist and Citizen* (1987). Press releases on Ramsey have been issued by the National Science Foundation. □

Petrus Ramus

The French humanist logician and mathematician Petrus Ramus (1515-1572) founded the anti-Aristotelian philosophical school of Ramism.

Petrus Ramus was born Pierre de La Ramée in the village of Cuth in Picardy. He worked and studied at the College of Navarre at Paris until he took his master of arts degree in 1536, having defended his thesis that "everything which Aristotle said is invented or contrived" ("quaecumque ab Aristotle dicta essent, commentitia esse"—the exact rendering in English of Ramus's dictum is still disputed, but the common translation of "commentitia" as "false" is now generally rejected). In 1543 he published his criticism of Aristotelian logic, called *Aristotelicae animadversiones*. This and further editions brought on Ramus the ire of his colleagues at the University of Paris, who accused him of heretical tendencies contrary to true religion and philosophy. Modern commentators do not see his departure from Aristotle as being as dramatic as his Parisian contemporaries did—his main differences with Aristotle are now considered to be more in pedagogical method than in logic. His case, however, was first taken before a civil magistrate, then before the Parlement of Paris, and eventually before Francis I, who in March 1544 issued a decree prohibiting Ramus's works and preventing his teaching of philosophy. Ramus left Paris and turned to mathematical studies until the decree was rescinded in 1547 by Henry II.

Ramus was a brilliant lecturer and the prolific author of more than 50 works. His adoption of Protestantism in 1561 rekindled his colleagues' hostility toward him, and he fled from Paris again in 1562. He returned in the next year, when Charles IX was able to conclude a tenuous peace with the Protestants. Ramus reclaimed his chair of philosophy and continued teaching until the religious civil wars resumed in 1567. This began a period of flight from France during which he traveled extensively and lectured at various universities throughout Europe. In August 1570 he returned to France. For 2 more years he lectured and published, but on April 24, 1572, his opponents seized the opportunity of the St. Bartholomew's Day Massacre to murder Ramus.

Ramus was a considerable influence in the humanist development of anti-Aristotelian, antischolastic, antimedieval thinking; he was a major contributor to the "new philosophy" then challenging the assumptions of the Middle Ages. His influence was especially strong (according to their own testimony) among the English and Scottish Ramists (including John Milton and Sir William Temple), in the German universities (Johann Sturm and Johann Friege), and among the Puritans of New England. Nonetheless, the controversies which he aroused in the 16th century now seem merely tendentious.

Further Reading

A readable biography of Ramus is Frank Pierrepont Graves, *Peter Ramus and the Educational Reformation of the Sixteenth Century* (1912). Indispensable for a thorough study of Ramus are the works of Father Walter J. Ong, *Ramus: Method, and the*

Decay of Dialogue (1958) and *Ramus and Talon Inventory* (1958). Wilbur Samuel Howell, *Logic and Rhetoric in England, 1500-1700* (1956), contains helpful chapters on the English Ramists. For Ramus's influence in colonial times see Perry Miller, *The New England Mind: The Seventeenth Century* (1939). □

A. Philip Randolph

The American labor and civil rights leader A. Philip Randolph (1889-1979), considered the most prominent of all African American trade unionists, was one of the major figures in the struggle for civil rights.

The son of an itinerant minister of the African Methodist Episcopal Church, A. Philip Randolph was born in Crescent City, Florida, on April 15, 1889. He attended Cookman Institute in Jacksonville, Florida, after which he studied at the City College of New York. Following his marriage in 1914 to Lucille E. Green, he helped organize the Shakespearean Society in Harlem and played the roles of Hamlet, Othello, and Romeo, among others. At the age of 21 Randolph joined the Socialist party of Eugene V. Debs. In 1917 he and Chandler Owen founded the *Messenger,* a radical publication now regarded by scholars as among the most brilliantly edited ventures in African American journalism.

Out of his belief that the African American can never be politically free until he was economically secure, Randolph became the foremost advocate of the full integration of black workers into the American trade union movement. In 1925 he undertook the leadership of the campaign to organize the Brotherhood of Sleeping Car Porters (BSCP), which would become the first African American union in the country. The uphill battle for certification, marked by fierce resistance from the Pullman Company (who was then the largest employers of blacks in the country), was finally won in 1937 and made possible the first contract ever signed by a white employer with an African American labor leader. Later, Randolph served as president emeritus of the BSCP and a vice-president of the American Federation of Labor and Congress of Industrial Organizations.

In the 1940s Randolph developed the strategy of mass protest to win two significant Executive orders. In 1941, with the advent of World War II, he conceived the idea of a massive march on Washington to protest the exclusion of African American workers from jobs in the defense industries. He agreed to call off the march only after President Franklin Roosevelt issued Executive Order 8802, which banned discrimination in defense plants and established the nation's first Fair Employment Practice Committee. In 1948 Randolph warned President Harry Truman that if segregation in the armed forces was not abolished, masses of African Americans would refuse induction. Soon Executive Order 9981 was issued to comply with his demands.

In 1957 Randolph organized the Prayer Pilgrimage to Washington to support civil rights efforts in the South, and in 1957 and 1958 he organized a Youth March for Integrated Schools. In August 1963, Randolph organized the March on Washington, fighting for jobs and freedom. This was the site of Martin Luther King Jr.'s famed "I Have a Dream," speech, and a quarter million people came in support to the nation's capital. Randolph was called "the chief" by King. And in 1966, at the White House conference "To Fulfill These Rights," he proposed a 10-year program called a "Freedom Budget" which would eliminate poverty for all Americans regardless of race.

The story of Randolph's career reads like a history of the struggles for unionization and civil rights in this century. He lent his voice to each struggle and enhanced the development of democracy and equality in America. Randolph always said that his inspiration came from his father. "We never felt that we were inferior to any white boys. . ." Randolph said. "We were told constantly and continuously that ('you are as able,' 'you are as competent,' and 'you have as much intellectuality as any individual.')" Randolph died on May 16, 1979.

However, Randolph's message lived on. Seventeen years after his death, Randolph's civil rights leadership and labor activism became the subject of a 1996 PBS documentary, *A. Philip Randolph: For Jobs and Freedom* . The tribute that took him from "obscurity" to a force that "moved presidents," was presented in conjunction with Black History Month, in February, telling his story through reenactments, film footage and photos.

Included were powerful images of the quest, including the formation of the National Association for the Promotion of Labor Unionism Among Negroes in 1919 and the 12-year battle to organize porters in spite of the Pullman Company's use of spies and firings to thwart it.

Throughout his years as a labor and civil rights leader, Randolph rocked the foundations of racial segregation, pressuring presidents and corporations alike to recognize the need to remedy the injustices heaped on African Americans. Embracing a nonviolent, forward looking activism, Randolph will be remembered as both a "radical subversive" and "Saint Philip."

Further Reading

There are two biographies available on Randolph. Jervis Anderson's *A. Philip Randolph: A Biographical Portrait* (1986) and Sally Hanley's *A. Philip Randolph* (1989), as well as Taylor Branch's *Parting the Waters: America in the King Years, 1954-1963* (1988) will provide good insight. There were two useful sites available through the internet. A guest editorial on Randolph's work was accessed at http://www.ai.mit.edu/people/ellens/ NCRA/randolph.html (July 29, 1997). Information on the aforementioned PBS special can be accessed at http://www2.pbs.org/weta/apr/aprprogram.html (July 29, 1997). His career and life were discussed in numerous books on African Americans and the labor movement. Among the older studies are Sterling D. Spero and Abram L. Harris, *The Black Worker* (1931); Bruce Minton and John Stuart, *Men Who Lead Labor* (1937); and Edwin R. Embree, *13 against the Odds* (1944). More recent studies are Saunders J. Redding, *The Lonesome Road: The Story of the Negro's Part in America* (1958); Herbert Garfinkel, *When Negroes March* (1959); Arna W. Bontemps, *100 Years of Negro Freedom* (1961); Russell L. Adams, *Great Negroes: Past and Present* (1963; 3d ed. 1969); and Roy Cook, *Leaders of Labor* (1966). □

Edmund Randolph

Edmund Randolph (1753-1813), American statesman and lawyer, was an exceedingly influential public figure from 1780 to 1800.

Edmund Randolph's father, of a family long prominent in Virginia, was king's attorney and returned to England before the American Revolution. Edmund, however, graduated from the College of William and Mary, and influenced by his uncle Peyton who was a firm patriot, broke with his father. In August 1775 he joined George Washington's army. When Peyton Randolph (president of the first Continental Congress) died a few months later, Edmund returned to Virginia. He served in the Virginia Convention of 1776, was mayor of Williamsburg, and was attorney general of Virginia before his twenty-fifth birthday. His marriage in 1776 to Elizabeth Nicholas, daughter of Robert Nicholas, consolidated his position in Virginia's public life.

In 1781 Randolph began serving as a delegate to the Continental Congress. There and in the Virginia Legislature he worked with James Madison to strengthen the union of the states. At the same time Randolph became one of Virginia's leading attorneys, distinguished for his learning and oratory. He was elected governor of Virginia in 1786.

Randolph's national service resumed in 1786 at the Annapolis Convention, and in 1787 he became a Virginia delegate to the Federal Constitutional Convention. Though not as thorough a nationalist as Washington or Madison, Randolph presented Madison's centralizing Virginia Plan to the Convention. He impressed the Convention with his "most harmonious voice, fine person, and striking manners," as well as with his keen sense of the dangers of tyranny. But his reservations about "energetic government," a concern for the special interests of Virginia, and a kind of indecisiveness caused him to refuse to sign the Constitution. Responding to Madison's tactful persuasion, though, he finally came out for the Constitution and played a key role at Virginia's ratifying convention.

Appointed attorney general of the United States (1789), Randolph soon became Washington's mediator in the bitter quarrels between Alexander Hamilton and Thomas Jefferson. As secretary of state (1794), he sought to maintain friendly relations with both England and France. He approved Jay's Treaty with England as well as the contradictory mission of James Monroe to conciliate republican France. Though he earned Washington's respect and gratitude, Jefferson declared him "a perfect chameleon," while Timothy Pickering aroused Washington's anger by alleging Randolph's subservience to France. Humiliated, Randolph resigned and wrote a *Vindication* of his conduct.

Randolph resumed his large law practice. In 1807 he was senior counsel for Aaron Burr in his treason trial. Randolph's health failed, however, and after writing a valuable manuscript history of the Revolution in Virginia, he died on Sept. 12, 1813.

Further Reading

The biography of Randolph by John J. Reardon, in progress, should become the standard work. Samuel F. Bemis, *Jay's Treaty: A Study in Commerce and Diplomacy* (1923; rev. ed. 1962), covers Randolph's career as secretary of state.

Additional Sources

Reardon, John J. *Edmund Randolph; a biograp,* New York, Macmillan 1975, 1974. □

John Randolph

John Randolph (1773-1833), half-mad, half-genius American statesman, foreshadowed John C. Calhoun, who developed Randolph's states'-rights premises into a political philosophy.

Scion of a great Virginia family, John Randolph was born on June 2, 1773, at his grandfather's plantation in Prince George County. Through his stepfather, St. George Tucker, he was indoctrinated with a worldly wisdom beyond his years. Before he was 12 he had read widely in Shakespeare and the Greek and Roman classics. His formal education was at Columbia and Princeton, and he read law in the office of his uncle, Edmund Randolph. As a schoolboy, he witnessed the inauguration of George Washington and early sessions of the first Congress, thus igniting his interest in politics.

At the age of 25, after a "great debate" with Patrick Henry, Randolph entered the U.S. House of Representatives. His genius was soon recognized. As floor leader for his cousin Thomas Jefferson and as chairman of the Ways and Means Committee, he cracked the whip over the House members. But his eccentricities soon caught up with him. He badly muffed the impeachment trial of Judge Samuel Chase (1804), and he disqualified himself as foreman of the Aaron Burr conspiracy trial (1807) because of his long-cherished prejudices against Burr.

Randolph broke openly with Jefferson in 1806 over the attempted Florida purchase, demanding a return to the principles of 1798 and emerging as founder of the first of America's "third" political parties, the Quids. Randolph was defeated for reelection in 1813 because of his opposition to the War of 1812. He served again in the House in 1815-1817, 1819-1825, and 1827-1829, and he also served a single term as U.S. senator from 1825 to 1827. During this time he was often ill and suffered from mental disorder.

Randolph's well-known opposition to the Missouri Compromise of 1820-1821 (though he hated slavery, he disapproved of interference with that institution), his fear of forced emancipation, and his brilliant defense of states' rights stirred the somber intellect of John C. Calhoun. Randolph was a delegate to the Virginia Convention of 1829-1830 and fiercely opposed any constitutional change. For a few months in 1830 he served as minister to Russia. He broke bitterly with Andrew Jackson over the nullification crisis of 1832 and wished that he could have his dying body strapped to his horse, Radical, and ride to the defense of South Carolina. On May 24, 1833, he died in Philadelphia.

Further Reading

The most comprehensive work on Randolph is William Cabell Bruce, *John Randolph of Roanoke* (2 vols., 1922). A good, brief biography is Gerald W. Johnson, *Randolph of Roanoke: A Political Fantastic* (1929), written in a popular style. Russell Kirk, *Randolph of Roanoke: A Study in Conservative Thought* (1951), a conservative view, is concerned primarily with Randolph's political principles. The 1964 edition of Kirk's work, *John Randolph of Roanoke: A Study in American Politics,* adds over 200 pages of letters and speeches by Randolph and an extensive bibliography.

Additional Sources

Adams, Henry. *John Randolph: a biography,* Armonk, N.Y.: M.E. Sharpe, 1996.

Dawidoff, Robert. *The education of John Randolph,* New York: Norton, 1979.

Kirk, Russell. *John Randolph of Roanoke: a study in American politics, with selected speeches and letters,* Indianapolis: Liberty Press, 1978. □

Charles B. Rangel

Charles B. Rangel (born 1930) was a Democratic member of the U.S. House of Representatives from New York City for more than 15 years. His major concern was the effects of narcotics on people and society.

Charles B. Rangel was born June 11, 1930, in Harlem in New York City. In 1948 he dropped out of high school to join the army. He was soon sent to Korea, where he received both a Purple Heart for being injured and a Bronze Star for bravery. The wounded Rangel led 40 of his comrades for three days behind enemy lines rather than surrender.

After his discharge from the army in 1952 Rangel worked in New York's garment district while completing high school. After receiving his diploma in 1953 he enrolled in New York University and graduated with a degree in accounting in 1957. In 1960 he received a law degree from St. John's University Law School and was soon admitted to the New York State Bar. From 1961 to 1962 Rangel served the southern district of New York as an assistant U.S. attorney.

Rangel was more interested in politics than in prosecuting criminals, and in 1966 he was elected to the first of two terms in the New York State Assembly. As an assemblyman Rangel was deeply concerned about the people in his district, which included Harlem. He walked the streets and talked with the people he represented. Rangel concluded that narcotics which threatened the stability and lives of thousands of youth were the major problem confronting his constituents, contending that "the country should treat this as a threat to national security. I don't think we should do anything less than we should do if missiles were pointed at our country." Rangel also advocated legalized gambling. He claimed that "for the average Harlemite, playing numbers . . . is moral and a way of life."

In 1970 Rangel sought the 19th district congressional seat held by Adam Clayton Powell. Rangel defeated the once powerful congressman in a close Democratic primary race. He did so with the endorsement of the Republican Party, and in the general election he defeated candidates representing the Liberal, Conservative, Communist, and Socialist Workers parties. As a congressman, Rangel continued his attack on the narcotics problem. He believed drugs to be the curse of the African American community and responsible for much of the crime there. In 1971 he attacked police corruption in New York City, accusing officers of drug trafficking. He also charged the U.S. State Department with "being involved in a conspiracy" with the French and Turkish governments which grew and processed narcotics "for the purpose of illegally importing" them into the United States. Later that year, President Richard Nixon telephoned Rangel to inform him that Turkey had agreed to end its production of opium poppies within a year.

Charles Rangel (speaking into microphones)

Rangel concentrated most of his energy on the drug problem. Education, housing, and health were all affected by drugs, he argued, and he proposed that economic aid to foreign countries who refused to act against the illegal drug traffic be ended. He was also influential in getting such a law passed. Rangel later chaired the House Select Committee on Narcotics Abuse and Control which examined the problems of drug abuse and trafficking.

With his appointment as deputy whip to the Democratic Steering and Policy Committee in 1983, Rangel joined the inner sanctum of the House Democratic leadership. He was appointed in 1974 as the first African American to serve on powerful Ways and Means committee. He also chaired the Subcommittee on Oversight and Investigations. As an influential member of the Ways and Means committee, he was instrumental in getting before the Congress the concept of economic aid for beleaguered cities in the from of "Enterprise Zones," a combination of grants and tax breaks for businesses that invest in inner cities. The concept was put into law in 1993.

In his many years of winning reelection as a U.S. representative, Rangel has become an influential and highly respected member of Congress. He is considered by some of his colleagues to be one of the most liberal members of the House. He is also the New York representative with the broadest power base. Although his power and influence increased in the nation's capitol, Rangel maintained close ties with his constituents. He regularly attends meetings on community problems with state legislators and city councilmen from his district. He ran on all three party lines in New York and attended the annual political dinners of the Democratic, Republican, and Liberal parties. In the congressman's Washington office hangs a portrait of Adam Clayton Powell as "a reminder of what can happen in Washington." Elected for his fourteenth term in 1996, he became the ranking Democrat on the Ways and Means committee. Rangel's ambition to be speaker of the U.S. House of Representatives might someday become a reality.

Further Reading

For additional information on Rangel's House career and voting patterns see the bi-annual editions of Barone, Ujifusa, and Matthews, *The Almanac of American Politics.* See also editions of Allen Ehrenhalt, *Politics in America.* □

Ranjit Singh

Ranjit Singh (1780-1839) was a ruler of the Punjab. His kingdom was so powerful that friendship with this "Lion of the Punjab" remained for 3 decades the sheet anchor of British policy in western India.

Ranjit Singh was heir to the Sukerchakia *misl,* one of the 12 *misls* which had been established by the warlike Sikhs during the 18th century and which ruled the greater part of the Punjab. Ranjit came into his own after the death of his widowed, dominating mother in 1796. Almost immediately he gathered a force of 10,000 to 12,000 horsemen.

At this time the Afghan king, Zaman Shah, was campaigning in the Punjab. The Afghans occupied but soon lost Lahore, traditionally the capital of a unified Punjab. Apparently acting in Zaman Shah's name but actually for himself, Ranjit captured Lahore in 1799. Soon he subjugated Jammu and Kasur, won the friendship of the strong Ahluwalia *misl,* the important Kanheya *misl* being already linked with him by marriage, and started on a career of expansion which by 1810 made him the supreme ruler of the Punjab north of the Sutlej.

To the south, Ranjit was checked by a treaty of mutual noninterference across the Sutlej with the British; the agreement, however, allowed Ranjit to consolidate his territories in the Punjab and systematically absorb Kashmir and much of the Punjab hills. In spite of fierce opposition from the Afghans, he also occupied areas beyond the Indus extending as far as the boundaries of Afghanistan proper, thus reversing a centuries-old pattern of military conquest in northwestern India.

Ranjit's success was primarily based on a large, loyal, well-drilled, excellently equipped, superbly led, and amazingly mobile standing army. He also pursued a wise civilian policy. He was genuinely motivated by the desire to unify the Sikhs in a Sikh state but one that would give equal participation and benefits to Sikhs and non-Sikhs. He gave his people a government under which living conditions improved noticeably. His dedication to the cause of good government won over most of the victims of his policy of absorption, and they served him loyally.

In his foreign policy, Ranjit was extremely cautious, never alienating a neighbor unless it involved certain improvement of his own position. Perhaps he practiced this policy to an excess, appeasing the English too long. Aware that war with the English was inevitable, he might have saved his kingdom from dissolving soon after his death had he risked a conflict.

Further Reading

Narendra Krishna Sinha, *Ranjit Singh* (Calcutta, 2d ed. 1945), and Khushwant Singh, *Ranjit Singh: Maharajah of the Punjab, 1780-1839* (1962), are the standard works on Ranjit. Older studies include William Godolphin Osborne, *The Court and Camp of Runjeet Sing* (1840), written by a contemporary of Ranjit, and Lepel Henry Griffin, *Ranjit Singh and the Sikh Barrier between Our Growing Empire and Central Asia* (1898). Extensive material on Ranjit is in Khushwant Singh, *A History of the Sikhs,* vol. 1 (1963). A succinct profile of Ranjit is in Ramesh Chandra Majumdar and others, *An Advanced History of India* (1946; 3d ed. 1967).

Additional Sources

Ahuja, Roshan Lal, *Maharaja Ranjit Singh, a man of destiny,* New Delhi: Punjabi Writers Coop. Society, 1983.

Duggal, Kartar Singh, *Ranjit Singh, a secular Sikh sovereign,* New Delhi, India: Abhinav Publications, 1989.

Hasrat, Bikrama Jit, *Life and times of Ranjit Singh: a saga of benevolent despotism,* Nabha: Hasrat; Hoshiarpur: local stockists, V. V. Research Institute Book Agency, 1977.

Khullar, K. K., *Maharaja Ranjit Singh,* New Delhi: Hem Publishers, 1980.

Kirapala Singha, *The historical study of Maharaja Ranjit Singh's times,* Delhi: National Book Shop, 1994.

Maharaja Ranjit Singh and his times, Amritsar: Dept. of History, Guru Nanak Dev University, 1980.

Singh, Gulcharan., *Ranjit Singh and his generals,* Jullundur: Sujlana Publishers, pref. 1976.

Singh, Harbans, *Maharaja Ranjit Singh,* New Delhi: Sterling, 1980. □

Otto Rank

The Austrian psychotherapist Otto Rank (1884-1939) taught and practiced a form of psychotherapy based upon his own trauma-of-birth theory and will therapy.

Otto Rank was born in Vienna on April 22, 1884, into a disintegrating lower-middle-class Jewish family. His father is said to have been indifferent to the family and to have drunk. As a child, Otto found solace in the music of Richard Wagner. For intellectual nourishment he read Henrik Ibsen, Arthur Schopenhauer, and Friedrich Nietzsche. Then he discovered the early works of Sigmund Freud. They were a revelation.

When Rank was 21 he met Freud, who persuaded him to attend the gymnasium and the University of Vienna and to study psychoanalysis. Freud read a manuscript which Rank had written; with the help of Freud's criticism, Rank rewrote it. The book, *Der Künstler* (1907; *The Artist*), was well received. He followed it with *Der Mythus der Geburt des Heldens* (1909; *The Myth of the Birth of the Hero*), a work strongly influenced by Freud. In *Das Inzest-Motiv in Dichtung und Sage* (1912; *The Incest Motive in Poetry and Legend*) Rank identified many motifs from myth and poetry with the Oedipus complex.

Rank saw service during World War I. The war transformed him from a shy over deferential person to "a wiry tough man with a masterful air." He became friends with Sándor Ferenczi, and together they published *Entwicklungsziele der Psychoanalyse* (1924; *The Development of Psychoanalysis*). In *Das Trauma der Geburt* (1924; *The Trauma of Birth*) Rank maintained that all anxiety, hence neurosis, came as a result of the infant's first shock at being separated from the mother. Freud was at first impressed by this new idea of his favorite disciple, but he later cooled considerably. One report states that Freud himself had planted this new idea in the head of Rank in the first place.

In 1924 Rank tore himself away from Freud and went to America. Because Freud represented a father image, Rank suffered fear, conflict, and illness at being separated from him. By 1926 he was recognized by some Americans as a psychoanalytic leader. His therapy (which he called psychotherapy rather than psychoanalysis) consisted mainly in having the patient reexperience the birth trauma, the psychological consequences of the separation of the child from the mother's womb. This trauma had in turn caused "separation anxiety," hence neurosis. Many if not all human activities, from thumb-sucking to lovemaking, were, as interpreted by Rank, substitutions for the original pleasures of existence in the mother's womb.

Between 1924 and 1936 Rank traveled extensively between New York and Paris for teaching and practicing psychotherapy. In 1936 he settled in New York City, where he had some influence among social workers. His influence was especially strong in Philadelphia, where at the Pennsylvania School of Social Work his methods were adopted to a large extent. Rank favored a short analysis which could take weeks or months instead of years.

Later in life Rank came to a realization that knowledge is not fundamentally curative. "It is illusions that cure," he contended, "but first of all the patient must learn to get along at all—to live; and to do this he must have illusions." Psychotherapy, far from removing illusions, should help the patient to sustain them.

Rank died in New York City on Oct. 31, 1939, five weeks after Freud had passed away in London.

Further Reading

A study of Rank's life is Jessie Taft, *Otto Rank: A Biographical Study Based on Notebooks, Letters, Collected Writings, Therapeutic Achievements and Personal Associations* (1958). Fay Berger Karpf, *The Psychology and Psychotherapy of Otto Rank* (1953), presents a three-part view of Rank: one section is devoted to his life and role in the psychoanalytic movement, one to the influences on his thought and work, and another to the essentials of his psychotherapy. An exposition of Rank's will therapy is the chapter "Rank's Will Psychology" in Lovell Langstroth, *Structure of the Ego* (1955).

Additional Sources

Lieberman, E. James, *Acts of will: the life and work of Otto Rank: with a new preface,* Amherst: University of Massachusetts Press, 1993.

Menaker, Esther, *Otto Rank, a rediscovered legacy,* New York: Columbia University Press, 1982. □

Leopold von Ranke

Leopold von Ranke (1795-1886) was a German historian and one of the most prolific and universal modern historians of his time. He imparted his expertise and methodology through the introduction of the seminar as an informal but intensive teaching device.

eopold von Ranke was born on Dec. 21, 1795, in the rural Thuringian town of Wiehe, which then belonged to electoral Saxony. Although Ranke was born into the era of the French Revolution, his bourgeois, small-town, generally well-ordered, and peaceful background and upbringing did not provide much contact with the violent events of the times. After receiving his early education at local schools in Donndorf and Pforta, he attended the University of Leipzig (1814-1818), where he continued his studies in ancient philology and theology.

In the fall of 1818 Ranke accepted a teaching position at the gymnasium (high school) in Frankfurt an der Oder. His teaching assignments in world history and ancient literature, for which he disdained the use of handbooks and readily available prepared texts, as well as the contemporary events of the period, led him to turn to original sources and to a concern for the empirical understanding of history in its totality.

Making use of materials from the Westermannsche Library in Frankfurt and from the Royal Library in Berlin, Ranke produced his first work, *Geschichten der romanischen und germanischen Völker* (1824; *Histories of the Romanic and Germanic Peoples*), which earned him a professorial appointment at the University of Berlin in 1825, where he was to remain for the rest of his life except for extended research trips abroad.

Although this first work was still lacking in style, organization, and mastery of its overflowing detail, it had particular significance because it contained a technical appendix

in which Ranke established his program of critical scholarship—"to show what actually happened"—by analyzing the sources used, by determining their originality and likely veracity, and by evaluating in the same light the writings of previous historians "who appear to be the most celebrated" and who have been considered "the foundation of all the later works on the beginning of modern history." His scathing criticism of such historians led him to accept only contemporary documents, such as letters from ambassadors and others immediately involved in the course of historical events, as admissible primary evidence.

With Ranke's move to Berlin, the manuscripts of Venetian ministerial reports of the Reformation period became available to him and served as the basis for his second work, *Fürsten und Völker von Süd-Europa* (1827; *Princes and Peoples of Southern Europe*), which was republished in his complete works as *Die Osmanen und die spanische Monarchie im 16. und 17. Jahrhundert* (vols. 35 and 36; *The Ottomans and the Spanish Monarchy in the Sixteenth and Seventeenth Centuries*).

Travels and Research

The limited collection in Berlin whetted Ranke's appetite to investigate other European libraries and archives, especially those of Italy. Armed with a travel stipend from the Prussian government, he proceeded at first to Vienna, where a large part of the Venetian archives had been housed after the Austrian occupation of Venetia. A letter of introduction brought acquaintance with Friedrich von Gentz, who, through intercession with Prince Metternich, not only opened the Viennese archives to Ranke but also brought him into immediate contact with the day-to-day politics of the Hapsburg court. During his stay in Vienna he wrote *Die serbische Revolution* (1829), republished in an expanded version as *Serbien und die Türkei im 19. Jahrhundert* (1879; *Serbia and Turkey in the 19th Century*).

In 1828 Ranke traveled to Italy, where he spent 3 successful years of study visiting various public and private libraries and archives, although the Vatican Library remained closed to him. During this period he wrote a treatise, *Venice in the Sixteenth Century* (published 1878), and collected material for what is generally considered his masterpiece, *Die römischen Päpste, ihre Kirche und ihr Staat im 16. und 17. Jahrhundert* (1834-1836; *The Roman Popes, Their Church and State in the 16th and 17th Centuries*).

Returning from Italy in 1831, Ranke soon became involved in the publication of a journal designed to combat French liberal influence, which had alarmed the Prussian government in the aftermath of the revolutionary events of 1830. Although the *Historisch-Politische Zeitschrift*, with Ranke as editor and chief contributor, contained some of the best political thought published in Germany during this time, it lacked the polemical quality and anticipated success of a political fighting journal and was discontinued in 1836. In the same year Ranke was appointed full professor and devoted the rest of his life to the task of teaching and scholarly work. A Protestant counterpart to his *History of the Popes* was published as *Deutsche Geschichte im Zeitalter der Reformation* (1839-1847; *German History during the*

Era of the Reformation), which was largely based on the reports of the Imperial Diet in Frankfurt.

Last Works

With the following works Ranke rounded out his historical treatment of the major powers: *Neun Bücher preussischer Geschichte* (1847-1848; *Nine Books of Prussian History*); *Französische Geschichte, vornehmlich im 16. and 17. Jahrhundert* (1852-1861; *French History, Primarily in the 16th and 17th Centuries*); and *Englische Geschichte, vornehmlich im 16. und 17. Jahrhundert* (1859-1868; *English History, Primarily in the 16th and 17th Centuries*). Other works, dealing mainly with German and Prussian history during the 18th century, followed in the 1870s.

During the last years of his life Ranke, now in his 80s and because of failing sight requiring the services of readers and secretaries, embarked upon the composition of his *Weltgeschichte* (1883-1888; *World History*), published in nine volumes. The last two were published posthumously from manuscripts of his lectures. He died in Berlin on May 23, 1886.

The complete work of Ranke is difficult to assess. Not many of his works achieved the artistic high point of *The Roman Popes* or its appeal for the general reader. Yet there is hardly a chapter in his total enormous production which could be considered without value. His harmonious nature shunned emotion and violent passion, and he can be faulted less for what he wrote than for what he left unwritten. His approach to history emphasized the politics of the courts and of great men but neglected the common people and events of everyday life; he limited his investigation to the political history of the states in their universal setting. Ranke combined, as few others, the qualities of the trailblazing scholar and the devoted, conscientious, and innovative teacher.

Further Reading

Considerable biographical information is in T. H. Von Laue, *Leopold Ranke: The Formative Years* (1950). A comprehensive and fair study which emphasizes an evaluation of Ranke's major works and provides a useful bibliography is G. P. Gooch, *History and Historians in the Nineteenth Century* (1913; rev. ed. 1952); it also discusses Ranke's critics and pupils and provides a chapter on the Prussian school of historical scholarship that paralleled Ranke's career. An assessment critical of Ranke as historian appears in James W. Thompson, *A History of Historical Writing*, vol. 2 (1942). Historian Pieter Geyl discusses Ranke in his *Debates with Historians* (1955; rev. ed. 1958). Carlo Antoni, *From History to Sociology: The Transition in German Historical Thinking* (1940; trans. 1959), and Ferdinand Schevill, *Six Historians* (1956), contain chapters on Ranke. For general background see Georg G. Iggers, *The German Conception of History: The National Tradition of Historical Thought from Herder to the Present* (1968).

Additional Sources

Krieger, Leonard, *Ranke: the meaning of history,* Chicago: University of Chicago Press, 1977. □

Jeannette Pickering Rankin

Jeannette Pickering Rankin (1880-1973) was the first woman elected to the U.S. Congress. She served two terms, one beginning in 1917 and the other in 1941. A pacifist, she was the only congressperson to vote against both World War I and World War II. She was active in the women's suffrage movement and in peace movements throughout her life.

Jeannette Rankin was born on a ranch near Missoula, Montana Territory, on June 11, 1880. She was the eldest of seven children of Olive Pickering, an elementary school teacher, and John Rankin, a successful rancher and lumber merchant. An indifferent student, she graduated from the University of Montana in 1902 with a B.S., but spent the next eight years casting about for a satisfying vocation. She taught school briefly, apprenticed as a seamstress, learned furniture design, and became a social worker. To qualify herself for social work, she studied at the New York School of Philanthropy in 1908 and briefly practiced in Montana and Washington state. However, feeling suffocated by social work, she quit and enrolled in the University of Washington. While a student she became involved in the successful 1910 campaign for women's suffrage in Washington, which proved to be a decisive event in her life. She became a suffrage worker, which led directly to her career as a social reformer and peace advocate.

Returning to Missoula for Christmas, Rankin learned that a suffrage amendment was being introduced in the Montana legislature in the session beginning January 1911. She quickly organized the Equal Franchise Society, asked to address the legislature on suffrage, and became the first woman to speak before the Montana legislature. Although the amendment narrowly failed, Jeannette Rankin had been launched on a political career. The national suffrage leaders noticed her, and in the next five years she was constantly involved in suffrage efforts across the nation, especially after becoming a field secretary for the National American Woman Suffrage Association (NAWSA). She was the driving force in the victorious Montana campaign in 1914, and the experience helped her to decide to run for Congress in 1916.

First Woman Elected to Congress

Montana had two congressional seats elected at large. Rankin always maintained that this arrangement made possible what seemed impossible for a woman in 1916. In the Republican primary she captured one of the two places on the ticket, far outdistancing the seven men who ran. She carried the women's vote and seemed to be the second choice of everyone else. Running at large in the general election also favored her as she had become one of the best known figures in the state. She campaigned for national woman suffrage, prohibition, child welfare reform, tariff revision, and staying out of World War I in Europe. But before she could take her seat in Congress Germany resumed

unrestricted submarine warfare and Wilson decided to ask Congress for a declaration of war.

She took her seat in the House of Representatives on April 2, 1917, and four days later voted against war with Germany. Fifty-six other members of Congress also voted against war, but her vote spoke the loudest: she was the first woman in Congress. She had evolved a peace position during her suffrage days. The leadership of the woman suffrage movement, social work, and child welfare campaigns had many women, such as Jane Addams, who were pacifists, and they helped to shape Rankin's views. Ironically, most of her suffrage friends urged her to vote for war. Carrie Chapman Catt, head of NAWSA, feared that Rankin's vote would damage the suffrage cause by seeming to prove that women were sentimental and irresponsible.

Rankin saw herself as the women's representative, and she pressed the social feminist agenda of suffrage, equal pay, child welfare, protection of working women, birth control, infancy and maternity protection, and independent citizenship. (A 1907 law stripped citizenship from American women who married aliens.) Although she voted for a later declaration of war on Austria-Hungary and for war expenditures and Liberty Bonds, her first anti-war vote eroded her support in Montana. In addition, she sided with the miners in a bitter struggle with the Anaconda Copper Company in 1917. The company-dominated legislature then divided the state into separate congressional districts and gerrymandered Rankin's district so that it was overwhelmingly Democratic. Seeing little chance to retain her seat in the House of Representatives in 1918, she ran for the

Senate instead. Losing in the Republican primary, she then ran a hopeless race in the general election on a third party ticket. After leaving Congress she was a delegate with Jane Addams and other peace activists to the 1919 Women's International Conference for Permanent Peace. Out of this came the Women's International League for Peace and Freedom (WILPF), and Rankin was named vice-chairwoman of its executive committee.

Activist for Social Reform and Peace

After her duties abroad she returned to the United States to become a field secretary for the National Consumers' League (NCL) under the direction of Florence Kelley. As such, she lobbied in Washington, D.C., for many of the reform measures that she had introduced in Congress. In 1921 she helped to bring about the passage of the Maternity and Infancy Protection Act, a bill that she had first introduced in 1918. She saw independent citizenship approved in 1922, and she worked to get the Child Labor Amendment passed in 1924. That autumn she resigned from the Consumers' League position to aid her brother's unsuccessful bid for the Senate. She could not know it, but her greatest accomplishments had all been made and her greatest frustrations were yet to come. Her energies, which had encompassed the broad range of social feminist reform, increasingly narrowed to the peace movement.

Discouraged with the militarism of Montana, she made a second home in Georgia, which she naively thought would be more receptive and responsive to her peace crusade. She organized the Georgia Peace Society in 1928 and tried to make Georgia a center of the peace effort, but she was to be sorely disappointed. She became a field secretary for the WILPF, but resigned within a year over disagreements with the national staff.

In April 1929 she became a paid lobbyist of the Women's Peace Union, a group trying to get a constitutional amendment to outlaw war, but soon resigned because of disagreements with the leadership. The National Council for the Prevention of War (NCPW) immediately engaged her as a Washington lobbyist. She remained with the NCPW from 1929 to 1939, resigning finally out of exasperation with the NCPW chairman and in disagreement with its tactics. In the 1930s she worked for the anti-war amendment, fought Navy appropriations, lobbied for U.S. adherence to the World Court, supported the neutrality laws, and whole-heartedly embraced the "devil theory of war," the view that the United States had been dragged into World War I by the "merchants of death"—the bankers and munitions makers.

Adamant Against All Wars

By the mid-1930s the guns of war had begun in China, Africa, and Spain. Rankin could see no justification for the United States to intervene in foreign wars, and she came to believe that President Franklin Roosevelt was plotting involvement. She strongly supported the America First Committee, and her passion for peace blinded her to the character of the likes of Father Charles Coughlin because he, too, opposed involvement. As the world slid into war, she concluded that lobbying efforts were ineffective, so she returned to Montana and ran for Congress in 1940.

Despite having been absent from Montana's political scene for 15 years, she won as a Republican pledged to keep America out of the war. In Congress, she fought a losing battle against military appropriations, the draft, and the war itself. This time, she stood alone, casting the only vote against the declaration of war against Japan after Pearl Harbor. She was the only person to have voted against war in 1917 and 1941, and the second time she experienced almost universal condemnation. Her political career was finished. She came to believe that Roosevelt deliberately provoked the Japanese attack.

From 1942 to 1968 she disappeared from the public's view. She travelled and tended to family affairs, but she was so forgotten that most people did not know that she was still alive. A reprise came during the Vietnam War when the leaders of the Women's Strike for Peace asked her to head the procession in the Jeannette Rankin Brigade in their march on Washington. Nearly 88 years old, she marched at the head and presented the women's petitions to the House and Senate leadership. In the following years she took part in many peace demonstrations, and, having regained the public's attention, she advanced her ideas about peace, preferential presidential elections, a unicameral Congress, and representation-at-large. She died in her sleep on May 18, 1973, almost 93 years old.

Further Reading

An admiring, rather uncritical biography of Jeannette Rankin is Kevin S. Giles, *Flight of the Dove: The Story of Jeannette Rankin* (1980). Hannah Josephson knew Jeannette Rankin for over 20 years before publishing *Jeannette Rankin: First Lady in Congress* (1974). Also see: Hope Chamberlin, *A Minority of Members: Women in the U.S. Congress* (1973), *Notable American Women: The Modern Period* (1980), and an obituary in the *New York Times* on May 20, 1973. □

Prince Norodom Rannaridh

Prince Norodom Rannaridh (born 1944) became first prime minister of Cambodia in 1993. He came to the government along with his father, Prince Sihanouk, restored to rule after 23 years in exile.

Prince Norodom Rannaridh's career was as a politician, lawyer, professor, journalist, military commander, and aide and confidant of his father, Prince (onetime King) Norodom Sihanouk. Having received much of his advanced education abroad, and with Cambodia falling under the control of rival communist regimes during much of the 1970s and 1980s, Prince Norodom Rannaridh seemed at one point inclined to accept a comfortable life in exile. By the late 1980s, however, international efforts provided a settlement that gave a new formal position and legitimacy to Prince Norodom Sihanouk as head of Cambodia. As a result, Rannaridh himself was increasingly drawn

into work on his father's behalf, including leading the political and combat organizations of Sihanouk supporters, known as the ANS (Armée Nationale Sihanoukiste). During the 1980s the ANS was a 30,000 member armed faction operating in Cambodia. Diplomatic, political, and—eventually—military experience allowed Rannaridh to enter more and more into domestic Cambodian politics and its internal rivalries for power.

Prince Norodom Rannaridh was born on January 2, 1944, in the royal palace in Phnom Penh. He was the second child and the first son of Prince Norodom Sihanouk and of Sihanouk's first wife, Neak Moneang Phat Kanhol (died 1969). Rannaridh's formative years were spent at the Royal Khmer court in the turbulent years at the end and during the aftermath of World War II. In 1941 King Monivong, Rannaridh's grandfather, had died. France, which since the 1860s had progressively imposed colonial power upon Cambodia, chose Prince Norodom Sihanouk to succeed him. Although in the royal line, he was only 20 years old and without government experience. But Sihanouk did not prove malleable to French rule, scheming early on to restore Cambodia's independence and upsetting the delicate power balances at the Cambodian court.

A Royal Family Beset with Problems

Some deep ambivalances in life values helped shape Rannaridh's youth. During his early years Cambodia saw much political turbulence, as his father, King Sihanouk, under Japanese occupation power, proclaimed Cambodia to be an independent nation on March 13, 1945. Then, as bitter fighting raged in nearby Vietnam, Cambodian and Vietnamese communists began pressing for the overthrow of Sihanouk and for the establishment throughout Indochina of a "people's democracy." Not until July 1953 did the French agree to grant Cambodia full independence (along with the other Indochinese states, Vietnam and Laos).

Despite widening Cambodian desire for complete freedom from French colonialism, the atmosphere in Rannaridh's family and at the Phnom Penh court remained heavily "Frenchified." Royal family members, like Cambodia's upper classes, more readily spoke French among themselves than the Cambodian language of Khmer. Their tastes and lifestyles generally mirrored those of the top classes of French society. There was no question that Rannaridh would further his education in France. Then too, Rannaridh was brought up in the opulent traditional Cambodian royal style and the almost religious veneration for the monarchy felt among the mass of Cambodians even today. This was a sharp paradox with the change in political atmosphere in Cambodia brought first by the Japanese occupation during World War II and subsequently by radical Cambodian and Vietnamese nationalists and communists as they battled to expel first the French and then the Americans from Indochina.

Rannaridh had a superb master of politics in the figure of his own father, who could seem ambivalent even toward the Cambodian communists. Sihanouk abdicated as king on March 1, 1955, and still, as Samdech (prince), retained his royal aura and influence among the mass of his countrymen.

As the neighboring Vietnamese war grew in intensity, Rannaridh plunged into the highly politicized print media of Cambodia, eventually becoming editor of the principal French-language daily in Phnom Penh, *Le Courier Khmer,* in 1967. The paper was the voice of the pro-Sihanouk Cambodian upper strata, nationalist but not radical, and distrustful of Vietnamese ambitions. There also was political training. In the middle 1950s when Cambodian reformers had begun calling for a more democratic government in which the king would be a constitutional monarch, Sihanouk had formed his own political party, the Sangkum. Rannaridh rose to a leadership position in the party. Rannaridh also was drawn to the good life, but his royal status protected him from scandal.

Rannaridh Leaves a Troubled Country

In the turbulent 1960s, as the struggle in Vietnam became ever more intense and Americanized, Rannaridh went as his father's personal representative to neighboring Southeast Asian countries (1967-1968). His concern was that the United States might enlarge its military operations and encroach further on Cambodia (quite justified, as it turned out). Sihanouk also feared that a coup by anti-communist, American-supported, Cambodian military would topple him from power. In the midst of these controversies, Rannaridh was appointed a delegate of the Cambodian mission to the United Nations General Assembly (1968-1969). This was to be his last excursion into affairs of state for a while.

Cambodia was now gradually unraveling. Sihanouk was beginning to lose the confidence of Cambodia's upper strata, the bureaucracy, and the educated. While he was temporarily out of the country (1967-1968), local Cambodian military attempted to crush peasant rebellions with great severity, producing renewed resistance. Rannaridh now moved in new directions. On September 14, 1968, he married Eng Marie, a member of an old aristocratic Cambodian family. She was an accomplished musician. They had three children, Prince Norodom Chakravuth (born 1970), Prince Norodom Sihariddh (born 1972), and Princess Norodom Rattana Devi (born 1974).

In January 1969 he began his studies for a doctorate of law at the University of Aix-en-Provence in France. It was a timely decision. On March 18, 1970, King Norodom Sihanouk was declared deposed in a coup d'état led by General Lon Nol, former prime minister. The coup was supported by senior Cambodian military commanders as well as by the United States.

As Sihanouk in exile embarked on creating a united front and a "royal government of national unity" in opposition to the new Lon Nol regime, Rannaridh seemed to withdraw from political life. He concentrated on maritime law and toyed with the idea of pursuing a maritime insurance career in France. Meanwhile, the war in Cambodia intensified, including U.S. bombing raids, giving added strength to the appeals for peace and freedom by Cambodian communist guerrillas known as the Khmer Rouge and their leader, Pol Pot (Saloth Sar). After the United States and the North Vietnamese signed the Paris Peace Accords on January 27, 1973, ending further American military involvement in the war, it was but a matter of time before the Khmer Rouge, aided by the Vietnamese, established their "democratic" government in Phnom Penh.

During the later 1970s a harrowing nightmare descended on Cambodia as first the blood-soaked Khmer Rouge regime (1975-1978) cost more than a million Cambodian lives through executions and mistreatment; and then a Vietnamese invasion (December 25, 1978) established a new communist, but Hanoi-dominated, People's Republic of Kampuchea (PRK). Most members of Rannaridh's family, including his father, Norodom Sihanouk, had escaped abroad. Rannaridh lost an uncle and three cousins during the blood-soaked Khmer Rouge regime.

Rannaridh Becomes Involved

As his father sought to restore his own government, Rannaridh seemed initially to turn to the life of the scholar. In 1974 he had acquired his doctorate in law and by 1979 he was a full professor of law at the University of Aix-en-Provence. Most of the Cambodians in France came from the better educated and higher social strata in Cambodian society. Some of them came to see Rannaridh as a younger, less mercurial, and more trustworthy leader than his father. Rannaridh also began to make contacts with the various pro-Sihanoukist resistance groups in Cambodia. Among these was the National Liberation of Kampuchea, known by its French acronym as Moulinaka.

By the early 1980s Rannaridh's scholarly career was shelved. He traveled to Bangkok and by mid-1983 had become his father's official representative in Thailand, a center of anti-communist Cambodian resistance groups. In 1981 Moulinaka merged with other pro-Sihanoukist factions into a broad-based, well-financed, and well-organized opposition, headquartered in Bangkok and called the National United Front for an Independent, Neutral, Peaceful and Cooperative Cambodia (FUNCINPEC). After serving on its executive committee for two years under his father's overall direction, Rannaridh in mid-1985 became secretary general of FUNCINPEC.

The struggle for power in Cambodia, meanwhile, increasingly turned to low-key civil war. As other Cambodian factions, including the Khmer Rouge and the government of the People's Republic of Kampuchea, maintained their own armed organizations, FUNCINPEC spawned a 15,000-member army of its own, the earlier-mentioned *Armée Nationale Sihanoukiste* (ANS). At the beginning of 1986 Rannaridh assumed the title of commander-in-chief and chief of staff of the ANS, although actual military tactics and planning was left to his subordinates. He was preoccupied with preparing for the time when the Sihanoukists might participate in United Nations supervised elections in Cambodia.

The prospect of such elections was becoming ever more likely toward the close of the 1980s. Finally, in Paris on October 23, 1991, as the last Vietnamese troops had already withdrawn three months earlier, a Cambodian Peace Agreement was signed by the principal Cambodian factions and with the approval of the U.N. Security Council.

The agreement called for a United Nations Temporary Administration in Cambodia (UNTAC) to control a cease-fire among the warring Cambodian factions and to ensure the holding of free and fair elections in Cambodia. The agreement also established a Supreme National Council (SNC) composed of representatives of all the warring Cambodian factions to be the official representative body of the Cambodian people during the transition period. Rannaridh was appointed a member of the SNC, which was headed by his father, Norodom Sihanouk, as head of state.

The United Nations Lends a Hand

Not until March 1992 did U.N. troops and support groups (eventually numbering nearly 16,000) arrive in Cambodia. During the next year and a half there were numerous outbursts of violence. Nevertheless, from May 23 to 28, 1993, as scheduled, some four million Cambodians went to the polls in a general election widely considered to have been free and fair. FUNCINPEC, led by Rannaridh, won a plurality, 58 of the 120 seats at stake in the new National Assembly, entitling the Sihanoukists to shape most of the government. The now defunct PRK government, led by its premier Hun Sen, won 51 seats, with a small third party winning most of the rest.

The Khmer Rouge, which had boycotted the elections, won no seats but said they would support Sihanouk as head of state. Within days the new National Assembly had granted Sihanouk broad powers as head of state (the title of king was studiously avoided). On June 14, 1993, the assembly accepted Rannaridh as first prime minister and Hun Sen as second prime minister. Most of the cabinet consisted of FUNCINPEC or CPP stalwarts (Rannaridh's younger brother, Norodom Siriwudh, was named foreign affairs minister). On September 21, 1993, the Constituent Assembly adopted a constitution creating a parliamentary monarchy, and Sihanouk was enthroned as king for the second time.

Things Fall Apart

The uneasy partnership between Rannaridh and Hun Sen began to unravel in 1996 as preparations began for national elections scheduled for 1998. The two prime ministers met less and less often and their parties attacked each other in the press. The Khmer Rouge, which had remained an armed opposition in remote parts of the country, split, with more moderate splinter groups announcing alignment with one party or the other. Each party courted the various Khmer Rouge leadership factions. In June 1997 came the surprising announcement that Pol Pot, the notorious hardliner who had led the Khmer Rouge for decades, had been deposed and taken in custody by other Khmer Rouge leaders.

Hun Sen brought the dual leadership to an end in July 1997 by sending troops against FUNCINPEC facilities and arresting key leaders. He accused Rannaridh of various crimes, most significantly, illegally negotiating with the Khmer Rouge. Rannaridh himself had been alerted and had left the country the day before the coup.

Further Reading

There is no published full-length biography of Norodom Rannaridh, but a useful summary of all the important events in the lives of the members of the royal Cambodian family, including Rannaridh, can be found in Justin J. Corfield, *The Royal Family of Cambodia* (Melbourne, Australia, 1990). A comprehensive survey of Cambodian history and politics, along with general information on the country and an extensive bibliography, is provided by Russell R. Ross, ed., *Cambodia. A Country Study* (1990). Other historical-political background accounts are: David P. Chandler, *The Tragedy of Cambodian History* (1991); Craig Etcheson, *The Rise and Demise of Democratic Kampuchea* (1984); Ben Kiernan, *Genocide and Democracy in Cambodia* (1993); and Justus M. van der Kroef, "Paths to a Solution in Cambodia: Problems and Prospects," *Asian Thought and Society. An International Review* (October-December 1991). For Rannaridh's own political outlook see his interview by Barbara Crosette in *The New York Times* (January 3, 1987) and in *Newsweek,* byline by Ron Moreau (June 14, 1993). Cambodian events, including Rannaridh's views and decisions, are reported regularly in the weekly *Far Eastern Economic Review* (Hong Kong; see especially its issues of June 3, 1993, and December 9, 1993). □

John Crowe Ransom

John Crowe Ransom (1888-1974), American poet, critic, and agrarian champion, was the center of the "Fugitive" group, of the Southern Agrarians, and of the New Critics.

John Crowe Ransom was born in Pulaski, Tennessee., on April 30, 1888. He received his bachelor of arts degree from Vanderbilt University in 1909. He was appointed a Rhodes scholar and was in residence at Christ Church, Oxford, from 1910 to 1913, earning a bachelor of arts degree. From 1914 to 1937 he was a member of the faculty at Vanderbilt, except for the World War I years, when he was a first lieutenant in the U.S. Army. In 1920 he married Robb Reavell; the couple had three children.

Vanderbilt and the Fugitives

As a young instructor at Vanderbilt, Ransom assembled a group of poets, calling themselves "Fugitives"; he created and edited the magazine for their expression, the *Fugitive.* They opposed both the traditional sentimentality of Southern writing and the increased pace of life that emerged during the war years and the early 1920s. Ransom's own poetry eventually appeared in the volumes *Poems about God* (1919), *Chills and Fever* (1924), *Grace after Meat* (1924), *Two Gentlemen in Bonds* (1927), and *Selected Poems* (1945, 1963). Ransom was much influenced by the ballad poetry of the romantic revival, though he totally altered it by irony and wit. His best-known poems are "Bells for John Whiteside's Daughter," "Captain Carpenter," and "The Equilibrists." He won the Bollingen Prize in 1951 and the National Book Award for his poetry in 1964.

Whether considered poet or critic, Ransom brought much to both fields through his teaching and writing. Ransom died on July 3, 1974 in Gambier, Ohio.

Further Reading

J. L. Stewart, *John Crowe Ransom* (1962), is the only study of the "whole man." Thomas Daniel Young, ed., *John Crowe Ransom: Critical Essays and a Bibliography* (1968), discusses Ransom as poet and critic. Ransom as poet is treated in Randall Jarrell, *Poetry and the Age* (1953). For information about the "Fugitives" see John M. Bradbury, *The Fugitives: A Critical Account* (1958), and Louise Cowan, *The Fugitive Group: A Literary History* (1959).

Additional Sources

Young, Thomas *John Ransom,* Steck, 1971.
Contemporary Authors: New Revision Series, Gale, Volume 34, 1991.
The New York Times, July 4, 1974.
National Review, August 2, 1974. □

Raphael

The Italian painter and architect Raphael (1483-1520) was the supreme representative of Italian High Renaissance classicism.

Raffaello Sanzio, called Raphael, was born on April 6, 1483, in Urbino. His father, Giovanni Santi, was a painter and doubtless taught Raphael the rudiments of technique. Santi died when his son was 11 years old. Raphael's movements before 1500, when he joined the workshop of Perugino, are obscure, but he evidently fully absorbed the 15th-century classicism of Piero della Francesca's paintings and of the architecture of the Ducal Palace at Urbino and the humanist tradition of the court.

During his 4 years with Perugino, Raphael's eclectic disposition and remarkable ability to assimilate and adapt borrowed ideas within a very personal style were already apparent. Many works of this period, such as the *Mond Crucifixion* (1502/1503), are in stylistic detail almost indistinguishable from Perugino's gentle sweetness, but they have an inherent clarity and harmony lacking in Perugino's work. Raphael's last painting before moving to Florence, the *Marriage of the Virgin* (1504), is primarily modeled on Perugino's version of the same subject, but the compositional design is reinterpreted with greater spatial sensitivity, the figures are more accurately built, and the dramatic significance is transmitted without the artificiality of pose and gesture of the prototype.

Florentine Period

When Raphael arrived in Florence late in 1504, it must have been evident to him that his Peruginesque style was dated and provincial compared with the recent innovations of Michelangelo and Leonardo da Vinci. It was to the latter's work that he was temperamentally more attracted, and

With the beginning of the Great Depression, Ransom joined the intellectual group of southerners, centered on Vanderbilt, who felt that the South could escape the ills of the times by rejecting the technology and financial complexities "imposed" by the North and by returning to antebellum agrarianism. Their views found expression in two symposia, *I'll Take My Stand* (1930) and *Who Owns America?* (1936).

The Kenyon Years

In 1937 Ransom became Carnegie professor of poetry at Kenyon College and there founded the *Kenyon Review,* which he edited until his retirement in 1958. He also founded the unit at Kenyon that became the Summer School of Letters at Indiana University. Ransom's leaving Nashville symbolized his achievement of a larger position in American literature. From the 1920s Ransom had mixed in the healthy discussions of criticism going on in the magazines, solidifying his position in *God without Thunder* (1930), *The World's Body* (1938), and *The New Criticism* (1941). He is given credit for applying the term "New Criticism" to the dedicated search for the intrinsic in poetry. In defining "New Criticism," Ransom and his fellow proponents contrasted their theory with romanticism's commitment to self expression and naturalism's deduction from fact as a basis of evaluating art. Instead, the New Critics looked upon art as an object in itself. They did not believe in outside influences such as the circumstances under which the art was created. Ransom's best-known essay on this subject is "Criticism as Pure Speculation," a lecture given at Princeton in 1940.

during the next 3 years he executed a series of Madonnas that adapted and elaborated compositions and ideas of Leonardo's, culminating in *La Belle jardinière* (1507). Here Raphael's own artistic personality was somewhat submerged in his fervent examination of the principles of Leonardesque design, modeling, and expressive depth. Raphael adopted Leonardo's *sfumato* modeling and characteristic pyramidal composition, yet the essential sense of clarity deriving from his 15th-century classical background was not undermined.

It was principally, however, Michelangelo's *Battle of Cascina* rather than Leonardo's companion piece, the *Battle of Anghiari,* that provided the dramatic ideas used by Raphael in his most ambitious Florentine work, the *Entombment* (1507). But perhaps unable yet to understand entirely the imaginative power of Michelangelo's works from which he borrowed, Raphael here failed to combine the figures, expressions, and emotions with the unforced balance and harmony of his later narrative works.

Stanza della Segnatura

Raphael left for Rome in 1508 and seems to have been at work in the Vatican Stanze by early 1509. Pope Julius II's enlightened patronage stimulated the simultaneous creation of the two greatest High Renaissance fresco cycles: Michelangelo's Sistine Chapel ceiling and Raphael's Stanza della Segnatura. Whereas Michelangelo's frescoes are a masterpiece of titanic creative imagination, Raphael's are the epitome of classical grandeur and harmony, disciplined in

overall conception, artistic thought, and clarity of individual compositions and figures.

The theme of the Stanza della Segnatura (completed in 1511), eminently suited to Raphael's thoughtful humanism, is divinely inspired human intellect in four spheres: theology, poetry, philosophy, and law. The earliest of the principal scenes to be painted, the *Disputà* (representing Theology), shows Raphael still developing from his Florentine style in the light of the enormous challenge of the stanza: never before had he undertaken a decorative scheme on this scale. It is not until the so-called *School of Athens* (representing Philosophy), the zenith of pure High Renaissance culture, that Raphael reaches complete, independent artistic maturity.

The disposition of each figure in this great fresco is so precisely calculated as, paradoxically, to achieve the impression of absolute freedom. The ingenuity with which the grand, harmonious space is mapped out by the figures, emphasized by the superbly rich Bramantesque architecture behind, is concealed by the overall compositional balance and the monumentally calm atmosphere. The compositional lines and the distant arch focus attention on the two central figures, which set the tone of the painting in their expressive contrast: the idealist Plato points heavenward, while Aristotle, the realist, gestures flatly toward the ground. Around them are grouped many other classical philosophers and scientists, each indicating clearly by expression and gesture the character of his intellect—yet never obtrusively, for detail is throughout subordinated to the total balanced grandeur of effect.

Stanza d'Eliodoro

Divine intervention on behalf of the Church was the theme of the Stanza d'Eliodoro (decorated between 1511 and 1514). This subject gave Raphael greater scope for dynamic composition and movement, and the influence of Michelangelo's Sistine Chapel ceiling, completed in 1512, is noticeable. Compositional unity is achieved in Raphael's *Expulsion of Heliodorus* by the balance of emotional and expressive contrasts. This fresco and the *Liberation of St. Peter,* a brilliant display of the dramatic possibilities of unusual light sources, witness the beginnings in Raphael's work of expansion away from the dignity and purity of the *School of Athens.*

During the progress of the second stanza Julius II died. He was succeeded in 1513 by Leo X, who appears in the *Repulsion of Attila,* the last of the Stanza d'Eliodoro frescoes, executed primarily by Raphael's pupils. At this stage Raphael's assistants began to play an increasingly important role in the production of work to his designs, partly because Leo X's dispatch of Michelangelo to work on a Medici project in Florence left Raphael undisputedly the major artist in Rome.

Late Paintings

Commissions of all sorts poured into Raphael's workshop during the last 6 years of his life. The frescoes in the Stanza dell'Incendio (1514-1517) were based on his design but executed almost entirely by assistants, as was the fresco and stucco decoration of the Vatican loggias (1517-1519).

The monumental cartoons (in the Victoria and Albert Museum, London) depicting the lives of Saints Peter and Paul, the decoration (begun 1519) of the Villa Farnesina in Rome, and Raphael's largest canvas, the *Transfiguration* (commissioned in 1517 but incomplete at his death), all show a new dynamism and expressiveness. The cartoons were sent to Flanders to be worked into tapestries for the Sistine Chapel and were partly responsible for the dissemination of Raphael's late style, with its emphasis on gesture and movement, throughout Europe.

His Portraits

In portraiture Raphael's development follows the same pattern. His earliest portraits closely resemble those of Perugino, whereas in Florence Leonardo's *Mona Lisa* was a basic influence, as can be seen in the portraits of Agnolo and Maddalena Doni (1505). Raphael adapted Leonardo's majestic design as late as 1517 in the portrait of Baldassare Castiglione, which, like most of his finest portraits, is of a close friend. Castiglione is portrayed with great psychological subtlety, a gentle, scholarly face perfectly suited to the man, who in *The Courtier* defined the qualities of the ideal gentleman. Descriptions of Raphael's urbane good humor and courteous behavior in fact recall the very qualities that Castiglione wished to find in his perfect courtier.

His Architecture

So Bramantesque is the architecture of the *School of Athens* that it seems probable that Raphael was working with Donato Bramante as early as 1509, perhaps in preparation for his succession to the post of *capomastro* of the rebuilding of St. Peter's after Bramante's death in 1514. During the next 6 years, however, progress on St. Peter's was very slow, and his only contribution seems to have been the projected addition of a nave to Bramante's centrally planned design.

As early as the *Marriage of the Virgin* (1504), Raphael's painted architecture shows the pure classical spirit epitomized in Bramante's Tempietto at St. Pietro in Montorio, Rome (1502). This same unadorned structural clarity characterizes Raphael's first architectural work, the chapellike St. Eligio degli Orefici, Rome, designed in collaboration with Bramante (1509). The Chigi Chapel in St. Maria del Popolo, Rome (ca. 1512-1513), however, shows a much more ornate decorative idiom, although structurally it is almost identical with S. Eligio. A similar development in richness of texture and detailing can be seen between Raphael's two Roman palaces. The Palazzo Vidoni-Caffarelli is directly dependent on Bramante's so-called House of Raphael, but the richly ornamented facade decoration of the Palazzo Branconio dell'Aquila (ca. 1520; destroyed) is essentially unstructural. As in Raphael's last paintings, the tendency in these late architectural projects is toward a form of mannerism and away from the serene classicism of Bramante.

At the time of his death in Rome on Good Friday, 1520, at the age of 37, Raphael's art was developing in new directions, paralleled in his own very different way by Michelangelo in his Medici Chapel sculptures. The zenith of classical harmony and grandeur, reached about 1510, had passed, and it was left to Raphael's pupils to interpret and exploit the trends toward mannerism in the last works of their great master.

Further Reading

Studies of Raphael in English are limited. An important monograph in English is Oskar Fischel, *Raphael* (1948). John Pope-Hennessy, *Raphael* (1970), an excellent introduction to Raphael's art, concentrates on his working methods and reproduces many drawings and large details. See also Ettore Camesasca, *All the Paintings of Raphael* (1963). A fine specialized study is John Shearman, *Raphael's Cartoons in the Royal Collection and the Tapestries for the Sistine Chapel* (1972). Sydney Freedberg, *Painting of the High Renaissance in Rome and Florence* (1961), is a very useful survey of the period in general. □

George Rapp

The German-American George Rapp (1757-1847) was the founder of the "Harmonist" sect and community, the most successful utopian association in America in the 19th century, and an inspiration for comparable ventures.

Born Johann Georg Rapp in Iptingen, Württemberg, Germany, on Nov. 1, 1757, Rapp followed his well-to-do father into farming. Rapp read earnestly in religious lore, the Swedish mystic Emanuel Swedenborg, among others, affecting his study of the Bible. Rapp's simple eloquence and fundamentalist views attracted followers, and by 1787 he was preaching. In a few years he counted some 300 families committed to attaining heavenly conditions on earth. Subjected to persecution by Lutheran clerics and magistrates, they looked abroad for friendlier surroundings.

In 1803 Rapp went to America and purchased 5,000 acres of unimproved land near Pittsburgh, Pa., and with additional followers prepared the site of "Harmony." By February 1805 they had organized the Harmony Society, with Rapp as leader. With a common fund, a simple and uniform style of dress and routine, and a mild approach to community offenders, the hardworking Rappites built a prosperous community.

Two years later the Rappites chose celibacy, a product of biblical interpretation. However, they enjoyed family life, food and wine (though no tobacco), art, singing, and other amenities. They did not separate men from women and emphasized cooperation rather than compulsion in most matters.

In 1814 the Rappites concluded that lack of water routes, limited space, and other conditions made moving necessary. They purchased some 38,000 acres in a southwest corner of Indiana on the Wabash River. Once again they prospered under their able leader and his adopted son Friedrich, sending wine, woolen goods, and other products as far as New Orleans.

Nevertheless, within several years they tired of the uncivilized area and early in 1825 sold their holdings to the British communitarian Robert Owen. They returned to Pennsylvania to build "Economy" on 3,000 acres on the Ohio River below Pittsburgh. Their fame as farmers and manufacturers, as well as their exemplary community life, brought distinguished visitors to view their homes and mills. Although celibacy precluded an indefinite career for the Harmonists, the group persisted even beyond its founder's death and counted 250 members as late as 1890. Rapp remained in full control of his faculties until his death on Aug. 7, 1847. In accordance with Harmonist traditions he was buried in an unmarked grave.

Further Reading

Studies of Rapp tend to be written as appendages to studies of Robert Owen and New Harmony, although Rapp's colonies were successful and Owen's were not. An exception is William E. Wilson, *The Angel and the Serpent: The Story of New Harmony* (1964). John S. Duss, *The Harmonists: A Personal History* (1943), best retains the flavor of the Rappite outlook. The treatment of Rapp in John Humphrey Noyes, *History of American Socialisms* (1870), is particularly interesting since Noyes's Oneida Community differed drastically from Rapp's colonies. □

Rashi

The Medieval scholar and commentator Rashi (1040-1105) wrote the greatest commentaries in Jewish exegeses on the Old Testament and the Talmud. His commentaries are still important in Jewish life.

Rashi was born Shelomoh Yitzhaki in Troyes, France. The name he is known by is an abbreviation of Rabbi Solomon bar Isaac. Rashi's father died when the boy was young, and his family's circumstances did not allow him to pursue his ambition of spending his life studying at Talmudic schools in Germany. After studies at Mainz and Worms, he returned to Troyes in 1065, when he was 25 years old. Forced by economic circumstances to manage his father's vineyards, Rashi limited his scholarly activities to reading and writing. In the next years he created his famous commentaries on the Old Testament (except for a few books) and on the Talmud. These exegeses were received and read with great attention, and Rashi's reputation was established by them.

After 1096 Rashi's commentaries became even more popular because during the zeal that surrounded the First Crusade rabbinic centers of learning in the Rhineland were destroyed, their teachers killed, and their students dispersed. Students gradually were attracted to Troyes, and Rashi then opened his own academy. It rapidly became one of the most important and celebrated rabbinic centers in Europe; simultaneously it became a rallying point for Ashkenazic Jewry and a center of Jewish scholarship.

Rashi then entered the high period of his achievement. He altered several rabbinic traditions of learning; he induced his students to commit many oral traditions to writing; he developed a personal style of exegesis; and he fostered many Jewish scholars who later spread across Europe. Rashi had no sons, but his three daughters married outstanding scholars. His students of special note included two sons-in-law, Rabbi Judah ben Nathan, commentator of the Talmud, and Rabbi Meir ben Semuel; his grandson Rabbi Semuel ben Meir, known as Rasbam, also a commentator; Rabbi Shemaiah, compiler of the *Sefer ha-Pardes* (The Book of Paradise); and Rabbi Simcha, compiler of the *Mahzor Vitry.*

Rashi's commentaries and tractates spread throughout Europe and the Near East after his death at Troyes on July 13, 1105. His commentary on the Talmud has been in universal use among Talmudic students and scholars since then. The text of the Talmud is usually printed side by side with Rashi's commentary and with the tosaphist additions dating from the two subsequent centuries. Rashi's commentary on the Pentateuch (printed 1475) has enjoyed a similar popularity. It has been the subject of numerous commentaries by both Jewish and Christian scholars. Nicholas of Lyra, whose work was one of Martin Luther's main sources in composing his Bible translation, used Rashi's commentary extensively. Rashi's school at Troyes produced custumals (collections and digests of customs and habits) and rabbinic tractates that maintained a wide influence among Jews of later generations.

Because of the wide range of Rashi's commentaries and the unique and personal character of his exegeses, he more than any other Jewish scholar has molded modern rabbinic commentary and interpretation of the Bible. He ranks as high as any ancient scholar as theologian, Bible commentator, and Talmudist.

Further Reading

An older study of Rashi is Maurice Liber, *Rashi* (trans. 1906). More recent studies include Samuel M. Blumenfield, *Master of Troyes: A Study of Rashi, the Educator* (1946), and Herman Halperin, *Rashi and the Christian Scholars* (1963). Harold Louis Ginsberg, ed., *Rashi Anniversary Volume* (1941), contains biographical material and commentary on Rashi. See also Meyer Waxman, *A History of Jewish Literature,* vol. 1 (1930; rev. ed. 1943).

Additional Sources

Pearl, Chaim, *Rashi,* New York: Grove Press, 1988.
Shereshevsky, Esra, *Rashi, the man and his world,* Northvale, N.J.: J. Aronson, 1996.
Shulman, Yaacov Dovid, *Rashi: the story of Rabbi Shlomo Yitzchaki,* New York: CIS Publishers, 1993. □

Knud Johan Victor Rasmussen

The Danish Arctic explorer and ethnologist Knud Johan Victor Rasmussen (1879-1933) was an authority on the folklore and history of the Greenland Eskimos.

Knud Rasmussen was born on June 7, 1879, in Jakobshavn on Disko Bay in southwestern Greenland. His father, Christian Rasmussen, was a Danish missionary who had been in Greenland 28 years and who had married a part-Eskimo girl. Knud learned both Danish and Eskimo ways and languages. He was sent to school in Copenhagen as a young man and hoped to become a writer.

In 1900 Rasmussen went as a correspondent for the *Christian Daily* on a trip to Iceland led by Ludwig Mylius-Erichsen and a year later took a trip to Swedish Lapland to gather material for literary works. He took part in Mylius-Erichsen's sledge journey to the Yap York district of west Greenland (1902-1904). Rasmussen became interested in the ethnology of the northern non-Christian Eskimos. His first book about the Eskimos was written in 1905. A book about Lapland, *People of the Polar North,* appeared in 1908, the year he married Dagmar Anderson.

Rasmussen established a trading station at North Star Bay in 1910 among the northern Greenland Eskimos, also called Polar Eskimos or Arctic Highlanders, and named it Thule, the classical word for the northernmost inhabited land. In 1912, with Peter Freuchen and two Eskimos, Rasmussen crossed the inland ice of Greenland from the Clements Markham Glacier at the mouth of Inglefield Gulf on the west coast to Denmark Fjord on the east coast in what he called the first Thule expedition.

There were seven Thule expeditions in all. Rasmussen's narrative of the fourth expedition is *Greenland by the Polar Sea* (1921). His books about the Eskimos include *Eskimo Folk Tales* (1921) and *The Eagle's Gift* (1932).

The most ambitious of the Thule expeditions was the fifth (1921-1924). It visited all of the existing northern Eskimo tribes. Several scientists accompanied the early part of the expedition to Greenland, Baffin Island, and vicinity, mapping, gathering ethnographic data, and taking movies. Rasmussen traveled across northern Canada and Alaska visiting Eskimo tribes; he always traveled and hunted as the Eskimos did. His narrative of this expedition is *Across Arctic America* (1927). On the seventh Thule expedition (1932-1933) he got food poisoning, contracted influenza and pneumonia, and died on Dec. 22, 1933, upon his return to Copenhagen.

Rasmussen was an outstanding leader. He had a unique ability for understanding the Eskimo mentality and being able to explain it to non-Eskimos. He did his ethnological studies at a critical time when it was still possible to record primitive Eskimo folklore and history. His mapping of parts of Greenland and crossing of its ice cap were valuable scientific contributions.

Further Reading

The only biography of Rasmussen in English is Peter Freuchen, *I Sailed with Rasmussen* (1958), which treats only his early years. For general background information consult L. P. Kirwan, *A History of Polar Exploration* (1960), and Paul-Émile Victor, *Man and the Conquest of the Poles* (1962; trans. 1963). □

Grigori Efimovich Rasputin

The Russian monk Grigori Efimovich Rasputin (1872-1916) gained considerable influence in the court of Czar Nicholas II.

Grigori Rasputin was born in the Siberian village of Pokrovskoe. His conduct in the village became so infamous that Bishop Anthony of Tobolsk commissioned the village priest to investigate it, with the result that the case was handed over to the civil authorities. In the meantime Rasputin disappeared into the wilderness of Russia. He wandered over all Russia, made two pilgrimages to Jerusalem, and roamed both in the Balkans and in Mesopotamia.

On Dec. 29, 1903, Rasputin appeared at the religious Academy of St. Petersburg. According to Illiodor, a student for the monkhood, Rasputin was a man who had been a great sinner but was now a great penitent who drew extraordinary power from his experiences. As such, Rasputin was welcomed by Theophan, inspector of the academy and, for a time, confessor to the Empress. Another of his early supporters was the vigorous bishop of Saratov, Hermogen. He soon had more powerful backing by one of the principal adepts of fashionable mysticism in St. Petersburg, the Grand Duchess Militsa. In St. Petersburg, Rasputin became a social favorite.

Rasputin was highly recommended to the royal family by Militsa and her sister Anastasia. It was the illness of the Czar's son, Alexis, that brought Rasputin to the palace. The date of Rasputin's entry into the palace is fixed by a note in the Czar's diary. He wrote on Nov. 14, 1905, "we have got to know a man of God—Grigori—from the Tobolsk Province."

Rasputin was able to stop Alexis' bleeding. Mosolov, an eyewitness to Rasputin's healing power, speaks of his "incontestable success in healing." Alexis' last nurse, Teglova, writes, "Call it what you will, he could really promise her [the Empress] her boy's life while he lived." Nicholas II was by no means always under Rasputin's influence. Dedyulin, at one time commandant of the palace, expressed to Nicholas his vehement dislike for Rasputin; the Czar answered him: "He is first a good, religious, simple-minded Russian. When in trouble or assailed by doubts I like to have a talk with him, and invariably feel at peace

with myself afterwards." Rasputin had greater influence on Empress Alexandra. He was a holy man for her, "almost a Christ."

At his first meeting with Nicholas II and Alexandra, Rasputin addressed them as if they were fellow peasants, and his relationship to them was as if he had the voice of God. In addition, Rasputin represented for the Czar the voice of the Russian peasantry. He informed him about "the tears of the life of the Russian people." Rasputin abhorred Russian nobility and declared that class to be of another race, not Russian.

Rasputin had experienced success in several of the big salons and took a peasant's delight in enjoying this world of luxury and extravagance. He made a point of humiliating the high and mighty of both sexes. There is not an iota of truth in the easy explanation that was so often given that Rasputin became the tool of others. He was far too clever to sell himself to anyone. Rasputin was showered with presents without his asking. On many occasions he took from the rich and gave to the poor.

Rasputin had already become a concern to the chief ministers. When Stolypin's children were injured by the attempt on his life in 1906, Nicholas II offered him the services of Rasputin as a healer. At his interview with Stolypin, Rasputin tried to hypnotize this sensible man. Stolypin made a report on Rasputin to the Emperor. In 1911 Stolypin ordered Rasputin out of St. Petersburg, and the order was obeyed. Stolypin's minister of religion, Lukyanov, on the reports of the police, ordered an investigation that produced abundant evidence of Rasputin's scandalous deeds. From this time on, the Empress detested Prime Minister Stolypin. After Stolypin was assassinated, the Empress brought Rasputin back to St. Petersburg.

Beletsky, the director of the police department, reckons that "from 1913 Rasputin was firmly established." Kokovtsev states that Rasputin had no political influence before 1908 but that he was now "the central question of the nearest future." Rasputin was constantly saying to the Emperor, "Why don't you act as a Czar should?" Only the autocracy could serve as cover for him; and he himself said, "I can only work with sovereigns." The strong movement for Church reform and the call for the summons of a Church council, which had accompanied the liberal movement of 1907-1910, had been opposed by Rasputin with the words "there is an anointed Czar," a phrase which constantly recurred in the Empress's letters. Rasputin was assassinated by a group of Russian noblemen on Dec. 31, 1916, in an endeavor to rid the court and the country of his influence.

Further Reading

A full study of Rasputin is by René Fülöp-Miller, *Rasputin: The Holy Devil,* translated by F. S. Flint and D. F. Tait (1928). An engaging if sensational and unreliable account is by Colin Wilson, *Rasputin and the Fall of the Romanovs* (1964). Rasputin is discussed in a useful background work by Bernard Pares, *The Fall of the Russian Monarchy* (1939). □

Taupotiki Wiremu Ratana

Taupotiki Wiremu Ratana (1870-1939) was the founder of the Ratana Church and a major force in the spiritual, political, and material development of the New Zealand Maori people.

Taupotiki Wiremu (Bill) Ratana was born on January 25, 1870, to Urukohai, or Wiremu Kowhai, a farmer reputedly possessed of prophetic powers, and Ihipera. His upbringing appears to have given little indication of the role he was later to play, although the formative influence of an aunt, Mere Rikiriki, should be noted. She was renowned as something of a prophet, and in 1912 she indicated that her nephew would become the focus of the aspirations and striving of his people.

His relative lack of formal education—he ended his school career in the fourth grade—served to distinguish him from other Maori leaders such as those active in the Young Maori Party, but this lack of a high level of European style education did not disadvantage him. The post World War I era saw some disillusionment with things European and with the traditional hierarchial structure of Maori society. Returning soldiers who had fought for a better society saw little in the way of change for the better. More Maori land had been alienated and little seemed likely to change. One of their concerns was to find a leader with a standing based upon achievement recognized within their own society rather than upon things European.

The outbreak of the influenza epidemic in 1918 produced a major shock to the society. It is said that the Maori mortality rate, at over 22 per thousand, was more than four times that of the European population. One result of the shock was to produce an audience whose mood was receptive to Ratana's accounts of religious experiences that he had at this time. War and influenza provided the catalysts which speeded the development of Ratana's influence.

The spiritual message he offered was timely for the many affected by the loss of family and friends. Ratana himself was only slightly affected by the epidemic although many of his close kin died. In November 1918 he experienced a vision when a cloud rose out of the Tasman sea and moved towards him. A voice told him:

Ratana, I appoint you as the mouthpiece of the God for the multitude of this land. He became convinced that the prophecy of his aunt and the earlier voices he had heard in the fields were sufficient to mark him as one who had been called to promote the causes of Christianity and unity among his people and to act against superstitions and tribal affiliations and structures.

He had many examples of previous leaders who had been held in awe as having religious standing as well as political. King Tawhiao, Te Ua Haumene, Te Kooti Rikirangi, and Te Whiti O Rongomai had all held power at least partially derived from their espousal of religious beliefs fundamentally based upon the Judaic-Christian message of the Bible.

Spiritualist faith healing formed a fundamental part of the way in which the early movement spread. Ratana's fame spread directly from the cure of his own son, Omeka, in 1918 to the cure of some one hundred at the Christmas 1920 gathering of 3,000 people. This took the form of a multi-denominational celebration under the control of his second cousin, Robert Tahupotiki Haddon, a minister of the Methodist Church.

The Ratana Church grew rapidly and initially attracted support from the established church. A settlement developed which became known as Ratana Pa, and at its peak the movement had approximately 20,000 members, about two-thirds of Anglican Church membership.

From an early date, however, political issues were woven in with the religious ones. Ratana's journey overseas in 1924 with a petition on the Treaty of Waitangi followed the steps of Parore in 1882 and Tawhiao in 1884. No interview with the British king or prime minister was achieved by Ratana, and a visit to Geneva found the League of Nations not in session.

By 1924 there was a break with the established church. Ratana Church matters were left increasingly to others, and from 1928 the political aims absorbed most of Ratana's energies. A dual role was always emphasized, both in statement and in the pictorial presentation of the movement. The Bible contained the spiritual message while the Treaty of Waitangi signed by Maoris and the British in 1840 represented the political one. The events of the Depression in the 1930s boosted support for the movement. An informal alliance was struck with the Labour Party, and this led to the exertion of some degree of influence as eventually all of the four Maori seats in the House of Representatives were won by Ratana members. Ratana himself took an active part in these events up until his death on September 18, 1939.

Ratana had associated himself with the ordinary people, rather than with the traditional leaders. His Christianity was couched in terms that were easily understood rather than cloaked in intellectual mystique, and it was a Christianity which was strongly tinged with socialist leanings. His movement had challenged the existing order. He saw, in the 1930s, the demise of both Coates, as representative of that order among the Europeans, and, in the political defeat of Sir Apirana Ngata in 1934, the demise of the more traditional alternative leadership among the Maoris.

Further Reading

Tauhupotiki Wiremu Ratana is listed in the standard works of history and biography on New Zealand, including: *A Dictionary of New Zealand Biography*, G. H. Scholefield, editor (1940), vol. 2; *New Zealand Encyclopaedia*, Gordon McLauchlan, editor-in-chief (1984); *The Oxford History of New Zealand*, W. H. Oliver, editor (1981); and *The New Zealand Book of Events*, Bryce Fraser, editor (1986). Longer accounts of his life are to be found in J. McLeod Henderson, *Ratana: The Man, the Church, the Political Movement* (1972) and in H. H. Bolitho, *Ratana, the Maori Miracle Man* (1921). □

Eleanor Rathbone

British politician and social reformer Eleanor Rathbone (1872-1946) was one of the first women members of Parliament, known principally for her successful advocacy of family allowances.

Eleanor Florence Rathbone was born in London on May 12, 1872, into a family of social reformist politicians. Her father was William Rathbone, heir to a family tradition of political commitment and social responsibility and for many years a reformist member of Parliament. Her mother, Emily Acheson Lyle, raised ten children, the next to youngest of whom was Eleanor. Her childhood was alternately spent in Liverpool, where the Rathbone family was rooted, and London, where she attended Kensington High School.

She matriculated at Oxford (at Somerville College) in 1893 in the field of humanities and received second class honors in 1896. After graduation she intended to pursue studies in philosophy, but soon found herself more interested in the real social, economic, and political problems of the Liverpool environment.

One of the first issues that attracted her attention was the plight of widows under the existing Poor Law. Her investigations led her to realize the need for family allowances (or social security allotments for needy children in families whose income was insufficient to support them). Her first book on the subject was *The Disinherited Family* (1924), which became known as a classic introduction to the topic. In 1940 she published *The Case for Family Allowances,* and throughout her political life she continued to agitate for this reform. In 1945 her efforts were rewarded when legislation establishing family allowances was passed.

In 1909 she was elected as an independent to the Liverpool city council. In that capacity she concerned herself primarily with housing problems. During World War I she held an administrative position managing military separation allowances. At the same time she became active in the women's suffrage campaign, which achieved limited success in 1918 when British women over 30 were granted the right to vote. (It was not until 1928 that the age limit was reduced to 21, the same as for men). In 1919 she became president of the constitutional branch of the suffrage movement, which came to focus primarily on various legislative reforms pertaining to women's legal status and economic well-being. Her feminist interests were long-standing. In 1917 she contributed an article, "The Remuneration of Women's Services" to Victor Gollancz's *The Making of Woman,* and in 1936 she authored a piece for Rachel Conn Strachey's *Our Freedom and Its Results,* published by Virginia and Leonard Woolf's Hogarth Press.

In 1929 she ran successfully for Parliament (she had run unsuccessfully in 1922). She was elected as an independent representing the Combined English Universities, a position she held for nearly two decades. She claimed that her

principal motivation for seeking office was her growing awareness of the unjust situation of women in other parts of the British commonwealth, particularly India. Thus, while she continued to be concerned with the interests of her university constituency, her primary focus from this point on was international. She worked intensely on extending Indian women's voting privileges and in 1934 published *Child Marriage: The Indian Minotaur,* an exposé that led to legislative reform in this area.

During the 1930s she took a strong position to the British government's policy of "appeasing" German dictator Adolf Hitler in his quest for territorial aggrandizement. In 1937 she published *War Can Be Averted,* which condemned the appeasement policy, as well as the Italian invasion of Ethiopia (or Abyssinia) in 1935 and the failure of the Western democracies to help the leftist forces in the Spanish Civil War (1936-1939) against the fascists headed by Francisco Franco. (The abject policy of the democracies was called "non-intervention.")

After World War II broke out in 1939 Rathbone became increasingly concerned about the plight of refugees. She organized numerous relief programs and performed many acts of assistance to individuals. Her encounters with Jewish exiles led her to an awareness of Nazi atrocities against Jews. In 1943 she published a commission report documenting this persecution entitled *Rescue the Perishing,* and in 1944 she put out *Falsehoods and Lies about the Jews.* By the end of the war she had developed strong sympathy for the Zionist cause. (At that time Palestine was a British protectorate; the state of Israel was not proclaimed until

May 1948.) Her own home in London was destroyed in the blitz.

Eleanor Rathbone died in London on January 2, 1946. She had left her mark as a tireless campaigner for social and economic justice and as a pioneer of women's participation in government.

Further Reading

The basic biography is Mary D. Stocks, *Eleanor Rathbone, A Biography* (1949). Other sources of information are Vera Brittain's *The Women at Oxford* (1960) and Jane Lewis's *Women in England (1870-1950)* (1985), which provides information on the political and social context in which Rathbone lived and worked. □

Walther Rathenau

The German industrialist and statesman Walther Rathenau (1867-1922) pioneered the public management of raw materials in his country during World War I. As postwar foreign minister, he inaugurated a new policy of reconciliation with Germany's former enemies.

Walther Rathenau, born in Berlin on Sept. 29, 1867, was the son of the famed German-Jewish entrepreneur Emil Rathenau (1838-1915), founder (1883) and president of AEG, the mammoth German General Electric Company. Trained as an electrochemist, he earned a doctorate in 1889. He served an apprenticeship as a researcher and manager from 1890 to 1900 before joining his father's company initially as a director, then in 1915 becoming successor to the older Rathenau as AEG president.

Vigorous and innovative as an entrepreneur associated with almost a hundred businesses, Rathenau wrote over a dozen books and many articles on philosophy, politics, and economics, in which the mechanization and suppression of modern man are overriding preoccupations. He saw the tyranny of technology and capital as fundamentally an irrational, chaotic one which he hoped would be replaced by an economy organized for the common social good without excessive politico-economic centralization (for which he believed inheritance in particular responsible) and the suppression of the working poor.

Concerned with Germany's insufficient economic preparation, Rathenau offered his services to the government at the outset of World War I and from September 1914 to March 1915 organized the German War Raw Materials Department, which was to become a crucial part of the German war effort. At the same time his inclinations and his intimate knowledge of Germany's potential made him a persistent advocate of an early, negotiated peace and a severe critic of the dominant military caste.

After the war Rathenau was brought into the government by Finance Minister Joseph Wirth in March 1920 as a member of the Socialization Committee and subsequently attended the Spa Conference on Disarmament as a technical assistant (July 1920). When Wirth became chancellor in May 1921, he appointed Rathenau to the Ministry of Reconstruction. Here Rathenau organized an extensive program of rationalization for German industry and launched his new "foreign policy of fulfillment," that is, reconciliation with the victorious powers by negotiating on the basis of the established peace treaty (Wiesbaden, October 1921; Cannes, January 1922). He became foreign minister in January 1922. The most memorable event of his brief tenure of office was a pact of peace with the Soviets, the Treaty of Rapallo, signed unexpectedly under the strain of failing reparations talks at the Genoa Conference in April 1922. The hope for international reconciliation was shattered, however, by the virulent attacks of a chauvinistic, anti-Semitic, and antirepublican right, which climaxed in the assassination of Rathenau by two young nationalists in Berlin on June 24, 1922.

Further Reading

Of Rathenau's own numerous writings, *In Days to Come* was translated by Eden and Cedar Paul (1921) and *The New Society* by Arthur Windham (1921). Several important volumes of personal writings remain untranslated. The best biographical studies of Rathenau in English are Count Harry Kessler, *Walther Rathenau: His Life and Work,* translated by W. D. Robson-Scott (1928) and by Lawrence Hyde (1930), a sensitive portrayal by a close friend; and the chapter on Rathenau in James Joll, *Three Intellectuals in Politics* (1961). An authoritative specialized study is David Felix, *Walther Rathenau and the Weimar Republic: The Politics of Reparations* (1971).

Additional Sources

Kessler, Harry, Graf, *Walther Rathenau: his life and work,* New York: AMS Press, 1975.

Loewenberg, Peter, *Walther Rathenau and Henry Kissinger: the Jew as a modern statesman in two political cultures,* New York: Leo Baeck Institute, 1980. □

Simon Denis Rattle

In resisting the present tendency among conductors to leave a post at the first attractive opportunity, Simon Denis Rattle (born 1955) transformed England's City of Birmingham Symphony Orchestra from second-rate to world-class status. His imaginative programming and brilliant performances made him, his orchestra, and the city of Birmingham the toast of the musical world.

Simon Rattle was born in Liverpool on January 19, 1955. Family members provided his earliest musical influences. His father, the managing director of an import-export company, played the piano, as did his mother. His sister, elder by nine years, taught him to read scores and introduced him through recordings to much music that would remain important in his musical life. But the music of both father and sister was not that which would normally serve in grooming the leader of a world-class orchestra; not the standard symphonic works from Haydn through Brahms. Instead, Gershwin or jazz on the piano and Bartok, Mahler, Schoenberg, and other early 20th-century masters on the phonograph served as Rattle's first musical encounters.

Rattle showed an early aptitude for music making and study, taking up percussion instruments at about the age of four, having been impressed by the tympani player at Merseyside Youth Orchestra rehearsals to which his father would take him. At age six or seven he took up the piano, which he would study seriously until his first year at the Royal Academy of Music, when he dropped it in order to devote more time to conducting. At about the same time that he began to play the piano he became intrigued by Berlioz's *Treatise on Instrumentation.*

His practice of playing the percussion part along with recordings, this often taking the form of "concerts" in the home for family and friends, furthered his progress. By the age of ten he had become a percussionist with the Merseyside Youth Orchestra. The following year he won a studentship from the Liverpool Education Authority allowing him to study the piano with a prominent teacher, Douglas Miller. Within two years he had mastered the Mozart piano concerto K488, which he played with orchestra in a concert of the Annual European Summer School for Young Musicians in Mödling, Austria (outside Vienna), in 1967. It was there that he also received some of his first opportunities to conduct.

Apart from musical talent, Rattle's conducting debut in England displayed in abundance his energies for organization and promotion when, at age 15, he pulled together a large *ad hoc* orchestra and conducted a charity concert at Liverpool College Hall. While attending Liverpool College, Rattle founded and conducted a percussion group, Percussionists Anonymous, but he was to remain there for only a short time before being accepted at the Royal Academy of Music. His conducting teacher at the latter was Maurice Miles.

He would not graduate from the Royal Academy of Music either. In 1974, after his third year, he won the John Player International Conductor's Award, sponsored by the Bournemouth Symphony Orchestra and engaging him with that orchestra until 1976. Although this must be regarded as the first major breakthrough in his career, he was at the same time becoming known through other channels. He had been conducting the Merseyside Youth Orchestra since 1971 and regularly since 1973, and his activities at the Royal College of Music had attracted the notice of Martin Campbell-White, an agent from the prestigious management company of Harold Holt Ltd.

The combination of an important award and enthusiastic management quickly threw him into the spotlight, but at the same time brought about a couple of serious problems. The first was that of repertoire. As was mentioned earlier, Rattle's taste was not that of the usual concert-going citizen, and he had insufficient experience with the staples of symphonic literature. Added to this was the fact that he had never conducted a professional orchestra of seasoned veterans, musicians who, as it turned out, resented his youth and inexperience. His early mentor, the conductor John Carewe, commented on Rattle's musicianship at the beginning of his career: "At that stage music just wandered for him—lovely sounds, but no appreciation of how it was actually built up." Rattle would spend years correcting the problem.

Following his tenure at Bournemouth he held posts as assistant conductor of the BBC Scottish Symphony Orchestra, Glasgow, and associate conductor of the Royal Liverpool Philharmonic Orchestra. Rattle first conducted the City of Birmingham Symphony Orchestra in May 1976 and accepted the post of principal conductor in September 1980. It was at first regarded by many as detrimental to the career of a young and gifted conductor that he should remain at the same post for so long rather than moving on to better-known orchestras. But in retrospect Rattle's decision benefitted not only his own career but all parties concerned.

Rattle deplored the modern tendency among conductors of switching orchestras frequently and of extensive guest conducting, claiming that the musical result in such cases will always be a compromise between what the orchestra has been previously taught and what the present conductor wishes. Budgeting considerations limit rehearsal time so that only standard works that the orchestra already knows can be performed, thus not allowing new or neglected pieces to enter the repertoire.

Rattle's commitment to the City of Birmingham Symphony Orchestra resulted in quite the opposite set of circumstances. When he assumed his post, the orchestra was failing both musically and financially, but he built it to compete with the best orchestras in the world. In 1989 Rattle stipulated that the renewal of his contract was contingent on the city of Birmingham meeting four demands: a new concert hall; enlargement of the orchestra's string section and the employment of additional experienced string principals; improved pay and working conditions for musicians; and the permission to undertake adventurous and enterprising tours and to explore the contemporary literature. With his exciting programming and the high level of performance, Rattle had already raised concert attendance to 98 percent capacity; this fact, coupled with the alternative prospect of losing him altogether, compelled the city to grant him all the terms of his contract.

This whole-hearted endorsement enabled Rattle to expand his already wide horizons. In addition to increasing his abilities in the standard repertoire, he ventured into historical performances of earlier masters such as Mozart and Haydn. Among his many accomplishments in the field of contemporary music were premiere performances of works by Oliver Knussen and Peter Maxwell Davies and the founding of the concert series "Toward the Millenium," which covered by decade works of the 20th century. A frequent performer in vocal works was his wife, the American soprano Elise Ross, whom he married in 1980.

While he received acclaim for performances of earlier masters, his greatest strength probably was with the moderns—Mahler, Bartok, Stravinsky, Britten, Janacek, Debussy, Messiaen, and others. He remained hesitant to accept guest engagements but was affiliated with the Aldeburgh Festival, the London Sinfonietta, and Age of Enlightenment Orchestra. Operatic successes included Gershwin's *Porgy and Bess* (recorded for his usual label, EMI) and Janacek's *The Cunning Little Vixen* and *Katya Kabanova*. The Rattle/City of Birmingham Symphony Orchestra recording of the film score for Kenneth Branagh's *Henry V* reached the top of the Billboard charts. In 1987 he was awarded the Commander of the Order of the British Empire, and in 1994 he was made a Knight Bachelor on the Birthday Honours List.

Further Reading

Rattle's activities continue to be charted by all classical music publications both in America and abroad. These publications include *American Record Guide, Stereo Review, Classic CD, Musical America,* and *Grammophone*. A particularly good, though short, essay by Herbert Kupferberg appeared in the November 1992 issue of *Stereo Review*. A full-length monograph on the conductor, *Simon Rattle: The Making of a Conductor,* by Nicholas Kenyon, was published in England in 1987. Though it received excellent reviews and contains a balance of praise and criticism in many interviews with colleagues, the book deals almost exclusively with his musical life so that one learns little of the person behind the baton. □

Friedrich Ratzel

The German geographer Friedrich Ratzel (1844-1904) was the author of several books on ethnology and human and political geography in which he described his observations during extensive travels in Europe and the Americas.

The father of Friedrich Ratzel was the manager of the household staff of the Grand Duke of Baden, and Friedrich was born on Aug. 30, 1844, at Karlsruhe. He went to a high school in Karlsruhe for 6 years before he was apprenticed to an apothecary in 1859. Ratzel stayed with him until 1863, when he went to Rappeswyl on the Lake of Zurich, Switzerland, where he began to study the classics. After a further year as an apothecary at Mörs near Krefeld in the Ruhr area (1865-1866), he spent a short time at the high school in Karlsruhe and became a student of zoology at the universities of Heidelberg, Jena, and Berlin. In 1868 Ratzel presented a thesis on the characteristics of worms and, a year later, a book on the work of Charles Darwin, whose *Origin of Species* had appeared in 1859. But Ratzel's work was overshadowed by Ernst Haeckel's.

Journalist and Geographer

Partly by good fortune Ratzel had the opportunity of traveling with a French naturalist, and he wrote up his experiences for a Cologne newspaper. Ratzel's travel and journalism were interrupted by a short but distinguished army career in the Franco-Prussian War of 1870-1871. In 1871 he went through the Hungarian plains, where he was fascinated by the signs of recent agricultural settlement, and the Carpathians, where he found German-speaking communities. In 1874 he went to North and Central America, where he once again saw successful German settlers. In 1876 he published a thesis on Chinese emigration, partly from his own experience in America, and in 1878 and 1880 he published two large books on North America.

In 1875 Ratzel joined the staff of the Technical High School in Munich, and in 1886 he moved to the University of Leipzig. Always an avid journalist, he also published several large books during these years, including *Völkerkunde* (2 vols., 1885-1888; Ethnology), *Anthropogeographie* (2 vols., 1882-1891; Human Geography), *Politische Geographie* (1897; *Political Geography*), and *Die Erde und das Leben* (2 vols., 1901-1902; Earth and Life).

Some of Ratzel's work was of uneven quality, for example, in the world survey of ethnology, but much of it was based on acute observation in his wide travels. He was anxious to interpret the observed movements of plant and animal life—and of people—to settle and establish themselves in a new environment, and he saw in biogeography the essential link between scientific and human phenomena. Immensely industrious throughout his life, he died of a stroke on Aug. 9, 1904, while on holiday with his wife and daughters in Ammerland, Bavaria.

Further Reading

A terse biography of Ratzel is Harriet Wanklyn, *Friedrich Ratzel: A Biographical Memoir and Bibliography* (1961). Background is in Robert H. Lowie, *The History of Ethnological Theory* (1937), and Marvin Harris, *The Rise of Anthropological Theory* (1968). □

Johannes Rau

Johannes Rau (born 1931) served as deputy chairman of the German Social Democratic Party (SPD), as minister-president of the powerful state of North Rhine-Westphalia, and in 1994 as candidate for chancellor and the federal presidency.

Johannes Rau was born on January 16, 1931, in Wuppertal-Barmen, the son of a businessman who became a Protestant minister and the grandson of a stonemason. He was one of five children, all of whom had close relationships with their parents. Early on, young Rau was attracted to the church and to the study of the Bible. His religious interest earned him, in his political career, the nickname "Brother Rau."

In 1949, after having attended secondary school, Rau became an apprentice in a publishing house. Three years later he was a sales representative for nine Protestant pub-

lishers. From 1954 to 1967 he served as executive director and director of a Protestant youth publishing house in Wuppertal.

In the early 1950s his interest in politics surfaced, especially when the conservative government led by Chancellor Konrad Adenauer decided to establish a German army. Opposed to the decision, Rau joined the newly-founded German People's Party, which stood for pacifism and neutrality in the East-West confrontation. The party was headed by Gustav Heinemann, who eventually became federal president and whom Rau admired for his devout Protestant and pacifist convictions.

When the small party was dissolved in 1957, Rau, following Heinemann's example, joined the Social Democratic Party (SPD), the chief left-of-center opposition party to Adenauer's government. Although initially Rau had some doubts about joining the SPD, which in the past had been anti-clerical, he and other applicants from the defunct German People's Party were assured that the party welcomed religious progressives who supported the SPD's moderate reformist and non-Marxist program, which was then being formulated.

As a result of his many acquaintances and friendships with politicians and religious leaders, Rau, as a new SPD member, rose swiftly in state politics. Already in 1958, less than one year after he joined the SPD, he won a seat in the state legislature. There he served for a time as chairman of the youth and cultural committees. In 1967 he was elected chairman of the SPD parliamentary group. From 1969 to

1970 he was also mayor of the Ruhr city of Wuppertal. In 1970, following a renewed victory of the SPD in the state election, the SPD minister-president appointed him head of the Ministry of Education and Research. As a result of severe overcrowding in universities in North Rhine-Westphalia, Rau founded six new universities, including an open university giving degrees to students studying by mail. In 1978 Rau became minister-president, a post that he had long coveted. Despite severe economic problems and high unemployment in the ailing coal and steel industries, Rau proved to be a popular minister-president who was repeatedly reelected to his post, gaining a sizable number of votes for his party. His record was the more remarkable when compared to the party's many electoral setbacks in other states.

Rau's climb up the ladder in the SPD was as swift as that in state politics. Soon after joining the SPD he served for four years as the chairman of the Young Socialists in Wuppertal and for six years as deputy chairman of the regional SPD. Beginning in 1968 he was a member of the party's national executive committee; from 1977 chairman of the North Rhine-Westphalia state branch of the SPD; from 1978 a member of the party's national presidium, the top policymaking body; and beginning in 1982—the period in which the SPD once again was in opposition at the national level—he served as one of the deputy chairmen of the party. Thus Rau, a pragmatic leader in the party's centrist-rightist wing who was an effective conciliator between the party's warring factions, remained one of the few party veterans still active in the inner circle of policymakers in the early 1990s.

The party nominated Rau to be its chancellor candidate for the 1987 election, but it lost the election, as it had in 1983, to the Christian Democratic Union/Christian Social Union (CDU/CSU), headed by Chancellor Helmut Kohl. Although Rau, a populist and folksy leader, was popular in his home state and among trade union members, whose backing the party needed, he could not gain enough support among the increasing number of "floating" voters, many of whom were civil servants and salaried employees. The party also could not recapture support from dissatisfied voters on the left who had voted for the environmentalist Green Party. Rau supported environmental protection but was a staunch opponent of the Greens, considered to be too radical. Thus, he opposed any national coalition with them should the two parties have enough parliamentary seats to form a government.

When Willy Brandt, former SPD chancellor and party chairman, resigned his party post in 1987, the SPD Old Guard, including Rau, carried on but groomed younger leaders to assume the top posts. After young Björn Engholm, newly-elected chairman in 1991, unexpectedly resigned his post two years later as a result of an earlier scandal, Rau for several months became acting chairman until the party selected Rudolf Scharping as new chairman. As a reward for Rau's dedication to the party and his national renown, SPD leaders chose him to become the party's candidate for federal president in 1994. But in a close election Rau lost to the CDU candidate, Roman Herzog. In 1995 he led his party to

a record fourth absolute majority in his state and so continued as Prime Minister of North Rhine-Westphalia.

Rau married in 1982. His wife, daughter of a factory owner and granddaughter of former federal president Heinemann, was a political scientist. They had three children. Rau was an excellent skat player, collected stamps, and appreciated fine literature and art.

Further Reading

For additional biographical information and personal recollections of Rau, see the edited book by Werner Filmer and Heribert Schwan, *Johannes Rau* (1986). A large selection of his speeches and essays can be found in *Johannes Rau: Ausgewählte Reden und Beiträge.* □

Robert Rauschenberg

The American painter and printmaker Robert Rauschenberg (born 1925) experimented freely with avant-garde concepts and techniques. His wild inventiveness and frank eclecticism were tempered by his almost unerring sense of color and design.

Robert Rauschenberg was born in Port Arthur, Texas, of German and Cherokee lineage. He attended the local public schools before becoming a naval corpsman. He began his formal art education at the Kansas City Art Institute in 1946. The following year he went to Paris to study at the Académie Julian.

In 1948 Rauschenberg returned to America to study with Josef Albers at Black Mountain College in North Carolina. Albers stressed design as a discipline, and Rauschenberg felt he needed such training. He later admitted that Albers was the teacher most important to his development. About 1950 Rauschenberg began to paint his all-white, then all-black, paintings. From these ascetic exercises in total minimalism he turned to making giant, richly textured and colored collage-assemblages, which he called "combines."

In 1952 Rauschenberg traveled in Italy and North Africa. The following year he was living in New York City and developing his concept of the combine. His best-known and most audacious combines are the *Bed* (1955), an upright bed, complete with a patchwork quilt and pillow, that has been spattered with paint; and the amazing *Monogram* (1959), a collagelike painting-platform resting flat on the floor, in the center of which stands a stuffed, horned ram with a rubber tire around its middle. About his art Rauschenberg explained: "Painting relates to both art and life. I try to act in the gap between the two." In the 1950s he participated in "happenings," an improvisational type of theater.

In 1958 Rauschenberg had an exhibition in New York City that catapulted him to prominence, and his paintings soon entered the collections of every large museum in America and abroad. Not satisfied with cultivating his ca-

reer as a painter, in 1963 he toured with the Merce Cunningham Dance Theater as an active participant. In 1964 Rauschenberg received first prize at the Venice Biennale. In the late 1960s he concentrated on developing series of silkscreen prints and lithographs. *Current* (1970), a set of giant silk-screen prints, was politically inspired.

Rauschenberg remains active in the art world. Started in the late 1980s, he created the Rauschenberg Overseas Cultural Exchange. The exchange was created to broaden cultural ties. In each county he visited, he would create art and leave one piece behind. The others were added to the ever growing collection.

Rauschenberg remained active with his art throughout the 1990s as well. In 1994, the World Federation of United Nations Associations selected his painting to appear on a stamp. He continues to create unique pieces of art.

Further Reading

The most extensive monograph on Rauschenberg is Andrew Forge, *Rauschenberg* (1969), which offers a comprehensive collection of illustrations, 47 of them in color, biographical material, and a brief autobiography. An essay on Rauschenberg and background material are in Calvin Tomkins, *The Bride and the Bachelors: The Heretical Courtship in Modern Art* (1965). □

Walter Rauschenbusch

The American clergyman Walter Rauschenbusch (1861-1918) broke the complacency and conservatism of late-19th-century American Protestantism, propounding a Social Gospel capable of responding to the challenges of an industrial, urban era.

Walter Rauschenbusch was born on Oct. 4, 1861, in Rochester, N.Y., the son of a German missionary, and reared in a pietistic environment. Years of study in his youth in Germany provided him with scholarly intellectual equipment and introduced him to the then revolutionary ideas shattering traditional dogmas. On graduation from the Rochester Theological Seminary in 1886, he was ordained to the Baptist ministry.

Rauschenbusch's first pastorate was on the edge of New York City's infamous Hell's Kitchen area, and daily observance of the terrible poverty of his block led him to question both laissez-faire capitalism and the relevance of the old pietistic evangelism with its simple gospel. As he observed during the depression of 1893, "One could hear human virtue cracking and crumbling all around." In these New York years he edited a short-lived labor paper; founded the Brotherhood of the Kingdom, a band of prophetic ministers; and formulated a theology of Christian socialism. In 1897 he left parish work for a professorship at Rochester Seminary, partly because deafness was reducing his ministerial effectiveness.

A series of books now came from Rauschenbusch's pen, most notably *Christianity and the Social Crisis, Christianizing the Social Order, A Theology for the Social Gospel,* and *Prayers of the Social Awakening*. These volumes, widely translated, reached hundreds of thousands. Penetrating in his critique of society, solidly grounded in theology, he towered above all the other prophets of the Social Gospel in the Progressive era.

Rauschenbusch believed that men rarely sinned against God alone and that the Church must place under judgment institutional evils as well as individual immorality. He held that men are damned by inhuman social conditions and that the Church must end exploitation, poverty, greed, racial pride, and war. The Church must not betray, as it had done since Constantine, its true mission of redeeming nations as well as men. But he was no utopian. He recognized the demonic in man, understood the power of entrenched interest groups, and predicted no easy or early establishment of God's reign of love. Therefore his theology, unlike that of so many bland modernists of the Progressive era, continues to speak for contemporary tragic conditions. Rauschenbusch died on July 25, 1918, deeply saddened by World War I, by the failure of pacifism to check the holocaust, and by the hatred poured out on all things German.

Further Reading

Dores Robinson Sharpe, *Walter Rauschenbusch* (1942), is a satisfactory but not definitive biography. Vernon Parker Bodein, *The Social Gospel of Walter Rauschenbusch and Its Relation to Religious Education* (1944), covers its limited subject well. Three fine studies of the Social Gospel are Charles H. Hopkins, *The Rise of the Social Gospel in American Protestantism, 1865-1915* (1940); Henry F. May, *Protestant Churches and Industrial America* (1949); and Robert T. Handy, ed., *The Social Gospel in America, 1870-1920* (1966). □

Maurice Joseph Ravel

The French composer Maurice Joseph Ravel (1875-1937) wrote works in an impressionistic idiom that are characterized by elegance and technical perfection.

Maurice Ravel was born on March 7, 1875, at Ciboure, Basses-Pyrénées. From his Swiss father, a gifted engineer and inventor of a petroleum engine and combustion machine, he seems to have inherited that feeling for precision which dominates his scores and which once prompted Igor Stravinsky to characterize them (not unsympathetically) as the products of a "Swiss watchmaker." From his Basque mother Ravel learned to love the Basque and Spanish cultures. In later life there would be the summers spent in Saint-Jean-de-Luz (twin city of Ciboure). There would also be, spanning his entire creative life, works on Spanish themes: *Habañera* (1895) for piano, later orchestrated and incorporated in the *Rapsodie espagnole* (1907); *Pavane pour une infante défunte* (1899); *Alborada del gracioso* (1905); the opera *L'Heure espagnole* (1907); and *Boléro* (1928), virtually synonymous with the composer's name.

Although Ravel was continually attracted to cultures outside his immediate sphere of acquaintance as sources of musical inspiration—Greece (*Mélodies populaires grecques,* 1907), the Near East (*Schéhérazade,* 1903), Palestine (*Mélodies hébraïques,* 1914), Vienna (*Valses nobles et sentimentales,* 1911; *La Valse,* 1920), and Africa (*Chansons madécasses* , 1925)—the imprint of Spain in his work has special significance. The Spanish elements in his music, although they did not alter his natural style, are an inseparable part of it.

Ravel grew up in Paris, where his family moved 3 months after his birth. It was natural for a boy of his talents to enter the conservatory at age 14, less natural to emerge at age 30. That Ravel, already the author of *Jeux d'eau* (1901) and the String Quartet (1903), chose to remain in Gabriel Fauré's composition class is testimony to a certain humility. But there were political reasons as well: his enrollment at the conservatory qualified him for the coveted Prix de Rome. Ironically, the prize was never to be his. After three unsuccessful attempts (1901-1903) he was denied the right to compete in 1905.

In the next few years Ravel wrote many of the works for which he is best remembered: *Ma mère l'oye* (1908), *Gaspard de la nuit* (1908), *Daphnis et Chloë* (1912), and the Piano Trio (1914). During World War I he served as an ambulance driver at the front. The war, coupled with the loss of his mother in 1917, left him physically and spiritually debilitated.

In 1921, sensing the need for further isolation in the interests of his work, Ravel moved to the village of Montfort l'Amaury. At this point his music changed radically. Unlike Claude Debussy, for whom understatement was a natural language capable of expressing the most elemental thoughts, Ravel had been an impressionist in sound only, not in spirit. The seductive sonorities of impressionism were now abandoned for a sparer texture, of which the Duo for Violin and Cello (1922) and the Sonata for Violin and Piano (1927) are the most austere examples. In spite of their less appealing surface, these pieces continued to enhance Ravel's reputation in France and abroad. His American tour of 1928 was a triumph, and that year Oxford awarded him an honorary doctorate.

In 1932 Ravel suffered a concussion in an automobile collision. After the accident he never finished another piece. The first symptoms of brain damage manifested themselves in his handwriting and then in his speech; the intelligence, unimpaired, continued to produce beautiful ideas, but the concentration necessary to put them together could not be sustained. In 1937 he consented to a brain operation; it was not successful, and he died on December 28.

An Evaluation

The case of Ravel remains something of an enigma. His position as a composer of the first rank is unquestioned, yet his achievement, viewed historically, had little consequence. His formal procedures, however masterfully they were realized, were not very innovative.

From the esthetic standpoint, Ravel's work poses a number of paradoxes. In 1912 he stated, "My aim is technical perfection . . . in my view, the artist should have no other goal." But in other places he spoke of the dependence of invention on instinct and sensibility and stressed the importance of emotionality over intellectuality in the creative process. In 1928 he wrote, "A composer . . . should create musical beauty straight from the heart and feel intensely what he composes."

Furthermore, according to Ravel a work of art exists in and of itself; the composer must take care not to write himself into it. However sincerely meant, this is something of a fallacy; an artistic creation is necessarily a reflection of its creator, if only in the sense that it owes its existence to him and is imbued with his esthetic intention. Ironically, Ravel may be present in his music much more than he would have wished—in the form of that "reticence" which was a determining factor in his emotional makeup. "People are always talking about my having no heart. It's not true. But I am a Basque and the Basques feel very deeply but seldom show it, and then only to a very few."

Opinion has traditionally refrained from conferring the epithet "great" on Ravel's total accomplishment. However, of the 60 works he wrote, perhaps not one is lacking in distinction. The works must finally speak for themselves: they continue, even the less famous ones, to be played; their powers of attraction seem not to have diminished over the years.

Further Reading

Rollo H. Myers, *Ravel: Life and Works* (1960), and Hans Heinz Stuckenschmidt, *Maurice Ravel: Variations on His Life and Work* (trans. 1968), are not intended as scholarly works, but they are dependable and useful. Material on Ravel and general background information are in Joseph Machlis, *Introduction to Contemporary Music* (1961).

Additional Sources

Demuth, Norman, *Ravel,* Westport, Conn.: Hyperion Press, 1979.

James, Burnett, *Ravel,* London: Omnibus Press, 1987.

James, Burnett, *Ravel, his life and times,* Tunbridge Wells, Kent: Midas Books; New York: Hippocrene Books, 1983.

Marnat, Marcel, *Maurice Ravel,* Paris: Fayard, 1986.

Nichols, Roger, *Ravel remembered,* New York: Norton, 1988, 1987.

Orenstein, Arbie., *Ravel: man and musician,* New York: Dover Publications, 1991. □

John Rawls

The American philosopher John Rawls (born 1921) was one of the most important political philosophers in the late 20th century. His *A Theory of Justice* developed principles of justice for a liberal society and challenged utilitarian political philosophy.

John Rawls, son of William Lee Rawls and Anna Abel Stump, was born in Baltimore, Maryland, on February 21, 1921. He graduated from the Kent School in 1939, completed a BA at Princeton University in 1943, and received his Ph.D. from Princeton in 1950. He was also a Fulbright Fellow at Oxford University (1952-1953). Rawls married Margaret Warfield Fox in 1949, and they had four children.

His academic career ranged from being an instructor at Princeton University (1950-1952) to serving as assistant and associate professor at Cornell University, where he became full professor in 1962. Beginning in 1979 he was James Bryant Conant Professor of Philosophy at Harvard University. His achievements included serving as president of the American Association of Political and Legal Philosophers (1970-1972) as well as of the Eastern Division of the American Philosophical Association (1974). He was also a member of the American Academy of Arts and Sciences. The author of numerous articles, Rawls was best known for his monumental *A Theory of Justice* (1971).

In *A Theory of Justice* Rawls returned to basic problems of political philosophy. He claimed to be working with the social contract tradition begun by such thinkers as John Locke, Jean Jacques Rousseau, and Immanuel Kant. Rawls held that justice is the first virtue of social institutions and that the good of the whole society cannot override the inviolability that each person has founded on justice. Given this, his position is a challenge to utilitarianism, which holds that the good of the community can override the claims to justice by the individual.

Rawls was concerned only with social justice in *A Theory of Justice.* As a contractarian, he claimed that the principles of justice which form the basic structure of society are ones won through agreement. In his words, they are "the principles that free and rational persons concerned to further their own interests would accept in an initial position of equality as defining the fundamental terms of their association." These principles, Rawls argued, are to regulate further agreements and associations. This way of understanding the principles of justice he calls "justice as fairness." Given this, Rawls developed an argument for justice as fairness and a "principle of equality" crucial to his contractarianism.

Rawls rejected traditional contractarian arguments about a primitive state of nature which generates the need for human political association. He developed an argument for what he called the "original position" noting that in "justice as fairness the original position of equality corresponds to the state of nature in traditional theory of the social contract." The original position is not then an actual historical state of affairs and even less a primitive social structure. Rather, it is a hypothetical notion characterized in order to lead to a certain idea of justice. Since it is not a primitive condition or historical reality, the original position can be entered conceptually any time in order to explore the principles of justice.

Rawls depicted the original position as one in which persons are ignorant of social status, differences in ability, fortunes, and even intelligence. Behind this "veil of ignorance," as he calls it, the principles of justice are chosen. Thus "justice as fairness" generates from that hypothetical situation wherein persons are asked to make decisions about what is just ignorant of the impact of these decisions and the possible benefits or cost to them. In such a situation of radical equality, the principles of justice as fairness are chosen. These principles, Rawls argued, are motivated by a "thin theory of good" since all are ignorant of specific character traits, abilities, or needs that would prompt one to argue for certain goods. Behind the "veil" that would be chosen as good are rational life plans and the conditions for self respect. The principles of justice regulate the distribution of these and other primary goods.

In the original position two principles of justice emerge. As Rawls noted, the first "requires equality in assignment of basic rights and duties, while the second holds that social and economic injustices . . . are just only if they result in compensating benefits for every one, and in particular for the least advantaged members of society." Having secured these principles, Rawls then explored institutions. His concern here was with distributive justice within the social good of liberty and the demands for justice as fairness. Given the demand for equality, the goods of society, and especially liberty, had to be distributed fairly. Finally, he explored the good for the political order entailed in justice as fairness. The crucial social good is self respect, and Rawls argued that justice as fairness furthers the equal distribution of the conditions necessary for this good.

In 1993 Rawls published *Political Liberalism,* based in part on lectures and work published since 1971 but much more than a collection of essays. The book refines and corrects some shortcomings of *A Theory of Justice,* but beyond that it gives a new focus to the central concerns of the earlier work. *Political Liberalism* does not depart from the principles put forth in the earlier work, but recasts them in a specifically political context. The question Rawls seeks to answer in this book is not the general one of how social justice can be established, but rather how a free, just and stable political order can be maintained in the present historical and social situation marked by pluralism of religious, philosophical and moral doctrines.

Not only is Rawls' work a seminal one in its own right, but *A Theory of Justice* also sparked a revival in political philosophy. *Political Liberalism* in turn generated additional discussion and debate. Given this, the contribution of his thought is difficult to assess. There is little doubt, however, that *A Theory of Justice* is one of the most important works in philosophy in the latter half of the 20th century. It is also a work that reached beyond the confines of the academy to help influence the reality about which it speaks: the world of our political order.

Further Reading

For helpful works on Rawls, see N. Daniels, *Reading Rawls* (Oxford, 1975); R.P. Wolff, *Understanding Rawls* (1977); and *John Rawls' Theory of Social Justice,* edited by H.G. Blocker and E.H. Smith (1980). □

Dixy Lee Ray

Dixy Lee Ray (1914-1994) was a marine biologist interested in environmental issues. Concerned about the energy supply, she was appointed to the Atomic Energy Commission. After also serving in the State Department, she was elected to one term as governor of Washington.

Dixy Lee Ray was born in Tacoma, Washington, on September 3, 1914. Her parents, Alvin Marion Ray, a commercial printer, and Frances (Adams) Ray, already had one daughter and could not decide on another girl's name. The birth certificate read simply "Baby Ray, female." As she grew up, she was affectionately called "the little Dickens," later shortened to Dick. When she turned 16 she chose her own name, taking Dixy in place of Dick and picking Lee for her Southern grandmother, who was related to General Robert E. Lee.

Dixy Lee Ray graduated from high school with an outstanding record and several scholarship offers. She picked Mill's College, a women's school in Oakland, California, where she paid her way waiting tables and painting fences and houses. A strong, sturdy girl, she relished jobs that called for muscle.

Although Ray began her college career studying drama and theater, she soon switched to science. Tide pools fascinated Ray, perhaps because as a child she had vacationed on Puget Sound. She earned her Bachelor's degree in zoology Phi Beta Kappa in 1935 and received a Master's degree and a teaching certificate the following year.

Ray liked teaching and remained in Oakland until 1942, teaching science in the public schools and working part-time on her doctoral degree by traveling to Stanford University's Hopkins Marine Biological Station in Pacific Grove on weekends. In 1942-1943 a fellowship allowed her to pursue her doctorate on a full-time basis. In 1945 she received her Ph.D. and took a position in the zoology faculty of the University of Washington in Seattle.

In her 27 years at the University of Washington, Ray addressed herself to environmental issues relating to the sea. She served on numerous scientific and governmental panels dealing with oceanography and sailed as chief scientist aboard the Stanford research ship *Te Vega* on the International Indian Ocean Expedition. In 1963 she became director of the Pacific Science Center in Seattle. Under her

mental and scientific affairs. But, frustrated in her attempts to gain a larger diplomatic role for scientists, she resigned after six months, got into her camper, and drove home to Washington state.

Convinced that scientists should take a more active role in politics, she ran in the Democratic gubernatorial primary in 1976. With limited funds but unlimited energy she barnstormed the state, urging the voters to fight bureaucracy and put a scientist in the governor's office. After a narrow victory in the primary she went on to become the first woman governor in Washington's history. Once in office, however, she soon made enemies. Her support for nuclear power plants, her enthusiasm for growth and development, and her insistence that huge oil tankers be allowed to dock in Puget Sound led environmentalists to call her Ms. Plutonium and to sport "Nix on Dixy" bumperstickers. A feud with Senator Warren Magnuson also cost her support. In 1980 Ray was defeated in the Democratic gubernatorial primary by State Senator James A. McDermott. She then retired to her 60-acre farm on Fox Island.

Following her retirement from active political life, Ray continued to write and speak. Her outspoken views on the lack of sound scientific knowledge demonstrated by environmental groups were expressed in two books, as well as in numerous magazine articles and television interviews. Ray died on January 3, 1994 at age seventy-nine of complications following a bronchial infection.

Further Reading

For a recent biography see Louis R. Guzzo, *Is It True What They Say About Dixy?* (1980). *TIME* magazine's cover story "Dixy Rocks the Northwest" (December 12, 1977) offers a glimpse of the controversy Governor Ray stirred in her state. See also *Newsweek*, "Can Dixy Rise Again?" (July 14, 1980). Ray is treated in Iris Noble, *Contemporary Women Scientists of America* (1979) and in Esther Stineman, *American Political Women: Contemporary and Historical Profiles* (1980). □

John Ray

The English naturalist John Ray (1627-1705) was an early botanical and zoological systematist who divided plants into monocotyledons and dicotyledons.

John Ray was born on Nov. 29, 1627, at Black Notley, Essex, where his father was the village blacksmith. At the age of 16 he entered Catharine Hall at Cambridge. In 1646 he transferred to Trinity College, where he graduated and was elected a fellow in 1649.

Early Exploration and Writing

In 1650 Ray fell ill, and, as he himself recounted, this led to a deepening of his interest in botany: "I had been ill, physically and mentally, and had to rest from more serious study and so could ride or walk. There was leisure to contemplate by the way what lay constantly before the eyes and were so often trodden thoughtlessly underfoot, the vari-

direction the center evolved into a multipurpose facility, including a museum, laboratories, and a center for scientific symposia. Ray also became a local television personality when she developed a weekly series called "Animals of the Sea," which proved a great popular success. In 1967 Seattle named Ray its Maritime Man of the Year in recognition of her success in bringing science to the people.

In 1972 President Richard M. Nixon appointed Ray to the Atomic Energy Commission (AEC). A marine biologist, not a nuclear physicist, Ray at first seemed an odd choice. But she was already deeply concerned about the nation's energy supply and brought to her new position a keen interest in nuclear power. On her way to Washington to accept her appointment she drove across the country so that she could inspect nuclear power stations.

In 1973 Ray became chairperson of the AEC. A colorful and often controversial figure, Ray championed the expansion of nuclear power facilities and often found herself at odds with environmentalists. Convinced that nuclear power could be made absolutely safe, she urged construction of more nuclear power plants. In Washington, D.C., Ray continued to be outspoken, blunt, and something of a maverick. She lived in her camper on a lot outside the city with her two dogs, a 100-pound deer-hound and a miniature poodle. At meetings and on the street she wore her usual comfortable attire, which often included knee socks.

When the AEC was abolished in 1974 and replaced by a new agency, Ray moved to the State Department as assistant secretary of state for oceans and international environ-

ous beauty of plants, the cunning craftsmanship of nature." For 6 years Ray studied the literature, explored the countryside around Cambridge, and grew plants in the garden by his room in college. Only then was he able to start on his book, which was finished in 1659 and called *Catalogus plantarum circa Cantabrigiam nascentium* (*Cambridge Catalogue*). This small, unpretentious pocketbook contained a great store of information and learning and was destined to initiate a new era in British botany.

During the writing of the *Cambridge Catalogue*, Ray had the encouragement of several friends at Cambridge, one of whom was Francis Willughby. In 1659, before the *Cambridge Catalogue* had been published, he had written to Willughby proposing a much more ambitious project: a complete British flora. However, life at Cambridge was becoming difficult for Ray because of religious controversies. In 1660 he was ordained as a priest, according to the requirements of the college statutes, but in 1662 he refused to accept the Act of Uniformity, resigned his offices in the college, and returned to his native village. Because of his integrity he was now unemployed, cut off forever from the resources of the university, and yet he was free; all he asked was that his friends should not desert him.

Earlier in 1662 Ray had visited Wales with Willughby, and the journey deepened their friendship. Both shared the conviction that, for the naturalist, museum studies and the literature must be subordinate to firsthand knowledge of the organism in its wild environment and that classification must take into account the way of life, the function as well as the structure.

For 3 years (1663-1666) Ray, Willughby, and two other friends traveled throughout Europe, studying and recording the flora and fauna. Ray's journeys gave him the data for his lifework and also introduced him to the centers of learning in Europe. The fruit of these researches was harvested at intervals during the next 30 years in the series of volumes which helped to lay the foundations of botany and zoology. His tours in Britain had a more immediate sequel, for in 1670 he published the *Catalogus plantarum Angliae et insularum adjacentium,* which was a flora of the British Isles, modeled on his earlier *Cambridge Catalogue*. It contained a long section on the medicinal use of plants, which denounces astrology, alchemy, and witchcraft and is ruthless in its demands for evidence. In 1671 Ray was elected a fellow of the Royal Society.

Willughby died in 1672, and for the next 10 years Ray concentrated on preparing books based on Willughby's material; these were *Ornithologia* (1676) and *Historia piscium* (1686). In *Ornithologia,* 230 species of birds personally observed by the authors are described and classified: the book laid the foundations of scientific ornithology.

Biotic Classification Schemes

In 1673 Ray married a girl of 20 who was to bear him four daughters. The following year Ray sent a paper to the Royal Society which laid the foundation for his classification of plants. The paper, "A Discourse on the Seeds of Plants," distinguished between plants with a single seed leaf and those with two such leaves. A second paper by Ray, also sent to the Royal Society in 1674, laid down the definition of a species in terms of the structural qualities alone. This was a highly original approach which was to bear fruit later.

Ray's first serious essay in classification, the *Methodus plantarum nova* (1682), raises his observations on seed leaves (soon to be called cotyledons) to a principle of great importance. He states that "from the difference in seeds can be derived a general distinction of plants, a distinction in my judgment the first and by far the best of all—that is into those which have a seed plant with two leaves, and those whose seed plant is analogous to the adult." This is the division into dicotyledons and monocotyledons which all subsequent botanists have adopted.

Following the publication of the *Methodus,* Ray decided to apply the principles he had discovered to a large-scale study of all the plants of the world. This occupied him for the rest of his life and was published in three volumes: *Historia generalis plantarum* (1686, 1688, 1704), each of about 1,000 pages. The book described about 6,100 species which he knew himself, but it was handicapped in its general appeal by having been written in Latin and having no illustrations.

Still inspired by Willughby's interest in zoology, Ray wrote an important work on mammals and reptiles (*Synopsis animalium quadrupedum et serpentini generis,* 1693) in which he rejected Aristotle's classification and introduced the names ungulates (animals in which the toes are covered with horny hoofs) and unguiculates (animals in which the toes are bare but carry nails). In about 1690 Ray began to collect insects, mainly Lepidoptera. He recorded his observations on some 300 species in *Historia insectorum* (1710), which was never completed and was published posthumously.

One of Ray's most famous books, *The Wisdom of God Manifested in the Works of the Creation,* was first published in 1691. In it Ray turns from the preliminary task of identifying, describing, and classifying to that of interpreting the significance of physical and physiological processes and the relations between form and function. He not only drew attention to these fascinating subjects but argued that this was a proper exercise of man's faculties and a legitimate field for Christian inquiry. He died at Black Notley on Jan. 17, 1705.

Ray's greatness as a scientist lies in his refusal to concentrate upon the study of one part of an organism to the exclusion of the whole and in his refusal to supplement his observations by speculation. He not only saw the need for precise and ordered knowledge but was able to provide, by his personal observations, classifications which form the basis of much of modern botany and zoology.

Further Reading

A biography of Ray is Charles E. Raven, *John Ray, Naturalist: His Life and Works* (1942). Ray is discussed in Charles Singer, *A History of Biology* (1931; 3d ed. 1959). See also Geoffrey Keynes, *John Ray: A Bibliography* (1951).

Additional Sources

Keynes, Geoffrey, Sir, *John Ray, 1627-1705: a bibliography, 1660-1970: a descriptive bibliography of the works of John Ray, English naturalist, philologist, and theologian, with introductions, annotations, various indexes, and a supplement of new entries, additions and corrections by the author,* Amsterdam: G. Th. van Heusden, 1976.

Raven, Charles E. (Charles Earle), *John Ray, naturalist: his life and works,* Cambridge Cambridgeshire; New York: Cambridge University Press, 1986. □

Man Ray

Man Ray (1890-1976), painter, photographer, and object maker, was the principal American artist in the Dada movement.

Man Ray was born in Philadelphia, Pa. on August 27, 1890. In 1908 he studied painting at the National Academy of Design in New York City. He made his first abstract painting in 1911 and held his first one-man show in 1912. Before meeting the Dadaist artist Marcel Duchamp in 1915, Ray worked in a quasi-cubist fashion. His oil painting *The Rope Dancer Accompanies Herself with Shadows* (1916) shows the influence of synthetic cubism in the way forms are put together; but the influence of Duchamp is evident in the concern with movement, as seen in the repetitive positions of the skirts of the dancer.

After 1917, the year that Ray became important in the New York Dada group, he gave up conventional methods of painting. He became an object maker and adopted various mechanical and photographic methods of image making. A 1918 version of the *Rope Dancer* combined a spray-gun technique with pen drawing. Among his "ready-mades" was the *Gift* (1921), a flatiron with metal tacks. His *Enigma of Isidore Ducasse* featured a mysterious object (a sewing machine) wrapped in a cloth tied with cord. At that time he was working, too, with airbrush on glass, as seen in the *Aerograph* (1919).

In 1920 Ray helped Duchamp make his first machine, the *Rotary Glass Plate,* which was composed of glass plates turned by a motor—one of the earliest examples of kinetic art. With Katherine Dreier and Duchamp in 1920 Ray was instrumental in founding the Société Anonyme, an itinerant collection which in effect was America's first museum of modern art. (The collection was given to the Yale University Art Gallery in 1941). Before settling in Paris in 1921, Ray teamed up with Duchamp to publish the one issue of *New York Dada* (1921).

Ray was interested in obtaining unusual effects through certain photographic processes. In 1921 he created his Rayographs, which were made without the use of a camera, by directly exposing to light sensitized papers on which various objects were placed. Strangely abstract forms resulted. He published an album of 12 Rayographs entitled *Les Champs délicieux* (1923). Ray also exploited the photographic technique of solarization, a process of over-and underexposing negatives which resulted in prints with

strange "bleached" effects. The photograph of André Breton (1931) is an example of this process.

By 1924 Ray was associating with many of the surrealists in Paris, and that year he contributed illustrations to the first issue of *La Révolution surréaliste*. In 1926 he had a retrospective exhibition of his paintings and objects at the Gallerie Surréaliste. In 1928 he made the film *L'Étoile de mer,* and, the following year, at the home of the Vicomte de Noailles, he filmed *Les Mystères du château de dés*. In 1933 Ray participated in the surrealist group show "Exposition Surréaliste." He participated in many major surrealist exhibitions, took up surrealist causes, and illustrated surrealist publications.

In 1940 Ray returned to America and settled in California, where he taught photography. He contributed to Hans Richter's film *Dreams That Money Can Buy* (1944). In 1947 Ray participated in the last major surrealist group show in Paris. After 1949 he maintained a studio in Paris, where he evolved new methods for printing color photographs.

From the early 1950s until his death in 1976, Man Ray lived in France. He spent that time working on a variety of different projects. He was one of the first artists to begin working with airbrush. He spent the last years of his life experimenting with photography, organizing exhibits and writing. He is still considered the pioneer of the 1960's style of pop art.

Further Reading

Ray's autobiography, *Self Portrait* (1963), is rich in personal and historical material. Los Angeles County Museum of Art, *Man Ray* (1966), contains texts by Ray and his associates. For Ray's early years see the chapter on him in George Wickes, *Americans in Paris* (1969), a vividly written study of the self-exiled American artists in Paris after World War I. □

Satyajit Ray

The Indian film director Satyajit Ray (1921-1992) was noted for his refined and subtly moving studies of native family life. His creations possess a humanistic warmth, crystalline purity, and mythic evocativeness which enable them to transcend the barriers of alien cultural sensibility.

Satyajit Ray was born in Bengal into one of the nation's most prominent artistic families. His grandfather was a painter, a poet, and a scientist who edited the first children's magazine in Bengal. Ray's father was the author of, among other works, Bengal's classic *Book of Nonsense*. In 1940 Satyajit Ray graduated with a degree in economics from the University of Calcutta. With the encouragement of Rabindranath Tagore, the great Indian writer-philosopher and close friend of the Ray family, the youth undertook graduate courses in painting and graphics at the Santiniketan Institute. Ray was subsequently hired as an art

director for the Calcutta branch of a British advertising agency in 1945. Sometime later he was transferred to the firm's London office, where, besides his regular assignments, he designed a new abridged edition of Bibhui Banerji's popular two-volume novel, *Pather Panchali*. With the cinematic version already germinating in his mind, Ray, a movie enthusiast from childhood, attended all the current films of John Ford and William Wyler; he was particularly impressed by Vittorio de Sica's *Bicycle Thief;* and, in addition, he studied the cinema theories of Sergei Eisenstein and Vsevolod Pudovkin.

When Ray returned to India in 1950, he met the French film maker Jean Renoir, who, while completing the location shooting of *The River,* gave Ray invaluable technical training. Stimulated by Renoir's personal interest, Ray began work on the scenario for the Banerji story. Produced on an extremely tight budget and employing such De Sica devices as the use of nonprofessional actors in their natural environs, Ray's sensitive visualization of the life of a poor Brahmin family, released in 1955, earned over 100 international film awards and fervent critical praise. Ray continued the events of Banerji's tale in his next production, *Aparajito,* a film as lyrical as the first, though more advanced technically and structurally. Before undertaking the concluding portion of the trilogy, the director shifted his focus from the physical hardships of the impoverished to the spiritual malaise of the declining aristocracy, creating *The Music Room* (1958). The final chapter in Ray's national epic, *The World of Apu* (1960), contrasting the joys of married life and childbirth with the desolation of defeat and bereavement, pro-

vided an ideal ending for a work of art which functioned with equal intensity on the particular and mythical levels. "It is fascinating to note," wrote critic Stanley Kauffmann (1966) of the trilogy, "how in the most commonplace daily actions—gesturing, walking, carrying a jug—these people move beautifully, how in the poorest homes the bowls and platters, the windings of the ragged shawls, have some beauty . . . not dainty aestheticism but an ingrained ethos."

With *Devi* (1960) Ray examined with intelligence and compassion the controversial problem of Hindu superstition, and in *Two Daughters* (1961) he explored the tension resulting from unyielding family ritual. *Kanchenjanga* (1962), the director's first color film, again dealt with domestic conflict.

In 1992 he was honored with a special Academy Award for Lifetime Achievement. He died on April 23, 1992. His funeral ceremony was conducted with full state honors and declared an official holiday by the government of West Bengal. Over one million mourners attended.

Further Reading

Ray gives his views in Hugh Gray's revealing interview with him, recorded in Andrew Sarris, ed., *Interviews with Film Directors* (1967). The most thorough and perceptive analysis of Ray's cinematography is in Erik Barnouw and S. Krishnaswamy, *Indian Film* (1963). See also sections of Pauline Kael, *I Lost It at the Movies* (1965); Eric Rhode, *The Tower of Babel* (1966); and Stanley Kauffmann, *A World on Film* (1966). □

duced and worked to get through Congress a substantial amount of progressive legislation, including bills to police stock market transactions under the Securities and Exchange Commission, to provide Federal aid to rural power cooperatives under the Rural Electrification Administration, and to break up the pyramiding of public utilities companies. In 1937 he became Democratic majority leader in the House and, 3 years later, Speaker.

Except for 4 years, Rayburn held the speakership for the next 21 years. During the two 2-year intervals of Republican House majorities (1947-1949 and 1953-1955), he resumed his duties as Democratic minority leader. He also served as permanent chairman of the Democratic national conventions of 1948, 1952, and 1956, relinquishing his post in 1960 to manage Lyndon Johnson's unsuccessful bid for the presidential nomination. Rayburn died on Nov. 16, 1961, in Bonham, Tex.

Further Reading

The only full-length biography of Rayburn is C. Dwight Dorough's laudatory *Mr. Sam* (1962). Rayburn's role in national politics and government is treated in Arthur S. Link, *Wilson* (5 vols., 1947-1965); Harry S. Truman, *Memoirs* (2 vols., 1955-1956); William E. Leuchtenburg, *Franklin D. Roosevelt and the New Deal, 1932-1940* (1963); Dwight D. Eisenhower, *Mandate for Change, 1953-1956: The White House Years* (1963) and *Waging Peace, 1956-1961: The White House Years* (1965); and Arthur M. Schlesinger, Jr., *A Thousand Days: John F. Kennedy in the White House* (1965).

Samuel Taliaferro Rayburn

Samuel Taliaferro Rayburn (1882-1961) served as Speaker of the U.S. House of Representatives longer than any man in the nation's history.

Sam Rayburn was born in Roane County, Tenn., on Jan. 6, 1882, the eighth of 11 children. When he was 5 years old, his family moved to northern Texas. At the age of 16 he entered Mayo Normal School (now East Texas State University) and graduated in 1903.

Following a 3-year stint teaching in nearby rural schools, Rayburn won election to the Texas House of Representatives. While serving in the legislature, he attended the University of Texas law school and passed the state bar exam in 1908. Two years later he was elected Speaker of the Texas House of Representatives. In 1912 he led a field of eight candidates for U.S. representative in the Democratic party primary, thus assuring his election in overwhelmingly one-party Texas. He was renominated and reelected 23 times.

Rayburn was above all a devoutly loyal party man. Although the national platforms of an increasingly liberal Democratic party often conflicted with the social prejudices and economic conservatism of his Texas constituents, he almost always fell into line behind his party's leaders. Yet over his many years in Washington, Rayburn himself intro-

Additional Sources

Champagne, Anthony., *Sam Rayburn: a bio-bibliography,* New York: Greenwood Press, 1988.

Champagne, Anthony, *Congressman Sam Rayburn,* New Brunswick, N.J.: Rutgers University Press, 1984.

Hardeman, D. B., *Rayburn: a biography,* Houston, Tex.: Gulf Pub. Co., 1990, 1987.

"Speak, Mister Speaker", Bonham, Tex.: Sam Rayburn Foundation, 1978.

Steinberg, Alfred, *Sam Rayburn: a biography,* New York: Hawthorn Books, 1975. □

3d Baron Rayleigh

The English physicist John William Strutt, 3d Baron Rayleigh (1842-1919), was one of the last of the great individual classical physicists whose interests spanned all disciplines.

John William Strutt was born in Maldon, Essex, on Nov. 12, 1842, the eldest son of the 2d Baron Rayleigh, a prosperous Essex farmer and landowner. His talent in mathematics was recognized early, and in 1861 he entered Trinity College, Cambridge. Under the tutelage of a great teacher, E. J. Routh, he captured in 1865 the coveted position of senior wrangler and also won the Smith's Prize. At Terling Place, the family seat in Essex, he converted the stables into a laboratory. There he commenced experimental studies in photography, optics, electricity, and acoustics, working alone for the next 50 years. He remained active in his laboratory until a few days before his death on June 30, 1919.

In 1870 Strutt derived theoretically, and verified experimentally, the mechanism of the scattering of light by small particles (Rayleigh scattering), thus explaining the blue of the sky and red of the sunset. In 1872 he spent 3 months in Egypt convalescing from an attack of rheumatic fever; and although far from any library, he occupied his mind by writing a large part of his book *The Theory of Sound* (1879), which is still considered the bible of acoustics. On the death of his father in 1873, Strutt became the 3d Baron Rayleigh. After the death of James Clerk Maxwell in 1879, Lord Rayleigh served as the second Cavendish professor of physics at Cambridge, from 1880 to 1885. There he commenced a series of experimental investigations in electricity which led to new standard definitions of the volt, the ohm, and the ampere.

In 1891 Rayleigh succeeded John Tyndall as professor of physics at the Royal Institution in London. In studying carefully the densities of several common atmospheric gases, including hydrogen, oxygen, and nitrogen, he observed that nitrogen separated from the atmosphere was very slightly (1 part in 2,000) heavier than "chemical" nitrogen obtained by the dissociation of ammonia. He suspected the presence of an impurity and cooperated with the chemist William Ramsay, though both worked separately and in great secrecy. They astonished the scientific world in

January 1895 by announcing that they had isolated a new element which they named argon (because of its inert chemical nature). They even proposed a new zeroth column for such elements in the periodic table. For this Rayleigh received the Nobel Prize in physics in 1904.

By his marriage to Evelyn Balfour, Rayleigh was brought close to high government circles: her uncle, the Marquis of Salisbury, was prime minister from 1885 to 1901, and her brother, Arthur Balfour, was also prime minister. Consequently, Rayleigh was influential in many government policies relative to science.

Rayleigh's honors are almost too numerous to mention. He was one of the original members of the Order of Merit and was secretary and later president of the Royal Society.

Further Reading

Robert John Strutt, 4th Baron Rayleigh, wrote *John William Strutt, Third Baron Rayleigh* (1924; rev. ed., 1968, entitled *Life of John William Strutt, Third Baron Rayleigh*). Biographical information on Rayleigh can be found in Nobel Foundation, *Physics* (3 vols., 1964-1967), a collection of Nobel laureates' lectures and biographies. Rayleigh's life and contribution to science are discussed in James Gerald Crowther, *Scientific Types* (1970). □

al-Razi

The Persian physician al-Razi (ca. 865-925), also known as Rhazes, prepared compilations that were influential in Western medicine for centuries. His monograph on smallpox and measles is still considered a medical classic.

Abu Bakr Muhammad ibn Zakariya al-Razi was born at Ray, a city not far from modern Teheran in northeastern Iran. He is believed to have devoted his early years to the study of music and philosophy. An accomplished lute player and singer, he enjoyed music throughout his life and even compiled an encyclopedia on the subject. According to one Islamic biographer, however, he never truly grasped the purpose of metaphysics and finally abandoned philosophy for more practical pursuits. He may even have earned his living for a time as a banker or money changer.

Authorities differ on precisely when al-Razi began to study medicine. Some maintain that he first left Ray and journeyed to Baghdad as a mature man, and others that he was still a youth when he arrived in the capital city of the Abbasid empire. As Baghdad at that time was the cultural and intellectual center of the Islamic world, there seems to be little doubt that he learned much about the healing art in Baghdad's well-equipped hospitals and remarkable libraries and in the research institutes that the Abbasid caliphs had richly endowed.

Returning to Ray, al-Razi was appointed chief administrator of the municipal hospital. He was soon summoned again to Baghdad, having been offered the post of chief physician and director of a great hospital in the capital. His appointment occurred during the caliphate of al-Muktafi, who reigned at Baghdad from 902 to 907.

His Practice

Al-Razi's success as chief physician of Baghdad is indisputable, and his services were in constant demand. Much of the remainder of his life was spent in traveling from city to city attending rulers and nobles as well as the poor, to whom he bestowed alms and ministered without charge.

Diet was a fundamental therapeutic procedure in al-Razi's medical methodology. He emphasized the importance of consulting the wishes of the patient concerning food, especially during the period of convalescence. Theoretically, no single factor in the treatment of the sick was more important to al-Razi than was the doctor-patient relationship. He stressed that a physician by a cheerful countenance and encouraging words should instill hopes of recovery in his patient even when the practitioner doubted that the case could terminate successfully. He also advised patients always to choose a physician in whom they had confidence and then to abide by his instructions exclusively. In practice, however, al-Razi's relations with his own patients were scarcely ever as placid as these calm injunctions would seem to indicate.

His Works

Al-Razi's writings, according to one authority, number over 230 and range in subject matter from medicine and surgery to mathematics, chess, and music. During the Middle Ages his most esteemed composition in the West was the concise handbook of medical science that he wrote for a ruler named Mansur, generally believed to be Mansur ibn Ishaq, who was appointed governor of Ray in 903. Called by al-Razi the *Kitab al Mansuri,* the Latin translation was known in Europe as the *Liber de medicina ad Almansorem or Liber Almansoris,* and its ninth book in particular formed part of the medical curriculum of almost every European university through the 16th century.

Al-Razi's most important medical work, the *Kitab al-Hawi,* is a compilation of the notes on his thoughts, reading, and practice that he amassed throughout his entire medical life. Perhaps never intended to appear as a single book, it was assembled posthumously by al-Razi's friends and students. In consequence, though the complete title of *al-Hawi* in Arabic means "System of Medicine," the book lacks the unity of design that only its author could have given it. Because of its immense size, copies of this medical encyclopedia were always rare, and even in the Islamic world it was not until modern times that a complete Arabic text was compiled for publication.

Since it is composed of extracts drawn from the writings of Greek, Islamic, and Hindu physicians enriched by al-Razi's own observations and comments, the book's utility was recognized early in the West, where a Latin version, entitled *Continens,* was prepared for Charles of Anjou, King of Sicily, in 1279 by the Jewish scholar Farj ibn Salim, who was known also by his Latin name, Farragut. The first Latin edition of the *Continens,* published at Brescia in 1486, is the largest and heaviest book printed before 1501. The *Continens* has been termed one of the most valuable and interesting medical books of antiquity, and al-Razi's reputation as the greatest Islamic clinician rests in large part on the case histories recorded in this work.

The most highly esteemed of al-Razi's works today is the monograph on smallpox and measles. Although smallpox had been described earlier, his account is astonishingly original and seems almost modern. Composed late in his life, the small work was translated from Arabic first into Syriac and Greek. The earliest Latin edition of the work, printed at Venice in 1498, was a translation from the imperfect Greek text, but in 1747 a more accurate version was prepared on which the first translation into English was based.

In his declining years, al-Razi was hindered by the slow deterioration of his sight. An anecdote relates that when urged to have the films removed from his eyes surgically, the old man rejected the proposal, replying that he had already seen enough of the world. Though the place and date of his death are uncertain, one rather reliable Islamic chronologer places it at Ray on Oct. 26, 925.

Further Reading

Biographical material on al-Razi is in Edward G. Browne, *Arabian Medicine* (1921), and Cyril Elgood, *A Medical History of Persia and the Eastern Caliphate* (1951). See also Donald Campbell, *Arabian Medicine and Its Influence on the Middle Ages* (2 vols., 1926); George Sarton, *Introduction to the History of Science,* vol. 1 (1927); and Henry E. Sigerist, *History of Medicine,* vol. 2 (1961). □

1st Marquess of Reading

The English lawyer and statesman Rufus Daniel Isaacs, 1st Marquess of Reading (1860-1935), known for his brilliant legal career, was an international figure during and immediately after World War I.

Rufus Isaacs, the fourth child and second son of Joseph and Sarah Davis Isaacs, was born on Oct. 10, 1860, in London. At 13 he entered the University College School and completed a year there.

At 15 years of age Rufus left school and entered the family business. His parents, however, desiring to instill a sense of discipline into his life, arranged to have him go to sea for several years. In 1876 he sailed as a shipboy on board the *Blair Athole.* He returned home 2 years later, having decided against a career at sea.

In the years following his adventure at sea, Isaacs returned to his father's business for a while and then spent 4 years at the stock exchange. Then in 1884 he unexpectedly decided to study law in order to pay off debts he had incurred during the financial slump of that year. Isaacs entered the Middle Temple in 1885, and 2 years later he was admitted to the bar. As a lawyer and later as a justice, he gained great repute for his tact, hard work, and suavity. He was attorney general from 1910 to 1913 and in 1913 was appointed lord chief justice. During these years Isaacs also actively engaged in politics and rose to prominence in the Liberal party. He was the first person to be knighted by George V when he became king; in December 1914 he was created a baron, Lord Reading of Erleigh.

Before and during World War I, Reading's counsel was sought frequently on financial questions; during the war he led several missions to the United States, and in January 1918 he became ambassador to Washington. Although he served as ambassador for just a little over a year, he quickly won the respect of high-ranking officials of both the United States and England and was a great champion of Anglo-American goodwill.

After the war Reading reached the pinnacle of his career when, in 1921, he was appointed viceroy of India. In the 1920s confusion and ill feeling were widespread in India. Mohandas Gandhi was advocating passive resistance, there was agitation against the dyarchy system, and the populace was aroused by the massacre of Indian nationalists in Amritsar in 1919. Throughout these troubled years Reading continued to display the dignity, sagacity, and

sense of duty for which he had gained international fame. In 1926 he returned to England and was made a marquess; he became the first commoner since the Duke of Wellington to be so honored. He played a leading role in the Round Table Conferences of 1930 and 1931, which attempted to resolve the Indian problem. In 1931 he served briefly as foreign secretary, and in 1934 he was appointed lord warden of the Cinque Ports. Reading died in London on Dec. 30, 1935.

Further Reading

The best biography of Reading is that by his son, Gerald Rufus Isaacs Reading, 2d Marquess of Reading, *Rufus Isaacs, First Marquess of Reading* (2 vols., 1942-1945). It is a detailed study of all phases of Reading's life; the chapters on his viceroyalty of India are of particular value. An older study is Stanley Jackson, *Rufus Isaacs, First Marquess of Reading* (1936). H. Montgomery Hyde, *Lord Reading* (1967), is a well-written and sympathetic recent biography. For his legal career see Derek Walker-Smith, *Lord Reading and His Cases: The Study of a Great Career* (1934). W. B. Fowler, *British-American Relations, 1917-1918* (1969), is also useful.

Additional Sources

Judd, Denis, *Lord Reading, Rufus Isaacs, First Marquess of Reading, Lord Chief Justice and Viceroy of India, 1860-1935,* London: Weidenfeld and Nicolson, 1982.

Sinha, Aruna., *Lord Reading, Viceroy of India,* New Delhi: Sterling, 1985. □

Ronald W. Reagan

Beginning as a radio sports announcer, Ronald W. Reagan (born 1911) enjoyed success as a motion picture actor and television personality before embarking on a political career. After two terms as governor of California (1967- 1975), he defeated incumbent Democrat Jimmy Carter for the presidency in 1980 and was easily re-elected over Walter Mondale in 1984.

Born on February 6, 1911, in Tampico, Illinois, Ronald Wilson Reagan was the second son of John Edward ("Jack") and Nelle Wilson Reagan. His parents were relatively poor, as Jack Reagan moved the family to a succession of small Illinois towns trying to establish himself in business. After living briefly in Chicago, the Reagans moved to Galesburg, Monmouth, and then—when Ronald was nine—to Dixon, where he grew to adulthood.

Nicknamed "Dutch," young Reagan liked solitude, but was popular; he enjoyed nature, reading, and especially sports. The elder Reagan's heavy drinking caused problems at home, but Nelle, a staunch member of the Disciples of Christ, exerted a powerful stabilizing influence. Ronald was raised a member of his mother's church. He graduated from Dixon High School in 1928 as a star athlete and student body president and enrolled the following fall at Eureka College, a small (250-student) Illinois school related to his church.

At Eureka Reagan held a partial athletic scholarship, earning additional income by washing dishes in his fraternity house, Tau Kappa Epsilon. He first demonstrated his skills in persuasive oratory as freshman representative in a successful student strike. Never a highly motivated student, he made an undistinguished record as an economics and sociology major but was well known on campus as a football player and swimmer. He also turned to theater—with such success that at least one faculty member urged him to turn professional. Reagan graduated from Eureka in 1932, later serving two terms on the school's board of trustees and receiving from it an honorary doctorate of humane letters.

On the Air and Screen

Graduating in the middle of the Great Depression, Reagan was unsuccessful in his job hunt in Chicago, but was finally hired by Davenport, Iowa, radio station WOC as a freelance sports announcer. His skill earned him a regular staff position at WOC in January 1933, and shortly afterward he moved to WHO in Des Moines, where one of his chief duties was to reconstruct Chicago Cubs baseball game broadcasts from telegraphic reports. In this role "Dutch" Reagan perfected a spontaneous speaking style and won at least a degree of fame throughout the Midwest. He sent a significant portion of his income home to his family, his father having suffered a series of heart attacks; he also helped pay his brother Neil's college expenses.

In 1937 Reagan persuaded the radio station to send him to cover the Cubs' spring training games in California. His real motive was to try to launch an acting career in Hollywood. A screen test with Warner Brothers netted him an initial seven-year contract. Unlike many performers, he chose to retain his own name.

As an actor Reagan received decent reviews, but not especially good roles. After a series of unmemorable films in which he typically played the innocent "good guy," in 1940 he landed a role which made him famous: that of Notre Dame football star George Gipp ("the Gipper") in *Knute Rockne—All American*. In January 1940 Reagan married starlet Jane Wyman. With her he had a daughter, Maureen, in 1941, and adopted a son, Michael, in 1945; another infant born to them died in June 1947.

The finest role of Reagan's movie career came in *King's Row* (1941), in which the character he played woke up to a double amputation crying out, "Where's the rest of me?" Reagan later used this line as the title for his autobiography, published in 1965; the role won him a new seven-year, million-dollar contract.

Reagan's film career was interrupted by World War II, which he spent as a second lieutenant in the Army Air Corps making training films (including one preparing pilots for the important bombing raids on Tokyo). Discharged in December 1945 as a captain, he resumed his film career, but with less artistic success. His income sufficient to sustain a playboy's life-style, Reagan encountered bad luck: in 1947 he contracted a nearly fatal viral pneumonia and, following his wife's miscarriage, his marriage failed. In June 1948 Jane Wyman divorced him on grounds of "extreme mental cruelty," winning custody of both children.

Actor-Politician

Part of the cause for the divorce was apparently Reagan's near-obsession in the late 1940s with the business of the Screen Actors Guild (he served as president from 1947 to 1952 and again in 1959), and particularly with its anticommunist activities. Reagan emerged from the ballyhooed hearings of the House Committee on Un-American Activities (HUAC) that produced contempt citations for (and "blacklisted") ten Hollywood figures in 1947 as a champion of civil liberties with strong anti-Communist views. He skirted the "blacklist" issue by denying that such a list existed.

In his acting career, Reagan found himself limited mainly to uninspired, unsuccessful comedies (including, in 1951, the unfortunately titled *Bedtime for Bonzo,* for which he was ridiculed in his later political career). Personally, however, Reagan achieved happiness with his marriage in March 1952 to actress Nancy Davis, who shelved her own career ambitions to be his full- time wife. They had two children, Patricia Ann (1952) and Ronald Prescott (1958).

Disillusioned by his diminishing movie opportunities and financially pressed, Reagan tried a stint as a Las Vegas nightclub entertainer, but soon found his preferred medium in television. (He continued to make occasional films, the last in 1957.) Signed by General Electric in 1954 as host and sometime star for the company's weekly half-hour dramatic series, *General Electric Theater,* Reagan was a success. Capitalizing on their television host's polish, popularity, and personableness, G.E. insisted that he go on personal appearance tours; during the shows' eight-year run, he spoke to about 250,000 workers at 135 G.E. plants.

Within a few years, he perfected "the speech": a paean to private enterprise and condemnation of the "rising tide of collectivism," combined with a salespitch for G.E. products. Though some critics later contended that his rightward political drift was due to the influence of Nancy (daughter of a strongly conservative Chicago physician), Reagan travelled the political path of many successful Americans in the post-World War II years: having voted Democratic through 1950, he backed Republicans Dwight Eisenhower in 1952 and 1956 and Richard Nixon in 1960. Then, in 1962, he formally registered as a Republican.

Avidly sought as a speaker by business and civic groups, Reagan became too controversial for G.E., and the show was cancelled in 1962. He continued as a television host on another series for a time, but gradually became a full-time political activist, narrating anti-Communist films, speaking at rallies, and becoming a member of the advisory board for Young Americans for Freedom. Reagan captured national attention and temporarily boosted Barry Goldwater's presidential campaign with an impressive televised speech in October of 1964.

By early 1965 a group of prominent California conservatives decided Reagan should run for governor of their state. Benefitting from massive financial support, shrewd

campaigning, and a strong conservative trend in the California electorate, Reagan easily won the Republican primary. Then, pressing the "law and order" issue by linking Democratic Governor Edmund G. (Pat) Brown with unrest in the cities and on California's campuses, he bested Brown in the 1966 gubernatorial election, receiving nearly 58 percent of the vote.

Governor and Presidential Candidate

Facing a state cash-flow shortage and large deficit, Reagan took immediate and dramatic action as governor, approving across-the-board budget reductions and a hiring freeze for state agencies. From the outset, the new governor jousted with higher education in the state, as he successfully sought increases in student fees and on several occasions detailed state troopers to quell campus antiwar protests. Combining the image of an ideological conservative with pragmatism in action, Reagan agreed to an increase in state income tax rates in 1967.

Re-elected with nearly 53 percent of the vote in 1970, Governor Reagan pressed for a major welfare reform act the next year. That law, the centerpiece of his second term, tightened eligibility requirements for welfare aid, strengthened family planning, and required the able to seek work, while increasing aid to the "truly needy." State spending increased more than inflation over the course of his eight years as governor, but Reagan firmly established a reputation for sound fiscal management as the state became solvent once again.

During his first term Reagan made a last-moment but energetic run for the 1968 Republican presidential nomination, and nearly managed to block Richard Nixon's victory by winning support in southern delegations. Though he did not contest Nixon's renomination four years later, Reagan's brief campaign of 1968 established him as a future presidential possibility, and in 1975—after rejecting at least two offers of cabinet posts from Nixon's successor, Gerald Ford—he once again declared his availability.

After a poor beginning in the 1976 primaries, Reagan gave President Ford a hard race for the nomination, campaigning as a strong conservative. He could not recover politically from his earlier ill-advised proposal for the massive transfer of federal programs to the states, however. Having been graceful in defeat at the GOP convention, Reagan became his party's frontrunner for the 1980 nomination after Ford was defeated by Democrat Jimmy Carter in the 1976 election. By means of his own syndicated newspaper column Reagan maintained high visibility during Carter's term, strongly attacking the Democrat on a wide range of issues.

Early White House Years

After announcing his candidacy once again in late 1979, Reagan defused the issue of his age (68) and campaigned aggressively and successfully in the primaries. Nominated easily, he selected his chief rival for the nomination, George Bush, as his running mate. Reagan's campaign against the incumbent Carter went well, despite some early gaffes, and his masterful performance in a televised debate with the president in late October sealed his victory. Taking 51 percent of the popular vote against Carter and Independent candidate John B. Anderson, Ronald Reagan became the nation's 40th president by an electoral vote of 489 to 49 for Carter. His election was viewed by many as a "new beginning," as the Republicans also won control of the Senate for the first time in 26 years.

As chief executive Reagan established an effective image of strong-mindedness tempered by occasional self-deprecation. Despite jibes by political opponents that he was lazy and lacked knowledge on many issues, he maintained generally high ratings in the public opinion polls. An assassination attempt by John Hinckley in March 1981 wounded him slightly, but served also to boost further his popular support.

Reagan appointed the first female Supreme Court justice, Sandra Day O'Connor, in July 1981. This particular move irritated his most conservative supporters, but he retained most of his following on the right through dogged adherence to the goals of reduced taxes and increased defense spending coupled with domestic program cuts ("Reaganomics"). Holding true to the precepts of the "supply-side economics" he had embraced since 1978, Reagan persuaded Congress to pass in 1981 a large, three-year reduction in income tax rates, even though federal deficits were well over $100 billion per year.

The skill displayed by Reagan with the media (which won him the nickname "the Great Communicator") enabled him to deflect most criticisms, including those aimed at his role in perpetuating huge federal deficits, his opposition to the Equal Rights Amendment and to abortion, and his seeming indifference to the issue of minority civil rights. His media talents also allowed him to become, more than any of his recent predecessors, the spokesman and symbol of the political movement that elected him.

Reagan's actions as president were not always as aggressive as his rhetoric. He did not launch an all-out assault on federal programs, for example, despite threats to do so. And—though he darkly characterized the Soviet Union as "evil"—he ended the Carter-imposed embargo on grain shipments to that country. He committed a large contingent of U.S. Marines to help police the civil war in Lebanon, but removed them, rather than escalating the effort, after a commando attack resulted in 240 American deaths. He launched a successful paratroop strike against Communist insurgents on the island of Grenada in late 1983—a feat generally applauded by the American public.

Despite suffering numerous setbacks in Congress (notably on his "social agenda" issues such as banning abortion and permitting school prayer), Reagan appeared difficult to beat for reelection in 1984. And so it proved, as Democratic challenger Walter Mondale was unable to capitalize on the ever-increasing deficit or criticisms of Reagan's policies in Central America and South Africa (where he refused to apply sanctions to oppose apartheid). In the 1984 election, Reagan defeated Mondale easily, with 58 percent of the popular vote and 525 of the 538 electoral votes.

Holding On—The Second Term

After his reelection, Reagan continued to talk a hard line against the Soviet Union, while simultaneously pursuing a new arms limitation agreement with that nation. Two summit meetings with Soviet leader Mikhail Gorbachev—in Geneva (1985) and Reykjavik, Iceland (1986)—accomplished little and Reagan pressed ahead with an aggressive (and costly) program of national defense, including the MX missile and the Strategic Defense Initiative ("Star Wars").

Economic problems proved intractable during Reagan's second term, as the deficit continued at record-high levels and the nation's negative trade balance grew steadily worse. Hoping to bring the deficit under control, Reagan endorsed a 1985 congressional measure mandating a series of large annual budget cuts (the Gramm-Rudman-Hollings Act), but the law had little real impact before its enforcement mechanism was voided by the Supreme Court the following year.

In late 1986, following substantial Democratic gains in the off-year elections, Reagan ran into serious problems due to the "Iran-contra" deal. At issue were the administration's secret sale of arms to Iran, apparently to gain the release of American hostages (and in contravention of Reagan's announced policy never to "yield to terrorist blackmail"), and subsequent diversion of the proceeds to the Nicaraguan "contras" (in seeming violation of a congressional ban on such aid). Joint congressional hearings on the Iran-contra episode captured headlines through the spring and summer of 1987, revealing significant misstatements by Reagan and, more damagingly, excessive arrogation of power by the president's national security adviser and others. Though the resulting decline in Reagan's public support was relatively slight, revelations from the hearings severely damaged his image, calling into question the degree to which he was in control of policy.

Despite these problems, in mid-1987 the resilient president seized the initiative from his detractors by means of three bold actions. The most controversial was his dispatch of American forces to the Persian Gulf in order to protect Kuwaiti oil tankers from attacks by the warring Iraqis and Iranians. Political opponents charged that the action called for invoking the 1973 War Powers Resolution, but neither Reagan nor Congress acted to do so. The president also kept his domestic critics busy by nominating a strongly conservative federal judge, Robert Bork, for a seat on the Supreme Court, and then—just as the divisive hearings on his confirmation were beginning—announcing a tentative agreement with the Soviets on limitation of intermediate range missiles. The Bork nomination backfired—the Senate rejecting the nomination by a vote of 58 to 42. But success in both of his other ventures held the potential of neutralizing any harm to Reagan's reputation produced by the hearings held earlier in the year.

As Reagan's second term drew to a close, with the Democrats once again in control of the Senate and looking optimistically to the 1988 presidential election, it was clear that he had not effected the "revolution" predicted in 1980. A number of domestic programs had been cut back, but aside from the 1981 tax cuts (and perhaps the Gramm-Rudman- Hollings Act), no truly significant legislation had been produced. The president even found himself in the ironic position of appearing to oppose reduction of the deficit, as he tried to fend off efforts by Congress either to cut defense spending or increase taxes. But an important part of Reagan's political legacy was the increased conservatism of the Supreme Court; although the Bork nomination failed, his ''replacement'' (actually the opening provided by the resignation of Justice Lewis Powell), Anthony Kennedy, represented Reagan's fourth conservative appointment to that body, following the appointments of Justices O'Connor and Antonin Scalia, and the elevation of William Rehnquist to be Chief Justice.

After his return to private citizenship in 1989, Reagan continued to be a popular and active public figure. Shortly after his retirement, the Ronald Reagan Presidential Library was opened in Simi Valley, California. By the mid-1990s Reagan had been diagnosed with Alzheimer's disease, an ultimately fatal degeneration of the central nervous system. He and Nancy publicized his condition in an attempt to create greater public awareness and to gain support for research into treatment. As his condition deteriorated, Reagan gradually withdrew from public appearances.

Through a mix of conservative dogma, pragmatic action, and mastery of the media, Ronald Reagan retained throughout his presidency a hold on public affection unequalled since Dwight Eisenhower's years in the White House. Paradoxically, he accomplished this feat even though polls showed that a majority of the voters consistently disagreed with his policies. Many people would agree that Ronald Reagan, whatever the verdict of history on his presidency, truly possessed that hard-to-define quality, political charisma.

Further Reading

Reagan's early life and film career are well covered in Anne Edwards, *Early Reagan: The Rise to Power* (1987), and in two comprehensive biographies: Lou Cannon, Reagan (1982) and Frank Van der Linden, *The Real Reagan: What He Believes, What He Has Accomplished, What We Can Expect From Him* (1981). Reagan's 1965 autobiography, *Where's the Rest of Me?*, written with Richard G. Hubler, does not deal with his political career but illuminates the character of the man. His 1990 autobiography, covers his personal and political life through the end of his second term in office. A second personal perspective is offered by Nancy Reagan's (1989). Solid treatments of the 1980 election include Elizabeth Drew, *Portrait of an Election: The 1980 Presidential Campaign* (1981), and John F. Stacks, *Watershed: The Campaign for the Presidency, 1980* (1981). Rowland Evans, Jr., and Robert D. Novak, *The Reagan Revolution* (1981), treats Reagan's political rise through his election to the presidency.
Strong assessments of Reagan's presidency may be found in John Palmer, editor, *Perspectives on the Reagan Years* (1986), and—though it covers only the first two years—Laurence I. Barrett, *Gambling With History: Ronald Reagan in the White House* (1983). Two critical appraisals, written from very different perspectives, are Garry Wills, *Reagan's America: Innocents Abroad* (1986) and Michael P. Rogin, *''Ronald Reagan,''* the Movie, and Other Episodes in Political Demonology (1987). □

Robert Recorde

Robert Recorde (1510-1558), the founder of the English school of mathematics, introduced algebra into England; he is also given credit for the introduction of the equals sign.

Robert Recorde was born in Wales. For a time, he taught mathematics at Cambridge and Oxford universities. He had first attended Oxford but received the medical degree from Cambridge in 1545. He then went to London, where he was court physician to Edward VI and Mary Tudor. The fact that Recorde graduated in medicine and was a practicing physician did not detract him from studies in mathematics; he published four books on that subject and only one on medicine.

Recorde's first book, *The Ground of Artes* (1540), was very popular. At the time of its publication, England had not made nearly the progress in mathematical books that was typical of the Continent, and his book served, in part, to close the gap. It was intended to be a basic arithmetic but has been described as a book of commercial arithmetic. It went through 18 editions in the 16th century and 12 in the 17th. In the preface Recorde introduces a dialogue between the teacher and the scholar in which the teacher explains the usefulness of arithmetic, mentioning, among other subjects, how much music, physics, and law depend on numbers and proportions. He also lists the number of occupations, such as those of merchant, steward, bailiff, army officer, and treasurer, in which, the master claims, a knowledge of arithmetic is an absolute necessity.

Recorde's other books included *The Castle of Knowledge* (1551), a work on astronomy which served to bring the Copernican hypothesis to the attention of the English reading public. *The Pathewaie to Knowledge* (1551) contains an abridgment of Euclid's *Elements of Geometry*. Of more importance was *The Whetstone of Witte* (1557), where the modern equals sign first appeared in print. The work also showed methods for extracting roots, the Cossike practice (algebra), the rule of equation, and ''the woorkes of Surde [irrational] Nombers.''

The *Ground of Artes,* Recorde's most important book, appeared at a time when commerce and finance were flourishing as never before. The England of Elizabeth I welcomed a book which told its merchants and investors how to compute with both Arabic numerals and with counting machines, how to establish proportions, the methods of fractions, and many other commercial forms and topics which had been established in Renaissance Italy well before Recorde's time.

For a time Recorde held the post of comptroller of mints and monies in Ireland, but his life ended in King's Bench Prison, Southwark, London. It is said that he was in prison for debt, but some evidence indicated that he was involved in a scandal concerning Irish mines.

Further Reading

A biographical sketch of Recorde, as well as a selection from *The Ground of Artes,* is in James R. Newman, ed., *The World of Mathematics,* vol. 1 (1956). The older work of David Eugene Smith, *History of Mathematics,* vol. 1 (1923), gives a concise discussion of English mathematics in the early modern period.

☐

Claro M. Recto

Claro M. Recto (1890-1960) was a Philippine nationalist leader and president of the 1934 constitutional convention. He was one of the most vocal advocates of Philippine political and social autonomy.

Claro M. Recto was born in Tiaong, Tayabas, on Feb. 8, 1890. He worked for a bachelor of arts at the Ateneo de Manila and finished a master of laws degree at the University of Santo Tomas in 1914. From 1916 to 1919 he served as legal adviser to the Philippine Senate. In 1919 he was elected as representative of the third district of Batangas and served as House minority floor leader. He was reelected in 1922 and 1925.

Framing of the Constitution

In 1924 Recto went to the United States as a member of a parliamentary independence mission. In the same year he was admitted to the U.S. bar by the Supreme Court. In 1934 a constitutional convention was held in accordance with the provisions of the Tydings-McDuffie Act, which required the drafting of a constitution as part of the steps leading to Philippine independence. Recto was elected president of the convention. It was due mainly to Recto's sagacity and intellectual acumen that the convention succeeded in framing and approving on Feb. 8, 1935, a constitution which would truly reflect the Filipinos' capacity to frame laws and principles that would govern their lives as free, responsible citizens in a democracy.

In 1931 Recto was elected to the Senate on the platform of the Democrata party. He acted as minority floor leader for 3 years. In 1934 he became majority floor leader and president pro tempore of the Senate. He subsequently resigned his Senate seat when President Franklin Roosevelt appointed him as associate justice of the Supreme Court. Recto left the Supreme Court in 1941 and was elected anew as senator. In 1949 he was reelected on the Nacionalista party ticket. In 1957 he ran for president but was defeated.

Apart from his numerous legal treatises and literary works in Spanish, Recto is noted for his staunch nationalist stand on questions regarding political sovereignty and economic independence.

World War II and Rehabilitation

Recto served in the wartime Cabinet of José Laurel during the Japanese occupation and was subsequently arrested and tried for collaboration. He wrote a defense and explanation of his position in *Three Years of Enemy Occupation* (1946), which convincingly presented the case of the "patriotic" conduct of the Filipino elite during World War II. Recto fought his legal battle in court and was acquitted.

On April 9, 1949, Recto opened his attack against the unfair impositions of the U.S. government as expressed in the Military Bases Agreement of March 14, 1947, and later in the Mutual Defense Treaty of Aug. 30, 1951, and especially the Tydings Rehabilitation Act, which required the enactment of the controversial parity-rights amendment to the constitution.

A Radical Gadfly

Recto's wit, irony, and sharp analytic powers exposed the duplicity of the diplomatic agreements with the United States and revealed the subservience of Filipino opportunists to the dictates of American policy makers. Recto opposed President Ramon Magsaysay on a number of fundamental issues, among them the Philippine relations with the Chiang Kai-shek regime in Taiwan, the Ohno-Garcia reparations deal, the grant of more bases to the United States, the American claim of ownership over these bases, the question of expanded parity rights for Americans under the Laurel-Langley Agreement, and the premature recognition of Ngo Dinh Diem's South Vietnam government. In all those issues, Recto's consistent stand in favor of Philippine sovereignty and security was proved right by the turn of events.

In perspective, Recto revived the tradition of the radical dissenter fighting against feudal backwardness, clericofascist authoritarianism, and neocolonial mentality and imperialism. He strove to reawaken the consciousness of the Filipinos to the greatness of their revolutionary heritage and emphasized the need to transform the character of the national life by reaffirming their solidarity as a sovereign, free people.

Recto was preparing to launch his Filipinist crusade in the tradition of the Propaganda Movement of the 1880s when he died of a heart ailment in Rome, Italy, on Oct. 2, 1960.

Further Reading

For Recto's ideas and attitudes see his own books, *Three Years of Enemy Occupation: The Issue of Political Collaboration in the Philippines* (1946); *My Crusade* (1955); and *Recto Reader,* edited by Renato Constantino (1965). The best biographical account from a nationalistic sociocultural point of view is Constantino's *The Making of a Filipino: Story of Philippine Colonial Politics* (1969). For other information about Recto's career consult Hernando J. Abaya, *The Untold Philippine Story* (1967). For a thoughtful appraisal of Recto's progressive tendencies by a young intellectual see José Maria Sison, *Recto and the National Democratic Struggle* (1969).

Additional Sources

Arcellana, Emerenciana Yuvienco, *Recto, nationalist,* Philippines: Claro M. Recto Memorial Foundation, 1988.

Arcellana, Emerenciana Yuvienco, *The social and political thought of Claro Mayo Recto,* Manila: National Research Council of the Philippines, 1981.

Claro M. Recto, 1890-1990: a centenary tribute of the Civil Liberties Union, Quezon City: Karrel, 1990?. □

Red Cloud

Chief of the proud Oglala Sioux tribe, Red Cloud (1822-1909) saw his people defeated and forced onto United States reservations.

Born on a tributary of the North Platte River in Nebraska, Red Cloud early distinguished himself as a warrior. By the 1860s Makhpiyaluta (his Native American name) was leading his own band of warriors and had gained an important reputation. In the Sioux War of 1865-1868 he was war chief of all the Oglala. In 1866 he learned of the U.S. government's intention to build the Bozeman Trail and to construct three forts along it; this road would run through land guaranteed by treaty to the Sioux. Red Cloud gathered 1,500 to 2,000 warriors and in December lured Capt. W. J. Fetterman and 80 soldiers into a trap and massacred them. Only the severe cold of winter prevented his overrunning the post itself.

Though at the famous Wagon Box Fight of August 1867 Red Cloud saw the deadly accuracy of the U.S. Army's new rifles, the government conceded defeat in 1868. The Bozeman Trail was closed and the forts abandoned. The Sioux happily set fire to these forts while Red Cloud went to Ft. Laramie, Wyo. Here on Nov. 6, 1868, he signed a treaty that, unknown to him, provided for reservations and the cession of certain tribal lands. Finding out the terms of the treaty, angry young warriors turned more and more to the militant leader Crazy Horse. In 1870 Red Cloud journeyed to New York and Washington, D.C., to clarify the treaty and to speak in defense of the Sioux. His speeches aroused public opinion to the extent that the government revised the treaty. A special agency for the Oglala Sioux was created on the North Platte River.

Thereafter Red Cloud counseled his people to remain peaceful. He frequently charged the government agents with fraud, graft, and corruption, but he advised the Oglala to be loyal to the U.S. government. During the final Sioux War, of 1875-1876, though he opposed the war faction led by Crazy Horse, he refused to cede the Black Hills. In 1881 Red Cloud was removed as chief. Thereafter he declined in prestige and importance. His tribe was moved to the Pine Ridge Agency in South Dakota following the final Sioux War. He became blind in his later years and died at the Pine Ridge Agency on Dec. 10, 1909.

Further Reading

The best account of Red Cloud is James C. Olson, *Red Cloud and the Sioux Problem* (1965). Still excellent is Earl A. Brininstool, *Fighting Indian Warriors* (rev. ed. 1953; original title, *Fighting Red Cloud's Warriors,* 1926). An assessment by a contemporary of Red Cloud is James H. Cook, *Fifty Years on the Old*

Frontier as Cowboy, Hunter, Guide, Scout, and Ranchman
(1923; new ed. 1957). □

Red Jacket

Red Jacket (1758–1830) was a Seneca Tribal Commander who lent support to the British during the Revolutionary War. He also fought to prevent conversions to Christianity among the Iroquios.

Red Jacket (1758-1830) supported the British during the American Revolution (1777-83) and later became a spokesman for his people in negotiations with the U.S. government. Red Jacket was also a staunch opponent of Christianity and worked to prevent Iroquois conversions to Christianity.

Although Red Jacket eventually allied himself with other Indian nations in support of the British during the American Revolution, he was originally hesitant about the affiliation. This ambivalence perhaps explains why he did little fighting during the conflict. According to a number of accounts, Red Jacket's reluctance to fight was perceived as cowardice by some Iroquois war leaders such as Cornplanter and Joseph Brant.

After the war, Red Jacket became a principal spokesman for the Seneca people. He was present at treaty negotiations in 1794 and 1797 in which major portions of Seneca land in upstate New York were ceded or partitioned into smaller reservations. During this era, Red Jacket also became an outspoken opponent of Christianity and an advocate for preserving traditional Iroquois beliefs. His efforts to protect traditional beliefs culminated in the temporary expulsion of all Christian missionaries from Seneca territory in 1824. Red Jacket and the so-called Pagan Party were undermined in the ensuing years, however, by accusations of witchcraft and Red Jacket's own problems with alcohol. In 1827, Red Jacket was deposed as a Seneca chief. He died three years later, after his own family had converted to Christianity.

Red Jacket is immortalized in a now-famous painting by Charles Bird King. In this historical painting, Red Jacket is depicted with a large, silver medal that was given to him in 1792 by President George Washington during a diplomatic visit to the then U.S. capital at New York City.

EXPANDED BIOGRAPHY

Red Jacket was an influential leader of the Seneca Indian Tribe and of the Iroquois confederation of tribes from the 1770s until the 1820s. He was primarily a political rather than a military figure. In fact, he was often accused of cowardice during the American Revolution. He was a very talented orator, in the opinion of both Indians and whites who heard him. Many of his speeches have been preserved in translations written down by whites. Partly because of problems of translation, the speeches, though undoubtedly impressive, often conceal as much as they reveal of the real

thought of the man. He acquired a reputation among both whites and Indians for deviousness and double-dealing. Contemporaries and later writers have differed greatly both on the basic character and personality of the man and on the interpretations to be placed on most of the major events of his life.

Various years from 1750 to 1758 have been given as that of Red Jacket's birth, but 1756 is the one most commonly cited. He was born somewhere in the territory occupied by the Seneca tribe, probably near either Seneca Lake or Cayuga Lake in the northwestern part of what is now the state of New York. He was a member of the Wolf clan of the Seneca tribe or "nation," which was the largest of the six closely related tribes that made up the confederation of the Iroquois. He was given the Seneca name Otetiani in his youth and that of Sagoyewatha when he later became a chief of the tribe. His English nickname "Red Jacket," by which he is usually known, was given to him after British army men had given him a red jacket during the American Revolution; he wore it or later replacements of it through most of his life. Nothing is known of his early life.

Urges Neutrality During American Revolution

Red Jacket first came to some prominence during the American Revolution. He participated in a council with British representatives at Oswego in the early summer of 1777, during which the Senecas and three other tribes of the Iroquois confederacy decided to abandon neutrality and enter the war on the British side. Red Jacket urged continued neutrality and was therefore pronounced a coward by the militant Mohawk war chief Joseph Brant. In fact Red Jacket seems to have been reluctant to participate in combat, and he was reported to have fled from the battle of Oriskany on August 6, 1777, after hearing the first sound of gunfire. He was also supposed to have refused to participate in the attack on the American settlement at Cherry Valley, New York, in 1778. When a large American army was assembled in 1779 to lay waste the villages and agricultural lands of the Iroquois confederacy, Red Jacket first urged that the Indians surrender and then once again fled the scene during a battle at Newtown. He had been correct in his belief that the Indians would suffer disaster during this campaign, but his actions did not enhance his reputation among the Iroquois leadership.

Red Jacket came into his own as a leader of the Seneca tribe in the years following the American Revolution, when he first displayed his talent as an orator. At some time during this period he became one of the principal civil chiefs of the Seneca and hence an influential figure in the Iroquois confederation. One of the most controversial questions about the role of Red Jacket in the 1780s and 1790s is in regard to his stand on the sale of Seneca and Iroquois lands in the state of New York to white Americans. In tribal councils and in negotiations with the whites, Red Jacket always argued strongly against such sales. However, after his fellow leaders agreed to the sales, he usually placed his mark on the written agreements. One biographer, Arthur C. Parker, believes that he did so merely in order to preserve the customary formal unanimity of the tribal chiefs. Other scholars, however, have maintained that he signed the agreements in order to curry favor with the whites.

Meets George Washington

An impressive example of the importance and influence which Red Jacket had obtained in the Seneca tribe and the Iroquois confederation was his inclusion among some fifty tribal chiefs who visited Philadelphia in March and April, 1792 to confer with President George Washington and other officials of the United States government. Speaking through interpreters, Red Jacket was one of the principal spokesmen for the Indian leaders during this meeting. Among other things, he expressed the desire of the chiefs for a closer friendship between their tribes and the United States. He also professed interest in and agreement with Washington's strong desire to have the Indians educated in the ways of white civilization. Washington was so impressed with Red Jacket's conduct during the conference that he presented the Indian leader with a large silver medal bearing an image of the American President extending his hand to an Indian. Red Jacket wore the medal proudly for the rest of his life.

In 1797, Red Jacket was heavily involved in the most controversial of all the sales of Seneca tribal land rights. The white American financier Robert Morris had acquired title to most of the land occupied by the Seneca tribe west of the Genesee River in western New York. He needed to eliminate all Seneca claims to a total of some four million acres

so that he could complete a sale of the land to a land company. Morris sent his son Thomas Morris to negotiate with the Senecas in August, 1797. The younger Morris proposed to buy the tribe's rights for $100,000. At first, Red Jacket and other Seneca political leaders refused to consider the offer, and Red Jacket at one point declared the meeting to be over. However, Morris and other white negotiators then persuaded the women of the tribe, who had the ultimate authority, to take the negotiations out of the hands of the political leaders and place them in the hands of the war leaders. The new negotiators agreed to Morris's terms. Red Jacket was reportedly in a stupor, perhaps induced by alcohol, at the end of the talks. At any rate, he once again signed the final agreement. The Seneca tribe was left with only a few small reservations within their former lands, including one where Red Jacket lived for the remainder of his life, located near the present Buffalo, New York.

After about 1800 Red Jacket became a strong traditionalist who wished to preserve as much as possible of the old Seneca way of life. He began to oppose the efforts of white Americans to educate the Indians in the ways of white civilization. He was particularly opposed to Christianity and to the attempts of white missionaries to spread the Gospel among the Seneca. His position was greatly complicated by the rise of a new Indian religion established by the Seneca prophet Handsome Lake. Red Jacket found himself caught in the middle between the new Indian zealot on the one hand and white and Indian Christians on the other. His opposition to the religious teachings of Handsome Lake led the prophet to charge him with witchcraft in about 1801. Handsome Lake also accused him of being primarily responsible for the sale of Indian lands to the whites. Red Jacket successfully defended himself against the charges, which could have resulted in his condemnation to death, in a Seneca tribal council.

Opposes Christianity and Cultural Assimilation

Despite the attacks of Handsome Lake and his followers, Red Jacket was probably at the height of his influence with his tribe at the time of the War of 1812. Though he was now strongly opposed to the introduction of American ways among the Indians, he consistently followed a policy of friendship toward the United States government. He opposed the efforts of the Shawnee tribal leader Tecumseh to create a new Indian confederation to halt the westward expansion of the United States. When war broke out between Great Britain and the United States in 1812, he urged the Seneca and the other tribes of the Iroquois confederacy to remain neutral. Later the Seneca Indians did go to war on the side of the United States. Red Jacket, though now approaching 60 years of age, fought bravely in several battles during this conflict.

By the 1820s, Christianity was gaining many adherents among the Seneca tribesmen, including many of its political leaders. Red Jacket's strong opposition to Christianity, as well as his increasing tendency to alcoholic excess, led the so-called "Christian party" to initiate a council in September of 1827 to remove his chieftainship. Twenty-five chiefs set their marks to the document that deposed him. Red Jacket then went to Washington, where he told his story to the Secretary of War and the head of the Indian Bureau. They advised him to return home and show a more conciliatory attitude toward the Christian party. He did so and a second meeting of the tribal council restored him to his leadership post.

Red Jacket's final years were not happy. His second wife and her children had become Christians. This so distressed Red Jacket that he left her for a time, though they were ultimately reconciled. He was once again commonly believed to be drinking heavily. He died on January 20, 1830, at his tribal village near Buffalo. His wife had him buried in a Christian cemetery following a Christian religious service, neither of which he would have approved. In 1884, his remains, along with those of other Seneca tribal leaders, were reinterred in Forest Lawn Cemetery in Buffalo, where a memorial now stands.

Further Reading

Dockstader, Frederick J., *Great North American Indians: Profiles in Life and Leadership,* New York, Van Nostrand Reinhold, 1977; 234-235.

Handbook of American Indians, edited by Frederick Webb Hodge, 2 volumes, Washington, D.C., U.S. Government Printing Office, 1907-1910; vol. 2, 360-363.

Parker, Arthur C., *Red Jacket: Last of the Seneca,* New York, McGraw-Hill, 1952.

Stone, William L., *Life and Times of Red-Jacket, or Sa-go-ye-wat-ha,* New York and London, Wiley and Putnam, 1841.

Wallace, Anthony F. C., *The Death and Rebirth of the Seneca,* New York, Knopf, 1969. □

an assistant professor. He was promoted to associate professor in 1930 and full professor in 1934, simultaneously becoming university dean of social sciences. The position as dean reinforced his broad conception of the integrated nature of the social sciences. Ties of the Chicago anthropology department to sociology encouraged him to concentrate on social anthropology, effectively excluding the archeology and linguistics which Franz Boas and his students considered integrally related to it. Redfield became chairman of the anthropology department in 1948 and Robert Maynard Hutchins distinguished service professor in 1953.

Redfield's fieldwork produced *Tepoztlan* (1930) and *Chan Kom: A Maya Village* (1934), the latter in collaboration with the village schoolteacher, Alfonso Villa. *Folk Culture of Yucatan* (1941) compared the effects of civilization on four Yucatan communities that shared a Mayan heritage but differed in amount of external communication. *Chan Kom: A Village That Chose Progress* (1950) dealt with the effort of Mexican peasants to adjust to the modern world.

Redfield's prevailing concern was with the effect of technological change on primitive peoples and the consequent responsibility of the social scientist for defining the resulting disruption of life-styles. He defined, within an established sociological tradition, two ideal types—"folk" and "urban" culture. *The Primitive World and Its Transformations* (1953) attempted to describe conflicts of the "moral order" accompanying the spread of civilization. Redfield's ideal types have been criticized primarily by students of Boas, who prefer to work with descriptions of particular

Robert Redfield

The American anthropologist Robert Redfield (1897-1958) specialized in Meso-American folk cultures. He was concerned with socially relevant applications of social-science skills and researches.

Robert Redfield was born on Dec. 4, 1897, in Chicago, Ill., the son of an attorney. In 1915 he entered the University of Chicago to study law. During World War I he served as a volunteer ambulance driver, returning to the university to receive his bachelor's degree in 1920 and his law degree in 1921. Although he then joined a Chicago law firm, he had already been drawn toward social science by Robert Park (whose daughter he had married in 1920) of the sociology department of the University of Chicago. A 1923 trip to Mexico confirmed Redfield's interest in primitive cultures. He became an instructor in sociology at the University of Colorado in 1925 and the following year received a fellowship for his first Mexican fieldwork.

In 1927 Redfield returned to Chicago to an anthropology department which had just attained independence from sociology. After receiving his doctorate in 1928, he became

culture histories rather than to find ways of comparing types of community.

The last book by Redfield, *The Little Community* (1955), drew on studies of Indian civilization. Although his own fieldwork in India was cut short by illness, he defined and contrasted a "great tradition" of urban intellectual life and a persistent "little tradition" of the villages. As in Mexico, communication rather than geography was crucial.

Redfield shared with Boas and many of his students a concern for social problems, maintaining that man and anthropologist were necessarily inseparable. During World War II he advised the War Relocation Authority; he participated in the initial UNESCO conferences in Europe; he became director of the American Council on Race Relations in 1948; and he served as president of the board of the American Broadcasting Company. He died on Oct. 16, 1958.

Further Reading

Although articles have appeared criticizing various aspects of Redfield's theoretical formulations, there is no significant biographical study of him. Some background is in Don Martindale, *The Nature and Types of Sociological Theory* (1960).

☐

Vanessa Redgrave

The British actress Vanessa Redgrave (born 1937) has had a well-celebrated career as a theater, film, and television actress of substance. She is also a controversial, committed political activist.

Vanessa Redgrave has been described as the "crown princess of a trans-Atlantic show business royal family." Her father was the noted classical actor Sir Michael Redgrave; her mother was a respected actress who performed under the name Rachel Kempson. Lynn Redgrave, the popular stage, screen, and television actress, and Corin Redgrave, an actor better known for his radical politics, were her siblings.

Born in London on January 30, 1937, Vanessa Redgrave was educated there, attending Queensgate School and later, 1955 to 1957, the Central School of Speech and Drama. (She joined the board of governors of the latter in 1963). Her first love was the dance. She initially trained for a career in ballet, but her height (she is nearly six feet tall) caused her to choose the stage instead. After some roles in stock she made her London theatrical debut in 1958 as the daughter of a schoolmaster, played by her father. Redgrave was married from 1962 to 1967 to the director Tony Richardson; they had two daughters, Joely and Natasha, both of whom became actresses. Redgrave also had a son Carlo, born in 1969. The father was the Italian actor Franco Nero, with whom she had a long relationship. He played Lancelot to her Guinevere in the film of the musical *Camelot* (1967).

During her acting career she undertook a wide variety of roles, including important parts in George Bernard

Shaw's *Major Barbara* and Anton Chekov's *The Seagull*. She played leads in various Shakespeare plays, including *The Taming of the Shrew,* and was for a time a member of the Royal Shakespeare Company. In 1966 she originated the title role in the well-received dramatization of Muriel Spark's novel *The Prime of Miss Jean Brodie.* During the 1970s her stage roles included Polly Peachum in *The Three Penny Opera* and Gilda in Noel Coward's *Design for Living* as well as parts in various Shakespeare plays. In the 1980s she again appeared in *The Seagull* and *The Taming of the Shrew* as well as other plays, including a dramatization of Henry James' *The Aspern Papers.* She also appeared in productions of Eugene O'Neill's *A Touch of the Poet* and a spirited revival of Tennessee Williams' *Orpheus Descending.*

Her reviews were not always euphoric, but generally she has been well-received by the critics, such as considering her as possibly "the greatest actress of the English-speaking theater." Her stage performances won her numerous awards, including the prestigious English *Evening Standard* Drama Award as Actress of the Year (1961, 1967) and the Laurence Olivier Award (1984).

Her screen career was more uneven, but not without distinction. Her film debut came in 1958, but she did not receive her first important movie role until 1966, as the dazzling ex-wife in *Morgan.* It was followed by an enigmatic role in Antonioni's *Blow-Up,* a confused blend of fantasy and reality set in "swinging London." She did not always choose her screen roles wisely, and among her more than 25 movies were pot boilers like *Bear Island* (1980), a weak adaptation of an adventure novel; *The Devils* (1971), an overheated version of an Aldous Huxley work about the excesses of religion in 17th-century London; and *Steaming* (1985), a failed attempt by Joseph Losey to film a feminist play. But Redgrave also had to her credit such films as *Julia* (1977), in which she played the fiery anti-Fascist eponymous heroine; *The Bostonians* (1984), a version of the James novel in which she played a betrayed feminist; *Prick Up Your Ears* (1987), a fascinating film about the career and death of homosexual writer Joe Orton in which she played his literary agent; and *The Ballad of the Sad Cafe* (1991), based on the novella of Carson McCullers.

Many of her directors commented on her ability before the cameras; Fred Zinneman said she "is *being* rather than acting." Redgrave garnered various awards for her film roles, including Academy Award nominations for her performances in *Morgan, Isadora,* and *The Bostonians;* an Academy Award as best supporting actress for *Julia;* and New York Film Critics Award, best supporting actress, for *Prick Up Your Ears.* She twice won the Cannes Film Festival Best Actress Award (*Morgan, Isadora*).

Her television credits also cover a wide range of roles and won her various awards. She appeared as the Wicked Queen in a "Faerie Tale Theatre" version of *Snow White* (1985), in a three-part "American Playhouse" dramatization of the Salem witchcraft trials (*Three Sovereigns for Sarah*, 1985), and in 1986 the nine-part miniseries *Peter the Great* (as his sister, for which she received an Emmy Award nomination). Redgrave also received an Emmy nomination for her role as a transsexual tennis pro and doctor (*Second Serve,* 1986). She won an Emmy for her performance in *Playing for Time* (1980) as Fania Fenelon, a Jewish musician who survives Auschwitz.

Jewish groups strongly criticized the casting of Redgrave as Fenelon because of her outspoken pro-Palestinian sympathies. In 1977 she had produced and narrated a tough anti-Israeli film, *The Palestinians,* and she had made clear her support for the Palestine Liberation Organization (PLO). A woman of definite political beliefs, Redgrave was also active in "ban-the-bomb" groups. A member of England's left Radical Workers Revolutionary Party, she stood as their candidate for Parliament from Moss Side in 1979. She described her "leisure interest" as "changing the status quo." Her politics led to a suit Redgrave filed in 1984 after the Boston Symphony Orchestra canceled her contract to narrate a performance of Stravinsky's *Oedipus Rex.* A jury awarded her $100,000 damages for breach of contract but rejected her charges that the dismissal was for political reasons.

Before her political notoriety surfaced she was made (1967) a Commander, Order of the British Empire (C.B.E.).

Her single-minded commitment to political causes was notorious. By Redgrave's account, her daughter Natasha once pleaded with her to stop traveling and spending time on political causes and spend more time at home. Redgrave said "I tried to explain that our political struggle was for her future and that all the children of her generation." Undaunted by her daughter's emotional plea, Redgrave continued to spend most of her time on activism. Her

theater and movie career suffered from her controversial causes leading to lesser and smaller roles being offered. Other acting assignments included: *Howards Way* (1995) with Emma Thompson; *Two Mothers for Zachary* (1996), a made for TV movie based on a famous child custody case, with Balerie Bertinellia; and *Sense of Snow* (1997), cameo role in Danish author Peter Hoeg's best-thriller of the same name. Redgrave demonstrated her vast theatrical talents, directing and acting in a 1997 Shakespearean mini-series, stagged at the Alley Theater in Houston, Texas. However one may respond to her political zealousness, she remains an actress of distinction.

Further Reading

She is included in various editions of *Who's Who, Who's Who in the Theatre,* and *Celebrity Register.* See also Benedict Nightingale, *New York Times* (September 17, 1989) and Frank Bruni, *New York Times Magazine* (Februray 1997). Redgrave wrote an autobiography, *Vanessa Redgrave: An Autobiography* (1995). □

Odilon Redon

The French painter and graphic artist Odilon Redon (1840-1916) was a leading symbolist and a forerunner of surrealism.

Odilon Redon was born on April 20, 1840, in Bordeaux. His father was a rich French colonist in the southern United States; his mother, of French descent, was from New Orleans. Odilon lived on his uncle's estate in Peyrelebade until 1851, and he spent summers there from 1874 to 1897.

Redon began to study drawing in 1855 with Stanislas Gorin in Bordeaux. At his father's wish Redon started to study architecture in 1860. Four years later he was accepted in the painting class of the École des Beaux-Arts in Paris. He exhibited some prints in the Salon of 1867. During 1870-1871 he served in the Franco-Prussian War.

In 1878 Redon visited Belgium and the Netherlands, studied the works of Rembrandt, and learned from Henri Fantin-Latour the technique of lithography. He produced his first lithographic series, *In the Dream,* in 1879; his second, *For Edgar Allan Poe,* in 1882; and his third, *The Origins,* in 1883. In 1884 Redon became known in avant-garde literary circles through J. K. Huysman's symbolist novel *Against the Grain,* in which Huysman said Redon's drawings "were outside of any known category; most of them leap beyond the boundaries of painting, innovating a very special fantasy, a fantasy of sickness and delirium." That same year Redon exhibited in the first Salon des Indépendants, which he had helped to create.

Redon's next lithographic series were *Homage to Goya* in 1885 and *The Night* in 1886. He exhibited with the impressionists in Paris and with "The Twenty" in Brussels in 1886. He did three series of lithographs for Gustave Flaubert's *The Temptation of St. Anthony*—1888, 1889,

1896—and a series for Charles Baudelaire's *Fleurs du mal* in 1890.

Not until 1890 did Redon produce his first pastels and oils. At this time he replaced Paul Gauguin as a mentor of the young Nabis. The lithographic series *Dreams* was produced in 1891, and his last series, the *Revelation of St. John,* in 1899. Redon also produced some fine portraits, decorative screens, and wall ornaments, and he executed designs for tapestries.

In 1900 Redon began a series of flower studies, turning away from the macabre subjects and nightmare visions of his black-and-white lithographs and drawings to paint in the most voluptuous colors, as in *Flowers in a Vase* (ca. 1905) and *Vase with Anemones* (1912-1914). He was more fully represented at the famous Armory Show of 1913 in New York City than any other artist. He died in Paris on July 6, 1916.

Further Reading

The outstanding work on Redon in English is Klaus Berger, *Odilon Redon: Fantasy and Colour* (1964). An earlier work is Walter Pach, *Odilon Redon* (1913). The definitive book on Redon's graphics is André Mellerio, *Odilon Redon* (1913; repr. 1968), the text of which is in French. Redon is discussed in John Rewald, *Post-Impressionism: From Van Gogh to Gauguin* (2d ed. 1962).

Additional Sources

Cassou, Jean, *Odilon Redon,* Deurne-Anvers: Plantyn, 1974.
Eisenman, Stephen, *The temptation of Saint Redon: biography, ideology, and style in the Noirs of Odilon Redon,* Chicago: University of Chicago Press, 1992.
Hobbs, Richard, *Odilon Redon,* London: Studio Vista, 1977.
Redon, Odilon, *To myself: notes on life, art, and artists,* New York: G. Braziller, 1986. □

John Silas Reed

John Silas Reed (1887-1920), American revolutionist, poet, and journalist, became a symbol in many American minds of the Communist revolution in Russia.

John Reed was born in the mansion of his maternal grandparents outside Portland, Ore., on Oct. 22, 1887. His father sold agricultural implements and insurance. Reed was a frail youngster and suffered with a kidney ailment. He attended Portland public schools and graduated from Harvard in 1910. Although he felt like an outsider, Reed had been active at the university.

Reed went to work for *American Magazine,* of muckraking fame, and *The Masses,* a radical publication. Journalists Ida Tarbell and Lincoln Steffens awakened his liberal feelings, but he soon bypassed them as a radical. In 1914 *Metropolitan Magazine* sent Reed to Mexico, where he boldly walked within the lines of Pancho Villa's army. Villa reportedly made Reed a staff officer and called the

journalist "brigadier general." Reed next gave sympathetic coverage to striking coal miners in Colorado. He went to Europe for *Metropolitan Magazine* when World War I broke out in 1914. He covered the battle fronts in Germany, Russia, Serbia, Romania, and Bulgaria.

Reed and his wife, Louise Bryant, were in Russia during the October Revolution. In reporting the Bolshevik effort to gain control, Reed won V. I. Lenin's friendship. Here Reed gathered materials for his most noted work, *Ten Days That Shook the World* (1919). It is generally recognized that the book lacks factual accuracy, but Bertram Wolfe (1960) contends that "as literature Reed's book is the finest piece of eyewitness reporting the revolution produced."

In 1918 Reed was named Russian consul general at New York, a status never recognized by the United States. In 1919, after he had been expelled from the National Socialist Convention, he formed the Communist Labor party in the United States. He was arrested several times for incendiary speeches and finally, after printing articles in the *Voice of Labor,* was indicted for sedition. He fled to the Soviet Union on a forged passport. The thing usually unreported about Reed among the Muscovites was his unrelenting contention that decisions should be made democratically and his opposition to a monolithic society under dictatorial control. Twice he tried to return to the United States but was unsuccessful. Stricken by typhus, he died on Oct. 19, 1920, in Moscow. He was given a state funeral and buried in the Kremlin.

Further Reading

Bertram D. Wolfe's brilliant introduction to the 1960 Modern Library edition of *Ten Days That Shook the World* takes note of Reed's inconsistencies in the epic, which is more literary than historical. The best work on Reed is Granville Hicks, *John Reed: The Making of a Revolutionary* (1936). A portrait of Reed is in the anecdotal-historical collection of essays of Bertram D. Wolfe, *Strange Communists I Have Known* (1965).

Additional Sources

Baskin, Alex, *John Reed: the early years in Greenwich Village,* New York: Archives of Social History, 1990.

Duke, David C., *John Reed,* Boston: Twayne Publishers, 1987.

Homberger, Eric, *John Reed,* Manchester; New York: Manchester University Press; New York: Distributed exclusively in the USA and Canada by St. Martin's Press, 1990.

Rosenstone, Robert A., *Romantic revolutionary: a biography of John Reed,* Cambridge, Mass.: Harvard University Press, 1990, 1975.

Tuck, Jim, *Pancho Villa and John Reed: two faces of romantic revolution,* Tucson, Ariz.: University of Arizona Press, 1984.
□

Thomas Brackett Reed

As Speaker of the U.S. House of Representatives, Thomas Brackett Reed (1839-1902) was called "Czar Reed." He was one of America's greatest parliamentarians.

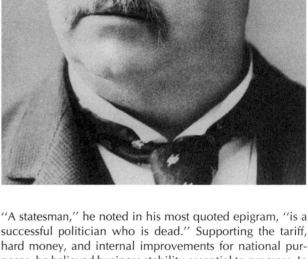

Thomas B. Reed was born on Oct. 18, 1839, in Portland, Maine, an origin stamped in the nasal drawl in which he delivered the corrosive witticisms for which he became famous. Graduating from Bowdoin College in 1860, he studied law, traveled to California, and taught school briefly. In 1865 he joined the Maine bar and entered politics, becoming state legislator (1867-1868), state senator (1869-1870), and attorney general (1870-1873). Elected congressional representative in 1876, he served in the House until 1899.

Congressman Reed's first important assignment was to the "Potter Committee," appointed in 1878 to investigate alleged fraud in the Hayes-Tilden presidential election of 1876. Representing the Republican minority, Reed demonstrated that his party was not alone in fraud and even managed to implicate the nephew of Democratic candidate Samuel J. Tilden. During the 1880s Reed emerged as a leading party regular. As Speaker of the House (1889-1891, 1895-1899), he struggled to revise House rules, especially those that allowed the Democratic majority to avoid action through filibustering or absenteeism. His physical appearance, a towering height of 6 feet 3 inches and a weight of almost 300 pounds, contributed to his impressiveness. Although later congresses lessened his power, he helped establish the principle of party responsibility.

Reed was fiercely partisan. Democrats, he said, never spoke without diminishing the sum of human knowledge.

"A statesman," he noted in his most quoted epigram, "is a successful politician who is dead." Supporting the tariff, hard money, and internal improvements for national purposes, he believed business stability essential to progress. In advance of his time, he opposed capital punishment and advocated woman's suffrage.

In his later years neither party nor country entirely pleased Reed. "The convention could do worse," he said of his presidential ambitions in 1896, "and probably will." He resigned from the House in the aftermath of the Spanish-American War and then practiced law in New York. He died on Dec. 7, 1902, in Washington.

Considered an archconservative by those who opposed his economic views, Reed displayed a genuine humanity and broad learning in his speeches and articles. As a master of the parliamentary skills that make representative government effective, he has rarely been equaled.

Further Reading

Samuel W. McCall, *The Life of Thomas Brackett Reed* (1914), although weak on Reed's political career, is useful for personal detail. William A. Robinson, *Thomas B. Reed, Parliamentarian* (1930), details Reed's political skills. Arthur Wallace Dunn, *From Harrison to Harding* (2 vols., 1922), and H. Wayne Morgan, *From Hayes to McKinley: National Party Politics, 1877-1896* (1969), place Reed's career in the context of "gilded age" politics. □

Walter Reed

Walter Reed (1851-1902), American military surgeon and head of the U.S. Army Yellow Fever Commission, is widely known as the man who conquered yellow fever by tracing its origin to a particular mosquito species.

Walter Reed was born on Sept. 13, 1851, at Belroi, Va., the son of a Methodist minister. After attending private schools, Reed entered the University of Virginia, where he received his medical degree in 1869, after completing only 2 years. He then went to New York, where he received a second medical degree from the Bellevue Hospital Medical College in 1870. After working for the Board of Health of New York and of Brooklyn, Reed was commissioned an assistant surgeon in the U.S. Army with the rank of first lieutenant in June 1875. Then followed 11 years of frontier garrison duty, further study at Johns Hopkins Hospital while on duty in Baltimore, and an assignment as professor of bacteriology and clinical microscopy at the newly organized Army Medical School in Washington in 1893.

When yellow fever made its appearance among American troops in Havana, Cuba, in 1900, Reed was appointed head of the commission of U.S. Army medical officers to investigate the cause and mode of transmission. After some months of fruitless work in searching for the cause of the disease, Reed and his associates decided to concentrate upon determining the mode of transmission. Carlos Juan Finlay first advanced the theory that yellow fever was transmitted by mosquitoes (he blamed it on the *Stegomyia fasciata,* later known as the *Aedes aegypti*) and proved it by experiments, but physicians generally did not credit the possibility. Walter Reed confirmed Finlay's findings by using human subjects. In fact, there was no alternative to experimentation with humans; Reed and his associates argued persuasively that the results would justify the procedure. Mosquitoes that had been fed on yellow fever-infected blood were applied to several of Reed's associates, including Dr. James Carroll, who developed the first experimental case of the disease.

Then followed a series of controlled experiments with soldier volunteers. In all, 22 cases of experimental yellow fever were produced: 14 by mosquito bites, 6 by injections of blood, and 2 by injections of filtered blood serum. At the same time, in order to eliminate the possibility of transmission by contact, Dr. Robert P. Cook and a group of soldiers slept in a detached building in close contact with the clothing and bedding of yellow fever patients from the camp hospital. Since no case of illness resulted from any of these contacts, the theory was conclusively proved.

The value of the commission's work quickly became evident. In 1900 there had been 1,400 cases of yellow fever in Havana; by 1902, after the attack, mounted because of the commission's report, on the mosquito had been under way for over a year in Cuba and the Panama Canal Zone, there was not a single case. Now that its mode of transmission is known, there is no danger of yellow fever in any country with adequate control facilities.

Reed returned to Washington, D.C., in February 1901 and resumed his teaching duties at the Army Medical School. In 1902 Harvard University and the University of Michigan gave him honorary degrees. Only a few days before his death in Washington on Nov. 22, 1902, he was appointed librarian of the Army Medical Library. The Walter Reed Hospital in Washington was named in his honor.

Further Reading

Howard A. Kelly, *Walter Reed and Yellow Fever* (1906; 3d ed. rev. 1923), includes a bibliography of Reed's writings. See also Albert E. Truby, *Memoir of Walter Reed: The Yellow Fever Episode* (1943).

Additional Sources

Bean, William Bennett, *Walter Reed: a biography*, Charlottesville: University Press of Virginia, 1982. □

Lloyd Frederic Rees

Australian artist Lloyd Frederic Rees (1895-1988) featured landscapes and architecture in his drawings and paintings.

Lloyd Frederic Rees was born in 1895 on the east coast of Australia in a small town named Yeronga near Brisbane in Queensland. His father, Owen Rees, was of Welsh ancestry, and his mother, Angéle Burguey, was of Mauritian and French descent.

When he was 21 years of age Rees was to visit Sydney in New South Wales for the first time, as well as Melbourne in Victoria. He worked in the Sydney studio of Smith and Julius at the invitation of Sydney Ure Smith, legendary art publisher and originator of "Art in Australia." After several years of this full-time employment, Rees visited Europe for the first time in 1923, returning to Australia the following year. He married Dulcie Metcalfe in 1926; she died in 1929. In 1931 he married Marjory Pollard.

In 1934 Rees' only child, Alan Lloyd Rees, was born, and the family moved to Northwood, a suburb of Sydney, where Rees was to spend almost 50 years, visiting Europe on several occasions in the 1950s, 1960s, and 1970s. Rees traveled to Tasmania in 1967, the first of many visits, and died there, in Hobart in December 1988.

Almost half of Lloyd Rees' life was spent drawing in different media. As a young man the earliest works were undertaken in Brisbane; then from 1917 creative drawing was cast done in many locations including Italy and Sydney, New South Wales. The focus tightened on Sydney in the 1930s, a passionate tribute to a city to which he remained devoted for the rest of his life.

During the next 20 years, until the mid-1950s, he was able to perfect a painting style that, by his own admission, was comparable to his drawing technique. Following various trips to Europe in the 1950s and 1960s, during which he drew extensively, he was able to develop these drawings into paintings subsequently completed in Australia. These later works are vigorous and brilliant, but with superb sensitivity, and all are redolent of a visionary regard and involvement with landscape and with architecture. Soft ground etchings and lithographs came later, adding as superb amalgamations to all that had been learned from the earlier drawings and the confident, muscular later paintings. The resultant totality expresses superbly a major artist's response to all that was held dear in the landscape about him.

Rees was honored by many exhibitions of his work in Australia as well as in Chicago and Paris. From 1946 to 1986 he was lecturer and instructor in art at the University of Sydney's School of Architecture. He was awarded an Honorary Doctor of Letters by the University of Tasmania in 1984 and a Companion of the Order of Australia (AC) the following year. During the Australian Bicentennial Rees was chosen as one of the "Two Hundred People Who Made Australia Great."

Further Reading

The fullest account of Lloyd Rees is in the two volumes of his memoirs—*The Small Treasures of a Lifetime* (1969) and *Peaks and Valleys* (1985). A similar volume of looking back is Renee Free's *Lloyd Rees—An Artist Remembers* (1987). Free published two earlier books on the artist—*Lloyd Rees* (1972) and *Lloyd Rees—The Later Works* (1983).

Additional Sources

Free, Renee, *Lloyd Rees,* Melbourne: Lansdowne Editions, 1979.
Rees, Jancis, *Lloyd Rees: a source book,* Sydney, N.S.W.: Beagle Press, 1995.
Rees, Lloyd Frederic, *Peaks & valleys: an autobiography,* Sydney: Collins, 1985.
Rees, Lloyd Frederic, *The small treasures of a lifetime: some early memories of Australian art and artists,* Sydney: Collins, 1984. □

Tapping Reeve

Tapping Reeve (1744-1823), an American jurist and founder of the Litchfield Law School, helped bring order to the law through systematic and integrated instruction.

Tapping Reeve, the son of a Presbyterian minister, was born in Brookhaven, Long Island, in October 1744. He entered the College of New Jersey (now Princeton) at 15 and graduated first in his class in 1763. In 1771 Reeve left his post as tutor at Princeton to read law in the traditional way in a judge's office in Hartford, Conn. In a year he was admitted to the bar, and he moved to the remote village of Litchfield, Conn., to begin his practice.

As his reputation grew, young prospective lawyers began to seek Reeve out to supervise their legal preparation. But he soon went beyond the usual procedures (which gave the clerks little or no overview in their reading and only a perfunctory knowledge of established legal forms) to introduce them to the substantive principles and concepts of law. In the absence of accessible textbooks and reports, he inaugurated in 1782 a series of formal and connected lectures which embraced the whole field of jurisprudence. Two years later, with students overflowing home and office, he erected a small frame building near his home and assembled his law library there. In this school he met his classes of from 10 to 20 men. On Saturdays the students were examined on the week's lectures, and Monday evenings were reserved for moot court sessions.

For 14 years Reeve conducted the school alone, but when, in 1798, he was appointed a judge of the superior court, James Gould began to share the teaching duties. The notes from their lectures, as the school catalog noted in 1828, "constitute books of reference, the great advantage of which must be apparent to every one of the slightest acquaintance with the . . . Law."

Before the school closed in 1833 because of increased competition from New York, New Haven, and Boston, Reeve and Gould graduated more than 1,000 lawyers. The roster of names reads like a "Who's Who in Nineteenth-century America," including 2 U.S. vice presidents, 3 Supreme Court justices, 6 Cabinet members, and 116 congressmen.

After 16 years on the state supreme court Reeve was elevated in 1814 to chief justice. He retired the next year, at the age of 70. He published *The Law of Baron and Femme* (1816), a legal analysis of domestic relations that went into four editions. Financially straitened and flagging with age, he withdrew from his school partnership in September 1820 and died in Litchfield on Dec. 13, 1823.

Further Reading

Samuel H. Fisher, *The Litchfield Law School, 1775-1833* (1933), contains a good description of the activities and alumni of Reeve's school and a sympathetic characterization of its teachers. □

Donald Regan

Donald Regan (born 1918) directed America's leading brokerage house (Merrill, Lynch, Pierce, Fenner, and Smith) to new heights of success in the 1970s, before serving consecutively as secretary of the treasury and White House chief of staff under President Ronald Reagan.

Born in Cambridge, Massachusetts, on December 21, 1918, Donald Thomas Regan attended Cambridge Latin School and Harvard University, graduating from the latter with a B.A. in English in 1940. While a student he ran a local guide service which netted him, in addition to his college expenses, savings of $2,000 by the time he graduated. Abandoning law school after less than a year, he enlisted in the Marine Corps and during World War II he served in five major campaigns, including Guadalcanal and Okinawa. After rising to the rank of lieutenant colonel, Regan left the corps in 1946; he subsequently credited his experience in the Marines for teaching him a sense of organization. In 1942 he married Ann Gordon; the couple had four children: Donna, Donald, Richard, and Diane.

Up the Business Ladder

In 1946 Regan was determined to join a corporation with an effective training program; narrowing his choices to two, he chose the nation's leading brokerage house, Merrill, Lynch, Pierce, Fenner, and Smith, Inc. He would spend his entire professional career at Merrill Lynch until entering the government 35 years later. Regan served for two years as a broker in the Washington office of Merrill Lynch, after which he was transferred to the New York office, where he was made manager of the over-the-counter department in 1952. Two years later he became a partner in the firm—at 35, the youngest in Merrill Lynch's history.

Regan's rise in the company continued at a rapid rate. From 1955 to 1960 he managed the Philadelphia office, then returned to New York in 1960. He served successively as director of the administrative division (1960-1964), executive vice president (1964-1968), president (1968-1971), and board chairman and chief executive officer (1971-1980).

Innovative Business Leader

During his years at the helm, Merrill Lynch diversified its services in a revolutionary way, entering into a wide range of financial services including money market funds, issuance of credit cards, and provision for check-writing by investors. Under Regan's leadership, the firm—which had originated the "chain-store" concept among brokerage houses—became a "supermarket" for financial services. Regan's performance in these years earned him a reputation as a corporate "maverick," a term he always rejected. (Mavericks, he contended, wander away from the herd, while it was always his purpose to lead.)

His leadership was profitable for the corporation and for himself. Merrill Lynch's annual revenues increased sixfold in the 1970s, while Regan amassed a personal fortune consisting of over 240,000 shares of the company's stock (estimated to be worth $8.5 million) by 1979.

Despite his prominence and formal membership in organizations of the nation's leading business executives (such as the Committee for Economic Development, the Council on Foreign Relations, and the Business Roundtable), Regan kept a low profile in national politics. Although a member of the influential 44-member Policy Committee of the Business Roundtable from 1978 on, his views on specific policy issues remained something of a mystery to the public. Even as a chief executive officer, Regan guarded his time and his privacy, earning a reputation as an "eight-to-five" executive and retreating with his wife to their colonial home in Mount Vernon, Virginia, for weekends.

Service in the Reagan Administration

When President-elect Ronald Reagan selected Regan to be secretary of the treasury in December 1980, press reaction was generally favorable but reserved. His reputation as a staunch supporter of the free market appealed to the financial community; yet many conservatives feared he would not give high priority to the tax reductions mandated by "supply-side" economic theory. As treasury secretary, however, Regan proved to be an effective advocate for tax reform, playing a key role in securing congressional passage of a three-year tax cut in August 1981. Recognized quickly as an effective agency head, Regan did not emerge immediately as the administration's chief economic spokesman. By 1982, however, he assumed that role, eclipsing the heads of the Office of Management and Budget and the Council of Economic Advisers.

Though Regan frequently offered blunt public comments suggesting internal disagreements in the administration (for example, blaming Federal Reserve Board policies for high interest rates and suggesting the need for tax increases in 1982 and 1984), his influence with Reagan rose steadily, culminating in his appointment as White House chief of staff (in an exchange of positions with James A. Baker, III) in early 1985. This appointment—and Regan's prominence, generally, in the Reagan White House—symbolized the power of non-economists in an administration which was almost certain to be remembered for its leadership in directions of economic change. True to his background as a Wall Street innovator, Donald Regan was positioned to play a major role in this revolutionary activity in the final four years of the Reagan presidency.

For almost two years of Reagan's second administration, Regan maintained a fairly high profile as a no-nonsense chief of staff. In this role he carried the president's support over those who disagreed on issues and personalities. But when the Iran-contra scandal broke in November 1986 Regan came under attack for not better advising/protecting the president. With the publication of the Tower report on the scandal (named for the committee's chairman John Tower, former senator from Texas) Regan saw his position as chief of staff so weakened that he resigned February 27, 1987. (He was replaced by another former senator, Howard Baker of Tennessee.)

In 1988 Regan published a memoir of his years in the government, *For the Record.* The book received mixed reviews. Perhaps the most valanced appraisal was given by Morton Kondracke in the *New York Times Review of Books* (May 20, 1988), who called it "a substantial (if self-serving) memoir of the reagan Presidency and a riveting tale of political downfall and human agony."

Further Reading

No biography of Regan has been produced, nor was there any systematic study of his tenure as secretary of the treasury and White House Chief of Staff apart from his own memoir *For the Record* (1988). The best sources on his personal history were *Fortune* (March 23, 1981) and several profiles that appeared when he was named to the Treasury position, including *U.S. News & World Report* (December 22, 1980) *and National Journal* (December 20, 1980). His impact on Merrill Lynch was best discussed in *Fortune* (March 23, 1981). □

Regiomontanus

The German astronomer and mathematician Regiomontanus (1436-1476) constructed the first European observatory and established trigonometry as a separate area of study in mathematics.

Regiomontanus, called after the Latinized form of his birthplace, Königsberg, in the duchy of Coburg, was born Johann Müller on June 6, 1436, the son of a miller. At the age of 12 he began the study of classical languages and mathematics at the University of Leipzig. In 1452 he moved to Vienna and became the favorite pupil of Georg Peurbach, astronomer and mathematician, who interested Regiomontanus in securing a truly reliable version of Ptolemy's *Almagest.*

A year after Peurbach's death in 1461, Regiomontanus went to Italy and established close contacts with Cardinal Bessarion, the leading Greek scholar of the time. Regiomontanus made quick progress in Greek and studied various Greek mathematical and astronomical texts in addition to Ptolemy's *Almagest.* The study of this latter work enabled him to complete Peurbach's *Epitome in Cl. Ptolemaei magnam compositionem,* but it saw print only in 1496.

The most important work of Regiomontanus, completed in 1464 but printed in 1533, was the first fullfledged monograph on trigonometry, *De triangulis omnimodis libri quinque* (Five Books on All Kinds of Triangles). The first two books dealt with plane trigonometry, while the rest were largely devoted to spherical trigonometry. Although Regiomontanus relied heavily on Arabic and Greek sources, such as al-Battani, Nasir al-Din al-Tusi, Menealos, Theodosius, and Ptolemy, his work was the starting point of a new development leading to modern trigonometry.

In 1468 Regiomontanus went to the court of King Matthias Corvinus of Hungary at Buda to serve as librarian of one of the richest collections of codices in existence in Europe. There he completed his *Tabulae directionum et projectionum,* the first European study of Diophantes' *Algebra.*

In 1471 Regiomontanus went to Nuremberg at the invitation of Bernhard Walther, a rich citizen who provided him with the means to set up the first observatory in Europe. It was equipped with instruments of Regiomontanus's own making, which he described in *Scripta de torqueto, astrolabio armillari,* first printed in 1544. His most important observations concerned the great comet of 1472 (probably Halley's comet). Walther also set up a printing press and published Regiomontanus's calendars and pamphlets.

Regiomontanus published Peurbach's planetary theory, *Theoricae novae planetarum,* and his own ephemerides for 1474-1506, which contained a method of calculating longitudes at sea on the basis of the motion of the moon. The book was used by the leading navigators of the times.

At the summons of Pope Sixtus IV, Regiomontanus, a newly appointed titular bishop of Ratisbon, journeyed to Italy in the fall of 1475 to undertake the reform of the calendar. He died on July 6, 1476, probably the victim of an epidemic.

Further Reading

There is a chapter on Regiomontanus in Lynn Thorndike, *Science and Thought in the Fifteenth Century* (1929). Also useful are J. L. E. Dreyer, *A History of Astronomy from Thales to Kepler* (1905; rev. ed. 1953); Lynn Thorndike, *A History of Magic and Experimental Science* vols. 5 and 6 (1941); and A. C. Crombie, *Augustine to Galileo: The History of Science A.D. 400-1650* (1953). □

William Hubbs Rehnquist

William Hubbs Rehnquist, (born 1924) one of the most Conservative members of the Supreme Court, became the court's Chief Justice when he succeeded Justice Warren Burger in 1986.

William Hubbs Rehnquist was born in Milwaukee, Wisconsin, on October 1, 1924. He grew up in the well-to-do Milwaukee suburb of Shorewood where his father, a first generation American of Swedish parentage, was a wholesale paper salesman. His mother, a graduate of the University of Wisconsin, was a housewife and a civic activist and, fluent in five foreign languages, worked as a freelance translator for local companies. At an early age he embraced his family's respect for such leaders of the Republican Party as Alf Landon, Wendell Wilkie, Herbert Hoover, and Robert A. Taft. As a child, he once told a teacher that his career plans were to "change the world."

Rehnquist attended public schools and as feature editor of the paper of the all-white Shorewood high school was critical of such news commentators as Walter Winchell whom he believed interpreted rather than reported the news. At 17 during World War II the young Rehnquist volunteered as a neighborhood civil defense officer. After attending one year of college on scholarship, he joined the Army Air Corps as a weather observer, serving principally in North Africa from 1943 to 1946. When he returned from Africa he first used his G.I. Bill benefits, then worked various part-time jobs to attend Stanford University in California. Rehnquist was an excellent student; majoring in political science he graduated Phi Beta Kappa in 1948. He received Master's degrees from Stanford and Harvard universities before completing a law degree at Stanford, where he was editor of the law review and graduated first in his class in 1952. His conservative views were solidly established by

this time and he was a willing and able debater on any political issues of the day. Such impressive accomplishments earned Rehnquist a prestigious 18-month clerkship in 1952-1953 with Associate Justice Robert H. Jackson of the U.S. Supreme Court. In 1953 he married Natalie Cornell, a fellow Stanford student.

Republican Activist and Assistant U.S. Attorney General

After completing his clerkship, the Rehnquists moved to Phoenix, Arizona, a city noted for its conservative bent. Once there, Rehnquist established a private practice and became increasingly involved in Republican politics. He soon achieved prominence and in 1958 was chosen as a special Arizona state prosecutor involved in bringing charges against several state officials accused of state highway frauds. He publicly opposed a number of legislative initiatives over the years, including one that would institute busing to achieve racial integration of the schools.

Rehnquist associated with conservative Senator Barry Goldwater and Richard G. Kleindienst, and who served as chairman of the state party and as national field director for the presidential campaigns of Goldwater in 1964 and Richard M. Nixon in 1968. Among the liberals he targeted for criticism during this period were Justices Earl Warren, William O. Douglas, and Hugo L. Black, whom he termed "left-wing philosophers" of the Supreme Court, accusing them of "making the Constitution say what they wanted it to say."

Following his election in 1968, Nixon appointed Kleindienst as deputy attorney general. Kleindienst then chose Rehnquist as assistant attorney general responsible for the Office of Legal Counsel. During his two and a half years at the Justice Department Rehnquist turned what had been an obscure position into a focus of publicity and a target for criticism from liberals and Democrats. Among other controversial positions, Rehnquist defended the constitutionality of the president's policies in Indochina, Nixon's orders barring disclosure of certain government documents, and the mass arrest of peaceful demonstrators. He strongly supported the administration's stringent law-and-order program, including "no-knock" entries, pretrial detention, wire tapping, and electronic surveillance, and repeatedly stated the view that the Supreme Court had been too vigilant in defending the rights of the accused. Such positions were consistent with Nixon's desire to appoint "judicial conservatives" to the Supreme Court, and the president nominated Rehnquist and Lewis F. Powell, Jr., a noted Virginia lawyer, to be associate justices on October 21, 1971.

A Conservative on the Supreme Court

A few liberal senators opposed Rehnquist, but after he softened his law-and-order image and admitted having acquired a more sympathetic attitude toward civil rights, he was confirmed. Rehnquist and Powell then filled the seats on the Court vacated by Justices Hugo L. Black and John M. Harlan.

Rehnquist was easily the most conservative member of the Warren Court. He joined a tribunal that was just beginning to reconcile years of judicial activism maintained under the leadership of Chief Justice Earl Warren with a more restrained approach to decisions symbolized by the new chief, Warren Burger. Even though Nixon had tried to fill the Court with "judicial conservatives," no radical shift to the right immediately occurred. Instead, the Court pursued an uneven course, sometimes adhering to a conservative position, at other times to a liberal one. There was, however, never a doubt about where Rehnquist stood. When the Court in *Roe* v. *Wade* (1973) overturned state laws against abortions, he dissented, arguing in favor of state power. Similarly, when the majority upheld bussing as a means to bring about desegregation in *Keyes* v. *School District No. 1, Denver, Colorado* (1973), Rehnquist wrote a stinging dissent. Often the only dissenter, he opposed school desegregation, women's rights, civil-service jobs for aliens, and health care for the poor, among others. Especially during the early years on the Court, his one-man dissents occurred so often that Rehnquist's law clerks presented him a Lone Ranger doll, referring to their boss as the "lone dissenter." He remained unpopular with liberals who argued that his unwavering support on such issues as states rights served to endorse blatant discrimination against minorities and women. Nevertheless, he was also recognized as an extremely intelligent and well organized addition to the Court, and some note that his lone dissents became important in later shaping majority decisions.

No decision illustrated better Justice Rehnquist's orientation than his remarkable decision in *National League of Cities* v. *Usery* (1976). The issue was whether the federal minimum-wage law applied to all state and local government employees. In an earlier case the majority of the Court had decided in favor of the federal government. Rehnquist alone had dissented, arguing against decades of opinions decided since the *New Deal* that the wage law violated state sovereignty. But in *National League of Cities* four justices accepted the reasoning of his previous dissent and Rehnquist wrote for a 5-4 majority that "this Court has never doubted that there are limits upon the power of Congress to override state sovereignty."

By the early 1980s Justice Rehnquist found himself more often in the majority. This occurred not because he changed, but because the Court did. With President Ronald Reagan's appointment of Justice Sandra Day O'Connor in 1981 Rehnquist and Chief Justice Burger gained a reliable third vote, which made it much easier to put together a majority whose views favored Rehnquist's views. Of 28 cases decided during the October 1984 term by a 5-4 vote, for example, the former "lone dissenter" was in the majority in 17. Slowly, the Court seemed to be shifting toward a discernibly conservative position more consistent with Rehnquist's views. Yet even so, the future was cloudy. Early in 1985 the Court overturned Rehnquist's *National League of Cities* opinion in *Garcia* v. *San Antonio* by a 5-4 vote.

When Chief Justice Burger resigned in 1986, President Reagan impressed with Rehnquist's intellect and conservative stances nominated him to be the nation's 16th chief justice, with Antonin Scalia named to the open associate justice slot. Liberals, and members of Congress who had long been at odds with Rehnquist were alarmed at the nomination. Allegations of past misdeeds (including a charge that he had harassed minority voters in Phoenix) were raised to try and thwart the confirmation, but nothing could stick in view of his years on the Supreme Court. The Senate confirmed both nominations.

Rehnquist proved an excellent administrator, lessening the Court's burgeoning case workload. Although he remained one of the most conservative justices, he also maintained a strong sense of independence. He had to endure charges that his opinions reflected his own personal politics more than actual judicial philosophy. However, when examined, it was noted that he often stood with the majority even if it crossed the established Republican line. In *Morrison v Olson* (1988) he upheld Congress' right to appoint independent counsel to investigate and prosecute government officials, over the strenuous objects of the Reagan administration, who had been responsible for his appointment to the Supreme Court. In 1996, he clashed openly with Republicans over their criticism of President Clinton's judicial appointments. As Chief Justice, Rehnquist brought order to the court and won striking support for judicial restraint from his colleagues. His belief that any move to weaken judicial independence would only serve to undermine the effectiveness of the federal courts was the cornerstone of his tenure at the Court. In a 1996 speech he said "Change is the law of life, and judiciary will have to change to meet the challenges which will face it in the future. But the independence of the federal judiciary is essential to its proper functioning and must be retained." Rehnquist was a pillar of conservative judicial thought on the nation's highest court.

Further Reading

The best treatment of Justice Rehnquist's role on the Supreme Court can be found in *The Burger Court: The Counter-Revolution That Wasn't,* Vincent Blasi, editor (1983). For Rehnquist's own views see his *The Supreme Court: How It Was, How It Is* (1987). An excellent article that covered both the course of Rehnquist's career and his ideas was "The Partisan: A Talk With Justice Rehnquist," by John A. Jenkins in *New York Times Magazine* (March 3, 1985). A specialized but nonetheless very good piece was Jeff Powell's "The Complete Jeffersonian: Justice Rehnquist and Federalism," *The Yale Law Journal* 91 (June 1982), which dealt especially with judicial theory and the *National League of Cities* opinion. Peter Iron's *Brennan vs. Rehnquist: The Battle for the Constitution* (1994) compared the conservative and liberal interpretations of the constitution and the courts. David Savage examined the rightward swing of the court in *Turning Right: The Making of the Rehnquist Supreme Court* Rehnquist's own views of the role of the federal judiciary can be found in a speech given May 1, 1996 in *Vital Speeches* May 1, 1996, p 418 *The Future of the Federal Courts.* □

Steve Reich

The American composer Steve Reich (born 1936) was the creator of "phase" and "pulse" music. A leading composer of minimalism in the 1960s and 1970s, Reich continued to expand his compositional resources to achieve striking expressiveness in his vocal pieces in the 1980s. His music, although very complex, was completely accessible.

One of the foremost composers of minimalism, Steve Reich was the creator of "phase" and "pulse" music, both of which rely on the gradual alteration of repetitive rhythmic patterns to create subtle changes in musical texture. Concerned with the manipulation of aural perception, he directed the listener to focus on one of the many rhythmic patterns occurring concurrently in his music by reinforcing one pattern through changes in dynamics and timbre. Although he was responsible for the invention of the "phase-shifting pulse gate," a device used to aid performers in measuring minute rhythmic changes, Reich avoided the use of electronic instruments in performance. Most of his pieces feature large percussion ensembles with the addition of standard concert string and wind instruments and voice. His later works required orchestras and large vocal ensembles.

Born in New York City on October 3, 1936, Reich spent most of his youth shuttling between the East and West coasts. His parents separated when he was very young, and although he spent most of his time with his father, an attorney in New York, Reich's interest in music may be attributed to the influence of his mother, a singer/songwriter who appeared in several musicals during the 1950s. He studied piano until the age of 14, when the influence of jazz compelled him to take up percussion with Roland Kohloff, the principal tympanist of the New York Philharmonic.

Reich's composition career began after his graduation in 1957 from Cornell University, where he received a degree with distinction in philosophy. During 1957 and 1958 he studied composition with Hall Overton, before entering the Julliard School of Music, where he received instruction from William Bergsma and Vincent Persichetti until 1961. He received an M.A. in 1963 from Mills College, where he studied with Darius Milhaud and Luciano Berio.

Creating "Phase" Music

Reich's first experiments with repetitive sounds occurred in 1965 and 1966 with the manipulation of taped voices. His method of rigging the tape recorders with tape loops that doubled back on one another resulted in the gradual dissection and reconstruction of the sounds called "phasing." Reich drew his material from voices that he found in the environment—*It's Gonna Rain,* which used a phrase from a Pentecostal minister delivering a sermon on Noah's flood, and *Come Out,* the text of which was derived from the testimony of a young African-American man injured in a public disturbance. Further experiments with phasing through live performance with the addition of taped sound proved unsatisfying, and the composer began to search for other musical materials.

Reich's interest in African music dated back to 1962, when he discovered A. M. Jones's *Studies in African Music.* With the aid of a travel grant from the Institute for International Education he studied drumming in Accra, Ghana, in 1970. He also acquired an interest in Balinese Gamalan and studied with Balinese masters in Seattle, Washington, and Berkeley, California, during the summers of 1973 and 1974. But Reich never felt comfortable using non-Western instruments or scales in his music. He retained Western tonality and musical instruments in all his works; he also did not consciously borrow the concepts of cyclic rhythms and ensemble playing found in non-Western cultures, for these were present in his music from the start. His acquaintance with non-Western music simply confirmed the validity of his musical intuition.

In 1966 the composer organized a performing group which later became known as the Steve Reich Ensemble. It was created out of necessity, for no existing ensemble was either capable of or interested in performing his early works. Reich composed *Piano Phase, Violin Phase, Phase Patterns,* and *Four Organs* between 1962 and 1970. These works, which explored the controversial "phasing" technique, provoked strong public reaction. A 1973 performance of *Four Organs* at Carnegie Hall divided the audience into two warring factions so vocal that the performers had to count out loud to keep their places in the music. Nevertheless, public acceptance grew steadily throughout the 1970s. The Steve Reich Ensemble, which at times numbered 18 or more musicians, performed over 300 tours across the United States, Canada, and Europe after 1971.

Drumming (1971) was the last and largest work which employed "phasing" techniques. One and one-half hours of music was divided into four parts, which were performed without pause. Each section used a different arrangement of instruments: section one featured four pairs of tuned bongo drums and male voice; the second used three marimbas and female voices; the third employed three glockenspiels, whistling, and piccolo; and the fourth used the entire ensemble of instruments and voices. However, the sections were unified by one rhythmic pattern which occured continuously throughout the piece. Reich systematically explored phasing by moving identical instruments playing the same pattern out of synchronization. He also introduced several new techniques: the gradual change of timbre while pitch and rhythm remained constant, the gradual substitution of rests for beats (or beats for rests) within the constant regular rhythmic pattern, and the imitation of the exact sounds of the instruments by the human voice.

Changing to "Pulse Music"

Several minor works followed *Drumming*. These included *Clapping Music* (1972), a work for two performers who clap their hands, and *Six Pianos* (1973), composed for performance in a retail piano store. Reich's next major work, *Music for 18 Musicians,* was composed in 1976. One critic cited it as one of the ten most important works to have emerged during the 1970s. Based on a cycle of 11 chords, the rhythmic patterns revolved around two underlying beats carried by the voices and the mallet instruments. Changes from chord to chord were triggered internally by the performers. In this way each member of the ensemble exercised a certain measure of control over the musical composition during performance.

Music for 18 Musicians was an excellent example of "pulse" music. All of the instruments or voices played or sang pulsing notes within each chord. At first only briefly introduced, the chords later returned to pulse for five or more minutes as the foundation for small musical pieces.

Reich's reliance on melody and harmony as well as rhythm in his later works indicated a move away from minimalism, which usually suppressed one or more of these. Indeed, *Tehillim* (1982), his successful vocal work, represented a significant change in his compositional style. A broad melodic structure supplanted the short repetitive patterns which characterized his earlier works. The four solo voices conveyed the five Jewish psalm texts in whole, much in contrast to his earlier works, which used voices only as a sonorous addition to the ensemble. Furthermore, the psalm texts clearly prescribed the musical direction. The final "hallelujah," for example, was exhilirating.

Desert Music (1984) was a later work in the solo vocal and orchestral idiom. Scored for 27 voices and an 88-piece orchestra, it was by far his most ambitious work to that point. Reich derived the text from the poems of William Carlos Williams. Although it was a somber commentary on nuclear war, Reich was still able to instill the music with joy, excitement, and humor.

Aside from his concert pieces, Reich collaborated with several choreographers, including Elliot Feld, Alvin Ailey, and Laura Dean. Jerome Robbins set his *Eight Lines* to dance for the New York City Ballet on 1985.Up to this point, Reich had avoided composing for the theater.

Music of Human Speech

The transformation of human speech into music shaped his work in the late 1980s and 1990s. For *Different Trains* (1988) he recorded the voices of Holocaust survivors, transcribed the most melodious phrases into musical motation, and developed the entire musical structure from this. In performance the taped voices stored in a sampling keyboard which enabled them to be precisely integrated with the live musicians.

Reich collaborated with his wife, the video artist Beryl Korot, to create *The Cave* (1993), a two-and-a -half hour multimedia opera for ensemble, voices, tape, and video. The cave in the title refered to the Cave of Machpelah, the traditional burial place of the Hebrew patriarchs and matriarchs, and so sacred to Jews, Muslims and Christians. Taped voices and video footage of Israelis, Palestinians and Americans were combined with graphics, songs and chants of Biblical and Koranic texts and the music of a 13 member ensemble. As K. Robert Schwarz wrote in *Opera News* (October 1993), "Reich and Korot have painstakingly constructed a unique hybrid - not quite music video, not quite docu-drama, not quite opera, but owing sonething to them all. [Audiences] may be glimpsing the face of music theater in the twenty-first century."

Steve Reich was the recipient of numerous grants and fellowships from the Rockefeller Foundation, the National Endowment for the Arts, and the Guggenheim Museum. He received commissions from Radio Frankfurt, the San Francisco Symphony, and the Ensemble Intecontemporain of Paris. His recordings can be found on CBS-Odyssey, Columbia Masterworks, Deutsche Grammaphon, ECM, Angel Records, and Elektra Nonesuch.

Further Reading

The reader is encouraged to consult Steve Reich's *Writings on Music* edited by K. Koenig (Halifax, Nova Scotia, 1974). Although not particularly well-written, this collection of essays provided insight into his compositional development as a journey of discovery rather than decision. Two interviews, one by M. Nyman in *Musical Times* 62 (1971), and one by E. Wasserman in *Art Forum* (May 1972), addressed his popular success in the 1970s. An article in the German periodical *Melos/Neue Zeitschrift für Musik* 1 (1975) examined his innovations in musical form and structure. Articles also appeared in the *New York Art Journal* 17 (1980) and *Virtuoso* (June 1981). A more detailed biographical essay can be found in David Ewen's *American Composers* (1982). □

Tadeus Reichstein

The Polish-Swiss organic chemist Tadeus Reichstein (1897-1996) shared the Nobel Prize in Physiology or

Medicine for his discoveries relating to the hormones of the adrenal cortex.

The son of Isidor Reichstein, an engineer, Tadeus Reichstein was born in Włocławek, Poland, on July 20, 1897. In 1914, shortly after his family moved to Zurich, he became a naturalized Swiss citizen. He began the study of chemistry at the State Technical College at Zurich in 1916, qualified in 1920, and in 1922 graduated as a doctor of philosophy in chemistry. For some years thereafter he investigated the cause of the flavor of coffee. In 1929 he became lecturer in organic and pharmaceutical chemistry at the Zurich Technical College, where in 1934 he was appointed titular professor, and in 1937 associate professor, of organic chemistry. In 1933 he synthesized ascorbic acid, independently of (Sir) Norman Haworth and by a different process.

In 1938 Reichstein was appointed professor of pharmaceutical chemistry, and in 1946 also of organic chemistry, in the University of Basel. From 1948 to 1952 he supervised the design of the new Institute of Organic Chemistry at Basel, of which, having meanwhile relinquished the chair of pharmaceutical chemistry (1950), he was director until 1960.

Chemistry of the Adrenal Cortex

In 1929 a long-standing rheumatoid arthritic was, because of an acute attack of jaundice, referred to Philip

Showalter Hench of the Mayo Clinic, Rochester, Minnesota. Within a few days most rheumatoid symptoms disappeared. During the next five years Hench saw 16 further cases, all of which were improved by the intercurrent jaundice. He concluded that the beneficial effect might be due to excess of a normal bile constituent or to an abnormal substance present in jaundice. He and his co-workers therefore administered bile and bile salts to rheumatoid arthritics, but no beneficial effects were observed. In 1931 Hench noted that female arthritics sometimes improved during pregnancy, and over several years he and his co-workers confirmed this fact. Hench now assumed that the improvement was due to the presence of a substance X, which was the same in jaundiced cases as in pregnant women. About 1938 he concluded that substance X was probably not derived from the bile but was a hormone found in both males and females.

About 1929 scientists first prepared extracts of the adrenal cortex which checked the symptoms following removal of the adrenals in animals and also those of Addison's disease in human patients. These extracts were named "cortin," and it seemed desirable to elucidate its composition and to prepare it in a pure state.

In 1934 E. C. Kendall, of the University of Minnesota, found that an extract thought to be pure cortin was really a mixture. In 1934 also Reichstein entered this field, and he and Kendall soon isolated about ten compounds from the adrenal cortex. Their detailed chemical investigation was mainly due to Reichstein. He soon proved that all such substances are steroids, and he continued to isolate new steroids from the cortex. By 1950, 29 were known.

The steroids were characterized by the presence of a complex nucleus, consisting of four rings bound together in a certain order to form a chain. This nucleus contained 17 carbon atoms, each bound to one or two hydrogen atoms. The nature of a particular steroid was determined by the nature of any substituent groups attached to carbon atoms in the nucleus. Of the 29 steroids isolated from the cortex by 1950, six were biologically active and not found in any other organ. They all contained 21 carbon atoms, that is, four additional to the 17 contained in the nucleus. The biological activity was dependent on the presence of a double bond. These cortical steroids were shown to influence the fluid balance of the body, the storage of sugar, and the metabolism of carbohydrates and proteins.

In 1934 both Reichstein and Kendall became interested in four of the active steroids, which Kendall called compounds A, B, E, and F. Compound E was isolated by Kendall in 1935 and about the same time by Reichstein. It was found to be 11-dehydro-17-hydroxycorticosterone. It was also found that it did not prolong the life of adrenalectomized animals but that it restored the power of their muscles to contract.

These substances were present in the adrenals in such minute amounts that to obtain enough for clinical purposes it was necessary to synthesize them. In 1937 Reichstein, starting with a bile acid, synthesized the simplest member of the group, deoxycorticosterone. Deoxycorticosterone acetate (DOCA) was soon available on an industrial scale and was satisfactorily used in treating Addison's disease.

For a long time other corticosteroids eluded synthesis. Manufacturers were not interested, as there were few patients with Addison's disease. In 1941 Hench and Kendall considered that Hench's substance X was probably Kendall's compound E, and they decided to administer compound E to rheumatoid patients as soon as a supply was available. In 1941 also the National Research Council of the United States, believing that the corticosteroids might be valuable in war, urged that attempts be made to synthesize compound A preparatory to the synthesis of compound E.

In 1943 Reichstein synthesized compound A from deoxycholic acid. His method could not be applied on a large scale, but in 1944 Kendall synthesized it by a more practical method. In 1947 Lewis H. Sarett, of the Merck Laboratories, synthesized a very small quantity of compound E from compound A. In August 1948 Hench, still searching for the hypothetical substance X, reaffirmed his decision to try Kendall's compound E on arthritics, and on September 4 he formally asked the firm of Merck for a supply sufficient for clinical trials. The small amount prepared was sent to Hench, and on September 21 his co-worker Charles H. Slocumb began to administer it to a rheumatoid arthritic. The excellent results led rapidly to the treatment of many other patients by Hench, Slocumb, and Howard F. Polley at the Mayo Clinic, and at the end of 1948 the name of compound E was changed to "cortisone." In February 1949 these workers obtained a small supply of the pituitary adrenocorticotropic hormone (ACTH), and this was also used successfully in treating rheumatoid arthritis, alone and in association with cortisone. Good results were also obtained in acute rheumatism, asthma, and the collagen diseases. The first report on the new treatment, by Hench, Kendall, Slocumb, and Polley, was presented on April 20, 1949. By the end of 1950 several thousand patients in many parts of the world had been successfully treated. In 1950 Reichstein shared with Kendall and Hench the Nobel Prize in Physiology or Medicine for their work in this field.

Later Life

After 1950 Reichstein discovered many other cortical steroids, including aldosterone, a hormone that regulates the salt balance of the body. He also worked on plant glycosides, especially the aglycones of the digitalis and strophanthus groups. His published work was entirely in the form of scientific papers.

In 1947 Reichstein became an Honorary Doctor of the University of Paris, and in 1951 he was awarded the Cameron Prize of the University of Edinburgh. In 1952 he was elected a Foreign Member of the Royal Society, and in 1968 he was awarded its highest honor, the Copley Medal.

By the late 1960s Reichstein had been hard at work for 45 years and the time had come to slow down. He stepped down from his post at the University of Basel, but had no intention of being completely idle. He continued to work in his laboratory until 1987, when his ninetieth year began. Then, his name appeared in print just once more before he died in 1996. Along with 62 other Nobel laureates in 1992, he signed an appeal to the worlds' governments to end the fighting in Bosnia and Herzegovina.

Further Reading

There was a biography of Reichstein in *Nobel Lectures, Physiology or Medicine, 1942-1962* (1964), which also included his Nobel Lecture, as well as those of Kendall and Hench. For an account of the earlier work see R. D. H. Heard, *The Hormones,* vol. 1 (1948). For related aspects of the corticosteroids see A. White, P. Handler, and E. L. Smith, *Principles of Biochemistry* (3d ed. 1964). Also see *New York Times* August 6, 1996. □

Thomas Reid

The Scottish philosopher, clergyman, and teacher Thomas Reid (1710-1796) originated the school of thought known as the philosophy of common sense.

Thomas Reid was the son of Lewis and Margaret Reid. He was born on April 26, 1710, at Strachan, Kincardineshire. Until he was 12 years old, he was educated at home and in the local parish school; he then entered Marischal College, from which he graduated in 1726. During the next decade he studied theology and read widely, and in 1737 he became a Presbyterian minister of the Church of Scotland. In 1740 Reid married his cousin Elizabeth Reid, and during their long life together they raised nine children. In 1752 he gave up his ministry at New Machar to become a professor of philosophy at King's College, Aberdeen. His best-known work, *An Inquiry into the Human Mind on the Principles of Common Sense* (1764), was derived essentially from material he had presented to the local philosophical society, which he had established.

Although David Hume claimed that his own major work, *A Treatise on Human Nature* (1739), "fell stillborn from the press," Reid seems to have been one of its few original readers. The two Scots, who were contemporaries, conducted an infrequent but complimentary correspondence, and Reid wrote, "I shall always avow myself as your disciple in metaphysics." In 1753 Reid succeeded Adam Smith, the famous economist, as professor of moral philosophy at Glasgow. He continued teaching until he retired at the age of 71. For the remaining 15 years of his life Reid published extensively. The two most important works of this period were *Essays on the Intellectual Powers of Man* (1785) and *Essays on the Active Powers of Man* (1788). Reid died on Oct. 7, 1796.

The philosophy of common sense took its point of departure from Hume's skepticism toward impressions and ideas. One of the chief tenets of modern classical philosophy is the representative theory of perception, which assumes that the immediate object of sensation is, in fact, a mental image that presents man with a world of material objects. Likewise, the relations between conceptual ideas are brought about by associations from past experience that are imaginatively projected into the future. Hume's skepticism led him to conclude that inferences on the basis of impressions and ideas are a matter of custom and belief rather than logical inference or demonstration. Reid's pur-

pose was to reject such analysis as "shocking to common sense" and to rely on a description of the way in which perception, conception, and belief work together to produce an instinctive conviction of the validity of man's sensations of the external world and of other selves.

Further Reading

Renewed interest in Reid's work is evident in Timothy Duggon's edition of Reid's *An Inquiry into the Human Mind* (1970). It partially supplements *The Works of Thomas Reid,* edited by Sir William Hamilton (2 vols., 1846-1863). This collection also contains Dugald Stewart's *Account of the Life and Writings of Thomas Reid* (1903). Studies of Reid include A. Campbell Fraser, *Thomas Reid* (1898), and Olin McKendree Jones, *Empiricism and Intuitionism in Reid's Common Sense Philosophy* (1927).

Additional Sources

Lehrer, Keith, *Thomas Reid,* London; New York: Routledge, 1991. □

William Ronald Reid

William Ronald (Bill) Reid (born 1920) was a Canadian artist who played a pivotal role in the resurgence of Northwest Coast Indian art, particularly that of the Haida.

B ill Reid was born January 12, 1920, in Victoria, British Columbia. He was the son of a Haida mother, Sophie Gladstone, from Skidegate Mission, Queen Charlotte Islands, and a Scottish-German American father, William Ronald Reid (Senior). During his childhood his family made several moves between Victoria and Hyder, Alaska; he later lived and worked in Vancouver, British Columbia.

Reid was the first artist born in this century to master the complex principles of northern Northwest Coast art—the art of the coastal Indian tribes of northern British Columbia. He began his task in the early 1950s, in a period when knowledge of the highly conventionalized formal structure that characterizes this art had largely been lost. The cumulative impact of colonization on the Haida, Northern Kwagulth, Tsimshian, and Tlingit peoples had meant the breakdown of these flourishing cultures by the late 1800s, destroying as well the traditional impetus for artistic expression.

With no knowledgeable practicing Haida artists to guide him, Reid had to search out the art far from his mother's and grandfather's native villages, in the museums that now house the finest works, and in the ethnographies written by anthropologists. By studying and sometimes copying these objects and images, he began to uncover the traditional design principles and understand the artistic process behind them. He was thus gradually able to create original images within Haida tradition, and later to extend the boundaries of that tradition by blending Northwest Coast iconography and Western naturalism.

Reid was raised entirely in the European/North American society of his father; as a teenager he first became aware of his Haida heritage. In 1943, when Reid was in his early twenties, he got to know his maternal grandfather, Charles Gladstone (1877-1954), the last in a direct line of Haida silversmiths who had learned their craft from their elders. Gladstone had lived and studied in his youth with his uncle, the renowned Haida artist Charles Edenshaw (c. 1839-1920). The work of Edenshaw, in turn, became Reid's initial artistic inspiration.

Reid's artistic career was preceded by a career in public broadcasting, first in commercial radio and from 1948 until 1958 with the Canadian Broadcasting Corporation (CBC). While working for the CBC in Toronto, Reid enrolled in a jewelry-making course offered by the Ryerson Polytechnical Institute. There, he spent two years studying conventional European jewelry techniques, followed by a partial apprenticeship at the Platinum Art Company.

Before leaving CBC, he wrote and narrated a television documentary that explored Totem Poles of the Queen Charlotte Islands and narrated a film documenting the "People of Potlach" Exhibition at the Vancouver Art Gallery. He returned to the Canadian west coast in 1951 to establish himself as a designer of contemporary jewelry. On a subsequent trip to the Queen Charlotte Islands, however, he saw a pair of bracelets engraved by Charles Edenshaw and decided to devote his creative energies to Haida jewelry, applying the European techniques he had learned.

In 1968 Reid spent a year at the Central School of Design in London, England, on a Canada Council senior fellowship to improve his goldsmithing techniques. Upon his return to Canada, he set up a workshop in Montreal and remained in that city for three years. His London experience strongly influenced all his subsequent production, which included pieces of both Haida and contemporary international design. Highly acclaimed works created during this period included his gold and diamond necklace (1969), the gold *Beaver, Human, and Killerwhale Box* (1971), the gold *Bear Mother Dish* (1972), and the intricate boxwood carving, *The Raven Discovering Mankind in a Clamshell* (1970). The 4.5-ton cedar version of the latter carving was completed ten years later for the University of British Columbia (UBC) Museum of Anthropology (*The Raven and the First Men*, 1980).

Reid considered himself primarily a goldsmith, but in addition to his jewelry he created massive and miniature works in wood, ivory, argillite, and bronze, as well as drawings, lithographs, and silkscreen prints. In 1958 Reid was commissioned by UBC to recreate a section of a Haida village, including two houses and seven poles. This allowed him to quit his broadcasting career and devote full time to his art. *Haida Village* was completed in 1962 with the assistance of Kwagulth carver Douglas Cranmer.

In 1978 Reid completed a 17-meter totem pole for the new Skidegate band council office, Queen Charlotte Islands. It was the first pole to be raised in his mother's village in more than a century. Reid's 15.2-meter ocean-going cedar canoe, *Lootas* ("Wave Eater"), was launched in 1986, and in 1989 it was paddled up the Seine River to be exhibited at the Musee de l'Homme in Paris, France. Among his large bronze works is *The Spirit of Haida Gwaii,* also called *The Black Canoe* (1991), at the Canadian Embassy in Washington, D.C. In creating his large sculptures, Reid utilized the skilled assistance of other Haida and non-Haida carvers and specialists, most notably sculptor George Rammell.

Through the 1990s Reid continued to be recognized for his tireless efforts to preserve the Haida art form. In 1990 he received the $100,000 Royal Bank Award for outstanding Canadian Achievement. Reid was the first recipient of the Lifetime Achievement award presented by the Canadian Native Arts Foundation in 1994. That same year he was inducted into the Order of British Columbia. The Canada Post Corporation issued a stamp on April 30, 1996 featuring "The Spirit of Haida Gwaii". He continued writing about Haida folklore and co-authored *The Raven Steals the Light: Native American Tales* (1996), with Robert Bringhurst. Reid received honorary doctoral degrees from the University of British Columbia, University of Victoria, Simon Fraser University and other schools as well.

Reid's role in recognizing and revitalizing the highest standards of traditional Haida craftsmanship was significant in helping to place Northwest Coast art on the world stage and in giving younger artists a foundation upon which to build their own understanding of Haida form. His acceptance as a 20th-century artist demonstrated the extent to which Haida iconography became for him a means of personal expression, no longer belonging only to the past. His

growing concern with social and environmental issues, particularly those affecting native peoples' self-determination, also found expression in his art and in his many publications.

Further Reading

Two biographies of Reid have been published: *Bill Reid* by Doris Shadbolt (1986) and *Bill Reid: Beyond the Essential Form* by Karen Duffek (1986). Both were accurate and contained many illustrations; Shadbolt's book was a larger and more extensive study. Much has been written about Reid in exhibition catalogues and popular media. Useful among these were *Bill Reid—A Retrospective Exhibition* (Vancouver Art Gallery, 1974) and "The Myth Maker" by Edith Iglauer (*Saturday Night,* 1982).

Reid himself wrote, illustrated, and collaborated on many books and essays. Two important examples in which he discussed Northwest Coast art include "The Art—An Appreciation" in *Arts of the Raven* (Vancouver Art Gallery, 1967) and *Indian Art of the Northwest Coast—A Dialogue on Craftsmanship and Aesthetics* by Reid and Bill Holm (1975). Reid's powerful and often witty poetry and prose was exemplified in three publications: *Out of the Silence* by Reid and Adelaide de Menil (1971); *The Haida Legend of the Raven and the First Humans* (UBC Museum of Anthropology, 1980); and *The Raven Steals the Light* by Reid and Robert Bringhurst (1984). For a general discussion on past and present Northwest Coast Indian art, including Reid's role, see *The Legacy* by Peter Macnair, Alan Hoover, and Kevin Neary (1980). Terren Iiana Wein, *The Black Canoe: Bill Reid and the Spirit of Haida Gwaii* (1996) provided a penetrating look at Reid and an in-depth analysis of his Haida masterpieces. □

Max Reinhardt

The talent and accomplishments of Max Reinhardt (1873-1943) contributed to the modern idea of the director as creative artist. He was an innovator and experimentor with both space and stage techniques and was one of the first directors to develop repertory companies.

Max Reinhardt was born Max Goldman in Baden, near Vienna, on September 9, 1873. His family moved to Vienna in 1877, and it was there he began acting under the name of Max Reinhardt in 1890. For the next ten years he played many roles, first in Vienna, then in Berlin under Otto Brahm at the Deutsches Theatre, and gradually established himself as a performer.

His first production as a director occurred in 1900 when he directed Ibsen's *Love's Comedy.* Shortly thereafter he opened his own cabaret in Berlin. He left Brahm and the Deutsches Theatre and became director of the Kleines Theatre and the Neues Theatre in 1903. During the next two years he would direct *Midsummer Night's Dream,* open an acting school, and purchase the Deutsches Theatre. These actions marked the beginning of a long career in which Reinhardt owned or managed many theaters, directed or produced over 500 plays in a variety of settings; toured

Germany, Europe, and the United States; and established himself as a most versatile and innovative director.

As a director Reinhardt was always in search of the "right" theater for each play he worked on. He used small cabaret and chamber theaters for intimate productions and arena theaters for his more spectacular ones. In the smaller spaces he presented such works as *Salome* and *The Lower Depths* because of the strong actor-audience proximity. The Neues and the Deutsches theaters were larger and better suited for such works as *The Merchant of Venice* or *King Lear*. In his famous playhouse, Kammerspiel, he directed *Ghosts, Man and Superman,* and *Lysistra*. But in his arena theater the Circus Schumann, which was later to become the Grosses Schauspielhaus, Reinhardt tried to realize his dream of a "Theatre of Five Thousand." He hoped to have a playhouse on the scale of the Greek and Roman theaters, one in which spectacle and ritual reached a large number of spectators who would be part of the communal-like event. The Grosses Schauspielhaus, which he built in 1919, was a vast domed arena that seated 3,000 people and had a giant thrust stage and a large revolve. There were no curtains, and behind the stage there was a permanent cyclorama. Such spaces were ideal for his productions of classics such as Aeschylus' *Oresteia*.

Among his other experiments with space were his spectacles such as *The Miracle,* a play for which he converted the interior of the Olympia theater in New York into a gothic cathedral; his outdoor productions such as *Faust,* for which a Faust City was built and added to each year when the play was produced; and his famous presentation of Hofmansthal's *Everyman* at the annual Salzburg festival. The play was staged in front of the cathedral and utilized buildings in the town as part of the production. Another spectacular work of Hofmannsthal's that Reinhardt directed at the festival was *The Salzburg Great Theatre of the World*. He also directed a production of *A Midsummer Night's Dream* at Oxford and used the natural outdoor setting to enhance the play.

Reinhardt was not only an innovator and experimentor with space, he was also an innovator and experimentor with stage techniques. An eclectic as a director, Reinhardt broke with those who favored realism and tried his hand at symbolic drama, impressionism, and naturalism. He also rejected the limitations of the proscenium stage. He favored more the freedom of the Elizabethan stage where actor and audience were in close contact with one another and where the stage could be used with great flexibility. He believed in the fluid use of set and symbolic use of lighting and was among the first to use the revolve for quick scene changes. He experimented repeatedly with the concept that a dramatic work was a total work of art, one that depended upon a mixing of the arts—of the visual, aural, scenic, and musical elements in drama.

Reinhardt also believed that the most important factor in the play was the actor. He was at the center of the art of the theater. Theater was at its best when the director, writer, designer, and composer had all imaginatively assumed the actor's part. While it is the case that Reinhardt held the actor in high regard and was one of the first directors to develop repertory companies, he was such a formidable force in the theater that he greatly enhanced the role of the director. His talent and accomplishments contributed to the modern idea of the director as a creative artist, a person capable of making aesthetic decisions. Reinhardt represented a controlling intelligence that guided the entire production in a vital and peculiarly identifiable manner.

In the early 1930s the Nazi regime forced Reinhardt to give up his theaters. In 1934 he signed a contract with Warner Brothers. He also directed *A Midsummer Night's Dream* in California and Chicago. Then in 1935 he made a film version of the play for Warner Brothers. He emigrated to the United States in 1937 and later opened the Max Reinhardt Actors Workshop for Stage, Screen, and Radio in Hollywood. He suffered a stroke in 1943 and died in New York City.

Further Reading

A critical biography is J. L. Styan, *Max Reinhardt* (1982). Other useful works include Huntley Carter, *The Theatre of Max Reinhardt* (1969) and Oliver M. Sayler, *Max Reinhardt and His Theatre* (1968).

Additional Sources

Reinhardt, Gottfried, *The genius: a memoir of Max Reinhardt,* New York: Knopf: distributed by Random House, 1979.
Styan, J. L., *Max Reinhardt,* Cambridge Cambridgeshire; New York: Cambridge University Press, 1982. □

Erich Maria Remarque

The German author Erich Maria Remarque (1898-1970) was a popular novelist whose "All Quiet on the Western Front" was the most successful German best seller on the subject of the soldier's life in World War I.

Erich Maria Remarque whose real name was Erich Paul Remark, was born on July 22, 1898, in Osnabrück. He attended the Teachers' Training College there and afterward the University of Münster. Toward the end of World War I he served in the army. After the war he worked variously as a press reader, clerk, and racing driver. The immense success of *Im Westen nichts Neues* (1929; *All Quiet on the Western Front*) established him as an author. This novel falls into a clearly distinguishable class of antiwar and antimilitary fiction that grew rapidly in Germany in the later 1920s—Arnold Zweig's *Sergeant Grischa* is another famous example. These books belong in general to that school known as neorealism and are characterized by a matter-of-fact, unpretentious, often colloquial style approximating the newspaper or magazine report.

Although Remarque conceals little of the squalor and bloodiness of life in the trenches, at the same time there is in this book an undeniable sentimental vein which is maintained strongly right through to the pathetic last pages, in which, following the death of his friend, the hero himself falls 2 weeks before the armistice, on a day when all is reported quiet at the front. This novel was translated into some 25 languages and has sold over 30 million copies.

Remarque continued in a similar vein with another war novel, *Der Weg zurück* (1931; *The Road Back*). *Drei Kameraden* (1937; *Three Comrades*) deals with life in postwar Germany at the time of the inflation and is also a tragic love story. By 1929 Remarque had left Germany and from that time lived abroad. The pacifism implicit in his works and their strong sense of pathos and suffering could scarcely endear them to the Nazi government. In 1938, in fact, Remarque was deprived of his German citizenship. In 1939 he arrived in the United States and became an American citizen in 1947. His next novel, *Liebe deinen Nächsten* (1940), was published in America under the title *Flotsam*. After World War II Remarque's productivity increased, and he turned more and more to the study of personal relationships set against a topical background of war and social disintegration. *Arc de Triomphe* (1946), the story of a German refugee surgeon in Paris just before World War II, reestablished his name in the best-seller lists. His later works include *Zeit zu leben und Zeit zu sterben* (1954; *A Time to Love and a Time to Die*), *Der schwarze Obelisk* (1956; *The Black Obelisk*), *Der Funke Leben* (1957; *Spark of Life*), *Der Himmel kennt keine Günstlinge* (1961; *Heaven Has No Favorites*), and *Die Nacht von Lissabon* (1962; *The Night in Lisbon*). All these novels are competent and gripping narratives and are skillful stories of personal crisis, escape, adventure, and intrigue. Remarque also had one play

produced, *Die letzte Station* (1956; *The Last Station*). He died in Locarno, Switzerland, on Sept. 25, 1970.

Further Reading

Despite his immense popularity there have been no general studies of Remarque in English or German. His career is briefly summarized in Harry T. Moore, *Twentieth-century German Literature* (1967). Useful for general background is Ernst Rose, *A History of German Literature* (1960). ☐

Rembrandt Harmensz van Rijn

Rembrandt Harmensz van Rijn (1606-1669) was the paramount artist of the great age of Dutch painting. In range, originality, and expressive power his large production of paintings, drawings, and etchings has never been surpassed.

In the attempt to grasp the full measure of the achievement of Rembrandt, the mistake has sometimes been made of interpreting his works as an autobiography. This they are not. His experiences are reflected in his works not directly, but transfigured into art. The events of art are different in nature from the events of life, and we understand very little about the relations between these two different realms of being. The few mundane facts we know about Rembrandt's life do not begin to explain his works or account for his extraordinary capacities.

Rembrandt was born in Leiden on July 15, 1606, next to the last of the nine or more children of the miller Harmen Gerritsz van Rijn and the baker's daughter Neeltgen Willemsd van Zuytbroeck. For 7 years Rembrandt was a student at the Latin school, and then, in 1620, he enrolled at the university. After only a few months, however, he left to become a painter. He was an apprentice for 3 years of the painter Jacob Isaacsz van Swanenburgh, who had studied in Italy.

In 1624 Rembrandt went to Amsterdam to work with Pieter Lastman, a painter of biblical, mythological, and historical scenes. In the 16th and 17th centuries art theory ranked "history painting" as superior to all other fields, and Lastman was one of the most respected specialists in this kind of subject matter in Holland at the time. Anecdotal painting like Lastman's came to be overshadowed in Rembrandt's time by other themes, such as landscape and still life. In fact, Rembrandt and his school were virtually the only painters of importance who continued to concern themselves with narrative subject matter, mainly based on biblical stories, through the second and third quarters of the century. Unlike Lastman, though, Rembrandt and his followers depicted a great variety of other subjects as well. Yet years later, even after Lastman's death in 1633, Rembrandt continued to borrow his teacher's subjects and motifs, for instance, in *Susanna Surprised by the Elders*. Rembrandt

made a drawing in red chalk after Lastman's 1614 painting of the subject, and in 1647 he freely adapted this composition in a painting.

Works of the Leiden Years

It was Lastman's ability to tell a story visually that impressed his youthful pupil. The earliest works by Rembrandt that we know, beginning with the *Stoning of St. Stephen* (1625), show an only partially successful imitation of Lastman's style, applied to scenes in which a number of figures are involved in a dramatic action.

By 1625 Rembrandt was working independently in Leiden. He was closely associated at this time with Jan Lievens, also a student of Lastman's. The two young men worked so similarly that even in their own lifetime there was doubt as to which of them was responsible for a particular painting. They used the same models and even worked on each other's pictures. Rembrandt's paintings were small in size and scale in these years, however, while Lievens preferred a larger format with life-size figures.

In addition to his narrative subjects, Rembrandt was practicing with pen, brush, and etcher's needle the depiction of emotions conveyed by facial expressions. Throughout his career he was his own most frequent model. Other sitters have been identified as members of his family, but this is conjectural, except in the case of a drawing inscribed with his father's name in a contemporary hand. Rembrandt liked to have his models wear such embellishments as gold chains and plumed hats, testing his skill at depicting varied textures.

By 1631 Rembrandt was ready to compete with the accomplished portrait painters of Amsterdam. His portrait of the Amsterdam merchant Nicolaes Ruts (1631) is a dynamic likeness executed with a degree of assurance that makes it clear why its author was in demand as a portraitist. A major commission soon came to him: *Dr. Nicolaas Tulp Demonstrating the Anatomy of the Arm* (1632). For this large canvas Rembrandt devised a new unified composition for the traditional "anatomy lesson."

Early Amsterdam Years

In 1631 or 1632 Rembrandt moved to Amsterdam, where he had already achieved some recognition as a portraitist. Both his career and his personal life prospered. On a charming silverpoint drawing of a pensive young woman holding a flower, he wrote, "This was drawn after my wife when she was 21 years old, the third day after our engagement—June 8, 1633." After an engagement of more than a year, he married this well-to-do young woman, Saskia van Uijlenburgh. In 1639 the young couple set themselves up in a fine house in the Breestraat, now maintained as a museum, the Rembrandthuis.

Like many prosperous men of his time, Rembrandt soon began to collect works of art, armor, costumes, and curiosities from far places. He used some of these objects as props in his paintings and etchings. The vast collection of drawings and prints that he amassed in the course of time made him familiar with works by artists distant in time and place, as well as by contemporaries. It was, in a way, a substitute for travel; he was quoted as saying, at the age of 23, that he could learn about Italian art without leaving Holland. He had the opportunity to see some Italian paintings in the flourishing mercantile city of Amsterdam, but he would have had to rely mainly on prints to bring Italian art to him. His works reflect his responsiveness to art of the most diverse types, from monumental painting of the High Renaissance to Mogul miniatures.

Rembrandt's works of the middle 1630s were his most baroque; indeed he seemed to be deliberately challenging the enormous prestige of Peter Paul Rubens. This is most explicit in the scenes from the *Passion of Christ* (1633-1639) that Rembrandt painted for the stadholder Frederick Henry. The etching *Angel Appearing to the Shepherds* (1634) shows how the same drama and excitement, the combination of fine detail with a grandiose new sweep based largely on unification of the composition through light and shadow, and the choice of the crucial moment—all characteristic of Rembrandt's baroque style—permeated his graphic works as well as his paintings in this period. The mysterious landscape that adds so strikingly to the emotional communication of this great etching had its parallels in the landscape paintings that also occupied Rembrandt about this time, such as the *Landscape with an Obelisk*.

Middle Period

The *Visitation* (1640) serves well to sum up Rembrandt's style at this transitional point in his development. The rather fussy large-leaved plants and birds in the left foreground are still reminiscent of Lastman. The architecture is pure fantasy; Rembrandt usually represented, in both exterior and interior views, structures that were never seen in reality and, indeed, in many cases could not be built because they were not based on a rational ground plan. The landscape, too, has nothing to do with the innovative Dutch realistic landscape of the 17th century. Its function is to suggest the long distance that Mary has traveled to visit her cousin. Instead of a baroque thrust into depth, the figures are deployed parallel to the picture plane, and prominent horizontal and vertical elements stabilize the composition in the "classicizing" manner that was to predominate in the works of Rembrandt, as in Dutch painting in general, in the middle of the century. Most significant is the fact that the picture dwells on the meaning of the story in a human sense. It demonstrates Rembrandt's unique ability to communicate the inmost emotions of the participants in the scene. The arbitrary use of light is a major expressive resource; this was the hallmark of his genius throughout his career.

One of Rembrandt's largest and most famous paintings is the group portrait known since the mid-18th century as the *Night Watch*. This is, in fact, not a night scene at all, and it is correctly titled the *Militia Company of Captain Frans Banning Cocq*. For this important commission, completed in 1642 but probably begun in the late 1630s, the artist devised an original, dynamic composition in the baroque style which he had already begun to abandon by this time. The painting was unfortunately cut down in the 18th century. Attempts have been made to relate this scene to an actual historical event, to a contemporary drama, and to

emblematic ideas. These different interpretations reflect the persistent impression that this is something more than a group portrait.

There is no foundation at all for the legend that Captain Cocq and his company were dissatisfied with their painting and that this failure initiated a decline in Rembrandt's fortunes that persisted until the end of his life. On the contrary, there is considerable evidence that the picture was highly praised from the start. Such difficulties as Rembrandt had were not caused by any rejection of his work.

Having had three children who died in infancy, Saskia gave birth to a fourth child, Titus, in September 1641. In June 1642 Saskia died. Acrimony entered Rembrandt's household with the widow Geertge Dircx, who came to take care of Titus. Hendrickje Stoffels, who is first mentioned in connection with Rembrandt in 1649, remained with him until her death in 1663. She left a daughter, Cornelia, who had been born to them in 1654.

About 1640 Rembrandt developed a new interest in landscape which persisted through the next 2 decades. A series of drawings and etchings show keen observation of nature, great originality in composing, and marvelous economy. The etched *View of Amsterdam* (ca. 1640) was the forerunner of the splendid panoramic landscape paintings of Jacob van Ruisdael. The tiny painting *Winter Landscape* (1646) has all the earmarks of having been painted from life, on the spot. This would be a rare case in 17th-century Dutch landscape, which customarily was painted in the studio from sketches.

In contrast with Rembrandt's dramatic religious compositions of the earlier period, those of the 1640s tend to be quiet, with exquisitely controlled light casting an almost palpable spiritual glow on scenes that might otherwise seem to depict humble everyday life. The painting *Holy Family* (1646) exemplifies this tender and compassionate quality, as does the *Hundred Guilder Print,* one of the most renowned of the master's etchings, on which he probably worked from about 1645 to 1648. Bustlength paintings of Christ, such as the one in Detroit, from the later 1640s, have a similar emotional tone. Richness of paint surface and warm, harmonious color add luster to the paintings of this period.

Later Years

The ruinous effect on commerce of the first Anglo-Dutch War (1652-1654) may have played a part in Rembrandt's financial difficulties, of which there is evidence from 1653 on. In 1656 he filed a petition of insolvency. In connection with this, an inventory was made listing all his possessions. This list of 363 items is an invaluable source of information as to the objects, and particularly the works of art, that Rembrandt had collected. It included numerous portfolios of drawings and prints. All these prized possessions were sold at auction, beginning in December 1657. In 1660 Rembrandt, Titus, and Hendrickje moved to a smaller house.

The idea that the formerly renowned artist was now friendless and neglected is a fiction. In fact the record shows that several prominent men who were his friends stood by

Rembrandt through these misfortunes. Though it is true that fashionable taste in art began to favor a more highly finished and elegant type of painting at this time, nevertheless Rembrandt continued to receive commissions and to work productively.

In 1652 a Sicilian nobleman who was a discerning collector commissioned a painting from Rembrandt. If the painting was satisfactory, two more were to be ordered. *Aristotle Contemplating a Bust of Homer* was completed in 1653 and shipped off to Sicily, and the two additional pictures were sent in 1661. The meaning of the *Aristotle* is not yet fully understood, but its quality is unquestionable. The lavish impasto, the scintillating white and gold contrasted with velvety blacks, and the quality of inwardness and self-communion are characteristic features of Rembrandt's style at this time.

Even commissioned portraits, such as the one Rembrandt painted of his old friend, the Amsterdam patrician Jan Six (1654), were built up of the bold patches of paint that invite the eye of the beholder to see the solid form beneath the surface. Another important commission for a group portrait came to Rembrandt in 1656: the *Anatomy Lesson of Dr. Joan Deyman,* of which only a fragment has survived. A pen drawing, however, shows the symmetrical composition, with the surgeon standing in the center behind the cadaver, which is seen in sharp foreshortening, perpendicular to the picture plane. Other figures are grouped symmetrically on either side. The difference between this composition and the diagonal in depth that unified the *Dr. Tulp* (1632) is a measure of the change not only in Rembrandt but in the dominant style in Dutch painting between the 1630s and the 1650s.

Rembrandt's regal *Self-portrait* (1658; Frick Collection, New York) shows the aging artist seated squarely before us, meeting our eyes with forthright gaze, and wearing a fantastic costume whose sharp horizontals and verticals stress the composition based on right angles that epitomizes this period. A number of admirable etched portraits also date from this time, as well as etchings of religious subjects, such as the impressive *Ecce homo* (1655), which reflects an engraving made in 1510 by the great Dutch graphic artist Lucas van Leyden.

It is noteworthy that even in his full maturity Rembrandt adapted features from many sources. It may be that making the inventory and facing the loss of his collection caused him to give special attention to the prints and drawings in his portfolios. In 1658, for instance, he painted the small and sensitive *Jupiter and Mercury Visiting Philemon and Baucis,* which was based on a painting by Adam Elsheimer, whose work had greatly impressed Rembrandt's teacher, Lastman, when he was studying in Rome. Rembrandt could have known the Elsheimer painting through an engraving made after it by Goudt in 1612.

In 1660-1661 Rembrandt painted an enormous canvas commissioned for the splendid new town hall in Amsterdam. It was the *Conspiracy of the Batavians,* or the *Oath of Julius Civilis,* known to us through the remaining fragment and a pen-and-wash drawing of the entire composition. The 17th-century Dutch, who in 1648, after 80 years of war, had

succeeded in finalizing their freedom from Spanish rule, considered themselves the descendants of the Batavians, who had rebelled against the Romans. The scene of the oath was painted broadly, to be viewed from a distance, and in the most luminous colors. For reasons not entirely understood, the painting was removed after hanging in the town hall for a time. Perhaps it was unacceptable because the style was too far from the traditional treatment of patriotic subjects for public places.

In any case, Rembrandt was even at this time held in high regard. In 1662 he painted the *Sampling Officials of the Drapers' Guild,* a group portrait whose vitality and psychological penetration certainly justified these dignified officials in their choice of a portraitist. The boldness of his brushstroke, the effulgence of his color, glowing like embers in a dark room, and the command of emotional content increased as he grew older. The beautiful pair of late portraits, *Man with a Magnifying Glass* and *Lady with a Pink,* have few peers in all the realm of art.

Hendrickje died in 1663. In February 1668 Titus married Magdalena van Loo; he died in September. The lonely Rembrandt continued to paint. His last *Self-portrait* (Mauritshuis, The Hague) is dated 1669. When he died, on Oct. 4, 1669, a painting, *Simeon with the Christ Child in the Temple,* was left unfinished on his easel.

Rembrandt the Teacher

Throughout his career Rembrandt was much sought after as a teacher, and the fees his pupils paid yielded considerable income. Even as early as the Leiden years students came to him; Gerard Dou was working in his studio by 1628, and it has been conjectured that it is Dou who is represented in Rembrandt's typical small painting of that year, the *Painter at His Easel.* Later pupils included Jacob Adriaansz Backer, Ferdinand Bol, Govaert Flinck, Phillips Koninck, Gerbrand van den Eeckhout, Samuel van Hoogstraten, Carel Fabritius, Abraham Furnerius, Lambert Doomer, Willem Drost, Abraham van Dyck, Heyman Dullaert, and Aert de Gelder.

It was common studio practice for the master to retouch or overpaint the drawings and paintings of his pupils and to sign works done in his studio even if they were not from his own hand. Rembrandt's students worked from life, but they also copied his works. These customs have added to the difficulties in attribution. Deliberate falsification has of course also contributed to the problems in determining the authenticity of Rembrandt's works.

Further Reading

Concise introductions to Rembrandt and his work are Christopher White, *Rembrandt and His World* (1964); Joseph-Émile Muller, *Rembrandt* (1969); and Henry Bonnier, *Rembrandt* (1970). Bob Haak, *Rembrandt: His Life His Work, His Time* (trans. 1969), has an excellent text and many reproductions. Scholarly studies of the artist include Jakob Rosenberg, *Rembrandt: Life and Work* (rev. ed. 1964), and Otto Benesch, *Rembrandt,* edited by Eva Benesch (1970).
The standard catalog of the paintings is Abraham Bredius, *Rembrandt: The Complete Edition of the Paintings,* revised by Horst Gerson (1969), although its reproductions leave much

to be desired. Far more satisfactory are the plates in Horst Gerson, *Rembrandt Paintings* (1968), which includes excellent essays on Rembrandt's life and his place in Dutch painting. The way in which our understanding of Rembrandt can best be increased, through the study in depth of individual works, is admirably demonstrated by Julius S. Held, *Rembrandt's "Aristotle" and Other Rembrandt Studies* (1969). Arthur M. Hind, *A Catalogue of Rembrandt's Etchings* (1923; 2d rev. ed. 1967), is the standard catalog of the prints; and Otto Benesch, *The Drawings of Rembrandt* (6 vols., 1954-1957), is the basic reference work on the drawings.

Recommended for general background are Paul Zumthor, *Daily Life in Rembrandt's Holland* (1959; trans. 1963); Pieter Geyl, *The Netherlands in the Seventeenth Century* (2 vols., 1961-1964); Jakob Rosenberg, Seymour Slive, and E. H. ter Kuile, *Dutch Art and Architecture, 1600-1800* (1966); and Johan H. Huizinga, *Dutch Civilization in the Seventeenth Century and Other Essays,* selected by Pieter Geyl (1968). □

Charles Lennox Remond

Charles Lennox Remond (1810-1873), African American leader, was one of the first black abolitionists and a delegate to the World Antislavery Convention held in London in 1840.

Charles Lennox Remond was born in Salem, Mass., on Feb. 1, 1810, the son of a free West Indian barber who had voluntarily emigrated to the United States. Remond was well educated and, like many of the free, middle-class African Americans of his day, was an ardent abolitionist and a major figure in the Antislavery Convention movement that served as a forum for black Americans after 1830.

Remond was one of the original 17 members of America's first Antislavery Society. The first African American to become a regular lecturer for the Massachusetts Antislavery Society, he was an ardent supporter of William Lloyd Garrison. In 1838 Remond was elected secretary of the American Antislavery Society and vice president of the New England Antislavery Society.

For several years Remond was the most distinguished black abolitionist in America. When his uniqueness was challenged by Frederick Douglass, Remond reacted bitterly. While he never got over his jealousy of Douglass, on several occasions the two found themselves allied. One occasion was the national antislavery convention at Buffalo, N.Y. (1843), at which Henry Highland Garnett challenged the slaves to liberate themselves by any means necessary. Remond and Douglass led the opposition that rejected the address as the sentiment of the convention. Neither man was at this time committed to violence, or even to political action, as a means of liberation.

As time passed, Remond grew increasingly frustrated over the injustice of color discrimination. He protested segregated travel in Massachusetts and was so incensed by the Dred Scott decision (1857) that he felt he could "owe no allegiance to a country . . . which treats us like dogs." For

African Americans to persist in claiming citizenship under the U.S. Constitution seemed to him "mean-spirited and craven." Eventually he moved very close to the radical position of the fiery Garnett. Speaking at the State Convention of Massachusetts Negroes in New Bedford (1858), he urged that the convention promote an insurrection among the slaves, declaring that he would rather see his people die than live in bondage.

During the Civil War, Remond recruited for the Negro 54th Massachusetts Infantry. After the war he served as a clerk in the Boston customhouse until his death on Dec. 22, 1873.

Further Reading

Useful information on Remond is offered by Herbert Aptheker, ed., *A Documentary History of the Negro People in the United States* (1951), and by August Meier and Elliot Rudwick, eds., *The Making of Black America: Essays in Negro Life and History* (2 vols., 1969). See also John Daniels, *In Freedom's Birthplace: A Study of the Boston Negroes* (1914; repr. 1968); Carter G. Woodson and Charles H. Wesley, *The Negro in Our History* (1922; 11th rev. ed. 1966); and Wilhelmena S. Robinson, *Historical Negro Biographies* (1967; 2d rev. ed. 1969). □

Ernest Renan

A French author, philologist, archeologist, and founder of comparative religion, Ernest Renan (1823-1892) influenced European thought in the second half of the 19th century through his numerous writings.

Ernest Renan grew up in the mystical, Catholic French province of Brittany, where Celtic myths combined with his mother's deeply experienced Catholicism led this sensitive child to believe he was destined for the priesthood. He was educated at the ecclesiastical college at Tréguier, graduating in 1838, and then went to Paris, where he carried on the usual theological studies at St-Nicolas-du-Chardonnet and at St-Sulpice. In his *Recollections of Childhood and Youth* (1883) he recounted the spiritual crisis he went through as his growing interest in scientific studies of the Bible eventually made orthodoxy unacceptable; he was soon won over to the new "religion of science," a conversion fostered by his friendship with the chemist P. E. M. Berthelot.

Renan abandoned the seminary and earned his doctorate in philosophy. At this time (1848) he wrote *The Future of Science* but did not publish it till 1890. In this work he affirmed a faith in the wonders to be brought forth by a science not yet realized, but which he was sure would come.

Archaeological expeditions to the Near East and further studies in Semitics led Renan to a concept of religious studies which would later be known as comparative religion. His was an anthropomorphic view, first publicized in

his *Life of Jesus* (1863), in which he portrayed Christ as a historical phenomenon with historical roots and needing a rational, nonmystical explanation. With his characteristic suppleness of intellect, this deeply pious agnostic wrote a profoundly irreligious work which lost him his professorship in the dominantly Catholic atmosphere of the Second Empire in France.

The *Life of Jesus* was the opening volume of Renan's *History of the Origins of Christianity* (1863-1883), his most influential work. His fundamental thesis was that all religions are true and good, for all embody man's noblest aspirations: he invited each man to phrase these truths in his own way. For many, a reading of this work made religion for the first time living truth; for others, it made religious conviction impossible.

The defeat of France in the Franco-Prussian War of 1870-1871 was for Renan, as for many Frenchmen, a deeply disillusioning experience. If Germany, which he revered, could do this to France, which he loved, where did goodness, beauty, or truth lie? He became profoundly skeptical, but with painful honesty he refused to deny what seemed to lie before him, averring instead that "the truth is perhaps sad." He remained sympathetic to Christianity, perhaps expressing it most movingly in his *Prayer on the Acropolis of Athens* (1876), in which he reaffirmed his abiding faith in the Greek life of the mind but confessed that his was inevitably a larger world, with sorrows unknown to the goddess Athena; hence he could never be a true son of Greece, any more than any other modern.

Further Reading

Little has been written in English about Renan. Two of the best studies are by Richard M. Chadbourne: *Ernest Renan as an Essayist* (1957) and *Ernest Renan* (1968).

Additional Sources

Mercury, Francis, *Renan,* Paris: O. Orban, 1990. □

Ruth Rendell

Ruth Rendell (born 1930) was one of the world's most skillful and popular writers of mysteries and suspense thrillers.

R uth Grasemann was born on February 17, 1930, in London, England, and was educated at Laughton High School in Essex. She worked as a newspaper reporter and sub-editor in West Essex from 1948 to 1952. In 1950 she married Donald Rendell, whom she later divorced, then remarried in 1977. They had one son.

Rendell was variously described as the "new Agatha Christie," the "new First Lady of Mystery," and the "British Simenon." While she was hailed primarily for her creation of character, she was also praised for her inventive plots, her keen social observation and incisive social criticism, her evocative settings, and her startling and often grim endings. But what especially raised her writing above the level of much detective fiction was her masterly control of elements of style (figurative language, dialogue, and irony) more often associated with "serious" fiction.

A prolific writer with consistently high standards, Rendell completed 27 novels and three short story collections. These works fall into two separate sub-genres of crime fiction. The first is the straightforward British police procedural, set in Kingsmarkham, which features Inspector Wexford as the central figure. The second is the individual psychological suspense thriller, with no detective and with no recurring characters. As noted by Francis Wyndham, Rendell excels equally in both forms: "Ruth Rendell's remarkable talent has been able to accommodate the rigid rule of the reassuring mystery story (where a superficial logic conceals a basic fantasy) as well as the wider range of the disturbing psychological thriller (where an appearance of nightmare overlays a scrupulous realism)."

The Kingsmarkham Series

It was in her first novel, *From Doon with Death* (1964), that Rendell introduced her central character, Detective Chief Inspector Reg Wexford of Kingsmarkham, a particularly murder-prone village in Sussex. In this and the 14 Wexford novels that followed the reader is given a realistic portrayal of an intelligent and admirable human being. Wexford is a great reader with a ready supply of literary quotations. Frequently these quotes are thematically or symbolically pertinent to the plot, and sometimes a quotation fragment serves as the book's title.

A civilized man with decent values, Inspector Wexford is unusually tolerant and compassionate. His success in case-solving is often based on his ability to see in people emotions and motivations that other detectives would overlook. In *Some Lie and Some Die* (1973), a novel centered around a rock music festival, it is Wexford's understanding of young people and his acceptance of their values which are instrumental to his solution of the case.

After his first appearance in the series at the age of 52, Wexford continued to grow, coping with domestic problems, conflicts with superiors, and personal illness. He is a vulnerable and thereby appealing character: a detective who transcends his crime-solving function.

To add texture and density to the series, Rendell created a "company of players" who were featured from novel to novel. Accounts of these characters (Wexford's family members, friends, and associates) are more than entertaining narrative digressions. They act as foils or provide frames for characters involved in the crimes, and they contribute to the development of the plot. For example, in the story "Inspector Wexford on Holiday," Dora, his supportive and sympathetic wife, plays an essential role in uncovering the clue which solves the mystery. In *A Sleeping Life* (1978), his daughter Sylvia's personal crisis serves as a catalyst for an examination of sexuality and the women's movement, both pertinent to the crime at hand. Wexford's loving relationship with his actress daughter Sheila offsets and highlights the selfish and unhealthy relationship of the Fanshawes, the key characters in *The Best Man To Die* (1969).

An important character in the series is Detective Inspector Michael Burden, Wexford's aide and friend. Though 20 years younger than Wexford, he is older in temperament. Rigid, prudish, and generally conservative at the outset, Burden matures and becomes more charitable as a consequence of his association with Wexford. An important stage in his growth takes place in *No More Dying Then* (1971), in which Burden's personal tragedy, the death of his wife, is central to the plot, and later, in *Put on by Cunning* (1981), there are signs that Burden may even have become a cultural match for Wexford.

Rendell's portrayal of the ongoing friendship between the two men creates a continuity in the series. In sharp contrast to the sick fantasies and perverse behavior they, as policemen, must deal with, their own psyches are normal, their view of life and humanity realistic, and their relationship with each other symbiotic and healthy.

The Suspense Thrillers

Rendell once stated that the creation of character was her primary interest, and it is characterization that invests the Wexford series with extraordinary richness and depth. Her fascination with character is even more apparent in the non-series books, the suspense thrillers.

Here she specialized in examining the inner guilt and darkness of her characters, whether they were drably commonplace or alarmingly aberrant. In fact, Rendell achieved suspense precisely by combining the more traditional elements of crime fiction with her rare gift for psychologically astute character study. In her muted, understated style, she

leads the reader into uneasy identification with a compulsive strangler (*A Demon in My View*, 1976), a failed writer (*The Face of Trespass*, 1974), an illiterate housekeeper (*A Judgement in Stone*, 1977), and a soulbartering teenager (*The Killing Doll*, 1984). The reader experiences the desperate alienation of these characters and is absorbed into the excitement of spotting and tracking the victims all the way to the murderous conclusions.

In 1986 two more novels were published—*Live Flesh*, a psychological suspense story in which the main character is a rapist and murderer, and *A Dark-Adapted Eye*, written under the pen name of Barbara Vine, which deals with intimations of various crimes within a conventional family. Two more "Barbara Vine" novels were published in 1987—*A Fatal Inversion* and *Talking to Strange Men*.

Rendell's mastery of crime fiction was widely recognized and honored. She received many awards, including the Mystery Writers of America's Edgar Allen Poe Award for short story and the Crime Writers Association's Gold Dagger Award. Her works have been translated into 14 languages. More than a million copies have been printed in English. Rendell continues to write mysteries from her home in Suffolk, England.

Further Reading

To date there are no biographical studies of Ruth Rendell. Reviews and critical articles abound; among the most helpful are Jane S. Bakerman's chapter in *10 Women of Mystery* (1981), edited by Earl F. Bargainnier, and an "Interview with Ruth Rendell," by Diana Cooper-Clark in the Spring 1981 edition of the *Armchair Detective*. □

Guido Reni

The Italian painter Guido Reni (1575-1642) is known for the gentle, highly decorative form of baroque classicism he developed.

Guido Reni was born in Bologna on Nov. 4, 1575. He began his apprenticeship under the mannerist painter Denis Calvaert and then entered the new, more progressive art school run by the Carracci. Their influence was to prove decisive. The Carracci opposed mannerism and urged instead a return to the generalized realism of the great masters of the High Renaissance, above all to Raphael, Titian, and Veronese.

Reni's personal life is a delight to those who insist that artists must be peculiar. He was, according to contemporary reports, neither heterosexual nor homosexual but absolutely sexless. His obsessive fear of women reached the point where he believed their slightest touch might poison him. The discovery of a woman's blouse that had found its way into his laundry left him terrified. Even in his own day there was thought to be a relationship between the asceticism of his life and the subdued, withdrawn quality of his art.

During the first years of the 17th century Reni spent much time in Rome. At first the fame of Caravaggio overwhelmed him. In the *Crucifixion of St. Peter* (ca. 1603) Reni tried as best he could to imitate Caravaggio's rough peasant types and deep shadows. At the same time, through the rather formal poses of the figures and the careful symmetry of the composition, he attempted to maintain his native Bolognese classicism.

But Reni soon abandoned this uneasy compromise. By 1609 he had replaced Annibale Carracci as the leader of baroque classicism in Rome. The *Aurora* fresco that Reni painted in the Casino of the Pallavicini-Rospigliosi palace in Rome (1614) is justly famous for its crisp, Hellenistic elegance.

After Reni returned to Bologna in 1614, his formalism became still more accentuated. In *Atalanta and Hippomenes* (ca. 1625) the coldly impersonal nude figures, though shown in the act of running a race, are frozen like fragments of ancient marble statues that have been cemented into a wall so as to form abstract linear patterns.

Late in life Reni developed what 17th-century critics called his second manner. In paintings such as *Cleopatra* and *Girl with a Wreath* (ca. 1635) we no longer see elaborate arrangements of poses or garment folds. Their place is taken by a play not of line but of color, of paint laid on thinly in loose, open brushstrokes. The many pale, commingled hues are all grayed over, so that their color harmonies, at times almost painfully delicate, can be read only with intensive study. Reni died on Aug. 18, 1642, in Bologna.

Further Reading

The standard work on Reni is in Italian. In English, see the sections on him in Rudolf Wittkower, *Art and Architecture in Italy, 1600-1750* (1962; 2d ed. 1965), and in E. K. Waterhouse, *Italian Baroque Painting* (1962; 2d ed. 1969). The chapter on Reni in Robert Enggass and Jonathan Brown, *Sources and Documents in the History of Art: Italy and Spain, 1600-1750* (1970), gives an interesting picture of Reni's strange personality as seen through 17th-century eyes.

Additional Sources

Malvasia, Carlo Cesare, conte, *The life of Guido Reni,* University Park: Pennsylvania State University Press, 1980. □

Karl Renner

The Austrian statesman and president Karl Renner (1870-1950) provided his nation with vigorous and able leadership after both world wars.

K arl Renner was born on Dec. 14, 1870, the eighteenth and last child of impoverished peasants in the Moravian village of Unter-Tannowitz near the Austrian border. Forced to leave home at age 14, he eventually studied law at Vienna, where he first became active in the Social Democratic party. Upon receiving a doctor of laws degree in the spring of 1896, he secured a position in the library of the Austrian Parliament, where he remained until his election to Parliament as a Social Democrat in 1907. He established his political reputation primarily in the theoretical realm with the publication of numerous significant treatises on the crucial issues of nationalities and constitution plaguing the Austro-Hungarian Empire at that time. Combining Socialist thought with national sentiment, he envisioned a democratic Austria as the nucleus and model for a Central European confederation of autonomous nationalities.

Always a pragmatic Marxist, Renner devoted himself during World War I primarily to questions of food supply, social security payments, and tax burdens for the lower classes—beyond a continued and impassioned plea for peace and a solution of the nationalities question. He was selected provisional chancellor on Oct. 30, 1918, and then permanent chancellor in February 1919. In this position, which he held until June 11, 1920, he prepared for the abdication of the Emperor, presided over the establishment of the republic, defended the young republic against virulent attacks from extreme left and right, led the Austrian delegation to the peace negotiations of Saint-Germain (1919), and—as chancellor and as foreign minister until October 1920—struggled in vain for unification with Germany.

With the Socialists out of power, Renner, with the exception of his tenure as president of the National Assembly from April 1931 to March 1933, faded increasingly into the background and, during the fascist era of Engelbert Dollfuss, was branded a traitor and briefly imprisoned in

1934. Withdrawn in seclusion during the Nazi occupation and World War II, he was recalled as provisional chancellor by the Soviet occupation authorities on April 27, 1945. Beyond restoring governmental functions in Austria, he used this position with great skill to preserve the unity of Austria and secure free parliamentary elections through difficult negotiations with the Soviets and the Western Allied authorities. As the Second Republic's first president from Dec. 20, 1945, he secured vital respect and legitimacy for the republic both at home and abroad. He died in office in Vienna on Dec. 31, 1950.

Further Reading

Neither Renner's memoirs nor the major biography of him has been translated into English. For background information on Renner and Austria see Richard Hiscocks, *The Rebirth of Austria* (1953); Friedrich Funder, *From Empire to Republic* (1956; trans. 1963); Wenzel Jaksch, *Europe's Road to Potsdam* (1958; trans. 1963); and Martin Gilbert, *The European Powers, 1900-45* (1965). ☐

Janet Reno

One of the most popular United States attorneys general in recent times, Janet Reno (born 1938) was identified as a major figure in the Clinton administration. With 15 years of experience as a state attorney in Florida, Reno sought new frontiers for the Justice

Department, which is the most powerful department in the Cabinet in terms of effecting social change.

Janet Reno, the 78th attorney general of the United States and the first woman ever to hold the nation's top law enforcement job, was born on July 21, 1938, in Miami, Florida. The eldest of the four children of journalists Henry and Jane (Wood) Reno, she grew up in a rather unconventional middle-class family in South Dade County. Her father, a Danish immigrant who is reported to have changed his surname from Rasmussen to one he selected from a map of Nevada, was a police reporter for the *Miami Herald* for 43 years before his death in 1967. Her mother, an investigative reporter for the now defunct *Miami News,* was described at her death in 1992 as an eccentric intellectual who wrestled alligators, read poetry, befriended the Seminole Indians, and built the family homestead on the edge of the Everglades with her own hands. It has been said that Janet Reno was deeply affected by her parents' strong attachment to the reporter's credo "to afflict the comfortable and to comfort the afflicted."

A product of the Dade County Public Schools, Reno attended Cornell University, where she earned an A.B. degree in Chemistry in 1960. Following graduation she enrolled at Harvard University Law School, becoming one of 16 women in a class of 500. As evidence of the road-blocks encountered by women in the legal profession, in 1962 Reno was denied a summer job "because she was a woman" by a prominent Miami law firm that 14 years later

would offer her a partnership. In 1963, however, with a law degree in hand, she entered a profession that was largely dominated by men and unfriendly to women interlopers.

Professional Background in Florida

Reno's earliest employment in the legal profession was with the Miami firm of Brigham and Brigham (1963-1967); this stint was followed by a junior partnership with the firm of Lewis and Reno (1967-1971). In 1971, adding political experience to her professional background, she was named staff director of the Judiciary Committee of the Florida House of Representatives (1971-1972), where she helped draft a revision of the state constitution that would make possible the reorganization of the court system in the state. In the spring of 1973 she served as counsel for the Florida Senate's Criminal Justice Commission for Revision of the Criminal Code. These experiences were followed by a job as assistant state attorney for the Eleventh Judiciary Circuit of Florida (1973-1976). In 1976 Reno returned to the private practice of law when she accepted a partnership in the firm of Steel Hector and Davis (1976-1978). Two years later Florida Governor Reubin Askew appointed Reno state attorney for Dade County, the first woman ever named to the position of top prosecutor for the county in Florida. Reno held the position for 15 years until nominated for the position of attorney general of the United States by President Bill Clinton in 1993.

As Dade County prosecutor, Reno was criticized for several early failures during her tenure. She was blamed for failing to obtain a conviction in a highly publicized case against four white Miami police officers accused in the beating death of an unarmed and handcuffed African-American insurance salesman. Riots followed in African-American sections of Miami, which resulted in deaths and destruction of property. Critics also cited a below-average rate of convictions and blamed her for what they deemed a lack of aggressiveness in pursuing public corruption cases at the local level, charging that she too often deferred to federal prosecutors in the investigation and prosecution of such cases. Reno's successes in prosecuting certain violent crimes and her fearlessness in dealing with Miami's crime problem helped to promote her reputation as a tough prosecutor and to win approval from opponents. She received praise from some in the minority communities for her efforts to use the prosecutor's office to tackle social ills affecting society.

A Lawyer for the People

Described as part social worker and part crime fighter who was "equally dogged about both," Reno advocated a holistic approach to law enforcement, a position that was not popular across all political spectrums. Juvenile justice emerged as her prime focus of reform. She became known for attempts to employ innovative alternatives to the incarceration of youth and to deal with troubled youths at the earliest possible age. Stressing the linkages between a nurturing childhood and the prevention of crime, she is said to have "identified with the problem of fighting crime in the early years and . . . struggled to get the resources for children and education."

She aggressively prosecuted child abuse cases; pursued delinquent fathers for child support; introduced innovations in drug courts; established a domestic crime unit; and worked with social agencies to provide nurturing environments for abandoned crack babies, to set up shelters for battered women, and to organize centers for the assessment of children experiencing or observing violence. In her opinion, "recreating families and community [was] the only way to break the cycle of poverty, ignorance, and rage that causes the everyday tragedies—child abuse, rape, domestic violence, drug addiction, senseless murder and mayhem—that afflict society."

Unanimously confirmed as U.S. attorney general by the Senate after smooth hearings, Reno took office on March 12, 1993. In this position she saw to the enforcement of policies on crime, race relations, immigration, corruption, and other legal issues that affect nearly every aspect of American life. In the area of crime and law enforcement, Reno's emphases represented a reorientation from the strategies of increased incarceration and rampant prison building stressed by Republican predecessors in the office. She focused on broad anticrime programs involving rehabilitation and treatment as well as gun control and hiring of additional police.

She argued that the Justice Department must see that the power of the federal government is harnessed in a way that ensures protection for the innocent and accords strict principles of due process and fair play in the prosecution and conviction of the guilty. She argued also for broad court reforms that provide ordinary citizens greater access to the justice system. Seeking to "revolutionize law enforcement (as well as) how America thinks about crime," Reno talked about addressing the root causes of crime and violence. She criticized mandatory sentencing for nonviolent offenses and advocated alternative sentences to permit the use of prison cells for dangerous offenders and persistent recidivists as well as major drug traffickers and distributors. She was reported to be personally opposed to the death penalty.

A National Agenda for Reform

The heart of Reno's agenda involves programs for the nation's children. As attorney general she pushed for reforms that would provide assistance to troubled youths at the earliest possible age, believing in the possibilities for redirecting children from careers in crime. For the youthful offender the idea was to use a measured carrot and stick approach that eliminated penal restrictions as increased responsibility was assumed for work, conduct, and education and that provided for coordinated reintegration into the community.

Reno advocated developing programs in the public schools that teach peaceful conflict resolution and proposed the development of teams of social workers, police officers, and public health officials to address the range of issues affecting youth. Reno's other concerns ranged broadly from commitments to aggressive civil rights enforcement in order to promote diversity and economic equity to the elimination of discrimination based on sexual preferences to tougher enforcement of environmental laws. The basic challenge Reno faced in her assignment involved translating her populist goals into real and substantive changes in the practice of law enforcement and the administration of justice.

As the first woman ever to hold the office of Attorney General, Janet Reno continues to make her mark in United States history. Her involvement in both the Branch Davidian seize in Waco, Texas and the Oklahoma City Bombing have brought her worldwide recognition.

Further Reading

Excellent coverage of Attorney General Janet Reno's personal background, law enforcement philosophy, and proposed programs is provided in a variety of news magazines and professional journals. These include the following: Elaine Shannon, ''The Unshakable Janet Reno,'' *Vogue* (August 1993); W. John Moore, ''The Big Switch,'' *National Journal* (June 19, 1993); and Stephanie B. Goldberg and Henry J. Reske, ''Talking with Attorney Janet Reno,'' *ABA Journal* (June 1993). See also Paul Anderson's *Janet Reno—Doing the Right Thing* (1994). □

Pierre Auguste Renoir

The French painter Pierre Auguste Renoir (1841-1919) was one of the central figures of the impressionist movement. His work is characterized by an extraordinary richness of feeling, a warmth of response to the world and to the people in it.

During the 1870s a revolution erupted in French painting. Encouraged by artists like Gustave Courbet and Édouard Manet, a number of young painters began to seek alternatives to the traditions of Western painting that had prevailed since the beginning of the Renaissance. These artists went directly to nature for their inspiration and into the actual society of which they were a part. As a result, their works revealed a look of freshness and immediacy that in many ways departed from the look of Old Master painting. The new art, for instance, displayed vibrant light and color instead of the somber browns and blacks that had dominated previous painting. These qualities, among others, signaled the beginning of modern art.

Pierre Auguste Renoir was a central figure of this development, particularly in its impressionist phase. Like the other impressionists, he struggled through periods of public ridicule during his early career. But as the new style gradually became accepted, during the 1880s and 1890s, Renoir began to enjoy extensive patronage and international recognition. The high esteem accorded his art at that time has generally continued into the present day.

Renoir was born in Limoges on Feb. 25, 1841. Shortly afterward, his family moved to Paris. Because he showed a remarkable talent for drawing, Renoir became an apprentice in a porcelain factory, where he painted plates. Later,

after the factory had gone out of business, he worked for his older brother, decorating fans. Throughout these early years Renoir made frequent visits to the Louvre, where he studied the art of earlier French masters, particularly those of the 18th century—Antoine Watteau, François Boucher, and Jean Honoré Fragonard. His deep respect for these artists informed his own painting throughout his career.

Early Career

In 1862 Renoir decided to study painting seriously and entered the Atelier Gleyre, where he met Claude Monet, Alfred Sisley, and Jean Frédéric Bazille. During the next 6 years Renoir's art showed the influence of Gustave Courbet and Édouard Manet, the two most innovative painters of the 1850s and 1860s. Courbet's influence is especially evident in the bold palette-knife technique of *Diane Chasseresse* (1867), while Manet's can be seen in the flat tones of *Alfred Sisley and His Wife* (1868). Still, both paintings reveal a sense of intimacy that is characteristic of Renoir's personal style.

The 1860s were difficult years for Renoir. At times he was too poor to buy paints or canvas, and the Salons of 1866 and 1867 rejected his works. The following year the Salon accepted his painting *Lise*. He continued to develop his work and to study the paintings of his contemporaries— not only Courbet and Manet, but Camille Corot and Eugène Delacroix as well. Renoir's indebtedness to Delacroix is apparent in the lush painterliness of the *Odalisque* (1870).

Renoir and Impressionism

In 1869 Renoir and Monet worked together at La Grenouillère, a bathing spot on the Seine. Both artists became obsessed with painting light and water. According to Phoebe Pool (1967), this was a decisive moment in the development of impressionism, for ''It was there that Renoir and Monet made their discovery that shadows are not brown or black but are coloured by their surroundings, and that the 'local colour' of an object is modified by the light in which it is seen, by reflections from other objects and by contrast with juxtaposed colours.''

The styles of Renoir and Monet were virtually identical at this time, an indication of the dedication with which they pursued and shared their new discoveries. During the 1870s they still occasionally worked together, although their styles generally developed in more personal directions.

In 1874 Renoir participated in the first impressionist exhibition. His works included the *Opera Box* (1874), a painting which shows the artist's penchant for rich and freely handled figurative expression. Of all the impressionists, Renoir most consistently and thoroughly adapted the new style—in its inspiration, essentially a landscape style—to the great tradition of figure painting.

Although the impressionist exhibitions were the targets of much public ridicule during the 1870s, Renoir's patronage gradually increased during the decade. He became a friend of Caillebotte, one of the first patrons of the impressionists, and he was also backed by the art dealer Durand-Ruel and by collectors like Victor Choquet, the Charpentiers, and the Daidets. The artist's connection with these individuals is documented by a number of handsome portraits, for instance, *Madame Charpentier and Her Children* (1878).

In the 1870s Renoir also produced some of his most celebrated impressionist genre scenes, including the *Swing* and the *Moulin de la Galette* (both 1876). These works embody his most basic attitudes about art and life. They show men and women together, openly and casually enjoying a society diffused with warm, radiant sunlight. Figures blend softly into one another and into their surrounding space. Such worlds are pleasurable, sensuous, and generously endowed with human feeling.

Renoir's ''Dry'' Period

During the 1880s Renoir gradually separated himself from the impressionists, largely because he became dissatisfied with the direction the new style was taking in his own hands. In paintings like the *Luncheon of the Boating Party* (1880-1881), he felt that his style was becoming too loose, that forms were losing their distinctiveness and sense of mass. As a result, he looked to the past for a fresh inspiration. In 1881 he traveled to Italy and was particularly impressed by the art of Raphael.

During the next 6 years Renoir's paintings became increasingly dry: he began to draw in a tight, classical manner, carefully outlining his figures in an effort to give them plastic clarity. The works from this period, such as the *Umbrellas* (1883) and the *Grandes baigneuses* (1884-1887),

are generally considered the least successful of Renoir's mature expressions. Their classicizing effort seems self-conscious, a contradiction to the warm sensuality that came naturally to him.

Late Career

By the end of the 1880s Renoir had passed through his dry period. His late work is truly extraordinary: a glorious outpouring of monumental nude figures, beautiful young girls, and lush landscapes. Examples of this style include the *Music Lesson* (1891), *Young Girl Reading* (1892), and *Sleeping Bather* (1897). In many ways, the generosity of feeling in these paintings expands upon the achievements of his great work in the 1870s.

Renoir's health declined severely in his later years. In 1903 he suffered his first attack of rheumatoid arthritis and settled for the winter at Cagnes-sur-Mer. By this time he faced no financial problems, but the arthritis made painting painful and often impossible. Nevertheless, he continued to work, at times with a brush tied to his crippled hand. Renoir died at Cagnes-sur-Mer on Dec. 3, 1919, but his death was preceded by an experience of supreme triumph: the state had purchased his portrait *Madame Georges Charpentier* (1877), and he traveled to Paris in August to see it hanging in the Louvre.

Further Reading

An intimate biography of Renoir is by his son, Jean Renoir, *Renoir: My Father* (trans. 1962). A standard monograph on the artist is Albert C. Barnes and Violette De Mazia, *The Art of Renoir* (1935). Renoir's drawings are richly represented in *Renoir Drawings,* edited by John Rewald (1946). For a complete survey of impressionism and Renoir's relation to the movement see Rewald's *The History of Impressionism* (1946; rev. ed. 1961). A more general survey, also of high quality, is Phoebe Pool, *Impressionism* (1967). □

James Renwick

The American architect James Renwick (1818-1895) designed churches, hotels, commercial buildings, and homes for the rich.

James Renwick was born on Nov. 1, 1818, in New York City. His father was a professor at Columbia College and an engineer. In 1836 James graduated from Columbia College. Following his father's example, he turned to engineering as a profession, taking a position with the Erie Railroad and then supervising construction for the Croton reservoir and aqueduct.

Renwick abruptly shifted to architecture by winning the competition for Grace Church (1843-1846) at Broadway and 10th Street in New York City. The design of the church, mainly late English Gothic in style, is remarkably coherent, except for the spire that was added later to replace the earlier wooden one. Following this success, he gained many commissions for churches in New York, such as Calvary

Church (1846), Church of the Puritans (1846), Saint Bartholomew's (1872), and Saint Patrick's Cathedral (1853, dedicated 1879, completed 1887). Saint Patrick's is generally considered his finest church. Its west facade is as well composed as any Gothic revival building in America.

The Smithsonian Institution (1846-1855), Washington, D.C., though burned in 1865 and repaired by another architect, is as interesting a design as any conceived by Renwick. In its complete lack of harmony with the established classical style of the Mall, this building has an aura of romance, of a colorful fairyland of picturesque angles, turrets, towers, and gingerbread decorations. Also in Washington, Renwick built the first Corcoran Gallery of Art (1859), which became the U.S. Court of Claims. Built of brick and brown stone, it is well proportioned and owes much to Jacques Lemercier's work on the Louvre in Paris. This is noticeable in the square dome, mansard roof, and imitative decoration.

Secure in his profession, Renwick was commissioned to build banks, hotels, and many private residences for well-to-do clients in New York, Staten Island, and Newport, R.I. In order to meet these obligations, he hired several young architects, among them John W. Root and Bertram Goodhue. (Both men were recognized as superior in the next generation.)

The Charity Hospital on Welfare Island in New York City (1858-1861), though esthetically unsuccessful, was considered otherwise by the Board of Governors, who commented that ''Its truly magnificent structure presents the appearance of a stately palace.'' Renwick based this design on the Tuileries Palace in Paris. Its gray stone was quarried by prisoners on Welfare Island; its quoins and lintels were of a lighter shade, and purple slate covered the roof. He designed the first major building for Vassar College, Poughkeepsie, N.Y. (1860-1861). Built of red brick, with blue stone trim and a green and purple mansard roof, the structure is chiefly noted for its fireproofing, central heating from a separate building, cast-iron columns, and colorful, though awkward, appearance. Renwick died in New York City on June 23, 1895.

Further Reading

There is no biography of Renwick, but some information on his life is in William R. Stewart, *Grace Church and Old New York* (1924). □

Ottorino Respighi

The rather conservative eclecticism of the music of the Italian composer Ottorino Respighi (1879-1936) made it immediately popular. His skill in writing for orchestra was unsurpassed.

The father of Ottorino Respighi was a professional musician and teacher at Bologna's Liceo Musicale, where Ottorino received his first musical training. He was a gifted violinist, and it was not until after his graduation from the conservatory that he definitely decided to be a composer rather than a violin virtuoso. Realizing that he needed a broader musical background than that supplied at home, he went to St. Petersburg to study with Nicolai Rimsky-Korsakov and later to Berlin to study with Max Bruch, a rather conservative German composer.

After his return to Italy, Respighi was appointed professor of composition at the prestigious Conservatory of Santa Cecilia in Rome, and in 1923 he became its director. Tours of Europe and the United States in 1925, 1928, and 1932, in which he conducted his compositions with leading orchestras, spread his fame.

Respighi is chiefly remembered as the composer of two tone poems, the *Fountains of Rome* (1916-1917) and the *Pines of Rome* (1924), brilliantly orchestrated evocations of the Eternal City. In a preface to the score of the former the composer wrote, ''In this symphonic poem the composer has endeavored to give expression to the sentiments and visions suggested to him by four of Rome's fountains, contemplated at the hour in which their character is most in harmony with the surrounding landscape, or in which their beauty appears most impressive to the observer.'' The *Pines* also has four sections, depicting the Villa Borghese, a catacomb, the Janiculum, and the Appian Way. These are very effective programs because they allowed the composer to write music of contrasting moods and varying associations, both pictorial and historical.

These compositions show Respighi's complete mastery of modern orchestration. His use of solo woodwinds and

brass reveals what he learned from Rimsky-Korsakov, but it is also apparent that he knew the scores of Claude Debussy, Maurice Ravel, Igor Stravinsky, and Richard Strauss as well. In the third section of the *Pines,* Respighi introduces a recording of an actual nightingale's song into the score.

Other compositions of Respighi are the operas *The Sunken Bell,* produced at the Metropolitan Opera in New York in 1928, *Maria Egiziaca* (1932), and *La Fiamma* (1934); a ballet commissioned by Sergei Diaghilev, *La Boutique fantasque* (1919), written on themes by Gioacchino Rossini; and a *Concerto Gregoriano* (1922) for violin and orchestra, based on Gregorian chant.

Further Reading

There is no biography of Respighi in English, but his wife, Elsa Respighi, wrote a memoir, *Ottorino Respighi* (trans. 1962). He is discussed in Paul Collaer, *A History of Modern Music* (1955; trans. 1961), and David Ewen, *The World of Twentieth-century Music* (1968).

Additional Sources

Alvera, Pierluigi., *Respighi,* New York, N.Y.: Treves Pub. Co., 1986.
Ottorino Respighi, Torino: ERI, 1985.
Respighi, Elsa, *Fifty years of a life in music, 1905-1955,* Lewiston: E. Mellen Press, 1993. □

James Barrett Reston

The American journalist James Barrett Scotty Reston (1909-1995) was one of the most important political commentators in the United States from the 1950s to the 1980s. His column in the *New York Times* was widely read by leading politicians and diplomats.

Born November 3, 1909, in Clydebank, Scotland, James Barrett ("Scotty") Reston was the second child of James and Johanna Reston. His family emigrated to the United States in 1920 and settled in Dayton, Ohio. Raised in a strict Presbyterian home, Reston thought seriously of becoming a preacher. He also considered a career as a professional golfer but ultimately went into journalism and became recognized as one of the nation's foremost political writers.

After graduating from the University of Illinois in 1932, Reston took a job as a sportswriter for the *Springfield* (Ohio) *Daily News.* He then worked for the Ohio State University sports publicity office and as a press secretary for the Cincinnati Reds baseball team. In 1934 he accepted a position with Associated Press in New York writing sports features and a column, "A New Yorker at Large." He was sent to London in 1937 to cover international sporting events and the British foreign office.

In 1939 Scotty Reston was hired by the *New York Times* to work in its London bureau. In 1941 he was covering the State Department in Washington, D.C. After publishing the book *Prelude to Victory* (1942), in which he stressed that the war effort must be a national crusade, he went to London to help organize the U.S. Office of War Information.

He returned to Washington, D.C., as the *Times'* diplomatic correspondent in 1944. While covering the Dumbarton Oaks conference which organized the United Nations, he obtained a full set of top-secret Allied position papers from an unhappy Chinese delegation. This major scoop earned him the 1945 Pulitzer Prize for national reporting.

A successful and valued reporter, Reston was named Washington bureau chief in 1953. He recruited a team of interns and young writers who formed an enterprising and powerful staff and developed into leading national journalists. While supervising the office he still managed to write about 5,000 words a week. In 1957 he received a second Pulitzer Prize for a series on America's lack of national purpose. Featured in a *Time* magazine cover story in early 1960, he was called "a crack reporter, a good writer, a thoughtful columnist and an able administrator of the biggest bureau in Washington."

In March 1960 Reston began the thrice-weekly political column which solidified his stature as one of Washington's most influential journalists. In the introduction to a collection of his essays, *Sketches in the Sand* (1967), he observed that columns are motivated by a wide range of objectives, from ideological interpretation to investigation. He saw his own purpose as if he were writing an informative letter to a thoughtful friend. *Life* magazine described it as "a highly intelligent summary of what policy makers are thinking and worrying about; Reston does not so much argue for or against their policies as clarify them with a readable prose style and stamp them with his own healthy point of view."

Distinguishing his style from another pre-eminent columnist, Walter Lippmann, who was known as a systematic thinker, Reston acknowledged that he did not profess a particular philosophy. "I'm a reporter of other men's ideas," he said. Critics and admirers both agree that Reston had the ability to cultivate powerful political figures such as Henry Kissinger.

Coming from a poor immigrant background, Reston saw America as a land of opportunity. Expecting its leaders to act in an exemplary manner, he was deeply disappointed after the bombings of Cambodia and the Watergate affair. Yet, a conservative man with traditional values, he was optimistic about the country's future.

Based on a moral outlook reflecting his Calvinist roots, Reston's message of hope appealed to the Sulzberger family which owned the *Times*. There was always mutual affection between the *Times* and Reston. According to one journalist, Reston "is not so much a man of the left or right as he is a man of the *Times*."

In 1960 Reston cautioned the *Times* not to print advance information it held about the imminent Bay of Pigs invasion. In 1965 Reston toured South Vietnam to take a personal look at the war. In 1967 he delivered a series of

lectures which were published as *The Artillery of the Press: Its Influence on American Foreign Policy* in which he advocated a more skeptical and less nationalistic role for the press. In 1971 he recommended that the *Times* publish the secret study of the Vietnam War, *The Pentagon Papers*. Later that year, at the height of his influence, he visited the People's Republic of China and conducted the first indepth interview of Premier Chou En-lai.

In 1964 Reston gave up his position as Washington bureau chief in order to become associate editor and devote more time to his column. In 1968 he served briefly as executive editor in New York before returning to Washington as vice president in charge of news production. After 1974 Reston was a director of the New York Times Company while continuing to write his column. In 1987 he gave up his regular column and retired except for writing a piece only now and then. In 1991, he wrote *Deadline,* a memoir of his life.

He was a stocky man with a square, reddish face. He married Sarah Jane Fulton in 1935 and they had three sons. They lived in Washington, D.C., but spent time in Fiery Run, Virginia, and in Martha's Vineyard, where Reston bought the weekly paper in 1968.

In addition to his Pulitzer Prizes Reston received many journalism awards and honorary degrees, including the Presidential Medal of Freedom, the Roosevelt Four Freedom medal, and the Commander, Order of the British Empire. James Reston died on December 8, 1995.

Further Reading

For Reston's own writings, see his collection of essays *Sketches in the Sand* (1967) and *The Artillery of the Press* (1967). He is frequently cited in two books about *The New York Times, The Kingdom and the Power* by Gay Talese (1966) and *Without Fear or Favor* by Harrison E. Salisbury (1980). He wrote his memoirs in a book titled *Deadline* (1991). □

Pieter Retief

Pieter Retief (1780-1838) was a South African emigrant leader. Some historians call him the first "president" of the Dutch-speaking people of South Africa. He gave expression to the racial policies of his people and formulated their republican ideals.

Pieter Retief was born on Nov. 12, 1780, at Wagenmakersvallei (modern Wellington, South Africa), strangely enough to pureblood French parents, although a century had elapsed since the Huguenot emigration. There was not much prospect of a livelihood for all 10 children on the family's wine farm, so Pieter became a clerk in a store. Later on, his employer entrusted him with a stock of goods, and he went trading eastward, reaching the border of the Cape Colony.

Retief's letters show him to have been an intelligent and refined person. He had an irrefutable record of moral integrity, honesty, and benevolence. He was a restless person, driven by an enterprising nature and boundless energy.

Life as a Frontiersman

In 1814 Retief married Lenie Greyling. He bought a farm on the Koega River but afterward moved to Grahamstown, where he became one of its wealthiest men. He eventually fell prey to his less scrupulous business partners and ended up bankrupt. Retief returned to farming—in the Great Winterberg. He soon regained solvency and proved himself a brave, respected, and esteemed commandant, a favorite with the authorities and trusted leader of his fellow citizens.

Spokesman for His People

As mediator in all dealings between citizens and the government, Retief was the embodiment of cooperative force, a man who did his utmost to procure permanent peace and safety on the frontier. As time went by, these attempts proved futile, and he eventually despaired. He then planned and prepared the orderly emigration of the dissatisfied Boers northward to the country beyond the Orange and Vaal rivers.

Retief summarized the reasons for this Great Trek and formulated the ideals of the emigrant farmers. To check the frequent losses and disturbances experienced on the eastern frontier, he visualized a Voortrekker government in the interior that would be the embodiment of an orderly state, where there would be "prospects for peace and happiness for their children" and where "with resoluteness, the principle of true freedom will be esteemed"—a government with "proper laws," based upon the fundamental concept of "righteousness." He issued a manifesto on Jan. 22, 1837, which was the declaration of independence of the Voortrekker farmers.

Retief was elected governor of the Voortrekker community then assembled at Thabanchu in the interior. In September he undertook to explore Port Natal and to barter with the Zulu king Dingane. He arrived in November at the laager. His ambition to reside in the promised land between the Tugela and Umzimvubu rivers was almost fulfilled. Upon Dingane's request, Retief punished Sekonyela in January 1838 for the latter's theft of Zulu cattle. Then he proceeded to the Zulu capital to settle the ceding of the territory in Natal to the emigrant farmers.

But tragedy awaited the man who had done so much for the betterment of his fellow citizens. On February 6, 1838 Zulu warriors—acting upon Dingane's command "Kill the wizards!"—slaughtered Retief and his company in the hills of Umgungundlovu.

An Evaluation

The death of Retief deprived the Voortrekkers of a talented, far-seeing statesman. Two letters illustrate his genius. On July 18, 1837, Retief wrote to native captains in the neighborhood. This letter not only outlined the Voortrekker principles of segregation, that is, the stillheld notion of separate development of European and non-European in South Africa, but also the all-important idea of the peaceful coex-

istence between nations. The racial policy of the Afrikaner had developed long before he wrote this letter, but Retief, as leader of the Voortrekkers, for the first time gave expression to these principles.

Three days later he wrote to the governor of the Cape Colony, declaring that the Voortrekker community desired to be acknowledged as "a free and independent people." This request was refused, but for the first time the republican notions of the Afrikaner were expressed at the international level. Perhaps Preller did not exaggerate when he concluded his biography on Retief by saying, "[It is] Retief's greatest virtue that in his deeds and in his death, he compelled the Dutch-Afrikaans Emigrants to believe that they were not merely isolated, roaming individuals, but that everyone was a participant in a great national bond, with one concern and one destination."

Further Reading

Major biographies of Retief are in Afrikaans. Recommended for general historical background are George M. Theal, *A History of South Africa* (1904); George E. Cory, *The Rise of South Africa* (1910); Manfred Nathan, *The Voortrekkers of South Africa* (1937); R. U. Kenney, *Piet Retief: the Dubious Hero* (1976) and Eily and Jack Gledhill, *In the Steps of Piet Retief* (1980). □

Johann Reuchlin

The German humanist and jurist Johann Reuchlin (1455-1522) was one of the greatest Hebraists of early modern Europe. He was involved in a great controversy concerning Hebrew literature that culminated in the famous "Letters of Obscure Men."

Johann Reuchlin was born at Pforzheim. He studied at Freiburg, Paris, Basel, and Rome; became a doctor of law; and began an impressive career as a public official and jurist. Reuchlin's studies in Italy had acquainted him with humanism, and his command of Greek and Latin was as accomplished as that of any scholar north of the Alps. A second journey to Italy, in 1492, caused Reuchlin to become interested in Hebrew, which he then studied intensely and described in a short book in 1494. Reuchlin soon became the most accomplished Gentile Hebraist of the Renaissance, and in 1506 he produced a grammar of Hebrew entitled *Rudimenta Hebraica*. His linguistic studies led Reuchlin to a genuine interest in Judaism and also into one of the most famous controversies in the history of anti-Semitism.

In 1506 a converted Jew named Johann Pfefferkorn began to produce a series of pamphlets in which he condemned Jewish "errors," ritual, and learning. He urged the forcible conversion of all Jews and obtained imperial permission to confiscate Jewish books. In 1509-1510 Pfefferkorn became more powerful, and Reuchlin's remarks in 1510 that Jewish books should not be burned but, indeed, chairs of Hebrew should be established in German universities made him a target not only of Pfefferkorn but also of the Dominican order at Cologne. In 1511, 1512, and 1513 Reuchlin issued pamphlets defending his own position and the value to Christian scholars of Hebrew literature. Although Reuchlin by no means believed that Jewish literature did not contain errors dangerous to Christians, his spirited defense of Hebrew and of the Jews remains one of the earliest modern Christian attacks on anti-Semitism. In 1514 Reuchlin was acquitted of charges of heresy by the bishop of Speyer, but his enemies then managed to transfer the case to Rome.

In 1514 Reuchlin issued a collection of letters in his defense written by the greatest humanistic scholars in Europe, the *Letters of Eminent Men.* In 1515 another collection of letters, the *Epistolae obscurorum virorum* (*Letters of Obscure Men*), appeared. Ostensibly serious letters from monks supporting the persecution of Reuchlin, the collection was in fact a withering satire on Reuchlin's opponents. The *Letters of Obscure Men* caused a furor: it was a superb example of humanist scorn not only of bigotry and stupidity but also of the ecclesiastical circles in which these traits dominated. Both Sir Thomas More and Erasmus applauded this work, written by Crotus Rubianus and Ulrich von Hutten.

Reuchlin's enemies, however, attacked him with even greater savagery, finally securing a papal condemnation of his position in 1520. Reuchlin was severely hurt by the final condemnation. He spent the last few years of his life teaching and lecturing, honored by some of his contemporaries for his courage and learning and viciously condemned by others for his persistent defense of Hebrew literature and the Jews.

Further Reading

Reuchlin's life and work are discussed in the historical introduction to Francis G. Stokes, trans. and ed., *Epistolae obscurorum virorum* (1909), and in Lewis W. Spitz, *The Religious Renaissance of the German Humanists* (1963). Particular aspects of Reuchlin's work are discussed in S. A. Hirsch, *A Book of Essays* (1905), and Joseph Leon Blau, *The Christian Interpretation of the Cabala in the Renaissance* (1944). □

Walter Philip Reuther

American labor leader Walter Philip Reuther (1907-1970) pioneered in unionizing the mass-production industries. In a movement traditionally preoccupied with bread-and-butter goals, he dedicated his career to broadening labor's political and social horizons.

Walter Reuther was born on Sept. 1, 1907. His father headed the central labor body in Wheeling, W.Va., and the five children spent their evenings earnestly debating social problems. Walter left school at the age of 15 to work in a steel mill; 4 years later he moved to Detroit, resumed his schooling, and worked at night as a tool-and-die maker in automobile factories.

Reuther began preaching unionism before President Franklin D. Roosevelt's New Deal put a legal foundation under collective bargaining. The result was Reuther's dismissal from the Ford Company in 1933. On a trip around the world he worked for over a year in a Soviet auto plant. Returning to Detroit, he helped build the United Automobile Workers (UAW), the union that became the launching pad for his influence in national affairs.

The dynamic redheaded Reuther slithered through national guard lines in the 1937 sit-down strikes at General Motors; he was beaten by Ford Company guards in a strike later that year. Even after the UAW was well-established, thugs made him a target. In 1948 a shotgun blast fired through a window of his Detroit home left his right hand permanently crippled. Later his brother, Victor, the union's education director, lost an eye in an almost identical attack.

Under Reuther's leadership the UAW grew to 1.5 million members. It pushed collective bargaining into innovative fields that provided workers and their families with cradle-to-grave protection as an adjunct of their regular pay. Perhaps the most spectacular success was a 1955 employer-financed program that gave auto workers almost as much take-home pay when laid off as when at work.

Reuther consistently fought corruption, communism, and racist tendencies within labor. Convinced in 1955 that the American Federation of Labor (AFL), led by George Meany, had also become a foe of such influences, he renounced the presidency of the Congress of Industrial Organizations (CIO) to accept a secondary role in a merged labor

movement. However, disenchanted by what he considered the AFL-CIO's standstill policies, he led his union out again in 1968.

The UAW joined the International Brotherhood of Teamsters, the biggest American union, in forming an Alliance for Labor Action. Its aim was to organize the working poor, especially in ghetto areas, and crusade for far-reaching social reforms. This venture reflected Reuther's social vision, but it died a year after his own death.

Reuther always looked forward to transforming the economy along lines of industrial democracy and social justice. He authored dozens of "Reuther plans" for the solution of problems ranging from housing and health to disarmament. Yet he found himself increasingly isolated from the general labor movement. He was killed in an airplane crash in Michigan on May 10, 1970.

Further Reading

A well-balanced study of Reuther is William J. Eaton and Frank Cormier, *Reuther* (1970). More specialized is Alfred O. Hero, *Reuther-Meany Foreign Policy Dispute* (1970). Older studies are Irving Howe and B. J. Widick, *The UAW and Walter Reuther* (1949), and the section on Reuther in Paul Franklin Douglass, *Six upon the World: Toward an American Culture for an Industrial Age* (1954).

Additional Sources

Barnard, John, *Walter Reuther and the rise of the auto workers,* Boston: Little, Brown, 1983.

Carew, Anthony, *Walter Reuther,* Manchester; New York: Manchester University Press; New York: Distributed exclusively in the USA and Canada by St. Martin's Press, 1993.

Lichtenstein, Nelson, *The most dangerous man in Detroit: Walter Reuther and the fate of American labor,* New York, NY: Basic Books, 1995. □

Bernard Revel

Bernard Revel (1885-1940), Talmudic scholar and educator, directed the Rabbi Isaac Elchanon Theological Seminary from its shaky beginnings to become the renown Yeshiva University with a comprehensive program of Judaic studies integrated with modern scholarship.

Bernard Dov Revel was born in 1885 in Kovno (now in Lithuanian S.S.R.), a center of traditional Jewish learning, the son of the second marriage of the scholar Nahum Shraga Revel of Pren (a son from the first marriage was Nelson Glueck, dean of the Reform Jewish seminary, the Hebrew Union College-Jewish Institute of Religion). As a youth he gained the reputation of a scholar and was influenced by the Musar movement, which offered an ethical and talmudic system of study to counteract the inroads of modernity among traditional Jews. Many of the

innovations which Revel brought to the Rabbi Isaac Elchanon Theological Seminary in New York were inspired by that movement.

Early Career as Rabbi

His rabbinic ordination occurred in 1901, and he combined this expertise with a sensitivity to the modern world. He qualified by passing the Russian gymnasium examinations, demonstrating a command of secular studies. His awareness of political concerns led him to join the Jewish Bund, a socialist revolutionary group, retaining his traditionalism all the while. Participation in the bund, however, led to his arrest and imprisonment in 1906. After his arrest he emigrated to the United States.

While in the United States he continued his combination of rabbinic and secular studies. As secretary to Rabbi Bernard Leventhal he was guided in his preparation for becoming a leading exponent of American Jewish Orthodoxy. He published articles in Jewish journals and was an associate editor and contributor to *Otzar Yisrael,* a Hebrew encyclopedia. His studies included a Master's degree from New York University, which included a thesis on the medieval Jewish ethical author Bachya Ibn Pakuda, and a Ph.D. from Dropsie University (a unique Jewish institution for graduate studies only begun in 1909 and from which Revel was the first Ph.D. graduate), for which he wrote a scholarly dissertation on the relationship between the heretical sect of the Karaites and earlier Jewish tradition.

His marriage in 1909 to Sarah Travis brought him into a wealthy family engaged in the oil business. For some time he too was active in the business, but in 1915 the Rabbi Isaac Elchanon Theological Seminary and the Yeshivat Etz Chaim merged and Revel was called to guide the new institution. It was said that he chose "Torah over oil" to accept the call. He broadened the curriculum of the rabbinical school, introducing such subjects as homiletics, pedagogy, and some secular instruction. In 1916 he founded the Talmudical Academy, which was the first Jewish high school to combine a complete secular curriculum with an in-depth program of Jewish learning. He set the institution on the road to becoming a fully modern Orthodox center of learning in which rabbis would be fully traditional, but trained to understand and respond to the needs of the American environment.

During the 1920s pressing problems in the family business caused him to relinquish his position. After a number of stopgap measures, however, the seminary called him back, and in 1923 he gave up his business endeavors to devote himself permanently to the upbuilding of the seminary. In 1928 he began Yeshiva College, which integrated secular studies and Judaica. Despite opposition from Reform Jews who opposed a Jewish college and traditionalists who opposed secular studies the college became a success. Revel's leadership brought many new facets to the school—he attracted European Jewish scholars (Roshei Yeshiva), introduced intercollegiate sports, and published the journal *Scripta Mathematica*, which became widely respected in its field. He continued teaching the higher level classes in Talmud to the seminary students. On November 19, 1940, he conducted his last class in Jewish codes; during that class he suffered a stroke from which he never recovered. He died on December 2, 1940, mourned by the entire Jewish community.

Struggles for American Jewish Orthodoxy

Revel's enduring importance lies in laying the foundations for a vital American Jewish Orthodoxy. His efforts often met with opposition, and the controversies in which he engaged are a guide to the development of American Jewish Orthodoxy. At first American Jews refused to believe that an institution for Jewish Orthodoxy was needed. The Jewish Theological Seminary of the Conservative Movement sought to speak for all traditional Jews. While Conservative Judaism still claims to be the true representative of traditional Judaism, many traditional Jews consider its innovations unacceptable. Later Revel faced opposition from traditionalists who were uncomfortable with his innovations. His use of non-Jewish workers in the Yeshiva cafeteria, the inclusion of such controversial subjects as the theory of evolution in Yeshiva's curriculum, and the giving of honorary degrees to non-Orthodox Jews (although Revel distinguished between the non-Orthodox and those identified with sectarian movements such as Reform or Conservatism) alienated many within his constituency.

Within the institution itself Revel faced problems. The presence of non-Orthodox students in both Yeshiva College and in the Teacher's Institute was problematic. Graduates of the seminary faced the dilemma of congregations in which men and women sat together. Questions arose when Jews formerly married to Gentile wives sought to reaffiliate with an Orthodox synagogue. Revel confronted these issues as a traditionalist firmly committed to Orthodox Jewish law. His replies to these dilemmas reveal a man who understood the needs of his time and the timelessness of his tradition.

Further Reading

Aaron Rothkoff has written a lively and vivid biography, *Bernard Revel: Builder of American Jewish Orthodoxy* (1972). Sidney B. Hoenig, who wrote the informative essay on Revel in the *Encyclopedia Judaica*, presents a scholarly investigation of Revel's writings in *Rabbinics and Research: The Scholarship of Bernard Revel* (1968). Useful references to Revel are found in Gilbert Klapperman, *The Story of Yeshiva University* (Toronto, Canada, 1969).

Additional Sources

Rakeffet-Rothkoff, Aaron, *Bernard Revel—builder of American Jewish orthodoxy*, Jerusalem; New York: Feldheim, 1981. ☐

Hiram Rhoades Revels

Hiram Rhoades Revels (1822-1901), African American clergyman and university administrator, was the first black American to sit in the U.S. Senate.

Hiram Revels was born of free parents on Sept. 27, 1822, in Fayetteville, N.C. His early education was limited, since it was illegal in North Carolina at that time to teach African Americans, slave or free, to read or write. As soon as he was able, he moved to Union County, Ind., to further his education at a Quaker seminary. After completing his work there, he moved to Ohio to attend another seminary. Eventually he moved to Illinois and graduated from Knox College at Bloomington. In 1845 he was ordained a minister of the African Methodist Episcopal Church in Baltimore, Md.

As a minister, Revels served African American churches in Ohio, Kentucky, Illinois, Indiana, and Tennessee. He finally settled in Baltimore, where he became minister of a church and principal of a school for blacks. When the Civil War began in 1861, he helped organize the first two regiments of black soldiers from the state of Maryland.

In 1863 Revels moved to St. Louis, established a school for African American freedmen, and recruited another regiment of black soldiers. In 1864 he joined the Federal forces in Mississippi as chaplain to an African American regiment. For a short time he was provost marshal of Vicksburg. For 2 years he worked with the Freedmen's Bureau and established several schools and churches for African Americans near Jackson and Vicksburg.

In 1866 Revels settled in Natchez, Miss. He joined the Methodist Episcopal Church in 1868, the year he was elected alderman. In 1870 he was elected as a Republican to fill an unexpired term in the U.S. Senate, where he served

fore the Revolutionary War to warn American patriots of a planned British attack. His silverware was among the finest produced in America in his day.

Paul Revere was born on Jan. 1, 1735, in Boston, Mass., the son of Apollos De Revoire, a French Huguenot who had come to Boston at the age of 13 to apprentice in the shop of a silversmith. Once Revoire had established his own business, he Anglicized his name. Paul, the third of 12 children, learned silversmithing from his father. On Aug. 17, 1757, he married Sarah Orne and eventually became the father of eight children.

As early as 1765, Revere began to experiment with engraving on copper and produced several portraits and a songbook. He was popular as a source for engraved seals, coats of arms, and bookplates, and he began to execute engravings which were anti-British. In 1768 Revere undertook dentistry and produced dental devices. The same year he made one of the most famous pieces of American colonial silver—the bowl commissioned by the Fifteen Sons of Liberty. It is engraved to honor the "glorious Ninety-two Members of the Honorable House of Representatives of the Massachusetts Bay, who, undaunted by the insolent Menores of Villains in Power . . . Voted not to rescind" a circular letter they had sent to the other colonies protesting the Townshend Acts. Revere's virtuosity as a craftsman extended to his carving picture frames for John Singleton

until March 1871. As a senator, he was dignified and respected; his political views, however, were somewhat conservative.

After retiring from the Senate, Revels returned to Mississippi to serve as president of Alcorn College (1871-1874). He was removed from his post for political reasons but was appointed president of Alcorn again in 1876. Following this second term, he returned to church work in Holly Springs, Miss. While attending a church conference at Aberdeen, Miss., he died on Jan. 16, 1901.

Further Reading

Revels's unpublished papers are in the Library of Congress. There is no full-scale biography of him. Biographical sketches are in Wells Brown, *The Black Man: His Antecedents, His Genius, and His Achievements* (1863; new ed. 1968); Benjamin Brawley, *Negro Builders and Heroes* (1937); and William J. Simmons, *Men of Mark* (1968). The best book for general reading on the Afro-American in Congress is W. E. B. Du Bois, *Black Reconstruction* (1935). Other useful sources of information on this period are Samuel Denny Smith, *The Negro in Congress, 1870-1901* (1940); Lerone Bennett, *Black Power, 1867-1877* (1969); and Maurine Christopher, *America's Black Congressmen* (1971). □

Paul Revere

Paul Revere (1735-1818), American patriot, silversmith, and engraver, is remembered for his ride be-

Copley, who painted the famous portrait of Revere in shirt sleeves holding a silver teapot.

Paul Revere's Ride

Revere became a trusted messenger for the Massachusetts Committee of Safety. He foresaw an attempt by the British troops against the military stores which were centered in Concord, and he arranged a signal to warn the patriots in Charlestown. During the late evening of April 18, 1775, the chairman of the Committee of Safety told him that the British were going to march to Concord. Revere signaled by hanging two lanterns in the tower of the North Church (probably the present Christ Church). He crossed the river, borrowed a horse in Charlestown, and started for Concord. He arrived in Lexington at midnight and roused John Hancock and Samuel Adams from sleep; the two fled to safety. Revere was captured that night by the British, but he persuaded his captors that the whole countryside was aroused to fight, and they freed him. He returned to Lexington, where he saw the first shot fired on the green. It is this ride and series of events which have been immortalized by Henry Wadsworth Longfellow in his poem "Paul Revere's Ride."

In the same year, 1775, the Massachusetts provincial congress sent Revere to Philadelphia to study the only working powder mill in the Colonies. Although he was only allowed to walk through the mill and not to take any notes about it, he remembered enough to establish a mill in Canton. During the Revolutionary War, he continued to play an active role. He was eventually promoted to the rank of lieutenant colonel.

After the war Revere became a pioneer in the process of copper plating, and he made copper spikes for ships. In 1795, as grand master of the Masonic fraternity, he laid the cornerstone of the new statehouse in Boston. Throughout the remainder of his life, he continued to experiment with metallurgy and to take a keen interest in contemporary events. He died in Boston on May 10, 1818.

The Silversmith

Revere is also remembered today as a craftsman. His work in silver spanned two major styles. His earliest work is in the rococo style, which is characterized by the use of asymmetric floral and scroll motifs and repoussé decoration; this was done before the Revolution. From this, he evolved a neoclassic style after the Revolution. This style, developed in England, was based on the straight lines and severe surfaces of Roman design. In 1792 Revere produced one of the acknowledged American masterpieces in this style—a complete tea set commissioned by John and Mehitabel Templeman of Boston. The type of ornamentation employed in this tea set was being used in Massachusetts architecture by Charles Bulfinch and Samuel McIntire.

Revere's silver is marked with the initials "P R" in a block. This was the usual type of marking on American silver of the 18th century. Revere commanded a very distinguished Boston clientele and was called on to make a number of memorial and commemorative pieces. Like many silversmiths of the period, he also worked in brass.

Master Engraver

Revere was also a master of engraving. An on-the-spot reporter, he recorded the events leading up to and during the Revolution with great accuracy. These engravings were advertised in Boston newspapers and were eagerly purchased by the public. In 1770 the *Boston Gazette* advertised for sale Revere's engraving *A View of Part of the Town of Boston in New England and British Ships of War Landing Their Troops, 1768*. Revere added to the print a description of the troops, who paraded "Drums beating, Fifes playing . . . Each Soldier having received 16 rounds of Powder and Ball." Today, all his silver and engravings are eagerly sought by collectors.

Further Reading

A full-length study of Revere is Esther Forbes, *Paul Revere and the World He Lived In* (1942). For information on his work see the publication of the Boston Museum of Fine Arts, *Colonial Silversmiths: Masters and Apprentices*, edited by Richard B. K. McLanathan (1956). □

Conde de Revillagigedo

Juan Vicente Güemes Pacheco y Padilla, Conde de Revillagigedo (1740-1799), was viceroy of New Spain and one of its ablest and most efficient administrators.

Juan Vicente Güemes Pacheco was born in La Habana, Cuba. His father was viceroy of New Spain from 1746 until 1755. The young and ambitious Juan Vicente joined the Spanish military service, gaining renown during the Spanish siege of Gibraltar against England.

Viceroy of New Spain

As viceroy of New Spain (1789-1794), Revillagigedo gained the respect and admiration of its people. He strove to make effective José de Gálvez's reforms and inaugurated the intendant system. He improved the administration of finances and justice, enlarged the school system, and reorganized the colonial militia. He founded the General Archives and inaugurated in 1793 the Museum of National History. To keep himself informed of the desires and grievances of the people, he placed a locked box in a public place for petitions and communications.

Perhaps one of Revillagigedo's most notable accomplishments was the transformation of Mexico from an unhealthy, filthy city into a modern metropolis. He ordered the principal streets paved, cleaned, and lighted. The great central plaza was cleared of street vendors, and new markets were set up in various parts of the city. He suppressed banditry, making Mexico a safer city. Concerned over the abuses being committed by some members of the clergy against the Indians, particularly in remote areas, he issued special instructions ordering that the Indians should not be compelled to perform personal services or to pay tribute to the clergy.

Administrative Reforms

Revillagigedo was particularly critical of the sale of public offices in New Spain and throughout the New World, for the system had led to corruption and inefficiency. Officials who came from Spain expected to recover at least a share of their investment, and many showed little interest in colonial affairs. Revillagigedo expressed his disapproval of the system, explaining that the greater efficiency of appointed officials would more than compensate for the loss of the royal treasury. The system, however, was not officially abolished until 1812, and even then the sale of offices continued for several years.

Revillagigedo was also critical of the complicated and overlapping system of taxation; he increased the major taxes and abolished the minor ones. An efficient and honest official, he increased revenues, and New Spain enjoyed years of prosperity. The budget, which suffered a deficit during the previous administration, enjoyed a surplus during his tenure of office. He used some of the funds to encourage the planting and growing of cotton and other textile fibers.

Revillagigedo also encouraged explorations of the California and northern Pacific coast as far as the Bering Straits. However, under his administration Spain was forced to yield to England—as a result of the Nootka Sound controversy—territories on the northwest Pacific coast, thus acknowledging that Spain could not claim territories not effectively occupied.

At the end of his enlightened administration in 1794, Revillagigedo left a more modern and prosperous Mexico with an efficient and honest government. He returned to Spain, where he died on May 12, 1799.

Further Reading

Valuable information on Revillagigedo's administration is in Donald E. Smith, *The Viceroy of New Spain* (1913), and C. H. Haring, *The Spanish Empire in America* (1947). Further background can be found in three works by Lillian E. Fisher: *Viceregal Administration in the Spanish American Colonies* (1926), *The Intendant System in Spanish America* (1929), and *The Background of the Revolution for Mexican Independence* (1934). □

Alfonso Reyes

Alfonso Reyes (1889-1959), one of Mexico's most distinguished men of letters, was especially well known as an essayist.

Alfonso Reyes was born on May 17, 1889, in Monterrey, Nuevo León. He attended the Escuela Nacional Preparatoria (National Preparatory School) and the Facultad de Derecho (Law School) in Mexico City. In 1909 he was one of the founders of the Ateneo de la Juventud (Athenaeum for Young People). He served as secretary of the Faculty for Advanced Studies, where he also taught the course on the history of the Spanish language and Spanish literature. His first book, *Cuestiones estéticas* (Esthetic Questions), appeared in 1911.

Reyes received his law degree in 1913, and that year he was appointed second secretary of the Mexican legation in France. In 1914 he went to Spain, where he devoted himself to literature and journalism, working in the Centro de Estudios Históricos (Center for Historical Studies) in Madrid. His book *Visión de Anáhuac* was published in 1917.

In 1920 Reyes was named second secretary of the Mexican legation in Spain. From that time on he occupied various diplomatic posts: chargé d'affaires in Spain (1922-1924), minister to France (1924-1927), ambassador to Argentina (1927-1930), ambassador to Brazil (1930-1936), and again ambassador to Argentina (1936-1937).

When Reyes returned to Mexico in 1939, he became president of the Casa de España en México (Spanish House in Mexico), which later became the Colegio de México. He was one of the founders of the Colegio Nacional. In 1945 he won the National Prize in Literature, and he was a candidate for the Nobel Prize. He served as director of the Academia Mexicana de la Lengua (Mexican Academy of the Spanish Language) from 1957 to 1959.

The works by Reyes that have enjoyed the greatest success are *Simpatías y differencias* (1921; Likes and Dislikes); *La experiencia literaria* (1942; Literary Experience); *El deslinde* (1944), a treatise on literary criticism which is

considered his masterpiece; and *La X en la frente* (1952; X on the Forehead). His works have been more frequently translated into foreign languages than those of any other contemporary Mexican author.

Reyes symbolizes the humanist par excellence. To his immense intellectual curiosity and his vast culture he added a gift of style which made his prose creations peculiarly his own. He was a wise and penetrating critic, a short-story writer prodigal in surprises, and a poet of delicate sensitivity; educated in the school of Góngora and Mallarmé, he was learned in both classical and modern writers.

Reyes died in Mexico City on Dec. 27, 1959. He was buried in the Rotonda de Hombres Ilustres (Rotunda of Illustrious Men).

Further Reading

Most biographical and critical work on Reyes is in Spanish. For English translations of his works see *The Position of America, and Other Essays* (1950) and *Mexico in a Nutshell and Other Essays* (1964), both translated by Charles Ramsdell with a foreword by Arturo Torres-Ríoseco. He is discussed in Carlos González Peña, *History of Mexican Literature* (3d ed., trans. 1968). □

Rafael Reyes

Colombian military and political leader Rafael Reyes (1850-1920) assumed the presidency following a disastrous civil war and established an absolutist regime which contributed to recovery from the excesses of the fighting.

Born in Santa Rosa, Rafael Reyes grew into a vigorous and robust youth addicted to outdoor life. At the age of 24, with two brothers, he undertook the exploration of the Putumayo River, which links Colombia with the upper Amazon Basin. For over a decade he charted jungle routes and located resources of rubber and quinine. One brother died of fever, and the other was killed by Native Americans.

Reyes distinguished himself in the civil wars of both 1885 and 1895. During the 3 years' bloody fighting which commenced in 1899, however, he was outside Colombia. In 1904, with the support of the Conservatives, he ascended to the presidency.

Coming to power in the wake of disastrous bloodletting and Colombia's loss of its province of Panama, Reyes first attempted to institute a policy of compromise, dedicating himself to the resurrection and strengthening of national unity. Unable to secure cooperation from dissident political elements, he established a highly centralized and authoritarian government which was committed to material change and economic development. Dissolving by executive decree an uncooperative Congress, he jailed many of its members, declared martial law, and assumed full dictatorial powers. Reyes sought the aura of legality by appointing a National Assembly whose task was to ratify his decisions. Impatient of dissent and uninterested in free elections or constitutional government, he turned to the improvement of material conditions.

Reyes adopted a series of stern measures. In 1905 he merged the finance and treasury ministrie s in order to tighten financial control and to reorganize the economy. The floating of foreign loans helped restore Colombian credit in world markets, and coffee production was encouraged. Public works included the building of highways and railroads, especially along the Magdalena River Basin.

In his early years in power Reyes encountered little opposition from a war-weary populace, but despite his efficiency the political situation grew stormy. He survived several attempts on his life, and the National Assembly voted to extend his term to 1914. In 1909 he negotiated treaties with Panama and the United States as final settlement of the independence movement in the former and was met by national protests and by student demonstrations. Although he withdrew the treaties, he was forced to resign in June 1909. After years of exile he returned home in 1919, where he died the following year.

Further Reading

The best analysis of Reyes's career within the context of national history is Jesús María Henao and Gerardo Arrubla, *History of Colombia,* translated by J. Fred Rippy (1938). A North American historical survey which also places Reyes in historical perspective is Hubert Herring, *A History of Latin America* (1955; 3d ed. 1968). □

Albert Reynolds

Albert Reynolds (born 1932) became prime minister of Ireland in 1992, reflecting a new generation of Irish leaders. Entering politics after success in business, he won leadership of the Fianna Fail Party and was able to build a governing coalition with a progressivist and socially liberal Labour Party.

Albert Reynolds was born in Rooskey, County Roscommon, on November 3, 1932, and was educated at Summerhill College in Sligo. He married Kathleen Coen, and they had two sons and five daughters. He became the owner of a chain of dance halls that flourished during Ireland's "show band" craze of the 1960s. Reynolds then got into the pet food business; next he purchased a local newspaper. The president of the Longford Chamber of Commerce from 1974 through 1978 and a member of the Longford County Council from 1974 through 1979, he was elected to the Irish parliament, Dail Eireann, in June 1977. He was part of the overwhelming majority won in that election by Fianna Fail, the Eamon de Valera-founded party that dominated Irish politics after 1932, as it again returned to power after four years in opposition.

In 1979 he was one of a group within the party that brought Charles J. Haughey to the leadership and to the post of taoiseach (prime minister). Reynolds occupied two positions, minister for post and telegraph and minister for transport, in that Haughey government, which lasted until June 1981. The election of that date, which was held while Irish Republican Army (IRA) prisoners were on hunger strike in Northern Ireland, resulted in Fianna Fail narrowly losing power to a fragile coalition headed by Garret FitzGerald of Fine Gael. That coalition government lasted only until early the next year when another election brought Haughey and Fianna Fail back into power, but with a plurality rather than a majority of seats in Dail Eireann, making them dependent on the votes of a handful of independent members.

Reynolds became minister for industry and commerce. However, that government fell in November 1982 and a Fine Gael-Labour coalition was returned in yet another election with enough support so as to govern until 1987. While in opposition, Reynolds served as front bench spokesman first on industry and employment and, from October 1984, on energy. Haughey and Fianna Fail were returned to power in March 1987, but again without an absolute majority. Reynolds again served as minister for industry and commerce until he became minister for finance in November 1988.

In June 1989 Haughey called an election, hoping to get an absolute majority for his party. He failed and, consequently, for the first time in the history of the Fianna Fail Party, had to form a coalition government. His partners were the Progressive Democrats, a party made up of many

ex-Fianna Fail members with a record of hostility toward Haughey, with a conservative economic position but a liberal social outlook.

Although he had considerable success in bringing Irish inflation and national indebtedness under control, Haughey remained plagued by allegations of scandal. In the fall of 1991 Reynolds led an unsuccessful effort within the party to replace Haughey and, naturally, then had to resign as finance minister. But a couple of months later charges about Haughey's awareness of the wire tapping of journalists a decade earlier prompted his resignation. Reynolds was then selected to replace him by the votes of 61 of the 77 Fianna Fail TDs (members of Dail Eireann), and he became taoiseach on February 11, 1992. In office he ousted many of the Haughey loyalists from the cabinet. The following June he successfully led the campaign for popular endorsement in a referendum of Ireland's signing of the Maastricht Agreement that further intensified the process of European political and economic unification.

Two matters did plague him. One was the controversy arising from an Irish Supreme Court ruling that allowed an unmarried 14-year-old girl to travel to Britain to have an abortion. The Supreme Court's logic was that the concern for the life of the mother expressed in the existing constitutional prohibition of abortion would permit the girl to travel to have the abortion, since she had threatened suicide because of her pregnancy. The other problem was increasing hostility from his coalition partners, the Progressive Democrats, especially from their leader, Desmond O'Malley. The latter had given testimony in a quasi-judical tribunal about alleged government favors for beef exporters, with the implication of responsibility on Reynolds' part, since he had been minister for industry and commerce. Reynolds went on the offensive against O'Malley, ultimately accusing him of dishonest testimony. O'Malley and colleagues thereupon resigned, provoking a national election in November 1992.

The election occurred the same day, November 25, as a referendum on a three-part amendment to the constitution that the Reynolds government had proposed to rectify confusion resulting from the court decision on abortion. Two parts, which permitted travel outside the state for abortions and the dissemination of information about the availability of abortion abroad, were approved by the voters. The other section, which continued the prohibition of abortion except where the life of the mother was endangered (for causes other than the threat of suicide), was defeated. The latter section was unsatisfactory to both opponents and advocates of the availability of abortion and left observers confused as to actual Irish opinion.

In the election Fianna Fail suffered substantial losses, while the only big gainer was the Labour Party, the former regular coalition partner of Fine Gael. Several weeks of negotiations finally resulted in a Fianna Fail-Labour coalition with a combined total of 101 votes in a Dail of 166 members. The numerical strength of the coalition suggested endurance; however, there remained potential internal disagreements between business-oriented, socially-conservative, and nationalist-populist Fianna Fail and progressivist, socially-liberal Labour.

Reynolds' government was noteworthy for its participation in a since-suspended conference with the British Government and the rival constitutional parties of Northern Ireland on the question of a political restructuring of that province. Later, on December 15, 1993, Reynolds issued jointly with British Prime Minister John Major an appeal to the men of violence in Northern Ireland to lay down their weapons and enter negotiations for a settlement in which the ultimate determiners of Irish unity would be the people of Ireland. Both premiers agreed, however, that such unification would be dependent on majority consent in both the Republic of Ireland and in Northern Ireland.

Reynolds continued efforts to depopularize the IRA's armed struggle for unification and to expand the peace dialog with the Major government. Reynolds' government fell during the delicate negotiations surrounding the Clinton peace initiative brokered by Special Advisor to the President and Secretary of State for economic initatives in Ireland, George Mitchell. The dark comic events resulting in Reynolds' ouster were precipitated by delays in the extradition of a priest to Northern Ireland on charges of child sexual abuse. A series of allegations emerged about Reynolds-appointed President of the High Court, Harry Whelehan, whom Reynolds had elevated to that post from Attorney-General in the midst of the affair. The charges implicated Whelehan, then serving as Attorney-General, in delaying the extradition to spare Reynolds the political embarrassment and risk likely to accompany compliance with the Northern Irish request.

Reynolds government fell shortly thereafter. One important effect of his demise was a delay in the peace process. In the months after Reynolds' fall, rumors surfaced in Dublin and Washington, based on likely CIA and FBI sources, that the entire affair had been orchestrated by British intelligence as a test to bring down Reynolds who was perceived as having too effective influence over Major. The priest in question was revealed to have paid four documented visits to the North with the the knowledge of authorities, yet no effort had been made to apprehend him.

In 1995, Reynolds was appointed to membership on the Board of Governors of the European Investment Bank and Governor for Ireland of the World Bank and the International Monetary Fund.

Further Reading

There is no biography of Reynolds. The best reporting would be in internationally circulating weeklies such as the *Economist* and the *New Statesman and Society*. Good introductions to modern Irish political history included J.J. Lee, *Ireland: 1912-1985* (1989), Terence Brown, *Ireland: A Social and Cultural History, 1922 to the Present* (1985), Padraig O'Malley, *The Uncivil Wars: Ireland Today* (1983), and Tim Pat Coogan, *The Troubles* (1996). ☐

Sir Joshua Reynolds

Sir Joshua Reynolds (1723-1792), the outstanding intellectual force among English artists of his age, vir- tually created a new type of portraiture by interpreting the humanity of his sitters in terms of the heroic tradition of Old Master history painting.

Joshua Reynolds was born on July 16, 1723, at Plympton, Devon, the third son and seventh child of the Reverend Samuel Reynolds, master of the Plympton Grammar School and sometime fellow of Balliol College, Oxford. Joshua was enabled by education, ability, and inclination to move all his adult life with ease and distinction in literary and learned circles. A vocation for art was confirmed by reading as a boy Jonathan Richardson's *Essay on the Theory of Painting* (1715), with its program for restoring portraiture to the dignity of high art, and at the age of 17 Joshua was apprenticed to Richardson's son-in-law, Thomas Hudson, in London.

Reynolds set up on his own in 1743 and practiced in Plympton and London. His work of this period shows the influence of Anthony Van Dyck and the innovations introduced by William Hogarth, then at the height of his powers.

In 1749 Reynolds sailed for Italy as the guest of Commodore Augustus Keppel. In Rome, Reynolds studied the Old Masters with a single-mindedness unmatched by any earlier English painter. His only diversion was a small number of caricature paintings in the manner of his fellow Devonian Thomas Patch. Raphael was Reynolds's hero, but on his way back to England he visited northern Italy and

came under the spell of the Venetian painters and Correggio.

Reynolds settled in London in 1753 and established his reputation as the foremost portrait painter with *Captain the Hon. Augustus Keppel* (1753-1754), the first of a long series of portraits ennobled by a borrowed pose, here taken from the *Apollo Belvedere.* He used borrowed attitudes in two ways: as a mode of elevation and as a species of wit. As Horace Walpole noted, both usages are controlled by intellect and taste, manifested in the aptness of his application to the sitter's character, achievement, or role in society.

After his election as foundation president of the Royal Academy in 1768 until his death in London on Feb. 23, 1792, Reynolds's life was too closely intertwined with the artistic, literary, and social history of his time for a summary to be adequate. A small group of portraits of men of genius with whom he was intimate, headed by Dr. Johnson, is unique in European art in that each is accompanied by a written character sketch which is a masterpiece of psychological assessment.

Reynolds delivered 15 discourses to the members and students of the Royal Academy between 1769 and 1790. They upheld the ideal theory in art and constituted the classic formulation of academic doctrine after more than 2 centuries of debate.

Reynolds's main types of portraiture commemorate naval and military heroes, civil and ecclesiastical dignitaries, the English landowning oligarchy in both its public and private aspects, actors and actresses, and children in fanciful roles, related in their vein of sentiment to "fancy pictures" like the *Age of Innocence* (1788). His most ambitious translation of a subject picture into a portrait is the group of the daughters of Sir William Montgomery, the *Graces Adorning a Term of Hymen* (1774), a Miltonian bridal masque in which the rite of worship to the God of Wedlock is performed by three famous beauties, one recently married, another preparing for marriage, and the third still to be betrothed. Among the finest of his heroicized military portraits in a battle setting are *Colonel Banastre Tarleton* (1782) and *George Augustus Eliott, Lord Heathfield* (1788).

A visit to Flanders and Holland in 1781 renewed Reynolds's enthusiasm for Peter Paul Rubens and was followed by a decade of prodigious creative energy. To this final phase belong most of Reynolds's history paintings, including those commissioned for John Boydell's Shakespeare Gallery and the *Infant Hercules* (1788), commissioned by the Empress of Russia. *Sarah Siddons as the Tragic Muse* (1784) shows the actress flanked by emblems of Open and Secret Murder and assembles motives borrowed from Michelangelo, with whose name he closed his last discourse.

As the foundation president of the Royal Academy, Reynolds guided its destinies in its momentous first phase, devoting his immense influence to the single goal of forming a national school of history painters choosing their exalted themes not only from the Bible and classical antiquity but also from Shakespeare and the national past. Courteous, affable, and open to new ideas, he steered a liberal and tactful course and stamped a character of devotion to high art on the institution that lasted into the age of J. M. W. Turner and even beyond.

Further Reading

The definitive edition of Reynold's *Discourses on Art* was edited by Robert R. Wark (1959). Frederick Whiley Hilles edited *Letters of Sir Joshua Reynolds* (1929) and Reynolds's *Portraits* (1952), which contains written character sketches of Oliver Goldsmith, Samuel Johnson, David Garrick, and others. The monumental study of Charles Robert Leslie and Tom Taylor, *Life and Times of Sir Joshua Reynolds* (2 vols., 1865), should be supplemented by Frederick Whiley Hilles, *The Literary Career of Sir Joshua Reynolds* (1936). See also Derek Hudson, *Sir Joshua Reynolds: A Personal Study* (1958). The best-illustrated and most critical study of Reynolds's art is Ellis K. Waterhouse, *Reynolds* (1941).

Additional Sources

Steegman, John, *Sir Joshua Reynolds,* Folcroft, Pa.: Folcroft Library Editions, 1977; Norwood, Pa.: Norwood Editions, 1978. □

Reza Shah Pahlavi

Reza Shah Pahlavi (1878-1944) was the founder of the Pahlavi dynasty. He rose from the ranks to become minister of war, prime minister, and then shah of Iran. As a reformer-dictator, he laid the foundation of modern Iran.

R eza Khan, later Reza Shah Pahlavi, was born in the Caspian province of Mazandaran. He was orphaned in infancy, and at the age of 14 he chose the military career of his father and enlisted in the Persian Cossack Brigade, which was under the command of Russian officers. A tall and rugged young man, Reza Khan rose by sheer courage and ability. He was highly intelligent without any formal education, had vision without much information, and was a champion of Westernization without having seen any other country but Iran.

Reza Khan was also very sensitive, and from his youth he must have been disgusted with the despicable condition of the country and also of the army. As a soldier, he took part in many engagements, but what bothered him most was the fact that he was under the command of foreign officers. After the Russian Revolution, some of the Russian officers in the brigade left, but the White Russians, who could not go, remained in command. In 1920 Reza led his fellow Persian officers in ousting the Russians, and he himself became commander of the brigade.

Coup d'Etat

On Feb. 21, 1921, he, together with Sayyed Ziya al-Din Tabatabai, a brilliant journalist, overthrew the government in Tehran. Sayyed Ziya became prime minister and Reza Khan minister of war and commander in chief of the armed forces. During the next 3 months it became evident that the civilian and the soldier could not agree on specific goals or methods. Since Reza Khan was the stronger of the two, it was Sayyed Ziya who was forced to leave the country. From 1921 to 1925, as minister of war and later as prime minister, Reza Khan built a strong modern army, subdued the rebellious tribes, and brought about a peace and security which the country had not experienced for a century.

Ahmad Shah, the last of the Qajar kings, was so overshadowed by the popular Reza Khan that he left for an indefinite stay in Europe. The creation of a republic in Turkey influenced many Persians, including Reza Khan. For a time there was a movement to create a republic, but it soon became evident that, although Persians did not mind changing kings, they were reluctant to do away with the monarchical principle. So on Oct. 21, 1925, the Majles (Parliament) deposed the absent Ahmad Shah and in December of the same year proclaimed Reza Khan as the shahanshah (king of kings) of Iran.

The Persian Revolution, which had started in 1906, had at last produced a leader to implement its ideals, even though some of the early revolutionaries had not envisaged the methods used by Reza Shah. He was at first popular among the masses and peasants because he gave them security. He was also popular among the educated classes because he was for modernization and reform.

In the field of foreign affairs he ended the system of capitulation; created an autonomous customs; terminated the right of the British Bank to issue currency notes; and in 1931 negotiated a new oil agreement with the Anglo-Persian Oil Company which, he believed, was more advantageous to Iran.

Internal Reforms

Reza Shah's main activity, however, was in internal reforms, which he carried out with the help of the army, which remained the object of his special devotion. He built roads, established a wireless service, and took over the management of the telegraph service from the British. He was rightly proud of the trans-Iranian railway from the Persian Gulf to the Caspian, which he had built without a loan from any foreign government. He set up trade monopolies, thus limiting the freedom of the merchants, and established the National Bank of Iran.

Like his predecessors Shah Abbas I and Nader Shah, Reza Shah tried to break down the power and prestige of the clergy. Islamic law was partially discarded; Islamic education was abandoned; religious processions were forbidden; the Islamic calendar was replaced by the old Persian-Zoroastrian solar calendar; mosques were modernized, and some of them were equipped with pews; the call to prayer was frowned upon; and pilgrimage to Mecca was discouraged.

All titles were abolished, and people were asked to choose family names; Persian men were ordered to don European attire and headgear, and Persian women were encouraged to discard the veil. Reza Shah founded the University of Tehran in 1934 and established the Persian Academy, whose task was to rid the Persian language of borrowed Arabic and other foreign words.

These and many other far-reaching and essential reforms in a country ridden with illiteracy, superstition, and vested interests could not be accomplished without the use of force. So, in order to silence the critics of the reforms, all criticism was banned. In order to have internal security, the army had to be strengthened, but this very act made tyrants of a number of officers who suppressed the masses.

Reza Shah's greatest weakness was his desire to amass wealth, especially real estate. In the acquisition of property he had to depend upon others, who in the process acquired wealth for themselves. Being a self-made man, he was loathe to delegate power to others. Unlike other reformers, he had no ideology, no party, and no well-defined program. Being in complete control of every aspect of life, he improvised and made decisions on the spot as he saw fit. Perhaps his ideas of modernization were superficial, but undoubtedly he forced the country to face the necessity of change, without which modernization would not be possible.

At the outbreak of World War II, Iran declared its neutrality. When Germany attacked the Soviet Union, Iran, already important to the allies for its oil, became the best supply route to Russia. Reza Shah failed to comply with the Russo-British plan of using Iran as a supply route and with their demand to deal effectively with the German agents active in Iran. On Aug. 26, 1941, Russian and British troops entered Iran; the Persian army put up a token resistance which lasted less than a week. Reza Shah abdicated the throne in favor of his son, Mohammad Reza Shah Pahlavi. Reza Shah died in exile in South Africa.

Further Reading

There is no adequate biography of Reza Shah. A sketch of his life is in his son's *Mission for My Country* (1961). Ramesh Sanghvi, *The Shah of Iran* (1969), is less a study than an enumeration of Reza Shah's political achievements. A brief, but probably the most sophisticated, treatment of him is in Richard Cottam, *Nationalism in Iran* (1964). The Shah is discussed in Peter Avery, *Modern Iran* (1965; 2d ed. 1967), and Yahya Armajani, *Middle East: Past and Present* (1970). □

Syngman Rhee

Syngman Rhee (1875-1965) was a leader in Korean independence movements. He was elected the first president of the Republic of Korea in 1948. His government was overthrown in 1960.

Yi Sŭng-man, who Westernized his name to Syngman Rhee, was born on April 26, 1875, only son of Yi Kyŏng-sŏn, a member of the local gentry in the village of Pyŏng-san in Hwanghae Province. Rhee's boyhood name was Sŭng-yong. When he was very young, the family moved to Seoul, the capital city of a dynasty in rapid decline. He studied Chinese readers and classics before enrolling in the Paejae Haktang (academy), a Methodist mission school, in 1894. Upon graduation from Paejae, he was employed by the academy as an English instructor. He became interested in Western enlightenment ideas and joined reform movements which bitterly criticized the anachronistic and impotent Korean government. He was arrested and imprisoned in 1897. His conversion to Methodism came while he was a political prisoner. He was released from prison in 1904.

In the winter of the same year, Rhee traveled to the United States with a hope of appealing to President Theodore Roosevelt for assistance to Korea in its desperate efforts to maintain its independence from Japan. The appeal was futile, as the American-Korean treaty of 1882 had lost meaning and as the U.S. government was eager to cooperate with the Japan that was emerging victorious from the Russo-Japanese War. The Portsmouth Treaty led to the Japanese protectorate over Korea, and the United States promptly withdrew the American legation from Seoul.

Education in the United States

While Syngman Rhee was pursuing his elusive goal of attempting to save Korean independence through hopeless appeals, he also enrolled, in the spring of 1905, as a student in George Washington University. Upon graduation in 1907, he decided to do postgraduate work in the United States and was admitted to Harvard University. He began to read extensively in international relations. When he received his master's degree in the spring of 1908, unstable conditions in his homeland prompted him to continue his education in the United States. He received his doctorate in political science from Princeton University in 1910, the year in which Japan formally annexed its Korean protectorate.

The topic of his dissertation was "Neutrality as Influenced by the United States."

Rhee returned to Korea in 1910 as a YMCA organizer, teacher, and evangelist among the youth of Korea. When an international conference of Methodist delegates was held in Minneapolis in 1912, Rhee attended the meeting as the lay delegate of the Korean Methodists. After the conference, Rhee decided to stay in the United States and accepted the head position at the Korean Compound School—later the Korean Institute—in Honolulu in 1913.

President of Provisional Government

On March 1, 1919, a Korea-wide demonstration for the independence of the country took place as 33 leading Koreans signed a declaration of independence which was then read to crowds in the streets. The Japanese reaction to the massive "Mansei Uprising," which was partly inspired by the Wilsonian doctrine of self-determination, was swift and cruel. An outcome of the "Samil movement" was that a group of independence leaders, meeting in Seoul in April 1919, formed a Korean provisional government with Syngman Rhee—still in the United States—as the first president. The provisional government was subsequently located in Shanghai, and Rhee continued to lead the independence movement mostly from the United States, where he was best known. When Kim Ku became the president of the "government in exile," Rhee acted as its Washington representative.

In early 1933 Rhee was in Geneva attempting to make an appeal on behalf of Korea to the delegates attending the League of Nations, where Japan's military conquest of Manchuria was under discussion. His mission was once again frustrating, as major powers were then unwilling and unable to check the expansionist Japan. It was in Geneva that Rhee first became acquainted with Miss Francesca Donner, the eldest of three daughters of a well-to-do iron merchant in Vienna. She was in Geneva serving as a secretary to the Austrian delegation to the League. After Rhee's return to the United States via Moscow, Miss Donner entered the United States under the Austrian immigration quota. They were married in October 1933, saying the vows in both Korean and English. He was then almost 58. Francesca shared his life as a devoted wife. (After Rhee's death in 1965, she lived in Vienna.)

Return to Korea

When Korea was liberated from Japanese colonial domination in 1945 by the Allied Powers, Rhee was flown back to the country that he had not seen for some 33 years. He was given a hero's welcome by the American military government that was ruling the southern half of Korea and by the Korean people, who were overjoyed with the prospect of independence. Rhee quickly became the leader of conservative, right-wing political forces in South Korea, thanks to his background as a leader of the "exile government." Rhee's only potential rival in South Korea politics, Kim Ku, who had led the "exile government" in China, was assassinated.

When the first general elections in Korean history, to elect the members of the National Assembly, were held on May 10, 1948, under the supervision of the UN Temporary Commission on Korea, Rhee's Association for the Rapid Realization of Independence won a plurality of seats. When the National Assembly convened for the first time, on May 31, 1948, Rhee was elected as Assembly chairman—a first step to the presidency of the Republic of Korea.

President of the Republic

The National Assembly adopted the 1948 constitution of Korea, providing for an essentially democratic, presidential system of government. As one of its first official acts under the new constitution, the National Assembly elected Rhee as the republic's first president. The Republic of Korea was proclaimed on the third anniversary of VJ-day, thus ending the 3-year administration of South Korea by the U.S. military government.

In the first few months of the Rhee administration, what may be called a "personalism" of the strong-willed president, as opposed to "institutionalism," was established in the republic. The crisis conditions under which the Rhee government had to function in the southern half of the divided peninsula tended to accelerate the process. Communist-inspired mutinies in the Yŏsu-Sunchŏn areas, for instance, made normal operations of the government difficult already in October—barely 2 months after the inauguration of the government. When the Communist army of North Korea invaded the Republic of Korea on June 25, 1950, the Rhee administration quickly adjusted to the wartime situation, and Rhee became increasingly autocratic.

While UN action led by the United States was being resolutely taken to repulse the armed aggression, and while numerous South Korean troops were engaged in fierce combat against Communist troops, the Rhee administration initiated a "political crisis" in and around the wartime capital of Pusan, which was placed under martial law.

The executive thoroughly intimidated the legislature in the early summer of 1952 to adopt a series of constitutional amendments that Rhee desired. By now, Rhee was unlikely to be reelected as president by the National Assembly according to the Constitution of 1948. The 1952 amendments provided, among other things, for a direct popular election of the president and vice president. Rhee and his running mate, Ham T'ae-yŏng, were elected by an overwhelming majority of south Korean voters in the Aug. 5, 1952, elections. By the time the Korean truce agreement was signed in a wooden hut in P'anmunjŏm in July 1953, the political position of President Rhee and his Liberal party was supreme.

After the victory of the Liberal party in the May 20, 1954, Assembly election, the Rhee administration again proposed on September 6 a long series of constitutional amendments. The more important provisions of these amendments, which were adopted on November 27, eliminated the two-term restriction on presidential tenure and abolished the office of the prime minister. Rhee won his third presidential term in the May 15, 1956, election. Rhee had won this election with only 56 percent of the vote, however, compared to 72 percent in the wartime election of 1952. Furthermore, Korean voters had elected Chang Myŏn (John M. Chang) of the opposition party as the vice president. Many commentators observed that the 1956 election was a partial repudiation by the people of Rhee's administration and his Liberal party, which were becoming increasingly more oppressive.

Aware of the mounting discontent of the people, the administration and the Liberal party extensively "rigged" the March 15, 1960, presidential election, although the opposition candidate, Cho Pyŏng-ok, had died of complications resulting from an operation at the Walter Reed Hospital. When all the votes were "counted" after March 15, it was announced that there were, astoundingly, no recorded "posthumous" votes for Cho; it was claimed by the government that Rhee had "won" 92 percent of the vote; the remaining votes were simply termed "invalid." The opposition groups in the National Assembly, the only public gathering where a semblance of free speech still remained under the Rhee government, protested the elections vigorously. They charged that a number of votes, equal to 40 percent of the total electorate, had been fabricated and used to pad the Liberal party vote.

Student Uprising

Pent-up frustrations of the Korean people at these political manipulations exploded in the April 19, 1960, "Student Uprising." The Rhee administration attempted to blame "devilish hands of the Communists" for disturbances throughout South Korea. President Rhee himself asserted that the Masan riot, which had touched off the uprising, was the work of communist agents. President Rhee declared martial law and made it retroactive to the moment when the police guarding his mansion fired against the demonstrators.

Heavily armed soldiers were moved into the capital. When bloody showdowns seemed imminent, the soldiers, under the martial law commander, Lt. Gen. Song Yo-ch'an, showed no intention of shooting at demonstrating students. In fact, the army seemed to maintain strict "neutrality" between the Rhee administration and the demonstrators. While the very life of the Rhee administration trembled in the balance, the coercive powers of the regime thus evaporated. President Rhee resigned on April 26, 1960. He flew to Hawaii in May to live out his life in exile. He died of illness on July 19, 1965.

Rhee's presidency for about 12 years was marked principally by his stern anti-communism, anti-Japanese policies, awesome "personalism," and paternalistic leadership. It was partly due to his prestige and leadership, however, that South Korea could maintain war efforts during the Korean conflict of 1950-1953. The first presidency of the Republic of Korea would have been an extremely difficult task for anyone; Rhee's evident obsession to prolong his regime turned it into a tragic one—for himself and for the country that he served so long.

Further Reading

An exceptionally thorough, well-researched biography that is extremely favorable to Rhee is Robert T. Oliver, *Syngman Rhee: The Man behind the Myth* (1954), although it is now dated. A fairly objective and sometimes critical biography is Richard C. Allen, *Korea's Syngman Rhee: An Unauthorized Portrait* (1960). For an analysis of Rhee as president of the Republic of Korea see John Kie-chiang Oh, *Korea: Democracy on Trial* (1968).

Additional Sources

Oliver, Robert Tarbell, *Syngman Rhee and American involvement in Korea, 1942-1960: a personal narrative,* Seoul: Panmun Book Co., 1978. □

Robert Barnwell Rhett

Robert Barnwell Rhett (1800-1876), American statesman, was a U.S. congressman and senator and the spokesman for Southern independence.

Robert Barnwell Rhett was born Robert Barnwell Smith on Dec. 21, 1800, in aristocratic Beaufort, S.C. His family had enjoyed a notable reputation in South Carolina history. At the age of 37 he changed his name from the plebeian Smith to the patrician Rhett. Although Rhett's schooling was irregular, at the age of 21 he was admitted to the South Carolina bar. He lived in the manner of the Carolina aristocracy throughout his life, owning two plantations and a succession of town residences.

In 1826 Rhett was elected to the state legislature, where he quickly became prominent in the protective tariff controversy. Initially he argued passionately for resistance, but he came to accept John C. Calhoun's theory of peaceful, constitutional nullification.

From 1837 to 1849 Rhett served in the U.S. House of Representatives. He worked closely with Calhoun, then senator from South Carolina, in propagating the notion that the Constitution, "rightly interpreted," protected the South. He also promoted Calhoun's plans for controlling the Democratic party. In 1844, when Calhoun failed to secure the presidential nomination, the Democrats deserted the South on the tariff issue; Rhett, defying Calhoun, led a movement for separate state action on the tariff.

When Calhoun died in 1850, Rhett was elected U.S. senator. By this time he had begun a campaign to promote South Carolina's secession from the Union. He was convinced that its withdrawal would encourage other Southern states to secede. The next year, however, South Carolina rejected Rhett's leadership by accepting the Compromise of 1850.

Although in political retirement throughout the 1850s, Rhett remained in contact with Southerners of secessionist persuasion. In the aftermath of the critical 1860 election, he was so influential in spreading secession ideas in South Carolina that he was called the father of secession. His most effective forum was the *Charleston Mercury,* a newspaper owned by his son after 1857. In early 1861 Rhett attended the Southern Convention at Montgomery. While not a member of the convention, he did lobby to defeat measures he deemed too conciliatory toward the North, and he was chosen by the convention to compose an address to the people of the slaveholding states. He failed, however, to secure the presidency of the Confederacy and was ignored in the Cabinet appointments.

Rhett attacked the Confederate administration for its attempts at centralization. He was twice defeated for a seat in the Confederate lower house and spent his last energies defending Southern civilization against the Confederate proposals to arm, and free, the slaves. On Sept. 14, 1876, Rhett died in Louisiana.

Further Reading

The best study of Rhett is Laura Amanda White, *Robert Barnwell Rhett: Father of Secession* (1931), a significant contribution to Confederate history, especially in its treatment of causative factors and immediate prewar events. □

Cecil John Rhodes

The English imperialist, financier, and mining magnate Cecil John Rhodes (1853-1902) founded and controlled the British South Africa Company,

which acquired Rhodesia and Zambia as British territories. He founded the Rhodes scholarships.

Cecil Rhodes was born on July 5, 1853, at Bishop's Stortford, Hertfordshire, one of nine sons of the parish vicar. After attending the local grammar school, his health broke down, and at 16 he was sent to South Africa. Arriving in October 1870, he grew cotton in Natal with his brother Herbert but in 1871 left for the newly developed diamond field at Kimberley.

In the 1870s Rhodes laid the foundation for his later massive fortune by speculating in diamond claims, beginning pumping techniques, and in 1880 forming the De Beers Mining Company. During this time he attended Oxford off and on, starting in 1873, and finally acquired the degree of bachelor of arts in 1881. His extraordinary imperialist ideas were revealed early, after his serious heart attack in 1877, when he made his first will, disposing of his as yet unearned fortune to found a secret society that would extend British rule over the whole world and colonize most parts of it with British settlers, leading to the "ultimate recovery of the United States of America" by the British Empire!

From 1880 to 1895 Rhodes's star rose steadily. Basic to this rise was his successful struggle to take control of the rival diamond interests of Barnie Barnato, with whom he amalgamated in 1888 to form De Beers Consolidated Mines, a company whose trust deed gave extraordinary powers

to acquire lands and rule them and extend the British Empire. With his brother Frank he also formed Goldfields of South Africa, with substantial mines in the Transvaal. At the same time Rhodes built a career in politics; elected to the Cape Parliament in 1880, he succeeded in focusing alarm at Transvaal and German expansion so as to secure British control of Bechuanaland by 1885. In 1888 Rhodes agents secured mining concessions from Lobengula, King of the Ndebele, which by highly stretched interpretations gave Rhodes a claim to what became Rhodesia. In 1889 Rhodes persuaded the British government to grant a charter to form the British South Africa Company, which in 1890 put white settlers into Lobengula's territories and founded Salisbury and other towns. This provoked Ndebele hostility, but they were crushed in the war of 1893.

By this time Rhodes controlled the politics of Cape Colony; in July 1890 he became premier of the Cape with the support of the English-speaking white and non-white voters and the Afrikaners of the "Bond" (among whom 25,000 shares in the British South Africa Company had been distributed). His policy was to aim for the creation of a South African federation under the British flag, and he conciliated the Afrikaners by restricting the Africans' franchise with educational and property qualifications (1892) and setting up a new system of "native administration" (1894).

Later Career

At the end of 1895 Rhodes's fortunes took a disastrous turn. In poor health and anxious to hurry his dream of South African federation, he organized a conspiracy against the Boer government of the Transvaal. Through his mining company, arms and ammunition were smuggled into Johannesburg to be used for a revolution by "outlanders," mainly British. A strip of land on the borders of the Transvaal was ceded to the chartered company by Joseph Chamberlain, British colonial secretary; and Leander Jameson, administrator of Rhodesia, was stationed there with company troops. The Johannesburg conspirators did not rebel; Jameson, however, rode in on Dec. 27, 1895, and was ignominiously captured. As a result, Rhodes had to resign his premiership in January 1896. Thereafter he concentrated on developing Rhodesia and especially in extending the railway, which he dreamed would one day reach Cairo.

When the Anglo-Boer War broke out in October 1899, Rhodes hurried to Kimberley, which the Boers surrounded a few days later. It was not relieved until Feb. 16, 1900, during which time Rhodes had been active in organizing defense and sanitation. His health was worsened by the siege, and after traveling in Europe he returned to the Cape in February 1902, where he died at Muizenberg on March 26.

Rhodes left £6 million, most of which went to Oxford University to establish the Rhodes scholarships to provide places at Oxford for students from the United States, the British colonies, and Germany. Land was also left to provide eventually for a university in Rhodesia.

Further Reading

Rhodes's letters and papers have not yet been edited and published, but Vindex (pseudonym for Rev. F. Verschoyle) published *Cecil Rhodes: His Political Life and Speeches, 1881-1900* (1900). There are a number of biographies: Sir Lewis Michell, *The Life of the Rt. Hon. Cecil John Rhodes, 1853-1902* (2 vols., 1910), comprehensive but eulogistic; Basil Williams, *Cecil Rhodes* (1921), which is still useful; Sarah Gertrude Millin, *Cecil Rhodes* (1933); and Felix Gross, *Rhodes of Africa* (1957), faulty in research, sometimes hostile, but suggesting interesting if often farfetched interpretations. J. G. Lockhart and C. M. Woodhouse, *Cecil Rhodes: The Colossus of Southern Africa* (1963), used the Rhodes papers and much new material, but the definitive biography remains to be written. A recent account of Rhodes's relationship to the Princess Radziwell and of the Jameson raid is Brian Roberts, *Cecil Rhodes and the Princess* (1969), an exciting piece of historical reconstruction.

Additional Sources

Baker, Herbert, Sir, *Cecil Rhodes: the man and his dream,* Bulawayo: Books of Rhodesia, 1977.

Davidson, A. B. (Apollon Borisovich), *Cecil Rhodes and his time,* Moscow: Progress Publishers, 1988.

Flint, John E., *Cecil Rhodes,* London: Hutchinson, 1976.

Gale, W. D. (William Daniel), *One man's vision: the story of Rhodesia,* Bulawayo: Books of Rhodesia, 1976.

Keppel-Jones, Arthur., *Rhodes and Rhodesia: the white conquest of Zimbabwe, 1884-1902,* Kingston Ont.: McGill-Queen's University Press, 1987.

Michell, Lewis, Sir, *The life and times of the Right Honourable Cecil John Rhodes, 1853-1902,* New York: Arno Press, 1977 c1910.

Roberts, Brian, *Cecil Rhodes: flawed colossus,* New York: Norton, 1988, 1987.

Rotberg, Robert I., *The founder: Cecil Rhodes and the pursuit of power,* New York: Oxford University Press, 1988. □

James Ford Rhodes

James Ford Rhodes (1848-1927), American historian, wrote an influential multivolume political narrative of the Civil War and Reconstruction.

James Ford Rhodes was born on May 1, 1848, in Ohio City, Ohio, now a part of Cleveland. His father was a prosperous businessman. After a year of education beyond high school, Rhodes went into business. The business proved to be very successful, and Rhodes, who had literary interests, was able to retire in 1884 to pursue his desire to write history. He had in mind a general history of the United States from 1850 to 1888. After completing the first two volumes, covering the period from 1850 to 1860, in Cleveland, he moved to Cambridge, Mass., in 1891, hoping to find more congenial surroundings and a more intellectual atmosphere.

When the first two volumes appeared in 1892, they received almost universal acclaim. Rhodes, being a thoroughly middle-class American, found it easy and natural to say what middle-class America wanted to hear. According

to Rhodes, the Civil War was a moral contest over slavery in which the North was entirely justified, although the South fought nobly to defend its views. Reconstruction was an unmitigated disaster; he believed, caused by the misguided attempt to elevate "inferior" African Americans to supremacy over superior whites.

Rhodes viewed history as a branch of literature, and he had an intensely personal view of the field. To Rhodes, the essence of history was the struggle between good people and bad people and not the result of conflicts between broad social forces. His historical views were attractive to the general reading public. As his subsequent volumes appeared, Rhodes came to be acknowledged as the leading authority on the Civil War and Reconstruction.

Despite declining health and his concern over World War I, Rhodes managed to publish the last two volumes of his history in the early 1920s, bringing his account up to the end of Theodore Roosevelt's first presidential administration. These books were not received as favorably as his earlier ones. Critics noted his exclusive preoccupation with political history, his failure to dig deeply into the forces causing historical change, his partiality for conservative business ideals, and his antipathy toward African Americans, immigrants, and workers.

Rhodes was one of the last men to write American history as a multivolume political narrative. He was also one of the last important amateurs in American historical writing. He died on Jan. 22, 1927.

Further Reading

The best book on Rhodes is Robert Cruden, *James Ford Rhodes: The Man, the Historian, and His Work* (1961), which contains biographical details and penetrating analyses of Rhodes's ideas and methods. Raymond Curtis Miller's essay on Rhodes in William T. Hutchinson, ed., *The Marcus W. Jernegan Essay in American Historiography* (1937), is brief but valuable. M. A. DeWolfe Howe, *James Ford Rhodes: American Historian* (1929), is adulatory and virtually ignores Rhodes's historical ideas but contains a large number of his letters. □

Jusepe de Ribera

Jusepe de Ribera (1591-1652) was a Spanish painter and etcher who worked in Naples. Stylistically, his paintings show the progression from the early to the late baroque.

Information concerning the life and personality of Jusepe de Ribera is sparse. He was born the son of a shoemaker in Játiva, Valencia Province. He appears to have gone to the city of Valencia while still a boy, but nothing is known of his possible artistic training there. As an adolescent, he traveled to Italy and spent time in Lombardy. Next he was in Parma, from which, it is said, he was driven by the contentious jealousy of local artists. He located himself in Rome until an accumulation of debts forced him to flee. Finally he settled in Naples, where in 1616 he married Caterina Azzolino, the daughter of a painter, by whom he had seven children between the years 1627 and 1636.

The Academy of St. Luke in Rome elected Ribera to membership in 1625, and 6 years later the Pope conferred upon him the Order of Christ. It is understandably speculated that Ribera revisited Rome for these events. Being sought after in Naples by the Church and the various Spanish viceroys who ruled there in the name of the Spanish monarchy, he dismissed the idea of returning to his homeland. He was quoted as saying that he was honored and well paid in Naples and that Spain was a cruel stepmother to its own children and a compassionate mother to foreigners. Nevertheless, he generally added his nationality when he signed his works. This practice inspired the Italians to nickname him "the Little Spaniard" (Lo Spagnoletto).

The last decade of Ribera's life was one of personal struggle. He suffered from failing health, the taunts of other artists that his fame was "extinct," and difficulty in collecting payments due him. Nevertheless, he kept it from being a tragic defeat by continuing to paint until the very year of his death in Naples. Actually, he was the victim of the local politics and finances. Naples was in the throes of a severe economic depression for which the foreign rulers, the patrons of Ribera, were naturally blamed, and the desperate citizenry was rioting in the streets. It is significant that Ribera continued to receive commissions in such a time, even if there was a dearth of payments.

Ribera was inventive in subject matter, ranging through visionary spectacles, biblical themes, genre, portraits, myth-

ological subjects, and portraits of ascetics and penitents. Three stylistic periods are pointed out by Elizabeth du Gué Trapier (1952): 1620-1635, dramatic chiaroscuro, dry and tight technique with the major influence from Caravaggio, as in the *Martyrdom of St. Andrew* (1628); 1635-1639, soft luminosity, sensitive line, and heavy impasto with influences from the Carracci, Guercino, Guido Reni, and Correggio, exemplified in the *Ecstasy of Mary Magdalene* (1636); and 1640-1652, looser brushstroke and less detail with a return to the Caravaggesque manner, for example, the *Communion of the Apostles* (1651). In etching he employed a painterly technique, refined and precise in the details.

Further Reading

The definitive work on Ribera is Elizabeth du Gué Trapier, *Ribera* (1952). See also George Kubler and Martin Soria, *Art and Architecture in Spain and Portugal and Their American Dominion, 1500-1800* (1959). □

David Ricardo

The English economist David Ricardo (1772-1823) was a founder of political economy. His economics armed reformers attacking the agricultural aristocracy's political, social, and economic privileges.

David Ricardo was born in London on April 19, 1772, the son of a Jewish merchant-banker émigré from Holland. Ricardo joined his father as a stockbroker at the age of 14. When he married a Quaker, his orthodox father cut him off. Ricardo became a Unitarian, and at 22, with a capital of £800 and support from the financial community, he became an independent stockbroker. At 42 he retired with a fortune of about £1 million and established himself as a landed proprietor.

Ricardo was an independent member of Parliament for the pocket borough of Portarlington from 1819 until his death. He supported a tax on capital to pay off the national debt; currency reform; abolition of the Corn Laws protecting British wheat; parliamentary, poor-law, legal, and military reform; a secret ballot; and Catholic emancipation; he also condemned political repression.

Ricardo's reputation rests upon *On the Principles of Political Economy and Taxation* (1817; rev. 3d ed. 1821), an analysis of the distribution of a fixed amount of wealth among three classes: the owner of land who receives rent, the owner of capital who earns profits, and the laborer who gets wages. Ricardo set out to "determine the laws which regulate this distribution" in relation to both the rate of capital growth and the yield of wheat per acre. Although the analysis is abstract, often ambiguous, and disorganized, seven related economic laws can be extracted.

First, prices are determined by the cost of production. Second, the value of any item is set by the quantity of labor used to produce it. In the revised edition of 1821, Ricardo

The sixth law argues the "diminishing returns" of profits, the earnings of the most useful class. As increasingly inferior land is cultivated, rent and food prices rise, and profits fall since the higher wages required for subsistence wages come out of the existing amount of circulating capital. The final law, the quantity theory of money, applies value theory to gold: the rise or fall in prices depends inversely upon the amount of money in circulation.

Ricardo's other important writings were *The High Price of Bullion* (1810); "An Essay on the Influence of a Low Price on Corn on the Profits of Stock" (1815); "Funding System" (1820), published posthumously in the *Encyclopaedia Britannica: Supplement* (1824); and the "Plan for the Establishment of a National Bank" (1824), also published posthumously. He died at Gatcombe Park, Gloucestershire, on Sept. 11, 1823.

Further Reading

The definitive edition of Ricardo's *Works and Correspondence* is edited by P. Sraffa with the collaboration of M. H. Dobb (10 vols., 1951-1955). A helpful guide through the intricacies and inconsistencies of the Ricardian system is Oswald St. Clair, *A Key to Ricardo* (1957). Mark Blaug, *Ricardian Economics: A Historical Study* (1958), deals with Ricardo within the general context of his time. A chapter on Ricardo in Robert Lekachman, *A History of Economic Ideas* (1959), provides a lucid, less technical discussion of Ricardo's ideas. ☐

suggested that value might also be influenced by the cost of production. A third law, a theory of rent, was based upon Malthus's prediction of increasing population. When population increases, more food is needed and less fertile land is planted. Rent is the difference in the price of wheat per acre between the most and least productive land. As population grows, rent increases at the expense of capital's profits and labor's wages. The interests of landlords were not only antithetical to the rest of the community, but landlords and capitalists were necessary enemies.

The fourth and fifth laws deal with the wages fund and the natural price of labor. These laws assumed that the price of labor, like other market prices, fluctuated with supply and demand; but at any given time there was a fixed supply of money for the payment of wages. This wages fund was the amount of capital in circulation. As capital increased, population grew, less fertile land was planted, rent increased, capital profits decreased, and wages dropped. Ricardo held that population will tend constantly to rise above the wages fund, especially in old countries like England, causing the working man's standard of living to fall. Disaster was arrested only by population reduction, essentially through infant mortality. Ricardo, like Thomas Malthus, never anticipated either population control or technological increase of food supplies. If wages fell below subsistence level, population decreased; when wages neither increased nor decreased the labor supply, they reached their "natural" or subsistence level. Popularizers of Ricardo's general model interpreted this to mean that most people were doomed inexorably to bare subsistence.

Matteo Ricci

Matteo Ricci (1552-1610) was an Italian Jesuit missionary who opened China to evangelization. He was the best-known Jesuit and European in China prior to the 20th century.

B orn at Macerata on Oct. 6, 1552, Matteo Ricci went to Rome in 1568 to study law. In 1571 he entered the Society of Jesus. After studying mathematics and geography at a Roman college, he set out for Goa in 1577 and was ordained there in 1580. In 1582 he was dispatched to Macao and started to learn Chinese.

Soon after the Jesuits established themselves at Chaoch'ing west of Canton, Ricci and a fellow Jesuit, Michele Ruggieri, went there on Sept. 10, 1583. When the Chinese governor general ordered the expulsion of the Jesuits in 1589, Ricci managed to acquire a place in Shaochou, north of Kwangtung, where he soon established amicable relations with the officials and with members of the educated elite.

Ricci's ambition, however, was to go to Peking and establish himself in the imperial capital. Early in 1595 he set out to the north but was halted in Nanking, as all foreigners were held under suspicion following the Japanese invasion of Korea; hence he retreated to Nanchang, Kiangsi. In 1598 he found another opportunity to go north when the Nanking minister of rites, Wang Hunghui, expressed willingness to escort him. They reached the gates of Peking but were again turned back due to the Sino-Japanese conflict. Ricci thereafter settled in Nanking, where he received warm welcome from the literate as a result of his broad knowledge of the Western sciences and deep understanding of the Chinese classics.

Ricci and his escort made another effort to go to Peking in 1600, but their entrance was delayed by the intrigue of the eunuch Ma T'ang, who had tried to take possession of the gifts brought for the Ming emperor. Eventually they arrived at the capital on Jan. 24, 1601, and subsequently received a warm welcome from the Emperor. This imperial favor provided Ricci with an opportunity to meet the leading officials and literati in Peking, some of whom later became Christian converts.

Finally, Ricci obtained a settlement with an allowance for subsistence in Peking, after which his reputation among the Chinese increased. Besides the missionary and scientific work, from 1596 on he was also superior of the missions, which in 1605 numbered 17. When he died on May 11, 1610, he was granted a place for burial in Peking. Some of the outstanding Chinese literati with whom Ricci had contact later became his converts, including the famous scholar-officials Hsü Kuang-ch'i, Li Chih-ts'ao, and Yang T'ing-yün. Ricci's writings include about 20 titles, mostly in Chinese, ranging from religious and scientific works to treatises on friendship and local memory. The most famous of these are the *Mappamondo* (World Map) and the *True Idea of God.*

Ricci owed his success, apart from his personality and learning, largely to his "accommodation method"—an attempt to harmonize the Christian doctrine with the Chinese tradition, which laid the foundation of the subsequent success of the Roman Catholic Church in China. Though the unhappy rites controversy (ca. 1635-1742) brought the mission to near ruin, the name of Ricci and his work left an indelible imprint on subsequent Chinese history.

Further Reading

Ricci's China journal was translated by Louis J. Gallagher as *China in the Sixteenth Century: The Journals of Matteo Ricci, 1583-1610* (1953), which unfortunately contains a number of errors. The standard biography of Ricci in English is Vincent Cronin, *The Wise Man from the West* (1955). For a scholarly estimation of Ricci's scientific contribution see Henri Bernard, *Matteo Ricci's Scientific Contribution to China* (trans. 1935). Recommended for general historical background are G. F. Hudson, *Europe and China* (1931), and George H. Dunne, *Generation of Giants* (1962).

Additional Sources

Spence, Jonathan D., *The memory palace of Matteo Ricci,* New York, N.Y.: Penguin Books, 1985, 1984. □

Anne Rice

In her fiction, Anne Rice (born 1941) seduces her readers through an ornate prose style and a painstaking attention to detail. With her careful blend of accurate historical elements with such themes as alienation and the individual's search for identity, she has acquired a legion of devoted fans.

Anne Rice was born in New Orleans, Louisiana, on October 4, 1941. She was originally named Howard Allen O'Brien (her father's first name was Howard and her mother's maiden name was Allen), but she disliked this name from an early age and it was legally changed when she was seven years old. Rice's father was a postal worker who also worked on sculpture and writing. Rice lost her mother, an alcoholic, when she was fourteen, and the family moved to Texas. Throughout her childhood Rice attended a Catholic church, but abandoned it when she was eighteen because she felt it was too repressive. She married her high school sweetheart, the poet Stan Rice, when she was twenty, and she held a variety of jobs, including cook, waitress, and insurance claims adjuster. She gave birth to a daughter, and wrote sporadically during these years; but when her daughter died of leukemia at the age of five, Rice channeled her grief into her first vampire novel, *Interview with the Vampire,* which she completed in only six weeks. The book was deemed a success, but Rice's depression was severe enough to cause her and her husband to drink heavily. Though she continued to write, and even completed *The Feast of All Saints,* their productivity was limited until their son was born. Finally overcoming her

Anne Rice (right)

Book-of-the-Month Club News, December, 1990.
Chicago Tribune Book World, January 27, 1980; February 10, 1980.
Globe and Mail (Toronto), March 15, 1986; November 5, 1988.
□

Elmer Rice

Elmer Rice (1892-1967) was an American playwright and novelist. Often innovative in style, his plays reveal a concern with individual freedom confronted by the tyranny of impersonal institutions and destructive passions.

Elmer Rice was born Elmer Reizenstein on Sept. 28, 1892, in New York City. After 2 years of high school, he began working at the age of 14. He passed the regents' examinations and entered the New York Law School, from which he graduated *cum laude* in 1912. He passed the bar examinations but decided to try writing instead. His play *On Trial* (1914) was a resounding success. In 1915 he married Hazel Levy. Although not a member of any political party, Rice inclined toward socialism. After World War I he spent 2 years in Hollywood before moving to East Hampton, Conn.

Following *On Trial,* he had several plays produced in New York, but it was not until *The Adding Machine* (1923), an expressionistic tragic-comic portrait of dehydrated man, that he showed his true power. Two more plays, written in collaboration, were produced before he directed his powerful *Street Scene* (1929), a realistic presentation of environmental influences on character relationships. It won the Pulitzer Prize. *The Subway* (1929), a rather underrated play much on the order of *The Adding Machine,* had a short run. In 1930 he published a novel, *A Voyage to Purilia,* and had an unsuccessful production of *See Naples and Die.* But in 1931 his *The Left Bank,* dealing with American expatriates, and *Counsellor-at-law* enlarged his reputation.

The impact of the Great Depression and Rice's trip to Russia and Europe in 1932 was manifested in the controversial *We, the People* (1933). After the production of *Judgment Day and Between Two Worlds* (1934), Rice excoriated New York critics and announced his retirement from the commercial theater. Nonetheless, between 1935 and 1938 he served with the Federal Theater Project, published a novel, helped organize The Playwrights' Company, and had his *American Landscape* produced.

After his divorce in 1942 Rice married Betty Field. During the war he worked for the U.S. Office of War Information, was active in the American Civil Liberties Union, and was president of the Dramatists' Guild. *Dream Girl* (1945), a psychoanalytical fantasy, was his final popular success. His novel *The Show Must Go On* appeared in 1949.

Rice's final work included essays, *The Living Theatre* (1959); an autobiography, *Minority Report* (1963); and ad-

alcohol problem, Rice continued to write more vampire novels, as well as several volumes of erotica, and a new series involving a sect of witches in New Orleans.

The success of *Interview with a Vampire* spurred more vampire books based on secondary characters in her original book; these include *The Vampire Lestat, Queen of the Damned, Tale of the Body Thief,* and *Memnoch the Devil.* Under the pseudonyms Anne Rampling and A. N. Roquelaure, she wrote several volumes of lightly sadistic erotica, including a trilogy based on the fairy tale of Sleeping Beauty.

Although some readers find Rice's subject matter disturbing, others take great interest in her treatment of otherworldly beings. Critics have compared her *Vampire Chronicles* favorably with Mary Shelley's *Frankenstein,* and several have commented on her ability to use language to convey different moods. Many reviewers have said that the popularity of Rice's books lies not only in her skill as a storyteller, but with the lurid fascination readers have with such creatures as vampires, mummies, and witches.

Further Reading

Contemporary Literary Criticism, Volume 41, Gale, 1987.
Ramsland, Katherine, *Prism of the Night: A Biography of Anne Rice,* Dutton, 1991.
Rice, Anne, *Interview with the Vampire,* Knopf, 1976.
Rice, Anne, *The Queen of the Damned,* Knopf, 1988.

ditional plays. He received an honorary doctor's degree from the University of Michigan in 1961. Divorced again, in 1966 he married Barbara Marshall. He died of a heart attack on May 8, 1967.

Further Reading

Rice's *Minority Report* (1963) gives autobiographical details and personal accounts of his plays. The major critical work is Robert G. Hogan, *The Independence of Elmer Rice* (1965). Joseph Mersand, *The American Drama since 1930* (1949), and Allan Lewis, *American Plays and Playwrights of the Contemporary Theatre* (1965), provide additional criticism.

Additional Sources

Vanden Heuvel, Michael, *Elmer Rice: a research and production sourcebook,* Westport, Conn.: Greenwood Press, 1996. □

Joseph Mayer Rice

Joseph Mayer Rice (1857-1934) was part of the Progressive education reform movement of the 1890s that sought to untangle the public school system from the web of political corruption in which it was floundering.

Joseph Mayer Rice was a Progressive education reformer of the nineteenth century who believed that the moral duty of society was to improve the conditions of those who were weak and underprivileged. Children were seen by many to be the most helpless of American citizens, and so education reform became one of the most pressing concerns of many Progressives.

Advocated Improving a Child's Environment

As American society had become more industrialized throughout the nineteenth century, schools were viewed by many as the training ground for the future industrial work force. As such they emphasized discipline, punctuality, and the rote memorization of facts, rather than personal growth. In addition, school systems had been modeled after corporations, centralizing power with school superintendents and principals trained in management techniques. Progressive reformers called for the separation of politics and education and for the implementation of the latest educational theories, which were grounded in experience and based on scientific principles of how the child's mind best develops.

As the son of German immigrants, Rice was himself educated in the public schools of Philadelphia and New York City. He studied at the College of the City of New York and later at the College of Physicians and Surgeons of Columbia, which granted him an M.D. in 1881. He practiced in the hospitals of New York from 1881 to 1884 and had a private practice there from 1884 to 1888. It was during this time that he became interested in the prevention of disease among children. He came to believe, in true Progressive fashion, that the improvement of the child's social environment could best ensure the child's resistance to disease. This gradually led him to give up his medical practice and launch an extensive eight-year study of the school systems in Europe and the United States.

Took Survey of Public Schools

From 1888 to 1890 Rice studied psychology and pedagogy at the German universities of Jena and Leipzig. In Jena he studied under Wilhelm Rein, an influential educational theorist who inspired many American reformers. Rein's philosophy of education placed greater emphasis on the building of moral character over the consumption of information, an idea which gained much currency among Progressive reformers. When he returned to the United States, Rice undertook an exhaustive survey of the public schools. The research lasted from January 7 to June 25, 1892 and took him from the East Coast to the Midwest. Taking stock of his observations, Rice published a series of muckraking articles on urban education in the magazine *The Forum* in 1892 and 1893 that proved to be his most influential work. His criticism mobilized parents against the corrupt politicians who, in practicing graft and patronage, had allowed many public schools to fall into lamentable disrepair.

The nine articles Rice published in *The Forum* were collected in the 1893 publication *The Public School System of the United States.* In this book, Rice presented the results of his study of the public schools in thirty-six cities. The foundation of his work, he wrote, was the idea that the school was meant to serve the best interests of the child, not school officials or teachers; therefore, the spirit in which the book was written was "the same as that in which an advocate pleads for his client." He made a special plea to parents, using language charged with the urgency he felt in pursuit of his cause: "It is indeed incomprehensible," he wrote, "that so many loving mothers . . . are willing, without hesitation, to resign the fate of their little ones to the tender mercies of ward politicians, who in many instances have no scruples in placing the children in class-rooms the atmosphere of which is not fit for human beings to breathe, and in charge of teachers who treat them with a degree of severity that borders on barbarism."

A Wake-Up Call to Parents and School Administrators

The book was essentially a wake-up call to parents and administrators, exposing the inhumane conditions of many schools and giving examples of some "progressive" schools which could provide models for improvement. Rice found gross inequalities among the schools, concluding that those of St. Louis were "the most barbarous schools in the country" and that those in Minneapolis, St. Paul, Indianapolis, and LaPorte, Indiana, met his highest standards. He also outlined the differences between the "old" and "mechanical" forms of instruction, which relied on rote memorization and the recitation of "cut-and-dried facts," and the "new" and "progressive" methods of education, which emphasized the development of the child "in all his faculties, intellectual, moral, and physical." Most importantly, according to Rice, the old methods precluded any sympathetic bond between children and their teachers, who tended to view their roles as that of "lord and master" rather than "friend and guide," as the proponents of the new education preferred. The book was ultimately optimistic that school conditions would improve—provided that those in charge were made aware of the cruel, demoralizing atmosphere of so many institutions. Rice's work rested on the Progressive belief that the authority's task is to expose inhuman conditions and instill the desire for betterment; it is thus that improvement will follow.

Rice was chosen as the chief editor of *The Forum* and served in that capacity from 1897 to 1907. In 1898, Rice published *The Rational Spelling Book,* based on his studies of how children learn to spell. He argued against the popular theory that the more time children spent on a particular subject, the more they would learn. Instead, he discovered that ten minutes of spelling a day was sufficient to produce the results of those who had spent the entire day on spelling exercises. On October 10, 1900, Rice married Deborah Levinson, daughter of private language tutor Ludwig Levinson; they had two children. He later published two more books: *Scientific Management in Education* (1913) and *The People's Government* (1915). Rice also founded the Society of Educational Research in 1903. He died on June 24, 1934, in Philadelphia.

Further Reading

Westbrook, Robert, *Dewey and American Democracy,* Cornell University Press, 1991.
Rice, Joseph Mayer, *The Public School System of the United States,* Arno Press, 1969. □

Adrienne Rich

Adrienne Rich (born 1929) perhaps more than any other contemporary poet crystallized in her work and life the deeply complex, awakening consciousness of modern women.

The daughter of Arnold Rich, a professor of medicine, and Helen, a trained composer and pianist, Adrienne Rich described her early upbringing as "white and middle-class . . . full of books, with a father who encouraged me to read and write." From her father's well-stocked library she was reading such writers as Rosetti, Swinburne, Tennyson, Keats, and Blake before officially attending grade school. In fact, since both her parents believed that they could educate their children better than a public school, neither she nor her sister was sent to class until fourth grade. However, by the time Rich graduated from high school she was writing concise and carefully constructed poetry.

In 1951, the year Rich turned 22 and graduated Phi Beta Kappa from Radcliffe College, *A Change of World* was published. Chosen by W. H. Auden for the Yale Younger Poets Award, it was praised for "its competent craftsmanship, elegance and simple and precise phrasing." Rich herself stated years later that being praised for meeting traditional standards gave her the courage to break the rules in her more mature work.

Rich won a Guggenheim fellowship in 1952 and began studying in Europe and England. In 1953 she married Alfred H. Conrad, a Harvard economist, and moved to Cambridge, Massachusetts. Two years later she gave birth to her first child, David, and saw the publication of her second volume, *The Diamond Cutters and Other Poems,* which received the Ridgely Torrence Memorial Award.

In 1957 and 1959 two more sons, Paul and Jacob, were born, and Rich, burdened already under the demands of motherhood, grew even more frightened by the sense that she was losing her grip on her art and her self. Those early years of motherhood are described with unflinching honesty and vivid detail in "When We Dead Awaken: Writing as Revision," an essay in which she chronicles her anger, fatigue, and frustration as a young mother who feared she had failed both as a woman and as a poet.

Despite her fears Rich did continue to write, publishing *Snapshots of a Daughter-In-Law* in 1963 and *Necessities of Life,* which won the National Book Award, in 1966. By then Rich's metamorphosis from housewife to active feminist was underway, and many of her new poems were illustrating that change. Gone were the traditional rhymed stanzas and the detached tone. In their place a new, bolder lan-

guage asserted itself, signalling a new and bolder Rich who was no longer reluctant to deal with personal issues or to express her outrage over social and political conditions. Poetry had become for her a means of changing people's ideas and attitudes about themselves and their world.

In the late 1960s Rich moved to New York City with her husband and began teaching at Swarthmore College, at the graduate school of Columbia University, and then in the open admissions program at the City College of New York. In 1969 *Leaflets,* a collection of poems about the political turmoil of the 1960s, was published, and Rich's reputation as an activist poet was established.

Throughout the 1970s Rich's work continued to reflect her deepening commitment to feminism, to nature, and to social involvement. Her collections *The Will To Change* (1971), *Diving into the Wreck* (1973), and *The Dream of a Common Language* (1978) all deal in some sense with these themes. Most critics agree, however, that the title poem "Diving into the Wreck" transcends any easy thematic labeling because of its sheer artistic beauty and metaphorical brilliance.

Of Woman Born: Motherhood as Experience and Institution, published in 1976, revealed another side of the poet. An historical and political study of immense scope, the book confirmed her ability as a competent scholar and researcher.

As Rich's confidence in her own abilities as a powerful poet and woman grew her poems became more open, sensual, and lyrical. In *Twenty-One Love Poems* she proved she was not afraid to express in clear, direct images her erotic love for another woman, and in "The Floating Poem, Unnumbered," her bold celebration of lovemaking becomes a tribute to her artistic honesty.

> Your travelled generous thighs
> between which my whole face has come and
> come-
> the innocence and wisdom of the place my
> tongue has found there-
> the live, insatiate dance of your nipples in my
> mouth-
> . . . Whatever happens, this is.

In 1979 Rich saw the publication of her next major work, *On Lies, Secrets, and Silence: Selected Prose 1966-1978,* a collection of essays on a wide range of subjects, including Emily Dickinson, Anne Bradstreet, Charlotte Bronte, Anne Sexton, Jane Eyre, motherhood, education, and writing. The work not only illustrates Rich's talents as a literary critic but also outlines her personal and poetic development and reemphasized the belief so central to her artistic philosophy that the poet is a seer who must speak a common language for those "who do not have the gift." Hers was the ancient concept of the poet and the ideal toward which she gave all her creative energy. In 1986 she won the first Ruth Lilly Poetry Prize, a $25,000 award believed to be the largest given to U.S. poets. In 1994 she was named a MacArthur Fellow. In 1997 Rich made headlines when she rejected a National Medal for the Arts. When growing numbers of people are being marginalized, impoverished, scapegoated and beleaguered, I don't feel I can accept an award from the government pursing these policies, Rich said, in the July 15, 1997 edition of *The News Journal* (Wilmington, DE).

In her varied roles as wife, mother, teacher, poet, radical feminist, lesbian, political activist, and essayist she explored those experiences that contributed to her growth as a woman and artist. In all her work, from her earliest collection of poetry, *A Change of World* (1951), to her later efforts as a political feminist determined to reject a suppressive patriarchal culture, the richness of her vision, her creativity, and her willingness to experiment with controversial themes are evident. But it was her ability to sense the shifting ideas, perceptions, and experiences of American women and to give them shape in language at once original and stark that transformed her into a popular and powerful poet.

Further Reading

An excellent source of commentary for a wide perspective on Rich's work is *Adrienne Rich's Poetry* (1975), edited by Barbara and Albert Gelpi. In addition to a selection of her poems and essays, this critical edition contains essays by several major writers, including W. H. Auden, Randall Jarrell, Erica Jong, Nancy Milford, and Robert Boyers. Judith McDaniel's *Reconstituting the World: The Poetry and Vision of Adrienne Rich* (1979) is a full-length study of the poet's work. *The New York Review of Books* (March 20, 1975) features an informative interview entitled "Susan Sontag and Adrienne Rich: Exchange on Feminism," and *The New Woman's Survival Sourcebook* (1975), edited by Susan Rennie and Karen

Grimstead, offers a dialogue between Adrienne Rich and Robin Morgan on poetry and women's culture. Both interviews reveal Rich as an informed and spirited conversationalist. Other sources of critical analysis are Robert Boyers' "On Adrienne Rich: Intelligence and Will," *Salmagundi* 22-23 (Spring-Summer 1973); Albert Gelpi, "Adrienne Rich: The Poetics of Change," in *American Poetry Since 1960,* edited by Robert B. Shaw (Cheadle, U.K., 1973); Randall Jarrell, "New Books in Review," *Yale Review* 46 (September 1956); David Kalstone, *Five Temperaments* (1977); Alicia Ostrike, "Her Cargo: Adrienne Rich and the Common Language," *American Poetry Review* 8 (July-August 1979); and Helen Vendler, "Ghostlier Demarcations, Keener Sounds," *Parnassus* 2 (Fall-Winter 1973). A recent work is *Dark Fields of the Republic: Poems 1991 - 1995.* □

Richard I

Richard I (1157-1199), called the Lion-hearted, reigned as king of England from 1189 to 1199. He is famous for his exploits on the Third Crusade.

B orn on Sept. 8, 1157, Richard I was the third son of Henry II of England and Eleanor of Aquitaine. From an early age he was regarded as his mother's heir and from 1168 lived with her in her duchy, chiefly at Poitiers. He was enthroned as duke in 1172; in the next year he and his brothers allied with the king of France against their father in a wide-ranging conspiracy. They were defeated, but Henry left Richard in Aquitaine, where he made his reputation as a soldier suppressing local risings. The death of his elder brother (1183) made Richard heir to the throne. He resisted by force his father's proposed transfer of Aquitaine to his brother John, being determined to keep for himself all his father's French lands. In November 1188 he did homage for them to Philip II of France and campaigned with him against Henry II. Henry was defeated and had to grant all their demands before his death (July 6, 1189).

Richard succeeded his father without difficulty; he was installed as Duke of Normandy (July 20) and crowned king of England on September 3. His principal object was now to raise money for a crusade; everything was for sale, including offices and privileges, and Richard even released the king of Scots from vassalage for 10,000 marks.

Leaving England to a council of regency, Richard set out in 1190, traveling through Sicily. There he recognized Tancred as king, offending Emperor Henry VI, who was claiming the throne in the right of his wife. On his way east Richard seized Cyprus from its Greek ruler and there married Berengaria of Navarre. Richard twice defeated Saladin, at Arsuf (Sept. 7, 1191) and Jaffa (July 1192), and twice got within 12 miles of Jerusalem, but his military skill was offset by his quarrels with the other leaders. The crusade failed to reestablish the Latin kingdom, and Richard, deeply disappointed, left Palestine (September 1192) after concluding a truce that gave the Christians a narrow coastal strip and access as pilgrims to the holy places. On his way home he was captured and handed over to the Emperor, who de-

manded £100,000 as ransom and kept him a prisoner till February 1194, when a large part of the money was handed over.

The last years of Richard's life were spent in France, meeting the attacks of the King. Philip made no headway against Richard's superior generalship, but Richard's early death (April 6, 1199) in a minor foray opened the way for the conquest of Normandy and Anjou a few years later.

Further Reading

The standard biography of Richard I is Kate Norgate, *Richard the Lion Heart* (1924). A popular account is by Philip Henderson, *Richard Coeur de Lion* (1959). Steven Runciman, *A History of the Crusades,* vol. 2 (1952), describes Richard's crusade. A contemporary account is translated by Merton Jerome Hubert, *The Crusade of Richard Lion Heart, by Ambroise* (1941). A short account of Richard's activities in France by F. M. Powicke is in *The Cambridge Medieval History,* vol. 6 (1929); and Austin L. Poole, *From Domesday Book to Magna Carta* (1955), describes the government of England. □

Richard II

Richard II (1367-1400) was king of England from 1377 to 1399. His reign, which ended in his abdication, saw the rise of strong baronial forces aiming to control the monarchy.

Richard II, known as Richard of Bordeaux from his birthplace, was born on Jan. 6, 1367, the younger son of Edward, Prince of Wales (the Black Prince), and Joan, daughter of Edmund, Earl of Kent. After his father's death, Richard became the heir apparent, was created Prince of Wales in the later part of 1376, and on June 22, 1377, succeeded Edward III, his grandfather, as king of England. While he was underage, the control of the government had been left to a regency that came increasingly under the influence of the Duke of Lancaster (John of Gaunt), one of his uncles. In 1381, during the revolt led by Wat Tyler, Richard showed his leadership potential by going out to meet the rebels and pacifying them after Tyler was killed.

After his marriage on Jan. 20, 1382, to Anne, the sister of King Wenceslaus and daughter of the emperor Charles IV, Richard attempted to end the regency's control of his minority and to take the leadership in national affairs, but Parliament was not eager to give up its powers. The following year, without consulting Parliament, Richard appointed Michael de la Pole as chancellor; and in 1384, hoping to check the opposition of his uncle Lancaster, he made his other uncles dukes of York and Gloucester.

As the barons under Gloucester's leadership hoped to rule Richard, he started to create a "new" nobility, raising Pole to Earl of Suffolk and Robert de Vare to Duke of Ireland, which resulted in Gloucester's forcing the King to accept a commission of 11 nobles with powers for reform in 1386. Using the law courts, Richard was able to have the commission declared unlawful in August 1387, but the barons were

determined to retain the upper hand, and in the "Merciless" Parliament, which met that winter, those who supported the King were attacked, and some were executed.

Although he was able to regain ministers of his own choosing in the spring of 1389, Richard hoped to win over the barons by a policy of conciliation, but this failed partly because of his own weakness and partly because of the death of his first wife in June 1394 and his second marriage to Isabella, daughter of Charles VI of France, in November 1396. This marriage to the traditional enemy caused a loss of popular goodwill, and Gloucester called for the resumption of the French war. Fearing that a second attempt might be made by the barons to limit his royal powers, Richard was able to get the leaders of the opposition, Gloucester, Arundel, and Warwick, in his power by July 1397, and in the Parliament that met in the autumn of the following year these men were condemned to death. This Parliament, after moving from Westminster to Shrewsbury in 1398, undid the acts of the Merciless Parliament. Now Richard was in full control and started to act in an arbitrary manner, alienating both barons and lesser subjects.

In February 1399, on the death of the Duke of Lancaster, Richard refused the inheritance to Lancaster's son, the exiled Henry of Bolingbroke; 2 months later Richard went to Ireland to avenge the death of the Earl of March, who had been killed on royal service. As soon as Henry of Bolingbroke heard of the King's absence, he landed in Yorkshire and raised a force to try to replace the King. Richard returned but, failing in an effort to raise an army, went into hiding in the north and after several months surrendered to Henry on Aug. 19, 1399, in North Wales. Henry, already acting as Henry IV, forced Richard's abdication on September 29 and imprisoned him. Richard died on Feb. 14, 1400, while at Pontefract.

Further Reading

Of the many biographical studies of Richard II, the most important is Anthony Steel, *Richard II* (1941). See also Harold F. Hutchison, *The Hollow Crown: A Life of Richard II* (1961). Gervase Mathew, *The Court of Richard II* (1969), is a scholarly and interesting study of the court life, the social milieu, and the arts of the time; and Richard H. Jones, *The Royal Policy of Richard II: Absolutism in the Later Middle Ages* (1968), plays down Richard's personality and emphasizes the political imperatives of the time. For general historical background see Sir James H. Ramsay, *Genesis of Lancaster, 1307-1399* (2 vols., 1913); May McKisack, *The Fourteenth Century, 1307-1399* (1959); and the excellent work of Arthur Bryant, *The Atlantic Saga*, vol. 2: *The Age of Chivalry* (1964).

Additional Sources

Bevan, Bryan, *King Richard II,* London: Rubicon Press, 1990.
Matthews, John, *Warriors of Christendom: Charlemagne, El Cid, Barbarossa, Richard Lionheart,* Poole, Dorset: Firebird Books; New York, NY: Distributed in the U.S. by Sterling Pub. Co., 1988.
Senior, Michael, *The life and times of Richard II,* London: Weidenfeld and Nicolson, 1981. □

Richard III

Richard III (1452-1485), last Yorkist king of England, reigned from 1483 to 1485 during the Wars of the Roses. He is generally considered a usurper and is suspected of the murder of Edward V and his brother.

Born on Oct. 2, 1452, at Fotheringhay Castle, Richard was the eleventh child and youngest son of Richard, Duke of York, and Cecily Neville. His father's 1454 and 1460 regencies for Henry VI caused Lancastrian opposition that brought York to his death in the Battle of Wakefield (Dec. 30, 1460). Richard and his brother George were fugitives until their 18-year old brother gained the throne as Edward IV in 1461. Thereafter George became a disloyal Duke of Clarence and Richard an able Duke of Gloucester. Richard shared command in the Yorkist victories at Barnet (April 14, 1471) and Tewkesbury (May 4).

Richard's 1472 marriage to 16-year-old Anne Neville caused disputes with Clarence, husband of Anne's older sister Isabella Neville, over the division of the estates of their late father, the Earl of Warwick. Clarence's treasonable habits led him to challenge the legitimacy of the King and his children, whereupon Edward's Parliament attained Clarence as "incorrigible," resulting in his execution in 1478 and the disinheritance of his son, Edward of Warwick. This reduced the contention for influence to a rivalry between Richard and the Woodville relatives of Edward's queen.

His Regency

The April 9, 1483, deathbed will of Edward IV left his 12-year-old heir, Edward V, to the regency and protectorship of Richard; yet the late king's children, treasure, and ships were in Woodville custody. At Middleham Castle in Yorkshire, Richard learned from Lord Hastings of the queen mother's attempts to dominate the council and of the preparations of Anthony Woodville, Lord Rivers, for bringing the new king from Wales to London with an escort of 2,000 men. Richard added the Duke of Buckingham's troops to his own, confronted the King at Stony Stratford on April 30, and persuaded Edward V to accept the arrest of Rivers and other leaders of the royal escort. Richard and Buckingham accompanied Edward to London House, while the queen mother and her other children sought sanctuary at Westminster.

As protector, Richard retained most government officials but moved to gain control of Woodville-held ships and forts. Buckingham's council motion removed Edward V to the Tower on May 19, 1483, "until his coronation," and on June 10, Richard wrote to the city of York for armed help against adherents of the queen mother. At a June 13 council in the Tower, Richard had Hastings killed, John Morton and former Chancellor Rotherham imprisoned, and Lord Stanley confined to quarters. A royal herald explained this to Londoners as suppression of a plot against the Protector and denounced the immoral liaison of Hastings and Jane Shore.

Accession to the Throne

On June 16, 1483, Richard invested Westminster with troops, and Queen Mother Elizabeth allowed 9-year-old Richard of York to join his brother in the Tower. Then commenced the "Richard for King" movement. From June 22 to 25, several meetings about London heard Buckingham and others claim the illegitimacy of Edward V and his brother and the need for the Protector to assume the crown. Richard was persuaded to occupy the throne on June 26, and on July 6 he was crowned with unusual ceremony as Richard III. Numerous pardons were given, although the June 25 execution of Lord Rivers, Lord Richard Grey, and Sir Thomas Vaughan showed little mercy for the Woodvilles. These deaths, the uncertain fate of the princes in the Tower, and the confinement of Clarence's son, Edward of Warwick, were evidence of at least some legal and moral confusion surrounding the new king.

In July, Richard commenced a royal progress through western and northern England, culminating in the September 8 ceremonies at York investing his only legitimate son, 10-year-old Edward, as Prince of Wales. At Lincoln on October 11, Richard learned that Buckingham was preparing a revolt in support of the exiled Henry Tudor on the claim that the princes in the Tower were dead by Richard's orders. Richard collected troops that dispersed Buckingham's forces and drove off Henry in October 1483. For this rebellion the duke was executed, but many of the rebels were pardoned.

In April 1484 Edward, Prince of Wales, died, leaving Richard with no successor who would have a clear title and the ability to continue the compacts of feudal loyalty beyond the King's lifetime. Richard eventually selected as his heir the Earl of Lincoln, son of the Duke of Suffolk and Richard's sister Elizabeth.

As Queen Anne declined with tuberculosis in 1484, Richard seems to have considered the possibility of a second marriage, to his niece, Elizabeth of York, already the object of Henry Tudor's political affections. However, Anne's death on March 16, 1485, started the canard that Richard had poisoned her in order to be free to marry again. Richard publicly denied all intention of marriage to his niece and sent her from the court.

On Aug. 7, 1485, Henry Tudor landed at Milford Haven with 2,000 men and gained swift support from his fellow Welshmen. From Nottingham, Richard ordered an array of troops, and on August 22 the opposing forces met at Bosworth Field. Richard led a charge on Henry's bodyguard in the hope of slaying his rival but was himself killed by Lord Stanley's soldiers. The victor was proclaimed King Henry VII, and Richard's corpse was stripped and carried on horseback to exposure at Leicester and burial at the Grey Friars.

Further Reading

The biography by Paul Murray Kendall, *Richard the Third* (1955), provides a thoughtful interpretation and comprehensive bibliography. Also useful is Sir Clements Markham, *Richard III: His Life and Character* (1906; repr. 1968). James Gairdner, *Richard III* (1898), is a fair appraisal, accurate in its use of sources. The biography attributed to Sir Thomas More in 1513, *The History of King Richard III* (1963), inspired much of the Tudor propaganda on Richard as "royal monster." Recommended general political histories for the period are E. F. Jacob, *The Fifteenth Century* (1961); S.B. Chrimes, *Lancastrians, Yorkists and Henry VII* (1964); J. R. Lander, *The Wars of the Roses* (1966); and A. L. Rowse, *Bosworth Field* (1966). □

Ann Willis Richards

Ann Willis Richards (born 1933) was elected Democratic governor of Texas in 1990, the second woman ever to hold that position in the state's history.

Ann Willis Richards was born in a one bedroom frame house in Lakeview, Texas, located eight miles from Waco. She was an only child of Iona Warren and Cecil Willis. When her father, who worked for a pharmaceutical company, was drafted during World War II, the family moved to San Diego to be near him. After the war they returned to Texas and moved to Waco. While attending Waco High School, Richards participated in debate and represented her school at Girls State, an annual gathering in which two representatives from each Texas high school came to Austin and set up a mock government. Fascinated by the elected officials whom she heard speak, Richards got

herself elected to Girls Nation, the national equivalent held in Washington, D.C. Upon graduating from high school in 1950, Richards attended Baylor University on a debating scholarship. Following her junior year at Baylor she married David R. Richards, a high school sweetheart. They had four children: Cecile, Dan, Clark, and Ellen.

Ann Richards graduated from Baylor in 1954 and moved to Austin so her husband could enroll in law school at the University of Texas. She earned her teacher certification at the University of Texas and taught social science studies at Fulmore Junior High School during this time. In addition, she became active in the liberal wing of the Texas Democratic Party. The couple moved to Dallas in 1957, where David Richards joined Mullinax, Wells, Morris & Mauzy, the premier labor law firm in the state of Texas.

After a brief stay in Washington, D.C., the Richards returned to Dallas in 1962. Ann divided her time between family and Democratic politics during these years. She serve as president of the North Dallas Democratic Women, and she helped organize the Dallas Committee for Peaceful Integration. Richards left Dallas in 1969 and returned to Austin with her husband and children. There she successfully managed Sarah Weddington's campaign for a seat in the Texas House of Representatives. In 1974 Richards joined Weddington's staff as an administrative assistant and worked for her for one legislative session. That same year she also participated in Wilhelmina Delco's successful campaign to become the first Black to represent Austin in the Texas legislature.

In 1975 Richards ran for the post of county commissioner in Travis County. Her effective grass-roots organization helped her to win the Democratic primary and to beat her Republican opponent easily. She continued to serve in that capacity until 1982. During her years as commissioner, Richards served on a variety of committees. On the state level, Lieutenant Governor Bill Hobby placed her on the Special Committee on the Delivery of Human Services; while on the national level, President Jimmy Carter appointed her to the President's Advisory Committee on Women. Richards also played an active role in the National Women's Political Caucus.

During the early 1980s Richards experienced some personal turmoil but also achieved political success. In 1980 she sought and successfully completed treatment for alcoholism. She and her husband of 26 years also separated that December. They divorced four years later. Despite these setbacks, Richards successfully ran for state treasurer of Texas in 1982, becoming the first woman to win a statewide office in 50 years in Texas.

As treasurer of Texas, Richards helped modernize the Treasury to earn the greatest possible interest for the state of Texas. According to one estimate, the Treasury under Richards made more than $1.8 billion for the state of Texas, a vast improvement over the past. During this time she also gained a reputation as a witty, engaging speaker and one of the most intriguing figures in Texas politics.

Richards also proved an effective state leader in formulating plans to bring water and sewers to the impoverished communities of the Lower Rio Grande Valley. For her public service efforts she was named to the Texas Women's Hall of Fame in 1985.

Richards came to national prominence in 1988 when she gave the keynote address at the Democratic National Convention in Atlanta. Two years later she secured the Democratic nomination for the governorship of Texas in what the *New York Times* called an "extraordinarily bitter campaign that revolved around allegations of drug use and personal attacks." To secure the Democratic nomination, Richards defeated former Governor Mark White and State Attorney General Jim Mattox. Strong support from the state's two largest urban centers, Houston and Dallas, gave Richards 57.1 percent of the vote against Mattox in the Democratic primary runoff.

In the general election in November of 1990, Richards defeated the Republican candidate, West Texas oil man Clayton Williams, in another rough-and-tumble campaign. Her narrow victory made her the only Texas woman governor besides Miriam A. (Ma) Ferguson, elected in 1924 as a stand-in candidate for her husband and former governor, James (Pa) Ferguson. She was known for her hands-on approach to governing. When asked about leading the state she said "I'm not afraid to shake up the system, and government needs more shaking up than any other system I know." After her election she marched into two state agencies unannounced and demanded resignations from what she deemed inept management. This was followed by unannounced midnight bus rides to nursing homes to get state agencies to improve a much neglected and scandalized state problem. Defeated by George W. Bush (son of President Bush) in 1994, Richards devoted time to her family, traveling and serving on corporate boards. In 1997 she was working with her daughter Cecile in the Texas Freedom Network to publicly denounce the extreme right.

Richards was known for her quick wit and humor. She once described President Bush as being "born with a silver foot in his mouth." In an interview with Evan Smith, appearing in Mother Jones (March-April 1996) Richards was asked about *Time* magazine's decision to name Newt Gringrich as Man of the Year. She replied, "If I had guessed who it was going to be, I wouldn't have thought of Newt Gringrich. I would have said O.J. Simpson." She was also known for her sincere and honest concern for the people of her state. In an interview appearing in *Texas Monthly,* Richards was asked about her memories of the Governor's Office, she said "Most of all, I remember those children in the classrooms and those kids who grabbed me around the knees, and I think of the old people who really need a voice when they're trapped in wheelchairs in dirty nursing homes. The person in this office really must have a conscience to know that how they direct this government dramatically affects the lives of those people."

Further Reading

More information about Richards' life can be found in her autobiography, *Straight from the Heart* (1989). For information on her early months in office see Richard Woodbury, "Winds of Change Sweep the Lone Star State" (*TIME,* April 29, 1991) and David Maraniss, "With 'Bubba' Mind" (*The Washington Post,* July 15, 1991). Articles on the former governor can be found in *Texas Monthly.* □

Ellen H. Richards

Ellen H. Richards (1842-1911), a chemist and leader in applied science, was instrumental in creating the field of home economics and in broadening opportunities for women in science education.

Peter and Fanny Swallow valued a good education, and they instilled in their only child Ellen ("Nellie") a passion for learning and meticulous attention to detail that later became the foundation for her life's work. Ellen Richard's parents met while attending New Ipswich Academy in New Hampshire and after their marriage, Peter Swallow combined teaching with farming. Born on the Swallow family farm in Dunstable, Massachusetts, on December 3, 1842, Richards, described as a tomboy, helped with the farm work from an early age. Though her father was said to have taken a keen interest in the way household tasks were performed, it was under the tutelage of her "deft and dainty" mother that she became proficient at housework, earning prizes as a 13-year-old at the country fair for an embroidered handkerchief and the best loaf of bread.

Richards was educated largely at home by her teacher-parents until 1859 when her father moved the family to Westford, Massachusetts. There, she assisted with her father's new business venture, the village store, and attended Westford Academy, studying, among other things, mathematics and Latin—subjects in which she later tutored to earn money for college. To enlarge his business, her father moved the family to nearby Littleton in 1863; while Richards focused her energy on assisting him in the store and fulfilling the social obligations of small town life, she remained determined to further her education. Though she taught school hoping to save money to attend college, her mother was often ill and caring for her frequently took precedence over teaching. "I am the same Nellie as of old," she wrote in 1865 to her cousin Annie, "full of business, never seeing a leisure hour, never finding time to study or read half as much as I want." Managing to attend lectures in Worcester during the winter of 1865-66, she had set her sights on receiving a higher education, only to find few doors open to ambitious women at that time. No colleges in New England were open to women (the two well-known women's colleges, Wellesley and Smith, were founded some ten years later), and Vassar, while a women's college, was so new that it was only just beginning to build a reputation. Frustrated by the seeming impossibility of realizing her goal, Richards experienced a period of ill health and deep depression: "I lived for over two years in Purgatory. . . . I was thwarted and hedged in on every side." Finally, in September 1868, at the age of 25, she entered Vassar College as a special student. The following year, she was admitted to the senior class.

A conscientious and enthusiastic student, Richards excelled at Vassar as her natural interest in science was encouraged and influenced by astronomer Maria Mitchell, the most important woman scientist in 19th-century America and one of the first women professors of science. It was, however, another Vassar scientist, chemistry professor Charles A. Farrar, whose influence ultimately led her into chemistry and developed in her the idea, advanced for the time, that science should help in the solution of practical problems.

After graduation, she had intended to teach in Argentina, but when war broke out there, she decided to continue her studies; again, however, she found opportunities limited. She wrote to a friend: "I have quite made up my mind to try Chemistry for a life study and have been trying to find a suitable opportunity to attempt it. . . . But everything seems to stop short at some blank wall." Then, in December 1870 good news arrived: Richards was accepted to the five-year-old Massachusetts Institute of Technology in Boston, the first woman admitted to that school, and, as she said, "as far as I know, any scientific school."

Her acceptance, however, did not constitute a signal that MIT was willing to open its doors to any woman who applied (the institute didn't begin admitting women directly until 1878). The university accepted her as a special student in chemistry, without charge, not because of financial need, as she assumed, but so that the president of MIT "could say I was not a student, should any of the trustees or students make a fuss about my presence. Had I realized upon what basis I was taken, I would not have gone."

While unaware of the underlying conditions of her acceptance, she nevertheless understood the important role she played as the only woman admitted to the institute, writing in 1870: "I hope in a quiet way I am winning a way which others will keep open. Perhaps the fact that I am not a Radical or a believer in the all powerful ballot for women to right her wrongs and that I do not scorn womanly duties, but claim it as a privilege to clean up and sort of supervise the room and sew things, etc., is winning me stronger allies than anything else." Three years later, she received a B.S. degree from MIT and an M.A. from Vassar. Continuing her studies at MIT for another two years, Richards never received a doctorate, because the institute—it has been said—did not want a woman to receive the school's first graduate degree in chemistry.

During her years at MIT, she worked as an assistant to Professor William R. Nichols who was engaged in water analysis, a new branch of chemistry, for the Massachusetts State Board of Health. She also met Professor Robert Hallowell Richards, who was developing the institute's metallurgical and mining engineering laboratories. Professor Richards proposed to Ellen Swallow, appropriately enough, in the chemistry laboratory shortly after she received her MIT degree; they were married on June 4, 1875. Both devoted scientists, Professor Richards supported his wife's work while she helped him prepare lectures and keep up with the many scientific journals that came to their Jamaica Plains home. She also acted as her husband's chemist for a project in which he experimented with methods of concentrating copper ores. Elected to the American Institute of Mining and Metallurgical Engineers, she was its first woman member.

The late 19th century saw a shift in women's roles, with the woman's suffrage movement gaining strength, and both educational and employment opportunities increasing for middle-class women. Science, however, was still viewed as the domain of men. Richards worked to change that image and to make scientific study more accessible to other women. While an MIT undergraduate, she helped teach an experimental course in chemistry, financed by the Woman's Education Association (a fledgling group devoted to promoting better education for women), at the Girls' High School in Boston to a class composed largely of teachers.

Then in November 1875, she received funds for the establishment of a women's laboratory at MIT; the following year, the Woman's Laboratory opened under the direction of Professor John Ordway, and Richards served as his assistant. The Woman's Education Association provided money for the laboratory apparatus, books, and scholarships, while Richards personally donated $1,000 annually for the seven years of the laboratory's existence. Clearly, not everyone at MIT supported the notion of women studying science; another MIT graduate recalled that the laboratory was "a sort of contagious ward located in what we students used to call the 'dump'." Nevertheless, Richards persisted, trying to provide her students with the individual attention required to learn the laboratory techniques that had been omitted during their previous education; she was also the unofficial "dean of women" at the Woman's Laboratory and, throughout her career at the institute, she made certain that these pioneering women did not in the words of one student, "do anything to give any setback to the status of women students at the Institute."

During her years at the Woman's Laboratory, Richards began stressing the importance of chemistry to the homemaker. Her consulting work for private industry included testing wallpapers and fabrics for arsenic, and she also looked at the adulteration of staple groceries for the State Board of Health while having her students in qualitative analysis assist in testing common household articles and cleaning materials. As a result of these efforts, in 1881 she published *The Chemistry of Cooking and Cleaning* which was followed in 1885 by *Food Materials and Their Adulterations*. Keenly aware of the lack of science education for middle-class women at home, in September 1876 she became head of the science section for the Society to Encourage Studies at Home, a correspondence school for women.

After MIT began admitting women directly in 1878, thus lessening the need for a separate Woman's Laboratory, Richards was suddenly out of a job. When the laboratory closed its doors in 1883, she wrote: "I feel like a woman whose children are all about to be married and leave her alone." But the feeling didn't last long. The following year, she was appointed an instructor of sanitary chemistry in MIT's new sanitation laboratory—probably the first such laboratory in the nation—and held the position until her death some 27 years later. In the sanitation laboratory, she assisted MIT professors in analyzing the state's water samples for the board of health, a monumental undertaking that became a classic in the field of sanitation and led to her position at MIT teaching the analysis of water, sewage, and air.

Richards's conviction, as stated by former pupil Dr. Alice Blood, "that if people knew better, they would do better," served as her driving force while seeking the practical application of scientific knowledge. In the late 19th century, this credo led her to concentrate on what came to be known as the home economics movement for which she coined the term "euthenics"—the "science of the controllable environment." In 1890, she opened the New England Kitchen which offered scientifically prepared food for home consumption at a low cost, with the cooking area open to the public for demonstration purposes. Though the New England Kitchen proved a failure, it led to other successful projects, including an exhibit at the 1893 Chicago World's Fair. The exhibit, "Rumford Kitchen," offered nutritious and scientifically prepared lunches to visitors for 30 cents. Again, the cooking area was open to the public, and food values—protein, fat, carbohydrates, and calories—were computed and noted on the bills of fare, a practice not followed by restauranteurs until nearly 100 years later. This interest led to Richards's work with the Boston School Committee, which in 1894 contracted with the New England Kitchen to prepare school lunches. Soon considered an expert on the subject of school lunches, she was consulted by other school systems, as well as other institutions, for information regarding food and nutrition. Her work laid the foundation for the now nationally accepted school lunch

program and helped create the field of dietetics as a vocation for women. Among her many books and articles are pamphlets written for the Department of Agriculture on nutrition and food chemistry.

In 1899, together with Melvil Dewey, director of the New York State Library and author of the "Dewey Decimal System" of book classification, Richards organized the first meeting of diverse individuals interested in what became known as home economics. As chair of these summer conferences in Lake Placid, New York, she helped determine the shape and objectives of this emerging field while developing model curricula. In 1908, at its tenth conference, the group formed the American Home Economics Association and elected Richards its first president, a position she held until 1910 when she insisted on retiring. She also helped found, and finance, the *Journal of Home Economics*.

During the last 15 years of her life, she was a prolific writer, publishing ten books and many scientific papers and magazine articles, and was in demand as a lecturer and consultant. Appointed to the council of the National Education Association in 1910, she was charged with supervising the methods of teaching home economics in schools.

Described by a colleague as "[s]mall, compactly built, and absolutely unafraid," Richards was a fighter. As one student recalled: "Mrs. Richards carried out in her own household all the principles of home economics which she was so vigorously and effectually promulgating." Her home was always open to her students. In addition to her work with the women students at MIT, in 1882 Richards was one of the founders of the Association of Collegiate Alumnae, later the American Association of University Women, and was a leader in the group's efforts to broaden women's opportunities for graduate education and develop physical education classes in colleges. She helped organize a school of housekeeping at the Woman's Educational and Industrial Union in Boston in 1899, which later became the department of home economics at Simmons College. In 1910, she received an honorary degree of doctor of science from Smith College and served as a trustee of Vassar.

Ellen Richards was active until the end of her life. Four days before her death, she presented a paper for the Baptist Society Union entitled, "Is the Increased Cost of Living a Sign of Social Advance?" She died at her Boston home on March 30, 1911, and is survived by the numerous home economics schools and clubs named for her and fellowships awarded in her name.

Further Reading

Hunt, Caroline L. *The Life of Ellen H. Richards*. American Home Economics Association, 1912, reprinted, 1980.
Journal of Home Economics. June 1911, October 1911, June 1929, December 1931, December 1942.
Rossiter, Margaret W. *Women Scientists in America, Struggles and Strategies to 1940*. The Johns Hopkins University Press, 1982. □

Ivor Armstrong Richards

Ivor Armstrong Richards (1893-1979), English-born American semanticist and literary critic, crusaded to have "Basic" English adopted as a fundamental English vocabulary.

On Feb. 26, 1893, Ivor Armstrong Richards was born at Cheshire. He was educated at Clifton College in Bristol and Magdalen College in Cambridge. In 1922 he became a lecturer in English and moral science at Cambridge and four years later was made a fellow of Magdalen. He had collaborated with C. K. Ogden and Charles Woods, Cambridge psychologists, on the *Foundations of Aesthetics* (1921). With Ogden he collaborated on *The Meaning of Meaning* (1923), a pioneer study in semantics, in which they established that what is known as "meaning" resides in the recipient as well as in the originator of the thought.

Richards's first independent book, *Principles of Literary Criticism* (1924), was revolutionary in the development of modern criticism. Deriding "bogus" esthetic terms, like "beauty" which has no "entity," Richards held that all value judgments reside in the communicant, not in the object or poem itself or in the communicator or poet. His principles of judgment are developed from this position. *Science and Poetry* (1925) treats, in terms of vocabulary, experiences that he terms "critical" and "technical." In 1926 he married Dorothy Eleanor Pilley.

In 1929 Richards published *Practical Criticism,* a report on the sad results of testing value judgments by presenting a class with specimens of writing whose authorship was not revealed. In 1929-1930 Richards was visiting professor at Tsing Hua University, Peking. He was a lecturer and later a professor at Harvard, retiring in 1963. During the 1930s he wrote *Mencius on the Mind* (1932) and *Coleridge on Imagination* (1935), careful examinations of the systems of these protean thinkers. He also completed *Interpretation in Teaching* and *How to Read a Page* (both 1934).

Richards joined his former collaborator C. K. Ogden in a crusade for the use of "Basic" English, which consisted of the 850 words most commonly used in the English vocabulary. To elaborate on his theories, Richards wrote three tracts: *Basic English and Its Uses* (1943), *Nations and Peace* (1943), and *So Much Nearer* (1968). His translations into "Basic" included *The Republic of Plato* (1942), *Tomorrow Morning, Faustus!* (1962), and *Why So, Socrates?* (1963). Two volumes of verse, *Good Bye, Earth* (1958) and *The Screens* (1960), won him the Loines Poetry Award in 1962.

Further Reading

The best treatment of Richards is W. H. N. Hotopf, *Language, Thought, and Comprehension: A Case Study of the Writings of I. A. Richards* (1965); see also Stanley Edgar Hyman, *The Armed Vision: A Study in the Methods of Modern Literary Criticism* (1948). For the English reaction to Richards see D. W. Harding and F. R. Leavis in Eric Bentley, ed., *The Importance of Scrutiny* (1948). Collections of his works include:

Internal Colloquies: Poems and Plays of I.A. Richards (1960-70) (1972); *Poetries: Their Media and Ends: a Collection of Essays by I.A. Richards* (1974), published to celebrate his 80th birthday; *Richards on Rhetoric: I.A. Richards, Selected Essays (1929-1974)* (1991); *New & Selected Poems by I.A. Richards* (1978); and *Complementarities: Uncollected Essays* (1976). □

Theodore William Richards

The American chemist Theodore William Richards (1868-1928) ushered in a new age of accuracy in chemistry by determining the atomic weights of many elements.

Theodore W. Richards was born on Jan. 31, 1868, in Germantown, Pa. His father, William Trost Richards, was a prominent landscape and marine artist; his mother, Anna Matlock Richards, was a poet and a woman of great cultivation. Until he entered college, his education was at home under his mother's direction. At age 14 he entered Haverford College as a sophomore, uncertain whether to become an astronomer or a chemist. He had defective eyesight, however, and by the time of his graduation he had decided on a career in chemistry.

In 1885 Richards entered Harvard as a senior and the following year was granted the bachelor's degree. Two years later he was awarded the doctorate with a dissertation on the atomic weights of hydrogen and oxygen. He won a Harvard grant for a year of travel and study in Europe. On his return to Harvard in 1889, he became an assistant and subsequently an instructor in analytical chemistry.

Atomic Weight Determinations

To Richards, atomic weights were the most fundamental constants in nature, and he associated them with deep questions about the universe. They offered more promise of contributing to the understanding of the universe than any other area of chemistry. By very thorough, painstaking work he published revised atomic weights for copper, zinc, barium, strontium, magnesium, and calcium.

In 1894 Richards introduced two new devices to overcome the two most prevalent sources of error in atomic weight work: the presence of moisture and the loss of traces of precipitate. His bottling apparatus enabled him to fuse, handle, and weigh solids under absolutely dry conditions. His nephelometer (cloud measurer) enabled him to determine traces of unrecovered precipitate by measuring the turbidity of the filtrate.

Along with his research Richards was teaching quantitative analysis. In 1894 he was promoted to assistant professor. Harvard sent him to Germany for a year of training in physical chemistry. On his return from Europe in 1896 he married Miriam Stuart Thayer.

Over the next few years Richards corrected the atomic weights of nickel, cobalt, iron, uranium, and cesium. In

every instance his results became the official ones of the International Commission on Atomic Weights. His revision of the atomic weights of J. S. Stas involved correcting for errors in purification, drying, and weighing of materials, and it inaugurated a new era of accuracy. His papers published from 1905 to 1910 exceeded in accuracy any chemical research ever published.

In 1901 Richards was promoted to full professor, and in 1912 he became Erving professor of chemistry and director of the new Wolcott Gibbs Memorial Laboratory (1913), which was the finest chemical laboratory in the world.

By 1913 the study of radioactive decay led to the possibility that an element may have more than one atomic weight. Richards analyzed radioactive samples of lead, and all of his determinations were below the atomic weight of ordinary lead, the lowest being 206.08. He concluded that there was no doubt that uranium transmuted itself into a light variety of lead. Frederick Soddy announced the isotope concept in 1913, and Richards's experiments were the first confirmation of the new theory and the only conclusive evidence for isotopes until the development of the mass spectrograph.

Atomic weights have remained the most frequently required units by chemists in quantitative measurements of all kinds. Richards determined the atomic weights of 25 elements. His students, Gregory Baxter at Harvard and Otto Hönigschmidt at Munich, continued his work and were responsible for 30 additional elements.

Physical Chemistry

Of Richards's almost 300 papers, about one-half deal with atomic weights, the remainder being concerned with several aspects of physical chemistry. He was a leader in introducing this new field into the United States, and his laboratory was a center which prepared a new generation of physical chemists. Richards made investigations in thermochemistry, electrochemistry, and the physicochemical study of the properties of matter. In physical chemistry, as in atomic weights, his work represented an advance in precision and accuracy.

One of Richards's most productive areas of research was thermochemistry. In 1905 he introduced the adiabatic calorimeter to prevent the loss or gain of heat to and from the surroundings. He published over 60 papers on thermochemistry and for many years was a pioneer in precision calorimetry.

In 1899 Richards began a study of the atomic volumes and compressibilities of the elements after noting that the constant b occurring in the Van der Waals equation $(p + a/V^2)(V - b) = RT$ was not a constant but varied with pressure and temperature. Since b was the space occupied by the molecule, Richards asserted that the concept of the atom as a hard, rigid particle was incorrect. He proposed that atoms were compressible, the forces of affinity and cohesion exerting a compressing effect on atoms resulting in enormous internal pressures. He devised methods to determine the compressibilities of the elements up to 500 atmospheres pressure and tried to correlate this property with the other fundamental properties of the elements in the hope of discovering important relationships. He never completed these studies; nevertheless, his experimental data proved to be invaluable to atomic physics.

His Character and Honors

Richards was primarily an experimentalist of exceptional ability. Yet his measurements were only a means to an end; with them he searched for an understanding of the material structure of the universe.

Richards received many honorary degrees and medals. A Harvard professorship was endowed in his name in 1925. He received the Nobel Prize in chemistry in 1914, the first American chemist to be so honored. He was a man of noble character who made a deep impression on those who met him. The guiding principles of his life he described as "kindliness and common sense." He died on April 2, 1928.

Further Reading

Richards presented his atomic weight research in *Determinations of Atomic Weights* (1910). In his Nobel Prize lecture, printed in Nobel Foundation, *Nobel Lectures: Chemistry, 1901-1921* (1966), he described both his research and his beliefs about the universe. Of the many biographical studies of Richards, the most informative are those in Benjamin Harrow, *Eminent Chemists of Our Time* (1927); Sir Harold Hartley, *Memorial Lectures Delivered before the Chemical Society* (3 vols., 1933); and Aaron J. Ihde, *Great Chemists* (1961). □

Henry Handel Richardson

Henry Handel Richardson was the pen name of Ethel Florence Lindesay Richardson (1870-1946), an expatriate Australian novelist. She based a series of novels on characters and incidents taken mainly from her life.

Born in Melbourne on Jan. 3, 1870, Ethel Richardson was the daughter of an Irish doctor who emigrated in the 1850s, living at first on the Victorian goldfields and later practicing in Melbourne. During a generally unhappy childhood she attended the Presbyterian Ladies' College, and after her father's death she taught briefly as a governess. At 17, she went abroad with her mother and sister; she studied music at Leipzig and in 1895 married a Scottish student, John G. Robertson, meanwhile studying the masters of the European novel.

Henry Handel Richardson began her literary career as a translator of *Niels Lyhne* by Danish novelist Jens Jacobsen; this was published as *Siren Voices* (1896). Jacobsen's style—"romanticism imbued with the scientific spirit, and essentially based on realism," in her view—profoundly influenced all her writing; imagery in character construction and meticulous realism in the detail of settings became her guideposts. Her first novel, *Maurice Guest* (1908), was autobiographical to the extent that the central character is an Australian girl studying music in Germany. The novel, somber and naturalistic, was coolly received, being stigmatized variously as dull, verbose, morbid, and erotic. However, because of its revealing attention to detail, it had a considerable influence among writers and was a forerunner of novels presenting amoral behavior dispassionately.

The *Getting of Wisdom* (1910) was an engaging study of school life; it won only limited praise. Nevertheless, proceeds from it made it possible for Henry Handel Richardson to visit Australia briefly in 1912 "to test memories" and to gather material for the first volume of the *Fortunes of Richard Mahony* trilogy.

The Trilogy

Marking a major expansion in Henry Handel Richardson's creative range, *Australia Felix* (1917) re-creates the mental climate as well as the sights and sounds of the goldfields life. Richard Mahony is portrayed as an intellectual groping for the unknown through spiritualism (just as the author's father had done) but unable to find contentment. Irony supplies much of the tension. Mahony voices his displeasure with life in the colony, which seems to have brought curses rather than blessings; the end of the novel marks his departure for England full of expectations.

In *The Way Home* (1925) Mahony's temporary pleasure at being able to relive the familiar within a richly civilized society turns quickly to disillusionment when he and his colonial-born wife experience its provincial narrowness. In Europe he learns of financial losses, which make it necessary for him to return to Australia. Back in Melbourne,

he finds his fortune restored; now he can build the mansion he has dreamed of so long—to be named Ultima Thule—but here his mental and physical deterioration begins.

In the final volume, *Ultima Thule* (1929), the author overlays her own psychological interpretations on the facts of her father's life and suggests that the emptiness and barrenness of the setting in which the fictional Mahony finds himself are powerful causes of his final mental disintegration. The trilogy has been described as an unusually thorough analysis of the "geographic disorientation" that sensitive immigrants suffered.

With the success of the *Richard Mahony* trilogy, the author's identity, previously concealed, was revealed. Her earlier novels were reprinted and reassessed. Her final work, *The Young Cosima* (1939), reconstructs the life of Franz Liszt's illegitimate daughter, Cosima. Fictionalizing the turbulent and massive influence of the life of Richard Wagner (whom Cosima married in 1870, after having left Hans von Bülow in 1865), this documentary novel is richly redolent with fact in its re-creation of the atmosphere of the period and its portraits of the great musicians.

In 1939 Henry Handel Richardson began writing her autobiography to 1903; she died before completing it, and it ends in 1895. It was published in 1948 as *Myself when Young*. She died at Hastings, Sussex, on March 20, 1946.

Further Reading

A comprehensive exposition, accompanied by some personal recollections and correspondence, is given in Nettie Palmer, *Henry Handel Richardson: A Study* (1950). An interesting review of Henry Handel Richardson's method is contained in Leonie J. Gibson, *Henry Handel Richardson and Some of Her Sources* (1954). Her writing style, as well as literary influences, is discussed in H. M. Green, *A History of Australian Literature* (2 vols., 1961). A telling analysis of the novels, with special attention to her aim of "scientific realism" in writing, is given by Leonie Kramer in Geoffrey Dutton, ed., *The Literature of Australia* (1964).

Additional Sources

Buckley, Vincent, *Henry Handel Richardson*, Philadelphia: R. West, 1977.
Clark, Axel, *Henry Handel Richardson: fiction in the making*, Brookvale, NSW: Simon & Schuster Australia: St. Peters, NSW: New Endeavour Press, 1990.
Green, Dorothy, *Henry Handel Richardson and her fiction*, Sydney; Boston: Allen & Unwin, 1986. □

Henry Hobson Richardson

Henry Hobson Richardson (1838-1886), American architect, helped set the standard for innovative design from which modern American architecture grew.

enry Hobson Richardson was born in St. James parish, La., on Sept. 29, 1838. He studied engineering at Harvard College (1854-1859). During 1859 he traveled throughout the British Isles, and the following year he entered the École des Beaux-Arts in Paris, enrolling in the atelier of Jules Louis André. Later, lacking funds as a result of the blockade of New Orleans during the Civil War, Richardson went to work for Théodore Labrouste and probably worked on the Hospice d'Ivry near Paris, begun in 1862. Richardson was the second American to study at the École. Following the lead of his predecessor, Richard Morris Hunt, he avoided using the architectural idioms of the French Second Empire when he returned to practice in the United States in 1865.

Richardson's early designs were an outgrowth of the High Victorian Gothic style as developed by English architects William Butterfield, Edward Godwin, and William Burges. The High Victorian Gothic influence was spread throughout the United States by the circulation of such English periodicals as the *Builder.* Godwin's Town Hall in Northampton, England (1861-1864), influenced Richardson's design for the Brookline, Mass., Town Hall (1870). It was also the basis for Richardson's American Merchants' Union Express Company Building, Chicago (1872), which introduced this style to the Midwest. Burges's entry in the competition for the London Law Courts (1866) influenced Richardson's Hampden County Courthouse, Springfield, Mass. (1871-1873). His Gothic style developed further in the Church of Unity, Springfield, Mass. (1866-1869); Grace Church, West Medford, Mass. (1867-1869); and the North

Congregational Church, Springfield, Mass. (1868-1873). The English influence is also seen in his Cheney Building, Hartford, Conn. (1875-1876).

In 1870, when he won a design competition for the Brattle Square Church in Boston, Richardson introduced suggestions of a Romanesque revival style. The architectural historian Henry-Russell Hitchcock noted of the Brattle Square Church that Richardson "had now definitely chosen certain lines, no longer French or English, but his own." This originality developed through Trinity Church, Boston, for which he won the design competition in 1872 (built 1873-1877), and culminated in his design for the Marshall Field Wholesale Store, Chicago (1885-1887; demolished).

Trinity Church has the centralized Byzantine Greek-cross plan of St. Mark's in Venice, a church that Richardson considered the "most beautiful . . . in the world" when he saw it during his European trip in 1882. The silhouette is also Byzantine, but the lantern is influenced by Spain's Salamanca Cathedral. The apse is typical of the Romanesque churches of the French Auvergne, and the western entrance and the porch (which was added in the 1890s) were taken from the Provençal church at Saint-Gilles-du-Gard. In the interior the wooden roof trusses show Burges's influence. Britishers William Morris and Edward Burne-Jones were commissioned to design some of the stained-glass windows, and other windows and murals were executed by John La Farge of the United States.

Richardson's domestic architecture, after initial mid-Victorian derivatives, became an American extension of the English Arts and Crafts movement as expounded by the British architect Norman Shaw. The F. W. Andrews House (1872), with its open plan, and the William Watts Sherman House (1874), both in Newport, R.I., have the American "shingle" and "stick" qualities in addition to the Shaw influence. The M. F. Stoughton House at Cambridge, Mass. (1882-1883), goes beyond stylistic associations and is comparable in its simplicity to the Marshall Field Wholesale Store.

Richardson's Marshall Field store, described by architect Louis Sullivan as "massive, dignified, simple . . . four-square and brown . . . a monument to trade," had an arcaded masonry skin over an iron skeleton frame. Richardson's work should be judged by this building, by the stark simplicity of the Allegheny County Jail, Pittsburgh (1884-1886), and by the J. J. Glessner House, Chicago (1885-1887). These were his ultimate architectural expressions at the height of his career. He died in Brookline, Mass., on April 27, 1886.

Richardson's influence spread far and wide. The work of the Burnham and Root architectural firm in the Monadnock Building in Chicago (1890-1891) and the whole span of Louis Sullivan's work captured the spirit of Richardson without copying his stylistic traits. Others who copied the "Richardson Romanesque" style designed buildings throughout the United States. His influence spread to Europe, where a host of architects took up his manner, adding local vernacular and sometimes historical traditions. From this great amalgam emerged modern architecture.

Further Reading

Mariana Van Rensselaer published a personal tribute to Richardson 2 years after his death, *Henry Hobson Richardson and His Works* (1888). Henry-Russell Hitchcock wrote *The Architecture of H. H. Richardson and His Times* (1936; rev. ed. 1961) and *Richardson as a Victorian Architect* (1966). See also Boston Museum of Fine Arts, *The Furniture of H. H. Richardson* (1962), an exhibition catalog of Richardson's furniture. Lewis Mumford revaluated Richardson in *Sticks and Stones* (1924; 2d rev. ed. 1955) and *The Brown Decades, 1865-1895* (1931; 2d rev. ed. 1955).

Additional Sources

Architect of the new American suburb, H. H. Richardson, Princeton, N.J.: Films for the Humanities, 1978, made 1977. □

Samuel Richardson

The English novelist Samuel Richardson (1689-1761) brought dramatic intensity and psychological insight to the epistolary novel.

Fiction, including the novel told in letters, had become popular in England before Samuel Richardson's time, but he was the first English novelist to have the leisure to perfect the form in which he chose to work. Daniel Defoe's travel adventures and pseudobiographies contain gripping individual episodes and an astonishing realism, but they lack, finally, the structural unity and cohesiveness characteristic of Richardson's lengthy novels. Unlike his great contemporary Henry Fielding, who satirized every echelon of English society in such panoramic novels as *Tom Jones,* Richardson chose to focus his attention on the limited problems of marriage and of the heart, matters to be treated with seriousness. In so doing, however, he also provided his readers with an unparalleled study of the social and economic forces that were bringing the rising, wealthy English merchant class into conflict with the landed aristocracy.

Born in Derbyshire, Richardson was one of nine children of a joiner, or carpenter. He became an apprentice printer to John Wilde and learned his trade well from that hard master for 7 years. After serving as "Overseer and Corrector" in a printing house, he set up shop for himself in Salisbury Court, Fleet Street, in 1720, where he married, lived for many years, and carried on his business. Within 20 years he had built up one of the largest and most lucrative printing businesses in London. Although he published a wide variety of books, including his own novels, he depended upon the official printing that he did for the House of Commons for an important source of income.

Richardson claimed to have written indexes, prefaces, and dedications early in his career, but his first known work, published in 1733, was *The Apprentice's Vade Mecum; or, Young Man's Pocket Companion,* a conduct book addressed to apprentices. *A Seasonable Examination . . .* (1735) was a pamphlet supporting a parliamentary bill to regulate the London theaters.

Pamela

In 1739, while at work on a book of model letters for social occasions proposed to him as a publishing venture by two booksellers, Richardson decided to put together a series of letters that would narrate the tribulations of a young servant girl in a country house. His first epistolary novel, *Pamela, or Virtue Rewarded,* was published in two volumes in November 1740 and became an instantaneous and enormous success. When its popularity led to the publication of a spurious sequel, Richardson countered by publishing a less interesting and, indeed, less popular continuation of his work in December 1741.

Richardson claimed in a letter to the Reverend Johannes Stinstra in 1753 that the idea for the story of Pamela had been suggested to him 15 years before, a claim he repeated to Aaron Hill. Regardless of the source for the story, however, Richardson's audience accepted and praised his simple tale of a pretty 15-year-old servant girl, the victim of the extraordinarily clumsy attempts at seduction by her young master, Squire B—(later named Squire Booby in the novels of Henry Fielding), who sincerely, shrewdly, and successfully holds out for marriage.

Richardson's use of the epistolary form, which made it possible for him to have Pamela writing at the moment, enabled him to give a minutely particular account of his heroine's thoughts, actions, fears, and emotions. Pamela's letters give the reader a continuous and cumulative impression of living through the experience and create a new kind of sympathy with the character whose experiences are being shared. But Richardson's decision to have the entire story told through Pamela's letters to her parents also raised technical problems that he was not to overcome until his second novel. Because she alone must report compliments about her charms, testify to her virtue, and relate her successful attempts to repulse Squire B—'s advances, she often seems coy and self-centered rather than innocent.

Richardson's continuation of *Pamela,* which describes her attempts to succeed in "high life" after her marriage to Squire B—, is a less interesting story, more pretentiously told and far less moving.

He followed his triumph with *Pamela* in 1741 by publishing the delayed *Letters Written to and for Particular Friends, Directing the Requisite Style and Forms . . . in Writing Familiar Letters,* a collection of little interest to the modern reader.

Clarissa

By the summer of 1742 Richardson had evidently begun work on what was to become his masterpiece. *Clarissa Harlowe* was published in seven volumes in 1747-1748. Although he had finished the first version of the novel by 1744, he continued to revise it, to solicit the opinions of his friends (and disregard most of their advice), and to worry about its excessive length. The massive work, which runs to more than a million words and stands as one of the longest novels in the English language, contains 547 letters, most written by the heroine, Clarissa Harlowe, her friend, Anna Howe, the dashing villain, Lovelace, and his confidant, John Belford. Letters of enormous length and incredible intensity follow Clarissa's struggle with her family to avoid marriage to the odious Mr. Soames, her desperate flight from her unbending and despicable family into the arms of Lovelace, her drugged rape, her attempts to escape from Lovelace by soliciting the aid of her unforgiving family, and her dramatic death. Before the final volumes of the novel were published, many of Richardson's readers had pleaded with him to give the novel a happy ending by allowing Clarissa to live. Richardson, however, had set out to show that in losing her innocence a girl might be ennobled rather than degraded, but that no matter how much of a paragon of virtue and decorum she might be in this world, she would find true reward for her virtue only in the next. The novel shows clearly the influence of the Christian epic, the English stage, and the funereal literature popular in the period. With specific debts to Nicholas Rowe's *Fair Penitent* and John Milton's *Paradise Lost,* it explores the problem of humanity desperately, if futilely, seeking freedom in a society where duty and responsibility are constant limitations upon that search. Although its great length has earned for it the title of "one of the greatest of the unread novels," it maintains a commanding place in the corpus of major English fiction because of its exploration of property marriages in the shifting social milieu of mid-18th-century England, its dramatic and cumulative power, and its clear tie to such other great Western mythical stories as Romeo and Juliet and Tristan and Isolde.

Sir Charles Grandison

Richardson toiled for 5 years to depict the perfect Christian gentleman, especially in order to answer criticisms that he had allowed Lovelace to become too attractive a figure in *Clarissa.* His third and final novel, *Sir Charles Grandison,* was published in 1753-1754. Richardson's contemporaries, who had found Lovelace a fascinating and dramatic villain, thought Sir Charles chilly and priggish. Richardson's story of the earnest Christian gentleman who must choose between the English maiden, Harriet Byron, and the more attractive and more interesting Clementina della Porretta pleases few readers. Because Sir Charles is too faultless and too moral, he does not win the reader's sympathies.

After this Richardson wrote no more novels. He died in London on July 4, 1761.

Further Reading

The major biography is T. C. Duncan Eaves and Ben D. Kimpel, *Samuel Richardson* (1971). Important studies of Richardson include Alan D. McKillop, *Samuel Richardson, Printer and Novelist* (1936); William M. Sale, *Samuel Richardson, Master Printer* (1950); Morris Golden, *Richardson's Characters* (1963); and Ira Konigsberg, *Samuel Richardson and the Dramatic Novel* (1968). Also useful are the chapters on Richardson in Alan D. McKillop, *The Early Masters of English Fiction* (1956); Ian P. Watt, *The Rise of the Novel: Studies in Defoe, Richardson, and Fielding* (1957); and Robert A. Donovan, *The Shaping Vision: Imagination in the English Novel from Defoe to Dickens* (1966). Recommended for general historical and social background are Louis Kronenberger, *Kings and Desperate Men: Life in Eighteenth-Century England* (1942); J. H. Plumb, *England in the Eighteenth Century* (1951); and A. R. Humphreys, *The Augustan World: Life and Letters in Eighteenth-Century England* (1954).

Additional Sources

Thomson, Clara Linklater, *Samuel Richardson: a biographical and critical study,* Philadelphia: R. West, 1977. □

Armand Jean du Plessis de Richelieu

The French statesman and cardinal Armand Jean du Plessis de Richelieu (1585-1642) devoted himself to securing French leadership in Europe and royal domination of the existing social order in France.

The policies and personal conduct of Richelieu were distinguished by self-restraint, flexibility in response to changing opportunities, and alertness to remote consequences. His long-range intentions could be achieved only at the expense of Spain abroad and of the King's family and the great noblemen at home.

In the early 17th century a precarious balance existed between reasons of state and religious sectarianism as principles for international action. A similar balance existed in France between the rights of the King and the particular rights of provinces, localities, classes, and persons. Each balance was tipped toward the first alternative during Richelieu's career. The alignments of European states shifted and their relative power changed. The French political system began to define anew the relation of each social group to the monarchy and thus to other social groups. These historical developments eventually went far beyond Richelieu's plans, but he played a significant part in them.

Armand du Plessis was born on Sept. 9, 1585, in Paris, fourth of the five children of François du Plessis, the lord of Richelieu, and Suzanne de La Porte. His father was provost of the King's central administrative establishment and grand provost of France under Henry III and conducted the investigation of the King's murderer in 1589; he remained in the same post serving Henry IV but in 1590 died of a fever. His mother, the self-effacing daughter of a learned, vain lawyer prominent in the Paris bourgeoisie, was placed in severe financial difficulties by early widowhood. She moved to the old stone manor house of Richelieu, a few miles east of Loudun in Poitou, to reside with her mother-in-law, a proud noblewoman originally of the Rochechouart family. About 4 years later, Armand returned to Paris to study grammar and philosophy at the College de Navarre, from which he went on to a military academy.

The Du Plessis family's plans appeared to be settled. The eldest son, Henri, was seeking to become established in the entourage of the new queen, Maria de' Medici. The second son, Alphonse, was destined to be bishop of Luçon;

the mother received the income of the benefice. But Alphonse declined the nomination and became a Carthusian monk. Armand was designated instead, and in 1603 he began serious study of theology. Younger than the canonical age to become a bishop, he went to Rome for a papal dispensation in 1607 and was consecrated there. He returned to Paris, obtained his degree in theology, and lingered to multiply his acquaintances among clergymen and among the associates of his brother Henri.

Career as Bishop

At the end of 1608 Richelieu arrived in Luçon, then little more than a village amid the marshes, a short distance from the Atlantic and north of La Rochelle. He found it "the most ignoble, mud-covered, unpleasant bishopric in France." He was an assiduous bishop, controlling his canons, carefully choosing parish priests, encouraging the preaching missions of the Capucin monks led by Father Joseph of Paris (François Le Clerc du Tremblay), and, while residing at his priory of Coussay between Loudun and Poitiers, cooperating with other active churchmen.

Richelieu's first important political opportunity came with the convocation of the Estates General in 1614. The clergy of Poitou elected him a deputy. At Maria de' Medici's suggestion he was chosen to speak for the clergy as a whole at the last session of the Estates (Feb. 23, 1615). He then went back to Poitou but a year later returned to Paris, served her in negotiations with the Prince of Condé, and was appointed secretary of state for foreign affairs and war. He held the post for only 5 months because Louis XIII seized power in April 1617 and dismissed his mother's councilors. Further steps against them followed, and in 1618 the bishop of Luçon was ordered into exile in the papal city of Avignon.

From Poitou, in 1617, Richelieu had joined in a pamphlet controversy between the King's Jesuit confessor and four Protestant ministers. In *Les Principaux points de la foi de l'église Catholique,* he employed moderate terms and rejected force as a means of conversion. He answered the Protestant ministers on several issues and told them, "You give to the people a power much greater than the one you deny to the pope, which is greatly disadvantageous to kings." In Avignon, in 1618, he finished a catechism he had been preparing in his diocese, *L'Instruction du Chrétien,* a calm, simple explanation of dogma and commandments which makes clear the sovereignty of God by comparing it to the sovereignty of the King.

Among Louis XIII's advisers, Father Joseph and others believed that Richelieu would be a moderating influence on the King's mother. Accordingly the King recalled him from Avignon in March 1619 and ordered him to resume serving her. Thereafter Richelieu's biography merges increasingly with the history of the monarchy. Representing the queen mother that spring, he negotiated an agreement with the King's commissioners that she would reside in Anjou. She designated his brother Henri de Richelieu as governor of the provincial capital; but 7 weeks later Henri was killed in a duel at Angoulême. This event, the personal sorrow of Armand de Richelieu's life, deprived him of a valued political ally.

The queen mother aspired to sit in the King's council. She also wanted the King to obtain Richelieu's nomination as a cardinal; for him this would mean undisputed political eminence, a voice in important decisions of state, and greater security than a bishop could expect. She hoped in the end to control royal policy through the influence Richelieu would exercise as a member of the King's council. These motives played an important part in the threat of an armed uprising in the summer of 1620 and in the tangle of duplicity and argument that ensued, with Richelieu in the role of mediator between the queen mother and her opponents. The resistance of the King and his ministers gradually crumbled. The queen mother was invited into the council at the beginning of 1622; in the following September, the Pope appointed Richelieu a cardinal; finally, the King called Richelieu to his council in April 1624 and designated him chief councilor 3 1/2 months later.

Position as Minister

Richelieu remained the King's principal minister until his death, and he was made a duke in 1631. He was never the only royal adviser, but he gradually built up in the council a group of men, his "creatures," loyal to him as well as to the King. He was never free from potential rivals. He relied on his family, which he extended by carefully arranging marriages of his nieces and cousins into great families. Thus he used intensively the kind of patron-client relation that had assisted his early career. He made clear that the King was his patron, and he made sure that Louis XIII knew that Richelieu was the King's creature.

From the first, Richelieu encountered a strong current of "devout" Catholic opinion that regarded Protestants everywhere as the enemy or as possible converts and insisted on reforms within France. The queen mother, Maria, the queen consort, Anne, and the keeper of the seals, Michel Marillac, shared that opinion. Richelieu partly satisfied it for a time, negotiating the marriage of the King's sister Henriette to Charles I of England, conducting the siege of the Huguenot city of La Rochelle, and cooperating with Marillac on a program of proposed reforms. But he firmly advised Louis XIII to intervene in northern Italy, against the Spanish king and the Emperor, in order to maintain a foothold on the route between Madrid and Vienna. Over this question the queen mother finally broke with Richelieu in 1630. The King eliminated her clientele and influence from his court.

Opposition to Richelieu and his policies arose also from ambitious, dissatisfied noblemen. This led to plots sanctioned by the King's brother Gaston (1626, 1632, 1636, and 1642), Queen Anne (1633), and a second cousin of the King, the Comte de Soissons (1636 and 1641). These all failed. Three scions of great families were beheaded (the Comte de Chalais in 1626, the Duc de Montmorency in 1632, and the Marquis de Cinq-Mars in 1642).

Foreign Policy

Richelieu gave first priority to foreign policy. He concluded, probably very early, that war against Spain in the long run would be unavoidable. He strove to delay it by encouraging German resistance to the Hapsburg emperor in

Vienna, thereby diverting into central Europe the resources and attention of the Hapsburg king in Madrid. In his German policy, he relied heavily on Father Joseph. He subsidized the Dutch Republic and the Swedish warrior king Gustavus Adolphus (Gustavus II) and in 1634 was prepared to aid the Bohemian general A. E. W. von Wallenstein against the Emperor.

From 1635 until his death Richelieu was preoccupied by an overt war against Spain and by the diplomacy it entailed. The fighting occurred principally on the northern and eastern frontiers of France, secondarily on the Mediterranean coast and in the Pyrenees. It was complicated by armed revolts of the populace, especially in western provinces. Richelieu negotiated often with emissaries of Spain but insisted on French control of Lorraine and French garrisons in northern Italy. The negotiations broke down. The war was still going on when Richelieu died on Dec. 4, 1642.

Further Reading

The best brief study of Richelieu in English is a thoughtful essay by Dietrich Gerhard in Leonard Krieger and Fritz Stern, eds., *The Responsibility of Power: Historical Essays in Honor of Hajo Holborn* (1968). A narrative concentrating on international relations is Daniel Patrick O'Connell, *Richelieu* (1968), with a good bibliography. A more personal treatment is provided in Carl J. Burckhardt's trilogy, *Richelieu and His Age* (1934-1966), of which two volumes have appeared in English: *His Rise to Power,* translated by Edwin and Willa Muir, and *Assertion of Power and Cold War,* translated by Bernard Hoy. Valuable special studies include Orest A. Ranum, *Richelieu and the Councillors of Louis XIII* (1963), and Aleksandra D. Lublinskaya, *French Absolutism: The Crucial Phase, 1620-1629,* translated by Brian Pearce (1968). □

Charles Robert Richet

The French physiologist Charles Robert Richet (1850-1935) was awarded the Nobel Prize in Physiology or Medicine for his discovery of the phenomenon of anaphylaxis.

Charles Richet, the son of Alfred Richet, a professor in the University of Paris, was born in Paris on Aug. 25, 1850. He studied medicine in Paris and intended to become a surgeon, but he soon abandoned surgery for physiology. He graduated at Paris as a doctor of medicine in 1869 and as a doctor of science in 1878. He became a lecturer in physiology in 1879 and in 1887 professor of physiology in the Faculty of Medicine at Paris.

Discovery of Anaphylaxis

In 1890 the phenomenon of antitoxic immunity was discovered, and in 1891 diphtheria antitoxin was first used in treating diphtheria. It was soon found that the guinea pigs used for testing diphtheria antitoxin became acutely ill if long intervals separated the test injections. About 1900, while cruising in tropical waters, Richet studied the poison of the tropical jellyfish, the Portuguese man-of-war. Working with Paul Portier, he found that injection of a glycerol solution of the poison produced the symptoms of poisoning by the jellyfish. On their return to France they studied the toxins of local jellyfish. They determined the minimum dose that was fatal for dogs several days after its injection. Smaller doses than this produced only transient effects. But if a dog that had been injected with a small dose received a similar small dose after an interval of several weeks, a violent reaction killed the dog.

By 1902 Richet had studied this phenomenon in different animals. Reactions produced by the injection of antitoxins or minute doses of toxins had already been called prophylactic, or protective. Richet realized that in this new phenomenon the first dose sensitized the animal, so that the second injection produced a violent reaction. The first dose was the opposite of prophylactic, and he therefore called the phenomenon anaphylaxis. He showed clearly that the first injection of an animal toxin sensitized the test animal to even a very small second injection, and that, with very small doses, the violent symptoms following the second injection were out of all proportion to the mild symptoms following the first. He also established that, to produce the violent reaction, there must be an interval of several weeks between the injections.

In 1903 Nicolas Maurice Arthus of Lausanne described the Arthus phenomenon. If a rabbit was injected subcutaneously with repeated doses of horse serum, no effect was produced by the subsequent injections at first, but as the interval from the first injection lengthened, the injection site became swollen, hardened, and ulcerous. In 1905 Richard Otto showed that it was not the toxin in the "diphtheria antitoxin" (at that time a mixture of toxin and antitoxin was used) that produced serious effects in guinea pigs injected with repeated small doses at long intervals, but the horse serum in which the toxin was contained. Further, the reaction depended not upon the dose but upon the time interval. It was soon shown that a guinea pig injected with horse serum showed no hypersensitivity to the serum of other animals, and also that specific reactions occurred after the injection of milk, egg, or muscle extract. It was thus conclusively demonstrated that Richet's anaphylaxis was due to the injection of any protein, whether or not it was toxic on the first injection.

In 1907 Richet showed that, if the serum of an anaphylactic dog was injected into a normal dog, the latter became anaphylactic. The anaphylactic state could therefore be passively transmitted, and it was an antigen-antibody reaction. He continued to study anaphylactic phenomena, and for his work he was awarded the Nobel Prize in 1913. Anaphylaxis is closely associated with serum sickness and allergy, and later investigations of allergic diseases stem from Richet.

Richet wrote numerous works on physiology and edited two journals. He retired from his chair in 1927 and died in Paris on Dec. 4, 1935.

Further Reading

There is a biography of Richet in *Nobel Lectures, Physiology or Medicine, 1901-1921* (1967), which also includes his Nobel Lecture. For his work in relation to the immunology of the period see C. Singer and E.A. Underwood, *A Short History of Medicine* (1962), and W. Bulloch, *The History of Bacteriology* (1938). □

Germaine Richier

The French sculptor Germaine Richier (1904-1959) explored the metamorphic dimensions of the insect-animal world. Technically, she exploited the deteriorating surface and the interior, felt structure of things.

Born in Grans near Arles, Germaine Richier enrolled in the School of Fine Arts in Montpellier in 1922. After completing her studies in 1925, she left for Paris, where she became a private pupil of the sculptor Antoine Bourdelle for the next 4 years. Her work of the 1930s won several awards, including the Blumenthal Prize of 1936, yet the forms were essentially extensions of the more classical sculpture of her teacher.

In the 1940s Germaine Richier began creating the sculptural vocabulary for which she is best known, the classical rendering of the figure undergoing dramatic changes. *L'Eau (L'Amphore,* 1944) is partially a female form and partially a Greek vase. Similarly, the working of the piece changes from skeletal support in the lower portion of the piece to full female shape in the upper portion. This metamorphosis was carried further in the Insect series (*Spider* and *Small Grasshopper,* 1946) and found full expression in the *Bat Man* (1946), possibly the most powerful image of her career. Projecting from a central core are gauzelike wings, thinly threaded planes that suggest decay. This method of construction—an approach that defies both the material and gravitational limits—is one of many experimental techniques she used.

A more traditional freestanding figure conventionally modeled can be seen in the male *Thunderstorm* (1948) and the related female *Hurricane* (1949). These large metaphors of violent natural forces are now tamed, the expressive qualities being revealed in the expressionistic surface and dangling appendages. Another figurative treatment, closer to the eviscerated skeletal structures of Alberto Giacometti, can be seen in the *Large Don Quixote of the Forest* and the *Shepherd of the Landes* (both 1951).

Germaine Richier's formal language continued to enlarge and develop during the 1950s. She worked in stone, carving compact shapes with angular projections, as in the *Shadow of the Hurricane* (1956), seemingly an outgrowth of the more abstract "Bird Man" series of the early 1950s. Another set of problems, that of creating a context in the form of a perpendicular plane acting as a background or foil for smaller shapes played off against this plane, also found currency in her work at this time. She died in Montpellier.

Further Reading

The most useful monograph on the sculptor, although narrow in scope, is Jean Cassou, *Germaine Richier* (1961). See also the catalog of the Arts Club of Chicago, *Germaine Richier* (1966). Further information is in Carola Giedion-Welcker, *Contemporary Sculpture: An Evolution in Volume and Space* (1956; rev. ed. 1961), and Michael Seuphor, *The Sculpture of This Century* (1960). □

Charles F. Richter

Charles F. Richter (1900-1985) was one of the developers of the Richter Scale which is used to measure the magnitude of earthquakes.

Charles F. Richter is remembered every time an earthquake happens. With German-born seismologist Beno Gutenberg, Richter developed the scale that bears his name and measures the magnitude of earthquakes. Richter was a pioneer in seismological research at a time when data on the size and location of earthquakes were scarce. He authored two textbooks that are still used as references in the field and are regarded by many scientists as his greatest contribution, exceeding the more popular Richter scale. Devoted to his work all his life, Richter at one time had a seismograph installed in his living room, and he welcomed queries about earthquakes at all hours.

Charles Francis Richter was born on April 26, 1900, on a farm near Hamilton, Ohio, north of Cincinnati. His parents were divorced when he was very young. He grew up with his maternal grandfather, who moved the family to Los Angeles in 1909. Richter went to a preparatory school associated with the University of Southern California, where he spent his freshman year in college. He then transferred to Stanford University, where he earned an A.B. degree in physics in 1920.

Richter received his Ph.D. in theoretical physics from the California Institute of Technology (Caltech) in 1928. That same year he married Lillian Brand of Los Angeles, a creative writing teacher. Robert A. Millikan, a Nobel Prize-winning physicist and president of Caltech, had already offered Richter a job at the newly established Seismological Laboratory in Pasadena, then managed by the Carnegie Institution of Washington. Thus Richter started applying his physics background to the study of the earth.

As a young research assistant, Richter made his name early when he began a decades-long collaboration with Beno Gutenberg, who was then the director of the laboratory. In the early 1930s the pair were one of several groups of scientists around the world who were trying to establish a standard way to measure and compare earthquakes. The seismological laboratory at Caltech was planning to issue regular reports on southern California earthquakes, so the Gutenberg-Richter study was especially important. They needed to be able to catalog several hundred quakes a year with an objective and reliable scale.

mic, so that a quake of magnitude 7 would be ten times stronger than a 6, a hundred times stronger than a 5, and a thousand times stronger than a 4. (The 1989 Loma Prieta earthquake that shook San Francisco was magnitude 7.1.)

The Richter scale was published in 1935 and immediately became the standard measure of earthquake intensity. Richter did not seem concerned that Gutenberg's name was not included at first; but in later years, after Gutenberg was already dead, Richter began to insist that his colleague be recognized for expanding the scale to apply to earthquakes all over the globe, not just in southern California. Since 1935, several other magnitude scales have been developed. Depending on what data is available, different ones are used, but all are popularly known by Richter's name.

For several decades Richter and Gutenberg worked together to monitor seismic activity around the world. In the late 1930s they applied their scale to deep earthquakes, ones that originate more than 185 miles below the ground, which rank particularly high on the Richter scale—8 or greater. In 1941 they published a textbook, *Seismicity of the Earth,* which in its revised edition became a standard reference book in the field. They worked on locating the epicenters of all the major earthquakes and classifying them into geographical groups. All his life, however, Richter warned that seismological records only reflect what people have measured in populated areas and are not a true representative sample of what shocks have actually occurred. He long remained skeptical of some scientists' claims that they could predict earthquakes.

Richter remained at Caltech for his entire career, except for a visit to the University of Tokyo from 1959 to 1960 as a Fulbright scholar. He became involved in promoting good earthquake building codes, while at the same time discouraging the overestimation of the dangers of an earthquake in a populated area like Los Angeles. He pointed out that statistics reveal freeway driving to be much more dangerous than living in an earthquake zone. He often lectured on how loss of life and property damage were largely avoidable during an earthquake, with proper training and building codes—he opposed building anything higher than thirty stories, for example. In the early 1960s, the city of Los Angeles listened to Richter and began to remove extraneous, but potentially dangerous, ornaments and cornices from its buildings. Los Angeles suffered a major quake in February of 1971, and city officials credited Richter with saving many lives. Richter was also instrumental in establishing the Southern California Seismic Array, a network of instruments that has helped scientists track the origin and intensity of earthquakes, as well as map their frequency much more accurately. His diligent study resulted in what has been called one of the most accurate and complete catalogs of earthquake activity, the Caltech catalog of California earthquakes.

Later in his career, Richter would recall several major earthquakes. The 1933 Long Beach earthquake was one, which he felt while working late at Caltech one night. That quake caused the death of 120 people in the then sparsely populated southern California town; it cost the Depression-era equivalent of $150 million in damages. Nobel Prize-

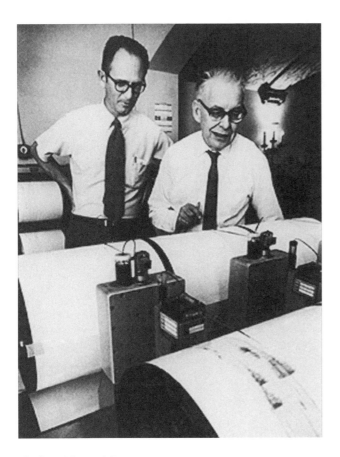

Charles Richter (right)

At the time, the only way to rate shocks was a scale developed in 1902 by the Italian priest and geologist Giuseppe Mercalli. The Mercalli scale classified earthquakes from 1 to 12, depending on how buildings and people responded to the tremor. A shock that set chandeliers swinging might rate as a 1 or 2 on this scale, while one that destroyed huge buildings and created panic in a crowded city might count as a 10. The obvious problem with the Mercalli scale was that it relied on subjective measures of how well a building had been constructed and how used to these sorts of crises the population was. The Mercalli scale also made it difficult to rate earthquakes that happened in remote, sparsely populated areas.

The scale developed by Richter and Gutenberg, which became known by Richter's name only, was instead an absolute measure of an earthquake's intensity. Richter used a seismograph—an instrument generally consisting of a constantly unwinding roll of paper, anchored to a fixed place, and a pendulum or magnet suspended with a marking device above the roll—to record actual earth motion during an earthquake. The scale takes into account the instrument's distance from the epicenter, or the point on the ground that is directly above the earthquake's origin. Richter chose to use the term "magnitude" to describe an earthquake's strength because of his early interest in astronomy; stargazers use the word to describe the brightness of stars. Gutenberg suggested that the scale be logarith-

winning physicist Albert Einstein was in town for a seminar when the earthquake struck, according to a March 8, 1981 story in the *San Francisco Chronicle*. Einstein and a colleague of Richter's were crossing the campus at the time of the quake, so engrossed in discussion that they were oblivious to the swaying trees. Richter also remembered the three great quakes that struck in 1906, when he was a six-year-old on the Ohio farm. That year, San Francisco suffered an 8.3 quake, Colombia and Ecuador had an 8.9, and Chile had an 8.6.

In 1958 Richter published his text *Elementary Seismology*, which was derived from the lectures he faithfully taught to Caltech undergraduates as well as decades of earthquake study. Many scientists consider this textbook to be Richter's greatest contribution, since he never published many scientific papers in professional journals. *Elementary Seismology* contained descriptions of major historical earthquakes, tables and charts, and subjects ranging from the nature of earthquake motion to earthquake insurance and building construction. Richter's colleagues maintained that he put everything he knew into it. The book was used in many countries.

In the 1960s, Richter had a seismograph installed in his living room so that he could monitor quakes at any time. He draped the seismographic records—long rolls of paper covered with squiggly lines—over the backs of the living room chairs. (His wife, Richter maintained, considered the seismograph a conversation piece.) He would answer press queries at any hour of the night and never seemed tired of talking about his work. Sometimes he grew obsessive about speaking to the press; when a tremor happened during Caltech working hours, Richter made sure he would be the one answering calls—he put the lab's phone in his lap.

Richter devoted his entire life to seismology. He even learned Russian, Italian, French, Spanish, and German, as well as a little Japanese, in order to read scientific papers in their original languages. His dedication to his work was complete; in fact, he became enraged at any slight on it. For instance, at his retirement party from Caltech in 1970, some laboratory researchers sang a clever parody about the Richter scale. Richter was furious at the implication that his work could be considered a joke. During his lifetime he enjoyed a good deal of public and professional recognition, including membership in the American Academy of Arts and Sciences and a stint as president of the Seismological Society of America, but he was never elected to the National Academy of Sciences. After his retirement Richter helped start a seismic consulting firm that evaluated buildings for the government, for public utilities such as the Los Angeles Department of Water and Power, and for private businesses.

Richter enjoyed listening to classical music, reading science fiction, and watching the television series *Star Trek*. One of his great pleasures, ever since he grew up walking in the southern California mountains, was taking long solitary hikes. He preferred to camp by himself, far away from other people. But being alone had its drawbacks; once, he encountered a curious brown bear, which he chased away by loudly singing a raunchy song. After his marriage Richter continued his solo hikes, particularly at Christmas, when he

and his wife would go their separate ways for a while. At these times Lillian indulged in her interest in foreign travel. The couple had no children. A little-known fact about them, according to Richter's obituary in the *Los Angeles Times,* is that they were nudists. Lillian died in 1972. Richter died in Pasadena on September 30, 1985, of congestive heart failure.

Further Reading

Current Biography, H. W. Wilson, 1975, November, 1985.
Los Angeles Times, October 1, 1985.
Los Angeles Times Home Magazine, May 11, 1980.
Pasadena Star-News, May 13, 1991.
San Francisco Chronicle, March 8, 1981. □

Conrad Michael Richter

Conrad Michael Richter (1890-1968), American novelist and short-story writer, depicted the nation's early frontier life and westward expansion. His works, based on his own adventures and research into American folklore, protest man's destruction of his environment.

C onrad Richter was born on Oct. 13, 1890, in Pine Grove, Pa. As a boy he traveled with his father throughout the farm settlements and was enchanted by the pioneer life-style and idiomatic speech. Graduating from high school, he determined to be a writer and began reporting for a local paper. After first working at random jobs—mechanics, coal breaking, farming—at the age of 19 he became editor of a country weekly. Following experience with the *Pittsburgh Dispatch* (1910) and the *Johnstown Leader* (1911) he moved to Ohio. His "Brothers of No Kin" was accepted by a magazine and selected by the *Boston Transcript* as the best short story of 1913. But discouraged by the low prices paid for fiction, Richter decided "to stick to business" and "write in my spare time only the type of story which would fetch a fair price, which I did."

After marrying Harvena M. Achenbach in 1915, Richter established a publishing firm. He started writing children's stories and then began his own juvenile periodical, *Junior Magazine Book*. During the next years his writing appeared under some 125 pseudonyms in various magazines. His short stories were collected in *Brothers of No Kin and Other Stories* (1924).

Richter was concerned with the vanishing frontier as well as the dubious benefits resulting from advancing technology. Desiring to escape encroaching industrial urbanization, he sold his business and moved his family to New Mexico in 1928. A collection of short stories, *Early Americana* (1936), structured with the minute details of daily living on the frontier, resulted from his painstaking search for diaries, journals, and artifacts of the Old Southwest. In *Sea of Grass* (1937), his first novel, he dramatized the cattleman-homesteader battle for the ranges of Texas and

New Mexico at the turn of the century. It was later made into a motion picture.

A family migrating west from Pennsylvania is portrayed in *The Trees* (1940), the first of a trilogy. A saga of 18th century pioneer heroics, this was a best seller. *The Fields* (1946) rather episodically traces the development of Ohio from its 18th-century wilds to the farms of the 19th century. Critic Orville Prescott noted that "seldom in fiction has the atmosphere of another age been so completely realized." *The Town* (1950) depicts the rise of industrialism in Ohio. The history is vivified in the simple and colloquial speech of the settlers.

Richter's novella *Tacey Cromwell* (1942), set in an Arizona mining town, effectively uses local color. *Always Young and Fair* (1947) is a sociopsychological exploration of a turn-of-the-century Pennsylvania town. Continuing the "wilderness" milieu, Richter produced nine novels in the next 17 years. *The Light in the Forest* (1953) and *A Country of Strangers* (1966) are critical of "civilized" man, contrasted with the "white child raised by Indians." *The Lady* (1957) returns to older tales of the Southwest. *The Waters of Kronos* (1960) portrays an Easterner who returns home after a satisfying stay in the West to find his residence under the waters of a hydroelectric plant. This novel takes a vigorous stand against man's heedless tampering with natural resources and, in effect, eternity.

Although afflicted with a serious heart ailment during his later years, Richter produced such novels as *A Simple Honorable Man* (1960), *The Grandfathers* (1964), *Individu-*

alists under the Shade Trees in a Vanishing America (1964), and *Over the Blue Mountain* (1967). *The Aristocrat* was published a month before his death on Oct. 18, 1968. With his protest against man's ecological destruction, his work has assumed increasing significance.

Further Reading

Richter's life and work are explored in Edwin W. Gaston, Jr., *Conrad Richter* (1965); Robert J. Barnes, *Conrad Richter* (1968); and the more specialized study by Clifford D. Edwards, *Conrad Richter's Ohio Trilogy: Its Ideas and Relationship to Literary Tradition* (1970).

Additional Sources

Gaston, Edwin W., *Conrad Richter,* Boston: Twayne Publishers, 1989.
Richter, Harvena, *Writing to survive: the private notebooks of Conrad Richter,* Albuquerque: University of New Mexico Press, 1988. ☐

Hans Richter

German-born artist Hans Richter (1888-1976) was responsible for pioneering several major areas of 20th-century art—both the Zurich and the Berlin phases of Dada, abstract cinema (in collaboration with Viking Eggeling), International Constructivism, and filmmaking. His presence exerted a significant influence on American art following World War II.

Hans Richter (Johann Siegfried Richter) was born in Berlin on April 6, 1888. Following a brief program in architecture at the University of Berlin in 1906, Richter attended the Hochschule für Bildende Kunst in Berlin and in Weimar in 1908 and 1909, respectively. His early commitment to the arts was interrupted by service in the German army between 1914 and 1916, at which point he was wounded on the Russian front and given his discharge.

Moving to Zurich, neutral capital and international haven for pacifists and war resisters, Richter encountered the Dadaists in 1916. Although his participation in the movement was limited, he did contribute to their journal, *Dada,* and occasionally participated in their events. Richter's early Zurich style betrays strong roots in Expressionism, especially that of Wassily Kandinsky, as well as the influence of Hans Arp who, like Richter, resided in Zurich at the time. By 1918 this tendency began to give way to a more abstract style in which any traces of naturalism were almost completely suppressed. It was in 1916, while living in Zurich, that Richter received his first one man show at the Galerie Hans Goltz in Munich. Exhibitions of his work in Zurich included two group shows, *Dada* and *Die Neue Kunst: Dada,* in 1917 and 1918 at the Galerie Corray and the Salon Wolfsburg.

In 1918 Richter was introduced to Viking Eggeling, also a Dada sympathizer, with whom he worked closely for the next seven years in the formulation of an abstract cinema. Although no films were actually made in Zurich, studies, often in the form of scrolls, were arranged contrapuntally. In their succession of images they suggested strong sources in and close analogies to music.

In 1918 Richter returned to Berlin, where Dada had preceded him by one year. In Kleinkolzig, near Berlin, he and Eggeling further pursued their work in the cinema. By the early 1920s Richter had produced his now-famous *Rhythm 21,* closely followed in time by *Rhythm 23* and *Rhythm 25.* Although loosely affiliated with the Berlin Dada group, his interests were quickly moving in the direction of International Constructivism, as were those of Raoul Hausmann and other members of the Berlin Dada group. Nevertheless, Richter clearly perceived Dada as an important part of his young career and in *Dada: Art and Anti-Art* (1965) provided the movement with one of its most complete and reliable memoirs.

Richter's new sympathies were clear from his substantial contributions to the Dutch journal *De Stijl.* Edited by Piet Mondrian and Theo van Doesburg, it became the publication organ of what was Western Europe's most systematic movement in the non-objective arts. These activities, spanning a period from 1921 to 1927, were paralleled by Richter's own publication, ''*G*'' (Gestaltung), in Berlin. For Richter, the Dada/Surrealist side of his nature was never in conflict with the Constructivist side. Thus in 1927 he worked on a film, never completed, with the Russian Suprematist Kasimir Malevich at the same time that he collaborated with the Surrealists on the film *Ghosts After Breakfast.* The latter was as full of typically irrational juxtapositions as the former was informed by rigor and discipline.

The 1920s and early 1930s were a time of intense activity for Richter's filmmaking. Following a short stay in Russia he returned to Switzerland in 1933 and began reinvestigating some of his earlier pictorial concerns. That same year his Berlin studio was raided by the Nazis and much of his work was destroyed. Richter's return to earlier concerns is partially reflected in his inclusion in 1937 in the exhibition *Konstruktivistern* in Kunsthalle, Basle.

In 1941 Richter emigrated to the United States. He was naturalized ten years later, in 1951, the year of his marriage to Frida Ruppel. Upon his arrival in America he joined the American Abstract Artists group—a distant cousin of De Stijl—and was exhibited in *Maitres de l'Art Abstrait* at the Helena Rubenstein Gallery in New York. From 1942 to 1956 Richter taught and served as director at the Institute of Film Techniques at the City College of New York. Richter's second one-man show was held in New York in 1946 at the Art of This Century Gallery, an organization founded by Peggy Guggenheim and of which Richter became president in 1948. One of his best works, *Dreams That Money Can Buy* (1946 to 1948), was made during these years in collaboration with Marcel Duchamp, Max Ernst, Fernand Leger, Man Ray, and Alexander Calder. Later in his career Richter, who always walked a fine line between spontaneity and structure, was much esteemed as one of the important founders of Concrete Art.

Among countless others, Richter received prizes at the Venice Biennale (1948) and at the Berlin International Film Festival (1971). He was awarded the Cross of Merit and the Grand Cross by the German government in 1964 and 1973 respectively. After a varied and important career, Richter died in Locarno, Switzerland, on February 1, 1976.

A major posthumous retrospective exhibition was held at the Akademie der Künst, Berlin (1982). Richter's work may be found in the collections of The National Gallery, Berlin; Museum 20 Jahrhunderts, Vienna; Galeria Nazionale d'Arte Moderna, Rome; Musée National d'Arte Moderne, Paris; and The Museum of Modern Art, New York, among many others.

Further Reading

Richter himself was an active and articulate author and began publishing in 1920; see *The Political Film* (1941), *Dada Art and Anti-Art* (1965), and *Hans Richter by Hans Richter* (1971). Besides these and other books, Richter wrote and published many articles on film history and theory and for extended periods worked as a film critic. *Hans Richter* (1965), introduced by Herbert Read, includes an extensive autobiographical text by the artist. Useful discussions of Richter are included in *The Pictorial Language of Hans Richter* by Roberto Sanesi (1975), although the best guide to his work is the catalogue for the Berlin exhibition *Hans Richter, 1888-1976: Dadaist, Film-pionier, Maler, Theoretiker* (1982). Additional material is readily available, including monographs, catalogues of various aspects of his work, and a large body of periodical literature.

Additional Sources

Fifield, Christopher, *True artist and true friend: a biography of Hans Richter,* Oxford England: Clarendon Press; New York: Oxford University Press, 1993. □

Johann Paul Friedrich Richter

The German humorist and prose writer Johann Paul Friedrich Richter (1763-1825), usually referred to as Jean Paul, achieved his greatest fame as a novelist.

On March 21, 1763, J. P. Richter was born at Wunsiedel, Fichtel Gebirge. As a boy, he went to school at the small town of Hof; then he moved to the University of Leipzig (1781-1784) to study theology. Financial difficulties forced him to become a tutor to various families. When he was 29, he called himself Jean Paul (after Jean Jacques Rousseau). Having given up the idea of entering the Church, he decided to become a writer. He was essentially a Platonist; Herder also had a profound influence on him, and they opposed Kant's speculative philosophy.

Jean Paul's early works were collections of satires about courtiers, society, and ladies: the *Grönländische Prozesse* (1783) and *Auswahl aus des Teufels Papieren* (1789). The first work that made him widely known and appreciated was *Die unsichtbare Loge* (1793), whose appendix contains the famous *Leben des vergnügten Schulmeisterleins Maria Wuz in Auenthal*. This story is a supreme example of an idyllic situation depicting happiness and complete contentment in a rustic existence. After that his great works followed in quick succession: *Hesperus* (1795), *Biographische Belustigungen unter der Gehirnschale einer Riesin* (1796), *Leben des Quintus Fixlein* (1796), *Blumen-, Frucht-und Dornenstücke, oder Ehestand, Tod und Hochzeit des Armenadvokaten Siebenkäs* (1796/1797), *Der Jubelsenior* (1797), and *Das Kampaner Thal* (1797).

After the death of his mother (1797), Jean Paul left Hof for Leipzig, Weimar, Berlin, Meiningen, and Coburg, and in 1804 he settled in Bayreuth. In the meantime (1801) he had married Karoline Mayer. From 1808 on, his financial situation improved considerably, as he received from the prince-primate Reichsfreiherr von Dalberg a yearly pension of 1,000 florins.

About the turn of the century Jean Paul had reached the height of his artistic achievements. He had developed an original poetic language. One of his favorite images is that of man's emerging from the chrysalis state into a new existence; another one is the (Platonic) image of shadows upon the wall, of the soul imprisoned in a shell, and the concept of *Hohe Menschen,* who are condemned to endure an earthly life but whose real home is a higher, unselfish world.

The theme of *Hohe Menschen* is the key problem in Jean Paul's masterpiece, *Titan* (1800/1803). According to him, this novel should bear the title *Anti-Titan,* as it proves that an artist's ruthless single-mindedness must destroy the ideal of harmony. In his self-centered vehemence, Roquairol spends all energy in a state of extravagant imagination and empties life of true human feeling. *Die Flegeljahre* (1804/1805), too, depicts a poetic Schwärmer who has to fulfill several practical tasks (as piano tuner, gardener, proofreader, and so on) and thus learn how to come to terms with life.

These two great works were followed by a number of novels in which the comic, satirical, and even grotesque elements are stressed: *Dr. Katzenbergers Badreise* (1809), *Des Feldpredigers Schmelzle Reise nach Flätz* (1809), *Das Leben Fibels* (1806-1811), and *Der Komet, oder Nikolaus Marggraf* (1820-1822). Moreover, there are the wealth and depth of his theoretical and critical writings on esthetics, education, society, and politics, which not until the 20th century received full appreciation: *Vorschule der Aesthetik* (1804), *Levana order Erziehungslehre* (1807), *Friedenspredigt* (1808), and *Politische Fastenpredigten* (1817).

The last years were overshadowed by illness, misfortune, and disappointments. In 1821 his only son, Max, died of typhus. Lonely and almost blind, Jean Paul died in Bayreuth on Nov. 14, 1825.

Further Reading

An authoritative and readable study of Richter's visionary pieces is John William Smeed, *Jean Paul's Dreams* (1966), which also has a useful selective bibliography. For briefer discussions of Richter's work see George P. Gooch, *Germany and the French Revolution* (1920); Lawrence M. Price, *English Literature in Germany* (1953); and August Closs, ed., *Introductions to German Literature* (4 vols., 1967-1970; 3d vol. by E. L. Stahl and W. E. Yuill). □

Flavius Ricimer

Flavius Ricimer (died 472) was a Romanized German political chief and the central power in the Western Roman Empire in the mid-5th century.

Ricimer came from royal Germanic stock on both sides of his family. His father was the king of the Suevians; his mother was the daughter of the Visigothic king Wallia. He was a Christian but, like most Goths, belonged to the heretical Arian sect of Christianity. Along with many other Germans, he decided to make his career in the service of Rome. Details of his early career are not preserved, but he must have been successful in both the political and military spheres. He formed important friendships such as that with Majorian, the future emperor, and he was selected in 456 by the emperor Avitus to stop a threatened attack of the Vandals on Sicily. He succeeded and was awarded the rank of *comes*. Shortly thereafter he was raised to the rank of master of soldiers.

His Political Force

At the same time, Ricimer began to display his political strength. In 456 he cooperated with Majorian to depose Avitus. After a short interval Majorian was recognized as emperor by the Eastern Roman Empire. Ricimer was raised to the rank of patrician in 457, and in 459 Majorian rewarded him with the consulship. However, Majorian and Ricimer began to draw apart, and when the former failed in his expedition against Gaiseric and the Vandals, Ricimer had him deposed and executed (461). In November 461 Ricimer made Livius Severus emperor, but the appointment failed to win approval either in the East or with Gaiseric, who had emerged as an independent political force. In 464 Ricimer defeated Beorger, the king of the Alans, who had invaded Italy. In 465 Severus died, and a political compromise was worked out. Leo, the Eastern Roman emperor, sent Anthemius to the West to become emperor. Ricimer agreed to the appointment when he received the hand of Anthemius's daughter in marriage.

Hostility soon developed, however, and by 470 the split was complete. Anthemius executed friends of Ricimer, and Ricimer in turn attacked Anthemius at Rome. In 472 Anthemius was defeated and killed by Ricimer. Ricimer's next candidate for the emperorship was Olybrius, who was satisfactory to Gaiseric. Olybrius was installed as emperor but soon lost the services of Ricimer, who died in 472.

Ricimer was the last strong man in the Western Roman Empire. His military skill kept Italy relatively free of invasion. Being both a barbarian and a heretical Arian, however, he was forced to act behind a screen of temporary emperors whose rapid succession added little to the strength and stability of the Western Empire.

Further Reading

Some information on Ricimer appears in the poems of Sidonius Apollinaris. Colin Douglas Gordon, *The Age of Attila: Fifth-century Byzantium and the Barbarians* (1960), collects some of the fragments of the ancient historians on Ricimer. For the background of Ricimer's era see J. B. Bury, *History of the Later Roman Empire: From the Death of Theodosius I to the Death of Justinian, A.D. 395 to A.D. 565* (1923). □

Edward Vernon Rickenbacker

Edward Vernon Rickenbacker (1890-1973), early automobile race driver and America's top fighter pilot in World War I, went on to manage giant Eastern Air Lines during its expansion era.

Eddie Rickenbacker was one of those rare heroes who enjoyed enduring fame. His remarkable victories as a fighter pilot in 1918, his many brushes with death throughout a long life coupled with the courage with which he confronted danger, his willingness to express his views openly, and his success in the airline business—all these made him a renowned popular hero in his day and beyond.

Born simply Edward Rickenbacher (later Rickenbacker) on October 8, 1890, in Columbus, Ohio, he was one of eight children in a poor Swiss immigrant family. After the death of his father, William, when Eddie was 13, his mother, Elizabeth Basler Rickenbacher, helped support the family with money earned by the older children. Eddie dropped out of school and moved rapidly through a succession of industrial posts. During the course of these ever better paying jobs, he embraced the values of the early 20th century—the ethical value of work, thrift, independence, and a distrust of government power.

As a teenager he developed a consuming passion for automobiles and gravitated to a car maker who, like many others, promoted his vehicle by racing. Eddie, riding as mechanic, took correspondence courses in engineering and acquired experience. He quickly rose into management while passing through a succession of companies. Moving behind the wheel, he began racing and competing against the greats of the day. His courage and ability were demonstrated around the United States, including Indianapolis Speedway, where he later owned a controlling interest. At Daytona Beach he set a new record of 134 miles per hour. Even the loss of much of his vision in one eye did not deter him; typically, he learned ways to compensate. Off the track he consciously molded himself along the lines of better educated, successful men that he met. In 1916 World War I unexpectedly gave him an even more hazardous occupation.

As soon as America took up arms Rickenbacker joined General Pershing and the first troops to go overseas. He was already interested in airplanes and used his opportunities, especially the support of Colonel Billy Mitchell, to move from the driver corps to the 94th Aero Pursuit Squadron and eventually to the cockpit of a fighter plane. At age 27 he was too old to be a combat pilot, but he falsified his age. He also lacked the gentleman's background expected of flyers, a deficiency that never showed itself in combat. The race track had provided him with experience that soon became apparent. In a little more than a month, a period that most new pilots did not survive, he was an "ace" with five kills to his credit. Between April and November 1918, he destroyed a remarkable toll of 26 enemy aircraft, becoming the United States' "Ace of Aces." These victories earned him the French Croix de Guerre and later the U.S. Congressional Medal of Honor. Lionized throughout America, he wrote a popular account of flying against Germany's pilots.

The well-known hero had to find a peacetime occupation, and he began establishing connections while looking for a high industrial position. He also took part in a number of adventures intended to put him in the headlines, ultimately gravitating back to the auto industry. These ventures led him to build and sell a car bearing the Rickenbacker name. Many new autos failed, and by 1927 the Rickenbacker was one of them. He then accepted a position at General Motors to sell cars. When GM entered the aviation business, he assisted and moved through several executive positions. He was presiding over Eastern Air Lines in 1938 when GM decided to sell it to some investors, possibly leaving him in the cold. Captain Eddie felt betrayed and sought his own financing, which would put him in charge.

That Eastern grew and made profits consistently in an unstable industry was largely due to his efforts. He carefully watched expenses and attended to operating details. He ruled omnipotent, as did most airline presidents at that time, and was popular with his growing mass of employees. Then came disaster. He barely survived a crash in one of Eastern's "Great Silver Fleet" in 1941. The good fortune for which he was already known had not abandoned him.

In 1934 he had made himself unpopular in Washington, D.C., for criticizing President Franklin D. Roosevelt's hostility to the aviation industry. Nevertheless, Washington called on him to help establish a military air transport system and to make several special missions during the course of World War II. He was to evaluate air operations and bear important messages. And, although he had once opposed American participation, the renowned "ace" now made morale-building appearances with the troops.

On one such mission his aircraft went down, and he spent more than three harrowing weeks adrift in the Pacific Ocean. While given up for dead at home, to Rickenbacker it seemed his fate-ordained duty to survive and save his small party. Once rescued, he would complete this mission. On a later trip Rickenbacker, without White House approval, wrote himself an extra mission to Russia. But his unrequested evaluation of the Soviets was largely ignored in Washington. After the war his impolitic remarks found him allied with conservative causes.

Rickenbacker, who had turned a money-losing Eastern Air Lines into a profitable venture, continued this role after the war. War gave Eastern the opportunity to expand, and Rickenbacker's attention to costs kept the firm profitable when most airlines were not. However, Eastern began losing ground to competitors. It experienced opposition in Washington and alienated customers, problems largely attributed to Captain Eddie. Eastern in the late 1950s flew into financial turbulence. Ultimately, "his" airline forced his retirement in 1963 at age 73 but still fell victim to its problems and went bankrupt.

Captain Eddie remained a popular figure speaking in behalf of conservative causes. He died on July 23, 1973, in Switzerland, leaving his wife, the former Adelaide Frost, whom he had married in 1922, and two adopted sons, David Edward and William Frost. His obituaries particularly noted his victories in the air during World War I.

Further Reading

Edward Rickenbacker is listed in *The Encyclopedia of American Business History and Biography* (1992). Hans Christian Adamson's *Eddie Rickenbacker* (1946) and Finis Farr's *Rickenbacker's Luck* (1979) plus an autobiography, *Rickenbacker* (1967), are basic sources. Rickenbacker also wrote *Fighting the Flying Circus* (1919) and *Seven Came Through* (1954), which describe remarkable experiences in two wars. Eastern Air Lines history is told in Robert J. Serling's *From the Captain to the Colonel* (1980).

Additional Sources

Farr, Finis, *Rickenbacker's luck: an American life,* Boston: Houghton Mifflin, 1979.
Rickenbacker, Eddie, *Fighting the flying circus,* Alexandria, Va.: Time-Life Books, 1990. □

Wesley Branch Rickey

Wesley Branch Rickey (1881-1965) was an innovative baseball executive who created baseball's farm system and integrated organized baseball when he signed Jackie Robinson in 1946.

Branch Rickey was born on December 20, 1881, in Stockdale, Ohio, and was raised in nearby Lucasville. Reared on his father's farm with a strict religious upbringing, young Branch excelled in academics and athletics. At the age of 19 Rickey enrolled at Ohio Wesleyan University, paying his way by playing semi-professional baseball and football and later coaching both sports. Upon graduation in 1904 he joined the Dallas baseball team in the Texas League. By the season's end the Cincinnati Reds of the National League purchased his contract, only to drop him from the squad when Rickey refused to play on Sundays. Over the next three years Rickey appeared as a catcher for the St. Louis Browns and for the New York Yankees, compiling a modest .239 life-time batting average.

Coaching and Managing

His playing career at an end, Rickey entered law school at the University of Michigan, once again financing his education by coaching. His legal career, however, proved short and unsuccessful. In 1912 St. Louis Browns owner Robert Hedges rescued Rickey from his failing Idaho law practice by offering him a position as his personal assistant. Two years later Rickey became the field manager of the team, and his emphasis on fundamentals and experimental training methods won him a reputation as a "Professor of Baseball." In 1917 Rickey transferred his allegiance to the crosstown St. Louis Cardinals, where he served as field manager until 1925 and as general manager from 1925 until 1942.

With the Cardinals Rickey perfected the "farm system," his first major contribution to the baseball industry. This ingenious scheme allowed a major league club to control a chain of minor league franchises through which it could develop young players before promoting the best to the parent team. The farm system allowed Rickey to assemble championship squads for the Cardinals as well as surplus players who were sold profitably to other teams. Under his leadership the Cardinals emerged as the most successful franchise in the National League.

Brooklyn Dodgers

In 1942, following a rift with Cardinal owner Samuel Breadon, Rickey became the general manager of the Brooklyn Dodgers. Rickey's early attempts to rebuild the Brooklyn

club by trading and selling older stars and creating a minor league chain like that of St. Louis met with derision from cynical Dodger fans and reporters. Rickey's intense moralism and sermonlike speeches led sportswriters to dub him the "Deacon" or the "Mahatma" (after Indian leader Mahatma Gandhi), and his office became known as the "Cave of the Winds." But by 1946 Rickey, now a part owner of the Dodgers, had once again constructed a pennant-contending team and his popularity soared.

Meanwhile, Rickey had embarked on a daring scheme to assure Dodger dominance in the post-World War II years. Since the late 1880s organized baseball had barred African Americans from participation. Rickey, who believed that segregation was immoral, correctly recognized that political pressures would soon bring about the integration of baseball and perceived that the first owner to tap this new source of players would benefit both in the standings and at the box office. In 1945, under the guise of creating a new Negro League, the Dodger organization secretly began scouting African American players. After carefully assessing the skills and background of dozens of players, Rickey chose Jackie Robinson, a former collegiate football star, to become the first African American major leaguer in the 20th century.

Rickey moved slowly and cautiously in bringing Robinson to the Dodgers. He studied the work of sociologists like Frank Tannenbaum and Dan Dodson and met with leaders of the African American community urging restraint in the enthusiasm of African American fans. He sent Robinson first to play for the Dodgers' top farm team, the Montreal Royals, in 1946 and started other talented African American players at lower levels of the Dodger minor leagues. Rickey's elaborate planning may have been unnecessary, but it reflected both his own complex personality and the racial perceptions of the era.

The choice of Robinson as his standard bearer proved an inspired one. Despite tremendous pressures and numerous instances of discrimination, Robinson led the International League in batting in 1946. The following year Rickey put down a rebellion among several Dodger players seeking to prevent Robinson's promotion and installed the African American athlete as the team's first baseman. Robinson led the Dodgers to the National League pennant and was named Rookie of the Year. His presence attracted record numbers of fans in every National League city. Over the next nine years Robinson established himself as one of the outstanding stars in baseball history, and the Dodgers, in large part due to Robinson and other African American players, became the dominant team in the National League.

In the aftermath of the Robinson experience Rickey became a prominent spokesman on behalf of civil rights. In the late 1940s he challenged Jim Crow laws by scheduling Dodger exhibitions throughout the South, forcing local officials to integrate their facilities or lose a sell-out crowd. In 1950 Rickey lost control of the Dodgers to Walter O'Malley and left the club. In subsequent years he worked for the Pittsburgh Pirates and the St. Louis Cardinals, but he was never able to recreate his earlier successes. In November 1965 he collapsed in Columbia, Missouri, while speaking on personal courage. He never regained consciousness and died on December 9, 1965.

Further Reading

The best biography of Branch Rickey is Arthur Mann, *Branch Rickey: American in Action* (1957). Other biographies include David Lipman, *Mr. Baseball: The Story of Branch Rickey* (1966) and Murray Polner, *Branch Rickey* (1982). See also Branch Rickey, *The American Diamond* (1965). For accounts of the integration of baseball see Jules Tygiel, *Baseball's Great Experiment: Jackie Robinson and His Legacy* (1983) and Carl T. Rowan and Jackie Robinson, *Wait Till Next Year: The Life of Jackie Robinson* (1960).

Additional Sources

Frommer, Harvey, *Rickey and Robinson: the men who broke baseball's color barrier,* New York: MacMillan; London: Collier MacMillan Publishers, 1982. □

Hyman George Rickover

Hyman George Rickover (1900-1986) was an officer in the U.S. Navy who played a significant and controversial role in ushering the Navy into the nuclear age. On active duty for almost 60 years, Rickover greatly influenced many nuclear power technicians who later served in the nascent military and civilian nuclear power industries.

Hyman George Rickover was born on January 27, 1900 (1898 according to school records), in the village of Makow, then in the Russian Empire, some 50 miles north of Warsaw. His father, Abraham, a tailor, emigrated to New York at the turn of the century. Around 1904 the senior Rickover sent for his family, wife Rachel (née Unger), daughter Fanny, and Hyman. Four years later they moved to the Lawndale neighborhood of Chicago, where Hyman attended public schools while working at various jobs as he grew older. He entered the U.S. Naval Academy in 1918.

Accounts of his years at Annapolis stress that he was a loner, perhaps because of anti-Semitism, but more likely because he preferred to concentrate on his studies. Commissioned an ensign in 1922, Rickover put in four years of sea duty before studying engineering at the Naval Postgraduate School. He then completed requirements for a Master's degree in electrical engineering at Columbia University in 1928. Promoted to lieutenant while at Columbia, Rickover met Ruth Masters, a student in international law and subsequently a scholar of some distinction. The two carried on a correspondence courtship and in 1931 were married by an Episcopal minister. They had one son, Robert Masters Rickover. Two years after his wife's death in 1972, Rickover married Eleonore Bednowicz, a navy nurse who retired thereafter and who survived him.

Sea Commands Elude Rickover

Accepted into submarine school in 1929, Rickover spent the next four years of his career in that branch of the navy. By the time his tour as engineer officer and then executive officer of *S-48* was completed in 1933 Rickover hoped to receive command of a submarine. Instead, he did a two-year tour at a naval facility in Philadelphia, after which he served two years in engineering on the battleship *New Mexico*. In 1937 Rickover was promoted to lieutenant commander and given command of the antiquated minesweeper *Finch*. His hard-driving ways seem to have caused resentment, and he was relieved after three months.

Convinced by his assignment to *Finch* that his aspirations for a conventional career of command at sea would not be fulfilled, Rickover had already requested a transfer to the status of "Engineering Duty Only." Since 1916 the navy had officially differentiated between unrestricted line officers and EDO officers. Line officers were trained to command ships, being rotated to a variety of duties at sea and on shore to familiarize them with many aspects of the navy. In contrast, an EDO officer could design, maintain, modernize, and repair ships but could not command one.

His first billet as an EDO was at the Cavite Navy Yard in the Philippines, where he spent nearly two years. From Cavite he returned to the United States for assignment to the Bureau of Engineering, consolidated with another shore establishment into the Bureau of Ships (BuShips) in 1940. The navy was expanding rapidly, and Rickover's duties as head of the Electrical Section of BuShips put him in a key post to develop and improve electrical apparatus. His style of command—which in time would become a major part of his public persona—was considered unconventional as he ignored rank among his section's personnel and thought nothing of working on Sundays and late into the evenings.

Rickover, after 1942 a (temporary) captain, appealed for duty in a combat zone and in 1945 went to Okinawa with orders to develop and operate a ship repair base. The war ended soon thereafter, and, like many other officers in a postwar navy due for retrenchment, Rickover's future was in doubt.

Father of the U.S. Nuclear Navy

Within a decade, however, Rickover was to become world-famous as the father of the nuclear navy. Although popular accounts credit Rickover alone with the founding of the nuclear navy, the idea of a nuclear-powered submarine had been batted around within the navy since 1939. His immediate superior, Admiral Earle Mills, was in favor of it, as were others. In 1946 Rickover was sent as one of a team of engineering officers to Oak Ridge, Tennessee, to learn about nuclear technology. Rickover then served as Mills' assistant for nuclear matters until 1948 when the navy made a firm commitment to develop nuclear propulsion. Rickover then received two choice assignments: head of the Nuclear Power Branch of BuShips and, in 1949, chief of the newly established Naval Reactors Branch of the Atomic Energy Commission (AEC).

These dual posts gave Rickover a great deal of autonomy in that he could initiate action from either his naval billet or from his post in the civilian-run AEC chain of authority. He gathered around him a group of bright and loyal officers who worked diligently to overcome the myriad problems in harnessing a nuclear reactor for shipboard power. By the early 1950s Rickover, still a captain, had succeeded in making himself known to the media and to influential congressmen as an officer who got things done, presumably indispensable to the navy's nuclear propulsion program. Although he was twice passed over for promotion to rear admiral—meaning that by navy regulations he would have to retire—pressure from congressional leaders led the secretary of the navy to order a reconsideration of Rickover's status, and he was promoted to rear admiral in 1953. Two years later *Nautilus*, the world's first nuclear submarine, was launched, and Rickover was about to become a living institution, compared most frequently to J. Edgar Hoover of the Federal Bureau of Investigation as a master of bureaucratic ways.

As the navy added more nuclear submarines to the fleet, and then surface ships, Rickover was retained on active duty through a series of special two-year reappointments that allowed him to serve long past the mandatory retirement age of 64. He was promoted to vice admiral in 1963 and a decade later to admiral. By insisting that safety considerations required him to personally approve officers of all nuclear-powered ships Rickover exerted influence far beyond his official position. As later assignments took these officers throughout the navy, Rickover's impact was felt in many quarters.

By no means was his reputation confined to the navy. His organization, with some private funding, developed the nation's first nuclear-powered electrical generating facility at Shippingport, Pennsylvania, in 1957. Rickover himself had little more to do with it following completion, but many men who learned their trade with the Naval Reactors Branch went on to become major figures in the growing nuclear power field in the 1960s. After the launching of Russia's Sputnik satellite called into doubt America's supremacy in science, Rickover for a while also gained recognition as an authority on American education. He wrote several books criticizing what he considered its shortcomings and calling for standards of excellence like those he had always imposed upon himself.

Not until 1981 was he retired from active duty, and even then he remained well-known, ironically making the news several times in 1984 when it was revealed that he had received—indeed requested—expensive gifts from many contractors he had dealt with. Regardless of those accusations—and Rickover did not deny them in their entirety—his naval career will rank as one of the most important and controversial of all time.

His detractors claim that by the 1960s Rickover had become a conservative force in the navy, hindering both innovation in submarine design and the adoption of gasturbine technology for surface ships by placing excessive emphasis on a comparatively few costly nuclear-powered ships at the expense of more numerous, less expensive, conventionally-powered ships which could perform many missions just as well. His admirers, however, were numerous and pointed to his role in ushering the navy into the nuclear age and his stress upon excellence at a time when laxness seemed to be pervading the armed forces and society as a whole. He summed up his own philosophy in the saying, "The more you sweat in peace the less you bleed in war."

Further Reading

Clay Blair, Jr.'s, *The Atomic Submarine and Admiral Rickover* (1954) is an interesting biography of Rickover, in part because it was written with his cooperation and because it presents an early version of what became the Rickover mystique. Other studies of Rickover, more balanced in approach, are Norman Polmar and Thomas B. Allen, *Rickover* (1982) and Eugene Lewis, *Public Entrepreneurship: Toward a Theory of Bureaucratic Political Power* (1980). For the navy's move into the nuclear age see Vincent P. Davis, *Postwar Defense Policy and the U.S. Navy, 1943-46* (1962) and Richard B. Hewlett and Francis Duncan, *Nuclear Navy, 1946-1962* (1974). The problem of gifts from contractors is discussed by Patrick Tyler in *Running Critical: The Silent War, Rickover and General Dynamics* (1986). Rickover authored several books. Perhaps the best known are the ones that deal with education: *American Education* (1963), *Education and Freedom* (1959), and *Swiss Schools and Ours: Why Theirs Are Better* (1962).

Additional Sources

Duncan, Francis, *Rickover and the nuclear navy: the discipline of technology*, Annapolis, Md.: Naval Institute Press, 1990.
Polmar, Norman, *Rickover*, New York: Simon and Schuster, 1982.

Rockwell, Theodore, *The Rickover effect: how one man made a difference,* Annapolis, Md.: Naval Institute Press, 1992.

Rockwell, Theodore, *The Rickover effect: the inside story of how Adm. Hyman Rickover built the nuclear Navy,* New York: J. Wiley, 1995. □

Paul Ricoeur

Paul Ricoeur (born 1913) was a leading exponent of hermeneutical philosophy. He developed a theory of metaphor and discourse as well as articulating a comprehensive vision of the relation of time, history, and narrative. Ricoeur's work influenced scholarship in virtually all of the human sciences.

Paul Ricoeur was born on February 27, 1913, in Valence, France, the son of Jules and Florentine Favre Ricoeur. He was married to Simone Lejas in 1935 and had five children. His education included a Licencié ès Lettres from the University of Rennes (1932), Agrégation de Philosophie from the Sorbonne (1935), and the Doctorat ès Lettres in 1950. He taught at the University of Starbourg (1948-1957) and the University of Paris-X, Nabterre, beginning in 1957; from 1971 to 1985 he was the John Nuveen Professor of the History of Philosophy at the University of Chicago. He won the Prix Cavailles in 1951 as well as the Hegel Prize for his *Temps et Récit III,* published in 1985. Ricoeur held numerous honorary degrees from universities around the world. In addition to his own writing he was editor of the collection *Éditions du Seuil,* the editor of *Revue de Métaphysique et Morale,* and a member of the Institut International de Philosophie.

Ricoeur's work is best understood as an interplay of three philosophical movements: reflexive philosophy, phenomenology, and hermeneutics. Reflexive philosophy reaches back to Plato, finding modern expression in Descartes' concern for the *cogito,* Kant's critical philosophy, and recent post-Kantian French philosophy. The central concern of this tradition is with the possibility of self-understanding. Reflexivity is the act of thought turning back on itself to grasp the unifying principle of its operation—that is, the subject or "I." Ricoeur continued the task of reflexive philosophy. His original intention was to develop a comprehensive phenomenology of the will. While not finished, this project was carried out through several works: *Freedom and Nature: The Voluntary and the Involuntary* (1966); *Fallible Man* (1965); and *The Symbolism of Evil* (1976). All of these works explore dimensions of human subjectivity and its world.

As a student of phenomenology, Ricoeur acknowledged that consciousness has an intentional structure; consciousness is always consciousness of something. Given this, there is no immediate self-transparency of the self to itself, even by a reflexive act. Thus the journey to self-understanding must involve, in Ricoeur's terms, a detour of interpretation. The "I think" knows itself only relative to the act of intending and the intended "sense," or what Husserl called the *noema.* That is, the self knows itself reflexively relative to intentional objects of consciousness which must be interpreted to disclose their import for self-understanding.

With the realization that understanding involves interpretation, Ricoeur follows Heidegger's hermeneutical turn of thought. Hermeneutical philosophy insists that the human way of being in the world is one of understanding. Humans understand themselves through the interpretation of the cultural and linguistic world in which they find themselves. Thus the journey to self-understanding is deepened yet again, since one must interpret the manifold signs, symbols, and texts which disclose the character of human life and its world. This led Ricoeur into studies of the problem of evil and the character of religious language, as well as numerous works on the philosophy of history.

Hermeneutical thinkers also argue that language is the primary condition for all experience and that linguistic forms (symbols, metaphors, texts) disclose dimensions of human beings in the world. To understand oneself, therefore, is to understand the self as it confronts a linguistic expression that discloses possibilities for existence. Ironically, then, while Ricoeur's work remains in the tradition of reflexive philosophy, he has qualified the focus on the self and any pretense to immediate self-knowledge. Self-understanding is always hermeneutical and is reached through interpretation within the medium of language.

Crucial to all of Ricoeur's works was the development of what he called the "hermeneutical arch" of understanding detailed in his *Interpretation Theory: Discourse and the Surplus of Meaning* (1976). By this "arch" he means that interpretation begins with the pre-reflective dimensions of human life. In order to reach an understanding of our pre-reflexive being in the world it is necessary to undertake the interpretation of the texts, symbols, actions, and events that disclose the human situation. At this level of interpretation Ricoeur, as opposed to some other hermeneutical thinkers, argued for the importance of various explanatory sciences. He explored the importance of psychoanalysis (*Freud and Philosophy,* 1970), structural linguistics and phenomenology (*The Conflict of Interpretations,* 1974), theory of myth and symbol (*The Symbolism of Evil,* 1967), and narrative theory (*Time and Narrative,* 1984 [Vol. I] and 1986 [Vol. II]), all as part of the hermeneutical task. However, Ricoeur was adamant that the moment of explanation, while necessary, is not sufficient for understanding. This is because understanding is an act of appropriation by the "reader" of what the text, symbol, or event discloses about human being in the world. Explanation of the human situation complements but does not answer the task of understanding.

Ricoeur's emphasis on the interpretive shape of understanding required reflection on the power of texts, symbols, and myths to disclose something about the human and its world. Central to his interpretation theory was work on the referential power of texts through studies of metaphor (*The Rule of Metaphor,* 1976) and narrative (*Time and Narrative*). Ricoeur's semantic theory escapes easy characterization. His main contention, however, is that meaning is generated when there is a clash of literal claims at the level of the sentence or when human time and action are configured as a whole through narration. Accordingly, texts refer to the world, but do so in an indirect way: they disclose a different vision of the world as possible for the reader. Ricoeur's theory of metaphor and text has had considerable import for the study of myth, literature, and religious language.

Ricoeur's thought was the creative convergence of dominant strands in modern philosophy. By exploring the hermeneutical arch and the manifold ways in which humans try to understand themselves (psychoanalysis, storytelling, myth, and so forth) he made substantive contributions to a wide array of disciplines. Moreover, Ricoeur's philosophy of metaphor and narrative continues to influence work in all of the human sciences. There is little doubt that Ricoeur's vast corpus of thought provides keen insight for the self-understanding of our age.

Ricoeur has kept up his pace in the publication of articles, mostly on the theories of justice of John Rawls and others and on the relation between ethics and politics. In the fall of 1995, he published two shorter books, one, entitled *Reflections accomplies,* contains his Intellectual Autobiography, along with several articles. The other, called *Justice,* is a collection of his recent articles on justice and its application in the modern world. His rediscovery in France is evidenced by the numerous interviews on television and in the newspapers. He was invited by President Mitterand to attend a state dinner at the Elysee Palace in honor of President and Mrs. Clinton in June of 1994. A book about his life, *Paul Ricoeur, His Life and His Work* was published by the University of Chicago Press in 1996.

Further Reading

For resources on Ricoeur's work see his own *Hermeneutics and the Human Sciences,* translated by John B. Thompson (Cambridge, 1981). Also see Don Ihde, *Hermeneutical Phenomenology: The Philosophy of Paul Ricoeur* (1971) and David E. Klemm, *The Hermeneutical Theory of Paul Ricoeur* (1983). □

Sally Ride

Sally Ride (born 1951) is best known as the first American woman sent into outer space. She also served the National Aeronautics and Space Administration (NASA) in an advisory capacity, being the only astronaut chosen for President Ronald Reagan's Rogers Commission investigating the mid-launch explosion of the space shuttle *Challenger* in January, 1986, writing official recommendation reports, and creating NASA's Office of Exploration.

B oth scientist and professor, Sally Ride has served as a fellow at the Stanford University Center for International Security and Arms Control, a member of the board of directors at Apple Computer Inc., and a space institute director and physics professor at the University of

California at San Diego. Ride has chosen to write primarily for children about space travel and exploration. Her commitment to educating the young earned her the Jefferson Award for Public Service from the American Institute for Public Service in 1984, in addition to her National Space-flight Medals recognizing her two groundbreaking shuttle missions in 1983 and 1984. Newly elected president Bill Clinton chose her as a member of his transition team during the fall of 1992.

Sally Kristen Ride is the older daughter of Dale Burdell and Carol Joyce (Anderson) Ride of Encino, California, and was born May 26, 1951. As author Karen O'Connor describes tomboy Ride in her young reader's book, *Sally Ride and the New Astronauts,* Sally would race her dad for the sports section of the newspaper when she was only five years old. An active, adventurous, yet also scholarly family, the Rides traveled throughout Europe for a year when Sally was nine and her sister Karen was seven, after Dale took a sabbatical from his political science professorship at Santa Monica Community College. While Karen was inspired to become a minister, in the spirit of her parents, who were elders in their Presbyterian church, Ride's own developing taste for exploration would eventually lead her to apply to the space program almost on a whim. "I don't know why I wanted to do it," she confessed to *Newsweek* prior to embarking on her first spaceflight.

The opportunity was serendipitous, since the year she began job-hunting marked the first time NASA had opened its space program to applicants since the late 1960s, and the very first time women would not be excluded from consid-

eration. NASA needed to cast a wider net than ever before, as *Current Biography* disclosed in 1983. The program paid less than private sector counterparts and offered no particular research specialties, unlike most job opportunities in academia. All it took was a return reply postcard, and Ride was in the mood to take those risks. This was, after all, a young lady who could patch up a disabled Toyota with Scotch tape without breaking stride, as one of her friends once discovered. Besides, she had always forged her own way before with the full support of her open-minded family.

From her earliest years in school, Ride was so proficient and efficient at once, she proved to be an outright annoyance to some of her teachers. Though she was a straight-A student, she was easily bored, and her brilliance only came to the fore in high school, when she was introduced to the world of science by her physiology teacher. The impact of this mentor, Dr. Elizabeth Mommaerts, was so profound that Ride would later dedicate her first book primarily to her, as well as the fallen crew of the *Challenger*. While she was adaptable to all forms of sport, playing tennis was Ride's most outstanding talent, which she had developed since the age of ten. Under the tutelage of a four-time U.S. Open champion, Ride eventually ranked eighteenth nationally on the junior circuit. Her ability won her a partial scholarship to Westlake School for Girls, a prep school in Los Angeles. After graduating from there in 1968, Ride preferred to work on her game full time instead of the physics program at Swarthmore College, Pennsylvania, where she had originally enrolled. It was only after Ride had fully tested her dedication to the game that she decided against a professional career, even though tennis pro Billie Jean King had once told her it was within her grasp. Back in California as an undergraduate student at Stanford University, Ride followed her burgeoning love for Shakespeare to a double major, receiving B.S. and B.A. degrees in tandem by 1973. She narrowed her focus to physics for her masters, also from Stanford, awarded in 1975. Work toward her dissertation continued at Stanford; she submitted "The Interaction of X-Rays with the Interstellar Medium" in 1978.

Ride was just finishing her Ph.D. candidacy in physics, astronomy, and astrophysics at Stanford, working as a research assistant, when she got the call from NASA. She became one of thirty-five chosen from an original field of applicants numbering eight thousand for the spaceflight training of 1978. "Why I was selected remains a complete mystery," she later admitted to John Grossmann in a 1985 interview in *Health*. "None of us has ever been told." Even after three years of studying X-ray astrophysics, Ride had to go back to the classroom to gain skills to be part of a team of astronauts. The program included basic science and math, meteorology, guidance, navigation, and computers as well as flight training on a T–38 jet trainer and other operational simulations. Ride was selected as part of the ground-support crew for the second (November, 1981) and third (March, 1982) shuttle flights, her duties including the role of "capcom," or capsule communicator, relaying commands from the ground to the shuttle crew. These experiences prepared her to be an astronaut.

Ride would subsequently become, at thirty-one, the youngest person sent into orbit as well as the first American woman in space, the first American woman to make two spaceflights, and, coincidentally, the first astronaut to marry another astronaut in active duty. She and Steven Alan Hawley were married at the groom's family home in Kansas on July 26, 1982. Hawley, a Ph.D. from the University of California, had joined NASA with a background in astronomy and astrophysics. When asked during a hearing by Congressman Larry Winn, Jr., of the House Committee on Science and Technology, how she would feel when Hawley was in space while she remained earthbound, Ride replied, "I am going to be a very interested observer." The pair were eventually divorced.

Ride points to her fellow female astronauts Anna Fisher, Shannon Lucid, Judith Resnik, Margaret Seddon, and Kathryn Sullivan with pride. Since these women were chosen for training, Ride's own experience could not be dismissed as tokenism, which had been the unfortunate fate of the first woman in orbit, the Soviet Union's Valentina Tereshkova, a textile worker. Ride expressed her concern to *Newsweek* reporter Pamela Abramson in the week before her initial shuttle trip. "It's important to me that people don't think I was picked for the flight because I am a woman and it's time for NASA to send one."

From June 18 to June 24, 1983, flight STS–7 of the space shuttle *Challenger* launched from Kennedy Space Center in Florida, orbited the Earth for six days, returned to Earth, and landed at Edwards Air Force Base in California. Among the shuttle team's missions were the deployment of international satellites and numerous research experiments supplied by a range of groups, from a naval research lab to various high school students. With Ride operating the shuttle's robot arm in cooperation with Colonel John M. Fabian of the U.S. Air Force, the first satellite deployment and retrieval using such an arm was successfully performed in space during the flight.

Ride was also chosen for *Challenger* flight STS–41G, which transpired between October 5 and October 13, 1984. This time, the robot arm was put to some unusual applications, including "ice-busting" on the shuttle's exterior and readjusting a radar antenna. According to Henry S. F. Cooper, Jr., in his book *Before Lift-off*, fellow team member Ted Browder felt that because Ride was so resourceful and willing to take the initiative, less experienced astronauts on the flight might come to depend upon her rather than develop their own skills, but this mission also met with great success. Objectives during this longer period in orbit covered scientific observations of the Earth, demonstrations of potential satellite refueling techniques, and deployment of a satellite. As STS–7 had been, STS–41G was led by Captain Robert L. Crippen of the U.S. Navy to a smooth landing, this time in Florida.

Ride had been chosen for a third scheduled flight, but training was cut short in January, 1986, when the space shuttle *Challenger* exploded in midair shortly after takeoff. The twelve-foot rubber O-rings that serve as washers between steel segments of the rocket boosters, already considered problematic, failed under stress, killing the entire crew.

Judy Resnik, one of the victims, had flown as a rookie astronaut on STS–41G. Ride remembered her in *Ms.* magazine as empathetic, sharing "the same feelings that there was good news and bad news in being accepted to be the first one." As revealed a few months later in the *Chicago Tribune,* program members at NASA began to feel that their safety had been willfully compromised without their knowledge. "I think that we may have been misleading people into thinking that this is a routine operation," Ride was quoted as saying.

Ride herself tried to remedy that misconception with her subsequent work on the Rogers Commission and as special assistant for long-range and strategic planning to NASA Administrator James C. Fletcher in Washington, D.C., during 1986 and 1987. In keeping with the Rogers Commission recommendations, which Ride helped to shape, especially regarding the inclusion of astronauts at management levels, Robert Crippen was eventually made Deputy Director for Space Shuttle Operations in Washington, D.C., as well.

As leader of a task force on the future of the space program, Ride wrote *Leadership and America's Future in Space.* According to *Aviation Week and Space Technology,* this status report initiated a proposal to redefine NASA goals as a means to prevent the "space race" mentality that might pressure management and personnel into taking untoward risks. "A single goal is not a panacea," the work stated in its preface. "The problems facing the space program must be met head-on, not oversimplified." The overall thrust of NASA's agenda, Ride suggested, should take environmental and international research goals into consideration. A pledge to inform the public and capture the interest of youngsters should be taken as a given. Ride cited a 1986 work decrying the lack of math and science proficiency among American high school graduates, a mere six percent of whom are fluent in these fields, compared to up to ninety percent in other nations.

While with NASA, Ride traveled with fellow corps members to speak to high school and college students on a monthly basis. As former English tutor Joyce Ride once told a *Boston Globe* reporter, her daughter had developed scientific interests she herself harbored in younger days, before encountering a wall of silence in a college physics class as a coed at the University of California in Los Angeles. As Joyce remarked, she and the only other young woman in the class were "nonpersons." Speaking at Smith College in 1985, Sally Ride announced that encouraging women to enter math and science disciplines was her "personal crusade." Ride noted in *Publishers Weekly* the next year that her ambition to write children's books had been met with some dismay by publishing houses more in the mood to read an autobiography targeted for an adult audience. Her youth-oriented books were both written with childhood friends. Susan Okie, coauthor of *To Space and Back,* eventually became a journalist with the *Washington Post. Voyager* coauthor Tam O'Shaughnessy, once a fellow competition tennis player, grew up to develop workshops on scientific teaching skills.

Ride left NASA in 1987 for Stanford's Center for International Security and Arms Control, and two years later she became director of the California Space Institute and physics professor at the University of California at San Diego. She has flown Grumman Tiger aircraft in her spare time since getting her pilot's license. The former astronaut keeps in shape, when not teaching or fulfilling the duties of her various professional posts, by running and engaging in other sports, although she once told *Health* magazine she winds up eating junk food a lot. Ride admitted that she didn't like to run but added, "I like being in shape."

Further Reading

Astronauts and Cosmonauts Biographical and Statistical Data, U.S. Government Printing Office, 1989.

Cooper, Henry S. F., Jr., *Before Lift-off,* Johns Hopkins University Press, 1987.

Current Biography, H. W. Wilson, 1983, pp. 318–21.

Hearing before the Committee on Science and Technology, U.S. House of Representatives, Ninety-eighth Congress, First Session, July 19, 1983, U.S. Government Printing Office, 1983.

O'Connor, Karen, *Sally Ride and the New Astronauts: Scientists in Space,* F. Watts, 1983.

Adler, Jerry, and Pamela Abramson, "Sally Ride: Ready for Lift-off," in *Newsweek,* June 13, 1983, pp. 36–40, 45, 49, 51.

Caldwell, Jean, "Astronaut Ride Urges Women to Study Math," in *Boston Globe,* June 30, 1985, pp. B90, B92.

Covault, Craig, "Ride Panel Calls for Aggressive Action to Assert U.S. Leadership in Space," in *Aviation Week and Space Technology,* August 24, 1987, pp. 26–27.

Goodwin, Irwin, "Sally Ride to Leave NASA Orbit; Exodus at NSF," in *Physics Today,* July, 1987, p. 45.

Grossmann, John, "Sally Ride, Ph.D.," in *Health,* August, 1985, pp. 73–74, 76.

Ingwerson, Marshall, "Clinton Transition Team Takes on Pragmatic Cast," in *Christian Science Monitor,* November 30, 1992, p. 3.

Lowther, William, "A High Ride through the Sex Barrier," in *Maclean's,* June 27, 1983, pp. 40–41.

Peterson, Sarah, "Just Another Astronaut," in *U.S. News and World Report,* November 29, 1982, pp. 50–51.

Roback, Diane, "Sally Ride: Astronaut and Now Author," in *Publishers Weekly,* November 28, 1986, pp. 42, 44.

Rowley, Storer, and Michael Tackett, "Internal Memo Charges NASA Compromised Safety," in *Chicago Tribune,* March 9, 1986, section 1, p. 8.

Sherr, Lynn, "Remembering Judy: The Five Women Astronauts Who Trained with Judy Resnik Remember Her . . . and That Day," in *Ms.,* June, 1986, p. 57.

Sherr, "A Mission to Planet Earth: Astronaut Sally Ride Talks to Lynn Sherr about Peaceful Uses of Space," in *Ms.,* July/ August, 1987, pp. 180–81. □

Matthew Bunker Ridgway

Matthew Bunker Ridgway (1895-1993), American Army officer, served as supreme Allied commander in Korea and immediately thereafter as supreme Allied commander in Europe.

Matthew B. Ridgway was born on March 3, 1895, at Fort Monroe, Va. He graduated from the U.S. Military Academy in 1917. Ridgway's early career took him to China, Nicaragua, and the Philippines, where in 1932-1933 he served as technical adviser to the governor general. In 1935 he attended the U.S. Command and General Staff School and in 1937 the Army War College.

When World War II broke out in 1939, Ridgway was in the War Department's War Plans Division. In 1942 he rose to commander of the 82d Infantry Division, which he converted into the 82d Airborne Division. He led the 82d in the invasions of Sicily and Italy and in 1944 parachuted with his troops into Normandy, France. Later that year he took command of the 18th Airborne Corps in Belgium, France, and Germany. In 1945 he became chief of the Luzon Area Command. Ridgway married Mary Anthony in 1947, and the couple had one son.

After the war Ridgway commanded the Mediterranean theater. From 1946 until 1948 he was chairman of the Inter-American Defense Board and from 1948 to 1949 chief of the Caribbean Command. In 1949 he returned to Washington as Army deputy chief of staff. Late in 1950, during the Communist Chinese offensive in South Korea, Ridgway assumed command of the U.S. 8th Army and organized the counteroffensive which drove the Chinese and North Koreans out of South Korea. In 1951 he succeeded Gen. Douglas MacArthur as supreme commander for the Allied Powers in Japan, as commander of United Nations forces in Korea, and as commander of all United States forces in the Far East.

Unlike the other generals who directed the Korean War, Ridgway rejected MacArthur's strategy for victory—an Allied advance to the Yalu River. Instead, he conducted a limited war until President Harry Truman transferred him to Europe to succeed Gen. Dwight Eisenhower as supreme commander of the Allied Powers in Europe in 1952. Ridgway served as chief of staff of the U.S. Army from 1953 until he retired in 1955.

Ridgway's many military decorations included the Distinguished Service Cross, the Distinguished Service Medal, the Legion of Merit, and the Silver Star. In civilian life, he became a business executive. He served as a member of the board of Colt Industries and as chairman of the board of trustees of the Mellon Institute of Industrial Research.

Further Reading

Ridgway's accounts of his career are in his *Soldier: The Memoirs of Matthew B. Ridgway* (1956) and *The Korean War* (1967). His activity in World War II is assessed in John S. D. Eisenhower, *The Bitter Woods* (1969) and Clay Blair, *Ridgway's Paratroopers: The American Airborne in World War II* (1985). His role in the Korean War is recounted in Harry J. Middleton, *The Compact History of the Korean War* (1965); Roy Appleman, *Ridgway duels for Korea* (1990). Also, Ridgway's own reflections on the Korean war and related events are in *The Korean War: How We Met the Challenge* (1986). An unsympathetic view of Ridgway is in Isidor F. Stone, *The Hidden History of the Korean War* (1952; with new appendix, 1969). □

Leni Riefenstahl

The German film director Leni Riefenstahl (born 1902) achieved fame and notoriety for her propaganda film *Triumph of the Will* and her two part rendition of the 1936 Olympic Games, *Olympia,* both made for Adolf Hitler's Third Reich.

Leni Riefenstahl was one of the most controversial figures in the world of film. A talented and ambitious dancer, actress, and director, she had already made a name for herself in her native Germany and abroad when Adolf Hitler came to power in 1933. She admired him, as he did her, and with his friendship and support became the "movie-queen of Nazi Germany," a position she much enjoyed but could not live down after the fall of the Third Reich. In spite of her energetic attempts to continue as a filmmaker and her protestations that she had done nothing but be an unpolitical artist, she never managed to complete another film. Eventually she turned to still photography, producing two books on the African tribe of the Nuba (*The Last of the Nuba,* 1974, and *The People of Kau,* 1976) and one of underwater pictures (*Coral Gardens,* 1978), for which she learned to scuba dive at the age of 73. These photographs continued her life-long fascination with the beauty and strength of the human body, especially the male, and her early interest in natural life away from modern civilization.

Early Career as Dancer and Actress

Helene Berta Amalie Riefenstahl was born in Berlin on August 22, 1902. Her father, Alfred Riefenstahl, owned a plumbing firm and died in World War II, as did her only brother, Heinz. Early on she decided to become a dancer and received thorough training, both in traditional Russian ballet and in modern dance with Mary Wigman. By 1920 Riefenstahl was a successful dancer touring such cities as Munich, Frankfurt, Prague, Zürich, and Dresden.

She became interested in cinema when she saw one of the then popular mountain films of Arnold Fanck. With characteristic decisiveness and energy she set out to meet Fanck and entice him to offer her the role of a dancer in his *Der heilige Berg* (*The Holy Mountain*, 1926). It was well-received and Riefenstahl made up her mind to stay with the relatively new medium of motion pictures. Over the next seven years she made five more films with Fanck: *Der grosse Sprung* (*The Great Leap*, 1927), *Die weisse Hölle vom Piz Palü* (*The White Hell of Piz Palü*, 1929), *Stürme über dem Mont Blanc* (*Storms over Mont Blanc*, 1930), *Der weisse Rausch* (*The White Frenzy*, 1931), and *S. O. S. Eisberg* (*S. O. S. Iceberg*, 1933). She also tried acting in another type of film with a different director, but *Das Schicksal derer von Habsburg* (*The Fate of the Hapsburgs*, 1929) turned out to be an unsatisfactory venture. In Fanck's films Riefenstahl

was often the only woman in a crew of rugged men who were devoted to getting the beauty and the dangers of the still untouched high mountains (and for *S. O. S. Eisberg,* of the Arctic) onto their action-filled adventure films. Not only did she learn to climb and ski well, she also absorbed all she could about camera work, directing, and editing.

The Blue Light

Eventually Riefenstahl conceived of a different kind of mountain film, more romantic and mystical, in which a woman, played by herself, would be the central character and which she herself would direct. *Das blaue Licht* (*The Blue Light,* 1932) was based on a mountain legend and was shot in remote parts of the Tessin and the Dolomites. It demanded—and received—a great deal of dedication from those involved, many of whom were former associates of Fanck's who continued to work with her on other films. She also obtained the help of the well-known avant-garde author and film theoretician Bela Balazs, a Marxist and Jew, who collaborated on the script and as assistant director.

The Blue Light tells the story of Yunta, a beautiful innocent mountain girl who falls to her death after greedy villagers find and take all the crystals in a grotto high up on a mountain where before only she had been able to climb. The crystals are the source of a mysterious blue light which sustained Yunta and fatally attracted the young men of the village. The theme, lighting, and camera angles of the film show the legacy of German Expressionism. Riefenstahl aimed at fusing the haunting beauty of the mountains with her legendary tale and, as she would continue to do, experimented technically with special film stock, special lenses, soft focus, and smoke bombs to achieve the desired mystical effect. *The Blue Light* won acclaim abroad, where it received the silver medal at the 1932 Biennale in Venice, and at home, where it also attracted the attention of Hitler.

Films for the Third Reich

When Adolf Hitler came to power he asked Riefenstahl to film that year's Nazi party rally in Nuremberg. *Sieg des Glaubens* (*Victory of Faith,* 1933) has been lost; presumably it was destroyed because it showed party members who were soon afterwards liquidated by Hitler. With his power consolidated he wanted Riefenstahl to do the 1934 rally as well, a task she claims to have accepted only after a second "invitation" and the promise of total artistic freedom.

Triumph des Willens (*Triumph of the Will,* 1935) is considered by many to be THE propaganda film of all times, even if its director later maintained that all she had made was a documentary. Carefully edited from over 60 hours of film by herself, with concern for rhythm and variety rather than chronological accuracy, it emphasizes the solidarity of the Nazi party, the unity of the German people, and the greatness of their leader who, through composition, cutting, and special camera angles, is given mythical dimensions. Filming Abert Speer's architechtural spectacle where the Nazi icons, swastika, and eagle are displayed prominently and, together with flags, lights, flames, and music, made a powerful appeal to the irrational, emotional side of the viewer, particularly the German of the time. Not surprisingly, the film was awarded the German Film Prize for 1935. But it was also given the International Grand Prix at the 1937 Paris World Exhibition, albeit over the protest of French workers.

Riefenstahl's next film, the short *Tag der Freiheit: Unsere Wehrmacht* (*Day of Freedom: Our Armed Forces,* 1935) was in a way a sequel, shot to placate the German Armed Forces, who were not at all pleased about having received little attention in *Triumph of the Will*.

Another major assignment from Hitler followed: to shoot the 1936 Olympic Games held in Germany. *Olympia,* Part 1: *Fest der Völker* (*Festival of Nations*) and Part 2: *Fest der Schönheit* (*Festival of Beauty*) premiered in 1938, again to great German and also international acclaim. Elaborate and meticulous preparation, technical inventiveness, and 18 months of laborious editing helped Riefenstahl elevate sports photography—until then a matter for newsreels only—to a level of art seldom achieved. From the naked dancers in the opening sequence and the emphasis upon the African American athlete Jesse Owens to the striking diving and steeplechase scenes, the film celebrated the beauty of the human form in motion in feats of strength and endurance.

Immediately after completing *The Blue Light* Riefenstahl had made plans to film *Tiefland* (*Lowlands*), a project that was to be interrupted by illness, Hitler's assignments, and the war. When it was finished in 1954 all fire had gone out of this tale of innocence and corruption, high mountains and lowlands, based on the opera by the Czech Eugene d'Albert. Many of Riefenstahl's other projects, most notably her plan to do a film on Penthisilea, the Amazon queen, were never completed at all. This was due partly to the fact that she was a woman in a man's profession but mostly to the war and the choices she made under the Nazis and for them. Ultimately, all her work, in spite of the great talent and dedication it so clearly demonstrates, is tainted by the readiness and skill with which she put her art at the service of the Third Reich, no matter whether it was from conviction, political naivete, ambition, or, most likely, a combination of all three.

Although her film career had come to a halt, Riefenstahl's attention focused on still photography. She visited Africa many times in hopes of making a film, but eventually these trips resulted in two books of photography (*The last of the Nuba, 1974,* and (*The People of Kau, 1976*. Once again her work was praised for its beauty and castigated for its fascist art. When she was 70, Reinstahl learned to scuba dive and concentrated her photography on underwater coral life, resulting in a new book *Coral Garden, 1976.*

In 1993, when she was 91 years old, German director Ray Mueller made a film biography (*The Wonderful, Horrible Life of Leni Riefenstahl.* The release of the film coincided with the English translation of her autobiography *Leni Riefenstahl: A Biography* In both the film and the book, Riefenstahl claims her innocence and mistreatment, never realizing the effect that her films had on promoting the Nazi cause. Ray Muller was quoted in (*Time Magazine* as declaring "she is still a 30's diva, after all and not accustomed to being crossed. By the second day, I was asking prickly

questions and she was having choleric fits." In his review of the film, *New York Times* film critic Vincent Canby concluded "Ms. Riefenstahl doesn't come across as an especially likable character which is to her credit and Mr. Muller's. She is beyond likability. She is too complex, too particular and too arrogant to be seen as either sympathetic or unsympathetic. There's the suspicion that she had always had arrogance and that it, backed up by her singular talent, is what helped to shape her wonderful and horrible life."

Further Reading

Kampf in Schnee und Eis (*Battle in Snow and Ice,* 1933), *Hinter den Kulissen des Reichsparteitagsfilms* (*In the Wings of the Party Rally Film,* 1935), and *Schönheit im Olympischen Kampf* (*Beauty in Olympic Competition,* 1937) are contemporary accounts, the first ghostwritten, by Riefenstahl on her work. They are available only in German. *The Last of the Nuba* (1974), *The People of Kau* (1976), and *Coral Gardens* (1978), her later books of still photography, exist in English editions as well. After the end of the war Riefenstahl wrote a number of statements and letters to editors defending herself. She also worked on an autobiography. She gave a lengthy interview for *Leni Riefenstahl Part I and II* (one half-hour each), produced by Camera Three for 1973 broadcast by the CBS Television Network. Three full-length books on her are: Renata BergPan, *Leni Riefenstahl* (1980); David B. Hinton, *The Films of Leni Riefenstahl* (1978), the most apologetic; and Glenn B. Infield's more gossipy *Leni Riefenstahl, The Fallen Film Goddess* (1976), all in English. The most important article by an American film critic is Susan Sontag's "Fascinating Fascism" in the *New York Review of Books* (February 6, 1975). □

Louis Riel

Louis Riel (1844-1885) was a Canadian rebel who led uprisings in the west in 1870 and 1884-1885 on behalf of the Métis people.

Louis Riel was born at Saint-Boniface, Manitoba, on Oct. 23, 1844, of Métis parents. His quickness of mind was early recognized by the priests at Saint-Boniface, and Riel was sent east to study at the Seminaire de St-Sulpice in Montreal. Riel decided not to become a priest, however, and he returned to the Red River area. In 1869 he became the secretary of the Comité National des Métis, an organization created by the population of Assiniboia, who were of mixed Native American and European heritage. He attempted to preserve their rights when the Canadian west was transferred from the Hudson's Bay Company to the Dominion.

As the brightest and best educated of the Métis, Riel soon became the unchallenged leader of his people, although he was only 25 years old. Proclaiming himself president of the provisional government of the Northwest Territories, he dispatched emissaries to Ottawa to negotiate with the Canadian government, and he was successful in securing the early grant of provincial status for the territory, now named Manitoba, and promises of fair treatment for the

Métis. Unfortunately Riel was somewhat overzealous in maintaining order in his domain, and he ordered the execution of Thomas Scott, a troublemaker from Ontario. The execution roused passions in Ontario, a military force was sent to Manitoba, and Riel was forced to flee.

For the next 14 years Riel was in limbo. Although he was three times elected to Parliament by Manitoba constituencies, he was never able to take his seat. In 1875, in fact, he was declared an outlaw. For part of the time he was in an insane asylum, and he was teaching school in the American West in 1884, when events again brought him to the fore.

Riel was approached by representatives of the Métis and other dissident groups in 1884 and asked to return to Canada. He leaped at the chance and was soon leading yet another rebellion against Ottawa. By this time he was clearly mad, believing himself the Messiah and certain that God was on his side. Unfortunately for his rebellion, the Canadian Pacific Railway was on the side of the government, and troops moved west with surprising speed. After a few skirmishes the second Riel rebellion was crushed, and Riel found himself a prisoner.

Soon the rebel was brought to trial by a completely English-speaking court and jury, and predictably Riel was found guilty of high treason. An insanity commission reported that he was sane, the Cabinet refused to commute the sentence, and Riel mounted the gibbet at Regina on Nov. 16, 1885. His death stirred animosity between French and English in Canada to fever pitch, and relations between the two peoples remained strained ever thereafter.

Further Reading

Of the numerous biographies of Riel the best is George F. G. Stanley, *Louis Riel* (1963). See also Joseph Kinsey Howard, *Strange Empire: A Narrative of the Northwest* (1952), and George F. G. Stanley, *The Birth of Western Canada* (1961).

Additional Sources

Charlebois, Peter, *The life of Louis Riel,* Toronto: NC Press, 1978.
Flanagan, Thomas, *Louis 'David' Riel: prophet of the new world,* Toronto; Buffalo: University of Toronto Press, 1979.
Neering, Rosemary, *Louis Riel,* Don Mills, Ont.: Fitzhenry & Whiteside, 1977. □

Georg Friedrich Bernard Riemann

The German mathematician Georg Friedrich Bernard Riemann (1826-1866) was one of the founders of algebraic geometry. His concept of geometric space cleared the way for the general theory of relativity.

On Sept. 17, 1826, Georg Riemann was born in Breselenz. Shortly afterward, the family moved to Quickborn, Holstein, where his father, a Lutheran minister, assumed the pastorate. Riemann senior quickly recognized his younger son's mathematical talent. When Georg was 10 years old, he was placed under a mathematics tutor who soon found himself outdistanced by his pupil.

Riemann had planned on a career in the Church in accordance with his father's wishes. In 1846 he entered the University of Göttingen as a student of theology and philology. But mathematics called, and he had probably already decided to change his mind, should his father consent. He may have strengthened his argument by a grand attempt to prove Genesis mathematically. The proof was hardly valid, but Riemann senior appreciated the effort and gave his blessing to the mathematical career. In 1847 Georg transferred to the University of Berlin, where such vigorous innovators as K. G. J. Jacobi, P. G. Lejeune-Dirichlet, J. Steiner, and F. G. M. Eisenstein had created a livelier atmosphere for learning. In 1849 Riemann returned to Göttingen to prepare for his doctoral examinations under Wilhelm Weber, the famous electrodynamicist.

Riemann Surfaces

Riemann's doctoral dissertation was, in Karl Friedrich Gauss's words, the product of a "gloriously fertile originality." Its novel ideas were further developed in three papers published in 1857. Here is a crude explanation of the principal novelty:

A complex number may be represented by a point in a plane. A function (single-valued) of a complex variable is a rule which pairs each point in one plane with a *unique* point in another plane. Imagine a fly wandering about the surface of a plate-glass window. As the fly moves from point to point, its shadow moves from point to point on the floor of the room. Each point which the fly occupies on the window determines a *unique* point that its shadow occupies on the floor.

Now suppose that the floor is a highly reflective surface. The incoming light strikes the floor and is reflected to the wall, and we see a *second* image of our wandering fly. Now each position of the fly on the window determines two shadows—one on the floor and one on the wall.

But that is not quite right. There are some positions in which the fly still casts only one shadow. These are the points which throw the shadow on the line of intersection between floor and wall. Let us call these points branch points.

Now suppose that we replace the plate-glass window with *two* parallel sheets of plate glass (like a double window for insulation against cold). We endow the sheets with the following magical properties: any object on the outside sheet will cast a shadow only on the floor, and any object on the inside sheet will cast a shadow only on the wall. Furthermore, we join the two sheets along the line of branch points, so that they now form a single surface. Our fly may crawl from one sheet to the other, but to each point that he occupies on the glass surface, there once again corresponds one unique location of his shadow.

This is what Riemann did for multiple-valued functions of a complex variable. His surfaces restore single-valuedness to functions and at the same time provide a method of representing these functions geometrically. Moreover, it turns out that the analytic properties of many functions are mirrored by the geometric (topological) properties of their associated Riemann surfaces.

His Göttingen Lecture

After successfully defending his dissertation, Riemann applied for an opening at the Göttingen Observatory but did not get the job. He next set his sights on becoming a privatdozent (unpaid lecturer) at the university. There were two hurdles to surmount before he could obtain the lectureship: a probationary essay and a trial lecture before the assembled faculty. The former, a paper on trigonometric series, included the definition of the "Riemann integral" in almost the form that it appears in current textbooks. The essay was submitted in 1853.

For his trial lecture Riemann submitted three possible titles, fully expecting Gauss to abide by tradition and assign one of the first two. But the third topic was one with which Gauss himself had struggled for many years. He was curious to hear what Riemann had to say "On the Hypotheses Which Lie at the Foundations of Geometry."

The lecture that Riemann delivered to the Göttingen faculty on June 10, 1854, is one of the great masterpieces of mathematical creation and exposition. Riemann wove together and generalized three crucial discoveries of the 19th century: the extension of Euclidean geometry to n dimensions; the logical consistency of geometries that are not

Euclidean; and the intrinsic geometry of a surface, in terms of its metric and curvature in the neighborhood of a point. In his synthesis Riemann demonstrated the existence of an infinite number of different geometries, each of which could be characterized by its peculiar differential form. Finally, he pointed out that the choice of a particular geometry to represent the structure of real physical space was a matter for physics, not mathematics.

The impact of the lecture was enormous but delayed. Riemann worked out some of the analytical machinery in a memoir of 1861 on the conduction of heat, but the lecture itself was not published until 1868. Twenty years later a respected historian noted simply that the paper "had excited much interest and discussion." By 1908 the same historian was calling it a "celebrated memoir" which had attracted "general attention to the subject of non-Euclidean geometry."

"Riemann Hypothesis"

Riemann spent 3 years as a privatdozent. In 1857 he was appointed assistant professor, and 2 years later, when Dirichlet died, Riemann succeeded him in the chair of Gauss. After 1860 the honors, including international recognition, came thick and fast. He died on July 20, 1866, in Selasca, Italy.

Riemann's special genius was the penetrating vision that enabled him to see through a mass of obscuring detail and perceive the submerged foundations of a theory intuitively. This uncanny talent was most obvious in his geometric work, but the most remarkable instance occurs in analytic number theory. In an 1859 paper on prime numbers, Riemann proved several properties of what came to be called "Riemann's zeta function." Several other properties of the function he simply stated without proof. After his death a note was found, saying that he had *deduced* these properties "from the expression of it (the function) which, however, I did not succeed in simplifying enough to publish."

To this day no one has the slightest idea of what this "expression" might be. All but one of the properties have since been proved. The last one, now called the "Riemann hypothesis," still awaits its conqueror, despite the efforts of several generations of talented mathematicians.

Further Reading

The best biography of Riemann in English is in Eric T. Bell, *Men of Mathematics* (1937). He is discussed in the first volume of Ganesh Prasad, *Some Great Mathematicians of the Nineteenth Century: Their Lives and Their Works* (1933). The place of Riemannian geometry in relativity theory is discussed in Jagjit Singh, *Great Ideas of Modern Mathematics: Their Nature and Use* (1959). For a nontechnical introduction to non-Euclidean geometries see Richard Courant and Herbert Robbins, *What Is Mathematics?* (1941).

Additional Sources

Riemann, topology, and physics, Boston: Birkhauser, 1987. □

Tilman Riemenschneider

Tilman Riemenschneider (1468-1531) was the most famous of all German late-Gothic sculptors. His style of carving is beautifully refined, with nervous, crackling drapery folds and superb surface finish of the alabaster, sandstone, or lindenwood with which he worked.

Tilman Riemenschneider was born in Osterode, Saxony. After traveling in the Rhineland and Swabia, he settled in the prince-bishopric of Würzburg in 1483. He became a citizen 2 years later and was mayor of the city in 1520-1521. As a Würzburg councilor, in 1525 he came into conflict with the Church authorities during the Peasants' War—an expression of the Reformation—and was imprisoned and tortured. He died in Würzburg on July 7, 1531.

Like his contemporaries at Nuremberg, notably Veit Stoss, Riemenschneider combined realism with picturesqueness. The figure groups on his altarpieces are crowded and expressively posed, and the folds of their garments are deep-cut and crisp. He developed a highly individual style characterized by a high-pitched sensibility and an intense seriousness. His figures are carefully posed and often seem to affect ungainly attitudes; their expressions are somewhat more restrained than the figures by Stoss.

Riemenschneider's chief early works are the wooden altarpiece of the parish church of Münnerstadt (1490-1492; portions are in Berlin and Munich, the rest are *in situ*); the stone figures of Adam and Eve carved for the portal of the Marienkapelle in Würzburg (1491-1493), which are among the earliest known realistically treated nude figure sculptures in Germany; and a sandstone Virgin for the Marienkapelle (all three in the Mainfränkisches Museum, Würzburg), of which many variations, generally in wood, made Riemenschneider the most famous sculptor of his day.

Between 1500 and 1520 Riemenschneider carved the superb *Assumption of the Virgin* wooden altarpiece for the little country church at Creglingen, the stone tomb of Bishop Rudolph von Scherenberg in the Cathedral of Würzburg, and the wooden Altar of the Holy Blood in the Jakobskirche in Rothenburg ob der Tauber (1501-1505). In the center of the Rothenburg altar is the *Last Supper;* on the wings are the *Entry of Christ into Jerusalem* and *Christ in Gethsemane,* brilliantly executed in low relief. Sensing the beauty of the wood itself, Riemenschneider frequently did not polychrome his altarpieces, a novelty at this time.

Riemenschneider's masterpiece of funerary sculpture is the monumental memorial of the emperor Henry II and his wife, Kunigunde, in Bamberg Cathedral (1499-1513), executed in marble. Relief carvings on the sides of the tomb depict legendary events from their lives in a style that reveals a new human understanding.

Further Reading

There is no monograph on Riemenschneider in English. Bernd Lohse and others, eds., *Art Treasures of Germany* (1958), contains some biographical information on Riemenschneider and reproductions of his works. See also Clara Waters, *Painters, Sculptors, Architects, Engravers and Their Works* (1899).

Additional Sources

Bier, Justus, *Tilmann Riemenschneider, his life and work,* Lexington, KY: University Press of Kentucky, 1982. ☐

Cola di Rienzi

The Roman popular leader Cola di Rienzi (1313-1354) was tribune of Rome during a period of the Avignonese papacy. He led a republican movement that restored for a time the dream, if not the reality, of Roman greatness.

Cola di Rienzo (incorrectly but popularly Rienzi; was born Niccola di Lorenzo Gabrini in Rome. His father was a tavern keeper whose Christian name, Lorenzo, had been shortened to Rienzo. As a boy, living at Anagni, Cola di Rienzi read voraciously of the heroes and deeds of ancient Rome. The poets and historians who told of the glories of the ancient city filled him with a burning zeal to restore its former greatness.

As a very young man, Rienzi attracted attention in Rome when, with eloquence and aided by the presence of monuments of antiquity all around him, he reminded his fellow citizens of the might of the empire. Rome had once bestowed order and justice first upon itself and then upon the world, and Rienzi believed it could do so again.

Rienzi became a notary and in 1343 was sent on a public mission to Avignon. In Avignon he won the favor of Pope Clement VI, whom he exhorted to return to Rome and to put an end to the corruption that prevailed there under the disorderly rule of the nobles. Rienzi returned to Rome in April 1344, and he then made plans for a general uprising, gathering ever greater support with a series of brilliant speeches.

On May 20, 1347, Rienzi appeared at the Capitol with the bishop of Orvieto, the Pope's vicar, and proclaimed to the Roman people that from that moment the republic was restored. Shouts of approval met his promises of equal justice and fair taxation, and he found himself at once in the possession of complete authority in Rome. The nobles fled in dismay, and Rienzi was given the title of tribune of the people.

Rienzi's rule began well. He dispensed justice impartially, gave attention to the storage of surplus food, and systematically drained nearby marshlands for cultivation. For a brief time, security and peace made the hearts of Roman citizens glad that the vicious and arbitrary rule of the aristocrats was past.

Cola di Rienzi (center, with arms extended)

On Aug. 1, 1347, representatives of the Italian cities, on Rienzi's invitation, met at Rome to consider the question of a united Italy. Many of the Italian communes, though not all, gave this plan and Rienzi's leadership their formal recognition. Dazzled by his own eloquence and apparent success, Rienzi then staged, on August 15, a ceremony of incredible pomp and ostentation in which he was installed and crowned tribune. Rienzi's extravagance led him to decree that all Italians were free and citizens of Rome and that only they had the authority to choose an emperor.

Pretensions such as these and the growing ostentation of Rienzi's habits soon caused popular enthusiasm to diminish, and the Roman barons, led by Stefano Colonna, made plans to overthrow him. Pope Clement VI, who had earlier supported Rienzi, was offended by his efforts to create a Roman empire based exclusively on the will of the people and was now most eager to be rid of him. On November 20 Rienzi set out boldly with a Roman militia and met and defeated the barons in a battle in which Colonna, his bitterest enemy, was killed.

This victory caused Rienzi to lose all moderation. He became more arrogant in behavior and more sumptuous in dress. He was deaf to all pleas of the papal vicar, with whom he supposedly shared authority. The exasperated pope issued a bull on December 3 branding Rienzi a criminal and calling upon the Roman people to drive him out. With opposition mounting, Rienzi lost his vaunted courage and

abdicated on December 15. He then secluded himself for more than 2 years, appearing in Prague in July 1350. There he begged Emperor Charles IV to restore Italy to liberty, but Charles imprisoned him and then handed him over to the Pope in August 1352.

Clement VI died in December of that year, and his successor, Innocent VI, pardoned Rienzi, hoping to use him against the barons in Rome. The former tribune returned to Rome in August 1354 accompanied by the papal legate, Cardinal Gil Álvarez Carrillo de Albornoz. Rienzi was acclaimed and restored to power, but again he succumbed to the fatal weakness of failing to recognize the limits of his power. He grew insufferably tyrannical, and on Oct. 8, 1354, he was murdered by a Roman mob at the Capitol, and his body was then dragged through the streets.

Further Reading

The best account of Rienzi's life is in Ferdinand Gregorovius, *History of the City of Rome in the Middle Ages,* translated by Annie Hamilton (8 vols., 1900-1909). For a lively recent treatment see Will Durant, *The Renaissance* (1953). ☐

David Riesman

The American sociologist, writer, and social critic David Riesman (born 1909) was a leading authority on higher education and on developments in American society.

D avid Riesman was born in Philadelphia, Pennsylvania, in 1909. His father, also named David Riesman, was a well-known physician and professor of clinical medicine and later of the history of medicine at the University of Pennsylvania Medical School. Young Riesman attended William Penn Charter School, Harvard College, where he was one of the editors of *The Crimson,* and Harvard Law School, where he was one of the editors of the *Harvard Law Review.* In the following year he was a research fellow and worked with Professor Carl Friedrich of the Harvard Government Department, and the next year he served as a law clerk to Justice Brandeis of the U.S. Supreme Court.

After a year of law practice in Boston he spent four years at the University of Buffalo Law School. Riesman's interests were, from the beginning wider than research in, and the practice of law. During his years in Buffalo he published important articles on civil liberties and a major series of articles on the law of defamation and slander. He discussed in the latter, among other things, the then key question of whether a right to suit for group libel should be recognized, as in the case of anti-Semitic writings attacking Jews. By the mid-1940s these articles had been widely noted. In a year as a research fellow at the Columbia Law School he was able to discuss his rapidly developing wide-ranging interests—in community studies, in the new culture and personality orientation in anthropology, and in change

What (1964), had wide influence. The latter volume in particular reflected his deep concern with the dangers of an uncontrolled nuclear arms race, which had led to his becoming one of the founders of the Committees of Correspondence in 1960, a group organized under the auspices of the American Friends Service Committee.

In 1958 Riesman moved from the University of Chicago to Harvard, where he became the first Henry Ford II Professor of Social Sciences. He made a deep and long-lasting commitment to undergraduate education at Harvard, teaching a famous course on "American Character and Social Structure," serving on the faculty committee supervising the undergraduate social studies program, and connecting himself, both in research and as a faculty associate, with the life of the undergraduate houses at Harvard.

He had begun to work on higher education even before going to Harvard. He published *Constraint and Variety in American Education* in 1956, and from then on was engaged almost continuously in research and publication on American higher education. He published (with Christopher Jencks) the important *Academic Revolution* in 1968, *Academic Values and Mass Education* (with Joseph Gusfield and Zelda Gamson) in 1970, *The Perpetual Dream: Reform and Experiment in the American College* (with Gerald Grant) in 1978, and *On Higher Education: The Academic Enterprise in an Era of Rising Student Consumerism* in 1980, *Choosing A College President: Opportunities and Constraints,* and he contributed to and edited many other volumes on higher education.

Riesman carved out for himself a unique role in American intellectual life. While his research for more than 30 years centered on higher education, and he became known as perhaps the leading authority on this subject, serving on many committees and often consulted on searches for college presidents and other high officials, this was only one side of his interests. As the writer of some of the most insightful works on American character and society, he was regularly asked for his views on developments in American society. And because of his permanent concern with what he saw as the greatest danger facing mankind—nuclear war—he maintained a strong interest in foreign affairs and the development of American politics. In all this, he escaped labels. If any label was suitable, it was that of old-fashioned liberal, but he enrolled under no banner and his distinctive voice could never be mistaken as being part of a crowd.

in American society—with Margaret Mead and Ruth Benedict and Robert and Helen Merril Lynd. In a further stay in New York during World War II as deputy assistant district attorney for New York County and with Sperry Gyroscope he was able to study psychoanalysis with Erich Fromm and Harry Stack Sullivan.

After the war Riesman joined the staff of the University of Chicago, then perhaps the most exciting enterprise in undergraduate education in America, and helped develop a course on culture and personality. In 1948, on a leave at Yale Law School, he began work on his first major book, *The Lonely Crowd* (with Nathan Glazer and Reuel Denney), followed by *Faces in the Crowd* (with Nathan Glazer). Riesman combined some new techniques in the social sciences, in particular long qualitative interviews, with analysis of popular culture, radio, and magazines and books to describe what was happening to American character. *The Lonely Crowd,* published in 1950, became (especially in a revised and shortened version published by Anchor Books-Doubleday in 1953) one of the seminal works of the 1950s and established Riesman as a leading commentator on trends in American life.

His style in inquiry was to take a conventional viewpoint and to question it sharply. He himself called his mode of analysis "counter cyclical." He continued to sharpen a unique and remarkably insightful view of American society in discussions of youth, the relations between men and women, American education, and American foreign relations. His essays on these and other subjects, collected in *Individualism Reconsidered* (1954) and *Abundance for*

Further Reading

The work of David Riesman is discussed in a volume published in his honor, *On the Making of Americans* (1979), edited by Herbert J. Gans, Nathan Glazer, Joseph R. Gusfield, and Christopher Jencks. This volume has a complete bibliography of his works up to 1979. Riesman wrote a number of autobiographical pieces, among them the essay "Two Generations," which appeared in *Daedalus* in Spring 1964, and "Becoming an Academic Man," which is to appear in a volume of autobiographical essays by sociologists edited by Bennett M. Berger. □

Gerrit Thomas Rietveld

Gerrit Thomas Rietveld (1888-1964), architect and furniture designer, was a member of the group of Dutch artists and architects known as de Stijl. He was the first to give its esthetic program visible form.

Gerrit Rietveld was born on June 24, 1888, in Utrecht and lived there most of his life. He was trained as a cabinetmaker by his father (1899-1906) and as a jewelry designer in the studio of C. J. Begeer (1906-1911). For the next 8 years he was self-employed as a cabinetmaker while studying and working with the architect P. J. Klaarhamer. Rietveld's career as an independent architect began in 1919.

A commission to copy from photographs furniture designed by the American architect Frank Lloyd Wright for a client of the Dutch architect Robert van't Hoff brought Rietveld into contact with de Stijl (the Style), founded in 1917. De Stijl advocated a "pure" artistic expression based upon the interrelationship in space of rectangles of primary colors. Rietveld was a member of this group from 1919 to 1931, but already in 1917-1918 he had designed the so-called Red-Blue chair. Composed of a modular grid of square or rectangular sticks painted black and with a sustaining seat and back of red and blue rectangular plywood planes, this design enabled each element to maintain its own absolute identity because of the color scheme and the joinery. It was the first executed object to exhibit the artistic principles of de Stijl.

Rietveld applied the same interplay of rectangles to an architectural design in his remodeling of the groundfloor shop front of the G. & Z. C. Jewelry Store, Amsterdam (1920; destroyed). In 1921 he began a period of collaboration with the designer Truus Schröder-Schräder, for and with whom he designed the paradigm of de Stijl architecture, the Schröder House, Utrecht (1924). The flexible design of the two-story house included an upper floor which could be made into one large room by sliding back the movable partitions. Its interior extended out into the surroundings through balconies, corner casement windows, projecting floor and roof planes, and large areas of glass. The exterior was a de Stijl composition of particolored, stuccoed brick planes and painted steel stanchions that suggested an inner volume dynamically defined by discrete lines and planes, but not actually enclosed. It set the standard for the progressive architecture of the 1920s in Europe.

De Stijl principles also formed the series of designs for shop fronts (1924-1929) which, with large-scale housing projects, comprised the bulk of Rietveld's work of the late 1920s. The only one exceptional design from this period was a garage and chauffeur's quarters in Utrecht (1927-1928; now altered). Here his concern was as much for technique as for form. He used precast concrete slabs held in place by a frame of steel I-sections expressed as a de Stijl grid on the exterior. In 1928 Rietveld was one of the cofounders of the CIAM (International Congress of Modern Architecture).

By the 1930s Rietveld's time seemed to have passed. Commissions became fewer, although he continued to design furniture (Zig-Zag chair, 1934) and buildings. Most of the latter were country houses displaying the canonical white stucco cubes, large areas of glass, and flexible, open planning of the mature International Style in Europe (Hillebrandt House, The Hague, 1935). With renewed interest in de Stijl following World War II, Rietveld continued to design private houses (Stoop House, Velp, 1951) and again received important commissions, including the Hoograven Housing complex, Utrecht (1954-1957), the Jaarbeurs, Utrecht (1956), and the De Ploeg textile factory, Bergeyk (1956). He died in Utrecht on June 25, 1964.

Further Reading

The only monograph on Rietveld is Theodore M. Brown, *The Work of G. Rietveld* (1958), which includes an illustrated catalog of Rietveld's work, a bibliography, and translations of some of his writings. Hans Ludwig C. Jaffé, *De Stijl* (1960), discusses Rietveld's connection with the group. □

Jacob August Riis

Jacob August Riis (1849-1914), Danish-born American journalist and slum reformer, created new standards in civic responsibility regarding the poor and homeless in his reporting of New York City slum conditions.

Jacob Riis was born May 3, 1849, in Ribe, Denmark, one of 14 children. His father was a school-teacher. Young Riis early showed a sensitive disposition and a faith in people that would sustain him through difficult days. Trained in carpentry, he emigrated to New York in 1870. Riis never forgot the bitter experiences with poverty and ill-treatment that followed, but they did not mar his hopeful outlook. In 1874 he became editor of the *South Brooklyn News* and began developing his skills as a reporter. In 1877 he joined the *New York Tribune* and was assigned to the Police Department in the slums of the lower East Side.

Although Riis was in some respects sentimental in outlook, he was able to investigate and report conditions that made cynics of less hardy journalists. Riis turned his energy and keen eye for human-interest stories into a weapon for rousing New Yorkers to the evil state of their slums. His articles for the *Tribune,* the *Sun* (which he joined in 1890), and elsewhere probed every aspect of human circumstances: sanitary conditions, family life, the fate of women and children, and even treatment of dead victims of hunger and cold. Riis's articles and exposés turned light on dark tenements, vice centers, lax police administration, firetraps, and other areas of civic neglect. *How the Other Half Lives* (1890) brought him fame and introduced him to his lifelong friend and associate Theodore Roosevelt, who termed him the most useful citizen in New York.

Although Riis never saw beyond the conditions to the causes, those conditions were so in need of correction that his reports constituted major reform. *Out of Mulberry Street* (1898), *The Battle with the Slum* (1902), and *Children of the Tenement* (1903) continued to report investigations which resulted not only in cleansing the city of sore spots but made Riis influential as writer and lecturer in cities throughout the land. Thanks to his efforts, Mulberry Bend, notorious for its crime and decay, became a park; its Jacob A. Riis Neighborhood House is symbolic of his benign crusades in behalf of children.

Riis married his childhood sweetheart in 1876 and raised a family. She died in 1905, and 2 years later he married his young secretary. Riis's energy and earnest concern took him about the country and finally cost him his health, which rest cures could not renew. He died May 26, 1914, at his summer house in Barre, Mass.

Further Reading

Riis's *The Making of an American* (1901; new ed. 1970) is a folk masterpiece. His childhood memoirs are in *The Old Town* (1909). A biography is Louise Ware, *Jacob A. Riis: Police Reporter, Reformer, Useful Citizen* (1938).

Additional Sources

Meyer, Edith Patterson., *"Not charity, but justice": the story of Jacob A. Riis,* New York: Vanguard Press, 1974.
Jacob A. Riis: photographer & citizen, London: Gordon Fraser, 1975.

Ware, Louise, *Jacob A. Riis, police reporter, reformer, useful citizen,* Millwood, N.Y.: Kraus Reprint Co., 1975, 1938. □

James Whitcomb Riley

American poet James Whitcomb Riley (1849-1916), often called the "People's Laureate" or the "Hoosier Poet," established a reputation for dialect poetry designed for recitation and easy reading.

James Whitcomb Riley was born on Oct. 7, 1849, in Greenfield, Ind. His father, a successful small-town lawyer, allowed him to shape his education by instinct rather than formal precedents. Oratory, drama, painting, and music took James's earliest attention. He idolized Charles Dickens. Poets Robert Burns, for dialect verse, and Henry Longfellow, for moral precepts, were his models. Young Riley wrote voluminously and saved every scrap, particularly the local-color sketches, incorporating anecdotes he heard from the country people around the courthouse. His musical ear was good; he played the violin, guitar, and banjo. His verbal ear was even better.

At the age of 16 Riley left school to become a "house, sign, and ornamental painter," wandering around Indiana. He read law for a while but took to the road with a traveling medicine man from whose wagon he learned to entertain the public with recitations in dialect. When he returned to Greenfield, he started a career in journalism, beginning with the local paper and expanding his horizons gradually. At one time he was local editor of the *Anderson Democrat.*

The *Indianapolis Journal's* invitation to join its staff was the door to success. Riley published his dialect poems under the name "Benjamin F. Johnson of Boone," and by 1883 the demand was enough to issue a pamphlet edition. Calling his first collection *The Old Swimmin' Hole and 'Leven More Poems,* he did not need a public-opinion poll to tell him he had found his métier. He sold more than half a million copies of this book, followed it with 40 more books before his death, and on platforms across the country entertained audiences with homely philosophy and dramatic monologues. *Old-Fashioned Roses* (London, 1888) captured an English audience. *Pipes o' Pan at Zekesbury* (1888), *Rhymes of Childhood* (1890), and *Here at Home* (1893) expanded his American reputation.

Riley's attractions were personal, not cerebral. His winsome nature was contagious in a public gathering, and he was determined to give his listener "simple sentiments that come from the heart." His poems were never burdened with ideas, complexities, ambiguities. He invented a whole gallery of Hoosiers; Riley was the first to admit that they spoke patent clichés in a dialect such as no real Hoosier ever spoke. At his best, he captured a tranquil America, wholesome, eccentric, sentimental, bucolic. "The Raggedy Man," "Little Orphant Annie," and "Nine Little Goblins" attest to his vitality within his limited range. He died on July 22, 1916.

Further Reading

The Complete Works of James Whitcomb Riley (6 vols., 1913) was edited by Edmund H. Eitel, and *Letters of James Whitcomb Riley* (1930) by William Lyon Phelps. Two biographical studies incorporate criticism with reminiscence: Jeannette Covert Nolan, *James Whitcomb Riley* (1941), and Richard Crowder, *Those Innocent Years: The Legacy and Inheritance of a Hero of the Victorian Era, James Whitcomb Riley* (1957). See also Marcus Dickey, *The Youth of James Whitcomb Riley* (1919). □

Rainer Maria Rilke

Rainer Maria Rilke (1875-1926) is considered the greatest lyric poet of modern Germany. His work is marked by a mystical sense of God and death.

Born in Prague on Dec. 4, 1875, Rainer Maria Rilke grew up in a middle-class milieu he called "petit bourgeois," of which he later felt ashamed. In spite of his sensitive, almost feminine nature, he was expected to become an army officer and was forced to spend 5 years (1886-1891) in the military academies of St. Pölten and Mährisch-Weisskirchen. After graduation from high school, he enrolled for a year as a student of literature at the German University of Prague (1895-1896) before moving away from his family. He continued his studies at the University of Munich for the next few years.

Early Works

At 19 Rilke began his literary career by publishing at his own expense a collection of indifferent love poems, *Leben und Lieder* (1894; *Life and Songs*), written in the conventional style of the Heine tradition. This was followed in 1895 by a collection of poems, *Larenopfer,* revealing a sentimental attachment to his native Prague. Both of these slim volumes as well as the next ones, *Traumgekrönt* (1896; *Dream-Crowned*), *Advent* (1897), and *Mir zur Feier* (1899; *Celebrating Myself*), fail to show the sharpness of observation that characterizes his later verse. His prose tales of this period, *Am Leben hin* (1898; *On the Rim of Life*), also contain little to foreshadow his later genius.

In his second, religious or mystic, period (1899-1903), Rilke, opposed to the naturalism of his time, became an esthetic symbolist and, above all, a religious prophet and humanitarian. In August 1900 he settled in the north German artist colony Worpswede near Bremen, met a young sculptress, Clara Westhoff, and married her. There he wrote a monograph, *Worpswede* (1902), about the painters whose work he observed, and contributed book reviews to the *Bremer Tageblatt.* His marriage, doomed almost from the start, remained a brief episode, although it was never formally dissolved. A few months after the birth (Dec. 12, 1901) of his daughter, Ruth, he departed for Paris, leaving behind his wife and child.

Two books of poetry, written for the most part during his time in the painters' colony, eventually brought Rilke fame. One was *Das Buch der Bilder* (1901, 1906; *The Book of Images*), a volume of individual poems without a common theme, marked by intense musicality and the ability to conjure up moods almost independent of the meaning of the words that are used. The other volume contains a cycle of religious poems, *Das Stundenbuch* (1905; *The Book of Hours*), consisting of three parts, each marking a stage in his development: *Das Buch vom mönchischen Leben* (1899), *Von der Pilgerschaft* (1901), and *Von der Armut und vom Tode* (1903). Its genesis was Rilke's two trips to Russia, undertaken in 1899 and 1900. His delightful, childlike stories, *Vom Lieben Gott* (1900; *Stories of God*), reveal a "circling around God," as he himself calls it, in which God and the believer are mutually interdependent. These early works are sincerely mystical, revealing his sense of humility and brotherhood, his simple faith and genuine compassion for the poor and exploited.

Life in Paris

Rilke's life in Paris (1902-1910) initiated a new phase, marked by the most significant turn in his poetic career: his new attitude toward objective reality and his attempt to apprehend the very essence of things, animate as well as inanimate. The commission to write a monograph on the great French sculptor Auguste Rodin had brought Rilke to Paris. He served Rodin for a while as secretary, and he admired him more than any other living artist. Rodin taught

Rilke not to wait passively for inspiration but rather to go out and look for subjects, to observe and study tangible objects. Rilke now developed a new concept of the artist as the hardworking craftsman. This new attitude manifests itself in those poems that appeared under the title *Neue Gedichte* (1907, 1908; *New Poems*). Here one finds his famous *Ding-Gedichte* (thing-poems), poetic re-creations of things he had seen and observed and which to him become impersonal symbols: animals and flowers, landscapes, and, above all, works of art.

During a trip to Sweden in 1904, Rilke composed the first version of *Die Weise von Liebe und Tod des Cornet Christoph Rilke,* a romantic, even melodramatic, sentimental account of the last hours of a young aspiring cavalry officer. Later he tried to disassociate himself from this poem that became his most popular work. After the publication of his *Neue Gedichte,* Rilke set about completing an autobiographical novel begun in Rome 4 years before. In this, his only major narrative work, *Die Aufzeichnungen des Malte Laurids Brigge* (1910 *Notebook of Malte Laurids Brigge*), he tells the story of his own inner suffering during his lonely Paris years.

With the completion of *Malte Laurids Brigge* in the winter of 1909/1910, Rilke's Paris time came to an end; he spent only 18 months of the next 4 1/2 years in Paris. These were the years of an inner crisis, and in his utter restlessness and despair he moved from country to country. Anxious to explore new territories, he traveled in the winter 1910/1911 to North African countries, Algiers, Tunis, and Egypt, and from November 1912 to February 1913 he lived in Spain. Amid the profound hopelessness and frustration of these years, however, was one event which was to change Rilke's whole literary career: Princess Marie of Thurn and Taxis offered him the hospitality of her Castle Duino, near Trieste, on the Dalmatian coast. Here in 1912 he began to compose a series of elegies that were to become his ultimate poetic achievement. They were not, however, completed until 10 years later.

Later Years

When the war broke out in August 1914, Rilke was caught in Leipzig and was forced to remain in Germany. Most of the next 5 years he spent in and around Munich, except for 7 months' service in the Austrian army. In the first days of the war, Rilke passed through a brief period of exaltation and wrote his patriotic *Fünf Gesänge* (Five Songs). But this initial enthusiasm and solidarity with his patriotic countrymen soon gave way to indifference and, finally, to outright opposition to the German war effort.

In June 1919 Rilke accepted an invitation for a lecture tour in Switzerland, where he remained, except for a few sojourns in Italy and France, including a 7-month stay in Paris in 1925, until the end of his life. During the first year or two, he searched desperately for a refuge where he could take up the cycle of poems that he had left unfinished for so long. He discovered in the summer of 1921 Muzot, a deserted medieval tower, hardly habitable, near Sierre in the canton of Valais. Here in February 1922 he completed within a few days the cycle of poems he had begun in Duino

in 1912. Dedicated to his hostess and benefactress, Princess Marie, he called them in gratitude *Duineser Elegien* (*Duino Elegies*). Their publication in 1923 marked the high point of his career, and even Rilke himself, critical of his own work, regarded them as his most important achievement. The great themes of the *Elegien* are man's loneliness, the perfection of the angels, life and death, love and lovers, and the task of the poet. They were followed by the *Sonette an Orpheus* (*Sonnets to Orpheus*), a total of 55 poems which represent the other aspect of Rilke's vision: his sense of joy, affirmation, and praise.

In his last years (1923-1926) Rilke turned more and more to French literature, not only translating André Gide and Paul Valéry, but also writing poems in French (*Poèmes français*). He died of leukemia on Dec. 29, 1926, in a sanatorium in Valmont above Montreux.

Further Reading

A truly satisfactory biographical study of Rilke cannot be undertaken until all his papers become available. A first serious attempt was made by Eliza M. Butler in her monograph, *Rainer Maria Rilke* (1941), and later by Jean Rodolphe de Salis in a book which covers only the last 7 years of Rilke's life, *Rainer Maria Rilke: The Years in Switzerland* (1964). For analysis of Rilke's writings, the works of two American scholars are recommended: Frank H. Wood, *Rainer Maria Rilke: The Ring of Forms* (1958), and Heinz F. Peters, *Rainer Maria Rilke: Masks and the Man* (1960). Useful background material is in Cecil M. Bowra, *Heritage of Symbolism* (1943), and particularly in the short work on German literature by Ronald Gray, *The German Tradition in Literature, 1871-1945* (1965), which includes an incisive interpretation of some of the key works of Rilke.

Additional Sources

Freedman, Ralph, *Life of a poet: a biography of Rainer Maria Rilke,* New York: Farrar, Straus & Giroux, 1995.

Hendry, J. F., *The sacred threshold: a life of Rainer Maria Rilke,* Manchester: Carcanet New Press, 1983.

Kleinbard, David, *The beginning of terror: a psychological study of Rainer Maria Rilke's life and work,* New York: New York University Press, 1993.

Leppmann, Wolfgang, *Rilke: a life,* New York: Fromm International Pub. Corp., 1984.

Nalewski, Horst, *Rainer Maria Rilke,* Leipzig: Bibliographisches Institut, 1976.

Prater, Donald A., *A ringing glass: the life of Rainer Maria Rilke,* Oxford; New York: Clarendon Press, 1993.

Tavis, Anna A., *Rilke's Russia: a cultural encounter,* Evanston, Ill.: Northwestern University Press, 1994. □

Jean Nicolas Arthur Rimbaud

Jean Nicolas Arthur Rimbaud (1854-1891), the marvelous boy-poet of French literature, established in a few short years his reputation for hallucinative verbal creation, only to give up poetry at the age of 19.

The tempestuous life of Arthur Rimbaud his relations with Paul Verlaine, his idea of the poet as seer and of the derangement of the senses are all part of the legend. His literary fame depends primarily upon the poem *Le Bateau ivre* and the remarkable volumes called *Les Illuminations* and *Une Saison en Enfer*. His abandonment of art and "the ancient parapets of Europe" has made Rimbaud a symptomatic and fascinating figure of alienation in the modern world.

A brilliant student in his native town of Charleville, Rimbaud published his first known French verses (*Les Étrennes des orphelins*) in *La Revue pour tous* for Jan. 2, 1870. Other early poems were *Sensation, Ophélie, Credo in Unam* (later called *Soleil et chair*), and *Le Dormeur du val*. *Les Chercheuses de poux* is a memorable example of beauty created from what seems at first a most unpromising subject; and *Voyelles,* with its coloring of the vowels ("A black, E white, I red, U green, O blue: vowels. . ."), aroused considerable interest in the aspect of synesthesia known as *audition colorée* (colored hearing).

On May 15, 1871, Rimbaud wrote his famous *Lettre du voyant* to a friend, Paul Demeny: "I say that one must be a *seer,* make himself a *seer.* The Poet makes himself a *seer* by a long, immense and reasoned *derangement* of *all the senses.* . . . He exhausts in himself all the poisons, to preserve only their quintessences. . . . For he arrives at the *unknown* . . . ."

In late September 1871 Rimbaud joined Verlaine in Paris, bringing with him the manuscript of *Le Bateauivre,*

one of the most remarkable poems of the century. It describes the adventures of a boat left free to drift down American rivers after its crew have been murdered by screaming Native Americans. The boat's progress is traced from its first exaltation at its freedom to its awakening on the stormy "poem of the sea," through a wild tumult of snows and tides and suns and hurricanes, amid vast imagery from the beginning of the world, until it becomes at last only a waterlogged plank, nostalgic for Europe and no longer worth salvaging. The poem is a marvel of hallucinative evocation and seems in a way to foreshadow Rimbaud's own strange life.

The turbulent relationship between Verlaine and Rimbaud ended finally with Verlaine in prison for shooting his friend in the wrist and with Rimbaud disoriented and restless. Rimbaud had *Une Saison en Enfer* printed in Belgium in 1873 and distributed a few copies, but he did not even claim the rest of the edition. *Les Illuminations* did not appear until Verlaine published the volume in 1886. Meanwhile, Rimbaud had given up poetry forever.

After years of wandering, Rimbaud lived as an African explorer, trader, and gunrunner. In 1888 he was at Harar working for an exporter of coffee, hides, and musk. A tumor of the knee forced his return to Marseilles in 1891, where his right leg was amputated. He died in the hospital there on Nov. 10, 1891, at the age of 37.

Critics have called Rimbaud one of the creators of free verse for such poems as *Marine* and *Mouvement* in *Les Illuminations.* Rimbaud had written in *Une Saison en Enfer:* "I believed I could acquire supernatural powers. Well! I must bury my imagination and my memories!" He apparently wrote nothing more after his farewell to letters at the age of 19.

Further Reading

Rimbaud's works have been extensively translated into English. Biographies in English are Enid Starkie, *Arthur Rimbaud* (1938; rev. ed. 1961), and Elisabeth M. Hanson, *My Poor Arthur: A Biography of Arthur Rimbaud* (1960). Useful critical studies of the poet include Cecil Arthur Hackett, *Rimbaud* (1957); Wilbur Merrill Frohock, *Rimbaud's Poetic Practice: Image and Theme in the Major Poems* (1963); John Porter Houston, *The Design of Rimbaud's Poetry* (1963); Gwendolyn Bays, *The Orphic Vision; Seer Poets from Novalis to Rimbaud* (1964); and Wallace Fowlie, *Rimbaud* (1966), a rewriting of his earlier *Rimbaud: The Myth of Childhood* (1946) and *Rimbaud's Illuminations* (1953).

Additional Sources

Borer, Alain, *Rimbaud in Abyssinia,* New York: William Morrow, 1991.

Carre, Jean Marie, *A season in hell: the life of Arthur Rimbaud,* New York: AMS Press, 1979.

Delahaye, Ernest, *Rimbaud,* Monaco: Editions Sauret, 1993.

Forbes, Duncan, *Rimbaud in Ethiopia,* Hythe, England: Volturna Press, 1979.

Hare, Humphrey, *Sketch for a portrait of Rimbau,* New York, Haskell House Publishers, 1974.

Petitfils, Pierre, *Rimbaud,* Charlottesville: University Press of Virginia, 1987.

Starkie, Enid, *Arthur Rimbaud,* Westport, Conn.: Greenwood Press, 1978, 1961. ☐

William Rimmer

William Rimmer (1816-1879) was probably the most individual and independent American sculptor in the 19th century. He was also a painter and a physician.

William Rimmer was born in Liverpool, England, on Feb. 20, 1816. At the age of 2 he was brought to Nova Scotia and at 10 to Boston, Mass., with which city he was primarily associated. In 1840 he began his artistic career as an itinerant portrait painter and also studied medicine, which he began to practice in the mid-1850s. At the same time he began carving directly in stone, producing such works as *St. Stephen,* a colossal granite head that is very personal in its display of fierce emotionalism and full of life. In his use of granite as a favored medium, he departed from the smooth, unbroken surfaces of the contemporary neoclassicists.

Falling Gladiator (1861), Rimmer's best-known sculpture, was done for his most important patron, Stephen Perkins. Although the work was classical in theme, the sense of strain and struggle in it was unlike any other sculpture done at the time, and here Rimmer's knowledge of anatomy was well utilized. The work, shown in the Paris Salon of 1863, appeared so lifelike that some thought it had been cast from a human model. In 1864 he received his one significant public commission, the statue of Alexander Hamilton for Commonwealth Avenue in Boston. Although rigorous and tense, this granite statue is more fussy and less vital than most of the artist's other works.

Rimmer lectured on art anatomy in Boston and conducted a school of drawing and modeling. From 1866 to 1870 he was director of the Cooper Union School of Design for Women in New York City. On his return to Boston, he taught at the school of the Boston Museum of Fine Arts. His last two surviving sculptures are *Fighting Lions* and the *Dying Centaur* (both 1871).

Rimmer has often been called the "American Michelangelo" because of his emphasis upon personal, tragic symbolism and his high standard of anatomical expressiveness. He had early come under the influence of the painter Washington Allston, whose personal, romantic classicism and sense of mystery undoubtedly contributed to the development of Rimmer's art. In the sensuous surfaces of his sculptures with their alternating patterns of light and dark, he anticipated the impressionistic sculpture of the French artist Auguste Rodin. Rimmer is considered primarily a sculptor, but his paintings are arousing interest today. He was also one of the greatest American draftsmen of the 19th century, and his book, *Art Anatomy* (1877), shows his ability as a draftsman and his anatomical knowledge. He died in South Milford, Mass., on Aug. 20, 1879.

Further Reading

Two studies of Rimmer are Truman H. Bartlett, *The Art Life of William Rimmer, Sculptor, Painter, and Physician* (1882), and Lincoln Kirstein, *William Rimmer, 1816-1879* (1946), published by the Whitney Museum of American Art. ☐

Nikolai Andreevich Rimsky-Korsakov

Nikolai Andreevich Rimsky-Korsakov (1844-1908), composer, conductor, and pedagogue, was a member of the Russian "Mighty Five." He was largely responsible for establishing the rigor and uncompromising professionalism of the Russian school of the turn of the century.

Nikolai Rimsky-Korsakov was born in the town of Tikhvin near Novgorod on March 6, 1844. His father had served prominently in the provincial government, and, although the boy showed an early musical talent, he was duly entered in the St. Petersburg Naval Academy at the age of 12. While there he took violoncello lessons and later piano lessons from Feodor Kanille (Théodore Canillé), who encouraged his efforts at composition.

About 1861 Kanille introduced the young cadet to the circle of talented dilettantes who depended on Mili Balakirev for professional advice and guidance. This "Balakirev Circle" sought a Russian-based expression on the model of Mikhail Glinka. Its prominent members— Balakirev, Rimsky-Korsakov, Aleksandr Borodin, Modest Mussorgsky, and César Cui, became what the critic Vladimir Stasov much later called the "Mighty Handful" or "Mighty Five."

From 1862 through 1865 Rimsky-Korsakov cruised around the world with the Russian navy. His First Symphony, composed during this trip, was performed upon his return by Balakirev, who conducted the orchestra of the Free Music School, which he had founded.

Rimsky-Korsakov now devoted less time to navy affairs. He composed the symphonic poem *Sadko* (1867), returning to the theme much later for an opera, and the Second (*Antar*) Symphony (1868). In 1871 he became a professor at the St. Petersburg Conservatory, and in 1873 he resigned his naval commission. From 1874 to 1881 he directed the Free School, and he served as director of navy bands until 1884. He became convinced of the need for professional training, professional mastery, and a professional attitude. He embarked on a thorough study of harmony, counterpoint, and especially orchestration and urged a similar course on his colleagues. He published a harmony text in 1884 and an orchestration text in 1896. He displayed his orchestral expertise in his Third Symphony (1874) and in the delightful tone poems *Capriccio español* (1887), *Scheherazade* (1888), and *Dubinushka* (1905). But most of his energy went

Further Reading

Rimsky-Korsakov's own *My Musical Life* (1909; trans. 1924; new ed. 1942) is basic. M. D. Calvocoressi and Gerald Abraham devote a chapter to Rimsky-Korsakov in their *Masters of Russian Music* (1936). Essentially the same chapter was published by Abraham as *Rimsky-Korsakov: A Short Biography* (1945). Any music history, especially with an account of the romantic era, will contain a section on Rimsky-Korsakov. The most recent reference is Mikhail Zetlin, *The Five,* translated and edited by George Panin (1959).

Additional Sources

Abraham, Gerald, *Rimsky-Korsakov: a short biography,* New York: AMS Press, 1976.
Reminiscences of Rimsky-Korsakov , New York: Columbia University Press, 1985.
Montagu-Nathan, M. (Montagu), *Rimsky-Korsakof,* New York: AMS Press, 1976.
My musical life, London: Ernst Eulenberg Ltd, 1974. □

Faith Ringgold

Faith Ringgold (born 1930) was known for paintings, sculpture, and performances which expressed her experience as an Afro-American woman.

into his operas, the most important of which are *Snow Maiden* (1882), *Sadko* (1898), *The Invisible City of Kitezh* (1907), and *The Golden Cockerel* (1909). The sources for these and other works were fairy stories, Eastern tales, and Russian folk epics.

During the political unrest of 1905 Rimsky-Korsakov vigorously protested police repression of the students. The conservatory was closed down and he was dismissed. Others, including Alexander Glazunov, resigned in protest. The conservatory eventually reopened on a more autonomous basis with Glazunov as director and Rimsky-Korsakov as head of the department of orchestration.

The orchestral color and the beguiling, if not authentic, "orientalisms" of Rimsky-Korsakov's work brought him considerable fame and popularity. He was by far the most prolific of the Five, with a long list of orchestral works, 15 operas, and a substantial amount of chamber and vocal music. Moreover, his major works were divisible with no great musical loss into small sections which could be put to utility concert and "background" use. Perhaps no less a contribution was his effort on the behalf of others' music: he finished, rewrote, and orchestrated many works of other Russian composers, including Alexander Dargomyzhsky's *Stone Guest,* Mussorgsky's *Khovanshchina* and *Boris Godunov,* and (with Glazunov) Borodin's *Prince Igor.*

Rimsky-Korsakov died on June 21, 1908. His establishment of professional mastery of technique as the exclusive route to musical legitimacy is a legacy still preserved in Russia.

Faith Ringgold was born Faith Jones on October 8, 1930, in Harlem Hospital, New York City, the daughter of city truck driver Louis Jones and Willi Posey Jones, a dress designer. She lived all her life in Harlem, where she studied education at the City College of New York in the 1950s. Yasuo Kuniyoshi and Robert Gwathmey, two exponents of figurative painting at that time, were her teachers. Ringgold taught art in the New York City public school system from her graduation until 1973. Married twice, she had two daughters and divided her time between New York and a teaching position at the University of California at San Diego after the mid-1970s.

In the early 1960s Ringgold began to make overtly political paintings, in part inspired by reading James Baldwin and Amiri Baraka (then LeRoi Jones), who wrote of their lives as black men within a white American culture. She made a series of paintings entitled *The American People,* followed by the mural *The Flag Is Bleeding* and a large painting, *U.S. Postage Stamp Commemorating the Advent of Black Power,* which consisted of 100 frames of human faces cropped to reveal only eyes and noses. Presented in a grid, like a sheet of postage stamps, ten percent of the faces were black, reflecting the percentage of black Americans in the population at large. In the early 1970s Ringgold completed a series of *Slave Rape* paintings in which female figures, the victims of rape, were presented in lush brocade frames, inspired by Tibetan wall hangings. All her work of this period was figurative, executed in a simplified, cubist-like style which Ringgold claimed to be a derivation of African art.

By the mid-1970s she was making masks, heads of women she had known, which then evolved into large full size portraits made of stuffed fabric entitled *The Harlem Series*. These were of prominent Harlem residents such as politician Adam Clayton Powell, Jr. and basketball player Wilt Chamberlain, as well as southerner Martin Luther King, Jr., who was by then dead. Her mother helped her sew these portrait-sculptures made of foam rubber, coconut heads and yarn wigs, which later became props and characters in performances she created in collaboration with her two daughters, who wrote stories and scripts. In 1981 Ringgold made an assemblage sculpture about the chain of slayings of Black children in Atlanta, Georgia, in which she placed small stuffed figures bound in wire, each with the name and photo of a victim, against a white background, suggesting a chess board on which the children were pawns.

Later she made a series of narrative quilts, in appreciation of traditional women's handiwork, which contain pictures accompanied by texts telling their stories. One is titled "Who's Afraid of Aunt Jemima?" and another "Street Story," which tells the story of a ghetto boy who goes through a series of family tragedies to finally become a wealthy writer in Hollywood, accompanied by pictures of the physical decline of the apartment building in which he grew up. She also worked on performances to accompany her story quilts.

Throughout her career as an artist Faith Ringgold was always politically involved in black and feminist issues. In 1966 she participated in the first black art exhibition in Harlem after its renaissance in the 1930s along with Romare Bearden, Ernie Crichlow, Norman Lewis, and Betty Blayton. In 1968 she joined the Art Workers' Coalition with critic Lucy Lippard and sculptor Carl Andre and demonstrated for the inclusion of Afro-American artists in exhibitions and purchases by major New York museums. In 1970 she participated in the Ad Hoc Woman's Art Group, which successfully pressured the Whitney Museum of American Art to include for the first time in its history the work of two black women artists—Barbara Chase-Riboud and Betye Saar—in its Sculpture Biennial. During that same year she was arrested for organizing "The People's Flag Show" at the Judson Church, which protested against laws governing the use of the image of the American flag. In 1985 she participated in the Guerrilla Girls all-woman exhibition at the Palladium in New York.

Although she always lived in New York and was knowledgable about contemporary art, Ringgold's work, like her life in Harlem, remained decidedly apart from what was generally considered mainstream American art. Because she was intent on using her life experience as a black woman living in a black subculture as the basis for her work, she was often overlooked or excluded by the art establishment, which was primarily white and male and whose aesthetics most often express these characteristics either directly or indirectly. This was especially true in the late 1960s when abstract art was the prominent manifestation of the notion of mainstream art.

The political ferment of the late 1960s caused considerable upheaval in the New York art world, and many artists collectively demanded that public institutions and museums expand their programs to include a broader range of art, to show and purchase artwork by artists outside the "mainstream." New galleries opened, often publically funded, whose intention was not to sell or buy art but to show significant art that existed outside of the established system of commercial galleries and museums, which were often closed to outsiders.

Faith Ringgold participated in many of these protest activities and usually showed her work in alternative places. In 1967 and 1970 she had one-person shows at Spectrum Gallery in New York, an artist-run gallery in which she was the first black to participate. She was the subject of a ten-year retrospective exhibition at Rutgers University in 1973 and of a 20-year retrospective at the Studio Museum in Harlem in 1984 and at the College of Wooster Art Museum in 1985.

She received numerous awards, including the John Simon Guggenheim Foundation Award in 1987, and the Moore College of Fine Art's Honorary Doctorate Award in 1986. In 1991 Crown Press published her book *Tar Beach*, which she wrote and illustrated, and the following year published her book *Aunt Harriet's Underground Railroad in The Sky*.

Further Reading

While there is no complete monograph on her work, a short catalog was published in conjunction with her show at the College of Wooster titled *Faith Ringgold: Painting, Sculpture, Performance* (1985). Chapters about her were included in

Lucy Lippard's *From the Center* (1976) and in Eleanor Munro's *Originals: American Women Artists* (1979). Ringgold published an essay, "Being My Own Woman," in *Confirmation: An Anthology of African American Women* (1983), edited by Amiri Baraka (LeRoi Jones) and Amina Baraka, and has been included in many documentary videotapes, including "Art Protest Movement," made by the Archives of American Art and the Smithsonian Institution, and "Black Artists in America," made by Oakley Holmes, Jr. Perhaps because of her position as an outsider in the art world and due to the fact that most of her exhibitions and performances have happened outside of established galleries and museums, critical response to her work is found in the general press rather than in art magazines. Articles on Faith Ringgold have appeared in *The Washington Post* (1979), *Ms. Magazine* (1979), the *Village Voice* (1981), the *New York Times Magazine* (1982), and the *Christian Science Monitor* (1984). □

Barão do Rio Branco

Jose Maria da Silva Paranhos, Barão do Rio Branco (1845-1912), was a Brazilian political leader whose success in defining Brazil's frontiers during the early years of the republic added extensive territory to the Brazilian patrimony and eliminated numerous causes of international friction.

Born in Rio de Janeiro, the Barão do Rio Branco is often confused with his equally famous father, the Viscount of Rio Branco, former minister of foreign relations and author of the "Law of Free Birth." Rio Branco attended the law academies of São Paulo and Recife, graduating from the latter in 1866. He was a war correspondent for the Parisian paper *L'Illustration* during the Paraguayan War and from 1869 to 1875 served with little distinction as deputy from Mato Grosso.

After earning a reputation as a bohemian and playboy, Rio Branco underwent a severe change of character after being appointed consul to Liverpool in 1876. In 1884 he was named counselor of the empire. In recognition of his distinguished foreign service, he was given the title of Barão (Baron) do Rio Branco in 1888. In 1891 he became the director of the Brazilian immigration service in Paris.

A longtime member of the Brazilian Geographical and Historical Institute, Rio Branco took advantage of his trips throughout the Continent to visit libraries and museums and regularly submitted historical articles to Brazilian journals. This experience was invaluable for later diplomatic work, for he developed language skills, social and official contacts, and an affinity for spending hours in study and research.

In March 1893 Rio Branco represented Brazil in an old boundary dispute with Argentina over the province of Misiones. On Feb. 6, 1895, the arbiter, U.S. president Grover Cleveland, awarded the 13,680-square-mile territory to Brazil. In December 1900, thanks to Rio Branco's meticulous research and presentation, Brazil was awarded the 101,000-square-mile Amapá territory on the Brazilian-

French Guianese border. He was appointed minister to Germany on March 28, 1901, but his stay there was a short one, for President Francisco Rodrigues Alves invited him to become minister of foreign relations in July of the following year. Apprehensively accepting the position, Rio Branco returned to Brazil for the first time in 26 years.

Yet Rio Branco's years in the foreign service had singularly well prepared him for his new task, and he had a profound understanding of Brazil's traditional diplomacy. His immediate task in 1902 was the demarcation of Brazil's 9,000-mile, ill-defined frontier, which touched all South American countries except Chile and posed a constant threat of international conflict. His most pressing problem was the dispute between Brazil and Bolivia over the rubber-rich area of Acre, where fighting had broken out just as he came to office. Obtaining a cease-fire, on Nov. 17, 1903, he negotiated the Treaty of Petrópolis, which gave Brazil 73,000 square miles of the rich territory. Between 1904 and 1909 Rio Branco won favorable decisions in boundary disputes with Ecuador, Venezuela, Surinam, Colombia, Uruguay, and Peru. In 15 years he had defined Brazilian boundaries, a cause of conflict for 4 centuries, and added almost 340,000 square miles to Brazilian national territory.

Besides his noted boundary successes, he jealously guarded Brazil's foreign coffee market and created numerous Brazilian diplomatic legations in all parts of the world. In 1905 he secured a cardinal for Brazil, which for 30 years was the only Latin American country that could boast of such a high Church official.

Rio Branco served four presidents and neither entered politics nor became involved in internal policies. He died in Rio on Feb. 10, 1912, after suffering a uremic attack.

Further Reading

The best work in English on Rio Branco is E. Bradford Burns, *The Unwritten Alliance: Rio Branco and Brazilian-American Relations* (1966), which includes more than the title suggests and gives a good biographical treatment. □

Richard Joseph Riordan

Richard Joseph Riordan (born 1930), a multimillionaire businessman and civic leader seeking public office for the first time, was elected mayor of Los Angeles on June 8, 1993. He had promised to revitalize the riot-torn city and put 3,000 more police on the streets. He won praise even from political adversaries for decisive leadership following the devastating January 17, 1994, Northridge earthquake.

Richard (Dick) Riordan was born to a wealthy family in Flushing, New York, on May 1, 1930, the youngest of eight children. Raised in comfortable surroundings in New Rochelle, he became an accomplished lawyer, businessman, and philanthropist.

Riordan attended Santa Clara, then transferred to Princeton, where he majored in philosophy and received his A.B. degree in 1952. Undecided between business and law, he made what he calls a "mental flip of the coin" and enrolled in the University of Michigan law school, graduating first in his class in 1956. That same year he was the sole recruit of the prestigious Los Angeles law firm of O'Melveny and Myers, where he became an expert in stock market and tax law. He founded his own firm in 1975 and parlayed an $80,000 inheritance into a $100 million fortune through the use of leveraged buyouts and vigorous investments in high-tech firms. Riordan's most notable business success came in rescuing financially troubled large firms such as Mattel Toys through restructuring.

At Princeton Riordan had become interested in the teachings of Jacques Maritain, an influential Catholic philosopher. Maritain taught the importance of "universal truth" and service to others. Riordan became highly active in philanthropic and service activities. He gave $3 million a year to charities, focusing on those that benefit children, and donated "Read to Write" computer labs to thousands of schools throughout the country. In East Los Angeles, where the population is overwhelmingly Latino, he financed purchase of the Puente Learning Center and then donated $1.5 million and 27 computers to the center to help children and adults learn to read and write English.

Riordan's life was marked by personal tragedies, and his friend and campaign manager Bill Wardlaw said that Riordan's generosity reflected a measure of "Irish guilt or Catholic guilt" as well as deep commitment to service.

Riordan lost a 5-year-old sister to a brain tumor, a 35-year-old sister to a fire, and a 41-year-old brother to a mudslide. His only son drowned while diving in the ocean. One of his four daughters died of bulimia. His first marriage of 23 years ended in annulment, and his second in separation.

Riordan was a political unknown when he sought the Los Angeles mayoralty. His experience consisted of service on the Los Angeles Parks and Recreation Commission (of which he became president) and the Coliseum Commission, posts to which he had been appointed by Mayor Thomas Bradley. Six months before his election a poll showed Riordan with support of only 3 percent of the voters.

But Riordan ran for mayor at a time when California was disenchanted with politicians and Los Angeles was reeling from a long recession and the deadly April 1992 riots triggered by acquittal of four Los Angeles police officers charged in the videotaped beating of Rodney King, an African American. Mayor Bradley's popularity declined sharply after the riots, and he decided to retire after four terms. Riordan, proclaiming he was "tough enough to turn L.A. around" and spending heavily to boost his name recognition, emerged as a leading candidate to replace Bradley in the nonpartisan office of mayor.

Los Angeles is a culturally diverse city where Latinos and Asians form a majority of the population but only 12 percent of the electorate. Whites are two-thirds of the voters, and Riordan led all candidates in a multi-candidate April primary. His opponent in the June runoff was Councilman Michael Woo, a Democrat who tried to capitalize on the heavy Democratic majority among Los Angeles voters by making the race a partisan test. Woo depicted himself as the legitimate heir of the coalition of African Americans, Jews, and business interests that had elected Bradley 16 years earlier. Riordan, a Republican, was described as a conservative throwback to the era when a white oligarchy ruled the city. But Riordan's promise to put 3,000 new police on the streets in four years struck a responsive chord with voters. He won with 54 percent of the vote, receiving overwhelming support from whites, conservatives, and Republicans plus 40 percent of Democrats, 43 percent of Latinos, and 31 percent of Asians. Only African Americans gave Woo solid support.

The new mayor's initial performance was mixed. Riordan proved an awkward speaker who found the bureaucratic process difficult, was embarrassed by rapid turnover among top appointees, and acknowledged a high degree of frustration in dealing with the city council. But Riordan won a major victory in his fight to raise landing fees at Los Angeles International Airport and devote the proceeds to beefing up the city's thinly-spread and over-worked police force. He surprised partisans by developing a close working relationship with President Clinton.

Riordan's political epiphany occurred when the San Fernando Valley was devastated by the Northridge earthquake, which killed more than 50 people, left scores of thousands homeless, and devastated the region's transportation network by cutting three major freeways. Working closely with Police Chief Willie Williams, in contrast to the hostility between Bradley and Police Chief Daryl Gates that hampered coordination during the riots, Riordan took charge of an emergency response that Housing and Urban Development Secretary Henry Cisneros called "the best-organized and best-executed . . . that we have seen." Even the mayor's opponents praised him for demonstrations of leadership that included frequent appearances at disaster sites and tireless efforts to cut red tape for quake victims. "I think people care about Los Angeles, and they're not going to give up on it," he said the day after the quake. "I believe in making decisions. It's easier to get forgiveness later than to get permission now."

Riordan's performance in this crisis put him in the forefront of the nation's mayors and gave him national visibility in a city that many, including Riordan, saw as a national harbinger of the multicultural society that the nation will become in the 21st century.

Riordan continues to draw attention as mayor of Los Angeles. He resides in the L.A. area.

Further Reading

For additional information on Riordan see "And Now for Something Completely Different," the *Los Angeles Times Magazine* (July 11, 1993); "Riordan Shows a Steady Hand in Leading a Rattled City," column by Bill Boyarsky in the *Los Angeles Times* (Jan. 23, 1994); "Richard Riordan '52: Mayor of L.A.," *Princeton Alumni Weekly* (Dec. 8, 1993); and "Richard Riordan on the Job," *Los Angeles Lawyer* (Dec. 1993). □

George Ripley

George Ripley (1802-1880), American clergyman and journalist, was a leader of the transcendentalist movement and a founder of the famous utopian community Brook Farm. He later became an able literary critic for the "New York Tribune."

George Ripley was born of Puritan ancestry on Oct. 3, 1802, in Greenfield, Mass., the son of a prosperous merchant. New England Congregationalism was bitterly divided in the years of his youth, and the Ripley family joined the Unitarian side. George attended Harvard College, where liberal religious views prevailed, and graduated at the head of his class in 1823. For 3 years he taught mathematics at Harvard and studied at the divinity school. In 1826 he was ordained minister of a new Unitarian church in Boston. In 1827 he married Sophia Willard Dana.

Ripley's years at Harvard had been years of what would now be called student unrest. Students found the instruction dry and unrelated to new romantic currents in European scholarship. They wanted more attention to the needs of mankind and less to inherited theological dogmas. By the mid-1830s Ripley was a recognized leader of the younger dissident ministers, some of whom were called transcendentalists. He wrote a series of brilliant attacks on conservatism in the *Christian Register*. He helped edit the

Specimens of Foreign Standard Literature (1838), a 14-volume work translating into English many important Continental authors. The transcendentalists moved steadily from religious to literary interests, and in 1840 Ripley began to help edit their magazine, the *Dial*. In 1841 he resigned from the ministry.

In April 1841 Ripley became president of the Brook Farm Association; he and his wife were devoted to establishing a utopian community. The community, outside Boston, sought to combine hard work with intellectual growth. In 1845 the community began issuing a journal, the *Harbinger*, edited by Ripley. But a bad fire in 1846 debilitated the struggling community, and in August 1847 it disbanded, with Ripley assuming the debts.

Ripley moved to New York City, where he continued publishing the *Harbinger* for 2 years. In 1849 he became literary critic for the *New York Tribune*, establishing himself as one of the most influential arbiters of American taste. He helped found and edit *Harper's New Monthly Magazine* (1850) and the *New American Cyclopaedia* (1858-1863). His wife died in 1861, and 4 years later he married Louisa Schlossberger. Ripley died on July 4, 1880, while writing an editorial for *Harper's*.

Further Reading

A good scholarly biography is Charles R. Crowe, *George Ripley: Transcendentalist and Utopian Socialist* (1967). Octavius B. Frothingham, *George Ripley* (1882), is an affectionate memoir, less detailed and accurate but containing many letters by Ripley. A brilliant introduction to transcendentalist writings is

Perry Miller, ed., *The Transcendentalists* (1950), which describes Ripley's role in the movement. William R. Hutchison, *The Transcendentalist Ministers: Church Reform in the New England Renaissance* (1959), is useful on the controversies within Unitarianism. A good approach to Brook Farm is through the documents in Henry W. Sams, ed., *Autobiography of Brook Farm* (1958).

Additional Sources

Golemba, Henry L., *George Ripley*, Boston: Twayne Publishers, 1977. □

Albrecht Benjamin Ritschl

The German theologian Albrecht Benjamin Ritschl (1822-1889) was an influential interpreter of the New Testament whose views were, for a time, an effective counterweight to the dominant romantic tendency of 19th-century German theology.

Albrecht Ritschl was born in Berlin on March 25, 1822, the son of a bishop and superintendent of the Evangelical Church in Pomerania. He studied philosophy and theology at Tübingen and other universities. His teaching career began at Bonn, where he was first lecturer (1846) and then professor (1852) of New Testament studies and patristics. In 1864 he accepted a call to Göttingen, where he remained as professor of theology until his death.

Early in his career, under the influence of Ferdinand Christian Baur, Ritschl subscribed to the speculative interpretation of the early Church introduced by G. W. F. Hegel and F. D. E. Schleiermacher. But he soon abandoned this in favor of an approach based solely on historical and theological interpretation of Scripture: no important Christian truth depends on metaphysical argument. At the same time, Ritschl firmly rejected all experiential approaches to religious truth as sheer sentimentalism: not what happens now in the subjective consciousness of the believer but what happened in history—this alone can be the starting point of theology. Ritschl therefore opposed all forms of mysticism, and in particular the Pietist movement, as being decadent relapses into pre-Reformation forms of piety.

Ritschl's historical work established, against the Baur interpretation, the important point that no sharp division exists between the account of St. Paul and the accounts of the other apostles. The tendency of Ritschl's constructive views, in spite of this emphasis on a historical basis, was toward regarding religion as a support, or a guarantee, for man's moral aspiration. Borrowing heavily from Immanuel Kant's moral philosophy, Ritschl asserts that ''in every religion what is sought . . . is a solution of the contradiction in which man finds himself as both a part of nature and a spiritual personality claiming to dominate nature.''

This theme is argued forcefully in Ritschl's major work, *Justification and Reconciliation* (3 vols., 1870-1874). The effect of faith is to free us from guilt consciousness, to restore harmony between God and man, and to reinforce man's spiritual dominion over nature. Critics like Sebastian Brunner and Karl Barth argue that this emphasis on inner-worldly moral ends does not sufficiently bring out the ''vertical,'' or transcendent, dimension of faith. Ritschl died in Göttingen on March 20, 1889.

Further Reading

Biographical studies of Ritschl are all in German. Interesting appraisals of him in English are in Hugh Ross Mackintosh, *Types of Modern Theology* (1937), and Karl Barth, *Protestant Thought: From Rousseau to Ritschl* (1959). A contemporary essay that draws heavily on themes from Ritschl is Philip J. Hefner, *Faith and the Vitalities of History* (1966).

Additional Sources

Ritschl in retrospect: history, community, and science, Minneapolis, Minn.: Fortress Press, 1995. □

David Rittenhouse

David Rittenhouse (1732-1796), American astronomer and instrument maker, was a noted amateur scientist who constructed the finest orrery made at that time.

David Rittenhouse was born on April 8, 1732, near Germantown, Pa., into a poor farming family. He was stimulated by some books and tools of his uncle's and evidently educated himself in mathematics and astronomy. With help and encouragement from an Episcopal clergyman, he continued to advance his mathematical knowledge. In 1763 his boundary survey for Pennsylvania was so accurate that it was later accepted by the English surveyors Charles Mason and Jeremiah Dixon.

In 1767 Rittenhouse began his masterwork, the finest and most accurate orrery of that period. This mechanical representation of the movement of the planets through the universe was used widely in teaching and demonstration in the 18th century and also served as a demonstration of the reasonableness of nature. Rittenhouse's first orrery was capable of reproducing the relations of the planets forward or backward 5,000 years and emitted music when in operation.

Rittenhouse was in demand over the next few years by colleges that wanted him to make orreries, and the Commonwealth of Pennsylvania awarded him £300 as an honor and £300 more to make an orrery "for the use of the public." The fame derived from his orrery guaranteed him support for his observations in 1769 of the transit of Venus, which was an opportunity to measure the solar parallax. Rittenhouse's observations, made in a specially constructed laboratory, with instruments of his own design, were highly accurate and were favorably considered by European scientists working on the same problem.

In 1770 Rittenhouse moved to Philadelphia, where he was able to pursue a more active scientific career. He became a member of the informal scientific circle presided over by Thomas Jefferson. With his own improved telescopes he continued to make astronomical observations and to produce scientific and surveying instruments for himself and others, while making his living as a clockmaker. There is some uncertainty as to whether he independently developed a system of calculus, but he did become mathematically sophisticated and made some contributions in this area.

During the Revolutionary War, Rittenhouse was an avid patriot, serving on councils and committees of public safety, devising harbor defenses and methods of saltpeter production for gunpowder, and substituting iron weights in pendulum clocks to get lead for bullets. His last public service was as director of the U.S. Mint from 1792 to 1795. He died of cholera on June 26, 1796. He is often cited as an example of the untutored genius springing from American soil.

Further Reading

The best biography is Brooke Hindle, *David Rittenhouse* (1964). Edward Ford, *David Rittenhouse: Astronomer-Patriot, 1732-1796* (1946), is also useful. For general background relating to Rittenhouse and the Jeffersonian circle see Daniel J. Boorstin, *The Lost World of Thomas Jefferson* (1948), and Brooke Hindle, *The Pursuit of Science in Revolutionary America, 1735-1789* (1956).

Additional Sources

Hindle, Brooke, *David Rittenhouse,* New York: Arno Press, 1980, 1964. □

Karl Ritter

Karl Ritter (1779-1859) was a German geographer of international fame and a founder of the modern school of German geography. His time is often called the "classical period" among geographers.

One of six children, Karl Ritter was born at Quedlinburg on Aug. 7, 1779, into the much-respected family of F. W. Ritter, a medical doctor. Two years later his father died. Young Karl entered a school in which the pupils were taken out to study nature. Apparently inspired by the theories of Jean Jacques Rousseau, this school left a permanent mark on Ritter, who retained an interest in new ideas on education, including those of Johann Pestalozzi.

Much of Ritter's writing was based on Pestalozzi's ideas of the three stages in teaching: the acquisition of the material, the general comparison of material, and the establishment of a general system. Ritter was largely concerned with comparison; some interesting general ideas emerged in his work, such as those of the water and land hemispheres, the contrast between the Northern and Southern Hemispheres, the contrast in form between the Old and the New World (the Old having great east-west length, and the New north-south), and the concept of the "space relations" of particular countries, meaning their position in relation to neighboring areas. Africa, he noted, had relatively the shortest and most regular coastline of all the continents, and the interior had little contact with the ocean. Asia was far better provided with sea inlets, but the interior was isolated from the margins. Europe was the most varied of all the continents, with a complex interpenetration of land and sea.

In 1796 Ritter went to Halle University for 2 years, and in 1798 he became a tutor for the Hollweg family, who were rich bankers in Frankfurt. He began to publish papers in 1802, and in 1804 and 1807 he published a two-volume work on Europe described as "geographical, historical [and] statistical." He traveled widely in Europe but only once went to Asia and then only to Smyrna. The first volume of his great *Erdkunde* (Geography), of some 10,000 pages, dealt with Africa and appeared in 1817; the second edition, revised, of 1822, was the first of 19 volumes published at intervals to 1859.

Having married in 1819, Ritter became a history teacher in Frankfurt, but in 1820 he went to Berlin as professor of geography at the university and the Royal Military Academy. He was a founding member of the Berlin Geographical Society in 1828. Active almost to the last, Ritter died on Sept. 28, 1859, in Berlin.

Further Reading

An old biography is William L. Gage, *The Life of Carl Ritter* (1867). An appreciation of Ritter by H. Bögekamp is in Ritter's *Geographical Studies* (1863). Ritter's work is discussed in Richard Hartshoren, *The Nature of Geography* (1939); Gerald R. Crone, *Modern Geographers* (1955; rev. ed. 1970); and Thomas W. Freeman, *A Hundred Years of Geography* (1971). □

Bernardino Rivadavia

Bernardino Rivadavia (1780-1845) was a leader in Argentina's efforts to secure independence and after the break with Spain introduced a vast body of reforms to provide a sound basis for the newly independent country.

Bernardino Rivadavia was born a citizen of Spain's colonial empire. Reared and educated in Buenos Aires, capital of the viceroyalty of the Rio de la Plata, he was an early advocate of independence. In 1810 he joined the meeting of leading citizens which ousted the Spanish viceroy and secured virtual independence.

Newly independent Argentina was groping for stable government, and in 1811 a triumvirate replaced the revolutionary junta. Rivadavia served first as a secretary and then as a full member of the governing body. He was a zealous innovator, introducing all manner of reforms and institutions into the sociopolitical vacuum left by the disintegration of the colonial edifice.

With phenomenal breadth of interest, Rivadavia offered a staggering array of proposals for the developing nation. Greatly concerned with human rights, he supported decrees designed to guarantee civil liberties for all citizens, male and female. Logically, then, he sought to strip both the Roman Catholic Church and the military of the special privileges he felt inappropriate in the envisioned egalitarian society. He realized that a responsive and viable government would protect and encourage national growth, so he implemented electoral and structural reforms, making Buenos Aires a model for other provinces. The average citizen, he believed, needed education in order to operate the hoped-for democracy, so he pressed for educational improvements on all levels. He felt that happiness depended on at least a modicum of material prosperity and insisted on commercial reforms, ranging from freer commerce to the introduction of new mining and agricultural processes. These are but a sampling of the innovations, none of them an unqualified success, which leaped from Rivadavia's fertile mind.

Rivadavia also served his nation in the field of diplomacy, twice traveling to Europe on delicate missions and filling the office of foreign minister. His successes included persuading both Great Britain and the United States to recognize Argentina's independence from Spain. Further, his trips to Europe gave him the chance to savor the concepts of

such thinkers as Bentham, Adam Smith, Jovellanos, and Campomanes.

In 1826 a constitutional congress named Rivadavia president of Argentina. Although that body's action was technically without legal sanction, Rivadavia carried out his duties to the fullest extent. But he soon ran into difficulties. An inconclusive war with Brazil drained the government's resources and stirred much resentment. His promulgation of a rather centralist constitution excited the wrath of jealous provincial chieftains. Faced with unrelenting opposition, he resigned in 1827.

Forced into exile by his enemies, Rivadavia wandered in Latin America and Europe for several years. He died in Cadiz, Spain. He left a rich heritage of reforms and institutions which, in more fortuitous times, Argentina would eagerly resurrect.

Further Reading

Hubert Clinton Herring, *A History of Latin America: From the Beginnings to the Present* (1955; 3d rev. ed. 1968), gives an excellent short sketch of Rivadavia, putting him in proper historical perspective. A section on him is in George Washington University, *South American Dictators during the First Century of Independence*, edited by Alva Curtis Wilgus (1937). An outstanding account of Rivadavia's political work is in José Luis Romero, *A History of Argentine Political Thought* (1946; 3d ed. 1959; trans. 1963). ☐

Diego Rivera

Diego Rivera (1886-1957), Mexico's most famous painter, rebelled against the traditional school of painting and developed his own style, a combination of historical, social, and critical ideas depicting the cultural evolution of Mexico.

Diego Rivera was born in Guanajuato, Guanajuato State, on Dec. 8, 1886. He studied painting at the National School of Fine Arts, Mexico City, under Andrés Ríos (1897), Félix Para, Santiago Rebull, and José María Velasco (1899-1901).

In 1907 Rivera received a grant to study in Europe and lived there until 1921. He first worked in the studio of Eduardo Chicharro in Madrid and in 1909 settled in Paris. He was influenced by the impressionists, particularly Pierre Auguste Renoir. Rivera then worked in a postimpressionist style, inspired by Paul Cézanne, Paul Gauguin, Georges Seurat, Henri Matisse, Raoul Dufy, and Amedeo Modigliani.

The series of works Rivera produced between 1913 and 1917 are in the cubist idiom, for example, *Jacques Lipchitz* (*Portrait of a Young Man;* 1914). Some of them have Mexican themes, such as the *Guerrillero* (1915). By 1918 he was producing pencil sketches of the highest quality, exemplified in his self-portrait. Before returning to Mexico he traveled through Italy.

Rivera's first mural, the *Creation* (1922), in the Bolívar Amphitheater at the University of Mexico, painted in encaustic, was the first important mural of the century. From the beginning he sought for, and achieved, a free and modern expression which would be at the same time understandable. He had an enormous talent for structuring his works and a great hand for color, but his two most pronounced characteristics were intellectual inventiveness and refined sensuality. His first mural was an allegory in a philosophical sense. In his later works he developed various historical, social, and critical themes in which the history and the life of the Mexican people appear as an epic and as a specific example of universal ideas.

Rivera next executed frescoes in the Ministry of Education Building, Mexico City (1923-1926). The frescoes in the Auditorium of the National School of Agriculture, Chapingo (1927), are considered his masterpiece. The unity of the work and the quality of the component parts, particularly the feminine nudes, show him at the height of his creative power. The general theme is man's biological and social development and his conquest of nature in order to improve it. This idea, which sprang from positivist roots, is complicated by Rivera's sociohistorical criticism and by a revolutionary feeling under the symbol of the red star. The murals in the Palace of Cortés, Cuernavaca (1929-1930), depict the fight against the Spanish conquerors.

In 1930 Rivera went to the United States. In San Francisco he did the murals for the Stock Exchange Luncheon Club and the California School of Fine Arts. Two years later

he had an exhibition at the Museum of Modern Art, New York City. One of his most important works is the fresco in the Detroit Institute of Arts (1933), which depicts industrial life in the United States. He returned to New York and painted part of a mural for Rockefeller Center (1933; destroyed) and a series of frescoes on movable panels depicting a portrait of America for the Independent Labor Institute.

When Rivera returned to Mexico City, he executed the mural for the Palace of Fine Arts (1934), a replica of the one he had started in Rockefeller Center, and completed the frescoes on the monumental stairway in the National Palace (1935), which interpret the history of Mexico from pre-Columbian times to the present and culminate in the symbolic image of Marx. Rivera later continued the frescoes along the corridors, but he never completed them. The four movable panels he executed for the Hotel Reforma (1936) were withdrawn from the building because of their controversial nature. During this period he did the portraits of Lupe Marín and of Ruth Rivera and two easel paintings, *Dancing Girl in Repose* and the *Dance of the Earth*.

In 1940 Rivera returned to San Francisco to do a mural for a junior college on the general theme of culture in the future, which he believed would consist of a fusion of the artistic genius of South America with the industrial genius of North America. His two murals in the National Institute of Cardiology, Mexico City (1944), portray the development of cardiology and include portraits of the outstanding physicians in that field. His mural for the Hotel del Prado, *A Dream in the Alameda* (1947), was based on a historical and critical theme.

In 1951 a great retrospective covering Rivera's 50 years of activity as an artist took place in the Palace of Fine Arts. His last works were the mosaics for the stadium of the National University and for the Insurgents' Theater and the fresco in the Social Security Hospital No. 1. In 1956 he made his second trip to Russia (his first was in 1927-1928). He died in Mexico City on Nov. 25, 1957.

Further Reading

Rivera's own writings include *Portrait of America,* written with Bertram D. Wolfe (1934), and *My Art, My Life,* written with Gladys March (1960). Biographies are Wolfe's *Diego Rivera: His Life and Times* (1939) and *The Fabulous Life of Diego Rivera* (1963). □

Fructuoso Rivera

Fructuoso Rivera (ca. 1788-1854) was the first president of Uruguay. Better known for his military spirit and leadership than for his statesmanship, he was a principal actor in the first 45 years of the country's history.

Fructuoso Rivera was a rancher in his youth. He volunteered for the army fighting for Uruguayan independence under José Gervasio Artigas in 1810. Rivera rose gradually to general, although he was not one of Artigas's principal lieutenants. When Artigas was forced into exile in 1820 by occupying Brazilian troops, Rivera fought on for a time. Brazil finally settled with him, however, recognizing his rank and granting him a pension.

In 1825 Juan Lavalleja and his "33 Immortals" landed in Uruguay from exile in Argentina. With Argentine support, including troops commanded by the Argentine general José Rondeau, they made the Brazilian claims to the region untenable. Rivera was closely associated with Lavalleja from the beginning, although there is disagreement as to whether Rivera joined voluntarily. A skilled opportunist, Rivera was commander of troops at two important battles, Rincón and Sarandí. Disagreements forced him to leave the country for a year, and he was not present at the final battle of Ituzaingó in 1828.

As the newly independent government was being formed, Rivera returned and engaged Lavalleja in bitter feuding. Rondeau briefly became the compromise provisional president. Rivera was elected constitutional president for the term 1830-1835 but spent at least half this period leading troops against Lavalleja.

In 1835 Rivera designated Gen. Manuel Oribe as his choice for the presidency. Rivera stepped aside to become commander of the armed forces. Within a year, Oribe found it necessary to break with Rivera; although the two had joined in the field to defeat another uprising by Lavalleja, Rivera refused to recognize his subordinate role. The official excuse was Rivera's profligate habits with official funds, from 1830 onward. Civil war broke out, and Oribe was

defeated in 1838 and forced to flee to Buenos Aires. It was at this time that Oribe's followers, wearing white identifying colors, became the so-called Blanco political party; similarly, Rivera's followers became Colorados, or reds.

Rivera regained the constitutional presidency for the term 1839-1843. In the meantime Oribe accepted a commission from the ambitious Argentine president-*caudillo* Juan Manuel de Rosas to invade and occupy Uruguay. Thus began the Guerra Grande, or Great War. Rivera spent most of his presidential term in the field, leading troops against Oribe and his allies. Finally, in December 1842, Oribe defeated Rivera in the battle of Arroyo Grande. Rivera fled to Montevideo; Oribe established a parallel government for the rest of Uruguay, just outside Montevideo's walls, at Cerrito. In effect Montevideo became "Colorado" and the rest of the country "Blanco."

Rivera remained de facto chief of government until 1847. His eccentric behavior made him many enemies, and he finally was forced into exile in Brazil, where he remained until 1853. In September the constitutional president of Uruguay, Juan Francisco Giró, was forced to resign after a troop mutiny. A triumvirate of officers—Lavalleja, Rivera, and Gen. Venancio Flores—was organized to take power. Lavalleja died almost immediately; Rivera died in northern Uruguay, en route to Montevideo, in January 1854.

Rivera's colorful personality, personal *machismo,* and popular support permitted him to indulge in many irregularities. Especially during the siege of Montevideo, he was virtually a law unto himself. On the other hand, his stubborn resistance to Rosas's ambitions preserved Uruguayan independence, and his leadership of the Colorado party gave stability to the political system at a period of national crisis.

Further Reading

Works in English referring to Rivera are Philip Bates Taylor, *The Executive Power in Uruguay* (1951), and John Street, *Artigas and the Emancipation of Uruguay* (1959). □

José Eustacio Rivera

José Eustacio Rivera (1888-1928) was a Colombian novelist. He brought fresh vision to national literature and with "La vorágine" wrote perhaps the finest novel of the Latin American tropics.

Born in the southern Colombian town of Neiva, José Eustacio Rivera came from a provincial family of modest means. After becoming one of the first graduates of the recently organized teachers' college, he took a degree in law. For several years Rivera combined a law practice with modest literary activities and became a recognized member of Bogotá's urban intelligentsia. Named legal adviser and member of the Venezuela-Colombia Boundary Commission, he traveled first to the plains and then to the Amazon region. Exposed to these less well-known regions of the country, he lived with the Indians, for a time was lost in the jungle, and eventually contracted beriberi. During a period of convalescence he wrote La vorágine (The Vortex), one of the greatest Latin American novels. Its publication in 1924 assured Rivera lasting fame throughout the hemisphere and beyond, and it was translated into English, French, German, and Russian.

The Vortex, a kind of romantic allegory, was also a novel of protest. It was the first realistic description by a Colombian of the cowherders of the plains and the jungle rubber workers. Rivera attempted to arouse humanitarian feelings concerning the exploitation of these people, and he reflected a cultured urban gentleman's frightened vision of the barbarism foisted on them. The story is dominated by the magnificent yet savage setting, in which there is no law other than survival of the fittest.

Arturo Cova, the protagonist of the novel, is an urban man of letters who, forced to flee from Bogotá, encounters the brutal reality of life in the rural areas. Rivera's experience in the Amazonian jungle permits him to describe the tragedy of rubber exploitation. In publicizing the condition of the workers and their degradation at the hands of Colombian and European adventurers, Rivera provides an impassioned image of decay, death, and violence. *The Vortex,* a work romantic in spirit and poetic in style, strongly suggests that the veneer of civilization is thin. For Rivera, civilization should not be taken for granted.

Gaining swift recognition with his novel, Rivera was widely hailed both at home and abroad. While still enjoying his literary triumph during a trip to the United States, he died

prematurely of pneumonia in New York City. He also authored one collection of poetry, *Tierra de promisión* (1921), and a volume of sonnets and at his death left an unpublished drama in verse.

Further Reading

The only extended critical treatments of Rivera are in Spanish. Literary surveys in English which include passages on Rivera are Arturo Torres-Ríoseco, *The Epic of Latin American Literature* (1942; rev. ed. 1946), and Jean Franco, *The Modern Culture of Latin America: Society and the Artist* (1967). □

Larry Rivers

Larry Rivers (born 1923) was an American artist who, in the course of his career, was also a jazz musician, writer, and filmmaker. His painting, primarily figurative, combined his origins in "action painting" with an often witty use of historical and pop icons.

Yitzroch Loiza Grossberg was born on August 17, 1923, in the Bronx, New York. His name was soon "anglicized" to Irving Grossberg, and it was not until age 18 that the future painter became known as Larry

Rivers. The change of name perhaps indicated the showmanship that would mark his life and artistic endeavors.

Rivers initially hoped to make it as a musician, studying piano, and later saxophone, during his formative years. From 1940 to 1942 he performed with various jazz bands, but interrupted his musical career by enlisting in the U.S. Army Air Corps. His military service was cut short by a nervous disorder which forced him to return to civilian life. He resumed his musical career and studied at the Juilliard School of Music in 1944 and 1945.

The year 1945 was a turning point for Rivers. While touring with a band in Old Orchard, Maine, he began to paint, encouraged by the artist Jane Freilicher, wife of a fellow bandmember. Also in that year Rivers married Augusta Berger. The marriage dissolved within the year, though Rivers fathered a son, Steven, as well as acquiring a stepson, Joseph. In a rather unconventional arrangement, Rivers and his two sons lived with his mother-in-law, Bertha "Berdie" Berger, in the mid-1950s.

Though he continued to support himself as a musician, Rivers' interest in painting grew. He studied with Nell Blaine in 1946 and with abstractionist Hans Hofmann in 1947 and 1948. Though teacher and pupil frequently clashed, Hofmann made art seem "glamorous" to Rivers, and this possibility sowed the seeds of his transition from professional musician to painter.

In 1948 Rivers studied art, with the hope of eventually teaching it himself, at New York University. At this time he

met William Baziotes (his teacher), Willem de Kooning, and other artists who were contributing to the birth of Abstract Expressionism and "action painting." A retrospective in 1948 at the Museum of Modern Art of Pierre Bonnard's Post-Impressionist painting clarified what Rivers called "the modern painter's ability to cope creatively with the tangible world." He began doing Bonnard-inspired pictures, such as the lushly colored *Interior, Woman at a Table* (1948). These representational pieces, at odds with the avant-garde style of his day, were exhibited in his first one-man show, at the Jane Street Gallery in 1949, and received favorable notices from several critics, including the influential Clement Greenberg.

Yet while Rivers became more entrenched in the downtown New York arts scene, meeting among others Franz Kline, Grace Hartigan, and Helen Frankenthaler, his confidence flagged. He spent much of his time with young contemporary poets, such as Kenneth Koch, John Ashbery, and, foremost, Frank O'Hara. In 1950 he left for eight months in Paris and found the large-scale history paintings in the Louvre an inspiration. *The Burial* (1951), a large oil canvas and his first to enter a public museum collection, drew on Jean Courbet's *Burial at Ornans* (1849), a grand treatment of a humble event. It also had as a source the funeral of Rivers' grandmother. This fusion of personal and public history, of nostalgia and grandeur, appears in much of Rivers' work.

The 1950s were years of experimentation as well as professional success for Rivers. He tried his hand at life-size plaster casts of figures that evoked ancient Roman statuary. He caused a sensation and much derision with his *Washington Crossing the Delaware* (1955), a heroic pastiche whose historical content and traditional draftsmanship deliberately flouted Abstract Expressionism. His mother-in-law was a frequent subject in the mid-1950s; the best known image of her is the candid nude, *Double Portrait of Berdie* (1955). Rivers divided his time during these years between New York City and Southhampton, Long Island.

Rivers was involved in many artistic collaborations dating back to 1952, when he designed sets for Frank O'Hara's play "Try! Try!" In 1957 he teamed again with O'Hara, this time on a lithographic series, *Stones*, produced by Tatyana Grosman's Universal Limited Art Editions. In 1960 Rivers worked with Kenneth Koch on several poetry-paintings. Other collaborators included Jean Tinguely (1961), LeRoi Jones (1964), and Terry Southern (1968-1977). In the late 1950s Rivers kept himself busy on many fronts, continuing to play jazz "gigs," appearing in the beat generation film "Pull My Daisy" (1959), and, in perhaps his most fabulous exploit, winning $32,000 on a television game show in 1957.

Rivers' style around 1960, with its anecdotal appropriations of current culture, anticipated the Pop movement. In 1961 and 1962 he did take-offs of various cigarette ad campaigns, while his *Civil War Veteran* series, begun in 1959, was based on photographs from *Life* magazine. *Parts of the Body* (1963) and its successors derive from foreign-language texts and illustrate Rivers' interest in verbal and visual alliance.

Rivers did not forsake the "big statement" of his earlier work. His 1963 billboard design for the first New York Film Festival encompasses an elaborate set of images, while his monumental *A History of the Russian Revolution* (1965) revives history painting of an earlier era. Later Rivers' look at Judaism with its tongue-in-cheek title, *History of Matzoh* (1982-1984), involved large-scale public statement.

Rivers' second marriage, to Clarice Price, lasted from 1961 to 1967. In 1966 his long-time friend O'Hara died tragically. During these years Rivers made increasing use of mechanical techniques of stencilling, projected images, and airbrush. He also began making mixed-media constructions. The casual quality of his earlier work was replaced by a slicker surface, though his content was strongly personal, as in the aggressive ideology of the *Some American History* pictures (1969) or the autobiographical reflections of *Golden Oldies,* a series commissioned in 1978. A strong dose of sexuality is often present. Expanding his artistic pursuits, Rivers travelled to Africa in 1967 to help work on a television film and then acted in several others. Film and video took on greater importance for Rivers, especially after 1970.

In 1972 he taught at the University of California in Santa Barbara, and in 1973 he had exhibitions in Brussels and New York. In 1974 he finished his Japan series. He was represented at the documentary 6 in 1977. And later in 1980-81 he was given his first Eurpean retrospective at Hanover, Munich and Berlin.

Larry Rivers' restlessness led to a career of remarkable diversity. His offbeat synthesis of high and low culture, his union of private and public expression, and his defiant stance made him a true "original."

Further Reading

For a discussion of the cultural climate from which Larry Rivers emerged see Irving Sandler, *The New York* (1978). Both Sam Hunter, *Larry Rivers* (1969) and Helen A. Harrison, *Larry Rivers* (1984) are fine surveys of the artist. Carol Brightman and Larry Rivers, *Drawings and Digressions* (1979) provides a comprehensive view of the artist's outlook in his own words. Additional information about Rivers can be found on the Internet at the following web addresses: http://www.fi.muni.cz~toms/PopArt/Biographies/rivers.html, and http://www.nga.gov/cgi-bin/psearch?. □

José Rizal

José Rizal (1861-1896) was a national hero of the Philippines and the first Asian nationalist. He expressed the growing national consciousness of many Filipinos who opposed Spanish colonial tyranny and aspired to attain democratic rights.

José Rizal was born in Calamba, Laguna, on June 19, 1861, to a well-to-do family. He studied at the Jesuit Ateneo Municipal in Manila and won many literary honors and prizes. He obtained a bachelor of arts degree with highest honors in 1877. For a time he studied at the University of Santo Tomas, and in 1882 he left for Spain to enter the Central University of Madrid, where he completed his medical and humanistic studies.

Gadfly and Propagandist

In Spain, Rizal composed his sociohistorical novel *Noli me tangere* (1887), which reflected the sufferings of his countrymen under Spanish feudal despotism and their rebellion. His mother had been a victim of gross injustice at the hands of a vindictive Spanish official of the *guardia civil*. Because Rizal satirized the ruling friar caste and severely criticized the iniquitous social structure in the Philippines, his book was banned and its readers punished. He replied to his censors with searing lampoons and diatribes, such as *La vision de Fray Rodriguez* and *Por telefono*. Writing for the Filipino propaganda newspaper *La Solidaridad*, edited by Filipino intellectuals in Spain, Rizal fashioned perceptive historical critiques like *La indolencia de los Filipinos* (The Indolence of the Filipinos) and *Filipinas dentro de cien años* (The Philippines a Century Hence) and wrote numerous polemical pieces in response to current events.

Of decisive importance to the development of Rizal's political thought was the age-old agrarian trouble in his hometown in 1887-1892. The people of Calamba, including Rizal's family, who were tenants of an estate owned by the Dominican friars, submitted a "memorial" to the government on Jan. 8, 1888, listing their complaints and grievances about their exploitation by the religious corporation. After a long court litigation, the tenants lost their case, and

Governor Valeriano Weyler, the "butcher of Cuba," ordered troops to expel the tenants from their ancestral farms at gunpoint and burn the houses. Among the victims were Rizal's father and three sisters, who were later deported.

Rizal arrived home on Aug. 5, 1887, but after 6 months he left for Europe in the belief that his presence in the Philippines was endangering his relatives. The crisis in Calamba together with the 1888 petition of many Filipinos against rampant abuses by the friars registered a collective impact in Rizal's sequel to his first book, *El filibusterismo* (1891).

Rizal's primary intention in both books is expressed in a letter to a friend (although this specifically refers to the first book): "I have endeavored to answer the calumnies which for centuries had been heaped on us and our country; I have described the social condition, the life, our beliefs, our hopes, our desires, our grievances, our griefs; I have unmasked hypocrisy which, under the guise of religion, came to impoverish and to brutalize us. . . ." In *El filibusterismo*, Rizal predicted the outbreak of a mass peasant revolution by showing how the bourgeois individualist hero of both novels, who is the product of the decadent feudal system, works only for his personal and diabolic interests. Rizal perceived the internal contradictions of the system as the source of social development concretely manifested in the class struggle.

Prison and Exile

Anguished at the plight of his family, Rizal rushed to Hong Kong for the purpose of ultimately going back to Manila. Here he conceived the idea of establishing a Filipino colony in Borneo and drafted the constitution of the Liga Filipina (Philippine League), a reformist civic association designed to promote national unity and liberalism. The Liga, founded on July 3, 1892, did not survive, though it inspired Andres Bonifacio, a Manila worker, to organize the first Filipino revolutionary party, the Katipunan, which spearheaded the 1896 revolution against Spain. Rizal was arrested and deported to Dapitan, Mindanao, on July 7, 1892.

For 4 years Rizal remained in exile in Dapitan, where he practiced ophthalmology, built a school and waterworks, planned town improvements, wrote, and carried out scientific experiments. Then he successfully petitioned the Spanish government to join the Spanish army in Cuba as a surgeon; but on his way to Spain to enlist, the Philippine revolution broke out, and Rizal was returned from Spain, imprisoned, and tried for false charges of treason and complicity with the revolution. His enemies in the government and Church were operating behind the scenes, and he was convicted. The day before he was executed he wrote to a friend: "I am innocent of the crime of rebellion. So I am going to die with a tranquil conscience."

The day of Rizal's execution, Dec. 30, 1896, signifies for many Filipinos the turning point in the long history of Spanish domination and the rise of a revolutionary people desiring freedom, independence, and justice. Rizal still continues to inspire the people, especially the peasants, workers, and intellectuals, by his exemplary selflessness and intense patriotic devotion. His radical humanist outlook forms part of the ideology of national democracy which Filipino nationalists today consider the objective of their revolutionary struggle.

Further Reading

Among the many books on Rizal, the following are reliable: Austin Craig, *Lineage, Life and Labors of José Rizal* (1913); Carlos Quirino, *The Great Malayan* (1940); Camilo Osias, *José Rizal: Life and Times* (1949); Rafael Palma, *The Pride of the Malay Race* (trans. 1949); Leon Maria Guerrero, *The First Filipino* (1963); Austin Coates, *Rizal* (1969); and Gregorio Zaide, *José Rizal* (1970). Recommended for general background is Gregorio Zaide, *Philippine Political and Cultural History* (1949; rev. ed. 1957).

Additional Sources

Abeto, Isidro Escare, *Rizal, the immortal Filipino (1861-1896)*, Metro Manila, Philippines: National Book Store, 1984.

Bernad, Miguel Anselmo, *Rizal and Spain: an essay in biographical context,* Metro Manila, Philippines: National Book Store, 1986.

Capino, Diosdado G., *Rizal's life, works, and writings: their impact on our national identity,* Quezon City: JMC Press, 1977.

Del Carmen, Vicente F., *Rizal, an encyclopedic collection,* Quezon City, Philippines: New Day Publishers, 1982.

Ocampo, Ambeth R., *Rizal without the overcoat,* Pasig, Metro Manila: Anvil Publishing, 1990.

Santos, Alfonso P., *Rizal in life and legends,* Quezon City: National Book Store, 1974.

Vano, Manolo O., *Light in Rizal's death cell: (the true story of Rizal's last 24 hours on earth based on eyewitnesses's testimonies and newspaper reports),* Quezon City: New Day Publishers, 1985.

Zaide, Gregorio F., *Jose Rizal: life, works, and writings of a genuis, writer, scientist, and national hero,* Metro Manila, Philippines: National Book Store, 1984. □

Alain Robbe-Grillet

The French novelist Alain Robbe-Grillet (born 1922) achieved fame for his innovative techniques in writing fiction. Influential in avant-garde Paris intellectual circles, his controversial critical theories regarding the concept of the modern novel were fulfilled in his own narratives.

Born in Brest, Alain Robbe-Grillet was educated at the Lycées Buffon and St. Louis in Paris and at the Lycée de Brest. Having received his engineering degree from the National Agricultural Institute of France, he pursued a scientific career as an officer at the National Institute of Statistics in Paris from 1945 to 1948. Later, as an agronomist for the French Institute of Colonial Agriculture, he traveled extensively in the tropics, particularly Morocco, Martinique, and French Guinea, for 3 years. Robbe-Grillet joined the publishing house of Minuit as a literary director in 1955, married 2 years after, and was subsequently named a

member of the High Committee for the Preservation and Expansion of the French Language.

Robbe-Grillet and his coterie—a select literary group composed of Nathalie Sarraute, Michel Butor, Bruce Morrissette, and Claude Simon—opposed the bourgeois, or Balzacian, novel of humanist tradition, preferring the geometrical precision and clinical exactitude of a scientific-literary approach. Robbe-Grillet, in particular, demonstrates a post-Sartrean sense of the alienated character and claims as the inspiration for his novels "the first fifty pages of Camus's *The Stranger* and the works of Raymond Rousset" (the latter is a little-known author who died in the 1930s). Critical analysis has also recognized the profound impact of the novels of Franz Kafka and Graham Greene on his work.

Known as the first "cubist" novelist and a "chosist," for his obsessive focus on inanimate objects, Robbe-Grillet initially described the *nouveau roman* and became the leading exponent of the New Wave in contemporary French literature. His revolutionary theories are based on the premise that man's perception of his milieu is distorted by his bourgeois background and its resulting emotionalism. Condemning the metaphorical phrasing of many existentialists, Robbe-Grillet attempts to illustrate in his fiction that all illusionary language falsely indicates a possible relationship between man and the material universe. The world is not man's domain, the novelist's essays and narratives insist, and objects exist independently of the transitory emotional content of human life. Characterized by an objective accuracy in its detailed descriptions, his writing is bare of intangible, inferential adjectives.

The Erasers (1953), Robbe-Grillet's first novel, appears to be a conventional detective thriller but thematically reworks Sophocles's *Oedipus Rex*. Intended as a comic parody, the narrative illustrates the chosist technique in its intense focus on the India rubber of the title as an antisymbol. *Le Voyeur* (1955) explores, without either conversation or interior monologue, the psychology of a rapist. The exaggerated realism of the physical descriptions imposes a dreamlike air of surrealism on this work.

The past, present, and future are juxtaposed in *Jealousy* (1957), an experiment with time and space elements, and humanity is characterized by mere behavior patterns, the identity of individuals being refined out of existence. The potential lushness of its tropical setting, based on Robbe-Grillet's equatorial travels, is deliberately reduced to a monochrome of color, measured distance, and tone and shape, with photographic precision. The antisymbol appears again, this time in the form of a centipede that to the nameless hero represents the image of jealousy itself. All indications of the subjective eye of the author are removed, resulting in a new literary mode. *In the Labyrinth* (1959) emphasizes the cinematic play of light and shadow over an endless expanse of snow. The Antonioni-like monotony of the landscape is reflected in the rhythm of language, and an unconventional attempt is made to suggest inner reality through the external vision.

At age 40 he embarked on a parallel career as screenwriter and director. Robbe-Grillet's finest effort may be the film scenario *Last Year at Marienbad* (1961), which reads like a novel and is written in the "continuous present." The film, directed by Alain Resnais, created considerable critical controversy and captured the Golden Lion Award at the Venice Film Festival. In this scenario, the most objectively pictorial of Robbe-Grillet's fiction, space has been created as a function of psychological time, and the internal conscious reality exists in terms of external objects with endless repetitions of long, empty corridors, baroque ceilings, mirrored walls, and formal gardens. The surprising commercial success of the film permitted its author to undertake other cinema efforts, notably *The Immortal* (1963), the first film he both wrote and directed and and winner of the Louis Delluc prize and *Trans-Europe Express* (1967).

A central figure in France's last literary movement, *Le Nouveau Roman* or *New Novel*, Robbe-Grillet published *Towards a New Novel* (1962), a widely acclaimed collection of essays in which he defends his literary thesis against those who say it lacks humanity; *Snapshots* (1962), a collection of short stories; *Topology of a Phantom City* (1976) and *Recollections of the Golden Triangle* (1978), which are primarily collages of collaborations with artists and photographers; and *Djinn: a red hole between disjointed paving stones* (1982), a light, humorous novel originally written as a textbook, titled *Le rendez-vous* (1981), with Cal State Domingues Hills Professor Yvone Lenard. Evolving from Robbe-Grillet's interest in film were two *cinematic novels, The House of Assignation* (1965) and *Project for a Revolution in New York* (1970), so called because they have the feel of a film, but are remarkably anti-visual. Robbe-Grillet also wrote and directed the films: *The Slow Sliddings of*

Pleasure (1974), *Playing with Fire* (1975), *The Fair Captive* ((1983), and *The Blue Villa* (1995).

Further Reading

A three-part imaginary autobiography of Robbe-Grillet includes: *Ghosts in the Mirror* (1991), *Angéleque, or the Enchantment* (1988), and *The Last Days of Corinthe* (1994). For Robbe Grillet in English, see *Understanding Robbe-Grillet* (1997); *The Erotic Dream Machine: Interviews with Alain Robbe-Grillet on his Films* (1992) by Anthony Fragola and Roch Smith; John Fletcher, *Alain Robbe-Grillet* (1983); Ilona Leki, *Alain Robbe-Grillet* (1983); Ben F. Stoltzfus, *Alain Robbe-Grillet and the New French Novel* (1964). See also Bruce Morrissette, *Alain Robbe-Grillet* (1965). Robbe-Grillet is discussed in John Sturrock, *The French New Novel* (1969) and Raylene Ramsay, *The French New Autobiographies* (1996). English criticisms of his work, include: Marjorie Hellerstein, *Inventing the Real World: the Art of Alain Robbe-Grillet* (1998); Lillian Dunmars Roland, *Women in Robbe-Grillet: a Study in Thematics and Diegetics* (1993); Raylene Ramsay, *Robbe-Grillet and Modernity: Science, Sexuality, and Subversion* (1992); Bruce Morrissette, *Novel and Film: Essays in Two Genres* (1985); Patricia Deduck, *Realism, Reality, and the Fictional Theory of Alain Robbe-Grillet and Anais Nin* (1982); and Victor Carrabino, *The Phenomenological Novel of Alain Robbe-Grille* (1974). □

Jerome Robbins

A major creative force on both the Broadway and ballet stages beginning in 1944, director/choreographer Jerome Robbins (born Rabinowitz 1918) extended the possibilities of musical theater and brought a contemporary American perspective to classical dance.

American director and choreographer Jerome Robbins was equally renowned for his work in musical theater and ballet and made auspicious debuts in both fields in 1944. On April 18, Ballet Theater (now American Ballet Theater) presented the world premiere of *Fancy Free,* which followed the exploits of three sailors on shore leave in New York. That ballet became the springboard for *On the Town,* a musical comedy which premiered eight months later and featured choreography by Robbins. Over the next 20 years, Robbins choreographed and/or directed 15 other musicals and "show doctored" five more. A partial list of his Broadway credits includes *High Button Shoes* (1947), *The King and I* (1951), *Pajama Game* (1954), *Peter Pan* (1954), *Bells Are Ringing* (1956), *West Side Story* (1957), *Gypsy* (1959), and *Fiddler on the Roof* (1964).

During and after the years he was active on Broadway he also earned a reputation as the greatest classical choreographer born in the United States. Working mostly with the New York City Ballet, he choreographed 61 ballets through 1989. Among his finest were *Interplay* (1945), *The Cage* (1951), *Afternoon of a Faun* (1953), *The Concert* (1956), *Dances at a Gathering* (1969), *The Goldberg Variations*

(1971), *In G Major* (1975), *Other Dances* (1976), *The Four Seasons* (1979), *Glass Pieces* (1983), and *Ives, Songs* (1988).

Robbins was born Jerome Rabinowitz in New York on October 11, 1918, to Russian Jewish parents who came to America to flee the pogroms. He grew up in Weehawken, New Jersey, and was in his late teens when he began studying at the Sandor-Sorel Dance Center in Brooklyn. He later took lessons in modern, Spanish, and Oriental dance.

Between 1937 and 1940 Robbins appeared in the chorus of four Broadway musicals and also danced at Camp Tamiment, a summer resort for adults where revues were staged by aspiring performers. It was there that he had his first opportunity to choreograph. In 1940 he joined the newly created Ballet Theater as a dancer and studied with the choreographers Antony Tudor and Eugene Loring. Ballet Theater had a particular penchant for Russian ballets—Robbins often said that he spent a good deal of time in "boots, bloomers and a peasant wig"—and *Fancy Free* was, in part, a reaction to that repertoire.

Successful Musicals and Ballets

The ballet—in which Robbins danced "the rumba" sailor—was set to a commissioned score by the relatively unknown Leonard Bernstein and was an instant masterpiece. It was not just the jazz inflections or familiar, everyday gestures incorporated into the choreography that made the piece special. A ballet portraying contemporary American characters behaving in contemporary American fashion

was virtually unheard of at the time, and wartime audiences recognized the people onstage at once.

Robbins then took his choreographic talents to Broadway with similar success. *On the Town* marked the first time that dance had been so fully integrated into a Broadway show, prompting one critic to suggest that it be called "a ballet comedy instead of a musical comedy."

For the next few years Robbins divided his time between Broadway and ballet. His choreography was singled out as the high point of *Billion Dollar Baby* (1946); *High Button Shoes* (1947); *Look Ma, I'm Dancin'* (1948), which he co-directed with George Abbott; *Miss Liberty* (1949); and *Call Me Madam* (1950). *High Button Shoes* earned him his first Tony award.

In 1949 George Balanchine invited Robbins to join the New York City Ballet as dancer, choreographer, and associate artistic director. During the next decade he created ten ballets for the company, and his moody, evocative dances were a wonderful contrast to Balanchine's plotless neo-classicism.

In 1951 Robbins choreographed Rodgers and Hammerstein's *The King and I*, the most sophisticated Broadway show of which he had thus far been a part. But the show that would forever cement his reputation as one of the most important figures in the history of Broadway was *West Side Story,* which opened in 1957 and continued to have an impact on the course of musical theater into the 1990s. This modern, updated Romeo and Juliet saga was the first musical conceived, choreographed, and directed by one man. It marked the culmination of many innovations that originally appeared in *On the Town* and earned Robbins his second Tony award for choreography.

Innovations in All His Work

In 1959 Robbins directed and choreographed *Gypsy,* another theatrical landmark. That same year he left City Ballet to devote his energies to his own company, Ballets: USA, which was formed in 1958 and disbanded in 1961. Among the works that came out of Ballets: USA was *Moves* (1959), a startling experiment in that it is performed without music. It was added to the repertory of City Ballet.

Robbins was back on Broadway with two shows in 1964. He was production supervisor on *Funny Girl* and director and choreographer of *Fiddler on the Roof. Fiddler* won nine Tony awards, with Robbins winning for both direction and choreography. It was Robbins who saw the universality in this simple tale about a milkman wrestling with his religious beliefs. He envisioned a work that depicted the dissolution of a community, which inspired lyricist Sheldon Harnick and composer Jerry Bock to write "Tradition," the song that informs the entire musical.

Two years after *Fiddler,* Robbins established the American Theater Laboratory, an experimental workshop designed to explore theater forms involving dance, song, and speech. It lasted through 1968, but none of the work done by the group developed into a project that was seen by the public. Among those to participate was Robert Wilson, who later became known for his avant-garde creations. Robbins won a Best Director Oscar for his work on the film version of *West Side Story* (1961) and also received a special Academy Award for his choreography. His work on the telecast of *Peter Pan* (1955) earned him an Emmy.

In 1969 Robbins returned to City Ballet as one of the company's ballet masters. The first work he choreographed was the hour-long *Dances at a Gathering,* which is set to various Chopin piano pieces and is regarded by many as his finest ballet. Ten dancers perform in various combinations—solos, duets, trios, quartets, and onward—expressing a range of moods and emotions, all the while suggesting a sense of community. The variety of the choreography is remarkable, and one critic called the piece "a celebration of dance."

Robbins was particularly productive during the 1970s, during which time he choreographed more than 20 pieces for City Ballet, including *The Goldberg Variations* (1971), a 90-minute exploration of the famous Bach score, and *Watermill* (1972), which borrows freely from Eastern theater techniques and elevates stillness to an art form. In 1976, for a non-City Ballet gala, he choreographed *Other Dances*—another Chopin ballet—for Mikhail Baryshnikov and Natalia Makarova. After Baryshnikov joined City Ballet for a year beginning in 1979, Robbins went on to choreograph two more works for him: *Opus 19, "The Dreamer,"* and *The Four Seasons* , in which Baryshnikov danced the fall section.

In the 1980s Robbins continued to expand his vision. Robbins was the recipient of a Kennedy Center Honor in 1981. In 1983 he was named co-ballet master-in-chief of City Ballet (with Peter Martins), shortly before Balanchine's death. Robbins' ballet *Ives, Songs* premiered several months before his 70th birthday in 1988 and poignantly depicted a man looking back at his life. That same year Robbins literally delved into his past: He went to work recreating and reconstructing some of the highlights from his 20 years in musical theater for archival purposes and wound up creating a new show, *Jerome Robbins' Broadway.* The musical opened in February 1989, marked Robbins' return to Broadway after a 25-year absence, and earned him his fifth Tony award.

Robbins retired from City Ballet in 1990, but continued his creative pursuits. In 1994 he premiered *A Suite of Dances,* a solo work performed by Mikhail Baryshnikov set to music from Bach's unaccompanied suites. That same year the School of American Ballet premiered his *2 + 3 Inventions,* another dance set to the music of Bach. The next January (1995) a major work by Robbins, *Brandenburg,* was preformed by the City Ballet. *Brandenburg* was described by critic Terry Teachout as the "missing link in Robbins's output."

Throughout his career Robbins combined theatrical savvy with an unerring sense of movement to create potent, moving panoramas. The diversity of his work is astonishing, but if there is one thread linking much of his art, it is his repeated exploration of community. His ballets have been danced by many of the world's major companies, including American Ballet Theater, Dance Theater of Harlem, Joffrey Ballet, Royal Danish Ballet, England's Royal Ballet, Paris Opera Ballet, National Ballet of Canada, San Francisco Ballet, and Australian Ballet.

Further Reading

His work is examined in *Repertory in Review* (1977) by Nancy Reynolds; Broadway Musicals (1979) by Martin Gottfried; *Broadway Song & Story* (1985), edited by Otis. L. Guernsey, Jr.; and "Robbin's 'Fancy'" by Tobi Tobias, which appeared in Dance Magazine in January 1980. A critical review of his choreography is provided by Terry Teachout in *DanceMagazine* (May 1997). □

Robert I

Robert I (1274-1329), or Robert Bruce, was king of Scotland from 1306 to 1329. Leader of the successful resistance to the threat of English domination of his country, Bruce is regarded as one of the great patriots of Scottish history.

Robert Bruce was the eighth male to bear that name in a direct line going back to the first Robert, who probably took part in the Norman conquest of England and died about 1094. The family subsequently gained considerable lands and prominence in Scotland. The fifth Robert Bruce (died 1245) married the niece of King William, "the Lion," thus establishing a possible claim, albeit a distant one, to the Scottish throne. This claim was advanced by the sixth Robert on the highly complicated succession quarrel that arose in Scotland in 1290. William the Lion's grandson, Alexander III, had died in 1286, leaving as direct heir only a 3-year old granddaughter, Margaret, the "Maid of Norway" (her father was king of Norway). The problems of how to manage the minority reign of a small girl were grave enough, but when she died suddenly in 1290, some 13 competitors claimed to be her rightful successor as monarch of Scotland.

In this situation the commanding nature of England's king, Edward I, was the decisive factor. Any choice opposed by Edward would most likely be untenable, and the question was submitted to him for arbitration. The claims of two competitors clearly stood out: John Balliol, great-grandson of a brother of William the Lion by an eldest daughter; and Robert Bruce (VI), grandson by a younger daughter. Edward decided for Balliol; but before issuing his decision, he took oaths of allegiance from all the claimants, including Robert Bruce (VI) as well as his son Robert (VII).

This seventh Robert was the father of the patriotic leader and future king of Scotland; but, as has been seen, the position of the Bruces was originally that of appellants to, and sworn men of, the English King. Edward's decision had by no means settled the situation in Scotland. Balliol, suspected by the Scots of being an English puppet and by Edward of forswearing his oath, could not rule effectively, and the situation was complicated by the alliance of Scotland with France, an enemy of England. From 1296 Balliol was no longer a factor, and the only choices were direct

English domination or Scottish independence, which meant war with England. William Wallace emerged as the leader of the Scottish resistance, winning a great victory at Stirling Bridge in 1297; but he was in turn defeated by Edward at Falkirk the following year, and though he kept up sporadic guerrilla warfare until his capture and execution in 1305, he was no longer a serious threat to the English. Besides, Wallace's movement was, nominally, to restore Balliol, a cause uncongenial to many of the leading Scots.

His Accession

Robert Bruce the eighth (hereafter called just Bruce) first emerged importantly as one of the "guardians" of the kingdom in December 1298, ostensibly on behalf of Edward I. The other principal guardian was John Comyn, nicknamed "The Red," whose affinity with the house of Balliol led to a lasting quarrel with Bruce from at least 1299. Bruce resigned as guardian in 1300, and though on the surface he was at peace with Edward, it is likely that he was thinking of the crown, especially after the death of his father (who had earlier transferred the Bruce claim to him) in 1304. He had apparently entered into a secret alliance with the patriotic Bishop Lamberton of St. Andrews, and perhaps through fear that his plans would be disclosed, he killed Comyn the Red in a church in Dumfries in February 1306. This violent and probably unpremeditated deed at once pushed Bruce to the head of the Scottish resistance. Within 6 weeks he was crowned as Robert I, King of Scotland.

In England, Edward I reacted strongly to the news and at the famous "Feast of Swans" swore to avenge Comyn's

death and destroy Bruce (who had also been excommunicated by the Pope for profaning the church at Dumfries). Bruce was immediately in trouble from the well-led English forces, as well as from the adherents of Comyn, and soon found himself a king apparently without a following, hiding in the western highlands, or even in Ireland. But the long final illness and death of Edward I in 1307 marked a turning point. The new English king, Edward II, was from the first unpopular with his nobility and, as a military leader, was beneath comparison with his father. From spring 1307 Bruce's fortunes began to revive. Edward II was vacillating and indecisive in his actions, and Bruce was able to make headway against both the English and his remaining Scottish enemies. In March 1309 a truce was made with England, whose holdings in Scotland were reduced to only a few castles.

In the next few years expeditions were made into the northern parts of England, and the last possession of the English in Scotland, Stirling Castle, was heavily besieged. In a concerted effort to remedy the situation, Edward II in 1314 led a large army to the relief of Stirling, but it was defeated by Bruce and his outnumbered Scots at the Battle of Bannockburn. The English fled in confusion, and Bruce was undisputed master of his country. Though tensions with England continued, there was no further major threat from the English in Bruce's lifetime; nor was there further serious dissension in Scotland.

From 1309 Bruce was holding parliaments and could attend in a systematic way to the government of the country. Parliament addressed itself to the succession problem in 1315, 1318 (when Bruce's brother and heir presumptive, Edward, was killed in Ireland), and 1326 (after the birth 2 years earlier of Bruce's first son and eventual successor, David). Bruce's relations with the papacy remained strained, until the papal refusal to recognize Bruce as king was reversed by John XXII in 1328. The Scottish hierarchy had consistently supported the King. In his later years Bruce suffered from what was called, and may have been, leprosy. He died at his country estate at Cardross in June 1329, just before the marriage of his son David to the sister of the new English king, Edward III, as the final provision of a peace treaty between the two countries.

Further Reading

John Barbour's long poem, *The Bruce* (ca. 1375; modern translation by Archibald A. H. Douglas, 1964), is the principal narrative source. The major modern work on Robert I is G. W. S. Barrow, *Robert Bruce and the Community of the Realm of Scotland* (1965). Older studies are Sir Herbert Maxwell, *Robert the Bruce and the Struggle for Scottish Independence* (1898), and Agnes Mure Mackenzie, *Robert Bruce: King of Scots* (1934). For historical background see William Croft Dickinson, *A New History of Scotland,* vol. 1 (1961; 2d ed. 1965).

Additional Sources

Barbour, John, *Barbour's Bruce: a fredome is a noble thing!,* Edinburgh: Scottish Text Society, 1980-1985.

Barrow, G. W. S., *Robert Bruce and the community of the realm of Scotland,* Edinburgh: Edinburgh University Press, 1976.

Mackay, James A. (James Alexander), *Robert Bruce: King of Scots,* London: Hale, 1974.

Scott, Ronald McNair, *Robert the Bruce, King of Scots,* New York: P. Bedrick Books, 1989, 1982; Carroll & Graf, 1996.

Tranter, Nigel G., *A traveller's guide to the Scotland of Robert the Bruce,* Harrisburg, PA, USA: Historical Times, 1985. ☐

Robert II

Robert II (1316-1390) was king of Scotland from 1371 to 1390. For many years heir presumptive to David II and frequently regent of the kingdom, Robert is important primarily for his role in Scottish affairs before he came to the throne.

R
obert Steward (or Stewart) was the son of Walter Steward (the third of that name in a line stretching back to Walter "the Steward," ca. 1158) and Marjorie Bruce (daughter of Robert Bruce, who had become Robert I of Scotland in 1306). As early as 1318 the Scottish Parliament declared Robert Steward heir presumptive if the male line of Bruce should die out.

Robert first came to prominence at the battle of Halidon in 1333, where he was one of the commanders of the losing Scottish side and was in consequence dispossessed of his estates by Edward Balliol, the English-supported rival to Robert Bruce's son David II (born 1324; reigned 1329-1371). Robert Steward was among the leaders of the successful resistance to the puppet regime of Balliol and, as principal regent from 1338, paved the way for David's return 3 years later.

However, no love was lost between the two men (Robert being David's nephew and heir presumptive as well as being older and having controlled the regency), and contemporaries suspected that Robert treacherously fled the field at the crucial battle of Neville's Cross in 1346, at which David was taken prisoner by the English. Robert was again regent, for 11 years, but David's release in 1357 (obtained by a promise to pay a crushing ransom to the English) put him out of power, and in 1363 Steward joined a conspiracy against the King. This was unsuccessful, however, and David's attempt to get his ransom lowered by settling the Scottish crown on the English royal family (thus effectively disinheriting Robert) sealed the enmity between the two. Parliament rejected David's proposal, and on the King's death in 1371 Robert succeeded to the throne as Robert II.

The new king seems to have played very little part in the important events of his reign, being overshadowed by two of his many sons, first the Earl of Carrick (the future Robert III) and then the Earl of Fife. Robert was uninterested in, and powerless to stop, the renewed and increasingly bitter hostilities between the English and the Scots (the latter egged on by the French) culminating in the burning of Edinburgh in 1385 and the Scottish victory at Otterburn 3 years later. It is conjectured that Robert, now an old man, suffered physical, and perhaps mental, decline; and he had been put under a guardianship, tantamount to deposition, a few

months before his death in 1390. He left a troubled succession, a quarrelsome and turbulent nobility, and a tradition of weak and largely ineffective kingship, all of which were to plague his country during the subsequent century.

Further Reading

There is no work solely on Robert II or his reign. The standard histories of Scotland give background information about his times: P. Hume Brown, *History of Scotland,* vol. 1 (1899), and William Croft Dickinson, *A New History of Scotland,* vol. 1 (1961; 2d ed. 1965). ☐

Robert III

Robert III (ca. 1337-1406) was king of Scotland from 1390 to 1406. Notable as king primarily for the weakness of his reign, he played a larger part in the affairs of the kingdom before his accession than as monarch.

T
he future Robert III (actually christened John) was born some years before the marriage of his parents, Robert Steward (who was to become king as Robert II in 1371) and Elizabeth Mure. The children of this union were subsequently legitimized, by papal dispensation, in 1347, the young John being styled Lord of Kyle. He was made Earl of Atholl by the King in 1367 and Earl of Carrick (as he is usually referred to) in 1368.

On the accession of Robert II in 1371, the Scottish Parliament, to forestall any possible doubts about legitimacy, firmly established the succession on Carrick and his line and, failing that, on his brothers. Carrick seems to have played an important part in the early years of his father's reign, negotiating with John of Gaunt in 1380 and being directed to restore order in the Highlands in 1384. But a kick from a horse, apparently sometime after 1385 (though some historians place it earlier), resulted in a disability and perhaps even a lifelong weakness, for in 1388 Carrick was relieved of his responsibilities in favor of his next surviving brother, Robert, Earl of Fife.

Nonetheless, on the death of Robert II, Carrick succeeded, taking as his regnal name Robert. The Earl of Fife continued, however, as the chief power in the kingdom. The new king's reign was constantly troubled by the lawlessness of great lords and the quarrels of clans, especially the celebrated combat between 30 men each of the clans Kay and Quele. Apparently, Fife's influence waned after 1393, and in 1399 the King's elder son, David, was appointed by the General Council as "lieutenant" of the kingdom for 3 years.

This young man had been created Duke of Rothesay the previous year, his uncle, the Earl of Fife, becoming Duke of Albany at the same time (the first dukes in Scotland). The rivalry between these two was a prime factor in the fortunes of the country during the next 3 troubled years. Resistance to the demands of the new English king, Henry IV, to have his overlordship of Scotland recognized was weakened by treachery and dissension among the leading magnates. Finally in 1402 Rothesay, whose profligacy had earned him many enemies, was arrested by order of his uncle and died in prison shortly afterward.

In all these events Robert III was virtually a cipher. Probably seeing, and fearing, the unbreakable ascendancy of Albany (lieutenant of the kingdom from 1402), the King sent his remaining son, James (born 1394), to France in 1406; but the young boy was intercepted by kidnapers and handed over to the English for a captivity that was to last 18 years. Robert's death followed quickly after the news reached him. He reportedly requested as his epitaph "Here lies the worst of kings and the most miserable of men."

Further Reading

There is no work solely on Robert III or his reign. Background information on his times is given in standard histories of Scotland; recommended is William Croft Dickinson, *A New History of Scotland,* vol. 1 (1961; 2d ed. 1965). ☐

Frederick Sleigh Roberts

The British soldier and filed marshal Frederick Sleigh Roberts, 1st Earl Roberts of Kandahar, Pretoria, and Waterford (1832-1914), made his reputation in India and South Africa and then became the last commander in chief of the British army.

Frederick Roberts was born in Cawnpore, India, on Sept. 30, 1832, the son of Gen. Sir Abraham Roberts, a British soldier in Indian service. His family was Anglo-Irish, long settled in Waterford. Roberts was sent to Eton in 1845, entered Sandhurst in 1847, and then attended the East India Company's college at Addiscombe. In 1851 Roberts joined the Bengal Artillery.

Roberts began by serving with his father, who was experienced in the affairs of the North-West Frontier. During the Indian mutiny, Roberts was at the siege of Delhi and at the second relief of Lucknow and won the Victoria Cross at Khudaganj in January 1858. During the years that followed, he rose steadily in rank, and he was involved in the 1860s and 1870s with the affairs of the North-West Frontier, although in 1868 he accompanied Sir Robert Napier on the British expedition to Ethiopia. During this time Roberts became an advocate of a "forward policy" toward Afghanistan, arguing for control of that country in order to check a supposed Russian threat to India.

In 1876 Lord Lytton became viceroy of India, and Roberts's influence increased. In 1878 he took command of the Punjab Frontier Force and in autumn headed one of the columns that invaded Afghanistan following the Emir's rejection of a British envoy while welcoming a Russian one. The Emir was deposed in 1878, and his successor signed a treaty with the British in 1879. In the previous year Roberts had been promoted to major general and knighted. In September 1879 Sir Louis Cavagnari was murdered while on a

mission to Kabul, and this led to the dispatch of Roberts and another British invasion of Afghanistan. Kabul was taken, and another Emir was installed on the throne. But the Afghans continued to resist, and in July 1880 they wiped out half a British brigade at Maiwand. Roberts force-marched his troops from Kabul and defeated the Afghans definitively at Kandahar in September, a victory that made him a popular hero in England, where he was feted after being given a baronetcy and made commander in chief of the Madras army (1881). Roberts tried unsuccessfully to persuade the government of William Gladstone to annex Kandahar.

In 1885 Roberts was named commander in chief in India. For the next 8 years he occupied himself with reorganizing military transport, increasing the training of troops, and developing obsessions about the Russian peril in the North-West Frontier. In 1892 he was created baron. From 1893 to 1895 Roberts held no official post, and he spent his time writing. In May 1895 he was given the rank of field marshal and appointed commander in chief in Ireland, where he served for the next 4 years.

In October 1899 the Boer War began, and the British soon suffered a series of disastrous defeats. Moreover, Roberts's son was killed at Colenso. In December, Roberts was appointed to command the British armies in the Boer War. He arrived in South Africa in January 1900 and immediately began reorganizing the poor transport, increasing the mounted troops, and planning a full-scale invasion of both Boer republics once reinforcements arrived. Roberts resisted pressures to scatter his troops in the relief of beleaguered garrisons, and the British advance began in

February. Almost everywhere that the Boers stood to fight they were defeated, and by mid-March Bloemfontein had fallen. On May 31 Roberts's forces entered Johannesburg, and Pretoria fell on June 5. By September the British had occupied most of the towns in the northern Transvaal, and in October President Paul Kruger fled to Europe. The war seemed won, and Roberts returned to a hero's welcome as the man who had quickly reversed the tide and won the war. His reputation was enormous. Queen Victoria gave him an earldom in one of her last acts, and he was made commander in chief of the British army.

In this post, which he held until 1904, Roberts's reputation began to dim. It soon appeared that the Boer War was far from won, and Gen. Kitchener had to face 2 years of guerrilla warfare led by Christian De Wet and Louis Botha. Roberts was then criticized for having concentrated on capturing Boer towns rather than on destroying the Boer armies in the field. At the War Office, Roberts—with his experience drawn entirely from India and his brief stay in South Africa—was put in charge of the organization of the British army. The Esher Commission on the organization of the War Office recommended the abolition of the post of commander in chief in 1903, and Roberts left the post in 1904.

Roberts then devoted his activity to the championing of conscription for home defense, becoming president of the National Service League in 1905. When World War I broke out in 1914, Roberts, then 82 years old, was appointed to command the Indian troops fighting in France. He did not live to reach the Western front, dying of a chill at Saint-Omer on Nov. 14, 1914. He was buried in St. Paul's Cathedral, London, as a national hero.

Further Reading

Among Roberts's own writings, the most important are his *Forty-one Years in India* (2 vols., 1897) and *Speeches and Letters on Imperial Defence* (1906). The best biography, based on Roberts's official and private correspondence, is David James, *Lord Roberts* (1954). □

Sir Dennis Holme Robertson

The English economist Sir Dennis Holme Robertson (1890-1963) was a major figure in the development of economic theory in the 20th century, particularly in the fields of monetary and business cycle theory and policy.

Dennis Robertson was born on May 23, 1890, the son of the Reverend James Robertson, clergyman and headmaster of Haileybury. Educated at Eton and at Trinity College, Cambridge, Robertson gained through his brilliance an abundance of medals, prizes, and honors. A large part of his first notable book, *A Study of Industrial Fluctuations* (1915), was written at the age of 22, when he was still in his third year of his economic studies. During World War I he served in Egypt and Palestine, win-

ning the Military Cross and, according to rumor, narrowly missing the Victoria Cross.

Robertson was elected fellow of Trinity College in 1914 and reader in economics at Cambridge University in 1930; he remained at Cambridge until 1938. At that time he was named the Sir Ernest Cassel professor of economics at the University of London. He resigned this post in 1944 to return to Cambridge as professor of political economy, a position that he held until his retirement in 1957. He died of a heart attack at Cambridge on April 21, 1963.

A brief assessment of the contributions of any one of the Cambridge economists of the immediate post-World War I period is singularly difficult. The source of the difficulty is in large part in the close working relationship and in the free sharing of ideas among men like Robertson, A. C. Pigou, R. G. Hawtrey, and John Maynard Keynes. Keynes himself remarked at the difficulty of distinguishing his own original ideas from those of his co-workers. Nevertheless, in Robertson's *Banking Policy and the Price Level* (1926) and a number of articles, most of which are collected in *Economic Fragments* (1931), are to be found, partially concealed by clumsy mathematics and confusing terminology, attempts to work real factors (such as saving and investment) into a discussion that had been previously dominated by purely monetary variables (such as the quantity of money). Also to be found are the origins of period analysis, which became so useful to economists in the following decade.

With the publication of Keynes's *Treatise on Money* (1930) a rift developed between Robertson and Keynes for reasons that are not entirely clear. From this time on, Robertson was particularly critical of and unwilling to accept either Keynesian theory or Keynesian policies. Although it might be argued that his contributions would have been greater had he not approached Keynesian thought as he did, his criticisms did produce positive results. His work contributed to the clarification of the inconsistencies in Keynes's definitions of saving and investment as well as to a better statement of the liquidity preference theory of interest. During World War II Robertson handled financial relations between Great Britain and the United States and played an important role in the Bretton Woods Monetary Conference.

Further Reading

Ben B. Seligman, *Main Currents in Modern Economics: Economic Thought since 1870* (1962), devotes a chapter to Robertson's life and work. Also useful is Terence Wilmot Hutchinson, *A Review of Economic Doctrines, 1870-1929* (1953). □

Pat Robertson

Marion G. "Pat" Robertson (born 1930) was a television evangelist who founded and led the Christian Broadcasting Network. In 1988 he ran for president, doing well in several primaries and caucuses and succeeding at getting his religious agenda into the arena of public discussion.

Pat Robertson was born on March 22, 1930, the son of A. Willis Robertson and Gladys Churchill Robertson, in Lexington, Virginia. His father was a congressman and later a senator, a staunch conservative known for his expertise in taxation and banking and for his die-hard segregationist views on issues of race. Robertson grew up largely in Lexington, finishing high school at the elite McCallie School in Chattanooga and then returning home to attend college at Washington and Lee University. Following military service in Korea he enrolled at Yale Law School, where he met Adelia "Dede" Elmer. They were married in August 1954.

Upon completion of law school Robertson took the New York Bar examination and failed it. He became a management trainee with the W.R. Grace Company and seemed destined for a career in international business; then he resigned and joined two law classmates in founding an electronics company. Leaving that business as well, in 1956 he enrolled at what is now New York Theological Seminary. Before graduating in 1959 he had become involved with a circle of fellow believers who were early participants in the neo-charismatic movement, many of them speaking in tongues. He remained in the largely noncharismatic Southern Baptist denomination, however, and was ordained a minister there in 1961. (He resigned his ordination in 1987 prior to announcing his candidacy for president.)

Launched CBN

Robertson's first experience in religious broadcasting came shortly after he had completed seminary when, during a visit to the family home in Lexington, he was asked to substitute for a vacationing minister on a daily 15-minute radio program. Soon thereafter he was informed by a minister-friend of his mother's of a bankrupt television station for sale at a bargain price in Portsmouth, Virginia. After extensive negotiating Robertson managed to buy the station and raise enough money to begin operations on WYAH-TV, the first television outlet for the Christian Broadcasting Network (CBN). Programming was launched on October 1, 1961. Radio broadcasting had been started in WXRI-FM two months earlier.

The shoestring operation slowly attracted viewers and financial contributions; among the early additions to the CBN staff were Jim and Tammy Bakker, whose initial responsibilities were in children's programming and who later left to start their own religious television operation. In 1963 the need to meet a $7,000-per-month budget with gifts from viewers led to a telethon in which 700 listeners were asked to pledge $10 per month each. These early supporters were called the "700 Club," a name that endured on CBN. By 1965 CBN was operating in the black, poised for a meteoric rise in support that reached some $240 million per year by the late 1980s.

Auxiliary enterprises were added as CBN grew. CBN University was established in 1978; it was followed in the 1980s by several other organizations, including a political education society known as the Freedom Council and a legal-assistance project for fundamentalist Christian causes called the National Legal Foundation. Various other counseling, benevolent, and outreach programs were developed in the United States and abroad.

Presidential Campaign

Robertson's background as a son of a successful politician and his strong moral drive came to a head with his 1988 candidacy for the presidency. In 1986 he announced a campaign to secure three million signatures on petitions urging him to run, a set of signatures that amounted to an enormous mailing list for fund-raising and volunteer services for the campaign. Claiming to have exceeded that goal, he formally announced his candidacy for the Republican nomination on October 1, 1987. His campaign embraced themes commonly voiced in conservative America, promoting, for example, fiscal conservatism, opposition to most abortions, moral conservativism on such issues as sexual conduct and pornography, and the return of religious observances to the public schools. For someone who had never previously run for public office, Robertson did very well in the various caucuses and primaries of the 1988 campaign, although he ultimately lost the nomination to George Bush.

During the presidential campaign some of the relatively unorthodox side of Robertson's theology came to light. The most prominent example involved his claim to have changed the course of a hurricane in 1985 by praying, on the air, "In the name of Jesus, we command you to stop where you are and move northeast, away from land, and away from harm." Indeed, Hurricane Gloria changed course and headed northeast, sparing the mainland. Later

Robertson suggested that his apparent success in averting bad weather helped confirm his decision to run for president: "It was extremely important because I felt, interestingly enough, that if I couldn't move a hurricane, I could hardly move a nation."

Controversy continued to follow Robertson after his 1988 run for the presidency (he declined to run in 1992). In 1993, for example, he was criticized when CBN invested $2.8 million of its nonprofit, donor-given monies in a for-profit vitamin and skin care company in which Robertson also had a substantial personal investment. Robertson, however, was never seriously damaged by controversy, and CBN continued its diverse operations in good health. Furthermore, Robertson was largely resposible for galvanizing the right-wing Christian movement, particularly the Christian Coalition. This small but well-organized group of fundamentalist Christians continues to be a powerful force in American politics.

Further Reading

An early autobiography, *Shout It from the Housetops* (1972), provides a good summary of Robertson's outlook. A relatively sympathetic biography is David Edwin Harrell's *Pat Robertson: A Personal, Religious, and Political Portrait* (1987). One of several critical works is *Salvation for Sale: An Insider's View of Pat Robertson* (1988), written by Gerard Thomas Straub, a former high-ranking CBN employee.

Additional Sources

Pat Robertson, *America's Date with Destiny,* Thomas Nelson, 1986.
Pat Robertson, *The End of the Age,* Word Publishing, 1996. □

Paul Leroy Robeson

Paul Leroy Robeson (1898-1976) was an American singer, actor, and political activist. He crusaded for equality and justice for black people.

Paul Robeson made his career at a time when second-class citizenship was the norm for all African-Americans, who were either severely limited in, or totally excluded from, participation in the economic, political, and social institutions of America.

Robeson was born on April 9, 1898, in Princeton, New Jersey. His father was a runaway slave who fought for the North in the Civil War, put himself through Lincoln University, received a degree in divinity, and was pastor at a Presbyterian church in Princeton. Paul's mother was a member of the distinguished Bustill family of Philadelphia, which included patriots in the Revolutionary War, helped found the Free African Society, and maintained agents in the Underground Railroad.

At 17 Robeson won a scholarship to Rutgers University, where he was considered an athlete "without equal." He won an incomparable 12 major letters in 4 years. His academic record was also brilliant. He won first prize (for 4

consecutive years) in every speaking competition at college for which he was eligible, and he was elected to Phi Beta Kappa. He engaged in social work in the local black community. After he delivered the commencement class oration, Rutgers honored him as the "perfect type of college man."

Robeson graduated from the Columbia University Law School in 1923 and took a job with a New York law firm. In 1921 he married Eslanda Goode Cardozo; they had one child. Robeson's career as a lawyer ended abruptly when racial hostility in the firm mounted against him. He turned to acting as a career, playing the lead in *All God's Chillun Got Wings* (1924) and *The Emperor Jones* (1925). He augmented his acting by singing spirituals. He was the first to give an entire program of exclusively African-American songs in concert, and he was one of the most popular concert singers of his time.

Robeson starred in such stage presentations as *Show Boat* (1928), *Othello,* in London (1930), *Toussaint L'Ouverture* (1934), and *Stevedore* (1935). His *Othello* (1943-1944) ran for 296 performances—a remarkable run for a Shakespearean play on Broadway. While playing opposite white actress Mary Ure, he became the first black ever to do the role in England's Shakespeare Memorial Theater (*Jet,* Feb. 6, 1995).

His most significant films were *Emperor Jones* (1933), *Show Boat, Song of Freedom* (both 1936), and *Proud Valley* (1939). Charles Gilpin and Robeson, as the first black men to play serious roles on the American stage, opened up this

aspect of the theater for blacks. Robeson used his talents not only to entertain but to foster appreciation for the cultural differences among men.

During the 1930s Robeson entertained throughout Europe and America. In 1934 he made the first of several trips to Russia. He spoke out against the Nazis, sang to Loyalist troops during the Spanish Civil War, raised money to fight the Italian invasion of Ethiopia, supported the Committee to Aid China, and became chairman of the Council on African Affairs (which he helped establish in 1937). The most ardent spokesman for cultural black nationalism, and militant against colonialism in Africa, Robeson also continued to fight racial discrimination in America. While World War II raged, he supported the American effort by entertaining soldiers in camps and laborers in war industries.

After the war, Robeson devoted full time to campaigning for the rights of blacks around the world. In the period of anti-Communist hysteria, the American government and many citizens felt threatened by Robeson's crusade for peace and on behalf of exploited peoples. The fact that for over 15 years he was America's most popular black man did not prevent Robeson's being barred from American concert and meeting halls and being denied a passport to travel abroad.

During the repressive 1950s Robeson performed in black churches and for trade unions. After 8 years of denial, he won his passport, gave a concert in Carnegie Hall, and published *Here I Stand* in 1958. He went abroad on concert, television, and theater engagements.. He received numerous honors and awards: the NAACP's Spingarn Medal, several honorary degrees from colleges, the Diction Award from the American Academy of Arts and Letters, numerous citations from labor unions and civic organizations, and the Stalin Peace Prize.

Robeson had used an "unshakable dignity and courage" learned from his father to break stereotypes, tradition and limitations throughout his life. He added 15 spoken languages, a law degree, an international career as singer and actor, and civil rights activist to his long list of accomplishments in his effort to be "the leader of the black race in America."

He returned to America in 1963 in poor health and soon retired from public life. Slowly detiorating and living in reclusiveness, Robeson died on January 23, 1976 in Philadelphia, after suffering a stroke.

However, it took him 77 years to win the respect of the college sports world. During his outstanding, four-year football career at Rutgers University, Robeson was named All-American consecutively in 1917 and 1918, the first African-American to do so. In 1995, after his color and politics were less of a detriment and the awards were based more on merit, he was inducted posthumously into the College Football Hall of Fame at the new $14 million museum's grand opening in South Bend, Indiana. *Sports Illustrated* (Jan.30, 1995) called it a "long-overdue step toward atonement."

In a report in *Jet* (February 6, 1995) magazine, Robeson's son, Paul, Jr., who accepted the honor, talked about his father's influence on other black men and his

dedication to causes. "He felt it was a job he had to do for his people and the world as a whole," said the younger Robeson.

His songs, such as his trademark Ol' Man River, and acting have remained available in videos and new releases of his vintage recordings (*Opera News,* July 1995).

Further Reading

Robeson's autobiography, *Here I Stand* (1958), remains the best statement explaining his political activism. All of the works on Robeson are somewhat inadequate. The best comprehensive account of his life is Marie Seton, *Paul Robeson* (1958). His wife, Eslanda Goode Robeson, wrote a short, colorful biography, *Paul Robeson, Negro* (1930), a personal account of Robeson's early years which strongly reflects her own biases and sentiments. An erroneous and distorted study is Edwin P. Hoyt, *Paul Robeson: The American Othello* (1967). Further information on Robeson can be found in *Opera News* (July 1995); *Jet* (February 6, 1995); and *Sports Illustrated* (January 30, 1995). □

Maximilien François Marie Isidore de Robespierre

The French Revolutionary leader Maximilien François Marie Isidore de Robespierre (1758-1794) was the spokesman for the policies of the dictatorial government that ruled France during the crisis brought on by civil and foreign war.

Maximilien de Robespierre was an early proponent of political democracy. His advanced ideas concerning the application of the revolutionary principle of equality won for him the fervent support of the lower middle and working classes (the *sans-culottes*) and a firm place later in the 19th century in the pantheon of European radical and revolutionary heroes. These ideas and the repressive methods used to implement and defend them, which came to be called the Reign of Terror, and his role as spokesman for this radical and violent phase of the French Revolution also won for him the opprobrium of conservative opponents of the Revolution ever since.

Career before the Revolution

Robespierre was born on May 6, 1758, in the French provincial city of Arras. He was educated first in that city and then at the Collège Louis-le-Grand in Paris. Upon completing his studies with distinction, he took up his father's profession of law in Arras and soon had a successful practice. But he had developed a sense of social justice, and as the Revolution of 1789 loomed, he assumed a public role as an advocate of political change, contributing to the pamphlet and *cahier* literature of the day, and being elected at the age of 30 a member of the Third Estate delegation from Arras to the Estates General, where he quickly associated himself with the Patriot party.

Role in Early Revolution

During the first period of the Revolution (1789-1791), in which the Estates General became the National (or Constituent) Assembly, Robespierre spoke frequently in that body. But his extremely democratic ideas, his emphasis on civil liberty and equality, his uncompromising rigidity in applying these ideas to the issues of the moment, and his hostility to all authority won him little support in this moderate legislature. He favored giving the vote to all men, not just property owners, and he opposed slavery in the colonies. On both of these issues he lost, being ahead of his time.

Robespierre found more receptive listeners at the Paris Jacobin Club, where throughout his career he had a devoted following that admired him not only for his radical political views but perhaps even more for his simple Spartan life and high sense of personal morality, which won for him the appellation of "the Incorruptible." His appearance was unprepossessing, and his old-fashioned, prerevolutionary style of dress seemed out of place. He lacked the warmth of personality usually associated with a popular political figure. Yet his carefully written and traditionally formal speeches, because of his utter sincerity and deep personal conviction, won him a wide following.

When his term as a legislator ended in September 1791, Robespierre remained in Paris, playing an influential role in the Jacobin Club and shortly founding a weekly political journal. During this period (1791-1792) he was an unremitting critic of the King and the moderates who hoped

to make the experiment in limited, constitutional monarchy a success. Robespierre, profoundly and rightly suspicious of the King's intentions, spoke and wrote in opposition to the course of events, until August 1792, when events turned in his favor with the overthrow of the monarchy and the establishment of the First French Republic.

Period in Power

A Convention was quickly elected to perform the task of drafting a constitution, this time for a democratic republic, and to govern the country in the meantime. Robespierre was elected a member for Paris. As a spokesman for the Mountain, the radical Jacobin faction in the Convention, he played a prominent role in the successive controversies that developed. He was an uncompromising antagonist of the deposed king, who was finally placed on trial, convicted, and executed in January 1793.

The moderate Girondin faction had incurred the enmity of Robespierre and the leaders of the Mountain in the process, and for this and other reasons, both personal and political, there followed months of bitter controversy, climaxed by the victory of the Robespierrist faction, aided by the intervention of the Parisian *sans-culottes,* with the expulsion from the Convention and arrest of the Girondins (June 2, 1793) and the execution shortly thereafter of their leaders.

The dual crises of foreign war, in which most of Europe was now fighting against the Revolutionary government in France, and civil war, which threatened to overthrow that government, had led to the creation of the crisis machinery of government, the Reign of Terror. The central authority in this government was the Committee of Public Safety. For the crucial months from mid-1793 to mid-1794 Robespierre was one of the dominant members of and the spokesman for this dictatorial body. Under their energetic leadership the crisis was successfully surmounted, and by the spring of 1794 the threat of civil war had been ended and the French army was winning decisive victories.

Political controversy had continued, however, as Robespierre, having prevailed against the moderate Girondins, now faced new opposition on both the left and the right. The Hébertists, a radical faction that controlled the Paris city government and was particularly responsive to the grievances of the *sans-culottes* concerning wartime shortages and inflation, actively campaigned for rigorous economic controls, which Robespierre opposed. Nor could he support their vigorous anti-Christian campaign and atheistic Religion of Reason. Robespierre and his colleagues on the committee saw them as a threat, and in March 1794 the Hébertist leaders and their allies were tried and executed.

Two weeks later came the turn of the Indulgents, or Dantonists, the moderate Jacobins who, now that the military crisis was ended, felt that the Terror should be relaxed. Georges Jacques Danton, a leading Jacobin and once a close associate of Robespierre, was the most prominent of this group. Robespierre was inflexible, and Danton and those accused with him were convicted and guillotined.

Robespierre and his associates, who included his brother Augustin and his young disciple Louis de Saint-Just, were now in complete control of the national government and seemingly of public opinion. He thus could impose his own ideas concerning the ultimate aims of the Revolution. For him the proper government for France was not simply one based on sovereignty of the people with a democratic franchise, which had been achieved. The final goal was a government based on ethical principles, a Republic of Virtue. He and those of his associates who were truly virtuous would impose such a government, using the machinery of the Terror, which had been streamlined, at Robespierre's insistence, for the purpose. Coupled with this was to be an officially established religion of the Supreme Being, which Robespierre inaugurated in person.

Downfall and Execution

Opposition arose from a variety of sources. There were disaffected Jacobins who had no interest in such a program and had good reason to fear the imposition of such high ethical principles. More and more of the public, now that the military crisis was past, wanted a relaxation, not a heightening, of the Terror. The crisis came in late July 1794. Robespierre spoke in the Convention in vague but threatening terms of the need for another purge in pursuit of his utopian goals. His opponents responded by taking the offensive against him, and on July 27 (9 Thermidor by the Revolutionary calendar) they succeeded in voting his arrest. He and his colleagues were quickly released, however, and they gathered at the city hall to plan a rising of the Parisian *sans-culottes* against the Convention, such as had prevailed on previous occasions. But the opposition leaders rallied their forces and late that night captured Robespierre and his supporters. In the process Robespierre's jaw was fractured by a bullet, probably from his own hand. Having been declared outlaws, they were guillotined the next day. With this event began the period of the Thermidorian Reaction, during which the Terror was ended and France returned to a more moderate government.

Further Reading

The best, and classic, work on Robespierre in English is the biography by James M. Thompson, *Robespierre* (2 vols., 1935; repr. 1968). A shorter and more popular study is Thompson's *Robespierre and the French Revolution* (1953). The imaginative fabrication by Henri Beraud, *My Friend Robespierre* (1938), provides a perceptive character analysis. Robespierre's role as a member of the Committee of Public Safety is summarized in Robert R. Palmer, *Twelve Who Ruled* (1941). Excerpts from widely differing assessments of Robespierre which have been written since the Revolution are compiled by George Rudé in *Robespierre* (1967). The best advocate for Robespierre's cause was Albert Mathiez, who devoted his scholarly career to Robespierre's defense but who never wrote a biography; see, however, his *The Fall of Robespierre and Other Essays* (1927) and *The French Revolution* (1928). A more balanced but not unfriendly estimate of Robespierre's place in the history of the Revolution is in George Lefebvre, *The French Revolution* (2 vols., 1962-1964); and his place in the history of political thought is analyzed in two essays in Alfred Cobban, *Aspects of the French Revolution* (1968). □

Edwin Arlington Robinson

Edwin Arlington Robinson (1869-1935), American poet and playwright, was a leading literary figure of the early 20th century.

E dwin Arlington Robinson was born in Head Tide, Maine, on Dec. 22, 1869. He grew up in nearby Gardiner, which became the "Tilbury Town" of his poems. The story is told that for many months after his birth his parents called him "the baby" because they had not wanted a boy. The name "Edwin" was pulled from a hat by a stranger who happened to live in Arlington, Mass. Robinson hated his name, for it signified to him the accidental nature of man's fate. After studying at Harvard from 1891 to 1893, he returned to Gardiner.

Robinson published his first volume of poetry, *The Torrent and the Night Before* (1896), at his own expense. His early verse was largely ignored. In 1905 the struggling poet was presented with a way out of his oppressive poverty when President Theodore Roosevelt, who admired *Captain Craig* (1902), secured him a clerkship in the New York City Customs House. He resigned from this post in 1910 to devote himself to writing.

Eventually Robinson found a patron in Mrs. Edward MacDowell, who owned the MacDowell Colony in New Hampshire; here, from 1911, Robinson spent his summers. His talent was finally recognized with *The Man against the Sky* (1916). His prose dramas, *Van Zorn* (1914) and *The Porcupine* (1915), which anticipate in many ways the plays of T. S. Eliot, are virtually unknown today, yet they are possibly more worthwhile than many of his celebrated long poetic narratives, such as *King Jasper* (1935).

Robinson's late poetry was both symbolic and experimental, but his reputation chiefly rests on the austere, ironic "Tilbury Town" portraits, which express his feeling that all men are "children of the night" who find no star to guide them and get no answers to their questions. "Luke Havergal," "Cliff Klingenhagen," "George Crabbe," "Miniver Cheevy," "Richard Cory," "Reuben Bright," "Bewick Finzer," "Eros Turannos," and "Mr. Flood's Party" remain incisive explorations of early-20th-century despair.

Robinson won the Pulitzer Prize for poetry three times. He died in New York City on April 5, 1935.

Further Reading

The standard edition of Robinson's verse is the *Collected Poems of Edwin Arlington Robinson* (1937). A shorter edition is *Selected Poems of E. A. Robinson* (1965). His letters are contained in *Selected Letters of Edwin Arlington Robinson* (1940); *Letters of Edwin Arlington Robinson to Howard George Schmitt* (1945); *Untriangulated Stars: Letters . . . to Harry deForest Smith, 1890-1905* (1947); and *Edwin Arlington Robinson: Selected Early Poems and Letters* (1960). Recommended studies of Robinson are Ellsworth Barnard, *Edwin Arlington Robinson: A Critical Study* (1952); Edwin S. Fussell, *Edwin Arlington Robinson: The Literary Background of a Traditional Poet* (1954); Wallace Anderson, *Edwin Arlington*

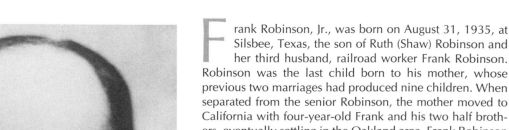

Robinson: A Critical Introduction (1967); and Louis Coxe, *Edwin Arlington Robinson: The Life of Poetry* (1969). See also the section on Robinson in Hyatt H. Waggoner, *American Poets from the Puritans to the Present* (1968).

Additional Sources

Burton, David Henry, *Edwin Arlington Robinson: stages in a New England poet's search*, Lewiston: E. Mellen Press, 1987.

Joan Robinson (1903-1983) and George Shackle (1903-1992), Aldershot, Hants, England; Brookfield, Vt., USA: E. Elgar Pub. Co., 1992.

The Joan Robinson legacy, Armonk, N.Y.: M.E. Sharpe, 1991.

Turner, Marjorie Shepherd, *Joan Robinson and the Americans*, Armonk, N.Y.: M.E. Sharpe, 1989.

Brode, Patrick, *Sir John Beverley Robinson: bone and sinew of the compact*, Toronto; Buffalo: Published for the Osgoode Society by University of Toronto Press, 1984. □

Frank Robinson Jr.

Frank Robinson, Jr. (born 1935), was the only base-ball player to win Most Valuable Player awards in each major league, the first African American player to manage a baseball team in each major league, and the first to be named Manager of the Year in the National as well as the American League.

Frank Robinson, Jr., was born on August 31, 1935, at Silsbee, Texas, the son of Ruth (Shaw) Robinson and her third husband, railroad worker Frank Robinson. Robinson was the last child born to his mother, whose previous two marriages had produced nine children. When separated from the senior Robinson, the mother moved to California with four-year-old Frank and his two half broth-ers, eventually settling in the Oakland area. Frank Robinson grew up in a poor, ethnically diverse neighborhood where he starred as an athlete. Excelling in baseball, the 15-year-old Robinson was a right-handed hitting and throwing out-fielder on Coach George Powley's 1950 American Legion team, which won a second consecutive national title. Rob-inson later played under Cowley at McClymonds High School, whose baseball program also developed future out-field stars Vada Pinson and Curt Flood.

After graduating in 1953, Robinson signed with the Cincinnati Reds for a $3,500 bonus. Assigned to Ogden, Utah, in the Pioneer League, outfielder Robinson batted .348. The following year, after playing eight games at sec-ond base with the Tulsa, Oklahoma, team of the Texas League, Robinson played with the Columbus, Georgia, team of the South Atlantic (Sally) League, batting .336 with 25 homers and 110 RBIs (runs batted in). Over the winter he injured his right arm playing in Puerto Rico. In the spring of 1955 Robinson trained with the Cincinnati Reds, but reinjured his arm and was reassigned to the Columbus team. In his three-year minor league stint Robinson learned to cope with the racial discrimination that also marred his early years in the majors.

Following a strong second half performance at Columbus, Robinson joined the Cincinnati Reds in the spring of 1956. In a brilliant debut he batted .290 with 38 homers and a league-leading 122 runs scored and won National League Rookie-of-the-Year honors. An established star with the Reds, over the next nine seasons the 6 foot 1 inch outfielder topped the .300 mark five times, struck 25 or more homers eight times, led the league in slugging percentage over the years 1960 to 1962, and four times drove in 100 or more runs. During those years Robinson's harddriving, aggressive style of play earned him a reputation as a "vicious" player, but Robinson endured frequent injuries and perennially led the league in being hit by pitched balls.

In 1961, after being arrested and fined $250 for wielding a gun in a pre-season lunch counter fracas in Cincinnati, the contrite Robinson led the Reds to their first National League pennant since 1940. For batting .323 with 37 homers and 117 RBIs, he won the league's Most Valuable Player award. On October 28, 1961, Robinson married Barbara Ann Cole of Los Angeles; an enduring union, it produced a son, Frank Kevin, born in 1962, and a daughter, Nichelle, born in 1965.

In the wake of contract disputes with Cincinnati general manager Bill DeWitt, who labeled him "an old 30 year old," Robinson was traded to the American League Baltimore Orioles following the 1965 season. In belying that judgment, Robinson's Triple Crown (.316-44-122) batting carried the Orioles to their first World Championship. After winning the World Series Most Valuable Player award, Robinson was voted the American League's Most Valuable Player, thus becoming the first player to win the honor in both major leagues. As a high-salaried star, Robinson's six years with the Orioles (1966-1971) saw his team win four pennants and two world titles; Robinson's contribution to these achievements included four .300 plus batting performances and five 25 plus homer seasons.

In 1972 Robinson was traded to the National League Dodgers, who dealt him to the American League California Angels in 1973. By then the aging Robinson was performing mostly as a designated hitter. In 1974 the Angels traded him to the American League Cleveland Indians, where Robinson soon realized his dream of becoming the first African American manager in the major leagues. In pursuit of that goal, over the past several winters Robinson had gained experience by managing the Santurce club of the Puerto Rican (winter) league.

Robinson's appointment as a manager of the Indians in October 1974 was a media event that drew a congratulatory telegram from President Gerald Ford. In his first game as playing manager in April 1975 Robinson homered in his first at bat to lead his team to victory. Robinson's 1975 Indians finished at 79-80, and the following year the team's 81-78 mark was Cleveland's first winning season since 1968. But when Cleveland faltered in 1977, Robinson became the first Black manager to be fired. By then Robinson's playing career had ended. As a player Robinson played 21 seasons in the majors, batting .294 with 2,943 hits. His 586 homers ranked him fourth among major league sluggers and his 1,829 RBIs ranked tenth.

After three seasons of coaching with the American League Angels and Orioles, including a 1978 managerial stint with the Orioles' Rochester, New York, club, Robinson became the National League's first African American manager in 1981 when he signed with the San Francisco Giants. In 1982 his team's 87-75 record won him National League Manager-of-the-Year honors; that year Robinson was also honored by election to the Baseball Hall of Fame. But after the Giants slumped in 1983 and in 1984, Robinson was fired.

Returning to the Orioles, Robinson coached under three managers, including Cal Ripken, under whose leadership the 1988 Orioles faltered badly. Replacing Ripken that year, Robinson directed the 1989 Orioles to a remarkable turnabout; mounting an 87-75 record, the Orioles finished a strong second in their division. That feat won Robinson recognition as National League Manager of the Year. But the following year (1990) the Orioles fell to 76-85 and when they started slowly, 13-24, in 1991 Robinson was replaced as manager by John Oates. The Hall-of-Famer then moved into the Oriole front office as assistant general manager. Robinson continues to remain active in the field of baseball.

Further Reading

Jules Tygiel's *Baseball's Great Experiment* (1984) surveys the struggles of Black players in gaining admission to the major leagues. David Q. Voigt's *American Baseball: From Postwar Expansion to the Electronic Age* (1983) and *Baseball: An Illustrated History* (1987) treat Black players both in the segregated leagues and in the era of integration in baseball's major leagues.

Robinson's three semi-popular autobiographies trace his major league baseball odyssey as a star player and as the first Black manager in both major leagues. The first, Frank Robinson with Al Silverman, *My Life in Baseball* (1968), covers his playing years to 1967 and offers important insights into his formative years, his encounters with racism in baseball, his views on hitting and fielding, and his aggressive style of play. A second volume, Frank Robinson with Russell Schneider, *The Making of a Manager* (1976), updates his playing career and furnishes a candid account of the trials and tribulations he encountered as the rookie manager of the Cleveland Indians. A third volume, Frank Robinson with Berry Stainback, *Extra Innings* (1988), covers Robinson's years as a manager of the Giants and offers forthright comments on problems of racial discrimination in major league baseball. □

Harriet Hanson Robinson

Harriet Hanson Robinson (1825–1911) wrote an account of her experince in the textile mills, helping to encourage women to flock to the mills for a chance to earn their own wages.

Harriet Hanson Robinson was born on August 2, 1825, in Boston, Massachusetts, the second of four children born to William and Harriet Hanson. When she was six years old, her father died, leaving her mother with the difficult task of feeding and caring for four young children. At the time, it was not unusual for a family to break up because of financial need, but Robinson's mother was determined to keep her family together. When a concerned neighbor offered to ease her burden by adopting young Harriet, Mrs. Hanson said, "No; while I have one meal of victuals a day, I will not part with my children." These words stayed with Robinson, who wondered for many years what the word "victuals" meant.

With help from her husband's friends, Mrs. Hanson set up a small shop in Boston, selling food, candy, and firewood. The family lived in a room behind the shop, sleeping in one bed, "two at the foot and three at the head." In spite of their poverty, the children went to school every day and Robinson also attended a sewing school on Saturdays.

Mrs. Hanson's struggle to support her family became increasingly difficult. When her sister suggested she join her in Lowell, a booming mill town about twenty miles northwest of Boston, to manage a boardinghouse for mill workers, Mrs. Hanson did not hesitate. In 1832, she piled her four children into a canal boat and traveled the short journey up the Middlesex Canal to Lowell.

New England mill towns

Samuel Slater's introduction of spinning technology, combined with advances in weaving technology, such as power looms, pushed the cotton spinning and cloth weaving industries to the forefront of American industry. As businessmen rushed to profit from the booming textile in-

dustry, new mills were quickly constructed. Large mill towns began to spring up all over the New England countryside, along the region's powerful rivers, especially the mighty Merrimack.

One of the most successful mill owners was Francis Cabot Lowell, a Harvard graduate from a wealthy Boston family. Taking advantage of the demand for cloth brought on by the War of 1812 and with financial help from his family, Lowell established the Boston Manufacturing Company. It was a mill complex that, under Lowell's guidance, used the power loom to its greatest advantage. Located at Waltham, the Boston Manufacturing Company was the first factory in which all processes from raw material to finished product were performed in one building. From the spinning of the cotton to the weaving of the finished cloth, all work was done in this one mill.

Young women over children

Instead of turning to very young children for labor, as Slater had done, Lowell believed that young women would suit his purposes perfectly. His employees did not need to be strong, only intelligent and hard working. Lowell knew, however, that in order to attract young women to the mills, he would have to offer safe, respectable working and living conditions. Single women living on their own feared for their safety and avoided circumstances that would stain their reputations. Lowell solved this problem by setting up boardinghouses run by responsible, trustworthy matrons, like Robinson's mother, and instilling a strict moral code in both the mills and the surrounding town.

Later, larger mills were built at Lowell, Massachusetts, along the Merrimack River. These mills used power looms, which required workers with nimble hands for smooth operation. The Merrimack Manufacturing Company employed both women and young girls, and the Hanson family moved to this new and larger city.

Life at the mills

In Lowell, Mrs. Hanson worked as hard as ever. She managed a house of forty boarders, taking care of all the cooking, cleaning, and shopping. Now her income was steady and secure. The children continued with their school, but also helped with the housework. Robinson washed many sinkfuls of dishes, standing on a crate to reach the sink.

At age ten, Robinson went to work in the mills. Her mother needed the extra income and Robinson wanted to help out. She was sent to work as a doffer—a worker who took full bobbins off the spinning frame and replaced them with empty ones. The work was fairly easy; doffers were needed only fifteen minutes out of every hour. "The rest of the time," she later wrote, "was their own, and when the overseer was kind, they were allowed to read, knit, or even to go outside the mill-yard and play."

Drawing-in girl

When she was older, Robinson became a drawing-in girl, one of the more desirable positions in the mill. Drawing-in girls drew in the threads of the warp through the harness and the reed, making the beams ready for the weaver's loom. (The warp is the thread that runs lengthwise in a fabric. The harness raises and lowers warp threads on the loom. The reed is a movable frame that separates the warp threads.) Though it required skill and a nimble and steady hand, this job was not very demanding. Since the drawing-in girls were paid by the piece, not by the hour, they could work at their own pace. If they chose to read, they could, and Robinson often took the opportunity to open a book while she worked. Throughout her childhood, books were extremely important to her. She spent much of the precious free time she had each day reading.

When she was fifteen, Robinson took two years off from working in the mills to attend Lowell High School. Here, in a wooden schoolroom located above a butcher shop, she learned French, Latin, and English grammar and composition. Her composition titles—including "Poverty Not Disgraceful" and "Indolence and Industry"—give a glimpse into her attitudes about life. She felt that hardworking poor people were just as worthy as wealthy people and she hated laziness. A photograph of her during this time shows a strikingly beautiful young women with piercing black eyes, ringlets in her long hair, and a brave, confident face.

After high school, Robinson joined in many of the literary groups that had sprung up around Lowell. She even began writing and publishing her own poetry. In fact she met her husband, William Robinson, when she took some of her poetry to the Lowell *Journal,* where he worked as an editor.

Chronicle of early mill life

Robinson left the mills at age twenty-three. She later wrote of her experiences in a book called *Loom and Spindle, or Life Among the Early Mill Girls,* published in 1898. Although many historians believe that Robinson paints an overly bright and rosy picture of life in the mills during this time, Robinson claimed that hers was an accurate account of her experiences and that working conditions did not worsen until after she left in 1848. It is important to keep in mind, however, that Robinson's circumstances may have been more favorable than most. She lived with her family (many girls had left homes far away to work in the mills); she held a skilled but relatively easy job that allowed time for reading; and she worked in the very early days of the industry, when workers were still allowed to perform at their own pace. Nonetheless, her account captures a time in history when women began to see their position in society change as they had the opportunity to become wage earners and to educate themselves.

Who were the mill girls?

Assured of a safe environment and attracted by the cash wages and the chance to earn a living for themselves, women from all over New England flocked to the mill towns to work. They called themselves mill girls.

According to Robinson, mill girls included farmer's daughters aching for city life, women from fine families who did not really need the money but wanted to be in a cultured and stimulating environment, "women with past histories," married women running away from husbands who had mistreated them, and unmarried women who had been dependent on relatives for their support.

Robinson's moving account of this last group gives a clear idea of how strongly women were affected by the opportunity to earn their own income: "How well I remember some of these solitary ones! . . . I can see them now, even after sixty years, just as they looked,—depressed, modest, mincing, hardly daring to look one in the face, so shy and sylvan had been their lives. But after the first pay-day came, and they felt the jingle of silver in their pockets . . . their bowed heads were lifted, their necks seemed braced with steel, they looked you in the face, sang blithely among their looms or frames, and walked with elastic step to and from their work."

Mills offered women the opportunity to make their own way in life. Becoming wage earners for the first time empowered these women with a new sense of confidence. Even the large numbers of women who worked in the mills to finance their brothers' education came away from the experience more confident and self-assured.

Working conditions

By today's standards, work in the mills during Robinson's time was demanding and difficult. Workers began their day at 5:00 in the morning and worked until 7:00 in the evening, with only two half-hour meal breaks in between. Robinson wrote that though she did not mind such a schedule, the worst part of it was having to get up so early: "I do not recall any particular hardship connected with this life, except getting up so early in the morning, and to this habit, I never was, and never shall be, reconciled, for it has taken nearly a lifetime for me to make up the sleep lost at that early age."

Inside the mills, the noise of so much machinery—pounding levers and grinding gears—could be deafening. As a drawing-in girl, Robinson worked in small rooms away from the busiest and noisiest part of the mill. In the early days of the mills, mill operators let workers progress at their own pace and did not force them to take on any more work than they could handle. As Robinson wrote, "We were not hurried any more than was for our good, and no more work was required of us than we were able easily to do." As the years passed, however, and textile manufacturing became more competitive, workers were forced to labor at a quick pace, churning out products as fast as was humanly possible.

"The mill girl's alma mater"

One of the most fascinating aspects of mill life was the urgency with which many girls went about educating themselves. Mill life, where books and ideas were shared and discussed on a daily basis, offered many mill girls their first opportunity at real learning. Many had come from faraway villages and farms where the only book available was the family Bible. Robinson recalled one boarder in her mother's boarding house who had traveled from her farm in Maine to work in the mills "for the express purpose of getting books."

This boarder read from two to four books per week, renting them for about six cents each at the local lending library. In exchange for running to the library and back, the boarder let Harriet and her siblings read the books, too.

With work consuming fourteen hours of each day, mill girls had precious little free time, yet many spent their free hours reading, writing, and learning. It was not uncommon for mill girls to spend their evening hours participating in reading groups, attending night school, and going to lectures. One lecturer, A. P. Peabody, gave a stirring picture of mill girls listening to a lecture: "The Lowell Hall was always crowded, and four-fifths of the audience were factory-girls. When the lecturer entered, almost every girl had a book in her hand, and was intent upon it. When he rose, the book was laid aside, and paper and pencil taken instead . . . I have never seen anywhere so assiduous note-taking. No, not even in a college class . . . as in that assembly of young women, laboring for their subsistence."

The Lowell Offering

In October 1840, some of the mill girls got together to produce and publish, in the words of editor Abel C. Thomas, "the first magazine or journal written exclusively by women in the whole world." The sixteen-page *Offering*, which sold for about six cents a copy, published poems, articles, and stories written by mill girls. Robinson contributed several poems to the journal and later became its historian. The *Offering* received praise from literary circles around the country and even the world. English novelist Charles Dickens claimed that it would "compare advantageously with a great many English annals." In France, female writer George Sands hailed the work.

Strikes

In spite of the educational advantages, the spirited fellowship, and the income that the mills offered, workers were not always happy with the treatment they received. Robinson witnessed two strikes during her younger years, and participated in one of them. In 1834, when she was nine, workers left their posts at 11:00 on a Saturday morning, turning out to the streets to protest a 15 percent wage cut. The mill owners were surprised by this show of female resistance and called the striking workers "Amazons." This strike was one of the first cases of organized protest in the history of the textile industry and did considerable damage. Some rooms in the mills were left completely empty and the town's banks were drained as fired workers withdrew their savings and returned home.

Two years later, when Robinson was eleven and working as a doffer, workers struck because of a proposed pay cut that would allow mill owners to pay more to the boardinghouse managers. This time, Robinson was directly involved in the strike, leading a room full of girls into the march. She wrote: "I, who began to think they would not go out, after all their talk, became impatient, and started on ahead, saying, with childish bravado, 'I don't care what you do, I am going to turn out,' and was followed by the others." This time, thousands—one-quarter of Lowell's working population—marched in the streets. This turnout, which

lasted a month, produced some effects; several of the mills reversed the wage cut. Only later did Robinson realize that her action hurt her mother, who, as a boardinghouse matron, could have used the extra income.

Worsening conditions

As early as 1841, when Robinson still worked in the mills, workers were complaining about the inhuman conditions, claiming they were treated like machines. The piece below, titled "The Spirit of Discontent," was published in *The Offering:* "I am going home, where I shall not be obliged to rise so early in the morning, nor be dragged about by the factory bell, nor confined in a close noisy room from morning to night. I shall not stay here. . . . Up before day, at the clang of the bell,—and out of the mill by the clang of the bell—into the mill, and at work in obedience to that ding-dong of a bell—just as though we were so many living machines."

As years passed, mills sped up production and gave workers increased work loads. Wages dropped and working conditions worsened. Reporters described mill hands as working endlessly and "when they can toil no longer, they go home to die." Housing became cramped as more and more workers moved to mill towns. In one home, reported the Lowell *Courier,* 120 people lived under the same roof; in another case, 22 people made their home in a basement.

Now, workers, with the support of the public, fought for a shorter working day (ten hours) and better wages. By the mid- to late 1800s, mill girls were replaced by immigrants—Irish, Italian, and Portuguese—who were willing to work for lower wages. As the twentieth-century approached, mill towns like Lowell, Lawrence, and Holyoke teemed with mill workers, many of them immigrant men. Housing became scarce and overcrowded. Cramped conditions, improper air circulation, and unclean surroundings caused outbreaks of tuberculosis, cholera, and typhoid. One out of every three spinners, many under the age of twenty-five, would die before completing ten years in the factory. It was a far cry from the dismal round of life in these mill towns to the pleasant, spirited days that Robinson wrote about.

Marriage and family

Robinson's marriage on Thanksgiving Day of 1848 to William Robinson ended her work in the mills. Her husband, who for a time published an antislavery newspaper, was politically active and his liberal views made him many enemies. The couple eventually moved to Malden, outside of Boston, and had four children, one of whom died in infancy. Robinson was content to live as a housewife while her husband worked. Later, however, after William's death, Robinson devoted much of her time to fighting for women's rights. She hoped to, but did not, see women get the vote in her own lifetime.

Suffragette

With her elder daughter, Hattie, Robinson joined the National Woman Suffrage Association, which promoted a woman's right to vote as well as her rights in the workplace and in the home. In 1881, Robinson published a book, *Massachusetts in the Woman Suffrage Movement.* At one point she testified before Congress on the subject of suffrage. Robinson and Hattie also formed a women's club in Malden.

In her later years, Robinson often was asked to lecture about her life as a mill girl. At these lectures she met women who were working in the mills of the late 1800s and soon learned that the conditions they labored under were far worse than anything she remembered. She wrote:

"The wages of these operatives are much lower, and although the hours of labor are less, they are obliged to do a far greater amount of work in a given time. They tend so many looms and frames that they have no time to think. They are always on the jump."

Robinson spent the last years of her life keeping active with her family, reading, writing, and sewing. She died on December 22, 1911, at the age of eighty-six. Death notices praised her contributions as a champion of women's rights. Years later, during the bicentennial celebration of the United States in 1976, Robinson's home in Malden was declared a landmark.

Further Reading

Bushman, Claudia, *"A Good Poor Man's Wife"; Being a Chronicle of Harriet Hanson Robinson and Her Family in Nineteenth-Century New England,* Hanover, New Hampshire: University Press of New England, 1981.

Dunwell, Steve, *The Run of the Mill: A Pictorial Narrative of the Expansion, Dominion, Decline and Enduring Impact of the New England Textile Industry,* Boston: David R. Godine, 1978.

Robinson, Harriet Hanson, *Loom and Spindle, or Life Among the Early Mill Girls,* Originally published, 1898; reprint, Hawaii: Press Pacifica, 1976.

Selden, Bernice, *The Mill Girls: Lucy Larcom, Harriet Hanson Robinson, Sarah G. Bagley,* New York: Atheneum, 1983. □

Jack Roosevelt Robinson

Jack Roosevelt Robinson (1919-1972) was the first African American of the 20th century to play major league baseball.

Jackie Robinson was born on Jan. 31, 1919, in Cairo, Ga., the son of a sharecropper. After his father deserted his mother, the family moved in 1920 to Los Angeles. Robinson attended Muir Technical High School, where his athletic feats opened college doors. At Pasadena Junior College and at the University of California at Los Angeles, he won acclaim in basketball, football, and baseball. In 1941, when family financial problems forced him to leave the University of California without a degree, he played professional football. In 1942 he enlisted in the Army and in 1943 was commissioned a second lieutenant. He served as

a morale officer, and his opposition to racial discrimination led to a court-martial for insubordination, but he was acquitted.

In 1944 Robinson began a professional baseball career, playing with the Kansas City Monarchs of the Negro Major League. His performance in the east-west championship games (1945) interested Branch Rickey, general manager of the Brooklyn Dodgers, who was scouting black players. A baseball innovator, Rickey knew that civil rights laws would soon end segregation in major league baseball, and he chose Robinson as a test case for integrating the sport. In 1946 Robinson signed a Dodger contract and was assigned to the Montreal team of the International League. Cautioned to prove himself worthy because other black players' futures depended on his success, Robinson maintained a subdued posture. He achieved stardom with the Dodgers, a team he joined in 1947, and in 1949 won the National League's batting championship and its Most Valuable Player Award.

With the admission of other African Americans to baseball, Robinson began to aggressively advocate more honest integration. His exposés of racial prejudice in baseball helped better the lot of black players but also branded him a troublemaker. He retired from the sport in 1956 and went into business. His lifetime batting average of .311 and his leadership prompted sportswriters in 1962 to vote him membership in Baseball's Hall of Fame.

As a businessman, Robinson fought for increased civil rights and economic opportunity for African Americans. For his civil rights work he received the Spingarn Medal from

the National Association for the Advancement of Colored People in 1956. He died suddenly on Oct. 24, 1972, in Stamford, Conn.

Further Reading

Five semiautobiographies deal with Robinson's career, of which Carl. T. Rowan with Jackie Robinson, *Wait till Next Year: The Life Story of Jackie Robinson* (1960), is a candid portrayal. With other sportswriters Robinson coauthored *Jackie Robinson: My Own Story* (1948); *Jackie Robinson* (1950); *Baseball Has Done It,* edited by Charles Dexter (1964); and *Breakthrough to the Big League* (1965). Rickey's role in Robinson's breakthrough is described in Arthur Mann, *Branch Rickey: American in Action* (1957), and Branch Rickey, *The American Diamond* (1965). Richard Bardolph, *The Negro Vanguard* (1959), places Robinson's contribution in the context of the black civil rights movement, and David Q. Voigt, *American Baseball* (2 vols., 1966-1970), places him in the general history of baseball. □

James Harvey Robinson

James Harvey Robinson (1863-1936), American historian, was the central figure in the New History movement, which attempted to use history to understand contemporary problems.

James Harvey Robinson was born on June 29, 1863, in Bloomington, Ill., the son of a local banker. He received his bachelor's and master's degrees from Harvard and did his doctoral work at the University of Freiburg. There he studied under Hermann von Holst, the constitutional historian, and wrote a dissertation on the Federal principle in the American constitution.

Robinson's first teaching position was in European history at the University of Pennsylvania, where the welfare economist Simon N. Patten, who had helped him secure the job, influenced him. After a year Robinson moved to Columbia University as an associate professor of European history and became active on the curriculum subcommittee of the National Education Association for history. In 1895 he became a full professor.

At Columbia, Robinson shared progressive, reformist views with colleagues like John Dewey and continued to develop his New History idea. This historiography movement believed in history as an instrument in helping solve contemporary problems, concentrated upon the life of the common man, and cooperated with other social sciences. Robinson's concepts appeared in his course, "The Intellectual History of Western Europe," which his students called "The Downfall of Christianity."

Robinson's first textbook, *An Introduction to the History of Western Europe* (1902), although quite popular, was more conventional than innovative. The ideas of the New History did not appear in significant text form until *The Development of Modern Europe* (1907), written in collaboration with his most famous student, Charles A. Beard. A group of Robinson's essays, all but one previously published, appeared in *The New History* (1912). This book brought together his ideas and remains the representative work in the movement.

In 1919 Robinson resigned from Columbia to help found the New School for Social Research. There he was chairman of the executive committee and taught one course. He continued to write, producing two popular polemical books—*The Mind in the Making* (1921), a best seller, and *The Humanizing of Knowledge* (1923). These books held that a just social order could be created by applied intelligence. Robinson's ideas remained constant until his death on Feb. 16, 1936, in New York City; this is obvious in the collection of his essays edited by his student Harry Elmer Barnes and published posthumously as *The Human Comedy* (1937).

Further Reading

Luther V. Hendricks, *James Harvey Robinson: Teacher of History* (1946), is short but good and includes a comprehensive bibliography of Robinson's writings. Harry Elmer Barnes's sketch of Robinson in Howard Odum, ed., *American Masters of Social Science: An Approach to the Study of the Social Studies through a Neglected Field of Biography* (1927), is the appraisal of an enthusiastic disciple. Harvey Wish's introduction to the paperback edition of Robinson's *The New History* (1965) is balanced and succinct. □

Joan Violet Maurice Robinson

The English economist Joan Violet Maurice Robinson (née Maurice; 1903-1983) was one of the foremost economists of her generation and the most accomplished, productive, and eminent female economist. She stood as the leading heterodox or dissenting economist of her time.

Joan Violet Maurice was born in Camberley, Surrey, England, in 1903 into a distinguished family in which individuals sought achievement in both the military and the church and remained firm in their beliefs. She was educated at St. Paul's Girls' School in London and then at Girton College of the University of Cambridge. In 1926 she married another English economist, E.A.G. Robinson. They spent the first two years in India where he was a tutor of the Maharajah of Gwalior and she a sometime teacher in a local school. They returned to Cambridge in 1928 and she commenced a career of serious contemplation, theorizing, research, and writing. Her gender, coupled with her husband having a position in the same faculty, hindered her promotion. She did not become a professor until 1965, having been a lecturer and reader during the interim, positions of considerably lower stature. The low level of academic recognition accorded her reflects the discriminatory treatment of women while underscoring the enormity of her achievements. That Joan Robinson did not receive the Nobel Prize in Economic Science may reflect both her gender and her outspoken criticisms of economic orthodoxy. She did leave a group of dedicated students who themselves became productive scholars, working generally along the lines she set down.

Robinson's first major work, *The Economics of Imperfect Competition* (1933), was largely within mainstream economics. It involved the working out of a theory of imperfect competition; that is, of competition limited because a firm may sell products which are not, in consumers' minds, perfect substitutes for those of its nominal competitors. Perfect competition is suggested to be a special case in the real world. Robinson intended for her analysis to eclipse or replace that of perfect competition, but economists, desiring to use the competition assumption to reach determinate equilibrium results, generally tended to pursue analyses using the assumption of perfect competition. This restricted Robinson's analysis, and the comparable analysis of certain other economists, to a separate analytical compartment, thereby rendering it relatively impotent.

Yet Robinson's work in the theory of imperfect competition had two remarkable, if substantially unintended, results. On the one hand, it helped redirect the theory of price and resource allocation toward the theory of the firm, rather than to markets as such; on the other hand, it established the mathematical techniques which came regularly to be used by economists working on price theory and the theory of the firm. Robinson therefore provided the geometrical mode of economic discourse but not the substitution of her particular theory for the mainstream focus on perfect competition.

Four decades later it became widely known that, during the same period in which she developed her theory of imperfect competition, Robinson was a member of an informal group, called the Circus, that served as a sounding board for John Maynard Keynes when he was developing the ideas contained in his epochal *General Theory of Employment, Interest and Money* (1936). Robinson subsequently became a leading interpreter of Keynes, on the one hand opposing more conservative economists whose own interpretations would have, in her view, severely restricted, if not destroyed, the messages for macroeconomic theory and policy which Keynes was trying to convey; and on the other urging that Keynes' type of analysis could be expanded and extended to other fundamental economic questions.

Together with other writers, most notably Piero Sraffa, Robinson attempted to develop a new approach to political economy, one whose emphasis was on growth and distribution. It questioned the coherence and completeness of the mainstream theories of production, growth, and distribution by calling attention to certain points, fundamental but hitherto neglected. These points concern the coherence of the concept of capital and the relations of the quantity of capital to both the rate of aggregate economic growth and the distribution of income, especially in a world of disequilibrium, uncertainty, capital accumulation, alternative combinations of inputs in producing goods (called production functions) and (re)switching from one combination to another, and the institutional and power structure factors underlying the operations of these factors. Her approach centered in part on a vision of a dual relationship between profitability and economic growth: growth depends on (actual and expected) profits, and profitability depends on growth, a fundamental relationship involving complexities not readily absorbed by conventional economic theory and thereby largely ignored by its practitioners.

Finally, Robinson was an incisive interpreter of the history of economic thought. She believed that economics was both (1) a branch of theology and a vehicle for the ruling ideology of each period—that is, an instrument of social control—and (2) an attempt to produce objective scientific knowledge. She felt that economics was inevitably characterized by tensions between these two aspects and that the careful analyst had to separate the two, a task that was not easily accomplished and that likely would be done differently (or to different effects) by different thinkers. Because economics is a serious subject, one needs to be cautious and self-conscious, even skeptical, in its practice.

In 1971 Robinson presented the prestigious Richard T. Ely Lecture to the American Economic Association. Among her many awards was an honorary doctorate from Harvard University in 1980. She and her husband had two children, Ann, born in 1934, and Barbara, born in 1937. Joan Robinson died in 1983.

Further Reading

There is no complete biography of Joan Violet Robinson. The closest to such a biography is Marjorie S. Turner's *Joan Robinson and the Americans* (1989). Detailed summaries and bibliographies of her technical and other work can be found in the entry by Luigi L. Pasinetti in *The New Palgrave: A Dictionary of Economics* (1987), volume 4, and the essay by Geoffrey Harcourt in Henry W. Spiegel and Warren J. Samuels, editors, *Contemporary Economists in Perspective* (1984), volume 2. For a discussion of her *Economic Philosophy* (1962), see Warren J. Samuels, "In Praise of Joan Robinson: Economics as Social Control," in *Society* (January/February 1989). □

Sir John Beverley Robinson

Sir John Beverley Robinson (1791-1863) was a leading member of the Family Compact and of the Tory party of Upper Canada and chief justice of Upper Canada for 33 years.

John Beverley Robinson was born on July 26, 1791, at Berthier in Lower Canada. He was the second son of the American loyalist Christopher Robinson and was educated for some years at Kingston and Cornwall under the tutelage of John Strachan, the future bishop of Toronto. Beginning in October 1807, Robinson read law for 3 years in the office of D'Arcy Boulton, then the solicitor general of Upper Canada.

In 1812 Robinson received a commission under Gen. Sir Isaac Brock and was present at the capture of Ft. Detroit and at the battle at Queenston, where Brock lost his life. From late 1812 until the end of the war in 1815, Robinson was the acting attorney general of Upper Canada, and for much of this period he was the only crown officer in the province. On Feb. 6, 1815, he became the solicitor general, and in September he sailed for England to study law in Lincoln's Inn and to qualify for admission to the English bar.

Robinson returned to Canada late in 1817 and was appointed attorney general on Feb. 11, 1818. In 1821 he entered actively upon a political career, being elected to the Legislative Assembly for York. He was appointed to the Legislative Council as well and from 1828 to 1840 was its speaker. Robinson had, by the mid-1820s, become one of the leaders of the Tory party and a prominent member of the Family Compact, an early Canadian power elite. On July 13, 1829, he was appointed the chief justice of Upper Canada and held this office until 1862.

Robinson opposed the union of the two provinces of Upper and Lower Canada, and in 1840 he published a book on the issue entitled *Canada and the Canada Bill*. Nevertheless he continued to hold the office of chief justice in the new union until, in 1862, he was appointed the first president of the Court of Error and Appeal. In 1853 he was elected chancellor of the University of Trinity College in Toronto and in 1854 was made a baronet.

Though often given to defending the status quo in political and social matters, Robinson acted in most cases with logic and common sense. A man of presence and of marked ability, he served the people of the colony ably for many years. He died at his home, Beverley House, in Toronto on Jan. 31, 1863.

Further Reading

The major biography of Robinson was written by his son, Charles W. Robinson, *The Life of Sir John Beverley Robinson, Bart.* (1904), which, although uncritical, contains valuable passages from many of Robinson's letters and journal entries. D. B. Read, *Lives of the Judges* (1888), is useful. For the earlier period of Robinson's life, Gerald M. Craig, *Upper Canada: The Formative Years, 1784-1841* (1966), offers a recent interpretation. □

Julia Robinson

Excelling in the field of mathematics, Julia Robinson (1919-1985) was instrumental in solving Hilbert's tenth problem—to find an effective method for determining whether a given diophantine equation is solvable with integers. Over a period of two decades, she developed the framework on which the solution was constructed.

In recognition of her accomplishments, Julia Robinson became the first woman mathematician elected to the National Academy of Sciences, the first female president of the American Mathematical Society, and the first woman mathematician to receive a MacArthur Foundation Fellowship.

Robinson was born Julia Bowman on December 8, 1919, in St. Louis, Missouri. Her mother, Helen Hall Bowman, died two years later; Robinson and her older sister went to live with their grandmother near Phoenix, Arizona. The following year their father, Ralph Bowman, retired and joined them in Arizona after becoming disinterested in his machine tool and equipment business. He expected to support his children and his new wife, Edenia Kridelbaugh Bowman, with his savings. In 1925, her family moved to San Diego; three years later a third daughter was born.

At the age of nine, Robinson contracted scarlet fever, and the family was quarantined for a month. They celebrated the end of isolation by viewing their first talking motion picture. The celebration was premature, however, as Robinson soon developed rheumatic fever and was bedridden for a year. When she was well enough, she worked with a tutor for a year, covering the required curriculum for the fifth through eighth grades. She was fascinated by the tutor's claim that it had been proven that the square root of two could not be calculated to a point where the decimal began to repeat. Her interest in mathematics continued at San Diego High School; when she graduated with honors in mathematics and science, her parents gave her a slide rule that she treasured and named "Slippy."

At the age of sixteen, Robinson entered San Diego State College. She majored in mathematics and prepared for a teaching career, being aware of no other mathematics career choices. At the beginning of Robinson's sophomore year, her father found his savings depleted by the Depression and committed suicide. With help from her older sister and an aunt, Robinson remained in school. She transferred to the University of California, Berkeley, for her senior year and graduated in 1940.

At Berkeley, she found teachers and fellow students who shared her excitement about mathematics. In December of 1941, she married an assistant professor named Raphael Robinson. At that time she was a teaching assistant at Berkeley, having completed her master's degree in 1941. The following year, however, the school's nepotism rule prevented her from teaching in the mathematics department. Instead, she worked in the Berkeley Statistical Laboratory on military projects. She became pregnant but lost her baby; because of damage to Robinson's heart caused by the rheumatic fever, her doctor warned against future pregnancies. Her hopes of motherhood crushed, Robinson endured a period of depression that lasted until her husband rekindled her interest in mathematics.

In 1947 she embarked on a doctoral program under the direction of Alfred Tarski . In her dissertation, she proved the algorithmic unsolvability of the theory of the rational number field. Her Ph.D. was conferred in 1948. That same year, Tarski discussed an idea about diophantine equations (polynomial equations of several variables, with integer coefficients, whose solutions are to be integers) with Raphael Robinson, who shared it with his wife. By the time she realized it was directly related to the tenth problem on Hilbert's list, she was too involved in the topic to be intimidated by its stature. For the next twenty-two years she attacked various aspects of the problem, building a foundation on which Yuri Matijasevic proved in 1970 that the desired general method for determining solvability does not exist. While working at the RAND Corporation in 1949 and 1950, Robinson developed an iterative solution for the value of a finite two-person zero-sum game. Her only contribution to game theory is still considered a fundamental theorem in the field.

Robinson's heart damage was surgically repaired in 1961, but her health remained impaired. Her fame from the Hilbert problem solution resulted in her appointment as a full professor at Berkeley in 1976, although she was expected to carry only one-fourth of the normal teaching load. Eight years later she developed leukemia and died on July 30, 1985.

Further Reading

"Julia Bowman Robinson, 1919–1985," in *Notices of the American Mathematical Society,* November, 1985, pp. 738–742.
Reid, Constance, "The Autobiography of Julia Robinson," in *The College Mathematics Journal,* January, 1986, pp. 2–21.
Smorynski, C., "Julia Robinson, In Memoriam," in *The Mathematical Intelligencer,* spring 1986, pp. 77–79. □

Mary Bourke Robinson

In 1990 Mary Bourke Robinson (née Bourke; born 1944) became the first woman to be elected president of Ireland. She was named United Nations commissioner for human rights in 1997.

Mary Robinson was born in May 1944 in Ballina, County Mayo. Her father, Dr. Aubrey Bourke, was a general practitioner in that area for 50 years. Her mother, Tessa O'Donnell, came from County Donegal.

The only girl in a family of five, she attended Mt. Anville, an exclusive Catholic girls' boarding school in Dublin. Next she studied at Trinity College at a time when the Irish Catholic hierarchy disapproved of Catholics attending that then predominantly Protestant university. She was admitted to the bar in 1967 after having attended the King's Inn. Subsequently she went to Harvard where she earned a Masters in Law. In 1969 she became the youngest professor of law at Trinity College. She married Nicholas Robinson, a Dublin solicitor, and they had three children. Her marriage at first met familial disapproval because her husband was a Protestant.

In 1969 she was elected to Seanad Eireann, the senate or upper house of the Irish legislature, as the youngest ever member. She represented the Dublin University (Trinity College) constituency and was a member of the Irish Labour Party, a socialist democratic party which in the 1970s and 1980s would be a governing coalition partner with the larger Fine Gael Party, one of the two essentially conservative nationalist parties dominant in Ireland. She was continually reelected and served for 20 years—until she became president in 1990.

Both as a senator and as a barrister Robinson championed numerous causes that could most appropriately be categorized as civil libertarian and feminist. In 1974 she introduced an unsuccessful private member's bill to liberalize Irish legislation on contraceptives. In various courts, Irish and European, she appeared on behalf of such causes as the ending of discriminatory treatment of women in selecting of Irish jurors, the granting of the franchise to 18 year olds, the protection of archaeological excavations from building developers, the equitable treatment of children born outside of marriage, and the restriction of wire taps on journalists.

She campaigned for the losing side in two constitutional referenda. The first, a "right to life" amendment that added constitutional permanence to the existing Irish legislation against abortion, was approved by about a two to one margin by the electorate in 1983. The second, a 1985 proposed amendment that would change the existing constitutional prohibition of the dissolution of marriage and allow divorce in certain circumstances, was defeated by a comparable margin.

Robinson took an independent position on the Anglo-Irish Agreement of 1985, which many regard as the most

significant development in Irish history in the second half of the 20th century. The accord, in which Britain and Ireland acknowledged that the status of Northern Ireland would not be changed without the consent of the majority of the province's population, was attacked by hardline Irish nationalists as the "copper-fastening" of the partition of the island. Northern Irish Unionists, on the other hand, saw the extending of a quasi-consultative role to the Irish government on the governance of Northern Ireland as the first step on the "slippery slope" towards their being abandoned into a united Ireland. Mary Robinson resigned from the Labour Party, which was part of the coalition government that had signed the treaty, to register her disapproval. She was convinced that any democratic reconciliation in Northern Ireland must have the consent of the Unionists, who had not been a party to the negotiations leading to the agreement. Furthermore, she believed it was incumbent on the Republic of Ireland to so amend articles two and three of its constitution, where a *de jure* claim for the whole island is made, so as to transform the wording from a claim into an aspiration.

Five years later she was selected as the presidential candidate of the same Labour Party. She also received the support of the more left-wing Workers Party and the environmentalist Green Party. She entered the campaign months before the voting, something very unusual in the election to the primarily honorific post, and was not given a serious chance at success by most knowledgeable observers.

The major opposition party, Fine Gael, had great difficulty in getting any of its major figures to agree to run in what was felt would be a certain victory by the governing Fianna Fail Party, whose candidates had won all previous contested presidential elections. Fine Gael finally settled on Austin Currie, a member of the Irish parliament whose earlier political career had been in Northern Ireland as a member of the Social Democratic and Labour Party, the moderate constitutional party of the Catholic minority.

Brian Lenihan, the former foreign minister, defense minister, and deputy leader of the Fianna Fail Party, was the candidate of the latter and was expected to be an easy victor, in no small part because of his own immense popularity and a general high level of sympathy as a consequence of his having undergone serious surgery a year before. However, in the closing stages of the campaign an embarrassing contradiction appeared between Lenihan's public denial that he had several years earlier tried to influence the then president to install a Fianna Fail ministry without benefit of a general election and his actual admission of the same on a tape made of a private interview he gave to a graduate student of political science. Many in the electorate were incensed more at the apparent lack of veracity than at the politically inappropriate but legal lobbying.

Lenihan still topped the polls on November 7, 1990, with 44 percent of the vote, with Robinson in second place with 38 percent, but the victor must have an absolute majority. Therefore, the second choices on ballots for the eliminated third place contestant, Currie, were distributed to the two front runners. The result gave Robinson a clear majority. She was expected to fully utilize the educational potential of the presidency to draw attention to numerous general concerns, particularly the socially and economically disadvantaged, the environment, and human rights in general. She stills holds this position in 1997.

Throughout her career as president, Robinson has had to deal with wars, internal government scandal and trying to overcome the stigmas applied to her for being a woman. To her credit she has tried to right some of the Irish historical wrongs. She took office asking for tolerance between the Catholics and the Protestants. She memoralized women who worked in laundries run by the Roman Catholic Priests (from 1766 to the 1960's) as pennance for their "immorality." She was present (Oct. 1996) when Gov. George Pataki signed a new law to make the Irish potato famine of the mid-19th Century a required lesson in New York public schools. And she was a key-note speaker at the 1996 International Women's Leadership Forum in Stockholm.

In 1997 Robinson was named the UN high commissioner for human rights, a move expected to invigorate the post created three years ago to promote civil liberties worldwide. Amnesty International, a critic of her predecessor Jose Ayala Lasso, welcomed the appointment and urged her to act quickly to confront human rights abuses in Congo, Sierra Leone, Colombia and elsewhere.

Further Reading

For an account of Mary Robinson's election victory see Glenn Frankel, "Socialist Feminist Wins Irish Presidency" in the (*Washington Post,* November 10, 1990). While there are no biographies of Robinson, excellent general histories of contemporary Ireland are J.J. Lee, *Ireland 1912-1988: Politics and Society* (1989) and Terence Brown, *Ireland: A Social and Cultural History, 1922 to the Present* (1985). Lively studies of prominent recent political leaders are Raymond Smith, *Garret: The Enigma* (1985) about Garret FitzGerald, and Joe Joyce and Peter Murtagh, *The Boss: Charles J. Haughey in Government* (1983). Updated information gathered from *LA Times* World in Brief, Ireland: "President Sworn In, Calls for Tolerance," Tuesday, December 4, 1990; *Chicago Tribune*, "Irish memorial," 05/12/96; "Schools Ordered to Study Irish Rights Commissioner," 06/13/97. Biographical information is also provided in *The Cambridge Biographical Encyclopedia* edited by David Crystal. ☐

Max Robinson

Max Robinson (1939-1988) broke racial barriers in the media industry when he became the first black television anchor in Washington, D.C., and again when he joined ABC's *World News Tonight* as a cohost in 1978. He fought for racial equality and more positive portrayals of African Americans throughout his career, making him a role model for many.

In 1981 noted media analyst Gerald Goldhaber wrote in *TV Guide* that "the paradox of network news is that the success of the show has far less to do with its informational content than with the charisma of the personalities that bring us the news." Oddly enough, one of the personalities anchoring the national news during that time was living his own paradox. Even though Max Robinson was heralded by the black community for fighting racism and injustice to become the first black network news anchor, he was constantly trying to overcome his own personal demons, which made his journey more difficult. "I think one of my basic flaws," he once told a *Washington Post* correspondent, "has been a lack of esteem . . . always feeling like I had to do more. I never could do enough or be good enough. And that was the real problem."

Robinson's quest to become a broadcast journalist and to overcome racial obstacles began in Portsmouth, Virginia, in 1959 when he applied for a "whites only" job at a local television station. The owner of the station courteously allowed him to audition for the job along with four white candidates. To his surprise, Robinson was given a job reading the news on the air, though his face was hidden behind a slide bearing the station's logo. "One night," Clarence Page wrote in *Chicago*, "[Robinson] ordered the slide removed so his relatives could see him. He was fired the next day. The station manager told him, 'Portsmouth isn't ready for

color television.'" Thus began the controversial broadcasting career of Max Robinson.

"A Great Presence on the Air"

The next job Robinson landed was as a cameraman-reporter trainee at WTOP-TV (now WUSA) in Washington, D.C. Once again, he was forced to accept the racial prejudices of the times—he was given a salary that was $25 less per week than his white counterparts. Robinson made the most of this opportunity, however, and was soon promoted to full-time reporter. "He had a great presence on the air," James Snyder, a co-worker at the time, told Burt Folkart of the *Los Angeles Times*. "He was very meticulous about his on-air performance. He rarely made a mistake. He was very conscious that he was a role model." But many people were also beginning to talk about the personal problems that seemed to haunt Robinson. "Friends said he labored under enormous pressure," Folkart continued, "both because of his race and his fears of inadequacy."

The troubles that plagued Robinson, though, didn't prevent him from furthering his career. It was less than a year after he began his career at WTOP that he was offered a job at another Washington, D.C., station, WRC-TV. Robinson wasn't looking forward to becoming the first black reporter at yet another station. Because he was unhappy with doing only traffic reports at WTOP, he took the job.

This move proved to be both a major stepping stone in Robinson's journalism career as well as a source of more racial prejudice. "I can remember walking down the halls and speaking to people who would look right through me,'' Robinson told Peter Benjaminson in *Contemporary Authors*. ''It was hateful at times . . . I've been the first too often, quite frankly. We firsts ought to get extra pay.''

Became Washington D.C.'s First Black Anchor

Even though Robinson was spending a great deal of time fighting racism, he was also being recognized as a consummate journalist. During his three and a half years at WRC he won six journalism awards for his coverage of such events as the 1968 riots after civil rights leader Martin Luther King, Jr.'s assassination, the antiwar demonstrations, and the national election. It was during this time that Robinson won two regional Emmys for a documentary he did on black life in Anacostia titled *The Other Washington*. Robinson, however, wanted more for his career; he aspired to be a television news anchor. The news director at WRC admitted to Robinson that he had the ability, but he wasn't convinced that Washington was ready for a black anchor. So, Robinson went back to his previous employer, WTOP, in search of an anchoring position. In 1969 he became the first black anchor in Washington, D.C., when he was given a job co-anchoring the midday newscast at WTOP. Two short years later, he was made co-anchor of the prestigious 6:00 pm and 11:00 pm newscasts with Gordon Peterson, the man that Robinson would later call the best partner he ever had.

Max Robinson had finally made it to the big time; he was now anchoring the top-rated newscasts in the city. ''On camera,'' Bart Barnes of the *Washington Post* wrote, ''Robinson had a quiet, authoritative delivery, a deep resonant voice and a serious demeanor that inspired trust and confidence in his viewers.'' But even with all the accolades that were being showered on him, there were those who worried about his mental health. *Washington Post* columnist William Raspberry observed, ''Even then, the demons had made themselves known. Indeed, it seemed to his friends that Max was forever the subject of some macabre competition between his demons and his manifest talent.'' In 1973 personal difficulties rendered Robinson a subject in the news, rather than just a reporter of it. Distraught over the death of his father, Maxie, Robinson fired a gun into the terrace of his apartment. A simple on-air apology, however, ended the incident and heightened his appeal as one of the city's premier media personalities.

A Controversial Figure at ABC News

In 1978 ABC News President Roone Arledge, impressed with the work that Robinson was doing, gave him the chance to be the first black network anchor, though it would not be a solo job. Arledge had decided to experiment with a new concept by offering America its first anchor trio featuring Frank Reynolds reporting from the Washington desk, Peter Jennings from the foreign desk in London, England, and Max Robinson from the national desk in Chicago, Illinois. So Robinson left his beloved Washington, where he was honored with a Max Robinson Day by the city council, to begin a new life in Chicago cohosting *World News Tonight*.

''Robinson arrived in Chicago triumphant,'' *Chicago'*s Page declared, ''with enough broadcast honors and viewer loyalty in Washington to make him a national hero. To all outward appearances, it was the top of Robinson's career, a time for enjoying his success, even for coasting.'' But, as Page concluded, ''it was to be a short ride.'' Almost immediately, Robinson took it upon himself to fight racism at every turn and at whatever cost he thought necessary. He was constantly embroiled with his network bosses over the way news stories portrayed black America and how they neglected to reflect the black viewpoint. Robinson's integrity as a journalist and his role as a leader in the fight against prejudice made him a mentor to many young black television journalists. Unfortunately, he never felt worthy of the admiration or satisfied with his accomplishments. It wasn't long before friends and coworkers began to notice a significant change in his behavior. He became stubborn and moody, began showing up late for work or not at all, and his fondness for alcohol took on epidemic proportions.

Management at ABC was getting frustrated with the image problems that Robinson was causing them. One particular incident, a 1981 speech for students at Smith College in Northampton, Massachusetts, began his fall from grace with network officials. ''He told an audience,'' Jeremy Gerard of the *New York Times* wrote, ''that the news media were 'a crooked mirror' through which 'white America views itself,' and that 'only by talking about racism, by taking a professional risk, will I take myself out of the mean, racist trap all black Americans find themselves in.''' Though Robinson later apologized for the remark and assured management that he wasn't trying to single out ABC, the damage had been done.

Two years later, when Robinson skipped the funeral of his co-anchor, Frank Reynolds, where he was supposed to sit next to former First Lady Nancy Reagan, management responded by returning their network newscast to a single-anchor program. Peter Jennings was given the prime spot, while Robinson was named a weekend anchor and Washington correspondent. Frustrated about his demotion, Robinson abandoned ABC in 1978 to become the first black anchor for WMAQ-TV, a local television station in Chicago.

Even though he was reportedly being paid twice his $200,000 salary at ABC, Robinson could not find success in his new role. The local press was constantly finding fault with both his personal and professional life, which in turn pushed Robinson to vent his anger and frustration on colleagues. He claimed he was being sabotaged by coworkers who tried to make his life difficult. On one occasion, the city of Chicago got a firsthand glimpse at the extent of Robinson's personal turmoil. ''Once, while the credits were rolling,'' Raspberry reported, ''Max lit into the crew in language that would curl a sailor's hair. But the [microphone] had 'accidentally' been left open, and those choice words went out all over Chicago.''

Things only worsened for Robinson after that. His excessive drinking and bouts with depression repeatedly kept him off the anchor desk. Many times it was by the choice of management, but for the most part it was because he simply never showed up for work. His co-anchors would make excuses for him at first. At one point the station announced to viewers that they had no idea where Robinson was. In 1985 his partnership with WMAQ ended.

Diagnosed With AIDS

Except for a few free-lance jobs, Max Robinson never again worked as a journalist. He spent a considerable amount of time in and out of treatment centers in the hopes of trying to recover from his alcoholism. Unfortunately, just when it appeared that he was about to put his life in order, he was hospitalized in Blue Island, Illinois, with pneumonia. It didn't take doctors long to figure out the cause of his ailment: acquired immunodeficiency syndrome (AIDS).

For the next year, Robinson was rarely seen in public, partly because of the shame he felt accompanied having the AIDS virus, but also because the illness had progressed quickly and powerfully. He did make an appearance in August of 1988 at the National Association of Black Journalists convention in St. Louis, Missouri. A few months later, he made his final public appearance when he spoke at a reception for Howard University's School of Journalism. Though his family and friends advised him to stay in Chicago, Robinson wanted to visit the city he loved one last time. Max Robinson died while in Washington, D.C., from complications of AIDS on December 20, 1988. Leaders in the black community, along with television news stars, including Peter Jennings and Dan Rather, joined civil rights activist Jesse Jackson at the Shiloh Baptist Church in Washington, D.C., to pay tribute to a man that had impacted both an industry and a culture. Bernard Shaw, co-anchor at Cable News Network (CNN) and one of the few blacks that has enjoyed a network anchor position, summed up his feelings for Judith Michaelson of the *Los Angeles Times:* "His impact will go on for generations. He was Engine No. 1."

Clarence Page offered a final tribute to his friend Max Robinson in *Chicago:* "Some journalists are remembered for the stories they covered. Robinson will be remembered for *being* the story. Like Jackie Robinson, who broke baseball's color bar in 1947, Max Robinson won't be applauded for his home runs, but for the fact that he ran the bases."

Further Reading

Contemporary Authors, Volume 124, Gale, 1990.
Broadcasting, December 26, 1988.
Chicago, June 1990.
Chicago Tribune, February 23, 1984; December 21, 1988.
Ebony, January 1979; August 1979; March 1981; August 1983.
Jet, January 9, 1989; January 30, 1989; May 1, 1989.
Los Angeles Times, December 21, 1988; December 23, 1988.
Newsweek, January 2, 1989.
New York Times, December 21, 1989.
People, December 28, 1982.
Time, January 11, 1988; January 2, 1989.
TV Guide, December 2, 1978; May 2, 1981.
Washington Post, December 31, 1987; December 21, 1988; December 23, 1988. □

Smokey Robinson

Motown star Smokey Robinson (born 1940), co-founder of the Tamla record label, has been a composer and performer for more than 30 years.

Smokey Robinson, the "poet laureate of soul music," has been composing and singing rhythm and blues hits for more than three decades. As the lead singer of the Miracles, Robinson, who moved to SBK Records later in his career, helped to put Detroit and its Motown Records on the music map; his solo performances have netted Grammy Awards and praise from pundits who usually shun the pop genre. *People* contributor Gail Buchalter labeled Robinson "one of the smoothest tenors in soul music," a romantic idol whose 60 million-plus in record sales "helped turn Motown into the largest black-owned corporation in the world."

According to Jay Cocks in *Time,* Robinson has written, produced, and performed "some of the most enduring rhythm and blues [songs] ever made. The church kept easy company with the street corner in his rich melodies, and his lyrics had a shimmering, reflective grace that, at his pleasure, could challenge or seduce. With the Miracles, Smokey helped make a kind of soul music that balanced ghetto pride and middle-class ambition. Some of the group's best tunes . . . stayed true to the R & B roots even as they beckoned, and found, a larger pop audience." In *Rolling Stone,* Steve Pond concluded that Robinson has written "some 4000 songs and recorded hundreds that have made him a true poet of the soul and a voice of the soul, too."

The Miracles's Success Spawned Motown Records

William "Smokey Joe" Robinson, Jr., not only rose from obscurity, he brought along a number of other now-famous black recording stars when he began to find success. He was born and raised in Detroit, in the rough Brewster ghetto, where, as he recalled in *People,* "you were either in a [music] group or a gang or both." Young Smokey grew up listening to his mother's records, including the works of B. B. King, Muddy Waters, John Lee Hooker, Sarah Vaughan, and Billy Eckstine. These black artists, he commented in *Rolling Stone,* were "the first inspirational thing I had." When Robinson was ten, his mother died, and his sister Geraldine took him in, raising him along with her ten children. The family was poor but close-knit, and Robinson spent his youth writing songs and singing in local bands.

Robinson would not consider a professional career until he graduated from high school, and even then he tried barber school and courses in dentistry before giving his full attention to music. In 1954 he formed a rhythm and blues group called the Matadors; the name was changed to the Miracles three years later to accommodate a female singer, Claudette Rogers, who married Robinson in 1959. At first the members of the Miracles—who were each paid five dollars per week by their agent, Berry Gordy—found the music business difficult. "For a while," Claudette Robinson related in *Essence,* "we lived basically in one bedroom. But we didn't stay in that house very long. Fortunately, the music started to happen.''

Robinson was lucky to have encountered Berry Gordy during an audition for another agent; Gordy, then a fledgling music producer on a shoestring budget, was equally fortunate to have found Robinson. Gordy began to produce the Miracles's singles in 1958, collaborating with Robinson on lyrics and tunes. Their first release, ''*Got a Job*'' —an answer to The Silhouettes's number one hit ''*Get a Job*'' — hit Number 93 on the nationwide Billboard Top 100 chart. The debut was encouraging, but nothing prepared Gordy and Robinson for the limelight they would attain in 1960. Late in that year they released an upbeat single, ''*Shop Around,*'' that became a chart-topping million-seller. The Miracles subsequently became a national phenomenon, and Gordy was able to launch Motown Records, a landmark production company that introduced such talents as Diana Ross and the Supremes, Stevie Wonder, Marvin Gaye, and the Temptations.

Became a Sought-After Songwriter

Robinson and the Miracles were Gordy's first star-quality group, and they continued their association with Motown as the company gained prestige. Indeed, Robinson wrote hit songs not only for his group but for other Motown headliners as well. He explained the Motown philosophy in *Rolling Stone:* ''We set out to make music for people of all races and nationalities. Not to make black music—we just wanted to make good music that would be acceptable in all circles. . . . All we were doing, man, was just putting good songs on good tracks, songs that anybody could relate to. We had good, solid songs that would fit your particular life situation if you were white or Oriental or Chicano or whatever you happened to be. And that made a world of difference.''

Throughout the 1960s, especially in the latter half of the decade, the Motown sound competed with the music of the British invasion for popularity among the young. Robinson and the Miracles were favorites among the Motown personnel, earning more than six gold records containing such hits as ''*The Tracks of My Tears,*'' ''*You've Really Got a Hold on Me,*'' ''*I Second That Emotion,*'' and ''*Ooo Baby Baby.*'' Still, Robinson was on the verge of quitting the group in 1968 when his son Berry was born. He reconsidered almost immediately, however, when the Miracles single, ''*Tears of a Clown,*'' became a Number One hit, first in England and then in the United States. Robinson noted in *Rolling Stone* that ''*Tears of a Clown*'' became the biggest record we ever had. It catapulted us into another financial echelon as far as what we made on dates, and I felt that the band was entitled to reap the benefits.'' The Miracles, a model group in terms of road behavior, endured until 1972, when Robinson quit.

For a time after leaving the Miracles, Robinson concentrated on his business duties as vice-president of Motown Records. He soon returned to recording, however, this time as a solo artist. His solo albums are, on the whole, more reflective and mellow than his work with the Miracles. All of them highlight the singer's particular talent—the creation

and performance of meaningful love songs at a time when many erstwhile romantics have become jaded cynics. Stephen Holden summed up the reason for the immense popularity of Robinson's music in *Rolling Stone:* ''Smokey Robinson is that rare pop singer whose rhapsodic lyricism hasn't diminished with approaching middle age. Indeed, time has added a metaphysical depth to his art. . . . Smokey Robinson's faith in the redemptive power of erotic love continues unabated. In Robinson's musical world, sexual happiness isn't the product of spiritual equilibrium but its source. . . . Don't think, however, that Robinson's songs aren't filled with sex. They are. But in this man's art, sex isn't a fast roll in the hay, it's sweet manna shared during a leisurely stroll into paradise. Smokey Robinson creates that paradise every time he opens his mouth to sing.''

Inducted Into the Rock and Roll Hall of Fame

Robinson's records of the late 1980s, when he was well into his third decade in the music business, continued to garner popularity and the approval of critics. A *People* magazine reviewer found that on his 1986 album *Smoke Signals*, for example, the singer ''remains a uniquely resilient performer.'' His 1987's album entitled *One Heartbeat* was termed ''another winning package of sharp, sophisticated soul'' by a reviewer from *Rolling Stone.* Robinson hits like ''*Cruisin',*'' ''*Just to See Her*'' —a Grammy Award winner—and ''*Being With You*'' became both rhythm-and-blues and pop hits and were rendered in a voice *Essence* contributor Jack Slater hailed as ''a hypnotic, airy aphrodisiac that puts tens of thousands in the mood for love.'' Coupled with his success with the Miracles and as a prolific Motown songwriter, Robinson's solo achievements in the music industry led to his 1986 induction into the Rock and Roll Hall of Fame, and in 1989 he was named a Grammy Living Legend.

Coping with such enormous fame has not always been easy for Robinson. He chronicles his personal struggles in his 1989 collaboration with David Ritz, *Smokey: Inside My Life. Musician* contributor Jon Young remarked that the autobiography ''documents everything from [Robinson's] family history and the early days of the Miracles to his extramarital affairs and, most striking, a graphic account of two years in thrall to cocaine in the mid-'80s.'' When asked why he chose to provide such candid details about his drug addiction, Robinson responded to Young, ''I wrote it because it was God's will. . . . I was saved from drugs in 1986 when my pastor prayed for me. I never went to rehab or to a doctor. It was a miracle healing from God, so that I could carry the message about the perils of drugs. At the time I was saved, I was already dead. You are now speaking to Lazarus.''

Left Motown for SBK Records

With the onset of the 1990s, Robinson's contract with Motown Records expired, and after a long and productive career with the record company, he moved to SBK Records. According to Gary Graff of the *Detroit Free Press,* the singer said simply, ''My contract with Motown was up, and I was just out of there.'' He also pointed to the sale of Motown

Records to MCA and Boston Ventures in 1988 as one of the reasons for his departure. "After we sold the company," he continued to Graff, "it was never really quite the same for me." With SBK Records, Robinson released a well-received LP he co-produced and recorded in less than six weeks, 1991's *Double Good Everything.* "It feels like a new day or something, man," he divulged to Graff. "This is the first thing I've *ever* done outside of Motown; that's a big deal to me. . . . I feel like a new artist, almost."

Also in 1991, Robinson ventured into previously un-chartered areas of the music world, considering an album of country-western tunes and penning the score for a Broadway musical titled *Hoops,* which presents the history of the Harlem Globetrotters basketball team. "I've written 22 pieces so far," Robinson told Young in February of 1992. "I want this to be like [the Broadway musical] *South Pacific* and produce several hits. The title track is a funk thing that I can envision being a halftime song for the NBA [National Basketball Association]." Robinson plans to continue his often hectic schedule of performing, comosing, and record-ing. "If the world lasts until the twenty-second century," the enduring singer-songwriter declared to Young, "I hope they're still playing my music."

Further Reading

Given, Dave, *The Dave Given Rock 'n' Roll Stars Handbook,* Exposition Press, 1980.

Robinson, Smokey, and David Ritz., *Smokey: Inside My Life,* McGraw-Hill, 1989.

The Rolling Stone Record Guide, Random House, 1979.

Detroit News, October 20, 1991.

Down Beat, June 1983.

Ebony, October 1971; October 1982; March 1989; May 1989.

Essence, February 1982.

High Fidelity, June 1980; May 1981; May 1982; July 1982; April 1986.

Jet, January 31, 1980; July 9, 1981; August 3, 1987; March 13, 1989; November 13, 1989; December 18, 1989; April 8, 1991; November 11, 1991.

Musician, February 1992.

New Republic, July 15, 1991.

Newsweek, January 27, 1986.

People, March 10, 1980; April 28, 1980; April 12, 1982; May 16, 1983; August 13, 1984; May 20, 1985; December 16, 1985; March 10, 1986; May 18, 1987; March 13, 1989; April 3, 1989.

Playboy, July 1985; June 1986.

Publishers Weekly, January 27, 1989.

Rolling Stone, April 16, 1981; September 17, 1981; February 12, 1987; April 23, 1987; December 17, 1987; February 9, 1989.

Stereo Review, July 1980; May 1982; January 1984; November 1986.

Variety, May 22, 1985; October 15, 1986; December 23, 1987; March 1, 1989. □

Theodore Robinson

One of the leading American impressionist painters, Theodore Robinson (1852-1896) was instrumental in introducing impressionism into American painting.

Theodore Robinson was born in Irasburg, Vt., on June 3, 1852. He grew up in Evansville, Wis., where his father, a Methodist minister, ran a clothing store. At the age of 18 Robinson went to Chicago to study at the Art Institute. Chronically afflicted with asthma, he was sent to Denver for his health, after which he studied at the National Academy of Design in New York City. He was one of the founders of the Art Students League, whose name he sug-gested.

In 1877 Robinson went to Paris and studied with J. L. Gérôme and then with C. E. A. Carolus-Duran. In 1879 Robinson was in Venice, where James McNeill Whistler gave him a little picture and probably influenced his style. Robinson's stay in Venice was important in his artistic de-velopment. He returned to the United States in 1880.

Robinson was active in the Society of American Artists, which was formed in protest against the National Academy of Design. He taught, worked for 3 years for a decorating firm in Boston, and helped John La Farge on the decoration of the Vanderbilt house at Tarrytown.

In 1884 Robinson returned to his beloved France. In 1887 he went to Giverny to see Claude Monet, the decisive step of his career. Impressionism was on the way, and Monet drew Robinson to nature; for him and for a large part of American painting this marked the decisive shift from the Barbizon school to impressionism. From then on Giverny was the fixed point of his life, and he always passed through there on his trips back and forth to the United States. But he was in no sense a pupil of Monet's and did not receive criticism from him as did some other Americans. Despite his shyness and lack of self-confidence, Robinson was fiercely independent and it is most unlikely that he would have welcomed advice on his work.

A great traveler, Robinson would often disappear, and his numerous friends would not know where he was. He lived very frugally, almost secretively, and never married. He died in New York City on April 2, 1896.

A pioneer of impressionism in the United States, Robin-son was one of the most brilliant and talented American artists of the period. It is a mistake to think of him merely as a follower of Monet, for he was a delicate and individual painter in his own right. Robinson said of himself that perhaps he was born to make sketches, but his fine and spirited little paintings have lasted far better than the monu-mental efforts of some of his contemporaries.

Further Reading

The only modern treatment of Robinson is John I. H. Baur, *Theodore Robinson, 1852-1896* (1946), which was responsi-ble for the current revival of interest in Robinson's work and has not been superseded. The best account by a contempo-rary is in Will H. Low, *A Chronicle of Friendships, 1873-1900* (1908). □

Julio Argentino Roca

Julio Argentino Roca (1843-1914) was an Argentine general and the leader of the oligarchy that held political control of Argentina from 1880 to 1916. He was a typical 19th-century caudillo.

Julio Roca was born of a prominent and wealthy Argentine family in Tucumán on July 17, 1843. He received a degree from the National College in Uruguay. When he was approximately fifteen, he volunteered to fight for the interior provinces in the struggle against the forces of Buenos Aires and was commissioned a sublieutenant; thereafter he remained on the military rolls for a period of 55 years of continuous service.

After graduation Roca took part in further fighting between the city and the provinces, this time on the side of the city. In the subsequent war against Paraguay he fought in several battles, and he achieved the rank of colonel in helping to put down the revolt of López Jordán in Entre Ríos. Roca finally reached the rank of general when he defeated and captured Gen. Aredondo, who had revolted in 1874.

Upon the death of the secretary of war, Adolfo Alsino, Roca undertook a successful campaign against the Indians in the south and added extensive land to the national domain, most of which fell into his and his friends' hands. Also, the Indian captives were to all intents and purposes forced into slavery under the application of old colonial laws. The results of the successful campaign made Roca popular in powerful circles, and he was elected president in 1880.

Rule by Oligarchy

Roca's administration ushered in a period of Argentine history known as the "era of the oligarchy," which lasted until 1916. Its core was made up of the great landowners, and it exerted its power through what has been called the most powerful farmers' organization in the Western Hemisphere, plus certain commercial elements with close ties with the British. On the credit side of the ledger, his government was powerful enough to end the many years of political chaos which had preceded his assumption of office.

Roca's platform proposed improvement in communications and a stronger army. Since the newly acquired Indian lands were useless without railroads, he spent vast sums during his administration to connect the area with the city of Buenos Aires. By diverting funds to the army he was able to count on its political support.

At the close of his administration, Roca left for Paris but soon returned to assist in the overthrow of his successor, Miguel Juárez Celmán. Roca was rewarded with the office of secretary of the interior, which enabled him to augment his personal fortune. He was once again elected president (1898-1904), having in the interim been president of the Senate. Roca's second administration is notable for the resumption of diplomatic relations with the Vatican, the settlement of the boundary dispute with Chile, and the pronouncement of the Drago Doctrine, an Argentine protest against intervention.

Roca retired from public life in 1904 until his appointment in 1913 as ambassador to Brazil. He was always a skillful politician and managed to cooperate better than most with leaders of both parties and was successful in smoothing over political quarrels. He was helped during both administrations by the universal prosperity resulting from the technological improvements of the time, and there is a great similarity between his administrations and those of President Ulysses S. Grant in the United States. Roca died in Buenos Aires on October 19, 1914.

Further Reading

There are no full-length biographies of Roca in English. Biographical material on Roca can be found in Ricardo Levene, *A History of Argentina* (trans. 1937); John W. White, *Argentina: The Life Story of a Nation* (1942); and Henry Stanley Ferns, *Argentina* (1969). See also Hubert Clinton Herring, *A History of Latin America: From the Beginnings to the Present* (1955; 3d rev. ed. 1968). □

Michel Rocard

Michel Rocard (born 1930) was one of the most respected politician on the French left in the period from 1965 into the 1990s.

Michel Rocard was born on August 23, 1930, in the outskirts of Paris. His father was a nuclear physicist who worked on France's first atomic bomb. Like many politicians of his generation, he got his start by attending the National School of Administration (ENA) and then beginning his career in the civil service.

He was a leader of the student wing of the socialist party (SFIO), but gradually grew disenchanted with its conservatism and support for French war policy in Algeria. In 1958 Rocard was part of a group of socialists who left the SFIO and with other activists formed the new Unified Socialist Party (PSU). Throughout the early 1960s the PSU remained small and lacked a firm identity. Many party leaders advocated merging with other non-communist left groups following François Mitterrand's surprisingly strong (but unsuccessful) presidential campaign in 1965.

Rocard, on the other hand, realized there was a need for a party like the PSU that could be an incubator for new ideas, especially regarding democratic socialism and decentralization. Therefore, he spearheaded a campaign to save the party and was named its national secretary in 1967.

Still, Rocard was primarily a theoretician who was little known outside of Parisian intellectual circles. Then came the uprising of May and June 1968. The PSU enthusiastically supported both the students and the workers in their protests against the Gaullist regime. By the end of 1968 the PSU started calling itself a revolutionary party and based its appeal on the issues and enthusiasm of the revolt, especially on the idea of *autogestion* or self-managed, decentralized

socialism. Rocard came to personify the ideas and enthusiasm that had burst into the open during those two months.

President Charles de Gaulle resigned in 1969. In the ensuing presidential elections, Michel Rocard did remarkably well, almost as well as the conventional socialist candidate, Gaston Defferre. That showing catapulted Rocard into the front ranks of French politicians. Public opinion polls for the next two decades showed him to be one of France's most popular politicians. Late in 1969 he won a seat in the National Assembly in a by-election in Paris' western suburbs.

Rocard began having troubles with the PSU at this time, however. The center of gravity of the party shifted further and further to the left. In the meantime, Rocard and his supporters came to the conclusion that revolution was not possible at the same time that a new reformist party (the Socialist Party [PS]) adopted many of the PSU's positions, including *autogestion*.

The PSU did quite poorly in the 1973 legislative elections. Rocard himself lost his seat in Parliament. On the other hand, the PS did extremely well, ending almost a generation of losses for social democratic parties. Rocard gave up the leadership of the party and returned to the civil service. Finally, in 1974, Rocard led his supporters into the PS, just after the presidential elections in which Mitterrand barely lost to Valéry Giscard d'Estaing.

Rocard became the PS national secretary for the public sector and saw his national popularity soar. In addition, as he began to grapple with both the economic and the electoral realities he shifted quickly to the right, shelving virtually all of his radical past except for *autogestion*.

Began His Ministerial Career

Rocard was reelected to the National Assembly in 1978. In 1980 public opinion polls showed him having the best chance of defeating President Giscard d'Estaing, but out of loyalty to François Mitterrand he withdrew his candidacy that October. When Mitterrand won the presidency the next May, Rocard began his ministerial career. Under Prime Minister Pierre Mauroy, Rocard served as minister of state for planning and regional development. Under Mauroy, and later Laurent Fabius, he also served as minister of agriculture. In both positions his influence was limited by his rivalry with President Mitterrand. Finally, in May 1985, Rocard resigned from the cabinet in opposition to the government's "expedient introduction of proportional representation" and the following month announced a tentative decision to run for the presidency when Mitterrand's term ended in 1988.

Appointed as Prime Minister

Rocard lost the 1988 presidential election to Mitterrand, but was named Prime Minister. Two days after his appointment, Rocard allocated 16 of the 26 cabinet posts to Socialists. This cabinet was the first minority government formed under the 30-year-old fifth republic. Rocard continued to be a popular politician with the public, winning a popularity poll in 1990 as the leader in whom the public had the most confidence. In May 1991 Mitterrand

replaced Rocard as Prime Minister with Edith Cresson, the first woman to claim the position. Rocard stated that he resigned the post to concentrate on the 1995 presidential campaign. In 1993 Rocard became the leader of the Socialist Party but resigned after only 14 months, when the party held a vote of no-confidence. This vote was due to poor election results for the Socialists, who received only 15% of the vote, the worst showing in two decades. This put an end to Rocard's presidential aspirations.

In 1995 Rocard was chosen to be one of the 15-member Canberra Commission for the Elimination of Nuclear Weapons, an international group formed by Australian Prime Minister Paul Keating and charged with helping to abolish nuclear weapons. He also was elected a board member of the International Crisis Group, founded in 1995 to help governments head off impending crises in unstable parts of the world.

Even though never achieving his goal to become president, Michel Rocard still had a remarkable influence in shaping French political life. He had a great ability to define issues and to set the agenda that politicians and intellectuals must discuss in confronting France's problems.

Further Reading

There is no biography of Michel Rocard in either French or English. On his PSU years, see Charles Hauss, *The New Left in France* (1978). On his years in the PS, see D.S. Bell and Byron Criddle, *The French Socialist Party: Resurgence and Victory* (1984). ☐

Virginia, but not both. They decided to have Adm. de Grasse sail from the West Indies to Chesapeake Bay to cut the British communications and prevent mutual support between Clinton and Cornwallis; to avoid Clinton; and to strike Cornwallis.

The French forces under Rochambeau joined the Americans at White Plains, N.Y., in June and marched to Williamsburg, Va., where they met the Marquis de Lafayette's army in September. Reinforced by 4,000 troops brought by De Grasse from Haiti, Washington and Rochambeau besieged the British forces under Cornwallis at Yorktown on October 2. De Grasse's naval forces turned back Adm. Graves's ships coming to Cornwallis's rescue and thereby prevented Cornwallis's escape or his reinforcement. On October 19 Cornwallis surrendered. Rochambeau spent the winter in Virginia, returned to Rhode Island in the fall of 1782, and went back to France in 1783.

In 1790, during the revolutionary period in France, Rochambeau commanded the Army of the North. He was made a marshal of France in 1791. In the following year, disenchanted with governmental policy and the conduct near Lille of poorly trained troops sent to him, he resigned his command and was succeeded by Lafayette. He was arrested for treason but escaped the guillotine.

In 1804 Napoleon made him a grand officer of the Legion of Honor. His two volumes of *Mémoires, militaires, historiques, et politiques* were published in 1809, after his death at Thoré on May 10, 1807.

Comte de Rochambeau

The Frenchman Jean Baptiste Donatien de Vimeur, Comte de Rochambeau (1725-1807), commanded the French expeditionary force in the American Revolution. He was with Gen. George Washington at the Battle of Yorktown.

The Comte de Rochambeau was born at Vendôme on July 1, 1725. Educated for the Church, he entered the army at the age of 17 and fought with bravery and skill in the War of the Austrian Succession, serving in Bohemia, Bavaria, and along the Rhine. A colonel by 1747, he took part in the Seven Years War as a brigadier general and achieved distinction in the expedition to Minorca and battles in Germany.

As a lieutenant general, Rochambeau was named commander of the French forces sent to America, and in July 1780 he landed at Newport, R.I., with about 5,500 troops. Although he was to launch combined operations with the Americans against New York, he was blockaded by a British fleet and was forced to spend a year entrenched while he awaited the arrival of French naval forces.

Rochambeau conferred with Washington in the spring of 1781, and they agreed that together they could overwhelm Henry Clinton at New York or Charles Cornwallis in

A striking figure, Rochambeau was simple in his tastes and dignified in his behavior. He eschewed ostentation and airs of self-importance. In America, he placed himself without reservation under Washington's orders and ensured the Franco-American cooperation that finally defeated the British in the American Revolution.

Further Reading

The latest work on Rochambeau is Arnold Whitridge, *Rochambeau* (1965). See also Allan Forbes, *Rochambeau* (1925), and Jean-Edmond Weelen, *Rochambeau: Father and Son* (1936).

Additional Sources

Le Comte, Solange, *Rochambeau,* Paris: Lavauzelle, c1976. ☐

George Rochberg

The American composer George Rochberg (born 1918) produced important works in several distinct styles, both tonal and atonal.

George Rochberg was born in Paterson, New Jersey, on July 5, 1918. He began studies in composition and counterpoint with Weisse, Szell, and Mannes at the Mannes School in 1939, after receiving a B.A. from Montclair State Teachers College. For a time in the 1930s he wrote popular songs under a pseudonym. In 1942 he interrupted his studies at Mannes for three years of military duty as a second lieutenant in the infantry. He was wounded in action. Resuming his education upon his return, he received degrees from the Curtis Institute (B.M., 1947), where he studied with Scalero and Menotti, and from the University of Pennsylvania (M.A., 1948).

Rochberg taught harmony, counterpoint, and form and analysis at Curtis from 1948 to 1954 and served first as editor and then as director of publications for the Theodore Presser Company from 1951 to 1960. In 1960 he accepted a post as chairman of the music department at the University of Pennsylvania. He resigned the chairmanship in 1968 to remain in the department in the 1980s as Annenberg Professor of Humanities. He also held several guest appointments, including those at the Temple Institute of Music (1969), the Oberlin Festival of Contemporary Music (1970), Testimonium, Jerusalem (1970-1971), and the Aspen Conference on Contemporary Music (1972). He retired from his position at the University of Pennsylvania in 1983.

Three Style Periods of Rochberg's Music

Rochberg's music falls into three distinct style periods, each major stylistic change being a response to a personal or social issue, rather than to a purely musical one. His first mature works reflect the influence of Bartók, Hindemith, and Stravinsky, but several of these works have either been considerably revised or withdrawn. Perhaps the best-known composition remaining in its original form is the Bartókian First String Quartet (1952).

The first major change in Rochberg's style resulted from his conversion to the principles of serialism after the war. Of this event, he wrote: "The war years were much more than an interruption of my musical studies. . . . The war shaped my psyche and precipitated my internal development. I came to grips with my own time. I came to the necessity of the twelve-tone method independently of the few other American composers who turned to it after the war." A meeting with Dallapiccola while in Italy on Fulbright and American Academy fellowships in 1950 strongly reinforced Rochberg's decision to pursue the serial method. He produced his first works in that idiom, the *Twelve Bagatelles* for piano, in 1952. These pieces, with their Schoenberg-like concentration and intensity, have remained among his most frequently played. He orchestrated them in 1964 and retitled the set *Zodiac*. Rochberg continued in this Schoenbergian vein until 1956 and produced other major works, including the *Chamber Symphony* (1953), *David the Psalmist* for tenor and orchestra (1954), the *Duo Concertante* for violin and cello (1955), the Second Symphony (1955-1956), and the *Sonata-fantasia* for piano (1956).

In adapting the serial method to suit his own compositional needs, Rochberg arrived at a means of organizing the harmonic material by hexachords. His important theoretical treatise, *The Hexachord and Its Relation to the Twelve-Tone Row,* codifies these principles. The serial works of the later 1950s and early 1960s, including the *Cheltenham Concerto* for small orchestra (1958), the Second String Quartet (with soprano, on a text by Rilke, 1959-1961), *Time Span* for orchestra (1962), and the *Blake Songs* for soprano and eight instruments (1961), all display the finely-detailed expressivity of Webern.

A fundamental change in the significance of musical duration also marked this phase of serial writing. What Rochberg referred to as "spatial music" replaced the concept of "becoming," achieved through development and final arrival at some musical objective in metered time, with that of "being," achieved through the initial statement of a completed idea in superimposed and changing meters and tempos. His extra-musical objective in this period was "to project the permanence of the world as cosmos, the cosmos as the eternal present."

Tragedy Altered His Music

The untimely death of his son in 1964 due to a brain tumor, marked the end of serial composition, which had proven "hollow . . . meaningless" for the expression of his grief. He grew increasingly discontent with modern music's self-conscious attempts to break from the past and with the idea of originality, in which the "personal style of the artist and his ego are the supreme values." As a means of realigning himself with what he felt to be the historical continuum, Rochberg resumed experiments with quotation. When he first borrowed this device from Charles Ives to quote a short segment of Schoenberg's Op. 23 No. 1 piano piece in his own *Sonata- fantasia* he was unaware that other composers were moving in similar directions. His first major effort in quotation, *Contra Mortem et Tempus* for flute, clarinet, piano, and violin (1965), utilizes material from Boulez, Berio, Varèse, Berg, Ives, and Rochberg himself. However, most of these excerpts are not readily identifiable because, except for the Ives, they are divested of their original rhythms and because they are all modern pieces and well-integrated by Rochberg into his own style. Later compositions would include quotations from earlier composers in more recognizable statements; *Music for the Magic Theater* for 15 instruments (1965) incorporates the music of Mozart and the third symphony, J.S. Bach and Heinrich Schütz.

In carrying this return to tonality to its logical conclusion, Rochberg has written several pastiche works, often in styles of 19th-century Austrian or German masters. His Third String Quartet (1972) contains stylistic references to Beethoven, Brahms, Mahler, and Bartók. The three *Concord Quartets* (1978) contain similar references plus quotations. Later still, his opera *The Confidence Man* (based on the Melville novel, 1982), *Between Two Worlds* for flute and piano (1983), and the Oboe Concerto (1983) rely less on other composers and are increasingly chromatic and angular.

Although he embraced a wide range of current means of expression, Rochberg resisted several others, again for humanistic reasons. He rejected the post-Webern aesthetic of total-serialism, saying that "music is not engineering, and I stick fast to my conviction that music retains a deep connection with existence as we feel, rather than think it." He responded to aleatoricism with "an unshakable aversion

to any type of art that ignores the human situation by avoiding responsible choice." He remained committed to acoustically produced sound, as he found electronic music lacking in passion. And he relied little on the new sounds being extracted from traditional instruments, with the exception of now-common devices such as flutter-tonguing or playing directly on the strings of a piano.

Awards and Recognition

Recognition of his work came early and continued without interruption, resulting in many prestigious awards, grants, and commissions. Among these were: The George Gershwin Memorial Award (1952) for *Night Music;* the Society for the Publication of American Music Award for the Bartókian First String Quartet (1952); a Koussevitzky Foundation commission (1956) for *Dialogues;* Guggenheim fellowships (1957, 1966); the Naumberg Recording Award (1961) for the second symphony; a National Institute of Arts and Letters grant (1962); a Lincoln Center Performing Arts commission (1966) for *Black Sounds;* a National Endowment for the Arts commission (1974) for the violin concerto; the Kennedy Center Friedheim Award (1979) for the fourth string quartet; a Chamber Music Society of Lincoln Center commission (1980) for the *Octet;* and the Brandeis Creative Arts Award (1985). Rochberg was elected into the American Academy and Institute of Arts and Letters in 1985. A television documentary was filmed of Rochberg in 1983 entitled "George Rochberg and His Music."

Further Reading

There is one biography on Rochberg titled, *George Rochberg: A Bio-Bibliographic Guide to his Life and Works* by Joan DeVee Dixon (1992). Another source is "Change and Continuity in the Music of George Rochberg," a doctorate thesis by Daniel P. Horn, Julliard School of Music (1987). Throughout his career Rochberg was quite verbal in matters both theoretical and aesthetic. Seventeen of his most important articles, written over 30 years and sometimes somewhat contradictory in statement, have been gathered into a volume, *The Aesthetics of Survival: A Composer's View of Twentieth Century Music* (1984). Theoretical writings in addition to this book include an important article, "The Harmonic Tendency of the Hexachord," in the *Journal of Music Theory* 3 (1959). Alexander Ringer has written articles on Rochberg for *The Musical Quarterly* 45 (1959), 47 (1961), and 52 (1966), of which the last contains especially thorough coverage to the end of his serial period. A dissertation entitled "The String Quartets of George Rochberg" was written by J. J. Smith (1976, Eastman School of Music). □

Kevin Roche

Kevin Roche (born 1922) was a brilliant designer best known for creating unique and distinctive images for corporate headquarters situated in urban and suburban areas.

Kevin Roche was born on June 14, 1922, in Dublin, Ireland. When he was 17 he received his first opportunity to design and build—a cheese warehouse for his father, a successful agricultural businessman in Mitchelstown, Ireland. During World War II he earned a Bachelors of Architecture degree (1943) from the National University of Ireland. In 1948, after working briefly for the Dublin architect Michael Scott and for Maxwell Fry in London, Roche decided to emigrate to the United States. In that same year he entered the Illinois Institute of Technology (ITT), studying under Mies van der Rohe and receiving his Masters of Architecture degree in 1949. In 1950 he joined the firm of Eero Saarinen and Associates where by 1954 he had become the principal associate in design, with basic authority for all their projects.

Following the death of Saarinen in 1961, Roche joined forces with John Dinkeloo, a partner in Saarinen's firm since 1956. Together the two men completed Saarinen's unfinished work, which included the Jefferson National Expansion Memorial, the TWA Terminal at JFK International Airport, and the Dulles International Airport Terminal in Northern Virginia. By 1966 the firm name was changed to Kevin Roche and John Dinkeloo and Associates. After the death of John Dinkeloo in 1978 Roche continued to use the firm name of Roche & Dinkeloo.

Roche's most important early design is the Ford Foundation Building (1967) in New York City. Here the architect employed Corten steel for the first time in the façade of an urban building. The 12-story structure consists of offices situated along two sides of a covered enclosed garden courtyard. The purity of the steel and glass walls are reminiscent of Mies van der Rohe and contrast with monumental granite-veneered supporting piers. Each office faces the courtyard, reinforcing a sense of community and family within the large corporate structure. The garden courtyard also functions as a public space, serving as a pedestrian link through the block. The concept of creating a community-oriented building and "adding something more" by making provisions of space for public use are recurring themes in Roche's work.

Another predominant theme in Roche's work is how his buildings respond to the automobile. He was one of the first architects to grasp the realities of an automobile society by consciously designing buildings with this view in mind. His design for the College Life Insurance Company (1967-1971) is a complex of identically designed blue-glassed pyramidal forms located on a rural site in Indiana at the intersection of two highways. These three 11-story tapered towers are composed on a monumental scale reminiscent of the visionary designs of the 18th-century French architect Claude Nicholas Ledoux. The simplicity and monumental scale of the pyramids make them visually effective for a person driving by in an automobile at 55 miles per hour.

This concern for architecture with a strong processional movement resulted in some of Roche's most successful designs. This concept was emphatically stated in his bold and simple composition for the Knights of Columbus building (1965-1969) in New Haven, Connecticut. Here Roche shared with his former mentor Saarinen the desire for strong

and simple imagery. However, rather than the romanticized representational imagery of Saarinen, Roche was more of a rational designer incorporating a certain degree of abstraction and geometric purity.

Roche also acquired from Saarinen the ability to work with big corporate complexes and to supply them with a dominant commercial image. These became the cornerstone to Roche's practice and made up the largest part of his ouevre. His later corporate commissions reflected a move toward an abstracted neo-classicism which was perhaps a response to the Post-modern acceptance of historical motifs. His design for the General Foods Headquarters (1977-1982) in Rye, New York, was a glistening white, symmetrically balanced building situated on an expansive suburban site.

General Foods was endemic of corporations in the 1970s and 1980s that escaped the chaos and skyrocketing real estate prices of the city and moved out to the comfortable surroundings of the suburbs. The juxtaposition of massive forms against steel and glass found in Roche's earlier work were replaced by pristine white panels and ribbon windows providing the building with a clean, delicate appearance. Classical devices such as the Palladian style atrium and pillared rotunda with a reflecting pool echo Roche's move toward a more formal architectural language. Again the automobile played a role in the design process. The visitor approaching by car is ceremoniously led down a central axis that leads directly underneath the main rotunda of the complex.

Roche continued to explore these themes in his later design for the Bouygues World Headquarters (1983-1989) outside Paris, France. Located a few minutes from Versailles, the Bouygues is symmetrically arranged and is approached by car along a formal axis with gardens, reflecting pools, a paved court enclosed by semi-circular wings, and symmetrical outlying buildings. Formal allusions to the Royal Palace are emphasized, with the president's office on the center point of the axis like that of the Sun King's at Versailles. Like the General Foods Headquarters, the Bouygues Headquarters (called "Challenger") is clothed in a thin skin of milky-white aluminum.

In addition to Roche's work as an architect, he was academician for the National Academy of Design; a member of the Academie d'Architecture; a trustee for the American Academy in Rome; and a trustee of the Commission of Fine Arts, Washington, D.C. He was also the recipient of numerous honors and awards, including the Academie d'Architecture Grand Gold Medal (1977) and the Pritzker Prize (1982), which is one of the most esteemed architectural awards. As the designer of such landmarks as California's Oakland Museum and the Ford Foundation headquarters in New York, he was named the winner of the 1993 American Institute of Architects' Gold Medal—one of architectrue's highest honors.

Spanning his career, Roche's accomplishment's also included, such well-known projects as the St. Louis Gateway Arch, the TWA building at New York's Kennedy Airport and Deer & Co. headquarters in Illinois; with the late Eero Saarinen. On his own, he was the architect for the master plan for the Central Park Zoo in New York and the Nations Bank Plaza in Atlanta.

Further Reading

The best source on Roche is Franceso Dal Co's book, *Kevin Roche* (1985), which includes an extensive interview, an incisive analysis of his buildings, and an excellent bibliography. Other sources which are particularly good for their illustrations are "Architecture and Urbanism" (1987) and Y. Futagawa's, *Kevin Roche John Dinkeloo and Associates, 1962-1975* (1975). Discussions about Roche can also be found in Paul Heyer, *Architects on Architecture: New Directions in America* (1966); Heinrich Klotz, *The History of Postmodern Architecture* (1988); and Robert A.M. Stern, *New Directions in American Architecture* (1977). Updated information gathered from *LA Times* Sunday, January 10, 1993; Roche Wins Architects' Gold Medal. □

David Rockefeller

David Rockefeller (born 1915), son of John D. Rockefeller, Jr., was the chairman of the Chase Manhattan Bank and became one of the most prominent bankers in the world.

D avid Rockefeller, the fifth and youngest son of John D. Rockefeller, Jr., and Abby Aldrich Rockefeller, was born in New York City on June 12, 1915. He received his elementary and secondary education at the Lincoln School of Columbia University's Teachers College. He graduated from Harvard University in 1936 with a B.S. in English history and literature and later did post-graduate work in economics at Harvard and at the London School of Economics. He received his Ph.D. in economics from the University of Chicago in 1940. Rockefeller's doctoral dissertation, *Unused Resources and Economic Waste,* was published in 1941 by the University of Chicago Press.

In September 1940 Rockefeller married Margaret Mc-Grath, and the couple eventually had six children: David, Abby, Neva, Margaret, Richard, and Eileen. To gain experience in city government, Rockefeller worked without salary for 18 months in 1940 and 1941 as one of 60 "interns" in New York City. He served as secretary to Mayor Fiorello H. LaGuardia. Rockefeller then became assistant regional director of the U.S. Office of Defense Health and Welfare Services in New York State. In 1942, after American entry into World War II, he joined the U.S. Army, enlisting as a private. In 1943 he attended the Engineer Corps Officers Training School and received further training in military intelligence. He served in North Africa and France, including six months as assistant military attache in Paris. He left the Army with the rank of captain in 1945 and was awarded the Italian Order of Merit, the French Legion of Honor, and the U.S. Legion of Honor.

Entry Into Business World

Rockefeller enjoyed politics and might have returned to it after the war, but instead decided to seek experience in business. In 1946 he joined the Chase National Bank, of which his maternal uncle, Winthrop W. Aldrich, had been chairman since 1933. Rockefeller began his banking career as assistant manager in the foreign department and rose to assistant cashier, second vice president, and vice president by 1949. As supervisor of the bank's business in Latin America he opened new branches in Cuba, Puerto Rico, and Panama and in 1950 established a quarterly economic publication, *Latin American Business Highlights*. Rockefeller's interest in foreign affairs in general and in Latin America in particular were reflected in his involvement in the Council for Foreign Relations and the Center for Inter-American Relations.

In 1951 Rockefeller became senior vice president and assumed responsibility for customer relations in the New York City area and for the economic research department. When Chase merged with the Bank of Manhattan in 1955, he was made executive vice president and given responsibility for the bank's development department. In 1956 he became chairman of the new New York Chamber of Commerce Committee on Lower Manhattan Redevelopment (now Downtown Manhattan Association, Inc.), concerned with the redevelopment of lower Manhattan. He was intimately involved in the bank's decision to remain and build a new headquarters in the area. In 1957 Rockefeller was promoted to vice chairman of the board with the responsibility for the overall administration and planning of the bank. He also served as vice president of Chase International Investment Corporation, a foreign financing subsidiary of the bank. In 1961 Rockefeller was made chairman of the board of Chase Manhattan Bank, a position he held for 20 years. He served simultaneously as president and chairman of the executive committee from 1961 to 1968 and as chief executive officer from 1969 to 1980. During the most active part of his career Rockefeller found time to write a book about his profession, *Creative Management in Banking* (1964), and to form the International Executive Service Corps, a group of volunteers who provide technical and managerial assistance to businesses in developing countries. He became a familiar figure to ministers and heads of state of various countries around the world and to heads of multinational corporations.

In 1981 Rockefeller retired from active management, but he remained as chairman of the international advisory committee and continued many of his outside activities. He served as chairman of the Americas Society, an umbrella group which coordinates the activities of a number of cultural, educational, and economic organizations concerned with the development of Latin America. Rockefeller was chairman of the Council on Foreign Relations and North American chairman of the Trilateral Commission, which he helped found in 1973 to promote understanding and cooperation between North America, Western Europe, and Japan. He also helped establish the Council of the Americas.

Philanthropic and Family Obligations

Rockefeller was a director of several corporations, including B. F. Goodrich, Punta Alegre Sugar Corp., and American Overseas Finance Corp. With his brothers, he was also active in the family's philanthropic organizations, it has been said that he held a strong feeling of obligation to the public. In 1940 Rockefeller became a trustee of the Rockefeller Institute of Medical Research (now Rockefeller University), founded by his grandfather, and he was elected its first chairman in 1953. He was a director of Rockefeller Center and a member of its executive committee, chairman of the board of trustees of the Rockefeller Brother's Fund, and a trustee and vice chairman of the executive committee of the Museum of Modern Art, which was founded by his mother. He also served as a life trustee of the University of Chicago and served for several terms on the board of overseers of Harvard University, including a term as chairman of the executive committee.

Trouble With Rockefeller Center

In 1995 Rockefeller at age 80, fought to preserve his family ties to Rockefeller Center. The Rockefeller Group, Inc. sold 80% of the Center to Japan's Mitsubishi Estate Co. in 1989 for $1.4 billion. David Rockefeller was against the sale, but was outvoted by the trustees. In 1995 when Mitsubishi was threatening to declare bankruptcy of the Center, Rockefeller resigned as chairman of the Rockefeller Group and gathered investors to make a bid for part of the property. This new group, including Rockefeller and Goldman Sachs & Co., eventually paid $1.2 billion for their share in the Center, bringing at least part of the Center back into the family.

Rockefeller has been described as representing the end of an era, as the Rockefeller family becomes more numerous. Rockefeller himself stated in a 1995 *New York Times* interview, "When a family multiplies the way ours has, it's hard to maintain the identity over time." He also stated that he "would like to be thought of as having seen that there was an important role for the private sector in world affairs and cooperating with governments for the benefit of both sides."

He has received honorary degrees from several universities and in 1994 was awarded the Hadrian Award of the World Mathematics Fund.

Further Reading

There is only one published biography, by William Hoffman, *David* (1971), but several studies of the Rockefeller family contain information on David Rockefeller, the best of which is Peter Collier and David Horowitz, *The Rockefellers: An American Dynasty* (1976). Another informative source is a profile from the *New York Times,* "Last of the Big Time Rockefellers: A Profile of David Rockefeller (12/10/95). □

John D. Rockefeller Jr.

John D. Rockefeller, Jr. (1874-1960), American philanthropist, utilized the family fortune to establish scores of philanthropic enterprises and participated actively in their management. He also became widely known as an expert in industrial relations.

Born to substantial wealth on Jan. 29, 1874, in Cleveland, John D. Rockefeller, Jr., was brought up in a rigorously puritanical atmosphere. The social life of the family centered in the Baptist Church, and young Rockefeller and his four sisters were taught to live upright, religious lives. Educated at Brown University, from which he graduated in 1897, he was shy and serious, determined to carry out what he felt were his duties to his God, his family, and society.

After graduation from college, young Rockefeller—largely to please his father, to whom he was devoted—entered the offices of the family's Standard Oil Company in New York City to prepare himself to administer his father's vast business interests. But because of his retiring and extremely moralistic nature he disliked the bruising business world and occupied himself increasingly with managing his father's estates and philanthropic enterprises. The Rockefeller Institute for Medical Research, the General Education Board, and the Rockefeller Foundation were financed by the elder Rockefeller, but his son participated actively in management. The education board was concerned chiefly with improving education for African Americans in the South; the foundation became a vast holding company for hundreds of philanthropies.

From 1900 to 1908 John D. Rockefeller, Jr., became more closely involved with his father's business interests. But allegations of unfair competitive practices used by Standard Oil led him to separate himself from active policy making in his father's corporations in 1910. In 1913, however, because of a large family stockholding in the Colorado Fuel and Iron Company, he was implicated in a strike that not only shut down the company but threatened to balloon into a domestic insurrection. Although keenly hurt by accusations from liberals and labor leaders that he had helped intensify the strife by siding with an arbitrary and unsympathetic management, Rockefeller worked out a plan for worker representation in company affairs that became a model for industrial relations during the 1920s. Elaborating this scheme in speeches and periodical articles, he came to be considered a leading liberal in labor affairs.

Among the best-known philanthropies occupying Rockefeller from 1915 until his death were conservation and national park projects in the West, the Cloisters art museum in New York, and the Williamsburg restoration. He also planned and constructed Rockefeller Center in New York City and donated the land upon which the United Nations building now stands.

Modest, unaffected, and unostentatious, Rockefeller did much to remove the "robber baron" stigma from big business and to awaken businessmen to social responsibilities. He died on May 11, 1960, in Tucson, Ariz.

Further Reading

A good source of information on Rockefeller is the sympathetic biography by his friend and colleague Raymond B. Fosdick, *John D. Rockefeller, Jr.* (1956).

Additional Sources

Schenkel, Albert F., *The rich man and the kingdom: John D. Rockefeller, Jr., and the Protestant establishment,* Minneapolis: Fortress Press, 1995.
Morrow, Lance, *The chief: a memoir of fathers and sons,* New York: Collier Books, 1986, 1984. □

John Davison Rockefeller

John Davison Rockefeller (1839-1937), American industrialist and philanthropist, founded the Standard Oil Company, the University of Chicago, and the Rockefeller Foundation.

John D. Rockefeller was born on July 8, 1839, in Richford, N.Y. His father owned farm property and traded in many goods, including lumber and patent medicines. His mother, a straitlaced puritanical woman, brought up her large family very strictly. The family moved west by degrees, reaching Cleveland, Ohio, in 1853, when it was beginning to grow into a city. John graduated from high school there and after three months of commercial college found his first job at the age of sixteen clerking in a produce commission house. In 1859, when he was nineteen, he started his first company with a young Englishman: Clark and Rockefeller. They grossed $450,000 in the first year of trading. Clark did the fieldwork; Rockefeller controlled office management, bookkeeping, and relationships with bankers.

Early Businesses

From the start Rockefeller revealed a genius for organization and method. The firm prospered during the Civil War. With the Pennsylvania oil strike (1859) and the building of a railroad to Cleveland, they branched out into oil refining with Samuel Andrews, who had technical knowledge of the field. Within two years Rockefeller became senior partner; Clark was bought out, and the firm Rockefeller and Andrews became Cleveland's largest refinery. A second refinery, the Standard Works, was opened in 1865 by another firm established by Rockefeller in his brother William's name; and a sales office was opened in New York City in 1866.

With financial help from S. V. Harkness and from a new partner, H. M. Flagler, who also secured favorable railroad freight rebates, Rockefeller survived the bitter competition in the oil industry. The Standard Oil Company, chartered in Ohio in 1870 by Rockefeller, his brother, Flagler, Harkness, and Andrews, had a capital of $1 million and paid a dividend of 40 percent a year later. Standard Oil controlled one-tenth of American refining, but competitive chaos re-

mained. The chief bottleneck was the transporting of the oil. Out of this situation came the controversial South Improvement Company scheme of 1872—a defensive alliance of Cleveland refiners to meet the bitter opposition of the oil producers of Pennsylvania. The sweeping freight rebate agreements in this scheme brought public opposition, and the plan was outlawed by the Pennsylvania Legislature. Meanwhile, a looser organization, a refiners' pool, also failed (1873).

Rockefeller still hoped to impose order on the oil industry. He bought out most of the Cleveland refineries, then acquired others in New York, Pittsburgh, and Philadelphia. He turned to new transportation methods, including the railroad tank car and the pipeline. By 1879 he was refining 90 percent of American oil, and Standard used its own tank car fleet, ships, docking facilities, barrel-making plants, draying services, depots, and warehouses. Strict economy and planning were enforced throughout. Rockefeller came through the Panic of 1873 still urging organization on the part of the refiners. As his control approached near-monopoly, he fought a war with the Pennsylvania Railroad in 1877, which created a refining company to try to break Rockefeller's control, but the bloody railroad strikes that year forced them to surrender to Standard Oil. Rockefeller's dream of order was near completion.

America's First Trust

By 1883, after winning control of the pipeline industry, Standard's monopoly was at a peak. Rockefeller created America's first great "trust" in 1882; since laws forbade one company's ownership of another's stock, ever since 1872 Standard had placed its acquisitions outside Ohio in the hands of Flagler as "trustee." All profits went to the Ohio company while the outside businesses remained nominally independent. In 1882 this was regularized. Nine trustees of the Standard Oil Trust received the stock of 40 businesses and gave the various shareholders trust certificates in return. The trust had a capital of about $70 million; it was the world's largest and richest industrial organization.

In the 1880s the nature of Rockefeller's business began to change; he moved beyond refining oil into producing crude oil itself and moved his wells westward with the new fields opening up. He pioneered in this by acquiring oil land in Ohio before it was certain that this sulfuric oil could be refined successfully; then he employed the scientist Herman Frasch, whose process (1886-1889) made these fields yield an enormous profit. Standard also expanded its marketing facilities and entered foreign markets in Europe, Asia, and Latin America. From 1885 a committee system of management was developed to control Standard Oil's enormous empire.

Attacking the Trust

Public opposition to Standard Oil grew with the emergence of the muckraking journalists; in particular, Henry Demarest Lloyd and Ida Tarbell published harsh exposés of the oil empire. Rockefeller was condemned for various alleged practices: railroad rebates (a system he did not invent and which many refiners used); price discrimination; industrial espionage and bribery; crushing smaller firms by unfair competition, such as cutting off their crude oil supplies or restricting their transport outlets. Standard Oil was investigated by the New York State Senate and by the U.S. House of Representatives in 1888. The rising tide of reform sentiment brought in the Sherman Antitrust Act (1890). Two years later the Ohio Supreme Court invalidated Standard's original trust agreement. Rockefeller formally disbanded the organization; though the trustees handed in their trust certificates, in practice the organization remained unified, and the four presidents of the state firms (John D. Rockefeller for Standard of Ohio, William Rockefeller for New York, Flagler for New Jersey, and J.A. Moffett for Indiana) still met regularly to fix overall policy. In 1899 Standard was re-created legally under a new form as a "holding company;" this merger was dissolved by the U.S. Supreme Court in 1911, long after Rockefeller himself had retired from active control in 1897.

Perhaps Rockefeller's most famous excursion outside the oil industry began in 1893, when he helped develop the Mesabi iron ore range of Minnesota. By 1896 his Consolidated Iron Mines owned a great fleet of ore boats and virtually controlled Great Lakes shipping. Rockefeller was now an iron ore magnate in his own right and had the power to dictate to the steel industry. He made an alliance with the steel king, Andrew Carnegie, in 1896: Rockefeller agreed not to enter steelmaking and Carnegie agreed not to touch transportation. In 1901 Rockefeller sold his ore holdings to the vast new merger created by Carnegie and J. P. Morgan,

U.S. Steel. In that year his fortune passed the $200 million mark for the first time.

Philanthropic Endeavors

From his first employment as a clerk, Rockefeller sought to give away one-tenth of his earnings to charity. His benefactions grew with his income, and he also gave time and energy to philanthropic causes. At first he depended on the Baptist Church for advice; the Church wanted its own great university, and in 1892 the University of Chicago opened under the brilliant presidency of a man Rockefeller much admired, William Rainey Harper. The university was Rockefeller's first major philanthropic creation. He gave it over $80 million during his lifetime and left the university entirely independent under Harper. Rockefeller chose New York City for his Rockefeller Institute of Medical Research (now Rockefeller University), chartered in 1901. Among the institute's many achievements were yellow fever research, discovery of serums to combat pneumonia, advances in experimental physiology and surgery, and work on infantile paralysis. In 1902 he established the General Education Board.

The total of Rockefeller's lifetime philanthropies has been estimated at about $550 million. Eventually the amounts involved became so huge (his fortune reached $900 million by 1913) that he developed a staff of specialists to help him; out of this came the Rockefeller Foundation, chartered in 1913, "to promote the wellbeing of mankind throughout the world."

Rockefeller's personal life was fairly simple and frugal. He was a man of few passions who lived for his work, and his great talent was his organizing genius and drive for order, pursued with great single-mindedness and concentration. His life was absorbed by business and later by organized giving. In both areas he imposed order, efficiency, and planning with extraordinary success and sweeping vision. He died on May 23, 1937, in Ormond, Fla.

Further Reading

Rockefeller's *Random Reminiscences of Men and Events* (1909) remains interesting and important. The definitive life of Rockefeller is Allan Nevins, *Study in Power: John D. Rockefeller* (2 vols., 1940; rev. ed. 1953). A sympathetic account is Jules Abels, *The Rockefeller Billions* (1965).

For general economic history see the readings in Peter d'A. Jones, *The Robber Barons Revisited* (1968). The history of Standard Oil of New Jersey is treated in R. W. and M. E. Hidy, *History of Standard Oil Company: Pioneering in Big Business, 1882-1911*, vol. 1 (1955), and Standard is considered comparatively in Alfred D. Chandler, Jr., *Strategy and Structure: Chapters in the History of Industrial Enterprise* (1962). Standard's history in California to 1919 is described in Gerald T. White, *Formative Years in the Far West* (1962). For a broader history see Harold F. Williamson and Arnold R. Daum, *The American Petroleum Industry* (2 vols., 1959-1963). □

Nelson Aldrich Rockefeller

Nelson Aldrich Rockefeller (1908-1979), an heir to the enormous Standard Oil fortune amassed by his grandfather, forsook business for a career in state and national politics, which included four terms as governor of New York, several attempts at the presidency, and a brief tenure as vice-president of the United States.

Nelson Aldrich Rockefeller was born in Bar Harbor, Maine, July 8, 1908. He was the third of six children of John B. Rockefeller, Jr., and Abby Greene Aldrich. His grandfathers were John D. Rockefeller, Sr., founder of the Standard Oil Company, and U.S. Senator Nelson Aldrich (Republican, Rhode Island).

Despite his family's great wealth, Rockefeller had a fairly frugal upbringing. He attended the Lincoln School, which was composed of students from diverse economic strata. For college, he attended Dartmouth, where he majored in economics, taught a Sunday school class, and occasionally worked in the school cafeteria to earn spending money. In 1930 he graduated Phi Beta Kappa and *cum laude* from Dartmouth and married Mary Todhunter Clark, a Philadelphia socialite, two weeks later. (They subsequently had five children.)

An Expert on Latin America

Rockefeller began his professional career working for his family's companies. By the age of 30 he was president of the New York Rockefeller Center. Business did not retain his interest, however. Several trips to Latin America in the late 1930s convinced him of the region's importance to national security, and in 1940 he accepted his first major governmental position as the head of the Office of Inter-American Affairs. The office strove, through advertising and trade agreements with Central and South American countries, to lessen the influence of the Axis powers in those areas. In 1944 he was promoted to assistant secretary of state in charge of Latin American affairs, but a year later he resigned and resumed a private career. Despite his brief tenure, many of the Latin American countries rewarded his efforts. President Rios of Chile inducted Rockefeller into his country's Order of Merit in 1945. The following year Brazil made him a member of the National Order Southern Cross, and in 1949 Mexico enrolled him in the Order of the Aztec Eagle.

Although removed from government, Rockefeller continued his efforts to promote a higher standard of living in underdeveloped areas of the world through the American International Association for Economic and Social Development, a private agency he created with the aid of his family's funds. In 1950 Rockefeller resumed his public career by accepting President Harry Truman's appointment as the chairman of the International Development Advisory Board, which combatted Communism in underdeveloped nations by encouraging economic growth in depressed areas.

President Dwight Eisenhower advanced Rockefeller's political ascent in 1952 by appointing him chairman of the Advisory Committee on Government Organization. Recommendations submitted by his committee helped to reorganize such basic government agencies as the Defense Department, the Office of Defense Mobilization, and the Agriculture Department. In addition, under Eisenhower's orders Rockefeller organized a new agency, the Department of Health, Education, and Welfare, and then became its first undersecretary. Rockefeller believed that good government meant efficient management of resources. He once stated, "The goal of society is to provide every individual with an opportunity to develop his highest potential as a citizen, as a productive member of society, and as a spiritual being."

Rockefeller served as undersecretary until 1954, when President Eisenhower made him one of his special assistants. As a special assistant Rockefeller aided the president with Cold War tactics, helping to develop such proposals as the "open skies" plan, the Atoms-for-Peace Plan, and the Aswan Dam program.

A Mixed Success in Politics

In 1956, frustrated with his ability as an appointed official to merely implement, rather than to initiate, government policy, Rockefeller resigned as special assistant and created, with his own monies, the Special Studies Project. The project, directed by Henry Kissinger, researched and suggested solutions to some of America's most demanding social problems. A book, *Prospect for America* (1961), recorded the proposed solutions.

At 5 feet, 10 inches Rockefeller was physically compact and forceful. He once noted, "nature gave me a strong body. I can keep going when a lot of other people fold up." He drew on his stamina heavily in 1958 during his successful campaign for governor of New York. His subsequent administration was notable for balancing the state budget and substantially reducing the state debt.

In 1961 Rockefeller divorced his wife. Despite some public disapproval of this, he maintained enough support in New York to win his second term as its governor the following year. In 1963 he married Margaretta Fitler "Happy" Murphy, who was 19 years younger than he and who would bear him two sons. Five weeks before marrying Rockefeller "Happy" Murphy had divorced her husband and had given him custody of their children. The remarriage caused so much public disenchantment with Rockefeller that a Gallup poll showed his decline after the remarriage from the frontrunner among the 1964 Republican presidential hopefuls to that of distant second behind Barry Goldwater. Rockefeller nonetheless announced his candidacy for the nomination. The Republican convention of 1964 chose Barry Goldwater, however, and Rockefeller continued his duties as governor.

Rockefeller won four gubernatorial elections in New York, but he lost three attempts for the presidency. On December 11, 1973, more than a year before his fourth term expired, Rockefeller resigned as governor in order to head the National Committee on Critical Choices for Americans and the Commission on Water Quality. He denied resigning to plan a rumored fourth presidential attempt.

Rockefeller once admitted to desiring the presidency "Ever since I was a kid. After all, when you think of what I had, what else was there to aspire to?" As early as 1967 he claimed to have lost his presidential cravings, but the political commentator Bill Moyers stated, "I believe Rocky when he says he's lost his ambition. I also believe he remembers where he put it."

Rockefeller nearly realized his presidential aspirations on December 19, 1974, when he was selected as vice-president under President Gerald Ford (who had moved to the White House following the resignation of Richard Nixon). After his two years as vice-president, however, Rockefeller began to substitute art for politics. Art had long intrigued him. The year of his college graduation he had become a trustee of the Metropolitan Museum of Art, and he served as president of the Museum of Modern Art in 1939. He founded the Museum of Primitive Art in 1957 and amassed extensive collections of modern paintings, sculpture, and all types of primitive art.

His own collections proved impressive enough to prompt the opening of a boutique which sold reproductions of his collected works. He also signed a contract with Alfred A. Knopf publishers to produce five books about his art collection. He only produced one of the contracted books, *Masterpieces of Primitive Art* (1978), before he died of heart failure on January 27, 1979.

Rockefeller wrote three other books: *The Future of Federalism* (1962), *Unity, Freedom and Peace* (1968), and *Our Environment Can Be Saved* (1970). In sum, Nelson Rockefeller's career in politics and philanthropy significantly contributed to the change in the family's reputation from that of avaricious manipulators to that of politically active philanthropists.

Further Reading

Among the extensive literature on Nelson Rockefeller is Stewart Alsop's *Nixon & Rockefeller: A Double Portrait* (1960). Robert H. Connery and Gerald Benjamin's *Rockefeller of New York: Executive Power in the Statehouse* (1979) documents Rockefeller's gubernatorial career. *The Rockefeller File* (1976) by Gary Allen harshly criticizes the Rockefeller wealth and power. *Nelson Rockefeller: A Political Biography* (1964) by James Desmond analyzes primarily the business and political aspects of Rockefeller's life. Frank H. Gervasi's *The Real Rockefeller: The Story of the Rise, Decline, and Resurgence of the Political Aspirations of Nelson Rockefeller* (1964) is one of the most favorable books about Rockefeller and chronicles his 1964 presidential attempt. *The Rockefeller Record* (1960) by James Poling anticipates a great political career for the then rising Rockefeller. *Rockefeller's Follies: An Unauthorized View of Nelson Aldrich Rockefeller* (1966) by William Rodgers portrays Rockefeller as a skilled administrator hindered by a shortsighted determination that his own will prevail. Michael Kramer and Sam Roberts *"I Never Wanted To Be Vice-President of Anything:" An Investigative Biography of Nelson Rockefeller* (1976) and *Nelson Rockefeller: A Biography* (1960) by Joe Alex Morris give additional political and character analyses.

Additional Sources

Persico, Joseph E., *The imperial Rockefeller: a biography of Nelson A. Rockefeller,* New York: Simon and Schuster, 1982; Thorndike, Me.: Thorndike Press, 1982.

Reich, Cary, *The life of Nelson A. Rockefeller, 1908-1958: worlds to conquer,* New York: Doubleday, 1996.

Rockefeller in retrospect: the governor's New York legacy, Albany, N.Y.: Nelson A. Rockefeller Institute of Govt., 1984.

United States. 96th Congress, *Memorial addresses and other tributes in the Congress of the United States on the life and contributions of Nelson A. Rockefeller,* Washington: U.S. Govt. Print. Off., 1979. □

2d Marquess of Rockingham

The English statesman Charles Watson-Wentworth, 2nd Marquess of Rockingham (1730-1782), as prime minister and leader of the Whig opposition, advocated leniency toward the American colonies.

Charles Watson-Wentworth was born on May 13, 1730. He was educated at Westminster School and at Cambridge. In 1745, at the age of 15, he ran away without parental permission to join the Duke of Cumberland's army, which was fighting against Prince Charles Edward Stuart, who was known as Bonnie Prince Charlie or the Young Pretender. Between 1748 and 1750, Watson-Wentworth completed the grand tour of Europe.

On the death of his father in 1750, Rockingham succeeded to the family estates in Yorkshire, Northamp-

tonshire, and Ireland, and in 1752 he augmented his inheritance by marrying Mary Bright, a Yorkshire heiress. In 1751 Rockingham also succeeded to his father's offices of lord lieutenant of the North and East Ridings of Yorkshire, was appointed a lord of the bedchamber, and took his seat in the House of Lords. For the next 15 years Rockingham divided his time between the Lords and his consuming passion for horse racing. In general he entered little into political issues, but in 1762, in protest against the signing of the Peace of Paris, he resigned his place in the bedchamber. In consequence, he was dismissed from his lieutenancies.

During the regency crisis of 1765 Rockingham and the elder William Pitt were approached by the Duke of Cumberland with a view to forming a coalition; and on Pitt's refusal to serve, Rockingham became prime minister. Rockingham was among those ministers inclined to act leniently on the American question. Nevertheless, it was not until the spring of 1766 that the government proposed and carried the repeal of the Stamp Act. The repeal was facilitated by a concurrent statutory declaration of the absolute supremacy of Parliament over the Colonies. George III, chagrined by the repeal of the Stamp Act, was further mortified by the coalition's refusal to grant an allowance to his brothers and by the passage of resolutions condemning general warrants. In July 1766 he dismissed Rockingham, and Pitt returned to power.

Disappointed, Rockingham, took little part in public affairs until the conclusion of the Franco-American alliance. Then he bitterly attacked Lord North's American policy, and in March 1778 he declared for the immediate recognition of

the independence of the Colonies. On the fall of North's administration in February 1782, Rockingham again became prime minister in a coalition government. This ministry conceded legislative independence to Ireland, and it considerably curtailed the political power of the Crown, chiefly by reducing the King's household. Rockingham's death on July 1, 1782, dissolved this short-lived administration. He was buried in York Minster.

Further Reading

Rockingham's relative unimportance in 18th-century politics is reflected by the absence of works devoted to his career. The only biographical study is short and deals with his life up to 1765: G. H. Guttridge, *The Early Career of Lord Rockingham, 1730-1765* (1952). A later study by Guttridge, *English Whiggism and the American Revolution* (1963), is important for the political philosophy of Rockingham and his associates. Recommended for general historical background is J. Steven Watson, *The Reign of George III, 1760-1815* (1960). □

Knute Rockne

Knute Rockne (1888-1931), a genius in the sport of football, became an American folk hero and left his stamp of greatness on the entire sport.

Knute Rockne was born on March 4, 1888, in Voss, Norway. In 1891 his father came to America to exhibit his carriage-building art at the World's Columbian Exposition in Chicago, and 18 months later he sent for his family. Swiftly absorbed in the Chicago melting pot, Knute played football and baseball (and had his nose permanently flattened by a carelessly swung bat). In high school he also ran on the track team and pole-vaulted.

Lacking the finances to enroll at the University of Illinois, Rockne worked in a post office for 4 years. For exercise he ran or vaulted. Two foot-racing buddies begged him to matriculate at Notre Dame University; he reluctantly joined them. Before he impressed athletic coaches with his physical prowess, Rockne dazzled professors with his brilliant mind. (He graduated *summa cum laude.*) His roommate was Gus Dorais, quarterback on the Notre Dame football team. In 1913 the two experimented with forward-passing techniques, a stratagem that was legal but little used.

That autumn top-ranking West Point invited little-known Notre Dame to fill a schedule opening: the result stunned the football world. Dorais passed to Rockne for the first touchdown; Notre Dame took the game. The forward-passing show revolutionized football.

After graduation Knute married Bonnie Skiles. Notre Dame named him assistant football coach, head track coach, and chemistry professor. By 1918 he was head football coach; a season later he had his first unbeaten team. As a strategist, Rockne was imaginative and inventive. With his Notre Dame team, he became the top-ranking coach in the history of intercollegiate football, with a winning average of .897. He produced five unbeaten and united teams. But it

was Rockne's witty, dynamic personality that dominated every gathering. He was not only a spellbinding orator but a funny one as well.

Rockne had not even approached his peak when he died in a plane crash on March 31, 1931. The nation mourned. The President of the United States sent condolences to his widow; so did the king of Norway. Knute's death was front-page news in every paper in America, and editorials lavished praise on the immigrant boy who had become one of America's best-loved figures.

Further Reading

Generally regarded as authoritative biographies are Arthur Daley, *Knute Rockne: Football Wizard of Notre Dame* (1960), and Francis Wallace, *Knute Rockne* (1960). A wealth of detail on Rockne is in Wallace's *The Notre Dame Story* (1949).

Additional Sources

Brondfield, Jerry, *Rockne, the coach, the man, the legend,* New York: Random House, 1976.
Knute Rockne, his life and legend: based on the unfinished autobiography of Knute Rockne, United States: October Football Corp., 1988.
Steele, Michael R., *Knute Rockne, a bio-bibliography,* Westport, Conn.: Greenwood Press, 1983. □

Norman Percevel Rockwell

Norman Rockwell (1894-1978) is remembered for his heartwarming illustrations of American life that appeared on covers of the *Saturday Evening Post* magazine for many decades. Marked by nostalgia and moral fortitude, the paintings remain popular with collectors.

When people use the expression "as American as apple pie" they could just as well say as American as a Norman Rockwell painting. Rockwell produced cover paintings for the *Saturday Evening Post,* a major magazine of its day, for several decades. In the process he became nationally renowned. His nostalgic vision and eye for detail brought him enormous popularity. "He created a moral myth in which people were reassured of their own essential goodness," art critic Arthur C. Danto told Allison Adato of *Life* magazine. "And that is a very powerful thing." Film director Steven Spielberg remarked to Adato, "Growing up, we always subscribed to the *Post.* He [Rockwell] saw an America of such pride and self-worth. My vision is very similar to his, for the most part because of him."

Summers in the Country

Rockwell was born on February 3, 1894, in New York City. His father worked for a textile firm, starting as office boy and eventually moving up to manager of the New York office. His parents were very religious and the young Rock-

well was a choir boy. Until he was about 10 years old the family spent its summers in the country, staying at farms that took in boarders. Rockwell recalled in his autobiography *My Adventures as an Illustrator,* "I have no bad memories of my summers in the country," and noted that his recollections "all together form[ed] an image of sheer blissfulness." He believed that these summers "had a lot to do with what I painted later on."

Rockwell enjoyed drawing at an early age and soon decided he wanted to be an artist. During his freshman year in high school, he also attended the Chase School on Saturdays to study art. Later that year he attended Chase twice a week. Halfway through his sophomore year, he quit high school and went full time to art school.

Started at Bottom in Art School

Rockwell enrolled first in the National Academy School and then attended the Art Students League. Because he was so dedicated and solemn when working at his art, he related in his autobiography, he was nicknamed "The Deacon" by the other students. In his first class with a live model, the location of his easel was not the best. The nude young woman was lying on her side and all Rockwell could see was her feet and rear end. So that is what he drew. Rockwell noted that, as Donald Walton wrote in his book *A Rockwell Portrait,* "he started his career in figure drawing from the bottom up."

At the Art Students League, Rockwell had two teachers who had a significant influence on him: George Bridgeman,

a teacher of draftsmanship, and Thomas Fogarty, a teacher of illustration. Besides their expert instruction, Walton wrote, they conveyed their "enthusiasm about illustration."

While still at the school, Fogarty sent Rockwell to a publisher, where he got a job illustrating a children's book. He next received an assignment from *Boys' Life* magazine. The editor liked his work and continued to give him illustration assignments. Eventually Rockwell was made art director of the magazine. He regularly illustrated various other children's magazines after that. "I really didn't have much trouble getting started," he remarked in his autobiography. "The kind of work I did seemed to be what the magazines wanted."

Paintings Made the *Post*

In March of 1916, Rockwell traveled to Philadelphia to attempt to see George Horace Lorimer, editor of the *Saturday Evening Post,* to show him some proposed cover paintings and sketches. It was his dream to do a *Post* cover. So he set out to sell Lorimer on his work. Since he did not have an appointment, the art editor came out and looked at his work, then showed it to Lorimer. The editor accepted Rockwell's two finished paintings for covers and also liked his three sketches for future covers. Rockwell had sold everything; his dream was not just realized but exceeded. This was the start of a long-term relationship with the *Post.*

His success with the *Post* made Rockwell more attractive to other major magazines and he began to sell paintings and drawings to *Life, Judge,* and *Leslie's.* Also in 1916 he married Irene O'Connor, a schoolteacher.

In 1917, shortly after the United States entered World War I, Rockwell decided to join the navy. He was assigned to the camp newspaper, related Walton, and he was able to continue doing his paintings for the *Post* and other publications. When the war ended in 1918, Rockwell got an immediate discharge.

Top Cover Artist

After the war, besides magazine works, Rockwell started doing advertising illustration. He did work for Jell-O, Willys cars, and Orange Crush soft drinks, among others. Also in 1920, he was requested to paint a picture for the Boy Scout calendar. He would continue to provide a picture for the popular calendar for over 50 years. During the 1920s, Rockwell became the *Post'*s top cover artist and his income soared. In 1929 he was divorced from his wife Irene.

In 1930, Rockwell married Mary Barstow. They had three sons over the next several years. In 1939, the family moved to a 60-acre farm in Arlington, Vermont. In 1941, the Milwaukee Art Institute gave Rockwell his first one-man show in a major museum.

Four Freedoms

After President Franklin Roosevelt made his 1941 address to Congress setting out the "four essential human freedoms," Rockwell decided to paint images of those freedoms, reported Maynard Good Stoddard of the *Saturday Evening Post.* With the U.S. entry into World War II. Rockwell created the four paintings during a six-month period in 1942. His "Four Freedoms" series was published in the *Post* in 1943. The painting portrayed Freedom of Speech, Freedom of Worship, Freedom from Want, and Freedom from Fear. The pictures became greatly popular and many other publications sent the *Post* requests to reprint.

Then the federal government took the original paintings on a national tour to sell war bonds. As Ben Hibbs, editor of the *Post,* noted in Rockwell's autobiography, "They were viewed by 1,222,000 people in 16 leading cities and were instrumental in selling $132,992,539 worth of bonds." Then, in 1943, his studio burned to the ground. Rockwell lost some original paintings, drawings, and his extensive collection of costumes. The family then settled in nearby West Arlington.

Wide Array of Work

Over the years Rockwell did illustrations for an ever-widening array of projects. He did commemorative stamps for the Postal Service. He worked on posters for the Treasury Department, the military, and Hollywood movies. He did mail-order catalogs for Sears and greeting cards for Hallmark, and illustrated books including *The Adventures of Tom Sawyer* and *The Adventures of Huckleberry Finn.*

In 1953, Rockwell and family moved to Stockbridge, Massachusetts. In the summer of 1959, his wife Mary suffered a heart attack and died. During the 1960s, Rockwell painted portraits of various political figures, including all of the presidential and vice-presidential candidates. Most of these were done for *Look* magazine. In 1961, he was presented with an honorary Doctor of Fine Arts degree from the University of Massachusetts. That same year he received an award that he especially treasured, wrote Walton. He was given the Interfaith Award of the National Conference of Christians and Jews for his *Post* cover paining of the Golden Rule. Also in 1961, Rockwell married a retired schoolteacher by the name of Molly Punderson.

Rockwell's last *Post* cover appeared in December of 1963. Over the years he had done 317 covers. The magazine's circulation was shrinking at that time and new management decided to switch to a new format. After Rockwell and the *Post* parted ways, he began a different assignment, painting news pictures for *Look*. He also started painting for *McCall's.*

People's Choice

In 1969 Rockwell had a one-man show in New York City. Art critics often were less than flattering toward Rockwell's work; if they did not knock him, they ignored him. But the public loved his paintings and many were purchased for prices averaging around $20,000. Thomas Buechner wrote in *Life,* "It is difficult for the art world to take the people's choice very seriously." Rockwell himself said to Walton, "I could never be satisfied with just the approval of the critics, and, boy, I've certainly had to be satisfied without it."

In 1975, at the age of 81, Rockwell was still painting, working on his 56th Boys Scout calendar. In 1976 the city of

Stockbridge celebrated a Norman Rockwell Day. On November 8, 1978, Rockwell died in his home in Stockbridge.

Buechner noted that Rockwell's art "has been reproduced more often than all of Michelangelo's Rembrandt's and Picasso's put together." In 1993, a new Rockwell museum was opened just outside of Stockbridge. Museum director Laurie Norton Moffatt cataloged his art in a two-volume book, wrote Landrum Bolling of the *Saturday Evening Post,* and listed over 4,000 original works. As Walton wrote, throughout his life, Rockwell followed the motto: "Don't worry; just work."

Further Reading

Life, November 13, 1970, p. 16; July 1993, pp. 84-91.
Newsweek, April 12, 1993, pp. 58-59.
Moline, Mary, *Norman Rockwell Encyclopedia: A Chronological Catalog of the Artist's Work 1910-1978,* Curtis Publishing Company, 1979.
Walton, Donald, *A Rockwell Portrait,* Sheed Andrews and McMeel, Inc., 1978.
Saturday Evening Post, 1994, pp. 40-43, 74-76; 1995, pp. 60-64.
    □

Alexander Mikhailovich Rodchenko

Alexander Mikhailovich Rodchenko (1891-1956) was a Russian abstract painter, sculptor, photographer, and industrial designer who, as an early pioneer in Russian Constructivism, believed that art must serve as an agent for social change.

Alexander Mikhailovich Rodchenko was born in St. Petersburg (Leningrad) on November 23, 1891. Rodchenko was of humble origin. His father, Mikhail, was a theater craftsman while his mother, Olga Yevdokimovna, was a laundress. Little is known concerning Rodchenko's early childhood. It is believed that he left school in 1905 before finishing his formal education.

In 1910 Rodchenko enrolled at the Kazan School of Art in the city of Odessa. His earliest works from this period are figurative and exhibit a marked influence from European trends, particularly the flat decorative quality found in the art of Aubrey Beardsley. Rodchenko's earliest subject matter was derived from the world of the theater, where his father worked, and the circus. Within a short time Rodchenko began to move toward abstract painting. By the time he left the Kazan School of Art in 1914 he had already begun to experiment with abstract design.

Rodchenko's first purely abstract works date from 1915 after he moved to Moscow and registered at the Stroganov School. He began with abstract designs drawn with a compass and ruler. He also worked in collage by arranging pieces of paper on canvas.

The following year was an important one for Rodchenko. In 1916 he met Vladimir Tatlin, who was later to play an important role in Russian Constructivism. Through Tatlin Rodchenko was introduced to many of the leading figures of the Russian avant-garde, including Kasimir Malevich, Liubov Popova, and the poet Vladimir Mayakovsky. He also met Varvara Stepanova, whom he later married. In March of 1916 Rodchenko exhibited some of his pictures at Tatlin's Futurist exhibition entitled ''The Store.'' Independent though struggling, Rodchenko began to embrace leftist political ideas.

Throughout the revolutionary period in Russia (1917-1921) Rodchenko experimented with both Cubistic and Futuristic tendencies. He was also greatly influenced by the work of his friend Tatlin and the Suprematist Malevich. From Tatlin Rodchenko acquired an interest in surface textures, while from Malevich he learned to work with flat geometric shapes. However, Rodchenko's own attitude toward abstraction digressed from that of many of his fellow artists. His interest in physics, math, and geometry led to a rather scientific approach whereby abstraction became both a scientific and a creative means of revealing reality. Therefore Rodchenko tended to avoid the spiritual aspects of Kandinsky as well as the metaphysical concerns inherent in the work of Malevich. He considered their art evidence of an avoidance of reality. For Rodchenko, art had to serve the function of social change and reform. He felt that his scientific approach was best suited to deal with the problems that reality presented.

After the revolution, Rodchenko played an active and spirited role in the reformation of Russian society and culture. In 1918 he worked for IZO, the Department of Fine Arts of the People's Commissariat of Education. Between 1918 and 1926 Rodchenko taught at the Proletkult School in Moscow and at the *vkhutemas* (technical workshops) throughout the 1920s. Rodchenko also held memberships in various institutes—for example, INKHUK (the Institute of Artistic Culture).

Between 1918 and 1921 Rodchenko's earlier interest in the arrangement of flat geometric shapes on a two-dimensional surface developed into ''spatial constructions'' where he broke free from the confines of the canvas to create three-dimensional sculpture. These constructions were made from various materials, including wood, tin, and cardboard. As in his drawings and paintings, Rodchenko abstracted flat, planar, geometric shapes from nature and assembled them in a process akin to the factory worker, often creating a series based on a single theme. Always an experimenter, Rodchenko's constructions grew more elaborate and sophisticated. His *Hanging Construction* (1920) was one of the first constructed sculptures in Russia to include moving parts. In this work Rodchenko arranged a series of intersecting and concentric circles of wood that hang freely to be moved by the natural circulation of air. Rodchenko became one of the earliest pioneers of the Constructivist movement in Russia.

The 1920s were the busiest and most productive years for Rodchenko. Apart from his busy teaching duties, Rodchenko embarked on a wide range of artistic pursuits.

He designed costumes and stage sets for the theater as well as designs in typography. In 1925 he designed the worker's club for the Soviet Pavilion at the Paris exhibition of decorative arts.

However, Rodchenko seemed to devote most of his energy in the 1920s to photography, a field in which he was most original. Known for his unique use of perspective and photomontage techniques, his photographs appeared on the covers of such Soviet magazines as *Lef* and *Novyi Lef* in the late 1920s. He also designed several photomontages for various editions of the Mayakovsky's poetry. Rodchenko's skills as a designer and photographer eventually led him to design numerous propaganda posters for the Soviet government. Such practical applications of Rodchenko's talents during the 1920s were indicative of the changes that Russia was experiencing. The revolutionary government began to discourage artists from working in the ''impractical'' mode of abstraction. Instead, artists were asked to serve the state and its ailing economy through more practical means. Rather than leave his homeland, as did so many other Russian artists during this period, Rodchenko chose to remain. His firm belief that art was created in the service of social reform was perfectly suited to a rapidly changing Russia.

By the 1930s Rodchenko's abstract painting and photography was increasingly losing favor as Russian taste grew even more conservative. Rodchenko's popularity began to wane. For the first time Rodchenko returned to the figurative painting and subjects of his youth.

During World War II Rodchenko was evacuated to Ochera, where he wrote articles and served as a photographer for several local newspapers while his paintings grew increasingly abstract and emotionally charged. The last years of his life were spent working on various literary projects with his wife. Alexander Mikhailovich Rodchenko died in Moscow on December 3, 1956.

Further Reading

Several excellent books on Rodchenko are available in English, including David Elliott, *Rodchenko and the Arts of Revolutionary Russia* (1979) and German Karginov, *Rodchenko* (1979). Background material may be found in Camilla Gray, *The Russian Experiment in Art: 1863-1922* (1962).

Additional Sources

Karginov, German, *Rodchenko,* London: Thames and Hudson, 1979.
Rodchenko: the complete work, Cambridge, MA: MIT Press, 1987, 1986. □

Richard Charles Rodgers

Richard Charles Rodgers (1902-1972), American composer, wrote the music for over 50 stage and film musicals and helped make the American musical a legitimate art form.

When Richard Rodgers, Lorenz Hart, and Dorothy Fields collaborated in 1925 on *Dearest Enemy,* "an American musical play" (as they called it), contributing respectively music, lyrics, and book, something new was added to the theatrical scene. Not only was the material original, charming, and witty, but the form and subject of the entertainment were distinctly unusual. Here was a play based on American history with unpredictable and pertinent musical sections. Rodgers and his lyricists, Hart and, later, Oscar Hammerstein II, were to repeat this sort of innovation on several occasions. Each occasion marked an important contribution to a more original, indigenous popular musical theater in the United States.

Richard Rodgers was born near Arverne, Long Island, New York, on June 28, 1902. His father was a successful physician and his mother, a well-trained amateur musician. Rodgers heard music in his home from earliest childhood and was regularly taken to the theater. He was especially delighted by the operettas of Victor Herbert and other popular composers. A little later he was inspired by the musicals of Jerome Kern, whose influence, Rodgers said, was "a deep and lasting one."

By the age of six Rodgers was playing the piano by ear and had begun receiving piano lessons. He attended secondary schools in New York. By the age of 14 he had written two songs in the popular vein (he was never interested in purely instrumental composition). His direction seemed fixed. Before he entered Columbia University in 1919, he had already written music for two amateur shows and had met Lorenz (Larry) Hart, a literate, amusing, somewhat

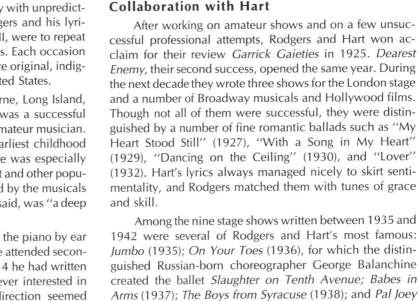

driven creator of verse, with whom Rodgers would collaborate for the next 24 years. Their first published song was "Any Old Place with You" (1919), and hundreds followed. Rodgers left Columbia at the end of his second year to devote full time to musical studies at the Institute of Musical Art, where he spent another two years.

Collaboration with Hart

After working on amateur shows and on a few unsuccessful professional attempts, Rodgers and Hart won acclaim for their review *Garrick Gaieties* in 1925. *Dearest Enemy,* their second success, opened the same year. During the next decade they wrote three shows for the London stage and a number of Broadway musicals and Hollywood films. Though not all of them were successful, they were distinguished by a number of fine romantic ballads such as "My Heart Stood Still" (1927), "With a Song in My Heart" (1929), "Dancing on the Ceiling" (1930), and "Lover" (1932). Hart's lyrics always managed nicely to skirt sentimentality, and Rodgers matched them with tunes of grace and skill.

Among the nine stage shows written between 1935 and 1942 were several of Rodgers and Hart's most famous: *Jumbo* (1935); *On Your Toes* (1936), for which the distinguished Russian-born choreographer George Balanchine created the ballet *Slaughter on Tenth Avenue; Babes in Arms* (1937); *The Boys from Syracuse* (1938); and *Pal Joey* (1940). A number of the songs written during this time are among Rodgers and Hart's most durable: "There's a Small Hotel," "Where or When," "My Funny Valentine," "This Can't Be Love," and "The Lady Is a Tramp." These are sophisticated pieces which display a firm control of the medium.

Collaboration with Hammerstein

After Hart died in 1943, Rodgers entered a period of unprecedented success with lyricist Hammerstein. Of their 10 musicals, 5 were among the longest-running and biggest-grossing shows ever created for Broadway: *Oklahoma* (1943), *Carousel* (1945), *South Pacific* (1949), *The King and I* (1951), and *The Sound of Music* (1959).

If the best work of Rodgers and Hart was marked by a considerable measure of wit and sophistication, the style of the Rodgers and Hammerstein collaboration was dominated by a basic, almost folklike, simplicity. In many songs both music and words seem stripped to the barest essentials. Romantic sentiment is a major ingredient.

Through touring productions, film versions, and recordings, the Rodgers and Hammerstein shows have become known around the world. Songs that have become standards in the popular repertory include "Oh, What a Beautiful Morning," "People Will Say We're in Love," "If I Loved You," "You'll Never Walk Alone," "Some Enchanted Evening," "Hello, Young Lovers," and "Climb Every Mountain." After Hammerstein's death in 1960 Rodgers for the first time served as his own lyricist for the score of *No Strings* (1962).

Rodgers's long association with the popular musical theater was an important one. His best projects were aimed at giving the musical play an ever more natural American expression. *Oklahoma,* especially, brought an engaging simplicity and earthiness to the form. On many occasions his choice of subject matter was unconventional, involving certain characters, situations, and themes of a seriousness seldom encountered previously in musical comedy. His work enriched and broadened a genre once regarded as little more than frivolous entertainment and helped make it into an authentic American art form.

Rodgers' death on December 30, 1972 didn't stop the popularity of his musical works, which enjoyed numerous revivals. Vintage original cast reissues and contemporary recordings, movies and videos, Broadway and community playhouse productions and even illustrated books abounded. They became the medium through which the timeless works credited with launching the 20th Century musical continued to exist.

Rodgers' shows didn't seem to lose dramatic impact. Their stories remained vividly current in *South Pacific,* encompassing the uncertainties of its World War II setting and *The King and I,* soon after, that began to deal with racism and the despotism of absolute authority.

Since music had to be hand-copied during most of Rodgers' lifetime, the musical scores from different productions did not always agree. Although there are some early recordings to follow for authenticity, it still left room for changes in interpretation or even omission of particular numbers during performances.

The original shows were lavished with honors, from an Academy Award for best song (*It Might as Well be Spring,* 1945 from *State Fair*) to another one 10 years later for best score for *Oklahoma!.* Three shows, *South Pacific* (1949); *The King and I* (1951); and *The Sound of Music* (1959) won Tony Awards for "Best Musical."

Later performances continued to bring notoriety and additional awards as top stars such as Julie Andrews and Patti LuPone starred in reissues and revivals. Rodgers himself was featured in one collection of vignettes on video in a scene of him conducting an orchestra on the fabled Ed Sullivan Show.

One of the biggest breakthroughs in perpetuating Rodgers' work was the transfer of a superior 1954 original movie of *Oklahoma!* to videotape. It surpassed a same-cast, second filming of inherently poorer quality and performance that had circulated for years. It took until 1994 when equipment finally was developed to transfer the "original edition" defunct Todd-AO process onto video for mass distribution.

Further Reading

David Ewen, *Richard Rodgers* (1957), a laudatory full-scale biography which contains lists of Rodgers's stage and film works, is quite comprehensive, although not without minor errors. Deems Taylor, *Some Enchanted Evenings* (1953), is a chatty, informal account of the Hammerstein collaboration and contains some musical analysis of Rodgers's songs and has numerous photographs. See also Stanley Green, *The Rodgers and Hammerstein Story* (1963). For additional information, see also *Publisher's Weekly* (July 18, 1994); *Entertainment Weekly* (January 20, 1995 and December 23, 1994); and *Newsweek* (May 15, 1995). □

Auguste Rodin

The French sculptor Auguste Rodin (1840-1917) conceived of his sculpture largely as volumes existing in space, as materials to be manipulated for a variety of surface effects. Thus he anticipated the aims of many 20th-century sculptors.

Auguste Rodin, the son of a police inspector, was born in Paris on Nov. 12, 1840. He studied drawing under Horace Lecoq de Boisbaudran and modeling under the sculptor Jean Baptiste Carpeaux at the School of Decorative Arts in Paris (1854-1857). Simultaneously Rodin studied literature and history at the Collège de France. Rejected three times by the École des Beaux-Arts, he supported himself by doing decorative work for ornamentalists and set designers.

In 1862, as a result of the death of his sister Maria, who had joined a convent, Rodin attempted to join a Christian order, but he was dissuaded by the perceptive father superior. Rodin continued as a decorator by day and at night attended a class given by the animal sculptor Antoine Louis Barye.

In 1864 Rodin began to live with the young seamstress Rose Beuret, whom he married the last year of his life. Also in 1864 he completed his *Man with a Broken Nose,* a bust of an old street porter, which the Salon rejected. That year he entered the studio of Carrier-Belleuse, a sculptor who worked in the light rococo mode of the previous century. Rodin remained with Carrier-Belleuse for six years and always spoke warmly of him. In 1870 he and his teacher went to Brussels, where they began the sculptural decoration of the Bourse. The next year they quarreled, and Carrier-Belleuse returned to Paris, while Rodin completed the work under A. J. van Rasbourg.

The Human Figure

In 1875 Rodin went to Italy, where he was deeply inspired by the work of Donatello and of Michelangelo, whose sculpture he characterized as being marked by both "violence and constraint." Back in Paris in 1876, Rodin made a bronze statue of a standing man raising his arms toward his head in such a way as to project an air of uncertainty, a figure held in a pose of slight torsion suggestive of Michelangelo's *Dying Slave.* Rodin originally entitled the piece the *Vanquished,* then called it the *Age of Bronze.* When he submitted it to the Salon, it caused an immediate controversy, for it was so lifelike that it was believed to have been cast from the living model. The piece was unusual for the time in that it had no literary or historical connotations. After Rodin was exonerated by a committee of sculptors, the state purchased the *Age of Bronze.*

In 1878 Rodin began work on the *St. John the Baptist Preaching* and various related works, including the *Walking Man*. Lacking not only moral and sentimental overtones but a head and arms as well, the *Walking Man* was an electrifying image of forceful motion. Derived partially from some of Donatello's late works, it was based on numerous poses of the model in constant motion. Rodin raised the very act of walking into a subject worthy of concentrated study.

Rodin's interests continued to broaden. Between 1879 and 1882 he worked at ceramics, and between 1881 and 1886 he produced a number of engravings. By 1880 his fame had become international, and that year the minister of fine arts commissioned him to design a doorway for the proposed Museum of Decorative Arts. The project, called the *Gates of Hell* after Dante's *Inferno,* occupied Rodin for the rest of his life, and particularly in the next decade, but it was never finished. The *Gates* were cast in their incomplete state in the late 1920s.

For Rodin, the study of the human figure in a variety of poses indicative of many emotional states was a lifelong preoccupation. In the *St. John* the artist caught the prophet at the moment when he was moved deeply, gesturing automatically by the strength of the idea he was presenting. The gestures of Rodin's figures seem motivated by inner emotional states. In his bronze *Crouching Woman* (1880-1882) an almost incredibly contracted pose becomes something beyond a mere mannerism. The cramped posture of the woman suggests humility, perhaps a conviction of debasement.

One of Rodin's most ambitious conceptions was the group commissioned by the municipality of Calais as a civic monument. The *Burghers of Calais* (1884-1886), a group larger than life size, commemorates the episode during the Hundred Years War when a group of local citizens agreed to sacrifice their lives to save their city. The pathos and horror of the subject accord with the romantic sentiments of the time. One of the figures clutches his head, another exhorts his companion, an older man walks stoically ahead. Each of the burghers is individualized, even while they all move ahead to a common purpose. The psychological interactions of the figures were acutely observed, and a lifelike immediacy was achieved. The group was finally installed in 1895.

Portrait Busts

From the late 1880s Rodin received many commissions from private individuals for portrait busts and from the state for monuments commemorating renowned people. Most of the state commissions exist in the state of models, such as the monument to Victor Hugo (begun 1889), which was to have been placed in the Panthéon in Paris, and the monuments to James McNeill Whistler, Napoleon, and Pierre Puvis de Chavannes. Among Rodin's portrait busts are those of George Bernard Shaw, Henri Rochefort, Georges Clémenceau, and Charles Baudelaire.

In the *Head of Baudelaire* (1892), as in his other portraits, Rodin went beyond mere verisimilitude to catch the inner spirit. Baudelaire's face looks ahead with rapt attention, and the eyes seem to be transfixed upon something invisible. Remarkably, Rodin used as his model not Baudelaire, who had died in 1867, but a draftsman named Malteste, who, for the sculptor, had all the characteristics of the Baudelairean mask: "See the enormous forehead, swollen at the temples, dented, tormented, handsome nevertheless. . . ."

In 1891 the Societé des Gens de Lettres commissioned Rodin to do a statue of Honoré de Balzac, a work that was subsequently rejected. It was not until 1939 that this work was placed at the Raspail-Montparnasse intersection in Paris. Here, too, Rodin went beyond the external appearance of the subject to catch the inner spirit. As is seen in a bronze of 1897, Balzac, wrapped in his dressing gown, is in the throes of inspiration. Details and articulations of the body are not indicated, all the better to call attention to the haughty yet grandiloquent pose of the inspired writer.

Almost single-handedly Rodin inaugurated the modern spirit in sculpture by freeing it from its dependence upon direct representation and conceiving of sculptural masses as abstract volumes existing in space. To conceive of his aims as being analogous to those of the impressionist painters is not entirely correct, for while the roughness of the surfaces of his sculpture may be connected with the loose handling of the painters, Rodin's painfully slow, intense realizations of the inward spirit of his subjects are foreign to the surface effects of most of the impressionists.

Rodin matured slowly, and his first principal work, the *Age of Bronze,* was not made until he was past 35, yet he achieved fame in his lifetime. After 1900 he knew intimately many of the great men of his time, and his apprentices included Antoine Bourdelle and Charles Despiau. In 1916 Rodin bequeathed his works to the state. He died in Meudon on Nov. 17, 1917.

Gates of Hell and Related Compositions

The *Gates of Hell* was conceived in the tradition of the great portals of Western art, such as Lorenzo Ghiberti's *Gates of Paradise* in Florence. Rodin was unable to plan the *Gates* as a total organized design, and they remained a loose federation of groups. Yet certain of the isolated figures or groups of figures, when enlarged and executed separately, became some of Rodin's finest pieces: *Three Shades* (1880), *Crouching Woman* (1885), the *Old Courtesan* (1885), the *Kiss* (1886), and the *Thinker* (1888).

The *Thinker* on the upper lintel of the Gates regards the debauchery and despair in the sections below. The *Thinker* was formally inspired by Michelangelo's *terribilità*, and the motif of the right elbow crossed over the left thigh derives from Michelangelo's Medici tombs. In this piece Rodin conceived of man as beset by intellectual frustrations and incapable of acting: the figure is self-enclosed, completely introverted.

The *Three Shades* on the top of the portal also derives from Michelangelo, especially from the figures of the Slaves, but instead of repeating the inner torment of Michelangelo's figures, they seem beset by languor and utter despair.

The *Kiss* was derived from one of the pairs of intertwined lovers on the *Gates*. The over-life-sized marble figures, sitting on a mass of roughhewn marble, seem to emerge out of the unfinished block in the manner of Michelangelo. But the surfaces of the bodies of the lovers are soft and fluid and suggest the warmth of living flesh. As seen in the *Kiss*, Rodin was capable of unabashed eroticism.

The *Old Courtesan*, based on a study of an aged Italian woman, may have been inspired by a poem of François Villon. Here Rodin showed through the sagging breasts, wrinkled skin, and phlegmatic gestures a completely different conception of the human female form, but the response of the observer is not one of revulsion. In this old, tottering body Rodin captured not ugliness but an uncommon sort of beauty.

Further Reading

Albert E. Elsen, *Rodin* (1963), is a well-documented study of Rodin as the great innovator in 19th-century sculpture, with particular emphasis on the *Gates of Hell*. Elsen's *Auguste Rodin: Readings on His Life and Works* (1965) contains writings about Rodin by the poet Rainer Maria Rilke, who was his secretary, and by Truman H. Bartlett and Henri Dujardin-Beaumetz. Other studies of Rodin include Rainer Maria Rilke, *Auguste Rodin* (1945), and Denys Sutton, *Triumphant Satyr: The World of Auguste Rodin* (1967). Sommerville Story, *Rodin and His Works* (1951), and Robert Descharnes and Jean-François Chabrun, eds., *Auguste Rodin* (1967), are valuable for their illustrations. For background consult Louis W. Flaccus, *Artists and Thinkers* (1916), and Sheldon Cheney, *Sculpture of the World: A History* (1968). □

Peter Wallace Rodino Jr.

Peter Wallace Rodino, Jr. (born 1909) was a Democratic member of the House of Representatives, first elected from New Jersey's 10th Congressional District in 1948 and finally retiring in 1988. He was chair of the House of Representatives' Judiciary Committee during two historic events: when it held hearings on the confirmation of Gerald Ford as vice president in 1973 and when it approved three articles of impeachment against President Richard M. Nixon in 1974.

Peter Wallace Rodino, Jr. was born June 7, 1909, in Newark, New Jersey, a city that was his life-long home base. His parents were Peter and Margaret (Gerard) Rodino. A product of the local schools, he graduated from the New Jersey School of Law (which later became Rutgers University), earning the LL.B. degree in 1937. He was admitted to the New Jersey State Bar shortly thereafter and practiced law in Newark.

Rodino volunteered for military service during World War II in 1941. He served with the First Armored Division in North Africa and Italy. Rodino was one of the first enlisted men to be commissioned as an officer overseas. He was discharged as a captain in 1946. Rodino received the Bronze Star and other decorations, including some from the Republic of Italy.

Began Congressional Career

Rodino's long legislative career began in 1948, when he won election to the House of Representatives from New Jersey's 10th Congressional District, which included most of Newark and parts of surrounding counties. He had first sought that office in 1946, at which time he was narrowly defeated. He was reelected over 20 times and became the dean of the New Jersey congressional delegation.

In Congress Rodino was active in sponsoring and working for many important laws. He was in the forefront of civil rights legislation (especially open housing and voting rights), immigration matters, and making Columbus Day and Martin Luther King's birthday national holidays. Generally, Rodino had a liberal voting record, but he voted for law and order measures and against government aid for abortions. He opposed constitutional amendments to ban abortion and busing and to restore school prayer. He was an assistant to the majority whip of the House between 1965 and 1972.

The congressman was appointed to the Committee on the Judiciary of the House of Representatives, having first served on the Veterans Affairs Committee. Rodino became chair of the committee in January 1973. He headed the committee's hearings on the confirmation of Republican House Minority Leader Gerald Ford to be vice president in late 1973 (replacing the resigned Spiro Agnew). This was the first instance of filling a vacancy in that office under the

25th Amendment to the Constitution. The amendment, ratified in 1967, provided for a president to nominate a vice president with the confirmation of a majority vote of both Houses of Congress. When Ford became president upon Nixon's resignation he named Nelson Rockefeller his successor. Rodino had to preside over the committee once again to hold confirmation hearings for the new vice-president during 1974.

Conducted Nixon Impeachment Inquiry

As the Watergate affair cover-up came to be linked closer to the White House in 1973, members of Congress began to call for the impeachment of President Nixon. Impeachment is the process of removing a president from office by a majority vote of the House, followed by a two-thirds vote of the Senate in agreement. The task of an impeachment inquiry was assigned to the Judiciary Committee in late October 1973.

During the first half of 1974 the committee moved slowly and cautiously as evidence was sought. Effort was spent on trying to obtain copies of relevant tapes of conversations discovered to have been secretly recorded in the presidential offices. These were sought to show whether or not Nixon was involved in any cover-up or obstruction of justice activities related to the Watergate break-in.

Getting the tapes was not an easy task. Having been refused its request for specific tapes by the White House, the committee took an unprecedented action to issue a subpoena to the president on April 11. The group of tapes were released within a few weeks. The tapes and accompanying transcripts were rejected by the committee as containing deletions and inaccuracies. Additional material was subpoenaed three more times by the committee, but the president refused to comply. The White House claimed that it was an escalating invasion into the confidentiality of presidential conversation that would compromise the institution of the presidency.

The committee held closed meetings during late spring and early summer to consider evidence. Beginning July 24, 1974, the meetings were open and televised. On July 27 the committee voted for the first of three articles of impeachment against Nixon: obstruction of justice. On July 29 the second article was approved: misuse of power. And on July 30 the third was voted for: contempt of Congress by defying its subpoenas. The full House was set to start impeachment proceedings in mid-August. Nixon, facing certain impeachment and removal from office, resigned on August 9, 1974.

Rodino also served as Chairman of the Intergovernmental Committee for European Migration, Chairman of the Scientific and Technical Committee of the North Atlantic Assembly, and as Chairman of the Immigration and Nationality Subcommittee of the House Judiciary Committee.

Honors Received

Rodino received numerous awards in recognition of his civic duty from civil rights, religious, and ethnic organizations and many honors from various governments. Seventeen honorary degrees were conferred on him. He was nominated for the office of vice president at the 1972 Democratic National Convention and was considered for that position again in 1976. In 1988 he announced that he would not stand for re-election. In 1992 Seton Hall University Law School (Newark, NJ) named its law library after Rodino. The Peter W. Rodino, Jr. Law Library contains a collection of personal and public papers of Rodino, including materials related to the Watergate investigation, personal correspondence, and speeches.

Rodino married Marianna Stango, December 27, 1941. They had one daughter and one son.

Further Reading

There is no published book length biography of Rodino. For an incisive analysis of Rodino and the historic period during which he served, read Theodore H. White, *Breach of Faith* (1975). A descriptive account, showing Rodino's role, is in Bob Woodward and Carl Bernstein, *The Final Days* (1976). □

George Brydges Rodney

The British admiral George Brydges Rodney, 1st Baron Rodney (1718-1792), by winning notable victories in Caribbean waters over French, Spanish, and Dutch forces, contributed substantially to British command of the seas in the late 18th century.

Born in February 1718, George Rodney attended Harrow before volunteering for naval service at the age of fourteen. Stationed in the Mediterranean, he became first a lieutenant and then a post captain. In October 1747, in command of the 60-gun *Eagle,* he took part in Adm. Edward Hawke's victory over the French off Ushant and was cited for gallantry. Two years later he was named governor and commander in chief of Newfoundland with the rank of commodore. In 1751 he was elected to Parliament.

During the Seven Years War, Rodney commanded the 74-gun *Dublin* and took part in the expedition against Rochefort in 1757; served under Adm. Edward Boscawen in 1758 at the siege and capture of Louisbourg, Nova Scotia; in 1759 and 1760 destroyed French transports collected along the Normandy coast for an invasion of Britain; was appointed commander in chief of the Leeward Islands station in 1761; and in 1762 reduced Martinique and forced the surrender of St. Lucia and Grenada.

Rodney was promoted to vice admiral of the blue and created a baronet. Governor of Greenwich Hospital from 1765 to 1770, he was appointed rear admiral in 1771. From then until 1774 he commanded the Jamaica station. Having fallen into debt, he lived in Paris for 3 years in order to escape his creditors.

Recalled to England in 1778, Rodney was promoted to admiral of the white. Late in 1779, named commander in chief of the Leeward Islands, Rodney was ordered to sail with 22 ships of the line and a large convoy of transports to the West Indies and on the way to relieve Gibraltar, which had been under Spanish siege since July 1779. In January 1780 he captured a Spanish convoy off Cape Finisterre and defeated Adm. Don Juan de Langara's 11 ships in the so-called Moonlight Battle, fought off Cape St. Vincent at night. These feats relieved Gibraltar and brought Rodney international fame.

In September 1780, leaving half of his fleet in West Indian waters, Rodney sailed to New York and foiled George Washington's designs for a Franco-American land and sea assault on the city. Returning to the Caribbean in February 1781, Rodney captured the Dutch islands of St. Eustatius and St. Martin and confiscated huge stocks belonging to British merchants trading illegally with American Revolutionists, thereby crippling a contraband trade on which the Americans depended. For the rest of his life he was involved in lawsuits with British merchants over this action.

In April 1782, after a running engagement with a fleet of 29 ships under Adm. François de Grasse, Rodney and his 34 ships defeated the French off Dominica by bursting in an unorthodox manner through the middle of the French formation and fragmenting it. Called the Battle of the Saints, this action was Rodney's greatest victory. Britain thereby won supremacy of the seas, but the action was too late to affect the outcome of the American Revolution.

When Rodney returned to England, he received a barony and a pension. A bold and irascible man who had been addicted to expensive tastes and to gambling, Rodney lived quietly in the country until he died in London on May 24, 1792. Dominating the waters of the West Indies during his periods of active service, Rodney personified the might of British naval power.

Further Reading

The standard biography is Donald Macintyre, *Admiral Rodney* (1962). Francis Russel Hart, *Admirals of the Caribbean* (1922), contains a chapter on Rodney. See also Alfred T. Mahan, *The Influence of Seapower upon History, 1660-1783* (1890). □

José Enrique Rodó

José Enrique Rodó (1872-1917) was a Uruguayan essayist and literary critic. A stylist and moralist, he aimed especially to maintain Latin American thought and society on a basis of respect for traditional European humanistic and ethical values.

José Enrique Rodó was born in Montevideo on July 15, 1872. The son of a Catalan father who died when José was twelve, he was largely self-taught. He attended primary school but left secondary school for part-time employment. He read broadly in the library left by his father and in the library of the Ateneo of Montevideo. An intellectual center in the arts and humanities, the Ateneo also provided the atmosphere that nourished Rodó's growth. He was greatly influenced by the works of French, Spanish, and British essayists and paid much attention to works on the United States.

Rodó's youth was a period of great, and occasionally violent, change in Uruguay. In March 1895, together with several other young men, Rodó founded the *Revista nacional de literatura y ciencias sociales.* Sixty issues appeared before its closing. Rodó had wanted to found an academy of literature and language, and this had been a compromise. Rodó's concerns for traditional values and proper use of the language were reflected in his publications. His work was unique to the extent that without signature it was recognized even in Spain for his control of ideas and of the *modernista* literary style.

The spiritual and intellectual unity of Latin America with Spain and Europe was Rodó's principal concern; he regarded even Brazil as a variation of this principle, and his main work, *Ariel* (1900), discussed his views in much detail. Latin America's peril lay in its enthusiasm for moral and intellectual change and the susceptibility to United States influence this produced.

Rodó admired some aspects of American life: its technology, spirit of personal liberty and open society, respect for useful labor, and rapid growth of political greatness. But these could entrap an uncritical society—and particularly the Latin masses. American materialism was an open challenge to Latin America.

Rodó praised the traditions of humanism and intellectual achievement of southern Europe's past and present. The

"hallowed cultural tradition and respect for genius" should combine with the Latin Americans' sense of liberty and material progress but never to the disadvantage of the superior minority which maintains its values alive. A leveling process should never occur through mass education or populist technical change.

In 1897 a revolution overthrew the President, and Rodó closed his journal in the interests of political peace and shortly after accepted a professorship in literature in the National University. Indicative of the open atmosphere was Rodó's recommendation by Samuel Blixen, publisher of an avowed anti-Catholic newspaper, for his own post.

In 1902 Rodó accepted election to the national Chamber of Representatives, where he served for 8 years. He opposed the government's open anti-Church position under José Battle but made no headway. Rodó returned to intellectual work and supported himself by teaching and newspaper work. On July 14, 1916, he left for Europe as foreign correspondent for publications in Montevideo and Buenos Aires. He died in Palermo, Italy, on May 1, 1917.

Rodó's influence on the young intellectuals and idealists of his time, and Latin Americans up to the 1940s, was enormous. Since he never visited the United States, many of his ideas were less than accurate. But he stated strongly the principle of Latin uniqueness in contrast with the United States and set a standard that has retained importance.

Ariel was the third in a pamphlet series entitled *La vida nueva.* Other titles were *El que vendrá* (1897) and *Rubén Darío* (1899); the latter is a critical analysis of the work of the famed Nicaraguan poet. In 1906, reflecting his political experience, Rodó wrote *Liberalismo y jacobinismo,* a pamphlet. In 1909 he published a book, *Motivos de Proteo.* A posthumous work is *El camino de Paros,* a collection of pieces written in 1916 and 1917.

Further Reading

The most complete studies of Rodó in English are in Isaac Goldberg, *Studies in Spanish-American Literature* (1920); William Rex Crawford, *A Century of Latin-American Thought* (1944; rev. ed. 1961); and Arturo Torres-Rioseco, *New World Literature: Tradition and Revolt in Latin America* (1949) and *Aspects of Spanish American Literature* (1963).

Additional Sources

Penco, Wilfredo, *José Enrique Rodó,* Montevideo: Arco, 1978. □

John Augustus Roebling

John Augustus Roebling (1806-1869), German-born American engineer, was noted for introducing the manufacture of wire rope to America and for constructing magnificent suspension bridges.

John Roebling was born in Mühlhausen, Thuringia (now part of Germany), on June 12, 1806. He obtained an excellent formal education, graduating from the Royal Polytechnic Institute at Berlin in 1826 with a degree in civil engineering. After working for 3 years on government road-building projects, he became dissatisfied with his life and opportunities in Germany. In 1831 Roebling and his brother, Karl, led a group of emigrants to the United States, where they established an agricultural community in western Pennsylvania.

Unsuccessful as a farmer, Roebling returned to engineering in 1837 and was employed by the state of Pennsylvania on various canal and railroad projects. He became interested in the Allegheny Portage Railroad linking the eastern and western sections of the Pennsylvania Canal, where he observed the difficulties involved in hauling bisected canal boats up and down the inclined planes of the railway. Roebling suggested using wire rope for hauling in place of the bulky and expensive fiber ropes which rapidly frayed and parted. He had read of experiments in Germany with ropes made of twisted wire but had not seen any. He made a number of experiments and eventually convinced the state Board of Public Works to test his idea; consequently, in 1841 Roebling manufactured the first wire cable in America. His small factory in Saxonburg, Pa., was equipped with machinery of his own design and fabrication. In the late 1840s the wire cable factory was relocated at Trenton, N.J., where Roebling subsequently made his home.

In 1844-1845 Roebling built his first structure utilizing his wire cables. He erected a wooden canal aqueduct across the Allegheny River. It consisted of seven spans, each 162 feet long, all supported by two 7-inch wire cables. Following this unprecedented achievement, Roebling built his first suspension bridge in 1845-1846; it was to carry a highway across the Monongahela River at Pittsburgh and consisted of eight spans of 188 feet each. Although he was anticipated in building wire suspension bridges by Charles Ellet, Jr., who in 1842 successfully introduced this type of design, Roebling achieved greater success and eminence in the field.

In many ways Roebling's most notable work was the pioneer railroad suspension bridge built at Niagara Falls between 1851 and 1855. This structure was begun in 1847 by Ellet, who withdrew from the job in 1849 after building a footbridge. Roebling built the railroad bridge, thus solidifying his reputation as the foremost suspension bridge builder in America. He subsequently built bridges over the Allegheny River at Pittsburgh (1860) and the Ohio River at Cincinnati (1867). Roebling's special building techniques included wrapping the numerous wires composing the cables. He also used special stiffening and bracing cables to protect against the weather and to add rigidity to the entire structure.

When plans for a bridge (the Brooklyn Bridge) over the East River connecting lower Manhattan and Brooklyn were revived in the 1860s, Roebling was appointed chief engineer of the mammoth project. His plans for the undertaking were approved in 1869, and work was about to begin when Roebling suffered the accident which cost him his life. On June 28, while he was working at the bridge site, a ferryboat rammed the piling on which Roebling was standing and crushed his foot. The injured toes were amputated, but tetanus set in and he died on July 22, 1869. The Brooklyn Bridge, completed 14 years later under the supervision of Roebling's son, Washington, remains an enduring monument to the Roeblings.

Further Reading

One of the best biography of Roebling is D. B. Steinman, *The Builders of the Bridge: The Story of John Roebling and His Son* (1945), a comprehensive, well-researched study presented with a lively style but with a partisan flavor; it is based on a book by Hamilton Schuyler, *The Roeblings: A Century of Engineers, Bridge-builders and Industrialists* (1931), which quotes from primary sources. A dated but useful work is Charles B. Stuart, *Lives and Works of Civil and Military Engineers of America* (1871). See also Gene D. Lewis's scholarly biography of another pioneer suspension bridge builder, *Charles Ellet, Jr.: The Engineer as Individualist, 1810-1862* (1968), and Carl W. Condit, *American Building Art: The Nineteenth Century* (1960), for the excellent chapters on bridges.

Additional Sources

Sayenga, Donald, *Ellet and Roebling,* York, PA: American Canal and Transportation Center, 1983. □

Washington Augustus Roebling

Washington Augustus Roebling (1837-1926), American engineer and manufacturer, was a noted bridge designer and builder.

Washington Roebling was born on May 26, 1837, in Saxonburg, Pa., where his father, an engineer, had settled in 1831 with a group of German colonists. The boy was raised in a strict home; both German and English were spoken daily. At the age of 13 he moved with his family to Trenton, N.J., where his father set up a factory to manufacture wire rope. Roebling was educated by private tutor, at an academy, and finally at Rensselaer Polytechnic Institute in Troy, N.Y., then the leading civil engineering school in the United States. After graduating in 1857, he went to work at his father's factory. During this period he also helped his father build the Allegheny River Bridge at Pittsburgh.

At the outbreak of the Civil War, Roebling enlisted and saw considerable service, mostly as an army engineer. He built several suspension bridges for use by the Union forces and at one time rode in a captive balloon to observe Confederate movements. After the war he returned to civil engineering, working with his father on the construction of a bridge across the Ohio River at Cincinnati. When it was opened in 1867, this was the longest suspension bridge ever built. Roebling spent a year abroad learning about European bridge-building techniques but returned in time to assist his father's work on the Brooklyn Bridge.

Roebling's father, John Roebling, had pioneered the manufacture of wire rope in the United States and had originated the application of such cables to the building of suspension bridges. The Brooklyn Bridge, connecting Brooklyn to Manhattan, was to be John Roebling's greatest feat. Then, just as the actual construction was beginning, he died. His son carried on the work for 3 years, but in 1872, after an attack of the bends in one of the caissons, his health was broken. Within a few months he retired to a house on the Brooklyn side of the East River, and from there he observed the work through a telescope and directed construction.

After completion of the bridge in 1883, Roebling largely withdrew from active engineering work and from the family manufacturing business, of which he had become president in 1876. He spent his last years in Trenton, occupied with philanthropic and scientific pursuits. He died on July 21, 1926.

Further Reading

The standard sources for Roebling's life and work are Hamilton Schuyler, *The Roeblings: A Century of Engineers, Bridgebuilders and Industrialists* (1931), and D. B. Steinman, *The Builders of the Bridge: The Story of John Roebling and His Son* (1945). A good study of the Brooklyn Bridge, which traces its importance in art and literature, is Alan Trachtenberg, *Brooklyn Bridge: Fact and Symbol* (1965). □

Theodore Roethke

American poet and teacher Theodore Roethke (1908-1963) is considered a major poet of his generation. He demonstrated a wide range of styles and growing awareness of how to transform his love of nature into a vehicle for expressing his mystical visions.

Theodore Roethke was born in Saginaw, Mich., on May 25, 1908. The family owned the largest greenhouses in the state. He called his home "a wonderful place for a child to grow up in and around"—25 acres under glass in town and "the last stand of virgin timber in the Saginaw Valley" out in the country.

Roethke claimed to have hated high school; nevertheless, he continued his education, earning a bachelor of arts degree at the University of Michigan (1929) and spending 1930-1931 at Harvard. He began teaching at Lafayette College (1931), later taught at Pennsylvania State College, then moved to Bennington as assistant professor of English (1943). By 1947 he had settled at the University of Washington in Seattle. In 1962 he was appointed poet in residence in addition to being professor of English. Awards and honors were frequent during these years, including a Pulitzer Prize (1953), the Bollingen Prize, the National Book Award (1958), and even a posthumous National Book Award for his last poems, *The Far Field* (1964).

Roethke began writing prose in high school but switched to poetry in graduate school (encouraged by Robert Hillyer and I. A. Richards). His first book, *Open House,* appeared in 1941. These short, intense lyrics demonstrated superior craftsmanship as well as a generous, ebullient personality: "My heart keeps open house,/ My doors are widely swung./ . . . I'm naked to the bone,/ With nakedness my shield./ Myself is what I wear:/ I keep the spirit spare." Years later Roethke said: "In those first poems I had begun, like the child, with small things and had tried to make plain words do the trick. Somewhat later, in 1945, I began a series of longer pieces which try, in their rhythms, to catch the movement of the mind itself, to trace the spiritual history of a protagonist (not 'I' personally but all haunted and harried men)."

The Lost Son and Other Poems (1948), a group of remarkable poems, traces Roethke's spiritual biography and celebrates growing up in the atmosphere of greenhouses. His moving elegy "Frau Bauman, Frau Schmidt, and Frau Schwartze" is almost equaled by "Big Wind," "Root Cellar," and "The Lost Son." *Praise to the End!* (1951) was followed by *The Waking* (1953) and *Words for the Wind* (1958). By this time Roethke's reputation was firmly established as a superb metaphysical poet. "I learn by going where I have to go," he wrote in an early poem, and in the

last years of his life he was taking his verse into the province of his master, W. B. Yeats: visionary lyrics, interior monologues, projected *personae,* transmuted life. He died on Aug. 1, 1963, of a heart attack. Had Roethke lived longer, he might well have surpassed his masters.

Further Reading

Roethke's *Collected Poems* appeared in 1966. Ralph J. Mills, Jr., edited *Selected Letters* (1968) and a volume of selected prose, *On the Poet and His Craft* (1965). The only biography of Roethke is Allan Seager, *The Glass House: The Life of Theodore Roethke* (1968). The major critical study is Karl Malkoff, *Theodore Roethke: An Introduction to the Poetry* (1966). Arnold Stein, ed., *Theodore Roethke: Essays on the Poetry* (1965), contains an introduction by the editor and essays by critics.

Additional Sources

Meyers, Jeffrey, *Manic power: Robert Lowell and his circle,* New York: Arbor House, 1987.

Seager, Allan, *The glass house: the life of Theodore Roethke,* Ann Arbor: University of Michigan Press, 1991.

Wolff, George, *Theodore Roethke,* Boston: Twayne Publishers, 1981. □

Roger II

Roger II (1095-1154), king of Sicily from 1130 to 1154, was the most able ruler in 12th-century Europe. He organized a multiracial, multinational kingdom in which Arabic, Byzantine, Lombard, Jewish, and Norman cultures produced a brilliant cosmopolitan state.

R oger II was the son of the "Great Count" Roger of Sicily and Adelaide of Savona, and the nephew of Robert Guiscard, the greatest Norman ruler of Apulia and Sicily. In 1101 Roger's father, who had been 64 when Roger was born, died, leaving his widow and two small sons to rule his turbulent and rebellious county of Sicily. Countess Adelaide managed to retain power in the county, and in 1105 her elder son, Simon, died, leaving Roger as sole heir. By 1112, when Roger II was knighted, he and his mother had made Palermo their capital. Roger, a member of the first generation of the Hauteville family to be born in their southern Italian domains, was raised in the cosmopolitan Arabic, Greek, and Norman culture of Sicily, and his subsequent character reflects that upbringing.

Adelaide died in 1118, and the 23-year-old Roger, his county somewhat pacified by the participation of many Norman knights in the First Crusade and in subsequent service in the Latin kingdom of Jerusalem, began to consider the exploitation of Sicily's strategic position along the Mediterranean trade routes. On the death of his cousin Duke William of Apulia in 1127, Roger claimed the mainland inheritance of his family as his own. In 1128 he was formally invested as Duke of Apulia by Pope Honorius II at

Benevento. By 1129 Roger had imposed his rule over the turbulent Norman barons of the mainland and had extracted from them a closely binding oath of personal loyalty to himself.

Norman Sicily and southern Italy had always been a subject of dispute between Normans, Byzantines, the German emperors, and the papacy. In the disputed papal election of 1130, Roger sided with the antipope Anacletus II against Innocent II. Therefore on Christmas Day, 1130, Anacletus crowned Roger king of Sicily at Palermo. The Norman adventure of the 11th century had reached its apex. At one stroke the dubiously gotten lands had been transformed into that most sacred of all Christian social structures, a kingdom. It was a kingdom, however, unlike any other European kingdom.

The first years of Roger's reign were spent in suppressing baronial revolts, countering the propaganda of Bernard of Clairvaux and Pope Innocent II, and defending his kingdom against the invading armies of the emperor Lothair. By 1139, however, Roger had succeeded in fending off all three dangers. The Emperor was dead, Roger was reconciled to Innocent II, and the last of the rebellious barons had been crushed. During the first 2 decades of his reign, Roger had begun to sponsor the architectural projects which were to make Norman Sicily one of the wonders of the world. The Cathedral at Cefalù, the Palatine Chapel at Palermo, and many other religious and secular buildings began to take on that unique combination of Greek, Arabic, and Norman artistic style which still fascinates the beholder. In 1140 Roger II promulgated the Assizes of Ariano, the most remarkable royal code of laws of the 12th century.

Not only did Roger and his officials patronize the arts and architecture, but they encouraged learning and literature. The great Arab geographer al-Idrisi dedicated his book to Roger, and Sicily, in continuous cultural contact with Byzantium, Islam, and Christian Europe, became not only a remarkable hybrid cultural meeting place but a center of Christian-Arab contacts from which much of Arabic and Greek learning would soon penetrate western Europe.

The old tensions among Sicily, Byzantium, and the German emperors were not, however, extinct. During the last years of his reign Roger had to counter a Byzantine-Western imperial alliance, and not until the death of the emperor Conrad III in 1152 was Roger able to cease his complex diplomatic efforts to neutralize this powerful threat to his independence. By 1153 Roger had once again vindicated his claims by his ability. In 1146 he had succeeded in establishing control of part of North Africa, and throughout his reign he succeeded in creating a stable political kingdom out of the most savagely opposed religious and racial factions which Christendom knew. His chancery issued documents in four languages: Arabic, Greek, Latin, and Hebrew, and his island and mainland kingdom knew a degree of racial and religious toleration and cross-cultural influence such as few societies have known before or since. Roger died on Feb. 26, 1154, leaving the kingdom to his son William; and his reputation as the most remarkable layman of the 12th century, to history.

Further Reading

The best work on Roger II in English is the two-volume study of John Julius Norwich, *The Normans in the South, 1016-1130* (1967) and *The Kingdom in the Sun, 1130-1194* (1970). David C. Douglas, *The Norman Achievement* (1969), surveys the entire Norman movement in France, England, and Sicily. Otto Demus, *The Mosaics of Norman Sicily* (1950), discusses the artistic style of Roger's period. □

Carl Ransom Rogers

Carl Ransom Rogers (1902-1987) was an American psychotherapist who originated person-centered, non-directive counseling.

Carl Rogers was born on January 8, 1902, in Oak Park, Illinois, the fourth of six children to Walter and Julia (Cushing) Rogers. His father, a successful contractor, engineer, and farmer, believed in the virtue of hard work. His mother had strong fundamentalist religious convictions and raised her six children (five boys) in a home where drinking, smoking, dancing, and playing cards were sinful. She believed that the elect people of God should not mingle with those whose actions indicated that they were otherwise.

Rogers later said that his attitude as a youth toward others outside the home "was characterized by distance and aloofness . . . taken over from . . . parents." (*A Way of Being,* 1980). He had only superficial contacts with others, "never having a real date in high school." He was a solitary boy who between numerous farm chores found time to read. His interests outside of school focused on science, reading his father's books on scientific farming, and studying systematically the life cycle of moths found in woods near his home.

From Seminarian to Education Student

Rogers' college years brought a break with the orientation of his parents and an end to his solitary life style. During those years at the University of Wisconsin (1919-1924) he began dating and soon developed a close relationship with his childhood friend Helen Elliot, whom he married upon graduation. During his sophomore year he changed majors from agriculture to history, thinking that the latter would be more suitable for a career in religious work. A six-month trip to China with other Christian youths during his junior year impressed upon him that sincere and honest people could hold divergent religious views.

The growing shift away from his parents' perspective was further evidenced by his choice of a liberal seminary for graduate studies, Union Theological Seminary in New York City (1924-1926). In a student initiated seminar at Union he came to the conclusion that although "the possibility of the constructive improvement of life for individuals [was] of deep interest to me, I could not work in a field where I would be required to believe in some specific religious

and facade diminishes. . . . he becomes more open. . . . and he finds that he is free to grow and change in desired directions.''

Advocate of Person-Centered Counseling

During mid-career, as a college professor, Rogers was able to apply his approach to counseling and further test the ideas that had grown out of earlier experiences. This also was a period of wide involvement in professional organizations and much writing effort. His theory and method quickly grew in popularity, but many established psychiatrists remained dubious as to their scientific rigor and applicability. He worked at three midwestern universities: Ohio State (1940-1945) in clinical psychology; University of Chicago (1945-1957) in psychology and as director of the student guidance center; and University of Wisconsin (1957-1963) in psychology and psychiatry.

Other activities during this period included visiting professorships at several universities and the receipt of many honorary degrees. Throughout his career he was active in professional organizations including being elected president of the American Association of Applied Psychology (1944), the American Psychological Association (1946), and the American Academy of Psychotherapists (1956). He received both the First Distinguished Professional Contribution Award and the Distinguished Scientific Contribution Award from the American Psychological Association, the only psychologist to be thus doubly honored. Rogers was named to the American Academy of Arts and Sciences in 1961.

Late in his career Rogers was named a fellow to the Center for Advance Study in the Behavioral Sciences at Palo Alto, California (1962-1963). He joined the Western Behavioral Sciences Institute in 1964 and later the Center for the Study of the Person in La Jolla, California, where he continued to work into the 1980s. Over his lifetime he published approximately 260 articles and 15 books, which have had a significant influence on the development of psychology in the 20th century. He was prominent in the human potential movement, and his book on encounter groups had an impressive impact.

After the mid-1970s Rogers was especially interested in facilitating groups involving antagonistic factions, whether the hostilities arose out of cultural, racial, religious, or national issues. He facilitated a group from Belfast containing militant Protestants and Catholics from Ireland and the English. He was involved in intercultural groups whose participants came from many nations, including participants from the Eastern European bloc countries. He facilitated Black-White groups in South Africa. He was deeply interested in applying the principles of the person-centered approach to international affairs in the interest of world peace.

Further Reading

Insightful autobiographical sketches with personal anecdotes are found in chapters 2, 3, and 4 of *A Way of Being* (1980) and in chapter 1 of *On Becoming a Person* (1961). A comprehensive biography by Howard Kirchenbaum is *On Becoming Carl Rogers* (1979). Also, a brief autobiography was published in *A*

doctrines'' (from his 1967 autobiography). As a consequence, he moved across the street to Teachers College-Columbia University, a move which was easily facilitated by the close affiliation of the two schools. He majored in clinical psychology and child guidance and graduated with a master's degree (1926) and a doctorate (1931). He characterized his education in psychology at Teachers College as having a markedly measurement and statistics approach to the understanding of behavior.

In 1928 the Rogers family (now including a two-year-old son and a daughter on the way) moved to Rochester, New York, where he began work as a psychologist for the Society for Prevention of Cruelty to Children. In contrast to Teachers College, many colleagues in Rochester emphasized a psychoanalytic approach to behavior. Through the practical and personal experiences in this clinic, however, he began to recognize that the results of both measurement psychologists and psychoanalysts were ''never more than superficially effective.''

Several incidents in the Rochester clinic helped him ''to perceive . . . that it is the client who knows what hurts, what direction to go, what problems are crucial, what experiences have been deeply buried. It began to occur to me that unless I had a need to demonstrate my own cleverness and learning, I would do better to rely upon the client for direction of movement in the therapeutic process.'' For effective counseling, the psychotherapist, Rogers believed, is ''to be genuine and without a facade. . . . and to be empathetic in understanding. As a result the client begins to feel positive and accepting toward himself. . . . his own defenses

History of Psychology in Autobiography, vol. 5, edited by Edwin G. Boring (1967). An overview of his person-centered therapy can be found in *On Becoming a Person* (1961), and an overview of his theory of education is in *Freedom To Learn* (1969).

Additional Sources

Evans, Richard I. (Richard Isadore), *Carl Rogers: the man and his ideas,* New York: Dutton, 1975.
Evans, Richard I. (Richard Isadore), *Dialogue with Carl Rogers,* New York, N.Y.: Praeger, 1981, 1975.
Kirschenbaum, Howard, *On becoming Carl Rogers,* New York: Delacorte Press, 1979. □

Edith Nourse Rogers

Edith Nourse Rogers (1881-1960) was the first woman from New England to be elected to Congress. Reelected 17 times, she worked tirelessly for veterans' concerns throughout her congressional career.

Edith Nourse Rogers, daughter of Franklin Nourse and Edith Frances Riversmith, was born March 19, 1881, in Saco, Maine. Her family was well-to-do and they moved to Lowell, Massachusetts, in 1895, when her father became the manager for the second largest textile mill in Lowell. Edith was educated by private tutors and then at Rogers Hall School, a private girls' boarding school, graduating in 1899. Her parents sent her to a finishing school at Madame Julien's School in Paris. Upon her return she plunged into the social whirl and was married to John Jacob Rogers in October 1907.

John Rogers began a successful law practice before turning to politics and being elected to Congress in 1912. He carried his district six more times before dying in March 1925. Edith Nourse Rogers was urged to run for her husband's seat in the special election and easily won on June 25, 1925, becoming the first woman from New England to be elected to Congress. She intended to remain in Washington for only a few years, but won reelection 17 times. As her 19th campaign began in 1960, she was unopposed. Her 35 years of service in the House of Representatives was the longest of any woman.

Although an ardent suffragist, Rogers was not an ardent feminist, and she became famous for her interest and advocacy of veterans' affairs. Her transformation from a socialite to a person deeply and enduringly interested in veterans' affairs occurred during World War I when she accompanied her congressman husband to Europe to visit base and field hospitals. Upon her return to Washington in 1918 she became a seven-days-a-week volunteer worker at Walter Reed Hospital, continuing there until 1922. In recognition of her interests, President Warren Harding appointed her a dollar-a-year inspector of veterans hospitals, a commission renewed by President Calvin Coolidge (1923) and Herbert Hoover (1929).

Her concern for veterans became her principal interest in the House of Representatives. Over the years she served on the House Committee on Veterans' Affairs, becoming the ranking member and twice chairing it when the Republicans held the House majority. Not surprisingly, she had a hand in many major veterans' bills. In 1930 she persuaded Congress to appropriate the money to construct a nationwide network of veterans hospitals. She was one of the major drafters of the G. I. Bill of Rights for veterans of World War II and sponsored the Korean War Veterans Benefits Bill. She introduced the legislation which established the Women's Army Corps in 1942 and created a permanent Nurse Corps in the Veterans Administration. In addition, she secured the passage of hundreds of private bills for pensions and disability allowances for veterans.

No rubber-stamp Republican, she often went her own way. In 1933 she was one of the first members of Congress to speak out against Nazi persecution of the Jews; subsequently she voted against the 1937 Neutrality Act, which the isolationist Republican leadership favored, and for the Selective Service Act of 1940, which they opposed. Her actions and dedication to her constituency made her unbeatable in elections. She always won by landslide proportions and was unopposed in three elections, although Massachusetts was increasingly Democratic-dominated.

Her health began to fail after 1954; but even at age 79 in 1960 when she approached her 19th election, she was invincible to all challengers except death itself. She died of a heart attack on September 10, 1960, three days before the primary election.

Further Reading

A gook sketch of Edith Nourse Rogers is Victoria Schuck's entry in *Notable American Women: The Modern Period* (1980). Also see the popularly-written sketch by Hope Chamberlin, *A Minority of Members: Women in the U.S. Congress* (1973). Other sources include the *Dictionary of American Biography, Supplement Six: 1956-1960* (1980) and obituaries in the *New York Times, Washington Post,* and *Boston Globe* on September 11, 1960.

Additional Sources

Konantz, Gail, *Edith Rogers,* Winnipeg, Man.: Peguis Publishers, 1981, 1980. □

John Rogers

John Rogers (1829-1904) was the most successful genre sculptor of mid-19th century America. His plaster groups sold by the thousands.

John Rogers was born in Salem, Mass., and spent his early life as a clerk in New England, New York, and the Midwest. He began to model sculpture before the middle of the century. In 1858 he went first to Paris and then to Rome for training. The ideals of contemporary neoclassicism, as practiced by both American and European sculptors in Italy, did not inspire him, however, and he turned his back upon his sculptural pursuits when he returned to Chicago.

However, Rogers was persuaded to continue modeling small genre figures of a type he had done previously. Their success led him to open a studio in New York City in 1859. A combination of his sculptural ability and shrewd marketing practices quickly made that venture a success too. His work consisted of small, very detailed sculptures in plaster, built around a metal armature, and painted a neutral earth color. His grasp of anatomy and sharp observation of details of costumes and accessories were combined with an ability at compositional massing of figures and an appealing, sympathetic expressiveness. Some of his earliest works related to the Civil War, appealing to patriotism and to the popular sentiment against deprivation, the horrors of war, and slavery.

The majority of Rogers's sculptures featured scenes of everyday life—in the schoolhouse, at the parsonage, in the home, more often rural or small town. Among his more ambitious works were scenes taken from literature, including three sculptures from Washington Irving's *Rip Van Winkle,* some from Goethe's *Faust,* and a number of Shakespearean interpretations; even these stressed anecdotal rather than dramatic qualities. There were a few small portrait sculptures, too, of Abraham Lincoln, George Washington, and Henry Ward Beecher. As time went on, Rogers's compositions tended toward greater looseness, and he also depicted more scenes of action. In all, there were about 80 so-called Rogers Groups, of which about 80,000 plaster reproductions were made. Rogers developed a mail-order business, and his works were often purchased as wedding presents. They cost about $10 or $15 each.

Rogers also executed a number of monumental sculptures, but these are far less significant than his plaster groups. They represent one phase of the reaction to the popular idealistic marbles, although in the 1850s some neoclassic sculptors were also producing genre works. Rogers had numerous imitators, but none achieved his renown.

Further Reading

Two full-length studies of Rogers are Mr. and Mrs. Chetwood Smith, *Rogers Groups: Thought and Wrought by John Rogers* (1934), and David H. Wallace, *John Rogers: The People's Sculptor* (1967). □

Richard Rogers

The British architect Richard Rogers (born 1933) was an avowed modernist who represented high tech architecture with his concern for advanced technology. He was best known for his joint design of the Centre Pompidou in Paris with Renzo Piano and for the Lloyd's of London Building in London.

ichard George Rogers was born in Florence, Italy, on July 23, 1933, to British parents. He served in the British Army (1951-1953) prior to attending the Architectural Association School (1953-1959) in London. He received the Diploma of Architecture in 1959 and in 1960 married the architect Su Brumwell. The following year he studied at the Yale University School of Architecture in New Haven, Connecticut on a Fulbright scholarship, and received the Master of Architecture degree in 1962. Returning from America, Rogers formed a partnership with Norman and Wendy Foster and Su Rogers (1963-1968) in London called Team 4. They completed an industrial building (1967) at Swindon, Wiltshire, England, for Reliance Controls Ltd. The Team 4 arrangement was followed by the partnership of Richard and Su Rogers (1968-1970).

Successful Collaboration With Renzo Piano

Rogers' collaboration with Renzo Piano began in 1970, and one of their earliest designs (1971-1973) was for the small office building located at the entrance to the B & B Italia factory in Novedrate, Como, Italy. Their use of chromatic effects, an open interior space that could be freely laid out and divided up, and the suspension of that space from an exterior trellis structure all look forward to the Centre Pompidou, or Beaubourg as it is more popularly known in Paris. Winning the competition for the Centre National d'Art et Culture Georges Pompidou (1971-1977) and then building it was an extraordinary achievement for Rogers and Piano. Criticism has been directed against the high tech

appearance of the building, but the public's acceptance and use of the building contradict this controversy. It has been said that Pompidou has attracted seven million visitors a year, "more than the Louvre and the Eiffel Tower combined." For Rogers, the aim of technology is to satisfy the needs of all levels of society. In Beaubourg the mechanical services and plant have been hung around the exterior of the building, thus leaving the interior spaces clear. These flexible spaces can accommodate new developments in information systems and communications. The multiple and varied functions of the Beaubourg are served well by the evolutionary nature of this building.

The most unique design to come from the Rogers and Piano collaboration was the one for the Institut de Recherche et Coordination Acoustique/Musique (IRCAM) in the center of Paris (1973-1977). This subterranean building with its roof at street level and improved acoustics contains studios, workshops, and an experimental concert hall. Scientific research and listening to music occur at IRCAM as scientists and musicians work side by side to explore the possibilities of abolishing the barrier that separates science and art.

Formed Richard Rogers Partnership

In 1973 Rogers married Ruth Elias and in 1977 formed the architectural firm of Richard Rogers Partnership with John Young, Marco Goldschmied, and Mike Davies. Lloyd's of London, the insurance underwriters, held a limited international competition in 1979 for a design to replace the 1925 headquarters designed by Sir Edwin Cooper. Richard Rogers & Partners presented the winning entry. Rogers' plan was a straightforward rectangular atrium office block, but by bringing the service elements (elevators, escape stairs, restrooms, and service ducts wrapped in gleaming stainless steel) out on to the facade, an ordinary building was dramatically altered. The technology of the Lloyd's building was not innovative, having been done before—mostly in the United States—but it was sophisticated. The design focus of the building is "The Room," which is lit and dominated by the central atrium. Several features from earlier Lloyd's buildings were saved for use in this scheme: Cooper's pedimented entrance and library, Lutyens' war memorial design, and Adams' committee room.

The Inmos microchip plant (1982) in Newport, Gwent, Wales, presented Rogers with an exacting task just as IRCAM had, but instead of refined acoustics, a high degree of environmental control was needed. The necessity of cleanliness in the production of microchip wafers was the controlling factor in the design. Inmos also wanted a friendly environment for its employees and maximum flexibility for an evolving industry. The design had to be responsive to any site and capable of being built in a range of sizes. The key organizing element in Rogers' plan was a wide corridor that acted as a central spine. The clean room for production was placed to the north of the spine and the offices, restaurants, and testing labs to the south. Through the use of a standard bay system pre-fabricated off-site, Rogers was able to give Inmos an eight-bay building with the potential for enlargement to 20 bays.

A natural evolution from the Inmos plant is seen in the research and development facility Rogers designed for Patscenter International (1983) in Princeton, New Jersey. Rogers and Piano had built a facility near Cambridge, England, in 1975 for the parent company based on an open plan, but here in Princeton Rogers repeated his idea of open space ranged on either side of a central spine. The smaller size of Patscenter and less rigorous environmental requirements allowed for a simplified structure. The different approaches of the British and American construction industries are also reflected in Inmos and Patscenter.

A later project of a somewhat different nature was Rogers' plan for the development of a site in the London borough of Hammersmith on the Thames River (1983-1985). It included a new studio for his firm, start-up spaces for innovative companies, and private housing. By refurbishing already existing structures and building new ones, while maintaining the residential character of the area, it was hoped that the qualities of the riverside would be preserved and enhanced. A new public riverwalk served as a unifying element and provided access to river views for pedestrians.

In 1997 the Richard Rogers Partnership received a contract to design the Millennium Exhibition—a 130-acre site on London's Greenwich Peninsula that will hold a year-long event in the year 2000. The center piece of the exhibit will be the Millennium dome, which the architects described as being able to hold "two Wembley Stadiums."

In spite of attacks on modern architecture, Rogers remained a committed modernist. He was interested most in the imagery of technology and concerned himself with advanced technology in architecture. There is a consistent development in his works so that those designs singled out are more or less typical. Even though devoted to technology, Rogers remained faithful to the environment. He thought that people should live closer to their workplace, so there would be no need to commute: thus, less pollution. He believed that people in the cities need open spaces. In a 1995 interview in the *Los Angeles Times,* Rogers said that urban design must contain squares and open spaces. "City squares are special," he said. "People come to them to talk, demonstrate and celebrate." Rogers was awarded the 1985 Royal Gold Medal for Architecture by the Royal Institute of British Architects (RIBA). He served as president of RIBA and was an honorary member of the American Institute of Architects (AIA). He was an internationally respected architect of the latter half of the 20th century.

In 1996, Rogers was introduced into the House of Lords, taking the title "The Lord Rogers of Riverside." He was given a Barony of the United Kingdom for life. In April 1997, Rogers received an honorary professorship from the Thames Valley University. He has written one book, *Architecture: A Modern View* (1991).

Further Reading

Books about Rogers and his work include: *Richard Rogers: A Biography* by Bryan Appleyard (1986); *The Architecture of Richard Rogers* by Deyan Sudjic (1995); *Lloyd's Building: Richard Rogers Partnership* by Kenneth Powell (1994); *Rich-*
ard Rogers Partnership: Works and Projects by Richard Burdett (1996); *Norman Foster, Richard Rogers, James Sterling: New Directions in British Architecture* by Deyan Sudjic (1986); and *Richard Rogers 1978-1988* (Architecture and Urbanism Extra Edition Series). There is also a collection of architectural monographs titled *Richard Rogers and Architects* edited by Barbie Campbell and Ruth Elias Rogers (1985). Numerous articles on Rogers may be found in international architectural journals such as *Architectural Review, The Architects' Journal, Building* , and *Architectural Design*. Rogers is listed in *Contemporary Architects,* edited by Muriel Emanuel (1980). Rogers, Piano, and others authored *The Building of Beaubourg* (1978). Current information can be found on the Richard Rogers Partnership Web site (www.richardrogers.co.uk/home.html). □

Robert Rogers

The colonial American Robert Rogers (1731-1795) was a frontiersman and army officer in the French and Indian War. Later he was extremely successful as a ranger, raider, and reconnaissance officer.

Robert Rogers was born in Methuen, Mass., on Nov. 18, 1731. He grew up in Dunbarton, N.H. Though formal education was slight in a frontier town like Dunbarton, his childhood in field and forest was ideal preparation for his career as a ranger officer.

Beginning service as a scout in King George's War (1744-1748), Rogers reentered service as a ranger officer when the French and Indian War (1755-1763) broke out, possibly because he was involved in alleged counterfeiting of the easily imitated colonial currency. Eventually, he commanded nine ranger companies and was promoted to major. He was in charge of reconnaissance, active in raiding around Lake Champlain, especially at Crown Point and Ticonderoga, and led the force that destroyed the St. Francis Indians (named after the Indian Village of St. Francis, northeast of Montreal), longtime terrors of the New England frontier. He was at the surrender of Montreal in 1760, which ended the French regime in Canada.

After the capitulation, Rogers led a party as far as Detroit to receive the surrender of the French garrison there and to persuade the Native Americans that they must henceforward look to the British as their "fathers." The popular hero was not completely successful. The Native Americans attacked in Pontiac's Conspiracy, and Rogers was with the British troops that moved to relieve Detroit, fighting in the defeat at Bloody Run and commanding the men who covered the British withdrawal to Detroit again.

After brief service in the South and a trip to England, Rogers became commandant at the northwestern Mackinac post. Here he was accused of illegal trading with the Native Americans and other offenses, including treason; but a court-martial triumphantly acquitted him. Rogers had been unfortunate in business; the exact nature of his business is not clear, but it certainly included ventures in Native American trading. He also had difficulty with vouchers for ex-

penses incurred during his Native American fighting, so that his debts eventually reached £13,000. When he returned to England in 1769, he was thrown into debtors' prison but was released with the aid of his brother James.

Returning to America in 1775 as a half-pay British lieutenant colonel, Rogers showed patriot sympathies, which may have been feigned. George Washington distrusted him, and Rogers eventually joined the service of the British with no great distinction. He died in poverty in London on May 18, 1795.

Further Reading

Rogers's *Journals* are the best source for his military exploits. Rogers's *Ponteach* (1914) contains a biography by the editor, Allan Nevins. An excellent biography is John R. Cuneo, *Robert Rogers of the Rangers* (1959). The second volume of the 1937 edition of Kenneth Roberts, *Northwest Passage,* contains documents and a lengthy bibliography.

Additional Sources

Cuneo, John R., *Robert Rogers of the rangers,* Ticonderoga, N.Y.: Fort Ticonderoga Museum, 1988.

Rogers, Robert, *Reminiscences of the French War: with Robert Rogers' journal and a memoir of General Star,* Freedom, N.H.: Freedom Historical Society, 1988. □

Will Rogers

One of the most celebrated humorists and public figures of his day, Will Rogers (1879-1935) offered dry, whimsical commentaries on a plethora of political, social, and economic issues. His aphoristic, satirical observations, which he voiced in magazine articles and nationally syndicated columns, revealed the foibles and injustices of American society and reaffirmed the humorist's role as the voice of the "average" citizen.

Born in Oklahoma into a prosperous ranching family of mixed Cherokee descent, the young Rogers was an expert rider and lariat stuntman. He appeared in Wild West shows throughout the world, and in 1905 he made his vaudeville debut. In vaudeville he enlivened his performances with off-the-cuff lectures on the art of roping. Rogers's humorous chatter, nonchalant delivery, and southwestern drawl proved a popular combination, resulting in an invitation to join the Ziegfeld Follies. His wife suggested that he vary and supplement his material with comments on contemporary personages and events. Following this advice, he delighted audiences with his homely philosophy and pungent remarks, becoming a renowned humorist and interpreter of the news. Rogers's first two books, *The Cowboy Philosopher on the Peace Conference* and *The Cowboy*

Philosopher on Prohibition, were drawn from his *Follies* monologues. His subsequent works, such as *The Illiterate Digest, There's Not a Bathing Suit in Russia,* and *Letters of a Self-Made Diplomat to His President,* were garnered from the newspaper columns "Will Rogers Says," "The Worst Story I Ever Heard," "The Daily Telegram," and also from his serialized correspondence from abroad appearing in *The Saturday Evening Post.* Rogers's death in a 1935 plane crash sent the entire country into mourning, prompting Carl Sandburg to reflect, "There is a curious parallel between Will Rogers and Abraham Lincoln. They were rare figures whom we could call beloved without embarrassment."

In his writings, as on the stage, Rogers affected a pose of ignorance, emphasizing his simple, rural background and lack of formal education. In reality he was a well-informed and thoughtful commentator, skilled in the use of the pun, metaphor, and hyperbole. By assuming the stance of a good-natured, naive country boy, Rogers was able to lampoon Congress, presidents, and foreign heads of state without occasioning offense or indignation. His *The Cowboy Philosopher on the Peace Conference,* for example, mocks the diplomatic stratagems of the Versailles talks, while *The Cowboy Philosopher on Prohibition* examines the futility and hypocrisy of the Volstead Act. Rogers's shrewd, fundamentally pessimistic point of view has been compared to Mark Twain's, as has his profound distrust of the motives and objectives of those in power. Unlike Twain, however, he was incapable of sustaining an idea at length. Rogers's forte was the pithy sentence—the short but highly suggestive statement calculated to effect an immediate response. While some critics no longer consider his topical humor relevant and find his intentional misspellings and grammatical errors excessive, others value his writings for the insight they provide into the concerns and opinions of the United States during the tumultuous 1920s and 1930s. Damon Runyon offered this assessment: "Will Rogers was America's most complete human document. He reflected in many ways the heartbeat of America. In thought and manner of appearance and in his daily life he was probably our most typical native born, the closest living approach to what we like to call the true American."

Further Reading

Alworth, E. Paul, *Will Rogers,* Twayne, 1974.
Brown, William R., *Imagemaker: Will Rogers and the American Dream,* University of Missouri Press, 1970, 304 p.
Croy, Homer, *Our Will Rogers,* Duell, Sloan and Pearce, 1953, 377 p.
Day, Donald, *Will Rogers: A Biography,* David McKay Company, Inc., 1962, 370 p.
Dictionary of Literary Biography, Volume 11, Gale, 1982.
Dockstader, Fredrick J., *Great North American Indians,* New York, Van Nostrand Reinhold Company, 1977; 243-45.
Feibleman, James, *In Praise of Comedy: A Study in Its Theory and Practice,* Allen & Unwin, 1939. □

Ruth Bryan Owen Rohde

Ruth Bryan Owen Rohde (1885-1954) was the first congresswoman from the South and the first woman to serve on a major congressional committee. In addition to championing women's issues in Congress, she was later active in international affairs, being the first American woman to hold a major diplomatic post.

Ruth Bryan Owen Rohde was born October 2, 1885, in Jacksonville, Illinois. Her father was William Jennings Bryan, three-time Democratic candidate for president. She grew up in a political atmosphere and learned politics and public speaking from her father, but she was deeply impressed by her mother, Mary Baird Bryan, a brilliant, college-educated woman who studied law and was admitted to the Nebraska bar in 1888. Ruth once declared that she wished to emulate her mother's mind and character. Ruth was five when her father was first elected to Congress, and she occasionally sat beside him on the House floor when he took part in congressional debates. The whole family travelled with him when he ran for president in 1896, and Ruth served as his secretary in his third run for the presidency in 1908.

She attended Monticello Female Academy in Godfrey, Illinois (1899-1901), before going to the University of Nebraska. She left college to marry a young artist, William Homer Leavitt, in October 1903; and they had two children before the unhappy marriage was dissolved in 1909. After the divorce Ruth Bryan went to Germany to study voice, where she met and married Reginald Altham Owen, a British officer in the Royal Engineers, in 1910. After three years in Jamaica the couple returned to England, where Ruth Owen gave birth to her third child in 1913. During World War I, while her husband campaigned in Palestine and Gallipoli, she worked for 15 months with Lou Henry Hoover in London as secretary-treasurer of the American Woman's War Relief Fund. She also studied nursing and in 1915 was posted to Cairo as an operating room nurse with the British Volunteer Aid Detachment.

Major Owen contracted a degenerative kidney disease in Gallipoli which ruined his health, so after the war the family returned to Florida, where Ruth Owen gave birth to her fourth child in 1920. Major Owen's failing health placed the responsibility for supporting the family upon his wife; therefore, she began lecturing on the Chautauqua and Lyceum circuits, becoming the highest paid woman lecturer on the circuit. She soon became a leader in various civic, cultural, educational, and patriotic organizations. In 1925 she was named vice-chairman of the board of regents of the newly established University of Miami and taught public speaking for the university extension service in 1927-1928.

In 1926 she entered the Democratic congressional primary; despite the complete opposition of the Democratic organization and the anti-suffrage prejudice of Florida, she lost by only 779 votes. Her husband died in December 1927. With the encouragement and help of her mother, she ran for Congress again in 1928. After an energetic campaign reminiscent of her father's campaigns, Owen won the Democratic primary and then swamped her Republican opponent by over 30,000 votes in the general election, becoming the first congresswoman from the South.

Her greatest legislative contributions derived from the controversy surrounding her being seated in Congress. Her defeated opponent challenged her right to the seat on the grounds that she had not been a citizen of the United States for seven years prior to her election, as required by the Constitution. Under a 1907 law, she had lost her American citizenship by marrying an alien, and she had not regained it until 1925 under the provisions of the 1922 Cable Act, an "independent citizenship" law demanded by the women's rights movement. The House Committee on Elections heard the challenge, and Ruth Owen presented her own case. She condemned the 1907 law as unfair in that it penalized only women for marrying aliens. No American man lost his citizenship by marrying a foreigner. In addition, she showed that the procedural flaws in the Cable Act itself had made it difficult for her, a woman supporting four children and a dying husband, to go through the process of repatriation. The Committee on Elections unanimously accepted her, and the entire House seated her without discussion or dissent. Her case focused attention on the defects of the Cable Act and led to corrective amendments which produced "independent citizenship" for women. She was reelected without opposition in 1930.

In 1929 she was appointed to the House Foreign Affairs Committee, making her the first woman to serve on a major congressional committee. In Congress she championed feminist issues, including the creation of a cabinet-level Department of Home and Child, the appointment of a woman to a cabinet office, and appropriations to send delegates to international conferences on health and child welfare. She came to grief over the prohibition issue in the 72nd Congress (1931-1933). She always voted "dry" on the question during the session, but the forces of repeal defeated her in the Democratic primary in 1932. In the lame-duck session that followed she accepted the wishes of her district and voted to repeal the prohibition amendment.

In 1933 President Franklin Roosevelt appointed her to be envoy extraordinary and minister plenipotentiary to Denmark, making her the first American woman to hold a major diplomatic post. Three years later she married Captain Borge Rohde of the Danish Royal Guards, which automatically made her a Danish citizen. This champion of independent citizenship found herself unable to continue in her diplomatic capacity because she now possessed dual citizenship. So she resigned and, with her husband and family, Ruth Rohde returned to live in the United States. She continued to lecture and write and in 1939 became a visiting professor at Monticello College.

In 1945 Roosevelt named her special assistant to the State Department to aid in the drafting of the United Nations Charter, and in 1949 President Harry Truman appointed her alternate delegate to the United Nations General Assembly. In 1954 she travelled to Denmark to accept the Order of Merit from King Frederick IX for her contributions to Danish-American friendship. While in Copenhagen, on July 26, 1954, Ruth Rohde died of a heart attack and was buried there.

Further Reading

A lively biographical sketch of Ruth Bryan Owen Rohde is found in Hope Chamberlin, *A Minority of Members: Women in the U.S. Congress* (1973). Her early life is described in a memoir by her parents, *Memoirs of William Jennings Bryan: By Himself and His Wife Mary Baird Bryan* (1925). The Cable Act and the citizenship question are discussed in J. Stanley Lemons, *The Woman Citizen: Social Feminism in the 1920s* (1973). Also see Paolo Coletta, *William Jennings Bryan. I. Political Evangelist, 1860-1908* (1964); *Notable American Women: The Modern Period* (1980); *Dictionary of American Biography, Supplement Five: 1951-1955* (1977), and an obituary in the *New York Times,* July 27, 1954. □

Roh Tae Woo

After serving as a rather obscure military leader for many years, Roh Tae Woo (born 1932) became active in the South Korean government following the coup by Chun Doo Hwan. It was his part in this coup which landed him with a 17-year prison sentence. In

1987 Roh was elected as the 13th president of the Republic of Korea.

Roh Tae Woo, as president of South Korea's Sixth Republic, wished to be remembered as "an ordinary man" in the era of "the common people." Although constitutionally elected as the 13th president of the Republic of Korea (ROK) on December 16, 1987, he received only 36.6 percent of the total popular votes. His ruling Democratic Justice Party also failed to capture the majority votes in the April 1988 National Assembly election, winning only 125 seats in the 299-member legislative body. As a result, President Roh's effectiveness as political leader was handicapped in the subsequent years.

Roh was a retired four-star general and a hand-picked successor to former President Chun Doo Hwan of the Fifth Republic (1980-1988). Roh was Chun's classmate in the 11th graduating class of the Korean Military Academy in 1955. Like Chun, Roh had his family roots in Taegu and served in Vietnam as commander of an ROK unit. When Chun carried out a coup on December 12, 1979, following President Park Chung Hee's assassination on October 26, Roh moved his 9th Infantry Division from the Demilitarized Zone to Seoul to support the coup.

Roh held several key army posts such as commander of the Capital Security Command in 1979 and commander of the Defense Security Command in 1980. After his retirement from the military in July 1981, Roh accepted Chun's

offer of the post of minister of state for national security and foreign affairs. Later he also served as sports minister, home affairs minister, president of the Seoul Olympic Organizing Committee, and, in 1985, chairman of the ruling Democratic Justice Party.

Despite this clear record of his past activities, Roh worked to distance himself from both his military background and his ties with his mentor, now-disgraced expresident Chun. The reason is that Roh worked to carry out his own agenda for democratic reform. By agreeing on June 29, 1987, to meet opposition demands for political reforms with his eight-point proposal, including direct presidential elections, Roh successfully upstaged Chun and thereby boosted his own image as reformer. In the December 1987 presidential election, the candidate Roh promised to submit his leadership to a mid-term "vote of confidence" soon after the 1988 Seoul Olympics (this pledge, however, was subsequently rescinded on March 20, 1989). Roh won the election and was inaugurated February 2-5, 1988.

Roh was born on December 4, 1932, into a farming family in a small village, Talsong, near Taegu, north Kyongsang province. His father, a low-echelon civil officer in the district, died in a car accident when Roh was seven years old. With his uncle's help, Roh first enrolled at the Taegu Technical School but transferred to the local Kyongbuk High School where he was an above-average student. His high school record describes him as a "gentle and hard-working student with a strong sense of responsibility."

During the Korean War (1950-1953) Roh joined the army as an enlisted man and later entered the Korean Military Academy, completing it in the first class of the four-year program in 1955. He fought in the Vietnam War first in 1968 as a lieutenant colonel and later as commander of the ROK unit. Roh was indeed an "ordinary man" unknown to the public until he plunged himself into politics by helping his classmate Chun Doo Hwan to carry out a coup.

Roh's stance as president was activist in diplomacy and steadfast in the push toward political and socio-economic reforms at home. Democratization of politics, economic "growth with equity," and national reunification were the three policy goals publicly stated by the Roh administration. Successfully hosting the 24th Summer Olympic in Seoul in 1988 was a major accomplishment, followed by his active diplomacy, including his address before the United National General Assembly in October 1988 and his meeting with U.S. President Ronald Reagan in the White House. During his subsequent U.S. trip in 1989, Roh also met with U.S. President George Bush and delivered a speech before a joint session of the U.S. Congress. He also conducted a five-nation European visit in December 1989.

On July 7, 1988, he launched an aggressive foreign policy initiative called the Northern Diplomacy, or Nordpolitik, which brought about benefits and rewards to his government. In 1989 Seoul established diplomatic relations with Hungary and Poland, followed by diplomatic ties with Yugoslavia, Romania, Czechoslovakia, Bulgaria, and Mongolia in 1990. South Korea's trade with China steadily increased, reaching the $3.1 billion mark in 1989 at the same time as South Korea's trade with the East European countries and the Soviet Union increased to $800 million. Seoul and Moscow exchanged full consular general's offices in 1990.

Roh's emphasis on "economic growth with equity," although well received by the public, led to the dwindling in the annual economic growth rate from the high of 12.3 percent in 1988 to 6.7 percent in 1989. As labor strikes and demands for higher wages intensified, the Roh government imposed an austerity plan to keep South Korea's export-oriented economy more competitive internationally. However, higher wages and the appreciation of the won in value against the U.S. dollar made Korean products less competitive internationally.

In order to overcome paralysis of governing due to lack of majority support in the National Assembly, the Roh government sought to attain "a grand compromise" in partisan politics. The surprising announcement of the party merger in January 1990 was an attempt to accomplish this political miracle. The ruling Democratic Justice Party merged with two opposition parties, Kim Young Sam's Reunification and Democracy Party and Kim Jong Pil's New Democratic Republican Party. The newly established Democratic Liberal Party, which commanded more than a two-thirds majority in the legislature, sought to establish political stability so as to enable socio-economic progress. On June 4 Roh Tae Woo, while visiting the United States, met with another presidential visitor, Mikhail Gorbachev of the U.S.S.R. The meeting ended 42 years of official silence between the two countries and paved the way for improved diplomatic relations.

The historical significance and legacy of Roh Tae Woo is the broad political reform which he helped to start rolling, steering the country toward greater democracy and pluralism.Yet, he may be just as well remembered for his "trial of the century".

On August 26, 1996, former South Korean President Chun Doo Hwan was sentenced to death, and former President Roh Tae Woo was given more than 22 years in prison, for seizing power in a 1979 mutiny. The sentences were later reduced to life and 17 years respectfully.

In addition, a three-judge panel confiscated war chests worth about $631 million illegally amassed by Chun and Roh during their dictatorships. They were convicted of masterminding a "creeping coup" which began with an army mutiny in 1979 and ended with a massacre of pro-democracy protesters in the southwestern city of Kwangju in 1980. At least 240 people were killed. Chun has insisted his actions were necessary to defend the country against a possible attack by North Korea in the unstable aftermath of the 1979 assassination of President Park Chung Hee.

Roh—designated Prisoner 1437—entered a Seoul courtroom on Dec. 19, 1995 without a hint of the power he once wielded as president. His head bowed and speaking in whispers, he answered more than 200 questions from prosecutors about the $650 million slush fund he admitted to amassing. "I have never, ever intended to accept any bribes," Roh insisted in an irritated tone. "I have received only donations. I have never swapped them for favors."

Roh did not make a final appeal to the Supreme Court against his convictions for mutiny, treason and bribery. He stated he didn't want to cause any more worries to the public over this incident. The appeals court cut his prison sentence to 17 years from 22 1/2 years.

Further Reading

Additional information on Roh Tae Woo can be found in Ilpyong J. Kim and Young Whan Kihl, editors, *Political Change in South Korea* (1988). Updated information was gathered from *LA Times* "S. Korea Court Overturns Ex-President's Death Sentence; Successor Roh Tae Woo's term cut by five years," Monday, December 16, 1996; "2 Ex-Leaders Guilty of Mutiny in S. Korea, Chun Given Death," Monday, August 26, 1996; World in Brief, South Korea: "Ex-Presidents Won't Appeal Convictions," Monday, December 23, 1996; *Chicago Tribune* "200 Questions for S. Korea's Roh," 12/19/95, and "Anger Flares at S. Korean Trial," 01/16/96. □

Gustavo Rojas Pinilla

Gustavo Rojas Pinilla (1900-1975) was a Colombian general and dictator-president. Though he interrupted briefly Colombia's civil war, his rule ultimately became an oppressive regime of terror.

Gustavo Rojas was born in ancient Tunja on March 12, 1900. After receiving his preuniversity education at Tunja Normal School, he began his military career in 1917, specializing in building airports. In 1927 he wrote a thesis at the Tri-State College of Engineering in Angola, Ind., on the building of airfields in Colombia. During the next 20 years, as he rose from lieutenant to general, Rojas was an engineer, building roads and airports. By 1945 he had become the director of civil aeronautics.

The *Bogotazo* riots of April 8, 1948, marked a turning point in Rojas's life and the start of his political career. He suppressed the Cali rioters with such efficiency and brutality that he won the hatred of the Liberals and the approval of the Conservative dictator, Laureano Gómez, who promoted him in 1950 to commander in chief of the armed forces and sent him in 1952 to Washington to represent Colombia on the Inter-American Defense Board and to Korea to inspect Colombian troops there.

In 1953, threatened with demotion and removal by Gómez, Rojas led a plot of army officers in a successful coup against the dictator and brought a brief stop to the bloody civil war in Colombia. Colombians were so thankful to Rojas for peace that they elected him president, but by June 8, 1954, Rojas had started his own violence.

Rojas used the army and police against all opposition in Colombia. Hundreds of thousands of Colombians fled burning villages for the comparative safety of mushrooming city slums. By the end of the Rojas regime, in 1957, over 300,000 Colombians were dead, and Rojas, the peacemaker and builder, had acquired a different reputation. Hubert Herring described him as a "sadist . . . one of the

Further Reading

A chapter on Rojas appears in Tad Szulc, *Twilight of the Tyrants* (1959). For further information on his role in the context of Colombian politics see Vernon Lee Fluharty, *Dance of the Millions: Military Rule and the Social Revolution in Colombia 1930-1956* (1957); John D. Martz, *Colombia: A Contemporary Political Survey* (1962); and Robert H. Dix, *Colombia: The Political Dimensions of Change* (1967). □

Madame Roland

Marie-Jeanne Roland (1754–1793) was a French writer and political figure, who presided over a salon and was influential in her husband's career during the early years of the French Revolution until she was arrested and executed for treason.

Marie-Jeanne "Manon" Philipon, better known as Madame Roland, was born in Paris sometime in 1754. The only surviving child of a master engraver, she was born into an age of reason and wit, the France of the *philosophes*. After spending the first two years of her life with a wet-nurse, Manon returned to her parents' middle-class household where she watched her father and his apprentices make decorated snuffboxes, jewel and watch cases, elaborate buttons, and picture frames. Taught to read at an early age, her intellectual curiosity was insatiable. She devoured books on virtually every subject including history, philosophy, poetry, mathematics, and religious works. From her mother, she learned the domestic duties of cooking and sewing. It was reading, however, that remained her greatest joy, and she spent the majority of her waking hours engaged in study. As she herself noted: "I need study as I need food." At the age of nine, Manon discovered Plutarch's *Lives* which made an indelible impression upon her. It was Plutarch, she later admitted, who made her a firm believer in the republican form of government.

Religion held a strong hold on the young girl who, at age 11, expressed an earnest desire to become a nun. Her parents agreed to a one-year trial and on May 7, 1765, she entered the Convent of the Ladies of the Congregation, in the Faubourg Saint-Marcel. Here, she met the Cannet sisters, Henriette and Sophie, who became her lifelong friends.

Convinced that the monastic life was not for her, Manon left the convent in the spring of 1776 to live for a year with her grandmother Philipon on the Ile Saint-Louis. It was during one of their infrequent social outings that Manon was introduced to Madame de Boismorel, a wealthy noblewoman who left an unfavorable impression on the young bourgeoisie. Madame Boismorel exhibited all of the pretentiousness and arrogance of the *ancien regime* aristocracy, and Manon maintained a critical and hostile attitude towards them for the rest of her life.

Upon her return home, Manon continued her extensive reading by making use of circulating libraries. Mastering Italian and with a good knowledge of English, she delighted

most savage and venal and altogether incompetent administrators in the history of the nation." Other historians were not so harsh. Vernon Lee Fluharty considered him a much-maligned reformer trying to modernize a semifeudal society which had been run for centuries by two small elite oligarchies. Fluharty saw these oligarchies as unwilling to give up their privileges or to "cope with long-smoldering social revolution." Fluharty excused the violence but incorrectly predicted that the two rival oligarchies would never cooperate.

The new military coup against Rojas came suddenly on May 9, 1957. After months of secret negotiations in Spain and Colombia, the Conservative and Liberal leaders jointly ousted Rojas and instituted their unique 16-year plan for "peace through alternation and parity." By this plan, Liberals and Conservatives alternated the presidency every 4 years after 1958, dividing the government jobs equally and giving Colombia years of comparative peace.

After a brief period of disgrace and exile, Rojas organized ANAPO, a rapidly growing party of left and right extremists who vowed to upset this "frozen democracy." In 1970 they claimed to have won a third of the votes and the presidency. When the Conservative Misael Pastrana was officially declared the winner, Rojas promised revolution and was held under house arrest. Bogotá was tense, but Pastrana became president.

in reading the works of English novelists and poets such as Fielding, Richardson, Pope, and Shakespeare. Voltaire became one of her favorite authors and, from the age of 14, she began to have serious doubts about her religion. She eventually chose to reject the staunch Catholicism of her childhood and instead relied on a sentimental form of deism. Nonetheless, she concluded that orthodox Christianity was useful and necessary for poor people in order to give them hope. Historian Gita May has concluded that "from her study of the *philosophes,* Manon came away a resolute optimist and a firm upholder of the dignity of the individual."

Her optimism was temporarily shattered by the death of her mother in June 1775. Estranged from her father, whose heavy financial speculations began to destroy his business, Manon kept to herself, spending more and more time alone. In 1776, at the age of 22, she resolved to remain a spinster for the rest of her life. Rejecting the young suitors her father suggested, she preferred the company of older men, with whom she could enjoy intellectual and social companionship without the burden of physical attraction. It was during this period that she first read Rousseau. Gita May asserts that "Rousseau . . . shaped her whole moral being and . . . determined her every important act both in her private and political life." In her *Memoirs,* Madame Roland discussed the philosopher's impact:

> Rousseau . . . made the same impression on me as had Plutarch when I was nine. . . . Plutarch had predisposed me to become a republican; he had inspired in me the true enthusiasm for public virtues and liberty. Rousseau showed me the domestic happiness to which I had a right to aspire and the ineffable delights I was capable of tasting.

Of all her elderly companions, Manon had not yet chosen a suitor whom she could consider marrying until January 1776 when she was introduced to Jean-Marie Roland de la Platière, an inspector of Commerce and Manufactures at Amiens. Twenty years her senior, M. Roland was a thin, slightly stoop-shouldered man who dressed like a Quaker and whose angular, sharp features gave him a somewhat striking appearance. Roland appeared more respectable than seductive, and Manon appreciated his broad range of interests and gravity of mind.

Their courtship was lengthy and often stormy. Roland spent long periods without visiting or corresponding with her. In addition, Manon's father disliked him intensely while Roland's family were wary of allowing their son to marry a dowerless bourgeoisie. In spite of these objections, they became engaged in April 1779 and, after Roland's procrastination, were finally married on February 4, 1780. As a couple the Rolands made an interesting sight. He looked more like her father than her husband while she, with her dark hair and pale complexion, radiated youth and vigor.

For the first six months of their marriage they lived in Paris even though Roland's office was in Amiens. During this time, he came to rely more and more upon his wife's literary and intellectual talents. Madame Roland helped him edit his writings, becoming not only his secretary, but also his copyist, editor, researcher, proofreader, and, finally, co-author. In Paris, she became acquainted with men of letters and scientists with whom she was to maintain lifelong friendships. Louis Bosc, a botanist, and François Lanthenas, a businessman, quickly became enamored of her lively wit and charming personality. It was with some regret that she left Paris for Amiens in the autumn of 1780. One year later, on October 4, 1781, she gave birth to the couple's only child Marie-Thérèse Eudora.

For the next four years, Manon's life remained uneventful. She continued to work along side her husband, providing him with invaluable assistance. In spite of her intellectual abilities and obvious talents, Madame Roland was no feminist. In a letter addressed to her friend Bosc she confessed:

> I believe . . . in the superiority of your sex in every respect. In the first place, you have strength, and everything that goes with it results from it: courage, perseverance, wide horizons and great talents. . . . But without us you would not be virtuous, loving, loved, or happy. Keep therefore all your glory and authority. As for us, we have and wish no other supremacy than that over your morals, no other rule than that over your hearts . . . . It often angers me to see women disputing privileges which ill befit them. . . . [Women] should never show their learning or talents in public.

Her quiet life in Amiens was interrupted when she embarked on a trip to Paris in March 1784 in order to obtain a patent of nobility for Roland. They both believed that his long service of duty entitled him to recognition and respect. Unfortunately, her charm, intelligence, and perseverance did not win over the hostile attitudes which the officials held about her husband, although she did manage to obtain for him a transfer from Amiens to Lyon and a promotion to general inspector. After a brief trip to England in July 1784, the Rolands moved to his family home at Villefranche-sur-Saone. Much of their time, however, was spent at their country retreat, Le Clos, which Manon greatly admired and enjoyed. In spite of the abject poverty she encountered, she was content and serene.

This was not the situation in the rest of the country. The French monarchy had become increasingly unpopular from the mid-18th century, and revolutionary language was circulating in France after the revolt of the American colonies. By 1787, the royal treasury was bankrupt from the wars with Great Britain, and a disastrous harvest in 1788 caused food shortages and subsequent bread and grain riots. Louis XVI, in order to alleviate the crown's financial difficulties, summoned a meeting of the Estates General which had not met since 1614. The Third Estate, made up of mostly lawyers, doctors, engineers, and merchants, demanded double representation which the king and his finance officer, Jacques Necker, granted. It was a fatal move. The delegates, who had drawn up a number of grievances, or *cahiers,* were disappointed when the Estates General met on May 4, 1789, and the king failed to address their concerns. More important, he chose to ignore the question of whether the assembly would vote by order, which usually ensured the dominance of the privileged estates, or by head, which would give the Third Estate control. Disappointed by the king's reluctance to decide upon this issue, the Third Estate took a momentous step and proclaimed itself the National Assembly on June 17. The king finally intervened by locking the delegates out of their meeting hall but, defying his will, they met in a nearby tennis court and bound themselves by a solemn oath not to separate until they had drafted a constitution for France. The French Revolution had begun.

Madame Roland's complacent and quiet life in the country was disrupted when news of the events taking place in Paris reached her. From the outset of the Revolution, she and her husband supported the goals of the insurgents. Convinced that the revolutionary movement would only be successful if it abolished the monarchy, she continued to suspect the King of plotting with counterrevolutionaries which turned out to be true. Remaining in Lyon, Manon and her husband became correspondents for a revolutionary newspaper, the *Patriote français* published by Jacques-Pierre Brissot, a lawyer whom they had met in 1787 and who was currently an active leader of the revolutionaries. In November 1790, sympathizers of the Revolution dominated the municipal council of Lyon, and Roland was subsequently appointed an officer.

The city was in the midst of an economic crisis due to its exorbitant debt, and Roland was appointed to negotiate for a loan from the National Assembly. Accompanying her husband to Paris in February 1791, Madame Roland opened her first political salon at the Hôtel Britannique in the rue Guénégaud. Many of the leading revolutionary figures attended, including Brissot, Petion, Robespierre, Buzot and Thomas Paine. Unlike other hostesses, she did not choose to be the center of attention, refraining from speaking until the meetings were finished.

By August 1791, with her husband's mission nearing its end, they decided to return to Le Clos. Their residence was short-lived. On September 27, the Inspectorate of Manufactures was abolished and Roland was consequently deprived of his profession. Having served for nearly 40 years, he felt that he deserved a pension and, as a result, the Rolands returned to Paris in December 1791 where they immediately became embroiled once again in revolutionary politics.

Louis XVI had signed the constitution on September 14, 1791, and from the first meeting of the Legislative Assembly on October 1, the question of war dominated its mood and work. The strongest advocates for war came from a group later known as the Girondists, whose unofficial leader was Roland's friend and fellow journalist Brissot. In speeches to the assembly and to the radical Jacobin Club, the Girondists advocated war with Austria as a means of rallying popular support for the Revolution, testing the loyalty of the king, and suppressing counterrevolutionaries. In March 1792, Louis XVI appointed a new cabinet which included Roland as minister of the interior. One month later, on April 20, war against Austria was finally declared.

Madame Roland, who had already proved a worthy partner to her husband, was now virtually indispensable.

She was often present when colleagues and friends brought up matters of state with her husband at home. Enjoying his fullest confidence, she wrote much of his correspondence and provided advice and support for his policies. With the reopening of her salon, Madame Roland found herself at the social and political center of the new government.

In spite of his earlier cooperation, Louis XVI became increasingly intractable by consistently refusing to endorse Girondist legislation. Military losses contributed to growing accusations that the king was secretly encouraging the Austrians. Distrust between the king and the government reached a climax in May 1792 when he vetoed three Girondist decrees. On June 10, Roland addressed a letter to the king, actually written by his wife, reprimanding him for his veto and encouraging him to become more patriotic. Madame Roland's dislike for the monarchy was clear: "I know that the stern language of truth is rarely welcomed by the throne, I know too that it is because truth is almost never heard there that revolutions become necessary."

Louis XVI not only ignored the letter but dismissed all of the Girondist ministers including Roland. His action led to an armed uprising of the Paris populace on June 20 and heightened anxiety throughout the country. Political excitement continued to increase until August 10 when a crowd of armed Parisians marched on the palace at the Tuileries, forcing the royal family to flee for protection to the National Assembly. The crowd, however, was in control, and the assembly had no choice but to suspend Louis XVI from his functions. As the monarchical constitution was clearly dead, they ordered elections for a new body, the National Convention. Roland and his colleagues were reappointed, and Danton was named minister of justice.

Madame Roland was once again in a position of influence as helpmate to her husband, although she fell increasingly under attack from Robespierre and his Jacobin allies. The Girondists were rapidly losing support in the French capital, and when the convention held its first meeting on September 21, 1792, the divisions were clear. On one side were the Girondists; on the other sat the Jacobin deputation from Paris which became known as the Mountain (*Montagne*) from the high seats it took at the back of the assembly. The rest of the deputies formed the Plain (*Plaine*) and were uncommitted to either faction.

The fate of the king led to a struggle for control of the convention itself. Roland became a favorite target of the opposition who accused him of royalist sympathies and secret correspondence. The slander directed against the Roland ministry included his wife who was summoned before the bar of the convention on December 7, 1792. After a dramatic defense of her politics, she was not only cleared of the charges brought against her but was voted honors of the session. Her husband was less successful. The convention voted in favor of the king's execution by a majority of one vote, and Louis XVI was guillotined on January 21, 1793. Roland handed in his resignation the following day.

Historians have debated upon the real reasons for Roland's decision to resign at this particular time and, until recently, were unaware of the personal crisis he and his wife were undergoing. Sometime before her husband's resignation, Madame Roland confessed to him her romantic attraction to the Girondist deputy from Evreux, François Leonard Buzot. Faced with a painful dilemma but realizing his dependence on her, Manon chose to remain with Roland. Thus, they continued to live and work together although their relationship was strained not only for personal reasons but by the uncertainty and growing danger of their political position.

In spite of repeated requests and petitions, they were prohibited from leaving Paris. Manon's sense of doom was realized when 21 Girondist deputies were expelled from the convention and arrested on May 31, 1793. Engineering her husband's escape, she did not elude the authorities. For the next five months, she spent her time in prison writing her *Memoirs* and her autobiography entitled *An Appeal to Impartial Posterity.* Throughout her imprisonment, she maintained a calm composure. After visiting Madame Roland in prison, an Englishwoman noted that:

> She conversed with the same animated cheerfulness in her little cell as she used to do in the hotel of the minister. . . . She told me she expected to die; and the look of placid resignation with which she spoke of it, convinced me that she was prepared to meet death with a firmness worthy of her exalted character.

During her imprisonment she refused to agree to several plans for her escape; her fate was sealed when the Girondists, after a seven-day trial, were found guilty of counterrevolutionary activities and were executed on October 31, 1793. Madame Roland's trial before the Revolutionary Tribunal was set for November 8. Dressed in a gown of white muslin, she listened to witnesses against her but was forbidden to speak in her own defense. Pronounced guilty of a "horrible conspiracy against the unity and indivisibility of the Republic, and the liberty and safety of the French people," she was ordered to be executed that very afternoon. On a bleak, wintry November day, Madame Roland traveled in a cart to the foot of the guillotine in the Place de la Revolution. Mounting the platform, her eyes fastened on the artist David's statue of Liberty as she exclaimed, "Oh Liberty, what crimes are committed in thy name."

Her death produced a grievous sense of loss in the two men who loved her. Two days after hearing the news of his wife's execution, Roland left his sanctuary at Rouen and was later found impaled upon his sword cane. Buzot, also heartbroken, met a similar fate when his body was found on June 25, 1794, half-devoured by wolves.

Further Reading

Clemenceau-Jacquemaire, Madeleine. *The Life of Madame Roland.* Longmans, Green, 1930.
May, Gita. *Madame Roland and the Age of Revolution.* Columbia University Press, 1970. □

John Rolfe

John Rolfe (1585-1622) was an English colonist who settled in Jamestown, Va., and pioneered in the cultivation of tobacco.

John Rolfe was born in the spring of 1585, the descendant of an old Norfolk family. His emigration to Virginia in 1609 was interrupted by a shipwreck on the newly discovered island of Bermuda. A child born to Rolfe's wife died while they were stranded in Bermuda. After almost a year the couple landed in Jamestown, Va.; the colony was in desperate condition. Apart from the danger of disease, which claimed Rolfe's wife shortly after their arrival, the province had no staple product, and there were constant threats of attack by the indigenous population.

Conceptions regarding colonization had proceeded no further in Rolfe's time than to think of plantations as trading ventures, places where quick returns might be won from a minimal investment. Finding neither precious metals nor other resources that could be exploited easily, the sponsors of Jamestown experienced continuing expense coupled with disappointment. The colony's settlers found the Native Americans growing and using tobacco, but its commercial possibilities seemed limited because the leaf tasted bitter.

Rolfe started to experiment with the cultivation of tobacco. In 1612 he planted seeds of tobacco plants that had been found originally in the West Indies and Venezuela and that offered a milder smoke. He also developed new methods of curing the leaf, thereby further enhancing its flavor and facilitating its shipment to England. Rolfe's experiments were very successful, and his first shipments to London in 1614 were the foundation of the staple production that underlay the southern economy before 1800.

Given the importance of Rolfe's contribution in the cultivation of tobacco, it is unfortunate that his fame is largely associated with his marriage in 1614 to Pocahontas, daughter of the chief Powhatan. Although Rolfe's marriage to Pocahontas grew out of mutual love, contemporaries also observed that it initiated an eight-year period of relative peace. A triumphant tour of England by Pocahontas and her entourage in 1616, during which she was received as a visiting princess, ended sadly in her death from consumption.

Rolfe's last years were busy and fruitful. He served as secretary of Virginia and as a member of the council, writing important letters describing the problems of Virginia. He was killed during the massacre of March 22, 1622, which was said to be perpetrated by the Native Americans. He left a third wife and daughter, as well as his son by Pocahontas, Thomas Rolfe.

Further Reading

In the absence of a biography, the best sources of information on Rolfe and the beginnings of Virginia are Richard L. Morton, *Colonial Virginia* (2 vols., 1960); Grace Steele Woodward, *Pocahontas* (1969); and Philip L. Barbour, *Pocahontas and Her World* (1970). Materials by contemporaries are in Lyon

G. Tyler, ed., *Narratives of Early Virginia, 1606-1625* (1907). A short, authoritative account of Virginia's tobacco economy is G. Melvin Herndon, *Tobacco in Colonial Virginia* (1957). □

Romain Rolland

The French writer Romain Rolland (1866-1944) was the author of many works, all reflecting the conscience of a great humanist.

omain Rolland was born on Jan. 29, 1866, in Clamecy (Burgundy). His family moved to Paris in 1880, where he graduated from the École Normale Supérieure in 1889 in history. During these years, disillusioned by the decadence of French society, having lost faith in Catholicism, but still looking for ideals, he turned toward the pantheism of Baruch Spinoza. In 1889 he arrived in Rome, where he discovered the Italian Renaissance and met Malvida von Meysenburg, who introduced him to the heroes of revolution and German romanticism; these various influences appear for the first time in his two unpublished dramas—*Empedocle* and *Orsino.*

Rolland returned to Paris in 1891, where he slowly turned toward the incipient socialism. In 1898, involved in the polemic aroused by the Dreyfus Affair, he wrote *Les Loups* (The Wolves), a play that transposed the case to 1793 and attempted to present objectively the arguments of both sides. The success of *Les Loups* encouraged him to write a whole cycle of plays on the French Revolution, whose spirit, he thought, must be carried into the future; among them were *Danton* (1900) and *Le Quatorze Juillet* (1902; The Fourteenth of July). Believing in the revolutionary role of culture, he wrote a series of essays in *Le Théâtre du peuple* (1903; The People's Theater).

In 1904 Rolland taught at the Sorbonne, inaugurating a course on the history of music. From 1904 to 1912 he wrote *Jean-Christophe,* a novel which shows the confrontation between an artist and a decadent society. Built like a symphony, *Jean-Christophe* is an affirmation of the German musical genius. *Colas Breugnon* (1914) is, on the contrary, a novel whose humor reminds one of François Rabelais. Meanwhile Rolland produced a series of biographies: *Beethoven* (1903), *Michel-Ange* (1906), and *Tolstoi* (1911).

Rolland spent the war years in Switzerland. He accused both France and Germany in a series of essays, *Au dessus de la melée* (Above the Battle). After the fall of Europe, only the Russian Revolution gave him some hope for the future. Opposing violence, he did not, however, join the Communist party. Throughout the 1920s he called for the unity of all truth-searching minds, regardless of political opinion, in *Déclaration d'indépendance de l'esprit* (1919; Declaration of the Independence of the Mind). His belief in nonviolence made him praise the Gandhian idea of revolution through his several books on Hindu thought.

Rolland meanwhile came back to his plays on the French Revolution; the last one was *Robespierre* (1939). In 1933 he published another novel, *L'Âme enchantée* (The Enchanted Soul), dealing with the problem of political action. Moved perhaps by the mounting fascism, he adhered more closely to communism; several essays show this evolution, in particular, *Quinze ans de combat* (Fifteen Years of Struggle).

In 1938 Rolland settled in Vézelay, where he composed his *Mémoires* and *Le Voyage intérieur* (Journey inside Himself), his spiritual autobiography. He died on Dec. 30, 1944.

Further Reading

Stefan Zweig, *Romain Rolland: The Man and His Work,* translated by Eden and Cedar Paul (1921), is one of the best studies but necessarily incomplete. William T. Starr, the specialist on Rolland who published the detailed and very useful *A Critical Bibliography of the Published Writings of Romain Rolland* (1950), also wrote *Romain Rolland: One against All—A Biography* (1971), based on Rolland's works, letters, notes, and diary.

Additional Sources

Kastinger Riley, Helene M., *Romain Rolland,* Berlin: Colloquium-Verlag, 1979. □

Richard Rolle of Hampole

The English prose and verse writer Richard Rolle of Hampole (ca. 1290-1349) gave the first formal expression to English mysticism and exerted a very important intellectual influence on the 14th century.

ichard Rolle of Hampole was neither a priest nor a monk but a simple layman. Born in the vicinity of Thornton-le-street, the son of William Rolle, a gentleman of Richmondshire, he was sent to Oxford by Thomas de Neville, who saw great intellectual promise in the boy. Rolle progressed well in his studies until at the age of 19 he had a deeply moving mystical experience of love and union with God. He returned home intent on serving God by contemplation as a hermit. He borrowed two gowns from his sister and a rain hood from his father to make a habit and tried to set up a hermitage in the nearby woods. He had an unsatisfactory time of it until one day he was recognized by John de Dalton, son of his former benefactor, as he donned a surplice in the Dalton chapel and, with ecclesiastical permission, preached a moving sermon. The Nevilles set him up on the estate with shelter, food, and suitable clothing.

It was not long before Rolle discovered that curious and intrusive friendship can destroy those essentials of a contemplative life, solitude and peace of mind. For a time he sought over the countryside for what he needed. At length he found a spot near the Cistercian convent of St. Mary's at Hampole. Here his freedom was unhampered, and he set-

tled down for a course of contemplative prayer. His experiences could not be contained, and they overflowed in passionate writing. At first he wrote in Latin, the language of the learned. Little by little, as his reputation for holiness spread, he was asked for advice and guidance. Since many who appealed to him were simple people, he turned to English, the vigorous, malleable Northumbrian dialect. His manuscripts were widely distributed and highly prized, some of the more than 400 extant being passed down in wills as family heirlooms.

Rolle died in Hampole in 1349, perhaps from the plague which was ravaging the country at the time. He had built an enduring reputation for holiness which encouraged the nuns at St. Mary's to write an office in view of a probable canonization. It is from this office that we learn most of the details of his life.

Rolle's writing was a stupendous achievement. Of the English prose tracts, some running to 10,000 words, the following are outstanding: *The Form of Perfect Living, Ego dormio et cor meum vigilat, A Commandment of the Love of God,* and the *Commentary on the Psalter.* With these, his Latin works, his many shorter prose tracts, and his many versified themes, he influenced people as dissimilar as the great mystic Walter Hilton and that bumbling seeker for true sanctity Margery Kempe. His style is passionate and personal but controlled by moderation, reasonableness, and a sense of humor.

Further Reading

Two indispensable works on Rolle are George C. Heseltine, *Selected Works of Richard Rolle, Hermit* (1930), which contains both prose and verse, and Hope E. Allen, *English Writings of Richard Rolle, Hermit of Hampole* (1931), which includes good biographical notes. Much background information about mysticism as a Christian phenomenon is in Gerard Sitwell, *Spiritual Writers of the Middle Ages* (1961), and David Knowles, *The English Mystical Tradition* (1961).

Additional Sources

Hodgson, Geraldine Emma, *The sanity of mysticism: a study of Richard Rolle,* Norwood, Pa.: Folcroft Library Editions, 1977.
□

The Rolling Stones

The Rolling Stones, having outlasted nearly all of their 1960s contemporaries, continue to belt out hits well into middle age. Original members included lead singer Mick Jagger (Michael Philip Jagger, born July 26, 1943, in Dartford, Kent, England); guitarist Keith Richard (surname sometimes listed as Richards, born December 18, 1943, in Dartford, Kent, England); guitarist Brian Jones (Lewis Brian Hopkins-Jones, born February 28, 1942, in Cheltenham, Gloucestershire, England, drowned, July 3, 1969); drummer Tony Chapman; bass player Dick Taylor; and pianist Ian Stewart. Drummer Charlie Watts (Charles Robert Watts, born June 2, 1941, in Islington, England) replaced Chapman c. 1962; bass guitarist Bill Wyman (William Perks, born October 24, 1936 [some sources say 1941]) replaced Dick Taylor c. 1962; guitarist Mick Taylor (born January 17, 1948, in Hertfordshire, England) replaced Jones, July 1969; guitarist Ron Wood (born June 1, 1947, in London, England) replaced Mick Taylor, 1975; bass guitarist Darryl Jones replaced Bill Wyman, 1993. Current members include Jagger, Richard, Watts, Wood, and Jones.

Often billed as "the world's greatest rock and roll band," the Rolling Stones have earned the title; if not for their musical prowess, then certainly for their longevity. Formation of the group began back as early as 1949 when Keith Richard and Mick Jagger, both from Dartford, England, went to school together. It would take another eleven years, however, before their paths would cross again. To their amazement, they discovered that both of them had grown up listening to the same great American bluesmen and rockers like Chuck Berry and Bo Diddley. The two formed a friendship that was based around one common interest: music.

The Rolling Stones (L-R Richard, Wood, Jagger, Watts)

At the time, Jagger was attending London's School of Economics while Richard was struggling at Sidcup Art College. Soon they found out about a local musician named Alexis Korner who held blues jams at the Ealing Club. After Jagger began to sing for Korner's Blues Incorporated, he decided to join a group that Richard was putting together. Other members included Ian Stewart, Dick Taylor, Tony Chapman, and a guitar player named Brian Jones.

Jones was quite different from the rest of the lads. Although only one year older than Jagger and Richard, he had already parented two illegitimate children by the time he was sixteen. And while Richard was more into the Berry school of rock guitar, Jones was pure blues and often referred to himself as Elmo Lewis (in reference to the slide guitarist, Elmore James).

Charlie Watts was already making a fair living drumming for a jazz combo when he was persuaded to replace Tony Chapman. The oldest member, a rocking bassist, Bill Wyman, hooked up immediately after to complete the rhythm section. With the shrewd talents of manager/publicist Andrew Loog Oldham, they began opening for Blues Inc. at London's Marquee Club in 1963, billed as '' Brian Jones and The Rollin' Stones'' (after a Muddy Waters tune). Dick Taylor was no longer in the band at this time.

With hair longer than any other group and an attitude that made the Beatles look like choir boys, the Stones took full advantage of their image as "the group parents love to

hate." "That old idea of not letting white children listen to black music is true," Jagger told Jonathan Cott, "cause if you want white children to remain what they are, they mustn't." Their negative public image was constantly fueled by Oldham, who also decided that Stewart's neanderthal presence did not fit in with the rest of the band and so delegated him to the background, never seen but often heard.

Oldham quickly secured the Stones a contract with Decca Records and in June of 1963 they released their first single, a cover of Chuck Berry's "Come On" backed with "I Want to Be Loved." Reaction was good and it would only take another six months for the group to make it big. Continuing their eight-month residence at the Crawdaddy Club in Richmond, they released their version of the Beatles "I Wanna Be Your Man" followed by Buddy Holly's "Not Fade Away," which made it to Number 3 in Great Britain. Their fourth single would climb all the way to the top in their homeland, "It's All Over Now" by Bobby Womack. Their next hit, "Little Red Rooster," likewise reached Number 1 but was banned in the United States.

Satisfaction

The Rolling Stones already had two albums out in England by the time they broke the U.S. Top 10 with "The Last Time," written by Jagger and Richard. And in the summer of 1965 they had a worldwide Number 1 hit with "Satisfaction." Propelled by Richard's fuzz-tone riff and Jagger's lyrics of a man who couldn't get enough, the song immediately secured a seat in rock history. Oldham had played up the outlaw image of the band to the point where they became the image, and he was no longer needed.

Allan Klein took over as manager and in 1966, after having relied on other artist's songs, they released their first all-originals LP, *Aftermath*. The band was plagued with drug busts during the psychedelic era and in 1967 recorded their reply to the Beatles' *Sgt. Pepper's Lonely Hearts Club Band*, titled *Their Satanic Majesties Request*. The album paled in comparison to the Beatles' masterpiece and is noted mainly as the last album Brian Jones truly worked on, having become too involved in drugs.

With Jones largely out for the count, Richard came into his own on 1968's *Beggar's Banquet*. His acoustic guitar sounded as full as an orchestra on "Street Fighting Man," and one of the most deadly electric solos of all time can be found on "Sympathy for the Devil." It was obvious the Stones didn't need Jones dragging them down anymore and he officially quit (or was booted out) on June 9, 1969. Less than one month later he was found drowned in a swimming pool with the official cause listed as "death by misadventure."

Two days later, the Stones had their replacement in Mick Taylor, former guitarist for John Mayall's Bluesbreakers. His first gig was a free concert in memory of Jones at Hyde Park. Taylor's influence would bring the level of musicianship up a few notches until he quit in 1975. Their first album after he joined was still mostly a Richard album, however. *Let It Bleed* was released to coincide with an American tour and contained two haunting tunes, "Midnight Rambler" and "Gimme Shelter." The latter became the title of the movie documenting the Stones' free concert at Altamont, California, at which Hell's Angels members (hired as security guards) stabbed a youth to death right in front of the stage. The group also released an album from that tour, *Get Yer Ya Ya's Out.*

Exiles

In 1971 The Stones formed their own label, Rolling Stones Records, and began to expand their musical horizons. *Sticky Fingers* contained jazz with "Can't You Hear Me Knockin," while the country-flavored "Dead Flowers" continued the trend of "Honky Tonk Women." Their next album, *Exile on Main Street,* oddly enough, was dismissed by critics when it came out, but over the years has come to be regarded as probably their finest recording. With Richard hanging out with Gram Parsons, the country influence was stronger than ever but the album also contains gospel ("I Just Want To See His Face"), blues ("Shake Your Hips"), and full-tilt rock ("Rip This Joint"). It is four sides of vintage Stones at their tightest, and loosest.

Their next two albums, *Goat's Head Soup* and *It's Only Rock and Roll,* contain both outstanding tracks and what some critics considered real dogs. "Time Waits For No One," with a beautiful solo by Taylor, shows just how much the Stones had changed, yet tracks like "Star Star" reveal just the opposite: the bad boys of rock just couldn't grow up. Five years was enough for Taylor and in 1975 he decided to walk away from one of the most sought-after positions in rock. "The fact is I was becoming stagnant and lazy with the Stones. I really got off on playing with them, but it wasn't enough of a challenge," he told *Rolling Stone.*

Rumors about who would take Taylor's place included such guitar greats as Roy Buchanan, Jeff Beck, Peter Frampton, and Rory Gallagher, but the obvious choice was Faces guitarist, Ron Wood. Wood fit the Stones mold perfectly, with the same musical roots and a look that was almost a carbon copy of Richard. Wood pinch-hit for Taylor on the 1975 tour of America, bounding back and forth with the Faces before finally joining the Stones full-time. The first full album he contributed to was *Black and Blue* in 1976. Once again the Stones stretched out by dabbling in reggae ("Cherry Oh"), disco ("Hot Stuff"), and a smoky lounge lizard treatment on "Melody." The group's future was in doubt in 1977 when Richard was busted in Toronto for heroin dealing, but his sentence did not include any jail time. "Drugs were never a problem," he told Edna Gundersen. "Policemen were a problem."

After 1978's classic *Some Girls,* the next Stones' records seem indistinguishable from each other. The songs are vehicles for Richard's guitar hooks with nothing equaling the emotion of previous hits like "You Can't Always Get What You Want" or "Moonlight Mile." Only the hit "Start Me Up" stands out from this period.

Everyone Was Hating Each Other

During the 1980s, rumors swirled constantly that the Rolling Stones would break up. Jagger would do nothing to dispel the rumors. Richard was reportedly not too happy when Jagger took time off to work on his solo album (even though Wyman and Wood both have records outside the group). Then Jagger refused to tour to support the Stones' *Dirty Work* LP, instead hitting the road to promote his own *She's The Boss.* "Touring *Dirty Work* would have been a nightmare," Jagger told *Rolling Stone,* "It was a terrible period. Everyone was hating each other so much; there were so many disagreements. It was very petty; everyone was so out of their brains, and Charlie was in seriously bad shape . . . It would have been the worst Rolling Stones tour. Probably would have been the end of the band." Richard, who had himself toured with Wood's New Barbarians in 1979, was outraged that Jagger would make the Stones a second choice. "I felt like I had failed. I couldn't keep my band together," he told the *Detroit Free Press.* Pursuing his own solo project, he stated that the Stones will "have to wait for me. They kind of pushed me into this solo thing, which I really didn't want, and now they're paying a price." Richard released his own album, *Talk Is Cheap,* with plenty of barbs for Jagger. "I'm enjoying myself too much to all of a sudden stop," Richard said.

And for a while in the 1980s, it seemed that the Stones had in fact broken up. Jagger was pursuing his solo career, barely speaking to Richard. The partners took turns sniping at each other through the press. As Jagger related in *Rolling Stone,* "Everyone was bored playing with each other. We'd reached a period when we were tired of it all. Bill [Wyman] was not enthusiastic to start with—there's a guy that doesn't really want to do much. . . . You've got Charlie overdoing it in all directions . . . Keith the same. Me the same . . . We just got fed up with each other. You've got a relationship with musicians that depends on what you produce together. But when you don't produce . . . You get difficult periods, and that was one of them."

Still the World's Greatest Rock and Roll Band

But rumors of the band's breakup had to be put on hold in 1989, when the Stones announced plans for a new album and a world tour. A favorite with critics, *Steel Wheels* quickly sold over two million copies. The tour, however, which was sponsored by Anheuser-Busch, was attacked by many for being blatantly over-commercialized. Despite the criticism, the *Steel Wheels Tour*—which reportedly raked in over $140 million—was a hit with music reviewers and fans. The 1990 *Rolling Stone* readers' and critics' polls selected the Stones as best band and artist of the year, and cited *Steel Wheels* as 1989's best tour.

The group's ability to overcome internal dissension and the toll of more than 25 years in rock and roll's fast lane to put together the industry's success story of the year surprised some observers, but not the Stones themselves. "The Stones, it's a weird thing, it's almost like a soap opera," Richard told *Rolling Stone.* "We needed a break to find out what you can and can't do on your own. I had to find myself a whole new band. . . . But then I realized maybe that's the way to keep the band together: leaving for a bit. . . . I never doubted the band, personally—but I'm an incredible optimist where this band is concerned. It never occurred to me that they might not be able to cut it. Absolutely not."

But *Steel Wheels* was to be Bill Wyman's last album and tour with the Stones—he announced his retirement in 1993. With Darryl Jones replacing Wyman, the Stones next released *Voodoo Lounge,* an album that in many ways was meant to recall the classic Stones sound of the early 1970s. The announcement for the subsequent tour was greeted with complaints from some critics that the Stones were simply too old, just going through the motions. But that album would go on to sell four million copies, and the supporting tour, which featured 22 songs from the band's 30-year history, went on to become the highest grossing tour of all time.

The years when a Rolling Stones breakup seemed a certainty have passed. As a change of pace from their usual mammoth concert tours, the Stones made a brief sweep of Europe, playing in far smaller venues, typically of less than 1,000 seats, such as the Paradiso in Amsterdam. For that tour, the Stones presented a more stripped down, more acoustic set, featuring songs like the Stones chestnut "The Spider and the Fly," "Shine a Light," from *Exiles,* and the Bob Dylan classic "Like a Rolling Stone." From that tour, the group released the live album "Stripped."

The experience seemed to bring new life to the band, and more certainty to the band's future, although the band remains noncommittal. "I don't think Charlie's wildly enthusiastic, nor am I," Jagger told *Rolling Stone,* "But I dare say the Rolling Stones will do more shows together . . . I don't know exactly what framework [that] would take . . . But I'm sure there will be Rolling Stones music and there will be Rolling Stones songs."

Selected recordings on London Records include *England's Newest Hit Makers—The Rolling Stones,* 1964; *12x5,* 1964; *The Rolling Stones Now!,* 1965; *Out of Our Heads,* 1965; *December's Children,* 1965; *Big Hits (High Tide and Green Grass),* 1966; *Got Live If You Want It!,* 1966; *Between the Buttons,* 1967; *Flowers,* 1967; *Their Satanic Majesties Request,* 1967; *Beggar's Banquet,* 1968; *Through the Past Darkly,* 1969; *Let It Bleed,* 1969; *Get Yer Ya Yas Out,* 1970. On Rolling Stone Records, except as noted: *Sticky Fingers,* 1971; *Hot Rocks: 1964-1971,* London Records, 1972; *Exile on Main Street,* 1972; *More Hot Rocks (Big Hits & Fazed Cookies),* London Records; *Goat's Head Soup,* 1973; *It's Only Rock 'n' Roll,* 1974; *Made in the Shade,* 1975; *Metamorphosis,* ABKCO, 1975; *Black and Blue,* 1976; *Love You Live,* 1977; *Some Girls,* 1978; *Emotional Rescue,* 1980; *Sucking in the Seventies,* 1981. On Virgin Records: *Tattoo You,* 1981; *Undercover,* 1983; *Dirty Work,* 1986; *Steel Wheels,* 1989; *Voodoo Lounge,* 1993; *Stripped,* 1995; *The Rolling Stones Rock & Roll Circus,* ABKCO, 1996.

Further Reading

Contemporary Musicians: Profiles of the People in Music, Gale Research, Detroit, Michigan.
Charone, Barbara, *Keith Richards, Life as a Rolling Stone,* Dolphin, 1982.
Christgau, Robert, *Christgau's Record Guide,* Ticknor & Fields, 1981.
Dalton, David, *The Rolling Stones, The First Twenty Years,* Knopf, 1981.
Allan Kozinn, Pete Welding, Dan Forte & Gene Santoro, *The Guitar,* Quill, 1984.
The Guitar Player Book, Grove Press, 1979.
The Illustrated Encyclopedia of Rock, compiled by Nick Logan and Bob Woffinden, Harmony, 1977.
David Dalton & Lenny Kaye, *Rock 100,* Grosset & Dunlap, 1977.
Rock Revolution, Popular Library, 1976.
The Rolling Stone Illustrated History of Rock & Roll, edited by Jim Miller, Random House/Rolling Stone Press, 1976.
The Rolling Stone Interviews, St. Martin's Press/Rolling Stone Press, 1981.
The Rolling Stone Record Guide, edited by Dave Marsh with John Swenson, Random House/Rolling Stone Press, 1979.
Sanchez, Tony, *Up and Down With the Rolling Stones,* Signet, 1979.
What's That Sound?, edited by Ben Fong-Torres, Anchor, 1976.
Detroit Free Press, December 4, 1988.
Detroit News, September 27, 1988.
Guitar Player, February 1980; April 1983; May 1986: January 1987.
Guitar World, March 1985; March 1986.
Metro Times (Detroit), December 7, 1988.
Oakland Press, December 4, 1988.
Rolling Stone, May 6, 1976; May 20, 1976; May 5, 1977; November 3, 1977; November 17, 1977; June 29, 1978; September 7, 1978; March 8, 1990; November 3, 1994; December 14, 1995. □

Rollo

The Viking adventurer Rollo (ca. 860-ca. 932) founded the line of the dukes of Normandy. He established Viking control of the lands at the mouth of the Seine River and thus began what became the most powerful French dukedom.

Probably born in Norway, Rollo, or Rolf, was the son of Rögnvald, Earl of Möre. Chronicle sources, which are not always reliable, note that he was exiled from Norway because of lawlessness, probably about 900. Rollo became a Viking raider and for a time was successful. He went to Scotland, where he married a Christian woman by whom he had a daughter; and possibly from this marriage his son, later known as William Longsword, his successor in Normandy, also issued. Rollo then may have gone to Ireland, but with the waning of Norse power in Ireland he probably followed his compatriots who traveled to France, where raiding parties could find richer opportunities for looting.

Rollo probably arrived in Gaul between 905 and 911. During these years he became famous, and stories about him circulated in his homeland: "Rolf [Rollo] was a great Viking: he was so big that no steed could bear him, so that he was called Rolf 'the Ganger.'" Rollo's name figured prominently in the treaty between King Charles the Simple of France and the Seine Vikings in 911. By that famous agreement, the Vikings received control of the territory at the mouth of the Seine in return for certain services to the King. Rollo himself was granted Upper Normandy (the territory between the Epte River and the sea), and he was converted to Christianity and baptized by the archbishop of Rouen. Rouen was the capital of the ecclesiastical province of Normandy, which Rollo's successors later added to their initial territory.

In 924 Rollo added the lands of Bessin and Maine to his holdings, and after his death his successor, William Longsword, completed the construction of the duchy by adding the lands of the Cotentin and the Avranchin to Rollo's acquisitions. Rollo's conversion to Christianity, however, and his gift of land from the king of France should not be misinterpreted. Very likely Rollo's Christianity was of a very limited character, and his supposed loyalty to the king of France could not be counted upon. Early Norman domination of the lower Seine Valley contributed to the disintegration of ecclesiastical and economic institutions in that area, but Rollo's able successors shaped a strong and flourishing duchy in the territory that their vigorous and bloodthirsty ancestor had conquered. Rollo was the great-great-great-great-grandfather of William the Conqueror (William I of England).

In 927 Rollo abdicated in favor of William Longsword,

Further Reading

There is no biography of Rollo in English. A good recent survey of the Normans is David C. Douglas, *The Norman Achievement, 1050-1100* (1969), recommended as an introduction for the general reader. See also Richard W. A. Onslow, *The Dukes of Normandy and Their Origin* (1947). □

Ole Edvart Rölvaag

The Norwegian-American writer Ole Edvart Rölvaag (1876-1931) was a powerful, realistic chronicler of the lives of Norwegian immigrants on the farms of the midwestern United States. His work is grimly pessimistic.

Ole Edvart Rölvaag was born on April 22, 1876, on the island of Dönne, Norway; his family had been fishermen and seafaring people for generations. After a meager education Rölvaag worked for several years as a fisherman, but in 1896 he emigrated to the United States to work on his uncle's farm in Elk Point, S. Dak. He worked his way through Augustana College, S.Dak., from 1897 to 1901 and through St. Olaf's College, Minn., where he received a bachelor of arts degree in 1905. He then returned to Norway to spend a year at the University of Oslo.

Returning to America in 1906, Rölvaag joined the faculty of St. Olaf's College. In 1908 he became a United States citizen and married Jenny Berdahl; they had four children. In 1910 Rölvaag received his master of arts degree from St. Olaf's.

Rölvaag had begun writing during his early teaching years. His first book, written in Norwegian, appeared in

1912 under the title *Amerika-Breve* (Letters from America); with a succeeding volume, *Pâ Glente Veie* (1914; On Forgotten Paths), it portrayed the life of the young immigrant in the Midwest. His next novel, *To Tullinger* (1920; Two Fools), is the study of a miser's temperament; it was translated into English a decade later under the title *Pure Gold* (1930). His most poetic and mystical work is *Laengselens Boat* (1921), which concerns a legendary vessel symbolic of the heartache caused by emigration. It was translated into English as *The Boat of Longing* (1933).

Rölvaag's artistic vision was doubtless shaped by the harshness of his life—the years of hard work and hard study and especially the tragic deaths of two of his children. His novels are strong reminders of life's severity, and this is nowhere truer than in his masterpiece, *Giants in the Earth* (1927), written with the assistance of a friend, Lincoln Colcord, who helped Rölvaag translate idiomatically from the Norwegian. Rölvaag dedicated the book "To Those of My People Who Took Part in the Great Settling, To Them and Their Generation." The *Nation* called *Giants in the Earth* "the fullest, finest and most powerful novel that has been written about pioneer life in America."

The last book by Rölvaag, *Their Father's God* (1931), consists of intensely dramatic projections of the Minnesota—South Dakota prairie and of the whole westward movement in America. Toward the end of his life, he was appointed head of the Norwegian department at St. Olaf's, where he hoped to institute a center of Norwegian culture, a plan that was aborted by his death on Nov. 5, 1931, from a heart attack.

Further Reading

Theodore Jorgenson and Nora O. Slocum, *Ole Edvart Rölvaag* (1939), is the standard biography.

Additional Sources

Moseley, Ann, *Ole Edvart Rölvaag*, Boise, Idaho: Boise State University, 1987. □

Archbishop Oscar Romero

Until his assassination by right-wing gunmen, Archbishop Oscar Romero (1917-1980) of San Salvador spoke out courageously in defense of human rights and social justice in strife-torn El Salvador.

Oscar Arnulfo Romero y Galdámez was born in Ciudad Barrios, El Salvador, on August 15, 1917. His father, the town postmaster and telegraph operator, apprenticed him to a carpenter when he was 13, but the younger Romero felt a vocation for the Roman Catholic priesthood and left home the following year to enter the seminary. He studied in El Salvador and in Rome and was ordained in 1942.

Romero spent the first two and half decades of his ministerial career as a parish priest and diocesan secretary in San Miguel. In 1970 he became auxiliary bishop of San Salvador and served in that position until 1974 when the Vatican named him to the see of Santiago de María, a poor, rural diocese which included his boyhood hometown. In 1977 he returned to the capital to succeed San Salvador's aged metropolitan archbishop, Luis Chávez y González, who had retired after nearly 40 years in office.

Romero's rise to prominence in the Catholic hierarchy coincided with a period of dramatic change in the Church in Latin America. The region's bishops, meeting at Medellín, Colombia, in 1967 to discuss local implementation of the recommendations of the Second Vatican Council (1962-1965), had resolved to abandon the hierarchy's traditional role as defender of the status quo and to side, instead, with the continent's poor in their struggle for social justice. This radical departure divided both the faithful and the clergy. Conservative laymen complained of "Communist" priests, while many clerics refused to accept the new role the Church was creating for itself in Latin American society.

In El Salvador, an extremely conservative society where the privileged few enjoyed great wealth at the expense of the impoverished majority, younger priests, among them many foreigners, grasped the new ideas enthusiastically, but the only prelate who encouraged them was Archbishop Chávez y González. During this period Oscar Romero's reputation was as a conservative, and on more than one occasion he showed himself skeptical of both the Vatican II reforms and the Medellín pronouncements. For this reason his appointment as archbishop in 1977 was not popular with the politically active clergy, to whom it appeared to signal the Vatican's desire to restrain them. To their surprise, Romero emerged almost immediately as an outspoken opponent of injustice and defender of the poor.

By Romero's own account, he owed his change of attitude to his brief tenure as bishop of Santiago de María, where he witnessed firsthand the suffering of El Salvador's landless poor. Increasing government violence against politically active priests and laypersons undermined his trust in the good will of the authorities and led him to fear that the Church and religion themselves were under attack. The assassination on March 12, 1977, of his longtime friend Jesuit Father Rutilio Grande brought a stinging denunciation from Romero, who suspended masses in the nation's churches the following Sunday and demanded the punishment of the responsible parties.

As Romero spoke out more and more frequently over the coming months, he gathered a large popular following who crowded into the cathedral to hear him preach or listened to his sermons over YSAX, the archdiocesan radio station. In his youth Romero had been a pioneer of broadcast evangelism in El Salvador, and he now turned the medium to great effect as he denounced both the violence of El Salvador's developing civil war and the deeply-rooted patterns of abuse and injustice which bred it. In a country whose rulers regarded dissent as subversion, Romero used the moral authority of his position as archbishop to speak out on behalf of those who could not do so for themselves. He soon came to be known as the "Voice of the Voiceless."

When a coup d'état overthrew the Salvadoran government on October 15, 1979, Romero expressed cautious support for the reformist junta which replaced it. He soon became disenchanted, however, as the persecution of the poor and the Church did not cease. In February 1980 he addressed an open letter to U.S. President Jimmy Carter in which he called upon the United States to discontinue military aid to the regime. "We are fed up with weapons and bullets," he pleaded.

Romero's campaign for human rights in El Salvador won him many national and international admirers as well as a Nobel Peace Prize nomination. It also won him enemies, however. On March 24, 1980, a group of unidentified gunmen entered a small chapel in San Salvador while Romero was celebrating mass and shot him to death. The archbishop had foreseen the danger of assassination and had spoken of it often, declaring his willingness to accept martyrdom if his blood might contribute to the solution of the nation's problems. "As a Christian," he remarked on one such occasion, "I do not believe in death without resurrection. If they kill me, I shall arise in the Salvadoran people."

Further Reading

An excellent account in English of Romero's career is James R. Brockman, S. J., *The Word Remains: A Life of Oscar Romero* (1982). On the role of the Roman Catholic Church as an advocate of social justice in Latin America, see Penny Lernoux, *Cry of the People,* 2nd edition (1982). □

Additional Sources

Brockman, James R., *Romero: a life,* Maryknoll, N.Y.: Orbis Books, 1989.

Erdozain, Placido, *Archbishop Romero, martyr of Salvador,* Maryknoll, N.Y.: Orbis Books, 1981. □

Carlos Romero Barceló

Carlos Romero Barceló (born 1932), Puerto Rican political leader, the fifth elected governor of the Commonwealth of Puerto Rico, and a representative in the U.S. Congress under territorial status, was one of the foremost advocates of U.S. statehood for his country.

Carlos Romero Barceló was born on September 4, 1932, in San Juan, Puerto Rico, and was reared in a family atmosphere in which public affairs and politics were considered important. His father, Antonio Romero Moreno, was a lawyer and engineer and served as a superior court judge. His maternal grandfather was Antonio R. Barceló, who had been one of Luis Muñoz Rivera's close associates, the first president of the Puerto Rico Senate (elected in 1917) and the founder of the Liberal Party in the early 1930s. His mother, Josefina Barceló, became the president of the Liberal Party shortly after her father's death.

Romero Barceló received his primary education in San Juan private schools and his high school education at Phillips Exeter Academy in Exeter, New Hampshire. He attended Yale University, from which he received his bachelor's degree in 1953, having majored in political science and economics. He then studied law at the University of Puerto Rico and received his law degree in 1956.

Founded the New Progressive Party

Upon graduation and until the mid-1960s he conducted a private law practice, specializing in civil cases, mainly damages and torts and corporate and tax matters. His long-nurtured interest in and aptitude for politics and his unswerving commitment to the cause of U.S. statehood for Puerto Rico soon led him into the public arena. In 1965 he joined an organization called Citizens for State 51 and later became its chairman. In 1967 this organization became a part of a new movement, founded by Luis Ferré, called United Statehooders, which was created to campaign for the statehood alternative in the status plebiscite held in July of that year. The following month Romero joined with Ferré in founding the New Progressive Party. Ferré became the party's victorious candidate for governor in 1968.

As a co-founder of the new pro-statehood party, and as one who proved to be a particularly aggressive, outspoken, and hard-working spokesman for the statehood ideology, Romero captured the party's nomination for mayor of San Juan in 1968 and won the post convincingly. During his stint as mayor of San Juan he was also elected second vice-president of the National League of Cities and in 1974 became its president. In 1972 Ferré was defeated by Popular Democrat Rafael Hernández Colón, but Romero handily won re-election in San Juan, and after serving three years as party vice-president he became the undisputed president in 1974. He held this position until 1984.

As head of the New Progressive Party, Romero ran for governor in 1976 and defeated the incumbent, Hernández Colón. In 1980 he won re-election after a hard-fought campaign by only about 3,000 votes. In 1981 Romero was elected chairman of the Southern Governors Association. In the elections of 1984 he lost to Hernández, but he continued as the chairman of the New Progressive Party.

The First Lady during Romero's administration was Kate Donnelly, from Baldwin, New York, whom Romero married in 1966. They had two children, born while Romero was mayor of San Juan. He also had two sons by a previous marriage.

Fought for Statehood for Puerto Rico

Throughout his political career Romero was an undaunted believer in statehood for Puerto Rico and in the compatibility of statehood with Puerto Rican cultural, linguistic, and psychological identity. He was a combative campaigner with a simple, direct, and unpretentious style. Under his direction the statehood cause became an important mass-based movement and the party system was transformed into something radically different from what it was during the time of the domination of the Popular Democratic Party and Luis Muñoz Marín.

After two terms as governor, Romero returned to private practice of law in 1985. One year later, he was elected to the Puerto Rico Senate, where he served until 1988. In 1989 he again was elected President of the New Progressive Party. Romero won a seat in the House of Representatives of the U.S. Congress in 1992 with the campaign theme, "On the Road to Equality." As a Representative of Puerto Rico, Romero had all the privileges of any other member of Congress, except the right to vote on the final passage of amendments. In the 104th Congress, he served on the Committee on Resources and the Committee on Economic and Educational Opportunities. As a delegate, he could vote and deliberate like any other member in those committees. In 1993 (the 103rd Congress) Romero became the first representative of the people of Puerto Rico to obtain limited voting rights in the House. However, this right was taken away by the Republican Party in the 104th Congress.

In 1997 House Bill 856 was proposed by Rep. Don Young of Alaska that would pave the path for Puerto Rican statehood, a dream come true for Romero, who is a co-sponsor on the bill. Entitled the "United States-Puerto Rico Political Status Act, it required that a referendum be held by December 31, 1998, on Puerto Rico's political status for either 1) retention of its Commonwealth status; 2) full self-government leading to independence; or 3) full self-government through U.S. sovereignty leading to statehood. Another inclusion in the bill, which Romero opposed, is that English should be the official language of the Federal Government in Puerto Rico. In a statement before the House in 1997, Romero declared that "It is time for Congress to permit democracy to fully develop in Puerto Rico, (Puerto Ricans) are citizens without political rights, including a vote in Congress."

Romero received an honorary doctorate from the University of Bridgeport in 1977, and received the James J. and Jana Hoey Award for Interracial Justice from the Catholic Interracial Council of New York that same year. In 1981 he was awarded the U.S. Attorney General's Medal.

Further Reading

There are no books in English dealing specifically with Romero Barceló or his administration. A good source for his activities in the U.S. Congress, including a biography, is the House of Representatives Web site (www.house.gov/romero-barcelo/). For more information on the issue of Puerto Rican statehood and Romero's involvement, refer to the Puerto Rico Statehood Web site (www.puertorico51.org/english/). Some good general works on Puerto Rico contain useful material on Romero and his activities. Examples are Kal Wagenheim, *Puerto Rico: A Profile* (1970); Jorge Heine and J. M. Garcia-Passalacqua, *The Puerto Rican Question,* Foreign Policy Association Headline Series #266 (Nov./Dec. 1983); Jorge Heine, ed., *Time for Decision* (1983), especially chapters 1, 8, and 9; and Raymond J. Carr, *Puerto Rico: A Colonial Experiment* (1984). Several of Romero's speeches have been published in *Vital Speeches of the Day*. □

Erwin Rommel

The German field marshal Erwin Rommel (1891-1944), known as the "Desert Fox," achieved fame as a brilliant desert-warfare tactician in World War II.

Erwin Rommel was born in Heidenheim near Ulm on Nov. 15, 1891, into an old Swabian middle-class family. After a traditional classical education, he joined the 124th Infantry Regiment as an officer cadet in 1910 and was commissioned as second lieutenant 2 years later. In World War I he served on the Western front in France and immediately distinguished himself as an outstanding soldier. In 1915 he was awarded the Iron Cross Class I. From autumn 1915 to 1918 he served in a mountain unit in Romania and on the Italian front, where, for unusual bravery in his capture of Monte Matajur, he was cited for the highest award offered in the German army, the Pour le Mérite, at the unprecedented age of 27.

After the war Rommel spent the 1920s as a captain with a regiment near Stuttgart. In the fall of 1929 he commenced his distinguished career as an infantry instructor at the infantry school in Dresden, where he stayed until 1933. After a two-year command of a mountain battalion, he continued his teaching career at the Potsdam War Academy in 1935 and finally—after the annexation of Austria in 1938—took over the command of the war academy in Wiener Neustadt as full colonel.

On the eve of the war Rommel was selected as commander of Hitler's bodyguard and served in that capacity in Hitler's first drives to the east into the Sudetenland, Prague, and finally Poland. His first field command in World War II was at the head of the 7th Tank Division, which swept toward the English Channel in May 1940.

Rommel's appointment in February 1941 as commander of the Afrikakorps with the rank of lieutenant general marked the beginning of his fame as a desert-war tactician. Initially he met with brilliant success. By June 1942 he had driven the British troops from his starting point in Libya all the way to El Alamein and was rewarded with a promotion to field marshal that same month—the youngest in the German armed forces. Because of lack of reinforcements he failed to take Alexandria and advance to the Suez Canal as hoped and was subsequently driven back by Field Marshal Bernard Montgomery's counterattack to Tunis, where he encountered fresh American troops under Gen. Dwight Eisenhower and lost the final, decisive battle at Médenine on March 5, 1943. Five days later he left for Germany on sick leave.

During the summer and fall of 1943 Rommel acted as a special adviser and troubleshooter for Hitler, a task which took him to Italy as commander of the newly formed Army Group B in a last effort to prop up the regime of Benito Mussolini. By December 1943 he was needed at the "Atlantic Wall," the coastal defenses along the coast from Norway to the Pyrenees, and in January 1944 he took over the command of all German armies from the Netherlands to the Loire River. He was unable to prevent the Allied landing in Normandy, however, and on July 17, 1944, was seriously wounded in an air raid, forcing him to return to his home in Herrlingen near Ulm.

Rommel had by this time become increasingly critical of Hitler and the Nazi party, of which he had never been a member. Although he disapproved of an assassination of Hitler, he maintained close contact with the officers who staged the unsuccessful coup of July 20, 1944, and he was to have succeeded Hitler as supreme commander in the event of success. Nazi investigators therefore sought him out at his home in Herrlingen on Oct. 14, 1944, and gave him the choice of taking poison or standing trial before the Nazi People's Court. Rommel chose the former. Hitler ordered national mourning and a state funeral with all honors.

Further Reading

Rommel's own draft narrative of the African campaign was edited by Capt. B. H. Liddell Hart, together with pertinent letters and notes by Rommel, under the title The Rommel Papers (1953). The best-known biography of Rommel in English, and still the standard work, is Desmond Young, Rommel, the Desert Fox (1950), a compassionate yet carefully researched work of a British brigadier general with considerable experience in desert warfare. It has been supplemented and updated by Ronald Lewin's work, Rommel as Military Commander (1968), which concentrates almost entirely on Rommel's most active years in the field, from 1940 to 1944. Paul Carell's beautifully written, exciting, and meticulously researched account of the African campaign, The Foxes of the Desert (1960), was skillfully translated by Mervin Savill. See also Hans Speidel, Invasion of 1944: Rommel and the Normandy Campaign (1950), and Siegfried Westphal, The German Army in the West (1951). □

George Romney

George Romney (1734-1802) was one of the most sought-after portrait painters in England. His portrait style is free, swift, and bold.

The son of a cabinetmaker, George Romney was born in Dalton, Lancashire. He was apprenticed in 1755 to Christopher Steele, a provincial portrait painter, but was largely self-taught. Romney's ambition was to become a history painter. In 1762 he moved to London, where he studied the Duke of Richmond's collection of casts of antique sculpture and established himself as a portraitist. He went to Italy in 1773, and after his return in 1775 he became the favorite painter of high society.

Morbidly sensitive and retiring, Romney kept aloof from the social world of his sitters and from the Royal Academy. By 1782 he was under the spell of Emma Hart, later Lady Hamilton and the mistress of Nelson, who sat for him as Circe, a Bacchante, Cassandra, the Pythian Priestess, Joan of Arc, St. Cecilia, Mary Magdalene, and other impersonations he suggested. In the 1780s he executed a number of Eton leaving portraits, which established him as the supreme interpreter of aristocratic adolescence in his age.

For much of his life in London, Romney was under the wing of the poet William Hayley, who encouraged him in the choice of subjects from Milton and Shakespeare as well as the Bible and Greek tragedy. Romney's history paintings are today chiefly known from engravings, like the dramatic Tempest (1787-1790) commissioned for John Boydell's Shakespeare Gallery. A large number of drawings for these projects survive.

Romney had married early in life an uneducated woman whom he did not bring to London but to whom he returned when his health finally gave way. Ill health and the facility with which he converted his early realistic style into a fashionable sketchlike formula for idealizing his sitters probably account for an unevenness of execution that has partially justified his critics.

Unlike Joshua Reynolds, Romney did not enter into the character of his sitters, unless they possessed nervous traits like his own, for example, the moving portrait William Cowper. But he was psychologically involved with the generalized charms of youth, beauty, and breeding that he admired in his aristocratic sitters, and by combining a neoclassic purity of line with free but masterly brushwork he achieved a number of incomparable images which transcend the realism of portraiture. This is exemplified in Mrs. Lee Acton (1791); with a faraway gaze which borders on the apprehensive, her fingers nervously clasped, she strays through a formless landscape menaced by storm clouds. In such paintings Romney is the "man of feeling" celebrated in Henry Mackenzie's novel (1771) with that title, just as the

best of his sketches earn him an honorable place in the neoclassic avant-garde headed by William Blake and Henry Fuseli. Romney died in Kendal, Westmorland.

Further Reading

The best biography of Romney is still Arthur B. Chamberlain, *George Romney* (1910), richly documented from the memoirs of the time. For one of the rare appreciations of Romney's history paintings see W. Moelwyn Merchant, *Shakespeare and the Artist* (1959). □

Carlos P. Rómulo

Carlos P. Romulo (1899-1985) was an author and the foremost diplomat of the Philippines. He was the only Filipino journalist to win the Pulitzer Prize and the first Asian to serve as president of the UN General Assembly (1949). He also gained prominence as America's most trusted Asian spokesman.

Carlos Romulo was born on Jan. 14, 1899, in Manila; but his well-to-do parents lived in Camiling, Tarlac. His father, Gregorio, was a Filipino guerrilla fighter with the Philippine revolutionary government of Emilio Aguinaldo during the Filipino-American War. Rómulo claimed to have witnessed his grandfather tortured by the water cure administered by American soldiers. After early

schooling in Tarlac, Rómulo entered the University of the Philippines, where he received a bachelor's degree in 1918. After getting a master of arts from Columbia University in 1921, he returned to work as professor of English and chairman of the English department of the University of the Philippines (1923-1928).

Rómulo became editor in chief of TVT Publications in 1931 and publisher and editor of the *Philippines Herald* (1933-1941). In 1929 he was appointed regent of the University of the Philippines. Previously he had served as secretary to Senate president Manuel Quezon (1922-1925) and as member of the Philippine Independence Mission, headed by Quezon. Rómulo belonged to the elite, the oligarchic stratum of the Filipino ruling class, by virtue of his role as defender of the interests of the propertied minority.

In 1941 Rómulo received the coveted Pulitzer Prize for a series of pioneering articles on the Southeast Asian political situation in which he recorded his extensive travels in China, Burma, Thailand, Indochina, Indonesia, and elsewhere. Nonetheless, in spite of his candid reporting, he confessed in an interview, "I held back a lot because as a writer I knew hatred is created by incidents." This revealed Rómulo's gift for shrewd diplomacy and somewhat "opportunistic" manner of dealing with people and events.

With the outbreak of World War II in 1941, Rómulo joined the staff of General Douglas MacArthur as press relations officer. He also served as secretary of information and public relations in Quezon's wartime Cabinet (1943-1944). He retreated with MacArthur from Bataan to Corregidor and

then to Australia (1941-1942). While in Corregidor he broadcast for the Voice of Freedom. He served as aide-de-camp to MacArthur and rose from the rank of colonel (1942) to brigadier general (1944).

In 1945 Rómulo acted as Philippine delegate to the United Nations Organization Conference in San Francisco. He was Philippine ambassador to the United Nations from 1946 to 1954. He distinguished himself as the first Asian to become president of the UN General Assembly (Fourth Session, Sept. 20, 1949). In 1950-1951 Rómulo acted as secretary of foreign affairs of the Philippine Republic and, from 1952 on (with some interruptions), as Philippine ambassador to the United States.

After serving as president of the University of the Philippines and secretary of education (1963-1968), Rómulo was appointed by President Marcos to the post of secretary of foreign affairs. Rómulo was the recipient of more than a hundred honorary doctorates, awards, and medals, given by American and Asian universities, organizations, and foreign governments.

Rómulo's prolific pen is attested to by his books, such as *I Saw the Fall of the Philippines* (1942), *Mother America* (1943), *My Brother Americans* (1945), *I See the Philippines Rise* (1946), *Crusade in Asia* (1955), *The Magsaysay Story* (1956), *I Walk with Heroes* (1961), and *Identity and Change* (1965).

Further Reading

Romulo's autobiography, with Beth Day Romulo, is *Forty Years: A Third World Soldier at the UN* (1986). His other books also are informative, since most of them are autobiographical in some sense. Full-length works on him are Grace S. Youkey (pseudonym: Cornelia Spencer), *Romulo: Voice of Freedom* (1953); Romulo figures prominently in Manuel Luis Quezon, *The Good Fight* (1946); Teodoro A. Agoncillo, *The Fateful Years: Japan's Adventure in the Philippines, 1941-45* (2 vols., 1965). □

Candido Mariano da Silva Rondon

Candido Mariano da Silva Rondon (1865-1958) was a Brazilian military man and Indianist. He explored much of the Brazilian interior and studied and helped the Indians of the region.

Candido Rondon was born in Cuiabá in the state of Mato Grosso on May 5, 1865. He entered the army in 1881 and by 1890 was substitute professor of mathematics in the Praia Vermelha Military School in Rio de Janeiro. That year he accepted a post with the Telegraphic Commission, which was extending telegraph lines into the deep interior of Brazil.

When Rondon began his career in the Amazonian region, the larger part of it had not been explored by civi-

lized man, and Brazil's claim to sovereignty in the region was largely symbolic. He and his coworkers established the first contacts with the outside world for many parts of the Brazilian interior. During his long service with the Telegraphic Commission, he studied intensively the flora and fauna of the Amazon region. He became an expert on the vegetation and inhabitants of the Brazilian interior.

Rondon's work brought him into close contact with the Indian tribes who lived isolated in the forests and plains of the Amazon Valley. He became outraged at the way in which some were being exploited and degraded by outsiders and how contacts with the outside world were tending to destroy the culture and sometimes the very existence of these tribes.

Rondon convinced the Brazilian government to establish the Servico Nacional de Proteção aos Indios (National Service for Protection of the Indians) to help save the indigenous peoples from exploitation and disintegration. He headed this service until 1940, and during his tenure the service gained an international reputation for its struggle on behalf of the tribes and for its efforts to introduce the Indians peacefully and slowly into modern civilization. However, a decade after Rondon's death the service was wracked by scandals surrounding its mistreatment of those it was supposed to protect.

In 1913 Rondon accompanied former U.S. president Theodore Roosevelt on his expedition of exploration in the Amazon Valley. From 1927 to 1930 Rondon conducted an inspection trip that completely covered the land frontiers of his country. In 1934 he was the Brazilian representative on a commission which successfully settled a long-standing border dispute between Peru and Colombia which had led to open warfare in that year.

During his career in the Telegraphic Commission and the Indian Service, Rondon rose steadily in military rank. In 1955, on his ninetieth birthday, the Brazilian Congress passed a special law raising him to the rank of marshal, the highest in the nation's military service. He received many honors from his own and foreign governments. The new Amazonian territory and its capital city were named Rondonia in commemoration of his work there. Rondon died on Jan. 19, 1958.

Further Reading

There is a good discussion of Rondon's career in Donald Emmet Worcester, *Makers of Latin America* (1966). Theodore Roosevelt recounts an expedition with Rondon in his *Through the Brazilian Wilderness* (1914). Some of Rondon's explorations are discussed in Charles E. Key, *The Story of Twentieth-century Exploration* (1938). □

Pierre de Ronsard

Pierre de Ronsard (1524-1585) was the greatest French poet of his day. His verse influenced French poetry well into the 17th century.

Pierre de Ronsard was born at La Poissonnière on Sept. 11, 1524. He was the son of Loys de Ronsard, an aristocrat whose nobility, if unquestionable, afforded him neither fame nor fortune. Pierre became a page in the royal house, where he attended briefly Francis I's eldest son and then the third son, Prince Charles. When James V of Scotland married Madeleine of France (1537), Charles gave the young page to his sister. Ronsard accompanied Scotland's new queen to her country but appears not to have stayed there more than a year. By 1540 he was acquainted with Lazare de Baïf, diplomat and humanist of distinction, who would help determine Ronsard's future. It began to take shape when an illness left the boy partially deaf and unsuited for a military career.

In 1543 Ronsard was tonsured. The act did not make the future poet a priest, but it did permit him to receive income from certain ecclesiastical posts—potentially an important source of revenue and one he would exploit. After his father died in 1544, Ronsard accepted an invitation from Lazare de Baïf to study in Paris with his son Jean Antoine under the direction of Jean Dorat. When Dorat became principal of the Collège de Coqueret in 1547, he took his pupils with him. Joined by Joachim du Bellay, the youths followed a strict but enlightened discipline that brought them into intimate contact with the languages, forms, and techniques of the ancient poets. In this way, the nucleus of that school of French poets known as the Pléiade was formed.

Odes and *Amours*

With the publication of *Les Quatre premiers livres des odes* (1550), the story of Ronsard's life is inseparable from the chronology of his works. Ronsard determined to open his career with éclat and chose to imitate the long, difficult odes of Pindar written in praise of Olympic heroes. The subjects of Ronsard's odes are the royal family and court dignitaries, but the length and difficulty remain.

With the *Amours* of 1552, Ronsard attempted to prove his ability to rival yet another great poet, Petrarch. Indeed, the *Amours,* addressed to Cassandra (identified as a Cassandra Salviati), so seek to capture the traits of the Italian's famous love poems to Laura that the existence of a woman named Cassandra at that time must be considered as incidental. Poetry in the 16th century was an affair of imitation and skill but rarely biography. The sonnets, in decasyllabic verse, are highly conventional, and whereas some critics find an appealing "baroque" quality in certain of them, many poems are so obscure, poorly constructed, and basely derivative that even Ronsard's contemporaries found fault with them.

During the remainder of the 1550s, Ronsard published his licentious *Livret de folastries* (1553, unsigned), his philosophical *Hymnes* (1555-1556), and more love poetry, the *Continuations des Amours* (1555-1556). The love sonnets of the cycles, addressed primarily to a Marie, are often no different in style from those of 1552. The greatest innovation lies in Ronsard's experimentation—the use of the Alexandrine and the increased quantity of nonsonnet material, for example. Yet even here, especially in the songs in imitation of Marullus, mannered phrases betray the relative simplicity of Ronsard's *style bas.*

The Wars and an Epic

Ronsard had official as well as personal reasons for becoming involved in the tensions that in 1562 brought Catholics and Huguenots to war. That year he composed his most important works on France's troubles: the *Discours des misères de ce temps,* the *Continuation du Discours des misères de ce temps,* and the *Remonstrance au peuple de France.* With eloquent virulence Ronsard depicts the desperate situation created by a divided France. He begs Beza, John Calvin's lieutenant, to help restore peace.

With the *Remonstrance,* Ronsard's tone rises to the satiric as he scourges Calvinism. Adhering to the principle of one king, one law, and one faith, he maintained that disregard for the last of these elements was bringing in its wake disobedience for the first two. Moreover, whereas he admitted that the Church needed reform, nothing he saw assured him that Calvinism was a more Christian, charitable sect. His personal feud with the Protestants stemmed from an attack by them on Ronsard as a pagan and a mediocre poet. Ronsard replied in his *Réponse aux injures et calomnies de je ne sais quels prédicants et ministres de Genève* (1563) with a proud (and revealing) defense supported by devastating satire.

In 1572 Ronsard published *Les Quatre premiers livres de la Franciade.* The remaining books were never written; it was obvious even to Ronsard that the poem was a failure. Why did this versatile poet fail in the epic when he had been so successful in numerous other genres? Critics have pointed to the verse form (decasyllabic verse, not the Alexandrine) and to the subject (a learned myth tracing France's royal house back to Troy). No less revealing are Ronsard's own words about the epic genre he published in a preface to the *Franciade*. Here the poet makes clear that only an epic written on the pattern set by Homer and Virgil is acceptable and that this pattern is to be followed in the greatest detail. Ronsard is so true to his own principles that the *Franciade* is often little more than a sustained reproduction of a traditional form.

Final Years

Ronsard's failure in the *Franciade* is more than offset by a new collected edition of his works printed in 1578. It contains two of his best-known sonnets, *Comme on voit sur la branche* and *Quand vous serez bien vieille*. The former was inserted among the previously published Marie poems but was most certainly written at the death of the King's mistress, Marie de Clèves. *Quand vous serez bien vieille* belongs to an entirely new cycle of love poems, the *Sonnets pour Hélène*, inspired in part by Hélène de Surgères, a lady of the court. The cycle reproduces much of the Petrarchan material used in 1552 and 1555. Its remarkable qualities—to be found also in *Comme on voit sur la branche*—lie in the poet's ability to manipulate the tradition and the sonnet form. The best sonnets of 1578 abandon the nervous style of 1552 and achieve with the same Petrarchan commonplaces a simplicity that is not without richness of expression and emotion.

Ronsard died on Dec. 27, 1585, at the priory of St.-Cosme near Tours. In his late works he was the forerunner of 17th-century French classicism.

Further Reading

Both the contemporary and modern biographies of Ronsard are unreliable mixtures of fact, fiction, and romance. Recent studies of his poetry include Isidore Silver, *Ronsard and the Hellenic Renaissance in France* (1961); Donald Stone, Jr., *Ronsard's Sonnet Cycles: A Study in Tone and Vision* (1966); and Elizabeth T. Armstrong, *Ronsard and the Age of Gold* (1968). Grahame Castor, *Pléiade Poetics: A Study in Sixteenth-century Thought and Terminology* (1964), discusses Ronsard's theoretical writings, and Richard A. Katz, *Ronsard's French Critics, 1585-1828* (1964), considers his influence. □

Wilhelm Conrad Röntgen

For the first two decades of his scientific career, Wilhelm Conrad Röntgen (1845-1923) studied a fairly diverse variety of topics, including the specific heats of gases, the Faraday effect in gases, magnetic effects associated with dielectric materials, and the compressibility of water. He is most famous, however, for his discovery in 1895 of X rays, which had a

revolutionary effect not only on physics but also on a number of other areas, particularly medicine, and for this he was awarded the first Nobel Prize in physics in 1901.

Wilhelm Conrad Röntgen was born in Lennep, Germany, on March 27, 1845. He was the only child of Friedrich Conrad Röntgen and the former Charlotte Frowein. His father was a textile merchant who came from a long line of metal workers and cloth merchants. His mother had been born in Lennep but then moved with her family to Amsterdam, where they had become wealthy as merchants and traders. When Röntgen was three years old, his family moved to Apeldorn, Holland. Otto Glasser speculates in *Dr. W. C. Röntgen* that the revolution of 1848 may have been a factor in this move because the family lost its German citizenship on May 23, 1848, and became Dutch citizens a few months later. In any case, Röntgen received his primary and secondary education in the public schools of Apeldorn and at a private boarding school in Middelann.

In December 1862, Röntgen enrolled at the Utrecht Technical School. His education at Utrecht was interrupted after about two years, however, when a childish prank went awry. He confessed to having drawn a caricature of an unpopular teacher for which another student had been responsible. As punishment, Röntgen was expelled from school, and his education was stalled until January 1865,

when he was given permission to attend the University of Utrecht as an irregular student. There he attended classes on analysis, physics, chemistry, zoology, and botany. His future still seemed bleak, however, and, according to Glasser, "both Wilhelm and his parents had become resigned to his seeming inability to adjust to the requirements of the Dutch educational system and to obtain the credentials necessary to become a regular university student."

A friend of Röntgen's told him about the liberal admission policies at the Swiss Federal Institute of Technology in Zurich. Röntgen applied and was admitted at Zurich, and he arrived there to begin his studies in the mechanical technical branch of the institute on November 16, 1865. Over the next three years, Röntgen pursued a course of study that included classes in mathematics, technical drawing, mechanical technology, engineering, metallurgy, hydrology, and thermodynamics. On August 6, 1868, he was awarded his diploma in mechanical engineering. His degree had come in spite of his rather irregular attendance at classes. He later told Ludwig Zehnder that the lake and mountains surrounding Zurich were "too tempting." As a result, he became a devoted mountain climber and boater but an undistinguished student. Only when one of his professors told Röntgen that he would fail his examinations did he settle down to his studies.

At Zurich, the most important influence on Röntgen was the German physicist August Kundt. Kundt suggested to him that he do his graduate studies in physics rather than engineering, and Röntgen took his advice. On June 22, 1869, he was granted his doctoral degree for a thesis entitled "Studies about Gases." Kundt then asked him to become his assistant, an offer he quickly accepted. A year later, when Kundt was offered the chair of physics at the University of Würzburg in Germany, he brought Röntgen with him as his assistant.

While still in Zurich, Röntgen had met his future wife, Anna Bertha Ludwig, the daughter of a German revolutionary who had emigrated to Switzerland. They were married on January 19, 1872, after his move to Würzburg. The couple never had children of their own, although in 1887 they did adopt his wife's six-year-old niece Josephine Bertha.

After two years at Würzburg, Kundt moved once more, this time to the newly established University of Strasbourg in France. Again, he asked Röntgen to accompany him as his assistant. At Strasbourg, in March 1874, Röntgen finally achieved a long-delayed ambition: He was appointed a privatdozent at the university, his first official academic appointment. The appointment was the result of more liberal policies at Strasbourg; his lack of the necessary credentials had prevented him from receiving a formal appointment in any German university.

In 1875, Röntgen accepted a position as professor of physics at the Hohenheim Agricultural Academy. Missing the superb research facilities to which he had become accustomed in Strasbourg, however, he returned there in 1876 as associate professor of physics. Three years later he was appointed professor of physics at the University of Giessen in Germany, where he remained until 1888. He then re-

turned to the University of Würzburg to take a joint appointment as professor of physics and director of the university's Physical Institute. Röntgen would remain at Würzburg until 1900, serving as rector of the university during his last six years there.

Röntgen wrote forty-eight papers on a diverse range of phenomena including the specific heats of gases, the heat conductivity of crystals, the Faraday and Kerr effects, the compressibility of solids and liquids, and pyroelectricity and piezoelectricity. Probably his most significant contribution during this period was a continuation of research originally suggested by James Clerk Maxwell's theory of electromagnetism. That theory had predicted that the motion of a dielectric material within an electrostatic field would induce a magnetic current within the dielectric material. During his last year at Giessen, Röntgen completed studies that confirmed this effect, a phenomenon for which Hendrik Lorentz suggested the name "röntgen current."

Yet there is no doubt that the discovery for which Röntgen will always be most famous is that of X rays. In 1894 Röntgen began research on cathode rays, which was then one of the most popular topics in physics. Much of the fundamental research on this topic had been carried out in the 1870s by the English physicist William Crookes. Crookes had found that the discharge of an electrical current within a vacuum tube produces a beam of negatively charged rays that causes a fluorescence on the glass walls of the tube. A number of scientists had followed up on this research, trying to discover more about the nature and characteristics of Crookes's cathode rays.

After repeating some of the earlier experiments on cathode rays, Röntgen's own research took an unexpected turn on November 8, 1895. In order to observe the luminescence caused by cathode rays more clearly, Röntgen darkened his laboratory and enclosed the vacuum tube he was using in black paper. When he turned on the apparatus, he happened to notice that a screen covered with barium platinocyanide crystals about a meter from the vacuum tube began to glow. This observation was startling, because Röntgen knew that cathode rays themselves travel no more than a few centimeters in air. It was not they, therefore, that caused the screen to glow.

Over the next seven weeks, Röntgen attempted to learn as much as he could about this form of energy. He discovered that its effect could be detected at great distances from the vacuum tube, suggesting that the radiation was very strong. He learned that the radiation passed easily through some materials, such as glass and wood, but was obstructed by other materials, such as metals. At one point, he even saw the bones in his hand as he held out a piece of lead before it. He also discovered that the radiation was capable of exposing a photographic plate. Because of the unknown and somewhat mysterious character of this radiation, Röntgen gave it the name *X strahlen,* or X rays.

On December 28, 1895, seven weeks after his first discovery of X rays, Röntgen communicated news of his work to the editors of a scientific journal published by the Physical and Medical Society of Würzburg. Six days earlier, he had made the world's first X-ray photograph, a picture of his wife's hand. Within weeks, news of Röntgen's discovery had reached the popular press, and the general public was captivated by the idea of seeing the skeletons of living people. On January 13, 1896, Röntgen was ordered to demonstrate his discovery before the Prussian court and was awarded the Prussian Order of the Crown, Second Class, by the Kaiser.

Röntgen actually devoted only a modest amount of attention to his momentous discovery. He wrote two more papers in 1896 and 1897, summarizing his findings on X rays, and then published no more on the subject. Instead, he went back to his work on the effects of pressures on solids. Röntgen chose not to ask for a patent on his work and refused the Kaiser's offer of an honorific "von" for his name. He did, however, accept the first Nobel Prize in physics, awarded to him in 1901. Even then, however, he declined to make an official speech and gave the prize money to the University of Würzburg for scientific research. His discovery had generated a surprising number of personal attacks, with many dismissing it as an accident or attributing it to other scientists. Glaser speculates that "Röntgen's reticence, bordering on bitterness with advancing years, was doubtless a defense against these attacks."

Röntgen had declined offers from other universities for many years, but in 1900, at the special request of the Bavarian government, he abandoned his chair at Würzburg in order to accept a similar position at the University of Munich. The decision was not an easy one for Röntgen because, as Zehnder later noted, "the nice quiet laboratory at Würzburg suited him so well." Röntgen remained at Munich until 1920 when he retired, a decision he made at least partly because of his grief over his wife's death a year earlier. She had suffered from a lingering disorder during which she became addicted to morphine. Zehnder was later to write that she was always "Röntgen's most understanding and truest friend."

Germany's defeat in World War I also had its effect on Röntgen: The inflationary period following the war resulted in his bankruptcy. He spent the last few years of his life at his country home at Weilheim, near Munich. He died there on February 10, 1923, after a short illness resulting from intestinal cancer. Among the many awards given to him were the Rumford Medal of the Royal Society (1896), the Royal Order of Merit, Bavarian (1896), the Baumgaertner Prize of the Vienna Academy (1896), the Elliott-Cresson Medal of the Franklin Institute (1897), the Barnard Medal of Columbia University (1900), and the Helmholtz Medal (1919).

Further Reading

Daintith, John, et al., *A Biographical Encyclopedia of Scientists*, Facts on File, Volume XX, 1981, p. 686.
Dibner, Bern, *Wilhelm Conrad Röntgen and the Discovery of X-Rays*, 1968.
Esterer, Arnulf K., *Discoverer of X-Ray: Wilhelm Conrad Röntgen*, 1968.
Gillispie, C. C., editor, *Dictionary of Scientific Biography*, Volume 1, Scribner, 1975, pp. 529–531.
Glasser, Otto, *W. C. Röntgen and the Early History of Röntgen Rays*, Charles C. Thomas, 1934.
Magill, Frank N., editor, *The Nobel Prize Winners—Physics*, Volume 1, *1901–1937*, Salem Press, 1989, pp. 23–32.
Nitske, Robert W., *The Life of W. C. Röntgen, Discoverer of the X-Ray*, University of Arizona Press, 1971.
Wasson, Tyler, editor, *Nobel Prize Winners*, Wilson, 1987, pp. 879–882.
Weber, Robert L., *Pioneers of Science: Nobel Prize Winners in Physics*, American Institute of Physics, 1980, pp. 7–9.
Zehnder, Ludwig, *Wilhelm Conrad Röntgen*, Basle University, 192?. □

Eleanor Roosevelt

Anna Eleanor Roosevelt (1884-1962), wife of the thirty-second president of the United States, was a philanthropist, author, world diplomat, and resolute champion of liberal causes.

Eleanor Roosevelt was born in New York City on Oct. 11, 1884, into an economically comfortable but troubled family. Her father was Elliott Roosevelt, the younger brother of Theodore Roosevelt, a future president of the United States. Although handsome and charming, Elliott was plagued by frequent mental depressions and by alcoholism. Her mother, beautiful but neurotic, was preoccupied with the family's image in upper-class society and embarrassed by Eleanor's homeliness. Eleanor's father entered a sanitarium for alcoholics when she was a child. When Eleanor was 8 years old, her mother died, and she and two younger brothers went to live with their maternal grandmother in New York. Shortly thereafter the older brother died, and when Eleanor was not yet ten, she learned that her father was dead. Her grandmother sheltered her from all outside contacts except for family acquaintances.

Eleanor Roosevelt began discovering a world beyond the family at Mademoiselle Souvestre's finishing school at South Fields, England, where she went at 15. Mademoiselle Souvestre taught a sense of social service and responsibility, which Eleanor began to act upon after her return to New York. She plunged into social work, but soon her tall, handsome cousin, Franklin Delano Roosevelt, began courting her. They were married in March 1905. She now had to contend with a domineering mother-in-law and a gregarious husband who did not really understand his wife's struggle to overcome shyness and feelings of inadequacy.

Beginnings of a Public Career

Between 1906 and 1916, the Roosevelts had six children, one of whom died in infancy. The family lived at their estate at Hyde Park, from which Franklin pursued his political ambitions in the Democratic party. He served a term in the New York State Senate before President Woodrow Wilson appointed him assistant secretary of the Navy in 1913. Although Eleanor did much Red Cross relief work during World War I and even toured the French battlefields shortly after the armistice, she remained obscure.

A major turning point in Eleanor's life came in 1921, when Franklin contracted polio and permanently lost the use of his legs. Finally asserting her will over her mother-in-law (who insisted that Franklin quietly accept invalidism), Eleanor nursed him back into activity. Within a few years he had regained his strength and political ambitions. Meanwhile, she entered more fully into public life. Speaking and working for the League of Women Voters, the National Consumers' League, the Women's Trade Union League, and the women's division of the New York State Democratic Committee, she not only acted as Franklin's "legs and ears" but began to acquire a certain notoriety of her own. During Franklin's New York governorship she saw the last of her children off to boarding school and kept busy inspecting state hospitals, homes, and prisons for her husband.

President's Wife

Roosevelt's election to the presidency in 1932 meant, as Eleanor later wrote, "the end of any personal life of my own." She quickly became the best-known (and also the most criticized) First Lady in American history. She evoked both intense admiration and intense hatred but almost never passivity or neutrality.

Besides undertaking a syndicated newspaper column and a series of radio broadcasts (the income from which she gave to charity), she traveled back and forth across the country on fact-finding trips for Franklin. She assumed the special role of advocate for those groups of Americans—working women, blacks, youth, tenant farmers—which Franklin Roosevelt's New Deal efforts to combat the De-

pression tended to neglect. Holding no official position, she felt she could speak more freely on issues than could Roosevelt, and she also became a key contact within the administration for officials seeking the President's support. In short, Eleanor became an intermediary between, on the one hand, the individual citizen and his government and, on the other, the President and much of his administration.

Of particular concern to her was securing equal opportunities for women under the New Deal's work relief projects; ensuring that appropriate employment for writers, artists, musicians, and theater people became an integral part of the Works Progress Administration (WPA) program; promoting the cause of Arthurdale, a farming community built by the Federal government for unemployed miners in West Virginia; and providing work for jobless youth, both white and black (accomplished under the National Youth Administration, set up in 1935). Much more than her husband, she denounced racial oppression and tried to aid the struggle of black Americans toward full citizenship. Largely because of her efforts, African Americans, for the first time since the Reconstruction years, had reason to feel that the national government was interested in their plight.

World Figure

As the United States moved toward war in the late 1930s, Eleanor Roosevelt spoke out forcefully in favor of the adminstration's policy of aiding antifascist governments. She accepted an appointment as deputy director in the Office of Civilian Defense. She applied herself diligently to her new job but proved inefficient as an administrator and resigned in 1942 in the face of growing congressional criticism. That was her first and last official position under Roosevelt. Once the United States formally entered the war, she made numerous trips to England, Europe, and the Pacific area to boost troop morale and to inspect Red Cross facilities.

After Roosevelt's death in April 1945, Eleanor was expected to retire to a quiet, uneventful private life. By the end of the year, however, she was back in public life. President Harry S. Truman appointed her American delegate to the United Nations Commission on Human Rights. As chairman of the Commission, she worked the other delegates overtime to complete the Universal Declaration of Human Rights, adopted by the UN General Assembly in 1948. She remained in her post at the UN through 1952. She became the target for virulent right-wing attacks during the presidential campaign of that year. After the election of Republican Dwight D. Eisenhower, she gave up her UN post, but continued to work for international understanding and cooperation as a representative of the American Association for the United Nations.

During the last decade of her life Eleanor Roosevelt traveled to numerous foreign countries, including two trips to the Soviet Union, and authored several books. She continued to articulate a personal and social outlook which, while never profound and sometimes banal and obtuse, still inspired millions. But by the early 1960s, although she had accepted three new government appointments from President John F. Kennedy (delegate to the U.N., adviser to the

Peace Corps, and chairman of the President's Commission on the Status of Women), her strength was waning. She died in New York City on Nov. 6, 1962.

Further Reading

Her candid autobiographical writings are invaluable: *This Is My Story* (1937); *This I Remember* (1949); and *On My Own* (1958). These works are combined with an additional updated chapter in Autobiography (1961). An even more intimate view of Eleanor can be gained from Joseph P. Lash, *Eleanor and Franklin: The Story of their Relationship Based on Eleanor Roosevelt's Private Papers* (1971) and *Eleanor: The Years Alone* (1972). Also helpful is Tamara K. Hareven, *Eleanor Roosevelt: An American Conscience* (1968). James R. Kearney, *Anna Eleanor Roosevelt: The Evolution of a Reformer* (1968), is less a biography than a topically organized analysis of various facets of Roosevelt's public life. Less critical though useful are Alfred Steinberg, *Mrs. R.* (1959); Joseph P. Lash, *Eleanor Roosevelt: A Friend's Memoir* (1965); and Archibald MacLeish, *The Eleanor Roosevelt Story* (1965). Information about Roosevelt's role in relation to her husband's career is in Frank Freidel's uncompleted biography *Franklin D. Roosevelt* (3 vols., 1952-1956); Alfred B. Rollins, *Roosevelt and Howe* (1962); and James MacGregor Burns, *Roosevelt: The Lion and the Fox* (1963). □

Franklin Delano Roosevelt

Franklin Delano Roosevelt (1882-1945), thirty-second president of the United States, led the nation out of the Great Depression and later into World War II. Before he died, he cleared the way for peace, including establishment of the United Nations.

Franklin Roosevelt was born on Jan. 30, 1882, of his father's second marriage, to Sara Delano, the daughter of a prominent family. The Roosevelts had been moderately wealthy for many generations. Merchants and financiers, they had often been prominent in the civic affairs of New York. When Franklin was born, his father was 51 years old and semiretired from a railroad presidency, and his mother was 28. Franklin was often in the care of governesses and tutors, until at the age of 14 he went to Groton School. Here he received a solid classical, historical, and mathematical training and was moderately good at his studies. His earnest attempts at athletics were mostly defeated because of his tall, ungainly frame.

Roosevelt wanted to go to Annapolis, but his parents insisted on preparation for the position natural for the scion of the Delano and Roosevelt families, so he entered Harvard University. He was a reasonably good student and found a substitute for athletics in reporting for the Harvard newspaper, of which he finally became editor. While seeming to be a Cambridge socialite, he spent an extra year studying public affairs. He also met and determined to marry his cousin, Eleanor, to his mother's annoyance. Eleanor was the daughter of Elliott Roosevelt, a weak member of the family who had died early. Raised by relatives, she received a lady's education but little affection. She was shy and retiring, but Franklin found her warm, vibrant, and responsive.

Despite his mother's opposition, they were married in 1905, and Franklin entered Columbia University Law School. He prepared for the bar examinations and without taking a degree became a lawyer and entered a clerkship in the Wall Street firm of Carter, Ledyard and Milburn. He took his duties lightly, however, and it was later recalled that he had remarked to fellow clerks that he meant somehow to enter politics and finally to become president. There was never any doubt of his ambition.

Roosevelt's chance came in 1910. He accepted the Democratic nomination for the New York Senate and was elected. Opportunity for further notice came quickly. Although his backing had come from Democrats affiliated with New York City's notorious Tammany Hall, he joined a group of upstate legislators who were setting out to oppose the election of Tammany's choice for U.S. senator. The rebels were successful in forcing acceptance of another candidate.

Much of Roosevelt's wide publicity from this struggle was managed by Albany reporter Louis McHenry Howe, who had taken to the young politician and set out to further his career. (This dedication lasted until Roosevelt was safely in the White House.) The Tammany fight made Roosevelt famous in New York, but it also won him the enmity of Tammany. Still, he was reelected in 1912. That year Woodrow Wilson was elected president; Roosevelt had been a campaign worker, and his efforts had been noticed by prominent party elder Josephus Daniels. When Daniels became secretary of the Navy in Wilson's Cabinet, he persuaded Wilson to offer Roosevelt the assistant secretaryship.

Assistant Secretary of the Navy

As assistant secretary, Roosevelt began an experience that substituted for the naval career he had hoped for as a boy. Before long he became restless, however, and tried to capture the Democratic nomination for U.S. senator from New York. Wilson and Daniels were displeased. Daniels forgave him, but Wilson never afterward really trusted the brash young man. This distrust was heightened later by Roosevelt's departure from the administration's policy of neutrality in the years preceding World War I. Roosevelt openly favored intervention, agitated for naval expansion, and was known to be rather scornful of Daniels, who kept the Navy under close political discipline.

America soon entered the war, however, and Roosevelt could work for a cause he believed in. At that time there was only one assistant secretary, and he had extensive responsibilities. Howe had come to Washington with him and had become his indispensable guardian and helper. Together their management of the department was creditable.

Though Roosevelt tried several times to leave his civilian post to join the fighting forces, he was persuaded to remain. When the war came to an end and Wilson was stricken during his fight for ratification of the Versailles Treaty, there was an obvious revulsion throughout the United States from the disappointing settlements of the war. It seemed to many that the effort to make the world safe for democracy had resulted in making the world safe for the old empires.

The Allied leaders had given in to Wilson's insistence on the creation of the League of Nations only to serve their real interest in extending their territories and in imposing reparations on Germany. These reparations were so large that they could never be paid; consequently the enormous debts the Allies owed to the United States would never be paid either. The American armies had saved Europe and the Europeans were ungrateful. Resentment and disillusion were widespread.

The Republican party had the advantage of not having been responsible for these foreign entanglements. In 1920 they nominated Warren G. Harding, a conservative senator, as their presidential candidate. The Democrats nominated Governor James Cox of Ohio, who had had no visible part in the Wilson administration; the vice-presidential candidate was Roosevelt.

It was a despairing campaign; but in one respect it was a beginning rather than an ending for Roosevelt. He made a much more noticeable campaign effort than the presidential candidate. He covered the nation by special trains, speaking many times a day, often from back platforms, and getting acquainted with local leaders everywhere. He had learned the professional politician's breeziness, was able to absorb useful information, and had an infallible memory for names and faces. The defeat was decisive; but Roosevelt emerged as the most representative Democrat.

Victim of Poliomyelitis

Roosevelt retreated to a law connection in New York's financial district again and a position with a fidelity and deposit company. But in the summer of 1921, vacationing in Canada, he became mysteriously ill. His disease, poliomyelitis, was not immediately diagnosed. He was almost totally paralyzed, however, and had to be moved to New York for treatment. This was managed with such secrecy that for a long time the seriousness of his condition was not publicized. In fact, he would never recover the use of his legs, a disability that seemed to end his political career. His mother, typically, demanded that he return to Hyde Park and give up the political activities she had always deplored. He could now become a country gentleman. But Eleanor, joined by Howe, set out to renew his ambition.

Roosevelt's struggle during the convalescence of the next few years was agonizing and continually disappointing. Not much was known then about rehabilitation, and he resorted to exhausting courses of calisthenics to reactivate his atrophied muscles. In 1923 he tried the warm mineral waters of Warm Springs, Ga., where exercise was easier. He was so optimistic that he wrote friends that he had begun to feel movement in his toes. It was, of course, an illusion.

Roosevelt invested a good part of his remaining fortune in the place. It soon became a resort for those with similar ailments. The facilities were overwhelmed, but gradually an institution was built up, and the medical staff began to have more realistic knowledge of aftereffects. There were no cures; but lives could be made much more tolerable. Meanwhile Roosevelt, realizing that cures were impossible, turned to the encouragement of prevention. (Ultimately, an effective vaccine was found.)

New York Governor

While at Warm Springs in 1928, Roosevelt was called to political duty again, this time by Al Smith, whom he had put in nomination at the Democratic conventions of 1924 and 1928. Almost at once, however, it became clear that Smith could not win the election. He felt, however, that Roosevelt, as candidate for governor, would help to win New York. Roosevelt resisted. He was now a likely presidential candidate in a later, more favorable year for the Democrats; and if he lost the race for the governorship, he would be finished. But the New Yorkers insisted, and he ran and was narrowly elected.

Roosevelt began the 4 years of his New York governorship that were preliminary to his presidency, and since he was reelected 2 years later, it was inevitable that he should be the candidate in 1932. Since 1929 the nation had been sunk in the worst depression of its history, and Herbert Hoover's Republican administration had failed to find a way to recovery. This made it a favorable year for the Democrats.

First Term as President

It would be more true to say that Hoover in 1932 lost than that Roosevelt won. At any rate, Roosevelt came to the presidency with a dangerous economic crisis at its height. Industry was paralyzed, and unemployment afflicted some

30 percent of the work force. Roosevelt had promised that something would be done, but what that would be he had not specified.

Roosevelt began providing relief on a large scale by giving work to the unemployed and by approving a device for bringing increased income to farmers, who were in even worse straits than city workers. Also, he devalued the currency and enabled debtors to discharge debts that had long been frozen. Closed banks all over the country were assisted to reopen, and gradually the crisis was overcome.

In 1934 Roosevelt proposed a comprehensive social security system that, he hoped, would make another such depression impossible. Citizens would never be without at least minimum incomes again. Incidentally, these citizens became devoted supporters of the President who had given them this hope. So in spite of the conservatives who opposed the measures he collectively called the New Deal, he became so popular that he won reelection in 1936 by an unprecedented majority.

Second and Third Terms

Roosevelt's second term began with a struggle between himself and the Supreme Court. The justices had held certain of his New Deal devices to be unconstitutional. In retaliation he proposed to add new justices who would be more amenable. Many even in his own party opposed him in this attempt to pack the Court, and Congress defeated it. After this there ensued the familiar stalemate between an innovative president and a reluctant Congress.

Nevertheless in 1940 Roosevelt determined to break with tradition and run for a third term. His reasons were partly that his reforms were far from finished, but more importantly that he was now certain of Adolf Hitler's intention to subdue Europe and go on to further conquests. The immense productivity and organizational ability of the Germans would be at his disposal. Europe would be defeated unless the United States came to its support.

The presidential campaign of 1940 was the climax of Roosevelt's plea that Americans set themselves against the Nazi threat. He had sought to prepare the way in numerous speeches but had had a most disappointing response. There was a vivid recollection of the disillusion after World War I, and a good many Americans were inclined to support the Germans rather than the Allied Powers. So strong was American reluctance to be involved in another world war that in the last speeches of this campaign Roosevelt practically promised that young Americans would never be sent abroad to fight. Luckily his opponent, Republican Wendell Willkie, also favored support for the Allies. The campaign, won by a narrow majority, gave Roosevelt no mandate for intervention.

Roosevelt was not far into his third term, however, when the decision to enter the war was made for him by the Japanese, whose attack on Pearl Harbor caused serious losses to American forces there. Almost at once the White House became headquarters for those who controlled the strategy of what was now World War II. Winston Churchill came immediately and practically took up residence, bringing a British staff. Together the leaders agreed that Germany

and Italy must have first attention. Gen. Douglas MacArthur, commander in the Pacific, was ordered to retreat from the Philippines to Australia, something he was bitterly reluctant to do. But Roosevelt firmly believed that the first problem was to help the British, and then, when Hitler turned East, to somehow get arms to the Soviets. The Japanese could be taken care of when Europe was safe.

Hitler's grand strategy was to subdue the Soviet Union, conquer North Africa, and link up with the Japanese, who were advancing rapidly across the Eastern countries. Roosevelt wanted an early crossing of the English Channel to retake France and to force Hitler to fight on two fronts. Churchill, mindful of the fearful British losses in World War I, instead wanted to attack the underbelly of Europe, cut Hitler's lines to the East, and shut him off from Africa. The invasion of Europe was postponed because it became clear that elaborate preparation was necessary. But Allied troops were sent into Africa, with Gen. Dwight Eisenhower in command, to attack Field Marshal Erwin Rommel from the rear. Eventually an Allied crossing to Sicily and a slow, costly march up the Italian peninsula, correlated with the attack across the English Channel, forced the Italian collapse and the German surrender.

Meanwhile MacArthur was belatedly given the support he needed for a brilliant island-hopping campaign that drove the Japanese back, destroyed their fleet, and endangered their home island. After the German surrender, the Pacific war was brought to an end by the American atomic bomb explosion over the Japanese cities of Hiroshima and Nagasaki. By this time Roosevelt was dead. He had not participated in that doubtful decision; but he had been, with Churchill, in active command during the war until then.

Roosevelt had gone to Warm Springs early in 1945, completely exhausted. He had recently returned from a conference of Allied leaders at Yalta, where he had forced acceptance of his scheme for a United Nations and made arrangements for the Soviet Union to assist in the final subjugation of Japan. The strain was visible as he made his report to the nation.

At Warm Springs he prepared the address to be used at San Francisco, where the meeting to ratify agreements concerning the United Nations was to be held; but he found himself unable to enjoy the pine woods and the gushing waters. He sat wan and frail in his small cottage, getting through only such work as had to be done. He finished signing papers on the morning of April 12, 1945. Within hours, he suffered the massive cerebral hemorrhage that killed him.

A special train carried Roosevelt's body to Washington, and there he lay in the White House until he was taken to Hyde Park and buried in the hedged garden he himself had prepared. His grave is marked by a plain marble slab, and his wife is buried beside him. He had given the estate to the nation, and it is now a shrine much visited by those who recall or have heard how great a man he was for his time.

Further Reading

Samuel I. Rosenman, ed., *The Public Papers and Addresses of Franklin D. Roosevelt* (1938-1950), includes selected messages to Congress, speeches, executive orders, and transcripts from press conferences. There is also a collection of Roosevelt's letters edited by Elliott Roosevelt, *F. D. R.: His Personal Letters* (4 vols., 1947-1950). Eleanor Roosevelt, *This I Remember* (1949), is a frank account by Roosevelt's wife. Frances Perkins, *The Roosevelt I Knew* (1946), and Samuel I. Rosenman, *Working with Roosevelt* (1952), personal accounts, are helpful in assessing Roosevelt's character and work methods.

The only full biography of Roosevelt is Rexford G. Tugwell, *The Democratic Roosevelt* (1957). Frank B. Freidel's biography, *Franklin D. Roosevelt* (3 vols., 1952-1956), was never completed. Rexford G. Tugwell's briefer *F. D. R.: Architect of an Era* (1967) studies the man and his work, and his *The Brains Trust* (1968) tells the part played in Roosevelt's presidency by a group of helpers, mostly from Columbia University. The presidential elections involving Roosevelt are covered in Arthur M. Schlesinger, Jr., ed., *History of American Presidential Elections* (4 vols., 1971). James MacGregor Burns, *Roosevelt: The Lion and the Fox* (1956), ranks Roosevelt among the great presidents. Basil Rauch, *Roosevelt: From Munich to Pearl Harbor, a Study in the Creation of a Foreign Policy* (1950), is a detailed, accurate history of events during this period. Written by an Albany newspaper correspondent when Roosevelt was governor, Ernest K. Lindley, *The Roosevelt Revolution: First Phase* (1933), helped establish Roosevelt as a progressive leader. An authoritative and readable history of Roosevelt's era is provided in the two volumes by Arthur M. Schlesinger, Jr., *The New Deal in Action, 1933-1939* (1940) and *The Crisis of the Old Order* (1957). Another account of the period is Basil Rauch, *The History of the New Deal, 1933-1938* (1944). □

Theodore Roosevelt

The first modern American president, Theodore Roosevelt (1858-1919) was also one of the most popular, important, and controversial. During his years in office he greatly expanded the power of the presidency.

A strong nationalist and a resourceful leader, Theodore Roosevelt gloried in the opportunities and responsibilities of world power. He especially enlarged the United States role in the Far East and Latin America. At home he increased regulation of business, encouraged the labor movement, and waged a long, dramatic battle for conservation of national resources. He also organized the Progressive party (1912) and advanced the rise of the welfare state with a forceful campaign for social justice.

Roosevelt was born in New York City on Oct. 27, 1858. His father was of an old Dutch mercantile family long prominent in the city's affairs. His mother came from an established Georgia family of Scotch-Irish and Huguenot ancestry. A buoyant, dominant figure, his father was the only man, young Roosevelt once said, he "ever feared." He imbued his son with an acute sense of civic responsibility and an attitude of noblesse oblige.

Partly because of a severe asthmatic condition, Theodore was educated by private tutors until 1876, when he entered Harvard College. Abandoning plans to become a naturalist, he developed political and historical interests, was elected to Phi Beta Kappa, and finished twenty-first in a class of 158. He also began writing *The Naval War of 1812* (1882), a work of limited range but high technical competence. Four months after his graduation in 1880, he married Alice Hathaway Lee, by whom he had a daughter.

Early Career

Bored by the study of law in the office of an uncle and at Columbia University, Roosevelt willingly gave it up in 1882 to serve the first of three terms in the New York State Assembly. He quickly distinguished himself for integrity, courage, and independence, and upon his retirement in 1884 he had become the leader of the Republican party's reform wing. Though his reputation was based on his attacks against corruption, he had shown some interest in social problems and had begun to break with laissez-faire economics. Among the many bills he drove through the Assembly was a measure, worked out with labor leader Samuel Gompers, to regulate tenement workshops.

Roosevelt's last term was marred by the sudden deaths of his mother and his wife within hours of each other in February 1884. After the legislative session ended, he established a ranch, Elkhorn, on the Little Missouri River in the Dakota Territory. Immersing himself in history, he completed *Thomas Hart Benton* (1886) and *Gouverneur Morris* (1887) and began to prepare his major work, the four-volume *Winning of the West* (1889-1896). A tour de force distinguished more for its narrative power and personality

sketches than its social and economic analysis, it won the respect of the foremost academic historian of the West, Frederick Jackson Turner. It also gave Roosevelt considerable standing among professional historians and contributed to his election as president of the American Historical Association in 1912. Meanwhile, he published numerous hunting and nature books, some of high order.

Politics and a romantic interest in a childhood friend, Edith Carow, drew Roosevelt back east. Nominated for mayor of New York, he waged a characteristically vigorous campaign in 1886 but finished third. He then went to London to marry Carow, with whom he had four sons and a daughter.

In 1889 Roosevelt was rewarded for his earlier services to President Benjamin Harrison with appointment to the ineffectual Civil Service Commission. Plunging into his duties with extraordinary zeal, he soon became head of the Commission. He insisted that the laws be scrupulously enforced in order to open the government service to all who were qualified, and he alienated many politicians in his own party by refusing to submit to their demands. By the end of his six years in office Roosevelt had virtually institutionalized the civil service.

Roosevelt returned to New York City in 1895 to serve two tumultuous years as president of the police board. Enforcing the law with relentless efficiency and uncompromising honesty, he indulged once more in acrimonious controversy with the leaders of his party. He succeeded in modernizing the force, eliminating graft from the promotion system, and raising morale to unprecedented heights. "It's tough on the force, for he was dead square . . . and we needed him," said an unnamed policeman when Roosevelt resigned in the spring of 1897 to become President William McKinley's assistant secretary of the Navy.

As assistant secretary, Roosevelt instituted personnel reforms, arranged meaningful maneuvers for the fleet, and lobbied energetically for a two-ocean navy. He uncritically accepted imperialistic theories, and he worked closely with senators Henry Cabot Lodge and Alfred Beveridge for war against Spain in 1898. Although moved partly by humanitarian considerations, he was animated mainly by lust for empire and an exaggerated conception of the glories of war. "No qualities called out by a purely peaceful life," he wrote, "stand on a level with those stern and virile virtues which move the men of stout heart and strong hand who uphold the honor of their flag in battle."

Anxious to prove himself under fire, Roosevelt resigned as assistant secretary of the Navy in April to organize the 1st U.S. Volunteer Cavalry Regiment (the "Rough Riders"). He took command of the unit in Cuba and distinguished himself and his regiment in a bold charge up the hill next to San Juan. In late summer 1898 he returned to New York a war hero.

New York's Governor

Nominated for governor, Roosevelt won election in the fall of 1898 by a narrow margin. His 2-year administration was the most enlightened to that time. By deferring to the Republican machine on minor matters, by mobilizing public opinion behind his program, and by otherwise invoking the arts of the master politician, Roosevelt forced an impressive body of legislation through a recalcitrant Assembly and Senate. Most significant, perhaps, was a franchise tax on corporations. As the Democratic *New York World* concluded when he left office, "the controlling purpose and general course of his administration have been high and good."

Roosevelt accepted the vice-presidential nomination in 1900. A landslide victory for McKinley and Roosevelt ensued. Then, on Sept. 14, 1901, following McKinley's death by an assassin's bullet, Roosevelt was sworn in. Not quite 43, he was the youngest president in history.

First Presidential Administration

Roosevelt's first three years in office were inhibited by the conservatism of Republican congressional leaders and the accidental nature of his coming to power. He was able to sign the Newlands Reclamation Bill into law (1902) and the Elkins Antirebate Bill (1903); he also persuaded Congress to create a toothless Bureau of Corporations. But it was his sensational use of the dormant powers of his office that lifted his first partial term above the ordinary.

On Feb. 18, 1902, Roosevelt shook the financial community and took a first step toward bringing big business under Federal control by ordering antitrust proceedings against the Northern Securities Company, a railroad combine formed by J. P. Morgan and other magnates. Suits against the meat-packers and other trusts followed, and by the time Roosevelt left office 43 actions had been instituted. Yet he never regarded antitrust suits as a full solution to the corporation problem. During his second administration he strove, with limited success, to provide for continuous regulation rather than the dissolution of big businesses.

Hardly less dramatic than his attack on the Northern Securities Company was Roosevelt's intervention in a five-month-long anthracite coal strike in 1902. By virtually forcing the operators to submit to arbitration, he won important gains for the striking miners. Never before had a president used his powers in a strike on labor's side.

Foreign Policy

Roosevelt's conduct of foreign policy was as dynamic and considerably more far-reaching in import. Believing that there could be no retreat from the power position which the Spanish-American War had dramatized but which the United States industrialism had forged, he stamped his imprint upon American policy with unusual force. He established a moderately enlightened government in the Philippines, while persuading Congress to grant tariff concessions to Cuba. He settled an old Alaskan boundary dispute with Canada on terms favorable to the United States. And he capitalized on an externally financed revolution in Panama to acquire the Canal Zone under conditions that created a heritage of ill will.

At the instance of the president of Santo Domingo, Roosevelt also arranged for the United States to assume control of the customs of that misgoverned nation in order to avert intervention by European powers. He had about the same desire to annex Santo Domingo, he said, "as a gorged boa constrictor might have to swallow a porcupine wrong-end-to." But he had already forestalled German intervention in Venezuela in 1902 and was anxious to establish a firm policy against it. So on May 20, 1904, and again in December he set forth what became known as the Roosevelt Corollary to the Monroe Doctrine. The United States, he declared, assumed the right to intervene in the internal affairs of the Latin American nations in the event of "chronic wrongdoing" or "impotence."

Roosevelt's first administration was also marked by a revitalization of the bureaucracy. The quality of appointees was raised, capable members of minority groups were given government posts (in 1906 Roosevelt named the first Jew, Oscar Straus, to a Cabinet position), and the civil service lists were expanded. At the same time, however, the President ruthlessly manipulated patronage so as to wrest control of Republican party machinery from Senator Mark Hanna and secure his nomination to a full term in 1904. "In politics," he disarmingly explained, "we have to do a great many things we ought not to do." Overwhelming his conservative Democratic opponent by the greatest popular majority to that time, Roosevelt won the election and carried in a great host of congressional candidates on his coattails.

Second Administration

Although the resentment of the Republican party's Old Guard increased rather than diminished as his tenure lengthened, Roosevelt pushed through a much more progressive program in this second term. His "Square Deal" reached its finest legislative flower in 1906 with passage of the Hepburn Railroad Bill, the Pure Food and Drug Bill, an amendment providing Federal regulation of stockyards and packing houses, and an employers' liability measure. Yet he probably did even more to forward progressivism by using his office as a pulpit and by appointing study commissions such as those on country life and inland waterways. Several of his messages to Congress in 1907 and 1908 were the most radical to that time. In the face of the Old Guard's open repudiation of him, moreover, he profoundly stimulated the burgeoning progressive movement on all levels of government.

Conservation Program

In conservation Roosevelt's drive to control exploitation and increase development of natural resources was remarkable for sustained intellectual and administrative force. In no other cause did he fuse science and morality so effectively. Based on the propositions that nature's heritage belonged to the people, that "the fundamental idea of forestry is the perpetuation of forests by use," and that "every stream is a unit from its source to its mouth, and all its uses are interdependent," his conservation program provoked bitter conflict with Western states'-rightists and their allies, the electric power companies and large ranchers. In the end Roosevelt failed to marshal even a modicum of support in Congress for multipurpose river valley developments. But he did save what later became the heart of the Tennessee

Valley Authority (TVA) by vetoing a bill that would have opened Muscle Shoals to haphazard private development.

By March 1909 Roosevelt's audacious use of executive power had resulted in the transfer of 125 million acres to the forest reserves. About half as many acres containing coal and mineral deposits had been subjected to public controls. Sixteen national monuments and 51 wildlife refuges had been established. And the number of national parks had been doubled. As Roosevelt's bitter enemy Senator Robert M. La Follette wrote, "his greatest work was inspiring and actually beginning a world movement for . . . saving for the human race the things on which alone a peaceful, progressive, and happy life can be founded."

Foreign Policy

Roosevelt's pronounced impact on the international scene continued during his second term. He intervened decisively for peace in the Algeciras crisis of 1905-1906, and he supported the call for the Second Hague Conference of 1907. But it was in the Far East, where he gradually abandoned the imperialistic aspirations of his pre-presidential years, that he played the most significant role. Perceiving that Japan was destined to become a major Far Eastern power, he encouraged that country to serve as a stabilizing force in the area. To this end he used his good offices to close the Russo-Japanese War through a conference at Portsmouth, N.H., in 1905; for this service he received the Nobel Peace Prize. He also acquiesced at this time in Japan's extension of suzerainty over Korea (Taft-Katsura Memorandum).

By 1907 Roosevelt realized that the Philippines were the United States' "heel of Achilles." He had also come to realize that the China trade which the open-door policy was designed to foster was largely illusory. He consequently labored to maintain Japan's friendship without compromising American interests. He fostered a "gentleman's agreement" on immigration of Japanese to the United States. He implicitly recognized Japan's economic ascendancy in Manchuria through the Root-Takahira agreement of 1908. (Later he urged his successor, President William H. Taft, to give up commercial aspirations and the open-door policy in North China, though he was unsuccessful in this.)

Progressive Movement

Rejecting suggestions that he run for reelection, Roosevelt selected Taft as his successor. He then led a scientific and hunting expedition to Africa (1909) and made a triumphal tour of Europe. He returned to a strife-ridden Republican party in June 1910. Caught between the conservative supporters of Taft and the advanced progressive followers of himself and La Follette, he gave hope to La Follette by setting forth a radical program—the "new nationalism"—of social and economic reforms that summer. Thereafter pressure to declare himself a candidate for the nomination in 1912 mounted until he reluctantly did so.

Although Roosevelt outpolled Taft by more than 2 to 1 in the Republican primaries, Taft's control of the party organization won him the nomination in convention. Roosevelt's supporters then stormed out of the party and organized the Progressive, or "Bull Moose," party. During the three-cornered campaign that fall, Roosevelt called forcefully for Federal regulation of corporations, steeply graduated income and inheritance taxes, multipurpose river valley developments, and social justice for labor and other underprivileged groups. But the Democratic nominee, Woodrow Wilson, running on a more traditional reform platform, won the election.

World War I

Within 3 months of the outbreak of war in Europe in 1914, Roosevelt began his last crusade: an impassioned campaign to persuade the American people to join the Allies and prosecute the war with vigor. He believed that a German victory would be inimical to American economic, political, and cultural interests. But he was also influenced, as in 1898, by his romantic conception of war and ultranationalism. As a result, he distorted the real nature of his thought by trumpeting for war on the submarine, or American-rights, issue alone. More regrettable still, he virtually called for war against Mexico in 1916.

Following America's declaration of war in April 1917, Roosevelt relentlessly attacked the administration for failing to mobilize fast enough. Embittered by Wilson's refusal to let him raise a division, he also attacked the President personally. He was unenthusiastic about the League of Nations, believing that a military alliance of France, Great Britain, and the United States could best preserve peace. He was prepared to support Senator Henry Cabot Lodge's nationalistic reservations to the League Covenant, but he died in his home at Oyster Bay, Long Island, on Jan. 6, 1919, before he could be effective.

Roosevelt's reputation as a domestic reformer remains high and secure. He was the first president to concern himself with the judiciary's massive bias toward property rights (as opposed to human rights), with the maldistribution of wealth, and with the subversion of the democratic process by spokesmen of economic interests in Congress, the pulpits, and the editorial offices. He was also the first to understand the conservation problem in its multiple facets, the first to evolve a regulatory program for capital, and the first to encourage the growth of labor unions. The best-liked man of his times, he has never been revered because his militarism and chauvinism affronted the human spirit.

Further Reading

Roosevelt can be studied through his own writings. Especially valuable are his *Letters,* edited by Elting E. Morison and John M. Blum (8 vols., 1951-1954), and a collection of his essays, books, and speeches, *The Works of Theodore Roosevelt,* edited by Hermann Hagedorn (24 vols., 1923-1925). A general collection, *Writings,* was edited by William H. Harbaugh (1967). Roosevelt's *An Autobiography* (1913) is revealing despite the usual deficiencies of such works.

William H. Harbaugh, *Power and Responsibility: The Life and Times of Theodore Roosevelt* (1961; rev. ed., entitled *The Life and Times of Theodore Roosevelt,* 1963), is a full-length biography. The best study of Roosevelt's early career is Carleton Putnam, Theodore *Roosevelt,* vol. 1: *The Formative Years* (1958); the best treatment of his governorship is G. Wallace Chessman, *Governor Theodore Roosevelt* (1965). John M.

Blum, *The Republican Roosevelt* (1954; new ed. 1962), is a penetrating essay. The roots of Roosevelt's imperialism are examined in David H. Burton, *Theodore Roosevelt: Confident Imperialist* (1968).

Howard K. Beale, *Theodore Roosevelt and the Rise of America to World Power* (1956), is a seminal study. Fine short accounts are George E. Mowry, *The Era of Theodore Roosevelt, 1900-1912* (1958), and G. Wallace Chessman, *Theodore Roosevelt and the Politics of Power,* edited by Oscar Handlin (1969). ☐

Elihu Root

Elihu Root (1845-1937), a U.S. secretary of war and secretary of state and a senator from New York, was the most constructive conservative of his times.

Elihu Root was born at Clinton, N.Y., on Feb. 15, 1845. His father was a college professor of old New England stock. Elihu attended Hamilton College during the Civil War, graduating as valedictorian in 1864. After taking a law degree at New York University in 1867, he went into private practice in New York City. He married Clara Frances Wales in 1878; they had two daughters and a son and were a devoted family.

Root was a junior counsel to William Tweed during the notorious boss's trial in 1873. A decade later Root served briefly as U.S. attorney for the district of southern New York. An astute and resourceful legal counselor, he afterward became one of the nation's preeminent corporation lawyers. He advised the Havemeyer Sugar Trust on the reorganization that enabled it to gain control of 98 percent of the market, and he represented the Whitney-Ryan traction interests and numerous other combines. "It is not a function of law," he explained, "to enforce the rules of morality."

Root opposed the encroachment of government upon individual rights, especially those involving property, but he never pursued the implications of corporate political and economic power. As he confessed in 1906, "The pure lawyer seldom concerns himself about the broad aspects of public policy.... Lawyers are almost always conservative.... Through insisting upon the maintenance of legal rule, they become instinctively opposed to change."

Secretary of War

Root accepted President William McKinley's urgent request in 1899 that he head the mismanaged War Department. His administration of the territories wrested from Spain was at once realistic and enlightened. In Puerto Rico, where the illiteracy rate was 90 percent, he instituted a highly centralized administration virtually devoid of popular participation. At the same time, he pushed public health measures and persuaded McKinley to exempt the colony from American tariff restrictions. In Cuba, Root arranged for almost immediate civil government but insisted that the United States maintain control of its foreign relations. This was accomplished through the Platt Amendment, which he drafted.

In the Philippines, Root also pushed civil government, including extension of the Bill of Rights. He formed the army that suppressed Emilio Aguinaldo's independence movement and was so sensitive to the honor of American troops that he failed to act promptly against American atrocities. Satisfied with the Philippine government that President William Howard Taft created under his broad direction, Root was unsympathetic in later years to the Democrats' insistence that it be liberalized in order to prepare the Filipinos for full independence.

Meanwhile Root reorganized the general staff, created the Army War College, and established the Joint Army-Navy Board. President Theodore Roosevelt valued him for his calm, incisive, and eminently practical judgment, and when Root resigned in 1904, the President wrote, "I shall never have, and can never have, a more loyal friend, a more faithful and wiser adviser."

Secretary of State

In 1905 Root returned to government service as secretary of state under Roosevelt. Continuing to complement Roosevelt admirably, he pacified the Senate, promoted friendly relations with Latin America, kept a wary eye on Germany, and otherwise comported himself with patience, tact, and cordiality. He supported the Second Hague Conference and worked hard and skillfully to maintain amicable relations with Japan. His crowning achievement was the negotiation of 24 bilateral arbitration treaties. He was awarded the Nobel Peace Prize in 1912.

Senator from New York

Root seemed unable to understand the nature or aims of the Progressive movement, and his 6 years (1909-1915) as a U.S. senator were among the least productive of his life. He disapproved much of the reform legislation under President Taft, and all of it under Woodrow Wilson. His attacks on Wilson's Mexican policy were also unfair and simplistic. Concluding that World War I was a struggle for "Anglo-Saxon" liberty, he was a strong proponent of American entry. In 1917 he headed an ineffective and imperceptive mission to Russia designed to keep the provisional government in the war.

During the fight over the League of Nations, Root was caught between his general approval of the League, his strong nationalistic strain, and his own and his party's partisanship. He tried, but failed, to play a constructive role by advocating American entry with nationalistic reservations. Root came out of retirement in late 1921 to serve on the American delegation to the Washington Conference. He also gave freely to the movement to adhere to the World Court and further invested himself in service to the Carnegie Endowment for International Peace and other Carnegie benefactions. He died on Feb. 7, 1937.

A charming, witty man in the company of intimates, Root lacked charisma in public. Aside from his obvious achievements in the War and State Departments, he is remembered for his embodiment of that which was wisest and most constructive in the conservative tradition.

Further Reading

Eight volumes of Root's writings and addresses up to 1923 were edited by Robert Bacon and James B. Scott and published between 1916 and 1925. The official biography is Philip C. Jessup, *Elihu Root* (2 vols., 1938), a full if somewhat adulatory account. It should be supplemented by Richard W. Leopold, *Elihu Root and the Conservative Tradition* (1954), a dispassionate work that benefits from recent scholarship. Considerable material on Root is contained in Julius W. Pratt, *America's Colonial Experiment: How the United States Gained, Governed, and in Part Gave Away a Colonial Empire* (1950), and in the biographies of Roosevelt, Taft, and other contemporaries.

Additional Sources

Leopold, Richard William, *Elihu Root and the conservative tradition,* Boston, Little, Brown 1954.
Root, Grace McClure Dixon (Cogswell) 1890-, *Fathers and sons* Clinton N.Y., 1971. □

Ned Rorem

Ned Rorem (born 1923) was widely regarded as the leading American composer of art songs. He was also well known as a diarist and essayist.

Ned Rorem was born in Richmond, Indiana, on October 23, 1923. He received his early music training in Chicago, where he took piano lessons and studied composition with Leo Sowerby at the American Conservatory in 1938 and 1939. He continued his studies at Northwestern University (1940-1942), the Curtis Institute (1943), and the Juilliard School of Music (1946, 1948), where he earned both Bachelor's and Master's degrees. In New York he also studied privately with Virgil Thomson, Aaron Copland, and David Diamond. In 1949 he went to Paris to study composition with Honegger. After a short stay in Paris he lived in Morocco for two years and then returned to Paris. Under the patronage of the Vicomtesse Marie Laure de Noailles he entered the musical circles of Paris and was befriended by Francis Poulenc, Georges Auric, Darius Milhaud, and Jean Cocteau, among others. In 1957 he returned to the United States, where he lived primarily in New York. From 1959-1961 he was composer-in-residence at the University of Buffalo and from 1966-1967 at the University of Utah.

Awards and Recognition

After first winning recognition in 1948 for *The Lordly Hudson* as "the best published song of the year," he won numerous awards and prizes: the Gershwin Prize (for an orchestral work from his student days), the Lili Boulanger Award, Fulbright and Guggenheim fellowships, the Prix de Biarritz, and Ford Foundation grants. He received the ASCAP-Deems Tayor Award three times: in 1971 for his book *Critical Affairs;* in 1975 for *The Final Diary;* and in

1992 for an article on American Opera in *Opera News.* In 1976 he won the Pulitzer Prize for his *Air Music* (1974), an orchestral work commissioned by the Cincinnati Symphony.

Rorem wrote about 300 songs for solo voice with piano accompaniment (including 17 song cycles), of which over 100 are unpublished. Some of his commissions for new works include: the Ford Foundation, the Lincoln Center Foundation, The Koussevitsky Foundation, the Atlanta Symphony, the Chicago Symphony, and Carnegie Hall. The Atlanta Symphony recording of the String Symphony, Sunday Morning, and Eagles, received a Grammy Award for Outstanding Orchestral Recording (1989).

Rorem's Songs

The considerable variety in his output-ranging from the short humorous *I Am Rose,* to the devotional *Cycle of Holy-Songs,* to the "jazzy" *Early in the Morning,* to the tragicomic *Visits to St. Elizabeth's*—results not only from the diverse compositional elements that make up his style, but also from his wide choice of texts. For his early songs he selected poetic texts from different literary periods, but after the mid-1950s he preferred the poetry of Walt Whitman and of 20th-century American poets such as Howard Moss, Paul Goodman, Theodore Roethke, and Kenneth Koch.

His songs are essentially lyrical, and their elegance, clarity, wit, and charm betray the influence of 20th-century French music, especially that of Ravel, Poulenc, and Satie. In his vocal writing Rorem showed a keen awareness of the capabilities of the human voice, and his melodies generally lie comfortably in the range of voice for which they were written. "Write gracefully for the voice—that is, make the voice line as seen on paper have the arched flow which singers like to interpret" was one of his mottoes for song-writing. In his melodies he was also able to capture the essential mood of the text.

In his early lyrical songs the melody was supported by full-textured chromatic accompaniment, while in the later ones a greater simplicity prevails, especially in the sparser, less chromatic accompaniments. In the Whitman songs and the dramatic songs of the late 1950s the vocal lines are more angular, have greater rhythmic variety, and alternate wide leaps with repeated-note passages. The piano parts of the more dramatic songs contain sharp contrasts in dynamics and texture and are as important as the voice in delineating the text.

In general, his songs are cast in the standard song forms, but some of the song cycles are unusual in structure. In *Poems of Love and the Rain* (1962), a cycle of 17 songs set to texts by American poets, Rorem set the same text (eight poems) twice, but in a contrasting manner. Each poem of the first half of the cycle receives a different setting in the second half and the poems appear in reverse order in the second half. The ninth poem is the central song and is set only once. In *Sun* (1967), for soprano and orchestra, the eight poems are presented as one continuous movement. Rorem's harmonic language, though basically tonal, was very much of the 20th century and showed the influence of Debussy, Stravinsky, and Hindemith. He used added-tone chords, chords based on superimposed thirds, chords arranged in fourths, polychords, and parallel chords. The extensive use of seventh, ninth, and eleventh chords gives some songs a jazz flavor. Contrapuntal techniques—ostinatos, imitation, contrary motion—also play an important part in many of the songs.

Rorem's Other Compositions

Although the songs occupy a central position in his output, Rorem also wrote operas, choral music, orchestral pieces (including three symphonies), chamber music, piano music, ballets, and incidental music for plays. Like his songs, his early instrumental works were also influenced by 20th-century French composers. In his later instrumental compositions he explored coloristic possibilities and the expansion of tonality through altered chords, modality, polymodality, and tone clusters. In works of the 1960s he used modified serial techniques. After 1958 he put aside sonata form in orchestral works and wrote instead semi-programmatic tone poems, variation forms, or multi-movement pieces.

In 1993 the premiere of Rorem's *Piano Concerto for Left Hand and Orchestra* received international attention and praise. In 1994 the New York Philharmonic debuted Rorem's *Concerto for English Horn and Orchestra,* a commission form for the orchestra in honor of its 150th anniversary.

In 1994 in several venues around the country there were celebrations of Rorem's 70th birthday. The New York Festival of Song presented a Rorem tribute; the New York Philharmonic premiered his *Concerto for English Horn and Orchestra;* Rorem accompanied soprano Angelina Reaux on piano in his seven-minute opera "Anna la Bonne;" St. Thomas Church in Manhattan presented his choral works weekly through the spring of 1994; and Robert Shaw (described as the "dean of American choral specialists) offered an overview of Rorem's choral music in Atlanta. Shaw stated that Rorem was "the most significant American song writer of the last half-century."

Literary Career

Rorem also enjoyed a distinguished literary career. He has authored thirteen books. As a writer he was best known for his diaries: *The Paris Diary of Ned Rorem* (1966), *The New York Diary* (1967), *The Final Diary* (1974), *The Later Diaries of Ned Rorem, 1961- 1972* (1983), and *The Nantucket Diary of Ned Rorem, 1973-1985* (1987). In these personal journals he recorded with great candor, wit, and elegance his observations of the world, people, friends, and culture and also offered a vivid and engaging portrait of himself. In a 1994 *New York Times* interview, Rorem (age 70) described himself as "mellowing." He stated that he lived monogamously with James Holmes for 27 years, this in contrast to his younger, "wilder" years, when he claimed to have slept with 3,000 men. In addition to the diaries, he wrote the following books: *Music from Inside Out* (1967), *Music and People* (1969), *Critical Affairs: A Composer's Journal* (1970), *Pure Contraption* (1973), *An Absolute Gift* (1978), *Setting the Tone* (1983), and *Knowing When to Stop*

(1994). He also contributed numerous articles to periodicals and newspapers. In spite of his abundant literary works, Rorem stated that he wanted to be remembered for his music. "No newspaper article can be me," he said. "My diaries have nothing to do with me, my music may be me."

Further Reading

Rorem wrote on autobiographical memoir titled, *Knowing When to Stop* in 1994. He also wrote a series of essays, *Settling the Score: Essays on Music* in 1988. The following articles discuss Rorem and his music: J. Oestreich, "At 70, an Enfant Terrible As Elder Statesman," *New York Times* profile (1994); G. Anderson, "The Music of Ned Rorem," *Music Journal* 21 (April 1963); B. Middaugh, "The Songs of Ned Rorem: Aspects of Musical Style," *National Association of Teachers of Singing Bulletin* 24 (May 1968); L.G. Rickert, "Song Cycles for Baritone," *National Association of Teachers of Singing Bulletin* 23 (November 1967); and P. L. Miller, "The Songs of Ned Rorem," *Tempo* (1978). Also recommended are Virgil Thomson, *American Music Since 1910* (1971) and John Gruen, *The Party's Over Now* (1972). □

Hermann Rorschach

Swiss psychiatrist Hermann Rorschach (1884-1922) was the developer of the inkblot personality test commonly known as the Rorschach test. The ten inkblot cards designed by Rorschach in the early twentieth century have continued to be used by mental health professionals as one of the standard means of compiling a subject's personality profile.

Swiss psychiatrist Hermann Rorschach was the developer of the widely-used personality evaluation method known as the Rorschach test. The Rorschach test involves the assessment by a psychiatrist or psychologist of a subject's responses when asked what he or she sees in a series of inkblots. Rorschach believed that this method could determine the amount of introversion and extroversion a person possessed, as well as clues about such characteristics as intelligence, emotional stability, and problem-solving abilities. In addition to general use in psychiatry and psychology, the test has come to be used by a wide-range of groups such as child development specialists, the military, prisons, and employers. Although the test was Rorschach's only contribution to the field of psychiatry, the popularity of the tool has made his name one that is recognized both inside and outside the profession.

Rorschach was born on November 8, 1884, in Zurich, Switzerland. He was the oldest of the three children of Ulrich Rorschach, an art teacher in Zurich schools; he also had a sister named Anna and a brother named Paul. His father's artistic interests may have been behind the young Rorschach's fascination with inkblots in his childhood. The boy's preoccupation with these random designs earned him the name "Kleck," German for "inkblot," from his classmates at school. In his adolescence Rorschach became an orphan after his mother died when he was 12 and his father died when he was 18. A year after his father's death, the young man graduated from the local high school with honors.

Focused on Psychiatry in Medical Career

After leaving high school, Rorschach went on to college with the goal of earning a medical degree. He spent time at a number of medical schools—in Neuchâtel, Zurich, and Bern in Switzerland and Berlin in Germany—completing his studies in Zurich after five years. While taking courses in Zurich, he had been a top student of Eugene Bleuler and had worked in the university hospital's psychiatric ward. Continuing to pursue his interest in psychiatry, he undertook a residency at a mental institution in Munsterlingen, Switzerland, in 1909. At the asylum he met Olga Stempelin, a Russian employee there, and the two began a relationship that resulted in their marriage in 1910. The couple had their first child, Elizabeth, in 1917; their second child, Wadin, was born in 1919.

Rorschach earned his doctor of medicine degree from the University of Zurich in 1912. The following year, he and his wife accepted posts at a mental institution in Moscow, Russia, where they remained for one year. In 1914, Rorschach secured a job as a resident physician at the Waldau Mental Hospital in Bern, Switzerland. He advanced to a higher position two years later when he was hired at the Krombach Mental Hospital in Appenzell, Switzerland. Respected as a leading psychiatrist in his native country, he was elected vice president of the Swiss Psychoanalytic Society in 1919.

Developed Inkblot Test

As early as 1911, Rorschach had begun research on the potential uses of inkblots in determining personality traits. He had done some early experiments using schoolchildren as subjects during his medical training at the University of Zurich, and he had also read about the inkblot experiments of other psychology researchers, including Justinus Kerner and Alfred Binet. He found, however, that his predecessors in this subject had not developed a consistent method of administering and evaluating such a test. Over the next decade, Rorschach conducted studies to develop such a method, using both patients in the mental hospitals where he was employed as well as healthy, emotionally stable people. Based on the information he gathered, Rorschach was able to devise a system of inkblot testing that provided a systematic way of testing and analyzing a subject that could produce meaningful results for understanding a person's personality traits.

Rorschach presented his new system in his book *Psychodiagnostik* (1921), which appeared in English translation as *Psychodiagnostics: A Diagnostic Test Based on Perception* in 1942. The book not only outlined Rorschach's famous inkblot test, but also discussed his wider theories of human personality. One of his primary arguments was that each person displays a mixture of the ''introversive'' personality, one motivated by internal factors, and the ''extratensive'' personality, or one more influenced by external factors. He believed that the amount of each trait in a person could be measured by using his ink-blot test, which could also reveal an individual's mental strengths or their abnormalities.

Planned Improvements on Testing Method

For his inkblot test, Rorschach designed 10 cards, each with a different symmetrical inkblot pattern. The designs, while not depicting any particular objects, do contain shapes suggesting physical items. The cards also vary in color: five are only in black and white, two are primarily black and white with some color, and three are in color. The person administering the test is to show each card to the subject without displaying any reaction to the subject's answers. The subject is instructed to describe what he or she sees in the inkblot, and the subject's answers are then analyzed in several different areas, including the part of the picture focused on, the length of time to generate a response, the content of the response, originality, and the subject's attention to such details as color, shading, and form. The value and accuracy of the test were based in large part on the ability of the person administering the test to interpret the results properly. But it still presented one of the most effective means of evaluating personality ever devised. Rorschach, however, looked upon *Psychodiagnostik* as a preliminary work that he intended to develop further.

Rorschach's book was not immediately given much attention when it appeared. Psychiatrists at that time did not think that personality could be tested or measured, so they initially ignored his work. By 1922, however, the ideas in Rorschach's book had become the subject of some discussion, but most psychiatrists remained wary of his new methods and did not feel that they could yield useful results, although they did acknowledge the potential value for the free-association thought that the inkblots generated. Rorschach discussed his plans to improve upon his inkblot system at a meeting of the Psychoanalytic Society that year, but this work was never completed. A short time later, Rorschach contracted appendicitis and died in Herisau, Switzerland, on April 2, 1922.

Rorschach did not live to see the great success that his testing methods would enjoy. His original ten inkblot designs were put into use by his students and colleagues and quickly gained a popularity that has continued to the present time. While detractors continue to exist, numerous studies have compiled statistical data about results of the Rorschach test, providing practitioners with an even greater degree of accuracy in interpreting results. Rorschach's inkblots are still in use in a number of areas, but those who use it now tend to look upon the results simply as indicators of potential psychiatric traits or problems, rather than an absolute diagnosis. But Rorschach's contribution to the fields of psychology and psychiatry is still considered a valuable procedure that remains one of the standard testing methods used to compile a personality profile by mental health professionals.

Further Reading

Klopfer, Bruno, and Douglas Kelley, *The Rorschach Technique: A Manual for a Projective Method of Personality Diagnosis,* World Book, 1942.
Larson, Cedric A., "Hermann Rorschach and the Ink-Blot Test," *Science Digest,* October, 1958, pp. 84-89. □

Richard Rorty

American philosopher and man of letters Richard Rorty (born 1931) gave new life to the pragmatist tradition and brought it into the public discussion of democracy and liberalism.

Richard Rorty had a major impact on American philosophy and culture. Within the world of academic philosophy he had the reputation of a thinker who, after mastering the most difficult challenges of analytic philosophy (in the tradition of G.E. Moore, Bertrand Russell, and Ludwig Wittgenstein), went on to challenge the notion of philosophy as an enterprise seeking truth in the manner of the sciences. He further suggested that philosophy was not so different from literature and so one need pursue no higher goals than making an edifying contribution to public conversation. From his perspective there could be no higher goal for philosophy to pursue. In a broader context, Rorty became known as a public intellectual, a man of letters more in the European mold rather than the American, insofar as he brought a wide and deep knowledge of history, philosophy, and literature to bear on questions concerning the nature of democracy, the relation between individuality and social cohesion, and feminism. Critics on the right attacked Rorty for being a relativist, while those on the left often claimed that he did no more than offer a bland defense of the status quo.

Born in New York City in 1931 to parents who were literate political radicals (they were followers of Trotsky), Rorty was intellectually precocious. He absorbed the Marxist theories and politics of his parents' circle, read voraciously, and developed aesthetic interests (for example, in wild orchids) that he feared were incompatible with the program for creating a classless society. As Rorty described himself, even after he outgrew Marxism, he felt a continuing tension between the literary and artistic cultivation of the self and the commitment to achieving social justice and articulating a conception of objective truth. On his account he was not able to reconcile these claims until relatively late in his career (and the achievement involved surrendering an objective notion of truth), but when he did so it was in a manner that was intended to be more than a mere individual solution.

Rorty enrolled at the University of Chicago when he was 15 (B.A. 1949) and received his Ph.D. in philosophy from Yale (1956). At Chicago Rorty absorbed the history of philosophy in an atmosphere where such thinkers as Leo Strauss and Richard McKeon wielded great influence. At

Yale and as a young professor at Wellesley (1958-1961) and Princeton (where he taught 1961-1982), Rorty also immersed himself in analytic philosophy of the sort that had been brought to the United States by such German and Austrian emigres as Rudolf Carnap, Hans Reichenbach, and Alfred Tarski. He became caught up in the project, in which American philosophers sought to assimilate the later thought of Ludwig Wittgenstein.

Rorty was quickly recognized for his contributions to analytical philosophy of mind and language. The anthology he edited, called *The Linguistic Turn* (1967; the title was borrowed from Gustav Bergmann), seemed to establish a set of thinkers and issues that would be canonical for future work in philosophy.

During the 1970s Rorty's views shifted in important ways. What was new was not his broad historical and cultural interests (which already distinguished him from most of his colleagues) but his definitive abandonment of the search for foundations in knowledge and ethics, which was marked by the publication of *Philosophy and the Mirror of Nature* (1979). He now brought together John Dewey, Martin Heidegger, and the later Wittgenstein as the heroes of a nonfoundationalist philosophy, who in different ways sought to redirect the discipline to focus on social and historical change or on language as a human practice rather than on the illusory pursuit of timeless truths. Philosophy was to be reconfigured in terms of hermeneutics so as to be devoted to the interpretation of history (including the history of thought) and culture.

While his views were stirring up philosophical controversy, Rorty was demonstrating that he could be an adroit academic statesman. He became president of the Eastern Division of the American Philosophical Association in 1979, at a time when a number of scholars, making common cause as "pluralists," claimed that Anglo-American analytic philosophy had attained a disproportionate and exclusionary power within the professional organization. As president, Rorty not only gave an address aimed at showing how his own perspective rendered a number of ostensibly different philosophical positions more compatible than the disputants supposed; he also took the lead in working out compromises and accommodations between the analysts and the pluralists that had a lasting effect on the American philosophical profession.

In 1981 Rorty was awarded a five-year fellowship from the MacArthur foundation. In 1982 he left Princeton to become university professor of the humanities at the University of Virginia. Both of these events marked Rorty's growing public status as a philosopher who had important things to say to an audience beyond the usual bounds of his discipline.

At the same time American intellectuals and academics were rapidly assimilating and confronting new waves of European thought, identified with thinkers such as Jürgen Habermas, Jacques Derrida, and Jean-Francois Lyotard. Rorty's critical essays on these figures became one of the primary means by which Americans who wanted to understand the significance of critical theory, deconstruction, and post-Modernism could inform themselves. His views were becoming widely known in Europe and Japan; his writings were translated, and he became a thinker of truly international interest.

Rorty, however, came to identify himself increasingly as an American, rather than as a disembodied philosopher. Having called himself a pragmatist for some time, he now addressed questions of culture and politics even more explicitly. In *Contingency, Irony, and Solidarity* (1988) Rorty moved from a powerful new statement of his anti-foundationalism (contingency) to a defense of individual freedom that combined traditional liberalism with the motif of self-creation in European high culture (as in Nietzsche and Proust) to an argument that democracy can exist without foundations and is compatible with self-creation (solidarity). In this and other writings of the late 1980s and 1990s, Rorty evinced a growing suspicion of the way in which, as he saw it, many American intellectuals were using European theory in order to argue for a politics of difference that would undermine a sense of national identity.

From Rorty's point of view, it was important to recognize that liberal democracy (specifically in the American form that he ironically referred to as "Postmodern Bourgeois Liberalism") was simply the best and most hopeful social arrangement yet devised. This despite the fact that it could be justified by no transcendental argument and that it continued to struggle with enormous challenges in a difficult and radically uncertain world.

Rorty's anti-objectivist view concepts such as truth and knowledge stresses the importance of community perceptions of what is and the language used within that community to configure the world. Rorty wrote frequently on political issues, attempting to clarify issues and strategies in the light of his approach. Thus, since people are members of many groups simultaneously, democratic liberal activism and advocacy become in significant part a matter of projecting outward the world view of a particular group to people not identifying themselves as members of that group. This approach eschews the strategy of the 90's left, which more commonly seeks recourse to claims of rights, which Rorty, borrowing from Harvard legal philosopher Mary Ann Glendon, describes as "unconditional moral imperatives," an approach which leads to a "blind alley," a pointless, distracting discussion of which rights exist and which do not. Instead, Rorty argues that what is really needed is a strategy by advocacy groups to get non-members to put themselves in their shoes, to see and understand the world from their perspective.

Further Reading

The best source for Rorty's thoughts are his own writings, including the essays collected in *Consequences of Pragmatism* (1982) and *Philosophical Papers* (2 vols., 1991) as well as those cited in the text. In addition, Rorty published a revealing autobiographical essay that gives its name to the collection *Wild Orchids and Trotsky*, Mark Edmundson, ed. (1993). Martyn Oliver of the University of Westminster conducted an interesting interview with Rorty, *Times Literary Supplement* (June 24, 1994). For an assessment and critique of Rorty''s overall approach, see Tibor Machan, "Indefatigable Alchemist: Richard Rorty's radical pragmatism," *American Scholar*

(Summer 1996). Rorty is exceptional among his peers in his willingness to write in publications more accessible to the non-academic reading public such as the *New York Review of Books,* the *London Review of Books,* the *New Leader,* the *New Republic, New York Review of Books, Dissent,* and in the op-ed pages of major U.S. and British dailies. See also "What's wrong with rights" (excerpt from a speech by Richard Rorty) (Transcript), *Harpers Magazine* (June 1996). □

Salvator Rosa

The Italian painter and poet Salvator Rosa (1615-1673) was one of the innovators of romanticism. His best-known paintings represent scenes of wild, untrammeled nature, populated with small genre figures.

Salvator Rosa was born in Naples on July 21, 1615. He first studied painting with his uncle, Domenico Greco, then with Jusepe de Ribera, and finally with Aniello Falcone. In 1640, after spending some time in Rome, Rosa moved to Florence, where he worked as a painter for the Medici court. In Florence he met Lucrezia, who became his mistress, and the poet Giovan Battista Ricciardi, who became his lifelong friend. Finding himself ill-adapted to court circles, in 1650 Rosa returned to Rome, this time permanently. There, on March 4, 1673, he married Lucrezia, with whom he had lived most of his adult life. Eleven days later he was dead.

Rosa emerges as a strangely touching figure, proud, melancholic, and fiercely independent. Alone among the major painters in the city, he had (by his own choice) no powerful patron. He rarely accepted commissions; instead, he tried to sell from his studio and to make himself known through public exhibitions, which were seldom and few. To a client who dared to suggest his own subject, Rosa said, "Go to a brickmaker, they work on order." In contrast, Pietro da Cortona, Rosa's enormously successful rival in Rome, boasted that he never chose the subject of any of his paintings and if asked would refuse to do so. In his stand for artistic independence Rosa was far ahead of his time.

Rosa's protest is still clearer in his satirical poetry. Here he ridiculed the official art of the papal court, especially the work of Cortona and Gian Lorenzo Bernini. Later Rosa's attacks extended to the papacy. His poetry won him a host of enemies, an entry in the Index of Forbidden Books that lasted for 2 centuries, and a place in the history of Italian literature, which, though small, appears to be permanent.

Grotto with Cascades is typical of Rosa's small landscapes, which his friends called "caprices." It is fully baroque in its painterly handling, open brushwork, dark shadows, and the silvery impasto that is used to suggest the sparkle of falling water. But it is also romantic. Above the tiny figures towers a gigantic natural bridge eroded by waterfalls. Man appears insignificant and irrelevant before the grandeur of nature.

L'umana fragilità is characteristic of the more serious current that imbues Rosa's later work. The young woman in the foreground wears a wreath of widely opened roses (which are fragile and impermanent). On her lap sits an infant who, guided by a winged skeleton, writes the words, "conceived in sin, born to pain, a life of labor, and inevitable death." Other symbols of impermanence are infants blowing soap bubbles and burning tufts of flax. In sharp contrast to his wild, untamed landscapes, the mood of these late works is one of quietude and resignation in the face of destiny; they reflect the then current revival of the philosophy of stoicism.

Further Reading

Selections in English from Rosa's correspondence and poetry are in Robert Enggass and Jonathan Brown, *Sources and Documents in the History of Art: Italy and Spain, 1600-1750* (1970). The standard work on Rosa, by Luigi Salerno (1963), is in Italian. Ellis K. Waterhouse, *Italian Baroque Painting* (1962; 2d ed. 1969), contains a good essay on Rosa.

Additional Sources

Scott, Jonathan, *Salvator Rosa: his life and times,* New Haven: Yale University Press, 1995. □

Juan Manuel de Rosas

Juan Manuel de Rosas (1793-1877) was an Argentine dictator. He was the prototype of the caudillo dictators of South America and ruled supreme in the Argentine Confederation from 1829 to 1852.

Juan Manuel de Rosas was born in Buenos Aires on March 30, 1793, and claimed descent from a noble Asturian family through Count Ortiz de Rosas. The first of his parents' 20 children, he detested school and spent most of his childhood on the family estancias, where he became one of the best horsemen in the Argentine and later excelled in all of the techniques of the gaucho frontiersman. His mediocre education led to his personal animosity toward his more highly educated contemporaries.

Rosas commenced his long military career at 15, when he volunteered in the Buenos Aires forces to combat the second English invasion of his homeland. This experience led him to mistrust the motives of any European powers dealing with his government.

He married Encarnación de Escurra despite the objection of his mother at a time when marriages were usually arranged by the parents. Under Juan Martin de Pueyrredon, he organized a cavalry troop to fight against the Indians and welded his men into a disciplined army completely subservient to his orders. He soon entered the power struggle between the urban commercial leaders of Buenos Aires (the

portenos) and the landed aristocracy of the interior provinces on the side of the latter. When Rosas was victorious in battle, he seized control of the Buenos Aires government in 1829.

Supreme Dictator

At first Rosas was just a senior partner of the federalist leaders of the other provinces, but as these were overcome or liquidated, he became almost supreme in the Argentine. He then became the prototype of more recent 20th-century dictators. He destroyed the liberty of the press, dissolved Congress, organized a secret police (the Mazorca Club), and inaugurated a reign of terror which lasted until his final overthrow in 1852. He was a natural leader and a master of efficiency and ran the government like a well-organized estancia or a well-disciplined army.

Near the close of his first term Rosas turned over his office to Juan Ramón Balcarce and led an expedition to fight the Indians to the south. He was visited at his bivouac by Charles Darwin, who gives a flattering account of Rosas at this time. The campaign allowed Rosas to train and maintain a large armed force under his personal command.

Foreign Wars

During his absence, his wife and his former tutor, Dr. Maza, held the real reins of the government. Rosas resumed control of the government upon his return and became embroiled in constant warfare. In 1837 he was involved in a war with Andrés Santa Cruz of Bolivia. Victorious in this costly encounter, he was faced with the necessity of defending his government against an uprising by the portenos, under Juan Lavalle and aided by the French, who blockaded Buenos Aires. The French soon pulled out, and Rosas was once more victorious. When the defeated invaders took refuge in Uruguay, Rosas intervened in the political turmoil in that country and was drawn into a siege of Montevideo which lasted for 9 years. Britain and France intervened jointly, and once again the ports of the Argentine were blockaded. The Europeans were forced to give up their blockade, but Rosas was forced to withdraw from the Uruguayan venture.

Ouster and Exile

The blockade had curtailed commerce and caused a loss of customs revenues from which the Rosas government never recovered. The other provinces had been equally hurt, and Justo José Urquiza, governor of Entre-Ríos and a former Rosas lieutenant, turned against him and, in 1852, at the battle of Caseros, Rosas was overthrown and fled to England aboard the British ship Locust. He never returned to his native land and died in England in relative obscurity.

The new government tried Rosas in absentia and found him guilty of tyranny, violating natural law, and endangering the republic to satisfy his personal ambition. His immense fortune, consisting of lands and cattle, was confiscated, and most of his personal records were destroyed. Until the Juan Perón era no man's memory was more uniformly hated in Argentina, and to this day there are no monuments to his memory in his native land. Yet Rosas

was the man who had done the most to keep Latin America free of European domination. Urquiza, who overthrew him, provided him with the necessary funds to enable him to sustain himself during his exile.

Rosas' life had been a series of contradictions. He had come to power as a federalist and had then centered the government in Buenos Aires and the power in his own hands. Lacking in imagination, he alienated all of the intelligentsia and instituted a reign of terror and bloodshed. Yet throughout, his love of country was unquestioned, and he served it in the only way he knew.

Further Reading

Rosas was hated by all contemporary Argentine intellectuals, most of whom he had exiled. The outstanding example of such vituperation is D. F. Sarmiento, *Life in the Argentine Republic in the Days of the Tyrants: or, Civilization and Barbarism* (trans. 1868). An extensive biography is "Juan Manuel de Rosas, Greatest of Argentine Dictators" in George Washington University, Seminar Conference on Hispanic American Affairs, *South American Dictators during the First Century of Independence,* edited by A. Curtis Wilgus (1937). An excellent volume on the economic aspects of the Rosas administration is in Miron Burgin, *Economic Aspects of Argentine Federalism* (1946). □

Julius and Ethel Rosenberg

Julius (1918-1953) and Ethel (1915-1953) Rosenberg were a nondescript couple accused in 1950 by the United States government of operating a Soviet spy network and giving the Soviet Union plans for the atomic bomb.

The trial of the Rosenbergs became a political event of greater importance than any damage they may have done to the United States. It was one of the most controversial trials of the twentieth century, and it ended with their execution.

The arrest of the Rosenbergs was set in motion when the FBI arrested Klaus Fuchs, a British scientist who gave atomic secrets to the Soviets while working on the Manhattan project. Fuchs's arrest and confession led to the arrest of Harry Gold, a courier for Soviet spies. Gold in turn led investigators to David Greenglass, a small-time spy who confessed quickly. Greenglass then accused his sister Ethel and brother-in-law Julius of controlling his activities.

Julius Rosenberg was a committed communist who graduated from the City College of New York in 1939 with a degree in electrical engineering. He had married Ethel Greenglass in the summer of that year. She was a headstrong woman, active in organizing labor groups. The couple had two sons, Michael, born in 1943, and Robert, born in 1947.

Espionage Activities

Julius had opened a mechanic shop with his brother-in-law, but the business soon began to fail, largely due to a lack

of attention from Julius, who had begun to spy for the Soviets. He began by stealing manuals for radar tubes and proximity fuses, and by the late 1940s had two apartments set up as microfilm laboratories. He had become the coordinator of a large spy network.

Julius immediately realized the implications of Harry Gold's arrest and began to make arrangements to get out of the country, but the FBI moved swiftly and he was arrested in July 1950.

His wife was arrested in August. The government had little evidence against her, but hoped to use the threat of prosecution as a lever to persuade Julius to confess. The couple was charged with conspiracy to commit espionage, and their trial began on 6 March 1951. The prosecutor was attorney Irving Saypol, the judge was Irving Kaufman, and the defense was led by Emmanuel Bloch.

From the beginning the trial attracted national attention. Saypol and his young assistant, Roy Cohn, decided to keep the scope of the trial as narrow as possible, with establishing the Rosenbergs's guilt the main target, and exposing their spy ring a lesser concern. Nonetheless, the trial was punctuated by numerous arrests of spies associated with the Rosenbergs, some appearing in court to testify against them.

Defense Incompetence

From the beginning the defense had problems. Bloch tried to downplay the importance of the information the prosecution claimed the Rosenbergs had stolen, and then turned around and requested that all spectators and reporters be barred from the courtroom when the information was discussed. Bloch later said he was trying to impress the jurors with a bold move, but what he actually did was impress them with the importance of the information.

Bloch also accused David Greenglass of turning on his sister and her husband because of their failed business, but his efforts only elicited sympathy for a man who had been forced to turn in a family member. Greenglass damaged the Rosenbergs by testifying that Julius had arranged for him to give Harry Gold the design of the atomic bomb used on Nagasaki (which differed considerably from the Hiroshima bomb). When Gold himself testified, he named Anatoli Yakovlev as his contact. This directly tied the Rosenbergs to a known Soviet agent.

International Protests

After months in prison, the Rosenbergs still maintained their innocence and began to write poignant letters, which were widely published, protesting their treatment. The case was followed closely in Europe, where many felt the Rosenbergs were being persecuted as Jewish (though Judge Kaufman was also Jewish). A movement began to protest the "injustice" of the Rosenberg trial. Passions both for and against the Rosenbergs grew so great that they even threatened Franco-American relations, as the french were particularly harsh in their condemnation of the trial as a sham.

By the end of the trial the defense had all but collapsed under the weight of the evidence and Bloch's incompetence. His summation appealed to the jurors' emotions, while prosecutor Saypol ran cooly through the testimony. Although the evidence against Ethel was slight, the jury and the public had come to believe that she was the mastermind of the operation. Both she and Julius were found guilty and sentenced to death, a punishment more fitting a treason conviction than the lesser charge of espionage.

In the months between the sentencing and execution, criticism of the trial grew more strident, and major demonstrations were held. Nobel Prize winner Jean-Paul Sartre called the case "a legal lynching which smears with blood a whole nation."

In spite of attempts at appeal and a legal stay issued by Supreme Court Justice William O. Douglas, Julius and Ethel Rosenberg were executed on 19 June 1953, both refusing to confess.

Years after the execution the case still stirs debate. It can now be seen as arising from the height of Cold War hysteria fed by the Korean War, which had broken out the summer before the trial. It must be remembered that, although the Rosenbergs were communists and spies, they did not spy for an enemy of the United States, as the sentence might indicate, but rather for its wartime ally. Recent studies of the couple's activities show that the evidence against them was overwhelming. It is difficult, however, to imagine the execution of a married couple without understanding of the hysteria that the Cold War produced.

Further Reading

Hanseman, Robert G., "Julius Rosenberg," in *The Cold War: 1945-1991*, Vol. 1, edited by Benjamin Frankel, Gale Research, Detroit, Michigan, 1992, pp. 427–428

Meeropol, Michael, and Robert Meeropol, *We Are Your Sons*, University of Illinois, Chicago, 1986.

Radosh, Ronald, and Joyce Milton, *The Rosenberg File*, Holt, Rinehart & Winston, New York, 1983.

Schneir, Walter and Miriam, *Invitation to an Inquest*, Doubleday, New York, 1965.

Sharlitt, Joseph, *Fatal Error*, Scribners, New York, 1989. □

Julius Rosenwald

The American retailer and philanthropist Julius Rosenwald (1862-1932) held executive offices in Sears, Roebuck and Company, America's leading mail-order house.

J ulius Rosenwald was born in Springfield, Ill., on Aug. 12, 1862. He was active in the wholesale clothing business from 1879 until he joined Sears, Roebuck in 1895, just as the modern history of the company began. Rosenwald became vice president and owner of one-third of the company's stock.

Rosenwald succeeded Richard Warren Sears as president of Sears, Roebuck in 1908. As chief executive, he emphasized administration, system, and order. He was a careful merchandiser concerned with merchandise selection and restrained selling. He had great faith in the mail-order business and looked for long-run advantages. The company expanded enormously and entered the retail chain-store business during the years Rosenwald was a dominant figure.

In 1916 Rosenwald testified on wage policy for sales clerks before the Illinois Senate Committee on Vice. A highly successful profit-sharing plan for Sears, Roebuck employees instituted in 1916 was partly his achievement.

However, the Panic of 1920-1921—when wholesale and retail prices declined precipitously—caught Sears, Roebuck with an excessive inventory bought at high prices during World War I. To bail the company out, Rosenwald advanced money to Sears, Roebuck in 1921, though he was under no legal or moral obligation to act in this fashion. He ended his term as president in 1924 and became chairman of the board of directors, a position he held until he died.

Rosenwald was active in public service between 1916 and 1919 and was absent from his company's affairs for about the same time. He was appointed a member of the Council of National Defense and chairman of its committee on supplies. Philanthropy became more important to him after the Panic of 1920-1921. Rosenwald's philanthropy aimed at social welfare, and his donations benefited the Young Men's Christian Association and the Young Women's Christian Association, among other agencies. He was also active in a variety of Jewish organizations.

The most distinctive feature of Rosenwald's philanthropy was his interest in African Americans; the breadth of his involvement was unmatched by any other contemporary philanthropist. The Julius Rosenwald Fund, organized in 1917, stressed education and aided all levels of education from grade school to the university. Rosenwald also aided the National Urban League. His gifts on behalf of African Americans served as a stimulant to other donors. He died in Chicago on Jan. 6, 1932.

Further Reading

Morris R. Werner, *Julius Rosenwald: The Life of a Practical Humanitarian* (1939), a general biography, provides some material on Sears, Roebuck but focuses on Rosenwald's philanthropic interests. Boris Emmet and John E. Jeuck, *Catalogues and Counters: A History of Sears, Roebuck and Company* (1950), places Rosenwald in the context of his enterprise. An account of Rosenwald's foundation is Edwin R. Embree and Julia Waxman, *Investment in People: The Story of the Julius Rosenwald Fund* (1949). Henry Allen Bullock, *A History of Negro Education in the South* (1967), notes Rosenwald's philanthropic role in African American education.

Additional Sources

Bachmann, Lawrence Paul, *Julius Rosenwald*, Waltham, Mass.: American Jewish Historical Society, 1976.

Jarrette, Alfred Q., *Julius Rosenwald, son of a Jewish immigrant, a builder of Sears, Roebuck and Company, benefactor of mankind: a biography documented*, Greenville, S.C.: Southeastern University Press, 1975. □

Franz Rosenzweig

The German-born philosopher and writer Franz Rosenzweig (1886-1929) was important for his formulations and definitions of Jewish-Christian relations.

Franz Rosenzweig was born at Kassel on Dec. 25, 1886. Rosenzweig first took up medicine; but, not finding this to his liking and discovering also a certain dichotomy in his life, he turned to the study of history and philosophy. He followed this with law studies. His early upbringing and education inclined him more and more to conversion to Christianity. However, in 1913 he attended an Orthodox Day of Atonement service and suddenly decided to halt his drift to Christianity and to adopt seriously the religion of his Jewish forefathers. It was these three themes, Christianity, Judaism, and Atonement (redemption), that formed the kernel of his life achievement in religious research.

While serving in the German army during World War I, Rosenzweig initiated a lively correspondence with Eugen Rosenstock concerning the relationship of Jewish and Christian theology. This correspondence was published (1935) only after Rosenzweig's death. He also started at this time one of his outstanding works—*Der Stern der Erlösung* (1921). In this he expressed his full thought on the nature of religion and the mutual relationship of Judaism and Christianity. Religion for Rosenzweig was a three-way relationship; he distinguished God, man, and the world as three distinct beings, none of which could be confused with the other. The point was important for Rosenzweig because on it he broke with the German idealism of his day and foreshadowed the position later taken up by the existentialist philosophers of the 20th century. He then proceeded to define the triple relationship: between God and the world, it is one of creator and created; between God and man, it is one of revelator to the recipient (man) of that revelation; and between man and the world, it is one of redemption. Man has a redemptive function for the world: he helps to save it.

Rosenzweig then proceeded to define Jewish-Christian relations. He spoke of two Covenants, one between God and the Jews, the other between God and other men (the Christian Covenant). He considered the two Covenants as complementary elements in God's overall plan of redemption for the world and for man. Yet, Rosenzweig held, the two Covenants were mutually exclusive. This was a bold step for a Jewish thinker; it involved an admission that some limitation had to be placed on the Jewish claim of being exclusively and uniquely the Chosen People. Consequently, it involved much protest and controversy.

Rosenzweig started off as an idealist philosopher; he broke, however, with this philosophic idealism because his religious beliefs and studies interfered. In 1920 he also established his Freies Jüdisches Lehrhaus, an adult study center, at Frankfurt am Main. Its academic excellence and religious commitment provided an example on which many such institutions were founded in Germany. Unfortunately, he was attacked by a progressive paralysis in 1921. In 2

years he lost his ability to speak, write, or move. With his wife's help, however, he turned out several important minor works published as his *Kleinere Schriften* in 1937 together with an annotated version of 92 poems of Judah Halevi. He undertook (1925) a German translation of the Bible with Martin Buber, but he did not see its completion and publication (1938). He died on Dec. 9, 1929, at Frankfurt.

Further Reading

A full-length work in English is Nahum Norbert Glatzer, ed., *Franz Rosenzweig: His Life and Thought* (1953; rev. ed. 1961). See also Bernard Martin, comp., *Great Twentieth Century Jewish Philosophers* (1969), and Eugen Rosenstock-Huessy, *Judaism despite Christianity* (1969). □

Ileana Ros-Lehtinen

Ileana Ros-Lehtinen (born 1952) is the first Hispanic-American woman to serve in the United States congress.

Being first has become something that Ileana Ros-Lehtinen does quite well. In 1982, she became the first Cuban-born female to be elected to the Florida state legislature. Seven years later, after a successful career as a state legislator, she won a special election held on August 29, 1989, to fill the seat left vacant by the death of long-time Miami political powerhouse Claude D. Pepper. A few days after her victory, Ros-Lehtinen was sworn in as the first Cuban American, as well as the first Hispanic woman, ever elected to the U.S. Congress. "As the first Cuban-American elected to Congress," *Boston Globe* commentator Chris Black noted, "she also will be likely to become one of the most visible, most quoted Cuban-born politicians in the nation."

Ros-Lehtinen (pronounced ross-LAY-teh-nin), who is known as Lily to her family and friends, was born July 15, 1952, in the Cuban capital city of Havana, to Enrique Emilio Ros, a certified public accountant, and Amanda Adato Ros. In 1960, she and her family—including her parents and a brother—fled to Miami from Cuba, a year after political leader Fidel Castro's revolution rocked that tiny island nation. Almost immediately, Ros-Lehtinen's parents became involved with other recent refugees in plotting the downfall of the Castro regime. But after the failure of an invasion attempt by anti-Castro forces at Cuba's Bay of Pigs in 1961, the possibility of returning to Cuba became more and more remote, and Ros vowed to raise his children as loyal Americans. His wife recalled in a *Boston Globe* article how strongly her husband felt about his decision: "He said you cannot educate two kids without a flag and a country. This is going to be their country and they have to love it."

Ros-Lehtinen earned her associate of arts degree from Miami-Dade County Community College in 1972 and her bachelor of arts degree in English from Miami's Florida International University in 1975. Eleven years later she completed requirements for a master of science in educa-

tional leadership from the same institution. Since then, she has continued her studies as a doctoral candidate in educational administration at the University of Miami. Before embarking on her political career, Ros-Lehtinen worked as a teacher and was principal for ten years at Eastern Academy, a school she founded. Her love of politics came as a legacy from her father who had concentrated so much of his life on the hope of restoring democracy to his native land. He is said to have been the chief architect of her political career and was at her side when she announced her victory in her U.S. Congressional race.

Launched Political Career as State Representative

Ros-Lehtinen's first elected office was in the Florida state legislature, where she served as a representative from 1982 to 1986 and as a state senator from 1986 to 1989. While in the state legislature she met her future husband, Dexter Lehtinen, who was also at the time a member of that legislative body. Although early in her career Ros-Lehtinen showed a tendency to focus on issues of a global nature rather than on those affecting her constituents in a personal way, Black wrote in the *Boston Globe* that Ros-Lehtinen eventually became "a politician of the opposite extreme, a pragmatic legislator focused almost exclusively on the most parochial of issues. One Miami political reporter now describes her as 'a pothole kind of legislator,' much more concerned with the specific needs of individuals and businesses in her district than broader changes in public policy."

When Ros-Lehtinen resigned her seat in the state senate shortly before the August 3, 1989, primary, it appeared—much to the dismay of the Miami area's non-Hispanic voters—that the race to fill Florida's 18th congressional district seat might be a head-to-head battle between two Cuban American women. Early favorites included Ros-Lehtinen on the Republican side and Miami City Commissioner Rosario Kennedy for the Democrats. However, the opponent who emerged from the primary was Gerald F. Richman, an attorney, a former president of the Florida Bar Association, and a Jew. The Ros-Lehtinen-Richman campaign was marked by deep cultural and racial tensions and came to be one of the most ethnically divided congressional races in Florida's history. A highlight of an otherwise brutal contest came from President George Bush who not only gave Ros-Lehtinen his personal endorsement, but made a special trip to Miami to deliver a speech on her behalf.

Most of the controversy surrounding the campaign grew out of a response to Republican party chair Lee Atwater's announcement that since the district was 50 percent Hispanic, electing a Cuban American to the seat was of utmost importance. Richman, the Democratic candidate, was quoted in a *Time* article as having countered Atwater's claim with the assertion, "This is an American seat." Cuban American and other Hispanic voters were deeply offended by Richman's reply and the implication it carried that Hispanics are not truly Americans. Spanish-speaking radio stations in the Miami area assured their listeners that a vote for Richman would be the equivalent of voting for Castro. Another source of division during the campaign came from the National Republican Congressional Committee (NRCC) which, according to reports in *National Review,* attempted to run Ros-Lehtinen's campaign from Washington. William McGurn explained the problem with a quote from a Republican insider: "The NRCC treated this district like a colony. . . . Their attitude was that they knew Florida's 18th better than the people who live here."

Won Turbulent Race for U.S. Congressional Seat

Triumphing over the bitterness of the campaign, Ros-Lehtinen emerged victorious from the race, capturing 53 percent of the vote. Post-election analysis showed that voters largely seemed to cast their ballot based on their ethnic heritage: 96 percent of blacks and 88 percent of non-Hispanic whites voted for Democratic candidate Richman; while 90 percent of Hispanics, who voted in record numbers, voted for Ros-Lehtinen. In her victory speech, the new congresswoman maintained that she would work to heal the wounds caused by the campaign. "It's been a terrible divisive campaign," she told the *New York Times.* "But now it's time for healing. I know that there are a lot of people out there who feel alienated." Ros-Lehtinen's win was also seen as a victory for the Republican party because the seat she had captured had belonged to the Democrats for 26 years. When Ros-Lehtinen's seat came up for election in 1990, she received 60 percent of the vote and a decisive mandate to continue her political career.

During her tenure, Ros-Lehtinen has been a member of the Foreign Affairs committee and has served on its subcommittee on Human Rights and International Organizations as well as its subcommittee on Western Hemisphere affairs. She has also been involved with the subcommittee on Employment and Housing, where she is the ranking minority member. In an article focusing on Hispanic political candidates, which appeared in *Hispanic,* Anna Maria Arias described Ros-Lehtinen's stand on issues important to voters in her district. According to Arias, Ros-Lehtinen supports bilingual education, is "in favor of a seven-day waiting period for the purchasing of guns, and voted for a bill that would improve veterans' benefits." Ros-Lehtinen is also vehemently anti-abortion, except to save a woman's life, favors a constitutional amendment to ban flag burning, and advocates the death penalty for convicted organizers of drug rings.

True to her ethnic roots, Ros-Lehtinen remains a staunch adversary of Castro and an equally outspoken champion of a free Cuba. In 1990, she expressed her strong opposition to South-African leader Nelson Mandela's visit to Florida during his eight-city tour of the United States. a trip that engendered a virtual hero's welcome for him in the other states to which he traveled. While there seemed to be a near unanimous outpouring of praise for Mandela and his efforts to end apartheid (racial segregation) in his native country, Ros-Lehtinen felt she could not honor a man who had not only publicly embraced such advocates of violent revolution as the Palestine Liberation Organization's Yasser Arafat and Libya's Muammar Gaddafi, but who also was on record as a strong supporter of Castro. She pointed out that Cuban Americans longing for a return to democracy in their country of origin could not forget that members of Mandela's African National Congress had received military training on Cuban soil.

Voiced Opposition to 1991 Pan American Games

Ros-Lehtinen again spoke out against Castro when she condemned participation in the Pan American Games, an Olympics-like international sports competition, held in Cuba during the first two weeks of August in 1991. She argued that Castro's bid to have the Games in his country was merely a ploy to bolster Cuba's ailing economy and to provide ready propaganda supporting his regime. In a *Christian Science Monitor* article on the topic, the congresswoman wrote: "Castro has his circus for now, but despite the fanfare of the Pan American Games, he is an anachronism in a world that values democracy and freedom. It will not be long till he follows the path of the dinosaurs into extinction. Cuba's economic crisis is so desperate that Castro would shave his own beard if that would give him the American dollars which he holds so dear."

The ethnic pride Ros-Lehtinen inherited from her father remains strong in the politician, and perhaps because of this, she is very conscious of her position as a role model for Hispanics. She also values the achievements made by other Hispanic women, and when presented with a special award from *Hispanic* magazine in 1992, she praised their suc-

cesses. "[The Hispanic woman] is an accomplished writer, or a computer programmer, or an attorney, or a doctor, as well as a loving wife and mother." She also believes that Hispanic women will continue to make contributions in the future. "Now, more than ever," she wrote in *Vista,* "we Hispanic women must re-energize and refocus our efforts to realize the vast potential that lies within our grasp."

Further Reading

Boston Globe, August 31, 1989, p. 3.
Christian Science Monitor, August 9, 1991, p. 18.
Hispanic, September 1990, p. S5; October 1990, p. 26; August 1992, p. 28.
Ladies' Home Journal, November 1991, p. 182.
National Catholic Reporter, April 19, 1991, p. 1.
National Review, November 24, 1989, p. 39.
New York Times, August 31, 1989, p. A16; October 22, 1996, p. A24.
Time, September 11, 1989, p. 31.
Vista, February 4, 1992, pp. 6, 22.
Washington Post, July 30, 1989, p. A4; August 17, 1989, p. A4. □

Antonio Rosmini-Serbati

The Italian philosopher and priest Antonio Rosmini-Serbati (1797-1855), who supported the Risorgimento, was one of the few churchmen of his day who endeavored to lay a philosophical and theological foundation for Roman Catholic involvement in national politics.

Antonio Rosmini-Serbati was born at Rovereto on March 24, 1797. After the usual studies, he was ordained a priest in 1821. Up to his time and for some time after, the Church forbade Roman Catholics in Italy to take part in national politics. Rosmini's studies led him to consider in what way Catholics could actively engage in politics, social reform, and the study of science without having to renounce the principles of their faith. He perceived that the educational methods of the Roman Church and its presentation of doctrinal matters were not suited either to the minds or to the tempers of his contemporaries. He also saw great deficiencies in the training of the clergy.

In 1828 Rosmini-Serbati established his Institute of Charity (Rosminians) at Monte Calvario near Domodossola. He modeled it on the Jesuit order, whose devotion to the Church and multifaceted activities he admired; it was approved by Pope Gregory XVI in 1839. The institute was established in England by Father Luigi Gentili, and there it played a part in the revival of Catholicism.

At this time the two major forces with which the Roman Catholic Church contended were nationalism and philosophic idealism. Nationalism was to change the face of Europe within a hundred years. Philosophic idealism supplied Karl Marx and Friedrich Engels with the bases of their theories and influenced the scientific thought of men such

as Charles Darwin and Sigmund Freud. To Rosmini's credit, he understood the importance of both movements. But in trying to change the minds of his contemporaries, he was like a man with his shoulder against a mountain.

The election of Pope Pius IX in 1848 seemed providential to Rosmini. The new pope was known as the "pope of progress" because of his liberal views. When war broke out between Italy and Austria in 1848, Pius declared the papacy to be neutral because of its universal significance for all men. By this time Rosmini was known for his views. The Piedmontese government empowered him to negotiate a settlement with Pius. Rosmini wrote an account of this mission called *Della missione a Roma . . . negli anni 1848-49* (1881). Pius soon changed from his earlier liberalism to a hard-core conservatism, and Rosmini fell into disfavor. He was attacked, his teachings were declared suspect, and he had to retire from all active participation in public life and teaching.

Rosmini's philosophy and teaching were based on an adaptation of current idealism. He placed at the center of his system what he called "ideal being." This was a hybrid sharing traits of the Neoplatonist ideal of Renaissance thinkers and the abstract Kantian idea of the unknowable *Ding-an-Sich*. Rosmini held that the "ideal being" was a reflection of God to be found in every man. He rescued the Kantian idea from its unknowability by declaring that not only was it most knowable but that it was the foundation of all else: the rights of the individual and man's concepts of truth and logic, and of his political and legal system. He expounded his theories in a series of books: *Maxims of*

Christian Perfection (1830); *New Essay on the Origin of Ideas* (3 vols., 1838); *Theodicy* (1845); and *Psychology* (1850). His political thought was expressed in his *Of the Five Wounds of the Holy Church* and *The Constitution according to Social Justice* (both 1848).

When Rosmini fell into disfavor, Pius IX had all his works examined for possible error. But on examination by the Roman Congregation of the Index, they were declared free from error. Rosmini died on July 1, 1855.

Further Reading

Biographical studies of Rosmini-Serbati include Giovanni Battista Pagani, *The Life of Antonio Rosmini-Serbati* (Eng. trans. 1907), and Claude Richard Harbord Leetham, *Rosmini: Priest, Philosopher and Patriot* (1957).

Additional Sources

Ingoldsby, Mary F., *A short life of Antonio Rosmini, 1797-1855,* Stresa, Italy: International Centre for Rosminian Studies, 1983.

Leetham, Claude, *Rosmini: priest and philosopher,* New York: New City Press, 1982. □

Betsy Ross

Although the evidence is not solid, most historians point to upholsterer Betsy Ross (1752-1836) as the woman who sewed the first U.S. flag.

On June 14, 1777, the Continental Congress, on a motion from John Adams, adopted the stars and stripes as the national flag. History leaves its students with very few clues as to who designed and created the original flag, but it has been long attributed to the Philadelphia seamstress and upholsterer Betsy Ross. So widely accepted is the story of this legendary flagmaker, the United States government issued a commemorative postage stamp in 1952 in celebration of the two hundredth anniversary of her birth.

Elizabeth Griscom was the eighth of 17 children born to Samuel and Rebecca Griscom. Her father operated a building business, which had been established by her great-grandfather Andrew Griscom, who had emigrated from England in 1680. Raised and educated as a Quaker, she was disowned by the Quaker church, the Society of Friends, in 1773 when she eloped to Gloucester, New Jersey, to marry John Ross, an Episcopalian.

Opened Upholstery Shop

Ross and her husband returned to Philadelphia, where they opened an upholstery and sewing shop on Arch Street, which also served as their home. John, a member of the state militia, was killed three years later in an explosion while on guard duty. After the death of her husband, Betsy continued the day-to-day operations of the shop.

boy, his grandmother told him of her involvement with the stars and stripes while on her deathbed. According to *Who Was Who in the American Revolution,* the legend stated: "(George) Washington, (George) Ross, and Robert Morris came to Mrs. Ross's house in June 1776 and asked her to make a flag for the new country that was on the verge of declaring its independence. She suggested a design to Washington, he made a rough pencil sketch on the basis of it, and she there upon made the famous flag in her back parlor. She is supposed also to have suggested the use of the five- rather than the six-pointed star chosen by Washington."

Although there is no written record to support this story, there is ample evidence, in the form of receipts, that she made numerous flags for the Pennsylvania State Navy, and many efforts to refute the legend have failed. The millions of members of the Betsy Ross Memorial Association would have one accept the story as fact, but until further evidence is revealed, it cannot be either proved or disproved.

Further Reading

Dictionary of American Biography, Charles Scribner's Sons, pp. 174-175.
Whitney, David C., *The Colonial Spirit of '76,* J. G. Ferguson Publishing Company, 1974, pp. 352-353. □

On June 15, 1777, Ross married Captain Joseph Ashburn, at Old Swedes' Church. Together they had two daughters. As with Ross's previous husband, Ashburn's military career once again made her a widow. The first mate of the brigantine Patty, he was captured at sea by the British Navy. He died on March 3, 1782, in the Old Mill Prison, Plymouth, England.

The news of her husband's death was brought to Ross by John Claypoole, a lifelong friend of both Ross and Ashburn. This friendship quickly grew into more, and the two were married May 8, 1783. Together, they continued to run the upholstery shop. Returning to her Quaker roots, Betsy and her husband joined the Society of Free Quakers. Before he died in 1817, he and Ross had five daughters.

After her third husband's death, Ross lived the remainder of her life with one of her daughters and continued to work in the shop until 1827, when she turned it over to her daughter. Upon her death on January 30, 1836, she was buried in Mount Moriah Cemetery, Philadelphia. The house where she purportedly made the flag was marked as a historical landmark in 1887.

Birth of a Legend

There is very little evidence to support the story that Ross was the creator of the original flag. The story of her contribution to the design and creation of the first flag of the United States was first put forth by her grandson, William Canby, in March of 1870 before a meeting of the Historical Society of Pennsylvania. He claims that as an 11-year-old

Diana Ross

Diana Ross (born 1944), once the lead singer for the Motown supergroup the Supremes, was the most successful female singer of the Rock 'n' Roll era. In the next few decades, she continued to enjoy success with a solo career and numerous television and film appearances.

Diana Ross was born on March 26, 1944, in Detroit, Michigan. She was the second of six children of Fred and Ernestine Ross, who lived in Brewster-Douglass, one of Detroit's low income housing districts. While her family was active in the Baptist church choir, Diana learned secular music from a cousin. She played baseball and took tap dance and majorette lessons at Brewster Center.

At age 14 Ross tried out for a part in a school musical, but was turned down. The brief failure turned into good fortune, as she was invited to sing with the Primettes, a girls' vocal group that included Florence Ballard and Mary Wilson among its members. She sang with the Primettes throughout her high school years at Cass Technical High School, where she took sewing and fashion design courses. The male counterparts of the Primettes were called the Primes, and their members included Paul Williams and Eddie Kendricks, who would later form part of the Motown superstar group the Temptations.

Yet another Motown superstar, Smokey Robinson, introduced Ross and the Primettes at Motown Studios, where they visited frequently until they met Motown producer Berry Gordy. Gordy instructed Ross and her friends to finish high school and come back, which they did in 1962. Ross, Ballard, and Wilson then signed a contract with Motown, and Ballard selected a name for the group—the "Supremes"—a name which Ross disliked.

The Supremes released a number of singles and often sang background vocals for Marvin Gaye and Mary Wells at local Detroit record hops. "Let Me Go the Right Way" became the first Supremes song to register on the national charts, and it enabled the group to join the touring Motor Town Revue. "Where Did Our Love Go?" was their first national number one hit, selling over two-million singles, and the Supremes became the Revue's opening act. Ross' ambition and talent helped the trio turn the fierce competition for recording songs at Motown in their favor, and she became the group's lead singer.

The Supremes proceeded to lead Motown and its outstanding artists into its heyday in the 1960s with a series of number one hits that included "Baby Love" (1964), "Stop! In the Name of Love" (1965), "Back in My Arms Again" (1965) and "I Hear a Symphony" (1966). A popular television group, the Supremes continued to skyrocket in popularity along with the Motown label, and their principal songwriting team—Eddie Holland, Lamont Dozier, and Brian Holland—produced many more of their number one songs, including "You Keep Me Hangin' On" (1966), "You

Can't Hurry Love" (1966), "Love Is Here and Now You're Gone" (1967), and "The Happening" (1967).

Holland-Dozier-Holland left Motown in 1967, and the Supremes entered their next phase with a new billing as Diana Ross and the Supremes. Florence Ballard was replaced by Cindy Birdsong, also in 1967. The year 1968 brought "Love Child," yet another top hit, this one written by themselves. By this time rumors had begun to circulate about Ross leaving the group, and they reached their peak when her performance in the 1969 television special "Like Hep" outdid co-stars Lucille Ball, Dinah Shore, and comedians Rowan and Martin. Diana Ross' last single with the group was, ironically, the number one hit "Someday, We'll Be Together" (1969). Indeed, she began her solo career after their last appearance together in January of 1970.

Things would only get better for Ross. Motown Records invested heavily in her new career, which debuted with "Reach Out and Touch (Somebody's Hand)" (1970). Many changes began to take place in her personal life as well. She had helped the Jackson 5 get its start with Motown with her well-developed business acumen that she had learned from Berry Gordy, and she had moved into her new Beverly Hills home. In 1971 Ross was married to Robert Silberstein, a pop-music manager, with whom she had three daughters— Rhonda, Tracee, and Chudney.

Diana Ross was cast as the legendary jazz singer Billie Holiday in the Motown film production *Lady Sings the Blues*. Her critically acclaimed performance earned her an Academy Award nomination for best actress. In 1973 she returned to her customary position atop the national record charts with "Touch Me in the Morning." Her next film was *Mahogany* (1975), from which her "Theme From Mahogany" (1976) was nominated for the Academy Awards' best song in a motion picture and topped the record charts again. After her third daughter was born in 1975 she and Silberstein were divorced.

Ross' hit parade continued with the number one "Love Hangover" (1976). She closed out the decade with a Broadway show entitled "An Evening With Diana Ross" (1976-1977); a March 6, 1977, television special that featured her alone; and a portrayal as Dorothy in Motown's film production of the Broadway show *The Wiz* (1978).

Ross continued to perform in concerts, in Atlantic City and Las Vegas casinos, and in charity functions. Her 1980 single "Upside Down" was her 16th number one hit, a record surpassed only by the Beatles. She moved to Connecticut with her three daughters and in 1985 married Norwegian shipping tycoon Arne Naess, Jr. In 1989, Ross made a return to Motown with a new album titled "Workin' Overtime", and in 1991 collaborated with Stevie Wonder and other artists to make "The Force Behind the Power", a group of contemporary ballads. In January of 1994, she received critical acclaim for her role as a schizophrenic in the ABC television movie *Out of Darkness*.

But tragedy marred Ross' new-found success in film in 1996 when her brother, Arthur Ross, and his wife, Patricia Ann Robinson, were found smothered to death on June 22, in Oak Park, Michigan. Ross and her family put up a reward of $25,000 for any information leading to an arrest. In September of 1996, two men, Ricky Brooks and Remel Howard, were charged with the killings. Police had no motive at the time, only to say that drugs were involved. "Like all survivors," quotes *The Harmony Illustrated Encyclopedia of Rock,* "Ross has adapted well, handling pop, soul, disco and rock masterfully." And as evident in a recent interview with Ross and her daughters, she was handling her life in that same fashion.

Further Reading

Tributes to the hard working Diana Ross' personification of the American dream are numerous. Her biographies include Lenore K. Itkowitz, *Diana Ross* (1974), Geoff Brown, *Diana Ross* (1981), J. Rand Taraborrelli's *Diana* (1985), and *Diana Ross* by James Haskins (1985). Her autobiography, *Secrets of a Sparrow,* was published in 1995. □

Edward Alsworth Ross

Edward Alsworth Ross (1866-1951), one of the founders of American sociology, is best remembered for his "Social Control."

Edward A. Ross was born in Virden, Ill., on Dec. 12, 1866. His father was a farmer, and his mother a schoolteacher. At 20 Ross graduated from Coe College in Cedar Rapids, Iowa; at 22, after two years as a teacher at the Ford Dodge Commercial Institute, he left for graduate study at the University of Berlin; and at 24 he received his doctorate in political economy at Johns Hopkins University.

In 1893 Ross was appointed full professor at Leland Stanford University, where he remained until his celebrated dismissal, in 1900, over the question of his right to speak out as a reformer on public issues. After five years at the University of Nebraska, he left in 1906 for the University of Wisconsin, famed for its Progressive-minded faculty and teachings. He spent the rest of his career at Wisconsin, first as professor of sociology and then as department chairman. He retired in 1937 and died in Madison.

Ross achieved national fame as a writer and popular lecturer. He authored 27 books and over 300 articles. His work can best be understood as the creative response of a reform-minded sociologist to the problems produced by the rapid industrialization and urbanization of the nation. *Social Control* (1901), a classic in American sociology, surveyed the institutions and values that would be needed to maintain individual freedom and social stability in an industrial order. *Social Psychology* (1908), the first textbook published in that field in the United States, similarly delineated the role of public opinion, custom, ceremony, and convention in maintaining social stability. *The Principles of Sociology* (1920, 1930, 1937), for many years one of the most popular texts in the field, stressed the role that the social processes can play in ensuring human progress.

More explicitly reformist in outlook were Ross's many books for the layman. *Sin and Society* (1907) established

Ross as a major figure in Progressive thought; other popular works advocating social reform include *Changing America* (1909) and *The Social Trend* (1922). He also published many books on social conditions in Europe, Asia, and Africa. In 1917 he went to Russia to report on the Bolshevik Revolution and for many years advocated recognition of the Soviet Union by the U.S. government and an appreciation of the improvements the Soviets brought to the economic and social life of the Russian people.

For a time Ross was active as a nativist. In his early career he espoused the superiority of the Anglo-Saxon peoples and advocated immigration restriction to prevent a large-scale influx of southern and eastern Europeans to the United States. In the 1920s his nativism included a program of eugenics and the nationwide prohibition of liquor. By 1930 Ross shed these notions and spent the greater part of his efforts promoting the New Deal reform and the freedoms of the individual. He served as the national chairman of the American Civil Liberties Union (1940-1950).

As a popularizer of the notion that the purpose of sociology is the reform of society, Ross had no peer among American sociologists in his lifetime. An erudite scholar, inspiring lecturer, courageous reformer, and uncompromising champion of freedom for the individual, he fulfilled the role he established for himself admirably.

Further Reading

Ross's autobiography is *Seventy Years of It* (1936). For his biography see Julius Weinberg, *Edward Alsworth Ross and the Sociology of Progressivism* (1971). His sociological theories are best explained by William L. Kolb, "The Sociological Theories of Edward Alsworth Ross," in Harry Elmer Barnes, ed., *An Introduction to the History of Sociology* (1948). Other works which place Ross in the history of sociology are Charles Hunt Page, *Class and American Sociology: From Ward to Ross* (1940); Howard W. Odum, *American Sociology: The Story of Sociology in the United States through 1950* (1951); and Heinz Maus, *A Short History of Sociology* (1956; trans. 1962).

Additional Sources

Ross, Edward Alsworth, *Seventy years of it: an autobiography,* New York: Arno Press, 1977, 1936. □

Harold Ross

Harold Ross (1892-1951) founded the *New Yorker* and remained at its helm for a quarter century. His idiosyncratic direction molded the magazine, with its blend of urbane wit and moral purpose.

Harold Wallace Ross was born November 6, 1892, in Aspen, Colorado, to George and Ida (Martin) Ross. His father was then in the lead mining industry and later worked at contracting and wrecking. Ross grew up in Salt Lake City and attended high school there, the whole extent of his formal education. At age 13 he went to work as a reporter for the *Salt Lake City Tribune.* In 1908 he and a friend left town, bumming their way west. Ross made it as far as Needles, California, where he briefly worked as a timekeeper before returning to Salt Lake City.

In 1910 he went back to California in earnest, working as a reporter, first for the *Marysville Appeal,* then for the *Sacramento Union.* By 1912 he was in the Panama Canal Zone, employed by the *Panama Star and Herald.* His itinerant journalistic career continued in New Orleans (for the *Item*), in Atlanta (for the *Journal*), and in San Francisco (for the *Call*). It was at the *Call* that he earned the nickname "Rough House." He was noted for such exploits as leading a former king of Siam on an incognito tour of the local night life and spiriting an excellent set of wicker furniture from the Danish pavilion at the Pacific Exposition, bestowing it on the local press club.

In 1917 Ross enlisted in the Army's Railway Engineer Corps, but he spent little time in those ranks, volunteering instead to work on *Stars and Stripes.* He was immediately made editor of that publication. His editorial board included a number of men who were to prove important in his later life, notably the belle-lettrist Alexander Woollcott. While in Paris with the army he married Jane Grant, the first of his three wives. She was a reporter for the *New York Times* and an ardent feminist. At that time Ross also founded a circle of wits he called the "Thanatopsis Literary and Inside Straight Club," which was publicized by Franklin Pierce Adams (F.P.A.) in his *New York World* column. This

cabal was eventually to mutate into the famed Algonquin Round Table.

Founding the New Yorker

Returning to New York, Ross made an unsuccessful attempt to continue *Stars and Stripes* in peacetime as the *Home Sector Magazine,* but he soon found himself working on various tasks for the Butterick Publishing Company. In 1921 he became editor of the *American Legion Weekly,* but he left two years later, feeling that the publication was becoming too politicized. He worked for a year (1924) as editor of the humor magazine *Judge.* Sometime that year Ross got together with yeast magnate Raoul Fleischmann, with the idea of starting a magazine. The proposal was drawn up in the winter and signed by a group of advisory editors: Ralph Barton, Heywood Broun, Marc Connelly, Edna Ferber, Rea Irvin, George S. Kaufman, Alice Duer Miller, Dorothy Parker, Laurence Stallings, and Alexander Woollcott. The *New Yorker* began publication in February 1925.

The cover of that first issue, the work of Rea Irvin, has become familiar to all who read the *New Yorker,* since the magazine revives it for a late February issue each year. It depicts a Regency dandy, whom humorist Corey Ford dubbed "Eustace Tilley," inspecting a butterfly through a lorgnette. Many of the magazine's features were new and startling, mostly in their insistence on the primacy of the text over the identity of its authors. There was, for example, no table of contents (although one was introduced in 1960 and remains to this day) and bylines appeared—in smallish type—at the end of pieces, rather than following the title. For all its innovation and wit, the *New Yorker* was not an initial success. Its humor was judged drab in comparison to the hilarity provided by the then-satirical *Life* and Ross's former vehicle, *Judge.* Circulation, which began at 15,000 for the first issue, had by that August plummeted to a mere 2,700. This was an impoverished period when, as James Thurber relates, Ross once inquired of Dorothy Parker why she had not come into the office to write a particular piece, and she replied, "Someone was using the pencil."

The *New Yorker* nearly met its death then, but somehow Ross persuaded Fleischmann to pour more money in, and by and by the publication stabilized. Ross' acquaintance with the members of the Round Table at the Algonquin Hotel did much both in terms of supplying writers and material and in terms of building a legend around the young magazine. The spirit of those famous wits—Parker, Woollcott, George Kaufman, Marc Connelly, Charles MacArthur, Robert Benchley, and Herman Mankiewicz, among others—permeated the *New Yorker's* style. Ross also had considerable success, both through acuity and luck, in hiring young talent. By the later 1920s he had engaged both James Thurber and E. B. White, who were to be mainstays of the magazine. Thurber, White, and Russell Maloney devised "The Talk of the Town," the magazine's flagship rubric, composed of anecdotes, overheard items, and miniature essays, all unsigned and distinguished by the editorial first person plural. White for many years was in sole charge of the "newsbreaks," the page-bottom items reprinting felicitous misprints and solecisms from other publications. Ross signed up a legion of young cartoonists, including Peter Arno, Helen Hokinson, Gluyas Williams, Mary Petty, Otto Soglow, and later Charles Addams and William Steig, whose various styles were also to be forever associated with the *New Yorker.*

Ross the Editor—Ross the Man

In spite of his good fortune in hiring contributors, Ross never really succeeded in finding his ideal managing editor. Such an enormous burden of expectation was placed on this post that its incumbents—who were variously referred to as "Jesuses," "geniuses," and "miracle men"—seldom occupied the chair for more than a few months. The long parade of "geniuses" under Ross included such otherwise famous names as Thurber, Ralph Ingersoll (later editor of *PM*), Ogden Nash, Joseph Moncure March, and James M. Cain. Ross was a perfectionist and a stickler for accuracy at the same time that he was idiosyncratic and often harebrained. He originated the *New Yorker's* ironclad fact-checking system (modeled on the one used by the *Saturday Evening Post*) and insisted on editing all copy and reviewing everything— including advertisements—himself.

Ross was a tall, awkward man who betrayed his western origins even while at the helm of the epitome of metropolitan sophistication. He split infinitives with abandon while enforcing the magazine's grammatical rigor and instituted a prohibition on anything even remotely sexual in implication while talking like the proverbial mule-skinner. He was noted for his "Rossisms," a species of inspired malapropism akin to Goldwynisms. He once exclaimed, "I don't want you to think I'm not incoherent," and one time leaned into a room at the office to enquire of the assemblage, "Is Moby Dick the whale or the man?" Ross had a mobile face; big lower lip; large, uneven teeth; and a mop of hair which, in his early days, stuck straight up, a phenomenon which he claimed to be the result of a stagecoach accident in childhood.

As an editor he was formidable, brilliant, unpredictable, and furiously dedicated. He insisted on making every sentence of copy clear to the least informed reader and could not abide suggestions that seemed contrary to logic. A well-known story concerns his struggle with a Peter Arno cartoon: a shower booth has completely filled up with water, and the man inside, holding his nose, his legs floating upward, tries to get his wife's attention. Ross long resisted publishing the cartoon because, he maintained, even if the door were stuck and the faucets jammed, there would still be a space at the door's bottom through which the water could escape.

Ross's contradictions inspired an odd mixture of exasperation and love in those around him. The English artist Paul Nash told Thurber, "He is like your skyscrapers. They are unbelievable, but they are there." Someone else once said, "His mind is uncluttered by culture. That's why he can give prose and pictures the clearest concentration of any editor in the world." Ross, in fact, was noted for reading few books and being deeply suspicious of high culture. Thurber himself wrote, "The *New Yorker* was created out of the

friction produced by Ross Positive and Ross Negative." The heat produced by this friction was impressive enough to raise the magazine's circulation to some 200,000 by the early 1940s, around that same period establishing the highest advertising revenues of any magazine in the country.

Meanwhile, almost every American writer of note had published in the *New Yorker* at least once. The magazine was equally shrewd about developing its local talent. Besides Thurber and White, there was the satire of S.J. Perelman, the reportage of Wolcott Gibbs and of Morris Markey, the "cliché expert" casuals by Frank Sullivan, the H*Y*M*A*N*K*A*P*L*A*N saga by Leonard Q. Ross (Leo Rosten), Ruth McKenny's stories of her sister Eileen, Richard Lockridge's tales of Mr. and Mrs. North, and Clarence Day's anecdotes about his father. After World War II the magazine became more serious, but without sacrificing its famous light touch. In 1946 an entire issue was devoted to John Hersey's long article on the bombing of Hiroshima, a major coup and a journalistic milestone. Ross earlier had solved the problem of "miracle men" by establishing a team of managing editors. The "fact editor" who urged Ross to publish *Hiroshima* was William Shawn, and he was soon to be named Ross' successor as editor-in-chief. After a bout with cancer, Ross died in Boston on December 6, 1951.

Further Reading

Ross never did write the autobiography he promised to call *My Life on a Limb.* The best source is unquestionably James Thurber's *The Years with Ross* (1959). Margaret Case Harriman's *The Vicious Circle: The Story of the Algonquin Round Table* (1951) provides some helpful anecdotes, as does Brendan Gill's *Here at the* New Yorker (1975).

Additional Sources

Kunkel, Thomas, *Genius in disguise: Harold Ross of the New Yorker,* New York: Carroll & Graf Publishers, 1996.
Thurber, James, *The years with Ross,* Harmondsworth, Middlesex, England; New York, N.Y.: Penguin Books, 1984, 1959. □

Sir James Clark Ross

The English admiral and polar explorer Sir James Clark Ross (1800-1862) is known for his discovery of the North magnetic pole and his magnetic surveys of the Antarctic.

James Clark Ross was born in London on April 15, 1800, the son of George Ross and a nephew of Rear Adm. John Ross. He entered the Royal Navy in 1812, serving with his uncle in four ships and accompanying him on his first Arctic voyage, in 1818. He was in William Edward Parry's four Arctic expeditions. The first was in 1819-1820 aboard the *Hecla;* the second was between 1821 and 1823 in H.M.S. *Fury.* Ross received a promotion on Dec. 26, 1822, and sailed as lieutenant of the *Fury* on Parry's 1824-1825

Arctic expedition. He was also with Parry in 1827-1828 during the latter's unsuccessful attempt to reach the North Pole by sledge from West Spitsbergen.

Ross was promoted to commander on Nov. 8, 1827. From 1829 to 1833 he again served on one of his uncle's Arctic expeditions. On this trip James Clark Ross led a party across Boothia Isthmus, reaching the North magnetic pole on May 31, 1831. After his return home in 1833, Ross was promoted to captain and undertook the relief of whalers in Baffin Bay in 1836 and conducted a magnetic survey of Great Britain from 1835 until 1838.

In September 1838, with Ross as commander, H.M.S. *Erebus* and *Terror* sailed to the Antarctic to discover the South magnetic pole, examine Antarctica, and conduct numerous scientific tests according to directions of the Royal Society. They penetrated the ice belt as far south as latitude 78°9'30'' in January 1841, reaching open water and discovering the Ross Sea. They continued to sail south and discovered Victoria Land (now part of New Zealand's Ross Dependency). The Ross Shelf Ice barred their way further south, and they were forced to turn back. In November 1841 they sailed again, from New Zealand, to solve the "Great Barrier Mystery" and failed owing to bad weather conditions. This time they wintered in the Falkland Islands, but they were no more successful on their third attempt. Finally they sailed for home and reached England in September 1843.

This voyage gave Ross "a distinguished place amongst the most successful votaries of Science, and the brightest

ornaments of the British Navy." He received gold medals from geographical societies in London and Paris; in 1844 he was knighted; and in 1848 he was elected a fellow of the Royal Society. He led the first naval expedition in 1848-1849 to search for Sir John Franklin, missing with H.M.S. *Enterprise* and *Investigator,* but this was unsuccessful. Until his death, Ross was frequently consulted as "the first authority on all matters relating to Arctic navigation." He died at Aylesbury, England, on April 3, 1862.

Further Reading

Ross's account of his expedition is *A Voyage of Discovery and Research in the Southern and Antarctic Regions, 1839-43* (2 vols., 1847). Laurence P. Kirwan, *A History of Polar Exploration* (1960), devotes a chapter to the expedition, largely based on Ross's own account. Ross's discovery of the North magnetic pole is told in Sir John Ross, *Narrative of a Second Voyage in Search of a North-West Passage . . .* (1835).

Additional Sources

Ross, M. J. (Maurice James), *Polar pioneers: John Ross and James Clark Ross,* Montreal; Buffalo: McGill-Queen's University Press, 1994. □

John Ross

John Ross (1790-1866), chief of the American Cherokee Indians, headed his tribe during the saddest era in its history, when it was removed from its ancestral lands to Oklahoma.

John Ross was born near Lookout Mountain, Tenn., on Oct. 3, 1790. His Indian name was Cooweescoowe. His father was a Scotsman; his mother was one-quarter Cherokee and three-quarters Scot. Ross was educated by private tutors and then at Kingston Academy in Tennessee.

Ross's rise to prominence began in 1817, when he was elected a member of the Cherokee national council. Two years later he became president of the council, a position he held until 1826. In 1827 he helped write the Cherokee constitution and was elected assistant chief. The following year he became principal chief of the tribe, and he remained in this position until 1839.

In 1829 the state of Georgia ordered the Cherokees removed. Ross became a leader of the faction of the tribe that opposed removal, and he led in challenging the state ruling before the U.S. Supreme Court. His appeal was successful, but Georgia officials refused to obey the higher court's ruling.

In 1835 the U.S. government signed a treaty of removal with a small faction of the Cherokee tribe. Ross drafted an appeal against this treaty, saying that it was obtained by fraudulent means, and addressed it to President Andrew Jackson. Jackson approved the policy of removal, however, as did Martin Van Buren, and when Gen. Winfield Scott arrived in Georgia with troops, Ross and the Cherokee were

forced to acquiesce. In 1838-1839 Ross led his people in the removal westward (known as the "Trail of Tears") to the Indian Territory (Oklahoma).

Once there, Ross was instrumental in drafting a Cherokee constitution that united the eastern and western branches of the tribe. That year he was also chosen chief of the united tribe, an office he held until his death. He settled near Park Hill in Oklahoma, where he erected a mansion and farmed, using his many slaves to cultivate his fields. His first wife, a Cherokee, Quatie, died in 1839. In 1845 he married a white woman who died in 1865.

Ross believed that the Cherokee Indians should not participate in the Civil War, and on May 17, 1861, he issued a proclamation of Cherokee neutrality. However, slave-owning Cherokee brought sufficient pressure to force a council resulting in a treaty of alliance with the Confederacy signed in October 1861. When Union troops invaded Oklahoma in 1862, Ross moved to Philadelphia and repudiated the Confederate alliance. This move caused some Confederate sympathizers in the tribe to dispute his right as chief. Ross lived in Philadelphia until the end of the Civil War. He died while negotiating a treaty for his tribe in Washington, D.C., on Aug. 1, 1866.

Further Reading

The major study of Ross is Rachel Caroline Eaton, *John Ross and the Cherokee Indians* (1914). For Ross's political career see Morris L. Wardell, *A Political History of the Cherokee Nation, 1838-1907* (1938), and Henry T. Malone, *Cherokees of the Old South* (1956). An overall study of the tribe and an evaluation of Ross as a leader are in Grace S. Woodward, *The Cherokees* (1963). □

Mary G. Ross

American engineer Mary G. Ross (born 1908) made notable contributions in aerospace technology, particularly in areas related to space flight and ballistic missiles.

Mary G. Ross was part of the original engineering team at Lockheed's Missile Systems Division, where she worked on a number of defense systems, and contributed to space exploration efforts with her work relating to the Apollo program, the Polaris reentry vehicle, and interplanetary space probes.

Born in Oklahoma in 1908, Ross took pride in her heritage as a Cherokee Indian. Her great-great-grandfather, John Ross, was the principal chief of the Cherokee Nation between 1828 and 1866. Ross was later to remark that she had been brought up in the Cherokee tradition of equal education for both boys and girls. She was, however, the only girl in her math class, which did not seem to bother her. Indeed, her early interests were math, physics, and science.

Armed with these interests and a sense of purpose, Ross graduated from high school when she was sixteen. She attended Northeastern State Teacher's College and graduated from there in 1928, when she was twenty. After graduating from college, Ross taught mathematics and science for nine and one-half years in public schools. She also served as a girls' advisor at a Pueblo and Navajo school for boys and girls. Ross returned to school herself, this time to Colorado State Teachers College (now the University of Northern Colorado at Greeley), where she graduated with a master's degree in mathematics in 1938.

With the growth of the aviation industry in the early part of World War II, Ross found a position in 1942 as an assistant to a consulting mathematician with Lockheed Aircraft Corporation in Burbank, California. Her early work at Lockheed involved engineering problems having to do with transport and fighter aircraft. Meanwhile, with the support of Lockheed, Ross continued her education at the University of California, Los Angeles, where she took courses in aeronautical and mechanical engineering.

When Lockheed formed its Missiles Systems Division in 1954, it selected Mary Ross to be one of the first forty employees, and she was the only female engineer among them. As the American missile program matured, Ross found herself researching and evaluating feasibility and performance of ballistic missile and other defense systems. She also studied the distribution of pressure caused by ocean waves and how it affected submarine-launched vehicles.

Her work in 1958 concentrated on satellite orbits and the Agena series of rockets that played so prominent a role in the Apollo moon program during the 1960s. As an advanced systems engineer, Ross worked on the Polaris reentry vehicle and engineering systems for manned space flights. Before her retirement from Lockheed in 1973, Ross undertook research on flyby space probes that would study Mars and Venus. After Ross retired she continued her interests in engineering by delivering lectures to high school and college groups to encourage young women and Native American youths to train for technical careers.

Ross authored a number of classified publications relating to her work in national defense and received several awards during her career. A charter member of the Los Angeles chapter of the Society of Women Engineers since 1952, Ross has received a number of honors. In 1961 she garnered the *San Francisco Examiner*'s award for Woman of Distinction and the Woman of Achievement Award from the California State Federation of Business and Professional Clubs. Ross was elected a fellow and life member of the Society of Women Engineers, whose Santa Clara Valley Section established a scholarship in her name. She has also been the recipient of achievement awards from the American Indian Science and Engineering Society and from the Council of Energy Resource Tribes. In 1992 she was inducted into the Silicon Valley Engineering Hall of Fame.

Further Reading

Ross, Mary G., *Interview with Karl Preuss,* conducted February 14, 1994. □

Nellie Tayloe Ross

American politician Nellie Tayloe Ross (1876-1977) gained fame in the 1920s when she was elected governor of Wyoming, becoming the first woman in the country to hold such a post. After leaving that office, she had an active career in national Democratic politics and was named director of the U.S. Mint by President Franklin D. Roosevelt in the 1930s, a position she held for nearly 20 years.

Although she had never planned a career in politics, Nellie Tayloe Ross became one of the best-known politicians of the first half of the twentieth century in the United States. After the death of her husband, William Bradford Ross, the governor of Wyoming, in 1924, Ross was elected to replace him, becoming the first woman to serve as a governor in the United States upon her inauguration on January 5, 1925. As a Democrat in a primarily Republican state, Ross did not accomplish much as governor, but she became active in the national Democratic Party after her term was completed. She was a strong supporter of Franklin D. Roosevelt during his presidential campaign of 1932; when he was elected to office, he named Ross to the federal post of director of the United States Mint, making her the first woman to hold that post.

Ross was born Nellie Davis Tayloe on November 29, 1876, in St. Joseph, Missouri. The daughter of James Wynn Tayloe and Elizabeth Blair Green Tayloe, she had distinguished ancestors on both sides of her family. Her father came from an influential Southern family that had included the builder of the famed Octagon House in Washington, D.C., the home of President James Madison and First Lady Dolley Madison after the burning of the White House in the War of 1812. Her mother's family boasted a distant relationship to President George Washington. Despite such a background, Ross's early years were not remarkable. She attended both private and public schools and in addition received some private instruction. After her family moved to Omaha, Nebraska, she entered a teacher training program for two years and then spent a short time teaching kindergarten.

Ross met the young lawyer William Bradford Ross while visiting relatives in Tennessee. The two fell in love, and after William Ross moved to Cheyenne, Wyoming, to begin a private law practice, they were married in 1902. A year later, the twin boys George Tayloe and James Ambrose were born to the couple. A third son, Alfred Duff, was born in 1905 but died before he was a year old. In 1912, their fourth son, William Bradford, was born. Ross was a devoted wife and mother who was content to spend her time at home and in assisting in educational self-improvement programs with the Cheyenne Woman's Club.

Husband Elected Governor

Her husband, however, was more active in the public sphere and his increasing interest in politics led him to run for various posts as a Democrat. Because the state was primarily Republican, however, he did not have much success. But his fortunes changed in 1922 when a group of Progressive Republicans joined the Democrats in supporting his nomination for governor and he was elected. Ross was not excited about the changes this created in her life, but she supported her husband's work and acted as a confidant who listened to his problems and ideas during his tenure as governor. The transition to her role as governor's wife may have been difficult, but the changes that were to occur over the next few years would prove to be even more of a challenge to Ross.

In September of 1924, William Ross underwent an appendectomy and developed complications from the surgery. He died on October 2, 1924. Because his death occurred only a few weeks before the November 4 general elections for the state, an election to name a successor to complete the last two years of the governor's term was required by Wyoming law. The Democrats asked Ross to run as their candidate; while she did not respond to their inquiry, it was assumed that by not answering, she was not declining their offer. She was named the Democratic nominee on October 14. The Republicans chose the attorney Eugene J. Sullivan as their candidate.

Elected First Woman Governor

Ross did not have any previous political experience, but she felt that she was the person who best understood what her husband had intended to do as governor and she wanted to carry on his work. She did not publicly campaign for office, but limited her efforts to two open letters to voters that outlined her plans as governor. She made it clear that a vote for her would be a vote for the programs begun by her husband. Wyoming residents sympathized with her role as a widow, perhaps her greatest advantage in the election. The idea that Wyoming could elect the nation's first woman governor also was attractive to the state's citizens. Wyoming had been the first state to legalize the vote for women, and the additional achievement of the first woman governor would be a source of pride for residents. The pressure to elect Ross was increased by the likely election of a female governor in Texas that year, Miriam A. Ferguson, wife of former governor James A. Ferguson, who had been impeached. The negative publicity attending Ross's competitor, Sullivan, due to his connections with the oil industry recently embarrassed by the Teapot Dome scandal, also helped Ross's chances in the election.

Although many other Democrats were defeated in Wyoming's 1924 elections, Ross emerged victorious. On January 5, 1925, she was inaugurated as governor, earning the distinction of being the nation's first woman in that office (Miriam Ferguson had also won her election, but was not sworn into office until January 25). Still wearing mourning clothes in memory of her husband, Ross addressed the crowd attending the ceremony with the message that the administration and policies of her husband would continue during her time in office. She began her term in a relatively strong position, with the advantages of having an administration in place and having the sympathy and support of many voters.

Received Nationwide Attention

Ross was aware that as the first woman governor she carried a special responsibility. She was careful not to do anything that would make people question whether women were able to hold such a post. Her role also brought her a great deal of notoriety; her office and the porch of her home were continually filled with people hoping to get a glimpse of the female governor. She even received such attention when she traveled to Washington, D.C., to participate in the inauguration day parade for president Calvin Coolidge—her presence drew the loudest applause from parade spectators that day. But despite numerous invitations to give lectures and appear across the country, she did not accept any of these offers, preferring to stay in Wyoming and focus on her political duties.

Her tenure as governor was not particularly fruitful, however. The Republican-dominated state house was reluctant to support her proposals, although she was able to reach some compromises on banking reform and other issues. Some of the other plans she initiated were assistance programs for the agricultural industry, legislation to protect women and children in the workplace, and cuts in state taxes and spending. One controversial move that she made was vetoing a bill calling for a special election to fill an unexpected vacancy in the U.S. Senate seats from Wyoming. Traditionally, the governor had appointed a replacement in these cases, but Republicans saw that an elderly Republican senator was not likely to survive his latest term and they wanted to avoid a Democratic appointee in the post. Ross later claimed that it was this issue that caused her to lose her bid for reelection in 1926.

Supported Democratic Presidential Candidates

Ross was renominated by Democrats in the gubernatorial election of 1926, but she no longer had the sympathy of voters that had overridden their party preferences in 1924. The Republican candidate, Frank C. Emerson, carried the election and Ross ended her only term in elected office. She began to give the lectures she had previously declined and also wrote a number of articles for magazines. She did not leave politics altogether, though. As a committee member from Wyoming for the Democratic National Committee (DNC), she joined in national political issues, later becoming a vice chair of the DNC. She worked with future first lady Eleanor Roosevelt in the 1928 presidential campaign of Alfred E. Smith, heading the Democratic Party's Women's Division's efforts in gaining support for the candidate and giving speeches around the country; she also was given the honor of seconding Smith's nomination at the Democratic convention that year. Smith was not elected, but Ross continued with her work for the Democratic Party in the 1932 elections, serving with the party's Women's Speaker's Bureau in campaigning for nominee Franklin D. Roosevelt.

After Roosevelt became president, he made it clear that he planned to name a number of women to high government posts. One of the women he selected for his administration was Ross, who received the assignment of directing the United States Mint. Ross was extremely successful in her new position. She cut costs and increased efficiency at the Mint by introducing automated processes, which also allowed her to reduce the Mint's staff by 75 percent. Her stellar performance in this position allowed her to remain in the post throughout all of Roosevelt's years in office and through the administration of president Harry S. Truman. It was not until the election of Republican president Dwight D. Eisenhower that Ross was finally replaced in 1952 after nearly 20 years at the Mint. Ross continued to live in the nation's capital for the rest of her life. She died on December 19, 1977, at the age of 101. While her most effective years in politics and government took place after her work in Wyoming, Ross's place in United States history still greatly rests on her role as the first woman in the country to serve as a governor.

Further Reading

"First U.S. Woman Governor Celebrates Her Centennial during the Bicentennial," *Aging*, February/March, 1977, pp. 13-14.

Tayloe, Nellie Ross, "The Governor Lady" (3-part series of articles), *Good Housekeeping*, August, 1927, pp. 30-31, 118-24; September, 1927, pp. 36-37, 206-18; November, 1927, pp. 72-73, 180-97. □

Christina Georgina Rossetti

The English poet Christina Georgina Rossetti (1830-1894) wrote poems of love, fantasy, and nature, verses for children, and devotional poetry and prose.

Christina Rossetti was born on Dec. 5, 1830, in London, the youngest of the four remarkable Rossetti children. Educated entirely at home, she spoke English and Italian with ease and read French, Latin, and German. Her first verses were written to her mother on April 27, 1842. Her first published poems were the seven she contributed in 1850 to the Pre-Raphaelite magazine, the *Germ,* under the pseudonym Ellen Alleyne.

When her father died in 1854, Christina became the close companion of her mother and followed her older sister's example in becoming a devout Anglican. Though mild and virtuous, she was frequently anxious about her self-presumed sinfulness. She is said to have pasted strips of paper over the more blasphemous passages in Swinburne's poetry. Yet she remained devoted to her brother, Dante Gabriel, whose life was far from a model of conventional virtue. At 18 she fell in love with James Collinson, a minor Pre-Raphaelite painter, but broke off her engagement to him 2 years later, when he became a Roman Catholic. In 1862 she fell deeply in love with Charles Bagot Cayley. But she again refused to marry, this time because Cayley had no firm religious faith. These two broken love affairs are reflected in many of her poems, especially the sonnet sequence *Monna Innominata.* In other poems a melancholy regret for lost love is mixed with a disturbing obsession with death. Because she suffered long and frequent periods of poor health, Rossetti came to regard life as physically and emotionally painful and to look forward to death both as a release and as the possible moment of joyful union with God and with those she had loved and lost.

Rossetti's three major volumes of poetry were *Goblin Market and Other Poems* (1862), *The Prince's Progress and Other Poems* (1866), and *A Pageant and Other Poems* (1881). She also published *Commonplace* (1870), a book of short stories; *Sing-song: A Nursery Rhyme Book* (1872), beautifully illustrated by Arthur Hughes and a favorite of Victorian children; and *Speaking Likenesses* (1874), a book of tales for children. But her poetry alone has secured her fame. Her poems, like those of the later Victorian poet Gerard Manley Hopkins, reveal a dual, self-contradictory sensibility. They express a sensuous attraction to physical beauty fused with a mystical and saintly religious faith. They are sometimes highly sentimental in tone yet scrupulously austere in diction and form. And throughout many of them one may find a quiet sense of humor that controls the sentimentality and keeps contradictions in balance. "Goblin Market" is certainly her finest poem and her most disturbing in its presentation of the conflict between sisterly love and destructive passion.

From 1871 through 1873 Rossetti was stricken by Graves' disease, which ruined her beauty and brought her close to death. When she recovered, she turned almost exclusively to religious writing, publishing a number of devotional books: *Annus Domini* (1874), *Seek and Find* (1879), *Called to Be Saints: The Minor Festivals* (1881), *Letter and Spirit* (1882), *Time Flies: A Reading Diary* (1885), *The Face of the Deep: A Commentary on the Revelation* (1892), and *Verses* (1893). In 1891 she began to suffer from cancer and died, after a long and painful illness, on Dec. 29, 1894, in London.

Further Reading

A wealth of biographical detail is in *The Family Letters of Christina Georgina Rossetti,* edited by her brother William M. Rossetti (1908; repr. 1968); Marya Zaturenska, *Christina Rossetti: A Portrait with Background* (1949); and *The Rossetti-Macmillan Letters,* edited by Lona M. Packer (1963). The best biography is Lona Packer, *Christina Rossetti* (1963). An interesting study of her poetry is Thomas B. Swann, *Wonder and Whimsy: The Fantastic World of Christina Rossetti* (1960).

Additional Sources

Battiscombe, Georgina. *Christina Rossetti, a divided life,* New York: Holt, Rinehart and Winston, 1981.

Birkhead, Edith. *Christina Rossetti & her poetry,* Philadelphia: R. West, 1977.

Jones, Kathleen. *Learning not to be first: the life of Christina Rossetti,* New York: St. Martin's Press, 1992.

Marsh, Jan. *Christina Rossetti: a life,* New York: Viking, 1995.

Proctor, Ellen A. *A brief of memoir of Christina G. Rossetti,* Philadelphia: R. West, 1978.

Sandars, Mary Frances. *The life of Christina Rossetti,* Westport, Conn.: Greenwood Press, 1980.

Sawtell, Margaret. *Christina Rossetti: her life and religion,* Philadelphia: R. West, 1977.

Shove, Fredegond. *Christina Rossetti: a study,* Norwood, Pa.: Norwood Editions, 1977. □

Dante Gabriel Rossetti

The English painter and poet Dante Gabriel Rossetti (1828-1882) was a cofounder of the Pre-Raphaelite Brotherhood. His works show an impassioned, mystic imagination in strong contrast to the banal sentimentality of contemporary Victorian art.

orn on May 12, 1828, of Anglo-Italian parentage, Dante Gabriel Rossetti was steeped throughout childhood in the atmosphere of medieval Italy, which became a major source of his subject matter and artistic inspiration. After 2 years in the Royal Academy schools he worked briefly under Ford Madox Brown in 1848.

Shortly after Rossetti joined William Holman Hunt's studio later that year, the Pre-Raphaelite Brotherhood was formed, in Hunt's words, "to do battle against the frivolous art of the day." An association of artists so varied in artistic style, technique, and expressive spirit as the Pre-Raphaelites could not long survive, and it was principally owing to Rossetti's forceful, almost hypnotic personality that the Brotherhood held together long enough to achieve the critical and popular recognition necessary for the success of its crusade.

His Paintings

Rossetti did not have the natural technical proficiency that is evident in the minute detail and brilliant color of a typical Pre-Raphaelite painting, and his early oil paintings, the *Girlhood of Mary Virgin* (1849) and the *Ecce Ancilla Domini* (1850), were produced only at the expense of great technical effort. In the less demanding medium of watercolor, however, Rossetti clearly revealed his intense, compressed imaginative power. The series of small watercolors of the 1850s culminates in such masterpieces as *Dante's Dream* (1856) and the *Wedding of St. George and the Princess Sabra* (1857), characteristic products of Rossetti's inflamed sensibility, with typically irrational perspective and lighting, glowing color, and forceful figures.

In almost all his paintings of the 1850s Rossetti used Elizabeth Siddal as his model. Discovered in a hatshop in 1850, she was adopted by the Brotherhood as their ideal of feminine beauty. In 1852 she became exclusively Rossetti's model, and in 1860 his wife. Beset by growing melancholy, she committed suicide 2 years later. Rossetti buried a manuscript of his poems in her coffin, a characteristically dramatic gesture which he later regretted. *Beata Beatrix* (1863), a posthumous portrait of Elizabeth Siddal, the Beatrice to his Dante, is one of Rossetti's most deeply felt paintings: it is his last masterpiece and the first in a series of symbolical female portraits, which declined gradually in quality as his interest in painting decreased.

His Poetry

Although early in his career poetry was for Rossetti simply a relaxation from painting, later on writing gradually became more important to him, and in 1871 he wrote to Ford Madox Brown, "I wish one could live by writing poetry. I think I'd see painting d———d if I could...." In 1861 he published his translations from Dante and other early Italian poets, reflecting the medieval preoccupations of his finest paintings. In 1869 the manuscript of his early poems was recovered from his wife's coffin and published the next year.

Rossetti's early poems under strong Pre-Raphaelite influence, such as "The Blessed Damozel" (1850; subsequently revised) and "The Portrait," have a sensitive innocence and a strong mystical passion paralleled by his paintings of the 1850s. As his interest in painting declined, Rossetti's poetic craftsmanship improved, until in his latest works, such as "Rose Mary" and "The White Ship" (both included in *Ballads and Sonnets,* 1881), his use of richly colored word textures achieves a sumptuous grandeur of expression and sentiment.

At his death on April 9, 1882, Rossetti had reached a position of artistic prominence, and his spirit was a significant influence on the cultural developments of the late 19th century. Although his technique was not always the equal of his powerful feeling, his imaginative genius earned him a place in the ranks of English visionary artists.

Further Reading

The most recent work on Rossetti is G. H. Fleming, *Rossetti and the Pre-Raphaelite Brotherhood* (1967), a detailed study of his relations with the Brotherhood, which like Oswald Doughty's *A Victorian Romantic: Dante Gabriel Rossetti* (1949; 2d ed. 1960) is a general biography, not a specialized work on the paintings. Fundamental on the Pre-Raphaelites is William Holman Hunt's firsthand account, *Pre-Raphaelitism and the Pre-Raphaelite Brotherhood* (2 vols., 1905). Also important are Robin Ironside, *Pre-Raphaelite Painters* (1948); T. S. R. Boase, *English Art, 1800-1870* (1959); and John Dixon Hunt, *The Pre-Raphaelite Imagination, 1848-1900* (1968).

Additional Sources

Ash, Russell. *Dante Gabriel Rossetti,* New York: H.N. Abrams, 1995.

Dobbs, Brian. *Dante Gabriel Rossetti: an alien Victorian,* London: Macdonald and Jane's, 1977.

Faxon, Alicia Craig. *Dante Gabriel Rossetti,* New York: Abbeville Press, 1989,

Nicoll, John. *Dante Gabriel Rossetti,* New York: Macmillan, 1976, 1975.

Waugh, Evelyn. *Rossetti, his life and works,* Norwood, Pa.: Norwood Editions, 1978. □

Aldo Rossi

A renowned Italian architect, Aldo Rossi (born 1931), was instrumental in the emergence of a renewed interest in architectural tradition after the 1960s. Examples of his work can be found in Italy, Germany, the United States, and Japan.

Aldo Rossi was born in Milan, Italy, on May 3, 1931. He entered the Polytechnic of Milan in 1949, graduating from the Faculty of Architecture in 1959. While still a student he began contributing to *Casabella-continuita,* the leading architectural journal in Italy, and served as editor of the magazine from 1960 to 1964. From this position Rossi participated in an ongoing Italian critique of the functionalism and progressivism of the Modern movement, particularly as embodied in the International Style.

In 1966 Rossi's research culminated in an influential first book, *The Architecture of the City,* which proposed a fundamental continuity between the principles of architecture and urban design. In contrast to a functionalist emphasis on political and economic forces, Rossi suggested a renewed focus on the description of the city as a constructed tangible artifact, an "urban science" founded on an important analytical tool, the concept of type. A typological system of classification was based on the identification, by formal and programmatic similarities, of archetypal urban institutions such as the courtyard, the street, and the house. In stressing traditional urban configurations, Rossi re-estab-

lished the study of architecture as a relatively autonomous discipline with a specific body of knowledge.

From the early 1960s he maintained an office in Milan and collaborated (most frequently after 1971 with Gianni Braghieri) on competitions for public buildings and housing. He completed the exhibition design for the 13th Milan Triennale (1964) and saw one of his competition-winning designs, a monumental fountain, built in Segrate, Italy (1965). These early designs showed a preoccupation with the axial arrangement of simple neo-classical elements such as bridges, courtyards, porticos, and towers.

In 1969 Rossi began work on a larger project, the Gallaratese 2 housing complex in Milan. Consisting of two contiguous slab blocks, the design's most significant feature was a colonnade which extended over five hundred feet in length, its relentless rhythm broken only by four cylindrical columns marking the break between the two blocks. Similar typological elements were used in an addition to the cemetery of San Cataldo in Modena, a 1971 competition-winner. Completed in 1984, the project involved a perimeter colonnaded columbarium enclosing a cubic shrine, a series of ossuary blocks, and a conical chimney-like tower marking the common grave.

An exhibition of Rossi's work with that of his contemporaries (known collectively as the neo-rationalists or *Tendenza*) at the 15th Milan Triennale (1973) brought them to international attention. Appointed chair of architectural composition by Venice University (1973), he accepted academic appointments at several U.S. universities, including Yale, Cornell, and Cooper Union. School buildings made up a significant part of his work at this time, including the elementary school of Fagnano Olona (1972-1976) and the more centralized secondary school at Broni (1979-1981), both organized around courtyards.

His continued interest in the institution of theater was reflected in the Teatro del Mondo, a floating theater and entrance portal he designed for the 1980 Venice Biennale. Seating an audience of 250 people, it was inspired by elements as diverse as the lighthouse and the barge. A steel structure clad in wood, it was towed from its construction site to a promontory in Venice where it remained only for the duration of the Biennale.

In 1981 Rossi published his second book, the episodic record of a decade of recollections entitled *A Scientific Autobiography.* Balancing his earlier emphasis on classification, here the private and poetic aspects of architecture were stressed. The rationale for design was now based on the connective logic of analogy, inspired by personal memory and evoking the collective unconscious. Confirming, in this autobiographical text, the power of "small things," Rossi expanded his activities to include product and furniture design, including a tea service (1980) and several coffee makers (1984-1988) for Alessi.

During the 1980s Rossi was increasingly awarded commissions outside his native country. Two housing projects completed in Berlin for the International Building Exhibition displayed a brick and steel vocabulary and similar concerns for maintaining the street edge and front/rear distinctions within units. The Rauchstrasse apartment building

(1983-1985) in the Tiergarten district was an urban villa on a corner site, and the Sudliche Friedrichstadt housing complex (1981-1988) formed a perimeter around a central urban garden. In 1988 Rossi won first prize in a competition for the design of the Museum of German History in Berlin.

Projects of increasing scale continued to be built in Italy. Public commissions ranged from a civic center and urban redevelopment for Perugia (comissioned in 1982) to a town hall for Borgorrico (1983-1988), both planned around entry courtyards. In a controversial strategy, Rossi's competition-winning project for the Carlo Felice Theater in Genoa (1983-1990) reconstructed the exterior of the original theater while inserting a new interior and an enlarged stage tower. Commercial projects included the Casa Aurora (Turin, 1984-1987); the GFT company headquarters, a street building with a large public arcade; and the Centro Torri, a shopping center in Parma (1985-1988) named after the monumental brick towers which advertise its presence.

In 1987 Rossi opened a small satellite office in New York to supervise projects in the United States and Japan. In non-European environments he sought to establish a source of urban coherence for his designs. In the University of Miami School of Architecture (begun in 1990) a campus lake with a library at the water's edge is connected to the main building by a palm-lined avenue. The hotel/restaurant complex in Fukuoka, Japan (1987-1989), a hotel tower entered from a plaza-topped public plinth, was oriented toward the nearby river.

The cumulative power of his achievements was recognized in 1990 with the award of the prestigious Pritzker Architecture Prize. As his career progressed his palette of materials expanded from the minimal stucco and bluepainted metal of his early work to a variety of masonry and metal textures. In both theoretical and built work, Rossi consistently rejected avant-garde experimentalism in favor of collective expression drawn from classical/vernacular sources. However, his architecture invokes, not a sentimental reconstruction of the past, but a continual obsessive reassemblage of a few small elements, the estranged enigmatic fragments of a lost order.

Rossi did not limit his designs to architecture. In 1994 he also designed a full five-piece setting of porcelain dinnerware. Designed for Rosenthal's Studio-Linie it resembles a lighthouse, or at least was inspired by the maritime tower's clean lines and geometric shape.

In 1995 Rossi began designing a $250-million timeshare resort for the Walt Disney Company. To be built along the Newport Coast, the resort would offer sweeping ocean vistas, gondola rides along quiet man-made canals and overnight camping for children.

The 76-acre hillside resort is designed as an Italian-style Mediterranean village of 650 condominiums and comes complete with two restaurants, several tennis courts, volleyball nets, pools and a golf course. The main entrance features a six-story "main estate" building flanked by twin 109-foot towers. The earth-tone buildings are to have tile roofs and a fake Roman aqueduct that spills into the swimming pool.

Further Reading

Books by Rossi include *The Architecture of the City* (1966) and *A Scientific Autobiography* (1981). The most comprehensive monograph on his work until 1985 is *Aldo Rossi Buildings and Projects* (1985), compiled and edited by Peter Arnell and Ted Bickford, with essays by Vincent Scully and Rafael Moneo. Rossi is listed in *Contemporary Architects,* edited by Muriel Emanuel (1980), and many of his drawings are reproduced in *Il Libro Azzuro: My Projects* (1981) and in *Aldo Rossi in America 1976-1979,* an IAUS exhibition catalogue with an essay by Peter Eisenman. Other useful English-language references are *Aldo Rossi: Projects and Drawings (1962-79),* edited by Francesco Moschandi, for documentation on the early projects; and *Aldo Rossi,* edited by John O'Regan, for translations of the early writings. Well-illustrated Italian texts on the early work include *l'architettura di Aldo Rossi* (Vittorio Savi) and *Aldo Rossi* (Gianni Braghiere). Selected projects have been published in several architectural journals, including *Casabella, Domus, Progressive Architecture,* and *Architectural Record.* Journals of special interest include *Aldo Rossi: Three Cities* (a *Lotus* document with an essay by Bernard Huet) and compilation issues of *Architecture and Urbanism* (November 1982) and *Architecture d'Aujourd'hui* (June 1989).Updated information was gathered from: *LA Times* Thursday, February 23, 1995, "Disney Unveils Newport Resort Plans; Development" and *The Chicago Tribune,* "That's Just Beachy," 07/24/94. □

Luigi Rossi

The Italian composer Luigi Rossi (ca. 1598-1653) wrote important works in the field of the chamber cantata.

Luigi Rossi was born in Torremaggiore, but records that could document his specific birthdate were destroyed in earthquakes of 1627 and 1638. He studied in Naples with Jean de Macque and was subsequently employed by the Duke of Traetta. Quite early in his career Rossi moved to Rome, and this became his permanent residence. He was first employed in Rome by Marc'Antonio Borghese.

In 1627 Rossi married Costanza de Ponte, a harpist and an outstanding musician in her own right. When the Rossis visited the Florentine court in 1635, Costanza de Ponte was highly acclaimed for her performances.

In 1633 Rossi took on the additional post of organist at the church of S. Luigi dei Francesi. Although he retained this post for the rest of his life, it was secondary to his main interests and activities, for he was essentially a composer of secular music who was suited to court life.

Of Rossi's several aristocratic patrons, the most important was Cardinal Antonio Barberini. The Barberini family was famous for its patronage of the arts, and Cardinal Antonio was the most lavish of all in his support of music. When Rossi entered the service of the cardinal in 1641, he joined a sizable musical establishment of brilliant singers and instrumentalists. Not only chamber music but theatrical music was presented at the Palazzo Barberini. Operas, complete with star singers and splendid productions, had been given there since 1632.

Soon after his appointment to the Barberini establishment, Rossi began work on his first opera, *Il palazzo incantato,* with a libretto by Giulio Rospigliosi, after Ariosto's *Orlando furioso.* This was performed several times at the Palazzo Barberini in 1642. Rossi's second and only other opera, *Orfeo,* with a libretto by Francesco Buti, was performed not in Rome but in Paris in 1647. Rossi went to Paris himself to organize the performances of *Orfeo.* It was performed six times and had a marked success. Two of the performances were in honor of the Queen of England, a guest of the French court at the time. One of the earliest operas given in France, it was highly influential on the subsequent development of French opera.

Rossi's chamber cantatas also proved to be very popular in French musical circles. Indeed, his success in France was so great that he was called to Paris again in 1648. He died in Rome on Feb. 19, 1653.

Rossi also wrote some Latin motets; probably some Italian oratorios (the authorship of these is uncertain); one harpsichord piece; and about 300 chamber cantatas, with Italian words, which represent his most important contribution. The great majority of the cantatas are composed for solo voice, usually soprano, accompanied by thorough-bass. Many others are written for two voices and thorough-bass. Some are for three or four voices and thorough-bass.

All sizes and varieties of the contemporary cantata appear in Rossi's output: short, simple pieces; long works in sophisticated forms; light airs; sorrowful laments; and pieces containing the most varied musical styles. His cantatas were copied and performed throughout Italy and abroad. They are outstanding examples of the Italian chamber cantata.

Further Reading

Rossi's music is discussed by Manfred F. Bukofzer, *Music in the Baroque Era: From Monteverdi to Bach* (1947); and by Claude V. Palisca, *Baroque Music* (1968). A thematic catalog of Rossi's cantatas, with a detailed introduction by Eleanor Caluori, entitled *Luigi Rossi,* is fascicle 3 of *The Wellesley Edition Cantata Index Series* (2 vols., 1965). Additional details of Rossi's life appear in *The New Grove Dictionary of Music and Musicians* (1980); and Nicolas Slonimsky, ed.,*Baker's Biographical Dictionary of Musicians* (1992). □

Gioacchino Rossini

The operas of the Italian composer Gioacchino Rossini (1792-1868), particularly those in the comic genre, were among the most popular works of the entire 19th century. His best-known work is "The Barber of Seville."

Gioacchino Rossini was born in Pesaro on Feb. 29, 1792, into a musical family: his father was a trumpeter and horn player; his mother became a successful operatic singer. When he was 4 years old, Gioacchino's mother took him to Bologna, where she sought and found singing engagements and where the child received instruction in singing, theory, keyboard, and several other instruments. By the time he was in his early teens, he was an accomplished accompanist, sometimes played horn with his father in the orchestra at the opera, and had begun writing music.

During Rossini's formal musical training at the Liceo Comunale in Bologna (1807-1810) he composed prolifically. His first opera was *Demetrio e Polibio,* written in 1809, but his first work to be put on the stage was the comic opera *La cambiale di matrimonio,* composed in 1810 and performed successfully at the Teatro di S. Moisè in Venice that year.

Success came quickly to the young composer. He wrote rapidly and fluently, in a style pleasing to singers and audiences alike. *La pietra del paragone* was staged to great acclaim at La Scala in Milan in 1812; Tancredi became a genuine international hit following its premiere in Venice the following year. Operas flowed from his pen at the rate of three or four a year. In 1815 the San Carlo and Del Fondo theaters in Naples engaged him as musical director, and his duties included writing a new opera every year for each theater. *Elisabetta, regina d'Inghilterra,* his first work for Naples, enjoyed enormous success. This was the first opera, incidentally, in which he wrote out the ornamentation he

expected from his singers rather than leaving this matter to them.

Rossini was in Naples until 1822; during this period he also composed works for such cities as Rome, Milan, Venice, and Lisbon. *Almaviva, ossia l'inutile precauzione,* based on Pierre Caron de Beaumarchais's *Le Barbier de Séville,* was poorly received on the occasion of its first performance in Rome in 1816, but soon (renamed *Il barbiere di Siviglia*) it enjoyed incredible success in Italy and all over the world, becoming one of the most widely sung works in the entire history of opera. *La Cenerentola,* based on the Cinderella story and premiered in Rome in 1817, was almost as successful; and these two comic operas established Rossini beyond question as the most successful operatic composer of the day.

The year 1822 was a critical one for Rossini in many ways. He went to Vienna for performances of several of his operas in German, married the famous singer Isabella Colbran, who had performed with great success in many of his operas, and worked with even greater care than usual on the new opera, *Semiramide,* for Venice. The poor reception of this work persuaded him that Italian audiences were no longer the proper ones for what he wanted to compose, and he resolved to write no more operas for performance in his native country. Later in the year he traveled—by way of Paris—to England, where he was royally received and realized a good profit from various performances of his works. He also sang some of his own vocal compositions.

In 1824 Rossini accepted an engagement as musical director of the Théâtre Italien in Paris. He revised a number of his earlier operas to suit the conventions of the French stage, presenting them to great acclaim. He wrote his last two operas for Paris: *Le Comte Ory* (1828) is one of the most brilliant and witty French comic operas of all time; and *Guillaume Tell* (1829), a spectacular five-act work integrating soloists, chorus, orchestra, dancers, and elaborate staging, became a model for an entire generation of French grand opera. He remained in Paris until 1836, when he returned to Bologna, where he served as honorary director of the Liceo Comunale. Political disturbances forced a move to Florence in 1847, the year after his marriage to his second wife, Olimpia Alessandrina Pélissier. In 1855 he returned to Paris, remaining there until his death on Nov. 13, 1868.

The most curious aspect of Rossini's later years is that he wrote no operas after 1829. He retained a lively interest in the musical scene, composed occasional cantatas, such religious works as the *Stabat Mater* and *Petite Messe solennelle* of 1864, and several hundred small "album" pieces for piano, voice and piano, and various instruments, but he never again attempted a work for the stage. He was a wealthy man, charming and witty, much in demand socially, and comfortable even with those men whose ideas about music were in conflict with his own. Much of his large estate went to the endowment of a conservatory of music in Pesaro. In 1887 he was reburied in the church of Sta Croce, Florence.

Rossini's 38 operas run the gamut from brief one-act comic works to the monumental and historic five-act *Guillaume Tell.* Some of his contemporaries and some histo-

rians, misled by the facility and speed of his writing, his habit of using portions of unsuccessful or forgotten works over again in new operas, and the easy charm of his solo arias and ensembles, have considered him a clever but superficial composer of no outstanding importance in the development of opera. But his works show remarkable craftsmanship, and in their brilliant integration of solo, ensemble, and orchestral writing and their sharp character delineation they are the most important link in the Italian operatic tradition between the late Italian works of Wolfgang Amadeus Mozart and the first works of Giuseppe Verdi. And Rossini's *Guillaume Tell* altered the entire course of French opera.

Further Reading

The standard work in English is Francis Toye, *Rossini: A Study in Tragi-comedy* (1934). An important contemporary study is Stendhal's *Life of Rossini* (2 vols., 1824; trans. 1869; new trans. 1957). A recent excellent study is Herbert Weinstock, *Rossini: A Biography* (1968). Rossini's life and career are discussed in Donald Jay Grout, *A Short History of Opera* (1947; 2d ed. 1965). Recommended for general background is Kenneth B. Klaus, *The Romantic Period in Music* (1970).

Additional Sources

Alvera, Pierluigi, *Rossini,* New York, N.Y.: Treves Pub. Co., 1986.

Kendall, Alan, *Gioacchino Rossini, the reluctant hero,* London: V. Gollancz, 1992.

Mountfield, David, *Rossini,* New York: Simon & Schuster, 1995.

Osborne, Richard, *Rossini,* Boston: Northeastern University Press, 1990.

Stendhal, *Life of Rossini / Richard N. Co,* London: J. Calder; New York: Riverrun Press, 1985.

Till, Nicholas, *Rossini,* London; New York: Omnibus Press, 1987.

Till, Nicholas, *Rossini, his life and times,* Tunbridge Wells, Kent: Midas; New York, NY: Hippocrene Books, 1983.

Toye, Francis, b. 1883., *Rossini, the man and his music,* New York: Dover Publications, 1987.

Weinstock, Herbert, *Rossini, a biography,* New York: Limelight Editions, 1987, 1968. □

Il Rosso

The Italian painter Il Rosso (1495-1540) was one of the leaders in the development of the mannerist style of painting, which he was the first to implant in France.

Giovanni Battista di Jacopo, known as Il Rosso or Rosso Fiorentino, was born in Florence. He began studying art as a boy but had difficulty finding a teacher to his liking since, as Giorgio Vasari tells us, "He had an opinion of his own in opposition to their styles." About 1512 he entered the workshop of Andrea del Sarto, where he met Pontormo.

Il Rosso and Pontormo brought Florentine mannerism into being. This new style, which contrasts dramatically with the order and calm of High Renaissance art, is well illustrated by Il Rosso's *Deposition* (1521). In this painting, sharply angular, emaciated figures climbing up and down ladders surround the twisted body of Christ, which has turned green in death. His *Moses Defending the Daughters of Jethro* (ca. 1523) is even stronger. Great muscular nudes (derived from his studies of Michelangelo's cartoon for the *Battle of Cascina*) fill the crowded canvas. Wildly they lunge and twist, falling in a contorted heap that fills the foreground.

In 1523 Il Rosso moved to Rome, where he met Michelangelo and members of Raphael's circle. In 1527, when the city was sacked by troops under the emperor Charles V, Il Rosso was captured by the dreaded Germans. On his release he fled to Perugia. The next 3 years he spent wandering from town to town in search of commissions. Following a brawl with some priests in Borgo San Sepolcro he fled to Venice, where he was befriended by the writer Pietro Aretino.

Il Rosso "always hoped to end his days in France," wrote Vasari, "and thus to escape the misery and poverty to which, so he said, those who work in Tuscany are exposed." The call to France came in 1530, and he became a success overnight. The king, Francis I, granted him a generous pension, a town house in Paris, and commodious quarters at Fontainebleau (then the chief seat of the French court), "where he lived like a lord."

Il Rosso executed frescoes (1532-1535; destroyed) for the Pavilion of Pomona at Fontainebleau. For the Grand Gallery of Francis I at Fontainebleau he and his assistant and successor, Primaticcio, created an entirely new style of palace decoration that combined paintings set into the wall with complex stucco reliefs and intricately carved wooden panels (1534-1537). The influence of these two major decorative projects on French art in the following centuries was enormous.

The painter died in Paris. Vasari tells us that, filled with remorse at having mistakenly accused a friend of theft, Il Rosso took his own life.

Further Reading

The only recent study of Il Rosso is in Italian: Paola Barocchi, *Il Rosso Fiorentino* (1950). By far the best account in English of his work at Fontainebleau is in Anthony Blunt, *Art and Architecture in France, 1500-1700* (1953). Giorgio Vasari, *Lives of the Most Eminent Painters, Sculptors and Architects* (many editions), contains a lively biography of Il Rosso. □

Medardo Rosso

Medardo Rosso (1858-1928), an Italian sculptor, broke with the prevalent classic and romantic attitudes of 19th-century sculpture and in doing so became one of the first truly modern sculptors. Rosso's work is viewed as being Impressionist, as well as being related to a lesser extent to Realism, Symbolism, and Expressionism.

Rosso was born in Turin, Italy, in 1858, the youngest of three children of a middle-class family. His attachment to his mother seems to have had a profound effect that later appeared in the tender, poetic way that he treated his favored themes—women, motherhood, and children. In 1870 the family moved to Milan, where Rosso spent much of his time in the workshop of a stonecutter. Because he had already decided to become an artist, this experience may have later influenced his having become a sculptor. The three year period of his enlistment in the army, 1879 to 1882, was unpleasant as Rosso was temperamentally unable to adapt to the necessary discipline.

Upon being discharged from the army Rosso immediately enrolled in anatomy and sculpture courses at Milan's Brera Academy. His earliest works, such as the *Hooligan* and the *Unemployed Singer,* both small bronzes of 1882, use his characteristic themes of that period, lower and lower-middle class life of the street. It may have been the example of Giuseppe Grandi (1843-1894), a Milanese sculptor noted for his small figures inspired by everyday life, which drew him in this thematic direction, as well as his own despondency and the impoverished conditions in which he lived.

Development of a Personal Style

In examples such as *Kiss Under the Streetlamp* (1882), Rosso captured what could be described as a snapshot effect. His figures were caught in telling but natural and unselfconscious poses, like random glimpses of life that are probably the most revealing. Under the streetlamp a young man with impetuous tenderness has stolen a kiss from his female companion. What Rosso captured was the emotion and gesture of the kiss without the details of the scene. It was an event momentarily viewed from a distance. In the recollection of this instant the artist remembered only what was to him most significant. This recollected vision characterized his sculpture thereafter. Rosso's technique was one of sketchiness and brevity. Only the lamppost and the kissing gesture are recorded. There is an awareness of the modeling of the clay (from which a mold was made and the bronze in turn cast) and a feel for the medium. Its manipulation is apparent in the varied, textured surfaces. This is related to Impressionist painting in its consciousness of the medium and the technique—paint, canvas, and individual brush strokes that have a meaning and visually pleasing effect aside from any representational quality.

In 1883 a disagreement and scuffle with a fellow student brought about his expulsion from the academy. The exhibition of four sculptures at the Exposizione di Belle Arti in Rome less than a month later must have given Rosso encouragement. Indicative of this was his productiveness and the emergence of a personal style.

The *Flesh of Others* (wax over plaster, 1883) is an early instance of Rosso's unprecedented use of these materials.

He normally worked initially in clay without the benefit of preparatory sketches. The clay was used as a model for a copy in plaster. From this a mold was made with duplicates being produced in bronze or plaster. Possibly when coating his plaster with wax in preparation for making the mold, Rosso was fascinated by the intermediary effects. He had created an image with subtle transitions of value as light reflects off its surfaces. There is a fluidity as forms lose distinctness and flow together. Instead of the solidity and opacity of traditional sculptural materials—stone, wood, and clay—Rosso created a translucent white surface that variedly reflected the light around it.

The "unfinished" quality of his bronze and wax over plaster figures can be thought of as following the esthetic of a sketch-like effect in which the figure is caught in the process of evolution. This is related to the "non finito" of many of Michelangelo's sculptures. One has the awareness of an image coalescing out of Rosso's manipulatable, translucent wax. Eugène Carrière's (1849-1906) monochromatic brown paintings, in which his figures emerge out of a dense atmospheric fog as if they are visions produced in a trance, come to mind. This striving for the essence of a spiritual or emotional reality would ally Rosso to the Symbolist movement emerging in the mid-1880s. In cases where more than one duplicate was made, in each wax-over-plaster he varied the details by allowing the working of the wax to direct the creative process rather than simply replicating earlier versions of the same sculpture.

Mixed Recognition in Paris

In 1884 Rosso went to Paris and worked in the studio of the sculptor Jules Dalou, where he met Rodin, whom Rosso would come to view as his major competitor for fame. The death of his beloved mother forced his return to Milan before the end of the year.

This next period in Milan proved to be personally and artistically beneficial. In 1885 he married Giuditta Pozzi, who by the end of that year bore him a son, Francesco. From 1886 to 1889 he received several commissions and had sculptures shown at both the official and "independents salons" in Paris. He also participated in a major show in Venice in 1887. In 1889 he returned to Paris for the honor of exhibiting his sculptures in the Universal Exhibition, but certainly also with the intention of staying there to secure his place in the art world. Emile Zola's purchase of his *Concierge* (1883) must have given hope to the near-penniless Rosso.

His *Sick Boy* (1893)—which was done in both wax-overplaster and bronze versions—with its indistinct or veiled features captures the mood of the Symbolist poetic trance found in his earlier work. Paris broadened his subject matter, as is evident in his *Conversation in the Garden* (1893, wax-over-plaster). This work consists of three forms which share a common base. Two of these forms appear to be seated, behatted ladies who have been talking; the third, upright, form presumably represents Rosso addressing one of the two ladies. What is obviously globs of wax equally appears to be three figures. There is a charge of mental communication between the standing figure and the central

form. Like most of his sculptures this is small—only 17 inches high. It has been observed in this instance and others that if a work is viewed from an elevated position with the light coming from above the mood and effect of the sculpture is much clearer. That Rosso often conceived his pieces to be viewed from a particular position and with specific lighting is also apparent in the duplication of this effect in photographs of his sculptures which he took himself or directed.

The importance given to visual perception as a factor of conception had appeared earlier, as in Rosso's *Impression in an Omnibus* (1883-1884). This consists of five seated, closely spaced figures whose clothing merges while their heads are silhouetted by what would be the light from the windows behind them. The two end figures are much less distinctly executed and suggest that he may have been thinking of a softening of focus in peripheral vision. While the theme recalls the realism of Honoré Daumier (1810-1879), the effect of a recollected glimpse is distinctly Rosso.

Starting in 1898 his productivity diminished to the point that Rosso rarely produced new works; he merely created copies and variations on older pieces. Conversely, it was in this period that he exhibited most extensively. In 1896 he was included in a Pre-Raphaelite show in London. An exhibition of his sculptures travelled through Germany in 1901, and in 1903 he showed at the Vienna Secession. In the same year he visited Leipzig, Berlin, and Brussels and returned to Paris, where he was one of the founding members of the Salon d'Automne, which had a one-man show of his work in 1904. Thereafter there were frequent exhibitions of his work in salons and galleries, particularly in Italy, where he was in effect discovered at last by his countrymen.

Madame X (wax-over-plaster), variously dated 1896 or 1913, is likely a sketch of 1896 which Rosso finished by coating and working wax over the earlier plaster. It is certainly his most simple piece, being only a ghost-image of a face. Periodically his creativity was resurrected, as in *Ecce Puer* (1906-1907, wax), the head of a child viewed as if with a softened focus. It is not so much the image of a pure, innocent child as it is the purity and innocence of a child that he captured. The controversy over Rodin's debt to him in regard to the *Balzac,* shown in 1898, and Rosso's general stylistic influence on his friend's work created such a bitterness over what Rosso felt was the lack of recognition of his genius that it seemingly inhibited further development.

A Growing Reputation

The poetic tone and Symbolist mood of his sculpture broke with the purely representational standards of the past. Ironically, by the time of his greatest fame during his lifetime—the first quarter of the 20th century—Rosso's work was no longer revolutionary, though the Italian Futurists praised his sculptures and drew upon his artistic experience. During his lifetime and after his death the significance of Rosso's sculpture and his place in the history of art was subject to debate. His work was always associated with that of the prolific French sculptor Auguste Rodin (1840-1917), whose reputation greatly exceeded that of Rosso and negatively affected the perception of Rosso's importance. Despite his having shown frequently and the support of critics and patrons, militating against Rosso's renown are his modest production as well as his having lived and worked so much of his career away from Paris, where Rodin was well established. Furthermore, Rosso had a volatile, bitter, and sometimes outrageous personality in contrast to Rodin's congeniality. A reappraisal of Rosso's work occurred after the 1960s, and his important contribution to the development of 20th-century sculpture has finally been acknowledged.

Rosso's uniqueness and importance in the history of sculpture is established by his having approached his medium as a way of seeing, feeling, and creating images that reject what to that point had been the concept of sculpture as solid and static. As Rosso said: "It is all a question of light. There is no matter in space."

Further Reading

Most of the writings on Rosso are in Italian. The best source to present him in relation to 20th-century sculpture is C. Giedioa-Welcker, *Contemporary Sculpture: An Evolution in Volume and Space* (1955, rev. ed. 1961). The most thorough study on Rosso is M. Scolari Barr's *Medardo Rosso* (1963). □

Michael Ivanovich Rostovtzeff

Michael Ivanovich Rostovtzeff (1870-1952), Russian-born American historian and the foremost classical scholar of his day, specialized in the social and economic movements of Greece and Rome.

Michael Rostovtzeff was born on Nov. 10, 1870, in Kiev, where he went through the university, earning master and doctorate degrees in classical philology. From 1895 to 1898 he traveled throughout the classical lands. He then became professor of Latin at the University of St. Petersburg, a post he occupied until 1918.

Rostovtzeff and his wife left their country in 1918 because of the Russian Revolution and went to England. His *Proletarian Culture* (1919), published under the auspices of the Russian Liberation Committee, showed his revulsion against the principles of the Russian Revolution. In 1920 he became professor of ancient history at the University of Wisconsin, a position he held until 1925, when he went to Yale as Sterling professor of ancient history and archeology. In 1928 he directed Yale's archeological expedition to Dura-Europos on the Euphrates River in Syria. He continued as director and remained as editor of the excavation reports after he retired from teaching in 1944.

At the same time, Rostovtzeff was writing monographs and more general books. Two of his studies, *A Large Estate in Egypt in the Third Century B.C.* and *The Iranians and Greeks in South Russia* (both 1922), showed his interest in economic and cultural development. His *Social and Eco-*

nomic History of the Roman Empire (1926) is considered one of the principal modern contributions to Roman historiography. In his popular text *A History of the Ancient World* (2 vols., 1926-1927) Rostovtzeff devoted considerable space to art and literature, and he extended this interest to Chinese art in his next book, *Inlaid Bronzes of the Han Dynasty in the Collection of C. T. Loo* (1927). He continued to write on topics such as Italy, Seleucid Babylonia, the animal style in Russia and China, and the art of Dura-Europos. The *Social and Economic History of the Hellenistic World* (3 vols., 1941) is his most famous work. He died in New Haven on Oct. 20, 1952.

Rostovtzeff believed that the past had meaning for the present. He thought the ancient world displayed features similar to the modern and argued that the economic development of the ancient world roughly approximated that of the present, although it did not reach the full stage of industrial capitalism. He favored the open Greek economic system in contrast to the closed Egyptian one and the urban middle class over a rural aristocracy. He attacked the notions that the ancient world was a stage from which modern economic development evolved and that economic factors were the sole cause of cultural change.

Further Reading

Rostovtzeff presents his ideas about history in the preface to his *A History of the Ancient World* (2 vols., 1926-1927). Herman Ausubel, *Historians and Their Craft: A Study of the Presidential Addresses of the American Historical Association, 1884-1945* (1950), considers Rostovtzeff the greatest classicist since Mommsen. □

Walt Whitman Rostow

Walt Whitman Rostow (born 1916) was an educator, economist, and government official.

Born in New York City on October 7, 1916, Walt Whitman Rostow was the son of Russian immigrants Victor Aaron and Lillian (Helman) Rostow. He attended Yale University, receiving a B.A. in 1936. Following graduation, Rostow continued his studies, first as a Rhodes scholar at Baillol College, Oxford University, 1936-1938, and then as a graduate student at Yale University, 1938-1940. After receiving a Ph.D. in economics from Yale University in 1940, Rostow taught for one year as an instructor in economics at Columbia University.

With the outbreak of World War II Rostow joined the Office of Strategic Services, soon achieving the rank of major. Stationed in London, one of his primary responsibilities was to recommend enemy targets to the U.S. Air Forces. For his additional work with the British Air Ministry in 1945 he was awarded the Legion of Merit and was made an honorary member of the Order of the British Empire.

Following the war he entered the Department of State as assistant chief of the German-Austrian Economic Division. In 1946-1947 Rostow was named the Harmsworth

Professor of American History at Oxford University. After a two year stint in Geneva as assistant to the executive secretary of the Economic Commission for Europe, an organ of the United Nations, he took another academic position in England serving as Pitt Professor of American History and Institutions at Cambridge University, 1949-1950. His first book, *The American Diplomatic Revolution* based on his inaugural lecture at Oxford University in November 1946, was published in 1947. The next year saw the publication of another book, *Essays on the British Economy of the Nineteenth Century.*

In 1950 Rostow was appointed professor of economic history at the Massachusetts Institute of Technology. The following year he was also named a staff member of the Center for International Studies at that university. Rostow continued in both posts until 1961. During those years Rostow wrote an impressive number of books, articles, and reviews on a wide range of topics. Among those works are: *The Process of Economic Growth* (1953, 2nd ed. 1960); *The Growth and Fluctuation of the British Economy, 1790-1850* (with others, 1953, 2nd ed. 1975); *The Dynamics of Soviet Society* (with others, 1953); *The Prospects for Communist China* (with others, 1954); *An American Policy in Asia* (with R. W. Hatch, 1955); *A Proposal: Key to an Effective Foreign Policy* (with M. F. Millikan, 1957); *The Stages of Economic Growth: A Non-Communist Manifesto* (1960); *The United States in the World Arena* (1960); *Rich Countries and Poor Countries: Reflections from the Past, Lessons for the Future* (1987); and *Theorists of Economic Growth from David Hume to the Present* (1990). These works helped establish

Rostow's reputation as an original and influential economic theorist as well as an astute observer of contemporary international affairs.

In *The Stages of Economic Growth,* perhaps his most influential work, Rostow advanced a theory that sought "to generalize the pattern of modern economic history in the form of a series of stages of economic growth": 1) traditional society, 2) the preconditions for take-off, 3) take-off, 4) the drive to maturity, and 5) the age of high mass consumption. As its subtitle—"a non-communist manifesto"—indicated, Rostow's book argued for the efficacy of the capitalist development model, an argument aimed especially at the newly developing nations of the Third World.

After serving as an aide to John F. Kennedy during the 1960 presidential campaign, Rostow was appointed deputy special assistant for national security affairs by the president-elect in 1961. Later that year he moved to the Department of State, where he remained until 1966 as chairman of the Policy Planning Council. From 1964 to 1966 he also served as a U.S. member of the Inter- American Committee for the Alliance for Progress with the rank of ambassador. In 1966 President Lyndon B. Johnson named Rostow to replace McGeorge Bundy as special assistant to the president for national security affairs. In that post Rostow became one of Johnson's principal foreign policy advisers, especially with regard to the Vietnam War. Beginning with a special mission that he undertook for President Kennedy in late 1961, Rostow had paid close attention to the deepening American involvement in Southeast Asia. His optimistic projections about the U.S. war effort and his consistent support for the use of air power to accomplish U.S. objectives embroiled him in much controversy. Even in later writings he continued to defend the American war effort as well as his own policy positions.

In 1969 Rostow returned to teaching, accepting an appointment at the University of Texas at Austin. In the 1980s he was Rex G. Baker Professor of Political Economy in the Departments of Economics and History at that university. He received the Association of American Publishers Award for outstanding book on social sciences in 1990. In 1992 Rostow was named Chairman of the Board and CEO of the Austin Project. This group's goal was to solve the problems of urban America, starting with the city of Austin, Texas. The idea of the project was to start with the expansion of public and private programs that are aimed at prenatal care and aiding disadvantaged children. Rostow's philosophy was to invest in the young people. He compared the problems of today's cities to Vietnam: "The way we fought the Vietnam War reminds me of the way we are trying to deal with the cities, running after all the symptoms and putting Band-Aids on them instead of going for the cause."

Rostow continued his prolific scholarship, writing a series of books during this period on history, economics, and international affairs. Among these are: *East-West Relations: Is Detente Possible?* (with William E.Griffith, 1969); *Politics and the Stages of Growth* (1971); *The Diffusion of Power* (1972); *How It All Began: Origins of the Modern Economy* (1975); *The World Economy: History and Pros-*

pect (1978); *Getting from Here to There* (1978); *Why the Poor Get Richer and the Rich Slow Down* (1980); *Pre-Invasion Bombing Strategy: General Eisenhower's Decision of March 25, 1944* (1981); *The Division of Europe After World War II: 1946* (1981); *Europe After Stalin: Eisenhower's Three Decisions of March 11, 1953* (1982); *Open Skies: Eisenhower's Proposal of July 21, 1955* (1982); *The Barbaric Counter-Revolution: Cause and Cure* (1983); *The United States and the Regional Organization of Asia and the Pacific, 1965-1985* (1986); and *Stages of Economic Growth: A Non-Communist Manifesto* (1991).

Further Reading

There is no full-length biography of Rostow, but references to his work can be found in numerous studies of economic development theory. In addition, Rostow's role within the Kennedy and Johnson administrations has been treated in a series of general studies of American foreign policy during those years, many focused specifically on the Vietnam War. Of the latter, David Halberstam's *The Best and the Brightest* (1972) contains a brief biographical sketch. □

Mstislav Leopoldovich Rostropovich

"A thorough going Romantic" describes the musicality of Russian-born Mstislav (Slava) Leopoldovich Rostropovich (born 1927). While also active as a pianist and composer, he achieved international renown as a cellist and conductor.

Mstislav Rostropovich was born in Baku, the capital of the Soviet Republic of Azerbaijan, on March 27, 1927. The family was musical, his father being a professional cellist, his mother an accomplished pianist, and his sister a violinist with the Moscow Philharmonic. Rostropovich received his first lessons on both the cello and piano from his parents while quite young and, when the family moved to Moscow, he attended the Gnesin Institute where his father taught.

In 1943 he entered the Moscow Conservatory, studying with Semyon Kozolupov (cello) and Dmitri Shostakovich and Vissaryon Shebalin (composition), among others. He graduated with the highest distinction.

Rostropovich had won competitions for his cello playing in Moscow, Prague, and Budapest by the late 1940s. In 1956 he received a post as cello professoshipr at the Moscow Conservatory. By now an international career was well established, documented by numerous prizes and tours of Europe and the United States. His American debut took place at Carnegie Hall, New York, in April 1956. During the same period he met his future wife, Galina Vishnevskaya, then a soprano with the Bolshoi Opera. He occasionally served as her piano accompanist in song recitals. Their two daughters are both musicians.

Rostropovich brought to his performances a complete command of the cello and a display of emotional intensity that were at once apparent to the audience. His technique maintained both accuracy of pitch and fullness of tone through the entire range of the instrument, and he excelled in producing a wide variety of tone colors. Flaws in his playing were more often of a musical, rather than technical, nature, such as his occasional tendency to overplay and his lapses in phrasing continuity. His repertoire extended from Bach to the moderns, several of whom wrote works for him. The list includes Shostakovich, Prokofiev, Penderecki, Lutoslawski, and Britten.

Beginning in 1975 Rostropovich played a cello, the "Duport," created by Antonio Stradivari in 1711. The instrument was in perfect condition except for a mark on its lower body, said to have been put there by Napoleon who, after hearing Duport play, asked to examine the instrument and accidentally bumped it with his spur.

Although Rostropovich had been interested in conducting since childhood, his career in this art did not pick up until after 1968, when he made his debut at the Bolshoi Theater in Moscow with Tchaikovsky's *Eugene Onegin*. He credited much of his ability to the observations he was able to make while performing as a soloist under various conductors. While he once made the statement that "no performer's identity is as important as the composer's," he was criticized for exaggerated and sometimes sentimental interpretations, tendencies also found in his cello playing. He was therefore most comfortable with music where these qualities are more appropriate—emotional works of the Romantic and Post-Romantic periods. He had, though, surprising success with some of the more "difficult" moderns, including Penderecki, Lutoslawski, and C. Halffter.

A defender of personal freedoms, Rostropovich ran afoul of the Soviet State for coming to the aid of his friend Alexander Solzhenitsyn, who was refused admittance into Moscow after the publication in the West of *The First Circle* and *Cancer Ward.* Rostropovich first allowed the writer to stay with him for an extended period and then, when Solzhenitsyn won the Nobel Prize for Literature in 1970 and was still not allowed to publish in Russia, wrote a letter to the press on his friend's behalf. The letter, which attacked Soviet censorship of the arts, the suppression of human rights, and the incompetence of those in administrative positions in the arts, remained unpublished in Russia but was picked up by foreign presses. Then began an official harassment of the careers of both Rostropovich and his wife. Their passports were confiscated and all tours outside the country canceled. At home they were limited to lesser engagements in remote places and when performances were broadcast their names were removed from the list of credits. A letter from Rostropovich to Brezhnev went unanswered. Finally, the intercession of several prominent people in the United States, including Leonard Bernstein and Senator Edward Kennedy, persuaded officials to allow Rostropovich and his family a two-year absence from the country during which they would be based in Britain. Both he and his wife were stripped of their Soviet citizenship in March 1978.

A successful concert he had given in Washington, D.C., with the National Symphony Orchestra led to a post as music director with that orchestra beginning in 1977. He was also a regular guest conductor with the London Philharmonic Orchestra for several years and it was with this orchestra that he made the first recording of Shostakovich's opera, *Lady Macbeth of Mtsensk,* his wife singing the role of Katerina. While with the London Philharmonic Orchestra he recorded the complete symphonies of Tchaikovsky, a composer he regarded more highly than do most musicians.

When he heard of the right-wing coup in the U.S.S.R. on August 19, 1991, Rostropovich flew immediately to Moscow. Continuing his dedication to freedom, he spent the next three days in the Russian parliament building while the coup collapsed around him. He called this time "the best days of my life." Those types of days became even more frequent. In May, 1997, wrapped in an emotional visit to his native Azerbaijan he offered his music or even his life to prevent new fighting in the region. During his five-day stay he offered to play for the presidents of Armenia and Azerbaijan for as long as it took to settle the long dispute over the enclave of Nagorno-Karabakh. Leaving for Moscow, he said, "If there is a new outbreak of hostilities in the conflict zone, I will go there, stand between the forces and say: Better kill me."

Although not originally known as a composer, Rostropovich retained an active interest in writing music throughout his career. He dismissed his student works as "bad imitations of Prokofiev," but occasionally included some later pieces in his own cello recitals. His compositions include two piano concertos, a work for a string quartet, various piano and cello pieces, and a satirical cantata.

His composing career has given him several widely acclaimed distinctions. In June, 1994, he conducted his last subscription concert as music director at the John F. Kennedy Center for the Performing Arts. The program, Verdi Requiem, more or less personified its leader: big, impassioned and extroverted and topped off his 17 seasons as the conductor of the National Symphony Orchestra.

In October, 1995, he returned to Russia to fight for a new cause-the costly and controversial reconstruction of Moscow's Christ the Savior Cathedral. It was said, that hundreds of wealthy and well-dressed Russians paid $1,000 apiece to hear Rostropovich conduct and play cello in the Moscow Conservatory.

April, 1997 gave Rostropovich the distinction of being the last conductor to play the Chicago Symphony Orchestra Hall before the $105 million renovation and expansion transformed the Orchestra Hall into Symphony Center.

Rostropovich did not give up his cello. In March of 1997, he, at age 70, played works by Marcello, Beethoven, Bach, Rachmaninoff and Shostakovich at the music festival in Monaco, dedicated to the memory of Princess Grace.

Among his numerous awards and distinctions were the Stalin Prize (1951); the Gold Medal of the Royal Philharmonic Society, London (1970); honorary doctorates from Harvard (1974) and Cambridge (1975) universities; Officer of the French Légion d'honneur (1982); the Anti-Defamation League Award (1985); and was made an honorary knight in 1987.

Further Reading

As Rostropovich divided his career between the cello and conducting, so the curious reader must consult different sources for either branch of his activities. The monthly periodical *The Strad* followed his life as a cellist very closely, scarcely an issue being without some mention of him. *The Washington Post* contained updates on his conducting engagements with the National Symphony Orchestra. This newspaper is indexed separately as well as in the *National Newspaper Index,* the latter being perhaps the more current. Helena Matheopoulos devoted a chapter to Rostropovich the conductor in her book *Maestro: Encounters with Conductors of Today* (1982). Rostropovich himself described the harassment of his and his wife's careers in an article in the *New York Times* (March 6, 1975). See also *Chicago Tribune,* "Grand Finale," 04/26/97; "CSO Announces 1996-97 Schedule," 02/09/96; "Famed Conductor Performs For Cathedral In Moscow," 10/23/95; "Verdi Requiem Is Swan Song For Rostropovich," 06/17/94. *New York Times* "Music Festival In Monaco," March 16, 1997. *LA Times* "World in Brief, Azerbaijan, Rostropovich Offers Music, Life for Peace," May 4, 1997. □

Philip Roth

The American author Philip Roth (born 1933) used his Jewish upbringing and his college days for the basis of many of his novels and other works.

Roth used his experiences in growing up in the Weequahic section of Newark, New Jersey, and his days as a college student in Rutgers and Bucknell as material for many of his works. He also employed his own writings and the public, and critical reaction to them, as the focus of much of his later material. For example, in two of his novels, *Zuckerman Unbound* (1981) and *The Anatomy Lesson* (1983), Roth expended thousands of words on the question of whether the novel he may be best known for, *Portnoy's Complaint* (1969), could be considered anti-Semitic.

Roth's critics found elements in his writing that reminded them of Saul Bellow, Norman Mailer, J.D. Salinger, and Bernard Malamud. He introduced Franz Kafka as a character in his essay-story "Looking at Kafka," in which he had the Czech writer coming to Newark to be his Hebrew teacher at the age of nine. In *Professor of Desire* (1977) Roth's character David Kepesh journeys to Prague to visit Kafka's home and discuss him with a Czech professor who is devoted to Melville. Henry James' *Portrait of a Lady* becomes a point at issue with the hero of *Letting Go* (1962) and the woman he is involved with, and *The Breast* (1972) concerns the overnight change of a professor of literature into a six-foot mammary gland, recalling Gogol's *The Nose* and Kafka's *The Metamorphosis*.

Born in 1933 to Herman Roth, an insurance salesman, and the former Bess Finkel, the writer grew up in a Jewish neighborhood in Newark, the city that was to serve as the home of the protagonist of his highly successful *Goodbye, Columbus* (1959), for which he won the National Book

Award when he was only 26 and which was later made into a film. It is the story of a poor young Jewish man from Newark, Rutgers, who has an affair with a wealthy young Jewish woman from the nearby New Jersey suburbs. The romance ends because of their differences in values. Alfred Kazin compared Roth's observations of the ways of the rich in this novella to F. Scott Fitzgerald's. Saul Bellow called him a virtuoso, and Irving Howe wrote that he had achieved the kind of a voice writers strive a lifetime to find. However, in "Philip Roth Revisited" (*Commentary*, 1972), Howe wrote a stinging assessment of the writer's works up to that point, declaring that he thought well of only one of his stories, "Defender of the Faith," which appeared with four other short stories in the *Goodbye, Columbus* collection. Later, in *The Anatomy Lesson*, Roth, through his alter ego, Nathan Zuckerman, describes an attack on his work by a Jewish intellectual whom critic Joseph Epstein names as Howe.

It was when he wrote of the suffocating restrictions of his Jewish youth in Newark in his best-selling *Portnoy's Complaint* that Roth leaped into public and critical scrutiny. He was praised for having written an amusing sex novel in the fashion of Henry Miller. It was described as hilariously lewd, capable of making the reader laugh out loud, although not without its touching moments. But, it had its detractors as well. Some found it obscene and revolting, declaring it pictured Jewish life in a degrading manner. Others thought it was a novel that led nowhere. Irving Howe, one of the major challengers to the value of Roth's work, said that "the cruelest thing anyone can do with *Portnoy's Complaint* is to read it twice." Later critics said that both of Roth's popular works, *Goodbye, Columbus* and *Portnoy's Complaint,* seemed somewhat dated by the end of the 1980s.

Many of the characters in his novels suggest Roth himself. In *My Life as a Man* (1970), which some critics hold as one of his best works, he depicts a novelist, Peter Tarnopol, recounting the sexual adventures of his fictional alter ego, Nathan Zuckerman, who will return as the author of *Carnovsky,* a sensational best-seller about sexual liberation that seems like *Portnoy's Complaint*. The Roth Tarnopol-Zuckerman character reappears in the Zuckerman trilogy—*The Ghost Writer* (1978), *Zuckerman Unbound,* and *The Anatomy Lesson*—as the hero confronts the relationship between life and literature and experiences the joys and sorrows of fame.

Not all of Roth's novels follow the theme of the male Jewish writer at work. In *When She Was Good* (1967) his main character is a Protestant female, and the novel is set in the Midwest. *Our Gang* (1971) is a political satire of the early 1970s opening with a quote from then President Richard Nixon that "the unborn have rights" that are "recognized in law, recognized even in principles expounded by the United Nations." Roth goes on to have his main character, whom he calls Tricky, argue that he "could have done the popular thing and come out against the sanctity of human life," but he decided to risk losing a second term by defending the rights of the unborn.

When Roth published *The Facts: A Novelist's Autobiography* in 1988, some of his readers though that the facts of his life might be here separated from the fiction he had been creating. But the form of the work helps to leave the issue in doubt. Roth begins by writing a letter to Nathan Zuckerman, hero of *The Counterlife* (1986) and so many of his previous novels, asking him for his candid opinion of the book. Then, 160 pages later, Zuckerman responds. He tells him not to publish it and, instead of trying to "accurately" report on the life of Philip Roth, to continue writing about Zuckerman. In *Deception* (1990) he challenged both reader and critic to decide what was fiction and what was autobiographical, when the male character (Philip) complains to the woman in the novel, "I write fiction and I'm told it's autobiography. I write autobiography and I'm told it's fiction, so since I'm so dim and they're so *smart,* let them decide."

Other major works published during the 1990's included: *Patrimony* (1991), a story about his 86-year-old father's struggle with an incurable brain tumor, received the National Book Critics Circle Award; *Operation Shylock: A Confession* (1993), winner of the 1994 Pen/Faulkner Award for Fiction and *Time* magazine's Best American Novel award; *Sabbath's Theater* (1995), National Book Award for Fiction; and *American Pastoral* (1997) an account of the effect that the Vietnam War had on the family of Seymour (Swede) Levov, a high school hero the fictional Zuckerman.

Further Reading

For additional information on Philip Roth from critics, including Roth himself, see Philip Roth, *Reading Myself and Others* (1975); Martin Green, "Introduction" in *A Philip Roth Reader* (1980); Sanford Pinsker, "Zuckerman's Success," *Mainstream* (December 1981); Julian Webb, "Nathan Agonistes," *The Spectator* (March 3, 1984); Joseph Epstein, "What Does Philip Roth Want?" in *Plausible Prejudices: Essays on American Writing* (1985); Jonathan Brent, "What Facts? A Talk With Philip Roth," and Justin Kaplan, "Play It Again, Nathan," both *The New York Times* (September 25, 1988); and Fay Weldon, "Talk Before Sex and Talk After Sex," the *New York Times* (March 11, 1990). Murray Baumgarten and Barbara Gottfried provided a critical review of major works in *Understanding Philip Roth* (1990, Columbia Univ Press). □

Mark Rothko

The American painter Mark Rothko (1903-1970) was one of the original abstract expressionists who emerged in New York after World War II. His mature painting emphasized pure color.

Mark Rothko was born on Sept. 25, 1903, in Gvinsk, Russia, and emigrated to the United States in 1913. He attended Yale University (1921-1923), and he began painting in 1925, when he studied with Max Weber at the Art Students League in New York. He later traveled extensively in Europe.

In 1935 Rothko cofounded "The Ten," an organization of expressionist artists in New York. During 1936 and 1937 he worked on the government's Federal Arts Project. In 1948 he joined Robert Motherwell, Barnett Newman, and William Baziotes in founding a New York art school called "Subjects of the Artist." For extensive periods throughout his career Rothko taught at colleges and universities, including the Center Academy in Brooklyn (1929-1952), the California School of Fine Arts in San Francisco (summers of 1947 and 1949), Brooklyn College (1951-1954), the University of Colorado (1955), and Tulane University (1956).

Rothko's first important one-man show in 1945 at the Art of This Century Gallery in New York City established him as a leading figure in postwar American painting. During the 1940s and 1950s he exhibited regularly. In 1958 his work was included in the Venice Biennale, and in 1961 the Museum of Modern Art in New York City held a retrospective exhibition. Among Rothko's special awards were his election to the National Institute of Arts and Letters in 1968 and the honorary degree of doctor of fine arts from Yale University in 1969. Rothko committed suicide in New York on Feb. 25, 1970.

Like nearly all the advanced American painters who matured during the 1940s, Rothko's early work was founded on the tenets of both cubism and surrealism. This meant that his art leaned both toward the problems of formal abstraction and toward a more traditional notion of conceptualized subject matter. By the late 1940s, however, he gradually broke through to a style that rejected both cubism and surrealism, and his work became linked with

the abstract expressionism of men like Jackson Pollock and Willem de Kooning. Rothko's bestknown paintings of the 1950s and 1960s continued to be associated with this general style.

But Rothko's art reveals a distinct and personal interpretation of the abstract expressionist style. From his first emergence as a mature artist, he eschewed the gestural brushwork and the dense, painterly surfaces that became celebrated in the work of De Kooning, Franz Kline, and others. Instead, Rothko concentrated on expression through color alone, and to this end he radically simplified his imagery. In his best paintings, the imagery consists of two or three rectangles of color that float within an abstract space. Generally, the areas of color dissolve softly into one another, denying all traces of either hard or tactile edges. The softness is a function of the artist's delicate, feathery brushstrokes, and it results in an expanding pictorial space that seems to consist of pure color rather than colored objects. In many of Rothko's paintings his colors appear to generate their own magical or divine light.

Further Reading

The catalog of Rothko's Museum of Modern Art retrospective exhibition, *Mark Rothko,* by Peter Selz (1961) is especially rich with illustrations. Rothko's place within the abstract expressionist movement is presented in Barbara Rose, *American Art since 1900* (1967). □

Johann Michael Rottmayr

Johann Michael Rottmayr (1654-1730) was the first native-born Austrian painter of the 18th century to achieve preeminence over the Italians, thus beginning the great century of Austrian baroque painting.

Johann Michael Rottmayr born in Laufen, a small town near Salzburg, on Dec. 10, 1654, probably learned the rudiments of his craft from his mother, who was a painter. About 1675 he went to Venice, entering the workshop of Karl Loth, an expatriate Bavarian, with whom he remained for 13 years. About 1688 he returned to Austria and soon entered the service of the prince-bishop of Salzburg, Johann Ernst Graf Thun, who favored German artists over the Italians, who still dominated art north of the Alps.

Rottmayr's lifelong friendship and collaboration with the architect Johann Bernhard Fischer von Erlach began in Salzburg. Rottmayr painted altarpieces and frescoes for most of Fischer's buildings in Salzburg—the Church of the Trinity (ca. 1702), the Church of the Hospital of St. John (1709), and the University Church (1721-1722)—as well as for the Residenz (1689, 1710-1714) and other secular and religious buildings in the city. The two men also collaborated at Frain Castle (Vranov) in Moravia (1695), creating, in the so-called Ancestral Hall, the first of their huge oval cupolas, where through painted illusionistic foreshortening

and perspective the impression is given of seeing the open sky filled with mythological beings glorifying, in this case, the family of the owner. Rottmayr's early style, though very much like that of his master, Loth, is characterized by his own bright local color, massive forms, and strong movement.

Rottmayr moved to Vienna about 1699, where he continued to work with Fischer on such projects as Schönbrunn Palace (1700). But Rottmayr also began to receive other commissions, notably the fresco decoration of the Jesuit Church in Breslau (1704-1706) and of the Liechtenstein Summer Palace outside Vienna (1706-1707), as well as paintings for the Council Chamber of the Vienna City Hall (1712).

In Vienna, Rottmayr's style became more fluid, with subtler, more ingratiating color and more harmonious compositions, suggesting the influence of the works of Peter Paul Rubens and Anthony Van Dyck available to him there; yet it retained the strong plasticity and dynamic movement of his early years. During the first 2 decades of the 18th century he was the leading painter of Vienna and the Hapsburg domains. Although he continued to work intermittently elsewhere in the Holy Roman Empire—Salzburg, Franconia, and Bohemia—his work from this time on was largely in Vienna and its environs. He decorated the interior of the church of the monastery of Melk with frescoes and altarpieces (1716-1722), and in the Karlskirche in Vienna, Fischer von Erlach's most famous creation, Rottmayr painted the *Glorification of St. Charles Borromeo* in the dome as well as the entire fresco decoration of the church (1725-1729). One of his last important commissions was the frescoes for the church of the monastery of Klosterneuburg outside Vienna (1729).

A painter of great imagination, Rottmayr imbued his essentially idealized figures with a robust liveliness and naturalism of great appeal. His color, especially in his maturity, is often of enchanting beauty and refinement. The visionary effect of his ceiling paintings is sometimes reduced by the massiveness of his figures, but all are eminently effective in their swirling compositions.

Rottmayr was ennobled in 1704 with the title "von Rosenbrunn." He died in Vienna on Oct. 28, 1730, almost literally with his brush in his hand.

Further Reading

There is no monograph on Rottmayr in English. He is discussed in Eberhard Hempel, *Baroque Art and Architecture in Central Europe* (1965). Edward A. Maser, *Disegni inediti di Johann Michael Rottmayer* (1971), in Italian, dealing with his drawings, is illustrated in color. □

Georges Rouault

Georges Rouault (1871-1958), a French painter and graphic artist, was one of the most outstanding religious painter of the modern movement.

Georges Rouault was born on May 27, 1871, in Paris. His father was a cabinet-maker, and the family had artistic interests. Between 1885 and 1890 Rouault worked as an apprentice to stained-glass painters on the restoration of medieval windows and attended evening classes at the École des Arts Décoratifs. His predilection for luminous colors and black outlines had its origin in these early experiences.

In 1890 Rouault entered the École des Beaux-Arts, and the following year Gustave Moreau became his teacher. Henri Matisse and Albert Marquet were fellow students. Rouault became Moreau's favorite pupil, and his early works (mainly religious themes, with some portraits and somber landscapes) were painted in a traditional manner very like his teacher's. Rouault competed twice for the Prix de Rome (1893 and 1895), both times without success. In 1894, however, the artist won both a prize and a competition.

In 1901 Rouault spent some time in the Benedictine abbey at Ligugé, where the author J. K. Huysman tried to organize a brotherhood of artists. In 1903 Rouault became the first curator of the Moreau Museum and participated in the foundation of the Salon d'Automne with Matisse and Marquet. In 1904 Rouault met the Catholic writer Léon Bloy and, influenced by him, sought to depict the tragedy of the human condition. At that year's Salon d'Automne a large number of Rouault's watercolors appeared, depicting prostitutes, clowns, and acrobats painted in gloomy colors. Although he exhibited with the Fauves in 1905, he did not belong to this or any other group.

Rouault's *Prostitute before Her Mirror* (1906) is depicted with fierce loathing and revulsion. The series of judges and politicians, in which he attacked injustice and hypocrisy, began in 1908 and continued to about 1916. He also painted the poor and the humble. His indignation was expressed not only in subject matter but also in his brushwork.

In 1908 Rouault married Marthe Le Sidaner; they had four children. His first one-man show took place in Paris in 1910. In 1911 he moved to Versailles, where the philosopher Jacques Maritain and his wife were neighbors. In 1917 Ambroise Vollard became Rouault's dealer and set him up in a large studio in Paris. Between 1917 and 1927 Vollard commissioned illustrations for several books (*Père Ubu, The Circus, Les Fleurs du mal, Miserere,* and *Guerre*). Rouault developed a new and complex technique in his graphic work and worked in etching, wood engraving, and color lithography.

In 1918, when Rouault abandoned watercolor and gouache for oil, his palette became lighter and more jewellike. The artist's fury was replaced by compassion, as in his tender faces of Christ. His mature work has a vibrant luminosity, and heavy black outlines define the forms. Masterpieces of this style are the *Old King* (1937) and the *Head of Christ* (1937-1938).

Rouault wrote both prose and poetry. He also published autobiographical books, such as *Souvenirs intimes* (1926) and *Stella Vespertina* (1947). He produced designs for tapestries, stained-glass windows (church in Assy), and enamels. In 1929 he executed the sets and costumes for Sergei Diaghilev's ballet *The Prodigal Son.*

Between 1940 and 1956 large restrospective exhibitions of Rouault's work took place in many European and American museums and even in Japan. He died in Paris on Feb. 13, 1958, and was given a state funeral.

Further Reading

The most comprehensive study of Rouault is Pierre Courthion, *Georges Rouault* (1962), which contains a classified catalog, bibliography, list of exhibitions, and index. A useful survey of his life and work is Lionello Venturi, *Rouault: Biographical and Critical Study* (1959). For reproductions and commentary on his work see the two publications of the New York Museum of Modern Art: *Georges Rouault: Paintings and Prints,* by James Thrall Soby (1945; 3d ed. 1947), and *Georges Rouault, Miserere,* with a preface by Rouault and an introduction by M. Wheeler (1952).

Additional Sources

Dorival, Bernard. *Rouault,* New York: Crown Publishers, 1984. □

Francis Peyton Rous

The American pathologist and virologist Francis Peyton Rous (1879-1970) received the Nobel Prize

in medicine for his pioneering work on the relation of viruses to cancer.

Peyton Rous was born in Baltimore, Md., on Oct. 5, 1879. He attended Johns Hopkins University in Baltimore, from which he received a bachelor's degree in 1900 and a medical degree in 1905. From 1905 to 1906 he served as resident house officer at the Johns Hopkins Hospital and from 1906 to 1908 was an instructor in pathology at the University of Michigan. In 1909 Rous went to the Rockefeller Institute for Medical Research in New York City, where he remained until his death on Feb. 16, 1970.

At the Rockefeller Institute, Rous began a series of studies of tumors in chickens. It was then widely believed that cancers were caused by chemical agents and that they could be transmitted from one animal to another only through the actual transplantation of cancerous cells. By 1911 Rous was able to show that tumors in chickens could be transferred from one chicken to another through a cell-free filtrate. The implication of this work was that the particular cancer being studied was caused by a virus. However, although Rous's observations were indicative of what would one day be a widely held belief, that is, that some cancers are virusinduced, his work was not well accepted in 1911.

Rous next attempted to show that a virus was present as a causative agent in mammalian tumors, but he failed, and it was not until the mid-1930s that he again turned to this line of research. In the interim he developed methods of cultivating cancer viruses in test tubes and in chick embryos, did research in liver and gallbladder physiology, and was a principal figure in the development of blood banks. The last-mentioned contribution was made during World War I, when, working with J. R. Turner, Rous found that whole blood could be preserved for many weeks under refrigeration when it was put in a citrate solution.

In the early 1930s Richard Shope, a member of the Rockefeller Institute and friend of Rous, demonstrated that a virus caused large warts in wild rabbits. Working with this fact, Rous and his laboratory associates were soon able to show that the virus causing these warts sometimes produced cancer. With this demonstration that viruses were associated with mammalian cancers, the virus theory made great progress. By the mid-1940s, that viruses were one cause of cancer was generally accepted; in 1966, at the age of 87, Rous was awarded the Nobel Prize in medicine. The prize was shared with Charles Brenton Huggins, a pioneer in the treatment of cancer.

Rous received many other awards and much public recognition. He was a member of the Board of Scientific Consultants of the Sloan Kettering Institute for Cancer Research and was coeditor of the *Journal of Experimental Medicine.*

Further Reading

Details on Rous's life and work are in George W. Corner, *A History of the Rockefeller Institute, 1901-1953* (1964). *McGraw-Hill Modern Men of Science,* vol. 1 (1966), includes an autobiographical sketch. Isaac Berenblum, *Men against Cancer* (1952), and Greer Williams, *Virus Hunters* (1959), are useful in placing Rous's work in an overall framework. □

Henri Rousseau

The Frenchman Henri Rousseau (1844-1910) was the greatest modern European primitive painter. His works are infused with fantasy of a naively charming character.

Henri Rousseau was born in Laval on May 21, 1844. At the age of 18 he enlisted in the army, where he played the saxophone in an infantry band. It is usually assumed by biographers, following Rousseau's own account, that he was stationed in Mexico from 1862 to 1866 as part of the French force supporting the emperor Maximilian.

Rousseau left the army in 1866, worked for a while as a clerk in a lawyer's office, and married in 1869. In 1871 he served as a corporal in the army in the Franco-Prussian War. Upon demobilization that year he took a minor position with the customs service (hence he is often called Rousseau le Douanier, "the Customs Officer"), where he remained until his early retirement in 1885.

Given a small pension, Rousseau settled in humble quarters and devoted himself to painting. In 1884 he had begun to copy in the Louvre. He studied briefly with the academic painter Jean Léon Gérôme at the École des Beaux-Arts. In 1886 Rousseau exhibited for the first time at the Salon des Indépendants, where he showed fairly regularly until his death. He helped support himself by giving lessons in painting, diction, and music—he was a skilled violinist. Though many ridiculed him, Paul Gauguin, Odilon Redon, Georges Seurat, Camille Pissarro, and Henri de Toulouse-Lautrec admired his work. Rousseau believed himself a great artist: in an autobiographical account of 1895 he wrote that he was becoming "one of France's best realist painters."

Of a generous and trusting nature, Rousseau was well liked by other artists, whom he invited to his soirées, but he was often made the object of practical jokes. In 1908 he was given a party by Pablo Picasso, whom he came to consider as one of the two greatest living painters, the other being himself. Rousseau died in Paris on Sept. 2, 1910, and Constantin Brancusi chiseled on his tombstone a eulogy composed by the poet Guillaume Apollinaire.

The power of Rousseau's paintings is derived from a remarkable combination of fantasy and actuality. His scenes are grounded in actuality, but even as he has tried to realize the concreteness of each event, they have been transformed into a quaint private world. Neither modeling nor atmospheric perspective, a technique in which objects are blurred to suggest distance from the observer, is used. He depicted weddings and family reunions of friends; cityscapes and landscapes of Paris and its suburbs, like the *Village Street* (1909); and, most remarkable of all, jungle scenes.

Rousseau's jungle pictures are an amalgamation of memory images of his Mexican trip (if, indeed, he ever was in Mexico), visual experiences from visits to botanical gardens and zoos, and depictions of plants and wild animals he had seen on postcards and in photographs. In the *Sleeping Gypsy* (1897) a Negress, in a picturesque costume, lies asleep in the midst of a desert with a mandolin and a pitcher beside her. The moon is shining (it echoes in form the curved mandolin), and a lion sniffs curiously at her. The *Dream* (1910) may be connected with a youthful romance of Rousseau, who had been enamored of a Polish girl named Yadwigah (he wrote a poem to her in connection with this work). A nude woman lies on a couch in the middle of jungle. About her grows lush foliage in which fierce animals, surprisingly tame, lurk. His jungle scenes, though based on real objects and perhaps certain events, in their totality clearly existed only in his mind's eye.

Further Reading

A study that takes into account most previous research on Rousseau is Dora Vallier, *Henri Rousseau* (1964). Other works on him include Daniel Cotton Rich, *Henri Rousseau* (1942; rev. ed. 1946), and Jean Bouret, *Henri Rousseau* (1961). For Rousseau and his times see Roger Shattuck, *The Banquet Years: The Arts in France, 1885-1918* (1958; rev. ed. 1968).

Additional Sources

Alley, Ronald. *Portrait of a primitive: the art of Henri Rousseau,* New York: Dutton, 1978. □

Jean Jacques Rousseau

The Swiss-born philosopher, author, political theorist, and composer Jean Jacques Rousseau (1712-1778) ranks as one of the greatest figures of the French Enlightenment.

Both Jean Jacques Rousseau the man and his writings constitute a problem for anyone who wants to grasp his thought and to understand his life. He claimed that his work presented a coherent outlook; yet many critics have found only contradictions and passionate outbursts of rhetoric. One interpreter has called Rousseau "an irresponsible writer with a fatal gift for epigram." In the eyes of others Rousseau was not a "serious thinker" but only a mere feeler who occasionally had a great thought. Still others have found Rousseau a mere juggler of words and definitions. Even those who turn to him as an innovating genius have been at odds concerning what he advocated. Rousseau has been variously applauded or denounced as the founder of the romantic movement in literature, as the intellectual father of the French Revolution, as a passionate defender of individual freedom and private property, as a socialist, as a collectivist totalitarian, as a superb critic of the social order, and as a silly and pernicious utopian. Some few critics notably Gustave Lanson and E. H. Wright—have taken Rousseau at his word and believe that he attempted to answer only one question: how can civilized man recapture the benefits of "natural man" and yet neither return to the state of nature nor renounce the advantages of the social state?

For Rousseau's biographers the man himself has been as puzzling as his work—a severe moralist who lived a dangerously "relaxed" life, a misanthrope who loved humanity, a cosmopolitan who prided himself on being a "citizen of Geneva," a writer for the stage who condemned the theater, and a man who became famous by writing essays that denounced culture. In addition to these anomalies, his biographers have had to consider his confessed sexual "peculiarities"—his lifelong habit of masturbation, his exhibitionism, his youthful pleasure in being beaten, his 33-year liaison with a virtual illiterate, and his numerous affairs—and, characteristic of his later years, his persecution suspicions that reached neurotic intensity.

Three major periods characterize Rousseau's life. The first (1712-1750) culminated in the succès de scandale of his *Discours sur les sciences et les arts*. The second (1750-1762) saw the publication of his closely related major works: *La Nouvelle Héloïse* (1761), *L'Émile* (1762), and *Du contrat social* (1762). The last period (1762-1778) found Rousseau an outcast, hounded from country to country, his books condemned and burned, and a personnage, re-

spected and with influential friends. The *Confessions, Dialogues,* and *Les Rêveries du promeneur solitaire* date from this period.

Youth, 1712-1750

Rousseau was the second child of a strange marriage. His mother, Suzanne Bernard, had at the age of 33 married Isaac Rousseau, a man less wellborn than she. Isaac, exhausted perhaps by his frequent quarrels over money with his mother-in-law, left his wife in 1705 for Constantinople. He returned to Suzanne in September 1711. Jean Jacques was born on June 28, 1712, at Geneva, Switzerland. Nine days later his mother died.

At the age of 3, Jean Jacques was reading and weeping over French novels with his father. From Isaac's sister the boy acquired his passion for music. His father fled Geneva to avoid imprisonment when Jean Jacques was 10. By the time he was 13, his formal education had ended. Apprenticed to a notary public, he was soon dismissed as fit only for watchmaking. Apprenticed again, this time to an engraver, Rousseau spent 3 wretched years in hateful servitude, which he abandoned when he found himself unexpectedly locked out of the city by its closed gates. He faced the world with no visible assets and no obvious talents.

Rousseau found himself on Palm Sunday, 1728, in Annecy at the house of Louise Eleonore, Baronne de Warens. She sent him to a hospice for catechumens in Turin, where among "the biggest sluts and the most disgusting trollops who ever defiled the fold of the Lord," he

embraced the Roman Catholic faith. His return to Madame de Warens in 1729 initiated a strange alliance between a 29-year-old woman of the world and a sensitive 17-year-old youth.

Rousseau lived under her roof off and on for 13 years and was dominated by her influence. He became her *Petit;* she was his *Maman.* Charming and clever, a born speculator, Madame de Warens was a woman who lived by her wits. She supported him; she found him jobs, most of which he regarded as uncongenial. A friend, after examining the lad, informed her that he might aspire to become a village curé but nothing more. Still Rousseau read, studied, and reflected. He pursued music and gave lessons. For a time he was a not too successful tutor.

First Publications and Operas

In 1733, disturbed by the advances made to Rousseau by the mother of one of his music pupils, Madame de Warens offered herself to him. Rousseau became her lover: "I felt as if I had been guilty of incest." The sojourn with Madame de Warens was over by 1742. Though she had taken other lovers and he had enjoyed other escapades, Rousseau was still devoted to her. He thought that the scheme of musical notation he had developed would make his fortune in Paris and thus enable him to save her from financial ruin. But his journey to Paris took Rousseau out of her life. He saw her only once again, in 1754. Reduced to begging and the charity of her neighbors, Madame de Warens died destitute in 1762.

Rousseau's scheme for musical notation, published in 1743 as *Dissertation sur la musique moderne,* brought him neither fame nor fortune—only a letter of commendation from the Académie des Sciences. But his interest in music spurred him to write two operas—*Les Muses galantes* (1742) and *Le Devin du village* (1752)—and permitted him to write articles on music for Denis Diderot's *Encyclopédie; the Lettre sur la musique française,* which embroiled him in a quarrel with the Paris Opéra (1753); and the *Dictionnaire de musique,* published in 1767.

From September 1743 until August 1744 Rousseau served as secretary to the French ambassador to Venice. He experienced at firsthand the stupidity of officialdom and began to see how institutions lend their authority to injustice and oppression in the name of peace and order. Rousseau spent the remaining years before his success with his first *Discours* in Paris, where he lived from hand to mouth the life of a struggling intellectual.

In March 1745 Rousseau began a liaison with Thérèse Le Vasseur. She was 24 years old, a maid at Rousseau's lodgings. She remained with him for the rest of his life—as mistress, housekeeper, mother of his children, and finally, in 1768, as his wife. He portrayed her as devoted and unselfish, although many of his friends saw her as a malevolent gossip and troublemaker who exercised a baleful influence on his suspicions and dislikes. Not an educated woman—Rousseau himself cataloged her malapropisms—she nonetheless possessed the uncommon quality of being able to offer stability to a man of volatile intensity. They had five children—though some biographers have questioned whether any of them were Rousseau's. Apparently he regarded them as his own even though he abandoned them to the foundling hospital. Rousseau had no means to educate them, and he reasoned that they would be better raised as workmen and peasants by the state.

By 1749 Diderot had become a sympathetic friend, and Rousseau regarded him as a kindred spirit. The publication of Diderot's *Lettre sur les aveugles* had resulted in his imprisonment at Vincennes. While walking to Vincennes to visit Diderot, Rousseau read an announcement of a prize being offered by the Dijon Academy for the best essay on the question: has progress of the arts and sciences contributed more to the corruption or to the purification of morals?

Years of Fruition, 1750-1762

Rousseau won the prize of the Dijon Academy with his *Discours sur les sciences et les arts* and became "l'homme du jour." His famous rhetorical "attack" on civilization called forth 68 articles defending the arts and sciences. Though he himself regarded this essay as "the weakest in argument and the poorest in harmony and proportion" of all his works, he nonetheless believed that it sounded one of his essential themes; the arts and sciences, instead of liberating men and increasing their happiness, have for the most part shackled men further. "Necessity erected thrones; the arts and sciences consolidated them," he wrote.

The *Discours sur l'origine de l'inégalité des hommes,* written in response to the essay competition proposed by the Dijon Academy in 1753 (but which did not win the prize), elaborated this theme still further. The social order of civilized society, wrote Rousseau, introduced inequality and unhappiness. This social order rests upon private property. The man who first enclosed a tract of land and called it his own was the true founder of civilized society. "Don't listen to that imposture; you are lost if you forget that the fruits of the earth belong to everyone and the earth to no one," he wrote. Man's greatest ills, said Rousseau, are not natural but made by man himself; the remedy lies also within man's power. Heretofore, man has used his wit and art not to alter his wretchedness but only to intensify it.

Three Major Works

Rousseau's novel *La Nouvelle Héloïse* (1761) attempted to portray in fiction the sufferings and tragedy that foolish education and arbitrary social conventions work among sensitive creatures. Rousseau's two other major treatises—*L'Émile ou de l'éducation* (1762) and *Du contrat social* (1762)—undertook the more difficult task of constructing an education and a social order that would enable men to be natural and free; that is, that would enable men to recognize no bondage except the bondage of natural necessity. To be free in this sense, said Rousseau, was to be happy.

Rousseau brought these three works to completion in somewhat trying circumstances. After having returned to the Protestant fold in 1755 and having regained his citizenship of Geneva that same year, Rousseau accepted the rather insistent offer of Madame Louise d'Épinay to install Thérèse and himself in the Hermitage, a small cottage on the

D'Épinay estate at Montmorency. While Rousseau was working on his novel there, its heroine materialized in the person of Sophie, Comtesse d'Houdetot; and he fell passionately in love with her. He was 44 years old; Sophie was 27, married to a dullard, the mistress of the talented and dashing Marquis Saint-Lambert, and the sister-in-law of Rousseau's hostess. Rousseau was swept off his feet. Their relationship apparently was never consummated; Sophie pitied Rousseau and loved Saint-Lambert. But Madame d'Épinay and her paramour, Melchior Grimm, meddled in the affair; Diderot was drawn into the business. Rousseau felt that his reputation had been blackened, and a bitter estrangement resulted. Madame d'Épinay insulted Rousseau until he left the Hermitage in December 1757. However, he remained in Montmorency until 1762, when the condemnation of *L'Émile* forced him to flee from France.

La Nouvelle Héloïse appeared in Paris in January 1761. Originally entitled *Lettres de deux amants, habitants d'une petite ville au pied des Alpes,* the work was structurally a novel in letters, after the fashion of the English author Samuel Richardson. The originality of the novel won it hostile reviews, but its romantic eroticism made it immensely popular with the public. It remained a best seller until the French Revolution.

The notoriety of *La Nouvelle Héloïse* was nothing compared to the storm produced by *L'Émile* and *Du contrat social.* Even today the ideas promulgated in these works are revolutionary. Their expression, especially in *L'Émile,* in a style both readable and alluring made them dangerous. *L'Émile* was condemned by the Paris Parlement and denounced by the archbishop of Paris. Both of the books were burned by the authorities in Geneva.

L'Émile and *Du contrat social*

L'Émile ou de l'éducation remains one of the world's greatest speculative treatises on education. However, Rousseau wrote to a correspondent who tried to follow *L'Émile* literally, "so much the worse for you!" The work was intended as illustrative of an educational program rather than prescriptive of every practical detail of a proper education. Its overarching spirit is best sensed in opposition to John Locke's essay on education. Locke taught that man should be educated to the station for which he is intended. There should be one education for a prince, another for a physician, and still another for a farmer. Rousseau advocated one education for all. Man should be educated to be a man, not to be a doctor, lawyer, or priest. Nor is a child merely a little man; he is, rather, a developing creature, with passions and powers that vary according to his stage of development. What must be avoided at all costs is the master-slave mode of instruction, with the pupil as either master or slave, for the medium of instruction is far more influential than any doctrine taught through that medium. Hence, an education resting merely on a play of wills—as when the child learns only to please the instructor or when the teacher "teaches" by threatening the pupil with a future misfortune—produces creatures fit to be only masters or slaves, not free men. Only free men can realize a "natural social order," wherein men can live happily.

A few of the striking doctrines set forth in *L'Émile* are: the importance of training the body before the mind, learning first through "things" and later through words, teaching first only that for which a child feels a need so as to impress upon him that thought is a tool whereby he can effectively manage things, motivating a child by catering to his ruling passion of greed, refraining from moral instruction until the awakening of the sexual urge, and raising the child outside the doctrines of any church until late adolescence and then instructing him in the religion of conscience. Although Rousseau's principles have never been fully put into practice, his influence on educational reformers has been tremendous.

L'Émile's companion master work, *Du contrat social*, attempted to spell out the social relation that a properly educated man—a free man—bears to other free men. This treatise is a difficult and subtle work of a penetrating intellect fired by a great passion for humanity. The liberating fervor of the work, however, is easily caught in the key notions of popular sovereignty and general will. Government is not to be confused with sovereignty of the people or with the social order that is created by the social contract. The government is an intermediary set up between the people as law followers and the people as law creators, the sovereignty. Furthermore, the government is an instrument created by the citizens through their collective action expressed in the general will. The purpose of this instrument is to serve the people by seeing to it that laws expressive of the general will of the citizens are in fact executed. In short, the government is the servant of the people, not their master. And further, the sovereignty of the people—the general will of the people—is to be found not merely in the will of the majority or in the will of all but rather in the will as enlightened by right judgment.

As with *L'Émile, Du contrat social* is a work best understood as elaborating the principles of the social order rather than schematizing the mechanism for those general principles. Rousseau's political writings more concerned with immediate application include his *Considérations sur le gouvernement de la Pologne* (1772) and his incomplete *Projet de constitution pour la Corse,* published posthumously in 1862.

Other writings from Rousseau's middle period include the *Encyclopédie* article *Économie politique* (1755); *Lettre sur la Providence* (1756), a reply to Voltaire's poem on the Lisbon earthquake; *Lettre à d'Alembert sur les spectacles* (1758); *Essai sur l'origine des langues* (1761); and four autobiographical *Lettres à Malesherbes* (1762).

Exile and Apologetics, 1762-1778

Forced to flee from France, Rousseau sought refuge at Yverdon in the territory of Bern. Expelled by the Bernese authorities, he found asylum in Môtiers, a village in the Prussian principality of Neuchâtel. Here in 1763 he renounced his Genevan citizenship. The publication of his *Lettres écrites de la montagne* (1764), in which he defended *L'Émile* and criticized "established" reformed churches, aroused the wrath of the Neuchâtel clergy. His house was stoned, and Rousseau fled to the isle of St. Pierre in the Lake

of Biel, but he was again expelled by the Bernese. Finally, through the good offices of the British philosopher David Hume, he settled at Wotton, Derbyshire, England, in 1766. Hume managed to obtain from George III a yearly pension for Rousseau. But Rousseau, falsely believing Hume to be in league with his Parisian and Genevan enemies, not only refused the pension but also openly broke with the philosopher. Henceforth, Rousseau's sense of persecution became ever more intense, even at times hysterical.

Rousseau returned to France in June 1767 under the protection of the Prince de Conti. Wandering from place to place, he at last settled in 1770 in Paris. There he made a living, as he often had in the past, by copying music. By December 1770 the *Confessions,* upon which he had been working since 1766, was completed, and he gave readings from this work at various private homes. Madame d'Épinay, fearing an unflattering picture of herself and her friends, intervened; the readings were forbidden by the police. Disturbed by the reaction to his readings and determined to justify himself before the world, Rousseau wrote *Dialogues ou Rousseau, Juge de Jean-Jacques* (1772-1776). Fearful lest the manuscript fall into the hands of his enemies, he attempted to place it on the high altar of Notre Dame. Thwarted in this attempt, he left a copy with the philosopher Étienne Condillac and, not wholly trusting him, with an English acquaintance, Brooke Boothby. Finally, in 1778 Rousseau entrusted copies of both the *Confessions* and the *Dialogues* to his friend Paul Moultou. His last work, *Les Rêveries du promeneur solitaire,* begun in 1776 and unfinished at his death, records how Rousseau, an outcast from society, recaptured "serenity, tranquility, peace, even happiness."

In May 1778 Rousseau accepted Marquis de Giradin's hospitality at Ermenonville near Paris. There, with Thérèse at his bedside, he died on July 2, 1778, probably from uremia. From birth he had suffered from a bladder deformation. From 1748 onward his condition had grown worse. His adoption of the Armenian mode of dress was due to the embarrassment caused by this affliction, and it is not unlikely that much of his suspicious irritability can be traced to the same malady. Rousseau was buried on the île des Peupliers at Ermenonville. In October 1794 his remains were transferred to the Panthéon in Paris. Thérèse, surviving him by 22 years, died in 1801 at the age of 80.

Further Reading

Rousseau himself is the best introduction to his own thought. Everyman's Library offers translations of *Emile* and a volume containing *The Social Contract* and the two *Discourses.* The *Confessions* is available in a Modern Library edition. The most accessible English version of Rousseau's novel is *Julie, or the New Eloise,* translated and abridged by J. H. McDowell (1968). A sampling of Rousseau's letters appears in *Citizen of Geneva: Selections from the Letters of J.-J. Rousseau,* edited by C. W. Hendel (1937). Useful biographies include Matthew Josephson, *J. J. Rousseau* (1931); R. B. Mowat, *Jean-Jacques Rousseau* (1938); and Lester G. Crocker, *Jean-Jacques Rousseau: The Quest, 1712-1758* (1968).

The literature on Rousseau is vast. An excellent introduction to his thought as a whole is E. H. Wright, *The Meaning of Rousseau* (1929). A critical study of Rousseau's life and writings is Frederick C. Green, *Jean-Jacques Rousseau* (1955), valuable for his life but less illuminating on the works. Ronald Grimsley, *Jean-Jacques Rousseau: Study in Self-awareness* (1961), focuses on Rousseau's attempts to answer the riddle of his personal existence. See also Grimsley's *Rousseau and the Religious Quest* (1968). Ernst Cassirer, *The Question of Jean-Jacques Rousseau* (1932), presents Rousseau as offering a non-Christian interpretation of the universe; and in his *Kant, Rousseau, Goethe* (1945), Cassirer suggests that Rousseau was a profound influence on Kantian thought. Roger Masters, *Political Philosophy of Rousseau* (1967), examines an important aspect of Rousseau's work. Frederika Macdonald, *Jean-Jacques Rousseau: A New Criticism* (2 vols., 1906), presents Rousseau as a victim of Madame d'Épinay's vilification. For a helpful review of fairly recent Rousseau literature see Peter Gay's chapter on Rousseau in his *The Party of Humanity* (1964). □

Théodore Rousseau

The French painter and draftsman Théodore Rousseau (1812-1867) was the most representative artist of the Barbizon school and an intermediary between the Dutch landscapists of the 17th century and the impressionist school.

Born in Paris, Théodore Rousseau seems to have been initially stimulated to paint landscape by a cousin. The example of Dutch painting supplemented the formal instruction that Rousseau received from minor artists of his own time. A precocious artist who was painting from nature at the age of 15, he combined an analytical eye with a romantic heart.

In the 1830s Rousseau established himself with a series of boldly painted and dramatic scenes from the Auvergne, such as the *Torrent* (ca. 1830). Among the pictures done in northern France, the *Forest of Fontainebleau, Bas-Bréau* (begun 1837-1839, completed 1867) is especially characteristic. The *Valley of Tiffauge* (1837-1841) is another outstanding illustration of an almost Flemish type of visual analysis.

Made controversial by his nonclassical bias, Rousseau was not able to exhibit at the Salon between 1837 and 1847. By that time he had settled at Barbizon, where he exploited the pictorial and "moral" qualities of oak trees and sunlight. At the same time, fine drawings such as *Country Road with Poplars* (1830-1840) reveal how sensitively he could interpret a flat, featureless plain like those of Berry, where he worked in the 1840s.

In spite of the fact that Rousseau did not show at the Salon for many years, he was widely acclaimed as a landscape artist. In the 1845 Salon the poet and critic Charles Baudelaire even went so far as to maintain that Rousseau was superior to Camille Corot. In 1864, however, Baudelaire modified his enthusiasm and remarked that the artist showed "too much love for detail, not enough for the architecture of nature."

Luminosity, which Rousseau considered the "great secret" of nature, is very much in evidence as early as 1842, when he painted the *Lowland Marsh* in surprisingly high-keyed, dramatically contrasted tones. The intensity of his response to nature is reflected repeatedly in active, dynamic scenes such as *Storm Effect, Road in the Forest of Fontainebleau* (1860-1865). But sometimes the painter of Barbizon, who, according to one critic, "never painted a stroke without thinking of Ruisdael," became dull in his "patient inventory of nature," heavy in his application of paint, and overripe in his use of color, as in *Sunset near Arbonne* (ca. 1865).

Rousseau's fundamentally romantic spirit is well expressed in one of his own statements: "I also heard the voices of the trees . . . whose passions I uncovered. I wanted to talk with them . . . and put my finger on the secret of their majesty."

Dependent though he was on Dutch and, to lesser degree, on English painting, Rousseau was also inspired directly by nature, as were his successors, the impressionists. Like them, he put a particular emphasis on light, but on a light that has a more symbolic and a less naturalistic character.

Further Reading

Little has been written about Rousseau in English. David Croal Thomson, *The Barbizon School of Painters* (1890), gives a 19th-century view of this group of artists. See also Charles Sprague Smith, *Barbizon Days* (1903). The most outstanding study is Robert C. Herbert, *Barbizon Revisited* (1962). □

Albert Roussel

Albert Roussel (1869-1937) was one of the most important French composers of his time. His early compositions reflect the main styles of the day; his later works were more advanced than those of his contemporaries.

Albert Roussel was born in Tourcoing, a town close to the Belgian border, where his grandfather was mayor. Destined for a career in the navy, he studied at the Collège Stanislas in Paris and joined the service in 1887. After he was commissioned, he served several years at sea, mostly in the Far East.

Roussel started composing while on his long voyages, and when he received encouragement for his efforts, he resigned his commission in 1894 and went to Paris to study composition at the relatively advanced age of 25. He entered the newly established Schola Cantorum, where he studied with Vincent d'Indy, its founder. D'Indy was conservative in that he held out against Claude Debussy's impressionism and based his instruction on a thorough knowledge of earlier musical styles.

Roussel's first published composition, a piano piece, appeared in 1898. In 1902 he became a teacher of counterpoint at the Schola, a post he held until 1914, when he resigned to enter the French army during World War I. He served as a transportation officer and saw duty at Verdun and the Battle of the Marne. When his health broke down, he returned to Paris, where he spent the rest of his life.

The best known of Roussel's early works is the ballet *Le Festin de l'araignée* (1912; The Spider's Feast), a skillfully orchestrated tone poem, somewhat reminiscent of Camille Saint-Saëns's music in the transparency of the writing. This was followed by a large ballet-opera, *Padmavati* (1914-1918), based on an Indian legend and employing Indian melodies and scales, a result of Roussel's visits to the East as a naval officer. His ballet *Bacchus et Ariane* (1930) reflects the sumptuousness of Sergei Diaghilev's Ballets Russes that influenced so many composers of the time. This rich score shows Roussel's mastery of the impressionist idiom.

Roussel's later compositions reveal other ideals. Already in the Suite in F (1926) and in his Third and Fourth Symphonies (1930 and 1934) he wrote neoclassic pieces, shown in their avoidance of programs, economy of means, clarity of form, 18th-century textures, and driving rhythms. Igor Stravinsky was the chief exponent of neoclassicism, and Roussel was one of its principal exponents. In these compositions the astringent harmonies, wide-ranging melodies, strong rhythms, and bitonality bring Roussel close to the younger composers of the time.

It has been said that Roussel "possessed every quality but that of spontaneous invention." Even though he was not a pathbreaker, he was one of the most important French composers of the first half of the 20th century.

Further Reading

Roussel is discussed in Aaron Copland, *The New Music, 1900-1960* (1941; rev. ed. 1968); Wilfrid Mellers, *Studies in Contemporary Music* (1947); and Joseph Machlis, *Introduction to Contemporary Music* (1961).

Additional Sources

Deane, Basil, *Albert Roussel,* Westport, Conn.: Greenwood Press, 1980, 1961.
Demuth, Norman, *Albert Roussel: a study,* Westport, Conn.: Hyperion Press, 1979. □

Carl T. Rowan

The journalist and author Carl T. Rowan (born 1925) was U.S. ambassador to Finland (1963-1964) and director of the U.S. Information Agency (1964-1965).

Carl Thomas Rowan was born on August 11, 1925, in Ravenscroft, Tennessee. He was one of five children (two boys and three girls) born to Thomas David and Johnnie B. Rowan and was raised in McMinnville, Tennessee. As a youth Rowan worked hoeing bulb grass for 10 cents an hour, later performing hard manual labor for 25 cents an hour when there was work available. Like many other African American youths, Rowan's childhood was deeply affected by the "Jim Crow" attitudes so prevalent in the South. While the economic and social situation was dismal, Rowan was determined to get a good education. He excelled in high school graduating from Bernard High School in 1942 as class president and valedictorian.

Rowan left McMinnville for Nashville with 77 cents in his pocket and the dream of a college education. In order to earn his tuition for college, he moved in with his grandparents and got a job in a tuberculosis hospital the summer before enrolling in the Tennessee Agricultural and Industrial State College in Nashville in the fall of 1942. During his freshman year Rowan participated in a training program that led to his becoming one of the first 15 African American persons in United States history to gain a commission as an officer in the U.S. Navy. He was trained at Oberlin College in northern Ohio and at the Naval Midshipmen School at Fort Schuyler, The Bronx. Following his service with the Navy during World War II where he was assigned sea duty (and excelled as deputy commander of the communications division), Rowan returned to complete his studies at Oberlin College. He earned his bachelor's degree in 1947 majoring in mathematics. He received his master's degree in journalism from the University of Minnesota, supporting himself by writing for two weekly newspapers, the Minneapolis *Spokesman* and the St. Paul *Recorder*. In 1950 Rowan married Vivien Louise Murphy, a public health nurse; their children were Barbara, Carl Jr., and Geoffrey.

Upon completion of his graduate studies Rowan joined the Minneapolis *Tribune* as a copyreader. He became a general assignment reporter in 1950. Among his early pieces were a series of columns entitled *How Far from Slavery?* which he wrote after returning to the South to study racial issues. The articles earned several local accolades and contributed to Rowan being the first African American recipient of the Minneapolis "Outstanding Young Man" award. The articles also served as the basis for *South of Freedom,* his first book (1952).

He then spent a year in India, Pakistan, and Southeast Asia writing columns during 1954. These led to a second well-received book: *The Pitiful and the Proud* (1956), which was based upon his observations while in the Orient. A third book, *Go South to Sorrow,* was published in 1957. While his books received favorable acclaim, Rowan's writing skills were most commonly acknowledged for his journalism. He was the only journalist to receive the coveted "Sigma Delta Chi" award for newspaper reporting in three consecutive years: for general reporting in 1954; for best foreign correspondence in 1955; and for his coverage of the political unrest in Southeast Asia in 1956.

In January 1961 Rowan accepted an appointment as deputy assistant secretary of state for public affairs in the Kennedy administration. He was responsible for press relations of the State Department. He was involved in the area of news coverage of increasing US military involvement in Vietnam and was also part of the negotiating team that secured the exchange of Francis Gary Powers, who was shot down over the Soviet Union. He accompanied then Vice President Johnson on a tour through Southeast Asia, India and Europe. During this time, Rowan became the center of controversy with the rejection of his application for membership in the prestigious Cosmos Club—whose membership qualifications included meritorious work in science, literature, the learned professions, and public service—on racial grounds. The Cosmos Club then passed a rule prohibiting discrimination on the basis of race, but Rowan's nomination was never resurrected. The controversy resulted in the withdrawal of President Kennedy's application to the club when Kennedy's sponsor resigned in protest.

Rowan went on to serve in both the Kennedy and Johnson administrations as ambassador to Finland (January 1963 to January 1964) and as the director of the U.S. Information Agency (January 1964 to July 1965). In serving as director of the U.S.I.A., Rowan became the first African American to hold a seat on the National Security Council. With a staff of 13,000, Rowan oversaw a vast government communications network that included the international Voice of America, the daily communiques to U.S. embassy personnel around the world, and a massive psychological warfare program to assist the Vietnam War effort. This last assignment brought him criticism, as it was felt that he was drawing away from other USIA activities. Rowan resigned from USIA in 1965 and returned to his first love—journalism, by accepting an offer to write a national column for the Field Newspaper Service Syndicate and to do three weekly radio commentaries for the Westinghouse Broadcasting Company.

As a national columnist and commentator, Rowan developed a reputation for being independent and often controversial. He publicly made statements, such as urging Dr. King to lessen his anti-war stance, because it was hurting the thrust of the Civil Rights movement and calling for the resignation of J. Edgar Hoover, the powerful FBI Director, citing abuses of power and corruption that brought him criticism. While Rowan has always been a spokesperson for civil and economic rights for African Americans, he has also been critical of those he feels should more aggressively address those issues affecting themselves.

Rowan received the George Foster Peabody Award for his television special "Race War in Rhodesia" and was awarded an Emmy for his documentary "Drug Abuse: America's 64 Billion Dollar Curse." His newspaper column was syndicated by the Chicago *Sun-Times* and reached nearly half of homes receiving newspapers in the United States. He was on numerous public affairs television programs and was a permanent panelist on "Agronsky and Company." He also aired "The Rowan Report," a daily series of commentaries on radio stations heard across the nation. He served as a roving reporter for the *Reader's Digest* and regularly published articles in that magazine. He was one of the most sought-after lecturers in the United States, speaking on college campuses and at conventions of teachers, business people, civil rights leaders, and community groups.

He once told Publisher's Weekly, "you gotta get tired before you retire" and went on to publish a number of books. They included: *New York Times* bestseller that "appeals to the whole spectrum of readers. *Dream Makers, Dream Breakers: The world of Thurgood Marshall* and *The Coming Race War in America: A Wake-Up Call*

Further Reading

For additional information, see Rowan's own works: *South of Freedom* (1952); *The Pitiful and the Proud* (1956); *Go South to Sorrow* (1957); and *The Coming Race War in America: A Wake-Up Call Breaking Barriers.* □

Henry Augustus Rowland

The American physicist Henry Augustus Rowland (1848-1901) made fundamental contributions to magnetism and to celestial physics.

Henry Augustus Rowland was born on Nov. 27, 1848, in Honesdale, Pa., the descendant of a long line of clergymen. He studied at Phillips Academy, Andover, Mass., and then graduated from the Rensselaer Polytechnic Institute with a degree in civil engineering. During the next 2 years he did some work in his profession and taught natural science at Wooster University, Ohio. In the spring of 1872 he returned to Rensselaer as instructor in physics. While at Rensselaer he published an important paper on magnetism which brought him favorable attention from the English physicist James Clerk Maxwell and an appointment as professor of physics at the newly established Johns Hopkins University, designed to be the model of a graduate school. This early paper brought lasting fame to Rowland, for it proved to be the starting point for all calculations for the design of dynamos and transformers.

One of Rowland's first actions upon arrival at Johns Hopkins was the development of a workshop in which the apparatus for fundamental research could be produced; the machines that he himself devised were among his most valuable contributions to science. Becoming interested, for example, in the spectrum of the sun and the spectra of the elements, he designed a ruling machine to produce gratings for spectrum analysis more accurate than any previously known. Dissatisfied with the results obtained with the plane gratings of Joseph von Fraunhofer and Ernest Rutherford, he combined the principle of the grating with that of the concave mirror, eventually producing concave gratings of about 100,000 lines of 6 inches in length. With these superb diffraction gratings which split light into its components, he mapped the solar spectrum more thoroughly than anyone before him had done. Making possible the direct photography and higher resolution of spectra of the heavenly bodies, this work started a new era in spectroscopy.

In the field of measurements, in addition to his work on spectra, Rowland obtained long-accepted values for the mechanical equivalent of heat, the ohm, and the ratio of the electric units and the wavelengths of various spectra. In most cases, he designed his own measuring instruments.

Although Rowland had an engineer's training and always remained interested in practical applications—among his inventions was a printing telegraph and several other commercial instruments—he was primarily known as an ardent campaigner for the importance of basic research, and from his post at Johns Hopkins he trained many students who were imbued with this viewpoint. He was the first president of the American Physical Society. Rowland was married to Henrietta Troup Harrison of Baltimore in 1890. He died of diabetes on April 16, 1901.

Further Reading

The only biographical account of Rowland is Thomas C. Mendenhall's memoir, which appears in Mendenhall's edition of *The Physical Papers of Henry Augustus Rowland* (1902), in the *Biographical Memoirs* of the National Academy of Sciences, vol. 5 (1905), and is reprinted in Bessie Zaban Jones, ed., *The Golden Age of Science: Thirty Portraits of the Giants of 19th-Century Science by Their Scientific Contemporaries* (1966). A profile of Rowland and an interesting selection of documents and letters are in Nathan Reingold, ed., *Science in Nineteenth-century America: A Documentary History* (1964). □

Manuel Roxas

Manuel Roxas (1892-1948) was the last president of the Commonwealth and the first president of the Republic of the Philippines. His administration demonstrated decisively that political sovereignty without economic independence encourages reaction, perpetuation of social injustices, and exploitation.

Manuel Roxas was born in Capiz, Capiz Province, on Jan. 1, 1892. In 1914 he graduated from the College of Law of the University of the Philippines. In 1916 he became provincial governor. In 1922 he was elected to Congress, becoming Speaker of the Philippine Assembly.

In December 1931 Roxas, together with Senate president pro tempore Sergio Osmeña, left for the United States to secure the Hare-Hawes-Cutting Act from the U.S. Congress, which would grant Philippine independence after a transition period of 10 years. This bill was rejected by the opposition forces led by Manuel Quezon. In 1934 Roxas was elected to the constitutional convention. In 1938 he was appointed secretary of finance by Commonwealth president Quezon and then became his trusted adviser. In 1941 Roxas ran for the Senate and won.

On Dec. 8, 1941, at the outbreak of the war, Roxas served as lieutenant colonel in the U.S. Army Forces in the Far East (USAFFE). He refused to join Quezon in fleeing to the United States because he wanted to preserve the morale of the Filipino soldiers fighting in Bataan and Corregidor. He was captured in 1942 by the Japanese forces in Malaybalay, Bukidnon, and was forced to serve in the puppet government of José Laurel. Roxas accepted the position of chair-

man of the Economic Planning Board in Laurel's wartime Cabinet. During the Japanese retreat he allegedly escaped from the Japanese high command in Baguio on April 15, 1945.

Because of Gen. Douglas MacArthur's unexplained intervention, Roxas was never tried as a collaborator, though he had served officially in Laurel's Japanese-sponsored administration. When the Philippine legislature convened during the liberation, Roxas was elected president of the Senate on June 9, 1945. He broke with President Osmeña and formed the Liberal party, which he led to victory as presidential candidate on April 23, 1946. Roxas thus became the last president of the Commonwealth and the first president of the Republic of the Philippines when it was inaugurated on July 4, 1946.

Owing to the unfair demands of the Bell Trade Relations Act of 1945, which called for a revision of the Philippine constitution to give parity rights to Americans in exchange for rehabilitation money, Roxas found himself surrendering his country's freedom and its right to determine its own destiny. Faced by the unified opposition of workers and peasants, the majority of the people, Roxas sided with the oppressive landlord class and the colonialistic merchants to put down by force the legitimate aspirations of the electorate.

It is public knowledge that most of Roxas's policies were dictated by Gen. MacArthur and U.S. high commissioner Paul V. McNutt. Not only did Roxas lack the vision to foresee the causes that would strain Philippine-American

relations later (for example, the Military Bases Agreement of March 14, 1947), but he also failed to sympathize with the plight of the majority of the poor.

Roxas was committing the Philippines to the side of the United States at the start of the cold war in a speech at the Clark Air Force Base when he suffered a heart attack on April 14, 1948. Loyal to the United States to the last, he died on American soil.

Further Reading

Two useful biographies of Roxas are Felixberto G. Bustos, *And Now Comes Roxas* (1945), and Marcial P. Lichauco, *Roxas* (1952). For Roxas's position in the collaboration issue see Hernando J. Abaya, *Betrayal in the Philippines* (1946), and David Joel Steinberg, *Philippine Collaboration in World War II* (1967). □

Lucille Roybal-Allard

Lucille Roybal-Allard is the first woman of Mexican American ancestry to be elected to the U.S. Congress.

She became the 33rd Congressional District's representative in November 1992. The oldest daughter of a political family, Roybal-Allard's father is the highly esteemed California Congressman Edward Roybal. After 30 years of Congressional service, Ed Roybal, often called the dean of California Latino legislators, retired in 1992. Congresswoman Roybal-Allard, a Democrat, previously served in the California State Assembly, representing the 56th District from 1987 to 1992. There she served on a number of influential committees, including the Assembly Rules committee and the very powerful Ways and Means committee, which oversees the distribution of public monies. She was also the chair of the Ways and Means subcommittee on Health and Human Services. Her political style, described as quiet and conciliatory, has contributed to her many legislative victories. She won passage of what some have hailed as landmark environmental legislation, as well as new laws in the areas of domestic violence and sexual harassment. Roybal-Allard is especially proud of her work to empower local communities. As she related in an interview with Diana Martínez: "People often don't know how their lives are impacted by what's going on in Sacramento or Washington, D.C. People can take control of their lives. They can be involved in the political process and make a difference."

Roybal-Allard was born and raised in the Boyle Heights section of Los Angeles, California, a predominately Mexican American area. She attended Saint Mary's Catholic School before she earned her B.A. from California State University, Los Angeles, in 1961. She has warm memories of working on her father's campaign; he was a great example to her, but Roybal-Allard is quick to give equal credit to her mother. "My mom has been a tremendous role model," she revealed to Martínez. "She's really the one who has helped to support and spearhead my father's career. She

used to run his headquarters, which used to be our home when we were kids because they couldn't afford a headquarters. So she has always been there, helping him get elected, walking precincts, registering voters, doing all the things that needed to be done. At the same time, she'd be at his side whenever he needed to be at public events. She's worked very hard and is greatly responsible for his success, because it really does take a partnership. In politics it takes the cooperation of your family; otherwise it's almost impossible to succeed.''

In an interview with the *Civic Center News Source,* Roybal-Allard says she remembers working on her father's political campaigns as early as age seven. ''We used to fold and stuff and lick stamps. When I got a little bit older they used to call us 'bird dogs,' and we would do voter registration. So I was a bird dog for a few years.''

There was a downside to political involvement as well. As Roybal-Allard explained to the *Civic Center News Source,* ''I think for me the main part of it was the lack of privacy and lack of personal identity. When my sister and I would go to a dance where people might not know who we were, we used to decide on a different last name so we could just be anonymous and have fun . . . I remember as a freshman in college in a political science class I raised my hand to answer a question and after I finished the professor said 'Well, now we know what you're father thinks,' and went on to the next student.''

Experiences such as these led Roybal-Allard to the conclusion that she did not want to be a politician. She

continued to be involved in her father's campaigns and those of other Latino politicians but chose a career of community and advocacy work for herself. As Roybal-Allard explained to Martínez, her decision to work in community service was a direct result of her upbringing. ''When I think you have a role model like both my father and my mother who have really dedicated their lives to the community and have taught human values and understand the value of people, it really has an impact on one's life.'' She served as the executive director of the National Association of Hispanic CPAs, in Washington, D.C., was the assistant director of the Alcoholism Council of East Los Angeles, and worked as a planning associate for United Way. She enjoyed community work, but as time went on she became more and more frustrated by the barriers created by political policy makers. In 1987 a combination of political opportunity and personal circumstances changed Roybal-Allard's mind about running for office.

Decided to Pursue Political Career

The 1987 election of Assemblywoman Gloria Molina to the newly created seat on the Los Angeles City Council left Molina's assembly position vacant. Roybal-Allard knew Molina through their mutual community activities and she had worked on the assemblywoman's campaign. Molina asked Roybal-Allard to consider running for the vacant assembly position. Her personal situation and the request of her friend led to her decision to run. As she explained to *Hispanic,* ''The timing was just right for me. My children were grown and my husband's job called for a lot of travel.'' Roybal-Allard's second husband, Edward Allard III, has his own consulting firm whose clients are mostly on the East Coast. Roybal-Allard told Martínez that she received no pressure from her father to run. ''I'm sure that his involvement in politics ultimately was one of the reasons . . . that I wound up getting involved in politics. But, he has always been one that believed that we needed to be independent and make decisions on our own, and if we need guidance he will be there.'' Once she decided to run for California's State Assembly, she received help from both her father and Gloria Molina. She easily defeated nine other candidates and won with 60 percent of the vote.

As a newly elected Assemblywoman, one of Roybal-Allard's first tasks was to continue the fight against building a prison in East L.A. A tremendous challenge for a new politician considering that her principal foe was the governor of California. In 1986, Governor George Deukmejian proposed a site near a heavily Mexican American residential area as the location for a State prison. Deukmejian tried to steamroll the opposition to get the prison built but had his plans flattened instead. For seven years Roybal-Allard, along with Gloria Molina and other local Latino politicians, worked with grassroots organizations, professional groups, and church leaders to prevent the prison from being built. As an expression of her philosophy of local empowerment, Roybal-Allard assisted community women in organizing ''The Mothers of East L.A.'' which was implacable in its opposition to the prison. A series of legal maneuvers halted construction of the prison but did not kill it. Deukmejian left office in 1990, but the struggle against the prison continued until September 1992 when Governor Pete Wilson signed a bill, amended by Roybal-Allard, which eliminated the funds for the construction of the East L.A. prison. This victory, coming as Roybal-Allard left the California Assembly for the U.S. Congress, gave her cause to reflect on her own feelings and what the political struggle meant to her community. As she stated in a press release, "I started my assembly career when the East Los Angles prison bill was approved and it feels great to be leaving the assembly on this victory note. . . . This is a victory for the entire community. For seven years our community has marched against the prison, we have fought in the courts and in [California capital] Sacramento—this fight has empowered us. This community was once viewed as powerless. However, the Mothers of East Los Angeles and other community groups have served notice to the state's powerbrokers that ignoring the desires of the East Los Angeles community will no longer be accepted."

The prison was not the only struggle Roybal-Allard waged to improve the quality of life in her district. She fought against a toxic waste incinerator, again aided by the highly respected grass roots organization, Mothers of East Los Angeles. As a result of that struggle Roybal-Allard authored a bill which entitles every community in California to an environmental impact report before a toxic incinerator is built or expanded, a protection that was often omitted prior to her efforts. This bill, along with her strong voting record on the environment, earned her the Sierra Club's California Environmental Achievement Award.

Took Action on Women's Issues

Roybal-Allard has also authored a series of laws which place her in the forefront of women's issues. Included is a requirement that the courts take into consideration an individual's history of domestic violence in child custody cases. She has also worked for legislation requiring colleges to provide information and referrals for treatment to rape victims and enacted two laws that strengthen the legal position of sexual assault victims by redefining the meaning of "consent." Another of her bills requires the California State Bar to take disciplinary action against attorneys who engage in sexual misconduct with their clients. This is the first such law adopted by any state in the country.

For her legislative efforts, Roybal-Allard has received a number of prestigious awards and commendations, including honors from the Los Angeles Commission on Assaults Against Women, the Asian Business Association, and the Latin American Professional Women's Association. Roybal-Allard was also honored in 1992 by the Mexican American Women's National Association (MANA) in Washington DC. She was presented with the "Las Primaras" Award for "her pioneering efforts in creating a better future for the community through the political process."

Ironically, when Roybal-Allard was first elected to the California Assembly many thought her to be too demure to be effective. But as she explained to *Hispanic* her conciliatory style is long-range effective, "People may be your enemies today on one issue, but they may be your allies tomorrow on another issue. So I've learned to work well

with groups on both sides of the aisle, even with those who I oppose bitterly on particular issues." Her track record on political effectiveness to date has been impressive. A number of community members, and political observers, have speculated that when the senior Royal left Congress in 1992, his daughter followed in his steps, continuing the Royal legacy of effective representation.

Further Reading

Civic Center News Source, January 13, 1992, pp. 1, 8, 12.
Hispanic, March 9, 1992, p. 20.
Los Angeles Times, February 7, 1997, p. A3.
News release from the office of Lucille Roybal-Allard, September 16, 1992. Roybal-Allard, Lucille, interview with Diana Martínez, September 2, 1992. □

Josiah Royce

The American philosopher Josiah Royce (1855-1916) was the last and the greatest spokesperson for systematic philosophical idealism in the United States.

Josiah Royce was born on Nov. 20, 1855, at Grass Valley, Calif. His forceful mother gave him his early education. He attended school in San Francisco, where the family moved when he was 11 years old. At the University of California the precocious youth's interests shifted from mining engineering to literature and philosophy.

When Royce graduated in 1875, his burgeoning intellectual powers won him a year of graduate study in Germany, where he immersed himself in philosophical idealism. On his return to the United States in 1876, he accepted a fellowship to Johns Hopkins University and took his doctorate in 1878. After teaching literature and composition at the University of California for 4 years, Royce was invited to teach philosophy at Harvard in 1882. The rest of his life as teacher and philosopher centered at Harvard.

His mother had impressed on Royce a concern for basic religious issues; his youth in California and his own solitary disposition had posed the problem of the relationship between the individual and the community. All of his philosophical writings revolved around these issues. His first major work, significantly entitled *The Religious Aspect of Philosophy* (1885), presented the central ideas that his later writings elaborated and refined. He developed this philosophy in a series of major works, the most important of which were *The Spirit of Modern Philosophy* (1892), *The Conception of God* (1897), *Studies of Good and Evil* (1898), *The World and the Individual* (2 vols., 1900-1902), and his summary statement, *The Problem of Christianity* (2 vols., 1913).

Royce's philosophy rested on the conviction that ultimate reality consisted of idea or spirit. "The world of dead facts is an illusion," he wrote. "The truth of it is a spiritual life." His central conception was the Absolute. The world

exists in and for an all-embracing, all-knowing thought, Royce explained. This amounted to a philosophical conception of God, the Absolute which united all thought and all experience. Given this reality, the individual's task is to understand the meaning of the Absolute and to adopt its purposes freely.

Royce's ethical theory rested on his striking principle of loyalty, which he presented most effectively in *The Philosophy of Loyalty* (1908). He argued that loyalty was the cohesive principle of all ethical behavior and of all social practice. The moral law, he thought, could be reduced to the precept "Be loyal." Loyalty also linked the individual to the community. The loyal man was one who gave himself to a cause, but each individual must choose his cause so that it would advance the good of all. He should act to further loyalty to the very principle of loyalty.

In his later years Royce's increasing concern about the practical bearings of philosophy was reflected in his *War and Insurance* (1914) and *The Hope of the Great Community* (1916). By the time of his death on Sept. 14, 1916, Royce had become one of America's most important philosophers. His influence on his contemporaries was a tribute to his intellectual power and to his concern with fundamental religious issues.

Further Reading

The Letters of Josiah Royce, edited by John Glendenning (1970), is the companion volume of Royce's *Basic Writings* (2 vols., 1969). Stuart Gerry Brown edited two collections of Royce's writings and provided excellent introductory essays: *The So-*

cial Philosophy of Josiah Royce (1950) and *The Religious Philosophy of Josiah Royce* (1952).
A fine presentation of Royce's complete ethical philosophy, using Royce's unpublished papers, is Peter Fuss, *The Moral Philosophy of Josiah Royce* (1965). Thomas F. Powell, in *Josiah Royce* (1967), argues that Royce's philosophy is relevant to contemporary religious thought. Vincent Buranelli, *Josiah Royce* (1964), gives considerable attention to Royce as a literary figure. For background see also Clifford Barrett, *Contemporary Idealism in America* (1932); and for a description of the rise of scientific methodology of inquiry during Royce's time at Harvard see Paul Buck, ed., *Social Sciences at Harvard, 1860-1902: From Inculcation to the Open Mind* (1965).

Additional Sources

Clendenning, John, *The life and thought of Josiah Royce,* Madison, Wis.: University of Wisconsin Press, 1985.
Hine, Robert V., *Josiah Royce: from Grass Valley to Harvard,* Norman: University of Oklahoma Press, 1992.
Kuklick, Bruce, *Josiah Royce: an intellectual biography,* Indianapolis, Ind.: Hackett Pub. Co., 1985. □

Agnes Maude Royden

As an internationally known British preacher, lecturer, and author, Agnes Maude Royden's (1876-1956) involvements spanned the issues of women's rights—political, social, and religious—social justice for the poor and disenfranchised, and world peace.

Born in Liverpool, England, in 1876, Agnes Maude Royden was the youngest of eight children and the sixth daughter. The family fortune was built on ships, and her eldest brother, Sir Thomas Royden, became chairman of Cunard Steamship Company. Intellectually more precocious than her elder sisters, Maude (as she would always be called) persuaded her parents to continue her education beyond high school. She graduated from Cheltenham Ladies College in 1896, and in 1897 went to Oxford University to continue her studies at Lady Margaret Hall. She read history and achieved second-class honors. It was here that she formed two important and enduring friendships, with Evelyn Gunter and Kathleen Courtney, who shared her strong desire to make a contribution to the world. The three of them worked together for the cause of women's suffrage and world peace.

In 1899, with her formal education at an end, Royden returned to her family home, Frankby, outside Liverpool to consider her future. She had no financial need to work but she longed to make herself useful. Maude suffered all her life from lameness, and when it was eventually diagnosed as dislocated hips there was little that could be done. Her success in conquering this handicap throughout her life was remarkable, but it did at times overtax her strength. Nevertheless, in 1900 she entered into settlement work and worked at the Victoria Women's Settlement in Liverpool for 18 months.

It was also during this period that she experienced something of a spiritual crisis. Like the rest of her family she was an Anglican, but she was attracted to Roman Catholicism, especially to the grandeur of its liturgy. While she was to remain within the Church of England, her love of the Roman liturgy can be seen in her writings on beauty in religion. This spiritual quest was the topic of many of the letters that crossed among the three friends, and it was Evelyn Gunter who suggested that she come to Oxford to take counsel with the Reverend Hudson Shaw. Hudson was an Anglican priest and a popular and dynamic lecturer for the University Extension Service, a continuing education service for ordinary citizens. The meeting with Hudson Shaw was the pivotal point in Royden's life.

Following their Oxford meetings they continued their conversations by mail, and within a few months of their meeting Shaw invited Royden to come and live with him and his wife, Effie, in his rural parish at South Luffenham. She would serve both as a parish assistant and as a companion to Effie while Hudson was away lecturing during the week. The triune bond of friendship which took shape in these first months was an unusual one. Years later, in 1947, when both Effie and Hudson were dead, Royden wrote the story of their friendship in the book entitled *A Threefold Cord*. She said that it was Effie who first understood the love between her husband and Maude, but she wished nothing more than that the relationship among the three of them continue. Effie was an unusual woman, intelligent and gifted, but mostly terrified of the world. Despite their love for each other, Hudson's and Maude's commitment to the

sanctity of marriage and their religious vocations meant that the relationship never became physical. Instead, they poured their energy into their work and into a mutual devotion to Effie. After Effie's death in the early 1940s Maude and Hudson married, but by this time Hudson was 84 years old and he lived only two months beyond the wedding day.

It was Hudson who was instrumental in enlisting Royden in the ranks of University Extension lecturers. Royden had an unusually good education for a woman and she was no stranger to the platform. Her "trial" lecture at the Summer Meeting in Oxford in 1903 was well received, and while there was some hesitation about listing A. Maude Royden—because she was a woman—among the staff of traveling lecturers, she proved a popular speaker and for the next two years maintained a steady schedule of lecturers. In 1905 she moved to Oxford, and this marked the beginning of her involvement in the suffrage movement.

Royden's work among settlement women had heightened her awareness of the situation of women in society, but it wasn't until 1905 that she embraced the suffrage movement as a whole, and this with a certainty of commitment which she had never known before. Royden anchored her belief in the suffrage movement in Christian belief. For her it was crystal clear that what Jesus taught was the equality of all persons regardless of sex. She believed that the women's movement was "the most profoundly moral movement . . . since the foundation of the Christian Church." She was strongly opposed to violence and could not condone many of the actions of the more militant Women's Social and Political Union headed by the Pankhursts. Indeed, she believed that women were natural pacifists, and that their goals would be achieved through a combination of prayer and education. Royden, along with Evelyn Gunter and Kathleen Courtney, joined the National Union of Women's Suffrage Societies, under the leadership of Millicent Fawcett. Royden was a tireless speaker for the cause, and she became editor and a major contributing writer to the NUWSS's weekly publication, *Common Cause,* a position she held until 1915. In the fall and winter of 1911-1912 she traveled to the United States, where she gave a series of lectures in several major cities and conferred with American suffrage leaders.

Royden's goals went beyond the vote. She sought better working conditions for women as well as equal pay for equal work; the protection of children; and equality of sexual standards for men and women. Her concern for society's sexual mores was at the same time both modern and staunchly Christian. She abhorred the "double standard" which, as she saw it, created two categories of women, the good (chaste wives) and the bad (prostitutes). The one was needed so that men could be assured both of the legality of their children and the sexual purity of their wives, but prostitutes were needed because males were not expected to control their passions. Prostitutes became society's "untouchables" and were treated with great cruelty. Royden insisted that if women must confine their sexual life to marriage so should men. She preached a positive approach to sexuality within marriage and, contrary to the Church of England's position, she approved of birth control.

Her book *Sex and Common Sense* was published in 1922, and she often addressed sexual issues in her lectures and sermons.

The outbreak of World War I brought a halt to most suffrage activity in England, and it also brought Royden into conflict with a number of her colleagues in the movement. Royden promoted the idea that the women's movement should stand for peace and refuse to support the war effort. She joined the Fellowship of Reconciliation and the Women's International League and wrote and spoke on pacifism. But pacifism was not a popular position in World War I, and Royden found herself both alienated from friends and under attack. After an especially ugly incident outside a small town in the Midlands, she changed her focus to one of structuring a peaceful society once the war was over.

In 1918 Royden adopted a baby girl (Helen) orphaned by the war, and as a response to the terrible plight of children in the postwar famine in Europe she also fostered a young Austrian boy, Friedrich Wolfe, for several years.

Her belief in the deep religious significance of the women's movement naturally propelled Royden to carry her cause for women's rights into the Church of England. In 1909 she became the first chair of the Church League for Women's Suffrage, which, following the passage of the suffrage act, would reform itself as the League of the Church Militant, dedicated to promoting women's equality within the church. As Royden revealed in her popular pamphlet *Women and the Church of England* (1916), not only were women barred from the priesthood but they were forbidden nearly every office in the church, despite the fact that they comprised the majority of the congregations and performed most of the parish work. There were many who supported her—lay and clergy—but a division existed between those who would accept women priests. Many, including Hudson Shaw, felt that the ordination of women was "premature." By 1919 the church had confirmed the rights of women as voting members on church councils, but the issue of "speaking" in churches was hotly debated.

Royden was in the forefront of these struggles and felt a deep commitment to the Anglican church, but she also felt she had a "calling" to the ministry, so when in 1917 the membership of City Temple, the famous nonconformist church in London, invited her to serve as a pulpit assistant, a position equivalent to associate pastor, she accepted. She was a gifted speaker and her sermons, many of which were later published in book or pamphlet form, always drew large audiences.

Several non-conformist Protestant churches then ordained women to the ministry, and this was a path that Royden could have chosen, but she refused because she wished to remain an Anglican. In 1920 she resigned her position at the City Temple in order to join with an Anglican cleric, Dr. Percy Dearmer, also chair of ecclesiastical art at King's College, London, to form a Christian fellowship that they called the Fellowship Guild. This was not a church, nor even an official arm of the Anglican church, but with its Anglican leadership and governing board it retained strong ties to the Church of England. Membership included both Anglicans and non-conformists, and it proved to be the kind of ecumenical venture which set an example for the reunion of Christendom which Royden and many of her friends sought. In addition to the popular Sunday evening worship services, the fellowship sponsored a variety of study groups on social and political issues. The fellowship "adopted" Albert Schweitzer's hospital in Lambarene, and Dr. Schweitzer once addressed the membership on a visit.

Royden's reputation as a preacher and spokesperson for peace grew to international proportions and she traveled to the United States in 1923 for the Women's International League. In 1928 Royden went on a round-the-world preaching tour, which took her again to the United States and then to China, Japan, New Zealand, Australia, and India, where she visited Gandhi. In 1930 she was awarded the Companion of Honour by the British Government.

In 1936 Royden, then 60 years old, resigned from the leadership of the fellowship but continued to travel widely and was one of the pioneers in religious broadcasting, carrying on a pastoral ministry over the BBC until the early 1950s. She died at the age of 80 in 1956.

Further Reading

Because of her varied involvements—in the suffrage movement, the peace movement, social issues, and as a religious feminist and pastor—there are sources for Maude Royden's life in the literature of these movements. *Common Cause,* the publication of the National Union of Women's Suffrage Societies, and church publications such as the *Church Militant* and the *Church Times* are good resources, as well as the newspapers of the period. Royden herself published over a dozen books and numerous pamphlets and articles. The breadth of her interests and involvements are represented in their titles: *The Church and Woman* (1924), *Women and the Sovereign State* (1917), *Woman's Partnership in the World* (1941), *Political Christianity* (1922), and *Sex and Common Sense* (1921). Her analysis and historical survey of the status of women anticipate the religious feminist movement of the 1970s and 1980s. Several of her books are more inspirational in nature, including *Prayer as a Force* (1922), *Beauty in Religion* (1923), and *I Believe in God* (1927). *The Guildhouse Monthly,* the periodical of the Fellowship Guild, 1928-1955, is an excellent source for information about Royden's life and work during this period. The letters between Royden and Kathleen Courtney are available at Lady Margaret Hall in Oxford, and the Fawcett library in London is another source for Royden correspondence. Brian Heeney's 1983 study *The Women's Movement in the Church of England* places Royden in the context of the larger movement. Royden's own "partial" autobiography, *The Threefold Cord* (1947), should be read in concert with a biography (1989) by Sheila Fletcher entitled *Maude Royden: A Life.* □

Mike Royko

Born into a tavern-owning family in a rough Polish neighborhood in the northwestern part of Chicago, Mike Royko (1932-1997) became one of America's premier political and social commentators.

I n their work *Chicago's Public Wits: A Chapter in the American Comic Spirit,* Kenny William and Bernard Duffy detail the writings of Chicago humorists. During the heyday of such humor Peter Finley Dunn, known to almost all American history students as "Mr. Dooley," and George Ade dominated the Chicago newspapers with their columns capturing the wit of the streets and the insight of the ethnic communities. Mike Royko, once feature writer for the Chicago *Sun-Times* and its syndicated wire service (until Rupert Murdoch bought the *Sun-Times*) and later columnist for the *Chicago Tribune,* followed in this tradition. He was a columnist who understood the language of the streets and the neighborhoods, a writer with a sense of what troubles and amuses the people. While Royko was at his best when commenting on the problems of ordinary people, those problems frequently called attention to larger issues.

Mike Royko was born on September 19, 1932, to Michael (a Ukrainian-American saloon keeper) and Helen Zak (a Polish-American saloon keeper) Royko. He grew up in a predominately Polish neighborhood on Chicago's northwest side. Reports on his early education range from his leaving school at 16 to his holding jobs as a bartender from the ages of 13 to 19 to his being sent to Montefiore High School after several arrests. He attended Wright Junior College, left when he was 19, and served in Korea as an Air Force radio operator. After reassignment near Chicago, he claimed to have been a writer for the *Chicago Daily News* and secured a job as editor of the base newspaper. This was the beginning of his newspaper career.

After discharge from the Air Force, Royko returned to Chicago and began a series of low-paying newspaper jobs, in time actually securing employment with the *Daily News.* In 1962 he was given a weekly column called "County Beat" with the assignment of commenting on local government and politics. This proved a popular feature, particularly as he made fun of the "payrollers," those who avoided ever working even though paid by Cook County or the city of Chicago. By 1963 he was awarded a daily column, "Mike Royko," where he could write on any subject that took his fancy. This column continued until 1978 when the *Daily News* ceased publication. Royko moved to the *Chicago Sun Times* until 1983 when he shifted to the *Chicago Tribune* where he wrote a daily column, three of which were syndicated each week by Tribune Media Services to nearly 600 newspapers.

Royko was ostensibly a liberal journalist, but a liberal journalist with a sense of the outrage of the common citizen. Therefore, he was at the forefront of those who questioned Gary Hart's judgment rather than his morals, had a nationally celebrated fight with AT & T, and wrote a column castigating those social workers who were attempting to get men in pool rooms to find regular jobs. Additionally, he was generally unsupportive of political correctness, of those who are young and fail to function within the political system, of police departments that fail to protect the average person, and of those politicians who see people as part of the problem. Royko was credited with first calling former California Governor Jerry Brown "Governor Moonbeam," and he rarely saw virtue in those who voiced the idea of the criminal as the victim.

Viewed as one of the few political or social journalists with "clout," Royko was seen as influential on both the Chicago and the national scenes. Despite this vision of influencing politics, Royko was at his best when writing through the voice of his *alter ego,* Slats Grobnik, the stereotypical beer-drinking, pool-playing, bar-sitting, white male Chicago ethnic. Slats spoke with Royko's concept of the common man, the person who cannot make sense of racism, ethnic purification, political correctness, the Chicago Cubs, police corruption, or television evangelists. Once when commenting on the problems of the governor of Alaska, who was accused of helping his friends, Slats questioned what politics was all about. It certainly wasn't about helping your enemies.

Royko retained his links to his own and other families. In 1954 Mike Royko married Carol Duckman. They had two sons, David, born in 1960, and Robbie, born in 1964. In 1979 Carol died of a cerebral hemorrhage. In 1985 Royko married Judy Arndt, and they had two children, a son Samuel and a daughter Katherine. John Culhane, a colleague from his days on the *Daily News,* noted that one of Royko's "funniest and saddest" columns was written after two men robbed Royko. Royko mused on the fact that his father had once kicked a robber in the face and had run over him with a truck. He wrote, "An hour after I was robbed I was depressed because I wasn't my father's son."

Royko published several books, mostly, as with *Slats Grobnik and Some Other Friends* or *Like I Was Saying,* these were collections of his columns. The exception was his 1971 work on Richard Daley, mayor of Chicago, *Boss: Richard J. Daley of Chicago. Boss* was a significant exploration of machine politics in a big city. Though the book received mixed reviews from both professional politicians and urban scholars, there is no doubt it was a valuable, insightful, amusing artifact of what might be the last of the great urban political machines.

In 1972 Royko received the Pulitzer Prize for commentary. He was actively involved as a writer for four decades and in the mid 1990s demonstrated no sign of future inactivity. He suggested that he might eventually write only about golf but, fortunately for the reader, he continued to pierce, with ridicule and humor, those who use and abuse authority.

By the mid-90s, Royko's earthy, blue collar perspective ran him afoul of activist identity groups. A number of his columns offended gays and lesbians, women, Mexican-Americans, and African-Americans. He also managed to offend Croatian-Americans and the police. He survived demands that he be fired and retained his intensely loyal reader base and his wide circulation.

Royke died at age 64, on April 29, 1997, while vacationing in Florida. In Chicago, his death was covered in a manner befitting a major public figure with television team coverage from his favorite hangouts and from the offices of the *Chicago Tribune*. The outpouring of tributes and accolades rank him with Ben Hecht, Ernest Hemingway, and Carl Sandburg, all of them Chicago journalists who earned national literary stature. Fellow Chicagoan Studs Terkel wrote of Royko on his death, "If somebody says, 'What was Chicago like in the last half of the 20th century?' you'd say read Royko. He captured the city like no one else has ever captured a city and Chicago was his metaphor for the rest of the country."

Further Reading

There is no single biographical work on Mike Royko. Some good individual articles are John Culhane, "The World According to Royko," *Reader's Digest* (April 1992); Tricia Drevets, "Commentary from a Chicago Columnist," *Editor and Publisher* (June 27, 1987); Rodger Schiffman, "He's Mr. Chicago," *Golf Digest* (June 1990); Daniel Le Duc, "Mike Royko remembered for capturing the essence of Chicago," *The Philadelphia Inquirer* (April 30, 1997); and Stephen McFarland and Corky Siemaszko, "Pulitzer Prize-winning Columnist Mike Royko dies," *New York Daily News* (April 29, 1997). ☐

Peter Paul Rubens

The Flemish painter and diplomat Peter Paul Rubens (1577-1640) was not only the unquestioned leader of the Flemish baroque school but one of the supreme geniuses in the history of painting.

During the last troubled decades of the 16th century the Flemish school of painting fell into a kind of tepid and uninventive mannerism which gave little promise of bringing forth a great master. Yet it was in this school that Peter Paul Rubens received his first training as an artist and acquired that belief in the humanistic values of classical antiquity that was to continue undiminished throughout his career.

Within his own lifetime Rubens enjoyed a European reputation which brought him commissions from Italy, Spain, France, England, and Germany as well as from his homeland, the southern Netherlands. His boundless imagination, immense capacity for work, and sheer productivity were legendary. In 1621, when he was not yet 45 years old, an English visitor to Antwerp described him as "the master workman of the world." And at almost the same moment Rubens said of himself, without boasting, "My talent is such that no enterprise, however vast in number and in diversity of subjects, has surpassed my courage." It reveals something of the many-sidedness of this extraordinary man that, without interrupting his artistic activity, he was able to engage in a demanding career of public service and also to conduct an extensive correspondence with learned men on scholarly and archeological matters.

Jan Rubens, the painter's father, was a lawyer of Antwerp who, because he was a Calvinist, fled to Germany in 1568 to escape persecution at the hands of the Spaniards. In Cologne he entered into an adulterous relationship with the wife of William the Silent, Prince of Orange, as a result of which he was thrown into prison. Released after 2 years

owing to the devoted and untiring efforts of his wife, Maria Pypelinckx, Jan Rubens was permitted to take up residence at Siegen in Westphalia. It was there that their second son, Peter Paul, was born on June 28, 1577. The family, which had now become Catholic, lived for some years in Cologne until Jan Rubens died in 1587, at which time his widow returned to Antwerp, bringing her three children with her.

After a period of schooling which included instruction in Latin and Greek, the young Rubens became a page to a noblewoman, Marguerite de Ligne, Countess of Lalaing. This early experience of court life, though he was glad to be released from it, was undoubtedly useful to the future artist, much of whose time was to be passed in aristocratic and royal circles. Returning to his home in Antwerp, he now decided to follow the profession of painter. He studied under three masters—Tobias Verhaecht, Adam van Noort, and Otto van Veen—and in 1598 was accepted as a master in the Antwerp Guild of St. Luke, the painters' guild.

Italian Period, 1600-1608

In 1600 Rubens set out on a journey to Italy, where within a short time he entered the service of Vincenzo Gonzaga, Duke of Mantua, whose palace housed a notable art collection. Since Rubens was not expected to remain always at the ducal court in Mantua, he found time to visit other cities in Italy, especially Rome, Florence, and Genoa. In Rome, Rubens completed his education as an artist, studying with unfailing enthusiasm the sculptures of antiquity and the paintings of the High Renaissance, especially those of Raphael and Michelangelo. During his first sojourn in the papal city (1601-1602) he painted three altarpieces for the Church of Sta Croce in Gerusalemme (now in the Hospital at Grasse).

In 1603 Duke Vincenzo sent Rubens on a diplomatic mission to Spain; here he made the impressive equestrian portrait of the Duke of Lerma and saw for the first time the Spanish royal collection, with its wealth of paintings by Titian.

Late in 1605 Rubens was again in Rome; he now contrived to remain there for almost 3 years. During this time he was commissioned to decorate the high altar of S. Maria in Vallicella—an extraordinary honor for a foreigner. His first solution, an altarpiece showing the Madonna and Child with St. Gregory and other saints (now in the Museum at Grenoble), did not make a good impression owing to unfavorable lighting conditions in the church, and he obligingly replaced it by a set of three pictures painted on slate. In October 1608, before this work had been unveiled, there came word that Rubens's mother was seriously ill, and the artist left at once for Antwerp. Though he did not know it at the time, he was never to see Italy again.

Antwerp Period, 1609-1621

Rubens arrived at his home to learn that his mother had died before he left Rome. Although it was surely his intention to return to Italy, he soon found reasons for remaining in Antwerp. The Archduke Albert and his consort, Isabella, the sovereigns of the Spanish Netherlands, appointed him court painter with special privileges. In October 1609 Ru-

bens married Isabella Brant, and a year later he purchased a house in Antwerp. The charming painting *Rubens and His Wife in the Honeysuckle Arbor* was painted about this time.

The humanistic atmosphere of Antwerp that appealed so strongly to Rubens is epitomized in the so-called *Four Philosophers.* In reality this is a commemorative picture representing the late Justus Lipsius, the eminent classical scholar, with two of his pupils, one of whom is Rubens's brother Philip (also recently deceased); the artist himself stands a little to one side, an onlooker rather than a participant in the symposium.

The first big project to be undertaken after Rubens's return from Italy was the *Raising of the Cross,* a triptych (1609-1611) for the church of St. Walburga (now in the Cathedral of Antwerp). With this bold and intensely dramatic work Rubens at once established himself as the leading master of the city. It was followed by another triptych, equally large and no less successful, the *Descent from the Cross* (1611-1614) in the Cathedral. Rubens's baroque imagination found new outlets in subjects chosen from both the sacred and profane worlds: in the *Great Last Judgment* he conjured up an apocalyptic vision of the torments of the damned; the same tempestuous energy is encountered in the artist's hunting pieces, with their ferocious combats of men and wild beasts.

Rubens's workshop was now in full operation, and he was able, with the aid of his pupils and assistants, to achieve an astonishing output of pictures. The ablest and most brilliant of these assistants was Anthony Van Dyck, who entered his studio about 1617/1618 and who undoubtedly helped in the execution of a number of important commissions. Nevertheless it must not be concluded that the master took no responsibility for his paintings but was simply content to let them be carried out by his studio. The principal works exhibit no falling off in quality. Indeed the masterpieces crowd so closely upon one another at this time that it is difficult to select a few representative examples. Of the mythologies the *Rape of the Daughters of Leucippus* is one of the most dazzling. Among the finest of the ecclesiastical works are the two altarpieces glorifying the first saints of the Jesuit order, the *Miracles of St. Ignatius of Loyola* and the *Miracles of St. Francis Xavier,* which fairly overwhelm the observer by their huge scale, richness of color, and depth of feeling.

In 1620 Rubens was commissioned to execute a series of 39 ceiling paintings for the Jesuit church in Antwerp. It was the largest decorative cycle that the artist had yet undertaken, and as such it called into play all his powers of invention and organization. The entire complex of ceiling paintings was destroyed by fire in 1718.

International Fame, 1621-1630

The Jesuit cycle was followed by an even larger commission from France. In 1622 Rubens was in Paris to sign a contract for the decoration of two great galleries in the Luxembourg Palace, the residence of the queen mother, Marie de Médicis. The first of these projects, the incomparable series of 21 large canvases illustrating the life of Marie (now in the Louvre, Paris), was finished in 1625. The subject matter was decidedly unpromising, but Rubens, undaunted as always, succeeded in transforming the dreary history of the Queen into one of the most brilliant and most spectacular of all baroque decorative programs. Work on the second cycle, which was to deal with the life of Marie's late husband, King Henry IV, was repeatedly delayed, and Rubens at length gave up the project in disgust.

There were other decorative schemes to occupy Rubens's attention during this period. For King Louis XIII of France he designed the tapestry series, the *History of Constantine the Great,* and several years later the Infanta Isabella commissioned him to design an even larger tapestry cycle, the *Triumph of the Eucharist,* for the Convent of the Descalzas Reales in Madrid.

Despite his being involved in these and other great undertakings, Rubens found time to paint important altarpieces for churches in Antwerp: the *Adoration of the Magi* (now in the Antwerp Museum) was made for St. Michael's Abbey in 1624; the *Assumption of the Virgin* for the high altar of the Cathedral in 1626; and—perhaps the most beautiful of all—the *Madonna and Saints* (sometimes called the *Mystic Marriage of St. Catherine*) for the church of the Augustinians in 1628. Some of his most memorable portraits also belong to these years. They range from the fresh and luminous *Susanna Fourment,* known as *Le Chapeau de paille,* to the stern and masterful *Thomas Howard, Earl of Arundel.*

In Windsor Castle is the famous *Self-portrait* (1623/1624) which Rubens painted at the request of the Prince of Wales, later King Charles I of England. It shows a strong and handsome face, with bold moustaches and curling hair and beard; the broadbrimmed hat not only lends animation by its sweeping oval shape but serves also to conceal the artist's baldness (about which he seems to have been rather sensitive).

Rubens's diplomatic activity, which had begun some time earlier, reached a peak in the years 1628-1630, when he was instrumental in bringing about peace between England and Spain. As the agent of the Infanta, he went first to Spain, where in addition to carrying out his political duties he found a new and enthusiastic art patron in King Philip IV and renewed his acquaintance with the works of Titian in the royal collection. His mission to England was equally successful. Charles I knighted the artist-diplomat, and the University of Cambridge awarded him an honorary master of arts degree. Rubens returned to Antwerp in March 1630.

Last Years, 1630-1640

Isabella Brant, Rubens's first wife, had died in 1626. In December 1630 he married Helena Fourment, a girl of 16. Though he had hoped, on returning to Antwerp, to withdraw from political life, he was obliged to act once more as confidential agent for the Infanta in the frustrating and unsuccessful negotiations with the Dutch. At length he succeeded in being released from diplomatic employment. In 1635 he purchased a country estate, the Castle of Steen, situated some miles south of Antwerp, and henceforth divided his time between this rural retreat and his studio in town.

In the last decade of his life Rubens's art underwent a surprising expansion in variety and scope of subject matter. The enchanting *Garden of Love,* with its complex interweaving of the classical and the contemporary, may serve as an illustration. A new interest in nature, inspired perhaps by his residence in the country, found expression in a series of magnificent landscapes, among them the *Castle of Steen.* The portraits of this period, especially those of his wife, Helena, and their children, are characterized by informality and tender intimacy.

A lyrical quality pervades even the traditional Christian and classical subjects. In the *Ildefonso Altarpiece* the scene of the saint receiving a vestment from the Virgin Mary is transfigured by a silvery radiance. The secular counterpart to this work is the *Feast of Venus,* in which Rubens pays tribute both to the art of antiquity and to the paintings of Titian. The almost dreamlike poetry of the late mythologies is beautifully exemplified by the *Judgment of Paris* and the *Three Graces,* in which the opulent nudes seem to glow with light and color.

Rubens continued to carry out monumental commissions during his last decade. For Charles I he executed the ceiling paintings of the Banqueting House at Whitehall—the only large-scale decorative cycle by the artist that still remains in the place for which it was designed. In the Whitehall ceiling, which is a glorification of King James I and the Stuart monarchy, the artist profited from the experience gained in the decoration of the Jesuit church some years earlier. In 1635, when the new governor of the Netherlands, Cardinal Infante Ferdinand, made his "joyous entry" into Antwerp, Rubens was given the task of preparing the temporary street decorations. Swiftly mobilizing teams of artists and craftsmen to work from his designs, the master created a stupendous series of painted theaters and triumphal arches which surpassed all expectations by their magnificence. His last great project was the provision of a vast cycle of mythological paintings for the decoration of Philip IV's hunting lodge near Madrid, the Torre de la Parada.

Toward the end of his life Rubens was increasingly troubled by arthritis, which eventually compelled him to give up painting altogether. One of the most moving documents of the last years is the *Self-portrait* in Vienna, in which the master, though already touched by suffering, wears an air of calm and serenity. He died in Antwerp on May 30, 1640.

Further Reading

Rubens's letters are available in a first-rate translation by Ruth S. Magurn, *The Letters of Peter Paul Rubens* (1955). The standard biography is Max Rooses, *Rubens,* translated by H. Child (2 vols., 1904), which, although dated in some particulars, remains unsurpassed as a detailed, authoritative, and readable account of the artist and his times. Two shorter biographies, both handsomely illustrated, are recommended: C. V. Wedgwood, *The World of Rubens, 1577-1640* (1967), and Christopher White, *Rubens and His World* (1968). Also enlightening is the lengthy essay by the 19th-century historian Jacob Burckhardt, *Recollections of Rubens,* translated by M. Hottinger, with an introduction and additional notes by H. Gerson (1950).

On Rubens's drawings, abundant information is in J. S. Held, *Rubens: Selected Drawings* (1959), and Ludwig Burchard and R.-A. d'Hulst, *Rubens Drawings* (2 vols., 1963). A scholarly discussion of the influences on Rubens is Wolfgang Stechow, *Rubens and the Classical Tradition* (1968). □

Helena Rubenstein

Polish-born beauty expert Helena Rubenstein (1870-1965) was among the first to establish cosmetics as essential to a woman's toilette. Rubenstein's business acumen enabled her to build a multi-million dollar empire based on the sale of beauty products.

Helena Rubenstein was born on December 25, 1870, in Cracow, Poland. The oldest of eight girls, she was raised in an upper middle class family. Her father favored Helena's intellect, her mother emphasized beauty and charm. Together, Rubenstein's parents shaped her career as the creator and financial genius of what was to become a multi-million dollar beauty empire.

In 1888, after rejecting both medical school and a suitor, Rubenstein travelled to Coleraine, Australia, to live with relatives. Elegant and fastidious, she introduced the neighbors to a special facial creme, the product of Hungarian chemist Jacob Lykusky. She soon moved to Melbourne and established a small beauty salon to which Australian women came to offset the drying effects of sun and wind. Within two years Rubenstein's reputation was assured. She had repaid an original $1,500 loan and was lured by the thought of greater financial success.

Returning to Europe, Rubenstein settled in London. She purchased Lord Salisbury's former residence on Grafton Street, a four-story house with 26 rooms. She redecorated in lavish color schemes influenced by theater designers Leon Bakst and Alexandre Benois. Shortly after her marriage to American newspaperman Edward William Titus, Rubenstein opened the "Salon de Beaute Valaze."

Rubenstein launched her salon at a time when make-up was worn only on stage. But society women once entertained by Lord Salisbury were curious about the Grafton Street establishment. Gradually, Rubenstein found them willing to pay ten guineas (about $50) for 12 beauty treatments. Her special product was a facial creme based on Lykusky's product, but she had developed other items, including face powder and rouge. Rubenstein planned for the time when conservative attitudes toward facial makeup relaxed and ladies considered it part of their daily toilette.

Rubenstein's treatments relied on her understanding of diet, skin anatomy, and body metabolism, all of which she had learned from French chemist Marcellin Berthlot of the University of Paris. One of Rubenstein's earliest staff members was Viennese doctor Emmie List, who introduced a skin peeling treatment for severely blemished complexions. But Rubenstein was not content to remain in the laboratory. She and her husband entered a social circle that included Margot Asquith, Baroness d'Erlanger, sculptor Jacob Epstein, and young pianist Artur Rubenstein.

In 1909 Rubenstein was expecting a child. She and Edward moved out of the Grafton Street apartment where they lived above the salon and purchased a separate residence. Simultaneously, Rubenstein opened a shop in the rue St. Honore in Paris, France. By now several of her sisters had joined the business—Ceska was in the Melbourne salon, Manka was part of the London establishment, and Pauline had responsibility for the Paris salon. Rubenstein's son Roy was born in late 1909 and another son, Horace, in 1912.

In 1914 they all moved to Paris, where Rubenstein threw herself into running the salon. Her ambition was rewarded, and soon society leaders and art and stage personalities crowded the appointment book. Rubenstein was an unqualified success.

World War I caused an abrupt, unanticipated change in the business. Due to her husband's nationality the family moved to the United States in January 1915. There Rubenstein discovered a new market. Most American women were just as reluctant to adopt facial make-up as their European counterparts had been. This untapped clientele represented a potential gold mine.

Greenwich, Connecticut, became home for the Titus family. Here Rubenstein planned new products based on the beauty needs of American women. Little more than a year after her arrival Rubenstein opened the first Maison de Beaute in New York City, located in a West 49th Street brownstone. She decorated the interior in dark blue velvet. The single salon soon proved inadequate and she rapidly opened salons in Boston, Chicago, Philadelphia, San Francisco, Washington DC, and Toronto, Canada.

In 1928, hoping to concentrate on her European business, Rubenstein sold controlling interest in her United States holdings to Lehman Brothers. They paid $7.3 million. One year later, deciding that Lehman could not maintain the quality she had established for her business, Rubenstein purchased back the controlling stock for $1.5 million.

Despite the Depression years, Rubenstein's beauty empire grew. An avid collector, she became famous for her collections of paintings, sculpture, and jewelry. In 1938 she and Edward Titus divorced, and later that same year Rubenstein married a Russian, Prince Artchil Gourielli-Tchkonia. Under his tutelage she met and mingled with the world's rich and titled. Together they established a gentlemen's product line through the House of Gourielli in New York City. In 1953 the Helena Rubenstein Foundation was established to help fund research and education and to support the America-Israel Foundation.

Widowed in 1955, Rubenstein maintained a demanding schedule. An early riser, she often conducted business meetings in her New York bedroom ensconced in a lucite bed with fluorescent head and footboard. Several times annually Rubenstein travelled to key cities throughout the world, alternately chiding and praising her agents there.

Rubenstein reportedly knew all the ingredients of every one of her beauty products. Her personal style was at once dictatorial and generous. At times parsimonius to the point of obsession, she reveled in her million-dollar jewelry collection while wearing $4.99 nightgowns. (She kept her jewelry in a dress box under her bed.)

In 1964 Rubenstein was burglarized in her Park Avenue apartment. Several servants were bound and gagged and Rubenstein was tied to a chair and threatened. She refused to reveal the location of a key to her safe, and the robbers left empty-handed as she shrieked for help.

Princess Gourielli—Madame Helena Rubenstein—died of natural causes in a New York hospital on April 1, 1965. She was 94 years old.

Further Reading

Patrick O'Higgins wrote a lively, impressionistic biography of Helena Rubenstein in *MADAME, an Intimate Biography* (1971). For a glimpse of Rubenstein's early years, a good source is her autobiography, *My Life for Beauty* (1964). Both volumes include extensive photographs showing Rubenstein in various settings throughout the world. □

Richard L. Rubenstein

Richard L. Rubenstein (born 1924) was an American Jewish theologian and writer who defined the agenda of post-Holocaust theology for Christians and Jews.

Richard Lowell Rubenstein was born on January 6, 1924, in New York City. The eldest son of an assimilated, educated, poor Jewish family, he did not have a Bar-Mitzvah, the traditional rite affirming a 13-year-old as an adult member of the Jewish community. Educated at the prestigious Townsend Harris High School, as a teenager Rubenstein considered converting to Unitarianism and becoming a minister. When the pastor advised him to change his last name, Rubenstein began his slow journey back to Judaism.

Ordained as a Rabbi

In 1942, during the height of the Holocaust, Rubenstein entered the Hebrew Union College in Cincinnati (Reform Judaism's rabbinical seminary) and simultaneously continued his studies at the University of Cincinnati. While millions of Jews were being slaughtered in Europe, Rubenstein was taught an anti-Zionist theology of religious liberalism, which spoke of the evolving perfection of man and enthusiastically welcomed modernity. Increasingly disillusioned, Rubenstein left the Hebrew Union College for the Jewish Theological Seminary. He was ordained a Conservative rabbi in 1952, prior to which he had also studied at an Orthodox yeshiva. The death of his infant son on the eve of the Day of Atonement triggered a personal and theological crisis for Rubenstein.

After ordination, Rubenstein worked as a pulpit rabbi and began a Ph.D. program at Harvard, completing his dissertation on a psychoanalytic understanding of rabbinic legends. Rubenstein served as the chaplain to Jewish students at Harvard (1956-1958) and later at the University of Pittsburgh (1958-1970), where he also was the Charles E. Merrill Adjunct Professor of Humanities (1966-1970). He subsequently moved to Florida State University, where he was the Robert D. Lawton Distinguished Professor of Religion and co-director of the Humanities Institute.

Literary Works

In 1966 Rubenstein published his first book, *After Auschwitz: Radical Theology and Contemporary Judaism.* An innovative, controversial work, it suggested that no Jewish theology could afford to ignore the twin revolutions of modern Jewish history—the Holocaust and the reborn state of Israel. Rubenstein argued that the Holocaust overturned traditional Jewish teaching regarding the God of history. To portray history as an expression of God's will is to maintain that God wanted Auschwitz—an idea which Rubenstein dismissed as thoroughly obscene. Like his teacher Mordecai Kaplan, Rubenstein rejected the concept of Jewish chosenness. Jews must recognize, Rubenstein argued, ''that we are, when given normal opportunities, neither more nor less than any other men, sharing the pain, the joy, and the fated destiny that Earth alone has meted out to all her children.''

Influenced by Freud's psychoanalytic theory, Rubenstein nevertheless affirmed the priestly functions of religious life. Religion is the arena in which people celebrate the joys and vicissitudes of life, its tragedies and triumphs. Though he denied the God of history, Rubenstein did not abandon the idea of divinity. He offered an ultimately tragic theological vision: "omnipotent nothingness is the Lord of all creation."

After Auschwitz took the Jewish community by storm. It was widely considered *the* Jewish contribution to the "death of God" theologies popularized in the 1960s. Yet, unlike other death of God theologians, Rubenstein viewed God's death not as an event in the divine life but as a mournful statement of the human condition. "We live in the time of the death of God," he wrote. *After Auschwitz* set the theological agenda of the Jewish community for the next period. It forced Christian theologians to confront the Holocaust but also reinforced Rubenstein's growing estrangement from the Jewish establishment.

Over the next eight years Rubenstein wrote four books: *The Religious Imagination* (1968), a psychoanalytic study of rabbinic myth which won the Portico d'Ottavia Literary Prize in Rome in 1977; *Morality and Eros* (1970), an examination of ethics in a permissive society; *My Brother Paul* (1972), a psycho-biography of Paul's struggles with Jewish tradition and his relevance for contemporary religious life; and *Power Struggle* (1974), Rubenstein's autobiography detailing his formative years, his failed first marriage, his happy remarriage to Betty Rogers Rubenstein, and his relationship to his three children. The memoir also deals with Rubenstein's struggles with Jewish tradition and authority.

In 1975 Rubenstein published *The Cunning of History*, in which the Holocaust is portrayed not as an aberration from Western tradition but an extreme expression of the deepest tendencies of civilization—demographic, religious, political, and economic.

According to Rubenstein, Western societies have been producing superfluous populations—people who could not find a place within the economic system—for the past 350 years. For most of that time, superfluous Europeans went to settle the new world or colonize Asia and Africa. Once the gates of the new world were shut, the Nazis undertook the next logical step: they murdered the people they deemed superfluous (Jews, Poles, Gypsies, homosexuals, and the retarded).

He felt that Christianity believes that it has superseded Judaism, a relic religion that will disappear in time. The Nazis took Christianity's target and sought to make the world *Judenrein*, free of Jews. On a political level, Nazism represented the perfection of bureaucracy. The Nazis could successfully destroy millions because they employed a highly disciplined bureaucratic system. Economically, I. G. Auschwitz, the corporately-sponsored slave-labor camp adjacent to the death camp, represented the perfection of human slavery. Human beings were reduced to a consumable raw material expended as a by-product of manufacturing. In *The Age of Triage* (1983) Rubenstein further developed the theory suggested in *The Cunning of History* and expanded his discussion of modernization. *The Cunning of History* had marked Rubenstein's transition from a Jewish theologian into a major theoretician of modernization and its consequences.

Rubenstein's works have been translated into Dutch, Swedish, Hungarian, Italian, and Japanese. As the president of the Washington Institute for Values in Public Policy (a conservative think-tank that explored religion and politics in the 1980s), Rubenstein traveled extensively in the Far East and Europe lecturing and consulting. Later he wrote on the crisis of modernization in the East and West.

In 1986 Rubenstein co-authored with John Roth *Approaches to Auschwitz* (1986), a scholarly and diverse text on the Holocaust. It is methodologically eclectic, incorporating history, ideology, theology, literature, philosophy, and the social sciences from a humanistic perspective. Other publications include *Modernization: The Humanist Response to Its Promises and Pitfalls* (1982); *The Dissolving Alliance: The United States and the Future of Europe* (1987); *Spirit Matters: The Worldwide Impact of Religion on Contemporary Politics* (1987); *The Dissolving Alliance: The United States and NATO* (1987); and *After Auschwitz: History, Theology and Contemporary Judaism* (1992).

Rubenstein retired from Florida State University in 1995 and became the president of the University of Bridgeport in Connecticut. He was a bold, innovative thinker whose approach to Judaism and religion was informed by the social sciences and then transformed by a fertile imagination.

Further Reading

Rubenstein's wife, B.R. Rubenstein and M. Berenbaum were the editors for a series of essays entitled *What Kind of God? Essays in Honor of Richard Rubenstein* (1997). Aside from reading Rubenstein's own work, the reader can find an understanding of Richard Rubenstein's early work in Michael Berenbaum's *The Vision of the Void* (1979); Steven Katz *Post-Holocaust Dialogues* (1983); and Eugene Borowitz's *Contemporary Jewish Theology*. William Styron's chapter "Hell Revisited" in *This Quiet Dust* (1982) deals with Rubenstein's later work. An advanced student might want to read a full length Ph.D. dissertation on Rubenstein: Jocelyn Hellig, *The 'Death of God' in the Thought of Richard L. Rubenstein* (The University of Witswatersrand, Johannesburg, South Africa, 1982). □

Jerry Rubin

Jerry Rubin (1938—1994), activist, writer, lecturer, and businessman, was best known as a leader of the counter-culture in the 1960s.

Jerry Rubin was born in Cincinnati, Ohio, on July 14, 1938. He was educated at the University of Cincinnati (B.A., 1961), Hebrew University, and the University of California at Berkeley. A journalist during his student years, Rubin became a full-time agitator in response to the Vietnam War. He was an organizer of Berkeley's Vietnam Day Committee (VDC) in 1965 which held the world's largest teach-in against the war. During a march on the Oakland Army Terminal, the VDC was attacked by both police and Hell's Angels (outlaw bikers who were extreme patriots and regarded the anti-war movement as a "mob of traitors").

In 1967, with Abbie Hoffman, he founded the Youth International Party. The party mixed political activism and the unbuttoned bohemianism of the period. The "yippies," as they were known, staged theatrical events and stunts that were intended to discredit authority and by means of cultural insurgency to bring on the social revolution. They failed in this, but succeeded in reaping a harvest of publicity that maddened and enraged the power structure. Rubin did much to further this process when he was called before the House Committee on Un-American Activities to explain his subversive ways. He was advised to rely upon his First Amendment right of free speech but explained that was not enough as the movement had to be "as exciting as the Mets." In that spirit Rubin attended the hearings dressed as a Revolutionary War soldier, subsequently appearing before committees as a bare-chested guerrilla and as Santa Claus.

Rubin showed himself to be a master organizer and publicist capable of transforming conventional protests into media happenings. In 1967 he was made project director of a flagging effort to demonstrate against the military in Washington. The novelist Norman Mailer later wrote that, "to call on Rubin was in effect to call upon the most militant, unpredictable, creative—therefore dangerous—hippie-oriented leader available to the New Left." What resulted was the celebrated March on the Pentagon, when some 75,000 protesters including Mailer, the poet Robert Lowell, critic Dwight Macdonald, Dr. Spock, Noam Chomsky, and many others rallied and railed against the war.

Jerry Rubin (foreground)

In 1968 Rubin and Hoffman, in connection with various peace groups, led what proved to be a far more violent anti-war protest. They planned to hold a yippie "Festival of Life" in Chicago during the Democratic National Convention. Crying out that "the streets belong to the people," yippie demonstrators made the streets unusable by setting fires, building barricades, and carrying out other acts of vandalism. This inspired the police (whom Rubin called "Czechago pigs") to beat and arrest them. It was a source of particular satisfaction to Rubin that bystanders and members of the press also fell victim to police enthusiasm. Whether the resulting publicity did the anti-war movement more harm than good is debatable. But Chicago authorities, led by the peerless Mayor Richard Daley, were not content with what they had accomplished, and Rubin and six others (including Hoffman and Tom Hayden of the Students for a Democratic Society), who came to be called the "Chicago Seven," plus Bobby Seale of the Black Panthers were tried for conspiracy to incite riot. The trial was scandalous in the extreme. The defendants vilified Judge Julius Hoffman, who at one point had Seale bound and gagged, finally separating his case from the others. Ultimately all eight—plus their lawyers—were found to be in contempt of court. Though convicted on lesser counts by a jury, none of the defendants went to jail as the trial had been a farce and the verdicts did not stand up on appeal.

Like most movement activists Rubin was "forcibly retired," as one interviewer put it, in the 1970s. Rubin differed from his colleagues by embarking on a relentless campaign of self-improvement, few therapies escaping his notice. Among the cults and techniques he sampled were EST, Esalen, meditation, massage, acupuncture, hypnotism, health foods, tantric yoga, and rolfing. He established, perhaps, a new record and certainly gave the phrase "open to experience" a new meaning. Never an intellectual, Rubin gave up reading anything that did not concern self-help. Even in his wildest days he had never been as radical or crazy as he used to seem, Rubin said over and over again, which anyone seeing the new, clean-cut, boyishly earnest Rubin of the post-revolutionary era could well believe. This was confirmed when he took up a new career as a stockbroker in 1980 with the brokerage firm of John Muir & Co., having discovered that capitalism was nicer than he had previously supposed.

Rubin continued his capitalistic pursuit with the creation of Business Networking Salons, Inc., a business in which Rubin and his wife, Mimi, would host weekly "parties" at New York's Studio 54 for the business crowd. For $8, patrons would receive a venue for swapping business cards, discussing deals, and socializing. In 1992 Rubin, living in California, joined a multilevel sales company called Omnitrition International, which sold powdered drink mixes. This company and Rubin were hit in 1992 with a class action suit claiming the company was involved with an illegal pyramid scheme.

In November, 1994, Rubin was hit by a car while jaywalking in Hollywood. He died 14 days later in a UCLA hospital bed. In a biography printed in the *Los Angeles Times* after Rubin's death, fellow Chicago Seven member and friend Tom Hayden stated: "Rubin was a great life force, full of spunk, courage, and wit. I think his willingness to defy authority for constructive purposes will be missed. Up to the end, he was defying authority."

Further Reading

With Abbie Hoffman and Ed Sanders, Rubin was the author of *We Are Everywhere* (1970). His *Doing It!* (1969) is autobiographical and liberally ornamented with nudes and four letter words, the tools of his trade at that time. *Growing (Up) at 37* (1976) is a more conventional memoir. He wrote *The War Between the Sheets* with Mimi Leonard in 1980. There is no biography of Rubin, but he has been the subject of numerous magazine and newspaper articles. An especially good one is John Leonard, "A New Jerry Rubin: Grown Up, Reflective," *New York Times* (February 11, 1976). □

Margaret Fogarty Rudkin

Entrepreneur of quality bakery products, Margaret Fogarty Rudkin (1897-1976) was founder and president of Pepperidge Farm Inc., the largest U.S. independent baking company.

The oldest of five children of Joseph and Margaret (Healey) Fogarty, Margaret Fogarty was born in New York City on September 14, 1897, during the time of cobblestone streets and gas lampposts. The family lived in a four-story brownstone with an Irish grandmother who taught ten-year-old Margaret about cooking, starting with biscuits, cream sauce, and chocolate cake. When she was 12 the family moved to Flushing, Long Island, where she attended public schools and graduated as valedictorian of her high school class.

Interested in a career in business, she went to work as a bookkeeper for a local bank and eventually was promoted to teller. Four years later, in 1919, she took a position with McClure, Jones & Co., a member of the New York Stock Exchange, where she met Henry Albert Rudkin, a partner in the firm. They were married on April 8, 1923, and had three sons—Henry Jr. (1924), William (1926), and Mark (1929), all of whom attended Yale University.

In 1926 the prosperous family purchased 125 acres of property near Fairfield, Connecticut, built a Tudor mansion, a garage for five automobiles, and stables for 12 horses. They named the estate Pepperidge Farm after pepperidge trees on the property. Her husband enjoyed golf and shooting and served for years as president of the Fairfield Hunt Club, whose polo grounds were called Rudkin Field. Margaret Rudkin lived the life of a woman of leisure, exhibiting at horse shows and winning many ribbons. Their life of ease and social grace was curtailed by the Depression and by a serious polo accident in 1932 which forced Henry Rudkin to remain at home for six months. Margaret Rudkin dismissed most of the servants, sold the horses and all but one automobile, and raised money for the farm by selling apples from their orchard of 500 trees and turkeys which they raised.

When her youngest son became ill with asthma at the age of nine, Margaret Rudkin developed an interest in proper food. She got out her Irish grandmother's recipe for whole wheat bread with its old-fashioned ingredients—stone-milled flour, honey, molasses, sugar syrup, milk, cream, and butter—and baked her first loaf of bread at the age of 40. The first loaf was "hard as a rock" but further experimentation produced a quality loaf. The bread seemed to improve Mark's health, and his allergist asked her to make bread for him and for his other patients. In 1937 Margaret Rudkin began making small batches with the help of a servant, later setting up a small bakery in an abandoned farm building and selling extra loaves to her own grocer. Expanding to an old-fashioned white bread made with unbleached flour, she tested it on the manager of Charles & Co., a specialty food store in New York City, who ordered 24 loaves daily, delivered at first by her husband on his way to Wall Street. Soon the order was 1,200 loaves a week, necessitating trucking. In a year the bakery was producing 4,000 loaves weekly.

Demand grew rapidly although the bread sold for twice the price of mass-produced bread. Enthusiastic articles in the *New York Journal and American, Herald Tribune,* and *World Telegram* promoted the products, and an article in the December 1939 *Reader's Digest* brought orders from all over the United States, Canada, and several foreign countries. To meet the demand, Rudkin had to borrow $15,000 in 1940 to move the bakery to Norwalk, Connecticut, where weekly volume exceeded 50,000 loaves of bread the first year. She refused to compromise on quality as business expanded.

In the years that followed, Pepperidge Farm grew into a major national firm. Margaret Rudkin served as president and looked after the daily production. Her husband gradually gave up his Wall Street position to handle finances, marketing, and sales as chairman. Two sons, Henry and William, were vice presidents of the firm. They moved to a bigger plant in Norwalk and later opened plants in Pennsylvania in 1947 and Illinois in 1953. Several restored grist mills stone-ground the flour, and Rudkin supplied her own top grade wheat bought in Minneapolis.

Initially, the firm had done little advertising, letting the products stand on their own merits and word-of-mouth reputation. In 1950 that policy changed with the appearance of Margaret Rudkin in television commercials. During this decade the list of products expanded as she purchased a frozen pastry line from a New Hampshire company and fancy cookie recipes from a firm in Belgium. Expansion eventually included 58 products including rolls, coffee cake, pound cake, Melba toast, herb-seasoned stuffing made from stale loaves returned by grocers, and fancy cocktail snacks called Goldfish.

The Rudkins sold the business to the Campbell Soup Company in 1960, exchanging the Pepperidge Farm assets for Campbell stock worth about $28 million. Even so, Margaret Rudkin continued to operate Pepperidge Farm as a separate company and, in addition, became a director of Campbell Soup. In 1962 she yielded the presidency to her son William and replaced her husband as chairman. Five months after her husband's death she retired in September 1966 and died on June 1, 1967 at the age of 69 of cancer. At that time the annual sales were 70 million loaves of bread.

Her interest in food led Margaret Rudkin to collect ancient cookbooks. She drew on her knowledge of food in writing *The Margaret Rudkin Pepperidge Farm Cookbook* (1963), which became a best seller. Her business acumen was recognized by invitations to lecture at the Harvard School of Business Administration. In later years the Rudkins maintained a home at Hobe Sound, Florida, and an ancestral manor house and 150 acres, purchased in 1953, at County Carlow, Ireland, where they spent summers.

Further Reading

Biographical information appears in Sicherman and Green's *Notable American Women: The Modern Period* (1980). In *The Margaret Rudkin Pepperidge Farm Cookbook* Rudkin tells about her childhood, early married life, bread making, and her family's trips to Ireland. Articles appear in *Reader's Digest* 35 (December 1939); *Time* 50 (July 14, 1947) and 75 (March 21, 1960); *Newsweek* 20 (September 21, 1942); *The New Yorker* (November 16, 1963); and *New York Times* (December 4, 1949); and her obituary appeared in the *New York Times* on June 2, 1967. □

Rudolf I

Rudolf I (ca. 1218-1291), or Rudolf of Hapsburg, was Holy Roman emperor-elect from 1273 to 1291. He was the first of a long line of Hapsburg emperors.

The struggle between the emperor Frederick II and Pope Innocent IV had shattered the power of the imperial office in both Germany and Italy. The "emperors" who reigned between 1250 and 1273—William of Holland, Alfonso X of Castile, and Richard of Cornwall—were powerless because of their absenteeism and the lack of cooperation they had received in Germany. When an imperial election was called in 1273, the German princes whose responsibility it was to elect the new emperor wanted neither a powerful nor an ambitious ruler, and their choice fell on Rudolf, a wealthy but not potentially dangerous German noble.

However, not only did Rudolph's reign enhance the wealth and power of the minor Hapsburg house, but it also gave his dynasty a foothold in the imperial office, which was eventually secured in the 15th century and not relinquished until the 19th. In the face of considerable opposition, Rudolf managed to impose a temporary peace upon the warring German Estates and princes, to subdue the powerful Premysl dynasty of Bohemia, and to heal the rift between the imperial office and the papacy, which had destroyed imperial power 25 years before.

Rudolf was a compromise candidate for the imperial office. In 1273 the strongest prince in the empire was the Premysl line's Ottocar II, King of Bohemia. In order to block Bohemian power, the electoral princes turned to Rudolf. Rudolf's first task as emperor was to quell Bohemian power, which he accomplished in 1276 at Vienna and again at the battle of Marchfeld in 1278, thus permanently defeating the possibility of Bohemian domination of Germany and the imperial office. After these victories, Rudolf made Vienna the Hapsburg capital, which it remained until the 20th century.

The Emperor's second step was to heal the wounds of the Church, still smarting after its long bout with the imperial Hohenstaufen dynasty. In 1279 Rudolf renounced many of the imperial claims in Italy, gave the Romagna to the Pope, and thoroughly subordinated the powers of the imperial office and its incumbent to the authority of the Church in matters spiritual and temporal.

Rudolf's accomplished effectiveness as both diplomat and general gave Germany nearly 2 decades of peace. His next undertaking—and that of the Nassau, Wittelsbach, and Luxembourg dynasties, which each provided emperors in the century following Rudolf's death—was the extension and increase of his family power and wealth, for only by this method could any imperial dynasty sustain itself in the troubled 13th and 14th centuries. Ecclesiastical fear of the public resources of the imperial office had grown so great, and the imperial office had become so fragmented, that only the private family resources of individual emperors could sustain imperial power. From 1282 to 1286 Rudolf worked for the increase of the house of Hapsburg. His favor toward his son Albert of Bavaria, his lack of sufficient resources to quench the rivalry between German princes and cities, and his rivalry over Burgundy with the French king Philip IV troubled the last years of his reign. His eldest son, Rudolf, died at the age of 20, and Rudolf I then turned toward the advancement of the fortunes of his second son, Albert, later King Albert I.

Rudolf's reputation as a capable and intelligent ruler, well aware of the limits of his real power, yet successful in the imposition of peace upon a torn Germany, stood him in good stead. Although his son did not succeed him directly, Rudolf worked for his succession up to the time of his own death. Rudolf died on July 15, 1291, at Speyer, attempting to the end to establish the house of Hapsburg on the throne, which it would, within 2 centuries, make a virtual family possession.

Further Reading

There is no biography of Rudolf I in English. Adam Wandruska, *The House of Habsburg* (1964), is a history of the dynasty with several chapters on early Hapsburg history, including one on Rudolf. *The Cambridge Medieval History,* vol. 7 (1936), gives considerable information, as do Geoffrey Barraclough, *The Origins of Modern Germany* (1946; 2d rev. ed. 1966), James Bryce, *The Holy Roman Empire* (1956), and Friedrich Heer, *The Holy Roman Empire* (1969). □

Paul Marvin Rudolph

The American architect Paul Rudolph (born 1918) sought to integrate into modern architecture a spatial drama, a concern for urbanism, and an individuality which he found lacking in his training under Walter Gropius.

The son of a Methodist minister, Paul Marvin Rudolph was born on October 28, 1918, in Elkton, Kentucky. He attended the architecture school at the Alabama Polytechnic Institute in Auburn, and after graduating in 1940 he entered the Harvard Graduate School of Design, where he studied under Walter Gropius, the former head of the Bauhaus in Germany. Rudolph's graduate studies were interrupted by a period of service as an officer in the U.S. Navy (1943-1946). He supervised ship construction in the Brooklyn Navy Yard, which provided a valuable learning experience in executing large building tasks within a bureaucracy. After receiving his master's degree from Harvard in 1947, he spent the next year traveling in Europe (on a Wheelwright Scholarship), where he began to develop a strong interest in urban design, a subject which he felt had been neglected in his education under Gropius.

Starting on a Small Scale, and Building

In 1948 Rudolph formed a partnership with Ralph Twitchell in Sarasota, Florida. On the modest scales of guest houses, Rudolph began to explore the lessons he had learned at Harvard. In such early works as his Healy Guest House (1949) in Siesta Key, Sarasota, the functions are carefully accommodated while the innovative structure (a centenary curved roof held in tension) is clearly articulated. However, during the 1950s he began to rebel against Gropius' teachings. Rudolph ended his partnership with Twitchell in 1952 and totally rejected Gropius' ideal of teamwork. Rudolph preferred a more personal and artistic approach to architecture. He also felt limited by Gropius' emphasis on function and structure. Through the siting, massing, silhouette, scale, and even decoration of Rudolph's first major building, the Jewett Arts Center (1955-1958) at Wellesley College in Massachusetts, he attempted to respond to the broader environmental context of the existing campus of collegiate gothic buildings. He also began to explore a richer approach to the spaces of architecture, as defined by planes rather than by linear structure, in such works as his Sarasota High School (1958-1959) in Florida.

Rise to Prominence

By attempting to expand the language and responsibilities of modern architecture, Rudolph quickly rose to prominence. From 1958 to 1965 he was chairman of the School of Architecture at Yale University in New Haven, Connecticut, where he built his most famous and controversial work, the Art and Architecture Building (1958-1964). This structure responded to its urban context by dramatically turning the corner on which it stands. It was also designed to allow for

future expansion, since Rudolph believed that architects should realize that their buildings will not be frozen in time. In an age characterized by the anonymous glass boxes of Ludwig Mies van der Rohe, Rudolph had created a highly dynamic and heroic monument which dominated its surroundings. He had combined the rough sculptural qualities of the late concrete buildings of Le Corbusier with the dramatic spatial flow of Frank Lloyd Wright's pinwheel plans. The intensity of Rudolph's orchestration of a building as a moving spatial experience reached a new extreme: labyrinth-like passages opened up to grand central spaces in this seven story building incorporating some 37 different floor levels. His distinctive use of vertically ribbed concrete created richly textured walls sensitive to light and shadow on a smaller scale, while avoiding the negative effects of weathering. (When the building later burned, Rudolph remarked that he felt as if someone had died.)

In his works after the late 1950s he consistently explored several themes. His desire to create psychologically stimulating spaces is perhaps best seen in his churches, where space is dynamically sculpted by the inner surfaces of the buildings and animated by natural light from above. Good examples of such works are his Interdenominational Chapel (1960-1969) at the Tuskegee Institute in Alabama and the William R. Cannon Chapel (1979-1982) at Emory University in Atlanta.

His fascination with the broader urban implications of architecture found early expression in New Haven with the expressway scale of his grandly monumental Temple Street Parking Garage (1959-1963) and the conscious arrangement of repetitive units into a village in his original design for married students' housing (1960-1961) at Yale. In 1965 Rudolph left Yale and moved his practice to New York City.

New York Megastructures

In New York, Rudolph combined his interests on an appropriate 20th-century urban scale with the potentials of cellular construction in his project for the Graphic Arts Center (1967), where prefabricated modules, trucked to the site like mobile homes, were to be suspended from the skyscrapers' superstructure in a terraced, pinwheel fashion providing great variety within the huge scale of this megastructure. The building was not built as planned due to clashes with local trade unions over his proposed use of modular-built structures from non-union factories outside the region, but Rudolph predicted the idea had an inevitability that would lead it to completion somewhere, sometime in the future. "The mobile home is the 20th century brick," Rudolph said, but the modules planned for this structure had little in common with the majority of factory-fabricated structures to roll down the highway by the end of that century. Rudolph's modules were designed to fit on a truck, yet be combined and unfolded into a variety of grand spaces. The modules would be hung in place, all wired, with completed bathrooms and kitchens. The roof of one would become a garden space for another, giving New York tenants more outdoor space and better views than they were accustomed to having. The megastructure was to include two high-rise office buildings, schools, restaurants, industrial space, recreational opportunities, traffic-free streets, and parking for 2,100 cars, all blended seamlessly with 4050 apartments next to the Hudson River . . . a steel city within the city.

"I want to put homes in the sky," said Rudolph of the ill-fated project. "Psychologically, it makes a great deal of difference for people living closely together in cities.

Rudolph further expanded his proposal of megastructure for New York in his study for a lower Manhattan expressway (1967-1972). In this project an A-framed structure spanned the air-rights of the two mile long expressway, resulting in a man-made terraced ridge into which modules for housing, schools, stores, and offices could be plugged.

Rudolph also undertook such large complexes as the uncompleted Boston Government Service Center (1962-1971), where a megastructure accommodating a variety of functions scaled up to the street along its perimeter and was scaled down, through terraces, to an interior pedestrian court. In his Southeastern Massachusetts Technological Institute (1963-1966) at North Dartmouth he organized interlocking buildings along a "spiraling mall," inspired by Thomas Jefferson's lawn at the University of Virginia. Rudolph respected the future in this design by leaving it open-ended, thereby assisting rather than hindering expansion.

Rudolph's work in the early 1980s included the City Center Towers (1982-1984) in Fort Worth, Texas. Rather than using the rough texture and monumental appearance of his most characteristic material, concrete, these towers had steel frames and glass curtain walls. Nonetheless, plasticity and a sculptural quality were achieved through the buildings' pinwheel plans. At the base of each building the curtain walls were set back, eroding the mass and exposing the steel structure. This served to address several urban concerns: a smaller scale was achieved, respecting the context of the older buildings in this historic district, and the more public oriented functions of the buildings' bases were acknowledged. This work summarized Rudolph's long held and pioneering concerns for an architecture with evocative spaces which was also responsible to its urban situation.

Rudolph made it clear that he was more interested in building than in collaboration or teaching, even within his own office. "Architecture is a personal effort, and the fewer people coming between you and your work the better." Despite this almost surly rejection of communication with colleagues, he focused much of his attention in his work to the "psychology of the building," the interactions of space and light with the human occupants, rather than merely on the lines of the building. His success in this endeavor led to many awards and accolades, including an Emmy Award in 1984 and a Creative Arts Award from Brandeis University in 1986.

Rudolph's later work included the Harbour Road mixed-use structure in Hong Kong, winner of an International Design Competition (1989), the Cheng Residence and Institution Hill condominiums in Singapore (1989), and the Wireless Road Project in Bangkok (1990).

Paul Rudolph's lasting effects in the field of architecture might be guessed from his statement: "Architecture, at least for me, is to a degree an art, and I feel fundamentally that it's the business of art to always question, to always turn everything upside down so that one sees it anew. It seems to me that this is the real business of art, though it is very disconcerting to most people; it gives them nothing to hold onto."

Further Reading

The best single work on Rudolph in English is Sibyl Moholy-Nagy (introduction by), Gerhard Schwap (captions by), and Paul Rudolph (comments by), *The Architecture of Paul Rudolph* (1970). Other books which are especially good for their illustrations are Rupert Spade, *Paul Rudolph* (1971), and Paul Rudolph, *Paul Rudolph: Architectural Drawings* Yukio Futagawa, rd., (1972). Rudolph's project for the Lower Manhattan expressway is presented in Peter Wolf, *The Evolving City: Urban Design Proposals by Ulrich Franzen and Paul Rudolph* (1974). Discussions of Rudolph can also be found in Paul Heyer, *Architects on Architecture: New Directions in America* (1966), and Robert A. M. Stern, *New Directions in American Architecture* (1977). An extensive interview with Rudolph can be found in John W. Cook and Heinrich Klotz, *Conversations with Architects* (1973).
Other information is available in Charles R. Smith, *Paul Rudolph and Louis Kahn: A Bibliography* (1987); "Architect of Grand Design" in *50 Plus* (Dec. 1985); an article about Rudolph's Graphic Arts Center appearing Dec. 13, 1968 in *The Daily Telegraph Magazine* and reprinted on an Internet site maintained by Frederick Clifford Gibson; and other descriptions of works at the same Internet site. □

Wilma Rudolph

Wilma Rudolph (1940-1994) became the first American woman runner to win three gold medals in the Olympic games.

Wilma Rudolph made history in the 1960 Summer Olympic games in Rome, Italy, when she became the first American woman to win three gold medals in the track and field competition. (At those same Olympic games, Rafer Johnson, winner of a silver medal at the 1956 Olympics and a gold medal at the 1959 Pan American Games for the decathlon, won a gold medal for the same event and was the first African American to carry the American flag during the opening ceremony.) Rudolph's brilliant accomplishments were all the more remarkable because she came from modest circumstances and endured a childhood of sickness and disability. Prior to her death on November 12, 1994, Rudolph was still busy coaching underprivileged children and encouraging minority interest in amateur athletics. "It's a good feeling to know that you have touched the lives of so many young people," the mother of four told the *Chicago Tribune.* "I tell them that the most important aspect is to be yourself and have confidence in yourself."

Rudolph's confidence may have flagged at times in her childhood, when it seemed she might spend a lifetime in leg braces or even a wheelchair. Through the efforts of her devoted family—and then her own steely determination to strengthen herself—she rose from disability to Olympic glory. Her victories in Rome in 1960 helped to set the stage for a life dedicated to the principles and practices that helped her to succeed. "Believe me, the reward is not so great without the struggle," she told the *Chicago Tribune.* "The triumph can't be had without the struggle. And I know what struggle is. I have spent a lifetime trying to share what it has meant to be a woman first in the world of sports so that other young women have a chance to reach their dreams."

Almost every circumstance was stacked against Rudolph from the day she was born on June 23, 1940. Her family was very large. Ed Rudolph had eleven children by a first marriage. His second marriage yielded eight more, of which Wilma was the fifth. At birth she weighed only four and one-half pounds. Her mother, Blanche, a domestic, feared for Wilma's survival from the outset. The family lived in tiny St. Bethlehem, Tennessee, a farming community about 45 miles southeast of Nashville.

Shortly after Wilma was born, the Rudolphs moved to nearby Clarksville, Tennessee, where they lived in town. Her father worked as a porter on railroad cars, and her mother cleaned house six days a week. Older siblings helped care for the sickly baby who had come into the world prematurely.

Wilma Rudolph (center)

At the age of four, Wilma contracted polio. The disease weakened her and made her vulnerable to pneumonia and scarlet fever. She survived the illnesses, but she lost the use of her left leg. Specialists in Nashville recommended a routine of massage for the limb, and Mrs. Rudolph learned it and taught it to some of the older children. Thus, Wilma's legs were massaged a number of times each day, helping her to regain strength. Medical history aside, she was a normal child. "When I was about 5, I spent most of my time trying to figure out how to get my [leg] braces off," she told the *Chicago Tribune*. "And you see, when you come from a large wonderful family, there's always a way to achieve your goals, especially when you don't want your parents knowing them. I would take off my braces, then station my brothers and sisters all through the house and they would tell me if my parents were coming and then I'd hurry and put the braces back on."

Once a week—on her day off—Blanche Rudolph would drive her daughter 45 miles to Nashville for physical therapy. The long drive provided Wilma with chances to daydream about her future, but the outlook was grim. "I would visualize myself in this gigantic white house on the hill and being married and having children," she said in the *Chicago Tribune*. "But as I began to understand life, those dreams vanished very quickly."

Staged a Comeback from Physical Disability

After five years of treatment, Wilma one day stunned her doctors when she removed her leg braces and walked by herself. She had been practicing—with the help of those siblings—for quite some time. Soon she was able to walk even better with the help of a supportive shoe. This she wore until she was eleven. After that, she not only left braces and orthopedic shoes behind, she confounded every prediction that she would be a disabled adult. Soon she was joining her brothers and sisters in basketball games in the Rudolph backyard and running street races against other children her age. "By the time I was 12," she told the *Chicago Tribune,* "I was challenging every boy in our neighborhood at running, jumping, everything."

Rudolph desperately wanted to play high school basketball, but she simply could not convince the coach to put her on the team. When she finally worked up the nerve to ask him for a tryout, he agreed to coach her privately for ten minutes each morning. Still she was cut in her freshman year. She finally earned a position on the roster at Burt High School in Clarksville because the coach wanted her older sister to play. Her father agreed to allow the sibling onto the team *only* if Wilma could be on it too.

Rudolph soon blossomed into a fine basketball player. As a sophomore she scored 803 points in 25 games, a new state record for a player on a girls' basketball team. She also started running in track meets and found that her greatest strengths lay in the sprint. She was only fourteen when she attracted the attention of Ed Temple, the women's track coach at Tennessee State University. Temple told her she had the potential to become a great runner, and during the summer recesses from high school she trained with him and the students at Tennessee State.

The Olympic Games were a far-off dream to a young black woman in Tennessee. She was a teenager before she even learned what the Olympics were. Rudolph caught on fast, though. In four seasons of high school track meets, she never lost a race. At the tender age of sixteen, she qualified for the Summer Olympics in Melbourne, Australia, and came home with a bronze medal. Rudolph told the *Chicago Tribune:* "I remember going back to my high school this particular day with the bronze medal and all the kids that I disliked so much or I thought I disliked . . . put up this big huge banner: 'Welcome Home Wilma.' And I forgave them right then and there. . . . They passed my bronze medal around so that everybody could touch, feel and see what an Olympic medal is like. When I got it back, there were handprints all over it. I took it and I started shining it up. I discovered that bronze doesn't shine. So, I decided I'm going to try this one more time. I'm going to go for the gold."

Rudolph entered Tennessee State University in the fall of 1957, with a major in elementary education. All of her spare time was consumed by running, however. The pace took its toll, and she found herself too ill to run through most of the 1958 season. She rebounded in 1959, only to pull a muscle at a crucial meet between the United States and the Soviet Union in Philadelphia. Ed Temple, who would prove to be a life-long friend, supervised her recovery and by 1960 Rudolph was ready to go to Rome.

Rudolph was not the first black woman to receive an Olympic gold medal: that distinction goes to Alice Coachman-Davis, who took first place in the high jump at the 1948 Olympic Games in London, England. A dozen years later at the 1960 Olympics, Rudolph won all three of her gold medals in very dramatic fashion. In both the 100-meter dash and the 200-meter dash, she finished at least three yards in front of her closest competitor. She tied the world record in the 100-meter and set a new Olympic record in the 200. Rudolph also brought her 400-meter relay team from behind to win the gold. The French called her "La Gazelle." Without question, Rudolph's achievements at the 1960 Olympic Games remain a stand-out performance in the history of Olympic competition.

The Price of Fame

Wilma Rudolph became an instant celebrity in Europe and America. Crowds gathered wherever she was scheduled to run. She was given ticker tape parades, an official invitation to the White House by president John F. Kennedy, and a dizzying round of dinners, awards, and television appearances. Rudolph remembered in *Ebony* magazine that the royal treatment she received was rather shallow—she was treated like a star, but not given the money to live like one. Today, beautiful young women athletes can count on endorsements for commercial products and hefty fees for personal appearances. That was not so in Rudolph's era, especially for a black athlete. She told *Ebony:* "You become world famous and you sit with kings and queens, and then your first job is just a job. You can't go back to living the way you did before because you've been taken out of one setting and shown the other. That becomes a struggle and makes *you* struggle.''

Rudolph made one decision that she stuck to firmly: she refused to participate in the 1964 Olympic games. She felt that she might not be able to duplicate her achievement of 1960, and she did not want to appear to be fading. She retired from amateur athletics in 1963, finished her college work, and became a school teacher and athletic coach. She also became a mother, raising four children on her own after divorcing two husbands.

Talent Didn't Go to Waste

For more than two decades, Wilma Rudolph sought to impart the lessons she learned about amateur athletics to other young men and women. She was the author of an autobiography, *Wilma,* that was published in 1977—and the subject of a television movie based on the book. She lectured in every part of America and even served in 1991 as an ambassador to the European celebration of the dismantling of the Berlin Wall. Rudolph helped to open and run inner city sports clinics and served as a consultant to university track teams. She also founded her own organization, the Wilma Rudolph Foundation, dedicated to promoting amateur athletics.

''I think the thing that made life good for me is that I never looked back,'' Rudolph told *Ebony.* ''I've always been positive no matter what happened.'' Rudolph added that she has always believed in herself and her abilities, and that the phrase *''I can't''* never applied to her.

Rudolph was a member of the United States Olympic Hall of Fame *and* the National Track and Field Hall of Fame. She traveled frequently and was well known for her motivational speeches to youngsters. ''I love working with kids. It's the motherly instinct in me,'' she told *Newsday.* And in an interview with *Ebony,* Rudolph claimed that her moment of Olympic glory ''sort of sent my way all the other positive things and feelings that I've had. That one accomplishment—what happened in 1960—nobody can take from me. It was something I worked for. It wasn't something somebody handed to me.''

Asked what she felt was her greatest achievement, Rudolph looked past 1960 to all the work she had done since. ''My thoughts about my life, my great moment, if I left the Earth today, would be knowing that I have tried to give something to young people,'' she commented in the *Chicago Tribune.* ''Hopefully, for the first time, I'm beginning to see that young black women in America are making a large contribution in sports. The impression is that together we can make a first. And that makes me very happy.''

On November 12, 1994, Wilma Rudolph died at her home in Brentwood, Tennessee of a malignant brain tumor. She is survived by two sons, two daughters, six sisters, and two brothers.

Further Reading

Rust, Edna, and Art Rust Jr., *Art Rust's Illustrated History of the Black Athlete,* Doubleday, 1985.
Chicago Tribune, January 8, 1989.
Ebony, February 1984; January 1992.
Jet, February 2, 1987.
Newsday, October 14, 1990.
Star-Ledger (Newark, NJ), August 18, 1991.
Time, September 19, 1960.
Upscale, October/November 1992.
USA Today, July 17, 1996.
Detroit Free Press, November 13, 1994. □

Abraham Ruef

An American political boss in San Francisco, Abraham Ruef (1864-1936) was convicted of bribery in a famous antigraft trial.

A braham Ruef, the son of French-Jewish immigrants, was born in San Francisco, Calif., Sept. 2, 1864. A precocious young man, he graduated in 1883 from the University of California with high honors. He studied at Hastings College of Law in San Francisco and was admitted to the bar in 1886. Cultivated, moderately well-to-do, and dynamic, he was first attracted to politics as a reformer, but reform proved too uncertain an avenue to power.

About 1888 Ruef shifted his loyalties to San Francisco's corrupt Republican political machine. As ''Boss Ruef,'' leader of the Latin Quarter (North Beach) district, he became an engaging campaign speaker and fully mastered the fine points of ward politics.

Ruef's desire for power and advancement led him to break with the Republican leadership in 1901. He first tried to defeat the organization in primary elections and, failing that, allied himself with the Union Labor party movement. San Francisco was a strong union town, but the party's leadership needed an experienced political ''kingmaker.'' Ruef was adept at just such behind-the-scenes services. After selecting Eugene Schmitz, the handsome president of the musicians' union, as the party's candidate for mayor, Ruef masterminded Schmitz's successful campaign in 1901 and his reelection in 1903 and 1905. The 1905 election was an especially triumphant one, since not only Schmitz but Ruef's handpicked board of supervisors were elected.

However, Ruef's triumph was also in large part the source of his downfall. Since Schmitz's first victory, large corporations had sought Ruef out as their ''confidential attorney,'' paying him lucrative fees as a way of assuring the administration's friendship. Initially, these fees were retainers, not outright bribes. After 1905, however, Ruef's greedy allies sought direct payment for their votes on many measures: restaurant licenses, street railway franchises, utility rates, permits for boxing matches. Ruef became the middleman in an alliance between influential corporations and political grafters, demanding huge sums of money to distribute to the pliant supervisors.

In 1906 a small group led by Fremont Older of the *San Francisco Bulletin* brought legal indictments against Ruef. After a spectacular, and sometimes bizarre, trial Ruef was convicted of bribery in 1908. When his appeals were turned down, he entered San Quentin Penitentiary in 1911. Largely

owing to the efforts of former enemies such as Older, Ruef was paroled in 1915 and pardoned in 1920. Avoiding politics, he tried his hand at real estate investments. He prospered in the 1920s but went bankrupt during the Depression years. He died in San Francisco on Feb. 29, 1936.

Further Reading

The colorful story of Ruef's career is told in vivid detail by Walton Bean, *Boss Ruef's San Francisco* (1952). See also Lately Thomas, *A Debonair Scoundrel* (1962).

Additional Sources

Bean, Walton, *Boss Ruef's San Francisco: the story of the Union Labor Party, big business, and the graft prosecution,* Westport, Conn.: Greenwood Press, 1981. □

Rosemary Radford Ruether

Rosemary Radford Ruether (born 1936) was an internationally acclaimed church historian, theologian, writer, and teacher specializing in the area of women and religion. She was a major voice in raising a feminist critique of the traditionally male field of Christian theology.

Rosemary Radford was born on November 2, 1936, in St. Paul, Minnesota, to Rebecca Cresap Ord and Robert Armstrong Radford. In 1957 she married Herman J. Ruether. They had three children: Rebecca, David, and Mimi. She resided in Evanston, Illinois.

Her collegiate career began at Scripps College where she received her B.A. in philosophy and history in 1958. At Claremont Graduate School she earned both her M.A. in ancient history in 1960 and her Ph.D. in classics and patristics in 1965. Her doctoral dissertation was entitled *Gregory Nazianzus Rhetor and Philosopher.* During her graduate work at Claremont, she was a Danforth fellow in 1960-1961 and held a Kent fellowship from 1962 to 1965.

Ruether was the Georgia Harkness Professor of Applied Theology at Garrett-Evangelical Seminary in Evanston, Illinois, and a faculty member in the joint doctoral program with Northwestern University. She previously taught at Immaculate Heart College in Los Angeles (1964-1965) and Howard University School of Religion (1965-1975). She was a visiting lecturer at Princeton Theological Seminary, Yale Divinity School, Harvard Divinity School, Boston College, Sir George Williams University, and Heythrop College, University of London. She was also a Danforth Lecturer at the Universities of Lund and Uppsala in Sweden. She held honorary degrees from St. Olaf's College, Minnesota; St. Xavier's College, Chicago; Wittenburg College, Ohio; Emmanuel College, Boston; Hamilton College, New York; Walsh College, Ohio; and Dennison College, Ohio.

Political Action

Active beginning in the early 1960s in civil rights and peace movements, and later in the feminist movement, Ruether was thoroughly Catholic and radically reformist in her scholarly approach to various topics essential to contemporary religious discussions. Her works in areas such as the history of women in Western religions, liberation theology, and the relationship between Judaism and Christianity were based on theological and historical data, utilized methods taken from the different liberation theologies, and drew upon a variety of personal experiences of and reflections on the condition of powerlessness. During the 1960s she worked in the Watts section of Los Angeles and with Delta Ministry in Mississippi. She traveled worldwide, including trips to Asia, Nicaragua, and the Middle East.

Ruether felt the church had two parallel traditions, one which identified with the state and institutions of the church and was inherently conservative, and another which traditionally defended the downtrodden. Feminist theology, liberation theology, and other forms of social activism fell solidly in the tradition of what she called prophetic faith. Indeed, she said, liberal causes, historically as well as currently, were often spearheaded by groups with strong religious convictions. Far from being on a political/religious fringe, Ruether felt she was firmly in one of two parallel mainstreams.

In a 1986 article in *America,* Ruether said Catholicism faced three major challenges: that of democratic values and human rights in the institution of the church, reacting to feminism and a crisis of sexual morality in church teaching, and responding to third world liberation struggles. "How the Catholic community responds to these three challenges will determine in large part whether Catholicism will be able to use its enormous human resources as a witness for truth and justice in this critical period of human history or whether it will lose its creative leadership and its opportunity for both its own renewal and its witness to the world." she wrote.

Publications

One of the most prolific and readable Roman Catholic theologians, she was the author of nearly 500 articles and more than 30 books. She also contributed to numerous anthologies. Ruether's work represents a significant contribution to contemporary theology, especially in the area of women and the church. Among her best known works are *The Church Against Itself* (1967); *Communion Is Life Together* (1968); *Liberation Theology: Human Hope Confronts Christian History and American Power* (1972); *New Woman/New Earth: Sexist Ideologies and Human Liberation* (1975); and *Mary—the Feminine Face of the Church* (1977). With Eugene Bianchi she co-authored *From Machismo to Mutuality: Essays on Sexism and Woman-Man Liberation* (1976).

Acting as both editor and contributor, Ruether produced two major anthologies on women and Western religious history: *Religion and Sexism: Images of Women in the Jewish and Christian Traditions* (1974) and *Women of Spirit* (1979) with Eleanor McLaughlin. In collaboration with Rosemary Skinner Keller, Ruether published a three volume docu-history, *Women and Religion in America* (1986). A contributing editor to *Christianity and Crisis* and *The Ecumenist,* Ruether was also published in such periodicals as *America, The Christian Century, Commonweal, Cross Currents, Dialog, Explor, Fellowship, National Catholic Reporter, Theological Studies,* and *Theology Today.*

Both the theory and the practice of religion came under her scrutiny as she spoke out against theologically based discrimination. For example, in *Faith and Fratricide: The Theoretical Roots of Anti-Semitism* (1979), she examined traditional Christology and discovered that it is inherently anti-Semitic in both theory and application. In *To Change the World: Christology and Cultural Criticism* (1981), Ruether's method was that of deconstructing traditional categories; in a later related work, *Sexism and God-Talk: Toward a Feminist Theology* (1983), she set out to reconstruct a new theology based on previously excluded women's sources and experience. In two later books, *Womanguides: Readings Toward a Feminist Theology* (1985) and *Woman-Church: Theology and Practice of Feminist Liturgical Communities* (1986), she moved beyond criticism and reconstruction of the past, seeking to create a new culture through women's stories and liturgies. In *The Wrath of Jonah* (1989), a book she co-authored with her husband, she cast her eye toward the origins of Zionism, Christian support for Zionism, and attempts to accommodate both Israeli and Palestinian claims to disputed lands in the Middle East.

Other recent books by this much-published author include *Contemporary Roman Catholicism: Crises and Challenges* (1987); *Disputed Questions: On Being a Christian* (1989); *Beyond Occupation: American Jewish, Christian and Palestinian Voices for Peace,* edited by Marc H. Ellis (1990); *Gaia & God: An Ecofeminist Theology of Earth Healing* (1992); *A Democratic Catholic Church: The Reconstruction of Roman Catholicism,* edited with Eugene C. Bianchi (1992); *'The Woman Will Overcome the Warrior':* *A Dialogue With the Christian/Feminist Theology of Rosemary Radford Ruether* (1994); *God and the Nations,* with Douglas John Hall (1995); *At Home in the World: The Letters of Thomas Merton and Rosemary Radford Ruether,* written with Merton and edited by Mary Tardiff (1995); and *In Our Own Voices: Four Centuries of American Women's Religious Writing,* edited by Rosemary Skinner Keller (1995).

Ruether was a member of numerous professional associations, including the Society for Religion in Higher Education, the American Theological Association, and the Society for Arts, Religion and Culture. She served with Ross Kraemer and Lorine Getz as national co-chair of the Women's Caucus: Religious Studies and was a board member of the Program of Women and Religion at Harvard Divinity School and of Chicago Catholic Women.

Further Reading

Rosemary Radford Ruether is listed in the *Who's Who of American Women.* No biographies of Ruether have appeared to date. However, she published an autobiographical essay under the title "Beginnings: An Intellectual Autobiography," in *Journeys,* Gregory Baum, ed., (1975). An introduction to her work by Mary Hembrow Snyder appeared in 1988, entitled *Christology of Rosemary Radford Ruether: A Critical Introduction.*

Among her hundreds of articles were these cited above: "Crises and Challenges of Catholicism Today" in *America* (March 1, 1986); and "Jerusalem's Future" in *The Christian Century* (Feb. 28, 1996). □

Edmund Ruffin

Edmund Ruffin (1794-1865), American editor and publisher, was a prominent scientific agriculturist as well as his period's most renowned advocate of establishing an independent Southern nation.

Edmund Ruffin was born in Prince George County, Va. Educated at home until he was 16, he attended the College of William and Mary for a year before he was dismissed. He saw brief military service in the War of 1812 and then began a life as a Southern planter. Agriculture in Virginia was in a depressed state, largely because of the dominant farming practices of the time. Ruffin developed methods of restoring the fertility of soils and described them in "An Essay on Calcareous Manures." This discovery and others, which Ruffin announced in his publication, the *Farmer's Register,* were adopted by large numbers of Virginia planters and led to an agricultural revival. Thereafter he contributed systematically to agricultural science—popularizing, distributing, writing, speaking, and informing Southern farmers of theoretical as well as practical, progressive agricultural methods.

In 1841 Ruffin was appointed a member of the Board of Agriculture of Virginia and became its secretary, and a year later he became agriculture surveyor of South Carolina. His detailed and clearly written *Report of the Commencement and Progress of the Agricultural Survey of South Carolina* became a landmark in the agricultural history of the state. On his estate, Malbourne, in Hanover County, Va., he applied his scientific farming ideas so successfully that the plantation became a showplace where record harvests were almost commonplace.

Ruffin is most widely known as a radical spokesman for Southern nationalism. Early in his career he became convinced that blacks were inferior and that a slave system was necessary and generally superior. He was the first outspoken advocate of Southern secession, viewing the competition of the North and South for advantage in the Union as one which would inevitably end in Southern defeat. The South as an independent nation would enjoy great advantages: direct trade with Europe, the end of the hidden subsidy by the South of Northern industries in the form of tariffs on imports, and a general strengthening of the slave society.

Ruffin announced his views in assorted publications which he sometimes printed and distributed at his own expense. He advocated secession at the Democratic con-

vention in Charleston in 1860; welcomed the election of Abraham Lincoln as a portent of the impending separation of the South from the Union; fired the first shot on Ft. Sumter to initiate the war; and fought in the Battle of Bull Run. He committed suicide when Confederate defeat became a fact.

Further Reading

The best biography of Ruffin is Avery O. Craven, *Edmund Ruffin, Southerner: A Study in Secession* (1932). His agricultural work is recounted in Albert Lowther Demaree, *The American Agricultural Press, 1819-1860* (1941).

Additional Sources

Allmendinger, David F., *Ruffin: family and reform in the Old South,* New York: Oxford University Press, 1990.

Craven, Avery Odelle, *Edmund Ruffin, southerner: a study in secession,* Baton Rouge: Louisiana State University Press, 1982.

Mathew, William M., *Edmund Ruffin and the crisis of slavery in the Old South: the failure of agricultural reform,* Athens: University of Georgia Press, 1988.

Mitchell, Betty L., *Edmund Ruffin, a biography,* Bloomington: Indiana University Press, 1981.

Ruffin, Edmund, *Incidents of my life: Edmund Ruffin's autobiographical essays,* Charlottesville: Published for the Virginia Historical Society by the University Press of Virginia, 1990. □

Harold Rugg

Teacher, engineer, historian, educational theorist, and student of psychology and sociology, Harold Rugg (1886-1960) was one of the most versatile educators associated with the progressive education movement.

Harold Ordway Rugg, son of Edward and Merion Abbie (Davidson) Rugg, was born in Fitchburg, Massachusetts, on January 17, 1886. His father was a carpenter. Following his graduation from high school in Fitchburg, Rugg worked for two years in a textile mill before he enrolled in Dartmouth College. At Dartmouth he earned his B.S. degree in 1908 and a graduate degree in civil engineering in 1909.

Upon leaving Dartmouth, Rugg worked briefly for the Missouri Pacific Railroad and then taught civil engineering for about a year at James Millikin University in Decatur, Illinois. In 1911 he entered the University of Illinois, where he taught engineering and did graduate work in education and sociology under the direction of William C. Bagley. On September 4, 1912, Rugg married Bertha Miller; they adopted two children. The marriage was the first of three for Rugg, two of which ended in divorce. Rugg completed his Ph.D. program in 1915 and in the fall of that year moved on to the University of Chicago, where he taught and carried on research in the fields of administration and educational statistics under Charles H. Judd. The experience Rugg gained at Chicago led in turn to a post with Edward L. Thorndike's U.S. Army Committee on the Classification of

Personnel during World War I. The work with Thorndike was noteworthy in that it was the first widespread attempt to test adults for aptitudes and intelligence.

Rugg returned to Chicago after the war and spent another year working with Judd. He left Chicago in January of 1920 to accept an appointment at Teachers College, Columbia University, and remained a member of the Teachers College faculty for some 30 years.

During his stint with the Thorndike committee, Rugg had become interested in the work of a number of contemporary social critics, and his intellectual interests began to shift from engineering and statistics to the social sciences. These new interests continued to develop during his early years at Columbia, and Rugg quickly gained national recognition, as well as lasting influence, as a leader in the field of curriculum design. He was noted both for his innovative efforts to unify the social sciences and for his empirical methods of selecting content for the social studies curriculum.

Many of Rugg's novel ideas concerning curriculum development were implemented in his 14-volume social studies textbook series, published under the general title "Man and His Changing Society" between 1929 and 1940. (Louise Krueger, who had become Rugg's second wife on August 25, 1930—they had one child—assisted with the preparation of eight of the books.) Rugg's attempt to provide an accurate account of the strengths and weaknesses of American society in the textbooks brought him a degree of notoriety rarely duplicated in academic circles. Although

the books were warmly received and widely read when they first appeared, the series was considered subversive in some conservative quarters and as a result was eventually dropped by most of the school districts that had used it. The controversy over the Rugg books led to one of the stormiest and most sensational cases of textbook censorship in the history of American education. It is still a highly instructive case study.

Apart from his professorship at Teachers College, where he also served as educational psychologist at the experimental Lincoln School, Rugg was involved in a number of other significant educational activities. He was, for instance, one of the charter members of the John Dewey Society and one of the founders of the National Council for the Social Studies. In 1934 he helped organize *The Social Frontier,* a journal highly regarded for its social and educational analysis from the liberal point of view. Rugg later edited the journal after it had been renamed *Frontiers of Democracy.* He also served for over a decade as social studies editor of *Senior Scholastic* and for 11 years as editor of the *Journal of Educational Psychology.* At various times in his career he was an educational consultant or visiting lecturer in the Middle East, the Far East, Western Europe, South Africa, Australia, and New Zealand. In addition, he came to be generally acknowledged as an unofficial delegate of the American Progressive Education Association to the international New Education Fellowship.

Rugg's work reflected most of the significant developments in American education during the first half of the 20th century, when progressive education was in its ascendancy. Early in his career—between 1915 and 1920, for example—he was involved in the pioneering attempts to apply the quantitative methods of science to educational problems. Then in the 1920s he was identified with the popular "child-centered" approach to teaching. His two most important books during this early phase of his career were *Statistical Methods Applied to Education* (1917), which became a standard in the field, and *The Child-Centered School* (1926, with Ann Shumaker), which historian Lawrence A. Cremin refers to as "the characteristic progressivist work of the twenties."

During and after the 1930s Rugg was a leading spokesperson for the reconstructionist point of view—that is, the view that formal education could, and should, be utilized as an agent of social change. Indeed, by virtue of his textbooks Rugg was the only reconstructionist who managed to present his views to significant numbers of students, at least temporarily. In 1947 he published *Foundations for American Education,* long the most comprehensive treatment of the subject, and the 1950s found him in the front rank of those searching for the secrets of the creative process.

Rugg is probably best remembered for his contributions to social reconstructionism during the Great Depression. In that period he published three of his most important books: *Culture and Education in America* (1931), *The Great Technology* (1933), and *American Life and the School Curriculum* (1936). All three were concerned with the problems of contemporary American society and the role of the school in solving them. Taken together, these three volumes are a comprehensive statement of Rugg's mature thought.

Due to his concern with creativity, Rugg's reconstructionism differed somewhat from that of his colleagues. Rugg was convinced that in addition to the social engineering endorsed by other reconstructionists, the good society required personal integrity on a large scale and, further, that integrity could be nurtured through creative self-expression. Consequently, he consistently sought to enlarge the scope of creative activities in the school curriculum.

Following his retirement in 1951, Rugg continued his study of creativity for the remaining nine years of his life. He died in 1960 at Woodstock, New York, his home since his marriage in 1947 to his third wife, Elizabeth May Howe Page.

Rugg's final book, *Imagination,* which represented the culmination of his career-long effort to understand the creative process, was published posthumously in 1963.

Further Reading

Although there is no full-scale biography of Rugg, his own *That Men May Understand* (1941) is a semi-autobiographical work. Biographical sketches may be found in *National Cyclopedia of American Biography* (1943-1946) and *Twentieth Century Authors: First Supplement* (1955). William H. Fisher provides a good overview of Rugg's career in *The Educational Forum* (March 1978), and Lawrence A. Cremin's *Transformation of the School* (1961) is an excellent background study. Peter F. Carbone, Jr., *The Social and Educational Thought of Harold Rugg* (1977), is the only book-length, published study of Rugg's work. Carbone also analyzes Rugg's theory of knowledge and views on creativity in *The Journal of Creative Behavior* (Spring 1969) and the *History of Education Quarterly* (Fall 1971). Franklin Parker describes the Rugg textbook controversy in the *Midwest Quarterly* (Autumn 1961), and Sanford W. Reitman discusses Rugg's reconstructionism in *Educational Theory* (Winter 1962). The July 1960 issue of *Educational Theory* contains a four-part memoir on Rugg. □

Jacob van Ruisdael

The Dutch landscape painter Jacob van Ruisdael (c. 1628-1682) raised to the highest level of quality and variety the painting of landscapes based on the observation of the visible world.

Jacob van Ruisdael was born in Haarlem, the son of the painter Isaak van Ruisdael, whose works are unknown to us, and the nephew of the gifted landscape painter Salomon van Ruysdael. Jacob's youthful works reflect the influence of his uncle and other painters of the Haarlem school, who played a leading part in the development of Dutch realistic landscape painting from the early years of the 17th century. He was already an independent master by 1648, when he became a member of the Haarlem guild. Paintings dated as early as 1645 and 1646 confirm that he was an accomplished painter while still very young.

The flat countryside around his native town provided subject matter for Ruisdael's brush again and again. Within the area of a small canvas, the level fields, on which the linen cloth that was a major product of Haarlem was stretched out to bleach, appear to extend on both sides as far as the eye can see. Cloud formations dapple the fields with sunlight. On the distant horizon, the buildings of the town join earth to sky. Such a picture is based on nature, but with the elements selected, emphasized, and reorganized so that the natural scene is transformed into an esthetic unity. It is a poetic transfiguration of reality.

Shortly after 1650 Ruisdael became familiar with a different kind of landscape, hilly and wooded, through travels in the border areas of eastern Holland and western Germany. Reminiscences of this experience appear in many of his paintings. In the *Wooden Bridge* (1652) a new monumentality is incorporated into a rugged landscape, whose structural strength is characteristic of Dutch painting about 1650. Ruisdael enriched the basic framework of the composition with a remarkable counterpoint of gently undulating contours, in which the curves of the meandering river, the paths, hills, clouds, and branches and crowns of trees underline, echo, and complete one another. The oak tree that dominates the left side of the composition is full of vitality and individuality. The richness of color and plasticity of forms of his mature works are evident here.

About 1656 Ruisdael moved to Amsterdam, where he seems to have spent the rest of his life. His extraordinary gift for evoking a higher reality in nature was embodied in a series of masterpieces. The brooding, emotion-filled *Ceme-*

tery, or Jewish Cemetery at Ouderkerk (ca. 1660; two versions), is unique in its explicitly allegorical intent. Death and the destruction of both natural and man-made objects is contrasted with the rainbow, symbol of resurrection. The preparatory drawings that he made for this painting show that the tombs were drawn from observation, the landscape background was imaginary, and the architecture was altered from a simple country church to a romantic ruin.

Paintings by his friend Allaert van Everdingen, who had traveled in Scandinavia, probably provided the vocabulary of rocky mountain streams and fir trees that began to appear in Ruisdael's paintings about 1660. These compositions tend to heroic grandeur, sometimes overstated. The *Waterfall with Castle* (mid-1660s) is an example of Ruisdael at his best in this type of theme, with an almost tangible differentiation of the textures of various materials, dramatic contrasts of light and dark, and intense local color, unified by firm compositional control.

Ruisdael painted as many as 50 seascapes, beginning in the mid-1660s. In these his energetic brushstroke and strongly contrasted values are particularly effective. This can be seen in *Stormy Sea* (ca. 1670), which might be called a portrait of the wind as it is reflected in sea and sky. He also painted forests, beaches, snow scenes, and town views. The figures in his paintings were often added by another artist. A number of drawings and some etchings by Ruisdael, mainly antedating 1650, have also come down to us.

By the mid-1670s Ruisdael's style had weakened. His most impressive pupil, Meindert Hobbema, carried on his tradition in a delightful but rather attenuated manner. Ruisdael's impact is seen in the great English landscapes of the 18th century, especially early works by Thomas Gainsborough, and in French landscapes of the 19th century, notably by Gustave Courbet.

Further Reading

The best book in English for the study of Ruisdael is Wolfgang Stechow, *Dutch Landscape Painting of the Seventeenth Century* (1966). See also Neil MacLaren, *The Dutch School* (1960). □

José Martínez Ruíz

The Spanish writer José Martínez Ruíz (1873-1967), who wrote under the name Azorín, was a spokesman for the Generation of 1898. He is famous for his impressionistic sketches and essays which evoke the essence of traditional and modern Spain.

José Martínez Ruíz was born on June 8, 1873, in Monóvar in Alicante Province. He spent his childhood in Yecla, later evoked in the autobiographical novel *Las confesiones de un pequeño filósofo.* He studied law in Valencia, Granada, and Salamanca but preferred literature and newspaper work. In 1896 he went to Madrid and wrote

for several republican, anticlerical newspapers. He soon became known as an outspoken republican with anarchist sympathies, symbolically expressed by his persistent use of a red umbrella.

In 1900 Ruíz published his first important work, *El alma castellana 1600-1800,* in which he revealed the essence of Spain, symbolized in Castilian towns and landscapes. Three novels followed: *La voluntad* (1902), *Antonio Azorín* (1903), and *Las confesiones de un pequeño filósofo* (1904). Their protagonist is Antonio Azorín, whose name Ruíz adopted in a kind of personal identification with his fictional character. The novels, which lack plot or any significant action, portray in three separate stages the anxieties and reminiscences of a hypersensitive intellectual surrounded by the decadence of modern Spain.

But Ruíz's lyrical, fragmentary style was much more suited to short sketches than to the longer novel form. Books such as *Los pueblos* (1905), *La ruta de don Quijote* (1905), and *Castilla* (1912) manifest his art in its purest form. Preoccupied with the past, Ruíz evoked poetically the beauty and inner life of familiar scenes and things, ultimately revealing the recurrence of the past in present life. The paradox of time visualized as eternal repetition became one of his chief concerns.

Ruíz also wrote literary criticism. He offers in *Lecturas españolas* (1912), *Clásicos y modernos* (1913), and *Almárgen de los clásicos* (1915) original views of the classics and many forgotten authors. He is the spokesman for the Generation of 1898, having defined that group of writers in a famous essay.

Gradually Ruíz became politically more conservative. He was elected deputy to the Cortes (1907, 1914) and served as undersecretary of education (1917, 1919). In 1924 he was admitted to the Spanish Academy but renounced membership when Gabriel Miró Ferrer was refused entrance. During the 1920s Ruíz wrote three more novels and a few unsuccessful plays, among them *Old Spain* (1926) and *Brandy, mucho Brandy* (1927). During the Civil War he lived in Paris, returning to Madrid in 1940. His subsequent works are inferior to his earlier works. He died on March 2, 1967, in Madrid.

Further Reading

The best work on Ruíz is Anna Krause, *Azorín, the Little Philosopher* (1948). His early novels are well analyzed in Katherine P. Reding, *The Generation of 1898 in Spain as Seen through Its Fictional Hero* (1936). □

Juan Ruiz

The Spanish poet Juan Ruiz (c. 1283-c. 1350), the archpriest of Hita, was the author of the "Libro de buen amor," one of the most extraordinary poetic creations of the Middle Ages.

Practically nothing is known of the life of Juan Ruiz except for what can be reconstructed from his poem. However, since the history of literature repeatedly proves that such a biographical technique is dangerous, it is best to carefully weigh all such evidence. In his poem he says that he was born in Alcalá de Henares (V: 1,510), a fact that agrees with the knowledge of geography shown in the poem. He gives an alleged self-portrait in stanzas 1,485-1,489, but scholars have pointed out that before these lines can be accepted as a physical picture of Ruiz, the weight of rhetorical tradition in literary portraiture—the physical correlates that medieval medical sciences attributed to psychological characteristics—and the fact that the description is made by a go-between, Trotaconventos, must be taken into consideration.

Lastly, the colophon to one of the manuscripts in which Ruiz's poem has survived explains that the work was composed while its author was in prison by order of Gil Álvarez Carrillo de Albornoz, Archbishop of Toledo. Since the poet also mentions a prison at the beginning of the *Libro de buen amor* (The Book of Good Love), scholars have argued that the reference in the poem is to the symbolic prison of Christian man and that this reference was interpreted literally by the scribe. Documentary proof gives evidence that by 1351 Ruiz was no longer archpriest of Hita. It is assumed that he died sometime earlier.

The *Libro* has survived in three main manuscripts, each one incomplete at different points. Two of the manuscripts represent a version of the poem finished in 1330. The third one represents an amplification of that version finished in 1343. Some fragments are also extant, including one of a Portuguese translation. Leaving aside the prose introduction (the *Libro* contains four different preliminary pieces before it expounds its *propósito,* or purpose), the poem has 1,728 stanzas, mainly narrative and in *cuaderna vía* (a learned 14-syllable poetic form) but with frequent lyrical outbursts in a variety of meters. The poem is supposedly an erotic autobiography written with a moral purpose, more in the medieval Ovidian tradition (as evidenced in the *Pamphilus de amore,* and mainly in the still-unpublished *De vetula*) than in the tradition of the Arabic and Hebrew works that have been pointed out as possible models. Spiritually, the poem is a hybrid product, typical of 600 years of coexistence of Christians, Moors, and Jews on the Iberian Peninsula.

Ruiz's poetic imagination and individualism were such, however, that no poetic tradition or literary theme employed by him has remained the same after his treatment of it. He was "one of the greatest poets of the Middle Ages, the equal of Chaucer," according to one modern critic.

Further Reading

E. K. Kane's notorious 1933 translation of *The Book of Good Love* was reissued in 1968. The *Libro* is analyzed at length in Anthony N. Zahareas, *The Art of Juan Ruiz, Archpriest of Hita* (1965). Américo Castro, *The Structure of Spanish History* (1948; trans. 1954), and María Rosa Lida de Malkiel, *Two Spanish Masterpieces* (1961), are good presentations of the case for Semitic influences; and Otis H. Green, *Spain and the Western Tradition,* vol. 1 (1963), presents the case for Occidental influences. □

Adolfo Ruiz Cortines

Adolfo Ruiz Cortines (1890-1973) was president of Mexico from 1952 to 1958. Not a flamboyant politician, he did lead Mexico on a steady course, the hallmarks of which were moderation and integrity. He believed in a "balanced revolution" in which private enterprise and the state would cooperate in the modernization process.

Adolfo Ruiz Cortines was born to a relatively poor family in the Gulf state of Veracruz on December 30, 1890. His father, a low ranking customs official in the port city, died when he was only a few months old. Although he did complete his primary education in his home state, he dropped out of school at the age of 16 to help support his family. Working for a short time as a bookkeeper's assistant and later in a textile mill, he did not abandon the idea of returning to school, but the outbreak of the Mexican Revolution in November of 1910 disrupted his plans for obtaining a university degree.

Ruiz Cortines played no major role in the early revolution. He did join the revolutionary army and served briefly in Venustiano Carranza's secret service in the fight against President Victoriano Huerta. When that movement succeeded in overthrowing Huerta, Ruiz Cortines became the personal aide to the newly named governor of the Federal District, Alfredo Robles Domínguez. For the next 20 years, 1920-1940, he served in various minor government positions, both civilian and military, and garnered a well-earned reputation for honesty and administrative efficiency.

Many Mexican political observers believed that Ruiz Cortines' inconspicuous career had culminated when, at the age of 54, he became governor of Veracruz, but during his governorship he cultivated a close personal relationship with Miguel Alemán, a rising political star, also from the state of Veracruz. Shortly after Alemán won the Mexican presidency in 1946 he decided to bring Ruiz Cortines into the cabinet as secretary of gobernación (government). He resigned his governorship to accept the cabinet post. It was a good decision, as he now had a strong patron and a national political base. Not at all characteristic of Mexican politicians in the post World War II period, as a cabinet minister Ruiz Cortines continued to live an austere life. He refused the government's offer of a chauffer and limosine and drove himself to work in his own car from his modest house. In 1952, with Alemán's backing, he won the presidential nomination of the Partido Revolucionario Institucional and in December of that year, at the age of 62, was inaugurated as president of Mexico.

Ruiz Cortines entered the Mexican presidency at a time when it was necessary to rekindle confidence in the country's political system. He proved to be most suited for this task as his personal honesty was above reproach. His predecessor and close friend, Miguel Alemán, had presided over an administration notorious for its widespread graft and corruption. Ruiz Cortines announced in his inaugural address that he would demand strict honesty from all public officials; high level government employees for the first time were required to publicly disclose their assets when they entered and left office. His own assets, public records disclosed, amounted to only $30,000. Hoping to instill a sense of professionalism in public servants, he authorized substantial increases in salary and benefits for government employees. Nevertheless, during his first three years in office he found it necessary to fire a number of bureaucrats found guilty of peculation. In another major political reform, in 1953 President Ruiz Cortines prodded his congress to pass legislation enfranchising the Mexican women in all elections. This long overdue political reform culminated years of active campaigning by women's organizations throughout the country.

Ruiz Cortines presided over a healthy Mexican economy. At a time when inflation was beginning to cripple other Latin American economies, he was able to keep it in check. He tightened monetary and fiscal policies and the Mexican gross national product responded by recording impressive gains during each year of his administration. The country weathered the world recession of 1952 with but few ill effects. Foreign capital and stepped up government financing encouraged rapid industrial growth. The exploitation of newly discovered oil fields provided a reliable source of government revenue, as did the exploitation of natural gas reserves. With the solid economic foundation in place and with improvements recorded in tax collection procedures the president was able to step up some important social services. Most significant was the expansion of the Instituto Mexicano de Seguro Social, Mexico's social security agency. Concerned that rural Mexico was not receiving its fair share of the benefits of a productive Mexican society, Ruiz Cortines extended social security coverage to the rural areas for the first time in the country's history. Throughout his administration relations with the United States were excellent.

Ruiz Cortines is not remembered for having initiated many new grandiose public works projects. Rather, he sought to consolidate the series of programs begun by his predecessors. Initial fears that he would be dominated by Miguel Alemán proved groundless. Not a man motivated by ideology, he set a good example with his own integrity and firmness. His years in the presidency were successful ones. In his own quiet way he restored confidence in the Mexican political system and brought an enviable measure of unity to his country. History remembers his presidency most kindly.

Further Reading

No adequate biography of Ruiz Cortines exists either in English or in Spanish. Political aspects of the presidential administration, however, can be traced in Frank Brandenburg, *The Making of Modern Mexico* (1964); Howard F. Cline, *Mexico: Revolution to Evolution, 1940-1960* (1964); and Robert E. Scott, *Mexican Government in Transition* (1959). Economic policies are treated in Raymond Vernon, *The Dilemma of Mexico's Development: The Role of the Private and Public Sectors* (1963).
□

Count Rumford

The American-born British physicist Benjamin Thompson, Count Rumford (1753-1814), is best known for his attacks on the caloric theory of heat.

Benjamin Thompson was born on March 26, 1753, in Woburn, Mass. He received only 2 years of formal education and at 13 was apprenticed to a local merchant. At the age of 19, while teaching in Concord, N.H., he married a wealthy widow, 14 years his senior. He thus acquired not only an extensive estate but social and political influence as well.

Thompson's open support of the British crown, however, made his position increasingly precarious as political tensions mounted in the Colonies. As a result of his loyalist activities, he was forced in December 1774 to flee to Boston, abandoning his wife and infant daughter. He spent the next 15 months actively spying for the British government, supplying them with detailed reports on the condition and activities of the assembling colonial forces. When the British abandoned Boston in March 1776, Thompson departed for London.

Thompson arrived in London a confident, aggressive young man with a very useful knowledge of the colonial military situation; within 4 years he had risen to the position of undersecretary of state for colonial affairs. He also found time to pursue his scientific interests, and he soon gained a reputation as a productive natural philosopher as well. He undertook a series of studies on the explosive force of gunpowder, and his published report of these experiments was influential in his election as a fellow of the Royal Society in 1781. In that year he suddenly left London and returned to the Colonies, where he spent an undistinguished 2 years as a commanding officer in the British forces. He then returned to London and from there set out for the Continent.

Social Reform

In 1784 Thompson settled down in Munich as an aide-de-camp and confidential adviser to Elector Karl Theodor of Bavaria. Thompson did much to advance the stature of the Bavarian court by promoting scientific and technological advances and by instituting reform in the military, educational, and economic structure of the country. His standing was such as to guarantee him both the financial and technical support necessary for his varied, and often grandiose, projects, and in return for his activities he was in 1793 made a count of the Holy Roman Empire. He chose as his title Count Rumford, Rumford being the original name of Concord, N.H.

While in Munich one of Rumford's chief responsibilities was reorganizing the Bavarian army. In an effort to find more efficient and economical means of feeding and clothing the troops, he undertook an extensive study of the thermal conductivity of various types of cloth, in the process discovering the principle of heat transfer through what are today known as convection currents. Unable to persuade

any commercial manufacturer to adopt the results of this research, Rumford set up what he called a "military workhouse" for producing the new military uniforms and in so doing became actively involved in social reform. Munich at the time was noted for its swarms of beggars, and on New Year's Day, 1790, Rumford had the Bavarian army arrest and jail every beggar in the city. These were then trained in his workhouse to manufacture the desired uniforms and in return for their labor received shelter, food, and education. The operation of this workhouse also involved Rumford in the associated practical problems of nutrition, heating, and lighting.

Theory of Heat

Rumford is best known today, however, for his contributions to the theory of heat. At the end of the 18th century the predominant theory of heat was the so-called caloric theory, according to which heat was a fluid substance that flowed into bodies when they were heated and flowed out of them as they cooled. The success of this theory in explaining then known phenomena is reflected in many terms, such as "heat flow" and "calorie," still used by physicists today. During his earlier gunpowder studies, however, Rumford had observed certain anomalies which the caloric theory seemed unable to explain, and for the remainder of his life he was constantly on the lookout for additional experimental evidence which might refute this theory.

Rumford's famous cannon-boring experiments present perhaps the most graphic evidence. One of his positions in Munich was inspector general of artillery for the Bavarian

army, and, in the course of supervising work in the Munich arsenal, he was struck by the large amount of heat produced in boring a brass cannon. He devised an experiment in which, by utilizing a blunt borer to maximize the heat produced, he was able to boil large quantities of water with the resultant heat. The important aspect of this experiment, as Rumford himself noted, was the seemingly endless supply of heat that could be thus produced. According to the caloric theory, the boring tool produced heat by squeezing the caloric fluid out of the bodies rubbed together, but, as Rumford pointed out, anything which could be produced without limitation could not be a material substance such as caloric fluid. It should be emphasized, however, that although Rumford also produced numerous other experiments to refute the caloric theory, these experiments did not alone disprove the caloric theory, and not until much later in the 19th century was the concept of heat as a mode of motion generally adopted.

Royal Institution and Later Life

Rumford's position in Munich had always been somewhat precarious. His privileged status, the rapidity and success of his numerous innovations, and his ruthless disdain for his political opponents did nothing to silence the clamor of his enemies, and in 1798 the elector found it expedient to appoint him minister plenipotentiary to England, a position of honor which nonetheless effectively removed him from Munich politics. Arriving in London, he discovered that George III refused to accept a British subject (which Rumford still was) as minister from a foreign country.

Finding himself without a job, Rumford settled down in London to the task of establishing the Royal Institution. Justly renowned today for its research and popular lectures, the institution at its founding was part science museum and part technical school, reflecting Rumford's concern for the practical application of his researches. In 1801, after financial and personality difficulties, Rumford dissociated himself from the institution.

In 1804 Rumford moved to Paris and there, the following year, married Madame Lavoisier, the widow of the famous French chemist. A fashionable, though discordant, marriage, it lasted but 2 years, and in 1807 Rumford retired to the village of Auteuil near Paris. He became a member of the National Institute of France, as the Academy of Sciences was then called, and was a frequent contributor to its sessions and debates, as well as actively working to adapt his theoretical researches to practical applications. He died at Auteuil on Aug. 21, 1814.

Further Reading

A new edition of Rumford's works is being edited by Sanborn C. Brown, *Collected Works of Count Rumford,* of which volume 1 is *The Nature of Heat* (1968). Of the full-length biographies the reader may most profitably consult W. J. Sparrow, *Knight of the White Eagle: A Biography of Sir Benjamin Thompson, Count Rumford* (1964). Sanborn C. Brown, *Count Rumford: Physicist Extraordinary* (1962), is an excellent, brief account. Other studies are James A. Thompson, *Count Rumford of Massachusetts* (1935), and Egon Larsen, *An American in Europe* (1953).

Additional Sources

Brown, Sanborn Conner, *Benjamin Thompson, Count Rumford,* Cambridge, Mass.: MIT Press, 1979.

Brown, Sanborn Conner, *Count Rumford, physicist extraordinary,* Westport, Conn.: Greenwood Press, 1979, 1962.

Dabney, Betty Page, *The silver sextant: four men of the Enlightenment,* Norfolk, Va.: B.P. Dabney, 1993.

Jones, Bence, *The Royal Institution, its founder and its first professors,* New York: Arno Press, 1975. □

Jalai ed-Din Rumi

The Persian poet and Sufi mystic Jalai ed-Din Rumi (1207-1273) was a brilliant lyrical poet who founded his own religious order, the Mevlevis. His poetry showed original religious and wonderfully esoteric forms of expression.

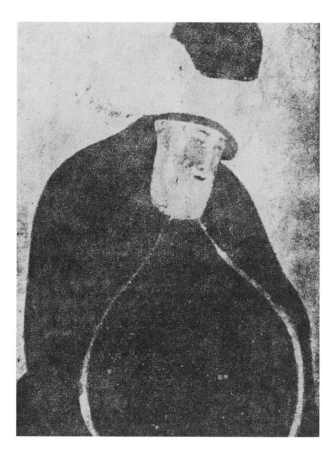

The unsurpassable peak of all Sufi thought was reached in the thought of Jalal ed-Din Rumi, born in Balkh. He migrated to Konya in Asia Minor at a young age with his father, fleeing the Mongol invader of his day, Genghis Khan. On this trip in the city of Nishapur the young Rumi was presented to the famous old poet Attar, who, according to legend, predicted his future greatness and gave him his *Book of Secrets.* Then Rumi and his father traveled through Baghdad, Mecca, Damascus, and Erzincan, finally reaching Konya about 1226 or 1227, where he resided for most of his remaining life. His father was appointed to a high post in the empire of the Seljuks of Rum. Rumi inherited this post in 1231, when his father died. Thus Rumi was a man of means and could devote his efforts to more esoteric fields.

Religious Inspiration

The event which had the greatest influence on Rumi's intellectual and moral life was his meeting with the Sufi mystic Shams ed-Din Tabrizi. The latter, in the course of his wanderings, visited Konya and thoroughly inspired Rumi with religious fervor. As a result of this friendship, Rumi dedicated most of his writings to this wandering Sufi. Because of this also, Rumi founded the Mevlevi order of dervishes—the dancing dervishes. The unique trait of this order was that, contrary to general Moslem practice, Rumi gave a considerable place to music (the drum and reed) in the ceremonies.

The principal work of Rumi is his massive *Mathnawi.* This work is a compendium of poems, tales, anecdotes, and reflections—all meant to illustrate Sufi doctrine, the result of 40 years of work by Rumi. He also wrote a shorter *Diwan* and a prose treatise entitled *Fihi Ma Fihi* (What Is Within Is Within).

Rumi was a poet of the first rank. His style was simple and colloquial. His tales possessed diverse qualities: variety and originality, dignity and picturesqueness, learning and charm, depth of feeling and thought. The *Mathnawi* is no doubt very disjointed; the stories follow one another in no apparent order. But it is filled with lyrical inspiration. Each small tale may be read separately, and one cannot help but be impressed with its succinctness.

As a philosopher, Rumi is less original than as a poet. His subject is Sufism, expressed with glowing enthusiasm. But it is not systematically expounded, and lyrical fervor seems to run rampant. But it can be said that just as Ibn Arabi summed up and gathered into a single system all that had been said on mysticism in Arabic before him, so Rumi in his famous *Mathnawi* comes the closest to this in Persian.

As with other Sufi poets, many Neoplatonic ideas abound in Rumi's writing. Ties to Christian mysticism can also be found. But in the last analysis, Rumi was a Moslem of very special interest. He was philanthropic and strongly emotional, and his writings seem easily to fit in with the excitement of the dance of the whirling dervishes.

Further Reading

A. J. Arberry's translation of Rumi's *Mathnawi* (2 vols., 1961-1963) contains short but useful introductions. Arberry also translated the *Discourses of Rumi* (1961) and *The Mystical Poems of Rumi* (1968), both with biographical introduction. Biographical studies of Rumi are Afzal Iqbal, *The Life and Work of Muhammad Jalal-ud-Din* (1956; 2d rev. ed. 1964), and A. Reza Arasteh, *Rumi, the Persian: Rebirth in Creativity and Love* (1965), an interesting psychological study. Also reliable is Khalifal Abdul-Hakim, *The Metaphysics of Rumi* (1933), a critical sketch. A classic background work is Edward G. Browne, *A Literary History of Persia* (2 vols., 1902-1906). For a comprehensive discussion of the Sufi thought of Rumi see A. J. Arberry, *Sufism: An Account of the Mystics of Islam* (1950), and Idries Shah, *The Sufis* (1964). □

Karl Rudolf Gerd Von Rundstedt

Field marshal Karl Rudolf Gerd von Rundstedt (1875-1953), the senior German field commander in World War II, directed the German war effort on the Western front from 1942 to 1945.

Gerd von Rundstedt was born on Dec. 12, 1875, in Aschersleben near Magdeburg. His family was of old Prussian nobility with a long military tradition dating back to the Middle Ages. His father was a general, and his brother was a major. Rundstedt received all of his education in military schools, and in 1891 he entered the Prussian infantry. In 1906 he received his first general-staff assignment.

In World War I Rundstedt took part in the Battle of the Marne in the autumn of 1914, and then he alternately served on the Eastern and Western fronts in army corps chief of staff positions. By the end of the war he had become the chief of staff of the 15th Army Corps with the rank of major. From 1919 to 1932 Rundstedt held several staff and command positions related to the secret rearmament of Germany. During the time of troubles preceding the take-over of Adolf Hitler, he held, as a lieutenant colonel, the politically sensitive position of commander of the Berlin Military District. In this capacity in July 1932 he executed the eviction of the duly elected Social Democratic government of Prussia on the order of the German chancellor, Franz von Papen. A few weeks later Rundstedt advanced to commander in chief of the entire Army Group I (Berlin and central Germany).

During his term as Army Group I commander in chief, Rundstedt did much to improve and reform the infantry, most notably through the reequipment and reorganization of infantry commands into small, self-sufficient units, or *Einheiten*. By 1938 he had become increasingly alarmed at Hitler's policies toward the general staff and at the growing war preparations, and he expressed these concerns by signing an officers' petition circulated by the chief of the general staff, Gen. Ludwig Beck. In October 1938 Rundstedt asked for and obtained permission to retire.

Even before the outbreak of World War II, however, Rundstedt was recalled from retirement. In the invasion of Poland (1939), he commanded the group of German armies in the south that swept through Galicia toward Warsaw with brilliant precision. In the German attack on France in May 1940, Rundstedt led the vital drive of the centrally located Army Group A through the Ardennes and behind the French fortifications of the Maginot Line. He was rewarded for his brilliant success with a promotion to the rank of field mar-

shal on July 19, 1940. In the summer of 1941, Rundstedt commanded the southern group of German armies in their rapid advance into Russia. He overwhelmed the army of Marshal Semyon M. Budyenny on the southern flank of the Soviets and subsequently occupied the mineral-rich Ukraine. Once again, however, the field marshal expressed disagreement with Hitler's plans and demanded a general retreat of his forces to the Mius Line. In the ensuing quarrel, Rundstedt offered his resignation, which was accepted in December 1941.

Following the entry of the United States into the war in December 1941 and the consequent increase in the likelihood of an Allied invasion of the Continent, Hitler once again turned to Rundstedt, and on March 1, 1942, Hitler appointed him commander in chief West. After the sinking of the French navy in November, Hitler added military commander of France to Rundstedt's titles. In this capacity Rundstedt prepared French defenses against an Allied invasion, which, however, he was unable to prevent. After the landing on June 6, 1944, Rundstedt withdrew German troops to the Seine River, which brought his dismissal and replacement on July 6. After his successor failed to reverse the situation and committed suicide, Rundstedt once again returned to the position of commander in chief West in September. In the following months he oversaw the declining fortunes of the German defense and watched with great consternation as Hitler's last gamble, the Ardennes offensive (Battle of the Bulge), failed in December 1944.

Thoroughly disenchanted and quite ill, Rundstedt entered final retirement on March 13, 1945. He was captured by American troops in Bavaria on May 1 and was turned over to the British for trial. Because of Rundstedt's poor health, his trial never took place, and on May 26, 1946, he was released from a British military hospital. He died in Hanover on Feb. 24, 1953.

Further Reading

One major biographical source on the field marshal is the work of an admiring friend, Gen. Guenter von Blumentritt, *Von Rundstedt: The Soldier and the Man*, translated by Cuthbert Reavely (1952). A section on Rundstedt is in Siegfried Westphal, *The German Army in the West* (1951).

Additional Sources

Messenger, Charles, *The last Prussian: a biography of Field Marshal Gerd von Rundstedt, 1875-1953*, London; Washington: Brassey's; N.Y., N.Y.: Macmillan (distributor), 1991. ☐

Rurik

The legendary Norman warrior Rurik (died ca. 873) was the founder of the first Russian state and of the dynasty that ruled in Russia until the death of Feodor I in 1598.

According to the first Russian annals, the *Primary Chronicle*, Rurik was a Scandinavian "from the tribe of the Rus" whom the people of Novgorod invited in 862 to assume rule over them, as they had been unable to govern themselves. Accompanied by his family and retinue, Rurik settled in Novgorod, and his brothers took control of adjacent regions. The area under their authority came to be called "the land of the Rus" and eventually Rus'. The descendants of Rurik continued to rule over this region following his death about 873.

Although this account of the origins of the first Russian state and dynasty enjoyed considerable credibility among older historians, modern scholars no longer accept it in its entirety and even question the actual existence of Rurik. The story of Rurik contains inconsistencies and information that cannot be confirmed from other sources. The origin of the name Rus' has never been satisfactorily explained. Scholars are certain only that the Scandinavians frequently invaded and migrated into Russia in the 9th century and that the origin of the names of early Russian princes, including the name Rurik, derives from the Normans. Though possibly reflecting earlier records or legends that have not been preserved, the *Primary Chronicle* has obviously used the story of Rurik to explain, justify, and antedate the rule of the Rurik dynasty, during which the chronicle was written and compiled (early 12th century).

The notion of Rurik's having been invited to rule in Russia seems in particular to be a product of such efforts. The original Rurik, if one existed at all, might have been one of the Norman chieftains who went to Russia from Scandinavia either as conquerors or as hirelings of local communi-

ties in which they often subsequently usurped power. At best, Rurik might have been invited to Novgorod as an auxiliary to one of several local parties competing for power. The establishment of his own power there under these circumstances was probably achieved through usurpation.

Further Reading

A standard translation of the *Primary Chronicle*, with a balanced commentary on its contents, is *The Russian Primary Chronicle: Laurentian Text*, edited and translated by Samuel Hazzard Cross and Olgerd P. Sherbowitz-Wetzor (1953). Compare with N. K. Chadwick, *The Beginnings of Russian History: An Enquiry into Sources* (1946). Varying interpretations of these events are reflected in a number of works on old Russia: Vilhelm Thomsen, *The Relations between Ancient Russia and Scandinavia and the Origin of the Russian State* (1877); V. O. Kliuchevskii, *A Russian History*, vol. 1 (1911); George Vernadsky and Michael Karpovich, *A History of Russia*, vol. 1 (1943); and Boris D. Grekov, *Kiev Rus* (trans. 1959). ☐

Benjamin Rush

Benjamin Rush (1745-1813), physician, patriot, and humanitarian, represented the epitome of the versatile, wide-ranging physician in America. He insisted on a theoretical structure for medical practice.

Benjamin Rush was born on Dec. 24, 1745, on a plantation at Byberry near Philadelphia. He graduated in 1760 from the College of New Jersey (now Princeton) and then studied medicine in Philadelphia until 1766. He completed his medical education at the University of Edinburgh, Scotland. Here he studied under many of the greatest medical teachers of the time, most notably William Cullen, proponent of the concept of rational rather than empirical medical systems. Rush received his doctorate in 1768, then returned to Philadelphia.

Rush practiced medicine and was soon made the first professor of chemistry in America at the College of Philadelphia. He joined the American Philosophical Society and became a permanent part of Philadelphia's scientific and medical circle, though his outspoken views made as many enemies as friends. In 1774 he helped organize the Pennsylvania Society for Promoting the Abolition of Slavery and became an outspoken defender of American rights in the brewing quarrel with Great Britain. In 1775 Rush suggested that Thomas Paine write a tract in favor of American independence under the title *Common Sense;* Paine did and the pamphlet was very influential in turning public opinion toward independence. Rush continued to be active in the American independence movement, was a member of the Continental Congress, and signed the Declaration of Independence.

Appointed surgeon general of the armies of the Middle Department in 1777, Rush found the medical services disor-

ganized and mounted an attack on William Shippen, the director general of medical services. When George Washington upheld Shippen, Rush resigned and resumed his medical practice. He began delivering lectures at the University of the State of Pennsylvania in 1780 and joined the staff of the Pennsylvania Hospital in 1783. By 1789 he was professor of theory and practice in the university. He became professor of the institutes of medicine and clinical practice in the University of Pennsylvania in 1792 and professor of theory and practice in 1796. From this base he developed a wide following.

Rush's great reputation as a teacher made him appear a more important innovator than he was. His major contribution was to introduce Cullen's concept of a rationally deduced medical system to replace empirical folk practice. He also supported the theory of John Brown of Edinburgh proposing a single cause for all disease—imbalance of the nervous energies. According to this theory, all illness was attributable to excesses or deficiencies in nervous energies; moderation in all things was the preventive medicine, but once illness occurred, either bleeding or purging was necessary. Rush was a zealot on bleeding and in extreme cases would remove as much as four-fifths of a patient's blood. His excesses in this brought much criticism, but his emphasis on moderation as a preventive was popular. He was thus led to advocate temperance, and he is sometimes regarded as the founder of the temperance movement in America.

Rush also became interested in the plight of the mentally ill and the poor, established the first free dispensary in the United States, and campaigned against public and capi-

tal punishment and for general penal reform. He also concerned himself with education, advocating education for women, less emphasis on classics and more on utilitarian subjects, and a national educational system capped by a national university. His ideas were behind the founding of Dickinson College in 1783.

The test of Rush's medical theories came during the yellow fever epidemic of 1793. His initial theory that the epidemic was partly caused by poor sanitation resulted in ostracism by fellow physicians. Rush bravely stayed in Philadelphia to treat yellow fever victims, while many other medical men fled. His treatment was bleeding, and he was charged with causing many more deaths than he prevented. Although Rush held to his theory, he was either unwilling or simply unable to keep records so that the theory could be checked against fact. However, his published accounts of the epidemic, especially his suggestion that poor sanitation was an ultimate cause, attracted attention in Europe.

Rush also did pioneering work relating dentistry to physiology and was influential in founding veterinary medicine in America. Both fields had been considered beneath the dignity of the professional. His observations on the mentally ill seem to presage modern developments in psychoanalytic theory, especially his *Medical Inquiries and Observations on the Diseases of the Mind* (1812).

Rush's insistence on a rational, systematic body of knowledge for the medical profession certainly helped set the stage for the later medical revolution in America. He died in Philadelphia on April 19, 1813.

Further Reading

Primary sources on Rush include *The Autobiography of Benjamin Rush,* edited by George W. Corner (1948); Rush's *Letters,* edited by L. H. Butterfield (1951); and John A. Schutz and Douglass Adair, eds., *The Spur of Fame: Dialogues of John Adams and Benjamin Rush* (1966). Although several books have been written about Rush, there is no definitive study. The only fully documented scholarly work is Nathan G. Goodman, *Benjamin Rush: Physician and Citizen* (1934). Carl A. L. Binger, *Revolutionary Doctor: Benjamin Rush* (1966), is fairly sound. A popularized work is Sarah R. Riedman and Clarence C. Green, *Benjamin Rush* (1964). For general background see Daniel J. Boorstin, *The Lost World of Thomas Jefferson* (1948), and Brooke Hindle, *The Pursuit of Science in Revolutionary America, 1735-1789* (1956).

Additional Sources

Blinderman, Abraham, *Three early champions of education: Benjamin Franklin, Benjamin Rush, and Noah Webster,* Bloomington, Ind.: Phi Delta Kappa Educational Foundation, 1976. □

William Rush

William Rush (1756-1833) was the most significant American sculptor to emerge from the folk-art and figurehead carving tradition of the early years of the republic.

William Rush was born in Philadelphia. His father was a ship carpenter, and as a boy William occupied himself by carving ship models. He was apprenticed to learn the trade of carving, probably before the Revolution; his earliest known commissions for figureheads date from about 1790. As time went on, Rush became famous as a carver, and he employed a number of apprentices. He was the only sculptor to become one of the founders, in 1794, of the short-lived Columbianum, the first art organization in America; and he was also one of the first directors of the Pennsylvania Academy of Fine Arts.

Probably because of his superior skill at figurehead carving, Rush was able to advance to a position beyond that of purely artisan work, and he received a number of significant commissions in the realm of "pure" sculpture. His first important works were the figures *Comedy* and *Tragedy* (1808) for the Chestnut Street Theater in Philadelphia. The following year he was commissioned to create what was probably his best-known sculpture, the *Water Nymph and Bittern.* In 1824, on the occasion of Lafayette's triumphal tour of the United States, Rush not only carved his portrait but also executed two monumental sculptures, *Wisdom* and *Justice,* which were placed atop a Philadelphia triumphal arch erected in Lafayette's honor. His last major works were two reclining figures, *Schuylkill River Chained* and *Schuylkill River Freed* (ca. 1828).

Rush executed a number of portraits. His subjects included Benjamin Rush, George Washington, Oliver Hazard Perry, Andrew Jackson, and Winfield Scott. Two of his finest works were portraits of himself and of his daughter, Elizabeth.

Rush was primarily a woodcarver, and the deep undercutting, broad planes, and general columnar form of many of his statues bear witness to his respect for his medium. He never worked in marble. Some of his portrait busts exist in plaster and some in terra-cotta, mediums in which he was also proficient. Stylistically, he was closer to the decorative rococo tradition of the 18th century than to the prevailing neoclassicism of his own time. Yet his allegories were not unlike those carved by European artists of his day, and his *Schuylkill River Chained* certainly relates to statues of classical river gods. While some critics have claimed that Rush was the first American sculptor, he really represents the apogee of the artisan tradition of woodcarving, for American sculpture would develop in the future along the lines of neoclassic marble carving.

Further Reading

A biographical study of Rush is Henri Marceau, *William Rush, 1756-1833: The First Native American Sculptor* (1937). □

Salman Rushdie

The Indian/British author Ahmed Salman Rushdie (born 1947) was a political parablist whose work often focused on outrages of history and particularly of religions. His book *The Satanic Verses* earned him a death sentence from the Iranian Ayatollah Ruhollah Khomeini.

Although he was called a writer to watch after the appearance of his first novel and was awarded one of the most prestigious literary prizes in Europe for his second, Salman Rushdie became a household word because of the enemies his fiction made rather than the admirers. *The Satanic Verses,* published in 1988, earned him a death sentence from Ayatollah Ruhollah Khomeini, then religious sovereign of Iran and spiritual leader to millions of fundamentalist Moslems worldwide.

Born Ahmed Salman Rushdie on June 19, 1947, to a middle-class family in Bombay, India, Rushdie was educated in England and eventually received his M.A. from King's College, Cambridge. After a brief career as an actor he made a living as a freelance advertising copywriter in England from 1970 to 1980. The experience of expatriation, which he shared with many writers of his generation who were born in the Third World, is an important theme in his work.

However, Rushdie's opus in particular expanded the meaning of the word "expatriate" to possibly its total linguistic limits. For instance, *Midnight's Children* (1981) is in part the story of a baby who was not only the result of an extramarital affair, but who was then switched at birth with a second illicit child. The hero of the novel is doubly removed from his true patrimony: His mother's husband is

not his father, and the Englishman with whom his Indian mother slept—who his mother thinks is his father—is not his real father either. In addition, the hero is caught between the two great religions of Indian, Islam and Hinduism, neither of which he can claim as his own. Finally, he spends his life being shunted back and forth by circumstance between the Indian republic and its antithesis, Pakistan.

Rushdie unfailingly took the stance of a lifelong member of the diaspora, which may be the most consistently autobiographical aspect of his work. Long before his hurried exile from the public eye, in an interview published after *Midnight's Children* received the Booker McConnell Prize, Rushdie presciently said: "I have a fear that it may, at some point, become necessary to make choices among [India, England, and America], and that it will be very painful."

Another characteristic of Rushdie's work is its reliance on the fantastic. In fact, Rushdie's first book, *Grimus* (1979), was classified as science fiction by many critics. It is the story of Flapping Eagle, an American Indian who is given the gift of immortality and goes on an odyssey to find the meaning of life. *Shame* (1983) has a Pakistani heroine, Sufiya Zinobia, who blushes so hotly with embarrassment at her nation's history her body boils her bath water and burns the lips of men who attempt to kiss her. The title *Midnight's Children* refers to the 1,001 infants born in the first hour of India's independence, all of whom have para-human powers. And *The Satanic Verses* opens with the miraculous survival and transfiguration of two Indian men who fall out of the sky after their jumbo jet to England is blown up in midair by Sikh terrorists.

Rushdie always used the element of the fabulous to make painfully incisive political commentary (among other varieties of observation). *Shame* is so thinly disguised a parody of recent Pakistani history as to be transparent, and the hero of *Midnight's Children* was described as a man "handcuffed to history" by the political journal *Commonweal*. Rushdie is often compared with Lawrence Sterne as well as Jonathan Swift as a political parablist, but according to *The New York Times Book Review*, "It would be a disservice to Salman Rushdie's very original genius to dwell on literary analogues and ancestors."

Rushdie also made a career out of poking fun at religious fanatics of every stripe. One technique of Rushdie's in furtherance of this aim was to infuse common objects with enormous symbolic significance. In *Midnight's Children*, for instance, pickled chutney is one of the main images for India's cultural and social maelstrom; in *The Satanic Verses*, bad breath plays a vital role in telling good from evil. Few other writers dare to found entire symbolic structures on items as replaceable as a sheet with a hole in the middle, but to Rushdie it undoubtedly seems a worse exercise in illogic to kill people over the contents of a so-called "holy" book.

Rushdie's habit of using the outrages of history—especially religious outrages and religious history—made *The Satanic Verses* (1988) a book of frightening precognition. In the novel, Rushdie has a writer sentenced to death by a religious leader. The writer in the book is a scribe meant to chronicle the life of a prophet who—as the writer of the book enjoys riddling—both "is and is not"

Mohammed. Creating this character, who exists within a psychotic dream of one of the two men who fell from the airplane, was a natural extension of Rushdie's personal horror at fundamentalist Islamic rule. It is this dream sequence which ignited fatal riots in India and garnered Rushdie the Ayatollah Khomeini's death sentence.

The title of the novel refers to verses from the Koran, which were struck out by later Islamic historians, describing an episode in which Mohammed briefly wavered in his adherence to belief in a single god and allowed mention to be made of three local goddesses. The dream section in the book details, from the point of view of a schizophrenic Indian actor who fancies himself an archangel, how the holy prophet yielded to temptation and then reversed himself. There are other "satanic" verses in the book, notably those a modern-day husband anonymously sings over the phone to drive his wife's lover insane with jealousy. But the contemporary aspect of the novel has been almost completely overlooked by the controversy surrounding it.

Khomeini's death threat extended not only to Rushdie himself, but to the publishers of *The Satanic Verses*, any bookseller who carried it, and any Moslem who publicly condoned its release. Several major bookstores in England and America had bomb scares, and the novel was temporarily removed from the shelves of America's largest book selling chains. Two Islamic clerics in London were murdered, ostensibly for questioning the correctness of Rushdie's death sentence on a talk show. Numerous book-burnings were held throughout the world.

Rushdie himself, and his possible disguises in hiding, became an established figure of black humor. During the 1990 Academy Awards presentation, which was seen worldwide by an estimated one billion viewers, comedian Billy Crystal joked that "the lovely young woman" who usually hands Oscar statuettes to their recipients "is, of course, Salman Rushdie."

Rushdie's wife of 13 months, author Marianne Wiggins, went into hiding with him when the death threat was announced. She soon emerged and indicated that their marriage was over.

In 1990 Rushdie released the fantasy novel *Haroun and the Sea of Stories*, written for his son (by a first marriage), Zafar. That same year Rushdie publicly embraced Islam and apologized to those offended by the *The Satanic Verses*. He made several appearances in London book-stores to autograph his newest work. But even after the Ayatollah's death, his successor, Iran's President Hashemi Rafsanzani, refused to lift the death edict. Rushdie continued to appear in public only occasionally, and then under heavy security.

Although the severity of the Ayatollah's sentence was at least partially a political gambit to aid his regime in its final days, it carried the force of gospel for many terrorists who regard America—and the freedom of speech espoused in the American Constitution—as the "Great Satan." Rushdie will live in danger until the last Khomeini loyalist has passed away. As if in a scene from one of his novels, the innocent speaker of a personal truth is surrealistically threatened with slaughter by his opposite, who claims a patent on universal truth. Rushdie has already been acclaimed as a supreme artist; one can only hope, for his sake as well as ours, that his life will no longer imitate his art.

Rushdie continues to live an isolated life. He has re-married, however, and become a father for the second time. Occasionally he makes radio appearances, but, they are usually unannounced. Rushdie's novel entitled *The Moor's Last Sigh* was published in 1995. This book drew hostile and negative reactions from Hindu militants in India.

Further Reading

Contemporary Authors, volume 111 (1984), edited by Hal May, contains selected reviews of *Grimus, Midnight's Children,* and *Shame,* as well as a comprehensive selection of reviews and news stories surrounding *The Satanic Verses.* A lengthy interview by Gerald Marzorati appeared in *The New York Times Magazine* (November 4, 1990). In 1991 Rushdie published *Imaginary Homelands: Essays and Criticism, 1981-1991,* a kind of intellectual autobiography. Rushdie was mentioned in ''People''*Time* (Septmeber 18, 1995) □

David Dean Rusk

America's 54th secretary of state and second only to Cordell Hull in length of service, Dean Rusk (1909-1994) presided over the Department of State during the turbulent Kennedy-Johnson years of the Vietnam War.

The life and career of David Dean Rusk, 54th Secretary of State of the United States, is a textbook case of barefoot poverty to black tie success. It must almost inevitably begin: ''Where else but in America . . . ?'' This judgment should be modified, however, by recognition of the family, character, and personality traits which marked his life and by the nebulous but indispensable final element luck which often accounts for greatness.

Early Years

On February 9, 1909, David Dean Rusk was born to school teacher Frances (Clotfelter) Rusk and her minister-farmer husband Robert Rusk. The latter, a Presbyterian minister, had taken up farming in Georgia's Cherokee county after a throat condition forced him to retire from his vocation. Four years after Rusk's birth, the family moved to Atlanta, where Dean's father became a postal worker. There, in the city's public school system, Dean Rusk was educated through secondary school. His two sisters and two brothers excelled in school and, as the fourth child of this family, Rusk profited from sibling example and parental encouragement.

By scrimping and with some scholarship assistance, he successfully matriculated in politics at North Carolina's Davidson College. At Davidson he was accepted into Phi Beta Kappa, participated in student government and other school activities including Reserve Officers Training Corps (R.O.T.C.), and graduated with honors in 1931.

Reception of a Rhodes scholarship gave Rusk three years at Oxford, where he earned a Master's degree in 1934. Specializing in international relations, he wrote an essay on Britain's international relations, thereby winning the coveted Cecil Peace Prize.

World War II Brings Career Change

On his return from Oxford he was hired as an assistant professor to teach international relations and politics at Mills College in Oakland, California. During the next few years he married, took up the study of law at the Berkeley campus of the University of California, and served as dean of faculty at Mills. So the war found him.

Rusk was commissioned a captain in December 1940, spending the year before Pearl Harbor performing a variety of military tasks. His qualifications and performance brought him transfer to Army Intelligence in Washington, where he specialized in Britain's Asian empire, then under Japanese siege.

Sent overseas in 1943 to the China-Burma-India Theater, he came to the attention of General Joseph Stilwell, serving as ''Vinegar Joe's'' deputy chief of staff. Already a skilled administrator, service with Stilwell sharpened his abilities further, bringing him to the attention of General George C. Marshall's recruiters, then assembling talented leaders for postwar duties.

Colonel Rusk, therefore, did not return to higher education after his 1946 discharge; instead he briefly joined the State Department and later that year moved to the War

Department. Less than a year afterward, in 1947, he returned to State as successor to Alger Hiss as of Director of the Office of Special Political Affairs, coming under the wing of Under Secretary Dean Acheson and his boss, newly named Secretary George C. Marshall.

Serving in the State Department

Rusk served in his first State Department post for five years, his work involving United Nations and Far Eastern affairs. When Acheson became secretary of state, Rusk moved up to the critical post of assistant secretary of state for Far Eastern affairs three months before the North Korean Communists crossed the 38th parallel. In this crisis Rusk played a significant role in every Korean War decision: the armed American response; U.N. Security Council involvement; Seventh Fleet protection for Taiwan; and the recall of MacArthur.

In 1952 he accepted the presidency of the Rockefeller Foundation. This choice reflected Rusk's deep commitment to an international policy of old fashioned Christian morality. His frequent speeches and articles were always based on the self-help ethic, government non-intervention in citizens' lives, a dedication to peace through international organization, and the desire to help the world's impoverished peoples. Permeating all this was a quiet but unyielding anti-Communism which made him a strong supporter of Chiang Kai-shek's Republic of China and a vigorous advocate of containment of Communism as developed and interpreted under Acheson.

When the John F. Kennedy administration began its staffing, several choices were considered for the post of Secretary of State, including Adlai Stevenson and J. William Fulbright. After much consideration, President-elect Kennedy invited Rusk for a meeting in December 1960 and selected him immediately.

Thus began a career which would make Rusk Secretary of State during one of the most turbulent and contentious eras in American history and for a length of service exceeded only by one other secretary, Cordell Hull. From January 21, 1961, to January 20, 1969, Rusk served Presidents Kennedy and Johnson, two of the most different and difficult bosses any public servant ever had. As their principal foreign policy adviser, Rusk made it a cardinal rule never to disagree with his boss in public and never to deny him the benefit of his advice in private, however much it diverged from the president's own views.

Rusk was not as much at home with the New Frontier as he became in the Great Society. Such men as Ambassador John Kenneth Galbraith, who served Kennedy in India, and Arthur M. Schlesinger, Jr., a Kennedy special assistant, led the so-called Eastern Liberal Establishment in their suspicion of him. At meetings, Schlesinger reported, "Rusk would sit quietly by, with his Buddha-like face and halfsmile . . . ." It was also reported by Schlesinger that the president called all cabinet members by their first names, with the single exception of Rusk.

Rusk disapproved of the Bay of Pigs invasion and played an important part in scaling down American air cover, a factor which brought him blame from conservative quarters. He opposed an air strike against Russian offensive weapons in 1962 during the Cuban missile crisis, supporting the naval quarantine alternative ultimately adopted. In these instances he was, a biographer noted," . . . the good soldier. He opposed the operation, expressed his dissent to the President privately, and accepted the President's decision. . . ."

Vietnam War Ends Public Career

It was in the Vietnam War that Rusk's instincts and loyalties were most tested. Initially he strongly opposed Kennedy's introduction of ground troops to South Vietnam in 1961 and disapproved of the regime of President Ngo Dinh Diem. Yet his loyalty to the chief executive and his strong anti-Communism caused him to support the war unwaveringly from that time until he left office in 1969.

The succession of Lyndon B. Johnson to the presidency dramatically changed Rusk's relationship with the White House. This alteration is remarkably recorded by historian Henry Graff, who sat in on the weekly luncheons held by L.B.J. and his top advisers. Flanked by Rusk and Secretary of Defense Robert McNamara, President Johnson at these "Tuesday Cabinet" sessions wrote " . . . the scenario for the conduct of the war. . . ."

Johnson's contribution to the Vietnam War was to magnify American involvement and to treat North Vietnam as a logical bombing target. Both of these decisions were initially privately opposed by Rusk, although he would advocate them once the decision became public. The vast "Americanization" and militarization of the war moved its locus of responsibility to the Defense Department. Yet Rusk was still totally involved and, like McNamara and the president himself, his movements around the country were marked by well-publicized and frequently ugly demonstrations.

During his career Rusk achieved eminence while remaining a somewhat enigmatic and unassuming person, regardful of others and their ideas and unfailingly civil to all. One insightful observer, journalist Joseph Kraft, saw his secret in " . . . a quality native to the pious poor of the South, . . . a quality of respect."

His day to day conduct of foreign relations was praised for its technical competence, and he won the respect of the American foreign policy apparatus. Nevertheless, as his biographer asserts, "Inevitably, he will be remembered as the man who defended the long and unpopular war in Vietnam."

Back to Academia

Upon leaving office Rusk returned to his homeland as the Samuel H. Sibley Professor of International Law at the University of Georgia, a post he held until his death in 1994. That institution honored Rusk in the summer of 1996 with the dedication of a campus building constructed in his name. The Dean Rusk Hall became home to the Dean Rusk Center for International and Comparative Law and the Institute of Continuing Judicial Education. The Center, first established in 1977, was pledged to the service of state, national, and international leaders.

With characteristic reserve, the elder statesman resisted temptations to tinker with historians' assessments of his State Department career, insisting his collected papers at the University of Georgia, the Lyndon B. Johnson and John F. Kennedy Presidential Libraries, and the National Archives should be left to speak for themselves, "If anyone is interested. . ."

Instead, Rusk chose in his later years to spin an optimistic world view for his audiences, sprinkled with a folksy wisdom borne of his humble origins and years of public service. Speaking in 1985 at his alma mater following Davidson's dedication of a new program of international studies in his name, Rusk asserted a faith in the ultimate sanity and good sense of world leaders, "frail human beings" though they might be. Admitting, "I have never met a superman or a demigod," Rusk still preferred to believe that those holding the ultimate fate of humanity in their hands would act responsibly.

Closing his Davidson address, Rusk predicted, "You will not have many dull moments in the decades that lie ahead. I shall not be able to go with you on that journey, but I have no doubt about how it is going to come out. You are going to make it. In any event, you carry with you the best wishes and the blessings of an old man."

Further Reading

Warren I. Cohen *Dean Rusk* (1981) is the most complete account of Rusk's life and career. Much information can be gleaned from Henry Graff, *The Tuesday Cabinet* (1970); Arthur M. Schlesinger, Jr. *A Thousand Days* (1965); Lyndon B. Johnson, *The Vantage Point* (1971); and memoirs of other principals. Some of Rusk's writings and speeches appear in Ernest K. Lindley, ed., *The Winds of Freedom* (1963); *The Owens-Corning Lectures 1968-69* (1969); and Alva Myrdal, Arthur J. Altmeyer, and Dean Rusk, *America's Role in International Social Welfare* (1967).

Rusk shared his later views on the abilities of world leaders to transcend human frailties in an address at Davidson College entitled, "The Threat of Nuclear War," reprinted in 1986 in *Vital Speeches of the Day* (January 15, 1986). Information about the Dean Rusk Hall and personal papers resides on the Internet on a site maintained by the University of Georgia, at www.libs.uga.edu/russell/ruskdoc.html. □

Ernst August Friedrich Ruska

The German engineer Ernst August Friedrich Ruska (1906-1988) designed and built the first electron microscope, for which he was awarded the Nobel Prize in Physics in 1986.

The electron microscope, like many other complex technological developments based upon current scientific research, cannot be associated exclusively with a single inventor. In the early 1930s several laboratories were at work on a super-microscope that would use electron waves, instead of light waves, to magnify a microscopic specimen. However, it is generally agreed that the German engineer Ernst Ruska designed and built the first working electron microscopes (1931-1933). Ruska's contribution to the science of physics, and to its applications in the fields of biology and medicine, was recognized in 1986 when he was awarded the Nobel Prize along with two other pioneers of modern microscopy, Gerd Binnig and Heinrich Rohrer.

Ernst August Friedrich Ruska was born in Heidelberg, Germany, on December 15, 1906. His immediate family and his closest relatives were all involved with the sciences in academic settings and it was assumed that Ernst would enroll at a German university in order to pursue a degree in science. But Ruska, who had long been fascinated by the technological progress of the early 20th century, had other plans. He entered technical colleges in Munich and Berlin to study first aeronautics and then electrical engineering. Ruska was awarded a Doctorate degree by the Berlin Institute of Technology in 1934. The topic of his doctoral dissertation was electron optics and the technology of electron microscopy.

For the next decade Ruska worked in engineering research for several German firms and in 1944 he received his *Habilitation,* the highest degree offered by the German university system. After World War II Ruska held a number of distinguished posts in German universities, including the directorship of the Institute of Electron Microscopy, Fritz Haber Institute, West Berlin (1957-1988).

Beginning in 1939 he had received numerous prizes and awards from German and foreign institutions, culminating in the 1986 Nobel Prize for Physics. He was honored for his contributions to physics, electronic technology, microscopy, and medicine. Ruska died in West Berlin on May 30, 1988.

The electron microscope is a technological device that draws upon the work of modern physicists, and Ruska possessed the ability to move easily between the worlds of physics and electrical engineering. As a student he was fortunate to have had professors who encouraged him in research projects that brought him close to the frontiers of modern physics. The invention of the electron microscope could only have been successfully completed by someone who had a deep understanding of the theoretical and practical aspects of electricity.

Quantum mechanics supplied the theoretical basis for electron microscopy. This theory was developed early in the 20th century to explain small-scale physical events such as the motion of electrons. In 1924 the French physicist Louis de Broglie claimed that electrons moving at very high speeds have a wave-like nature. De Broglie's wave particle hypothesis opened the way for the establishment of wave mechanics in physics and suggested that a microscope might be built using electron waves. Because the wavelength of an electron is about 12,500 times smaller than the wavelength of visible light, an electron microscope is much more powerful than a magnifying system using ordinary light. Specifically, a visible light microscope magnifies an object up to 2,000 times its original size; an electron microscope, 1,000,000 times its original size.

The first order of business for a designer of an electron microscope is the construction of a set of "lenses" to focus the beam of electrons. In 1928 Ruska's professor, Max Knoll, assigned him this task. Within three years Ruska constructed an electron microscope using two specially-designed magnetic coils to focus the electron beam for the purposes of magnification. Ruska's primitive model of 1931 was able to magnify a mere 17 times, but it yielded a sharp image and proved that an electron microscope could be built.

Within a few days after Ruska announced his new microscope one of his German competitors, Reinhold Rüdenberg, applied for several patents covering electromagnetic and electrostatic magnification of electron beams. Although Ruska was forestalled from obtaining the first patent for his invention this did not stop him from embarking upon plans to develop a commercial model of an electron microscope. By 1938 Ruska, working with a team at the Siemens electrical company, had constructed prototype electron microscopes capable of magnifying 30,000 times.

As the electron microscope moved towards commercialization and eventual mass-production, there were several problems that had to be overcome. First, there was the need to improve the magnification and resolution of the instrument in order to produce sharp images that revealed the fine details of the specimen under observation. Second, it was necessary to devise ways to expose biological specimens in the electron microscope without their being de-stroyed. The intense electron beam incinerated samples of living matter placed in its path.

Solutions to these and other problems were undertaken by Ruska, but groups of physicists, biologists, and engineers in Europe and America joined in the work of improving electron microscopes. These groups refined the electron microscope, making it a standard instrument in advanced laboratories of biology, medical science, metallurgy, and crystallography. Although the modern electron microscope has been put to many different uses, it has proved to be crucial in the investigation of the cellular structures of living material.

Further Reading

Some information on Ernst Ruska can be found in Frank N. Magill, *The Nobel Prize Winners: Physics,* volume 3 (1989) and in Bertram Schwarzschild, "Physics Nobel Prize Awarded for Microscopes Old and New," *Physics Today* (January 1987). Dennis Gabor, *The Electron Microscope* (1944); L. Marton, *Early History of the Electron Microscope* (1968); and Peter W. Hawkes, editor, *The Beginnings of Electron Microscopy* (1985) cover the history of electron microscopy and Ruska's contributions to its development. □

John Ruskin

The English critic and social theorist John Ruskin (1819-1900) more than any other man shaped the esthetic values and tastes of Victorian England. His writings combine enormous sensitivity and human compassion with a burning zeal for moral value.

John Ruskin's principal insight was that art is an expression of the values of a society. Though he sometimes applied this insight in a narrow—even a bigoted—way, it nevertheless gave him an almost messianic sense of the significance of art to the spiritual wellbeing of a nation. Ruskin awakened an age of rapid change, uncertain taste, and frequently shoddy workmanship to the meaning of art. But because art was for Ruskin the evidence of society's underlying state of being, he gradually turned his attention, with a reformer's zeal, more and more from art to the transformation of society itself. Though his prose tracts were much abused, they were important and influential contributions to radical criticism of the dominant social and political philosophy of the age. Ruskin's art criticism found the most likely focus to interest a people whose leading concerns were more moral than esthetic.

Ruskin was born on Feb. 8, 1819, in London. His parents were of Scottish descent and were first cousins. His father was a well-to-do wine merchant with a fondness for art. His mother was stern and devout. Both parents lavished attention and supervision on their only child, recognizing his precociousness, but Ruskin's childhood was isolated and his education irregular. He was encouraged in reading, however, and received some instruction in art. In 1837 Ruskin matriculated at Christ Church, Oxford, but his studies were interrupted by ill health and consequent travel abroad so that he did not receive his degree until 1842.

"Modern Painters"

Ruskin had early begun to write both poetry and prose, and by the time he left Oxford he had already published articles on architecture and on other subjects. After leaving Oxford, he undertook his first major work, *Modern Painters;* it testified to his love of nature, especially of Alpine scenery, and to his reverence for J.M.W. Turner as the supreme modern interpreter of "truth" in landscape. The first volume of *Modern Painters,* published anonymously in 1843, was a success with the discerning public, but it was attacked by professionals, who spotted the author's tendency to dogmatize on an insufficient foundation of experience and technical study. Ruskin then set about to remedy his deficiencies through a firsthand study of the Italian painters, particularly those of the Florentine and Venetian schools. Ruskin's Italian tour of 1845 culminated in his discovery of Tintoretto, who, together with Fra Angelico, displaced Turner to become the heroes of volume 2 of *Modern Painters* (1846).

In 1848 Ruskin married Euphemia Chalmers Gray. The parents of the bridal couple were old friends, and the match was arranged without any bond of deep affection on either side. Ruskin and his bride honeymooned in Normandy, where he studied the Gothic cathedrals. The pair, unfortunately, were not suited to one another, and the marriage was annulled in 1854. Euphemia Ruskin had by then fallen in love with the painter John Everett Millais, whom she subsequently married.

Architectural Criticism

The weight of Ruskin's interest had now shifted to architecture as the most public of the arts. If, as Ruskin thought, all art expresses the spirit of its maker, architecture then most fully expresses the whole spirit of a people. His religious emphasis was implicit in the title of his next book, *The Seven Lamps of Architecture* (1849), as well as in his emphasis upon "truth of expression" in materials and in structure. This book and its successor, *The Stones of Venice* (1851-1853), a great Protestant prose epic of the decline and fall of the Venetian Republic, became the bibles of the Victorian Gothic revival. Ruskin's style in this period was powerfully evocative and readily expanded into sermonic flourishes that cloaked many historical inaccuracies. Once again professionals, though fascinated by his works, were moved to demur on many points where theory had replaced a concrete knowledge of the facts of architectural practice. Perhaps Ruskin's most enduring contribution to the development of modern style was his hostility to classicism. He himself was too devoted to ornament and too hostile both to the machine and to standardized construction ever to figure as a grandfather of functionalism. However, his celebrated chapter on the nature of Gothic in *The Stones of Venice* can be taken as the main testament of Victorian esthetic values.

Social Criticism

Ruskin had interrupted the composition of *Modern Painters* for his architectural studies. He now returned to the

earlier work, completing it with volumes 3 and 4 in 1856 and volume 5 in 1860. He also lectured on art and defended the Pre-Raphaelites, but his concerns were inevitably drifting further toward social criticism as a way of transforming society. In reality, he had dropped the integument of art from his sermons, and following the lead of Thomas Carlyle, he began to inveigh directly against the values of the political economists. The year 1860 marks the official turning point in his interests, for Ruskin published a series of social essays in the *Cornhill Magazine* that he later collected as *Unto This Last.* Ruskin's attack on the dehumanized ethic of modern industrial capitalism drew a bitter response from readers, but it influenced the thinking of many reformers in the developing Labour movement.

Another series of articles on economic subjects, published in *Fraser's Magazine* (1862-1863) and collected as *Munera pulveris* (1872), drew a similar outcry from the public. Ruskin now began to lecture frequently, and he later published two collections derived from his lectures, *Sesame and Lilies* (1865) and *The Crown of Wild Olive* (1866). Both volumes circulated widely and brought him a popular following. In 1869 Ruskin was appointed the first Slade professor of art at Oxford, a post that he held with some interruption until 1885. These years, however, were turbulent and troublesome for Ruskin. His religious faith had been undermined, and he was tormented by frustrated love for Rose LaTouche, a girl 30 years his junior, whom he had first met when she was a child.

Last Years

On the death of his father Ruskin became independently wealthy. The variety and fever of his activities were an indication of his deeply disturbed condition. In 1871 he began to publish *Fors clavigera,* a periodical that lasted until 1884. An attack on James McNeill Whistler in *Fors* in 1887 occasioned a celebrated libel suit which was decided against Ruskin. He also endowed and led a variety of welfare and socialist schemes, thereby consuming most of his inheritance. In 1878 Ruskin suffered his first clear attack of mental illness. Seizures recurred until 1888, when he fell victim to a severe mental breakdown which confined him to his house at Brantwood in the Lake District until his death. In lucid intervals between 1885 and 1889 Ruskin worked on his unfinished autobiography, *Praeterita,* one of the most moving and revealing of his works. He died on Jan. 20, 1900.

Further Reading

The standard biography of Ruskin is E. T. Cook, *The Life of John Ruskin* (2 vols., 1911). Important, more recent works are Derrick Leon, *Ruskin: The Great Victorian* (1949), and Joan Evans, *John Ruskin* (1954). The best introductions to Ruskin's thought and work are R. H. Wilenski, *John Ruskin: An Introduction to Further Study of His Life and Work* (1933), and John D. Rosenberg, *The Darkening Glass: A Portrait of Genius* (1961). The chapter on Ruskin in Graham Hough, *The Last Romantics* (1947), is very helpful. For intellectual and social background see G. M. Young, *Victorian England: Portrait of an Age* (1936; 2d ed. 1953), and Jerome Hamilton Buckley, *The Victorian Temper* (1951). □

Bertrand Arthur William Russell

The British mathematician, philosopher, and social reformer Bertrand Arthur William Russell, 3d Earl Russell (1872-1970), made original and decisive contributions to logic and mathematics and wrote with distinction in all fields of philosophy.

ertrand Russell was born at Ravenscroft, Monmouthshire, Wales, on May 18, 1872, into an aristocratic family with many distinguished and some eccentric members. By the time he was 4 years old, his parents were dead, and his paternal grandparents, overturning his parents' will specifying that the child be reared by two atheist friends, became his guardians. Russell's grandfather, Lord John Russell, twice prime minister to Queen Victoria, died 3 years later, and young Bertrand was left in the care of his grandmother, a lady of strict puritanical moral views who nevertheless gave him great affection and "that feeling of safety that children need."

Early Life and Education

Russell's early education was provided at home by tutors, and in retrospect he found his childhood a happy one. In adolescence, however, he experienced intense loneliness, relieved by "one of the great events of my life, as dazzling as first love." His brother introduced him to the *Elements* of Euclid. "I had not imagined there was anything so delicious in the world. From that moment until [Alfred North] Whitehead and I finished *Principia Mathematica,* when I was 38, mathematics was my chief interest and my chief source of happiness."

At Trinity College

When he was 18 years old, Russell entered Trinity College, Cambridge. Alfred North Whitehead was the first to sense Russell's extraordinary talent, and he quickly undertook to sponsor Russell among the Cambridge literati. In his second year at Cambridge Russell was elected to the Apostles, a weekly discussion group that since 1820 has included among its members many of the people of intellectual eminence at Cambridge. There he met and formed close friendships with, among others, G. Lowes Dickinson, G. E. Moore, and John McTaggart, and a little later with John Maynard Keynes and Lytton Strachey. Of his generation at Cambridge, Russell later wrote, "We believed in ordered progress by means of politics and free discussion."

After graduation Russell stayed on at Cambridge as a fellow of Trinity College and lecturer in philosophy. In 1916 he was dismissed because of a scandal over his conviction and fine for writing about the case of a conscientious objector in World War I. His association with Cambridge meant a great deal to Russell, and he was deeply wounded by its abrupt termination.

First Marriage and Mathematical Writings

In 1894, after overcoming the opposition of his family, Russell married an American girl, Alys Pearsall Smith. The first years of their marriage were largely spent traveling in Europe and in the United States, where Russell gave some lectures. From this period his first book, comprising a set of lectures on German socialism, and his fellowship dissertation, *An Essay on the Foundations of Geometry,* date. The latter work established Russell's reputation. The year 1900 was another turning point for Russell, for at the International Congress of Philosophy, he met Giuseppe Peano, the Italian mathematical theorist, and immediately saw the significance of Peano's work. Enormously stimulated, he began to rethink his own ideas about the fundamental notions of mathematics, and during the fall of 1900 he finished most of his first major work, *The Principles of Mathematics.* "Intellectually," he later wrote, "this was the highest point of my life."

A few years later Russell's views on mathematics deepened further, and he became "reluctantly convinced" that mathematics consists of tautologies. With Whitehead he undertook the enormous project of trying to show that mathematics—in particular, arithmetic, but in principle, all mathematics—was an extension of logic, that no underived concepts and no unproved assumptions need be introduced other than those of pure logic. The results were published as *Principia Mathematica* in three volumes (1910-1913). Russell and Whitehead each had to put up £50 toward publication costs. In spite of mistakes and later improvements, the work remains a landmark in the history of mathematics.

While serving a 6-month prison term in 1918 for writing an article about the British government and the American army that was judged libelous, Russell wrote his *Introduction to Mathematical Philosophy*. But Russell's interest was deflected from these abstract topics by the "vast suffering" caused by World War I; in the face of this tragedy his earlier work now seemed to him "thin and rather trivial." Increasingly thereafter, Russell's work showed a marked reformist bent. Seldom, indeed, has a philosopher shown such a sense of social responsibility.

Theory of Knowledge and Metaphysics

Russell's views in epistemology and metaphysics, though influential, show less originality than his work on logic and on social questions. His views in these fields constitute, in effect, refinements or further developments in the tradition of British empiricism. Following a principle that he called the supreme maxim in scientific philosophy, "Wherever possible substitute constructions out of known entities for inferences to unknown entities," Russell argued that one's own private sense-data were the things most directly known. In *Our Knowledge of the External World* Russell tried to show that physical objects are logical constructions out of actual and possible sense-data. In his *Analysis of Mind* (1921) Russell went still further to argue that from sense-data, regarded as neutral elements, one can construct both mind and matter.

In his *Inquiry into Meaning and Truth* and *Human Knowledge: Its Scope and Limits,* Russell offered provocative opinions about the ways truth claims can be assessed, and he outlined a set of principles for use in defending the validity of inductive reasoning.

Travel and Controversy

After World War I Russell visited China and the Soviet Union. Initially sympathetic to the Bolshevik Revolution, he quickly saw its threat to the value he prized above all others—liberty—and he wrote a book, *The Practice and Theory of Bolshevism,* that proved prophetic regarding the developing course of the Russian Revolution. Russell also stood three times for election to Parliament, each time unsuccessfully.

In 1927, with his second wife, Dora, Russell founded a progressive school at Beacon Hill. There he tested the educational theories propounded in his books *Education Especially in Early Childhood* and *Education and the Social Order* (1932).

In the late 1930s Russell lectured frequently in the United States, and in 1940 he was appointed to teach at the College of the City of New York. Immediately he was subjected to a barrage of criticism in the American press by clergymen and city officials. These worthies had been offended by Russell's advocacy, in *Marriage and Morals* (1929), of temporary marriages for college students. A New York Supreme Court judge voided Russell's appointment on the grounds that he was an alien and an advocate of sexual immorality.

In the wake of this scandal Russell was offered a lectureship by the Barnes Foundation in Merion, Pa. The lectures prepared for this position formed the basis of Russell's *History of Western Philosophy* (1945), perhaps his most widely circulated book. However, in 1943 Russell was summarily dismissed from his Barnes post under circumstances that enabled him to bring a successful suit for redress of grievances.

Radical Sage

In 1944 Russell returned to England and was reelected a fellow of Trinity College, Cambridge. Honors began to pour in upon him. He was made an honorary fellow of the British Academy in 1949, and in the same year he received the Order of Merit. In 1950 Russell won the Nobel Prize for literature, being cited for "his many-sided and significant writings, in which he appeared as the champion of humanity and freedom of thought."

Russell had abandoned his pacifism at the outset of World War II, but immediately thereafter he resumed his activities in the peace movement. He led the "Ban the Bomb" fight in England, taking part in a sit-down demonstration at the age of 89, for which he served a 7-day jail sentence. Russell tried to intervene in the Cuban missile crisis, and he vigorously opposed American involvement in Vietnam.

Russell was an essentially shy man, yet brilliant and witty in conversation. He had a remarkable capacity for friendship. Though unhappy in his first three marriages, he finally found, late in life, "ecstasy and peace" in his fourth marriage, to Edith Finch in 1952. Although frail in appearance, he was vigorous and active throughout most of his life, embroiled in social and political controversies to the very end. He died at Penrhyndendraeth, Wales, on Feb. 2, 1970.

Further Reading

Perhaps the most useful introduction to Russell's work is his *Basic Writings, 1903-1959,* edited by Robert E. Egner and Lester E. Dennon (1961), and his *My Philosophical Development* (1959). The most interesting accounts of his life are by Russell himself: a half-dozen earlier autobiographical essays were crowned by his *The Autobiography of Bertrand Russell* (3 vols., 1967-1969). Biographies include Alan T. Wood, *Bertrand Russell: The Passionate Sceptic* (1957), and Herbert Gottschalk, *Bertrand Russell: A Life* (1965). Russell published a great deal, and critical commentary on his work is considerable. An excellent bibliography is in Paul Schilpp, ed., *The Philosophy of Bertrand Russell* (1944; rev. ed., 2 vols., 1963), which also includes a large number of critical essays by eminent authors together with Russell's replies. □

Charles Edward Russell

Charles Edward Russell (1860-1941), American writer and reformer, was a leading Socialist and muckraker.

Charles Edward Russell was born in Davenport, Iowa, on Sept. 25, 1860, the son of the abolitionist editor of the *Davenport Gazette*. Charles learned newspaper skills and attended the St. Johnsbury (Vt.) Academy, from which he graduated in 1881. He then returned to become the *Gazette*'s managing editor. He later became an editor in Minneapolis and Detroit and then moved on to New York City. In 1894 he was city editor of Joseph Pulitzer's *World* and then a Hearst editor in New York and Chicago.

During his newspaper years Russell was interested in democratic politics; in Populist, single-tax, and other causes; and in music, theater, and poetry. In 1902 his health broke, and he left newspaper work. After traveling abroad, he returned to begin a literary career. His first book, *Such Stuff as Dreams* (1902), was a volume of verses. *Thomas Chatterton: The Marvelous Boy* (1908) retraced the writings and career of the English poet.

Meanwhile a literature of protest (muckraking) had appeared on the American scene, and Russell found himself part of it. *The Greatest Trust in the World* (1905) muckraked the beef trust in Chicago. In the popular magazines he effectively exposed a wide range of social evils, from New York church-owned slums to southern prison camps. *The Uprising of the Many* (1907) and *Lawless Wealth* (1908) summed up some of the reasons why he joined the Socialist party. His writings earned him a national reputation. He campaigned for governor, mayor, and U.S. senator in New York State. In 1916 he declined the Socialist party's presidential nomination.

Russell sided with the Allied Powers during World War I and was expelled from the Socialist party. An admirer of Woodrow Wilson, he became a member in 1917 of the American diplomatic mission to revolutionary Russia. *Unchained Russia* (1918), *After the Whirlwind* (1919), and *Bolshevism and the United States* (1919) were earnest but perishable efforts to interpret the revolution. *The Story of the Non-partisan League* (1920) and *The Outlook for the Philippines* (1922) were Russell's efforts to rejoin the reform movement. As early as 1912, he had begun his memoirs in *The Passing Show. Julia Marlowe: Her Life and Art* (1926) was an outgrowth of his interest in the arts, as was *The American Orchestra and Theodore Thomas* (1927), for which he won the Pulitzer Prize.

Russell was eventually reconciled with the right wing of the Socialist party. He was a member of Clarence Darrow's National Recovery Administration Review Board and a staunch defender of oppressed people. He died in Washington, D.C., on April 23, 1941.

Further Reading

Russell's autobiography, *Bare Hands and Stone Walls: Some Recollections of a Sideline Reformer* (1933), throws light on his causes and attitudes. He figures significantly in Louis Filler, *Crusaders for American Liberalism* (1939; new ed. 1950). □

Charles Marion Russell

Charles Marion Russell (1864-1926), American painter, left one of the most extensive and accurate pictorial records of the Old West.

Charles Marion Russell was born on March 19, 1864, in St. Louis, Mo., to a comfortable family. As he was hard to control, his parents sent him to military school in Burlington, N.J. In 1880 he left for Montana and for the next twelve years worked as a sheepherder and cowpuncher. In 1888 he spent six months with the Blood Indians in the Northwest Territory. All the while, he drew and painted, seldom selling his work, more often giving it away.

Starting in 1890-1891 in Lewiston, Mont., Russell began to sell his paintings; he also executed a mural for a bank there for which he received $25—the most money he had ever earned for a single work. In 1891 a bartender in Great Falls, Mont., contracted for all of Russell's work. The following year he ceased riding the range.

In 1896 Russell married, and in 1903 he established his studio in Great Falls. That year he went to New York City to sell some of his paintings. As a result of the trip, his pictures were published in *McClure's, Leslie's Illustrated Weekly,* and other magazines. By 1906 he was known throughout Montana, and his work was featured in the Mint in Great Falls, an old-time saloon that functioned as a museum. Russell's first major show in New York was held in 1911. By the early 1920s he was so successful that a single small painting could fetch a price of over $10,000. He was also a gifted writer, and his *Rawhide Rawlins Stories* are among the finest sagas in western literature. He died in Great Falls on Oct. 24, 1926.

Russell vividly caught the blood-stirring action of the Old West in his paintings of Native American war parties, brawling cowboys, Native American buffalo hunts, and bucking broncos. A *Tight Dally and a Loose Lattice* (1920) depicts the movement called the dally: the half hitch a cowboy took around his saddle horn after lassoing a steer. *Loops and Swift Horses Are Surer than Lead* (1916) portrays cowboys lassoing a bear which was chasing a pack of horses. In the *Holdup* (1899) Russell memorialized the last crime of the notorious outlaw Big Nose George—the holdup of a stagecoach. *When Horse Flesh Comes High* (1909) pictures a posse charging two outlaws who fire while crouching behind their horses.

Russell also executed many small bronze sculptures of cowboys, Native Americans, and animals and modeled a few small groups in wax. One of these, the *Poker Game* (ca. 1893), depicts a Chinese person, a cowboy, and a Native American sitting on the grass around a blanket on which the cards are placed.

Further Reading

A readable, anecdotal biography of Russell was written by his nephew: Austin Russell, *C.M.R., Charles M. Russell: Cowboy*

harles Taze Russell was born on Feb. 16, 1852, in Pittsburgh. His parents awed him at an early age with grim tales of hellfire and damnation. While helping his father build the family's chain of clothing stores, Russell began to question the validity of including the concept of eternal damnation in Christian dogma. Bible study, fascination with the Millerite, or Adventist, movement, and his own inability to reconcile hell with the Christian concept of mercy caused him to develop a personal theology which he began to teach others.

Unlike other Adventists, Russell believed that Christ's Second Coming might be invisible. When others were disappointed because Christ's much-predicted advent did not seem to occur in 1874, Russell, who believed it had happened invisibly, wrote *The Object and Manner of Our Lord's Returning.* He and a like-thinking Adventist, N. H. Barbour, published *Three Worlds or Plan of Redemption* (1877), which declared that a 40-year harvest of souls had begun which would end in 1914 with the termination of the time of the Gentiles and the coming of God's Kingdom. In 1879, having broken with Barbour, Russell started his magazine, *The Watch Tower and of Herald of Christ's Presence,* destined to become a major voice in religion in the United States and abroad. In ensuing years he wrote his major theological work, the six-volume *Studies in the Scriptures,* which served as the dogma for Russellites during his lifetime.

After 1900 Russell encountered agonizing problems. His wife, Maria Frances Ackley, left him in 1897, after 18 years of childless marriage, amid tension over her role as

Artist (1957); it is rather short on the paintings themselves. Beautifully illustrated and copiously annotated is the catalog of the Amon G. Carter Museum of Western Art, *Charles M. Russell: Paintings, Drawings, and Sculptures* (1966), which also includes a biographical essay.

Additional Sources

Hassrick, Peter H., *Charles M. Russell,* New York: Abrams; Washington, D.C.: National Museum of American Art, Smithsonian Institution, 1989.

Morris, Patricia M., *Charles M. Russell, man of the West,* Casper, WY: P.M. Morris, 1987.

Russell, Charles M. (Charles Marion), 1864-1926., *Trails plowed under,* New York: Doubleday, 1990, 1927.

Taliaferro, John, *Charles M. Russell: the life and legend of America's cowboy artist,* Boston: Little, Brown, 1996.

Tucker, Patrick T., b. 1854., *Riding the high country,* Seattle: Fjord Press, 1987. □

Charles Taze Russell

Charles Taze Russell (1852-1916), American religious leader, founded a sect known as Russellites or Millennial Dawnists, which provided the nucleus for the Jehovah's Witnesses sect.

associate editor of the *Watch Tower*. In 1903 she sued for divorce, and a scandalous case involving accusations of alleged affairs between Russell and women parishioners was dragged through the courts. In 1909 Russell moved his headquarters to Brooklyn, New York City. In 1911 the *Brooklyn Eagle* charged the "Pastor" with profiteering in the church's sale of "miracle wheat" to members, who were told it would produce fantastic yields. In 1914 the long-awaited end of the age of the Gentiles did not materialize, forcing Russell to revise his texts.

Russell was still popular in many quarters and was something of a hero to Zionists, whose cause he championed. He traveled widely to visit his many congregations and while in Texas on Oct. 31, 1916, died of a heart attack. His last request, to die in a toga, was adhered to by using Pullman sheets.

Further Reading

There is no standard biography of Russell, but he is discussed in a number of studies of Jehovah's Witnesses, some laudatory, some denunciatory, few balanced. Some useful sources are Milton S. Czatt, *The International Bible Students: Jehovah's Witnesses* (1933); Herbert Stroup, *The Jehovah's Witnesses* (1945); and William J. Whalen, *Armageddon around the Corner* (1962). □

Elizabeth Shull Russell

Through the efforts of Elizabeth Shull Russell (born 1913), laboratory mice populations—which include dozens of strains exhibiting particular characteristics that make them desirable for research—are available to scientists worldwide. Russell has also used the mice for her own ongoing research in mammalian genetics and the study of such conditions as hereditary anemias, muscular dystrophy, cancer, and aging.

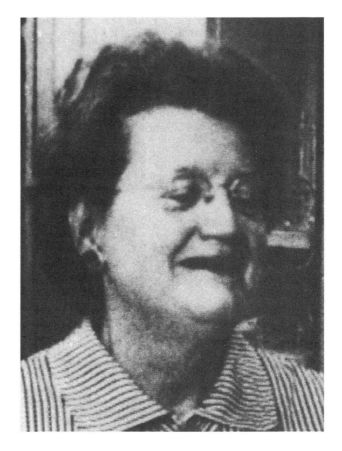

The Roscoe B. Jackson Laboratory in scenic Bar Harbor, Maine, has been the professional home of geneticist Elizabeth Shull Russell since the late 1930s. For the last five decades it has also been the birthplace of millions of laboratory mice which have been meticulously bred and characterized by Russell and the center's staff.

Russell was born on May 1, 1913, in Ann Arbor, Michigan. Her mother, Margaret Jeffrey Buckley, held a master's degree in zoology and was a teacher at Grinnell College in Iowa during an era when few women even attended college. Her father, Aaron Franklin Shull, was a zoologist and geneticist who taught at the University of Michigan. Both the Buckleys and the Shulls had scientists in their families. Elizabeth's uncle on her mother's side was a physicist, and on her father's side there was a geneticist, a plant physiologist and a botanical artist. Her parents met in 1908 when both attended a summer course at the laboratory in Cold Spring Harbor on Long Island, New York. It seemed quite natural that Russell became interested in the plants and animals in her surroundings; as a girl she carefully catalogued every flowering plant near their summer home.

Entering the University of Michigan at the age of sixteen, Russell graduated in 1933 with a degree in zoology. This was during the midst of the Great Depression, however, and few jobs were available teaching science. Upon hearing of a scholarship program at Columbia University, her father convinced her to participate in it. Russell's coursework at Columbia included genetics, which was to prove her greatest interest. She became influenced by a paper written by Sewall Wright of the University of Chicago, entitled "Physiological and Evolutionary Theories of Dominance." He proposed that the specific way in which characteristics are inherited must be from either the nucleic acids or proteins on the chromosomes (geneticists now know that inheritance is controlled by the nucleic acid DNA). Upon receiving her master's degree, Russell went to the University of Chicago where she obtained an assistantship and did further graduate work under Wright. Her doctoral thesis explored the effect of genes in the pigmentation of guinea pigs.

Russell received her Ph.D. at Chicago in 1937 and married a fellow graduate student, William L. Russell. They moved to Bar Harbor, Maine, when he was appointed to a position at the Roscoe B. Jackson Memorial Laboratory. As was the general practice of most institutions at the time, only one member of a family could be employed by the laboratory, so she was invited to work as an independent investigator, which she did from 1937 to 1946.

While pursuing her research, Russell spent much of her time at the laboratory working with precollege, college and graduate students that came to Jackson each summer. That first summer of 1937 she had twelve summer students. As several other members of the Jackson family were also named Elizabeth, she soon became known as Tibby, a name that stuck. Over the next several years, the Russells started a family. They would eventually have three sons and a daughter together.

Although Russell had begun her investigations into how a gene controls characteristics by using fruit flies, during the 1940s she helped build up a population of laboratory mice that could be used in researching many more genetic questions. She characterized each strain, whether it be by coat color or the presence of a hereditary disease. With great precision Russell managed the genetically controlled inbred populations, and in 1946 she officially became a member of the research staff. The following year, she and her husband divorced. Russell—with four young children—now pursued her career in earnest even as the lab was starting to appreciate her great potential as a researcher.

In October, 1947, a devastating fire spread across Bar Harbor, destroying the Jackson Laboratory. Almost one hundred thousand laboratory mice perished—animals which had been carefully bred by Russell and others. In the years following, however, the team helped to once again build up the mouse population.

One day in 1951, while studying the source of mouse skin pigmentation, Russell looked in a cage and observed a most unusual mouse, a female that was dragging its feet in a peculiar way. The mouse was not injured. It appeared that it was born with some kind of muscular defect and Russell named it "Funnyfoot." By breeding Funnyfoot's brothers and sisters, the same trait cropped up in subsequent generations, leading the team to conclude that Funnyfoot and her related offspring had a genetic disease similar in some ways to muscular dystrophy in humans. This particular fact became of great interest to other researchers working on muscular dystrophy. At once, scientists flooded the lab with requests for mice with the funnyfoot trait. There was a big problem, however—the funnyfoot females were unable to reproduce and the mice died young.

Russell devised a plan for breeding more funnyfoot mice, transplanting the ovaries of funnyfoot females into those of normal females without the characteristic. The ovaries contained egg cells (ova) in which the chromosomes carried the faulty gene. When the normal females mated, many funnyfoot offspring were produced, which were then sent to researchers. Alongside the cages of funnyfoot mice were many other strains that were meticulously bred by Russell and her team. Each group of mice and its ancestry were clearly labeled and recorded. Some strains, for instance, had hereditary diseases like anemia, while others had characteristics that made them sterile or prone to tumors. Other mice were to be used for research on blood disease, the immune system, the endocrine system, diabetes, nutrition, or aging.

By 1953, Russell was named staff scientific director at the Jackson Laboratory. The following year she organized a conference at the laboratory where—for the first time—scientists from around the globe were invited to contribute what they were studying about mammalian genetics and its relationship to cancer. The conference was a success and in 1957 Russell became senior staff scientist. The following year Russell was awarded a Guggenheim Fellowship to review what was currently known about mammalian physiological genetics; the grant provided time and money to compile all the current research in one place, resulting in reference material useful to scientists the world over.

During her directorship, Russell's responsibilities were twofold—to provide the research mice that helped support the lab financially and to work on her areas of interest. One very important area of research at the lab under Russell involved studying blood cells of mice, especially the cells which provide the immune response (the ability to fight off invading foreign substances). This research became very important in an era in which there were a growing number of organ transplants. These mice were used in experiments that determined when tissue is accepted or rejected by an organism.

Russell also took an avid interest in blood hemoglobin—a substance which carries oxygen to all parts of a mammal's body—and was especially curious about how the hemoglobins develop. A mammal fetus inside its mother (including humans) has hemoglobin from a very early stage; after birth, however, that hemoglobin changes both its structure and the site of its production. Some of Russell's work concerned the processes of these developmental changes.

Other research topics Russell investigated include different kinds of cancers, blood diseases, and the process of aging. She has written or collaborated on over a hundred scientific papers and several books. Since 1978, Russell has been senior staff scientist emeritus. Throughout her long active career, Russell's role has also been one of mentor to many of the students that have come through the Jackson Laboratory, either as permanent staff working together on biochemistry and microbiology or the many summer graduate students that come from all over the world.

Russell has been made a member of the American Academy of Arts and Sciences and the National Academy of Sciences. During the 1970s she was an active member of the Academy's Council, acting to edit and evaluate scientific papers. She was also a member of the Genetics Society of America, becoming its vice president in 1974 and president from 1975 to 1976. In 1983 she was made a member of the American Philosophical Society. Russell holds an honorary degree from Ricker College and was a trustee of the University of Maine and the College of the Atlantic. Because of her work on the aging of mice she was asked to be a member of the advisory council to the National Institute of Aging. By attending discussion groups at the laboratory, she continued to closely monitor trends in genetics research.

Further Reading

Noble, Iris, *Contemporary Women Scientists of America*, Messner, 1979, pp. 123–137.

Russell, Elizabeth Shull, *Telephone interview with Barbara A. Branca,* conducted February 18, 1994. □

James Earl Russell

An early 20th-century educator and college dean, James Earl Russell (1864-1945) from 1897 to 1927 developed Teachers College into the nation's leader in the advanced training of elementary and secondary school teachers, administrators, and supervisors.

James Earl Russell was born at Hamden, New York, to Charles and Sarah (McFarland) Russell on July 1, 1864. The only son and eldest of nine children, Russell grew up on a farm and attended the one-room country school in the community. Young Russell was never close to his struggling but unsuccessful father, but was very fond of his mother Sarah, who urged him to seek an education beyond the common school.

Because of limited funds, the only realistic choice of a secondary school was the Delaware Academy, a private school in nearby Delhi. It was here that Russell prepared for college. Although his personal relations with his teachers while at the academy were pleasant, Russell was later to remember his "academical training as a 'veritable nightmare' with considerable emphasis on learning the answers to former examinations." This early sensitivity to the "rigid formalism" of traditional secondary education was to influence Russell's later efforts to improve teaching at the secondary level.

College Studies Lead to Teaching Career

In 1883 Russell won the New York State Regents' scholarship for his district and enrolled at Cornell University, Ithaca, New York, in the face of some opposition from his home community, for "every good Scotch Presbyterian of the community protested . . . that I would turn out an infidel if allowed to go to Cornell." In the 1880s Cornell was regarded in some quarters as an extremely liberal institution. It was co-educational and the scientific studies were equated with the classical studies. Students were even allowed to select their own pattern of work through the elective system.

At Cornell Russell came under the influence of two great teachers—Jacob Gould Schurman and Benjamin Ide Wheeler. It was Schurman who introduced him to Locke's *Essay on Human Understanding,* and Wheeler, the philologist, gave Russell an appreciation of Greek life and literature. Both teachers left a lasting impression on the young scholar with their "radical concepts of education."

Russell took the A.B. degree in 1887 with first honors in philosophy and decided on teaching as a career. He taught preparatory Latin and Greek for three years and became headmaster of the Cascadilla School, a private academy in Ithaca, New York. While in Ithaca he became review editor of the *School Review,* an educational journal established by Schurman. His first contribution as editor was a summary of an article from the London *Journal of Education* on the education of teachers in Germany. As a result of this publication and other similar work on the *Review,* Russell began to be recognized as an authority on European education.

In 1893 Russell, becoming increasingly dissatisfied with the rigid formalism of American secondary education, resigned his position at Cascadilla and made plans to study in Germany. There he studied pedagogy with Wilhelm Rein at Jena and in 1894 went to Leipzig and took his Ph.D. under Volkelt in philosophy and Wilhelm Wundt in psychology. He also studied secondary schools in Germany, France, and England. Russell was to retain a lasting but favorable impression of the training given to German teachers and the way the German system of education prepared students for their roles in society. He was, however, fundamentally distrustful of the anti-democratic tendencies and the authoritarian character of Germany's system of universal education. In spite of these misgivings Russell returned to the United States in 1895 convinced that a high degree of professional training was necessary and desirable for teachers and that education was an important subject for study and research at the university level.

Back in the United States, Russell accepted a position as professor of philosophy and pedagogy at the University of Colorado. He remained there for two years expanding the university's program for teacher training. While in Colorado Russell was beginning to achieve a national reputation through his increasing activity in professional organizations and numerous publications.

Move to Teachers College

In 1897 Russell accepted an invitation to join the faculty of Teachers College in New York City as head of the Department of Psychology. The invitation had been extended by his old teacher Benjamin Ide Wheeler, who had temporarily accepted the presidency. Teachers College at that time was a struggling normal school whose loose affiliation with Columbia University was in danger of termination because of philosophical and jurisdictional disputes between the two institutions. To resolve the controversy, Russell offered an organizational plan in which Teachers College would become a professional school and a part of the university structure having the same rank as the law and medical schools. The president of Columbia was to become ex officio president of Teachers College. The plan was approved with some modification and the young educator, within three months of his arrival in New York, became dean of the newly structured school.

By 1900 Russell had developed a basic conception of professional education that would guide the school during its formative years. There would be four goals of teacher education: general culture (liberal education); special scholarship (the content area of teaching); professional knowledge (theory, psychology, and history of education); and technical skill (study and practice of pedagogy). Russell had returned from Europe recognizing that democracy requires a type of education closely linked to everyday life. Teacher education must not be confined to public education but must prepare leaders in such fields as nursing, scouting, adult education, rural education, and vocational education.

Important Contributions to Education

Very early Russell began to assemble a faculty of outstanding men and women still relatively unknown who would rise to national prominence in their respective fields. Among them were Edward L. Thorndike in psychology, David Snedden in educational sociology, Paul Monroe in history of education, George D. Strayer in educational administration, and William Heard Kilpatrick in philosophy of education. Although a member of Columbia's philosophy department, John Dewey lectured at Teachers College. Some have observed that Dewey's focus on educational liberalism, also found in Russell's philosophy, resulted in Teachers College becoming the "intellectual crossroads" of the Progressive movement.

Russell's strong convictions concerning the importance of research in education led to the establishment of two experimental schools: the Speyer School (1902) and the Lincoln School (1917). In 1921 the Institute of Educational Research was created to promote the scientific study of education in cooperation with several departments of Teachers College. Two other research institutes were established during Russell's tenure: the International Institute funded in 1923 by the International Education Board and the Institute of Child Welfare Research established in 1924.

Through Russell's leadership and efficient management, the enrollment of Teachers College grew from 169 students in 1897 to almost 5,000 in 1927. During this period the budget expanded tenfold and the physical plant grew from two buildings to 17.

Russell was married twice, first in 1889 to Agnes Fletcher, with whom he had four sons, and in 1929 to Alice Forman Wyckoff. When he retired as dean in 1927 he was succeeded by his son, William Franklin Russell.

Russell enjoyed a long and fruitful retirement. He was influential in organizing the American Association of Adult Education and served as its first president. A special avocational interest in the scientific breeding of cattle was maintained throughout his retirement. He remained active with the Boy Scouts, Girl Scouts, and 4-H clubs.

Russell died of cancer at the age of 81 in 1945. His ashes are buried in the cemetery at Lawrenceville, New Jersey.

Further Reading

Russell is listed in the *Dictionary of American Biography* (Supplement 3); *Biographical Dictionary of American Educators* (vol. 3); and *Who's Who in America,* (vol. 22, 1905). Two good critical treatments of Russell's contributions are found in Lawrence A. Cremin, David A. Shannon, and Mary Evelyn Townsend, *A History of Teachers College, Columbia University* (1954) and in Lawrence A. Cremin, *The Transformation of the School: Progressivism in American Education, 1876-1957* (1961). Numerous tributes to Russell appeared in *Teachers College Record* around the time of his retirement in 1927 and again at his death. A useful obituary filled with facts about his life and career appeared in the *New York Times* on Nov. 5, 1945.

Russell's numerous publications in periodicals and his *Annual Report of the Dean of Teachers College, 1898-1927* reveal much about his educational philosophy. Especially helpful are his books, which include *The Extension of University Teaching in England and America* (1895), *The Function of the University in the Training of Teachers* (1900), *German Higher Schools: The History, Organization, and Methods of Secondary Education in Germany* (1898), *Industrial Education* (1912), *The Trend in American Education* (1922), and *Founding of Teachers College* (1937). His last book, *Heredity in Dairy Cattle* (1945), reflected an avocational interest in the breeding of dairy cattle. □

John Russell

The English statesman John Russell, 1st Earl Russell of Kingston Russell (1792-1878), was the author of the Great Reform Bill of 1832 and one of the founders of the British Liberal party.

John Russell was born on Aug. 18, 1792, in London. He was the third son of the 6th Duke of Bedford. Russell was educated primarily by private tutors and at Edinburgh University.

Russell's parliamentary career began in 1813, when he was elected Whig member of Parliament for Tavistock. In poor health during his early parliamentary career, Russell rarely spoke in the Commons. His vanity was great, and he was easily disturbed by criticism. But he was a man of courage and conviction. In the 1820s he emerged as a champion of parliamentary reform and religious toleration. He worked for repeal of the Test and Corporation Acts and supported Catholic emancipation in 1829.

Russell was largely responsible for preparing the first Reform Bill and introduced it in the Commons in March 1831; the bill passed the Lords in June 1832. Russell was a member of the Whig Cabinets of Lords Grey and Melbourne in the 1830s, first as home secretary and then as secretary for war and the colonies (1839-1841). The Municipal Corporation Act of 1835, which expanded the electorate for town councils, was one of his contributions.

After the fall of Sir Robert Peel's second ministry in 1846 Russell became prime minister. He held this office for the next 6 years (1846-1852). During this period he faced the Great Famine in Ireland, but his relief measures were too cautious to succeed. The Ten Hours Act of 1847 was a turning point in the history of labor legislation. Russell sympathized with the popular outcry against the papal bull that restored a Roman Catholic hierarchy in England in 1850, and he sponsored the Ecclesiastical Titles Bill (1851), which forbade the assumption by Roman Catholic clergy of titles within the United Kingdom. A more liberal attitude characterized his actions in imperial affairs. The Australian Colonies Act of 1850 extended self-government to New South Wales.

Lord Palmerston was the most controversial figure in the Russell Cabinet, and relations between the two were frequently strained. Palmerston was dismissed by Russell in December 1851 for having conveyed to the French ambassador Russell's approval of Louis Napoleon's coup d'etat. Two months later, however, Palmerston had his revenge when he successfully led the opposition in defeating the government's Militia Bill, and Russell resigned in 1852.

Russell served as foreign secretary for a few months in 1852-1853 in Lord Aberdeen's coalition and as colonial secretary for 5 months in Palmerston's Cabinet in 1855. He returned to the Foreign Office 4 years later in the second Palmerston ministry (1859-1865) and did much to preserve British neutrality during the American Civil War. Russell became prime minister for a second time in 1865, but he resigned the following year in a dispute over the specifics of a second Reform Bill. He then retired to a private life of writing, and he died on May 28, 1878.

Russell was known as "Finality Jack" to the British working classes, as one who opposed all further reform after 1832. This, however, was not true. He was active in the reform movement to the end of his life, and he helped to move the Whigs toward the new Liberal party under his immediate successor as party leader, William Gladstone.

Further Reading

The standard biography of Russell is Spencer Walpole, *Life of Lord John Russell* (2 vols., 1889; repr. 1968). A more recent, concise study is A. Wyatt Tilby, *Lord John Russell: A Study in Civil and Religious Liberty* (1930). Norman Gash, *Politics in the Age of Peel* (1953), is a penetrating study of the machinery of politics during the period of Russell's activities. □

John Brown Russwurm

John Brown Russwurm (1799-1851), African American and Liberian journalist, educator, and governor, was co-editor of the first African American newspaper. After he emigrated to Africa, he became governor of Maryland-in-Liberia.

John Russwurm was born on Oct. 1, 1799, in Jamaica, British West Indies, of a Creole woman and a white American father. When his father returned to the United States in 1807, the boy was sent to Canada for schooling. His father's new wife brought John to their Maine home and insisted that he be fully educated. He graduated from Bowdoin College in 1826, one of the first two blacks to graduate from any college.

Russwurm declined a position in Liberia and in 1827 joined Samuel Cornish, another free black, to edit *Freedom's Journal*, the first newspaper published by and for blacks. At first, following Cornish's lead and in line with the opinions of most articulate free blacks, the paper opposed the American Colonization Society (ACS), sponsor of Liberia as a home for blacks. When Cornish left, Russwurm began shifting editorial policy concerning emigration. In February 1829 he announced support for colonization; antagonistic black subscribers let the newspaper die and heaped verbal abuse on Russwurm. By the end of the year he had settled in Liberia.

In 1830 Russwurm became superintendent of schools, and he also edited the *Liberia Herald*. Elected to office by the Liberian settlers, he served as secretary of the colony until ACS officials in the United States dismissed him in 1836. Angered by this refusal to let black men govern themselves, he left Monrovia and became governor of Maryland-in-Liberia, the African settlement sponsored by the Maryland Colonization Society.

Russwurm governed the colony from 1836 until 1851, ruling wisely although with a strong hand. He enabled the colony to survive by keeping peace with surrounding Africans. He found remedies for problems of finance, trade, agriculture, justice, representative government, and relations with American supporters of the colony. After Liberia became an independent republic in 1847, Russwurm worked to unite the two settlements, but differences between the settlers and between their two supporting societies in the United States prevented unification until after his death.

Russwurm was a man of administrative ability and intellectual accomplishment. He had a proud sense of destiny for the African race, maintaining that they were equals of all men and should govern themselves. He left a clear mark on African American history. Like other black nationalists, he despaired of gaining equality in the United States and rejected that nation for Africa. He died on June 17, 1851.

Further Reading

Mary Sagarin, *John Brown Russwurm* (1970), is a full, carefully researched biography. Accounts of Russwurm's Liberian career are in John H. B. Latrobe, *Maryland in Liberia* (1885), and Charles H. Huberich, *The Political and Legislative History of Liberia* (2 vols., 1947). His early life is briefly described in Nehemiah Cleaveland, *History of Bowdoin College,* edited by Alpheus Spring Packard (1882). Background on the attitudes of free blacks concerning emigration to Africa is in Howard Holman Bell, *A Survey of the Negro Convention Movement, 1830-1861* (1953; repr. 1969). □

Bayard Rustin

The pacifist Bayard Rustin (1910-1987) was committed to nonviolent strategies for working toward racial equality and economic justice. He worked through a variety of groups organizing demonstrations for civil rights and for peace.

One of 12 children, Bayard Rustin was born on March 17, 1910, in West Chester, Pennsylvania, a small town near Philadelphia where the Quakers had established a colony of Black freedmen before the Civil War. Raised by his grandparents, he acquired a gourmet appreciation of fine food from his grandfather, a caterer, and a lifelong commitment to nonviolence and racial equality from his grandmother, a dedicated member of the Society of Friends and local leader of the National Association for the Advancement of Colored People (NAACP). After graduating from West Chester High School as an honor student and three-letter star athlete, he drifted about the United States doing odd jobs and periodically studying history and literature at Cheney State Teachers College and Wilberforce University. In the mid-1930s, seeking an organization that shared his opposition to war and racism, he joined the Young Communist League (YCL). In 1938 he moved to Harlem as an organizer for the league, enrolling in the City College of New York and earning his livelihood by singing in nightclubs with Josh White and Huddie Ledbetter ("Leadbelly").

In 1941 Rustin left the YCL and began a 12-year association with the Fellowship of Reconciliation (FOR), a pacifist, religious organization devoted to solving world problems through nonviolent means. As the FOR youth secretary, and then as director of its Department of Race Relations, Rustin served as an organizer for A. Philip Randolph's 1941 March on Washington. The demonstration convinced President Franklin D. Roosevelt to issue Executive Order 8802, which stipulated that all employers and unions with government defense contracts must cease racial discrimination and es-

tablished a Committee on Fair Employment Practices to enforce the order. The following year, with James Farmer, he helped to form the Congress of Racial Equality (CORE) to challenge Jim Crow by nonviolent direct action. A conscientious objector to military service, Rustin was imprisoned for resisting the draft in 1943 and served nearly two and a half years in the Ashland Correction Institute and Lewisburg Penitentiary.

After the end of World War II Rustin became chairman of the Free India Committee and later went to India to study the Gandhi movement's nonviolent civil disobedience. In 1947 he organized a Journey of Reconciliation to 15 cities in the South to publicize segregation in interstate transportation and to encourage African Americans to insist on the rights they had won in the courts. Arrested in North Carolina, Rustin served 22 days on a chain gang. (Two years later North Carolina abolished chain gangs.) In 1948 he directed A. Philip Randolph's Committee Against Discrimination in the Armed Forces, which helped to persuade President Harry S. Truman to issue an executive order banning racial segregation in the military.

Early in the 1950s Rustin became active in the movement of African nationalists seeking independence from European colonialism and also headed the pacifist War Resisters League. As a peace activist he mobilized the first Aldermaston march for nuclear disarmament in England and joined a ban-la-bombe march in the Sahara to protest the first French nuclear-test explosion.

Joining Martin Luther King, Jr. first in the 1955 bus boycott in Montgomery, Alabama, Rustin served for a half dozen years as a special assistant to King and played a major role in planning the establishment of the Southern Christian Leadership Conference (SCLC). A master logistician, Rustin organized many of the key civil rights demonstrations of the late 1950s and early 1960s, and A. Philip Randolph again turned to him to orchestrate the massive March on Washington for Jobs and Freedom of August 28, 1963, which brought nearly a quarter of a million Americans to the Lincoln Memorial to petition for African American rights. In 1964, in the largest civil rights demonstration ever, he mobilized a boycott of the New York City public schools to protest racial imbalance. The eruption of violent race riots in the African American ghettoes of the nation and the emergence of the Black Power movement in the mid-1960s, however, forced Rustin from the forefront of African American protest and demonstrations.

After 1966 Rustin used his presidency of the A. Philip Randolph Institute to promote his Democratic-Socialist politics, particularly his belief that African American progress depends on a political coalition of African Americans and progressive whites united in their support of "A Freedom Budget for All Americans." This was designed to cure the basic economic ills of the nation through federal programs for full employment, the abolition of slums, and the reconstruction of the educational system. Elegant in diction and dress, with the poise and manners of an aristocrat, Rustin was a connoisseur of African art and European antiques. He was the author of *Down the Line* (1971), *Strategies for Freedom* (1976), and *Which Way Out? A Way Out of the Exploding Ghetto* (1967). Rustin received numerous honors, including the Eleanor Roosevelt Award, Liberty Bell Award, Eugene V. Debs Award, Howard University Law School J.F.K. Award, and Man of the Year Award from the Pittsburgh chapter of the NAACP. He also chaired such notable organizations as the Social Democrats, U.S.A.; the Leadership Conference on Civil Rights; and the Black Americans to Support Israel Committee.

In his nearly half a century struggle for peace, civil rights, and economic justice, Rustin was arrested more than 20 times. He never softened his principles. As late as 1980 he said, "You cannot give respectability to one terrorist group [meaning the Palestine Liberation Organization] without other groups benefiting from that respectability." Rustin died in New York City of a heart attack August 24, 1987.

Further Reading

Although Bayard Rustin has not yet been the subject of a full biography, many of his protest activities are chronicled in Jervis Anderson, *A. Philip Randolph* (1972); August Meier and Elliot Rudwick, *CORE: A Study in the Civil Rights Movement, 1942-1968* (1973); David L. Lewis, *King* (1970); and Harvard Sitkoff, *The Struggle for Black Equality, 1954-1980* (1981). His own views are best expressed in his books *Which Way Out? A Way Out of the Exploding Ghetto* (1967); *Down the Line* (1971); and *Strategies for Freedom* (1976). □

George Herman Ruth Jr.

George Herman Ruth, Jr. (1895-1948), American baseball player, was the sport's all-time champion, its greatest celebrity, and most enduring legend.

Geoorge Herman Ruth was born on Feb. 6, 1895, in Baltimore, one of eight children of a saloonkeeper. Judged as incorrigible at the age of 7, Ruth was committed to the St. Mary's Industrial School for Boys, where he learned baseball from a sympathetic monk. His left-handed pitching brilliance prompted Jack Dunn of the Baltimore Orioles to adopt him in 1914 to secure his release. That same year Dunn sold him to the American League Boston Red Sox. Ruth pitched on championship teams in 1915 and 1916, but his hitting soon marked him as an outfielder. In 1919 his 29 home runs set a new record and heralded a new playing style. Baseball had been dominated by pitching and offense; by 1920 Ruth's long hits inaugurated the "big bang" style.

In 1920 Babe Ruth was sold to the New York Yankees for $100,000 and a $350,000 loan. This electrifying event enhanced his popularity. His feats and personality made him a national celebrity. An undisciplined, brawling wastrel, he earned and spent thousands of dollars. By 1930 he was paid $80,000 for a season, and his endorsement income usually exceeded his annual income.

Ruth led the Yankees to seven championships, including four World Series titles. He was the game's perennial home run champion, and the 60 he hit in 1927 set a record for the 154-game season (Roger Maris hit 61 home runs in 1961, but on the extended game schedule). His lifetime total of 714 home runs is unsurpassed. With a .342 lifetime batting average for 22 seasons of play, many rate him the game's greatest player.

When his career ended in 1935, Ruth's reputation as being undisciplined frustrated his hopes of becoming a major league manager. In 1946 he became head of the Ford Motor Company's junior baseball program. He died in New York City on Aug. 16, 1948.

Further Reading

So much has been written about Ruth, both in his lifetime and since his death, that it is surprising to find no adequate biography of him. A popular biography of his playing career is by sportswriter Thomas Meany, *Babe Ruth: The Big Moments of the Big Fellow* (1947). Also useful is Ruth's *The Babe Ruth Story as Told to Bob Considine* (1948). An intimate, iconoclastic account of Ruth's personal life was written by his wife, Claire M. Ruth (with Bill Slocum), *The Babe and I* (1959). A Pulitzer Prize—winning sketch of Ruth, written at the height of his career, is included in Laurence Greene, *The Era of Wonderful Nonsense: A Casebook of the Twenties* (1939). Ruth's impact on baseball history is assessed in David Q. Voigt, *American Baseball* (2 vols., 1966-1970). □

Ernest Rutherford

The British physicist Ernest Rutherford, 1st Baron Rutherford of Nelson (1871-1937), discovered transmutation of the elements, the nuclear atom, and a host of other phenomena to become the most prominent experimental physicist of his time.

In searching for an experimental physicist to compare with Lord Rutherford, it is natural to think of Michael Faraday. Like Faraday, Rutherford instinctively knew what experiments would yield the most profound insights into the operations of nature; unlike Faraday, however, Rutherford established a school of followers by training a large number of research physicists. One of his colleagues observed that Rutherford always appeared to be on the "crest of the wave." Rutherford, with no sense of false modesty, replied, "Well! I made the wave, didn't I?" Then, after a moment's reflection, he added, "At least to some extent." Most physicists would agree that it was to a very large extent.

Ernest Rutherford was born on Aug. 30, 1871, in Spring Grove (Brightwater), near Nelson, New Zealand. His father, a Scot, was a wheelwright, farmer, timberman, and large-scale flax producer. Rutherford attended Nelson College, a secondary school (1886-1889), and then studied at Canterbury College in Christchurch, receiving his bachelor's de-

gree in 1892. The following year he took his master's degree with honors in mathematics and physics.

First Research

Rutherford's interest in original research induced him to remain at Canterbury for an additional year. Using the rather primitive research facilities available to him, he proved that iron can be magnetized by the rapidly oscillating (and damped) electric field produced during the discharge of a Tesla coil. This indicated that electromagnetic (Maxwellian or Hertzian) waves might be detectable if they were allowed to demagnetize a magnetized wire, and by the end of 1894 he was sending and receiving these "wireless" signals in the laboratory.

In 1895 Rutherford arrived in Cambridge, where he became the first research student to work under J. J. Thomson at the Cavendish Laboratory. He improved his earlier instrumentation and was soon transmitting and receiving electromagnetic signals up to 2 miles' distance, a great achievement in those days. Thomson asked Rutherford to assist him in his own researches on the x-ray—induced conduction of electricity through gases. Within a year these studies led Thomson to his discovery of the electron.

Rutherford then explored still another recent find, A. H. Becquerel's 1896 discovery of radioactivity. Rutherford soon determined that the uranium rays were capable of ionizing gases. He also discovered something new, namely, that uranium emits two different types of radiation, a highly ionizing radiation of low penetrating power, which he

termed alpha radiation, and a much lower ionizing radiation of high penetrating power, which he termed beta radiation.

Rutherford remained with Thomson at the Cavendish Laboratory until 1898; he was therefore extremely fortunate in being at precisely the right place at precisely the right time. His scientific horizons broadened enormously during these years; and his confidence increased greatly owing to Thomson's open recognition of his exceptional ability.

Radioactive Transformations

Rutherford's first professorship was the Macdonald professorship of physics at McGill University in Montreal. In 1900 he married Mary Newton; the following year their only child, Eileen, was born.

Concerning research, Rutherford knew precisely the area he wished to study: radioactivity. On his suggestion, R. B. Owens, a young colleague in electrical engineering, had prepared a sample of thorium oxide to study the ionizing power of thorium's radiations. Owens found, oddly enough, that the ionization they produced apparently depended upon the presence or absence of air currents passing over the thorium oxide. Nothing similar had ever been observed with uranium. It was this mystery that Owens, going on vacation, left for Rutherford to solve.

Rutherford designed a series of masterful experiments from which he concluded that thorium somehow produces a gas, which he called "thorium emanation." It was this gas that Owens's air currents had transported, thereby influencing the recorded ionization. Rutherford also found that any thorium emanation produced soon disappeared before his very eyes! By passing some thorium emanation through a long tube at a constant rate, Rutherford discovered that half the amount present at any given time disappeared ("decayed") roughly every minute—its "half-life." He also found that, if thorium emanation came into contact with a metal plate, the plate would acquire an "active deposit" which also decayed but which had a half-life of roughly 11 hours. Further studies revealed that pressure or other external conditions did not influence these half-lives. In addition, the "activities" of the substances as a function of time decayed exponentially, which Rutherford realized was possible only if the activity was directly proportional to the number of "ions" (atoms) present at any given time. In this way Rutherford discovered the first known radioactive gas, thorium emanation, and explored its behavior.

In 1900 Rutherford was joined by Frederick Soddy, a member of McGill's chemistry department. Together they resolved to isolate the sources of thorium's radioactivity by chemical separation techniques. By the end of 1901 their most important conclusions were, first, that thorium emanation is an inert gas like argon and, second, that thorium emanation is produced, not by thorium directly, but by some unknown, and apparently chemically different, element which they termed "thorium X." This was a key insight into the understanding of radioactivity, for it suggested that one element, thorium, can decay into a second element, thorium X, which in turn can decay into a third element, thorium emanation.

Item after item now fell into place. Soddy, turning from thorium to uranium, found that it decayed into a new radioactive element, "uranium X." Next, Rutherford came to understand the crucial fact that each radioactive transformation is accompanied by the *instantaneous* emission of a single alpha or beta particle. Rutherford also proved by a simple calculation that in radioactive transformations enormous quantities of energy are released, which, he argued could be derived only from an internal atomic source.

Although some links were still missing, Rutherford's revolutionary theory of radioactive transformations was essentially complete by early 1904. He summarized the results of all of his own researches, as well as those of the Curies and other physicists, in his Bakerian lecture, "The Succession of Changes in Radioactive Bodies," of May 19, 1904, which he delivered before the Royal Society of London. In this lecture, one of the classics in the literature of physics, he presented the complete mathematical formulation of his theory, identified the four radioactive series—uranium, thorium, actinium, and radium (neptunium)—and established the principle, albeit tacitly, that any radioactive element can be uniquely identified by its half-life.

Rutherford also delivered a lecture at the Royal Institution in which he dwelled at some length on an important consequence of his theory—its implications for the age of the earth. He realized that lead, a stable element, is the end product of each radioactive series. This meant that, by determining the relative amounts of, say, uranium and lead in a sample of rock, its age can be calculated—which is the basis of the radioactive dating method.

Rutherford's researches attracted a number of scientists to McGill. His activities there—teaching, experimenting, writing his famous book *Radioactivity*—were prodigious. Recognition came to Rutherford early: he was elected a Fellow of the Royal Society in 1902, was awarded the society's Rumford Medal in 1905, and delivered the Yale University Silliman Lectures and received his first honorary degree in 1906. In 1908 he received the Nobel Prize—in *chemistry!* Rutherford later remarked that he had in his day observed many transformations of varying periods of time, but the fastest he had ever observed was his own from physicist to chemist. He refused to disappoint the Nobel Committee, however, and titled his Nobel lecture "The Chemical Nature of the Alpha-Particles from Radioactive Substances."

Nuclear Atom and Artificial Transmutations

In 1907 Rutherford arrived at the University of Manchester to succeed Sir Arthur Schuster as Langworthy professor of physics. Rutherford seems to have enjoyed teaching at Manchester more than at McGill. As he later wrote to his friend B.B. Boltwood of Yale University: "I find the students here regard a full professor as little short of Lord God Almighty.... It is quite refreshing after the critical attitude of Canadian students."

By early 1908 Rutherford was ready to test some new ideas. One of the first questions he wanted to settle was the nature of alpha particles. He devised a very simple scheme for capturing alpha particles, from purified radium emanation, in a glass enclosure. There the alpha particles acquired free electrons and formed a gas which spectroscopic analysis proved to be helium. This work took on much broader significance as a result of another observation, namely, that alpha particles can be scattered by various substances. His coworkers, H. Geiger and E. Marsden, allowed alpha particles to strike various metal foils (for example, gold and platinum) and counted that between 3 and 67 alpha particles per minute—or about 1/8000 of those present in the incident beam—were scattered backward, that is, through more than a right angle.

Two years elapsed before Rutherford achieved the insights necessary for a satisfactory explanation of Geiger and Marsden's experiments. He had to realize that the alpha particle is not of atomic dimensions but that it can be considered to be a point charge in scattering theoretical calculations and that the number of electrons per atom is relatively small—on the same order of magnitude, numerically speaking, as the atom's atomic weight. He also had to realize the extreme improbability of obtaining Geiger and Marsden's results if the alpha particle was multiply scattered by presumably widely separated electrons in the atom, as a 1904 atomic model, as well as a 1910 scattering theory, of Thomson's suggested. In early 1911 Rutherford became convinced, through rather extensive calculations, that Geiger and Marsden's alpha particles were being scattered in hyperbolic orbits by the intense electric field surrounding a dense concentration of electric charge in the center of the atom—the nucleus. The nuclear atom had been born.

No one, however, noticed the new arrival. It was apparently not even mentioned, for example, at the famous 1911 Solvay Conference in Brussels, which Rutherford, Albert Einstein, Max Planck, and many other prominent physicists attended. Whatever novelty contemporary physicists attached to Rutherford's paper seems to have been to his scattering theory rather than to his model of the atom—which was only one of many models present in the literature. Only after Niels Bohr exploited the nucleus in developing his famous 1913 quantum theory of the hydrogen atom, and only after H.G.J. Moseley attached to the nucleus a unique atomic number through his well-known 1913-1914 x-ray experiments, was the full significance of Rutherford's nuclear model generally appreciated. Only then, for example, did the concept of isotopes become generally and clearly recognized.

The researches that Rutherford fostered at Manchester—partly for which he was knighted in 1914—were not confined to alpha scattering and atomic structure. For example, he and his coworkers studied the chemistry and modes of decay of the radioactive elements; the scattering, the wavelengths, and the spectra of gamma rays; and the relationship between the range of alpha particles and the lifetime of the elements from which they are emitted.

Most of this immense activity was brought to a halt at the outbreak of World War I. Rutherford became associated with the Admiralty Board of Invention and Research early in the war, and he carried out experiments relating to the detection of submarines, devising a variety of microphones, diaphragms, and underwater senders and receivers to study underwater sound propagation. He supplied American scientists with a vast amount of information when the United States entered the war in 1917.

In 1919 Rutherford and William Kay found, as the culmination of a long series of investigations, that when alpha particles strike hydrogen—or, in a more famous experiment, nitrogen—recoil "protons" (Rutherford's term) are produced. Rutherford realized at once that he had achieved the first artificial nuclear transmutation (alpha particle + nitrogen to proton + oxygen) known to man. He gave a full account of his and Kay's work in 1920 in his second Bakerian lecture, "Nuclear Constitution of Atoms." One surprising prediction he made in this lecture was that of a "kind of neutral doublet," perhaps a faint premonition of the neutron. Rutherford's discovery of artificial transmutation was, in general, a fitting capstone to his brilliant career at Manchester.

Cambridge and Honors

In 1919 Rutherford became Cavendish Professor of Physics and Director of the laboratory and, a bit later, Fellow of Trinity College, Cambridge. As the occupant of the most prestigious chair of physics in England, and, concurrently, as the holder of a Professorship of Natural Philosophy at the Royal Institution (1921), Rutherford was more and more called upon to deliver public lectures and serve in various professional offices. In 1923 he was elected President of the British Association for the Advancement of Science; in 1925, the same year in which he gained admittance into the coveted Order of Merit, he became President of the Royal Society for the customary 5-year term. In 1933 he accepted the presidency of the Academic Assistance Council, formed to aid Nazi-persecuted Jewish scholars. He died on Oct. 19, 1937, in Cambridge.

Portrait of the Man

C. P. Snow has provided the following portrait of Rutherford in mature life: "He was a big, rather clumsy man, with a substantial bay window that started in the middle of the chest. I should guess that he was less muscular than at first sight he looked. He had large staring blue eyes and a damp and pendulous lower lip. He didn't look in the least like an intellectual. Creative people of his abundant kind never do, of course, but all the talk of Rutherford looking like a farmer was unperceptive nonsense. His was really the kind of face and physique that often goes with great weight of character and gifts. It could easily have been the soma of a great writer. As he talked to his companions in the streets, his voice was three times as loud as any of theirs, and his accent was bizarre. . . . It was part of his nature that, stupendous as his work was, he should consider it 10 per cent more so. It was also part of his nature that, quite without acting, he should behave constantly as though he were 10 per cent larger than life. Worldly success? He loved every minute of it: flattery, titles, the company of the high official world."

Further Reading

Rutherford's scientific papers, together with introductory notes by James Chadwick and other physicists, were assembled in *The Collected Papers of Lord Rutherford of Nelson* (3 vols., 1962-1965). Selections from his papers are in J. B. Birks, ed., *Rutherford at Manchester* (1962), and Alfred Romer, ed., *The Discovery of Radioactivity and Transmutation* (1964). Lawrence Badash edited *Rutherford and Boltwood: Letters on Radioactivity* (1969).

Arthur S. Eve, *Rutherford: Being the Life and Letters of the Rt. Hon. Lord Rutherford* (1939), is a full-length biography; Eve and James Chadwick wrote the obituary notice of Rutherford in the Royal Society of London, *Obituary Notices of Fellows of the Royal Society,* vol. 3 (1936-1938). Three other full-length biographies are Ivor B. N. Evans, *Man of Power: The Life Story of Baron Rutherford of Nelson* (1939); John Rowland, *Ernest Rutherford: Atom Pioneer* (1955); and Edward N. da C. Andrade, *Rutherford and the Nature of the Atom* (1964). A brief biography is C. M. Focken, *Lord Rutherford of Nelson* (1938). Extremely interesting recollections by H.R. Robinson, J. D. Cockcroft, M.L. Oliphant, E. Marsden, and A.S. Russell were published between 1943 and 1951 and separately reprinted in 1954 by the Physical Society of London under the title *Rutherford: By Those Who Knew Him* (1954). For help with questions on physics see W.E. Burcham, *Nuclear Physics: An Introduction* (1963). □

John Rutledge

John Rutledge (1739-1800), American jurist and statesman, was Revolutionary War governor of South Carolina. He exemplified the conservative views of the mercantile and planter aristocracy.

John Rutledge was born in Charleston, S.C., into an affluent and politically active family. He was tutored at home and then went to England at 18 to study law. After being admitted to the English bar in 1760, he returned to Charleston, where he developed a successful practice. He served as the province's attorney general (1764-1765), but as a member of the Commons House of Assembly (1761-1776), he was more often in vigorous opposition to the royal administration.

At the Stamp Act Congress, Rutledge vigorously defended American rights. In 1769 he fought for the Commons' appropriation of funds in support of the English radical John Wilkes. In the general quarrel with Britain, however, Rutledge was a moderate. At the First Continental Congress he approved the Galloway Plan for a constitutional accommodation with the mother country, although he joined the movement for independence; in the Second Congress he urged the establishment of new state governments. He helped to frame the South Carolina constitution of 1776 and was immediately chosen president (governor) of the state, but his innate conservatism caused him to resign 2 years later.

When South Carolina was confronted by a British invasion in 1779, the state again chose Rutledge as governor,

and for the next 3 years he provided energetic leadership in the war effort, with such broad emergency powers that he was called "Dictator Rutledge." Resigning in 1782, he was elected to the state legislature and in 1784 was named to the state's chancery court. At the Constitutional Convention he resisted restrictions on the slave trade, urged property as a basis for representation, and sought election of the president by Congress, and of the Congress by state legislatures.

President George Washington named Rutledge to the Supreme Court when it was organized in 1789, but he resigned 2 years later, without ever having attended a single session of the Court, to become chief justice of South Carolina. In 1795 Washington appointed him chief justice of the United States, but Rutledge's violent speech against the Jay Treaty resulted in a Senate rejection of the nomination, even though he had presided at one term of the court. The ferocity of his tirade was symptomatic of a mental deterioration which had commenced a few years earlier upon the death of his wife. He died on July 18, 1800.

Further Reading

The only full-length biography of Rutledge is Richard H. Barry, *Mr. Rutledge of South Carolina* (1942); it is based on extensive sources and is highly readable. His political career in South Carolina may be traced in Edward McCrady, *History of South Carolina* (4 vols., 1897-1902), and David D. Wallace, *History of South Carolina* (4 vols., 1934-1935; rev. ed., 1 vol., 1951). Rutledge's career on the Supreme Court in discussed in Charles Warren, *The Supreme Court in United States History* (3 vols., 1923; 2 vols., rev. ed. 1935), and in Leon Friedman

and Fred L. Israel, eds., *The Justices of the United States Supreme Court, 1789-1969* (4 vols., 1969).

Additional Sources

Barry, Richard, b. 1881. *Mr. Rutledge of South Carolina,* Salem, N.H.: Ayer, 1993.
Haw, James. *Founding brothers: John and Edward Rutledge of South Carolina,* Athens: University of Georgia, 1997. □

Jan van Ruysbroeck

The Flemish mystic Jan van Ruysbroeck (1293-1381) was the most important spiritual writer and mystic in the Low Countries in the 14th century.

Jan van Ruysbroeck was born in the village of Ruysbroeck a few miles from Brussels. For his education and religious training he was sent to Brussels at the age of 11 to live with his uncle, John Hinckaert, a priest and canon of the Cathedral of St. Gudule. There he also came under the spiritual influence of another canon, Francis van Coudenberg, who was a friend of his uncle, and these two men had a strong effect on the young man's career and religious development.

Ruysbroeck's personal inclinations as well as his environment eventually persuaded him to adopt the religious life, and in 1317 he was ordained to the priesthood. For more than a quarter century he lived in the area of St. Gudule in Brussels and attained a reputation as a preacher and orthodox religious thinker. In order to recapture the quiet, contemplative life of his early years, in 1343 Ruysbroeck retired with his two aging spiritual advisers, Hinckaert and Coudenberg, to a hermitage in the forest of Soignes called Groenendael on the southeast edge of Brussels. With the disciples that joined them, they formed themselves into a community in 1349 according to the rule of Augustinian canons. In this place of solitude Ruysbroeck wrote the mystical treatises on which his reputation is based, and he remained there until his death in 1381, at the age of 88.

Most of Ruysbroeck's writings describe how the soul of man can be joined with God in mystical union. He was careful to avoid heresy. He rejected pantheistic doctrines that did not distinguish clearly enough between God and the creature; he rejected the overly optimistic evaluation that man could approach God apart from grace; and he rejected quietistic tendencies that obliterated human activity in the mystical union or seemingly prolonged the experience.

In one of his most important works, however, written early in his stay at Groenendael, *The Adornment of Spiritual Marriage,* Ruysbroeck suggested the possibility of an intuitive vision of the divine essence as well as the idea that part of the soul might be uncreated. Although stated more cautiously in his later writings, these ideas led to an attack on Ruysbroeck not long after his death. His writings, however, have been judged orthodox by most. He forms a link between the Rhenish mystics of the early 14th century, especially the Dominican mystics like Meister Eckhart, Heinrich Suso, and Johannes Tauler, and the Devotio Moderna, the major spiritual movement of the 15th century in the Low Countries, northern France, and the Rhine Valley.

Further Reading

Most of Ruysbroeck's writings have been translated into English. Biographical studies of Ruysbroeck in English are Vincent Scully, *A Medieval Mystic* (1911), and Alfred Wautier d'Aygalliers, *Ruysbroeck the Admirable* (1923; trans. 1969). Additional material on Ruysbroeck is in Stephanus Axters, *Spirituality of the Old Low Countries* (trans. 1954). Almost any survey of medieval thought or late medieval mysticism includes a description of Ruysbroeck's thought, such as the work by Etienne Henry Gilson, *History of Christian Philosophy in the Middle Ages* (1955). □

Nolan Ryan

Nolan Ryan (born 1947) is considered one of the best pitchers of all time, known both for his fastball and as a role model for players and fans alike.

Ranked among the greatest pitchers of all time, Nolan Ryan struck out a record 5,714 batters and had 61 shutouts over a career that spanned from 1966 through 1993. Ryan's career saw 324 games won and 292 games lost. 1973 marked the beginning of what would later become a baseball legend when Ryan set a major league record of 383 strikeouts for a single season. However more important than his incredible blazing fast ball or his fantastic durability, Ryan brought back to baseball a concept that had been sorely missing—the idea of an American hero. Ryan was not only a player that others in the game could look up to as a professional role model, but he was also someone that mainstream America could look to as a role model as well. Ryan, unlike others who play the sport today, was never concerned with money. Although he was the first pitcher to earn a million dollar annual salary, Ryan played for the love of the game and it was this love that endeared him to the American populace.

Early Years

Lynn Nolan Ryan was born January 31, 1947, in Refugio, Texas. Ryan grew up in Alvin, Texas, where his father worked for an oil company and delivered papers for the *Houston Post*. Ryan credits his father for instilling in him the value of the work ethic. As mentioned earlier, Ryan never played baseball for the money even though he was the first million dollar pitcher. Ryan played the game for what he felt it was, a sport that required hard work and intense dedication. It was this spirit that permeated Ryan's game and allowed him to endure criticism and the tough times without making excuses that other players routinely did. Ryan was disgusted when other players blamed management decisions, biased reporting, lack of other players' skills, or a

variety of other excuses for their own shortcomings. Ryan became a willing role model through his 27-year career and is probably the last who played or will play the game with the old-style courage and skill reminiscent of early baseball.

Baseball Beginnings

Ryan moved away from Alvin, Texas, in 1965 to Greenville, South Carolina, to begin playing a game that even he did not realize would become his career. Ryan was selected by the New York Mets during the 1965 free-agent draft and played in the West Carolinas League beginning on September 11, 1966. During Ryan's stint with this league, his teammates began to respect his fast ball. Before his playing, his teammates thought his fast ball was just a high school fantasy. Although Ryan lacked true ball control, he nonetheless frightened batters and catchers alike with his scorching fast ball. At times, his pitches had been recorded at speeds well over 90 miles per hour. Even with lack of ball control, it was enough for the Mets that Ryan possessed such pitching skill and as a result they called him up to play in the major leagues at the end of the 1966 season. Ryan had already won 17 games by the start of his major league career. The Mets at that time were in sore need of great players, because until 1969, the Mets had finished last or next to last in every season since the team was founded in 1962. Unfortunately for the Mets, the 1967 season did not bring the great plays expected. Ryan was often homesick and therefore missed much of the 1967 season due to illness, an arm injury, and service with the Army Reserves.

Marriage and Career Upswing

Ryan married his high school sweetheart, Ruth, in 1968. She moved to New York City to be closer to Ryan and help ease his homesickness. Her actions helped to improve Ryan's game during the 1968 season. Along with the improved playing ability Ryan achieved during that season, the New York Mets also improved as a team. The Mets added two key people to their pitching staff, Jerry Koosman and Tom Seaver, a strikeout leader in his own right from whom Ryan learned a great deal. This would later prove to be a valuable and much needed management contribution. With these two incidents, the Mets became positioned for their first-ever bid for the World Series in 1969. During the 1969 season, Ryan played as both a starting and relief pitcher, finishing the season with a six win and three loss record. This type of finish soon became the norm for Ryan as he concentrated more on striking out batters than on winning games. Regardless, it was primarily Ryan's pitching abilities that took the New York Mets to the league championships that year and later the World Series. Ryan saved the Mets' bid for the World Series title when in the third game of the series, Ryan made the crucial plays needed to earn the win. The Mets went on to upset the Baltimore Orioles after five games. The New York Mets had finally done the impossible; what no professional commentator thought they could do. With the help of Ryan, the New York Mets had won their first World Series title since arriving in the National League.

Team Movements

Even with a world championship title to his credit Ryan still felt uncomfortable and disillusioned in New York, and requested to be traded in 1971. Without much discussion, the Mets agreed to Ryan's request and traded him along with three other players to the California Angels. Because of this move, he was able to distance himself from the East and a climate and location he was never fond of. For Ryan and those three players, the New York Mets received Jim Fregosi, a third baseman. Looking back as players and managers often do, this trade is often considered the worst in the history of the Mets. Once in California, Ryan blasted his way into superstar status. He stayed with the Angels for eight seasons, from 1972 through 1979.

Team Accomplishments

With the help Ryan received from both the Mets and the Angels, he began to pitch in a much more controlled and compact fashion allowing for an unbelievably fast delivery across the plate. Ryan had finally reigned in his pitch to a truly skilled perfection of speed and balance. As a result he also struck out more than three hundred batters for the first time. To be more specific, Ryan finished the 1972 season with 19 wins, 16 losses, and 329 strikeouts. With this feat accomplished, Ryan became only the second right-handed pitcher since 1946, when Bob Feller accomplished it, to strike out three hundred or more batters in a single season. With the close of the 1973 season, Ryan became the first-ever pitcher to have back-to-back over three hundred strikeout seasons. Striking out 383 hitters, Ryan set an all-

time major league record. This achievement is now challenged only by Roger Clemens of the Boston Red Sox. Additionally in the 1973 season, Ryan became only the fifth pitcher in baseball history to pitch two no-hit games in one season. His first no-hitter came against the Kansas City Royals on May 15. On July 15 against the Detroit Tigers, Ryan pitched his second no-hit game of 1973. The 1974 and 1975 seasons were also quite good for Ryan stat-wise. In the 1974 season, Ryan pitched his third no-hit game and completed a third season of over three hundred strikeouts. The 1975 season saw Ryan complete his fourth no-hit game. Ryan now became only the second pitcher in major league history to achieve this feat. This accomplishment was first achieved by Sandy Koufax during the 1960s while playing for the Los Angeles Dodgers. Critics and opponents of Ryan and his games believed his career was all but over when in 1975 he underwent elbow surgery. This surgery usually spells the end for a pitcher, therefore such criticism was expected. Not wanting to stay away from the game he loved, Ryan reappeared on the baseball season larger than life in 1976. Ryan closed the 1976 season with 17 wins, 18 losses, and 327 strikeouts. Impressing doubters even more, Ryan closed his 1977 season with 19 wins, 16 losses, and 341 strikeouts. Again Ryan completed back-to-back over three hundred strikeout seasons.

Move to Texas and Desperation

Although Ryan played some of his best games with the California Angels, he still longed for his native Texas. His break came when at the end of the 1979 season when he became a free agent. Ryan was immediately signed with the Houston Astros and became baseball's first pitcher to earn a million dollars a year. Although this amount is common by today's standards, when it was awarded to Ryan, such a sum was unheard of. After taking some time to readjust to a newer pitching style introduced by the National League, Ryan showed off his adjustment by pitching his fifth no-hit game in 1981. Effectively breaking Koufax's record, Ryan, it was widely thought, was well on his way to setting even more major league records. Unfortunately for Ryan, rather than setting records, he failed to even match his own prior performances. Essentially, from 1984 until the 1987 season, Ryan was continuously placed on the disabled or the injured reserve list. Ryan rarely pitched a game during this time and has always felt that it was the worst time of his professional career. He was especially concerned about his fellow teammates who had to make the difference even without Ryan to pitch his all-star games.

Game Picked Up

The 1987 season saw not only a rejuvenated Ryan, but new records as well. His legendary durability and willingness to play despite great personal discomfort, landed him his second ERA (Earned Run Average) title with a 2.76 average. Ryan's first ERA title was in 1981 in which he attained a 1.69 average. Additionally, Ryan became the first pitcher in baseball's history to attain 2,000 strikeouts in both the American League and the National League. After completing his contract with the Astros, Ryan again became a free agent at the end of the 1987 season. He again was quickly picked up, this time by the Texas Rangers in time for the 1988 season. Ryan had hoped that perhaps with the Rangers, despite his age, he might again have a chance at playing the World Series again. With only four and one-half games separating the Rangers from the division leader, Chicago, this possibility seemed probable. This desire had followed Ryan since his departure from the Mets. Although, Ryan would not see a championship playoff with the Rangers, he did attain his sixth no-hit game and led the American League in strikeouts by the close of the 1990 regular season. Additionally, while playing for the Rangers, Ryan attained his record setting seventh no-hit game against the Toronto Blue Jays.

Called it Quits

On September 22, 1993, on Nolan Ryan Appreciation Day in Seattle, Washington, all that Ryan dreamed of and played for came to an abrupt halt. For the pitcher that was to strikeouts what Hank Aaron was to home runs, for the man who pitched more strikeouts and no-hitters than anyone who had played the game to that point—the final call was made for Ryan. Although he planned to retire at the end of the 1993 season, he expected to do so with the grace and dignity deserving of his accomplishments. Instead fate or should one prefer, Father Time, took that from Ryan. After feeling his right elbow pop with pain from a torn ligament in the middle of the Rangers game against the Seattle Mariners, Ryan knew his chances at the World Series were over. Ryan was sidelined for the rest of the game, giving him ample time to reflect on his 27-year career. Although Ryan had technically done little to help the Rangers in their bid for the American League West title, especially with his 115 days on the injured reserve list, he still felt somehow personally responsible. When it finally settled in on Ryan he was crushed. At 46, Ryan walked off the field that day giving to baseball and its fans something that will not be seen again. As an athlete, Ryan defined his own class and style. He attained the 5,000 strikeout mark at the age of 42, when most professional sports players had long since retired. A physical wonder, Ryan was still throwing out his legendary fast balls, clocked at 95 miles per hour at the age of 46. Fast ballers, so it was thought, were supposed to lose their edge, break down, and rely on deceptions to keep the ball "unhittable," but not Nolan Ryan. Age only appeared to perfect his ability.

Further Reading

Sports Illustrated, October 4, 1993, p. 46; September 19, 1994, p. 132.

"Monument to Greatness," in *The Sporting News,* October 11, 1993, p. 31.

USA Today, February 15, 1996.

Sullivan, George, *Pitchers: Twenty-seven of Baseball's Greatest,* Atheneum, 1994.

Reiser, Howard, *Nolan Ryan: Strikeout King,* Children's Press, 1993.

Briggs, Jennifer, *Nolan Ryan: The Authorized Pictorial Biography,* The Summit Group, 1991.

Libby, Bill, *Nolan Ryan: Fireballer,* Putnam, 1975. □

Albert Pinkham Ryder

The painter Albert Pinkham Ryder (1847-1917) was the most original romantic artist of 19th-century America. His highly personal art, at the opposite extreme from the literal naturalism of his period, anticipated the expressionist and fantastic trends of modern art.

Albert P. Ryder was born on March 19, 1847, in New Bedford, Mass., then the world's busiest whaling port. His ancestors on both his father's and mother's sides were of old Cape Cod families. Many had been sailors, and his childhood was intimately associated with the sea. His education went no further than grammar school, as his eyes were oversensitive. Without professional training he began to paint landscape outdoors.

About 1870 Ryder moved with his family to New York, where he lived the rest of his life. At 23 (relatively late) he entered the National Academy of Design, where he studied for four seasons, mostly drawing from casts; but more important was the informal teaching he received from the portraitist and romantic painter William E. Marshall. This limited art education contrasted with the thorough academic training usual at the time.

Ryder's early paintings were landscapes, often including horses, cows, and sheep—memories of the country around New Bedford. Small in scale and relatively naturalistic in style, they were already marked by a dreamlike poetry and by extremely personal form and color. They were generally rejected by academy juries, and in 1877 Ryder was one of the founders of a new liberal organization, the Society of American Artists, with which he exhibited for the next decade.

By contrast with that of most American artists of his generation, Ryder's European experience was small. His first trip abroad was in 1877, when he spent a month in London. The next and longest trip was in the summer of 1882, when he visited France, Spain, Tangier, Italy, and Switzerland. In 1887 and 1896 he crossed and recrossed the Atlantic, for the sea voyages, spending only 2 weeks in London each time. These limited foreign contacts had little effect on his art.

About 1880, in his early 30s, Ryder embarked on the imaginative paintings which were his greatest achievements. They were based on the Bible, classical mythology, Chaucer, Shakespeare (his favorite poet), and 19th-century romantics such as Lord Byron, Thomas Campbell, Alfred Lord Tennyson, and Edgar Allan Poe. Two of his major paintings were based on Richard Wagner's operas. But Ryder's works were quite different from the "literary" pictures of the period. They were not illustrations but original works of art—great themes transformed by his imagination into highly personal visions. Nature always played an essential part. Youthful memories of the sea were embodied in his frequent image of a lone boat sailing the moonlit waters. But his major conceptions were more than simple nature po-

ems; their central motif was the human being in relation to superhuman powers. Ryder's art was fundamentally religious; he was one of the few artists of his time to whom religion was not mere conformity but intense, profound belief.

Ryder's art was never bound by the literal naturalism of his time. For him painting was not mere representation but creation in the language of color, form, and rhythmic movement. As he said, "What avails a storm cloud accurate in form and color if the storm is not therein?" He used the elements of nature far more freely than any American contemporary painter, shaping them to his creative sense of design.

Ryder worked long over his pictures, building them in layer on layer of pigment, often keeping them for years, so that his total production numbers only about 165 paintings. Unfortunately he had no sound technical knowledge, and many of his pictures have deteriorated to some extent. Because of the small number of his works and their increasing value, forgeries began to appear in his last years; and after his death the production increased until there are now about five times as many fakes as genuine works.

As a person, Ryder was completely unworldly. He cared nothing for money or reputation. As he said, "The artist needs but a roof, a crust of bread and his easel, and all the rest God gives him in abundance. He must live to paint and not paint to live." He never married, and in later life he became a recluse except to a few old friends. He was utterly unable to cope with housekeeping, and the two rooms in

which he lived were in a condition of incredible disorder, piled waist-high with all kinds of objects. After a serious illness in 1915, he lived with friends in Elmhurst, Long Island, where he died on March 28, 1917.

Though Ryder's art had little to do with the prevailing trends of his day, it had much to do with future trends. His freedom from literal naturalism, his relation to the subconscious mind, and the purity of his plastic creation were prophetic of much in modern art.

Further Reading

Three monographs on Ryder have appeared. Frederic Fairchild Sherman, *Albert Pinkham Ryder* (1920), is a sympathetic study, now outdated by recent research, especially as regards forgeries. Frederic Newlin Price, *Ryder* (1932), is unreliable, a considerable proportion of the works listed and illustrated being forgeries. Lloyd Goodrich, *Albert P. Ryder* (1959), gives the most complete biographical and critical account to date; all 81 works illustrated and referred to are unquestionably genuine. □

Adolphus Egerton Ryerson

Adolphus Egerton Ryerson (1803-1882) was a Canadian Methodist clergyman and educator. One of the leading Methodists in Upper Canada, he opposed the pretensions of the Anglican Church.

Egerton Ryerson was born on March 24, 1803, at Charlotteville, Norfolk County, Upper Canada. His father, Joseph, was a United Empire loyalist. Ryerson was educated at the district grammar school and then worked for a time on his father's farm. In 1821 he joined the Methodist Church and taught in the London district grammar school. In 1823 he returned to work on his father's farm once more, but in 1825 he was ordained a Methodist minister and assigned to the Niagara circuit. He was soon transferred to the Yonge Street circuit, which included York (Toronto), and he immediately entered into a strenuous campaign in opposition to the claims of the Church of England in Upper Canada to the income of the clergy reserves.

In 1829 he began to edit the *Christian Guardian* and remained its editor, with several interruptions, for the next decade. In 1833 he was sent as a delegate to the Wesleyan Methodist Conference in England and was a key figure in bringing about the uniting of the Wesleyans and the Methodist Episcopal Church in Canada. He returned to England in 1835 in search of financial support for a Methodist college in Upper Canada, and in 1841 Victoria College was incorporated, with Ryerson as its first president.

Ryerson at first favored the Reform cause in politics, but in the early 1830s he became disillusioned with many of the Reformers, and with William Lyon Mackenzie in particular, and increasingly gave his support to the governor's party. In the general election of 1844 he worked effectively on behalf of the administration of the new governor, Sir Charles Metcalfe.

In the same year he was appointed as the second superintendent of education for Upper Canada and thus began what, in effect, was the second of his careers. He studied schools and teaching methods in the United States, in England, and on the Continent and used his findings to remodel the educational system of Upper Canada.

In 1846 a school bill which incorporated many of Ryerson's ideas was passed by the legislature. After the Reformers obtained control of the government in 1848, they attempted to alter his system, but with the cooperation of Robert Baldwin, the attorney general for Canada West, Ryerson was able to maintain the basic structure intact.

Ryerson continued to administer the school system in the United Province of Canada and then, under confederation, the schools in the province of Ontario until he retired as superintendent in 1876. He died at Toronto on Feb. 19, 1882.

Further Reading

Ryerson's autobiography, *The Story of My Life,* was edited and published posthumously by J. George Hodgins (1883). The definitive biography of Ryerson is C. B. Sissons, *Egerton Ryerson: His Life and Letters* (2 vols., 1937-1947).

Additional Sources

Damania, Laura. *Egerton Ryerson,* Don Mills, Ont.: Fitzhenry & Whiteside, 1975. □

theories.'' In his Tanner Lectures, published as *Dilemmas* (1954), he showed how certain philosophical impasses could be dissolved by a clearer understanding of the concepts employed by the apparently contradictory views.

In his major work, *The Concept of Mind* (1949), Ryle mounted a devastating attack on Cartesian dualism and, in particular, on the view of mind as a separate substance apart from the body. He caricatured this view as the ''myth of the ghost in the machine'' proposed by Descartes. Ryle's own view of mental reality is that it consists in dispositions to behave in certain ways. He tried to show that mental concepts do not refer to private, unwitnessable events, maintaining against critics that his view was not identical with behaviorism.

In *Plato's Progress* (1966) Ryle exhibited an unexpected talent for ingenious speculation in an attempt to reconstruct the historical genesis of Plato's dialogues. Ryle, a bachelor, lived most of his life in college rooms. Friends said that ''the Common Room atmosphere fits him like a glove.'' Quick and formidable in debate, Ryle was also the writer of clear and witty prose. He took particular delight in exploding pompous views and in inventing fresh metaphors and vivid aphorisms. Though professing to dislike erudition and intellectual matters, Ryle was both learned and highly intellectual. He was said to distrust imagination and its works, but he had a typically British love of gardening.

Gilbert Ryle

The English philosopher Gilbert Ryle (1900-1976) ranked among the leaders of the contemporary analytic movement in British philosophy. His most original work was his analysis of the concept of mind.

Gilbert Ryle was born on Aug. 19, 1900, in Brighton, the son of a prosperous doctor. He was educated at Brighton College and then entered Queen's College, Oxford, where he took first honors in two subjects: classical honor moderations and the school of philosophy, politics, and economics. He was also captain of the Queen's College Boating Club.

As a result of his brilliant academic work, Ryle was appointed lecturer in 1924 and a year later tutor in philosophy, both appointments at Christ Church, Oxford. In 1940 he was commissioned in the Welsh Guards, serving for the duration of World War II and ending his military career as a major.

Ryle returned to Oxford to become Waynfleete professor of metaphysical philosophy, a post he held from 1945 to 1968. In 1947 he inherited from G. E. Moore the editorship of *Mind,* the most influential journal of English philosophy.

Early in his philosophical career, Ryle decided that the task of philosophy was ''the detection of the sources in linguistic idioms of recurrent misconceptions and absurd

Further Reading

Ryle's works are eminently readable even for the general reader. *The Concept of Mind* (1949) and *Dilemmas* (1954) are the most important. The only study of any length is the highly critical one by Laird Addis in *Moore and Ryle: Two Ontologies* (1965). Also see William Lyons, *Gilbert Ryle: An Introduction to his Philosophy,* (1980) and Ira Altman, *The Concept of Intelligence: A philosophical Analysis* (1997). Collections of Ryle's works include: *Modern Studies in Philosophy* (1971) and *Logic and Language* (1978). □

S

Mem de Sá

Mem de Sá (1504-1572) was a Portuguese jurist and a governor general of Brazil who served from 1558 to 1572 and helped to bring a new stability and prosperity to Portuguese America.

Mem de Sá was born in Coimbra, Portugal. He studied law at the University of Salamanca. After receiving his law degree in 1528, he served as a judge in several of the highest courts of Portugal. A learned and able jurist, he enjoyed special favor with King João III. The Crown appointed him to be the third governor general of Brazil.

The cultured Sá brought peace and a certain degree of prosperity to Brazil after he assumed his duties in January 1558. Among others, the eminent Jesuit missionary Manuel da Nóbrega sang his praises: "As soon as Mem de Sá took the reins of government, he began to show his prudence, zeal, and virtue both in the good government of the Christians and the Indians by putting everything in order as Our Lord showed him." To increase the base of economic prosperity, Sá encouraged agriculture in general and sugar culture in particular. The number of sugar mills multiplied, particularly in the captaincies of São Vicente, Rio de Janeiro, Espírito Santo, Bahia, and Pernambuco, where the huge sugar plantations and their mills quickly became powerful agricultural, industrial, and social organizations.

The Indians had proved to be an unsatisfactory answer to the labor shortage which plagued the colony, but they were pressed into service as the only available workers. The Church, most vocally the Jesuits, regarded the enslavement of the Indians as contrary to the Christian intentions of the King, and they intensified efforts to save them both physically and spiritually by gathering them into the Church-administered villages. The colonists loudly criticized the interference with their labor supply. Sá desired to bring the Indians within the pale of empire. On the one hand, he maintained close relations with the Jesuits and approved the continuation of the mission villages. On the other, he fought fiercely to pacify those Indians who had rebelled against Portuguese authority.

The perennial French threat demanded much of the governor's attention and resources. In 1555, Vice Admiral Durand de Villegaignon had founded France Antartique around Guanabara Bay. The French colony there threatened the Portuguese king's claims to the entire Brazilian coast. Sá attacked the French invaders on several occasions. On March 1, 1565, he established Rio de Janeiro as a base to fight against the stubborn French and after prolonged siege expelled them in 1567. After the defeat of the French, Rio de Janeiro grew rapidly in size and importance. The Crown manifested its delight with the accomplishments of Sá by retaining him as governor general long after his 4-year appointment expired. He stayed on until he died in office on March 12, 1572, in Salvador da Bahia.

Further Reading

Sá is referred to in several useful background works on Latin America: Hubert Herring, *A History of Latin America* (1955; 3d rev. ed. 1968); Charles R. Boxer, *Four Centuries of Portuguese Expansion, 1415-1825: A Succinct Summary* (1961); and Helen M. Bailey and Abraham P. Nasatir, *Latin America: The Development of Its Civilization* (2d ed. 1968).

Additional Sources

Sá, Mem de, *Tempo de lembrar: memorias,* Rio de Janeiro: Livraria J. Olympio Editora, 1981. □

Saadia ben Joseph al-Fayumi

The Jewish scholar Saadia ben Joseph al-Fayumi (882-942) ranks as the most important medieval Jewish scholar of literature and history.

L ittle is known of the early life of Saadia ben Joseph except that he was born in Egypt, lived for sometime in Palestine, and finally settled in the Jewish communities of Babylonia. Saadia became affiliated with the academy at Sura, Babylonia, and became the *gaon* (head) of the academy in 928. Deposed in 930, he again became gaon in 936, holding this office until his death in 942. During this period the academy became the highest seat of learning among the Jews.

Saadia's numerous works were written for the most part in Arabic, which had become the vernacular and literary language of eastern Jews. When the Babylonian schools ceased to function in the middle of the 11th century and the Jews were expelled from Spain, Saadia's works ceased to be widely known until the late 19th and early 20th centuries. Their importance, however, cannot be exaggerated. In bulk, in range of interest, in breadth of knowledge, and in pioneer thinking, his works are a monument between the close of the Talmudic period in the 6th century and the rise of the Jewish Enlightenment in the 18th century.

At least 20 major works, apart from Saadia's translations and commentaries, exist. Saadia translated the Bible into Arabic and added a commentary. He composed a Midrashic work on the Decalogue, translated the five Megilloth (Song of Songs, Ruth, Lamentations, Ecclesiastes, and Esther), and also translated the Book of Daniel and added a commentary.

Saadia's major works divide into five categories: polemical tracts, exegetical writings, grammatical treatises, works on Talmudic subjects, and philosophic works. His polemical writings arose principally from his position in Sura. His *Book of the Festivals* was written against Ben Meir of Palestine in 922, when the latter attempted to make alterations in the Jewish calendar. Other writings were directed against the Karaite sect and against the skeptic Hivi of Balkh, David ben Zakkai, and others.

Of Saadia's grammatical works, only his treatise on the *hapax legomena* (words used once in the Bible) and a poem on the letters of the alphabet survive. His liturgical writings and poems survive in greater quantity. One poem, *Azharoth,* is a practical enunciation of the 613 Precepts. Saadia's philosophical works display his wide knowledge of Aristotle and of Christian, Moslem, and Brahmin teachings. In his *Kitab al-Amanat wal-Itiqadat* (933) Saadia expressed his views of religion and human destiny. He maintained that revealed religion and human reason do not clash but complement each other.

Saadia's health was broken by the continual controversies which surrounded his leadership of the Sura Academy, and he died in 942. His importance can be measured by the fact that without his extant works there would be no direct knowledge of the inner development of Judaism and Jewish literature between the 7th and the 10th century.

Further Reading

David Druck, *Saadya Gaon: Scholar, Philosopher, Champion of Judaism* (trans. 1942), and Solomon Leon Skoss, *Saadia Gaon: The Earliest Hebrew Grammarian* (1955), are biographical studies. Various aspects of Saadia's life and career are discussed in two studies published on the thousandth anniversary of his death by the American Academy for Jewish Research, *Saadia Anniversary Volume,* edited by Boaz Cohen (1943), and by the Jewish Quarterly Review, *Saadia Studies,* edited by Abraham A. Neuman and Solomon Zeitlin (1943). Background information is in Heinrich H. Graetz, *History of the Jews* (trans. 1891-1898), and the highly technical work by Paul Ernst Kahle, *The Cairo Geniza* (1947; 2d ed. 1959). □

Eliel and Eero Saarinen

Eliel (1873-1950) and Eero (1910-1961) Saarinen, father and son, were Finnish-American architects and industrial designers. Eliel had a profound interest in the total idea of the city. Eero developed new structural techniques for his eclectic works.

E liel Saarinen was one of a small band of architects who rejected the architectural styles of the 19th century, stating, "Architecture has gone astray; something has to be done about it; now is the time to do things." His designs show a continuous progression, and all bear his unmistakable stamp. Eero Saarinen borrowed from a wide range of sources; he lacked the unifying philosophy of design which can be discerned in his father's architecture. Eero defined architecture as a "fine art" and the architect as a "form giver."

Eliel Saarinen

Eliel was born in Rantasalmi on Aug. 20, 1873. He studied painting and architecture at the University and the Polytechnic Institute of Helsinki, respectively, and in 1896, a year before graduating, he entered into partnership with two other institute graduates, Herman Gesellius, brother of Eliel's wife-to-be, Loja, and Armas Lindgren.

Finnish architecture at the turn of the century reflected national romanticism verging upon Art Nouveau. Eliel's design for the Finnish Pavilion at the 1900 Paris Exposition, with its bulging tower and Art Nouveau decorations, reflects this trend. The flowing line of Art Nouveau was replaced in Eliel's own home at Hvittrask (1902) by a more geometricized decor.

That Eliel was influenced by the later English architects of the Arts and Crafts movement there can be no doubt. His own house bespeaks the idioms, which lingered in his work until the 1920s. The handmade bricks and tiles, bay windows with leaded lights, lead rainwater pipes, wrought-iron decoration, and hand-carved woodwork and furniture are the trademarks of the Arts and Crafts movement.

Eero Saarinen

The American Arts and Crafts developments, especially Henry Hobson Richardson's "Romanesque revival" and its outgrowth in the functionalism of Louis Sullivan, had also reached the Scandinavian countries. In 1904 Eliel won the competition for the Central Railroad Station, Helsinki (built 1910-1914). The building is antitraditional, with spacious interiors and monumental proportions, similar in character to the smaller buildings of Richardson and Sullivan.

In 1922 Eliel won the second prize in the Chicago Tribune Tower competition. His design, with a strong vertical emphasis and the upper portion set back, had the monumentality of a classical Mayan pyramid. That year he moved to the United States. He taught for a short while at the University of Michigan and then was invited to Bloomfield Hills, Mich., where he built the Cranbrook Academy of Art (1926-1943) in the Arts and Crafts tradition. He also headed the department of architecture and city planning there.

Eliel's later works, executed in collaboration with his son, include the Kleinhans Music Hall, Buffalo (1938-1940), the Tabernacle Church of Christ, Columbus, Ind. (1940-1942), the Christ Lutheran Church, Minneapolis (1949), and the projected Smithsonian Art Gallery, Washington (1939). All have a simple monumental dignity, with unadorned wall surfaces and a spacious light openness.

Eliel was always interested in city planning, and he became planning consultant to Budapest and to Estonia. He submitted an entry in the Canberra, Australia, competition

and projected plans for Helsinki and other Finnish cities. Although his projects stressed organic informality, they usually included the mannerist and baroque motif of a long axis, terminated by a round point incorporating a monumental structure. Eliel abhorred skyscraper construction as the basis for increasing the value of the land, and he felt that low-cost housing was poorly constructed and thus expensive to maintain. He demanded social research, adequate and appropriate means and methods, and an architecture created to enhance the total environment.

Eliel's books, *The City: Its Growth, Its Decay, Its Future* (1943) and *Search for Form* (1948), as well as his "Proposal for Rebuilding Blighted Areas" and "Outline for a Legislative Program to Rebuild Our Cities," prepared for discussions at Cranbrook in 1942, contained concepts far ahead of their time. He died at Bloomfield Hills on July 1, 1950.

Eero Saarinen

Eero was born in Kirkkonummi on Aug. 20, 1910. He studied sculpture in Paris (1930-1931) and architecture at Yale, earning a bachelor of fine arts degree in 1934. He worked for, and in collaboration with, his father from 1936 to 1950. The leadership of Eliel seems to have been dominant. "As his partner," said Eero, "I often contributed technical solutions and plans, but only within the concept he created."

The two Saarinens designed the group of 25 buildings that make up the General Motors Technical Center, Warren, Mich. (1945-1956). Independently, in 1948, Eero won the competition for the Jefferson National Expansion Memorial, St. Louis (built 1962-1965). The memorial is a stainless-steel arch in the shape of an inverted weighted catenary curve. Eero designed the Kresge Auditorium and Chapel at the Massachusetts Institute of Technology, Cambridge (1953-1956); the auditorium was the first major shell construction in the United States.

In Eero's Trans World Airlines terminal at Kennedy Airport, N.Y. (1956-1962), the flow of space is dynamic. The quality of space is lost in the Dulles International Airport, Chantilly, Va. (1958-1962), where internal clutter negates the expression. The exterior of Dulles, however, has the splendor and grandeur of Versailles. At this airport Eero was attempting to solve the complex problem of passenger movement and access to aircraft by means of a mobile lounge system. His Morse and Stiles colleges at Yale University, New Haven, Conn. (1958-1962), are successfully integrated with the older buildings of the campus. Stylistically, the two colleges are dominated by the current trends.

Eero also designed the so-called womb chair (1948) and free-flowing plastic pedestal furniture (1958) capable of being mass-produced. He died in Bloomfield Hills on Sept. 1, 1961.

Further Reading

Albert Christ-Janer, *Eliel Saarinen* (1948); Alan Temko, *Eero Saarinen* (1962); and Aline B. Saarinen, ed., *Eero Saarinen on His Work* (1962), are well-illustrated, comprehensive discussions of the total contribution to architecture of the two Saarinens.

Additional Sources

Christ-Janer, Albert, *Eliel Saarinen: Finnish-American architect and educator,* Chicago: University of Chicago Press, 1979. □

Angel de Saavedra

The Spanish poet, dramatist, and statesman Angel de Saavedra, Duque de Rivas (1791-1865), is best known for his drama "Don Álvaro, or the Force of Destiny," which marked the triumph of romanticism in Spain.

Angel de Saavedra, later the Duque de Rivas, was born on March 10, 1791, in Cordova, the second son of a family of grandees. In 1800 the family moved to Madrid, where Saavedra studied at the Seminario de Nobles. In 1808, at the outbreak of the War of Independence against Napoleon, he joined the Castilian army. Badly wounded in 1809, he went to Cadiz, where he met Quintana and Martinez de la Rosa, two major literary figures. Between 1814 and 1820 he wrote drama and poetry in the classical manner, publishing various poems with the title *Poesías* in 1814.

By 1823 Saavedra had joined the liberals against the despotic rule of Ferdinand VII. He became a deputy and secretary of the Cortes and was among those who imprisoned the King at Cadiz. When Ferdinand regained power, Saavedra was condemned to death but escaped, emigrating with other Spanish intellectuals to London in 1823. For the next 10 years he lived abroad in England, Italy, Malta, and France. In Malta in 1825 he met John Hookham Frere, a noted English Hispanist who introduced him to the British romantics and urged him to search for poetic themes in Spanish history. In 1828 Saavedra wrote his poem *El faro de Malta* and in 1829 began writing the first successful Spanish *leyenda, El moro expósito,* published in 1834. It is a long epic poem in 12 cantos that reworks the medieval story of the Siete Infantes de Lara and their Moorish half brother Mudarra. In keeping with the romantic spirit, Saavedra changed Mudarra into an exotic hero and sought to recreate the atmosphere of the days of chivalry.

In 1830 Saavedra witnessed in Paris the premiere of Victor Hugo's *Hernani,* which formally established romanticism in France. Saavedra was back in Spain when amnesty was granted in 1834, the year that his elder brother died without issue. Saavedra inherited the family fortune and title by which he is generally known. He adopted more conservative political views and in 1835 became minister of the interior.

The performance of Rivas's play *Don Álvaro, o la fuerza del sino (Don Álvaro, or the Force of Destiny)* in 1835 signaled the advent of romanticism in Spain. Don Álvaro is a typically romantic hero, and the play is charged with violent action and melodrama. Yet Rivas balanced these romantic elements with expertly designed stage settings and scenes of local color in which minor characters enact realistic, often comic, situations.

In 1837 Rivas was exiled again, this time for being a conservative. He returned in 1838 and in 1841 published *Los romances históricos,* poems inspired by Spanish ballad literature and ancient chronicles. During 1844-1860 Rivas served as ambassador in Naples, Paris, and Florence, and in Spain he was elected president of the Cortes and Consejo de Estado. After 1860 he withdrew from politics but continued as president of the Spanish Academy until his death on June 22, 1865, in Madrid.

Further Reading

The best book on Rivas's life and work is Edgar Allison Peers, *Rivas and Romanticism in Spain* (1923). Rivas is discussed in two general background works: Gerald Brenan, *The Literature of the Spanish People* (1951; 2d ed. 1953), and Richard E. Chandler and Kessel Schwartz, A *New History of Spanish Literature* (1961).

Additional Sources

Lovett, Gabriel H., *The Duke of Rivas,* Boston: Twayne, 1977. □

Paul Sabatier

The French chemist Paul Sabatier (1854-1941) is best known for his work in the field of catalyzed gas-phased reactions.

Paul Sabatier was born in Carcassonne on Nov. 5, 1854. After graduating from the École Normale Supérieure in 1874 and teaching a year in the lycée at Nîmes, he became a laboratory assistant at the Collège de France in 1878. Two years later he received his doctoral degree with a thesis on the thermochemistry of sulfur and the metallic sulfides. After serving as *maître de conference* in physics in the faculty of sciences at Bordeaux for a year, he took charge of the course in physics in the faculty of sciences at Toulouse, the school at which he remained for the rest of his life. He became professor of chemistry in 1884 and went on to become one of the most brilliant representatives of the French chemical school.

After completing his thesis, Sabatier turned his attention to a host of inorganic and physical problems related to the thermochemistry of sulfides, chlorides, and chromates. A detailed study of the rate of transformation of metaphosphoric acid, studies on absorption spectra, and measurement of the partition coefficients of a base between two acids were included in the first 2 decades of his work.

Sabatier's efforts in the field of organic chemistry began about 1897 and led to the enunciation of a theory of catalytic hydrogenation over finely divided metals such as nickel, copper, cobalt, iron, and platinum. With the help of his colleagues he not only carried out a large number of experimental studies on catalytic hydrogenation but also proposed a theory of catalysis that is still useful and sound.

He suggested that reactants combine with each other over catalysts as a result of forming unstable complexes or compounds with the catalyst surface. For this hypothesis and for his numerous experimental catalytic studies, science and industry will be eternally grateful.

The chemist received many honors. He was elected a member of the French Academy of Sciences, commander of the Légion d'Honneur, and an honorary member of the Royal Society of London, the Academy of Madrid, and the Royal Netherlands Academy of Sciences. He was awarded many prizes and medals as well, and "for his method of hydrogenating organic compounds in the presence of finely divided nickel" he received the Nobel Prize in chemistry in 1912.

Sabatier is described as being reserved and detached. He was fond of art and gardening. From his marriage to Mademoiselle Herail there were four daughters, one of whom married the Italian chemist Emile Pomilio. Sabatier died on Aug. 14, 1941.

Further Reading

Biographical information on Sabatier is in Eduard Farber, *Nobel Prize Winners in Chemistry, 1901-1950* (1953); Eduard Farber, ed., *Great Chemists* (1961); and Nobel Foundation, *Chemistry: Nobel Lectures, Including Presentation Speeches and Laureates' Biographies* (3 vols., 1964-1966). □

Ernesto Sábato

The novelist and essayist Ernesto Sábato (born 1911) was one of Argentina's most challenging 20th-century intellectuals, concerned with both surrealist and real interpretations of phenomena, in real and imagined life.

Ernesto Sábato was born in Rojas, a provincial town of Buenos Aires Province, on June 24, 1911. One of 11 children of immigrant Italian parents, he received secondary and university training in La Plata, the provincial capital. Receiving a university degree in physics in 1937, he worked on a scholarship at the Joliot-Curie laboratory in Paris in 1938 and at the Massachusetts Institute of Technology in 1939. In 1939 he published a professional paper on his specialty, cosmic radiation. From 1940 to 1945 he taught at the University of La Plata but was forced to resign by the Perón dictatorship as politically undesirable.

As a student, Sábato had been deeply involved in protest against the corrupting military manipulation of the country, and after discarding anarchism as a philosophy he became a leader of the Communist party's youth movement. In 1935 he attended the international Antifascist Congress in Brussels but refused to go to Moscow for indoctrination. After many months of traumatic self-examination in Paris, he broke with the party and returned to Argentina. To a degree, he remained a political iconoclast thereafter.

Simultaneously, Sábato became much interested in philosophy and literature. He credited Pedro Henríquez Ureña, the noted Mexican philosopher and writer, who was his teacher, with being the greatest early influence in his life. Sábato read with extraordinary breadth and increasingly skimped on his scientific work. By 1938 he already was doubted by his professional colleagues to some extent, and his expulsion from teaching in 1945 therefore was not a shock except to family income.

Sábato endured the Perón dictatorship through work for publishers and writing essays and articles. In 1955, when Perón fell, Sábato became director of *Mundo Argentino,* a reputable intellectual journal, but was removed when he took a dogmatic position against the torture of political opponents of the post-Perón military government of Pedro Aramburu. Sábato returned briefly to public life in 1958-1959, under Arturo Frondizi, but soon resigned.

Sábato's three novels, which have been translated into more than 30 languages, are in English *The Tunnel* (1948); *On Heroes and Tombs* (1961); and *The Angel of Darkness* (1974). His principal essays are *Uno y el universo* (1946); *Hombres y engranajes* (1951); *Heterodoxia* (1953); *El otro rostro del peronismo* (1956); *El escritor y sus fantasmas* (1963), and *Apologías y rechazos* (1979).

El túnel, a very short novel, is concerned with a figure unable to establish his own identity or effective relationships with others. Some autobiographical elements are suggested by the figure's anomie. Eventually the person resorts

to violence against others, seeking a general understanding and awareness. *Sobre héroes y tumbas* is a longer and sweeping work and examines a variety of Argentine types, mores, and scenes. Critics find Sábato's novels influenced to some degree by the torment and anxiety of prerevolutionary Russian works. He employs imaginative metaphors and many asides in narration, in the style of romantic German novels. On the other hand, his scientific and epistemological training seems to have effected a precision and use of clarifying comparisons, especially in his novels.

Sábato's essays derive from his social and political concerns for the most part. At first he dealt with man's search for self and identity in a technocratic and indifferent society. His work of the Perón period was aphoristic, sarcastic, and critical of political abuses, but his later political essays show greater maturity of understanding and emphasize social morality and the need for consensual action to establish the responsibility and dignity of the society as well as of the individual.

In his later years, Sábato's work yielded to public appearances throughout the world and to popular television activity in Buenos Aires. In 1985 he received the prestigious Cervantes Prize for a lifetime of literary achievement. In 1996 Sábato was presented an Honorary Doctorate Degree by the University of the Republic. He had married Matilde Kusminsky-Richter, a fellow student, and they had two children.

Further Reading

A work on Sábato in English is in the *Twayne World Authors* series, Harley Oberhelman, *Ernesto S&aacute* (1970). For discussions of his work see Enrique Anderson-Imbert, *Spanish-American Literature: AHistory* (1954; trans. 1963; 2d ed., 2 vols., 1969), and Jean Franco, *The Modern Culture of Latin America: Society and the Artist* (1967). A collection of his essays in English is *Selections: The Writer in the Catastrophe of Our Time*, Ernesto Sábato (1990) □

Sabbatai Zevi

The Jewish mystic and pseudo-Messiah Sabbatai Zevi (1626-1676), or Sebi, was the founder of the Sabbatean sect.

Sabbatai Zevi was born in Smyrna (modern Izmir), Turkey, of Spanish-Jewish parentage. At an early age he adopted the mysticism of Isaac ben Solomon Luria and began to lead an ascetic life. Sabbatai's continual prayer, prolonged ecstasies, and Messianic prophecies secured for him by the age of 22 a large and enthusiastic following.

Sabbatai's father was the local agent in Smyrna for an English firm. Perhaps through his father, Sabbatai heard excited talk about the English Fifth Monarch Men, a group that with Christian millennialists had fixed upon 1666 as the year of the Messiah and of millenarian fulfillment. The Jewish Cabalists had already proclaimed 1648 as the year of salvation. In that year Sabbatai announced himself as the coming Messiah, pointing to his birthday (the ninth day of the month Av) as the traditional birthday of the Messiah.

Sabbatai left Smyrna in 1651, lived at the Cabalist school of Salonika, and then proceeded to Constantinople, where he met a man who claimed to have been told by angelic voices of Sabbatai's coming as the Redeemer. From Constantinople he traveled to Palestine and Cairo. The treasurer of the Turkish governor of Egypt, Raphael Halebi, gave Sabbatai moral support and funds. In Cairo he married a girl named Sarah who had survived the Chmielnicki massacre; he attributed a mystical value to his marriage, basing it as much on his wife's survival as on her name.

Sabbatai returned to Jerusalem to organize his movement. In the summer of 1665 Nathan of Gaza recognized Sabbatai as the Messiah, and he proclaimed that Sabbatai would win the longed-for Messianic victory "riding on a lion with a seven-headed dragon in his jaws."

The rabbis of Jerusalem, however, did not accept Sabbatai, and they also feared that his activities would arouse the anger of their Turkish overlords. Privately they threatened him with excommunication; publicly they could do nothing to stem the delirium of expectation that swept the Jewish communities of Egypt, Palestine, and Turkey and even those of Europe.

Sabbatai returned to Smyrna in the autumn of 1665, as the year of salvation approached. Jews in Venice, Amsterdam, London, Hamburg, southern Europe, and North Africa began to sell their belongings in expectation of being transported miraculously back to the restored Holy Land. At the beginning of 1666 Sabbatai went to Constantinople. Some reports say he was summoned by the Turkish authorities, who feared a popular uprising throughout their empire. He was arrested and imprisoned for 2 months in Constantinople and then transferred to the island of Abydos. Sabbatai's followers still believed in him, and in prison he held court, directed his movement, and lived like a king.

Denounced to the sultanate, Sabbatai was summoned to appear before the Sultan. To save his life he renounced Judaism and accepted Islam. Afterward, he was appointed doorkeeper to the Sultan. Later he was sent to Albania, where he died in complete obscurity. Long after his death many of his followers continued to believe in him. The influence of the Sabbatean movement survived into the 18th century.

Further Reading

A study of Sabbatai is Julius Katzenstein (pseudonym: Josef Kastein), *The Messiah of Ismir: Sabbatai Zevi* (1930; trans. 1931). He is discussed in Israel Zangwill, *Dreamers of the Ghetto* (1898), and Solomon Schechter, *Studies in Judaism* (1958). □

Albert Bruce Sabin

The Polish-American physician and virologist Albert Bruce Sabin (1906-1993) developed the first effective and widely used live virus polio vaccine.

Born in Poland, Sabin emigrated to the United States with his parents in 1921 in order to avoid persecutions directed against Jews. After attending New York University as a pre-dental student he switched to medical school and to an interest in microbiology. Upon receiving his medical degree in 1931, Sabin immediately began research on the nature and cause of polio, an acute viral infection that could result in death or paralysis. This disease had reached epidemic proportions affecting people around the world. During his internship at Bellevue Hospital in New York City, Sabin successfully isolated the B virus from a colleague who had died after a bite from a monkey. Sabin was soon able to prove the B virus's relation to the herpes simplex virus, the cause of herpes in humans.

Sabin joined the staff of the Rockefeller Institute in New York City in 1935 and four years later left for a post at the Children's Hospital Research Foundation in Cincinnati, Ohio. It was there that he proved that polio viruses not only grew in nervous tissue, as was generally assumed, but that they lived in the small intestines. By introducing the idea of *enteroviruses* —viruses that lived in the gut—Sabin established that poliomyelitis was essentially an infection of the alimentary tract. This discovery indicated that poliomyelitis might be vulnerable to a vaccine taken orally.

Sabin's work on a poliomyelitis vaccine was interrupted by World War II. In 1941 he joined the U.S. Army Epidemiological Board's Virus Committee and accepted assignments in Europe, Africa, the Middle East, and the Pacific. During this phase of his career Sabin developed vaccines for encephalitis (sleeping sickness), sand-fly fever, and dengue fever. At the war's end Sabin returned to Cincinnati and to his research on the polio virus.

Convinced that the polio virus in nature lived primarily in the intestines, Sabin resolved to make the human gut a hostile environment for it. This he intended to accomplish by isolating a mutant form of the polio virus that was incapable of producing the disease. The *avirulent* virus would then be propagated and introduced into the intestines, where it would reproduce rapidly, displacing the lethal *virulent* forms of the polio virus and protecting the human host from the disease. Sabin's goal from the outset was to find a live and safe variant polio virus that could be administered orally to combat poliomyelitis.

After an intensive investigation during which he discovered a number of new enteroviruses, Sabin managed to isolate the viruses he sought. Sabin and his research associates first ingested the live avirulent viruses themselves before they experimented on other human subjects. For two years (1955-1957) he gave the vaccine to hundreds of prison inmates with no harmful effects. At this point Sabin was ready for large-scale tests, but he could not carry them out in the United States. A rival polio vaccine developed by Dr. Jonas Salk in 1954 was then being tested for its efficacy in preventing the disease among American school children.

Whereas Sabin thought an attenuated live virus diluted and weakened would be effective, Salk was determined to create a vaccine using a killed form of the virus.

Some foreign virologists, especially those from the U.S.S.R., were convinced of the superiority of the Sabin vaccine, and hence it was first subjected to widespread tests outside the United States from 1957 to 1959. Millions of Russians, and millions more living in Latvia, Estonia, Czechoslovakia, Poland, Hungary, and East Germany, gained protection from poliomyelitis with Sabin's vaccine. A much smaller group of persons living in Sweden, England, Singapore, and the United States received Sabin's vaccine by the end of 1959.

In the meantime the Salk vaccine experienced some problems that made the American medical community more receptive to the solution proposed by Sabin. Salk's vaccine, which utilized killed virulent polioviruses, was accidently contaminated with some live virulent polioviruses which subsequently brought death or severe illness to several hundred school children. In addition, the Salk vaccine was somewhat difficult to administer (it was necessary to inject it into the body) and it was effective for a relatively short time (less than a year).

Sabin took advantage of this situation by vigorously promoting his vaccine. It was, he said, free of virulent viruses, easily administered orally, and effective over a long period of time. The battle that ensued between the supporters of the Salk and Sabin vaccines was finally won by the Sabin forces and hence it was a live virus vaccine that was used in the United States and the rest of the world to eradicate poliomyelitis. The battle between Salk and Sabin went on for years. Salk denounced Sabin's vaccine in 1973 as being unsafe and tried to persuade the public to use his vaccine again. But he was ignored by many, and by 1993 health organizations reported the near-extinction of the polio disease in the Western Hemisphere.

The success of his polio vaccine brought Sabin many honors at home and abroad. Always a tireless researcher, Sabin did not rest upon his laurels but moved on to a new field of study—the viral origins of human cancer. After more than a decade of work he was forced in 1977 to conclude that cancers were not caused by viruses as he had first assumed. During this time he served as research professor at the University of South Carolina until taking an emeritus status in 1982. In 1980 he traveled to Brazil to deal with a new outbreak of polio, and retired from medicine in 1986. Until his death on March 3, 1993, of heart failure, Sabin continued to add wood to the fire, speaking out against many ideals, including his doubts that a vaccine should be developed to fight the human immunodeficiency virus, or HIV, which causes AIDS.

Further Reading

Sabin's life and scientific achievements are treated in chapter 5 of Theodore Berland, *The Scientific Life* (1962) and in chapter 14 of Roger Rapoport, *The Superdoctors* (1975). The Salk-Sabin controversy is covered in Richard Carter, *Breakthrough: The Saga of Jonas Salk* (1966). *The Miracle Finders* by Donald Robinson and *The Health Century* by Edward Shorter are encouraged reading for learning of many other contributors to the world of virology. □

Florence Rena Sabin

Florence Rena Sabin's studies of the central nervous system of newborn infants, the origin of the lymphatic system, and the immune system's responses to infections—especially by the bacterium that causes tuberculosis—carved an important niche for her in the annals of science. She also researched and taught at Johns Hopkins School of Medicine and Rockefeller University.

In addition to her contributions to science, Florence Sabin's later work as a public health administrator left a permanent imprint upon the communities in which she served. Some of the firsts achieved by Sabin include becoming the first woman faculty member at Johns Hopkins School of Medicine, as well as its first female full professor, and the first woman to be elected president of the American Association of Anatomists.

Sabin was born on November 9, 1871, in Central City, Colorado, to George Kimball Sabin, a mining engineer and son of a country doctor, and Serena Miner, a teacher. Her early life, like that of many in that era, was spare: the house where she lived with her parents and older sister Mary had no plumbing, no gas and no electricity. When Sabin was four, the family moved to Denver; three years later her mother died.

After attending Wolfe Hall boarding school for a year, the Sabin daughters moved with their father to Lake Forest, Illinois, where they lived with their father's brother, Albert Sabin. There the girls attended a private school for two years and spent their summer vacations at their grandfather Sabin's farm near Saxtons River, Vermont.

Sabin graduated from Vermont Academy boarding school in Saxtons River and joined her older sister at Smith College in Massachusetts, where they lived in a private house near the school. As a college student, Sabin was particularly interested in mathematics and science, and earned a bachelor of science in 1893. During her college years she tutored other students in mathematics, thus beginning her long career in teaching.

A course in zoology during her junior year at Smith ignited a passion for biology, which she made her specialty. Determined to demonstrate that, despite widespread opinion to the contrary, an educated woman was as competent as an educated man, Sabin proceeded to chose medicine as her career. This decision may have been influenced by events occurring in Baltimore at the time.

The opening of Johns Hopkins Medical School in Baltimore was delayed for lack of funds until a group of prominent local women raised enough money to support the institution. In return for their efforts, they insisted that

women be admitted to the school—a radical idea at a time when women who wanted to be physicians generally had to attend women's medical colleges.

In 1893 the Johns Hopkins School of Medicine welcomed its first class of medical students; but Sabin, lacking tuition for four years of medical school, moved to Denver to teach mathematics at Wolfe Hall, her old school. Two years later she became an assistant in the biology department at Smith College, and in the summer of 1896 she worked in the Marine Biological Laboratories at Woods Hole. In October of 1896 she was finally able to begin her first year at Johns Hopkins.

While at Johns Hopkins, Sabin began a long professional relationship with Dr. Franklin P. Mall, the school's professor of anatomy. During the four years she was a student there and the fifteen years she was on his staff, Mall exerted an enormous influence over her intellectual growth and development into prominent scientist and teacher. Years after Mall's death, Sabin paid tribute to her mentor by writing his biography, *Franklin Paine Mall: The Story of a Mind.*

Sabin thrived under Mall's tutelage, and while still a student she constructed models of the medulla and midbrain from serial microscopic sections of a newborn baby's nervous system. For many years, several medical schools used reproductions of these models to instruct their students. A year after her graduation from medical school in 1900, Sabin published her first book based on this work, *An Atlas of the Medulla and Midbrain*, which became one of

her major contributions to medical literature, according to many of her colleagues.

After medical school, Sabin was accepted as an intern at Johns Hopkins Hospital, a rare occurrence for a woman at that time. Nevertheless, she concluded during her internship that she preferred research and teaching to practicing medicine. However, her teaching ambitions were nearly foiled by the lack of available staff positions for women at Johns Hopkins. Fortunately, with the help of Mall and the women of Baltimore who had raised money to open the school, a fellowship was created in the department of anatomy for her. Thus began a long fruitful period of work in a new field of research, the embryologic development of the human lymphatic system.

Sabin began her studies of the lymphatic system to settle controversy over how it developed. Some researchers believed the vessels that made up the lymphatics formed independently from the vessels of the circulatory system, specifically the veins. However, a minority of scientists believed that the lymphatic vessels arose from the veins themselves, budding outward as continuous channels. The studies that supported this latter view were done on pig embryos that were already so large (about 90mm in length) that many researchers—Sabin included—pointed out that the embryos were already old enough to be considered an adult form, thus the results were inconclusive.

The young Johns Hopkins researcher set out to settle the lymphatic argument by studying pig embryos as small as 23mm in length. Combining the painstaking techniques of injecting the microscopic vessels with dye or ink and reconstructing the three-dimensional system from two-dimensional cross sections, Sabin demonstrated that lymphatics did in fact arise from veins by sprouts of endothelium (the layer of cells lining the vessels). Furthermore, these sprouts connected with each other as they grew outward, so the lymphatic system eventually developed entirely from existing vessels. In addition, she demonstrated that the peripheral ends (those ends furthest away from the center of the body) of the lymphatic vessels were closed and, contrary to the prevailing opinion, were neither open to tissue spaces nor derived from them. Even after her results were confirmed by others they remained controversial. Nevertheless, Sabin firmly defended her work in her book *The Origin and Development of the Lymphatic System.*

Sabin's first papers on the lymphatics won the 1903 prize of the Naples Table Association, an organization that maintained a research position for women at the Zoological Station in Naples, Italy. The prize was awarded to women who produced the best scientific thesis based on independent laboratory research.

Back at Hopkins from her year abroad, she continued her work in anatomy and became an associate professor of anatomy in 1905. Her work on lymphatics led her to studies of the development of blood vessels and blood cells. In 1917 she was appointed professor of histology, the first woman to be awarded full professorship at the medical school. During this period of her life, she enjoyed frequent trips to Europe to conduct research in major German university laboratories.

After returning to the United States from one of her trips abroad, she developed methods of staining living cells, enabling her to differentiate between various cells that had previously been indistinguishable. She also used the newly devised "hanging drop" technique to observe living cells in liquid preparations under the microscope. With these techniques she studied the development of blood vessels and blood cells in developing organisms—once she stayed up all night to watch the "birth" of the bloodstream in a developing chick embryo. Her diligent observation enabled her to witness the formation of blood vessels as well as the formation of stem cells from which all other red and white blood cells arose. During these observations, she also witnessed the heart make its first beat.

Sabin's technical expertise in the laboratory permitted her to distinguish between various blood cell types. She was particularly interested in white blood cells called monocytes, which attacked infectious bacteria, such as *Mycobacterium tuberculosis,* the organism that causes tuberculosis. Although this organism was discovered by the German microbiologist Robert Koch during the previous century, the disease was still a dreaded health menace in the early twentieth century. The National Tuberculosis Association acknowledged the importance of Sabin's research of the body's immune response to the tuberculosis organism by awarding her a grant to support her work in 1924.

In that same year, she was elected president of the American Association of Anatomists, and the following year Sabin became the first woman elected to membership in the National Academy of Sciences. These honors followed her 1921 speech to American women scientists at Carnegie Hall during a reception for Nobel Prize-winning physicist Marie Curie, an event that signified Sabin's recognized importance in the world of science.

Although her research garnered many honors, Sabin continued to relish her role as a professor at Johns Hopkins. The classes she taught in the department of anatomy enabled her to influence many first-year students—a significant number of whom participated in her research over the years. She also encouraged close teacher-student relationships and frequently hosted gatherings at her home for them.

One of her most cherished causes was the advancement of equal rights for women in education, employment, and society in general. Sabin considered herself equal to her male colleagues and frequently voiced her support for educational opportunities for women in the speeches she made upon receiving awards and honorary degrees. Her civic-mindedness extended to the political arena where she was an active suffragist and contributor to the Maryland *Suffrage News* in the 1920s.

Sabin's career at Johns Hopkins drew to a close in 1925, eight years after the death of her close friend and mentor Franklin Mall. She had been passed over for the position of professor of anatomy and head of the department, which was given to one of her former students. Thus, she stepped down from her position as professor of histology and left Baltimore.

In her next position, Sabin continued her study of the role of monocytes in the body's defense against the tubercle bacterium that causes tuberculosis. In the fall of 1925, Sabin assumed a position as full member of the scientific staff at the Rockefeller Institute for Medical Research (now Rockefeller University) in New York City at the invitation of the institute's director, Simon Flexner . At Rockefeller Sabin continued to study the role of monocytes and other white blood cells in the body's immune response to infections. She became a member of the Research Committee of the National Tuberculosis Association and aspired to popularize tuberculosis research throughout Rockefeller, various pharmaceutical companies, and other universities and research institutes. The discoveries that she and her colleagues made concerning the ways in which the immune system responded to tuberculosis led her to her final research project: the study of antibody formation.

During her years in New York, Sabin participated in the cultural life of the city, devoting her leisure time to the theater, the symphony, and chamber music concerts she sometimes presented in her home. She enjoyed reading nonfiction and philosophy, in which she found intellectual stimulation that complemented her enthusiasm for research. Indeed, one of her co-workers was quoted in *Biographical Memoirs* as saying that Sabin possessed a "great joy and pleasure which she derived from her work . . . like a contagion among those around her so that all were stimulated in much the same manner that she was. . . . She was nearly always the first one at the laboratory, and greeted every one with a *joie de vivre* which started the day pleasantly for all of us."

Meanwhile, she continued to accrue honors. She received fourteen honorary doctorates of science from various universities, as well as a doctor of laws. *Good Housekeeping* magazine announced in 1931 that Sabin had been selected in their nationwide poll as one of the twelve most eminent women in the country. In 1935 she received the M. Carey Thomas prize in science, an award of $5,000 presented at the fiftieth anniversary of Bryn Mawr College. Among her many other awards was the Trudeau Medal of the National Tuberculosis Association (1945), the Lasker Award of the American Public Health Association (1951), and the dedication of the Florence R. Sabin Building for Research in Cellular Biology, at the University of Colorado Medical Center.

In 1938 Sabin retired from Rockefeller and moved to Denver to live with her older sister, Mary, a retired high school mathematics teacher. She returned to New York at least once a year to fulfill her duties as a member of both the advisory board of the John Simon Guggenheim Memorial Foundation and the advisory committee of United China Relief.

Sabin quickly became active in public health issues in Denver and was appointed to the board of directors of the Children's Hospital in 1942 where she later served as vice president. During this time she became aware of the lack of proper enforcement of Colorado's primitive public health laws and began advocating for improved conditions. Governor John Vivian appointed her to his Post-War Planning

Committee in 1945, and she assumed the chair of a sub-committee on public health called the Sabin Committee. In this capacity she fought for improved public health laws and construction of more health care facilities.

Two years later she was appointed manager of the Denver Department of Health and Welfare, donating her salary of $4,000 to the University of Colorado Medical School for Research. She became chair of Denver's newly formed Board of Health and Hospitals in 1951 and served for two years in that position. Her unflagging enthusiasm for public health issues bore significant fruit. A *Rocky Mountain News* reporter stated that "Dr. Sabin . . . was the force and spirit behind the Tri-County chest X-ray campaign" that contributed to cutting the death rate from tuberculosis by 50 percent in Denver in just two years.

But Sabin's enormous reserve of energy flagged under the strain of caring for her ailing sister. While recovering from her own illness, Sabin sat down to watch a World Series game on October 3, 1953, in which her favorite team, the Brooklyn Dodgers, were playing. She died of a heart attack before the game was over.

The state of Colorado gave Sabin a final posthumous honor by installing a bronze statue of her in the National Statuary Hall in the Capitol in Washington, D.C., where each state is permitted to honor two of its most revered citizens. Upon her death, as quoted in *Biographical Memoirs,* the Denver *Post* called her the "First Lady of American Science." Sabin's philosophy of life and work might be best summed up by words attributed to Leonardo da Vinci, with which she chose to represent herself on bookplates: "Thou, O God, dost sell unto us all good things at the price of labour."

Further Reading

Bluemel, Elinor, *Florence Sabin: Colorado Woman of the Century,* University of Colorado Press, 1959.

Kronstadt, Janet, *Florence Sabin,* Chelsea House, 1990.

McMaster, Philip D. and Michael Heidelberger, "Florence Rena Sabin," in *Biographical Memoirs,* Columbia University Press, 1960.

Yost, Edna, *American Women of Science,* Frederick A. Stokes, 1943.

Rocky Mountain News (Denver, CO), March 1, 1951. □

Sacajawea

In the early 1800s, Sacajawea accompanied Meriwether Lewis and William Clark on their historical expedition from St. Louis, Missouri, to the Pacific Ocean. Sacajawea is responsible in large part for the success of the expedition, due to her navigational, diplomatic, and translating skills.

Sacajawea was an interpreter and guide for and the only woman member of the Lewis and Clark Expedition of 1804-1806. She was born somewhere between 1784 and 1788 into the Lehmi band of the Shoshone Indians who lived in the eastern part of the Salmon River area of present-day central Idaho. Her father was chief of her village. Sacajawea's Shoshone name was Boinaiv, which means "Grass Maiden." The primary documentation of Sacajawea's life is contained in the journals of Meriwether Lewis and William Clark, a lawyer and a clerk of a fur trading company who led an expedition authorized by President Thomas Jefferson in 1803 to explore the recently purchased Louisiana Territory. In addition, the Shoshone Indians have many stories in their oral tradition about Sacajawea, and many living Shoshone trace their ancestry to her. Nevertheless, there is much controversy surrounding the life of this intrepid woman.

Captured by Hidatsa War Party

In 1800, when the Shoshone girl, Boinaiv, was about 12 years old, her band was camped at the Three Forks of the Missouri River in Montana when they encountered some Hidatsa warriors. The warriors killed four men, four women and a number of boys. Several girls and boys, including Boinaiv, were captured and taken back to the Hidatsa village. At the Hidatsa camp, Boinaiv was given the name Sacagawea by her captors, which means "Bird Woman." There is more than a little argument over the derivation and

Sacajawea (woman, second from left)

spelling of Sacajawea's name. Sacajawea is a name meaning "Boat Launcher" in Shoshone. The *Original Journals of Lewis and Clark* support a Hidatsa origin. On May 20, 1805, Lewis wrote of "Sah-ca-ger-we-ah or Bird Woman's River" as a name for what is now Crooked Creek in north-central Montana. Sometime between 1800 and 1804, Sacajawea and another girl were sold to (or won in a gambling match by) trader Toussaint Charbonneau, a French-Canadian who was residing among the Hidatsa. He eventually married both girls.

Joins the "Corps of Discovery"

In 1803, Jefferson and the U. S. Congress authorized a "Voyage of Discovery" by which a group of men would explore the territory between the Mississippi and Columbia Rivers and attempt to find a water route to the Pacific Ocean. Jefferson's secretary and confidante, Lewis, and Lewis's friend Clark were assigned to lead the corps of explorers. The expedition of some 45 men left St. Louis, Missouri, on May 14, 1804. They arrived at the Mandan and Hidatsa villages near the mouth of the Knife River in North Dakota on October 26, 1804. There, they built cabins in a clearing below the villages and settled in for the winter.

On November 4, 1804, Clark wrote in his journal: "a Mr. Chaubonie [Charbonneau] interpreter from the Gross Ventre nation came to see us . . . this man wished to hire as an interpreter." Clark's field notes for the same day state that both Charbonneau and Sacajawea were hired: "a french man by name Chabonah who speaks the Big Belley language visited us, he wished to hire and informed us his 2 Squaws were Snake [Shoshone] Indians, we engaged him to go on with us and take one of his wives to interpret the Snake language." Lewis and Clark realized that they would need someone to help interpret and help secure supplies from the Shoshone when they passed through their territory. As it later turned out, the process of interpretation was a cumbersome matter. Sacajawea conversed with her husband in Gros Ventre. Charbonneau then passed on Sacajawea's words in French to another individual in the party who spoke French and English; that individual then relayed the information along to Lewis and Clark in English. Sacajawea also made extensive use of sign language, which many in the party could interpret.

At the time the party had come to the Mandan villages, Sacajawea was pregnant. Lewis duly noted in his journal the birth on February 11, 1805, of a "fine boy," although Sacajawea's "labor was tedious and the pain violent." The boy was named Jean Baptiste Charbonneau. Even with an infant, Sacajawea and her husband were hired as interpreters. On April 7, 1805, Sacajawea—carrying her infant in a cradleboard—accompanied the expedition out of the Mandan villages for the trek west. Clark listed among the 32 members of the party "my servant, York; George Drewyer, who acts as hunter and interpreter; Sharbonah and his Indian squaw to act as Interpreter and interpretess for the Snake Indians . . . and Shabonah's infant."

Sacajawea quickly demonstrated her knowledge of edible plants along the course. Lewis wrote on April 9 that when the expedition stopped for dinner Sacajawea "busied

herself in search for the wild artichokes. . . . This operation she performed by penetrating the earth with a sharp stick about some collection of driftwood. Her labors soon proved successful and she procured a good quantity of these roots." At many other points in the trip, Sacajawea gathered, stored, and prepared wild edibles for the party, especially a plentiful root called *Year-pah* by the Shoshones.

On May 14, the party encountered heavy winds near the Yellowstone River. Charbonneau was at the helm of the pirogue, or canoe, which held some supplies and valuables gathered during the expedition. Lewis noted that "it happened unfortunately for us this evening that Charbono was at the helm of this perogue . . . ; Charbono cannot swim and is perhaps the most timid waterman in the world." Both Lewis and Clark were on shore and could only watch in horror at what occurred next. Clark wrote: "We proceeded on very well until about 6 o'clock. A squall of wind struck our sail broadside and turned the perogue nearly over, and in this situation the perogue remained until the sail was cut down in which time she nearly filled with water. The articles which floated out were nearly all caught by the squaw who was in the rear. This accident had like to have cost us dearly; for in this perogue were embarked our papers, instruments, books, medicine, a great proportion of our merchandise." Lewis noted in his journal: "The Indian woman, to whom I ascribe equal fortitude and resolution with any person on board at the time of the accident, caught and preserved most of the light articles which were washed overboard." About a week later, Lewis recorded that a recently discovered river was named in Sacajawea's honor, no doubt in recognition of her important service to the party. According to Lewis: "About five miles above the mouth of Shell river, a handsome river of about fifty yards in width discharged itself into the Shell river on the starboard or upper side. This stream we called Sah-ca-ger-we-ah or 'Bird Woman's river,' after our interpreter, the Snake woman."

On June 10, Sacajawea became ill and remained so for the next several days. This event is discussed at length in the journals of both Lewis and Clark, who were extremely concerned for her welfare. Both took turns tending to her. On June 16, Clark wrote that Sacajawea was "very bad and will take no medicine whatever until her husband, finding her out of her senses, easily prevailed upon her to take medicine. If she dies it will be the fault of her husband." Lewis wrote that Sacajawea's illness "gave me some concern as well for the poor object herself, then with a young child in her arms, as from the consideration of her being our only dependence for a friendly negotiation with the Snake [Shoshone] Indians on whom we depend for horses to assist us in our portage from the Missouri to the Columbia River." Sacajawea recovered from this illness, but a few days later, on June 29, she, her infant son, Charbonneau, and the servant York nearly drowned in a flash flood. Fortunately, Clark hurried the group to safer ground and all were spared.

Reunion with the Shoshones

On July 30, 1805, the party passed the spot on the Three Forks of the Missouri where Sacajawea was taken from her people some five years previously. A little over one week later, at Beaverhead Rock, Sacajawea recognized her homeland and notified the expedition that the Shoshones had to be near. On August 13, Lewis took an advance party on ahead to find and meet the Shoshone while Clark remained behind with Sacajawea and the rest of the group. The next day, Charbonneau was observed by Clark on two occasions to strike his wife, for which Clark severely reprimanded him.

On August 17, Clark, Sacajawea, and the rest of the party came upon Lewis who had met the Lehmi-Shoshone chief Cameahwait. Clark described what happened: "I saw at a distance several Indians on horseback coming towards me. The interpreter and squaw, who were before me at some distance, danced for the joyful sight, and she made signs to me that they were her nation." The Biddle edition of the journals of Lewis and Clark notes that Sacajawea was sent for to interpret between Lewis and Clark and Cameahwait: "She came into the tent, sat down, and was beginning to interpret, when in the person of Cameahwait she recognized her brother; she instantly jumped up and ran and embraced him, throwing over him her blanket and weeping profusely . . . ; after some conversation between them she resumed her seat, and attempted to interpret for us, but her new situation seemed to overpower her, and she was frequently interrupted by tears." Sacajawea learned that her only surviving family were two brothers and a son of her eldest sister, whom she immediately adopted. She also met the Shoshone man to whom she had been promised as a child; however, he was no longer interested in her because she had borne a child with another man. While among her people, Sacajawea helped to secure horses, supplies, and Shoshone guides to assist in the expedition's trip across the Rocky Mountains.

Leaving her adopted son in the care of her brother Cameahwait, Sacajawea and the rest of the party traveled on, eventually following the Snake River to its junction with the Columbia, and on toward the Pacific Ocean. On October 13, 1805, Clark again commented on the value of having Sacajawea as a member of the expedition: "The wife of Shabono our interpreter we find reconciles all the Indians as to our friendly intentions a woman with a party of men is a token of peace." In November 1805, a lead party from the expedition reached the ocean. Having heard that this group had discovered a beached whale, Sacajawea insisted that Lewis and Clark take her to see the ocean. Lewis wrote on January 6, 1805: "The Indian woman was very importunate to be permitted to go, and was therefore indulged; she observed that she had traveled a long way with us to see the great waters, and that now that monstrous fish was also to be seen, she thought it very bad she could not be permitted to see either."

When the party separated on the return trip in order to explore various routes, Sacajawea joined Clark, directing him through the territory of her people, pointing out edible berries and roots, and suggesting that Clark take the Bozeman Pass to rejoin the other members at the junction of the Yellowstone and Missouri rivers. Clark noted on July 13, 1806, that "The Indian woman, who has been of great

service to me as a pilot through this country, recommends a gap in the mountains more south which I shall cross."

Two days after the parties were rejoined, on August 14, 1806, the expedition arrived back at the Mandan villages. Here Charbonneau and Sacajawea decided to remain. Clark offered to adopt their son Jean Baptiste, whom he had affectionately called "Pomp" on the trip. They accepted Clark's offer for a later time after the infant was weaned. On the return trip to St. Louis, Clark wrote a letter to Charbonneau, inviting him to come live and work in St. Louis and commenting: "your woman, who accompanied you that long dangerous and fatiguing route to the Pacific Ocean and back, deserved a greater reward for her attention and services on that route than we had in our power to give her at the Mandans." While Charbonneau was paid for his services, Sacajawea, as his wife, received no financial remuneration separate from her husband.

Controversy Remains over Sacagawea's Later Years

There is strong evidence to indicate that Sacajawea lived for only a few short years after parting ways with the Lewis and Clark expedition. It may be that Charbonneau accepted Clark's invitation to come to Missouri and farm land. On April 2, 1811, a lawyer and traveler named Henry Brackenridge was on a boat from St. Louis to the Mandan, Arikara, and Hidatsa villages of North and South Dakota. He noted in his journal for that day (cited in Ella E. Clark's and Margot Edmonds's *Sacagawea of the Lewis and Clark Expedition*): "We have on board a Frenchman named Charbonet, with his wife, an Indian woman of the Snake nation, both of whom had accompanied Lewis and Clark to the Pacific, and were of great service. The woman, a good creature, of a mild and gentle disposition, was greatly attached to the whites, whose manners and dress she tried to imitate; but she had become sickly, and longed to revisit her native country; her husband, also, who had spent many years amongst the Indians, was become weary of a civilized life."

It is believed by many scholars that Charbonneau and Sacajawea, having left their son Jean Baptiste with Clark to raise in St. Louis (Jean Baptiste later became a respected interpreter and mountain man) took their infant daughter named Lizette, and traveled to the Missouri Fur Company of Manuel Lisa in South Dakota. An employee of the fur company, John C. Luttig, recorded in his journal on December 20, 1812: "this Evening the Wife of Charbonneau, a Snake Squaw died of a putrid fever she was a good and the best Woman in the fort aged abt 25 years she left a fine infant girl." Sacajawea was buried in the grounds of the fort. In addition, William Clark published an account book for the period of 1825-1828, in which he listed the members of the expedition and whether they were then either living or dead. He recorded Sacajawea as deceased.

Another theory of Sacajawea's life, supported among others by an early biographer, Dr. Grace Hebard of the University of Wyoming, relates that Sacajawea actually left her husband, took her son Jean Baptiste and adopted son— named Bazil—and went to live with the Comanches. There she married a man named Jerk Meat and bore five more children. Later, Sacajawea returned to her homeland to live with her Shoshone people at what was now the Wind River Agency. She was called Porivo ("Chief") at Wind River and became an active tribal leader. She was reported by some Shoshones, Indian agents, and missionaries to have died at the age of about 100 in 1884 and to have been buried at Fort Washakie. Opponents of this theory argue that the woman who called herself Sacajawea was actually another Shoshone woman.

The Shoshones of Fort Washakie have started a project to document the descendants of Sacajawea. As of mid-1993, more than 400 Shoshones who can trace their ancestry to Sacajawea have been counted. Many among them believe that she indeed lived a long and full life.

From the time of her marriage, Sacajawea's life became inextricably bound to a group of Anglo explorers and their quest for westward expansion. In spite of separation from her people, illness, physical abuse from her spouse, and an infant to care for, Sacajawea made key contributions to the success of the Lewis and Clark Expedition. Her skills as an interpreter and as liaison between the Shoshone and the expedition, her knowledge of the flora and fauna and of the terrain along much of the route, and her common sense and good humor were key elements that contributed to the successful resolution of the journey.

Sacajawea has become one of the most memorialized women in American history. A bronze statue of her was exhibited during the centennial observance of the Lewis and Clark Expedition in St. Louis in 1904. Another statue was commissioned by a women's suffrage group in Oregon, with the unveiling set to coincide with the Lewis and Clark Centennial Exposition in Portland in 1905. Statues also reside in Idaho, Montana, North Dakota, Oklahoma, and Virginia. In addition to the river in Montana named for Sacajawea by Lewis and Clark, other memorials include three mountains, two lakes, and numerous markers, paintings, musical compositions, schools, and a museum.

Further Reading

Biographical Dictionary of Indians of the Americas, Newport Beach, CA, American Indian Publishers, Inc., 1991, Vol. II; 642-647.

Clark, Ella E., and Margot Edmonds, *Sacagawea of the Lewis and Clark Expedition,* Berkeley, University of California Press, 1979.

Dictionary of American Biography, edited by Dumas Malone, New York, Scribner's, 1935, Vol. XVI; 278.

Dockstader, Frederick J., *Great North American Indians: Profiles in Life and Leadership,* New York, Van Nostrand Reinhold, 1977; 248-249.

Dye, Eva Emery, *The Conquest: The True Story of Lewis and Clark,* Chicago, A. C. McClurg, 1902.

Hebard, Grace Raymond, *Sacajawea: A Guide and Interpreter of the Lewis and Clark Expedition, with an Account of the Travels of Toussaint Charbonneau, and of Jean Baptiste, the Expedition Papoose,* Glendale, CA, Arthur H. Clark Company, 1933.

Howard, Harold P., *Sacajawea,* Norman, University of Oklahoma Press, 1971.

Letters of the Lewis and Clark Expedition, with Related Documents, 1783-1854, edited by Donald Jackson, Urbana, University of Illinois Press, 1962.

Lewis, Meriwether, and William Clark, *Original Journals of the Lewis and Clark Expedition, 1804-1806,* 8 vols., edited by Reuben Gold Thwaites, New York, Dodd, Mead, 1904-1905.

Lewis, Meriwether, William Clark, and Nicholas Biddle, *History of the Expedition Under the Command of Captains Lewis and Clark, to the Sources of the Missouri, Thence Across the Rocky Mountains and Down the River Columbia to the Pacific Ocean, Performed During the Years 1804-5-6, by Order of the Government of the United States,* 3 vols., New York, A. S. Barnes, 1904.

Liberty's Women, edited by Robert McHenry, Springfield, MA, Merriam, 1980; 362-363.

Native American Women: A Biographical Dictionary, edited by Gretchen M. Bataille, New York, Garland, 1993; 219-222.

Native North American Almanac, edited by Duane Champagne, Detroit, MI, Gale Research Inc., 1994; 1151.

Notable American Women, 1607-1950: A Biographical Dictionary, edited by Edward T. James, Cambridge, MA, Harvard University Press, 1971, Vol. III; 218-219.

Reader's Encyclopedia of the American West, edited by Howard R. Lamar, New York, Thomas Y. Crowell, 1977; 1055.

Reid, Russell, *Sakakawea: The Bird Woman,* Bismark, ND, State Historical Society of North Dakota, 1986.

Remley, David, "Sacajawea of Myth and History," in *Women and Western American Literature,* edited by Helen Winter Stauffer and Susan J. Rosowski, Troy, NY, 1982; 70-89.

Ronda, James P., *Lewis and Clark among the Indians,* Lincoln, University of Nebraska Press, 1984.

Waldman, Carl, *Who Was Who in Native American History,* New York, Facts on File, 1990; 309-310.

Weatherford, Doris, *American Women's History,* New York, Prentice Hall, 1994; 303-304.

Anderson, Irving, "Probing the Riddle of the Bird Woman," *Montana, the Magazine of Western History,* 23, October 1973; 2-17.

Chuinard, E. G., "The Bird Woman: Purposeful Member of the Corps or Casual 'Tag-Along'?" *Montana, the Magazine of Western History* 26, July 1976; 18-29.

Dawson, Jan C. "Sacagawea: Pilot or Pioneer Mother?", *Pacific Northwest Quarterly,* 83, January 1992; 22-28.

Morrison, Joan, "Sacajawea's Legacy Traced," *Wind River News* 16, June 22, 1993; 4.

Schroer, Blanche, "Boat-Pusher or Bird Woman? Sacagawea or Sacajawea?" *Annals of Wyoming* 52, Spring 1980; 46-54. □

Sacco and Vanzetti

Nicola Sacco (died 1927) and Bartolomeo Vanzetti (1888-1927), Italian-born anarchists, became the subject of one of America's most celebrated controversies and the focus for much of the liberal and radical protest of the 1920s in the United States.

The execution of Nicola Sacco and Bartolomeo Vanzetti in Boston in 1927 brought to an end a struggle of more than 6 years on the part of Americans and Europeans who had become convinced that they were innocent of the crimes of robbery and murder. For a sizable portion of the American intellectual community their case symbolized the fight for justice for ethnic minorities, the poor, and the politically unorthodox. The case had a catalytic influence on the subsequent development of leftist thought in America.

Sacco was born in Torremaggiore. When he was 17, he immigrated to the United States. He learned the trade of shoe edge-trimming and settled in Milford, Mass., working for a local shoe company. He married, fathered a son, and seemed to be building a stable and secure life.

Vanzetti, by contrast, was a bachelor and a wanderer. Born in Villafalletto, he went to the United States in early adulthood. He worked as a kitchen helper in New York, then at various menial jobs in the Boston area. There Vanzetti, already committed to anarchist principles, met Sacco. When the United States entered World War I, they fled to Mexico to escape military conscription. Within a few months Sacco returned to his family; Vanzetti traveled around the American Midwest for a year.

Returning to New England, Vanzetti worked at a succession of jobs and renewed his friendship with Sacco, who was employed at a shoe factory. Vanzetti spent much time reading and reflecting on prospects for the revolutionary transformation of industrial society. Sacco, though little interested in books and ideas, also accepted the anarchist vision of brotherhood, peace, and plenty without government. The two moved in a circle of anarchists and sometimes distributed revolutionary literature.

Arrest, Trial, Conviction

Such were the ostensible circumstances of the two men's lives in May of 1920, when they were arrested and charged with participating in the robbery of a shoe factory in South Braintree, Mass., on April 15 and murdering the plant's paymaster and payroll guard. They were arrested shortly after going to a garage to claim an automobile which had supposedly been seen near the South Braintree crime. Both were armed but protested they knew nothing of the crime and had planned to use the automobile to distribute anarchist literature.

Vanzetti, also charged with taking part in an attempted mail truck robbery the previous December, was speedily indicted, tried, convicted, and sentenced to 12 to 15 years' imprisonment. It was almost a year before Vanzetti and Sacco went on trial in Dedham for the South Braintree robbery and murders. Their trial turned into an extraordinarily vigorous and complicated legal struggle between the prosecutor and Fred H. Moore, who managed the Sacco and Vanzetti defense. After more than 6 weeks of listening to witnesses, to the presentation of ballistics evidence which supposedly matched a bullet from one of the victims with bullets from Sacco's pistol, and to grueling cross-examinations and closing speeches, the jury returned verdicts of guilty for both.

Posttrial Strategy

The Dedham trial received almost no publicity outside Boston while in progress; the anarchist issue was apparently of minor importance. But over the next 6 years Moore, William G. Thompson (who became chief defense counsel after Moore left), and the Sacco-Vanzetti Defense Committee (an array of anarchists, Boston free-thinkers from prestigious families, and middle-class liberals and radicals) reshaped the public image of the case into a political and ideological rather than a legal controversy. The thesis of the defense's campaign was that the trial had been conducted in an atmosphere of fear and repression and that the jury and especially Judge Webster Thayer had been prejudiced against the defendants. Therefore Sacco and Vanzetti stood convicted not because of the evidence but because of their radical political beliefs.

This strategy increasingly mobilized public sentiment as years passed and doubts multiplied regarding portions of the evidence. Some prosecution witnesses repudiated their identifications, then repudiated their repudiations. Another convicted murderer confessed that he had taken part in the South Braintree crime and that Sacco and Vanzetti had not been in the gang, but his story was sketchy and inconsistent. The defense lawyers repeatedly but unsuccessfully presented motions for a new trial. On April 9, 1927, after the Massachusetts Supreme Judicial Court affirmed the convictions, Judge Thayer sentenced Sacco and Vanzetti to die in the electric chair.

Sacco (left) and Vanzetti (right)

Final Failure

The fight to save Sacco and Vanzetti's lives continued. Governor Alvan T. Fuller, harassed on all sides, appointed a three-man panel to review the documents accumulated since 1920. The committee concluded that Sacco and Vanzetti should die. Desperate efforts to convince the U.S. Supreme Court to hear the case failed. On Aug. 22, 1927, as hundreds of heavily armed police faced crowds of demonstrators outside Boston's old Charles-town Prison, and as tens of thousands protested in the streets of New York and in many cities abroad, Sacco and Vanzetti were electrocuted.

The Sacco-Vanzetti case furnished a public cause around which American intellectuals of widely variant beliefs could unite. The case inspired a voluminous literary outpouring and seemed to dramatize the intolerance and injustice of American society. The movement to save Sacco and Vanzetti presaged the greater involvement of intellectuals with social issues that would mark the 1930s.

The Sacco and Vanzetti case remains a tragic chapter in United States history. The case has come to stand for the type of racial bigotry and breach of human rights the United States Constitution is to protect against. The legacy of Sacco and Vanzetti serves to protect others from racial and political prosecution.

Further Reading

Published material on the Sacco-Vanzetti case is voluminous. The classic brief for the defense is Felix Frankfurter, *The Case of Sacco and Vanzetti* (1927). G. Louis Joughin and Edmund M. Morgan, *The Legacy of Sacco and Vanzetti* (1948), an almost exhaustive résumé and analysis of the evidence, strongly upholds their innocence. Robert H. Montgomery, *Sacco-Vanzetti: The Murder and the Myth* (1960), concludes they were guilty, while Francis Russell, *Tragedy in Dedham* (1962), accepts the state's ballistics evidence and the guilty verdict for Sacco but exonerates Vanzetti. David Felix, *Protest: Sacco-Vanzetti and the Intellectuals* (1965), is more concerned with describing the development of the Sacco-Vanzetti "myth" and its impact on American intellectuals in the 1920s. Much of the atmosphere of the Sacco-Vanzetti protest movement can be gleaned from Upton Sinclair's novel *Boston* (1928) and John Dos Passos' *The Big Money* (1936) and *U.S.A.* (1937). □

Hans Sachs

The German poet Hans Sachs (1494-1576) made Nuremberg famous in his time as a center of Meistergesang.

Born in Nuremberg, the son of a tailor of the upper middle class, Hans Sachs was apprenticed to a shoemaker in 1508. As a journeyman, he traveled from one German town to another between 1511 and 1516 learning his trade. Simultaneously, he studied *Meistergesang* in the Singschulen, his principal teacher being Leonhard Nunnenbeck. *Meistergesang* is the German art of singing original poems to usually original tunes, according to the rules of the pedestrian craft of burgher poets; it was revived in the 19th century in parody form (as sung by Beckmesser in Richard Wagner's opera *Die Meistersinger*).

In Nuremberg in 1517 Sachs attained the rank of master in the shoemakers' guild and in *Meistergesang*. He declared himself in favor of Martin Luther in the poem *Die wittenbergische Nachtigall* ("The Nightingale of Wittenberg") in 1523 and also in prose dialogues.

Sachs produced works in profusion: more than 4,000 *Meisterlieder;* 208 dramas, according to his own count; 85 Shrovetide plays; and many rhymed orations and other verses. During his lifetime three volumes of his verse appeared, and two more were issued posthumously. Other works remain unpublished in a collection in Zwickau, Saxony. His themes, derived from his reading in anecdotal and farcical literature of the time and from popularized and trivialized hero lore, cover a wide range from classical (Lucretia), biblical (Cain and Abel), and medieval (Siegfried) times to later periods. No matter what the subject or era, the time and locale are always those of Sachs's own Nuremberg; his characters talk like upright burghers of his age.

Sachs's so-called meistersinger dramas, a genre originating with his predecessor Rosenplüth, are merely dramatized dialogues, weak and heavy in the tragic mood, sprightly in the comic. Sachs excelled in the didactic-satiric manner. His best works are his later, exuberant Shrovetide plays, such as *Der fahrende suchüler im Paradies* (1550; *The Itinerant Scholar in Paradise*) and *Das heisse Eisen*

(1551; *The Hot Iron*), and such narrative skits as *St. Peter mit der Geis* (*St. Peter with the Goat*), all in rhymed doggerels.

Sachs's satire is good-natured, his humor never unduly coarse. He had a healthy moral instinct and a realistic bent, best employed on familiar ground. His comedies, performed in taverns and halls, though lacking dramatic quality, have influenced folk drama. Eclipsed after his death, Sachs's work was revived and popularized by Johann Wolfgang von Goethe in a poem of 1776; and in the opening scene of *Faust,* Goethe resuscitated Sachs's free doggerels. Sachs is the only German writer of his time whose short, witty, unsophisticated narrative poems and humble, jolly, dramatic Shrovetide skits can hold an audience today.

Further Reading

Some of Sachs's writings are in *Selections from Hans Sachs,* chosen by William M. Calder (1948). His work is discussed in Walter French, *Medieval Civilization as Illustrated by the Fastnachtsspiele of Hans Sachs* (1925). ☐

Nelly Sachs

The German-born poet and playwright Nelly Sachs (1891-1970), winner of the Nobel Prize, is noted for her austere but moving work, which constitutes a solemn monument to the hardships and sorrows of the Jewish people.

Born on Dec. 10, 1891, into a wealthy Jewish family, Nelly Sachs grew up in Berlin. After having studied dance and music with private tutors, she began at the age of 17 to write poetry. Her first collection of legends and sagas from the Middle Ages was published in 1921; this work reflected her fascination with the mystical elements of Christianity. Despite the influences of her own religious tradition, which can be traced throughout her poetry, in the years before the overt political persecution of the Jews accompanying Hitler's rise to power, she was not particularly concerned with her own religious origins. But with the advent of anti-Semitism, she turned to Orthodox Hasidism, where she discovered many of those occult aspects which had earlier attracted her to Christianity.

With the aid of Selma Lagerlöf, a well-known Scandinavian novelist, Sachs and her mother fled Germany in 1940 and settled in Sweden. While still working on her own poetry, she acquired sufficient knowledge of Swedish to earn a living translating Swedish works into German. Her postwar anthology of Swedish verse, *Wave and Granite* (1947), brought some well-deserved acclaim to little-known writers. Her first collection of poetry was *But Even the Sun Has No Home* (1948). Both this volume and *Eclipse of the Stars* (1951), which were written during her flight from Germany, deal with the annihilation of 6 million Jews under the Third Reich; for diverse reasons they received little critical attention.

In 1950 a group of Swedish friends issued a private edition, 200 copies, of Sachs's *Eli: A Miracle Play of the Suffering Israel,* which eventually found its way into Germany, where it became a widely acclaimed radio play. Like the other 11 plays written in this period, *Eli* was created in memory of those who had suffered and perished in Nazi concentration camps. Structurally the work has the simplicity of a medieval miracle play, but thematically it depicts a world devoid of trust and goodness, where innocence falls victim to evil.

Recognition of Nelly Sachs's gift as a lyric poet came in the late 1950s after the publication of *And No One Knows Where to Go* (1957) and *Flight and Metamorphosis* (1959). Once again the focus is on the black theme of the victims of the holocaust, as well as the author's personal loneliness. In the following decade she was the recipient of numerous honors, among which were the 1961 Nelly Sachs Prize, established by the city of Dortmund, and the Peace Prize of the German Book Trade at the Frankfurt Fair of 1965. In honor of her seventieth birthday, a Frankfurt publisher issued her collected works, containing a new series of poems, "Journey to the Beyond," which was dedicated by the author to "my dead brothers and sisters."

Despite the esteem in which she was held by many German-language readers, Nelly Sachs was little known to the rest of the European and American public when she received the Nobel Prize for literature in 1966. She died in Stockholm on May 12, 1970.

Further Reading

There is no substantial study of Nelly Sachs in English. A chapter in Paul Konrad Kurz, *On Modern German Literature,* vol. 1 (1967; trans. 1970), provides biographical information and comments on her work; and Harry T. Moore, *Twentieth-century German Literature* (1967), includes brief biographical data. A recent, important background study is Peter Demetz, *Postwar German Literature: A Critical Introduction* (1970)

Additional Sources

Jewish writers, German literature: the uneasy examples of Nelly Sachs and Walter Benjamin, Ann Arbor: University of Michigan Press, 1995. □

Anwar Sadat

Anwar Sadat (1918-1981) was Egypt's president from 1970 until his assassination. He launched a surprise attack on Israel in 1973, then became the first Arab leader to sign a peace treaty with Israel. He shifted from Soviet to American patronage and relaxed Egypt's internal economic and political system.

Anwar Sadat

Mohamed Anwar El-Sadat was born in 1918. His village, Mit Abul Kom, is about 40 miles north of Cairo in the Nile delta. Sadat lived with his grandmother while his father, a minor civil service clerk, was away in the Sudan with his Sudanese wife. The boy attended a village Quran (Moslem) school, then went briefly to a Coptic (Christian) school.

His parents returned to Egypt in 1925, and Sadat went to live with them in Cairo. In later years he relished visits to his village and spoke nostalgically of his humble rural origins. Sadat's father struggled to support 13 children on his modest salary. Poor grades led Sadat to shift from government to private secondary schools on two occasions, but in 1936 he earned the coveted secondary school certificate.

Plotting against British Rule and King Farouk

As a schoolboy, Sadat frequently demonstrated against the British, who occupied Egypt at that time. His heroes were all nationalists: Mahatma Gandhi, Adolf Hitler, Ataturk, and Egyptians Saad Zaghlul, Mustafa Kamil, and Mustafa Nahhas. He also admired a peasant martyr from Dinshaway (near Mit Abul Kom) whom the British had executed in 1906.

One result of the 1936 treaty which Prime Minister Nahhas signed with the British was the opening of the military academy to lower middle class youths like Sadat and Gamal Abdel Nasser. Sadat graduated from the academy in 1938 and was posted to Manqabad in Upper Egypt. There he first met Nasser, a natural leader, serious and somewhat aloof. The idealistic young officers talked politics, debating the best way to rid their country of the British.

In 1939 Sadat entered the Signal Corps. While Nasser was off in the Sudan, Sadat plotted direct action against the British. Occasionally he met with Hassan Al-Banna, the Supreme Guide of the Muslim Brotherhood, a group of religious zealots who wanted to root out Western and secular influences and turn Egypt into a theocracy.

Axis forces based in Libya pushed into Egypt in 1941, hoping to seize the vital Suez Canal. In the following year the British arrested Sadat for plotting with two German spies who were living in a Nile houseboat and trying to send information to Rommel's army. Escaping from jail in October 1944, Sadat hid out until the end of the war made it safe for him to resurface. He then participated in an unsuccessful attempt on the life of former prime minister Nahhas, who had cooperated with the British during the war. Sadat's role in the killing of Amin Osman, an Anglophile politician, landed him back in jail in January 1946. Sadat's friendship with King Farouk's private doctor linked him to the Iron Guard, a secret palace organization which struck at the king's enemies.

The trial of Sadat and others in the Amin Osman case was overshadowed by the outbreak of the 1948 Arab-Israeli war. The principal defendant escaped; Sadat and the others were acquitted and released. After dabbling in business schemes for a year or two Sadat won reinstatement in the army. He reestablished contact with Nasser's circle, who were now calling themselves "Free Officers" and planning to overthrow the corrupt and inept government. The riots of January 1952 destroyed foreign-owned businesses throughout Cairo and completed the public's disillusionment with the playboy king and the old politicians.

Nasser summoned Sadat to Cairo from his post in Sinai on the evening of July 22, 1952. But finding no further message from his chief, Sadat took his family to the movies and nearly missed the coup. However, it was Sadat who broadcast the news of the coup to the public on the morning of July 23. King Farouk was sent into exile and Brigadier Mohamed Naguib served as the Free Officers' front man until Nasser broke with him and put him under house arrest in 1954.

The posts Sadat held during the Nasser years were not quite at the center of power. He edited the regime's newspaper, *al-Gumhuriya*. He served as secretary-general of the Islamic Congress and of the National Union, the forerunner of the Arab Socialist Union and Egypt's only political party. During the 1960s he was speaker of the National Assembly. Sadat, along with Field Marshall Abdel Hakim Amer, bears much of the responsibility for Egypt's disastrous involvement in the Yemeni civil war (1962-1967). Then Egypt's defeat by Israel in the 1967 Six-Day War nearly destroyed Nasser's regime. Aware of his ill-health and of plots against him, Nasser named Sadat vice president at the end of 1969. Nicknamed "Major Yes-Yes" for his acquiescence to Nasser's wishes, Sadat had outlasted most of the other Free Officers who might have inherited the presidency.

Sadat Takes Command

Nasser died of a heart attack on September 28, 1970. A plebiscite quickly confirmed Sadat as his successor. Ali Sabri and others in the Arab Socialist Union, the army, and the intelligence organizations assumed Sadat could soon be shouldered aside. But Sadat's "Corrective Revolution" of May 1971 sent the plotters to jail and consolidated his grip on power. A treaty of friendship reassured the nervous Soviets a few days later.

Sadat liked to govern by surprises. In February 1971 he unexpectedly extended a ceasefire with the Israelis on the Suez front and announced plans to reopen the canal even though the enemy was entrenched on the opposite bank. Unable to obtain enough Soviet support for a military showdown and under increasing domestic pressure to act, Sadat pulled off another surprise in the summer of 1972. He expelled the numerous Soviet military advisers from Egypt.

Failing to win American attention as he had hoped, Sadat now openly declared his intention to fight Israel. No one took him seriously, so the Syrian-Egyptian attack on October 6, 1973, came as a surprise. Egypt's successful crossing of the Suez Canal contrasted with the 1967 fiasco, but the Israeli counter crossing under General Sharon left Egyptian forces in a critical position by the time U.S. and Soviet intervention produced a ceasefire. Sadat always portrayed the Yom Kippur War as an unqualified victory, calling himself "The Hero of the Crossing."

President Nixon and Henry Kissinger were paying attention at last. Sadat abandoned his Soviet option and risked all on Egyptian alignment with the United States. Kissinger's

shuttle diplomacy produced limited Israeli pullbacks in Sinai in 1974 and 1975. Thereafter progress toward a settlement bogged down until Sadat's astonishing visit to Jerusalem in November 1977 to meet Prime Minister Menachem Begin and address the Knesset. President Jimmy Carter's personal diplomacy brought Begin and Sadat together at Camp David in September 1978. They signed two "framework" agreements, one providing for an Israeli-Egyptian peace treaty within three months, the other for a five-year transition toward autonomy and Palestinian self-government in the Israeli-occupied West Bank and Gaza Strip. Begin and Sadat signed the final treaty in March 1979, and they shared the Nobel Peace Prize for 1978. The Palestinian part of the agreement remained a dead letter, however, with Begin pursuing hardline policies toward the Palestinians and the other Arab states.

In renaming the United Arab Republic the Arab Republic of Egypt, Sadat signaled his intention to put Egyptian interests ahead of the Pan-Arabism of the Nasser era. Nothing practical became of the Federation of Arab Republics (Egypt, Libya, and Syria), a scheme he had inherited. The impetuous young Gaddafi of Libya, who saw himself as Nasser's true heir, turned hostile and plotted to overthrow Sadat. In July 1977 open warfare flared for a time on the Libyan-Egyptian border.

Syria, Jordan, Saudi Arabia, and the Palestinians saw the Camp David agreement as being made at Arab expense. Other Arab states agreed, and at an Arab League meeting in Baghdad the Arab states decided to withdraw their ambassadors from Egypt, sever political and economic ties, and move the headquarters of the league from Cairo to Tunis. The United States compensated somewhat for the loss of Egypt's Arab ties by massively increasing its aid to Sadat.

The October 1973 war made Sadat his own man in economic policies and domestic politics as well as in foreign affairs. In 1974 he turned sharply toward economic liberalization, in contrast to the statist policies of Nasser. He proclaimed an "open door" economy, hoping it would attract private investment from Western, Arab, and Egyptian businessmen. He returned some of the lands and businesses nationalized under Nasser to their former owners. A new class of free-wheeling entrepreneurs quickly made fortunes in land speculation, luxury apartment construction, and consumer imports.

Sadat's Regime Becomes Controversial

Sadat also planned his political liberalization with American audiences in mind. Abandoning Nasser's single-party system, he encouraged "left" and "right" splinters to break off from the Arab Socialist Union's "center" in 1976. He made sure, however, that his own center party (called the National Democratic Party since 1978) kept over-whelming control in the People's Assembly. Manipulation of the laws and government harassment kept the Progressive Unionist left, the New Wafd right, and the religious purists from mounting all-out public challenges to the regime.

Even before the signing of the treaty with Israel, the early hopes for the Sadat era were fading inside Egypt. The "open door" had brought in foreign banks, tourism, and luxury imports, and it had encouraged many Egyptians to earn quick fortunes in Egypt's oil-rich Arab neighboring countries. But there was little investment in productive industries. A contractor named Osman Ahmad Osman, whose son had married one of Sadat's daughters, came to symbolize the nepotism and opportunism of the new rich whom the public labeled "fat cats." Student and worker opposition flared into full-scale riots in January 1977 when the government, acting under pressure from the International Monetary Fund, cut back the food subsidies which cushioned poverty for the average Egyptian.

The lifestyle of Sadat and his wife Jihan also aroused concern. Sadat divorced his rustic first wife on emerging from prison in 1948. His new wife, Jihan, was half-British, good looking, and considerably younger than himself. The couple developed a taste for the good life, ordering clothes from Paris designers. Sadat's first wife had followed Middle Eastern custom by remaining in the background, but Jihan enjoyed the limelight. She spoke up for women's rights, visited hospitals, and presided at official ceremonies. Reporters abroad were delighted with the couple's Western manner and their ready accessibility for interviews. Many Egyptians were not.

In his last years the Islamic religious groups which he had at first encouraged to balance off other opponents came back to haunt Sadat. The Muslim Brotherhood and its more radical offshoots deplored the Westernization and corruption of Egyptian public life. They opposed the treaty with Israel. The example of the Iranian revolution of 1979 and their own dismal career prospects also turned educated urban youths to fundamentalist Islamic groups in large numbers. The fears of the Coptic minority mounted simultaneously, and violence between Christians and Muslims broke out on several occasions.

In September 1981 Sadat struck out wildly at his diverse opponents. He arrested hundreds of politicians of all stripes, banned journals, stripped the Coptic Pope of his temporal power over his community, and expelled the Soviet ambassador.

Sadat had lost his political touch. On October 6, 1981, Muslim religious radicals shot him down as he reviewed a military parade commemorating the 1973 war. The shocked West paid tribute to Sadat by dispatching three former U.S. presidents and other prominent statesmen to his funeral. Prime Minister Begin also attended. Egyptians and Arabs reacted differently. The streets of Cairo, which millions of mourners had jammed when Nasser died, remained eerily silent. President Nimeri of the Sudan was the only Arab head of state to attend the funeral. Sadat had left a difficult legacy to his successor, Vice President Hosni Mubarak.

Further Reading

For Sadat's own story, see his *Revolt on the Nile* (1957) and *In Search of Identity: An Autobiography* (1978). The first book defers to Nasser, while the second plays up Sadat's own role in the 1952 revolution. Jimmy Carter's *Keeping Faith: Memoirs of a President* (1982) discusses his negotiations with Sadat and Israel's Begin. David Hirst and Irene Beeson, *Sadat* (1981)

and Mohamed Heikal, *Autumn of Fury: The Assassination of Sadat* (1983) provide unfavorable interpretations. P. J. Vatikiotis, *Nasser and His Generation* (1978) analyzes the generation of army officers to which Nasser and Sadat belonged. *My Father and I* (1986) by Camelia Sadat provides more intimate glimpses of the personal, as well as political, aspects of his life. □

Jihan Sadat

Jihan Sadat (born 1933), the second wife of Anwar Sadat, she pioneered for women's rights in her country.

The woman who would become the second wife of Egyptian president Anwar Sadat was born near Cairo to an Egyptian father and an English mother. Her father was a surgeon and her family was upper-middle class. Sadat was raised as a Moslem according to her father's wishes. She attended a Christian school for girls and a secondary school in Cairo. It was in Cairo that Sadat met her future husband, Anwar Sadat. Her parents objected to the idea of their daughter marrying a divorced revolutionary; nonetheless, Jihan and Anwar were married in May 1949.

Jihan was the devoted wife of a rising political man and mother of their four children, but she was more than that. Although while a teenager she had been almost obsessed with Sadat as a local hero, even before meeting him, she always had an activist cosmopolitan streak. This led her to take bold (for a Muslim woman) initiatives, and, after her husband attained the presidency, controversial ones.

Jihan Sadat pioneered the cause of women's rights in her country. She set up cooperatives in Egyptian villages for peasant women. During her husband's presidency, two laws that gave women greater rights were issued. One law allowed for thirty seats to be filled by women in the Egyptian parliament. The second law provided women with the right to sue for divorce and retain custody of their children. Sadat was also concerned with various humanitarian causes. She established orphanages and a facility for rehabilitating the handicapped veterans of war in Egypt.

Sadat traveled outside the country on her own, something unprecedented for the wife of a Muslim leader. She returned to the university in 1974. In 1980 she earned a master's degree from the University of Cairo in Arabic literature. She received a doctorate in 1987, six years after her husband's death.

While many admire Jihan Sadat for her independent nature and activism, she has had her share of critics. Fundamentalist and traditionalist Arabs were scandalized by her Western mannerisms and willingness to grant personal interviews in Western magazines. One such interview was published in *Playgirl* although she seems to have been misled by her interviewer about where the article would appear. Others have found her typically bourgeois with more than a little taste for luxury and comfort.

Sadat's presence in the academic world has given her a place to continue her life following the death of her husband. She has taught in both Egypt, at the University of Cairo, and in the United States. Her pursuits in the U.S. have taken her to the American University in Washington, D.C., the University of South Carolina, Radford University in Virginia, and the University of Maryland. She has taught classes and led seminars on women's issues, Egyptian culture, and international studies. Sadat has also written a book on her life titled *A Woman of Egypt.*

Further Reading

Sadat, Jehan. *A Woman of Egypt* (1987). □

Saddam Hussein

Saddam Hussein (born 1937), the socialist president of the Iraqi Republic beginning in 1979 and strongman of the ruling Ba'th regime beginning in 1968, was known for his political shrewdness and ability to survive conflicts. He led Iraq in its long, indecisive war with Iran beginning in 1980. He was defeated in the six week Persian Gulf War in 1990 which was a result of his invasion of Kuwait.

Saddam Hussein al-Tikriti was born in 1937 to a peasant family in a village near Tikrit, a town on the Tigris River north of Baghdad. His father died before his birth and his mother died in childbirth. He was raised by his uncles, particularly his maternal uncle Khairallah Talfah, a retired army officer and an avid Arab nationalist who influenced his political leanings and served as a role model for Hussein. (In 1963 Saddam married Talfah's daughter Sajida.) In 1956 he moved to his uncle's house in Baghdad, where he was caught up in the strong Arab nationalist sentiments sweeping Iraq in the wake of the Suez war that year. In 1957 he joined the Arab Ba'th Socialist Party, founded in Syria in 1947 and dedicated to Arab unity and socialism. The party spread to neighboring Arab countries in the 1950s (including Iraq where it was an underground party) and was especially popular with students. From 1957 on Saddam's life and career were inextricably bound up with the Ba'th Party.

In 1959 Saddam Hussein was one of the party members who attempted to carry out the unsuccessful assassination of the Iraqi dictator, Major General Abdul Karim Qasim (Kassem). Although wounded, he was subsequently able to stage a daring escape to Syria and then Egypt, where he remained in exile until 1963. In Egypt he continued his political activities, closely observing the tactics and movements of Gamal Abdel Nasser and his politics.

In February 1963 a group of Nasserite and Ba'thist officers in Iraq brought down the government of Qasim, and Saddam returned to his country. However, this Ba'thist government did not survive in power past November of the

same year, and Saddam was once again forced underground. Between 1963 and 1968 he was involved in clandestine party activities and was captured and jailed, although he later escaped. In 1966 he became a member of the Iraqi branch's regional command and played a major role in reorganizing the Ba'th Party in preparation for a second attempt at power. It was during this period that he formed a close alliance with Ahmad Hasan al-Bakr—a retired officer, a distant relative, and a leading spokesman of the party. It was in this period, too, that Saddam acquired his reputation as a tough, daring Ba'th Party partisan.

The Dual Rule: Bakr and Hussein

In July 1968, after two coups d'etat in short succession—in both of which Saddam played a key role—the Ba'th came back to power in Iraq, temporarily governing through the Revolutionary Command Council (RCC). Ahmad Hasan al-Bakr was elected president of the republic by the RCC and Saddam was elected vice president of the RCC in 1969. Between 1969 and 1979 Iraq was ruled outwardly by al-Bakr and behind the scenes by Saddam. Saddam who proved to be a shrewd manipulator and survivor. No major decisions in this decade were taken without his consent.

In domestic affairs the Ba'th regime implemented its socialist policy by bringing virtually all economic activity under the control of the government. In 1972 Iraq nationalized the foreign-owned oil company IBC, the first Middle Eastern government to do so. Minorities were given cultural rights, generally modeled on the Yugoslav experiment in this field, and the Kurdish area of northern Iraq was given some self-rule in 1974.

Saddam Hussein also oversaw the rapid economic and social development of Iraq which followed the oil price increases of the 1970s. The country received major infusions to the infrastructure, especially schools and medical facilities. A major campaign to wipe out illiteracy was started in 1978 and compulsory schooling was effectively implemented. The status of women was substantially improved through legislation. Petrochemical and iron and steel industries were built.

In international affairs, Iraq improved relations with the Soviet Union and the socialist bloc, signing a treaty of friendship with the U.S.S.R. in 1972; at the same time Iraq distanced itself from the West, except for France. Iraq took a hard line on Israel and attempted to isolate Egypt after Anwar Sadat signed the Camp David agreements with Israel's Menachem Begin.

Between 1974 and 1975 Saddam was involved in a major Kurdish insurrection in northern Iraq; the Kurds were seeking more autonomy and were receiving support from the Shah of Iran. In an effort to bring the conflict to a close, in March 1975 Saddam signed an agreement with Iran, arranged by Algeria, which ended Iranian support for the Kurds in return for rectification of the border with Iran.

Saddam Hussein as President

Iraq was the country most affected by the Islamic revolution in Iran in 1979. Iraq needed more energetic leadership than that provided by the aging and ailing President Bakr. On July 16, 1979, al-Bakr resigned and Saddam was elected president of the Iraqi Republic. One of the first things he ordered were posters of himself scattered throughout Iraq, some as tall as 20 feet, depicting himself in various roles: a military man, a desert horseman, a young graduate. He carefully concocted an image of himself as a devoted family man. All in order to win the trust and love of the Iraqi people. He held the titles of Secretary General of the Ba'th party and Commander in Chief of the Armed Forces.

Throughout 1979 and 1980 relations with Iran had deteriorated, as Ayatollah Khomeini called on Iraq's Shi'ites to revolt against Saddam and the secular Ba'thist regime. (Iraq is about equally divided between members of the Shi'ite and Sunni branches of Islam.) Secret pro-Iranian organizations committed acts of sabotage in Iraq, while Iranians began shelling Iraqi border towns in 1980. In September 1980 the Iraqi army crossed the Iranian border and seized Iranian territory (subsequently evacuated in the course of the war), thus initiating a long, costly, and bitter war, which continued into the late 1980s.

With the continuation of the war, Saddam adopted a more pragmatic stance in international affairs. Relations with conservative countries such as Kuwait, Saudi Arabia, and Egypt improved since they provided Iraq with either financial or military aid. Diplomatic relations with the United States, cut in 1967 in protest against U.S. support for Israel in the Six-Day War, were restored in November 1984. However, Iraq did not change its friendly relations with the U.S.S.R. which, together with France, was the main source

of its arms. In 1987 the United Nations formally called for a cease-fire, but the fighting continued.

Saddam Hussein was a man with the reputation for ruthless suppression of opposition. When he assumed power, he purged his party of officials and military officers due to an alleged Syrian plot to overthrow his government. He executed another 300 officers in 1982 for rebelling against his tactics in the war with Iran. In order to protect himself, Saddam surrounded himself with a coterie of family and friends in positions of trust and responsibility in the government. This however did not ensure that these individuals were safe from his rages. After Saddam had a much publicized affair with another woman, his brother-in-law, first cousin and childhood companion, and Minster of Defense Adnan Talfah was killed in a "mysterious" helicopter crash for standing by his sister (Saddam's wronged wife). He ordered the murders of his sons-in-law after they defected to Jordan in 1996. His image of a devoted family man was shattered with these acts.

On several occasions (1969, 1973, 1979, and 1981) the regime uncovered plots against it, and at least seven unsuccessful assassination attempts were made against Saddam. The main opposition came from the Kurds, the Communists, pro-Khomeini Shi'ites, and, on occasion, elements within the Ba'th Party itself.

In 1990, Saddam Hussein brought the wrath and combined power of the West and the Arab world down upon Iraq by his unprovoked invasion of Kuwait. The Persian Gulf War lasted for six weeks and caused Iraq's leader worldwide condemnation. However, there are still a great many proponents of Saddam scattered throughout the world. They see him as "someone who is shaking an unacceptable status quo." Despite the sanctions imposed upon Iraq in the years subsequent to the war, Saddam maintained absolute power over his country. In 1997, citizens of Baghdad feared to overtly criticize Saddam and rumors abounded that he had put his wife under house arrest after his son Uday was shot. Whatever the case, Saddam Hussein remained a powerful strongman, in spite of an ongoing embargo of his country's oil, goods and services.

Further Reading

Majid Khadduri, *Socialist Iraq, A Study in Iraqi Politics Since 1968* (1978); Phebe Marr, *The Modern History of Iraq* (1985); Christine Helms, *Iraq, Eastern Flank of the Arab World* (1984); and Fuad Matar, *Saddam Hussein, the Man, the Cause and the Future* (London, 1981) provide information on Saddam's role in the leadership of Iraq. Stefoff's *Saddam Hussein: Absolute Ruler of Iraq* provides valuable insight into the operation of Iraq since the Persian Gulf War. Bob Simon's *Forty Days* is an excellent memoir of the war. □

Comte de Sade

The French writer of psychological and philosophical works Donatien Alphonse François, Comte de Sade (1740-1814), was also a libertine, debaucher,

pornographer, and sadist—a term derived from his name.

The Marquis de Sade has been traditionally viewed as the greatest incarnation of evil that ever lived. Recently, however, new interpretations of his life and writings have begun to appear. It is now generally agreed that despite his reputation, his works, which were ignored for over a century, must be considered as of the first rank. Sade has been termed the "most absolute writer who has ever lived."

Born on June 2, 1740, to Marie Elénore de Maille de Carman, lady-in-waiting to and relative of the Princess de Condé, and Jean Baptiste Joseph François, Comte de Sade, who traced his ancestry to the chaste Laura of Petrarch's poems, the Marquis de Sade may be the most typical and the most unusual representative of the other side of the Enlightenment, the side at which the *philosophes* railed.

Very little is known of Sade's life. He graduated from the Collège de Louis le Grand, was commissioned as a coronet in the French army, and later sold his commission. He was forced to marry the eldest daughter of a leading magisterial family, Renée Pélagie de Montreuil, who bore him three children. Because of his libertinage, which included the seduction of and elopement with his wife's sister, Anne Prospère, he incurred the unending enmity of his mother-in-law, who eventually had him imprisoned in 1781. Sade had tasted imprisonment before for libertinage

and indebtedness, and he spent half of his adult life in prisons and asylums. Only three public scandals can be proved against him, and none of these seems to merit the punishment meted out to him, reinforcing his claim that he was an unjust victim of his reputation and others' hatreds.

During the Revolution, Sade was released from prison, served as secretary and president of the Piques section of Paris, and represented it at least once before the National Convention, where he addressed a pamphlet calling for the abolition of capital punishment and the enfranchisement of women. His attitudes and actions gained the hatred of Maximilien de Robespierre, who had him imprisoned (1793). He was saved only by the death of the "Incorruptible." Released in 1794, Sade was arrested in 1801 for being the supposed author of a scandalous pamphlet against Napoleon. He spent the rest of his life at Charenton insane asylum, where he died on Dec. 8, 1814. His best-known books include *Justine; ou, Les Malheurs de la vertu* (1791) and its sequel, *Histoire de Juliette; ou, Les Prospérités du vice* (1797).

Thus the life of the Marquis de Sade. Who was he? Why did he acquire the unique reputation he possesses? There are no simple answers regarding the life of any man. For Sade, there is possibly no answer at all. Recent works on his life have justly sought answers in his literary works, and because of this most commentators tend to psychoanalyze him. Although many of these works have offered brilliant insights into the character of the man, none of them is definitive and most treat him out of context, as though his life and aberrations were apart from life. Most Sadean scholars tend to agree that his hostility to religion, to the established social and political order, and to the despotism of existing law was similar in many ways to that of the *philosophes*. Some writers believe that he carried the beliefs of the *philosophes* to the rational conclusions, which in the end negated the conclusions and opened for succeeding generations a moral abyss. Others focus on what is termed a philosophy of destruction found in Sade's writings. Sade's atheism is viewed as the first element in a dialectic which destroys divinity through sacrilege and blasphemy and raises to preeminence an indifferent and unfolding nature which destroys to create and creates to destroy. Nature itself is then destroyed by being constantly outraged because it takes on the same sovereign character as God. What emerges is the "Unique One," the man who rises above nature and arrogates to himself the creative and destructive capacities of nature in an extreme form, becoming solitary, alone, unique in the conscious awareness that he is the creative force and all others are but the material through which his energy is expressed.

Further Reading

Many of Sade's works are available in English. Biographies include Geoffrey Gorer, *The Life and Ideas of the Marquis de Sade* (1934; rev. ed. 1953), and Gilbert Lély, *The Marquis de Sade* (trans. 1962). Recommended for literary background is Mario Praz, *The Romantic Agony* (trans. 1933; 2d ed. 1956).

Additional Sources

Gorer, Geoffrey, *The life and ideas of the Marquis de Sade,* Westport, Conn.: Greenwood Press, 1978, 1963.

Hayman, Ronald, *De Sade: a critical biography,* New York: Crowell, 1978.

Lever, Maurice, *Sade: a biography,* San Diego: Harcourt Brace & Co., 1994.

Thomas, Donald, *The Marquis de Sade,* Secaucus, NJ: Citadel Press, 1992. □

Sa'di

The Persian poet Sa'di (ca. 1200-ca. 1291) was the author of the classic literary works *Bustan* (translated as *The Orchard*) and *Gulistan* (translated as *The Rose Garden*). Moralistic books that contain teachings and stories on love, religion, and other aspects of life, these volumes by Sa'di are central to the literature of Iran and are the source of a number of popular proverbs in that culture.

The thirteenth-century poet Sa'di (pronounced SAH-dee) is regarded as one of the greatest figures in Persian literature. He is best-known for his major works *Bustan,* or *The Orchard* and *Gulistan,* or *The Rose Garden.*. Both of these works are filled with semi-autobiographical stories, philosophical meditations, pieces of practical wisdom, and humorous anecdotes and observations. The books are valued not only for their elegant language and entertaining style, but also for their role as a rich source of information about the culture in which Sa'di lived and worked. He is considered as having an influence on the culture and language of Iran that equals in significance the role of playwright and poet William Shakespeare in the history of English language and literature.

What is known about the life of Sa'di is primarily drawn from folk legend and his own semi-autobiographical stories, which were likely embellished to suit his literary needs. Therefore, the information that exists is somewhat suspect. It is generally believed, however, that the writer was born around the year 1200 in the town of Shiraz, Persia (now Iran). Shiraz was located in the region of Fars Province, which was known in antiquity as Persis, a name the Greeks used for the entire country, bringing about the name Persia. The popular name Sa'di was actually an assumed pen-name for the author, whose given name may have been Masharrif al-Din ibn Moslih al-Din, or some similar form of this name. The pseudonym was drawn from the names of the leaders who ruled Fars Province during his lifetime: Sa'd ibn Zangi, his son Abu Bakr ibn Sa'd, and grandson Sa'd ibn Abu Bakr. Sa'd ibn Zangi played an important role in Sa'di's life, taking the boy into his care and providing him with an education after the death of Sa'di's father, a court official for the ruler. After completing his studies in Shiraz, Sa'di was sent to Baghdad to attend Nizamiya College, possibly the finest institution of learning in the world at that time. But the young man was not much interested in academics; in his later writings he recalled his duties as a teaching assistant to be a tiring chore. He much preferred to spend his time in a more celebratory fashion and devoted a great deal of energy to socializing and enjoying himself.

Wandered Middle East for Thirty Years

After leaving the college, Sa'di entered a lengthy period in which he traveled extensively, simply traveling to various towns and countries in search of adventure. This phase of his life probably lasted about 30 years, and his wanderings led him all over the Middle East and to parts of Asia and Northern Africa, including such countries as Iraq, Syria, Palestine, Egypt, Arabia, Turkey, and perhaps India. It is thought that he began this style of life in order to escape the Mongol forces that were invading and conquering large parts of his homeland; it may also be that he was a follower of the Sufi dervishes, a nomadic mystical Moslem order that engaged in chanting and dancing to achieve religious ecstasy. Whether he was truly committed to Sufi doctrine or not, he benefitted from traveling with them, as it insured him a greater amount of safety and hospitality during these years.

Sa'di's books are filled with tales that are supposedly based on incidents from his itinerant years. In *The Rose Garden* he relates how he was captured in Palestine by Christian Crusaders and forced into manual labor digging moats. He was only released after a friend passed by and, upon recognizing Sa'di, bought his freedom from the captors for ten dinars. The friend later engaged his daughter to the writer with a dowry of 100 dinars. Sa'di's new wife was apparently a nagging woman and he probably left her. But she did provide him with good material for his book. He wrote that during one argument she attempted to put him in his place by reminding him that her father had saved him. Sa'di's quick response was that while it only cost his father-in-law 10 dinars to rescue him, it took 100 dinars to marry off his daughter. Sa'di is reported to have had another wife in Arabia, with whom he had a child who died. There is no indication that he remained with her either.

Wrote Classic Persian Texts

After a number of other troublesome adventures, including being run out of India for his insults to religious figures there, Sa'di finally ended his rambling life around 1250 and settled in his home town. There he lived a secluded life and engaged in writing the works that would make him famous. His first major work, *The Orchard,* was completed in 1257. This book is designed as a kind of guide on morality and other aspects of life and draws upon literary, religious, and folk themes to create pithy maxims and philosophical reflections. It is written mostly in verse form, utilizing the *mathnavi* style of rhymed couplets. His next and last important book was *The Rose Garden,* a 1258 work that also touches on ethical issues, but in a more informal, light-hearted manner than *The Orchard.* *The Rose Garden* contains verse, mostly written in quatrains, as well as prose writings such as humorous stories and instructive homilies. Both of the books are organized into chapters on topics applying to specific areas of life, ranging from "On Love, Intoxication, and Delirium" to "On the Advantages of Silence."

Around 1258 Mongol invaders conquered the city of Baghdad, killing its entire population of more than one million people. While Sa'di was safe from such a threat, thanks to an arrangement made with the Mongols by the leader of Fars Province, he mourned the loss of the great center of Islamic culture and composed a lament on the occasion. This period also seemed to mark the end of Sa'di's literary prowess; while his two major works earned him great acclaim in his later years, he did not compose anything more of note. But his place as a literary icon was well secured. Copies of *The Orchard* and *The Rose Garden* began to be circulated throughout Persia and he was celebrated by his contemporaries as "the Shaykh" or "wise old man." He was even invited to stay at the court of Abu Bakr ibn Sa'd, but Sa'di opted to continue his quiet private life. More than thirty years after the appearance of his best-known works, Sa'di died in Shiraz, probably around 1291.

Works Translated in the West

While the writings of Sa'di have been a central part of the literature of Iran for seven hundred years, English translations of his works did not appear until Victorian times. Western readers have since come to enjoy the wisdom and witticisms of Sa'di, but have also had some hesitation over his blatantly sexual content. Another aspect that may disturb modern readers is Sa'di obvious racism regarding Jews and blacks (a typical attitude for people of his culture during his time). But despite these cultural barriers to a complete appreciation of his work in the West, Sa'di remains a cultural treasure in Iran, where his sayings permeate the language to such a degree that it is said only the Koran is quoted more often. For the rest of the world, the writings of Sa'di serve as a lively means of studying the cultural beliefs and practices of thirteenth-century Persia, which in turn can illuminate the modern culture of that land.

Further Reading

Arberry, A. J., *Classical Persian Literature*, Macmillan, 1958.
Levy, Reuben, *An Introduction to Persian Literature*, Columbia University Press, 1969. □

Shaikh Muslih-al-Din Sadi

The Persian poet Shaikh Muslih-al-Din Sadi (ca. 1184-1291) is known in Iran today as its greatest ethical and worldly-wise poet. His works have a poignancy seldom equaled in world literature.

Born in Shiraz, Sadi was the son of a minor poet. His father's patron was Sad ben Zangi, from whom the younger poet took his *takhallus,* or poetical pseudonym, of Sadi.

Unfortunately, all our knowledge of Sadi must be derived from his own writings. Generally his life is broken into three main periods. First, he is thought to have studied in Shiraz, his birthplace, and in Baghdad until 1226, leaving these cities only to go on pilgrimages to different religious shrines. While in Baghdad, he studied under the well-known Sufi Shaikh Shihabud-Din Suhrawardi, of whose unselfish piety Sadi makes mention in his first major work, the *Bustan.* He proved to be a very fine student and soon gained fame as a wit and poet of short descriptive passages. His early poetry on the whole represented well the clever, half-pious, half-worldly side of the Persian character.

It was during the second period, from 1226 to 1256, that Sadi traveled widely and gained the experiences that were to be expressed so cogently later in his works. He left Shiraz largely because the old social and political infrastructure was breaking down. This was a period of warring and chaos in Persia. Sadi visited central Asia, India, Syria, Egypt, Arabia, Ethiopia, and Morocco.

Major Works

Sadi then returned home to his native town of Shiraz in 1256 to record his many experiences. This marks the third distinct period in his life. A year after his return he finished the *Bustan (Fruit Garden).* This is a collection of poems on ethical subjects always evidencing a practical train of thought. Then, in 1258, he finished the *Gulistan (Rose Garden),* which is a collection of moral stories in prose interspersed with verse. His last major work, the *Diwan,* was

completed near the end of his life and is more biographical in nature.

Much has been said of the "ethical" nature of Sadi's writing, but this is so in a unique sense. The moral of the first story in the *Gulistan* is that "an expedient falsehood is preferable to a mischievous truth." The fourth story tries to show that the best education of a man is useless if he has inherited criminal tendencies. The eighth warns that a cornered cat will scratch out the eyes of a leopard. The ninth reiterates the sad truth that often a man's worst enemies are the inheritors of his wealth. And the fourteenth commends a soldier who deserted because his pay was in arrears.

As a moralist, Sadi gained much from the vicissitudes of life that he experienced on his travels. His knowledge of the world adds much to his cosmopolitan view. He seems to look upon the world with sympathetic humor and not harsh satire. And yet he is sometimes Machiavellian. Revenge is sometimes recommended in place of mercy, insincerity in place of veracity. Above all, man is encouraged to keep his independence from other people.

The different aspects of Sadi's morality make it difficult to believe in his sincerity. However, with a Persian poet it is often difficult to separate what belongs to the poet himself and what are concessions to his patrons. In any case, his popularity in the Eastern world should not be overlooked. Sadi has shown himself in all his humanity, and he has satisfied the predilections of the Persians for moralizing, a trait they have had since pre-Islamic times.

Finally, when speaking to the philosophy of his day—mysticism—there is no doubt that Sadi was a diligent student and believer. But when referring to the Sufis of his day, he is always more of a moralizer than a mystic. It was precisely the perishability of the world that made it of value for Sadi. He preached a this-worldliness with only a moderate fatalism, and he disapproved of extreme piety.

Further Reading

Edward Rehatsek's translation *The Gulistan, or Rose Garden of Sa'di* (1964), includes an excellent biographical preface by W. G. Archer and a fine introduction by G. M. Wickens. There is no definitive full-length biography of Sadi. The best sources are Edward G. Browne, *A Literary History of Persia* (4 vols., 1906-1909), which discusses the full range of Persian literature and relates Sadi to many of his contemporaries, and Philip K. Hitti, *History of the Arabs* (1937; 10th ed. 1970). For good discussions of the Sufism of Sadi see A. J. Arberry, *Sufism: An Account of the Mystics of Islam* (1950), and Idries Shah, *The Sufis* (1964). □

Musa al-Sadr

Musa al-Sadr (1928-circa 1978), known as Imam Musa, was a Shi'ite Moslem religious and political leader who was instrumental in improving the lot of the ordinary Shi'ites in South Lebanon while reducing the power of the Shi'ite elites. Al-Sadr disap-peared in 1978 under mysterious circumstances and is presumed dead.

Musa al-Sadr was born in Qum, Iran, in 1928, the son of an important Shi'ite Muslim religious leader, Ayatullah Sadr al-Din Sadr. He attended secondary and primary school in Qum and college in Tehran. He did not intend to study religion, but upon the urging of his father he discarded his secular ambitions and pursued an education in Islamic jurisprudence (*fiqh*). Initially, he studied in a Qum *madrasah* (religious school), and while still in Qum he edited a magazine, *Makatib-i Islami* (Islamic Schools), which is still published in Iran. One year after his father's death in 1953, he moved to Najaf, Iraq, where he studied under Ayatullah Muhsin al-Hakim.

Imam of Tyre

Al-Sadr first visited Lebanon, which was his ancestral home, was in 1957. During this visit he made a strong impression on his fellow Lebanese Shi'ites. Following the death of the Shi'ite religious leader of the southern Lebanese coastal city of Tyre, he was invited to become the Imam, or senior religious authority, in Tyre. In 1960 he moved to Tyre, with the active support of his teacher and mentor, Muhsin al-Hakim.

One of his first significant acts was the establishment of a vocational institute in the southern town of Burj al-Shimali. The institute, constructed at a cost of half a million Lebanese pounds (about $165,000), would become an important symbol of Musa al-Sadr's leadership. Today it still provides vocational training for about 500 orphans.

A physically imposing man of intelligence, courage, personal charm, and enormous energy—one of his former assistants claims that he frequently worked 20 hours a day—al-Sadr attracted a wide array of supporters. Imam Musa, as his followers referred to him, set out to establish himself as the paramount leader of the Shi'ite community, which was most noteworthy at the time for its poverty and general underdevelopment.

Imam Musa helped to fill a yawning leadership vacuum that resulted from the increasing inability of the traditional political bosses to meet the cascading needs of their clients. From the 1960s on, the Shi'ites had experienced rapid social change and economic disruption, and the old village-based patronage system was proving to be ever more an anachronism. Musa al-Sadr was able to stand above a fragmented and victimized community and see it as a whole. He reminded his followers that their deprivation was not to be fatalistically accepted. He felt that as long as they could speak out through their religion they could overcome their condition. As he once observed, "Whenever the poor involve themselves in a social revolution it is a confirmation that injustice is not predestined."

As a Political Leader

He shrewdly recognized that his power lay in part in his role as a custodian of religious symbols. But above all else he was a pragmatist. It is both a tribute to his political skill and a commentary on his tactics that one well-informed Lebanese should have commented that nobody knew the position of Imam Musa.

He was often a critic of the Shah of Iran, but it was only after the Yom Kippur (October) War of 1973 that his relations with the Shah deteriorated seriously. He accused the Shah of suppressing religion in Iran, denounced him for his pro-Israel stance, and described him as an "imperialist stooge." As Imam Musa's relations with Iran deteriorated after 1973, he improved his relations with Iraq, from which he may have received significant funding in early 1974.

Like the Maronite Christians, the Shi'ites are a minority in a predominately Sunni Muslim Arab world, and for both sects Lebanon was a refuge in which sectarian identity and security could be preserved. It is not surprising that many Maronites saw a natural ally in Imam Musa. He was a reformer, not a revolutionary. He sought the betterment of the Shi'ites in a Lebanese context. He often noted, "For us Lebanon is one definitive homeland."

Musa al-Sadr recognized the insecurity of the Maronites, and he acknowledged their need to maintain their monopoly hold on the presidency. Yet he was critical of the Maronites for their arrogant stance toward the Muslims, and particularly the Shi'ites. He argued that the Maronite-dominated government had neglected the south, where as many as 50 percent of the Shi'ites lived.

Musa al-Sadr was anti-Communist, one suspects not only on principled grounds but because the various Communist organizations were among his prime competitors for Shi'ite recruits. While the two branches of the Ba'th Party (pro-Iraqi and pro-Syrian) were making significant inroads among the Shi'ites of the south and of the Beirut suburbs, he appropriated their pan-Arab slogans. Although the movement he founded, Harakat al-Mahrumin (the Movement of the Deprived), was aligned with the Lebanese National Movement (LNM) in the early stages of the Lebanese civil war (1975-1976), he found its Druze leader, Kamal al-Jumblatt, irresponsible and exploitative of the Shi'ites. As he once noted, the LNM was willing "to combat the Christians to the last Shi'ite." He imputed to Jumblatt the prolongation of the war.

Thus, he deserted the LNM in May 1976, when Syria intervened in Lebanon on the side of the Maronite militias and against the LNM and its Palestinian allies. He was a friend and confidant of Syrian President Hafez al-Assad, yet he mistrusted Syrian motives in Lebanon. It was, in Imam Musa's view, only the indigestibility of Lebanon that protected it from being engulfed by Syria. Nonetheless, the Syrians were an essential card in his serious game with the Palestinian resistance.

He claimed to support the Palestine resistance movement, but his relations with the Palestine Liberation Organization (PLO) were tense and uneasy at best. During the 1973 clashes between the PLO and the Lebanese army, Imam Musa reproached the Sunni Muslims for their chorus of support for the guerrillas. On the one hand he chastised the government for failing to defend the south from Israeli aggression, but on the other he criticized the PLO for shelling Israel from the south and hence provoking Israeli retalia-tion. He consistently expressed sympathy for Palestinian aspirations, but he was unwilling to countenance actions that exposed Lebanese citizens, and especially Shi'ite citizens of the south, to additional suffering.

After the 1970 PLO defeat in Jordan, the bulk of the PLO fighters relocated to south Lebanon, where they proceeded to supplant the legitimate authorities. Imam Musa prophetically warned the PLO that it was not in its interests to establish a state within a state in Lebanon. It was the organization's failure to heed this warning that helped to spawn the alienation of their "natural allies" the Shi'ites" who actively resisted the Palestinian fighters in their midst only a few years later. But his unremitting opponent was Kamil al-As'ad, the powerful Shi'ite political boss from the south, who quite accurately viewed al-Sadr as a serious threat to his political power base.

Chairman of the Supreme Shi'ite Council

In 1967 the Chamber of Deputies (or parliament) had passed a law establishing a Supreme Shi'ite Council, which would for the first time provide a representative body for the Shi'ites independent of the Sunni Muslims. The council actually came into existence in 1969, with Imam Musa as its chairman for a six year term—a stunning confirmation of his status as the leading Shi'ite cleric in the country, and certainly one of the most important political figures in the Shi'ite community. The council quickly made itself heard with demands in the military, social, economic, and political realms, including: improved measures for the defense of the south, the provision of development funds, construction and improvement of schools and hospitals, and an increase in the number of Shi'ites appointed to senior government positions.

One year after the formation of the Supreme Shi'ite Council, Musa al-Sadr organized a general strike "to dramatize to the government the plight of the population of southern Lebanon vis-a-vis the Israeli military threat." Shortly thereafter the government created the Council of the South (Majlis al-Janub), which was capitalized at 30 million Lebanese pounds and was chartered to support the development of the region. Unfortunately, the Majlis al-Janub quickly became more famous for being a locus of corruption than for being the origin of beneficial projects.

By the early 1970s the existing social and economic problems of the Shi'ites were compounded by a rapidly deteriorating security environment in the south. While the Supreme Shi'ite Council seemed a useful vehicle for the promotion of the community's interests (as mediated by Musa al-Sadr, of course), the council was ineffectual in a milieu that was quickly becoming dominated by militias and extralegal parties. Hence in March 1974, Imam Musa launched a popular mass movement, the Harakat al-Mahrumin (the Movement of the Deprived). With this movement he vowed to struggle relentlessly until the social grievances of the deprived in practice, the Shi'ites were satisfactorily addressed by the government.

Lebanese Civil War

Just one year later, al-Sadr's efforts were overtaken by the onset of civil war in Lebanon. By July 1975 it became known that a militia adjunct to Harakat al-Mahrumin had been formed. The militia, *Afwaj al-Muqawama al-Lubnaniya* (the Lebanese Resistance Detachments), better known by the acronym AMAL (which also means "hope"), was initially trained by al-Fatah (the largest organization in the PLO), and it played a minor role in the fighting of 1975 and 1976. Musa al-Sadr's movement was affiliated with the LNM and its PLO allies during the first year of the civil war, but it broke with its erstwhile allies when the Syrians intervened in June 1976 to prevent the defeat of the Maronite-dominated Lebanese Front.

Four months before the Syrian intervention President Sulaiman Franjiya (Suleiman Franjieh) accepted a "Constitutional Document" that Imam Musa indicated was a satisfactory basis for implementing political reform. The document "which called for an increase in the proportion of parliamentary seats allocated to the Muslims, as well as some restrictions on the prerogatives of the Maronite president[APM1]" seemed to offer a basis for restoring civility to Lebanon. When it was combined with the prospect of bringing the PLO under control through Syrian intervention, there appeared to be a prospect for a new beginning. Unfortunately, the opportunity to stop the carnage was more apparent than real. While the pace of fighting had decreased by the end of 1976, the violence continued.

The growing influence of Musa al-Sadr prior to the civil war was certainly proof of the increased political importance of the Shi'ites; however, it bears emphasizing that Imam Musa led only a fraction of his politically affiliated co-religionists. It was the multi-confessional parties and militias that attracted the majority of Shi'ite recruits and many more Shi'ites carried arms under the colors of these organizations than under AMAL's. Even in war the Shi'ites suffered disproportionately; by a large measure they incurred more casualties than any other sect in Lebanon. Perhaps the single most important success achieved by al-Sadr was the reduction of the authority and the influence of the traditional Shi'ite elites, but it was the civil war and the associated growth of extralegal organizations that conclusively rendered these personalities increasingly irrelevant in the Lebanese political system.

Whatever he may have been, despite his occasionally vehement histrionics, the Imam was hardly a man of war. (He seems to have played only a most indirect role in directing the military actions of the AMAL militia.) His weapons were words, and as a result his political efforts were short-circuited by the war. He seemed to be eclipsed by the violence that engulfed Lebanon.

Disappearance and Presumed Death

In August 1978 he flew from Beirut to Tripoli with two aides to attend ceremonies commemorating Libya's Muammar Gaddafi's ascent to power in 1969. When he was not seen in Tripoli, it was said he had left for Italy. Airline crews could not confirm he had ever flown from Libya to Italy, and he was never seen after that on either side of the Mediterra-

nean. While his fate is not known, it was widely suspected that he was killed at the behest of Gaddafi, who may have viewed him as a religious rival. The Libyan government quickly claimed it had evidence that al-Sadr had left the country. The PLO, however, countered it had found al-Sadr's baggage in a Tripoli hotel and had uncovered no evidence of his arrival in Rome.

Other rumors surfaced, one saying al-Sadr had secretly returned to Qum to fight for the overthrow of the Shah of Iran. Another rumor had him kidnapped by the Shah. As months passed with no resolution to the mystery, tensions rose between Lebanon, Libya, and Iran, but no word surfaced to reveal al-Sadr's fate and he was presumed dead.

Ironically, it was al-Sadr's disappearance in 1978 that helped to retrieve the promise of his earlier efforts. Musa al-Sadr became a hero to his followers, who revered his memory and took inspiration from his words. The movement he founded, later simply called AMAL, became, after his disappearance, the most important Shi'ite organization in Lebanon and one of the most powerful.

Further Reading

There is an excellent political biography of Musa al-Sadr entitled *The Vanished Imam* by Fouad Ajami (1986). Other important references are: Edward Azar, et al., *The Emergence of a New Lebanon* (1984); Karim Pakradouni, *Stillborn Peace* (1985); Juan Cole and Nikki Keddie, editors, *Shi'ism and Social Protest* (1986); and Augustus R. Norton, *Amal and the Shi'a: Struggle for the Soul of Lebanon* (1987). A news account of al-Sadr's disappearance appeared in *Time* on October 9, 1978. □

William Safire

The American journalist William Safire (born 1929) was one of the most influential political columnists in the United States into the 1990s. A former public relations executive and President Richard Nixon speechwriter, Safire contributed a conservative perspective to the *New York Times*.

Born December 17, 1929, in New York City, William Safire was the youngest of three sons of Oliver C. and Ida (Panish) Safir. (Safire later changed the spelling of the family name while in the army to ensure correct pronunciation.) His father, a successful thread manufacturer, died when Safire was four, and he was raised by his mother in Los Angeles and New York.

After graduating from the Bronx High School of Science in New York, Safire attended Syracuse University for two years. Through the help of his older brother Leonard, he got a job as a copyboy for Tex McCrary, a personality columnist for the *New York Herald Tribune* who also hosted a radio show and was involved in Republican politics. McCrary's "kids" included future media celebrities such as Barbara Walters, but Safire was regarded as the brightest of the bunch, interviewing leading figures of the day. In 1952 he spent time as a correspondent in Europe and the Mid-East before entering the army. Assigned to public relations, he persuaded NBC to televise a July 4th ceremony awarding military decorations staged at the floor of the Statue of Liberty.

After leaving the army in 1954, Safire got a job with NBC producing a television and radio show featuring Mc-Crary and his wife. In 1955 he was named vice-president of the Ted McCrary, Inc. public relations firm. In 1959, representing a household products firm at the American Exhibition in Moscow, he helped arrange the famous "kitchen debate" between Vice-President Richard Nixon and Soviet Premier Nikita Khrushchev, shooting the Associated Press photo of the event.

Through McCrary, Safire had organized in February 1952 an Eisenhower for President rally at Madison Square Gardens. He later received a political education from Wall Street lawyer Jack Wells, who introduced him to William Casey, Nixon's 1960 campaign manager. Much later, Casey, serving as President Ronald Reagan's director of the Central Intelligence Agency, became a target of Safire during the Iran-Contra affair.

In 1960 Safire acted as chief of special projects for Nixon's presidential bid. In the early 1960s he worked on a number of other Republican campaigns in New York City and state, and in 1964 he supervised public relations for New York Governor Nelson Rockefeller's presidential campaign.

In 1961 Safire opened his own public relations firm. In 1963 he wrote his first book, *The Relations Explosion,* followed by *Plunging into Politics* in 1964 (written with Marshall Loeb) which offered candidates advice on organizing, staffing, and financing campaigns.

In 1965 Safire volunteered as an unpaid speechwriter for Nixon and wasassigned to help Patrick Buchanan with Nixon's syndicated newspaper column. In 1968 he wrote the victory speech following Nixon's election and in 1969, after selling his company for a reported $335,000 cash, he joined the White House staff. As a presidential assistant he represented the moderate wing of the Republican Party and was responsible for major statements on the economy and Vietnam War. On loan to Vice-President Spiro Agnew in 1970, he was credited with coining such well-known phrases as Agnew's labeling of the liberal media as "nattering nabobs of negativism."

During Nixon's 1972 reelection campaign Safire wrote a series of signed articles for *The Washington Post* which ran as a debate with Senator George McGovern's campaign coordinator, Frank Mankiewicz. After the election Safire was courted by the *Post* to become a columnist, but then met *New York Times* publisher Arthur Punch Sultzberger at a charity dinner. Safire accepted Sultzberger's offer to become a columnist for the *Times,* an offer greeted with scorn by other *Times* editors and reporters, especially when Safire defended Nixon during the Watergate crisis.

He proved a hard-working reporter and in 1978 won a Pulitzer prize for commentary for exposing questionable financial dealings of President Jimmy Carter's budget director Burt Lance. But Safire, who espoused the philosophy "kick them when they're up," later became a friend of Lance's after he was found innocent by a jury.

A self-labeled "libertarian conservative," Safire showed tremendous loyalties to the Nixon White House and Israel, but he criticized friends if he felt they strayed from his sense of right. A militant on foreign policy—"I am a hard-liner and a hawk"—he once called Nixon soft on Communism for favoring detente. He attacked President Reagan for not being tough enough early in his administration, but also held him responsible for the Iran-Contra scandal, upsetting many on the political right.

Over the years Safire earned the admiration of other journalists, such as *Washington Post* editor Bob Woodward of Watergate fame, and even respect from early critics such as *New York Times* executive editor Max Frankel, who later believed opposing the hiring of Safire was his biggest mistake.

Described as "a master of both puckish wit and earsplitting indignation" by one critic, Safire was called "America's best practitioner of the art of calumny."

In addition to his twice-a-week political column, which appeared in over 300 papers, he was also known as a literary stylist, a pop grammarian, and the author of a weekly column, "On Language," which appeared in the *New York Times Sunday Magazine* section.

In 1968 he published *The New Language of Politics,* a dictionary of words and slogans in the political arena, and later he published several revisions as well as numerous other books on language.

He also turned his pen to fiction, writing *Full Disclosure* (1977) and *Freedom* (1987), a massive story about President Abraham Lincoln and the Civil War between 1860 and the signing of the Emancipation Proclamation.

Safire hoped to continue the column until he was 80. "I have the greatest job in the world," he said. At 68, he's still cranking out weekly columns for the *Times* on politics, language usage and the way things ought to be. In 1996, as a token of his appreciation, he donated a number of books from his private collection to the E.S. Bird Library at New Yorks' Syracuse University.It was his way of paying the school back for a 1949 scholarship he'd received. He was living in a suburb of Washington, D.C., in 1997 with his British-born wife Helene. They had two children.

Further Reading

William Safire's column can be read in the *New York Times*. He is also the author of numerous books on politics and language: *The Relations Explosion* (1963), *Plunging into Politics* (1964), *The New Language of Politics* (1968), and again, *The New Language of Politics* (1972), *Before the Fall: Inside View of the Pre-Watergate White House* (1975), *Full Disclosure* (1977), *Safire's Political Dictionary,* (updated 1978), *Safire's Washington* (1980), *On Language* (1980), *What's the Good Word* (1982), *Good Advice* (1982), *I Stand Corrected: More on Language* (1984), *Take My Word for It: More on Language* (1986), *Freedom* (1987), *You Could Look It Up: More on Language* (1988), *Words of Wisdom: More Good Advice* (1989), *Language Maven Strikes Again* (1990), and *Leadership* (1990).
He was also featured in a couple of magazine profiles: Lally Weymouth, "From Nixon to Lincoln," *New York* (August 31, 1987) and Walter Shapiro, "Prolific Purveyor of Punditry," *TIME* (February 12, 1990). □

Carl E. Sagan

The American astronomer and popularizer of science Carl E. Sagan (1934-1996) studied the surfaces and atmospheres of the major planets, conducted experiments on the origins of life on earth, made important contributions to the debate over the environmental consequences of nuclear war, and wrote a number of popular books explaining developments in astronomy, biology, and psychology.

Carl Edward Sagan was born November 9, 1934, in New York City. Pursuing a boyhood fascination with the stars, he studied astronomy at the University of Chicago, receiving his undergraduate degree in 1954 and hisdoctorate in 1960. After holding teaching and/or research posts at the University of California-Berkeley, Harvard University, the Smithsonian Astrophysical Observatory, and Stanford University, Sagan became director of Cornell University's Laboratory for Planetary Studies and David Duncan Professor of Astronomy and Space Science (1970). In addition to his academic appointments Sagan served as a consultant to the National Aeronautics and Space Administration (NASA) and was closely associated with the unmanned space missions to Venus, Mars, Jupiter, and Saturn. Sagan's work in the popularization of science, which brought him public recognition as author, lecturer, andtelevision personality, won for him the Pulitzer Prize in 1978.

Carl Sagan's main contributions to science were made in the fields of planetary studies and the origin of life. His first major research effort was an investigation of the surface and atmosphere of Venus. In the late 1950s the prevailing scientific view was that the surface of Venus was relatively cool, life of some sort might exist on the planet, and the observed Venusian radio emissions had their origins in the activity of charged particles located in an atmospheric layer. Sagan (1961) overturned this by showing that the emissions could be explained by simply assuming that the Venusian surface was very hot, over 300 degrees Centigrade, and therefore hostile to life. He accounted for the high temperatures by positing the existence of a "greenhouse effect" that resulted from the sun's heat being trapped between the Venusian surface and the planet's carbon dioxide cloud cover. This hypothesis was confirmed by an exploratory space vehicle sent to Venus by the Soviet Union in 1967.

Solar System Research

The physical characteristics of the surface of Mars have long interested astronomers and science fiction writers. Tel-

escopic observation of the planet revealed distinctive bright and dark areas on its surface. This led some to speculate that large regions of Mars were covered with vegetation subject to seasonal changes. So matters stood until the mid-20th century, when radar and other new means of surveillance were used to gather information on the topography, temperature, wind velocities, and atmosphere of Mars. Reviewing this newly collected data, Sagan concluded that the bright regions were lowlands filled with sand and dust blown by the wind and that the dark areas were elevated ridges or highlands. Hence there was no need to assume the existence of extensive Martian plant growth.

Sagan's scientific interest in planetary surfaces and atmospheres led him to investigate the origins of life on earth and to champion the study of exobiology (the biology of extraterrestrial life). In the mid-1950s Harold Urey and Stanley Miller successfully produced key organic compounds in the laboratory by simulating the physical and chemical conditions that prevailed upon earth shortly before the first forms of life appeared. Building upon this research, Sagan irradiated a mixture of methane, ammonia, water, and hydrogen sulfide. In these experiments he was able to produce amino acids and adenosine triphosphate (ATP), complex chemical compounds which are crucial to living cells. Sagan's foray into biochemistry contributed to a better understanding of the nature and origins of terrestrial life and testified to his competence in fields of science beyond astronomy.

Popular Writing

It is not his scientific achievements but his popular books and his television appearances that have made Sagan a well-known public figure. In 1973 he published *The Cosmic Connection,* a lively introduction to space exploration and the search for extraterrestrial life. Four years later there appeared his Pulitzer Prize winning book on the evolution of human intelligence, *The Dragons of Eden.* Drawing upon recent work in neuro-physiology and exploring the brain-computer analogy and studies of sleep and dreaming, as well as interpretations of mythology, Sagan created a highly readable, original, and witty account of the development of the human intellect. Another of Sagan's books, *Cosmos* (1980), deserves notice because it was written in conjunction with his well-received television series of the same name. In this work Sagan offered a summary history of the physical universe, showed how the cosmos came to be understood with the help of modern science, and warned that the earth was in danger of being destroyed by a nuclear holocaust.

In December of 1983 Sagan, with colleagues R. P. Turco, O. B. Toon, T. P. Ackerman, and J. B. Pollack, published "Nuclear Winter: Global Consequences of Multiple Nuclear Explosions," an article which transformed the world-wide public debate over nuclear policy. The authors claimed that in a nuclear war tremendous quantities of soot and dust would be injected into the atmosphere to form a gigantic black cloud covering most of the Northern Hemisphere. This cloud would reduce the incoming sunlight by more than 95 percent for a period of several weeks and

affect the climate on earth for a number of years thereafter. During the cold, dark nuclear winter the vegetation which animals and humans need for sustenance would be seriously depleted and great harm would be done to the ecosystem and to human society. In this instance, as so often during the course of his career, Sagan drew upon his extensive knowledge of the forces operating in the atmosphere. However, that knowledge was not used to explain the features of some remote planet but to send a message warning the entire human race of the terrible consequences of nuclear warfare.

Sagan continued to work and proselytize for the furtherance of science until his death in Seattle on December 20, 1996, of pneumonia brought on by a rare bone marrow disease. In July of the following year, upon successful touchdown and deployment on the surface of Mars, the Pathfinder Lander was renamed The Dr. Carl Sagan Memorial Station.

Further Reading

Sagan's career in science and public life to the mid-1970s is covered in Henry S. F. Cooper, Jr., "Profiles (Carl Sagan—I, II)," *The New Yorker,* June 21 and 28, 1976. Among Sagan's many publications see: *Communication with Extraterrestrial Intelligence* (1973), *The Cosmic Connection* (1973), *The Dragons of Eden* (1977), *Broca's Brain* (1979), *Cosmos* (1980), *Comet* (1985), and *Contact* (1985).

Additional Sources

Rae Goodell, *The Visible Scientist,* Little, Brown, 1975.
Carl Sagan, and Richard Turco, *A Path Where No Man Thought: Nuclear Winter and the End of the Arms Race,* Random House, 1990.[/bibcit.composed
Carl Sagan, *Pale Blue Dot: A Vision of the Human Future in Space,* Random House, 1994.
Carl Sagan, *The Demon-Haunted World: Science as a Candle in the Dark,* Random House, 1996.
Carl Sagan, *Billions and Billions: Thoughts on Life and Death at the Brink of the Millennium,* Random House, 1997. □

Ruth Sager

Ruth Sager devoted her career to the study and teaching of genetics. She conducted groundbreaking research in chromosomal theory, disproving nineteenth-century Austrian botanist Gregor Johann Mendel's once-prevalent law of inheritance —a principle stating that chromosomal genes found in a cell's nucleus control the transmission of inherited characteristics.

Through her research beginning in the 1950s, Ruth Sager revealed that a second set of genes (nonchrosomomal in nature) also play a role in one's genetic composition. In addition to advancing the science of nonchromosomal genetics, she has worked to uncover various genetic mechanisms associated with cancer.

Born on February 7, 1918, in Chicago, Illinois, Ruth Sager was one of three girls in her family. Her father worked as an advertising executive, while her mother maintained an interest in academics and intellectual discourse. As a child, Sager did not display any particular interest in science. At the age of sixteen, she entered the University of Chicago, which required its students to take a diverse schedule of liberal arts classes. Sager happened into an undergraduate survey course on biology, sparking her interest in the field. In 1938, she graduated with a B.S. degree. After a brief vacation from education, Sager enrolled at Rutgers University and studied plant physiology, receiving an M.S. in 1944. Sager then continued her graduate work in genetics at Columbia University and in 1946 was awarded a fellowship to study with botanist Marcus Rhoades. In 1948 she received her Ph.D. from Columbia, and in 1949 she was named a Merck Fellow at the National Research Council.

Two years later, Sager joined the research staff at the Rockefeller Institute's biochemistry division as an assistant, working at first in conjunction with Yoshihiro Tsubo. There she began her work challenging the prevailing scientific idea that only the chromosomal genes played a significant role in genetics. Unlike many of her colleagues of the time, Sager speculated that genes which lay outside the chromosomes behave in a manner akin to that of chromosomal genes. In 1953 Sager uncovered hard data to support this theory. She had been studying heredity in Chlamydomonas, an alga found in muddy ponds, when she noted that a gene outside the chromosomes was necessary for the alga to survive in water containing streptomycin, an antimicrobial drug. Although the plant—which Sager nicknamed "Clammy"—normally reproduced asexually, Sager discovered that she could force it to reproduce sexually by withholding nitrogen from its environment. Using this tactic, Sager managed to cross male and females via sexual fertilization. If either of the parents had the streptomycin-resistant gene, Sager showed, the offspring exhibited it as well, providing definitive proof that this nonchromosomal trait was transmitted genetically.

During the time she studied "Clammy," Sager switched institutional affiliations, taking a post as a research associate in Columbia University's zoology department in 1955. The Public Health Service and National Science Foundations supported her work. In 1960 Sager publicized the results of her nonchromosomal genetics research in the first Gilbert Morgan Smith Memorial Lecture at Stanford University and a few months later in Philadelphia at the Society of American Bacteriologists. Toward the end of the year, her observations were published in *Science* magazine. As she continued her studies, she expanded her knowledge of the workings of nonchromosomal genes. Sager's further work showed that when the streptomycin-resistant alga mutated, these mutations occurred only in the non-chromosomal genes. She also theorized that nonchromosomal genes differed greatly from their chromosomal counterparts in the way they imparted hereditary information between generations. Her research has led her to speculate that nonchromosomal genes may evolve before the more common DNA chromosomes and that they may represent more closely early cellular life.

Sager continued announcing the results of her research at national and international gatherings of scientists. In the early 1960s Columbia University promoted her to the position of senior research associate, and she coauthored, along with Francis J. Ryan, a scientific textbook titled *Cell Heredity*. In 1963 she travelled to the Hague to talk about her work, and the following year she lectured in Edinburgh on nonchromosomal genes. In 1966 she accepted an offer to become a professor at Hunter College of the City University of New York. She remained in New York for nine years, spending the academic year of 1972 to 1973 abroad at the Imperial Cancer Research Fund Laboratory in London. The following year she married. Harvard University's Dana-Farber Cancer Institute lured her away from Hunter in 1975 with an offer to become professor of cellular genetics and head the Institute's Division of Cancer Genetics.

In the past twenty years, Sager's work centered on a variety of issues relating to cancer, such as tumor suppressor genes, breast cancer, and the genetic means by which cancer multiplies. Along with her colleagues at the Dana Farber Institute, Sager researched the means by which cancer multiplies and grows, in an attempt to understand and halt the mechanism of the deadly disease. She has likened the growth of cancer to Darwinian evolution in that cancer cells lose growth control and display chromosome instability. In 1983 she told reporter Anna Christensen that if researchers discover a way to prevent the chromosomal rearrangements, "we would have a potent weapon against cancer." She speculated that tumor suppressor genes may be the secret to halting cancer growth.

Sager continued to publish and serve on numerous scientific panels. In 1992 she offered scientific testimony at hearings of the Breast Cancer Coalition. A member of the Genetics Society of America, the American Society of Bacteriologists, and the New York Academy of Sciences, Sager was appointed to the National Academy of Sciences in 1977. An avid collector of modern art, she was also a member of the American Academy of Arts and Sciences.

On March 29, 1997, Sager died of cancer. At her death, she was chief of cancer genetics at the Dana-Farber Cancer Institute in Boston, which is affiliated with the Harvard Medical School.

Further Reading

Christensen, Anna, *Potential Weapon in War on Cancer,* United Press International, February 7, 1983.
The New York Times, April 4, 1997, p. A28. □

Saicho

Saicho (767-822) was a Japanese Buddhist monk who bore the posthumous title Dengyo daishi. He was the founder in Japan of the Tendai sect, which he imported after a period of study in China.

n 783 the emperor Kammu decided to remove his capital from the city of Nara, where it had been since 710. By training, Kammu was Confucian and generally anti-Buddhist. He was opposed to the great power that the six Nara sects had amassed. He had been particularly alarmed when, in 764, the monk Dokyo had almost succeeded in having himself declared ruler of Japan. Kammu's decision to move was based on his desire to preserve the prerogatives of the imperial court. To counterbalance the influence of the old, still powerful Nara sects on his new capital of Heian (Kyoto), which he founded in 794, he encouraged the founding of two new sects, which were to maintain a close relationship with the new government: Tendai, established by Saicho and Shingon, by Kukai.

Of Chinese descent, Saicho was born in Shiga in the province of Omi, entered the priesthood at the age of 14, and was ordained in 785. He was, however, disenchanted with the worldliness of the Nara priesthood and was convinced of the need for a new location if there was to be a moral and ethical awakening. Thus, in 788, he founded a small temple, later called the Enryaku-ji, on Mt. Hiei. In 788 the area around Mt. Hiei was uncultivated marshland, but in 794 it was chosen as a site for the new capital of Heian. Perhaps Saicho was instrumental in the choice, for he enjoyed the patronage of the Emperor. He was asked to hold a ceremony for purification of the new emplacement, and in 797 the Emperor is said to have referred to Mt. Hiei as the true guardian of the empire.

Travel to China

In 804 Saicho was sent to China, forming part of the ambassadorial party of Fujiwara Kadonomaro. The Shingon master Kukai was a member of the group, but on a different ship, and it is not certain that the two men met. The purpose of this trip was most especially to obtain sanction for his temple on Mt. Hiei, Chinese approval being considered necessary for standing vis-à-vis the Nara sects. Saicho returned to Japan in 805.

It does not appear at first that Saicho wanted to found a new sect. His temple enshrined the Buddha of Medicine (Yakushi), as did many of the temples at Nara, but after a year abroad he was drawn to the universality of the T'ien-t'ai sect, which was flourishing at the time. The Tendai he introduced into Japan was essentially the same as the mother sect and was based on the Lotus Sutra. Nara sects, with the exception of Kegon, were all based on secondary sources—the commentaries—and Saicho considered Tendai superior to them, for it was based on the Buddha's own words, that is, a sutra. Tendai, for Saicho, was true Mahayana Buddhism.

Saicho's teaching was universal in that it claimed enlightenment for all. This universality stood against Hosso beliefs, for example, that some beings were excluded from Buddhahood by virtue of inborn defects. Tendai claimed that all men had the innate possibility of enlightenment. It also stressed the basic unity of the Buddha and other beings; even the wicked man is Buddha. For Saicho, Buddhist perfection was a life of moral purity and contemplation, and he strongly stressed moral perfection over metaphysics. In 807

Saicho held an ordination ceremony on a *Kaidan* (ordination platform) erected on Mt. Hiei. But such was the opposition of the Nara sects that further permission was denied until 827, five years after his death.

Tendai Sect

In contrast to Nara practice, Saicho demanded a severe discipline of the monks under him. In 818 he codified the rules for monks on Mt. Hiei. There they were obliged to remain 12 years, during which time they received the "training of a bodhisattva." This meant study of Mahayana sutras, most especially the Lotus, and a kind of mystic concentration called *shikan*. It was Saicho's intent that Mt. Hiei should supply the nation with teachers and leaders.

There were three classes of monks who received training. The first was the "Treasure of the Nation," those particularly gifted in actions and words. They would remain on Mt. Hiei and serve the country by religious practice. The less gifted would leave to serve the state: some would teach; others would engage in agricultural and engineering pursuits. Thus, unlike Nara Buddhism, the new sect was at the service of the court, and the Enryaku-ji was called the "Center for the Protection of the Nation."

Saicho's writing shows a streak of nationalism. His *Defense of the Country (Shugo kokkai sho)* considers Tendai teachings as a protection for Japan. He felt very strongly about the prestige of the court, and despite his Chinese origins he admired the "Country of great Japan" (*dai nippon koku*). Tendai monks were obliged to swear an oath which included acknowledgment of the sect's debt to the Emperor.

Kukai and Saicho

In 806 the emperor Kammu died, and Saicho and his sect were at once threatened, first by the Nara monks, who questioned his authority, and then by the return in the same year of Kukai, the Shingon ecclesiastic who gained the favor of Kammu's successor.

Relations between Kukai and Saicho were at first friendly. Saicho sincerely wanted to learn what Kukai had acquired and brought back with him from China. Indeed, Saicho was much impressed with Esoteric teachings. He went so far as to receive baptism from Kukai, and he borrowed works on Esotericism from him. Relations changed, however, when Saicho sent his favorite disciple, Taihan, to study with Kukai, for the latter refused to honor Saicho's request that his pupil return to Mt. Hiei. And when Saicho requested a loan of certain Esoteric sutras, Kukai's response was plainly impolite, if not insulting, and he suggested that if Saicho wished to learn he should become a regular student. Relations between the two men remained bitter until Saicho's death.

Saicho's contribution to Japanese Buddhism lies more in organization than in doctrine. His writing tends to be heavy and repetitious, lacking the distinction of Kukai's. His most winning feature, however, is his sincerity, his desire to know the truth, not only as it was propounded by his own sect but by others as well.

Further Reading

Examples of Saicho's writings and an essay on his impact on Japanese Buddhism may be found in Ryusaku Tsunoda and others, eds., *Sources of the Japanese Tradition* (1958). There is no full-length biography of Saicho. However, Sir Charles Eliot, *Japanese Buddhism* (1935), discusses Saicho and the Tendai sect. An excellent book depicting the times when Saicho lived is Ivan Morris, *The World of the Shining Prince: Court Life in Ancient Japan* (1964).

Additional Sources

Groner, Paul, *Saicho: the establishment of the Japanese Tendai School*, Berkeley: Center for South and Southeast Asian Studies, University of California at Berkeley: Institute of Buddhist Studies, 1984. □

Seyyid Said

Seyyid Said (1790-1856) was the energetic and resourceful sultan of Oman who transferred his capital from Arabia to Zanzibar, where he initiated clove production and greatly expanded the East African slave trade.

S eyyid Said became sultan of the Persian Gulf state of Oman in 1806. Although the area was neither rich nor easy to govern, Omani fortunes rose during the Napoleonic Wars, when European merchants relied heavily on Arab shipping throughout the northern and western Indian Ocean. This prosperity proved short-lived after Britain gained control of Indian Ocean ports, thereby enabling British companies to monopolize shipping in that "English lake"; simultaneously the British navy worked to eliminate piracy in the Persian Gulf. Said's prolonged struggles with the fierce Wahhabis from the desert marshes of Oman finally convinced him of the futility of attempting any expansion of his power within the Arabian peninsula. Oman quickly descended to the depths of poverty as unemployment rose and discontent spread.

A flexible and ambitious man, Said sought alternatives to improve the lot of his countrymen and agreed to a treaty with Britain in 1823 that forbade slave trading between his Moslem subjects and any Christian power, at least in the Persian Gulf. The British in return offered friendship and support for Said's commercial interests elsewhere, especially on the East African coast, where he tried to reassert dynastic claims to govern that region of long-standing Omani trading activity.

Move to Zanzibar

Devoting more energy to his African dominions in the 1830s, Said eventually relocated his capital from the city of Masqat to Zanzibar in 1840 and thus became an East African ruler with possessions in Arabia. Although Said never entirely abandoned Oman, it thereafter ranked as an unruly distant province rather than as the heart and soul of his realm. Said used military and naval expeditions, diplomatic scheming, and the personal appointment of governors to exploit local dynastic disputes among the East African Mazrui rulers; thus by 1841 the establishment of his authority over all main coastal towns made him the first ruler ever to control the coast from Mogadishu (Somalia) to southern Tanzania.

A merchant prince rather than a soldier, Said depended on mercantile and maritime resources for his power in both Oman and Zanzibar. Recognizing the suitability of Zanzibar climate and soil, he initiated large-scale cultivation of cloves—an essential meat preservative in Europe prior to the advent of refrigeration—and soon after sought slaves as cheap labor to plant and harvest the biennial crop. In order to reach potential slaving areas in the African interior, it was necessary to finance and equip caravans for this egregious activity; resident Indians long active in Indian Ocean business ventures were attracted by possible high returns on labor investments and not only extended credit to Arab-led caravans but henceforth supplied most loans for slave purchases at Zanzibar.

Said functioned as a skillful liaison, bringing together the available Indian capital for use by his Arab adventurers. He stood between these two disparate groups, preventing wasteful arguments and quarrels, protecting Arabs from arbitrary exactions by Indians, and requiring the moneylenders to make loans only to caravans and plantations controlled by men who had Said's personal approval. Despite Arab prestige and commercial power in the interior, Said never actually ruled over any sizable number of Africans there; and in fact, wherever Arabs offended powerful tribes such as the Nyamwezi and Shambaa of Tanzania, they were often expelled.

Said's creation of the Zanzibar sultanate brought renewed prosperity to his Omani followers, and by 1850 he reported an annual income exceeding £100,000. Zanzibar Town developed into an important international entrepôt exporting slaves and ivory from regions of present-day Mozambique and Tanzania, and the mainland north of the island witnessed the major development of grain and coconut plantations. This entire pattern of economic growth was continually underwritten by Indian capitalists at Zanzibar and coordinated largely by Said's government at the coast. Seyyid Said ruled the East African coast in this way until his death in 1856; afterward the Arab-Indian alliance slowly collapsed because of British interference, succession disputes, and political squabbles.

What was Seyyid Said's contribution to East Africa? If the answer is based on what he left behind, then undoubtedly the increase in the Islamic faith and the spread of Swahili as the lingua franca of the coast and interior are the most enduring monuments of his rule. Although his economic revival helped launch the first sustained contact between the East African coast and interior, the Sultan must also be remembered for his part in at least a century-long pattern of domination and exploitation established, maintained, and encouraged by him and his successors.

Further Reading

Said's years in Oman and Masqat are thoroughly examined in J. B. Kelly, *Britain and the Persian Gulf, 1795-1880* (1968). Reginald Coupland, *East Africa and Its Invaders: From the Earliest Times to the Death of Seyyid Said in 1856* (1938), is an exhaustive historical survey of the East African coast, but many of its assumptions have been questioned and revised in Roland Oliver and others, eds., *History of East Africa,* vol. 1 (1963), and B. A. Ogot and J. A. Kieran, *Zamani: A Survey of East African History* (1968). A succinct statement on the slave trade is Edward A. Alpers, *The East African Slave Trade* (1967); and J. Spencer Trimingham, *Islam in East Africa* (1964), serves as a useful introduction to Moslem activity throughout the region. □

Takamori Saigo

The Japanese rebel and statesman Takamori Saigo (1827-1877) was the military leader of the Meiji restoration. His eventual revolt against the Meiji government in 1877 represented the resistance of the old warrior class to the swift and often ruthless policy of Westernization of Japan.

Takamori Saigo was born the eldest son of a lower-ranking samurai family on Feb. 7, 1827, in Kagoshima, the castle town of the Satsuma domain. As a youth, he showed much interest in both Wang Yang-ming Confucianism and Zen Buddhism, both of which stressed the importance of acting on individual conscience. After briefly attending the domain academy, he became a minor domain official. A huge man, physically powerful with a dark penetrating gaze and a commanding presence, he attracted the attention of the lord of the domain, Nariakira Shimazu, who agreed with his views that major domestic reforms were necessary to meet the challenge of the West. He acted as courier and confidant to Nariakira until the latter's death in 1858.

After an abortive attempt at suicide in 1858, Saigo remained in retirement until 1864, when he reemerged as a military leader in the domain. He led Satsuma troops in skirmishes with Choshu forces at Kyoto in 1864 and later in the shogunate's expedition against Choshu. Gradually, however, he became convinced that it was in the interest of both his domain and the country that Satsuma act in concert with Choshu to bring an end to continued domination of the country by the Shogun. In 1868 Saigo served as field commander of the imperial forces in campaigns against the military resistance of the shogunate. As a result of this experience, he won a reputation as a great military hero and the universal respect of the samurai who served under him.

Discontent with Meiji

Once the Meiji restoration was accomplished, Saigo found himself in growing disagreement with the leaders of the new imperial government. Although he was appointed minister of war in 1871 and became a field marshal and court councilor in 1872, he opposed the growing centralization of the government, the trimming of the legal and social privileges of the samurai class, and the rapid pace of Westernization. In 1873 he finally broke with the government when some of its members, who had returned from an extended trip to Europe, rejected his plan for an invasion of Korea to provide military glory for former samurai and to enhance Japan's international position.

Saigo returned to his native province, where there was much samurai discontentment with the abolition of their privileges and the shift of power from the feudal domains to the central government. Saigo seems to have remained politically inactive and even resisted pressure by discontented elements in other domains to revolt. But in 1877, when an army of former Satsuma samurai rebelled against the central government's attempts to end Satsuma's semi-autonomous administrative status, he agreed to lead them. On Sept. 24, 1877, he took his life in traditional samurai fashion during the final battle with government troops, which ended the rebellion.

Further Reading

One biography of Saigo in English is a translation of a work by a well-known novelist, Saneatsu Mushakoji, *Great Saigo: The Life of Takamori Saigo* (1942), which is romanticized and eulogistic. The story of Saigo's involvement in the rebellion of 1877 is treated in a contemporary journalistic account by Augustus H. Mounsey, *The Satsuma Rebellion: An Episode of Modern Japanese History* (1879).

Additional Sources

Yates, Charles L., *Saigo Takamori: the man behind the myth,* London; New York: Kegan Paul International; New York: Distributed by Columbia University Press, 1995. □

Arthur St. Clair

Arthur St. Clair (1736-1818), Scottish-born American soldier and politician, was the first territorial governor in United States history.

Arthur St. Clair was born on March 23, 1736, in Thurso. He attended the University of Edinburgh and had some training with the prominent London anatomist William Hunter. St. Clair joined the British army as an ensign in 1757 and served with Col. Jeffery Amherst in Canada. Three years later he married Phoebe Bayard, who bore him seven children. In 1762 he resigned his army commission and bought 4,000 acres of land in western Pennsylvania, which made him the largest resident landholder in that area.

This distinction brought St. Clair local responsibilities. He served as the agent for Governor William Penn in 1771 and justice of the Westmoreland County Court 2 years later. For several years he represented Pennsylvania in its fight with Virginia over the territory at Pittsburgh, but he had little success.

In 1775 St. Clair became a colonel in the American army, and a year later he became a brigadier general, serving with George Washington's forces in the American Revolution. By the spring of 1777 St. Clair had been promoted to major general and received command of Ft. Ticonderoga. When he evacuated that post, Congress recalled him. Although a court-martial cleared him in 1778, he received no further army assignments.

Returning to civilian life, St. Clair reentered politics. He was a member of the Pennsylvania Council of Censors in 1783; in 1785 he was elected to the Continental Congress, becoming president of that body 2 years later. When Congress established the Northwest Territory in 1787, St. Clair was appointed territorial governor.

St. Clair's career as governor was stormy. His territorial militia was dealt disastrous defeats by the Indians in 1790 and 1791. Meanwhile, his efforts to govern the territory caused considerable difficulty. He used his authority to obstruct legislation designed to curtail his power and democratize the territorial government. He opposed the move for statehood and, to delay it, tried to split the territory into smaller political units. When he denounced the Ohio Enabling Act as null, President Thomas Jefferson removed him from office. St. Clair then retired to his home near Ligonier, Pa., where he died on Aug. 31, 1818.

Further Reading

The most recent and only book-length biography of St. Clair is Frazer Ellis Wilson, *Arthur St. Clair: Rugged Ruler of the Old Northwest* (1944), which presents a laudatory account of his checkered career. William Henry Smith, *The St. Clair Papers: The Life and Public Services of Arthur St. Clair* (2 vols., 1882), ignores St. Clair's weaknesses, presenting only his virtues. For general studies of the problems encountered in settling the Northwest Territory see Richard L. Power, *Planting Corn Belt Culture* (1953), and John D. Barnhart, *Valley of Democracy* (1953). Randolph C. Downes discusses frontier Indian affairs in *Council Fires on the Upper Ohio* (1940). □

Ruth St. Denis

Ruth St. Denis (1878?-1968), American dancer and choreographer, was one of the founders of modern dance. Her work was characterized by its religious and Far Eastern content.

Ruth St. Denis, whose name was originally Ruth Dennis, was born in Newark, N.J., on January 20, probably in 1878, the daughter of an inventor father and a physician mother. At the age of 10 Ruth started dancing and gave her first solo performance in 1893 in a play produced by her mother.

Professional dance at this time presented two equally uninspiring alternatives: the world of vaudeville and the moribund classical ballet of opera. Miss St. Denis was delivered from this dilemma when she discovered an advertising poster for Egyptian Deities cigarettes showing the goddess Isis sitting on a throne. Immediately she saw the possibility of developing a dance on an Egyptian theme. While doing research on the culture and dance of Egypt, she discovered the dances of India.

With the help of some Indian friends, Miss St. Denis danced the *radha,* a freestyle Indian dance. She was the first in the Western world to introduce to a legitimate audience Oriental and Eastern dancing. The dances were accompanied by European music performed on Western musical instruments. American audiences were hostile to her experiments, labeling her the "Jersey Hindoo" and comparing her with the belly dancers at the local burlesque houses.

Miss St. Denis toured in Europe from 1906 to 1909, and her dances proved a great success. Like the dancer Isadora Duncan, Ruth St. Denis was also preoccupied with mysticism and was not concerned with steps but with the expressive movement of the body. But her style was more exotic and more lavishly theatrical—combining lights, scenery, costumes, music, and story in one unified experience—and her dances were much more religious.

In 1910 Miss St. Denis became the first solo dancer to play a New York theater as the evening star attraction. She continued to experiment with new dance forms. In 1913 she presented her *Egypta* dances and gave the first performance of *O'Mika,* a Japanese ballet based on her study of Japanese No theater.

In 1914 Miss St. Denis married her dancing partner, Ted Shawn, and they set up the Denishawn School of Dancing, the first serious school of dance in America with a

standard curriculum. From 1915 to 1931 it was *the* training ground for America's leading dancers and choreographers. Thirteen Denishawn tours of America helped create a basic audience for modern dance and establish dance in America as an accepted art form. The school's approach was eclectic and experimental. In 1925, for example, Miss St. Denis created *Tragica,* the first dance without music. In 1930 she and Shawn separated, and the school disbanded.

As a result of her study of Oriental systems of thought, Ruth St. Denis extended the religious implications of her dancing. In 1931 she founded the Society of Spiritual Arts to establish the dance as an instrument of worship. In 1947 she formed a Church of the Divine Dance in Hollywood, where she conducted dance masses and rituals. She continued to dance and experiment until her eighties. She died on July 21, 1968.

Further Reading

Ruth St. Denis's own account is *An Unfinished Life: An Autobiography* (1939). The authorized and most comprehensive biography is by a lifelong friend and dance critic, Walter Terry, *Miss Ruth: The "More Living Life" of Ruth St. Denis* (1969). An early appraisal was written by Ted Shawn, *Ruth St. Denis: Pioneer and Prophet* (1920). See also Walter Terry, *The Legacy of Isadora Duncan and Ruth St. Denis* (1959).

Additional Sources

Shelton, Suzanne, *Divine dancer: a biography of Ruth St. Denis,* Garden City, N.Y.: Doubleday, 1981. ☐

ment. For Saint-Exupéry there are higher values than human life, and the novel achieves an almost tragic intensity.

During the following years Saint-Exupéry pursued his flying career, despite several crashes, but published no more books until 1939, when he brought out *Terre des hommes* (*Wind, Sand and Stars*). Less a novel than a series of essays containing the pilot's meditations, poetic in tone, on the spiritual aspects of the adventure of flight, it brought Saint-Exupéry to the height of literary fame.

In 1939 Saint-Exupéry rejoined the French air force and was decorated for bravery in 1940. After the French defeat, he went to the United States, where he wrote *Pilote de guerre* (*Flight to Arras*), published in 1942. This is the record of a reconnaissance mission in May 1940, during the German invasion of France, and the author's almost miraculous survival against enormous odds. In 1943 he rejoined his unit in North Africa, fighting with the Free French; although now overage, he insisted on undertaking reconnaissance missions. On July 31, 1944, his aircraft disappeared near Corsica, probably shot down by a German fighter; no trace was ever discovered.

Other works of Saint-Exupéry include a children's story, *Le Petit prince* (1943; *The Little Prince*); a long philosophical work published posthumously, *Citadelle* (1948; *The Wisdom of the Sands*); and volumes of correspondence and notebook jottings.

Antoine de Saint-Exupéry

The French novelist and essayist Antoine de Saint-Exupéry (1900-1944), a pioneer commercial pilot, more than any other writer can be regarded as the poet of flight.

Antoine de Saint-Exupéry was born in Lyons on June 29, 1900; he attended Jesuit schools in France and Switzerland. He was a poor and unruly student but took great interest in the rapidly developing science of flight. In 1921 he began military service and learned to fly, later being commissioned as an air force officer. After 3 years in business, Saint-Exupéry became a commercial pilot in 1926, flying first from France to Morocco and West Africa. From his experiences he drew the novel that launched his literary career in 1929, *Courrier Sud* (*Southern Mail*). Here he portrays the pilot's solitary struggle against the elements and his sense of dedication to his vocation, stronger even than love.

In 1929 Saint-Exupéry was transferred to Buenos Aires, and he married in 1931. The same year he published his second book, *Vol de nuit* (*Night Flight*). Again the theme is the pilot's devotion to duty, and although, as in *Courrier Sud,* it ends in his death, this is seen not as defeat but as victory, a step forward in man's conquest of his environ-

Further Reading

Curtis Cate, *Antoine de Saint-Exupéry: His Life and Times* (1970), is an excellent biography. Other studies, biographical as much as literary, include Richard Rumbold and Lady Margaret Stewart, *The Winged Life* (1955); Maxwell A. Smith, *Knight of the Air: The Life and Works of Antoine de Saint-Exupéry* (1956); and Marcel Migeo, *Saint-Exupéry* (trans. 1961). A good short study of him is in Henri Peyre, *French Novelists of Today* (1967).

Additional Sources

Saint-Exupéry, Antoine de, *Wind, sand and star,* London, Heinemann, 1970.

Nicolson, Harold George, Sir, *Sainte-Beuve,* Westport, Conn.: Greenwood Press, 1978. □

Augustus Saint-Gaudens

Augustus Saint-Gaudens (1848-1907), the leading American sculptor of the late 19th century, is best known for his bronze historical memorials.

Augustus Saint-Gaudens was born in Dublin, Ireland, on March 1, 1848, and taken to America as an infant. He grew up in New York City. At the age of 13 he was apprenticed to a cameo cutter, and he later attended classes at Cooper Union and the National Academy of Design. In 1867 he went to Paris, where he studied at the École des Beaux-Arts, and in 1870 he left for Rome. His marble *Hiawatha* and *Silence,* carved in Rome, were his only significant works in the still prevalent neoclassic style.

Shortly after Saint-Gaudens returned to the United States in 1875, he received the commission for the Adm. Farragut monument in Madison Square, New York City. This work, which was completed in 1881, is imbued with the spirit of the early Renaissance, and it established his reputation. It was the first of a number of memorials relating to the Civil War. In the Farragut monument he combines the idealistic sense of the heroic with vivid portraiture. The base is adorned with extremely delicate low-relief sculptures, a form which Saint-Gaudens revived from the Renaissance. He had already achieved success in low-relief portraits.

Saint-Gaudens next executed a sculpture of Abraham Lincoln standing in front of a Renaissance chair (1887) for Lincoln Park, Chicago. As in the Farragut, he was associated with the architect Sanford White in constructing the base. Saint-Gaudens's *Puritan* (1887), a memorial to Deacon Samuel Chapin in Springfield, Mass., is an eloquent embodiment of early New England Puritanism. His next major Civil War monument was the complex memorial to Robert Gould Shaw (1884-1897), who had led the first regiment of Negro troops from Massachusetts and died during the conflict in 1863. This monument, opposite the State House in Boston, has a high-relief equestrian statue and other figures in varying depths of relief.

Probably Saint-Gaudens's best-known work is his memorial to Gen. Sherman (1892-1903) in Central Park, New York City, a work which blends realism and idealism. The figure of Victory is based on the ancient Victory of Samothrace, and the great equestrian statue is related to Donatello's 15th-century *Gattamelata.* Diana (1892; now in the Philadelphia Museum of Art) is Saint-Gaudens's one ideal nude. Perhaps his most moving and affecting sculpture is the figure sometimes entitled Grief (1891-1893), the monument to Mrs. Henry Adams in Rock Creek Cemetery, Washington, D.C. The inscrutable, enigmatic form is a touching embodiment of personal grief and tragedy, the greatest of all the allegories of death of the period.

Saint-Gaudens was eminently successful in his own time. He was the leader in the artistic community which grew up around his estate at Cornish, N. H. He died there on Aug. 3, 1907, and his house and studio have been preserved as the Saint-Gaudens Memorial.

Further Reading

A definitive study of Saint-Gaudens by John Dryfhout was in preparation as of 1972. Useful works are Royal Cortissoz, *Augustus Saint-Gaudens* (1907), and *The Reminiscences of Augustus Saint-Gaudens,* edited by Homer Saint-Gaudens (2 vols., 1913).

Additional Sources

Wilkinson, Burke, *The life and works of Augustus Saint Gaudens,* New York: Dover; Gerrards Cross, England: C. Smythe, 1992. □

Louis Antoine Léon de Saint-Just

Louis Antoine Léon de Saint-Just (1767-1794), a radical political leader during the French Revolution, was a member of the ruling Jacobin group in Paris during the Reign of Terror.

Louis de Saint-Just was born on Aug. 25, 1767, in Decize, the son of an army officer. After a period of schooling, he ran away from home to Paris, taking with him part of the family silver. He studied law for a time and also published a burlesque epic which was a mixture of the crudely erotic and of sharp criticism of the government and society of his day.

When the Revolution broke out in 1789, the youthful Saint-Just gave it his enthusiastic support, and he published in 1791 *The Spirit of the Revolution and of the Constitution of France*. He was too young to be elected to the Legislative Assembly that year, but in September 1792 he was elected a member of the Convention, whose task it was, now that the King had been deposed, to draft a new constitution and to govern France in the meantime. Saint-Just, handsome, proud, and self-possessed, spoke with the zeal of a dedicated revolutionist. He ruthlessly and brilliantly urged the trial and execution of the King; he participated actively in drafting the Constitution of 1793; and in the feverish atmosphere of foreign and civil war, he became the spokesman for the Jacobins in demanding the death of their moderate opponents, the Girondins.

In June 1793 Saint-Just became a member of the Committee of Public Safety, the executive body that ruled France in dictatorial fashion, using the so-called Reign of Terror as a means of repressing opposition. In October he was sent as a representative to the Army of the Rhine in Strasbourg, where the war was going badly and factionalism and opposition to the government in Paris were at their height. He was twice sent on similar missions to the Army of the North.

Back in Paris, Saint-Just defended the Terror in speeches and proposed a redistribution of the property of the disloyal rich, a plan that was never implemented. As spokesman for the Robespierrist faction, he denounced the extremist Hébertists; he also denounced Georges Jacques Danton and the Indulgents; and each time the objects of his scorn were sent to the guillotine.

Although a determined terrorist, Saint-Just was also an idealist. His unpublished *Fragments concerning Republican Institutions* reveals his Rousseauistic and Spartan utopianism. He and Robespierre were determined to fashion a new France, a "Republic of Virtue," and for that goal the continuation of the Terror was essential. But a moderate trend had begun, prompted in part by the military victory of Fleurus, to which Saint-Just had contributed during his last mission to the army. For this and other reasons, a fatal split took place.

Saint-Just prepared a report denouncing his and Robespierre's opponents, to be delivered to the Convention on July 27, 1794. But he was interrupted by the opposition, and he, Robespierre, and their colleagues were arrested. Released by their supporters, they gathered at the city hall, hoping to prevail over their enemies with the aid of the Parisian populace. But shortly after midnight they were captured and executed. Saint-Just's youthful beauty and his terrible virtue have earned him the sobriquet of "archangel of the Revolution."

Further Reading

The most comprehensive and best biography, although sometimes unnecessarily detailed, is Eugene Newton Curtis, *Saint-Just: Colleague of Robespierre* (1935). A short and perceptive study is Geoffrey Bruun, *Saint-Just: Apostle of the Terror* (1932). Both studies are reasonably objective in their estimate of the man. Saint-Just's role as a member of the Committee of Public Safety is described in the excellent history of that organization by R. R. Palmer, *Twelve Who Ruled* (1941).

Additional Sources

Hampson, Norman, *Saint-Just,* Oxford, UK; Cambridge, Mass., USA: Blackwell, 1991.
Mazzucchelli, Mario, *Saint-Just,* Milano: Dall'Oglio, 1980.
Vinot, Bernard, *Saint-Just,* Paris: Fayard, 1985. □

Louis Stephen St. Laurent

Louis Stephen St. Laurent (born 1882) was a Canadian statesman. He was prime minister and leader of the Liberal party of Canada, and during his efficient government Canada experienced an economic boom.

L ouis St. Laurent was born in Compton, Quebec, on Feb. 1, 1882, of French-and Irish-Canadian parents. Completely bilingual, St. Laurent was educated at Laval University, where he did brilliantly in legal studies. Until 1941 he was content to be a lawyer, building a large practice and earning a reputation for integrity and honesty.

In 1941, however, World War II was under way, and Ernest Lapointe, the minister of justice and French Canada's spokesman in Ottawa, had just died. Prime Minister Mackenzie King selected St. Laurent to be Lapointe's successor, and after giving serious consideration to the request, St. Laurent decided to accept for war service only.

The relations between French Canadians and English Canadians had always been delicate, but in wartime they were more so. St. Laurent played a major role in reconciling Quebec to conscription, and he quickly established himself as the Prime Minister's right-hand man. With the end of the war, he was persuaded to remain in the Cabinet as secretary of state for external affairs, and in this post he became one of the architects of the North Atlantic Treaty.

When Mackenzie King retired in 1948, St. Laurent was selected as his successor at a leadership convention, and in the next year he led the Liberals to a sweeping victory in a general election. St. Laurent's administration was fortunate to be in office in boom times, and with C. D. Howe, his English-Canadian lieutenant, St. Laurent opened the doors to foreign investment. The results in the short term were astonishing: Canada's gross national product climbed; population increased; the standard of living rose; and resources development proceeded apace. In 1953 the government was again victorious in a general election.

Although the boom continued, charges of arrogance and contempt for Parliament soon were leveled against the St. Laurent government, particularly after the extraordinary measures employed in the House of Commons during the great "pipeline debate" of 1956. St. Laurent's angry attacks on the policies of Britain and France during the Suez crisis of 1956 did little to improve matters, and in the general election of 1957 the government was defeated. St. Laurent continued as leader of the Liberal party until January 1958, after which he entered retirement. St. Laurent was a manager rather than a leader, and although he and his government were undoubtedly efficient, there were few tears shed over the end of his regime.

Further Reading

There are few serious studies of St. Laurent or his administration. The only biography, Dale C. Thomson, *Louis St. Laurent, Canadian* (1967), is uncritical. William Kilbourn, *Pipeline:*

Transcanada and the Great Debate (1970), sheds interesting light on the pipeline debate of 1956. □

Abbé de Saint-Pierre

The French political and economic theorist Charles Irénée Castel, Abbé de Saint-Pierre (1658-1743), was an early philosophe of the Enlightenment. His pamphleteering expressed the intellectual upheaval and fascination with affairs of state which marked this era.

O f noble lineage, in 1680 Charles Irénée Castel, who is known as the Abbé Saint-Pierre, left his native Normandy and boyhood dreams of a monastic vocation for the ebullient intellectual atmosphere of Parisian university studies. For 5 years he followed every course available in the physical sciences, drifting further and further away from preoccupations with his ecclesiastical state as well as from what remained of his faith. After 1685 he experienced a brief return to the concerns of ethics and moral theology before abandoning the divine again for what would be the area of his real intellectual vocation— political theory. Henceforth his religion and his "consecration" to Holy Orders provided him with a comfortable living in sinecures which left him free to speculate on the art of government.

In 1712 Saint-Pierre composed his first important treatise, the *Project for an Everlasting Peace in Europe,* a text he would refine for years to come. He envisioned a confederation of European sovereigns who would renounce the use of arms and submit their differences to a council of arbitration. He was in fact simply modernizing a 1624 treatise of Henry IV's minister the Duc de Sully.

The basic political principle of Saint-Pierre's work was his refusal to accept as either inevitable or rational the divine right of kings. His treatise *La Polysynodie* (1718) represented, at the height of the regent's liberalization policies, an outright attack on individual sovereignty, suggesting rule by multiple councils and offering many unfavorable comparisons drawn from the recently ended rule of Louis XIV. The French Academy, to which he had been elected in 1694, was scandalized, and when Saint-Pierre refused to recant, he was summarily dismissed. His political influence was growing, however; the previous year he had issued *Mémoire sur la taille tarifiée,* suggesting tax reforms which amounted to the first version of proportional, declared revenue taxation. Historians consider this his most important contribution to governmental affairs, since some of its provisions actually found limited application after 1832.

In the ensuing years Saint-Pierre became a habitué of the salon of Madame de Tencin and a regular contributor to meetings of the Club de l'Entresol; it was here that the Baron de Montesquieu, who called Saint-Pierre his master, met him. The Abbé was very likely responsible for this progressive group's dissolution, however, when in 1731 A. H. de

Fleury suggested that he and others like him should refrain from discussing politics. In the last years of his life Saint-Pierre continued to write assiduously on governmental practice and management while pursuing his *Annales politiques,* a comprehensive, chronological treatment of the affairs of France eventually covering the years from 1658 to 1739; critics have compared this last work favorably to the *Siècle de Louis XIV* of Voltaire.

Curiously, Voltaire and most of the later *philosophes,* including Jean Jacques Rousseau, disdained the Abbé, readily placing him with cranks and inventors and remembering his chimerical *Trémoussoir* (a therapeutic chair which jolted its user like a carriage) better than his insightful projects for public assistance to orphans and the aged and infirm, the maintenance of highways in winter (complete with statistical evidence of its economic advantage), and Parisian postal reform. But Saint-Pierre lacked the doctrinaire assurance of the next generation; avoiding grandiose plans for human betterment, he continued to the end refining his practical suggestions, a modest reformer who died in 1743, before the age of prerevolutionary visions.

Further Reading

In English, a recent treatment of Saint-Pierre is Merle L. Perkins, *The Moral and Political Philosophy of the Abbé de Saint-Pierre* (1959), which contains an extensive bibliography. Partial studies of him appear in E. V. Souleyman, *The Vision of World Peace in Seventeenth- and Eighteenth-century France* (1941); Carl Joachim Friedrich, *Inevitable Peace* (1948); and Francis Harry Hinsley, *Power and the Pursuit of Peace: Theory and Practice in the History of Relations between States* (1963). □

Charles Camille Saint-Saëns

The French composer Charles Camille Saint-Saëns (1835-1921) wrote music in almost every form and medium, characterized by polish and skill although lacking in ultimate depth or passion.

Born in Paris into a moderately poor family, Camille Saint-Saëns began his musical education by studying piano with his grandaunt. As a child, he exhibited considerable talent in performance and composition. He made his official concert debut as a pianist at the age of 11 and 2 years later was admitted to the Paris Conservatory. He studied composition with Jacques Fromentin Halévy and won prizes in organ in 1849 and 1851. Saint-Saëns's dexterity at this instrument, coupled with his ability to improvise, led in 1853 to his appointment as organist at the church of St-Merry and 5 years later at the Madeleine. From 1861 to 1865 he taught piano at the École Niedermeyer.

In 1871 Saint-Saëns helped found the National Society of Music, an organization devoted to the encouragement of young French composers, but he withdrew 5 years later as his essentially conservative nature had come into conflict with the changing interests of the younger composers. He

resigned from his position at the Madeleine in 1877 and spent the following years touring North and South America, England, Russia, and Austria, conducting and performing his own compositions. Highly honored in his lifetime, he was admitted into the French Legion of Honor in 1868, gaining its highest order, the Grand-Croix, in 1913. He was outspoken against the music of Claude Debussy and the French impressionist school.

The compositions of Saint-Saëns include five Piano Concertos, of which the Second (1868) and the Fourth (1875) hold a secure place in the repertoire today. His *Introduction and Rondo Capriccioso* for violin and orchestra (1870) is better known than his other concertos. Among his symphonic poems the *Danse macabre* (1874) is probably his most popular composition. Its charm lies not only in its melodic appeal but in the delightful way in which Saint-Saëns imitates Death playing his out-of-tune violin and the rattling of the bones as the skeletons dance. Another composition that reveals his sense of humor is the *Carnival of Animals* (1866); the lovely cello solo ''The Swan'' comes from this work. More impressive than these occasional compositions is the Third Symphony (1886), the orchestration of which includes an organ as well as piano. His only operatic success, *Samson et Dalila* (1877), contains the well-known aria ''My heart at thy sweet voice'' and a colorful bacchanale.

In addition to his activities as composer and performer, Saint-Saëns was also the general editor of the complete works of Jean Philippe Rameau. The English conductor Sir

Thomas Beecham, in an oft-quoted statement, called Saint-Saëns the greatest second-rate composer who ever lived.

Further Reading

Considerable biographical information is in Saint-Saëns's autobiographical book, *Musical Memories* (1913; trans. 1919). James Harding, *Saint-Saëns and His Circle* (1965), is the most important study of the composer in English. Saint-Saëns is one of the subjects of Donald Brook, *Five Great French Composers* (1946).

Additional Sources

Smith, Rollin, *Saint-Saëns and the organ,* Stuyvesant, NY: Pendragon Press, 1992. □

Duc de Saint-Simon

The French writer Louis de Rouvroy, Duc de Saint-Simon (1675-1755), provides in his classic "Memoirs" a major source of information on the court of the "Sun King," Louis XIV.

The Duc de Saint-Simon was born on Jan. 16, 1675, in Paris. As a young aristocrat, he studied horsemanship and fencing as much as letters and entered the elite King's Musketeers at the age of 16. Three years later, apparently inspired by the memoirs of Marshal Bassompierre and others, which he read in the field, he began making notes for memoirs of his own.

Passed over for promotion in 1702, Saint-Simon abandoned his military career and went to live at the court of Versailles. He apparently continued to make notes and read extensively in the works of other memorialists and historians, to the point that his fellow courtiers often consulted him on questions of history, genealogy, and court etiquette. However, both his resignation from the army and his sometimes unwelcome knowledge of court traditions irritated Louis XIV, who excluded him from any official post for the rest of his reign.

After the death of Louis XIV in 1715, Saint-Simon played an important role as public and private counselor to the regent, Philippe II d'Orléans, retiring upon the death of the latter in 1723. After spending several years on such other historical projects as his *Notes on the Dukedoms and Peerages* and his *Additions* to the Marquis of Dangeau's *Journal,* he began revising and writing out his *Memoirs* in 1739.

In the *Memoirs,* Saint-Simon's observations allowed him to describe vividly both the elegance and the corruption of the court of Versailles. Despite some errors of fact and interpretation, his knowledge of history made him aware of the breakdown of traditional checks and balances that underlay Louis XIV's royal absolutism and which was to lead, in the next century, to the French Revolution. Saint-Simon's intensely written accounts of court intrigues and such events as the deaths of the Grand Dauphin, the Duke of Burgundy, and Louis XIV himself—as well as his incisive

word portraits of his fellow courtiers—make him perhaps the world's greatest writer on the prestige, the ambitions, the uncertainties, and the ironies of public life. He completed his *Memoirs* in 1752. Saint-Simon died on March 2, 1755, in Paris.

Further Reading

Saint-Simon's *Memoirs* have never been completely translated into English. The most recent partial translation is by Lucy Norton, *Historical Memoirs of the Duc de Saint-Simon* (2 vols., 1967-1968). The best study of Saint-Simon in English is Edwin Cannan, *The Duke of Saint Simon* (1885). □

Comte de Saint-Simon

The French social philosopher and reformer Claude Henri de Rouvroy, Comte de Saint-Simon (1760-1825), was one of the founders of modern industrial socialism and evolutionary sociology.

The Comte de Saint-Simon was born in Paris to the poorer side of a prominent noble family. From childhood on he was filled with great ambitions that took him on many different paths. First commissioned into the army at 17, he served 4 years, during which he fought with some distinction in the American Revolution.

On his return to Europe, Saint-Simon tried a series of bold commercial ventures but had limited success before the French Revolution. During the Terror of 1793-1794 he was imprisoned for a year and barely escaped execution. This experience left him deeply opposed to revolutionary violence. After his release, for a short time he obtained a sizable fortune by speculating in confiscated properties, which he spent on a lavish Paris salon that attracted many intellectual and government leaders. But his funds were soon exhausted, and he lived his remaining years in constant financial difficulties.

In 1802 Saint-Simon turned to a new career as writer and reformer. In numerous essays and brochures written during the chaotic years of Napoleon's rule and the Bourbon restoration that followed, he developed a broad-ranging program for the reorganization of Europe. Although many of its ideas were commonplace, his program is distinctive for its blending of Enlightenment ideals, the more practical materialism of the rising bourgeoisie, and the emphasis on spiritual unity of restorationists.

All three strands are joined in Saint-Simon's evolutionary view of history—as a determined progression from one stable form of civilization to another—which gave his program a distinctive rationale. Each higher form was thought to be based on more advanced "spiritual" as well as "temporal" (that is, political-economic) principles, reflecting a more general process of cultural enlightenment. But each in turn also is destined to become obsolete as further cultural progress occurs.

Saint-Simon argued that all of Europe had been in a transitional crisis since the 15th century, when the established medieval order (based on feudalism and Catholicism) began to give way to a new system founded on industry and science. He wrote as the new system's advocate, urging influential leaders to hasten its inception as the only way to restore stability. In this he was one of the first ameliorators to argue for reform as an evolutionary necessity.

Saint-Simon's earlier writings, during Napoleon's reign (*Introduction aux travaux scientifiques du XIX siècle,* 1807-1808; and *Mémoire sur la science de l'homme,* 1813), stress the spiritual side of the transitional crisis. He argued that disorder was rampant because theistic Roman Catholicism, the spiritual basis of medieval society, was being undermined by the rise of science and secular philosophies. Although the trend was inevitable, Saint-Simon was highly critical of many scientists and intellectuals for their "negativism" in breaking down an established creed without providing a replacement. Instead, he called for the creation of an integrative social science, grounded in biology, to help establish a new "positive" credo for secular man in the emerging social order. This "positivistic" notion was developed by his one-time disciple Auguste Comte.

After Napoleon's downfall Saint-Simon shifted his attention from the ideology of the new system to its temporal structure and policies in a series of periodicals: *L'Industrie* (1816-1818); *La Politique* (1819); *L'Organisateur* (1819-1820); and *Du Système industriel* (1821-1822). These contain his main socialist writings, but his doctrines often are closer to venture capitalism and technocracy than to Marxism or primitive communalism. Saint-Simon's future society is above all one of productive achievement in which poverty and war are eliminated through large-scale "industrialization" (a word he coined) under planned scientific guidance. It is an open-class society in which caste privileges are abolished, work is provided for all, and rewards are based on merit. Government also changes from a haphazard system of class domination and national rivalries to a planned welfare state run by scientific managers in the public interest.

Saint-Simon's final work, *Le Nouveau Christianisme* (1825), inspired a Christian socialist movement called the Saint-Simonians, who were devoted to a secular gospel of economic progress and human brotherhood. After his death, his ideas were reworked by followers into the famous *Doctrine de Saint-Simon* (1829). This was the first systematic exposition of industrial socialism, and it had great influence on the Social Democratic movement, Catholic reforms, and Marxism.

Further Reading

F. M. H. Markham edited and translated *Selected Writings of Saint-Simon* (1952). The best account of Saint-Simon's life and work is Frank E. Manuel, *The New World of Henri Saint-Simon* (1956). Other accounts include Mathurin M. Dondo, *The French Faust: Henri de Saint-Simon* (1955), and the section on Saint-Simon in Manuel's *The Prophets of Paris* (1962). For his place in socialist thought see volume 1 of G. D. H. Cole, *A History of Socialist Thought* (1953). □

Charles Augustin Sainte-Beuve

The French literary critic Charles Augustin Sainte-Beuve (1804-1869), who developed a very personal technique of literary criticism, remains the most important literary arbiter of his century.

B orn in Boulogne-sur-Mer, Charles Augustin Sainte-Beuve went to Paris in 1824 to study medicine. But by 1826 he was contributing actively to the *Globe,* where an article favorable to Victor Hugo won him the young poet's confidence and a place in his *Cénacle,* or coterie, among the most innovative literary talents of the time. Saint-Beuve's *Tableau historique et critique de la poésie française et du théâtre français au XVI siècle* (1828) not only rehabilitated the neglected Pléiade poets (Pierre Ronsard, Joachim du Bellay) but laid a claim to respectability for his contemporaries, "romantic" descendants of those forgotten giants of lyricism.

Saint-Beuve's own elegiac efforts in *Vie, poésies et pensées de Joseph Delorme* (1829) and Consolations (1830) enhanced a prestige among his peers that was not echoed by the public; his unhappy affair with Hugo's wife, Adèle (allusively chronicled in his novel *Volupté,* 1834), led to an open break with his most ardent supporters and initiated a period (mid-1830s) of spiritual upheaval during which he sought guidance in Saint-Simonism and even in the renewed Catholicism of Félicité Robert de Lamennais. His interest in the Jansenist community of Port Royal dates from these years, although he continued producing critical articles for the *Revue des deux mondes,* which would be collected in *Portraits littéraires, Portraits de femmes,* and *Portraits contemporains.* The *Histoire de Port-Royal* (3 vols., 1840-1848; originally a lecture series given in Lausanne in 1837-1838) remains his most important single contribution, however, and is often termed the most valuable and original work of literary criticism in the 19th century. Here his ideal role as "naturalist of human spirits," seeking to classify by "families" and "generations" those writers whose interior lives he deliberately pursues, is clearly expressed. Sainte-Beuve sought here, as he would throughout his career, that "relative truth of each thing" by which literature remained for him a domain of vital and infinite variety.

The second half of Sainte-Beuve's career (1849-1869), marked by a hasty and widely criticized rallying to the regime of Napoleon III, saw his elevation to a place in the French Academy and finally (1865) a seat in the Senate. These were his most productive years, during which the *Causeries du lundi* ("Monday Chats" in the *Moniteur*) regularly confirmed his official status as arbiter of national taste under the Second Empire. *Chateaubriand et son groupe littéraire* (1861; dating from a course given at Liège in 1848-1849) stands with *Port-Royal* as a major, unitary contribution. The *Lundis* and *Nouveaux Lundis,* however, best reveal that shifting, curious, always allusive talent with which he attempted to join "physiology" and "poetry" in an art of evocation and critical appraisal. Sainte-Beuve, by abandoning the dogmatic evaluations of his predecessors, made of criticism an inductive process based on detailed examination of the author's character, his life, and so his literary work. This historical, biographical method established Sainte-Beuve as the first "modern" literary critic.

Further Reading

There is no complete edition of Sainte-Beuve's works in either French or English, although many of his works have been translated. Two particularly useful critical biographies and appraisals are Harold Nicolson, *Sainte-Beuve* (1957), and Andrew George Lehmann, *Sainte-Beuve: A Portrait of the Critic, 1804-42* (1962). □

Kimmochi Saionji

Kimmochi Saionji (1849-1940) was the last elder statesman, or genro, of Japan. Catapulted by birth into high position, he played a major role in the Japanese government both during and after the Meiji restoration of 1868. He made the final recommendations for premiers until his death.

Born on Oct. 23, 1849, the second son of Kinzumi Tokudaiji, Kimmochi was adopted at the age of 2 by the Saionji family, who were court nobles (*kuge*) close to the imperial family. He served Emperor Komei as boy chamberlain and imperial guard and knew Mutsuhito as prince. When the latter became the Meiji emperor, Saionji at 19 was made a councilor (*sanyo*) and later was appointed a commander, assisted by Aritomo Yamagata, 10 years his senior.

After 10 years in France, imbibing liberal ideas, Saionji returned home in 1881 and was happy to find the Freedom and People's Rights movement in progress. He consented to head the *Toyo Jiyu Shimbun* (Oriental Liberal Newspaper) but was quickly ordered by the Emperor to step down.

Government Career

In 1882 Saionji accompanied Hirobumi Ito to Europe on his constitutional research mission and later spent 6 years as minister to Austria-Hungary, Germany, and Belgium. Returning home, Saionji became president of the Bureau of Decorations, then vice president of the House of Peers, and, when he was 46, during the Sino-Japanese War, minister of education in the second Ito Cabinet. It was thus natural for Saionji to assist Ito in founding the Seiyukai party in 1900 and later, after a turn at the presidency of the Privy Council, to follow Ito as party president. This in turn led to two premierships alternating with those of Taro Katsura, Yamagata's protégé. Yet on Yamagata's recommendation Saionji became *genro* in 1916 and was appointed chief delegate to the Paris Peace Conference in 1919, where he

took part in founding the League of Nations. For this he was raised from marquis to prince.

With the death of Masayoshi Matsukata in 1924, Saionji became the only living *genro* and thus the ultimate "Cabinet maker." Although he was partial to the idea of a Cabinet based on a majority party, he could not find statesmen of real stature to choose from. This he blamed on the poor quality of the parties and the low level of the people's political understanding. As pressure from the military and support for aggression grew, Saionji lost confidence and considered resigning.

Fearing that civilians would be assassinated, Saionji recommended military men as premiers. In 1937 Saionji mistakenly thought that he had found an ideal premier in Prince Fumimaro Konoe, who could control the military. Saionji died on Nov. 24, 1940, still faintly hoping Japan could negotiate with Chiang Kai-shek and avoid war with the United States. Theoretically a bachelor, Saionji had three common-law wives and successive mistresses; he adopted a son who married his eldest daughter and became his heir, Hachiro Saionji. Saionji also distinguished himself as an author, a translator, and a musician on the biwa.

Further Reading

A scholarly study, *Prince Saionji* (trans. 1933), was written by Yosaburo Takekoshi, a noted Japanese historian. A fascinating fictionalized biography published before Saionji's death is Bunji Omura, *The Last Genro: Prince Saionji, the Man Who Westernized Japan* (1938), which contains glossaries. Although generally accurate and offering much background and personal detail, Omura did not have available the great amount of material that has since been published in Japanese by persons who knew Saionji personally. They include Sakutaro Koizumi, who edited Saionji's autobiography in 1949, and Kumao Harada, his personal secretary and official spokesman, who published a nine-volume work on him between 1950 and 1956, volume 1 of which, *Fragile Victory: Prince Saionji and the 1930 London Treaty Issue* (trans. 1968), is introduced and annotated by the translator, Thomas Francis Mayer-Oakes.

Additional Sources

Connors, Lesley, *The emperor's adviser: Saionji Kinmochi and pre-war Japanese politics,* London; Wolfeboro, N.H.: Croom Helm; Oxford, Oxfordshire: Nissan Institute for Japanese Studies, University of Oxford, 1987. □

Andrei Sakharov

Andrei Sakharov (1921-1989), one of the Soviet Union's leading theoretical physicists and regarded in scientific circles as the "father of the Soviet atomic bomb," also became Soviet Russia's most prominent political dissident in the 1970s . From 1980 to 1986 he was banished from Moscow to Gorky and cut off from contact with family, friends, and scientific colleagues.

ndrei Sakharov was born in Moscow on May 21, 1921, the son of a physics teacher. A brilliant student, he studied at Moscow University under Igor Tamm, winner of the Nobel Prize for theoretical physics. During World War II Sakharov served as an engineer in a military factory. In 1945 he entered the Lebedev Institute in Physics and soon joined the Soviet research group working on atomic weapons. Author of numerous scientific articles in this period, his achievements were broadly recognized inside Soviet Russia and out. In 1953, at the age of 32, he became the youngest person ever elected to the Soviet Academy of Sciences.

Between 1950 and 1968 Sakharov conducted top secret research on thermonuclear weapons in a secret location. He also developed an acute awareness of the dangers of nuclear testing activity and the irreversible consequences of nuclear war. His activities as a dissident can be dated from the period of relative intellectual freedom under Nikita Khrushchev in the late 1950s, when Sakharov began to send letters to Soviet leaders urging a halt to nuclear testing. In November 1958 *Pravda* allowed him to publish a lengthy article criticizing a plan to send children talented in mathematics and physics to the countryside for farm work. He also published several prominent articles in *Atomnaia Energiia* and other Soviet journals arguing against continued nuclear testing and the arms race. His views apparently carried weight with Khrushchev and others, with whom Sakharov

communicated directly, and influenced the Soviet decision to sign the first test ban treaty in 1963.

The freedoms Sakharov and others enjoyed in these relatively liberal years had enormous effect. The ability to think and write openly about critical social issues was not easily repressed, despite the concerted efforts of Khrushchev's conservative successor, Leonid Brezhnev. In 1966 and 1967 Sakharov openly warned against efforts to rehabilitate Stalin and pressed for civil liberties. With the Soviet invasion of Czechoslovakia in 1968 and the brutal repression of the Prague Spring, Sakharov and others became more militant, expressing their criticism more openly and sometimes standing vigil at trials of those arrested for protest activities. It was at this time that Sakharov published his most prominent and eloquent political essay, *Reflections on Progress, Peaceful Coexistence and Intellectual Freedom,* urging cooperation between East and West, civil liberties, and an end to the arms race.

It was while standing vigil at one such trial in 1970 that Sakharov, a widower, met Elena Bonner, who soon became his second wife and strongest supporter. The publication of *Reflections* in the West resulted in Sakharov's removal from most of his scientific projects and his dismissal as principal consultant to the Soviet Atomic Energy Commission. It soon became difficult for him to publish scientific works as well, although he continued his research and writing. In these difficult circumstances, Sakharov, assisted by Bonner, rapidly assumed a leading role in the Soviet dissident movement.

His writings and protests throughout the 1970s generally touched four themes: the treatment of individuals, particularly other dissidents arrested or otherwise harassed for their political views; the suppression of civil liberties in the U.S.S.R. and elsewhere; attacks on Soviet "totalitarianism," as he described it, and demands for political freedom in Russia; and the grave dangers of the arms race and nuclear development and testing plus the likely consequences of nuclear war. Sakharov's great international prestige as a nuclear physicist (and his particular knowledge of the Soviet Union's nuclear weapons program) gave special significance to his views and also for a time helped protect him from arrest and expulsion.

Toward the end of the 1970s Sakharov became increasingly alarmed about the Soviet arms build-up. A strong advocate of East-West parity in nuclear weapons, he saw the development of new Soviet missiles as a reflection of aggressive and expansionist designs. He frequently expressed his views to foreign reporters, and much of his *samizdat* writing appeared in the West. His outspoken criticism of the Soviet invasion of Afghanistan in late 1979 reflected these concerns and led, finally, to his detainment and expulsion from Moscow. In a celebrated incident, Sakharov was banished by administrative order to Gorky, a small city 250 miles east of Moscow, and cut off from open contact with friends and colleagues. Thus began a period of almost total isolation and constant harassment by the KGB (secret police).

Sakharov's plight became in the 1980s a constant sore in Soviet-American relations. In 1983 he reportedly consid-

Andrei Sakharov (holding child)

ered emigration, but was refused because of his knowledge of Soviet state secrets. Continued protests against Soviet militarism resulted in new threats and warnings to him and to family members. On several occasions Sakharov engaged in hunger strikes to call attention to these threats and to gain the right of family members to go abroad. In 1983 President Reagan proclaimed May 21 "National Sakharov Day" in recognition of his courage and his contribution to humanity.

Sakharov was detained in Gorky for almost seven years, released at last by Mikhail Gorbachev in 1986. The remaining three years of his life were spent traveling abroad—something he had never previously done, despite his international fame. He died of a heart attack on December 14, 1989, in Moscow.

Three times named "Hero of Socialist Labor" (1953, 1956, 1962), winner of the Order of Lenin, the Stalin Prize, and the Lenin Prize, Sakharov also received the Nobel Peace Prize in 1975 for his tireless work for nuclear disarmament and his outspoken criticism of human rights violations everywhere, especially in his homeland. He was for many, inside the Soviet Union and out, a noble symbol of courage, intelligence, and humanity.

Further Reading

Articles by Andrei Sakharov can be found in translation in various places, including the journals *Chronicle of Human Rights, Russia;* and *New York Review of Books.* An important article, "A Letter from Exile," was also published in the *New York Times Magazine* on June 8, 1980. Sakharov's major books in English are *Progress, Coexistence and Intellectual Freedom* (1972); and *Alarm and Hope* (1978). There is also a collection of essays, *Sakharov Speaks* (1974), edited by Harrison Salisbury.

Numerous articles about Sakharov have appeared in Western newspapers and journals, particularly *The Bulletin of Atomic Scientists* (1971, 1978, 1981, 1982, 1983, and 1984); *Science* (1973, 1975, 1981, and 1984); and *TIME;* and *Newsweek.* His activities as a dissident are chronicled in *Biographical Dictionary of Dissidents in the Soviet Union, 1956-75* (1982). Readers interested in examining particular aspects of his career more closely should consult the *New York Times* through its annual index. An "Autobiographical Note" appears in *Russia* (1981), but there is as yet no adequate biography.

Additional Sources

Sakharov Andrei, *Reflections on Progress, Peaceful Coexistence, and Intellectual Freedom,* Norton, 1968.

Sakharov, Andrei, *My Country and the World,* Knopf, 1975.

Sakharov, Andrei, *Collected Scientific Works,* Dekker, 1982.

Sakharov, Andrei, *Memoirs,* Knopf, 1990.

Sakharov, Andrei, *Moscow and Beyond, 1986 to 1989,* Vintage Book, 1992.

Babyonyshev, Alexander, editor, *On Sakharov,* Knopf, 1982.

Bonner, Yelena, *Alone Together,* Knopf, 1986. □

Saladin

Saladin (1138-1193), a Kurdish ruler of Egypt and Syria, is known in the West for his opposition to the forces of the Third Crusade and for his capture of Jerusalem.

From about 1130 Zengi, the Turkish atabeg (regent) of Mosul and his son, Nur-ad-Din (Nureddin), who succeeded him in 1146, undertook a holy war to unify Syria. Saladin Arabic, Salah-ad-Din Yusuf ibn Aiyub) served with his uncle, Shirkuh, under Nur-ad-Din and was strongly impressed with the need to complete the unity of Islam under orthodox rule.

After several expeditions into Egypt, where the Fatimid dynasty remained the most important of the successor kingdoms established after the fall of the Abbasid empire, Saladin assumed full military power on the death of Shirkuh in 1168. He was successful in repulsing the combined French-Byzantine invasion of Amalric, King of Jerusalem, a victory which opened the way for him to move his armies up into the Transjordan area. The Fatimid caliphate was crushed by 1171, and on the death of Nur-ad-Din 3 years later, Saladin began the conquest of the Frankish lands and of the old Zengid empire. He shortly occupied Damascus and married the widow of Nur-ad-Din. He thus faced increased hostility from two sides: from the Zengid rulers at Mosul, who were in no way enthusiastic about his conception of the *jihad,* or holy war, and from the Latin forces under Baldwin IV, the Leper King. The complexities of operating on two fronts at the same time were reduced somewhat by diplomatic negotiations with Baldwin and Raymond of Tripoli as well as with the Byzantine emperor

and certain of the Italian maritime cities. In the former case the result was essentially negative. A series of provisional treaties served to forestall an attack on the vulnerable western side, for Baldwin proved to be quite capable of containing Saladin, although he was unable to do him any damage. But in the latter case not only were assurances of nonintervention given, but material aid was obtained.

By the end of 1185 Saladin had imposed his authority in northern Syria and Mesopotamia, and he was ready to turn his full attention to the crusading kingdom. After the unfortunate betrayal of a peace treaty by a Western knight, the *jihad* was declared in the beginning of 1187. Drawing troops from Syria as well as from Egypt, Saladin brought his combined forces to face the Latin army at Hattin near Tiberias in July. The star-crossed monarchy in Jerusalem, born of the antagonisms among the leaders of the First Crusade, was never able to operate from a position of strength, and once again personal jealousies were responsible for the overwhelming defeat by the Moslem forces. Saladin set a trap for the crusaders; they marched into it and were annihilated. By any measure Hattin was a disaster for the West, and in rapid sequence most of the other important towns, Acre, Sidon, Jaffa, Caesarea, Ascalon, fell into Moslem hands. Finally, Jerusalem was occupied on October 2. Further campaigning reduced the extent of Frankish power in Syria to Tyre, Antioch, and Tripoli.

The kings of western Europe responded to the fall of Jerusalem by taking the cross and then by gathering their knights together in the expeditions known to history as the Third Crusade. Their chief victory was the successful siege and relief of Acre, which capitulated in July 1191. King Richard I of England defeated Saladin at Arsuf and then concluded an armistice in the fall of 1192 without having been able to retake Jerusalem. Nevertheless, Richard's presence in the East clearly prevented Saladin from capitalizing fully on his victory at Hattin. After 12 days of illness, Saladin died on March 4, 1193.

Saladin is described in the pages of his biographer, Baha ad-Din, as one who was entirely committed to the justice of the *jihad* against the unbelievers. Of medium height and gentle manners, courageous, even ruthless, but generous and humane, he was respected by his followers and by his adversaries for the steadfast manner in which he kept his promises. Strong in his faith, he was orthodox to the point of intolerance, as in the summary murder of as-Suhrawardi, a heretical preacher of Aleppo. It should be remembered that it was Saladin who carried on the work of Nur-ad-Din and completed the unity of Islam, although his success did not long survive him.

Further Reading

The fundamental full-length treatment of Saladin is S. Lane-Poole, *Saladin and the Fall of the Kingdom of Jerusalem* (1898; rev. ed. by H. W. C. Davis, 1926). Other works on him are Charles J. Rosebault, *Saladin, Prince of Chivalry* (1930), and G. E. T. Slaughter, *Saladin, 1138-1193* (1955). An important chapter on his early career by Sir H. A. R. Gibb is in Kenneth M. Setton, *A History of the Crusades,* vol. 1 (1969). □

António de Oliveira Salazar

The government of the Portuguese statesman António de Oliveira Salazar (1889-1970) once was considered to be the very model of a modern authoritarian political system.

Antóntio de Oliveira Salazar was born on April 28, 1889, in Vimieiro near Santa Comba Dão in the province of Beira Alta. His parents, owners of several small estates, as well as innkeepers, were António de Oliveira and María de Resgate Salazar, who, despite financial problems, saw to it that Salazar was well educated. He entered the seminary of Viseu in 1900, but after 8 years of religious training he decided to teach. In 1910 he began to study economics at the University of Coimbra, spending 4 years there as a student and another 7 as an economics professor. He obtained a chair of political economy in 1918. A knowledge of economics was valuable in underdeveloped Portugal, and soon Salazar was well known by the government for his monetary skills.

The emergence of Salazar as a national figure came at a difficult moment in Portuguese history. After more than a century of economic difficulties tied to imperial decline, political life had degenerated badly. The double assassination of Carlos I and the crown prince in February 1908 and the overthrow of Manuel II in October 1910 had led to creation of a republic which in the 16 years of its existence went from crisis to crisis. The University of Coimbra furnished many republican leaders in the first phase of the period, but spread of a deeper radicalism engendered a conservative reaction led by António Sardinha. He sought an "organic monarchy" that would be traditionalist and antiparliamentary, but chaos prevented any success.

Economic Policies

In the stalemate after 1918 Salazar's star rose. His economic thought was strongly influenced by Catholic corporatism and Leo XIII's *Rerum novarum*. He favored joint labor-management industrial commissions, compulsory arbitration, and Catholic trade unions. In January 1921 Salazar was one of three Catholic deputies elected to the Parliament, but turmoil was still so great that he attended only a few sessions before returning to the university. However, in May 1926, when a military dictatorship overthrew the republic, Salazar was offered the Ministry of Economic Affairs. He refused the position until 1928, when he received great powers which made him the most important figure in the government.

Salazar's reforms brought some national stability by prohibiting the import of foreign goods, cutting the state budget, and developing a new tax system. Soon he turned to a revision of the structure of government itself. "In an administrative system in which lack of sincerity and clarity were evident," he said, "the first requirement is a policy of truth. In a social order in which rights were competitive and unaccompanied by equivalent duties, the crying need is for a policy of sacrifice. And in a nation divided against itself by

groups and clashing interests which threatened its unity, the main need is a national policy.''

Ruler of Portugal

The national policy emerged during 1929 in the wake of Portugal's newfound stability, when Salazar's reforms stood the test of the Depression. The military leaders of the dictatorship no longer had as much prestige or interest in ruling, and Salazar informally became the strongest man in the regime. He immediately began to write a new constitution which was approved by plebiscite on March 19, 1933. It created a corporative state divided by levels into *sindicatos* (government unions by industry), *gremios* (guilds of employers), and *ordens* (white-collar organizations). Each of these handled welfare arrangements, employment of their members, and vocational training and negotiated national wage agreements. Each was also guided by special government secretariats that dictated policy. A fourth level was made up by the armed forces, although here there was more autonomy in honor of the role played by the services in establishing the new regime. All four levels elected representatives who then chose deputies for the national Parliament, giving the franchise to the corporative institutions rather than to the national electorate—a variation of the indirect franchise. Salazar's motto was ''control by stability,'' which was facilitated further by the provision that only his National Union party had official status. The president of the party became president of the republic with enormous executive powers, not the least being control of the newly established secret police, the PIDE.

Much of this structure had been modeled on Mussolini's Italy, and Salazar remained diplomatically close to Mussolini in the 1930s. He intrigued several times against the Spanish Republic, and when the Civil War broke out in Spain, he recognized Franco's Nationalists in December 1937. Portugal supplied funds and arms to the Burgos government until the end of the war, and on March 17, 1939, a pact of friendship and nonaggression was signed between the two countries which pledged eternal opposition to communism and created an ''Iberian bloc'' linking them together against outside attack. For Portugal it was the first time since 1640 that it had cooperated directly with Spain, but even so Salazar was restrained by long-standing treaties with Great Britain, which kept him from closer cooperation with either Franco or Mussolini. Portugal, as a result, remained correctly neutral during World War II until 1943, when Salazar granted the Allies bases in Portuguese territory. His anticommunism brought Portugal into NATO in 1949 and won him backing to join the United Nations at the same time.

Postwar Period

The postwar period, despite these successes, was troubled, first because of domestic economic difficulties and then because of colonial unrest in Angola and Mozambique. Government mismanagement of both problems led to renewal of opposition to Salazar's dictatorship in 1956. Two years later, an opposition candidate, Humberto Delgado, polled a quarter million votes for the presidency, which Salazar had occupied since 1951. The PIDE became more active, but the opposition continued to grow until 1965, when Delgado was assassinated in Spain. By that time Draconian measures in the colonies diminished the drive for independence to the point where there was less unrest in metropolitan Portugal, although vestiges of opposition continued to manifest themselves spasmodically until September 1968, when Salazar was incapacitated by a massive brain hemorrhage. His 36-year rule thus came to an end on September 27, when Marcelo Caetano of the National Union replaced him in the premiership. Salazar died on July 27, 1970, in Lisbon.

Further Reading

A biography of Salazar is Christine Garnier, *Salazar: An Intimate Portrait* (1952; trans. 1954). See also Gowan Pinheiro, *Oldest Ally: A Portrait of Salazar's Portugal* (1961). □

'Ali' Abdallah Salih

After rising through the military ranks and following a series of military coups, 'Ali' Abdallah Salih (born 1942) was elected president of the Yemeni Arab Republic (North Yemen) in 1978. After several years in which the legitimacy of his government grew along with his reputation as a consensus-builder, Salih became the first president of the United Republic of Yemen in 1990.

Brigadier General 'Ali' Abdallah Salih became the first president—officially, chairman of the Presidential Council—of the Arab world's newest state, the Republic of Yemen, in May 1990. With 13 million people, the fledgling republic was the Arabian peninsula's most populous country. It united the former Marxist, Russian-aligned People's Democratic Republic of Yemen (SouthYemen) with the more moderate tribal-and military-oriented Yemeni Arab Republic (North Yemen), over which 'Ali' Abdallah Salih had presided since July 1978.

Salih's rise to the presidency of a country which combined southwestern Arabia into one political entity was the culmination of a remarkable career. He was born in modest circumstances in 1942 in the small agricultural town of Bayt al-Ahmar. He was a member of the Sanhan tribe, a numerically and politically insignificant segment of the powerful Zaydi Muslim Hashid tribal confederation that had long dominated extensive districts southwest of the Yemeni capital of Sana'a. Salih's formal education was limited to a Koranic primary school in Bayt al-Ahmar.

He began his military career as a teen-aged private soldier in the Hashid tribal levies attached to the army of the Zaydi imams who had ruled Yemen for a thousand years. However, when the Hashid shaykh supported the military coup that toppled the royalist government in September 1962, Salih's allegiance was transferred to the new republican regime. But Imam Badr did not accept his deposition and ignited a six-year civil war in an ultimately unsuccessful attempt to restore royal rule. Nevertheless, Salih's career profited from the conflict because influential Hashid pa-

trons secured him a commission as a second lieutenant in the republican army in 1963. The most important of these patrons was Colonel Ahmad Husayn al-Ghashmi, who was destined to become the army's chief-of-staff and, briefly in 1977-1978, the Yemeni Arab Republic's president.

As an al-Ghashmi protege, 'Ali' Abdallah Salih's star rose steadily. Active in the civil war, he matured into a tough, effective soldier willing to take personal risks. He attended various service schools and successively advanced from junior officer to armored company commander, armored battalion commander, staff officer in the Armored Division, and chief of armaments in the Armored Corps. As his career progressed, Salih was increasingly drawn into Yemen's political affairs, especially after the 1974 coup when Ibrahim al-Hamdi took over as president. Salih's mentor, Colonel al-Ghashmi, one of the coup organizers, became Hamdi's army commander and arranged for his client's appointment to the twin-posts of brigade commander and military governor of the strategically important Ta'iz province with the rank of major. In 1977 Salih played a major role in the events which led to al-Hamdi's assassination and al-Ghashmi's subsequent assumption of the presidency. But after an eight-month rule, in June 1978 al-Ghashmi himself was killed by a bomb smuggled into his office. The Yemeni Arab Republic's fifth president—its third in less than a year—was about to take office.

Given the chaotic situation, the power to select the new president was essentially in the hands of the military. Salih, although seemingly little qualified for the presidency either by seniority, political experience, or education, had been promoted to lieutenant colonel and army deputy commander in the wake of al-Ghashmi's assassination. He was well-placed to bid for the post as the military's candidate. Thus, on July 17, 1978, after aggressive political maneuvering, 'Ali' Abdallah Salih was elected North Yemen's president and army commander-in-chief.

Salih's initial year in office was not promising. Dismissed by many as an opportunistic, rude-speaking, tribal fighting-man who could not master the rough-and-tumble of North Yemen's traditional politics, he barely survived assassination plots, coup attempts, and military disaster in border fighting with South Yemen. To stay in control, he relied heavily upon members of his tribe, close relatives, and especially his seven brothers, whom he placed in sensitive posts in the national security apparatus, the army, and the air force.

Nevertheless, eventually he converted North Yemen's chaotic political environment into a comparatively stable one. Like many in the military, Salih was an authoritarian nationalist and statist by nature. But he also championed the cause of national reconciliation. Thus, his leadership style tended to be center-oriented and friendly to compromise and consensus building. In time, this linked the aspirations of the military to those of left leaning statists, middle-of-the-road technocratic, professional, and business interests as well as conservative tribal and religious leaders. Moreover, because he allowed educated technocrats to operate the bureaucracy, the administrative effectiveness of the government rose significantly. Meanwhile, although Salih believed in a "no-party" government, he also encouraged carefully controlled popular political participation through the thousand-member General People's Congress that met regularly after 1982. The enhanced legitimacy of Salih's regime plus his record as a consensus-building nationalist were among the chief reasons that South Yemen, after a decade of inconclusive talks, was willing in 1989 to address its increasingly discouraging internal political problems by uniting with North Yemen. Another stimulus for unification was the promise of economic benefits that would accrue to both parts of Yemen if they joined to cooperatively exploit the large oil deposits that were discovered in the mid-1980s along their common border. The South Yemenis were not disappointed in Salih, for after unification he moved leftward to accommodate them.

Initially, President Salih was unsure of himself when dealing with foreign leaders, but this changed as he gained experience. His extensive travels included visits to both the Soviet Union and, in January 1990, the United States. Family ties strongly influenced the course of President Salih's career, and his own marriage produced five children. In historical terms, however, 'Ali' Abdallah Salih's chief accomplishment was to surmount Yemen's traditional family-oriented factional politics to promote the political stability that allowed realization of his countrymen's long-held dream to unify all of southwestern Arabia into a single state.

In 1994, war broke out again. In June of that year, under his leadership, the war with South Yemen came to end after only two months and the two sides agreed to an eventual reunion. As late as 1997, Salih still held the position as President.

Further Reading

Outside of brief official sketches there is no biography of President Salih. Information is found in various newspapers such as the (London) *Times;* the *New York Times,* specialized magazines such as *The Middle East Journal,* and scattered in a few books such as Robert D. Burrowes, *The Yemen Arab Republic, The Politics of Development* (1987); J. E. Peterson, *Yemen, The Search for a Modern State* (1982); Brian Pridham (editor), *Contemporary Yemen; Politics and Historical Background* (1984); and Richard Nyrop (editor), *The Yemens, Country Studies* (1986).Updated information gathered from the *LA Times* North Reverses Self, Supports Truce in Yemen, Friday, June 3, 1994; U.N. Demands Yemen Halt Attack on Rebel City Aden, Thursday, June 30, 1994. □

Carlos Salinas de Gortari

Carlos Salinas de Gortari (born 1948) was elected president of Mexico in 1988. He quickly moved toward an economy based more on free market principles than on state control and toward better economic relations with the United States. He is, perhaps, best known for his role in negotiating the North American Free Trade Agreement (NAFTA).

Born on April 3, 1948, in the small town of Agualeguas, Nuevo León, only about 25 miles from the United States border, Carlos Salinas de Gortari was raised in a politically active Mexican family. His father, Raul Salinas Lozano, had served the state of Nuevo León in the national Senate and in 1958 became Mexico's secretary of industry and commerce, a position he held for six years. The younger Salinas, after having received his undergraduate degree in economics at the National Autonomous University of Mexico, entered the graduate program at Harvard University. Compiling an excellent academic record and writing a dissertation on "Production and Political Participation in the Mexican Countryside," he was awarded a Ph.D. in political economy in 1978.

In 1982, Miguel de la Madrid, one of Salinas' former economic professors, became president of Mexico and appointed his ex-student to a major cabinet position secretary of planning and budget. After a few years of observing his young cabinet minister's high level of performance, the president also began grooming Salinas to succeed him in the nation's highest office. In the summer of 1988, Carlos Salinas de Gortari, then only 40 years old, won the Mexican presidency in the closest presidential election of the 20th century. With strong opposition from both the right and left, Salinas, the candidate of the Partido Revolucionario Institucional (P.R.I.), won the office with less than 51 percent of the popular vote. Some political analysts argued that the election had been fraudulent and that the winning candidate in reality had not received the constitutionally required majority vote.

Inheriting a country in which the government's political legitimacy was in question and which many believed was on the verge of economic collapse, Salinas had an inauspicious start. Like many of his predecessors, he asked his citizenry to tighten their belts and accept a new round of austerity measures in the effort to bring about some semblance of economic stability. In effect, he was asking the poor to accept their miserable squalor. But he did have a plan, and within a year he had begun to depart noticeably from the more timid approaches of his immediate predecessors.

While never relinquishing the mantle of "Revolutionary" leadership, Salinas de Gortari demonstrated clearly that he planned to move his country in a more conservative direction during his first two years in office. He surprised many with an early announcement that Mexico, a country with a long history of anti-clericalism, should seek to normalize its relations with the Roman Catholic Church. In February 1990, the president named a personal representative to the Vatican and a few months later, during Pope John Paul II's visit to the country, indicated Mexico should establish formal diplomatic relations with the Holy See.

In an even more startling change of direction, President Salinas, observing the collapse of socialism in the Soviet Union and Eastern Europe, also let it be known that he would place his presidential faith less in continued statism and more in the dynamics of the free market. The new economic policy saw his government strike out against organized labor and adopt a strong stand against even the powerful petroleum workers and copper miners unions. The president also wanted the government to divest itself of costly, inefficient, and bureaucracy-laden government companies, the so-called parastatal corporations. He began selling off dozens of them to the private sector, including the government-owned airline, Aeromexico, and the large Cananea Copper Mines in the northern state of Sonora. A new, more lenient attitude to foreign capital became integral to government policy. Salinas believed that foreign capital should be encouraged, not feared, and had his congress enact legislation easing the 1973 foreign investment law which restricted foreigners to 49 percent ownership of Mexican enterprises.

The most dramatic shift of all was Salinas' announcement in the spring of 1990 that Mexico would enter into negotiations with the United States for the purpose of establishing a free trade agreement. This policy was in direct conflict with the economic model embraced by every Mexican president since the revolution. The historical tradition had been one of economic nationalism and the subsidizing of Mexican products for the purpose of keeping foreign competition out. Now, for the first time, a Mexican president, seeing trade barriers and international suspicions recede in Western Europe, admitted publicly that his country's economic future would inevitably be linked to that of the United States and that Mexico's interests could be best served by eliminating barriers to the free flow of goods and services across the international line that separated the two countries. It was a calculated gamble and one which

precipitated a lively debate within the country. But many political realists agreed with the president's assessment. The idea of a Latin American common market continued to be no more than a chimera and Mexico found herself with few alternatives to stimulate badly needed economic development. Integrating Mexico's economy with that of the United States, Salinas concluded, was reasonable, prudent, and potentially beneficial.

Salinas' policy of restructuring the economy, providing social programs, and attacking corruption in government and some labor unions proved popular with the Mexican electorate. *Salinastroika* was the word coined to describe the transformation in Mexican economy when Salinas took office.

In the mid-term congressional elections of 1991 the P.R.I. candidates won by a margin far greater than the vote that put Salinas into office.

Salinas' critics belittled his attempts to improve the living for the Mexican populace. In 1993, statistics claimed more than 70 percent of the population earned less than needed to purchase food and meet basic nutritional requirements and about 30 percent had little or no access to health care. In 1994, these numbers were paired with the peso and foreign debt crisis that occurred shortly after he left his post, giving critics more fuel for their fire.

On March 23, 1994 presidential candidate and Salinas' rival Luis Donaldo Colosio was assassinated. Salinas has denied any involvement with the murder and rejected rumors he argued with Colosio days before the shooting. He alleged the death of Colosio was a personal and political blow against him.

Nov 30, 1994 was the last day of Salinas' presidential term . Less than one month later, the peso devaluation began, marking Mexico's most debilitating economic crisis to date.

Salinas' predecessor, President Ernesto Zedillo, exiled Salinas from Mexico in March of 1995. Since that time, reports and rumors of the ex-president in New York, Boston, Canada, Cuba, the Bahamas and Dublin, Ireland remain ambiguous.

The Mexican government moved against Salinas' brother, Ral Salinas, who allegedly stashed $83.9 million in Swiss bank accounts under false names while working in the government. Ral's wife, Paulina Castañón, was also jailed in Switzerland in a narcotics money-laundering investigation. Swiss authorities suggested the money in Rual Salinas' accounts might have come from drug traffickers, according to the *New York Times* . It is also alleged that Salinas' sister, Adriana, is under investigation for fraud that may have made her millions richer.

Salinas denied any involvement in the money scandal. "My brother Raul's deception is unacceptable to me," Salinas said in a *New York Times* interview.

Further Reading

There is no English-language biography of Mexican president Carlos Salinas de Gortari. Two recent studies of Mexican politics, Judith Adler Hellman, *Mexico in Crisis* (2nd ed.,

1983); and Daniel Levy and Gabriel Székely, *Mexico Paradox of Stability and Change* (2nd ed., 1983), provide context for his economic policies. Michael C. Meyer and William L. Sherman's *The Course of Mexican History* (4th ed., 1990) contains a brief section on the Salinas administration. ☐

J. D. Salinger

Best known for his controversial novel *The Catcher in the Rye* (1951), Salinger is recognized by critics and readers alike as one of the most popular and influential authors of American fiction to emerge after World War II. Salinger's reputation derives from his mastery of symbolism, his idiomatic style, and his thoughtful, sympathetic insights into the insecurities that plague both adolescents and adults.

Salinger's upbringing was not unlike that of Holden Caulfield, the Glass children, and many of his other characters. Raised in Manhattan, he was the second of two children of a prosperous Jewish importer and a Scots-Irish mother. He was expelled from several private preparatory schools before graduating from Valley Forge Military Academy in 1936. While attending a Columbia University writing course, he had his first piece of short fiction published in *Story,* an influential periodical founded by his instructor, Whit Burnett. Salinger's short fiction soon began appearing in *Collier's, The Saturday Evening Post, Esquire,* and other magazines catering to popular reading tastes. Salinger entered military service in 1942 and served until the end of World War II, participating in the Normandy campaign and the liberation of France. He continued to write and publish while in the Army, carrying a portable typewriter with him in the back of his jeep. After returning to the States, Salinger's career as a writer of serious fiction took off. He broke into the *New Yorker* in 1946 with the story "Slight Rebellion Off Madison," which was later rewritten to become a part of *The Catcher in the Rye.* Salinger quickly became one of the top contributors to the prestigious magazine. After *The Catcher in the Rye* was published, Salinger found himself at the center of a storm of controversy. His novel was lauded by many, but condemned by others for its language and social criticism. When it began to find its way onto the recommended reading lists of educational institutions, it became the target of numerous censorship campaigns. Salinger reacted to all the publicity by becoming increasingly reclusive. As years passed, and his continuing work on the Glass family saga drew increasing critical attacks from even those corners of the literary establishment that had once accorded him an almost cult-like reverence, he withdrew from publishing and public life altogether. His novella-length story "Hapworth 16, 1924," which once again revolved around an incident in the Glass family, appeared in the *New Yorker* in 1965; it was his last published work. Since the early 1960s, he has lived in seclusion in New Hampshire. Reportedly, he continues to write, but only for his own satisfaction; he is said to be completely unconcerned with his standing, or lack of it, in the literary world.

The Catcher in the Rye and much of Salinger's shorter fiction share the theme of idealists adrift in a corrupt world. Often, the alienated protagonists are rescued from despair by the innocence and purity of children. One of the author's most highly-acclaimed stories, "For Esme—With Love and Squalor" (collected in *Nine Stories*) concerns an American soldier, also an aspiring writer, who encounters a charming young English girl just before D Day. Almost a year later, suffering serious psychic damage from his combat experiences, the soldier receives a gift and a letter from the girl. Her unselfish gesture of love heals him and he is once again able to sleep and write. In *The Catcher in the Rye,* Holden Caulfield is driven to the brink of a nervous breakdown by his disgust for the "phoniness" of the adult world which he is about to enter. He finds peace only in the presence of Phoebe, his young sister. Much like Holden, Franny Glass (whose story "Franny" is half of *Franny and Zooey*) undergoes a physical and nervous collapse due to the conflict between her involvement with a crude, insensitive boyfriend and her desire for a pure, spiritual love experience. In the "Zooey" section of *Franny and Zooey,* Franny's older brother attempts to help her resolve her confusion by discussing with her the worldly nature of religious experience. But for some of Salinger's characters, like Seymour Glass, the only relief from the anguish of living in the hellish modern world is the ultimate escape. In "A Perfect Day for Bananafish" (collected in *Nine Stories*), Seymour encounters an innocent young child on the beach and converses with her; later that evening, he shoots himself in the head in his hotel room.

Beginning with *The Catcher in the Rye,* Salinger's work has provoked considerable comment and controversy. Critic James Bryan summarized the positive response to the work when he observed: "The richness of spirit in this novel, especially of the vision, the compassion, and the humor of the narrator reveal a psyche far healthier than that of the boy who endured the events of the narrative. Through the telling of his story, Holden has given shape to, and thus achieved control of, his troubled past." The book has also been praised retrospectively for its author's early depiction of dissatisfaction with the repression and smugness that characterized post-World War II America. *The Catcher in the Rye* has recurrently been banned by public libraries, schools, and bookstores, however, due to its presumed profanity, sexual subject matter, and rejection of traditional American values. *Nine Stories* also drew widely varied response. The volume's first story, "A Perfect Day for Bananafish," has been read alternately as a satire on bourgeois values, a psychological case study, and a morality tale. *Franny and Zooey,* along with several of the pieces in *Nine Stories,* stands as Salinger's most highly acclaimed short fiction. Critics generally applauded the satisfying structure of "Franny," as well as its appealing portrait of its heroine, while "Zooey" was praised for its meticulous detail and psychological insight. *Raise High the Roofbeam, Carpenters and Seymour: An Introduction* proved less satisfying to literary commentators, who began to find the Glass clan self-centered, smug, perfect beyond belief, and ultimately boring. It was after publication of *Raise High the Roofbeam* that the cult of Salinger began to give way to an increasing perception that the author was too absorbed in the Glass saga to maintain the artistic control necessary for literary art. Whatever the flaws detected, however, few deny the immediacy and charm of the Glasses, who are so successfully drawn that numerous people over the years have reportedly claimed to have had personal encounters with relatives of the fictitious family. In the decades since Salinger has stopped publishing, a more balanced reading of his work has emerged—one that acknowledges the artistic value of much of his canon, his influence on the style and substance of other writers, and, above all, his place of honor among young readers who have continued to identify with the confusion and ideals of Holden Caulfield.

Further Reading

Alsen, Eberhard, *Salinger's Glass Stories as a Composite Novel,* Whitson, 1983.
Authors and Artists for Young Adults, Volume 2, Gale, 1989, pp. 201-10.
Belcher, W. F., and J. W. Lee, editors, *J. D. Salinger and the Critics,* Wadsworth, 1962.
Bloom, Harold, editor, *J. D. Salinger: Modern Critical Views,* Chelsea House, 1987.
Carpenter, Humphrey, *Secret Gardens: A Study of the Golden Age of Children's Literature,* Houghton, 1985.
Children's Literature Review, Volume 18, Gale, 1989, pp. 171-94.
Concise Dictionary of American Literary Biography: The New Consciousness, 1941-1968, Gale, 1987, pp. 448-58.

New York Times, February 20, 1997, p. C15. □

3d Marquess of Salisbury

The English statesman and diplomat Robert Arthur Talbot Gascoyne-Cecil, 3d Marquess of Salisbury (1830-1903), was prime minister of Great Britain in 1885-1886, 1886-1892, and 1895-1902. His life spanned the period of England's greatest affluence and power.

Lord Robert Cecil was born at Hatfield on Feb. 3, 1830, the second son of James Brownlow William Gascoyne-Cecil, 2d Marquess of Salisbury, Lord Privy Seal and Lord President of the Council, and of his wife, Frances Gascoyne, an heiress. Educated at Eton and at Christ Church, Oxford, where he received a fourthclass in mathematics, he was elected in 1853 to a fellowship at All Souls College, Oxford, and in the same year was elected unopposed to the House of Commons for Stamford.

In July 1857 Cecil married Georgina Alderson, a woman of great ability. His father, however, objected to the marriage and cut off funds, so Cecil became partly dependent on his pen. He wrote for the *Standard* and the *Saturday Review,* but his most famous articles, such as "The Conservative Surrender," were published in the *Quarterly.* Cecil revealed in these articles his deep distrust of democracy, considering the poor as subject to more temptations. Cecil reached a wide public with his articles, and his style was "a rare model of restrained, pungent, and vigorous English."

On the death of his elder brother in 1865, Cecil became Lord Cranborne, and in July 1866 he was appointed secretary of state for India. On the death of his father in 1868, he entered the House of Lords as Marquess of Salisbury and in 1869 became chancellor of Oxford University. In 1874 the Conservatives were back in office, and Lord Salisbury was again at the India Office, where he was censured for refusing to check the export of wheat during a famine in Bengal.

After Lord Derby resigned from the Foreign Office in April 1878, Salisbury was appointed in his stead. Twentyfour hours later he issued the "Salisbury Circular," requiring all articles of the Treaty of San Stefano to be submitted to the proposed Berlin Conference. This speech did not prevent Salisbury from concluding a secret negotiation with the Russian ambassador to London by which the Balkans were to be divided. This secret convention was balanced by the Cyprus convention with Turkey, which secured for Britain the semblance of a diplomatic success at the Congress of Berlin (June 13-July 13, 1878). By the treaty provisions, Austria was to administer Bosnia and Herzegovina; the idea of a big Bulgaria was abandoned; and Russia received Kars, Ardahan, and Batum on condition it make Batum a free port.

In 1880 the Conservatives were defeated, and Salisbury became their leader in the Lords. In 1881 Benjamin Disraeli

died, and on June 12, 1885, the Liberals fell. Salisbury became prime minister and foreign secretary. He made the protocol of Sept. 18, 1885, securing the Zulfikar Pass to the emir of Afghanistan, and he secured the eastern frontier of India against the French by the annexation of Burma. In Parliament he promoted a bill for the housing of the working classes that penalized landlords for renting unsanitary tenements.

In December 1885 the general election left the Irish members in command, and the government was defeated. Later that year Gladstone was defeated on home rule. Salisbury said in a speech that some races, such as the Hottentots and the Hindus, were unfit for self-government. A month later he became prime minister again, making Lord Randolph Churchill his chancellor of the Exchequer. In December, Churchill left the government, thinking thereby to force Salisbury's hand on the army estimates, but the latter appointed George Goschen in Churchill's place. In 1887 Salisbury initiated the first colonial conference, and in 1888 he granted a royal charter to the British East Africa Company by which England recovered its hold over the upper sources of the Nile.

In 1890 Germany acknowledged a British protectorate of Zanzibar; in exchange Salisbury gave up Helgoland. In 1899 he encouraged the British South Africa Company under Cecil Rhodes to colonize Rhodesia. The Portuguese claimed Matabeleland, but Salisbury sent an ultimatum to Lisbon, and Portugal yielded. In 1888 Salisbury introduced the Life Peerage Bill, which was withdrawn, and in 1891 he got the Free Education Act passed. In 1895 a coalition of

Salisbury and Joseph Chamberlain won a majority. In 1897 the Working Men's Compensation Act was passed.

From 1895 to 1900 Salisbury pursued a policy of brinkmanship with each of the four Great Powers. In the United States, President Grover Cleveland declared that the British refusal of arbitration between British Guiana and Venezuela was a violation of the Monroe Doctrine, but the U.S. Commission decided in favor of Britain. Salisbury allowed the United States a free hand in Cuba, surrendered British rights in Samoa to the United States, and abrogated the Clayton-Bulwer Treaty of 1850 by allowing the United States to build the Panama Canal under American control. He had to deal with the Germans in 1896 over the Kaiser's telegram to Paul Kruger congratulating him on suppressing the Jameson Raid, and with the French from 1897, when Gen. Horatio Kitchener dislodged the French flag from Fashoda after his victory at Omdurman, until 1899, when they abandoned all designs on the Sudan. In 1899 the Czar's rescript led to the Hague Conference.

In 1900, after Salisbury had refused foreign mediation, the largest army ever assembled by England set off to fight the Boers. In 1902 Salisbury negotiated the Anglo-Japanese Treaty, and on May 31 peace was signed with the Boers. In July, Salisbury resigned, and he died on Aug. 22, 1903.

Further Reading

Salisbury's life is recounted in Samuel Henry Jeyes, *Life and Times of the Marquis of Salisbury* (4 vols., 1895-1896), and in Aubrey Leo Kennedy, *Salisbury, 1830-1903: Portrait of a Statesman* (1953). Aspects of his career are covered in Rose L. Greaves, *Persia and the Defense of India, 1884-1892: A Study in the Foreign Policy of the Third Marquis of Salisbury* (1959); J. A. S. Grenville, *Lord Salisbury and Foreign Policy: The Close of the Nineteenth Century* (1964); Cedric J. Lowe, *Salisbury and the Mediterranean, 1886-1896* (1965); and Michael Pinto-Duschinsky, *The Political Thought of Lord Salisbury, 1854-1868* (1967). □

Harrison Evans Salisbury

The American journalist Harrison E. Salisbury (born 1908) was well-known for his reporting and books on the Soviet Union. A distinguished correspondent and editor for the *New York Times*, he was the first American reporter to visit Hanoi during the Vietnam War.

Born November 14, 1908, in Minneapolis, Minnesota, Harrison E. Salisbury was the son of Percy and Georgiana Salisbury. His family was descended from English emigrants to the United States in 1640. Departing from a long line of craftsmen and farmers, Salisbury's grandfather, after whom he was named, was a doctor in Minneapolis. His father had a harder life, working for a company which made bags for the flour milling industry. Salisbury grew up in a neighborhood with a large concentration of poor Russian Jews and, with one foot in that culture, he eventually established his reputation as a writer on Russian affairs.

The Cub Reporter

A solitary child, Salisbury spent much of his time alone reading and writing. He graduated at age 16 from North Side High School where he edited the weekly newspaper. Enrolling at the University of Minnesota in 1925, he intended to study chemistry. After becoming editor of the campus daily and working as a reporter for the *Minneapolis Journal* he decided to pursue a career in journalism.

Expelled from school after attempting to set up a test case, with 20 comrades, of the library's no-smoking rule, Salisbury found a job working with United Press (UP) in St. Paul. He quickly became a star of the news service's eager but underpaid staff. He circulated through other UP bureaus in Chicago; Washington, D.C.; and New York before being sent to Europe in 1942. In London—a training ground during World War II for influential American journalists of the coming decades one of his fellow correspondents and friends was Walter Cronkite.

Dateline Moscow

In 1944, following a short tour of North Africa, Salisbury received his first assignment to Moscow, where he covered the Russian army's victory over the retreating German troops. After the war he returned to New York as the foreign-news editor of UP. His initial view of life in Russia appeared in a series of articles for *Colliers* magazine and

later as a book entitled *Russia on the Way* (1946), the first of over 20 books Salisbury would write relating to Russian history and politics.

Dissatisfied working with UP, he sought a position at the *New York Times*. He did not want to return to the Soviet Union, but when the *Times* offered him a job as their Russian correspondent in 1949 he accepted. His reports coming out of Moscow were heavily censored, and in the McCarthy anti-Communist atmosphere prevailing in America at the time were seen as controversial.

In the spring of 1954 he traveled extensively through Siberia. His observations formed the basis for a 14-part report, written after his return to the United States and printed in the *New York Times* as "Russia Re-viewed." The series received the 1955 Pulitzer Prize for international reporting.

When Salisbury returned to New York, he was placed on the *Times*' metropolitan beat. He turned an assignment on garbage collection in New York City into a major investigative story. An examination of teen-age gangs in Brooklyn was later republished in book form as *The Shook-Up Generation* (1958).

By the end of the decade Salisbury was focusing on the growing civil rights movement. Sent to cover race relations in the South in 1960, his reports led to a six million dollar libel suit against the *Times* which wasn't resolved in the *Times*' favor until 1964. In a landmark Supreme Court decision, the Sullivan case established a strict standard for the judgment of libel regarding a public figure.

Although barred from the Soviet Union for five years after receiving the Pulitzer Prize, Salisbury was able to tour Poland, Bulgaria, Rumania, and Albania in 1957, and his report on the deterioration of Communism in Eastern Europe led to a George Polk Memorial award for foreign news coverage. Allowed to visit the Soviet Union in 1959 and 1961-1962, Salisbury wrote several books describing the changes in the post-Stalin era. He also published *Moscow Journal: The End of Stalin* (1961), which included the censored dispatches from his earlier five-year residence in Moscow. His knowledge of Stalin's regime provided the background for his well-received first novel, *The Northern Palmyra Affair* (1962).

His Rise at the *Times*

In 1962 Salisbury was named national news editor of the *Times*. He supervised the paper's excellent coverage of President Kennedy's assassination and in 1964 became assistant managing editor.

As the United States became more heavily involved in the Vietnam War, Salisbury was eager to travel to North Vietnam, where no American journalists had visited. His patience and inquiries were finally rewarded in late 1966 when he received an invitation and a visa. In a two-week trip to Hanoi he surveyed the extent of property damage and civilian casualties inflicted by American bombing, which contradicted the benign impression presented by the Johnson administration. His reports were given the Overseas Press Club and George Polk Memorial awards. He elaborated his experience in North Vietnam in the book *Behind the Lines* (1967).

While serving as *Times* editor Salisbury remained a prolific writer of books. He wrote *Orbit of China* (1967), the best-seller *The 900 Days: The Siege of Leningrad* (1969), and *War Between Russia and China* (1969).

In 1970 Salisbury became the first editor of the *New York Times*' Op-ed page. In 1972 he was elevated to the rank of associate editor. At the end of 1973 he reached the *Times*' mandatory retirement age.

Retirement

Leaving the *Times,* he continued to churn out books, publishing 12 of his 29 books after his retirement. Salisbury wrote about the Soviet Union in a series of books including *Black Night, White Snow* (1978); *One Hundred Years of Revolution* (1983); and *A Journey for Our Times: A Memoir* (1983), which also narrates his boyhood and early career as a journalist. His memoirs were elaborated in another book published in 1988, entitled *A Time of Change.* The retired Salisbury also took several trips to China and wrote a book describing following the course of the Long March [*/The Long March: The Untold Story,* (1985)].

Salisbury wrote an authorized but independent history of the *New York Times* which was published as *Without Fear or Favor* (1980). It discusses the shift in the paper from reporting the news to becoming more actively engaged in political events. Salisbury focuses his story on the decision of the *Times* to print the secret study of the Vietnam War, the *Pentagon Papers,* which provoked a confrontation with the Nixon administration.

Salisbury had two sons from his first marriage, which ended in divorce. In 1964 he married Charlotte Young Rand, and they lived in Manhattan and Taconic, Connecticut.

Salisbury donated his 600-box collection of papers and archival materials to Columbia University, which mounted a retrospective exhibit in the spring of 1997 chronicling Salibury's years as a reporter, from his coverage of Al Capone's trial to his presence at the 1989 Tianamen Square uprising [described in *Tianamen Diary: Thirteen Days in June* (1988)].

Further Reading

A prolific writer, Salisbury authored 29 books in addition to pursuing a full career as a newspaper correspondent. For a sampling of Salisbury's work a reader should see his novel *The Northern Palmyra Affair* (1962); his best-seller *The 900 Days: The Siege of Leningrad* (1969); his account of his experience in North Vietnam, *Behind the Lines* (1967); his memoirs, *A Journey for Our Times* (1983); and *A Time of Change: A Reporter's Tale of Our Time* (1987); and his history of the making of the Chinese Red Army, *The Long March: The Untold Story* (1985). Those interested in the inner workings of the *New York Times* should see *Without Fear or Favor* (1980); and *The Kingdom and the Power* (1966), Gay Talese.
Other books written after his retirement included *Russia in Revolution* (1979); *The New Emperors: China in the Era of Mao and Deng* (1992); and his last, *Heroes of My Time* (1993). Multiple tributes to Salisbury can be found on the Internet at sites maintained by Columbia University and the Minnesota News Council. □

Jonas Edward Salk

The American physician, virologist, and immunologist Jonas Edward Salk (born 1914) developed the first effective poliomyelitis (polio) vaccine.

Jonas Salk was born in New York City on Oct. 28, 1914. At the age of 16 he entered the College of the City of New York with the thought of studying law. He decided instead to study medicine and in 1934 enrolled in the College of Medicine of New York University, from which he graduated in 1939. He interned at New York's Mount Sinai Hospital from 1940 to 1942, when he went to the University of Michigan, where he helped develop an influenza vaccine. In 1944 he was appointed research associate in epidemiology, and in 1946 he was made assistant professor.

In 1947 Salk accepted a position at the University of Pittsburgh as associate professor of bacteriology, where he carried out his researches on a polio vaccine. Polio vaccines had been attempted before but without success because, as was apparent by 1949, there were three distinct types of polio viruses. This provided a starting point for Salk, who, working under a grant from the National Foundation for Infantile Paralysis, prepared a killed-virus vaccine effective against all three types. Testing began in 1950, and the preliminary report on the vaccine's effectiveness was published in the *Journal of the American Medical Association* for 1953. National field trials were held in 1954, and in 1955 the vaccine was determined safe for general use.

Acceptance of the vaccine was not without problems for Salk. Fear, skepticism, opposition from medical colleagues who favored a live-virus vaccine, improper production of the vaccine by some pharmaceutical companies, and a glaring Hollywood-like promotion for the vaccine caused much scientific criticism of Salk. Many also felt that the National Foundation had improperly favored him. Although the Salk vaccine was effective, it was replaced largely by the Sabin oral vaccine, a live-virus vaccine which, unlike the Salk vaccine, provides permanent protection.

During his polio researches Salk was made research professor of bacteriology at Pittsburgh (1949-1954) and professor of preventive medicine (1954-1957). In 1957 he was named Commonwealth professor of experimental medicine. In 1963 he opened the Salk Institute for Biological Studies in San Diego, where he and his colleagues studied problems relating to the body's autoimmunization reaction; that is, why the body rejects foreign material, for example, an organ transplant.

Jonas Salk died in June 1995 at the age of 80 from heart failure. In his lifetime he was able to see the effects of his life's work. By the time Salk died, polio had been virtually disappeared from the United States.

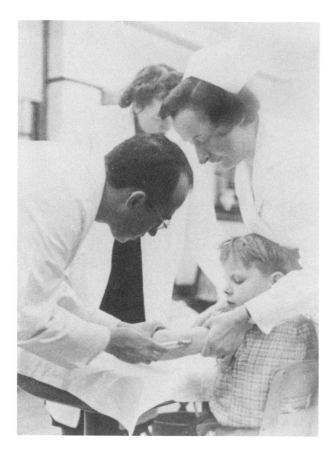

Jonas Salk (left)

Further Reading

Richard Carter, *Breakthrough: The Saga of Jonas Salk* (1966), details the development of the vaccine and emphasizes Salk's dedication to humanity. A harsher view of Salk's role in developing the vaccine is John R. Wilson, *Margin of Safety* (1963). Several books contain well-balanced sections on Salk, such as Greer Williams, *Virus Hunters* (1959), and H. J. Parish, *A History of Immunization* (1965). Information regarding Salk's life and death can be found by reading "The Good Doctor," *Time* (July 3, 1995) and "When the Vaccine Causes The Polio," *Time* (October 30, 1995). □

David Salle

The American artist David Salle (born 1952) combined the human figure with abstract forms in many of his works, presenting disturbing meditations on our modern existence.

David Salle was born in Norman, Oklahoma, in 1952 and spent much of his youth in Wichita, Kansas, before going to California to study art at the age of 18. He received both his B.F.A. (1973) and M.F.A. (1975) from the California Institute of the Arts while study-

ing under the artist John Baldessari. In 1975, at the age of 22, he moved to New York to embark on a career as a painter. His early years in New York, where he still resided in the early 1990s, were financially difficult ones, so much so that in 1976 he declared bankruptcy. As a result, he was forced to support himself by taking on odd jobs working alternately as a cook, teacher, and even a paste-up artist in the art department for *Stag* magazine, a pornographic publication.

Nevertheless, Salle's rise to the top of the art world was rapid and his success made him one of the most widely known artists of the 1980s. His first artistic triumph was in 1979 at an exhibition staged by a private dealer in New York. Once he was discovered by Mary Boone, one of the most prominent art dealers in New York, his career accelerated at a feverish pace. At the relatively young age of 37, Salle had participated in countless one man and group exhibitions throughout the world.

If the Post-Modern era can best be characterized by the term "pluralism," then David Salle was the 1980s most representative artist. Salle's imagery and the unique manner in which he drew from a variety of sources sets his painting apart from the work by other artists clamoring for public and critical attention. He drew from such widely disparate artistic traditions as Pop Art, Minimalism, Abstract Expressionism, Cubism, and Realism as well as images from popular culture. Though his paintings often conformed to the 1980s call for a return to the figure and representational art, he often combined the figure with abstract forms and this juxtaposition typically resulted in a mode of painting that was at once accessible and unfamiliar.

One relatively early example was his *How To Use Words as a Powerful Aphrodisiac* (1982). Typical of Salle's style was the inclusion of the human form, usually monochromatically rendered and erotically posed, upon which he will often superimposed hastily sketched images drawn either from popular culture or works of art from both the recent and distant past. In this case, Salle, in the center panel of his unequally proportioned triptych, superimposed Picasso's *Cubist Head of a Woman* over a quickly painted monochromatic copy after a Coney Island scene painted by Reginald Marsh (1940). In the left panel Salle painted a vertically posed, academically rendered right arm and shoulder of a model. Were it not for the shocking red background one might think this was an anatomical study pulled from the portfolio of Salle's painted studies from life he made during his student days. The right panel, curiously cut off at the bottom, was completely non-representational and in the tradition of the best of the Abstract painters from the 1950s. The painting was therefore an odd juxtaposition of artistic modes of expression familiar to any student of art in the 20th century: the abstract or non-representational, the experimental, as well as the figurative.

Salle was not merely interested in the problems of the Post-Modern era's coming to terms with viable means of expression after the Modern period, but he was also interested in the phenomenon of mass consumption, mass media, and the objectification of intimate human contact and relationships, as was quite clear in his painting entitled *His*

Brain (1984). Here Salle presented us with a graphic image of a nude woman bent at the waist with her buttocks to the beholder. Again, superimposed upon this erotic image were sketches of Monet's floating studio, the ghostly image of a woman with her fingers in her mouth, and what seemed to be faint silhouettes of Abraham Lincoln. The left quarter of the canvas was dominated by a vertical strip of abstract painting that consists of repeating clusters of crisply delineated multicolored crescent shapes separated by vaguely zoomorphic forms. Pained over this pattern was a suggestively phallic form. This painting was typical of Salle's style through his seemingly haphazard combination of various images. The image was jarring and confrontative yet strangely distanced from our experience. It was this dichotomy that was the core of Salle's work. Yet the attempt to fathom the meaning in Salle's paintings often resulted in frustration. Salle's paintings refered to so many images and themes outside themselves that his art has been described as "intertextual." As a result, his paintings tended to be discursive, passing from one subject to another in quick fashion, resulting in message that is not usually immediately forthcoming.

The notion of the impersonal nature of contemporary life and culture was also fertile ground for Salle and was best expressed in his characteristic use of coolly rendered grisaille figures, particularly those that bordered on the pornographic, as does the woman in *His Brain*. Though she offered herself to the viewer, she was rendered with such coldness and detachment as to stifle any romantic impulse. In this sense Salle seemed to be working in the tradition of Degas in the 19th century, detached and remote in his relationship to the subject. The absence of both color and human interaction made Salle's women mere objects—a consumer item, a commodity for the eyes like a pornographic photograph or an urban billboard. His pictures demanded a reaction and begged us to discover. His sketchy borrowings from the past, were strident comments on tradition, both historical and artistic. He called into question the very foundations of our own time and pondered with a certain cynicism the validity of the Modern era.

In the mid 1980s Salle's work became increasingly complex both in its formal construction and intellectual implications, as he often included real objects. Witness the light fixture in his *The Trucks Bring Things Home* or the wooden panel studded with pegs in his equally enigmatic *The Disappearance of the Booming Voice* of 1984. The upper portion of the latter painting consisted of a wooden panel with projecting dowels whose ends have been painted with green acrylic. Given the subject of the lower panel, the foreshortened raised legs and buttocks of a prone nude woman, there can be no doubt that these pegs carry a phallic meaning. Again, Salle combined the familiar and unfamiliar, along with the artistic and the erotic, in such a way as to pique our curiosity while at the same time purposely discouraging our efforts to ascertain his meaning.

Salle may be considered a kind of Post-Modern Pop artist with fangs as he repeatedly borrowed from artists like Andy Warhol, Jasper Johns, and James Rosenquist. He differed from them in that his paintings were introspective, enigmatic, often brooding and vaguely disturbing meditations on the contemporary world and our desperate search for meaning. In a society fixated on images and image making, Salle presented us with an unsettling mirror of our own existence.

Salle turned to stage decoration and in 1986 was awarded a Guggenheim Fellowship to create paintings for the theater and ballet. In December 1985 he devised the settings and costumes for the play *Birth of the Poet,* by Kathy Acker, which was performed at the Brooklyn Academy of Music. In the spring of 1986 the American Ballet Theatre premiered Karol Armitage's *The Mollino Room,* with sets and costuming by Salle. Some of the costumes resembled the garb of circus performers, while others were whimsical variations of ordinary street clothes. For example, Mikhail Baryshnikov, the lead character, wore a blue polo shirt with a smiling fish design. The sets (which some found striking) differed from his paintings in their lack of multipanel format and erotic content. Three of the five drops contained but a single image, the fourth was simply a monochromatic expanse of orange and the fifth was painted with an abstract rectangular design. Significantly, the title of the ballet refered to Carlo Mollino, a modern Italian architect whose belief that bad taste merited serious attention, may have lead the fascination of pop culture. Though not heralded as his finest accomplishments, his set designs were better received than his cinematography directing debut—*Search and Destroy,* 1995.

"The idea of a painter becoming a filmmaker is an intriguing one," John Petrakis, of the Chicago Tribune, wrote, "and perhaps someday modern artist David Salle will direct an enticing piece of cinema. But he'll need a much better script than the one provided for him here by writer Michael Almereyda, based on Howard Korder's stage play. To put it bluntly, this movie is a mess." Though much ado was made about the opening and that this was his first attempt, little good was said about the production. Although it had infomercial hosts, closet scriptwriters —for slasher flicks, drug dealers, gangsters and a bit of love thrown in for good measure; some of the actors were "dangerously out of control, the tell-tale sign of a rookie director."

Further Reading

In a paperback volume, *David Salle* (1986), Janet Kardon traced the transition of the artist from the 1970s to the 1980s.

There were many critical articles and numerous museum catalogues concerned with the art of David Salle. Some excellent sources containing background material that place Salle within his historical context are H.H. Arnason, *History of Modern Art,* 3rd edition (1986), and Howard Smagula, *Currents: Contemporary Directions in the Visual Arts,* 2nd edition (1989). See also *Chicago Tribune* "Puzzling 'Search' Self-Destructs," 05/12/95 and *Current Biography Yearbook* (1986), pages 488-491. □

Sallust

Sallust (86-ca. 35 B.C.), or Gaius Sallustius Crispus, was a Roman statesman and historian. Rejecting the annalistic method of writing history, he concentrated with improved accuracy and narrative technique on critical stages in the decline of the Roman Republic.

Sallust was born of plebeian stock in the small Sabine town of Amiternum. Joining the Popular faction, he was elected tribune of the people in 52 B.C. When Clodius was murdered by Milo, Sallust was instrumental in arousing public outrage against Milo. Sallust's motives probably went beyond loyalty to Clodius and certainty of Milo's guilt to revenge arising from the whipping Sallust endured for an adulterous relationship with Milo's wife. In 50 his immoral life and factionalism caused Sallust's name to be stricken from the senatorial roll.

With the outbreak of civil war in 49 B.C., Sallust joined Julius Caesar, who secured for him a quaestorship and command of a legion in the unsuccessful campaign against Pompey in Illyricum. Sallust continued to serve Caesar as praetor in Africa and was rewarded with a proconsular governorship of Numidia. Sallust plundered the province to amass his great wealth, but he either was not brought to trial or was acquitted. In 44 B.C. Sallust retired to Rome and the splendor of his residence, situated amid the famous Gardens

of Sallust (Horti Sallustiani). The estate later was the residence of several Roman emperors. His last years were devoted to elegant leisure and the writing of history. He died in 35 or 34 B.C.

Sallust's first historical monograph, *The Conspiracy of Catiline* (*De Catilinae coniuratione*), was apparently published in 43 B.C. The work begins with a grave account of the moral decline of the Romans and narrates the career of Catiline with emphasis on the detection and suppression of the conspiracy. Despite Sallust's knowledge of the facts from personal experience and contemporary records, the work is more notable for brilliant speeches and character sketches.

The Jugurthine War (*Bellum Iugurthinum*), was published about 41 B.C. After a philosophical introduction and an account of the career of Jugurtha, Sallust narrates the war of the Romans against the Numidian king (111-106 B.C.). Sallust drew upon his own knowledge of Africa and literary sources which included translations of Punic documents, but he does falter on chronology and topography.

Probably after 39 B.C. Sallust composed his *Histories* (*Historiae*), in five books, devoted to the critical period from the death of Sulla in 78 B.C. to Pompey's rise to power in 67 B.C. Unfortunately, only fragments, including two letters and four speeches, survive.

Sallust was judged by Quintilian to rival Thucydides, and Martial ranked him as Rome's foremost historian. Some critics allege that Sallust's works are politically inspired in favor of Caesar. Whatever his biases may be, Sallust's avowed ambition was an impartial and trustworthy narrative. Rather than writing general or annalistic history, he deliberately selected subjects and portions of history on the basis of their interest and value. Like Thucydides, he fathoms character and motivation; thus his works are never dreary or monotonous but are dramatic, colorful, and concentrated. Sallust's polished, vigorous, and varied style shows a fondness for concise expression, neatly turned phrases, figurative language, archaisms, and colloquialisms.

Further Reading

Sallust, translated by John Carew Rolfe (1921), contains the major works. An excellent, incisive critique of Sallust, his work, and his cultural milieu is Ronald Syme's scholarly *Sallust* (1964). Also useful is D. C. Earl, *The Political Thought of Sallust* (1961). A brief but clear account of Sallust for the general reader is in Stephen Usher, *The Historians of Greece and Rome* (1970), which, since it reports the conclusions of modern scholarship, is more useful than the older works by J. B. Bury, *The Ancient Greek Historians* (1909), and Max Ludwig Wolfram Laistner, *The Greater Roman Historians* (1947). □

Charlotte Salomon

Charlotte Salomon (1917-1943), a young German artist, painted her autobiography in the midst of World War II.

During the war a German Jewish artist named Charlotte Salomon recorded the story of her life. She was 24 years old when she began her autobiography, a refugee from Nazi Germany living on the French Riviera. As autobiography, there is nothing like Salomon's work: *Life or Theater?: An Operetta.* It unfolds in 1,350 paintings of astonishing vividness and force, with acts and scenes, captions and narrative texts, dialogues, commentaries, and musical accompaniments. The characters, based on her own family and friends, have fictional names, and the whole work takes the form of a painted play. After 1980 it achieved international renown through publications, film, drama, and popular exhibits in Amsterdam, Berkeley, Los Angeles, Miami, Tel Aviv, Berlin, and elsewhere.

On April 16, 1917, Salomon was born in Berlin to a family distinguished in the medical profession. But the family kept secret the fact that five of its members, including Salomon's mother, had taken their lives before her birth or in her childhood. Her father, Albert Salomon, professor at Berlin University's Medical School, married again in 1930. Through her stepmother, Paula Lindberg, a well-known mezzosoprano, Salomon first experienced the demands of love, the commitment to art, the crisis for Jews. Through Alfred Wolfsohn, an impoverished and charismatic voice coach employed by her stepmother, Salomon discovered passion, artistic conviction, and faith in self-disclosure. These influences from her stepmother and her mentor inspired her later work.

When the Nazis came to power in 1933, Paula Salomon-Lindberg began working with the Jewish Cultural Association, the sole sponsor permitted for Jewish performers. Salomon was admitted to the famous Berlin Fine Arts Academy in 1935, a rarity for a Jewish student. Developing her considerable talent, she found affinities with artistic movements the Nazis were working to suppress—Expressionism, poster art, caricature, and avant-garde theater. *Life or Theater?* registers the impact of Nazi power on one family: her grandparents decide to leave Germany; her stepmother is banned from the public stage; her father is fired from the university and thrown into a concentration camp; she herself is forced to leave the academy in 1938, then in 1939 to leave her family and Germany.

Salomon joined her grandparents in Villefranche, near Nice in southern France, where they were suffering the stresses of exile. There in 1940 at age 23 she witnessed her grandmother's suicide and suddenly learned the whole truth about her relatives. Uncovering the legacy of suicide from her family and culture brought her to "the question," as she put it: "whether to take her own life or undertake something crazy and unheard of"—an autobiography in art. Reflecting back on events of the 1930s in Berlin, the autobiography helped redeem her losses by creating what she called a "song of farewell to my native land." Her thousand-part self-portrait granted substance to a life that the German "master race" presumed expendable—merely young, female, Jewish.

Probably this work would not have come into being in 1941 and 1942 if Salomon had not faced the possibility of suicide in herself, had not known the danger of a Nazi-dominated Europe, and had not settled in one of its safer corners. On the French Riviera thousands of Jewish refugees found sanctuary, especially after the Italian occupation in late 1942, for the Italian authorities rejected Nazi demands to deport Jews to the deathcamp of Auschwitz in Poland. When Salomon finished the 1,300 paintings and hundreds of texts for *Life or Theater?* she gave them to a friend in Villefranche for safekeeping. Marrying another refugee, Alexander Nagler, she lived in relative security until the Germans occupied the Riviera in September 1943. Under the command of SS Captain Alois Brunner, the Gestapo conducted one of the most brutal roundups in Western Europe. Along with thousands of other Jews, she was arrested and sent by cattle transport to Poland.

Giving *Life or Theater?* away, she had said: "Keep this safe: it is my whole life." Her whole life ended in October 1943 at the age of 26 in Auschwitz.

After the war her father and stepmother, who had survived hidden in the Netherlands, found *Life or Theater?* in Villefranche and brought it back to Amsterdam. The original paintings now reside in Amsterdam's Jewish Historical Museum.

Further Reading

Two books have reproduced Charlotte Salomon's work: a selection of 80 paintings in *Charlotte: A Diary of Pictures* (1963) and 769 paintings in *Charlotte: Life or Theater? An Autobiographical Play* (1981). The former includes an account of Charlotte's life in France by Emil Straus, and the latter includes excellent introductions by Judith Belinfante, Gary Schwartz, and Judith Herzberg. A film, "Charlotte" (BBC, 1981) by Judith Herzberg and Frans Weisz, shows both the work and the life. Articles about Salomon and her work include those by Gary Schwartz in *Artnews* (October 1981) and by Mary and John Felstiner in *Moment* (May 1982). A study by Mary Felstiner of Charlotte Salomon's life, work, and times is in progress.

Additional Sources

Felstiner, Mary Lowenthal, *To paint her life: Charlotte Salomon in the Nazi era,* New York, NY: HarperCollins, 1994.
Salomon, Charlotte, *Charlotte, life or theater?: An autobiographical play,* New York: Viking Press; Maarssen, The Netherlands: G. Schwartz, 1981. □

Gaetano Salvemini

The Italian historian and journalist Gaetano Salvemini (1873-1957) introduced economic and social analysis into Italian historiography. He spent his later years combating the Fascist dictatorship.

Gaetano Salvemini was born in Molfetta on Sept. 8, 1873, the second of nine children in a poor peasant family. As a child, he had little to read but the Bible and the novels of Alexander Dumas and Eugène Sue.

But his success on his school examinations led him to try for a scholarship at the Institute for Higher Studies at Florence, which he barely won.

In Florence he was soon caught up in the Socialist movement. His thesis on the Florentine knighthood in the Renaissance was followed by *Magnati e popolani nelle commune di Firenze 1280-1295* (1899), in which he described the origins of the Florentine Republic as the product of class conflict. Salvemini saw the history of this period as one of conflict between the aristocracy and the great merchants, in which economic change brought institutional change in its wake. Though the book sold very few copies, it was considered the manifesto of the new Italian historiography. The work won Salvemini a professorial chair in 1901 and a prize from the Accademia dei Lincei that allowed him to marry Maria Minervini, whose acquaintance he had made as a student.

In 1897 Salvemini had begun to contribute to the Socialist journal *Critica sociale*. After his professorial appointment he helped organize secondary school teachers and joined a campaign to promote universal suffrage and universal education. At the same time he wrote *La Rivoluzione francese* (1905; *The French Revolution*), introducing to the Italian reading public the work of the French historian Alphonse Aulard, and a study *Mazzini* (1905), the first major analysis of this Italian statesman's ideas in the European context. These productive years were brought to a sudden end when an earthquake at Messina killed Salvemini's entire family in 1908, a tragedy from which he only slowly recovered.

In 1910 and 1913 Salvemini stood for election to Parliament but was defeated by government-instigated electoral fraud. Meanwhile he founded a new socialist journal, *L'unità*, on whose pages he fought the exacerbated nationalism of the war and immediate postwar years. In 1919 he was elected to Parliament by a large majority. But parliamentary government was already in deep trouble; in 1921, after the Fascists had gained power, he withdrew from politics. Though this move probably saved him from an assassin's bullet, it deprived the opposition of one of its most courageous leaders.

In 1925, after being arrested for clandestine anti-Fascist activities, Salvemini managed to escape and flee the country. He went first to France and England, then in 1933 to the United States to teach the history of Italian civilization at Harvard. He worked to awaken the English and American world to the dangers of fascism. He returned to Florence in 1947 and died there on Sept. 6, 1957.

Further Reading

Salvemini's own works, which give considerable insight into his character, include *The Fascist Dictatorship in Italy* (1927) and, in collaboration with George LaPiana, *What To Do with Italy* (1943). Also of interest is his *Under the Axe of Fascism* (1936). For background see Charles F. Delzell, *Mussolini's Enemies: The Italian Anti-Fascist Resistance* (1961). □

Samory Touré

The African ruler and state builder Samory Touré (1830-1900) held the French at bay for 15 years and created one of the most powerful, best-organized states in the western Sudan. His military and administrative genius was compared to Napoleon's.

Samory Touré was born in the Milo Valley of the western Sudan. His family owned cattle and traded, but their once strong ties to Islam had been loosened for over a century. Traveling widely over western Africa in 1846-1851, Samory came into contact with Islam and was reconverted to the faith.

From 1870 to 1875 Samory succeeded in creating a large empire through military victories. Influenced by the example of African empire builders like al-Hajj Omar, in 1880 he began a new *jihad* (holy war) to convert the pagans and push out the Europeans if necessary. His first armed conflict with the French occurred in February 1882.

As the result of a series of battles lasting until 1885, Samory negotiated a treaty ending hostilities. He agreed to send his son to France as a hostage. In addition, Samory agreed not to cross the Niger River in search of further conquests. In 1891 war broke out again between Samory and colonialists, and this time hostilities continued bitterly for 7 years until the fall in 1898 of Sikasso, a great walled city of 40,000 inhabitants. Samory, captured alive, was exiled to Gabon, where he died on June 2, 1900.

By the time of his fall Samory had created an administrative structure of 162 former chiefdoms organized into 10 provinces. He invented tactics of guerrilla warfare reminiscent of modern insurgent tactics and also opened an arms factory with 300 to 400 men turning out modern weapons that supplemented those from Europe. He maintained an intelligence network that kept him informed of developments from what is today Mauritania to Nigeria at a time when other great African leaders were driving independently in holy wars against the Europeans. Had princes of the caliber of the sultan of Sokoto, to this day a power in Nigeria, accepted Samory's proffered invitation to unite, the story of colonial conquest in Africa might indeed have been quite different.

Further Reading

Although there is no good biography of Samory Touré, a good, brief summation of his significance is in Michael Crowder, *West Africa under Colonial Rule* (1968). A less sympathetic account is in John D. Hargreaves, *West Africa: The Former French States* (1967). See also Roland Oliver and Anthony Atmore, *Africa since 1800* (1967). □

Samudragupta

Samudragupta (reigned 350-375) was the second emperor of the Gupta dynasty of India. His reign ushered in the Golden Age of India, and he is remembered both as a benevolent imperial conqueror and as a patron of the arts and letters.

A detailed record of the reign of Samudragupta is preserved in the shape of an inscription—a *prasasti,* or panegyric, composed by the poet Harisena and engraved on the same pillar on which Emperor Asoka, centuries before, had had an edict carved. The two inscriptions make a contrasting reading: Asoka's, written in simple Pali, speaks of peace and righteousness; Samudragupta's, written in elegant and classical Sanskrit, glorifies war.

At the time of his accession, Samudragupta's territories comprised present-day north Bihar and north and west Bengal. Acting on his father's dying behest, the young ruler embarked upon *digvijaya,* a lofty Hindu political ideal to conquer the four quarters of the Aryan universe. The *prasasti* divides Samudragupta's opponents into four categories: rulers slain, whose dominions Samudragupta annexed outrightly; rulers defeated, but reinstated as tributaries; "frontier" kings, who were forced to pay homage; and "distant" kings, who acknowledged Samudragupta as an emperor by sending him embassies. Among the first were independent potentates of the Gangetic Basin; their extermination made Samudragupta the ruler of all territories from the Ravi in the west to the Brahmaputra in the east, and from the Himalayan foothills in the north to the Narbada in the south. In the second category were 12 potentates with territories between the Mahanadi and the Godavari. In the third category came more than a dozen tribal leaders of Assam, Malwa, Gujarat, and western Punjab and Rajputana. Lastly, Saka satraps of western India and Kushan rulers of northwest India and Afghanistan seem to have paid him homage. The ruler of Ceylon sent an embassy to secure privileges for Sinhalese monks at Bodhgaya. About 365 Samudragupta offered the horse sacrifice, the traditional symbol of lordship over Aryan India.

Samudragupta issued gold dinars: they weigh as much as 123 grains and have a gold content of 87 percent. One shows him performing the horse sacrifice; another shows him playing a harp. He was a gifted musician, a poet, and a person who took part in religious discussions. None of the many buildings he appears to have erected has survived. Though personally a Hindu, he extended his patronage to other religions, and one of his chief courtiers appears to have been the great Buddhist philosopher Vasubandhu. Not much is known of his administrative system, but he must have been an ideal ruler as is evidenced by the introductory portion of a late Javanese text, the *Tantri Kamandaka,* which refers to him in eloquent terms.

Further Reading

The best biography is Balkrishna Govind Gokhale, *Samudra Gupta: Life and Times* (1962). Information is also in John F. Fleet, ed., *Inscriptions of the Early Gupta Kings and Their Successors* (1888; rev. ed. 1963). □

Samuel

The prophet Samuel (ca. 1056-1004 B.C.) was the last judge of Israel and the first of the prophets after Moses. He inaugurated the monarchy by choosing and anointing Saul and David as kings of Israel.

S amuel was the son of Elkanah and Hannah, and he was born at Ramathaim-zophim in the hill country of Ephraim. Brought to the Temple at Shiloh as a young child to serve God in fulfillment of a vow made by his mother, he succeeded Eli as the high priest and judge of Israel. Because the Philistines had destroyed Shiloh, Israel's religious center, Samuel returned to Ramah, making it the center of his activity.

Samuel made annual circuits through the cities of Bethel, Gilgal, and Mizpah, judging the people, exhorting them to stop worshiping idols, and using his influence to hold the tribes together. He seemed able to penetrate the future, and the people looked upon him as a prophet.

Israel at this time was subjected to Philistine domination, constant threats from the Ammonites, and disunion among its own tribes. The people lacked respect for Samuel's corrupt sons, Joel and Abijah, whom he appointed to judge Israel in his stead. The elders urged Samuel to seek a forceful national leader to become king. Samuel acceded and chose Saul, son of Kish of the tribe of Benjamin, and he took an active role in Saul's coronation.

Samuel later broke with Saul because Saul twice disobeyed him. Samuel then proclaimed that Saul was rejected as king of Israel and that his dynasty would not continue on the throne. The prophet transferred his support to David, selecting him and secretly anointing him king of Israel. Samuel's last days are obscured by the conflict between Saul and David. The Bible makes a brief reference to his death and to his burial at Ramah.

Samuel, though counted among the greatest of the judges, like Moses, is also numbered among the prophets. He was not a warrior but, like Moses, was a hero who rallied the spirit of his people in the midst of oppression, keeping alive their hope and faith.

Further Reading

Although there is no single authoritative biography of Samuel, there are numerous volumes of fiction, making it difficult to distinguish between the historical and the legendary. The best short essays are in Rudolph Kittel, *Great Men and Movements in Israel* (trans. 1929), and James Fleming, *Personalities of the Old Testament* (1939). The best treatment of Samuel is, of course, in the Holy Scriptures, with commentaries published by each of the major religious groups. Recommended for the historical background are Max I. Margolis and Alexander Marx, *A History of the Jewish People* (1944); William Foxwell Albright, *From the Stone Age to Christianity* (1940; 2d ed. with new introduction, 1957); Salo Wittmayer Baron, *A Social and Religious History of the Jews,* vol. 1 (2d ed. 1952; 2d rev. ed. 1969); and Martin Noth, *The History of Israel* (trans. 1958; 2d ed. 1960). □

Paul Anthony Samuelson

The American economist Paul Anthony Samuelson (born 1915) was the most distinguished of the economists who entered the profession during and after the mid-1930s—the "Keynesian generation." He was frequently referred to as the last of the generalists.

Paul Samuelson was born on May 15, 1915, in Gary, Indiana. He graduated from the University of Chicago in 1935 and pursued graduate study in economics at Harvard University, where he received the master's degree in 1936 and the doctorate in 1941 and was made a member of the prestigious Harvard Society of Junior Fellows. In 1940 he joined the faculty of the Massachusetts Institute of Technology.

Samuelson's *Foundations of Economic Analysis* and numerous pioneering articles on economic theory, statistics, mathematical economics, and the important postwar policy issues placed him among the select few of the world's leading economists by the 1940s. In 1947, he was awarded the John Bates Clark Medal, which acknowledged him as the outstanding American economic scholar under the age of 40.

A continuing steady stream of scientific books and articles and the appearance of Samuelson's textbook, *Economics: An Introductory Analysis* (1948), made him not only the most respected but also the best-known economist of his time. His *Economics* had been the standard textbook in the United States and throughout the world for more than two decades. Its unprecedented success was of course attributable to its overall greatness. However, high on the list of specific reasons were Samuelson's concern with the big, vital economic issues, his changing of these issues as appropriate with each new edition, and his sparkling and lucid writing style, which made these issues come alive to both teacher and student. He also wrote *Economics from the Heart: the Samuelson Sampler* (1983); and co-authored with William D. Nordhaus, *Microeconomics* (1989) and *Macroeconomics* (1989).

Samuelson was president of the Econometric Society (1951), the American Economic Association (1961), and the International Economic Association (1965-1968). In 1970 he was awarded the Nobel Memorial Prize in Economics, the first American economist to be so honored. In 1991 MIT established the Paul A. Samuelson Professorship in Economics in his honor. In 1996 Samuelson received the Medal of Science, the nation's highest award in science and engineering, for his contributions to economic science, education and policy and for establishing both the agenda of modern economics and scientific standards for economic analysis. He received honorary degrees from a host of colleges and universities. He delivered, among many other prestigious lectures, the Stamp Memorial Lecture (London, 1961), the Wicksell Lectures (Stockholm, 1962), and the Franklin Lecture (Detroit, 1962).

Samuelson, a leading figure in the new, more activist intelligentsia, was an advisor to President's Kennedy, Johnson and their Councils of Economic Advisers, government agencies, and other public and private institutions. His frequent appearances on television and radio and in the printed media made Samuelson's name, and his economic views on vital economic issues, widely familiar. He, along with several other MIT faculty members, made President Nixon's "enemies list" for his harsh criticism of the economic policies of the Nixon administration. The economics profession became accustomed, over three decades, to hearing MIT students proclaim, with justifiable pride, that they were taught by Professor Samuelson. In a much broader sense, he taught more economics to more of the world's citizenry than any other economist of the 20th century.

Further Reading

Information on Samuelson was in Lawrence Boland, *The Methodology of Economic Model Building: Methodology After Samuelson* (1989); John Cunningham Wood and Ronald

Woods, *Paul A. Samuelson: Critical Assessments* (1989); E. Cary Brown and Robert M. Solow, *Paul Samuelson and Modern Economic Theory* (1983); George Feiwel, *Samuelson and Neoclassical Economics* (1982); Marc Linder, *The Anti-Samuelson* (1977); Ben B. Seligman, *Main Currents in Modern Economics: Economic Thought since 1870* (1962); and in Robert Lekachman, *The Age of Keynes* (1966). □

Sanctorius

The Italian physician and physiologist Sanctorius (1561-1636) is noted for his application of quantitative methods to the study of human physiology and pathology.

Sanctorius, the Latin name of Santorio Santorio, was born on March 29, 1561, at Capo d'Istria. The University of Padua, the leading medical institution of the period, provided his medical education between 1575 and 1582. After receiving his medical degree, he practiced as a physician up to 1599 in Croatia (Yugoslavia), where he had been invited by some Croatian nobility. In 1611 he assumed the chair of theoretical medicine at Padua and held this distinguished post until 1624, when he went to Venice. He died in Venice on Feb. 22, 1636. He endowed an annual lectureship at Padua, which is still continued.

As is typical of many pioneers, Sanctorius, without realizing the full value of his ideas, recognized the necessity of measurement in medicine. Therefore he directed all his energies toward one goal: the development of instruments and appliances which would permit the physician investigator to quantify all known facts about the body.

Sanctorius's classic experiment was carried out over a period of 30 years, during which he spent as much time as possible seated in a chair rigged up to a balance so that he could weigh himself frequently. He also weighed all the food he ingested and all the excreta that he passed. These measurements provided convincing evidence for the existence of the then controversial "insensible perspiration," by which volatile substances were supposed to leave the body. He published his results in *De medicina statica aphorismi* (1614), of which there were 32 editions up to 1784 and many translations into modern languages. Sanctorius's constant endeavors to conduct systematic measurements entitle him to rank among the founders of experimental medicine.

Sanctorius gave impetus to the iatrophysical school of medicine, that is, the school which explained all body processes and diseases and their treatments within a numerical and geometrical context. However, iatrophysics began to flourish outside of Italy only in the early 18th century, three-quarters of a century after Sanctorius's death.

Among the instruments Sanctorius invented or perfected for use in physiology and pathology are the balance, the thermometer, the hygrometer, the trocar (for removing excess water from the abdomen and the chest), and a catheter for removing kidney stones. The best-known of these instruments is the thermometer described by Sanctorius in his commentary on Arab medicine. He also developed an apparatus for measuring pulse rates by comparing them to the swings of a pendulum on strings of different lengths. Then, by comparing the string lengths, the pulse rates were calibrated as a function of time. Thus, medieval medicine and Renaissance physics were combined in the imaginative mind of Sanctorius to develop this important instrument.

Further Reading

There are no books on Sanctorius in English. Most biographical accounts are in Italian. The closest to a definitive biography is in Serbian by Mirko Drazen, *Santorio Santorio* (Zagreb, 1952); it includes a few pages of summary in English. For background see Henry E. Sigerist, *The Great Doctors: A Biographical History of Medicine* (trans. 1933); Ralph H. Major, *A History of Medicine,* vol. 1 (1954); and Katherine B. Shippen, *Men of Medicine* (1957). □

George Sand

The French novelist George Sand (1804-1876) was the most successful woman writer of her century. Her novels present a large fresco of romantic sentiment and 19th-century life, especially in its more pastoral aspects.

George Sand was born Armandine Aurore Lucille Dupin in Paris on July 1, 1804. On her father's side she was related to a line of kings and to the Maréchal de Saxe; her mother was the daughter of a professional bird fancier. Aurore's father, Maurice Dupin, was a soldier of the Empire. He died when Aurore was still a child.

At the age of 14, tired of being the "apple of discord" between her mother and grandmother, Aurore went to the convent of the Dames Augustines Anglaises in Paris. Though she did her best to disrupt the convent's peaceful life, she felt drawn to quiet contemplation and direct communication with God.

To save Aurore from mysticism, her grandmother called her to her home in Nohant. Here Aurore studied nature, practiced medicine on the peasants, read from the philosophers of all ages, and developed a passion for the works of François René Chateaubriand. Her eccentric tutor encouraged her to wear men's clothing while horseback riding, and she galloped through the countryside in trousers and loose shirt, free, wild, and in love with nature.

Marriage and Lovers

When her grandmother died, Aurore became mistress of the estate at Nohant. At 19 she married Casimir Dudevant, the son of a baron and a servant girl. He was goodhearted but coarse and sensual, and he offended her lofty and mystical ideal of love. Aurore soon began to seek her idealized love object elsewhere. For a time she maintained a platonic relationship with Aurélien de Sèze, but eventually this affair languished. She had begun to realize

that it was impossible to sustain love without physical passion.

At the age of 27 Aurore moved to Paris in search of independence and love, leaving husband and children behind. She began writing articles to earn her living and met a coterie of writers. Henri de Latouche and Charles Sainte-Beuve became her mentors.

Aurore fell in love with Jules Sandeau, a charming young writer. They collaborated on articles and signed them collectively "J. Sand." When she published her first novel, *Indiana* (1832), she took as her pen name "George Sand."

George Sand made a home for Sandeau and for her daughter, Solange, but eventually she wearied of his jealousy and idle disposition. He, in turn, realized that he could never overcome her essential frigidity. She felt as though she had failed in marriage as well as in adultery. Several novels of disillusioned love were the fruit of this period of her life. Then she met the young poet Alfred de Musset, and they became lovers.

George Sand legally separated from her husband; she gained custody over Solange, while her husband kept the other child, Maurice. She now came to enjoy great renown in Paris both as a writer and as a bold and brilliant woman. She had many admirers and chose new lovers from among them. Her lovers included the Polish composer Frédéric Chopin and the doctor who attended Musset in Venice. Perhaps it was her inability to be aroused to physical passion that drove her from one lover to another. She compensated for this deficiency by the spiritual intensity of her love.

Political Views

George Sand was a democrat; she felt close to the people by birth, and she often praised the humble virtues of the urban and country poor in her novels. She was a Christian of sorts and advocated a socially conscious religion. Like Jean Jacques Rosseau, she believed that inherently good man was corrupted by civilization and faulty institutions.

Despite her own feminist leanings, George Sand never advocated political equality for women. It was in love that she demanded equality, in the free choice of the love object; the inequality of men and women before the law seemed to her a scandal.

Last Years

As she grew older, George Sand spent more and more time at her beloved Nohant and gave herself up to the intoxications of pastoral life, the entertainment of friends, the staging of puppet shows, and most of all to her grandchildren. Though she had lost none of her vital energy and enthusiasm, she grew less concerned with politics. Her quest for the absolute in love had led her through years of stormy affairs to the attainment of a tolerant and universal love—of God, of nature, of children. She died in Nohant on June 9, 1876.

Early Novels

Every night from midnight until dawn, George Sand covered her daily quota of 20 pages with her large, tranquil writing, never crossing out a line. All her novels are love stories in which her romantic idealism unfolds in a realistic setting. The characters are people she knew, although their sentiments are idealized.

The early works by George Sand are novels of passion, written to alleviate the pain of her first love affairs. *Indiana* (1832) has as its central theme woman's search for the absolute in love. *Valentine* (1832) depicts an aristocratic woman, unhappily married, who finds that a farmer's son loves her. *Lélia* (1854) is a lyrical but searching confession of the author's own physical coldness. Lélia is a beautiful woman loved by a young poet, but she can show him only maternal affection.

Socialist Novels

During the 1840s George Sand wrote a number of novels in which she exposed her socialist doctrine joined with a humanitarian religion. *Le Compagnon du tour de France* (1840), *Consuelo* (1842-1843), and *Le Péché de Monsieur Antoine* (1847) are typical novels of this period. Her socialism was of an optimistic, idealistic nature. She sympathized in these novels with the plight of the worker and the farmer. She also wrote a number of novels devoted to country life, most produced during her retreat to Nohant at the time of the 1848 uprising. *La Mare au diable* (1846), *La Petite Fadette* (1849), and *Les Maîtres sonneurs* (1852) are typical novels of this genre. They celebrate the humble virtues of a simple life and offer idealized portraits of the peasants of Berry.

George Sand's last works show a tendency to moralize; in these novels the characters become incarnated theories rather than human beings.

Further Reading

George Sand's appeal to biographers has inspired a number of good works. Elizabeth W. Schermerhorn, *The Seven Strings of the Lyre: The Romantic Life of George Sand, 1804-1876* (1927), is authoritative and carefully compiled. Felizia Seyd, *Romantic Rebel: The Life and Times of George Sand* (1940), is a straightforward account. André Maurois, *Lélia: The Life of George Sand* (1952; trans. 1953), is readable and emotionally compelling. Two books that emphasize George Sand's love life are Marie J. Howe, *George Sand: The Search for Love* (1927), and Frances Winwar, *The Life of the Heart: George Sand and Her Times* (1945). □

Carl Sandburg

An American poet, anthologist, singer of folk songs and ballads, and biographer, Carl Sandburg (1878-1967) is best known for his magnificent biography of Abraham Lincoln and his early "realistic" verse celebrations of Chicago.

The legend of Carl Sandburg as a raw, folksy poet of midwestern democracy has overshadowed his later development. From the time he wrote his moving elegy on the death of Franklin D. Roosevelt, "When Death Came April Twelve 1945," until his final volume of poetry, *Honey and Salt* (1963), he exhibited a newly achieved depth and originality that far surpassed his earlier work. His youthful career as an impassioned revolutionary socialist has largely been forgotten, and he died one of America's best-known and best-loved poets.

Sandburg was born in Galesburg, Ill., on Jan. 6, 1878, of a poor Swedish immigrant family. At the age of 13 he quit school to work as a day laborer. He traveled extensively through the West, where he began developing a lifelong devotion to his country and its people. Following Army service during the Spanish-American War, he entered Lombard (now Knox) College in Galesburg. Here he wrote his first poetry.

After graduation Sandburg worked as a newspaperman in Milwaukee, Wis. In 1907 and 1908 he was district organizer for the Social Democratic party in Wisconsin and served as secretary to Milwaukee's Socialist mayor (1910-1912). Later he moved to Chicago, becoming an editorial writer for the *Daily News* in 1917. Meanwhile his verse began appearing in the avant-garde *Poetry* magazine; his first volume, *Chicago Poems,* was published in 1916. His reputation as vital poet of the American scene was solidified with *Cornhuskers* (1918), *Smoke and Steel* (1920), and *Slabs of the Sunburnt West* (1922).

Early Writings

Sandburg's early poetry was as close to being "subliterary" as the work of any American poet of comparable stature. Meant to illustrate his humanitarian socialist ideology, his early verse is scarcely above the level of political oratory. "I Am the People, the Mob" from the *Chicago Poems* is characteristic. The ending of the poem is reminiscent of Walt Whitman at his most prosaic: "When I, the People, learn to remember, when I, the People, use the lessons of yesterday and no longer forget who robbed me last year, who played me for a fool—then there will be no speaker in all the world say the name: 'The People,' with any fleck of a sneer in his voice or any far-off smile of derision. The mob—the crowd—the mass—will arrive then."

Neither in use of language nor in metrics does this qualify even as free verse; in style it is closer to John Dos Passos' contemporary experiments in prose than to poetry. The revolutionary naturalistic esthetic of the time called for a poetry of direct imitation; but Sandburg's "imitations" exhibited little artistry.

Sandburg's early poetry not only tended toward excessively unshaped imitation of reality but also copied other poets as well. T. S. Eliot's "The Love Song of J. Alfred Prufrock" had appeared the year before Sandburg's "Fog" was published. Eliot's image of the fog as a cat has profound implications in the context of the rest of his poem; "Fog," which was hailed as a fine example of an imagist poem, has no context whatsoever and hence no meaning. In terms of imagist poetics, "Fog" might be considered successful, but Sandburg had never counted himself a member of that movement; nor had he ever seriously considered its esthetic.

Similarly, Sandburg's "Happiness" compares unfavorably with Ezra Pound's "Salutation," and his "Buffalo Bill" expresses mere nostalgia in relation to E. E. Cummings's more penetrating "Buffalo Bill's." Some of the poems in *Cornhuskers* are more original and fully realized than those discussed here, but none meets the standards of the best of his contemporaries.

Later Work

From 1926 to 1939 Sandburg devoted himself primarily to writing the six-volume biography of Abraham Lincoln, presenting Lincoln as the embodiment of the American spirit; he received a Pulitzer Prize in history for this work (1939). He also was collecting the folk songs that made up *The American Songbook* (1927).

Honey and Salt (1963), a remarkable achievement for a "part-time" poet in his 80s, contains much of Sandburg's best poetry. Here the mellowness and wisdom of age are evident; the sound of an American idiom echoes through these poems more effectively than in the earlier "realistic" verse. By this time Sandburg had moved from his dependence on ideology to a deeply felt sympathy and concern for actual people. Tenderness replaces sentimentality; emotional control replaces defensive "toughness." There is an explicitly religious consciousness in these last poems, only implicit in the earlier work, where it was often submerged in political ideology and naturalistic poetics.

Sandburg also published a collection of children's stories, *Rootabaga Stories* (1922). Other volumes of poetry are *Good Morning, America* (1928); *The People, Yes* (1936); *Collected Poems* (1950), which won a Pulitzer Prize; and *Harvest Poems, 1910-1960* (1960). *Remembrance Rock* (1948), an epic panorama of American history, was his only novel. He died in Flat Rock, N.C., on July 22, 1967.

Further Reading

Sandburg's autobiography is *Always the Young Strangers* (1953). A biography is Harry L. Golden, *Carl Sandburg* (1961). Good critical commentary includes "Carl Sandburg's Complete Poems" in William Carlos Williams, *Selected Essays* (1954); Newton Arvin's "Carl Sandburg" in Malcolm Cowley, ed., *After the Genteel Tradition: American Writers since 1910* (1959); Roy Harvey Pearce, *The Continuity of American Poetry* (1961); and Hyatt H. Waggoner, *American Poets: From the Puritans to the Present* (1968). □

Augusto C. Sandino

Augusto C. Sandino (1894-1934) was the leader of a Nicaraguan guerrilla movement which opposed United States Marine intervention in that country from 1927 to 1933. His opposition galvanized anti-American feeling throughout Latin America and helped convince U.S. policy makers that military intervention was often self-defeating.

Augusto Calderón (later he adopted César for his middle name) Sandino was born in the village of Niquinohomo on a date variously given but probably May 18, 1894, to Gregorio Sandino and Margarita Calderón, a servant girl. For several years Gregorio neglected his illegitimate son, who lived with his mother in poverty. At age 11 Augusto went to live in the house of his father, who had married América Tíffer. He attended primary school in his village and an institute in Granada, Nicaragua, after which he became a produce merchant. When he had trouble with a local political chief he left home for Honduras and Guatemala, eventually arriving in Mexico in 1923, where he worked in the oil industry around Tampico. There he observed Mexican nationalism, and when Mexicans chided Nicaraguans for their lack of patriotism he began thinking about United States interference in his native land. He formed a social and political philosophy that Nicaragua's problems lay in politicians and American imperialism.

Sandino returned to Nicaragua in 1926 during the political disturbances following Conservative Emiliano Chamorro's ouster of President Carlos Solorzano and Vice President Juan B. Sacasa (supported by the Liberals). He worked briefly for an American-owned gold mine, where he talked with workers about the need for a government to protect them from exploitation by captialists and foreign-owned

companies. According to one account he told them he was not a Communist but a socialist.

Sandino's decision to take up arms may have been influenced initially by his strong Liberal background reacting against Conservative control as much as by a reaction against the intervention. When his attempt at independent military action in the revolution against the Conservatives failed, he decided to join forces with the Liberals headed by Juan B. Sacasa, a claimant for the presidency who had returned from forced exile and set up a government on Nicaragua's east coast. Sandino's relationship with the Liberal military and political leadership was not close, but according to his own account he gave valuable service to the cause, even at one time preventing rout of the main Liberal force.

In April 1927 Henry L. Stimson, special representative of President Calvin Coolidge, arrived in Nicaragua to stop the fighting and, through threatened forcible disarmament, arranged a settlement in talks at Tipitapa with General José María Moncada, Sacasa's minister of war. The settlement provided for United States supervision of the next presidential election to meet the Liberal complaint that revolution was the only way for them to regain power since Conservative-controlled elections would not be fair. Despite general Liberal acceptance of the Tipitapa terms, Sandino refused them and escaped with a few followers to northern Nicaragua, where he launched a guerrilla campaign against U.S. Marines and the Nicaraguan government. Trying to hold his small force together, Sandino moved to San Rafael del Norte, where, on May 18, 1927, he married Blanca Arauz, a young telegrapher whom he had met earlier in the revolution.

At first Sandino's moves did not cause alarm because most of the revolutionaries surrendered their arms and the American military did not believe the others would offer effective resistance. Sandino's failure to stop Marine and Nicaraguan national guard occupation of northern towns seemed to confirm this view. Nonetheless, Sandino's attack on the Marine garrison at Ocotal on July 16, 1927, alarmed Washington and brought international attention to the Nicaraguan nationalist who might have won the battle but for the timely intervention of U.S. warplanes. Sandino's attack on a well-fortified enemy was a mistake and led his followers, the Sandinistas, to develop more refined methods of guerrilla warfare. Although the guerrilla leader was unable to prevent American supervision of the Nicaraguan elections of 1928, 1930, and 1932 or formation of an American-trained national guard, he was never captured and was able to win support in Latin America and the United States as he continued his hit and run tactics. Sandino's activities led Washington to reconsider the issue of military intervention and helped lay the groundwork for the principle of nonintervention in the Good Neighbor policy.

During Sandino's resistance, the Communists looked upon him as an important leader in the anti-imperialist struggle and sought to influence him. The relationship, one of convenience only, was strained when Sandino temporarily left for Mexico (1929-1930) and later, when Sandino made peace with Managua, there were charges of betrayal.

After U.S. Marines withdrew from Nicaragua in January 1933, Sandino and the newly-elected Sacasa government reached an agreement by which he would cease his guerrilla activities in return for amnesty, a grant of land for an agricultural colony, and retention of an armed band of 100 men for a year. There followed a growing hostility between Sandino and Anastasio Somoza Garcia, chief of the national guard, which led to Sandino's abduction and death during a visit to Managua on February 21, 1934. Sandino's death removed a major block to Somoza's drive for power and a Somoza family dictatorship which lasted from 1937 to 1979. Years later, Sandino's anti-imperialism influenced opposition to the Somozas and inspired formation of the Sandinista Front of National Liberation, which brought the downfall of the dictatorship in 1979.

Further Reading

Neill Macauley's *The Sandino Affair* (1967) details U.S. Marine activities against Sandino. Lejeune Cummins in his *Quijote on a Burro: Sandino and the Marines* (1958) reflects that Sandino crystallized Latin American sentiment against the United States and forced reexamination of policy. *A Search for Stability: United States Diplomacy Toward Nicaragua, 1925-1933* (1968) by William Kamman puts Sandino in the context of U.S.-Nicaraguan relations.

Additional Sources

Macaulay, Neill, *The Sandino affair,* Durham, N.C.: Duke University Press, 1985.
Sandino, the testimony of a Nicaraguan patriot: 1921-1934, Princeton, N.J.: Princeton University Press, 1990.
Selser, Gregorio, *Sandino,* New York: Monthly Review Press, 1981. □

Sir Edwin Sandys

Sir Edwin Sandys (1561-1629), a great figure in the British Parliament during the turbulent first quarter of the 17th century, was important in the English colonization of America.

Born on Dec. 9, 1561, in Worcestershire, Edwin Sandys was the son of an archbishop of the Church of England and thus a member of the English nobility. He was educated at Oxford University and the Middle Temple.

Sandys entered Parliament in 1586 and distinguished himself as an energetic legislator. He also traveled much and found time to write about religious matters, early displaying his liberalism. He was among James I's first supporters; under his patronage Sandys emerged as a prime mover in parliamentary circles.

Within a decade, however, Sandys deserted the Crown and took leadership of the opposition. He had come to believe that a king ruled *under* law and this imposed limitations on the rights of both the Crown and its subjects, and that if the former trespassed the latter's rights, he could legally be overthrown. Thus it was that Sandys contributed immensely to the active leadership of the budding Whig (parliamentary) cause and to the dogma opposing the king's prerogative that grew out of it.

When the Crown suspended Parliament in 1613 (a suspension lasting 6 years), Sandys turned his attention to the growing colonial empire. He appeared first as a power in the East India Company, but the contributions for which he is remembered were to the Virginia Company. For several years treasurer of that overseas joint stock company, Sandys was in a position to influence policies both in London and the New World.

One historian has noted that Sandys "was virtually managing" the company from 1617 on. The Virginia Company's operations, then, became a natural source of enmity between the Crown and the Whigs during the 1620s, for the King "cherished a grudge against Sandys" and in 1624 dissolved the company. By that time, however, the Virginia Colony had been successfully established; Sandys had been instrumental during the colony's crucial years in settling large numbers to repopulate Virginia after the "starving time." Sandys also gained a monopoly in England for Virginia's tobacco and tried to introduce manufactures into the colony.

However, with Virginia's economic well-being and population restored, Sandys became dispensable to the Crown; over the protests of the shareholders he was removed from the company's management by James I. "It was the manipulations of Sandys," a historian has written, that

played a crucial part in establishing the "supremacy of Parliament [that] was embodied in the unwritten constitution" of England. He was one of the few Englishmen who contributed significantly both to the establishment of the rule of law in the British Isles and to the expansion of England's overseas empire. He died in October 1629.

Further Reading

There is no modern acceptable biography of Sandys. For the period as a whole and for insights into Sandys's career see Wallace Notestein, *The English People on the Eve of Colonization, 1603-1630* (1954). □

The Sangallo family

The Sangallo family (active late 15th-mid-16th century) was a large and important clan of Florentine artists. The three most prominent figures were architects and military engineers.

Descended from the woodworker Francesco Giamberti, the family received the name Sangallo from its residence near the Porta S. Gallo in Florence. The chief members were Francesco's sons, Giuliano (ca. 1443-1516) and Antonio the Elder (ca. 1453-1534), and their nephew, Antonio the Younger (1483-1546). Giuliano, as leader of the second generation of Florentine Renaissance architects, refined the architectural style of Filippo Brunelleschi to suit the less heroic and more sensuous age of Lorenzo de' Medici. His brother, Antonio the Elder, who often assisted him, was more concerned with military engineering, but his late church at Montepulciano reflects the High Renaissance architectural style inaugurated by Donato Bramante.

Giuliano da Sangallo

Giuliano was trained as a woodcarver in the shop of Il Francione, a local woodworker and military engineer. Giuliano probably accompanied his master to Rome and was certainly there in 1465, as he notes on the title page of his large sketchbook of antiquities (in the Vatican Library). Although there has been some uncertainty about his identification in Roman documents, he was probably active in several of the papal building projects, such as the Palace of S. Marco (1469-1470), St. Peter's (1470-1472), and the benedictional loggia (1470) which once stood in front of old St. Peter's.

After Giuliano returned to Florence, he aided Il Francione with the fortification of Colle Val d'Elsa (1479) and prepared a model for the church of the Servi (1480). With Antonio the Elder, he completed a model for the church and monastery of the Badia (1482) and carved a crucifix for SS. Annunziata (1481-1483).

By the mid-1480s Giuliano was the most prominent architect in Florence and in favor with Lorenzo de' Medici. Nearby at Prato he designed the Church of the Madonna

Giuliano da Sangallo

delle Carceri (1485-1491) on a Greek-cross plan of four equal arms with an interior melon-shaped dome over the crossing. The interior with its contrast of dark architectural moldings against the light wall surface is a reflection of the influence of Brunelleschi. The green-and-white marble revetment of the exterior conveys that element of elegance so characteristic of Giuliano. At the same time he built the villa at Poggio a Caiano (ca. 1485) for Lorenzo de' Medici. Organized with separate apartments at the corners of the large central salon, the living quarters of the villa are set in two stories above a great arcaded podium which serves as a terrace around the building. The rectangular mass of the villa is relieved by an entrance loggia designed as a temple front set into the center of the first floor. In 1488 Lorenzo de' Medici sent Giuliano to Naples to deliver to King Ferdinando I the model of a palace, whose plan is in the Vatican sketchbook.

On his return to Florence in 1489 Giuliano prepared the model for the Sacristy of Sto Spirito, and from September 1489 to February 1490 he was paid for the model of the Strozzi Palace. This massive palace was begun in 1490 by Benedetto da Maiano with some minor changes, particularly in the rustication of the stone, from Giuliano's model (preserved in the palace). The Gondi Palace, begun in 1490 after his designs, is a very refined descendant of Michelozzo's Medici Palace in Florence. In 1492 Giuliano traveled to Milan with the model of a palace for Duke

Lodovico Sforzo, and the same year he designed the church of S. Maria dell'Umiltà at Pistoia.

Giuliano followed Cardinal Giuliano della Rovere to Lyons, France, in June 1494. By August, Giuliano had returned to Italy, probably to the cardinal's native city of Savona, where he designed a palace for the cardinal. With his appointment in 1497 as military engineer of Florence, Giuliano's activity was primarily in Tuscany.

The election in 1503 of his patron, Cardinal della Rovere, as Pope Julius II soon attracted Giuliano to Rome, where he remained until 1507. During this second residence in Rome he was involved in expanding the papal hunting lodge at La Magliana. In 1506 the Pope sent him and the great Florentine sculptor Michelangelo to view the ancient sculpture *Laocoon*, which had just been discovered, in anticipation of the Pope's acquisition of it for his collection in the Vatican Palace.

By November 1507 Giuliano was again in his native city of Florence, where he was principally active with fortifications at Pisa and Leghorn. When Leo X of the Medici family became pope in 1513, Giuliano immediately returned to Rome. In July he designed for the new pope a tremendous palace near the Piazza Navona which was never executed. On Jan. 1, 1514, Giuliano was appointed supervisor of work for the new St. Peter's, which the architect Bramante was building, and in April he continued in that position with Raphael, who succeeded Bramante.

Giuliano returned to Florence in July 1515. He prepared several unexecuted designs, preserved among his drawings, for the completion of the facade of Brunelleschi's S. Lorenzo. He died on Oct. 20, 1516. His son, Francisco (1494-1576), was a sculptor who was particularly known for his tomb monuments.

Antonio da Sangallo the Elder

Antonio the Elder was active with fortifications in and near Rome in the early 1490s. He worked on the Castel Sant'Angelo in Rome (1492-1493) and designed the citadel of Civita Castellana (1494). In 1517 he collaborated with Baccio d'Agnolo on the design of the loggia on the Piazza dell'Annunziata in Florence, matching that of Brunelleschi's Ospedale degli Innocenti.

Antonio's most important independent commission was the Church of the Madonna di S. Biagio at Montepulciano (1518-1529). The centralized Greek-cross plan of the church with independent towers in the reentrant angles of the facade and the tall dome on a drum over the crossing obviously reflect Bramante's ideas for St. Peter's.

Antonio da Sangallo the Younger

Antonio the Younger, whose real name was Cordini, was the son of a sister of Giuliano and Antonio the Elder. Accompanying Giuliano to Rome in 1504, Antonio the Younger soon assisted Bramante and served as master carpenter on the work of St. Peter's. In 1516 Antonio was appointed chief assistant to Raphael at St. Peter's. Antonio designed the Farnese Palace in Rome for Cardinal Alessandro Farnese. Work on the palace began in 1517 but was interrupted about 1520, when Antonio succeeded Raphael as chief architect of the new St. Peter's.

For the next decade Antonio undertook numerous papal commissions, although little was executed because of the political and religious upheavals of the period. The Mint, or Zecca, in Rome (1523-1524; now the Banco di Sto Spirito) was designed with a slightly concave facade modeled on a triumphal arch motif above a rusticated ground floor. In 1525 Antonio was concerned with fortifications for Parma and in the following year for Piacenza. At Orvieto he built an amazing public well, the Pozzo di S. Patrizio (1528-1535), with double spiral ramps penetrating to the base of the well around an open core.

The election in 1534 of Cardinal Farnese as Pope Paul III brought renewed architectural activity for Antonio. He redesigned and enlarged the Farnese Palace, resulting in a tremendous three-story building arranged around a square central court. The palace was completed by Michelangelo after Antonio's death. Antonio practically rebuilt the Farnese town of Castro with fortifications, a ducal palace, and the Zecca (all destroyed in 1649). For the entry into Rome of the emperor Charles V in 1536, Antonio organized the artists of Rome to prepare the festival decorations, including temporary triumphal arches near the palace of S. Marco and at the entrance to the Vatican Borgo. Under the threat of Turkish attacks Antonio began in 1537 to prepare new fortifications for Rome, which work continued until his death, including the unfinished Porta di Sto Spirito near the Vatican.

Although Antonio had continued since 1520 to be the architect of the new St. Peter's, assisted by Baldassare Peruzzi, it was only with the Farnese pope that extensive work was accomplished. Antonio built a great wooden model (1539-1546) for a new design for the church (preserved in St. Peter's). The design is of a tremendous Greek-cross plan with a large additional entrance vestibule and twin-towered facade with a benedictional loggia. His actual work on the church was principally concentrated on the southern arm, but he also raised the floor level, changing the interior spatial proportions. In the Vatican Palace from 1539 Antonio was architect for the Sala Regia, where the Pope received royalty, and the adjacent Pauline Chapel. Antonio died at Terni on Aug. 3, 1546.

Further Reading

There are no monographs in English on the Sangallos. Biographical information on them is in Giorgio Vasari, *Lives of the Most Eminent Painters, Sculptors and Architects* (many editions), and in André Chastel, *The Studios and Styles of the Renaissance, Italy 1460-1500* (1966). □

Frederick Sanger

The English biochemist Frederick Sanger (born 1918) was awarded the Nobel Prize in Chemistry for his discovery of the chemical structure of insulin.

Frederick Sanger, son of Frederick Sanger, a medical practitioner, was born at Rendcombe, Gloucestershire, on Aug. 13, 1918. Entering St. John's College, Cambridge, in 1936, he graduated with the degree of bachelor of arts (in natural sciences) in 1939. In 1943 he received his doctorate of philosophy (in chemistry) with a thesis on lysine. He held a Beit Memorial Fellowship from 1944 to 1951 and then joined the staff of the Medical Research Council. He later became director of the Division of Protein Chemistry in the Council's Laboratory for Molecular Biology at Cambridge.

Sanger worked entirely on the chemical structure of the proteins, especially insulin. About 1900 Emil Fisher had succeeded in breaking down proteins into polypeptides, consisting of their ultimate constituents, amino acids. About 25 different amino acids occur in nature, and of these 20 are found in most mammalian proteins.

By 1943 it was known that proteins consisted of long chains of amino acid residues bound together by peptide linkages. A. C. Chibnall and others knew the 51 amino acid residues that composed insulin; they also knew that phenylalanine was at the end of one of the chains. The insulin molecule appeared to consist of a large number of polypeptide chains, and it was held that what was important biologically was the sequence in which the amino acids followed each other in the chains. This sequence was unknown for any protein.

Sanger introduced the reagent fluorodinitrobenzene (FDNB), which reacted with the free amino acid at the end

of a chain to form a dinitrophenyl derivative (DNP) combined with that amino acid. The DNP acids were bright yellow. If the chains were then split by hydrolysis, the colored terminal acid of each link could be identified by chromatographic and electrophoretic methods. Sanger at first thought that the insulin molecule contained four long chains; but he later concluded that it consisted of only two chains containing 21 and 30 amino acids respectively. He then split the bridges joining the chains by oxidation with performic acid and dealt with each chain individually. The chain was separated into successively shorter links, and in each link the terminal amino acid was identified. He was able to determine the exact sequence of amino acids in each chain.

Sanger then determined that the two chains were linked by two disulfide bridges of cystine residues, with a third bridge linking two parts of the short chain. The determination of the exact positions of these bridges enabled Sanger, after over 12 years of research, to give a diagram for the structure of insulin. For this work he was awarded the Nobel Prize in Chemistry in 1958.

In 1951 Sanger was awarded the Corday-Morgan Medal of the Chemical Society. In 1954 he was elected a Fellow of the Royal Society and a Fellow of King's College, Cambridge; and in 1958 he was elected a Foreign Honorary Member of the American Academy of Arts and Sciences.

In 1980 Sanger shared the Nobel Prize for Chemistry with two other scientists for work determining the sequences of nucleic acids in DNA molecules. Their combined work has been lauded for its application to the research of congenital defects and hereditary diseases. It also proved vitally important in producing the artificial genes that go into the manufacture of insulin and interferon, two substances which are used to treat a variety of diseases. Sanger retired from research in 1983.

Further Reading

There was a biography of Sanger in *Nobel Lectures, Chemistry, 1942-1962* (1964). This work also included his Nobel Lecture, which gave an admirable summary of his work. For the chemical background see P. Karrer, *Organic Chemistry* (4th ed. 1950). See also the article "Sequences, Sequences, and Sequences" in *Annual Review of Biochemistry* (1988, pages 1-28), and *Nobel Prize Winners* (H. W. Wilson, ed. 1987, pages 921-924). □

Margaret Higgins Sanger

The pioneering work of Margaret Higgins Sanger (1884-1966), American crusader for scientific contraception, family planning, and population control, made her a world-renowned figure.

Margaret Higgins was born on Sept. 14, 1884, in Corning, N.Y. Her father was a thoroughgoing freethinker. Her mother was a devout Roman Catholic who had eleven children before dying of tubercu-

losis. Although Margaret was greatly influenced by her father, her mother's death left her with a deep sense of dissatisfaction concerning her own and society's medical ignorance. After graduating from the local high school and from Claverack College at Hudson, N.Y., she took nurse's training. She moved to New York City and served in the poverty-stricken slums of its East Side. In 1902 she married William Sanger. Although plagued by tuberculosis, she had her first child, a son, the next year. She had another son by Sanger, as well as a daughter who died in childhood.

Margaret Sanger's experiences with slum mothers who begged for information about how to avoid more pregnancies transformed her into a social radical. She joined the Socialist party, began attending radical rallies, and read everything she could about birth control practices. She became convinced that oversized families were the basic cause of poverty. In 1913 she began publishing a monthly newspaper, the *Woman Rebel,* in which she passionately urged family limitation and first used the term "birth control." After only six issues, she was arrested and indicted for distributing "obscene" literature through the mails. She fled to Europe, where she continued her birth control studies, visiting clinics and talking with medical researchers.

Sanger returned to the United States in 1916 and, after dismissal of the indictment against her, began nationwide lecturing. In New York City she and her associates opened a birth control clinic in a slum area to give out contraceptive information and materials. This time she was arrested under state law. She spent a month in prison, as did her sister.

Leaving prison in 1917, Sanger intensified her activities, lecturing, raising money from a group of wealthy patrons in New York, and launching the *Birth Control Review,* which became the organ of her movement for 23 years. Encouraged by a state court decision that liberalized New York's anti contraceptive statute, she shifted her movement's emphasis from direct action and open resistance to efforts to secure more permissive state and Federal laws. Although regularly in trouble with New York City authorities, she continued lecturing to large crowds and keeping in touch with European contraceptive research. Her brilliantly successful visit to Japan in 1922 was the first of several Asian trips. A year later she and her friends opened clinical research bureaus to gather medical histories and dispense birth control information in New York City and Chicago. By 1930 there were 55 clinics across the United States. Meanwhile Sanger obtained a divorce and married J. Noah H. Slee.

Margaret Sanger's fame became worldwide in 1927, when she helped organize and spoke before the first World Population Conference at Geneva, Switzerland. She and her follower continued to lobby for freer state and Federal laws on contraception and for the dissemination of birth control knowledge through welfare programs. By 1940 the American birth control movement was operating a thriving clinic program and enjoying general acceptance by the medical profession and an increasingly favorable public attitude.

For most Americans, Margaret Sanger *was* the birth control movement. During World War II her popularity continued to grow, despite her opposition to United States participation in the war based on her conviction that wars were the result of excess national population growth. In 1946 she helped found the International Planned Parenthood Federation. This was one of her last great moments. She was troubled by a weak heart during her last 20 years, although she continued traveling, lecturing, and issuing frequent statements. She died in Tucson, Ariz., on Sept. 6, 1966.

Further Reading

Margaret Sanger: An Autobiography (1938) incorporates much of Sanger's earlier *My Fight for Birth Control* (1931). The most recent biography is Emily Taft Douglas, *Margaret Sanger* (1969), a carefully researched and sympathetic account. See also Lawrence Lader, *The Margaret Sanger Story and the Fight for Birth Control* (1955). David M. Kennedy, *Birth Control in America: The Career of Margaret Sanger* (1970), focuses on her public career and examines the whole controversy over birth control. Less solid but of possible interest is the fictionalized biography by Noel B. Gerson, *The Crusader* (1969). Brief treatments of her are in Mary R. Beard, *Woman as a Force in History* (1946); Mark H. Haller, *Eugenics: Hereditarian Attitudes in American Thought* (1963); and Donald K. Pickens, *Eugenics and the Progressives* (1968). □

José de San Martín

The South American soldier and statesman José de San Martín (1778-1850) played an important role in winning the independence of several South American countries from Spain.

José de San Martín was born at Yapeyú, a village on the northern frontier of Argentina, where his father was an official of the Spanish colonial government. At the age of 7, San Martín returned to Spain with his parents. He entered the Royal Academy as a cadet and was educated there with sons of the nobility of Spain. As a member of the Spanish army, he fought in some of the campaigns against French forces in the Peninsular War and by 1811 had acquired the rank of lieutenant colonel.

Hearing of the revolt against Spain in his native Argentina, San Martín resigned from the Spanish army in 1812 and sailed for Buenos Aires to join the patriot forces. He took a prominent part in organizing Argentine troops and soon became military governor of the north to organize defense against Spanish troops in Upper Peru. In 1814 he secured the governorship of the province of Cuyo at the foot of the Andes. Here for 3 years he recruited and trained his Army of the Andes, since he believed that Argentina could not be safely independent unless Spanish forces were dislodged from Chile, Peru, and Bolivia.

In January 1817 San Martín led his army of Argentines and fugitives from Chile over the Andes and surprised the Spanish army in Chile. After having captured and occupied Santiago on February 15, San Martín was offered the supreme dictatorship of Chile but declined in favor of his

friend and colleague Bernardo O'Higgins. He made Chile completely free of Spanish troops by May 15, 1818, and began planning for an invasion of Peru.

San Martín was 2 years assembling a fleet which, under the able command of Lord Cochrane, swept Spanish shipping from the west coast of South America. In August 1820 the army of San Martín was transported toward Peru, convoyed by warships under Lord Cochrane. Within a year San Martín was able to occupy the capital, and on July 28, 1821, he proclaimed the independence of Peru from Spain. On August 3 he accepted the position of supreme protector of Peru.

However, considerable fighting was still needed before Peruvian independence was assured, since the bulk of the Spanish army had merely withdrawn into the mountains and was still a viable fighting force and a threat. San Martín considered that he did not have enough force to meet the Spaniards and would need the aid of the armies of Simón Bolívar, who had just liberated the areas of Venezuela, Colombia, and Ecuador. For that purpose, San Martín and Bolívar met at Guayaquil; that conference is one of the most disputed points in South American history.

Possibly they disputed over Guayaquil, which Bolívar had just occupied and which San Martín wanted to be a part of Peru. Possibly they disagreed on the type of government to be instituted in South America. San Martín did not believe that the South Americans were ready for democracy, and he probably preferred a constitutional monarchy, whereas Bolívar believed, at that time, in complete democracy. Possibly they disagreed on the terms by which the armies of Bolívar would be brought into Peru. At any rate, San Martín left the conference in a precipitous manner, returned immediately to Peru, resigned his power and positions to the Congress, and left Bolívar in undisputed leadership.

San Martín made his way to Argentina and then to Europe, where he spent the rest of his life. He died on Aug. 17, 1850, at Boulogne-sur-Mer.

Further Reading

The standard biography of San Martín is Bartolome Mitre, *The Emancipation of South America* (trans. 1893; new introduction, 1969), a good starting place for understanding the liberation of Chile and Peru. A popular short biography by an Englishman is John C. J. Metford, *San Martín: The Liberator* (1950). Other biographies include Anna Schoellkopf, *Don José de San Martín, 1778-1850: A Study of His Career* (1924); Margaret H. Harrison, *Captain of the Andes* (1943); and Ricardo Rojas, *San Martín: Knight of the Andes* (trans. 1945).

Additional Sources

The Liberator General San Martín: a bicentennial tribute, 1778-February 25-197, Washington: General Secretariat, Organization of American States, 1978?.

San Martín, José de, *The San Martín papers,* Washington, D.C.: Full Life: San Martín Society, 1988. □

Michele Sanmicheli

The Italian architect and military engineer Michele Sanmicheli (ca. 1484-1559) introduced to north Italy the Roman High Renaissance style of architecture. His work is generally characterized by a boldness and strength inspired by his military interests.

Born in Verona, Michele Sanmicheli went to Rome about 1500. With the counsel of the architect Antonio da Sangallo the Elder, Sanmicheli served from 1509 as supervisor of the completion of the facade of the Cathedral at Orvieto. His first involvement with military architecture was in 1526, when he inspected the papal fortifications in the Romagna with Antonio da Sangallo the Younger.

Returning to Verona about 1527, Sanmicheli began the Pellegrini Chapel (ca. 1528) attached to S. Bernardino. The interior of this circular, domed chapel is very richly decorated with relief sculpture and elegant Corinthian columns, some with spiral fluting. In 1529 he commenced work on the nearby fortifications of Legnago and was soon charged with the fortifications of many of the cities controlled by Venice, such as Verona (from 1530), Chioggia (from 1541), and Udine (from 1543). In 1535 he was appointed engineer of the state for lagoons and fortifications by the Venetian Senate, and from 1537 to 1539 he traveled to Corfu, Crete, and Dalmatia to design fortifications. Incorporated in these fortifications were powerful gates combining heavily rusticated stonework with massive Doric columns and prominent keystones, as in the Porta Nuova, Verona (1533-1550), the Forte di S. Andrea a Lido, Venice (1543-1549), and the Porta Palio, Verona (1548-1557).

The chronology of Sanmicheli's architecture in Verona is controversial. The spiral fluting of the half columns and the relief sculpture on the upper story of the Bevilacqua Palace resemble the interior of the Pellegrini Chapel, suggesting a date of about 1530 for the palace. The Canossa Palace (ca. 1530-1537) is much more planar and reveals the influence of Giulio Romano's work in Mantua. In the 18th century the roof was raised, drastically changing the character of the facade. The Pompei Palace (ca. 1550; now the Museo Civico) marks a return to the severe classicism of Donato Bramante, but the robust Doric order and large keystones resemble Sanmicheli's Porta Palio.

Sanmicheli designed two imposing palaces in Venice: the Cornaro a S. Polo Palace (after 1545-1564) and the Grimani Palace (ca. 1556-ca. 1567). On the mainland near Castelfranco Veneto he built the Villa La Soranza (ca. 1545-1550), of which only a portion of the service buildings is preserved. Originally the villa consisted of a casino flanked by separate one-story, arcaded service buildings. Built of brick covered with stucco lined in imitation of stone, it had a rustic character emphasized by the simplicity of architectural detail and omission of the classical orders.

The Lazzaretto, or pesthouse, outside Verona (1549-1603), attributed to Sanmicheli, was a large, rectangular, arcaded court lined with cells. In the center of the court was a circular chapel with dome on a high drum. At his death in August 1559 he had just begun another circular, domed church, the Madonna di Campagna (1559-1561) near Verona.

Further Reading

The only monograph in English on Sanmicheli is Eric J. Langenskiöld, *Michele Sanmicheli, the Architect of Verona: His Life and Works* (1938). Piero Gazzola edited *Michele Sanmicheli* (1960), a fully illustrated catalog for an exhibition of Sanmicheli's architectural work which contains a complete bibliography to 1960. Sanmicheli is discussed in Peter Murray, *The Architecture of the Italian Renaissance* (1963), and T. A. West, *History of Architecture in Italy* (1968). □

Jacopo Sansovino

The Italian artist Jacopo Sansovino (1486-1570) executed sculpture and architecture in Venice whose quality and extent create much of the effect of the city today.

Trained in Florence and active in Rome and Florence in the crucial early decades of the 16th century, Jacopo Sansovino became the man of destiny for Venetian architecture and trained so many young sculptors that Giorgio Vasari credited him with virtually running an academy. In his 40 years of service as principal architect to the city of Venice, Sansovino profited by his early Florentine training in his skillful use of sculpture to enrich and animate buildings distinguished by a breadth, grandeur, and structural harmony surely based on his close study and understanding of ancient and current Roman architecture.

Jacopo Tatti was born in Florence, the son of Antonio Tatti. In 1502 Jacopo entered the workshop of the sculptor and architect Andrea Sansovino and adopted his master's name. Jacopo followed Andrea to Rome in 1505; he may have assisted his teacher in the Rosso and Sforza tombs in S. Maria del Popolo, but he also worked independently restoring antiques and making one of the first copies of the newly excavated *Laocoon*.

Sansovino's earliest major commissions came shortly after he returned to Florence in 1511: the large statue *St. James* for the Cathedral of Florence and the nearly lifesize statue *Bacchus*. Both works reveal his technical facility; the ease in handling drapery invests the spare figure of St. James with a needed surface enrichment, and the graceful, swinging movement and dextrous carving makes the Bacchus instantly attractive.

After collaborating on the decorations for Pope Leo X's triumphal entry into Florence, Sansovino was disappointed in hopes for a share in the project to complete the facade of the Medici church of S. Lorenzo. He returned to Rome in 1518 and executed such varied works as the idealized *Madonna* in S. Agostino, the more taut and complex *St. James* in S. Maria del Monserrato, and the elaborate tomb of Cardinal St. Angelo in S. Marcello. He was also consulted on the preliminary designs for the Florentine church in Rome, S. Giovanni dei Fiorentini.

The violent disaster of the sack of Rome in 1527 proved ultimately a blessing for Sansovino, who, fleeing Rome for France, found in Venice a city that stimulated his full development as an artist and provided a totally congenial atmosphere. His first work there was the utilitarian but crucial problem of strengthening the dangerously weakened fabric of S. Marco. This led to his appointment as protomagister to S. Marco in 1529 and his decision to stay in Venice. While he soon became a leading figure in Venice, the friend of such men as Titian, Tintoretto, and Pietro Aretino and the easy associate of noble patrons, Sansovino never felt himself above a concern for the countless practical details that together affected the appearance of his adopted city.

Appointed principal architect of Venice in 1529, Sansovino also continued to execute sculpture, creating works ranging from the fluent precision and richness of his bronze sculpture for S. Marco (tribune reliefs, 1530s; statues of the Evangelists, 1553; doors, 1563) to the harsh colossal figures *Mars* and *Neptune* on the Scala dei Giganti of the Ducal Palaco (1550s). A more chilly and disciplined classicism characterizes his marble reliefs for the church of S. Antonio in Padua (1562).

Sansovino's most formidable assignments as an architect were centered in and near the Piazza di S. Marco. The Library, designed to provide handsomely for the collection left to the city of Venice by Cardinal Bessarion, the Mint, and the Loggetta involved different functions, but all demanded a careful adjustment to the preexisting buildings. The memorable impression of all these buildings in their relation to each other and to the one large open space in Venice, the Piazza di S. Marco demonstrates Sansovino's brilliance and originality as an architect. The Mint (1537-1554) is deliberately compact in its use of the severe Doric order and heavy rustication to emphasize its function as a secure treasury. The Library (1536-1554; completed by Vincenzo Scamozzi in 1588), with its long, horizontal facade kept low to harmonize with the Ducal Palace on the opposite side of the Piazzetta, is far richer in its architectural and sculptural detail and strong contrasts of light and shadow. The small Loggetta received the greatest amount of sculptural adornment in the form of a triumphal arch to act as a firm base for the soaring bell tower.

In addition to his major public buildings, Sansovino also regulated the markets, improved the city, and executed countless designs for churches, private dwellings, and mainland villas. While some of his designs were never executed or were completed by other architects, Sansovino's presence and the ideas expressed in his drawings and buildings exerted a strong and lasting influence on contemporary and later Venetian architects. His grand Corner Palace (begun 1537), for example, was decisive in its transformation of the lighter arcades and ornamental patterns of the persistent Venetian Gothic into the measured balance of the larger, simpler forms of Donato Bramante and current Roman architecture, adapted to Venetian requirements.

Sansovino died in Venice; one son was a distinguished writer. The quality of Sansovino's life is touchingly conveyed by Vasari, who wrote that he was ''very dear both to the great and to the small and to his friends'' and that ''his death was a grief to all Venice.''

Further Reading

The fullest and most important study of Sansovino remains that by Giorgio Vasari in *Lives of the Most Eminent Painters, Sculptors, and Architects,* edited by Gaston du C. de Vere, vol. 9 (1915; abr. ed. 1959). There is no modern biography in English, but John Pope-Hennessy, *Italian High Renaissance and Baroque Sculpture,* vol. 2 (1963), includes a discerning presentation of Sansovino's work as a sculptor. For a discussion of his architecture see Peter Murray, *The Architecture of the Italian Renaissance* (1963), and T. A. West, *A History of Architecture in Italy* (1968).

Additional Sources

Howard, Deborah, *Jacopo Sansovino: architecture and patronage in Renaissance Venice,* New Haven: Yale University Press, 1975. □

Antonio López de Santa Ana

The Mexican general and statesman Antonio López de Santa Ana (1794-1876) was often called the "man who was Mexico." An unprincipled adventurer, he dominated Mexico for some 25 years, during which he served as president six times, switching parties and ideologies at will.

The Mexican struggle for independence was as bloody and destructive as any in the Western Hemisphere. The struggle, a bitter civil war, destroyed trade, farming, communications, and commerce. The ultimate victors, conservative churchman and soldiers, had no intention of sharing their power or wealth with their millions of poor countrymen, of either Indian or mixed blood.

The three decades following independence (1821) saw a continuation of civil war as the small ranchers and farmers of the north and west tried to break the economic, political, and social stranglehold of the colonial elites. Virtually the only beneficiary of this struggle was the United States, which violently seized over 50 percent of Mexico's territory. Gen. Antonio López de Santa Ana did not cause this tragic situation or Mexico's varied problems. A vain, pompous man with great leadership qualities, he only used the contemporary chaos to personal advantage. His very character epitomized one of the most unfortunate periods in Mexican history.

Early Career

Antonio López de Santa Ana was born in Jalapa, Veracruz. His family was Spanish and Caucasian. His father, a well-to-do Veracruz mortgage broker, had estates in Jalapa. When Santa Ana was 16, the family sent him to the military academy, from which he graduated in time to serve in the royalist army against the forces of independence. He fought against Miguel Hidalgo, the priest and original leader of the independence movement, in Texas and distinguished himself in battle. Apparently a gambling scandal delayed his promotion, and by 1821, despite a distinguished record in the Spanish army, Santa Ana had reached only the rank of captain. In that year he defected to the conservative but proindependence army of Gen. Agustín de Iturbide. The grateful rebels made him first a colonel and later a brigadier general.

Santa Ana did not remain loyal for long; he was one of the first to pronounce against Iturbide's empire, seizing the port of Veracruz in the name of the 1823 revolt which ended Iturbide's short-lived imperial experiment. In 1823 Santa Ana endorsed a republic but later admitted that a Jalapa lawyer had only briefly explained to him all that he knew about republicanism. He remained a political illiterate all his life, one year a rabid Jacobin liberal, the next a monarchist.

In the late 1820s the "republican" general Santa Ana served various Mexican governments as an officer first in Yucatán and later in Veracruz. In 1827 he was one of the principal supporters of the presidential bid of independence hero Vicente Guerrero. The same year at Tampico he took the surrender of a small yellow fever-ridden Spanish force from Cuba which had attempted to invade Mexico. Now the "hero of Tampico," he became an important figure in the chaotic world of Mexican politics. The liberal Congress elected him president, and he took office in 1833 with the determined anticlerical Valentín Gómez Farías his vice president.

Presidential Career

Santa Ana's first presidency never even got started. The newly elected president pleaded sick and remained on his hacienda, Magna de Clavo, in Veracruz, leaving Gómez Farías as provisional president. The latter attacked Church and military legal privileges and attempted to reduce the army's size. Santa Ana then posed as the champion of traditional interests and overthrew Gómez Farías. Calling himself "liberator of Mexico," he assumed a dictatorship, dismissed Congress, restored military and ecclesiastical prerogatives, and exiled the leading liberals.

The result was a period of confusion: revolts and counterrevolts, with Santa Ana resigning and again taking office. In 1836 he led a Mexican army into Texas, and after some initial successes his forces were annihilated by Sam Houston at San Jacinto on April 21, 1836. Santa Ana, a prisoner of the Texans, signed the Treaty of Velasco, granting the withdrawal of Mexican troops and the "independence" of Texas. During a short sojourn as a prisoner in Washington, he conferred with President Andrew Jackson and returned to Mexico in February 1837.

While imprisoned in the United States, Santa Ana had been deposed by the conservative Congress, which had abrogated his agreement with the Texans and recalled former president Anastasio Bustamante. Still somehow a national hero, Santa Ana retired to Magna de Clavo for 18 months. In November 1838 he emerged to lead a Mexican force against a French squadron bombarding San Juan de Ulúa in the "pastry war." Caught in a cannonade, he lost a leg to the invaders, a sacrifice which apparently greatly increased his political appeal. He was now the "hero of Veracruz."

In 1839, faced with a liberal revolt, President Bustamante named Santa Ana interim president, a post which he held from March to July. In a period of further confusion and fiscal bankruptcy, Santa Ana doggedly maneuvered through various alliances. By October 1841 he had returned to Mexico City, where he was once again president of Mexico by virtue of a conservative junta. This time his government lasted until 1842. He raised revenue by taxation but spent lavishly on festivals and a private army. In March 1843 he again resumed the executive and ruled until July 1844. He apparently began to see the possibilities of a monarchy as the solution to Mexico's problems.

Overthrown in 1844, Santa Ana again retreated to Veracruz. In 1845 the government captured him and exiled him to Cuba. He solicited aid from the United States, promising to amicably settle the Texas boundary dispute if he returned to power. Permitted to pass through the American blockade of the Mexican coast, he broke his promise and began to prepare Mexico for war. In December 1846 he became Mexico's president. In 1847 he once more led Mexican troops against American forces. The Mexicans, badly beaten owing in part to Santa Ana's incompetence and in part to internal quarrels, lost much valuable territory. In 1847, fleeing both his Yankee and Mexican enemies, the general took refuge on the British Island of Jamaica, but his incredible career had not yet closed. He spent 2 years in Venezuela, devoting his time to farming while Mexico sank further into chaos.

In 1853 the conservatives again seized power. Their leader, Lucas Alamán, sponsored Santa Ana as an interim president until a suitable monarch could be found. In April 1853 Santa Ana again returned as president of Mexico. But Alamán's constructive influence ended with his death in June, and Santa Ana continued to dissipate government funds. In April 1854 he signed the Gadsden Treaty, selling Arizona to the United States for $10 million. In August 1855 the liberals, led by Juan Álvarez, revolted against the increasingly corrupt regime. Santa Ana again fled. A decade later he attempted to stage yet another comeback during the European intervention, but he no longer had any following. He again went into exile but was allowed to return in 1873 to Mexico. No longer a danger, he lived out his last days in semipoverty, dying in Mexico City in June 1876.

Further Reading

Santa Ana's own account is *The Eagle: The Autobiography of Santa Ana*, edited by Ann Fears Crawford (trans. 1967). There is no definitive work on Santa Ana. The basic biography, although dated, is Wilfrid Hardy Callcott, *Santa Ana* (1936; repr. 1964); also useful is Callcott's general study *Church and State in Mexico, 1822-1857* (1926). Oakah L. Jones, *Santa Anna* (1968), scholarly and well written, is not distinctly different from Callcott's account. Useful for a flavor of the times are the memoirs of Frances Erskine Calderón de la Barca, *Life in Mexico* (1843; new ed. 1966). The war with the United States and Santa Ana's role are best related in George Lockhart Rives, *The United States and Mexico, 1821-1848* (2 vols., 1913; repr. 1969), and Justin H. Smith, *The War with Mexico* (2 vols., 1919). For life in Mexico during the war see José Fernando Ramírez, *Mexico during the War with the United States*, edited by Walter V. Scholes (trans. 1950). □

Andrés de Santa Cruz

The Bolivian military leader Andrés de Santa Cruz (1792-1865) was a supporter of a united Peru-Bolivia and was president of a short-lived confederation of the two.

Andrés de Santa Cruz was born on Dec. 5, 1792, in La Paz, the mestizo son of a Peruvian Creole and a Bolivian Indian heiress. After receiving a Church-directed education in La Paz and Cuzco, he elected to follow his father's army career. He was commissioned in a militia unit in 1809 and began active duty a year later, with the onset of the Wars of Independence. His royalist service lasted until early 1821 and included military action in Bolivia (then Upper Peru) and Peru, as well as an interval as a prisoner of war in Argentina. In January 1821, when once again a captive, he volunteered for the patriot army and served the cause of liberation through the remaining 3 years of fighting.

Santa Cruz commanded units under both José de San Martín and Simón Bolívar, became chief of staff for the Peruvian units under the latter, and then was given a series of administrative assignments, first military and then, with the end of fighting, civilian ones.

In July 1825 Santa Cruz became prefect of Chuquisaca (now Sucre), the capital of the newly created Bolivia. He had opposed this Bolívar-designed transformation of Upper Peru, favoring a continued union with Peru. He nevertheless accepted a series of assignments, both in Bolivia and in Peru, given him by Bolívar. Santa Cruz was, in fact, serving in Lima as president of the Peruvian Council of State when, in September 1826, Bolívar left Peru to return to Colombia. In June 1827 Santa Cruz surrendered that office to an elected successor but, after a brief period in Chile, became the chief executive of Bolivia in early 1829. Until 1835 he gave his full attention to governing that country. Under his stern authority, order was restored and some economic gains were achieved.

Meanwhile, Peru was nearly torn apart by the rivalries of political and military factions. In 1835 Santa Cruz was invited to intervene and, with the help of Peruvian allies, established the Confederation of Peru and Bolivia. The new nation was to have three states, each with a large measure of autonomy but with overall control exercised by Santa Cruz, now named to the office of supreme protector.

The union was maintained, although shakily, until early 1839, when it was brought to an end by the united efforts of Argentina, Chile, and its Peruvian opponents. Santa Cruz, forced out of both Peru and Bolivia, spent the next 6 years, mostly in Ecuador, plotting a return to power. In 1845, when it was clear that Chile and the other nations would not allow this, he left for Europe, where he remained for the rest of his life.

Further Reading

There is no biography of Santa Cruz in English, although his career is partially discussed in several general histories of Peru and Bolivia, most notably Frederick B. Pike, *The Modern History of Peru* (1967), and Robert Barton, *A Short History of the Republic of Bolivia* (1968). For an understanding of Chile's opposition to the confederation see Robert N. Burr, *By Reason or Force: Chile and the Balancing of Power in South America, 1830-1905* (1965). See also Charles W. Arnade, *The Emergence of the Republic of Bolivia* (1957). □

Bartholomew Augustine Santamaria

Bartholomew Augustine Santamaria (born 1915), a Roman Catholic publicist and organizer in Australia, founded the Catholic Social Movement.

Bartholomew Santamaria was born in Brunswick, Victoria, on Aug. 14, 1915, the son of Italian immigrants. He was educated at the University of Melbourne and soon became prominent as a Roman Catholic ideologist and organizer in Victoria. In 1937 he became assistant director and, in 1947, director of the National Secretariat of Catholic Action. This organization had been founded to enlist the support of the laity in the pastoral work of the Roman Catholic Church and existed in all parts of the world under the patronage of the Pope. In 1943 Santamaria created, and became president of, the Catholic Social Movement, which was organized and largely recruited by the members of Catholic Action.

By the 1940s Santamaria's principal concern was the advance of communism in the Australian Labour party, and to counter it he sought to organize the Catholics in the trade union movement. He and his followers in the Labour party in Victoria regarded communism rather than capitalism as the enemy. They attempted to secure the elimination of communists from the leadership of the trade unions.

The Catholic Social Movement supported efforts of the non-Labour federal government of Robert Gordon Menzies to proscribe communism. Fearing socialism as a potential menace to the property of the Catholic Church, the organization was vigorously antagonistic to some of the more radical and dogmatic ideas of the Labour party. Santamaria's influence within the ranks of the Victoria Labour party steadily increased, causing much sectarian bitterness. In October 1954 the federal leader of the Australian Labour party, Herbert Vere Evatt, publicly denounced what he called "a small minority of Labour members located particularly in the state of Victoria" who, he said, had become "increasingly disloyal to the Labour movement and the Labour leadership."

This public accusation split the Labour party in Victoria; the supporters of Santamaria resigned from the party and formed themselves into what was termed the Anti-Communist Labour party and, later, the Democratic Labour party. In the elections in Victoria in May 1955, these dissident elements campaigned and voted independently of the Australian Labour party and contributed to the defeat of the state's Labour government. Similarly, in Queensland the split in the party resulted in the defeat of a state Labour government.

In the federal sphere, the Democratic Labour party, though never in a position to secure a substantial number of seats in Parliament, helped to destroy the Australian Labour party's chances of regaining office for the next decade and more. Santamaria himself, however, dropped out of public prominence, but he remained an important contributor to public debate on political problems facing Australia. He became a regular political columnist for *The Australian* and wrote several books on Australian politics and political leaders, including: *Archbishop Mannix: His Contribution to the Art of Public Leadership in Australia* (1978); *Against the Tide* (1981); *Daniel Mannix, the Quality of Leaderhship* (1984; and *Australia at the Crossroads: Reflections of an Outsider* (1987).

Further Reading

Santamaria's own account of the Catholic Social Movement can be found in his *The Price of Freedom* (1968) and in his contribution to Henry Mayer, *Catholics and the Free Society* (1961). *Point of View* (1969) was a collection of his commentaries on Australian foreign policy and domestic affairs. Tom Truman, *Catholic Action and Politics* (1960), was a detailed discussion of the entire subject. □

Pedro Santana

The Dominican Republic military leader and president Pedro Santana (1801-1864) inflicted several decisive defeats on Haitian forces, at one time or another quarreled with all sectors of his country's society, and finally led the Dominican Republic into annexation by Spain.

Born in Hincha, Pedro Santana appears, from his portraits, to have been of mixed Caucasian, African, and Indian ancestry. Unlike his contemporary Buenaventura Baez, he was uneducated, rough, and uncouth; but like Baez, he did not lack for personal courage.

Fresh from military triumphs over the Haitians, on July 12, 1844, only 5 months after the Dominican declaration of independence, Santana and his troops deposed his country's provisional government. He called a convention which drafted the Dominican Republic's first constitution. It was promulgated on Nov. 6, 1844, and according to one of its provisions, that the convention select the president for the first two terms, Santana became his country's first constitutional president.

Baez acceded to the presidency after Santana's handpicked successor refused to serve. Beset by financial problems and the ever present possibility of revolt, Baez resigned on Aug. 4, 1848, but was recalled to inflict still another defeat on the Haitians, who were trying to reconquer the Dominican Republic. Santana then again deposed a president and was given the title of "Liberator."

From the ensuing electoral confusion, on Dec. 24, 1849, Baez was chosen president. At the end of his term, on Feb. 15, 1853, he passed the power back to Santana. This was one of the rare occasions when a Dominican president served out his term and constitutionally and personally delivered up the office to his successor. However, Santana and Baez soon fell out, and the next decade of Dominican history revolved around their quarrels.

By July 1853 Santana had exiled Baez, accusing him of treason. Baez countered with accusations of despotism, which appeared to be accurate as Santana constantly fought with his Congress, banishing or shooting his opponents. In 1854 Santana called another constitutional convention, extended his own term to 6 years, and established the office of vice president.

Under Santana's second presidency, on Dec. 22, 1855, the final Haitian invasion was defeated. Nevertheless, by March 26, 1856, he had again resigned. This paved the way for the return of Baez, who promptly exiled Santana. But by mid-1857 he was back, and after prolonged strife he was instrumental in toppling the Baez government on June 12, 1858. Using the 1854 Constitution, Santana had himself declared president on Jan. 31, 1859, repudiated many outstanding European debts, and appealed to Spain to annex the Dominican Republic. This was arranged, and on March 18, 1861, while the United States was distracted by its Civil War, the Dominican Republic again became a Spanish colony. Santana was named governor and captain general, with the rank of lieutenant general in the Spanish army.

True to form, Santana soon quarreled with his Spanish subordinates, who opposed his increasingly harsh methods of rule. He resigned on Jan. 7, 1862, and was granted a title and a lifetime pension.

By August 1863 the Dominicans revolted against the Spaniards. To help crush the revolt, Santana was given command of a Spanish force but because of insubordination was removed from this command. On the verge of being shipped off in disgrace to Cuba, Santana died in the capital, Santo Domingo, on June 14, 1864. The revolt, known as the War of the Restoration, culminated in the final retreat of all Spanish forces on July 11, 1865, and the Dominican Republic was once again independent.

Further Reading

Probably the classic work on the Dominican Republic is Sumner Welles, *Naboth's Vineyard* (2 vols., 1928; new foreword, 1966), which explains and interprets the history, culture, and society of that nation. Another valuable work is Otto Schoenrich, *Santo Domingo* (1918). Current useful studies include Robert D. Crassweller, *Trujillo* (1966), and John Bartlow Martin, *Overtaken by Events* (1966). □

Franciso de Paula Santander

Francisco de Paula Santander (1792-1840), a Colombian general and statesman, was one of the leaders of Spanish American independence. He later served as first constitutional president of the Republic of New Granada.

Francisco de Paula Santander was born on April 12, 1792, at Rosario de Cúcuta near the Venezuelan border. His family were cacao planters, members of the local gentry. When the independence movement began in 1810, he was a law student at Bogotá, but he soon left his books to join the patriot forces. Although the first independent government was crushed in 1816, Santander escaped to the eastern plains, or *llanos,* and there helped organize a base of continuing patriot resistance.

Accepting the leadership of the Venezuelan Simón Bolívar, Santander took part in the expedition that climbed the Colombian Andes, won the decisive victory of Boyacá (Aug. 7, 1819), and finally expelled the Spaniards from Bogotá. Bolívar placed him in charge of administering the liberated provinces, and 2 years later he was chosen vice president of the new nation of Gran Colombia, which included present-day Venezuela, Colombia, Panama, and Ecuador. Since Bolívar, as president, preferred to continue fighting at the head of his armies, Vice President Santander became acting chief executive.

Administrator of Gran Colombia

Though he held the rank of general, Santander is chiefly remembered as a vigorous civil administrator. He lacked Bolívar's magnetism but was a man of impressive personal bearing and dignity. Highly conscious of his own prerogatives, he nevertheless generally respected legal formalities: Bolívar dubbed him the "Man of Laws." As ruler, furthermore, he promoted a series of liberal reforms designed to curb clerical influence, aid economic development along lines of free enterprise, and extend public education.

Conflict with Bolívar

The stability of Gran Colombia was shaken in 1826 by the outbreak of a revolt in Venezuela under José Antonio Páez. Even more serious was a growing conflict between Santander and Bolívar, who later that year returned from Peru. Santander suspected Bolívar of seeking to change the constitution by illegal means and also resented his leniency toward Páez in finally settling the Venezuelan revolt. When Bolívar reassumed full control of the government in 1827, Santander drifted into open opposition, and in 1828 he was exiled on the charge, never really proved, of complicity in a plot against Bolívar's life.

After the dissolution of Gran Colombia in 1830, Santander's supporters gained control of the new Republic of New Granada, corresponding to modern Colombia plus Panama. Santander returned to serve as president from 1832 to 1837. He now showed greater caution in pressing liberal reforms, but he energetically repressed would-be conspirators, and he succeeded in organizing the national administration on a sound basis.

Santander retired briefly from public life on leaving the presidency, but he soon emerged to win a seat in the lower house of Congress. There he joined the opposition to his successor, the moderate liberal J. I. Márquez, whose election he had opposed. He was still serving in Congress at the time of his death in Bogotá on May 5, 1840.

Further Reading

Santander's political and administrative career, roughly from 1819 to 1827, is related in detail in David Bushnell, *The Santander Regime in Gran Colombia* (1954). He is also discussed in Jesús María Henao and Gerardo Arrubla, *History of Colombia* (1938). □

George Santayana

George Santayana (1863-1952), Spanish and American philosopher, developed a personal form of critical realism that was skeptical, materialistic, and humanistic.

George Santayana was unique among American and European philosophers during his long lifetime. While others strove to make philosophy "scientific" and to apply philosophy and science to society, Santayana proclaimed, "My philosophy neither is nor wishes to be scientific." He rejected the inherited genteel tradition in American thought as well as his contemporaries' pragmatism, idealism, and positivism. He openly disliked the liberal and democratic drift of Western civilization. In his philosophy he strove to combine philosophical materialism and a deep concern for spiritual values. A prolific writer with a graceful style, he also published several volumes of poetry, and his most popular book was a novel, *The*

Last Puritan (1936). He is singular among American philosophers for the special flavor of his thought and for his treatment of religion and art.

Life, Career, and Personality

As a girl Santayana's mother was taken to the Philippines, where she met and married George Sturgis, a Bostonian. Santayana later observed that this "set the background for my whole life." After being widowed, she tried to settle in Boston with her children but soon returned to Spain and remarried. The only child of this marriage was born in Madrid on Dec. 16, 1863, and christened Jorge Agustin de Santayana. He lived until the age of 9 in Ávila with his father, a lawyer and student of painting, then joined his mother, who was raising the children of her first marriage in Boston. Although he visited his father in Ávila and traveled in Europe frequently, Santayana lived and wrote in America for the next 40 years. As a boy he was quiet, studious, and lonely.

In spite of his connection to the Boston Sturgises and his American education, Santayana never felt fully at home in the United States. Indeed, he never felt fully at home anywhere. Dark-eyed, gentle, unobtrusive, witty, and very detached, he described himself as "a stranger at heart." His philosophy is clearly marked by a sense of detachment. "I have been involuntarily uprooted," he explained without regret. "I accept the intellectual advantages of that position, with its social and moral disqualifications."

Santayana's years at Harvard College, which he attended after Boston Latin School, were generally happy and satisfying. After graduating from Harvard in 1886, he studied philosophy in Germany. He returned to America in 1888 and completed the work for his doctorate in philosophy under the direction of Josiah Royce at Harvard. In 1889 Santayana joined Harvard's department of philosophy, with the apparent intention of retiring as soon as it was financially possible. When he inherited a modest legacy, he resigned his professorship in 1912.

Santayana lived the remainder of his life in Europe, traveling extensively and eventually settling in Italy. He spent his final years in Calvary Hospital, Rome, under the care of the Sisters of the Little Company of Mary. He died on Sept. 26, 1952.

His Philosophy

Santayana's true life was intellectual. "My career was not my life," he wrote. "Mine has been a life of reflection." His philosophy reflected the diversity of his own experience. Spanish Catholic by cultural inheritance and personal inclination, Protestant American by education and environment, disengaged by circumstances and temperament, he regarded his philosophy as a synthesis of these traditions. It is not surprising that his philosophy is full of ironies and ambiguities. At the same time, he was consistent in his concerns, if not in his opinions, and in the mood and tone of his philosophy. His primary orientation was spiritual, although not in the conventional sense, and his primary interest was moral, in the broadest sense.

The philosophy of Santayana is characterized by its skepticism, materialism, and humanism. His skepticism is evident throughout his writings: "My matured conclusion has been that no system is to be trusted, not even that of science in any literal or pictorial sense; but all systems may be used and, up to a certain point, trusted as symbols." His materialism or naturalism was "the foundation for all further serious opinions." Unlike that of so many contemporaries, Santayana's materialism depended not on science but on his own experiences and observations, for which he found philosophical confirmation in the works of Democritus, Lucretius, and Spinoza. In addition, in Greek ethics he found a vindication of order and beauty in human institutions and ideas. His systematic reading and thought culminated in the writing of his masterwork, *The Life of Reason* (5 vols., 1905-1906), which he intended as a critical history of the human imagination. He developed his philosophy further in *Scepticism and Animal Faith* (1923), which served as an introduction to his philosophical consummation, *Realms of Being* (4 vols., 1927-1940).

Santayana's materialism, the foundation of his philosophy, was the conviction that matter is the source of everything; he held that there are purely natural or materialistic causes of all the phenomena of existence. Consequently, thought is the product of material organization and process. Throughout *The Life of Reason* he assumed that the whole life of reason was generated and controlled by the animal life of man in the bosom of nature. One critic has described him as a nondeterministic fatalist who believed that dark, irrational, impersonal powers determined events. The human mind could not affect nature. Santayana wrote, "We are creatures and not creators." This important feature of his thought is clear in his conception of essences, which he defined as the obvious features that distinguish facts from each other. Apart from the events they may figure in, essences have no existence. Ironically, the mind cannot know existence; it can know only essences. This means that there is no necessary relation between what is perceived (or thought) and what exists. Consequently, "The whole life of imagination and knowledge comes from within." It is no wonder that Santayana was thoroughly skeptical about the possibility of attaining genuine knowledge.

It is also no wonder that Santayana believed that the works of the imagination "alone are good; and [that] the rest—the whole real world—is ashes in its mouth." Religion, science, art, philosophy were all works of the imagination. But religion he regarded as "the head and front of everything." In spite of his sympathies, Santayana was not a practicing Catholic and did not believe in the existence of God. He considered religion a work of the imagination: "Religion is valid poetry infused into common life." The truth of religion was irrelevant, for all religions were imaginative, poetic interpretations of experience and ideals, not descriptions of existing things. The value of religion was moral, as was the value of art.

Beauty, to Santayana, was a moral good. He valued the arts precisely because they are illusory. Like religion, he explained, genuine art expresses ideals that are relevant to human conditions. "Of all reason's embodiments," Santayana exulted, "art is . . . the most splendid and complete." "This is all my message," he wrote by way of summary, "that morality and religion are expressions of human nature; that human nature is a biological growth; and finally that spirit, fascinated and tortured, is involved in the process, and asks to be saved."

His Influence

Santayana had few disciples, but his philosophy has attracted considerable critical attention since his death. The grace and beauty of his prose and the strength of his intellect partly account for this interest. In addition, in the intellectual climate of the years following World War II his philosophy of disillusion struck a sympathetic chord. Santayana, like others of his generation, found himself confronted with a choice between Catholicism and complete disillusion. He did not hesitate or complain: "I was never afraid of disillusion, and I have chosen it."

Further Reading

Santayana's autobiography, *Persons and Places* (3 vols., 1944-1953), reveals his personality, character, and some of his key ideas. It is supplemented by his Letters, edited by Daniel Cory (1955). An excellent anthology is Irwin Edman, ed., *The Philosophy of Santayana: Selections from All the Works of George Santayana* (1936; rev. ed. 1953).
Valuable critical and descriptive essays on his philosophy and Santayana's replies are in Paul Arthur Schilpp, ed., *The Philosophy of George Santayana* (1940; 2d ed. 1951). Although there is no full intellectual biography of Santayana, Mossie M.

Kirkwood, *Santayana: Saint of the Imagination* (1961), is a pleasant introduction. Willard E. Arnett, *George Santayana* (1968), compares Santayana's philosophy with that of his contemporaries. □

Alberto Santos-Dumont

Alberto Santos-Dumont (1873-1932) was a Brazilian inventor of dirigibles and airplanes. He was the first man to successfully combine the internal combustion engine with ballooning, and Europeans long believed him to be also the first to fly a heavier-than-air motorized plane.

Alberto Santos-Dumont the grandson of a French emigrant to Brazil, was born in the state of Minas Gerais. His father was an engineer, entrepreneur, and coffee planter, married to the daughter of a distinguished Brazilian family. In 1891 Alberto was sent to Paris to study mechanics and other sciences, more or less on his own. His father's death the next year left Alberto a fairly wealthy young man. After 4 years of desultory studies, the alternately dreamy and practical Brazilian began to devote all his money and energy to his inventions.

The idea of flight had long exerted a strange fascination for the boy; and as a wealthy and daring young man, he was also one of the first Parisians to invest in a gasoline-driven automobile. He made his first balloon flight in the spring of 1898, blown by the wind and depending for ascent and descent on the careful balancing of ballast and gas-produced lift. Like many others at the time, he was struck by the possibility of attaching a gasoline motor with propeller to a balloon and thus being able to drive against the wind as well as to change altitude by pointing the craft upward or downward. He was the first to succeed in doing so (fall 1898), 2 years before the successful flight of the rigid dirigibles later known as Zeppelins. In 1901, after several setbacks, he won the Deutsch de la Meurthe Prize of 100,000 francs and much acclaim for the first airship to complete a specified circuit around the Eiffel Tower and back within a half hour.

A few years later Santos-Dumont turned his attention to manned flight in craft that were heavier than air. In September 1906 he flew the "14-bis," an awkward machine resembling a box kite, for a few feet, and within the next 2 months he won prizes for the first aircraft to fly 25 meters and the first to do 100. Three years earlier the Wright brothers had flown in the United States, but their feat had been at first ignored and then systematically denied by most of the American press, so that Europeans hailed Santos-Dumont as the first man to fly. As often happens with inventors, others were fast on his heels, and his own achievement hastened their work. A few months later he himself flew all over Paris in a new and graceful instrument of his design that resembled a modern airplane.

In 1910 Santos-Dumont retired from aviation, apparently because of the onset of multiple sclerosis. He then

entered a period of slow physical and mental decline ending in his suicide in Brazil at the age of 59.

Further Reading

Santos-Dumont's autobiography is *My Airships: The Story of My Life* (1904). Peter Wykeham, *Santos-Dumont: A Study in Obsession* (1963), is a balanced, fair account that avoids both adulation and deprecation, but it is inadequately documented. An older account is Henrique Dumont Villares, *Santos-Dumont: The Father of Aviation* (trans. 1956).

Additional Sources

Wykeham, Peter, *Santos-Dumont,* New York: Arno Press, 1980, 1962. □

Edward Sapir

Edward Sapir (1884-1939) was a distinguished American linguist and anthropologist who developed a basic statement on the genetic relationship of Native American languages and pioneered in modern theoretical linguistics.

E dward Sapir was born in Lauenburg, Germany, on Jan. 26, 1884, and emigrated in his early childhood to the United States, first living in Richmond, Va., and then moving to New York City, where he spent the greater part of his youth. As a student at Columbia University, he first studied Germanics, but under the influence of Franz Boas, the founder of modern American anthropology, Sapir switched to anthropology and linguistics. His main contributions concerned Native American, Indo-European, and general linguistics; American Indian and general anthropology; and what has come to be called culture and personality, or psychological anthropology. Beyond these scientific pursuits Sapir also made numerous contributions to American letters by publishing reviews and poems in such journals as *Poetry, the Dial, Freeman,* and the *Nation.*

Study of Native American Languages

Upon receiving a doctorate at Columbia, Sapir obtained his first important position, as head of the division of anthropology at the Canadian National Museum in Ottawa, in 1910. During the 15 years spent in Canada, Sapir studied the Native American languages of western Canada. This work, coupled with previous studies in the United States of Takelma, Chinook, Yana, and Paiute, permitted Sapir, in collaboration with his colleagues, to simplify and considerably clarify the earlier genetic classification of American languages.

Two important works were published during the Canadian years. The first, *Time Perspective in Aboriginal American Culture: A Study in Method* (1916), was a succinct account of the techniques available to ethnographers for the reconstruction, in the absence of written sources, of culture history. This short monograph represented a position paper, one of a number produced in those years by Franz Boas and his students, in counter-statement to the rather facile historiography promulgated by the various schools of evolutionary determinism that had been current from the 19th century until well into the first decades of the 20th.

The second work, Sapir's only full-length book, was an introduction to scientific linguistics *Language* (1921)—in which with great brilliance he delineated the full range of what the study of language, both structure and history, entails. *Language* included a discussion of phonetics as it was practiced at that time and a particularly subtle grammatical typology that took into account the great diversity of natural languages. In this book he also introduced the concept of linguistic drift, a theory arguing that grammatical change in language is never random but, rather, the result of certain systematic trends followed through in the course of a language or language family's history. He took as his main example the drift apparent in many Indo-European languages away from complex case systems in favor of syntactic position; that is, the grammatical function of a word tends to be indicated less by inflection than by its position in the overall sentence.

Linguistic and Cultural Theory

In 1925 Sapir accepted a teaching position in the newly created department of anthropology at the University of Chicago. During this period Sapir began publishing his most important papers in linguistic and cultural theory. The ideas and viewpoints set out in these papers had a deep and lasting influence on the subsequent development of linguistics and anthropology.

In "Sound Patterns in Language" (1925) Sapir demonstrated that the sounds of language are not merely physical but also mental or psychological phenomena, in that for all languages any sound is part of a system of discrete contrasts that are altered and combined in ways determined by shared linguistic conventions rather than physical necessity. That the systematic and conventional nature of sounds is available to the intuitions of a native speaker was set out in a paper published a number of years later ("The Psychological Reality of the Phoneme," 1933).

These two papers, especially the first, laid the groundwork for much that was to follow in the field of phonemics (the study of conventionally relevant sounds) and in large measure converged with, and to a certain extent anticipated, similar discoveries made by European linguists who had been working under the inspiration and influence of the Swiss linguist Ferdinand de Saussure.

Recognizing the unconscious reality of both the phonological and grammatical aspects of language led Sapir to argue that culture should be considered as patterns of individually learned conventions (both conscious and unconscious) rather than external facts ("The Unconscious Patterning of Behavior in Society," 1927). That is, in more current phrasing, culture is best defined as learned rules for behaving rather than the results of conventional behavior.

Two other important ideas already implicit in earlier work were succinctly formulated by Sapir during his Chicago years in his short paper "The Status of Linguistics as a Science" (1929). First, language, because of its central place in culture, acts as a "guide to 'social reality'" and to a large extent shapes, if not completely determines, an individual's and a culture's understanding and perception of the "external world," or reality. Second, language, which yields to systematic analysis, can in its study provide tools for the systematic investigation of other, more elusive aspects of culture.

Last Years

In 1931 Sapir was offered and accepted a position at Yale University as Sterling professor of anthropology and linguistics. At Yale he continued refining aspects of his theoretical positions, writing a series of papers on language and various aspects of culture for the *Encyclopaedia of Social Sciences*. He also, more than previously, devoted time and interest to the relationship between culture and the individual personality, always arguing that both must be taken into account if meaningful statements about one or the other are to be made. The exploratory papers written as a result of these interests had great influence in defining the general subject of culture and personality.

During these last years of his life, Sapir continued to find time for detailed work on particular languages, though at this time his interest shifted (though never completely) away from Native American languages to problems of Indo-European and Semitic linguistics. He died on Feb. 4, 1939.

Further Reading

A chapter-length portrait of Sapir is in Thomas A. Sebeok, ed., *Portraits of Linguists,* vol. 2 (1966). For general background see Hoffman R. Hays, *From Ape to Angel: An Informal History of Social Anthropology* (1958).

Additional Sources

Darnell, Regna, *Edward Sapir: linguist, anthropologist, humanist,* Berkeley: University of California Press, 1990. ☐

Sappho

Sappho (ca. 625-570 B.C.), a Greek lyric poet, was the greatest female poet of antiquity. Her vivid, emotional manner of writing influenced poets through the ages, and her special quality of intimacy has great appeal to modern poetic tastes.

The poetry of Sappho epitomizes a style of writing evolved during the 7th and 6th centuries B.C. At that time the main thrust of Greek poetry turned away from the epic form, which was concerned mainly with telling the stories of heroes and gods, utilizing the traditional and highly formulaic dactylic hexameter. The poets of the 7th and 6th centuries wrote choral songs, which were sung and danced by a choir, and solo songs, in which the poet was accompanied by a lyre or flutelike instrument. Doubtless these types of composition had existed side by side with the epic tradition, but after 700 B.C. poets refined the techniques of the choral and solo song, employing a variety of meters and a wide range of subject matter. Among the most prominent features of this kind of poetry were the infusion of the poet's personality and a concentration on his own inner feelings and motivations. No poet of this period displays the personal element more than Sappho.

Her Life

Despite the highly personal tone of her poetry, Sappho gives very few details of her life. She was born either in the town of Eresus or in Mytilene on the island of Lesbos in the northern Aegean Sea and lived her life in Mytilene. She is said to have married a wealthy man named Cercylas, and she herself mentions a daughter, Cleis. Apparently Sappho came from one of the leading noble families in Mytilene, and, although she herself never mentions politics, tradition has it that her family was briefly exiled to Sicily shortly after 600 B.C.

Sappho had three brothers: Larichus, who served as a wine bearer in the town hall of Mytilene (an honor reserved for youths of good family); Charaxus, a merchant, whom Sappho scolds in her poetry for loving a prostitute in Egypt; and Eurygyus. There is some evidence that she lived to a fairly old age. Tradition relates that she was not beautiful but "small and dark." A more charming description is a one-line fragment from another Aeolian poet, Alcaeus: "Violet-haired, pure, honey-smiling Sappho." The legend that she

of polite "finishing school" which prepared young ladies for marriage or that she was the leader of a *thiasos* (religious association), sacred to Aphrodite, in which girls were taught singing and other fine arts, with no hint of sexual irregularity. The precise nature of this circle of young women remains unclear. From the poems themselves it is clear that Sappho associated with girls, some of whom came from long distances, to whom and about whom she wrote poems detailing her frankly erotic feelings toward them.

Sappho's poetry is characterized by its depth of feeling and delicacy and grace of style. She wrote in her native Aeolian dialect, using ordinary vocabulary; her thoughts are expressed simply and unrhetorically but with exquisite care. Her grace and charm together with her technical skill in handling language and meter are most fully realized in the several longer fragments which have survived. One poem, "He appears to me like a god," a masterpiece of erotic lyric poetry, was closely imitated by the Roman poet Catullus over 500 years later and suggests the esteem in which the ancients held Sappho. Plato called her "the tenth Muse."

Further Reading

An excellent modern translation of Sappho with Greek text and notes is Willis Barnstone, *Sappho* (1965). The best general account in English of Sappho's life and poetry is Sir Cecil M. Bowra, *Greek Lyric Poetry from Alcam to Simonides* (1936; rev. ed. 1961). A more detailed analysis of Sappho's works is Denys L. Page, *Sappho and Alcaeus: An Introduction to the Study of Ancient Lesbian Poetry* (1955; rev. ed. 1959). □

killed herself by leaping from the Leucadian Rock out of love for a young man named Phaon is one of many fictitious stories about her.

Her Works

We can only estimate how much Sappho actually wrote, but her output must have been large because her works were collected in nine books (arranged according to meter) in the 3d century B.C. Although she enjoyed great popularity in antiquity, changes in literary fashion, the general decline of knowledge in the early Middle Ages, and Christian distaste for a poet who was considered vile resulted in the loss of most of her poetry. Book 1 alone contained 1,320 lines; yet a total of fewer than 1,000 lines survive, many of them preserved by ancient grammarians citing peculiarities of the Aeolian dialect. Since the late 19th century many new fragments have been recovered from papyrus finds in Egypt.

Except for a few wedding songs and some narrative poems, most of what remains of Sappho's poetry may be termed "occasional pieces," addressed to some person or to herself, very personal in content and manner. The subject is nearly always love and the attendant emotions—affection, passion, hatred, and jealousy—which Sappho felt toward the young girls who made up her "circle" or her rivals in love. Much scholarly controversy rages over the relationship between Sappho and the women about whom she wrote. On the one hand, it has been maintained that she was a corrupter of girls and instructed them in homosexual practices; on the other hand, it is said that she headed a kind

Sir Tej Bahadur Sapru

Sir Tej Bahadur Sapru (1875-1949) was an Indian lawyer and statesman. His career aptly illustrates the significance of the legal profession in the political and constitutional development of India.

Tej Bahadur Sapru was born in Aligarh into an aristocratic Kashmiri Brahmin family living in Delhi. He attended high school in Aligarh and matriculated at Agra College, where he took his law degree. After an apprenticeship at Moradabad he joined the Allahabad High Court in 1898. He was knighted in 1923 for outstanding legal contributions. He set impeccable standards in his personal and professional life and possessed a scholarly knowledge of Persian and Urdu as well as English.

Sapru was appointed a member of the governor general's executive council and served on the Round Table Conferences in London and on the Joint Parliamentary Committee. As a liberal favoring moderate change within the constitutional and legal framework, Sapru worked untiringly in the role of mediator between the British authority and Indian nationalists and between Hindu and Moslem leaders. He sought, for example, to mediate between the Congress and the British in the Round Table Conferences but was unable to exact concessions from either side. In other instances he was successful, as with the Gandhi-Irwin

Pact in 1931. He objected equally to Congress tactics of civil disobedience as prejudicial to compromise and to government imprisonment of Congress leaders.

Most notably he was chairman of the Sapru Committee, appointed in November 1944 by the Standing Committee of the Non-party Conference. The committee was charged with examining the whole communal question in a judicial framework following the breakdown of the Gandhi-Jinnah talks on communal problems. Sir Tej selected 29 committee members representative of all communal groups. The committee submitted proposals to the viceroy, Lord Wavell, in an attempt to break the political deadlock ensuing on the collapse of the Gandhi-Jinnah talks.

The committee's report contained a detailed historical analysis of proposals and claims of each community and a rationale for its constitutional recommendations. On the critical question of partition, the Sapru Committee made a final but fruitless plea to avert the creation of Pakistan. Sapru was also a member of the defense committee in the 1945 trials of Indian National Army officers for treason. The defenses argued that as the INA was an independent army representing an independent government-in-exile, its officers could not be prosecuted for treason.

Throughout the constitutional debates Sapru played a key moderating role, appealing at each stage to Hindu and Moslem and to Englishman and Hindu to conciliate their differences. He sought in the process to safeguard the rights of each communal group. He died on Jan. 20, 1949.

Further Reading

An excellent source of information on Sapru's career is an article about him by Donald Anthony Low in *Soundings in Modern South Asian History,* edited by Low (1968). Aspects of his career are also discussed in Cyril Henry Philips and Mary Doreen Wainwright, eds., *The Partition of India: Policies and Perspectives, 1935-1947* (1970). For general historical background see Romesh Chandra Majumdar and others, *An Advanced History of India* (1946; 3d ed. 1967).

Additional Sources

Bose, Sunil Kumar, *Tej Bahadur Sapru,* New Delhi: Publications Division, Ministry of Information and Broadcasting, Govt. of India, 1978.

Mohan Kumar, *Sir Tej Bahadur Sapru: a political biography,* Gwalior: Vipul Prakashan, 1981. □

John Singer Sargent

John Singer Sargent (1856-1925) was America's most technically brilliant portrait painter. His work profoundly influenced his generation.

Born on Jan. 20, 1856, in Florence, Italy, of American parents, John Singer Sargent spent the greater part of his life in Europe but made frequent short visits to the United States. His father was a doctor from Gloucester,

Mass.; his mother, who came from Philadelphia, preferred Continental life and persuaded her husband to give up his medical practice. Sargent was a born artist, very precocious, and fortunate in having his mother's encouragement. At the age of 9 he was sketching animals at the Paris Zoo. In 1868-1869 he worked in the studio of Carl Welsch in Rome, then attended school in Florence and took courses at the Accademia delle Belle Arti.

In 1874 the family settled in Paris, and Sargent worked at the École des Beaux-Arts, but in October he entered the studio of Carolus-Duran, a skillful portrait painter. In 1876 Sargent made his first trip to America, to establish his American citizenship. In 1877 he exhibited a portrait of Miss Watts, his first appearance at the Paris Salon. After an early period of realism he went through an impressionist phase, as seen in the two versions of *Luxembourg Gardens at Twilight* (1879). His most brilliant early portrait was of Mrs. Charles Gifford Dyer (1880). The tragic beauty of the face shows the artist's intuitive faculties. The *Pailleron Children* (1880) shows great sophistication and an almost Jamesian sinisterness. His great early success, more liked by fellow artists than by critics, was the *Daughters of Edward Darley Boit,* shown at the Salon of 1883. Four little girls are placed asymmetrically in a composition as remarkable for its subtle balances as for its luminous effect.

Sargent's most daring and brilliant portrait, known as *Madame X,* was of Madame Gautreau, one of the most elegant and fashion-conscious beauties of Parisian society. He painted her standing, wearing an extremely lowcut evening gown, and he made effective use of the contrast of her

white skin with the black dress. When the picture was shown at the Salon of 1884, the public as well as her family were shocked, and Sargent was forced to withdraw it. Largely because of this, he left Paris and established himself in London, where he remained for the rest of his life.

In the mid-1880s Sargent painted two portraits of Robert Louis Stevenson, both brilliant, spontaneous, and sensitive portrayals of this frail and talented man. In 1887 Sargent went to America to paint the Marquands and a stark and commanding portrait of the austere matriarch Mrs. Adrian Iselin. By 1890 he was so firmly established that all the peeresses and notables of England clamored for the privilege of having him do their portraits. In 1898 Asher Wertheimer, a famous London art dealer, commissioned him to paint all the members of his family. One of the finest of this group is the portrait of Mrs. Wertheimer, which is elegant and impervious but facile and penetrating. His portrait of the great beauty Lady Sassoon, dressed in the highest fashion, is sparkling and vivacious and a technical tour de force. Although he painted men less often than women, one of his most dashing achievements was of Lord Ribblesdale in riding costume. The Duchess of Devonshire, the Duchess of Sutherland, the Countess of Warwick, and dozens of others were all painted with the same facile elegance. He also did groups such as the Marlborough family, the Sitwell family, and the Wyndham sisters.

Some of Sargent's greatest accomplishments were in watercolor, which he undertook mostly during summer trips to the Tirol, Italy, and Spain. These works are transparent, luminous, and brilliantly executed. In 1890 he was commissioned to do murals for the Boston Public Library (completed in 1916), the finest of which is the series of prophets. In 1916 he executed murals for the rotunda of the Museum of Fine Arts, Boston. He died in London on April 15, 1925.

Further Reading

Biographies of Sargent include W. H. Downes, *John S. Sargent* (1925); Frederick A. Sweet, *Sargent, Whistler and Mary Cassatt* (1954); and Charles Merrill Mount, *John Singer Sargent* (1955). See also David McKibbin, *Sargent's Boston* (1956).

Additional Sources

Fairbrother, Trevor J., *John Singer Sargent,* New York: Abrams, 1994.
Olson, Stanley, *John Singer Sargent, his portrait,* New York: St. Martin's Press, 1986.
Ratcliff, Carter, *John Singer Sargent,* New York: Abbeville Press, 1982.
Weinberg, H. Barbara (Helene Barbara), *John Singer Sargent,* New York: Rizzoli International: Distributed by St. Martin's Press, 1994. □

Sargon II

The Assyrian king Sargon II (reigned 722-705 B.C.) was one of the chief architects of the late Assyrian Empire and the founder of its greatest line of kings.

Sargon II, upon his accession, took the name Sharrukin (Sargon is the biblical form), after the illustrious founder of the Akkadian dynasty, who had died 1,600 years before. This name and the fact that his predecessor, Shalmaneser V, reigned very briefly suggest that Sargon may have been a usurper. His first task was to restore order and overcome opposition at home; he then turned to the problems facing his army on the frontiers of the empire. He captured Samaria, the Israelite capital, and deported its inhabitants; next he defeated the rebel Syrian vassels at Qarqar. In the northeast, the turbulent Iranian tribes had been stirred into revolt by Assyria's old enemy, the Kingdom of Urartu. Punitive campaigns between 719 and 717 B.C. restored order, but trouble broke out again, and in 715 Sargon, in a demonstration of strength, marched round Lake Urmia to Van, Urartu's capital. Van held out, however, creating a stalemate on Assyria's northern frontier.

In 717 Sargon was faced with a revolt in the west encouraged by King Midas of Phrygia. Sargon's army overran northern Syria and the Taurus region, and by 710 all Syria and Palestine had submitted to Assyrian rule with the exception of Judah; Egypt was friendly. Only the Babylonians enjoyed virtual independence under their Chaldean leader, Merodach-Baladan; but when Sargon marched south in 708, Merodach-Baladan fled to Elam, and Sargon was crowned king of Babylon. The king of Bahrein sent gifts, and so did seven kings of Cyprus. Like his ancient namesake, Sargon could claim sway from the Upper Sea (the Mediterranean) to the Lower Sea (the Persian Gulf).

Sargon lived in Calah (modern Nimrud), the military capital, which he fortified and embellished. He also created a new residence city, Sargonsburg, 15 miles northeast of Nineveh, near modern Khorsabad. The city, which was inaugurated in 706, took 10 years to build. It was laid out in a rectangle, and its walls were pierced by eight gates. The great palace and temple, which stood on a 50-foot-high citadel platform, contained spacious halls decorated with stone reliefs. Colossal figures of man-headed bulls stood at the doorways. Early in 705 Sargon was called to the northwest, where he fell in battle against the nomadic Cimmerians.

Further Reading

Contemporary sources are collected in *The Inscriptions of Sargon II, King of Assyria,* translated and edited by A. G. Lie (1929). For the University of Chicago's excavation of Sargonsburg consult Gordon Loud, *Khorsabad,* vol. 1 (1936), in which references are given to the publications of the 19th-century French excavators. Many of the sculptures from Khorsabad are now in the Louvre in Paris. Volume 3 of *The Cambridge Ancient History* (12 vols., 1925) contains a reliable general account of Sargon's reign by Sidney Smith. A. T. Olmstead, *Western Asia in the Days of Sargon of Assyria* (1908), is still of use.

Additional Sources

Kristensen, Anne K. G. (Anne Katrine Gade), *Who were the Cimmerians, and where did they come from?: Sargon II, the Cimmerians, and Rusa I,* Copenhagen: Det kongelige Danske videnskabernes selskab, 1988. □

Sargon of Agade

Sargon of Agade (reigned ca. 2340-2284 B.C.) was the first Semitic king of Mesopotamia. He founded the Akkadian dynasty and was the first ruler in history to win and hold an empire. He became a heroic figure of literature.

Sargon was born, according to legend, in the city of Saffron on the banks of the Euphrates. His father was a nomad, his mother a temple votary who set him, like Moses, afloat in a basket. He was found by a peasant who adopted him and brought him up. He became cupbearer to the king of Kish, and later he himself became king. He founded Agade, or Akkad (the site of which is not known), as his new capital and, by defeating the paramount ruler of the Sumerian city-states, became master of all Mesopotamia. In 34 battles he conquered ''as far as the shore of the sea.''

In the first year of his rule Sargon marched northwest up the Euphrates to conquer Hit and Mari (near Deirez-Zor), and in the eleventh year he reached the Mediterranean coast, claiming dominion over the Cedar Forest (Lebanon or Amanus, the latter now called Alma Dag) and the Silver Mountain (perhaps the eastern Taurus). Legends credit him with the conquest of the land of Tin and the island of Crete and also with a successful expedition to central Anatolia. The text relating this incident, called the ''King of Battle,'' may be based on stories handed down by trading colonies established by the Akkadians in this rich mining area. Whether or not Sargon went as far as the Salt Lake (Tuz Lake, or Tuz Gölü), he undoubtedly reached the Mediterranean and could with right claim territories ''from the Lower Sea [the Persian Gulf] to the Upper Sea'' and from the rising to the setting sun.

In other remarkable campaigns, Sargon went east to conquer the lands of Elam and Barakhshe, in the Plain of Khuzistan and the Zagros Mountains, and north to Assyria. The king lists say that he reigned for 56 years. In later ages his name was synonymous with success, and his adventures became legend. An itinerary which survives in a late Assyrian version credits him with further conquests, including the lands around the Persian Gulf and Bahrein and, perhaps, the coast of Makran.

Further Reading

For a recent study of the Akkadian period, with an ample bibliography, see C. J. Gadd's ''The Dynasty of Agade'' (1921) in the revised edition of volume 1 of the *Cambridge Ancient History* (12 vols., 1967). The contemporary inscriptions are translated by George A. Barton in *Royal Inscriptions of Sumer and Akkad* (1929); and the later legends are discussed in Sidney Smith, *Early History of Assyria* (1928). □

Sarit Thanarat

The Thai army officer and prime minister Sarit Thanarat (1908-1963) overthrew the government of Phibun Songkhram in 1957 and was responsible for initiating major programs of economic development and social welfare.

The son of Maj. Luang Rüangdetanan (Thongdi Thanarat), an army officer whose career was spent mainly on the eastern frontier and who is remembered for his translations from Cambodian, Sarit was born in Bangkok on June 16, 1908. His youth was spent with maternal relatives in the remote frontier district of Mukdahan in Nakhon Phanom Province, an experience which gave him a lifelong interest in and affinity for the Lao provinces of northeast Thailand. He attended a monastery school in Bangkok and entered the royal military academy in 1919. Completing his studies there only in 1928, he was commissioned a second lieutenant in 1929.

Sarit at first rose slowly in the army ranks. The first decade of his military career was spent in infantry regiments and training schools in Bangkok and nearby Lopburi. A major at the outbreak of war in 1940, he saw service in northern Thailand and at the conclusion of the war was in command of Thai occupation troops in the Federated Shan States of northeast Burma.

Political Career

Unlike many of his fellow officers, Sarit did not take a prominent role in politics until 1947, when, as a colonel commanding an infantry battalion in Bangkok, he assumed a leading role in the military coup which overthrew civilian parliamentary government. This was the turning point in his public life. He was jumped in rank to major general and placed in command of the troops of the Bangkok military region and in 1949 was primarily responsible for crushing a navy and marine rebellion on behalf of Pridi Phanomyong. He then took charge of the 1st Army in Bangkok, which after 1932 always retained particular political significance. In that position he was responsible for suppressing a further attempted coup by the navy and marines in 1951.

Sarit's promotion in rank to lieutenant general in 1950 and general in 1952 served to confirm power he already had. The restoration of Phibun by the 1947 coup was in effect the assumption of power by a generation of army officers which, unlike Phibun and the leaders of prewar governments, had not had foreign training. They were slow in developing their own political leadership, and the coups and countercoups of the late 1940s and early 1950s saw a jockeying for power which by 1951 had resulted in a rivalry centering on two figures: Sarit—who became deputy commander of the army and deputy minister of defense in 1951 and commander in chief of the army in 1954—and Police Gen. Phao Siyanon, who became director general of the paramilitary police department in 1951 and acted as the strong arm of the regime.

Leader of a Coup

Phibun's power slipped rapidly in the 1950s as economic conditions worsened after the Korean War boom; official corruption became more blatant; and Phao's ruthless attacks on political rivals, the Chinese business community, and civilian political figures got out of hand. Sarit, having become a field marshal in 1956, was increasingly aloof from the regime, although he kept the loyalty of the armed forces and gained some popular support. When Phibun, in a bid for popular support to counterbalance his rivals, attempted a return to parliamentary government in 1957, Phao blatantly managed the elections in Phibun's favor. Sarit capitalized on the publicly displayed royal displeasure with Phibun, public outrage, and student demonstrations to call out his troops and overthrow the Phibun government in September 1957.

Leaving the government in the hands of a newly elected parliamentary regime under his deputy, Gen. Thanom Kittikachorn, Sarit flew hurriedly to the United States for urgently needed medical treatment. In his absence, representative government almost ground to a halt for lack of consensus and leadership, and economic conditions worsened. Returning quietly to Bangkok, Sarit staged a second coup in October 1958 and, with Thanom's consent, seized power.

The revolutionary government Sarit established then, legitimized by a new constitution styled on those of Gaullist France and the United Arab Republic, moved quickly and with great force to execute positive policies of economic development and social reform and services. A commanding executive, he early gained a reputation for getting things done, as when he personally wielded an ax to smash opium dens and arrested arsonists. He encouraged King Bhumibol Aduldej to travel, and he revived neglected royal ceremonies to bolster national identity.

Sarit traveled widely himself, often swooping down on remote villages in an army helicopter to chat with peasants. He attempted to restore some of the authority of specialist bureaucrats in the important ministries, though, through his army, he retained control of the Ministry of Interior. He promised an eventual return to parliamentary democracy but moved only slowly to implement this intention.

Economic Reformer

Sarit will be remembered for his effective policies of economic development, which brought the country rapidly to an annual growth rate of 8 percent in the gross national product, for his strong promotion of education, especially in rural areas, and for the special attention he devoted to the impoverished northeast, which had long been neglected by Bangkok governments. The statistics were only beginning to show the success of these policies when he died suddenly on Dec. 8, 1963.

An unusually tall, heavyset, and dark-complexioned man, with a booming, growling voice, Sarit is said to have been genuinely concerned that he be remembered in Thai history as one who revived the kingdom and gave it a clear direction. The successful continuance of his policies, and

the beginning of a return to parliamentary democracy in the late 1960s, reflected favorably on his intentions and hopes.

Further Reading

There is no full biography of Sarit in any Western language, although numerous popular accounts of his life appear in Thai. The important events of his time are recounted in David A. Wilson, *Politics in Thailand* (1962), and Frank C. Darling, *Thailand and the United States* (1965). □

Domingo Faustino Sarmiento

The Argentine statesman, educator, and gifted journalist Domingo Faustino Sarmiento (1811-1888) was known as the "Teacher President" for his unremitting efforts to foster education in his country. He was also an intuitive writer with a prophetic gift who created a classic of Argentine literature.

Domingo Sarmiento was born on Feb. 15, 1811, in San Juan, an old and primitive town of western Argentina near the Andes, of humble, hardworking parents living in near poverty. His formal education was scanty, and he was largely self-taught, reading whatever came within his reach. Benjamin Franklin's *Autobiography* exercised a powerful influence on his young mind, and in later life he wrote, "No other book has done me more good than that one." At the age of 15 Sarmiento taught in a country school; later he clerked briefly in a general store with little success, tried his hand at surveying, and entered politics at a youthful age, thus emulating Abraham Lincoln's early life. Sarmiento's features, about which he often joked, were also rugged and homely. Indeed, these statesmen from opposite ends of the Western Hemisphere had a certain affinity, and in the last decades of his life, Sarmiento always kept near him plaster busts of his "household divinities"—Lincoln and the New England educator Horace Mann.

Sarmiento turned to politics with passionate dedication. The independent provinces of Argentina had lapsed into general anarchy, from which emerged the classic Latin American dictatorship of the cruel and despotic Juan Manuel de Rosas. Liberal and constructive elements of society fled into exile, and Sarmiento's opposition soon obliged him to seek asylum in Chile. In that hospitable land he promoted public schools and, with equal passion, assailed the dictator of Argentina with fiery pamphlets and newspaper articles. In the heat of this fray he wrote the classic *Civilization and Barbarism; or, The Life of Juan Facundo Quiroga* (1845), more succinctly known as *Facundo*.

This anomalous work in three parts is neither history, biography, a novel, nor sociology, yet it partakes of the characteristics of all of these. The first part is a geographical and social description of the vast pampas, or plains, of

Argentina. Isolated cities are oases of civilization in the empty wilderness, over which wild gauchos roam in semibarbarism. The influence of James Fenimore Cooper, particularly his novel *The Prairie,* is apparent in these pages, and it is of interest to note that neither writer at the time of composition had actually seen the region that he described with intuitive genius. The second part is a melodramatic biography of the *caudillo* Facundo, who symbolizes the barbarism of the pampas and the tyranny of the despot Rosas. The third part is a program of social and political reorganization after the overthrow of the dictator.

From 1845 to 1848, while Sarmiento was still an expatriate, the Chilean government enabled him to travel in Europe and the United States to study educational systems, and these journeys inspired some of his finest descriptive writing, in *Travels in Europe, Africa, and the United States* (1849-1851). On returning to Chile he wrote his nostalgic *Hometown Memories* (1850) to defend himself from political slander, and this work, describing his childhood and early home life, contains some of his most moving pages.

The comments on North American life and ways in his travel book are both humorous and penetrating. They clearly reveal his profound and unfailing admiration for all things American, particularly public education. His veneration for Horace Mann approached adoration and later extended to the Massachusetts educator's widow, Mary Tyler Mann, who became Sarmiento's confidante and correspondent for the remainder of his days.

With the fall of the Rosas dictatorship in 1852, Sarmiento returned from exile to devote his energies with ceaseless intensity to bringing unity and a sense of nationality to his people. From 1865 to 1868 he was again in the United States as minister plenipotentiary of Argentina, during which time he met Emerson, Longfellow, Ticknor, and many other North American notables. The most prized distinction that he received was an honorary doctorate from the University of Michigan in June 1868, on the eve of his return to Argentina to assume the presidency.

Sarmiento's term as chief executive, from 1868 to 1874, was one of frustration owing to the exhausting war with Paraguay and to other circumstances unfavorable for a cherished program of reform. Nevertheless, he did much to advance learning and to promote public schools, including arrangements for American women schoolteachers to go to Argentina under contract to give instruction in the newly established teacher-training institutions and in the primary schools of provincial towns and cities.

Despite a strong reluctance to step down from his high office at the end of his term, Sarmiento patriotically turned over the presidency to an elected successor. Then, in minor positions, he continued to work to unify his countrymen and to prepare them for civic participation. Deafness and ill health saddened his last years. compelling him to spend his winters in the milder climate of Paraguay, where he died on Sept. 11, 1888. Shortly before his death he wrote to a friend: "I must soon start on one last journey. But I am ready . . . for I carry the only acceptable passport, because it is written in every language. It says: Serve mankind!"

Further Reading

A good selection of Sarmiento's writings is in Allison Williams Bunkley, ed., *A Sarmiento Anthology,* translated by Stuart Edgar Grummon (1948). Bunkley is also author of a full-length biography, *The Life of Sarmiento* (1952). Mary Tyler Mann provided a biographical sketch in the translation of Sarmiento's *Life in the Argentine Republic in the Days of the Tyrants; or, Civilization and Barbarism* (1868; repr. 1960).

Additional Sources

Patton, Elda Clayton, *Sarmiento in the United States,* Evansville, Ind.: University of Evansville Press, 1976.

Sarmiento, Domingo Faustino, *Life in the Argentine Republic in the days of the tyrants: or, Civilization and barbarism,* New York: Gordon Press, 1976. □

David Sarnoff

The American pioneer in radio and television David Sarnoff (1891-1971) was chairman of the board of the Radio Corporation of America.

David Sarnoff was born on Feb. 27, 1891, in the Russian-Jewish community of Uzilan close to Minsk. In 1895 his father left to try his luck in the United States; 5 years later he sent for his family. When the father died in 1906, David, as the eldest son, became the family provider. He started as a messenger boy for the Commercial Cable Company. Six months later he became an office boy for the Marconi Wireless Telegraph Company of America.

Studying in his spare time, Sarnoff finally was promoted to wireless operator. While working at Sea Gage, N.Y., he completed a course in electrical engineering at Pratt Institute and later acquired practical experience as a marine radio operator on various ships. He then became the operator for John Wanamaker's New York station, where he was the first to pick up the distress call of the S.S. *Titanic* on April 12, 1912. This unfortunate incident proved rewarding for Sarnoff, for his dedicated work in the disaster won him an appointment as a radio inspector and instructor at the Marconi Institute. By 1914 he had risen to contract manager, and in 1919, when Owen D. Young's Radio Corporation of America (RCA) absorbed American Marconi, Sarnoff was commercial manager. In 1917 he married Lizette Hermant, who bore him three sons.

By 1921 Sarnoff was general manager of RCA and had revived an earlier idea to send music over the air. RCA's directors were reluctant to invest much money, but after Sarnoff broadcast the 1921 Dempsey-Cartier fight, they quickly changed their minds. Sarnoff became a vice president in 1922 as RCA began the manufacture of radio sets. He also was responsible for the creation of the National Broadcasting Company (NBC) in 1926.

Sarnoff is known as the father of American television. From the initial experiments in the early 1920s, he pushed its development to commercial feasibility. As president of RCA (since 1930), he appeared on the first public demonstration of television, in April 1939. Although NBC launched commercial telecasting in 1941, World War II retarded its growth. Sarnoff served as communications consultant to Gen. Dwight D. Eisenhower and emerged as a brigadier general.

In 1947 Sarnoff became chairman of the board of RCA, which grew into one of the world's largest corporations, its activities including leadership in black-and-white and color television and many other associated industries. He received honorary degrees from over 26 universities and numerous awards from foreign governments and technical institutes. He died on Dec. 12, 1971, in New York City.

Further Reading

For the serious student of communications, Sarnoff's own *Looking Ahead: The Papers of David Sarnoff* (1968) is valuable for its predictive glances into the future of electronics and masterful coverage of the history of broadcasting. A biography is Eugene Lyons, *David Sarnoff* (1966).

Additional Sources

Bilby, Kenneth W., *The general: David Sarnoff and the rise of the communications industry,* New York: Harper & Row, 1986.

Dreher, Carl, *Sarnoff, an American success,* New York: Quadrangle/New York Times Book Co., 1977.

Lewis, Thomas S. W., *Empire of the air: the men who made radio,* New York, NY: Edward Burlingame Books, 1991.

Sobel, Robert, *RCA,* New York: Stein and Day/Publishers, 1986. □

William Saroyan

The skill of William Saroyan (1908-1981), American short-story writer, dramatist, and novelist, in evoking mood and atmosphere was noteworthy, and his imaginary world, peopled with common men, was warm and compelling.

William Saroyan was born in Fresno, California, on August 31, 1908, the son of Armenian immigrants. After his father's death in 1911, William spent four years in an orphanage. Selling newspapers at the age of eight, he attended public schools in Fresno until, as he said, "I had been kicked out of school so many times that I finally left for good when I was fifteen."

In 1928 Saroyan decided to become a writer, but it was 1934 before his short stories began appearing consistently in major magazines. His first book was *The Daring Young Man on the Flying Trapeze and Other Stories* (1934). At this time he concentrated on short stories. Seven collections appeared, from *Inhale and Exhale* (1936) to *My Name Is Aram* (1940). The works centered on memories of San Francisco and Fresno and show his joy in living. *My Name Is Aram* was particularly lyrical.

From 1939 through 1943 Saroyan was among America's most active playwrights. In *My Heart's in the Highlands* (1939) he departed from the current dramatic practice, for he believed that "it is folly for emotionality to be prolonged as a means by which to achieve drama." Completely episodic, bonded by a tenuous mood deriving from free spirits, the play was distinctive. He created a similar piece in *The Time of Your Life* (1939). Awarded the Pulitzer Prize and the Drama Critics' Circle Award for this play, Saroyan rejected the former. *Love's Old Sweet Song* (1940) was less effective, but his firm grip was evident again in *The Beautiful People* (1941). *Hello Out There* (1942), atypical of Saroyan, was an effective realistic one-act play of human isolation. Another dark play, *Get Away Old Man* (1943), failed, but his film *The Human Comedy* (1943) won an Academy Award.

During World War II Saroyan served in the Army. In 1943 he married Carol Marcus. Divorced in 1949, they remarried in 1951 and were again divorced in 1952. Although he continued to write plays, his work was mainly novels, autobiographies, film and television scripts, short stories, and even songs. His most praised novels are *The Human Comedy* (1943), *The Assyrian* (1950), *Tracy's Tiger* (1951), *The Laughing Matter* (1953), and *Mama I Love You* (1956). He also wrote *I Used To Believe I Had Forever, Now I'm Not So Sure* (1968); *Escape to the Moon* (1970); and *The Tooth and My Father* (1974). He died on May 18, 1981 in Fresno, California.

Further Reading

Saroyan's autobiographies were *The Bicycle Rider in Beverly Hills* (1952), *Here Comes: There Goes: You Know Who* (1961), *Not Dying* (1963), and a more extensive one, *Places Where I've Done Time* (1972), in which he recalled 68 key places in his life. Carol Matthau, former spouse of Saroyan, wrote about him in her memoir, *Among the Porcupines* (Publishing Mills, 1992). See, also, Saroyan, Aram, *William Saroyan* (Harcourt, 1983). A major critical work on him was Howard R. Floan, *William Saroyan* (1966). A major bibliographical work was David Kherdian, *A Bibliography of William Saroyan, 1934-1964* (1965). Useful insights were in John Mason Brown, *Broadway in Review* (1940); Brooks Atkinson, *Broadway Scrapbook* (1947); and George Jean Nathan, *The Magic Mirror: Selected Writings on the Theatre* (1960). □

Paolo Sarpi

The Italian prelate and statesman Paolo Sarpi (1552-1623) was one of the greatest historians of early modern Europe and a founder of the modern historical method.

Paolo Sarpi was born in Venice, the son of a merchant. His early education was supervised by a family friend, a member of the Servite order of friars. In 1565 Sarpi himself joined the Servites, and in 1574 he was ordained a priest. His intellectual gifts brought him into contact with some of the most important people and cities in Italy. He spent 3 years as court theologian in Mantua and then traveled to Milan. He returned to Venice, where he taught philosophy while studying at the nearby University of Padua, the intellectual center of Italy in this period. In 1579 he became provincial of the Venetian province of the Servites, and in 1584, at the age of 32, he moved to Rome as procurator general of the whole order.

Between 1588 and 1606 Sarpi lived in studious retirement in Venice, participating in the vigorous scientific life of Venice and Padua and making friends with such men as Galileo. In 1606 he was called out of retirement and made theologian and canon lawyer of the Republic of Venice. It was a critical moment in Venetian history: the republic had been laid under an interdict by Pope Paul V, and Sarpi's duties entailed the defense of the Venetian cause against the weight and authority of the Counter Reformation papacy. His role in the defense of Venice led him directly to the most important phase of his career, that of skilled and penetrating historian of the medieval and Renaissance Church.

Sarpi's first historical work was a long memorandum, intended for private circulation, of the events in Venice between 1605 and 1607. His second work was the great *History of Benefices* (1609), in which he relied upon his access to the secret archives of Venice and expressed his conviction that individuals and circumstances, political as well as economic, influenced this important chapter of ecclesiastical history. By 1616 Sarpi had completed his

greatest work, *History of the Council of Trent,* which was published in Italian in London in 1619.

In these original historical works, Sarpi deals with limited topics, opens his analysis of causality to economic and political influences, and tries wherever possible to base his conclusions upon documentary evidence. His perception of complex human background made his *History of the Council of Trent* a landmark in the technique of ecclesiastical and institutional history.

During his lifetime Sarpi was honored and protected by the Republic of Venice, a popular and well-known figure. After his death, he became a revered civic hero, not only of the republic but of all Europe.

Further Reading

The introductory remarks that preface the selections from Sarpi's writings in translation by Peter Burke, *Sarpi: History of Benefices and Selections from the History of the Council of Trent* (1967), provide an excellent introduction to Sarpi's method. The best study of his life and ideas is William Bouwsma, *Venice and the Defense of Republican Liberty* (1968).

Additional Sources

Wootton, David, *Paolo Sarpi: between Renaissance and Enlightenment,* Cambridge Cambridgeshire; New York: Cambridge University Press, 1983. □

Nathalie Tcherniak Sarraute

Nathalie Sarraute (born 1900) was one of the seminal figures in the emergence of France's "Nouveau Roman" ("New Novel") in the 1950s. Her work included not only novels but also plays and influential essays on literary theory.

Nathalie Tcherniak was born in Ivanovo-Voznessensk, Russia, the daughter of a chemist father and a writer mother. The date of her birth was July 18, 1900, but at one point in her career, evidently wishing to cut some years from her age, she gave the year of her birth as 1902, a figure still found in some reference works.

In 1902 her parents were divorced. She left Russia and lived with her mother in Paris, visiting her father for two months each year. In 1906 she and her mother returned to St. Petersburg; for the next two years she spent each summer with her father in France and Switzerland. In 1908 went to live with him and his second wife in Paris.

In 1920 she received a *licence* (equivalent to a degree) in English from the Sorbonne and began work toward a B.A. in history at Oxford, a project she abandoned. In 1922 she enrolled in the law school of the University of Paris, where the following year she met fellow student Raymond Sarraute. In 1925 she received her *licence* in law, was admitted to the Paris bar, and married. She practiced law from 1925 to 1939.

In 1932 and 1933 Sarraute composed two sketches described by some as prose poems, by others as experimental fiction. She titled these pieces *Tropismes* (*Tropisms*), and they were subsequently incorporated into her first book, which bore the same title and was published in 1939, receiving only one review.

Tropisms

The word *tropism* was taken from biology and was defined as the movement which, in response to an external stimulus, caused an organism or part of an organism to turn in a determined direction. As to her technique in applying this concept to literature, Sarraute wrote, "What I tried to do was to show certain inner 'movements' by which I had long been attracted. . . ."

She continued,

These movements, of which we are hardly cognizant, slip through us on the frontiers of consciousness in the form of undefinable, extremely rapid sensations. They hide behind our gestures, beneath the words we speak and the feeling we manifest, all of which we are aware of experiencing, and are able to define. They seemed, and still seem to me to constitute the secret source of our existence, in what might be called its nascent state.

"Anti-Novels"

Her next two works were novels in which she put theories into practice: *Portrait d'un inconnu* (1948, published in the United States in 1958 as *Portrait of a Man Unknown*) and *Martereau* (1953, published in the United States in 1959 under the same title). The former novel received great attention because it was preceded by an introduction contributed by Jean-Paul Sartre, the foremost philosopher in France at the time and the father of the existentialist school.

Characterizing the work as an "anti-novel," Sartre observed, "She takes her characters neither from within nor from without, for the reason that we are, both for ourselves and for others, entirely within and without at the same time." He continued, " . . . for her the human being is not a character, not first and foremost a story, nor even a network of habits, but a continual coming and going between the particular and the general." Sartre concluded that by " . . . tenaciously depicting the reassuring, dreary world of the inauthentic, she has achieved a technique which makes it possible to attain human reality in its very *existence*."

Viewed from the standpoint of the conventional novel, little happened in these books. In *Portrait of a Man Unknown* we watched the alienation of the participants from their own family, while in *Martereau* an orphan observed an unexceptional family as Martereau, who may or may not be the wife's lover, swindled them.

With these two works and the essay collection *L'ère du soupçon* (1956, published in the United States in 1963 as

The Age of Suspicion), Sarraute took her place in the forefront of the practitioners of the so-called "Nouveau Roman" ("New Novel"). This literary school also included Alain Robbe-Grillet, Michel Butor, Samuel Beckett, Marguerite Duras, Claude Simon, and Robert Pinget and was strongly influenced by Dostoevski, Kafka, Joyce (particularly the stream-of-consciousness technique in *Ulysses*), and American novelists Dos Passos and Faulkner (especially *The Sound and the Fury*). As critic Henri Peyre wrote in *The Contemporary French Novel,* they were interested in the "more dramatic models of interior monologue provided by Faulkner." He added that the " . . . novelists of 1940-50 who have resorted to it . . . have avoided taking it overseriously and using it, as it were, pure and unadulterated."

Sarraute's next novel was *Le planétarium* (1959, published in the United States in 1960 as *The Planetarium*). Although hailed as a classic example of the New Novel, this work had more plot than most of her fiction as Alain, a vague, weak intellectual, and Gisele, his wife, were allowed to occupy an apartment by their Aunt Berthe.

This was followed by her most successful work, *Les fruits d'or* (1963, published in the United States in 1964 as *The Golden Fruits*). This novel concerned an author who has published a novel titled *Les fruits d'or,* which was both acclaimed and attacked by some rather superficial critics. Such action as there was involved a man holding a shawl for a lady and the forgetting of an umbrella. *The Golden Fruits* won the International Prize for Literature in 1964.

Sarraute turned to drama in 1964 with her radio play *Le silence* (*The Silence*), which was broadcast in Germany, Switzerland, and Scandinavia. Two years later her second radio play, *Le mensonge* (*The Lie*), was broadcast simultaneously in French and German. In 1967 France's most famous actor-director, Jean-Louis Barrault, selected these two plays to open his new theater, the Petit Odéon. Other plays followed: *Isma* in 1970, *C'est beau* (*It's Beautiful*) in 1973, and *Elle est là* (*She Is There*) in 1975. All these dramatic works were collected in *Le théâtre de Nathalie Sarraute* (1978, published in the United States in 1981 as *Collected Plays*). Another play, *Pour un oui ou pour un non* (*For a Yes or for a No*), was written in 1982.

Sarraute did not abandon fiction, however, releasing *Entre la vie et la mort* in 1968 (published in the United States in 1969 as *Between Life and Death*); *Vous les entendez?* in 1972 (published in the United States in 1973 as *Do You Hear Them?*); "*disent les imbéciles*" in 1976 (published in the United States in 1977 as "*fools say*"); and *L'usage de la parole* in 1980 (published in the United States in 1983 as *The Use of Speech*), a collection of short pieces around a unifying theme.

Later Works

Sarraute's literary output continued into ripe old age, as *Enfance* was published in 1983 and *Ici* followed in 1995. Interviewing her for the *New Yorker* (June 27, 1983), Jane Kramer wrote, "Old age seems to have distilled her, leaving only the radiant, essential qualities that small children and great beauties have. Speaking about *Enfance* in a radio interview recorded in the late 1980s while she completed *Tu ne t'aimes pas,* Sarraute said, "It's the first time that I am speaking in my own name, so that makes it much easier for the reader. I didn't want to write an autobiography to say 'This is all my life.' I just tried to show certain moments separated from each other; it was just that I tried to show certain feelings, inward movements that I found interesting, because they gave birth to a certain way of writing."

Elsewhere, Sarraute likened her work to poetry rather than prose. "For me, the poetry in a work is that which makes visible the invisible," she wrote. "You ask me whether I think my own works are poetic. Given what my view of poetry is, how could I possibly be expected not to think so?" [Valerie Minogue's *Nathalie Sarraute and the War of the Words: A Study of Five Novels* (1981].

Critical opinion on Sarraute, as on all of the New Novelists, varied considerably. Among her supporters the most enthusiastic was Claude Mauriac, who declared in *The New Literature* that she was "the only living author who has created anything new after Proust." In *Nathalie Sarraute* René Micha observed, "She descends into the depths of the psyche, strives to seize something of it, especially the movement, to designate it, to retain it for an instant, when already it is half escaping her, transforming itself, disguising itself, to bring it to the light of day and to share it." Gretchen Besser commented, "It is because she has used the medium of tropisms as a lens through which to view fundamental issues of human concern that Sarraute's work has attained a panoramic dimension. It is the recapitulation of certain universal themes. . . ."

Peyre, however, dissented, calling *Portrait of a Man Unknown* "a failure, though an interesting one . . . an honest, pedestrian, and fumbling search for authenticity." He added, "But good intentions count scantly in literature." He adjudged *Martereau* "not a much better performance" and labeled *The Age of Suspicion* "overpraised." His summary: "She is a serious but hardly an inventive or revolutionary novelist . . . ," although he conceded that she had a "fine intellect."

Further Reading

The best biography in English was *Nathalie Sarraute* by Gretchen R. Besser (1979). There were mentions and/or analyses in *The Contemporary French Novel* by Henri Peyre (1955), *French Novelists of Today* by Peyre (1955), and *The New Literature* by Claude Mauriac (1959). Excerpts from her writing can be found in *The French New Novel* by Laurent LeSage (1962). Other works of critical analysis included *Nathalie Sarraute (Collection Monographique Rodopi: En Literature Francaise Contemporaine Sous La Direction De Michael Biship, No 24* by Bettina Knapp (1994); *Nathalie Sarraute: Metaphor, Fairy-Tale and the Feminine of the Text (Writing About Women Feminist Literary Studies, Vol 13* by John Phillips (1994); and *Nathalie Sarraute and the Feminist Reader: Identities in Process* by Sarah Barbour (1993). □

George Sarton

The Belgian-born American historian of science George Sarton (1884-1956) founded the history of science in America.

George Sarton was born in Ghent on Aug. 31, 1884, the son of one of the directors and chief engineers of the Belgian national railroad system. Sarton studied philosophy at the University of Ghent and then turned to science, winning his doctorate in mathematics in 1911. He had, however, already become known as an author and scientist for his published novels and poems and his award-winning essay on chemistry (1908). Sarton emerged from his training with admiration for the insights of Auguste Comte and Henri Poincaré and a conviction that the basis of scientific philosophy was the history of science.

Sarton married an English artist, Eleanor Noble Elives, in 1911. In March 1913 he published the first issue of *Isis,* a journal of the history of science. At the beginning of World War I he fled to Holland, then to England, and, finally, to the United States. He arrived in 1915 and lectured at Harvard from 1916 to 1918, the first academic year in philosophy and the second in history of science. The appointment was not a regular one, and he was supported in the main by friends. The Lowell Lectures at Harvard in 1916 started Sarton on his lifetime project of tracing the history of science to Leonardo da Vinci.

The Carnegie Institution in Washington appointed Sarton a research associate in 1918, thus making him economically secure. He remained at Cambridge and, beginning in 1920, gave a course on the history of science in exchange for library space at Harvard. Meanwhile, he had published the second issue of *Isis* in September 1919. Sarton became an American citizen in 1924 and helped found the History of Science group the same year.

Sarton's major work, *Introduction to the History of Science,* consists of *From Homer to Omar Khayyam* (1927), *From Rabbi Ben Ezra to Roger Bacon* (1931), and *Science and Learning in the 14th Century* (1947-1948). During this time he went to North Africa and the Near East (1931-1932) to study Arabic and Islam; founded *Osiris* (1936), a journal designed for articles longer than those in *Isis;* and wrote and lectured.

In his writings Sarton used the model of a map maker. He combined biography and science, using secondary sources. As a result, he slighted Egyptian and Babylonian sources and relied heavily on Greek and medieval Arabic ones, which were more available to him. All of his works emphasized the continuity of science and its close affinity with magic.

Sarton officially became professor of the history of science at Harvard in 1940 and retired in 1951. He continued to lecture and write until his death on March 22, 1956.

Further Reading

Sarton's most important theoretical essays were collected in *Sarton on the History of Science,* edited by Dorothy Stimson (1962). May Sarton in *I Knew a Phoenix: Sketches for an Autobiography* (1959) treats her father sympathetically and poetically. His contributions to the history of science are critically analyzed in Joseph Agassi, *Towards an Historiography of Science* (1963). □

Jean Paul Sartre

The French philosopher and man of letters Jean Paul Sartre (1905-1980) ranks as the most versatile writer and as the dominant influence in three decades of French intellectual life.

Jean Paul Sartre was born in Paris on June 21, 1905. His father, a naval officer, died while on a tour of duty in Indochina before Sartre was two years old. His mother belonged to the Alsatian Schweitzer family and was a first cousin to Albert Schweitzer. The young widow returned to her parents' house, where she and her son were treated as "the children." In the first volume of his autobiography, *The Words* (1964), Sartre describes his unnatural childhood as a spoiled and precocious boy. Lacking any companions his own age, the child found "friends" exclusively in books. Reading and writing thus became his twin passions. "It was in books that I encountered the universe."

Sartre entered the École Normale Supérieure in 1924 and after one failure received first place in the *agrégation* of philosophy in 1929. The novelist Simone de Beauvoir finished second that year, and the two formed an intimate bond that endured thereafter. After completing compulsory military service, Sartre took a teaching job at a lycée in Le Havre. There he wrote his first novel, *Nausea* (1938), which some critics have called the century's most influential French novel.

From 1933 to 1935 Sartre was a research student at the Institut Français in Berlin and in Freiburg. He discovered the works of Edmund Husserl and Martin Heidegger and began to philosophize in the phenomenological vein. A series of works on the modalities of consciousness poured from Sartre's pen: two works on imagination, one on self-consciousness, and one on emotions. He also produced a first-rate volume of short stories, *The Wall* (1939).

Sartre returned to Paris to teach in a lycée and to continue his writing, but World War II intervened. Called up by the army, he served briefly on the Eastern front and was taken prisoner. After nine months he secured his release and returned to teaching in Paris, where he became active in the Resistance. During this period he wrote his first major work in philosophy, *Being and Nothingness: An Essay in Phenomenological Ontology* (1943).

After the war Sartre abandoned teaching, determined to support himself by writing. He was also determined that his writing and thinking should be *engagé.* Intellectuals, he thought, must take a public stand on every great question of their day. He thus became fundamentally a moralist, both in his philosophical and literary works.

Sartre had turned to playwriting and eventually produced a series of theatrical successes which are essentially dramatizations of ideas, although they contain some finely drawn characters and lively plots. The first two, *The Flies* and *No Exit,* were produced in occupied Paris. They were followed by *Dirty Hands* (1948), usually called his best play; *The Devil and the Good Lord* (1957), a blasphemous, anti-Christian tirade; and *The Prisoners of Altona* (1960), which combined convincing character portrayal with telling social criticism. Sartre also wrote a number of comedies: *The Respectful Prostitute* (1946), *Kean* (1954), and *Nekrassov* (1956), which the critic Henry Peyre claimed "reveals him as the best comic talent of our times."

During this same period Sartre also wrote a three-volume novel, *The Roads to Freedom* (1945-1949); a treatise on committed literature; lengthy studies of Charles Baudelaire and Jean Genet; and a prodigious number of reviews and criticisms. He also edited *Les Temps modernes.*

Though never a member of the Communist party, Sartre usually sympathized with the political views of the far left. Whatever the political issue, he was quick to publish his opinions, often combining them with public acts of protest.

In 1960 Sartre returned to philosophy, publishing the first volume of his *Critique of Dialectical Reason.* It represented essentially a modification of his existentialism by Marxist ideas. The drift of Sartre's earlier work was toward a sense of the futility of life. In *Being and Nothingness* he declared man to be "a useless passion," condemned to exercise a meaningless freedom. But after World War II his new interest in social and political questions and his rapprochement with Marxist thought led him to more optimistic and activist views.

Sartre has always been a controversial yet respected individual. In 1964, Sartre was awarded but refused to accept the Nobel prize in Literature. Sartre suffered from detrimental health throughout the 1970s. He died of a lung ailment in 1980.

Further Reading

Sartre's *The Words* (trans. 1964) gave a highly unusual account of his childhood, subjecting his early years to the same "existential psychoanalysis" that he applied to Baudelaire and Genet. The autobiography of Simone de Beauvoir, *The Prime of Life* (trans. 1962), contained a detailed and intimate account of Sartre. Mary Warnock, *The Philosophy of Sartre* (1965), was a readable account of the philosophical writings. Philip Thody, *Jean-Paul Sartre: A Literary and Political Study* (1960), gave a thoughtful appraisal of the literary works. □

Sassetta

The Italian artist Sassetta (ca. 1400-1450), the greatest painter of the Sienese school in the 15th century, is noted for the gentle piety of his art.

The place and date of birth of Stefano di Giovanni, known as Sassetta are unknown. He may have been born in Cortona, the home of his father, Giovanni di Consolo. A baptismal record preserved in Siena dated Dec. 31, 1392, for one Stefano di Giovanni is widely accepted as evidence that he was born in Siena that year. Some scholars, however, would suggest a birth date not before 1400 on the basis of Sassetta's earliest dated work of 1423.

Sassetta's style was wholly Sienese in character, suggesting that he was trained in the shop of some Sienese master. Whether or not that master was Paolo di Giovanni Fei, as suggested by some critics, is unknown. In 1440 Sassetta married Gabriella di Buccio di Biancardo. The eldest of their three children was the sculptor Giovanni di Stefano. Sassetta died in April 1450, after contracting pneumonia the previous month while frescoing the Porta Romana, Siena.

On July 1, 1423, the wool guild (Arte della Lana) commissioned an altarpiece (now disassembled) from Sassetta for its chapel next to the church of S. Pellegrino, Siena. From 1426 to 1431 he was associated with the Cathedral Works, Siena. Among the documents from this period are records of payment dated December 1427 for a drawing of the baptismal font "in the shape that it ought to take." This suggests that he may have collaborated with Jacopo della Quercia, the sculptor who built the font.

On March 25, 1430, Sassetta was commissioned to paint an altarpiece of the Madonna with Saints with the legend of the founding of S. Maria Maggiore, Rome, in the predella. The *Madonna of the Snow*, as it is called, was finished by mid-October 1432. His style in this work betrays the influence of Masaccio, especially in the broad modeling of the Virgin and Child and in the arrangement of figures in the predella. Little is known of Sassetta's activities between 1433 and 1436, though this is the period when he probably painted the *Crucifixion* for S. Martino (of which fragments remain) and the altarpiece for S. Domenico, Cortona.

The altarpiece of the Madonna with Saints Jerome and Ambrose, dated 1436, in the Church of the Osservanza, Siena, formerly attributed to Sassetta, is now generally attributed to another artist, the so-called Osservanza Master. Some critics would extend the oeuvre of the Osservanza Master to include the *Birth of the Virgin* in Asciano and the group of panels with the life of St. Anthony Abbot from an altarpiece dedicated to the saint. These panels still have advocates who attribute them to Sassetta.

Two small panels, the *Journey of the Magi* and the *Adoration of the Magi,* were probably once part of a single composition. The most important extant later work by Sassetta is the altarpiece (now dismembered) commissioned on Sept. 5, 1437, and completed by June 5, 1441, for the church of S. Francesco, Borgo San Sepolcro. His style in these panels is somewhat flatter and more decorative than in the *Madonna of the Snow*. When Sassetta died, he left at least two major works unfinished: the fresco decoration of the Porta Romana, Siena, and the *Assumption of the Virgin*.

Further Reading

John Pope-Hennessy's monograph *Sassetta* (1939) gives the facts of the artist's life. See also Bernhard Berenson, *A Sienese Painter of the Franciscan Legend* (1909). □

Siegfried Sassoon

The English poet Siegfried Sassoon (1886-1967) wrote a group of dramatic, intense lyrics in reaction to the horrors of World War I. His six volumes of partly fictionalized memoirs are a detailed record of the sensibilities of his age.

Siegfried Sasson was born in Brenchley, Kent, on Sept. 8, 1886, and spent his childhood at the family home in Weirleigh, in the protected and somewhat rarefied atmosphere of a family near the center of the late Victorian and Edwardian literary and artistic world. He was formally educated at Marlborough School and at Clare College, Cambridge, and began publishing poems privately in 1906. However, Sassoon's distinctive voice was not heard until the publication of his war poems—in *The Old Huntsman* (1917) and *Counter-attack* (1918). He was the first of the younger Georgian poets to react violently against sentimentally patriotic notions of the glories of war; these poems have an extraordinary vigor—a stridency of tone, in fact—expressing with unconcealed irony and in colloquial terms a passionate hatred of the horrors of war. Some of Sassoon's contemporaries produced poems that addressed more seriously the confusion of values that World War I revealed; but none responded with such passion or with such hatred of the ignorance and folly that permitted such pain.

Sassoon's poems of the 1920s—represented in *Satirical Poems* (1926 and 1933) and in *The Road to Ruin* (1933—although they set out to satirize the corruptions and the pretensions of a disintegrating and confused materialistic society, were more controlled, artificial, less intense—and vastly less effective than the war poems.

Perhaps Sassoon's reputation will ultimately rest on his prose works. *The Memoirs of George Sherston* (1937), his three-volume fictional autobiography, describes, on one level at least, the way of life and the decline in influence of the educated, cultivated, English country gentry during the first quarter of the 20th century. More significantly, it delineates the decay of a culture and the character of an age. It is composed of *Memoirs of a Foxhunting Man* (1928), *Memoirs of an Infantry Officer* (1930), and *Sherston's Progress* (1936).

Sassoon later wrote three volumes of direct autobiography to complement his Sherston trilogy. They are brilliant evocations of characters and patterns of life in one period, but they remain fundamentally the explorations of a man whose own experience, whose own alienation, is by no means representative. These volumes are *The Old Century and Seven More Years* (1938), *The Weald of Youth* (1942), and *Siegfried's Journey* (1945).

The latter half of Sassoon's life was lived in semiretirement from the world of pressing public issues and changing literary values. His critical biography of George Meredith, published in 1948, valued Meredith largely for his "freedom of spirit" and for his unimpaired, instinctive love of nature. Sassoon died in Warminster, Wiltshire, on Sept. 1, 1967.

Further Reading

The absence of any full-scale biography of Sassoon is offset, to a degree, by his memoirs. Much incidental criticism of his work is available in periodicals, and his war poetry is evaluated in the many studies of Georgian and war poetry. Early evaluations are in Frank Swinnerton, *The Georgian Literary Scene* (1934; rev. ed. 1951), and Edmund Blunden, *The Mind's Eye: Essays* (1934), reprinted in *Edmund Blunden: A Selection of His Poetry and Prose,* edited by Kenneth Hopkins (1950). Joseph Cohen, in a sound and comprehensive critical essay, *The Three Roles of Siegfried Sassoon* (1957), distinguished three phases of Sassoon's poetry, but the only book-length study is Michael Thorpe, *Siegfried Sasson: A Critical Study* (1966). Geoffrey Keynes prepared *A Bibliography of Siegfried Sassoon* (1962). □

Satanta

Satanta (1830–1878) was a leader of the Kiowa tribe who fought an endless war to protect his tribe's land from being taken away from the U.S. government.

I n the 1860s and 1870s, the Kiowa Indians waged an ongoing battle to protect their land and way of life from U.S. encroachment. Satanta (1830-1878), also known as White Bear, was a major Kiowa leader in favor of resistance. Besides his prowess as a warrior, Satanta was also a famed orator—a fact attested by his American-given nickname "The Orator of the Plains."

Satanta was born on the northern Plains, but later migrated to the southern Plains with his people. His father, Red Tipi, was keeper of the tribal medicine bundles or Tai-me. Much of Satanta's adult life was spent fighting U.S. settlers and military. He participated in raids along the Santa Fe Trail in the early 1860s, and in 1866 became the leader of the Kiowa who favored military resistance against U.S. military forces. In 1867, he spoke at the Kiowa Medicine Lodge Council, an annual ceremonial gathering, where, because of his eloquent speech, U.S. observers gave him his nickname. At the council, Satanta signed a peace treaty that obligated the Kiowa to resettle on a reservation in present-day Oklahoma. Shortly thereafter, however, he was taken hostage by U.S. officials who used his imprisonment to coerce more Kiowa into resettling on their assigned reservation.

For the next couple of years, Satanta participated in a number of raids in Texas where cattle ranchers and buffalo hunters were steadily pushing Kiowa and Comanche Indians onto reservations. It was one of these raids that eventually led to Satanta's capture. In May 1871, Satanta planned an ambush along the Butterfield Stage Route on the

Salt Creek Prairie. After allowing a smaller medical wagon train to pass, Satanta and his warriors attacked and confiscated the contents of a larger train of ten army freight wagons. Unfortunately for Satanta, the train he had allowed to pass was carrying General William Tecumseh Sherman, the famous Civil War general, then commander of the U.S. Army. Sherman took the attack as a sign that a more militant and coordinated offense was needed to subdue the Kiowa and Comanche, who were unwilling to settle permanently onto reservations. A short time later Satanta was lured into a peace council and then arrested and was sentenced to death. Humanitarian groups and Indian leaders protested the harsh sentence. In 1873, Satanta was paroled on the condition he remain on the Kiowa Reservation.

In 1874, during the Comanche and United States conflict called the Red River War, Satanta presented himself to U.S. officials to prove that he was not taking part in the hostilities. His demonstration of loyalty was rewarded with imprisonment. Four years later, an ill Satanta was informed that he would never be released. He jumped to his death from the second story of a prison hospital. □

Erik Satie

Erik Satie (1866-1925) was an eccentric but important French composer. His works and his attitude toward music anticipated developments of the next generation of composers.

Erik Satie was born in Honfleur to a French father and a Scottish mother. Because he showed musical talent, he was sent to the conservatory, but his real interest lay in the cafés of Montmartre, where he played the piano and for which he composed sentimental ballads.

From the beginning Satie had a flair for novel musical ideas, and his first serious compositions reveal this originality. The *Gymnopédies* for piano (1888) avoid all the clichés of the time and strike a note of chasteness, quite different from the feverish and sentimental music of the day. His *Three Sarabandes* for piano (1887) include some very interesting parallel ninth chords that later became an important feature of the styles of Claude Debussy and Maurice Ravel. In some of his compositions of the next few years Satie used Gregorian modes as well as chords built in fourths, again anticipating musical idioms that would be extensively developed in the next 25 years.

In 1898 Satie "withdrew" to Arcueil, a suburb of Paris, where he spent the rest of his life. He lived quietly, spending a day each week with Debussy, writing café music, and studying counterpoint. He gave the piano pieces he wrote at this time ridiculous, almost surrealistically humorous titles, such as *Three Pieces in the Shape of a Pear*, *Three Flabby Preludes for a Dog*, and *Desicated Embryos*—perhaps parodying the elaborately evocative titles Debussy sometimes

gave his compositions. Satie also included in his scores such puzzling directions as "play like a nightingale with a toothache," "with astonishment," "from the top of the teeth," and "sheepishly."

Satie's tendency to underplay the importance of his compositions reached its climax in the music he wrote in 1920 for the opening of an art gallery. The score, for piano, three clarinets, and a trombone, consists of fragments of well-known tunes and isolated phrases repeated over and over, like the pattern of wallpaper. In the program he stated, "We beg you to take no notice of the music and behave as if it did not exist. This music . . . claims to make its contribution to life in the same way as a private conversation, a picture, or the chair on which you may or may not be seated."

This violently antiromantic attitude toward music attracted the attention of the group of young French composers who were to become known as "Les Six" and of Jean Cocteau, their poet-artist-publicity agent. Another group acclaimed Satie as the leader of the "School of Arcueil." Serge Diaghilev commissioned Satie to write the music for a surrealist ballet, *Parade* (1917). Cocteau wrote the libretto, and Pablo Picasso designed the cubist sets and costumes. Satie's *Mercure* (1924) and *Relâche* (1924), again with the collaboration of Picasso, anticipated surrealism with their noticeable lack of connection between the action on the stage and the mood of the music. A surrealist movie, part of the ballet, is accompanied by music that alternates between two neutral, "wallpaper" compositions.

Socrate (1919), for four solo sopranos and chamber orchestra, is a serious work. The words are fragments from three Platonic dialogues, one having to do with the death of Socrates. *Socrate* is distinguished by its atmosphere of calm and gentle repose. It is completely nondramatic, for one of the sopranos sings Socrates's words. The music consists of simple melodic lines and repetitive accompaniment figures. It is this simplicity, this avoidance of the big gesture that made Satie's music important and prophetic of an important branch of 20th-century musical developments.

Further Reading

Two studies of Satie's life and music are Pierre-Daniel Templier, *Eric Satie* (1932; trans. 1969), which contains many photographs of Satie's friends and family, and Rollo H. Myers, *Eric Satie* (1948). Roger Shattuck, *The Banquet Years* (1958), contains an interesting chapter on Satie in the context of Paris in the early years of the century.

Additional Sources

Gillmor, Alan M., *Erik Satie,* Boston: Twayne Publishers, 1988.
Harding, James, *Erik Satie,* New York: Praeger, 1975.
Satie remembered, Portland, Or.: Amadeus Press, 1995.
Templier, Pierre-Daniel, *Erik Satie,* New York: Da Capo Press, 1980, 1969. □

Eisaku Sato

Eisaku Sato (1901-1975) was a Japanese political leader who served as prime minister longer than anyone else in Japanese history. Under his leadership Japan gradually began to translate its immense economic strength into enhanced political power in the international environment.

Eisaku Sato was born on March 27, 1901, in Yamaguchi Prefecture into a family of samurai descent. His home province, Choshu, provided much of the leadership (including Sato's great-grandfather) in the movement that overthrew the Tokugawa shogunate in 1868 and established the new imperial government. During the first century after the Meiji restoration, Yamaguchi provided more premiers than any other prefecture.

Sato therefore grew up in an atmosphere highly charged with political concerns; his mother was reported to have impressed upon her sons a sense of obligation to serve the state. Sato's eldest brother, Ichiro, became a rear admiral, retiring just prior to World War II. Another older brother, Nobusuke Kishi, served in the Hideki Tojo Cabinet as minister of commerce and industry during the war and subsequently, after serving 3 years in prison as a Class A war criminal, became a leader of the Liberal Democratic party and served as Japanese prime minister from 1957 to 1960.

Career in the Bureaucracy

Like Kishi, Sato attended Tokyo Imperial University, a ladder to success in Japanese society, and graduated in 1924 after studying German law. For a time he was interested in working for the N.Y.K. steamship line or the Ministry of Finance, but neither yielded him an opportunity, and he eventually ended up in the Transportation Ministry. His rise in the bureaucracy was not meteoric in the way Kishi's was in the Ministry of Commerce and Industry. Starting in a minor provincial post, he slowly rose through the ministerial hierarchy to become director of the Automobile Bureau. He was reportedly demoted after an argument with the deputy minister and sent to Osaka. The fact that he was not at ministerial headquarters saved him from the postwar purge.

Immediately after the war Sato was named general director of the Railway Administration and was soon promoted to deputy minister of transportation, the highest rank a civil servant could aspire to. At this juncture he made a decisive departure from his bureaucratic career.

Career in Politics

The Occupation's purge of large numbers of the prewar political elite left room for new people to enter parliamentary politics. Shigeru Yoshida, the prime minister, was in the midst of building up a strong personal following in the Diet, composed mainly of former bureaucrats. One who came to his attention was Sato. It is said that Sato's handling of troublesome new labor unions caught the attention of Yoshida. However that may be, Yoshida asked Sato, in 1948, to become his chief Cabinet secretary, a position of considerable importance in running the affairs of the Cabinet and supervising relations with the party. Sato accepted and soon after won a seat in the Diet.

Sato's association with Yoshida lasted for several years, and he was intensely loyal to the old man. Yoshida suffered public criticism in the spring of 1954, when he rescued Sato from legal charges growing out of a scandal that involved shipping interests and many top leaders of Yoshida's Liberal party. Sato, who was serving as secretary general of the party, was accused of having received political bribes from shipbuilding executives. Yoshida employed the powers of his office to intervene and prevent the arrest of Sato, who thereafter always maintained his innocence.

Rise to Prime Minister

In late 1954 Yoshida, whose position had been weakened by the scandal and more basically by increasing factionalism among the conservatives, was unseated by Ichiro Hatoyama. The following year Yoshida's Liberal party merged with Hatoyama's conservatives to form the Liberal-Democratic party. Behind the thin facade of party unity, factional strife continued unabated. Sato had by this time built up a strong personal following which he threw behind his brother Nobusuke Kishi, who with Sato's help became prime minister from 1957 to 1960. Sato entered the Cabinet as minister of finance. The immense popular disturbances that attended the Security Treaty crisis in 1960 toppled Kishi, who was succeeded by Hayato Ikeda.

Sato himself gradually built up his own claims to the premiership. Ikeda defeated him in a bitter struggle for the party presidency in 1964; but later in the year Ikeda, dying of cancer, was forced to retire, and Sato succeeded to the party presidency and the premiership by acclamation.

The crisis in the universities and continuing problems of Japanese-American relations were two of the major challenges confronting Sato during his term as prime minister. To deal with campus disorders, which wracked nearly all the universities in Japan, Sato's response was a bill that would allow the Ministry of Education to take over a school if the disruption persisted more than nine months. It was evident in elections that Sato's party benefited from a hard line on student disorders.

In November 1969 Sato flew to Washington seeking to conclude negotiations for the reversion of Okinawa to Japanese sovereignty by 1972. Upon returning to Japan, he dissolved the House of Representatives, and in the general elections held on December 27 his party won a resounding victory. In June 1971 the United States and Japan signed a treaty to restore Okinawa and the other Ryukyu Islands to Japanese sovereignty in 1972; the accord was ratified by both countries in March 1972. In July the 71-year-old premier resigned. He was awarded the Nobel Peace Prize in 1974, along with Sean MacBride, for his policies on nuclear weapons that contributed to stability in the geographic area. He died the following year, on June 2, 1975, in Tokyo.

Further Reading

There was no reliable biography of Sato. For a perceptive analysis of the workings of Japanese politics see Donald C. Hellmann, *Japanese Foreign Policy and Domestic Politics* (1969). Another useful book for understanding the intricacies of the politics in Sato's party was Nathaniel B. Thayer, *How the Conservatives Rule Japan* (1969). Sato's policies were also discussed in Edwin O. Reischauer's *Japan: The Story of a Nation* (1989). □

Carl Ortwin Sauer

Carl Ortwin Sauer (1889-1975) was an American geographer and anthropologist with a strong interest in historical fieldwork and other forms of geographical research.

On December 24, 1889, Carl Sauer was born in Warrenton, Missouri. His father taught at the Central Wesleyan College, a German Methodist enterprise, since closed. His parents sent young Sauer to a school at Calur, Württemberg, and he gained his first degree from Central Western College before his nineteenth birthday. In 1915 he earned a doctorate of philosophy from the University of Chicago, and from 1915 to 1922 he served on the staff at the University of Michigan. In 1923 he went to the University of California, Berkeley, where he remained to his retirement in 1957.

Sauer's first paper was an "outline for fieldwork" in geography, published in 1915 and developed further in 1919 and 1921 in the *Geographical Review* and the *Annals of American Geographers*. Physical geographers in America already had a long and distinguished record of field survey, but Sauer, with a few other vigorous young men in the University of Chicago, saw the potential of land-use mapping, possibly with a view to evaluation of the most suitable use. In time he saw the fascination of human settlements and other patterns in relation to the culture of the people who established them.

Sauer recognized the difficulty of reconstructing past landscapes, even in America, where some areas had been settled only for a very few generations, and he turned with admiration to such studies as the 10-volume *Corridors of Time* series (1927-1956) of H. J. E. Peake and H. J. Fleure. Perpetually concerned with the human imprint on the landscape, he said in 1956 that the geographer need not fear the expression of a value judgment, for the use of resources will influence the lives of future generations for good or evil. He also organized the international Symposium on Man's Role in Changing the Face of the Earth, held at Princeton, New Jersey, in 1955.

Agricultural dispersals, the origins of various cultures, the destruction of plant and animal life, the strivings of man for life under adverse conditions, and the effects of climatic change all attracted the scholarly attention of Carl Sauer. Apart from a school text, *Man in Nature: America before the Days of the White Man* (1939); the Bowman Memorial Lectures, published as *Agricultural Origins and Dispersals* (1952); and *The Early Spanish Main* (1967); and *Seventeenth Century North America* (1971), virtually all his writing was in the form of articles, scholarly, fascinating, persuasive, and well documented, if at times arousing the opposition of readers. He died on July 18, 1975 and was interred in his hometown of Warrenton, Missouri.

Further Reading

Sauer's *Land and Life,* edited by John Leighly (1963), was a selection of his papers with an introduction by Leighly. Sauer's work was briefly discussed in Richard J. Chorley and Peter Haggett, eds., *Models in Geography* (1967), and Robert E. Dickinson, *The Makers of Modern Geography* (1969). □

Henri Sauguet

Henri Sauguet (1901-1989) was one of the most important composers, writers, and thinkers on French art and music in the latter half of the 20th century. He contributed notable works in all musical genres, particularly ballet and opera. He was the most important heir of the compositional style of Erik Satie, which was characterized by clarity and simplicity.

Henri Sauguet was born in Bordeaux, France, on May 18, 1901. As a young child Sauguet studied piano and was attracted to the music of Bizet, Schumann, and Debussy. He received organ lessons from Paul Combes, and after a brief appointment as an organist at a local church he studied composition under J. P. Vaubourgoin and Joseph Canteloube. He soon became interested in the music of Igor Stravinsky and Erik Satie.

After reading Jean Cocteau's *Le Coq et l'arlequin,* the most important work of this literary Dadaist, Sauguet organized the Bordeaux counterpart to the Parisian "Les Six." "Les Trois" consisted of Sauguet, the composer J. M. Lizotte, and the poet Louis Emié. Sauguet actively corresponded with Darius Milhaud, who encouraged his compositional endeavors. In 1923 he produced his first collection, *Trois Françaises* for piano, which reflected the influence of Satie with its spontaneity, simple lines, and tender emotions.

Later that year Sauguet relocated to Paris, where he became involved with the "*École d'Arcueil,*" a collaborative group whose members included Cliquet-Pleyel, Maxime (Don Clement) Jacob, and Desormière. The group, named in honor of Satie's place of birth, gave their inaugural concert at the Sorbonne with the assistance of both Satie and Cocteau. As a result of this successful presentation, Sauguet received his first major commission for stage. When *Le Plumet du colonel* was presented on a double bill with Stravinsky's *L'Histoire du soldat* at the Théâtre des Champs-Elysées, Stravinsky congratulated the young Sauguet: "22 years old; that's good. . . . Don't search for yourself. You've already found yourself . . . but work hard, and *seriously.*"

Sauguet excelled as a writer for the stage. His second commission, *Les Roses* (1924), was technically cohesive and critically successful. *La Chatte* (1927), danced by Balanchine, was a major success for Sergei Diaghilev and considerably furthered Sauguet's reputation as a composer. It was followed by *David,* written and danced by Ida Rubinstein, and *La Nuit* (1930), presented in London, based on a scenario by Kochno, with choreography by Lifar and scenery by Bérard. These led to the culmination of his stage work, *Les Fourains* (1945), first performed by Petit's company. Based on the story of a melancholy yet hopeful troop of traveling players, the work captured the playful manner of Chabrier.

Sauguet also wrote notable operatic works. After *Le Plumet du colonel,* Sauguet produced *La Contrebasse* in 1930, an opera buffa by Troyat, after a story by Chekhov. It was successfully revived in 1981. His *La Chartreuse de Parme* (1927-1936) remains his best work in this genre. While it has been described as a somewhat "featureless" work, it was directly emotional, containing the simple, flowing, melodic lines which perfectly embody the French sentiment of that period. *La Chartreuse de Parme,* revised for the Winter Olympic Games in Grenoble, France, in 1968, was well received.

Sauguet's chamber and orchestral works tended to be programmatic. The first of his four symphonies, *Expiatoire* (1945), was a heartfelt lament for the victims of World War II; *Concert des mondes souterrains* (1961-1963) suggested the dripping water and strange lights of an underground grotto; *Melodie concertante* (1964), written for the famous cellist Mstislav Rostropovich, tried to recapture the vision of a young female cellist whose expressive interpretation of Debussy's music touched the composer in his youth; and *Suite Royale,* written and performed by Sylvia Marlowe in 1962, was reminiscent of the harpsichord suites of the 18th century and recalls the brief and tragic life of Marie Antoinette. The themes were tender and moving.

Satie was an important link in the genesis of the modern French symphony. Except for the two symphonies by Dom Clement Jacob (Maxime Jacob's name after he received religious orders), Sauguet's four works were the only embodiment of Satie's style in this genre.

Sauguet's career was marked by individuality. A neoromantic, he continued to write emotional music of unusual expressivity throughout his career. Sauguet avoided complicated and cluttered structures, preferring clarity and simplicity to create mood. According to the composer, art was saying something in everyday words that no one had ever said before.

Sauguet continued as a strong voice in the arts until his death in 1989.

Further Reading

Sauguet remained active as a composer, writer, and thinker of French art and music as an octogenarian. A member of the Académie des Beaux-Arts beginning in 1975, Sauguet contributed articles to the *Courrier de Musique France* (no. 38, 1972) and *Revue de Musicologie* (nos. 316-317, 1978). Two biographies were available, one by M. Schneider (Paris, 1959) and one by F. Y. Bril (Paris, 1967). Information on the composer may also be obtained from *Henri Sauguet: A Bio-Bibliography (Bio-Bibliographies in Music, No 39)* by David L. Austin (1991). □

Saul

The first king of Israel, Saul (reigned ca. 1020-1000 B.C.) was a man of valor who brought the virtues of modesty and generosity to his office.

The youngest son of Kish of the tribe of Benjamin, Saul was a modest shepherd boy, a resident of Gibeah, when the prophet Samuel, after a chance meeting, secretly chose and anointed him king of Israel. It was a period of national humiliation, for the Philistines had defeated the Israelites at Shiloh and captured the Ark of the Covenant, which symbolized the presence of God in their midst. This calamity convinced the Israelites that they must either strive for national unity with a king as leader or face complete and permanent subjugation.

Saul succeeded in freeing Israel of its enemies and extending its boundaries. He fought successfully against the Philistines, Ammonites, Moabites, Edomites, Arameans, and Amalekites. He also succeeded in drawing the tribes of Israel into a closer unity.

Saul's initial conflict with Samuel occurred after Saul offered a sacrifice to God, thereby assuming Samuel's office. Samuel rebuked Saul and proclaimed that Saul's dynasty would not be continued on the throne of Israel. Their second disagreement took place after Saul retained the war booty of the defeated Amalekites, Israel's traditional enemy, and spared the life of their king, Agag. Samuel publicly pronounced Saul's deposition from the throne. Saul fell into a state of melancholia that developed into an emotional disorder.

Saul's fits of depression and his moody, suspicious temperament caused him to attack the lad David, who had been brought into his household to soothe him by playing music. Jealous of David, Saul persecuted him, attacked him, sent him on perilous expeditions, and finally made him into an outlaw.

The Philistines then renewed their attack on Israel. Without David's support and depressed by the feeling that God had deserted him, Saul consulted a witch of Endor, seeking to recall the spirit of the dead Samuel. He was reproached and advised of his impending doom. In a battle against the Philistines Saul fought valiantly but vainly. His forces routed and his three sons slain, Saul died by his own hand. The tragic tale is told by David in an exquisite elegy lamenting the death of Saul and Jonathan. It is one of the most beautiful poems in the Bible.

The affection in which Saul was held is reflected in the action of the men of Yabesh-gilead, whose city he had saved in his first act as monarch. They risked their lives to rescue his body from the Philistines and gave it an honorable burial.

Further Reading

Although there is no single authoritative biography of Saul, there are numerous volumes of fiction, making it difficult to distinguish between historical and legendary accounts. An excellent short essay on him is in Rudolph Kittel, *Great Men and Movements in Israel* (trans. 1929). For historical background the following works are recommended: William Foxwell Albright, *From the Stone Age to Christianity* (1940; 2d ed. with new introduction, 1957); Max I. Magolis and Alexander Marx, *A History of the Jewish People* (1944); Salo Wittmayer Baron, *A Social and Religious History of the Jews,* vol. 1 (2d ed. 1952; 2d rev. ed. 1969); and Martin Noth, *The History of Israel* (trans. 1958; 2d ed. 1960). □

Sir Charles Edward Saunders

Sir Charles Edward Saunders (1867-1937) was a Canadian cerealist who developed early-maturing hard spring wheat—in particular, Marquis wheat, an early high-protein variety.

Charles Edward Saunders was born in London, Ontario, on Feb. 2, 1867, son of William and Sarah Agnes Robinson Saunders. He received his early education in the elementary and collegiate system in London and his university education at the University of Toronto, Johns Hopkins University, and the Sorbonne. He married Mary Blackwell of Toronto in 1892.

Saunders began an academic career as professor of chemistry and geology at Central University, Ky., in 1893. Within 2 years, however, he turned to a musical career in Toronto, where, in addition to acting as an agent, he gave lessons in singing and flute playing and wrote as music critic in a newspaper. His musical career was not a financial success, however, and in 1903 he accepted appointment as Dominion cerealist at the Experimental Farm in Ottawa. The new work was not a break with family tradition, for Saunders's father had founded the system of experimental farms established in Canada, and his brother, Percy, had done considerable work in cross-breeding strains of wheat.

Saunders turned enthusiastically to his new tasks. Following up his brother's research, he developed Marquis wheat in 1904, a variety which showed marked superiority in milling quality for bread flour over other varieties popular in western Canada. Marquis had the advantage of maturing 10 days earlier than its competitors—a factor of great importance in the Canadian wheat belt. The Indian Head Experimental Farm in Saskatchewan raised Marquis wheat for seed, and by 1909 its use was widespread. By 1920 90 percent of the wheat grown in western Canada was Marquis. However, Marquis was not resistant to stem rust. In seeking newer and better varieties Saunders developed three other strains of wheat—Ruby, Garnet, and Reward—specifically adapted to prairie conditions. He was also responsible for improved varieties of oats and barley.

In 1922 Saunders retired and turned to the study of French, a subject which had always attracted him. He spent the years 1922-1925 at the Sorbonne, returning to Canada to write a book, *Essais et vers,* in 1928. In recognition of his work in the French language he was decorated by the French government and was presented with the Medaille de l'Académie Française.

Saunders won honor in his own country also. He was elected a fellow of the Royal Society of Canada in 1921 and won the society's Flavelle Medal in 1925. He was knighted in 1933. He died on July 25, 1937.

Further Reading

The best book on Saunders and his family is Elsie M. Pomeroy, *William Saunders and His Five Sons* (1956). □

Augusta Christine Savage

Augusta Christine Savage (1892–1962) was a renowned sculptor and teacher who also fought for the civil rights of African Americans.

Despite a lifetime spent combatting the effects of racism and sexism, Augusta Savage's accomplishments were many. She was a talented sculptor, an admired teacher, and a fighter for the rights of African Americans. Her circumstances were never easy, though she was afforded financial help and artistic encouragement from several sources. In addition to her achievements in sculpture, she contributed to the history of art in America by helping to launch the careers of a number of other artists during the 1930s and 1940s.

The topsoil in the area where Augusta Christine Fells (later Savage) grew up in Florida was made of red clay, and the major industry there was brick making. It was in her own backyard that Savage learned to model with clay. Her family was very poor. She and her 13 brothers and sisters had no toys. But Savage found that she could amuse herself and others by making clay ducks, pigs, and other animals. She loved working the clay so much that she sometimes missed school to visit the town's clay pit. Savage's father was a minister, a deeply religious and very strict man. He did not approve of his daughter making images of "God's creatures" out of clay.

When Savage was about 15, her family moved to West Palm Beach, Florida. Their life improved greatly there. The principal of Savage's new school discovered her modeling talents and offered her a dollar a day to teach clay modeling classes. During this time Savage married John T. Moore and the couple had a daughter, born in 1908. Moore died a few years later. Savage continued to live with her parents. She

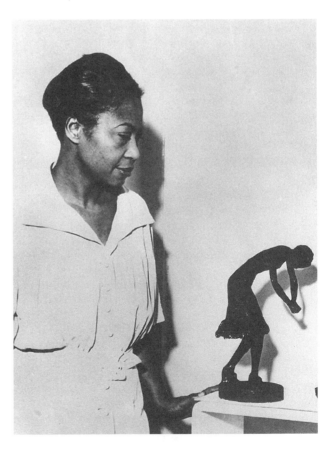

was married again around 1915, to James Savage, a carpenter. They were divorced in 1921.

Wowed county fair with clay animals

During this period Savage attended a state teacher's school (now Florida A & M University) for one year in Tallahassee, Florida. To earn money she convinced the superintendent of the local county fair, George Currie, to let her set up a booth to sell her animal sculptures. Fair officials at first objected to a black woman having her own booth, but they finally agreed. Savage's animals were very popular and she made about $150, more money than she'd ever had. Fair officials also awarded her a $25 prize for the most original exhibit.

Currie believed that Savage had a lot of talent. He encouraged her to go to New York and gave her a letter of introduction to a sculptor he knew in the city. Savage arrived in New York in 1921 with less than five dollars. But Currie's friend arranged for her to take art classes at a tuition-free school called the Cooper Union. She landed a job as an apartment caretaker to cover living expenses. Three months later, though, she lost her job and soon found herself penniless. Recognizing her talent, the Cooper Union Advisory Board voted to supply funds to meet Savage's living expenses. This was the first time the school sponsored a student.

Sculpted bust of W. E. B. DuBois

In New York Savage became interested in African art and spent a lot of time at the public library reading and doing research. She befriended the librarian there. When the librarian found out about Savage's dire financial straits, she arranged for the library to hire Savage to sculpt a bust of the famous African American thinker and writer W. E. B. Du Bois. This was Savage's first commission; several others followed, including one of another black leader, Marcus Garvey. These works earned Savage considerable recognition among the important figures of the Harlem Renaissance. Harlem was the predominantly African American neighborhood of New York. During the 1920s and 1930s this community was experiencing a particularly active and exciting period of creativity in the arts.

Stung by racism

In 1923 Savage's career received a setback when she encountered a fierce incident of racial prejudice. The French government was offering scholarships to 100 American women to study at a summer art school in Paris. Savage applied for the $500 scholarship and gathered pledges from friends and acquaintances to pay for her travel and other expenses. Her application was returned when the committee learned she was of African descent. Savage was disappointed and outraged. She decided to fight the rejection and gathered many prominent people behind her. Her cause garnered considerable publicity. In an article in the *New York World,* Savage explained that she was not raising a fuss just for herself. "Other and better colored students might wish to apply sometime. . . . I don't like to see them establish a precedent." Still, Savage felt personally stung. "My

brother was good enough to be . . . [in a] regiment that saw service in France during the war, but it seems his sister is not good enough to be a guest of the country for which he fought. . . . How am I to compete with other American artists if I am not to be given the same opportunity?"

This experience inspired Savage to become active in the political and social issues concerning African Americans. Eventually, some factions of the art world began to consider her a "troublemaker"; a few historians have even surmised that she was purposely excluded from exhibits and galleries because of the flap over the scholarship. But through the efforts of W. E. B. Du Bois, Savage was awarded a scholarship in 1925 to study in Italy. She desperately longed to go, knowing that European study would refine her sculpting techniques. But the little money she was earning working in a laundry was needed to feed her family, who had left Florida to join her in New York. This time she was not able to raise money from those who had supported her in the past.

Work earned needed scholarships

In the meantime, Savage continued to develop her style. She produced many small clay figures of people around the city. One became especially popular and is considered among her best works. It is the head of a boy, with his hat turned at a jaunty angle and a streetwise expression on his face. Savage called this piece *Gamin.* When it was featured on the cover of a magazine, it caught the eye of the head of the National Urban League. He asked the Julius Rosenwald Fund, a philanthropic organization established by the founder of the department store Sears Roebuck, to award Savage a scholarship. The grant afforded her enough money to cover living and travel expenses for two years. When her scholarship awards were announced, other groups raised money for her as well, including African American women's groups and teachers at her former school, Florida A & M. They understood the discrimination she had suffered at the hands of the French scholarship board and wished to support her.

Nurtured careers of budding artists

Savage's dream to study in Europe finally came true. In 1930 and 1931 she studied sculpture in Paris and traveled throughout the Continent. Her works were shown in numerous exhibitions and won awards from two. Moreover, an African figure she designed was selected to adorn a medal for an important French exposition. Savage continued sculpting on her return to New York in 1931. The Great Depression was making life very hard then, especially for African Americans. Nonetheless, the early 1930s were a very busy time for Savage; they found her creating portraits of many prominent African Americans, including abolitionist Frederick Douglass, poet James Weldon Johnson, composer W. C. Handy, and others. It was also during this period that she founded the Savage Studio of Arts and Crafts in Harlem, where she taught many classes, several for children. This studio became the focus of her career in the 1930s. She encountered many talented young people in Harlem and was instrumental in starting their careers. Her students described Savage as a very inspirational teacher, while also acknowledging that she could be very stern and demanding. Jacob Lawrence, Gwendolyn Knight, and Norman Lewis are just three who benefited from Savage's help and encouragement.

As the 1930s continued, Savage spent less and less time on her own artworks and more on teaching and community activities. In 1937 she was appointed the first director of the Harlem Community Art Center, where she organized classes in art, education, and recreation. She also became an important figure in the government-sponsored programs of the Works Progress Administration, which were designed to help artists financially during the Depression. In 1939 Savage opened the Salon of Contemporary Negro Art, a gallery specializing in the art of African Americans. Despite her growing prominence in the community, it closed after a few years.

Created sculptures for World's Fair

The last major commission Savage received came when she was one of four women, and the only African American, asked to create sculptures for the 1939 New York World's Fair. She took as inspiration a line from a song known as the "Negro National Anthem." Called *Lift Every Voice and Sing,* the huge sculpture bore the shape of a harp, each string a figure of a child with his or her mouth open in song. The piece became one of the most popular attractions at the fair. Nonetheless, the plaster cast displayed there was never rendered in stone or metal. It was destroyed after the event. This was the fate of many of Savage's works as her meager funds rarely enabled her to permanently cast them. Only a few of her many creations survive.

Around 1940 Savage moved to a farm in upstate New York; she cut all ties to friends and the art world. She produced few works, preferring to spend her hours laboring on the farm or teaching an occasional art class for local children. Perhaps the years of financial and artistic struggle, much of it the result of racism, exhausted her. When her health declined in the early 1960s, she returned to New York to live with her daughter. She died there in 1962.

At an exhibition of African American art in 1967, the largest ever held up to that time, Savage's spirit could be detected. Many of the artworks were by her former students. According to collage artist Romare Bearden, the work that "attracted the most attention, the most favorable comments, was *Gamin* . . . created by Augusta Savage." Though often thwarted in her own artistic desires, her refusal to bow to the racism she encountered and her commitment to the black community, as well as the beauty of her sculpture, have remained an inspiration to artists of all colors.

Further Reading

Bearden, Romare, and Harry Henderson, *A History of African-American Artists: From 1792 to the Present,* Pantheon, 1993, pp. 168-80.
Bibby, Deirdre L., *Augusta Savage and the Art Schools of Harlem,* Schomburg Center for Research in Black Culture, 1988.
Ebony, August 1966, pp. 90-94; February 1968, pp. 116-22. □

Michael Joseph Savage

Michael Joseph Savage (1872-1940) was a prime minister of New Zealand and a labor leader. He won a high place in his nation's esteem for the social and political leadership he offered in a time of depression and economic insecurity.

Michael Joseph Savage was born on March 23, 1872, near Benalla in Victoria, Australia. His parents were among the first Irish settlers of the colony. Educated up to the age of 14 at the local state school, Savage worked as a store hand for some years, during which he and his family experienced the full weight of the depression of the 1890s. After a period of unemployment and farm laboring in New South Wales, Savage returned in 1900 to Victoria, where he took up gold mining for a living. Already known as a fine debater, he helped establish and manage a cooperative and a local labor league.

In 1907 Savage emigrated to New Zealand in order to join friends who had moved there from Victoria. Instead of going to the mining areas on the west coast, he stayed on in the North Island working as a miller and later as a cellarman. He never married.

Union Leader

Savage represented Auckland at the National Conference of Trades and Labour Councils of 1910 and in the next year stood as a parliamentary candidate of the New Zealand Socialist party for the seat of Auckland Central. He was unsuccessful, and he again failed as a candidate for the Social Democratic party in 1914. Despite the splintering of the unionist groups, the burly Savage was emerging as a popular figure.

When the New Zealand Labour party was formed in 1916, he became a member and was eventually elected national secretary in 1919. In the general election of December 1919 he won the seat of Auckland West and kept this seat for the rest of his life. In 1923 he was voted deputy leader of the parliamentary Labour party.

Prominent for his championing of the working man, Savage concentrated during his political career on social questions. When Harry Holland died in October 1933, Savage had become sufficiently trusted by his colleagues to be elected leader of the Labour party, and in the depression years from 1933 to 1935 he made a great impression on the New Zealand public with his sympathetic manner, humane sincerity, and common sense.

His Government

The election of 1935 was a spectacular victory for Labour, which under Savage's leadership had gained a moderate, or middle-of-the road, reputation with the electorate. As prime minister, Savage bore responsibility also for external affairs, native affairs, and broadcasting. He had a flair for publicity and in 1936 introduced the broadcasting of parliamentary proceedings.

In 1937 Savage went to London to attend the Imperial Conference and sought guarantees from the British for defense against possible Japanese attack. On his failure to obtain specific agreements he initiated a defense conference with Britain and Australia at Wellington in April 1939. Reluctantly he became concerned that New Zealand should rearm heavily, and he threw his considerable influence behind the recruiting campaign which preceded the outbreak of war in September.

During Savage's time as prime minister the foundations were laid for a very comprehensive social security scheme. He was not by any means a doctrinaire socialist, and he referred to his Social Security Bill as "applied Christianity." In 1938 his popularity assured the Labour party of an even more significant electoral victory than that of 1935.

In 1938 Savage's health deteriorated, however, and divisions within the party further sapped his strength and taxed his considerable skill in public relations. By August 1939 he was forced to hand over his duties to Peter Fraser, who became acting prime minister. Savage died in Wellington on March 27, 1940.

Not as well read or as able as Holland or Fraser, Savage was nevertheless an affable, popular, and shrewd father figure for a small democracy which seemed intent on giving high priority to personal and social security. His simplicity appealed to the plain man in the street and gave New Zealand government a human touch.

Further Reading

John A. Lee, *Simple on a Soap-box* (1964), is an autobiography by a former colleague of Savage and contains extensive material on him. His career is well covered in Bruce M. Brown, *The Rise of New Zealand Labour* (1962). For background material see Frederick L. W. Wood, *The New Zealand People at War* (1958), and Keith Sinclair, *A History of New Zealand* (1959; rev. ed. 1969).

Additional Sources

Gustafson, Barry, *From the cradle to the grave: a biography of Michael Joseph Savage*, Auckland: Reed Methuen, 1986. □

Friedrich Karl von Savigny

The German jurist Friedrich Karl von Savigny (1779-1861) advocated the doctrine of historical continuity, according to which historical rather than natural rights and actual historical facts rather than legal theory were the bases for legal systems.

Friedrich Karl von Savigny was born on Feb. 21, 1779, in Frankfurt am Main, one of 13 children. By the time he reached the age of 13, he had lost all his brothers and sisters and his parents.

In 1795 Savigny entered the University of Marburg, and in 1800 he received his doctor of laws degree. He began a teaching career as privatdozent (unpaid lecturer) the same

year. His first major work, *Das Recht des Besitzes* (1803; *The Law of Possession*), was well received by other jurists.

In 1804 Savigny married Kunigunde Brentano, the sister of Clemens Brentano, the poet, and the young couple set out on an extended study tour through France and southern Germany to collect legal materials for Savigny's planned work on the history of medieval law. Upon their return in 1808, he accepted a professorship in Roman law at the University of Landshut in Bavaria. Two years later, at the instigation of Wilhelm von Humboldt, who was assembling a faculty at the new University of Berlin, Savigny moved to the Prussian capital as professor of Roman law. He joined the commission for the establishment of the university and organized the law faculty and a *Spruch-Collegium* as an extraordinary tribunal for the purpose of delivering opinions on cases submitted by lower courts.

In 1814 Savigny issued a protest pamphlet, *Vom Berufunserer Zeit für Gesetzgebung and Rechtswissenschaft* (On the Vocation of Our Age for Legislation and Jurisprudence), where he spoke out against the pamphlet by the famous Heidelberg jurist A. F. J. Thibaut entitled *On the Necessity of a General Code for Germany* (1814). Thibaut had advocated the establishment of a completely new civil and criminal code of German law, pointing out that the presently used chief sources were based on Roman law, "the work of a nation which was very unlike us, and from the period of the lowest decline of the same." Savigny maintained that "law comes into being through custom and popular acceptance, through internal, silently working forces and not through the arbitrariness of a law giver." The

historical continuity prevalent in the sources of Roman law was a better foundation for a legal system than the arrogance and shallow philosophy of the so-called "natural law."

In 1815 Savigny, Karl Friedrich Eichhorn, the author of the multivolume *History of German Law and Institutions,* and the publisher Johann Friedrich Ludwig Göschen founded the *Zeitschrift für geschichtliche Rechtswissenschaft,* which became the organ of the new historical school of jurisprudence. The same year Savigny published the first volume of his monumental *Geschichte des römischen Rechts im Mittelalter* (6 vols., 1815-1831; *History of Roman Law in the Middle Ages*). He described the survival of Roman law in western Europe and stimulated at the same time historical writing based on actual source materials.

Between 1817 and 1822 Savigny served on various legal boards. Because of a serious nervous illness he sought relief and recuperation in travel, spending more than a year in Italy, where he completed a number of smaller writings while continuing work on his *History of Roman Law.* In the late 1830s he undertook another major research project which culminated in the publication of *Das System des heutigen römischen Rechts* (8 vols., 1840-1849; The System of Contemporary Usage of Roman Law).

In 1842 Savigny's teaching career came to an end when he was appointed *Grosskanzler* (high chancellor), a position which put him in charge of the Prussian Ministry of Legislation, which was being separated from the administration of justice. The main legal concerns during his tenure dealt with bills of exchange, divorce regulations, and questions of civil and criminal court procedures. He retired from office in 1848. In 1853 he added to his earlier writings on contemporary Roman law with the treatise *Das Obligationenrecht* (*The Law of Obligations*). He died on Oct. 25, 1861, in Berlin.

Although Savigny was not the founder of the historical school of jurisprudence, he was its most famous representative. Many of his interpretations were challenged during his lifetime and later, but by reintroducing the juridical methods of Roman law he provided an important impetus for the study of modern law.

Further Reading

There is no full-length biography of Savigny in English. A short but useful introduction to Savigny's work is in G. P. Gooch, *History and Historians in the Nineteenth Century* (1913). The Thibaut-Savigny controversy is described in A. W. Small, *Origins of Sociology* (1924), which also deals with other German historians and writers and their impact on the social sciences. □

Jonas Malheiros Savimbi

Jonas Malheiros Savimbi (born 1934) was a founder and the leader of UNITA (National Union for the Total Independence of Angola) which first fought **against Portuguese rule in Angola and later against the socialist government led by the Popular Movement for the Liberation of Angola (MPLA).**

Jonas Malheiros Savimbi was born on August 3, 1934, at Munhango, in the Moxico province of central Angola. His father was a longtime employee of the Benguela railroad. Savimbi attended the Protestant missionary school in his father's home village in Bie province and later transferred to another missionary school at Dondi. He then attended secondary school, first at Silva Porto (now called Bie), the largest town in central Angola, and then at Sa da Bandeira (now called Lubango) in the south.

Savimbi had already received far more education than most Angolans, who under Portuguese colonial rule had little opportunity of going to school. In 1958 his abilities were further recognized when he won a scholarship from the United Church of Christ to study in Lisbon. In 1960 he transferred to Fribourg University and then to the University of Lausanne in Switzerland, where he studied political science.

The Struggle for Independence

He was soon to put his knowledge to practical use as one of the leaders of Angolan resistance to Portuguese colonialism. Savimbi, however, maintained that his real training in politics came through his participation in the struggle for independence itself.

Savimbi credited the Kenyan nationalist leader Tom Mboya, whom he met at a students' conference in 1961, with persuading him to enter politics full-time. He joined a liberation movement called the Popular Union of Angola and within a year had been appointed first as general secretary and later as foreign minister of the government in exile. Disillusioned with the leadership of this group, Savimbi broke away and started to lay the groundwork for a new liberation front which was to draw most of its support from the people of central Angola, the Ovimbundu, to whom Savimbi himself belonged. In 1966 his work culminated in the founding of UNITA (National Union for the Total Independence of Angola) at a secret meeting in the remote bush country of eastern Angola. From this time Savimbi launched the armed struggle of UNITA against the Portuguese government in the Angolan capital, Luanda.

After the Portuguese dictatorship was overthrown in a military coup in 1974, Savimbi emerged from the guerrilla war to conclude a cease-fire with the new Portuguese leaders. He also signed an agreement with the two other Angolan liberation parties in 1975 in the hope that the three groups might come together and lead their fellow citizens in a peaceful transition to independence. This was not to be, however. Civil war broke out, and Jonas Savimbi then entered into one of the most controversial periods of his political career.

Civil War

Savimbi continued this war from 1975 into the 1990s. His enemies maintained that UNITA was a puppet organization in the hands of South Africa, the most hated regime on the African continent. UNITA also received arms and medical supplies from the United States and other Western powers. Savimbi claimed that he had a great deal of popular support among Angolans, especially in the central region of the country where the Ovimbundu live, a people downtrodden and dominated by their compatriots to the north during colonial rule. The success of UNITA early in the guerrilla war fluctuated. At times it controlled about one-third of the country, but mostly in thinly-populated regions in eastern and southeastern Angola. The most serious threat to the MPLA government was UNITA's sabotage of the Benguela railroad, which was crucial to the Angolan economy.

A Controversial Figure

Savimbi attracted some admiration throughout his career, for he was a natural politician, dynamic, charismatic, and a first-rate orator. He spent most of his time in the bush country of eastern and southern-eastern Angola, at his headquarters at Jamba, or traveling about in order to rally villagers to his party and to his guerrilla army. He also traveled in search of external support, as he did in 1986 when he was received at the White House and by some American congressional leaders who supported his resistance to the Cuban-supported government of MPLA. The burly, bearded guerrilla chief was seldom seen without his combat fatigues, beret, and swagger stick, in keeping with his image as a resistance fighter. In spite of his ability to gain foreign support (including from the United States during President Reagan's second term), the potential long-term success of Savimbi and UNITA was doubtful as a result of its association with the racist South African regime.

Still, Savimbi enjoyed considerable support among conservatives in the United States and other western countries, who saw UNITA as a foil to communist ambitions, here embodied by Cubans aiding the MPLA. Arms flowed to UNITA, despite U.S. leaders' reluctance to support the war effort openly for fear of antagonizing surrounding African countries. According to Savimbi, U.S. interests also subsidized the MPLA through $2 billion per year in oil revenues flowing into Luanda.

Critics of U.S. support for Savimbi argued he was a strange bedfellow for a country which purportedly despised tyrants. Savimbi was described variously as an opportunist and a butcher by those who found it strange that a former self-described Marxist would befriend a white racist South Africa, that a follower of Mao Tse-tung and Ché Guevara would be welcomed in the United States by conservative senator Jesse Helms. Savimbi, meanwhile, thundered that his Angolan opponent, Eduardo do Santes, was a puppet of Russian and Cuban imperialism.

Human rights watchers throughout the world worried that Savimbi was reported to participate actively in the execution of supposed witches, some of whom, coincidentally, were his opponents in UNITA. In September 1983, Savimbi allegedly participated in the burning of twelve women and three children accused of witchcraft, purportedly firing his trademark ivory pistol at one woman attempting to escape.

Elections

In December 1988, the logjam was temporarily broken by a tripartite agreement in which South Africa assented to granting independence to Namibia, Cuba agreed to pull out of Angola, and the warring sides in Angola began talks leading to elections. Zambian President Kenneth Kaunda hinted that Savimbi would go into voluntary exile, a report that proved incorrect as the UNITA leader went on the campaign trail instead after a cease-fire was negotiated to end the decade. For 17 months, a 16-year civil war which had left 350,000 people dead came to a standstill.

Savimbi's speeches were marred by threats of violence and statements, that by definition, an election would be unfair if he did not win. Despite the word of 300 foreign observers that the 1992 elections were indeed fair, Savimbi refused to accept a loss at the polls and resumed fighting six weeks later.

The civil war thus entered a particularly tragic chapter, during which another 150,000 people died and tremendous damage was done to what remained of a potentially prosperous country. Western support for Savimbi crumbled, though he was able to obtain enough weapons to regain control of about 70 percent of the country at first. By the mid-1990s, Savimbi's grip on the country weakened, however, and he once again entered talks with Dos Santos, agreeing to end 19 years of hostilities and demobilize

UNITA forces in exchange for a power-sharing arrangement between UNITA and the MPLA.

Further Reading

For general background on Angola see Lawrence W. Henderson, *Angola: Five Centuries of Conflict* (1979), and Basil Davidson, *In the Eye of the Storm* (1972). On Savimbi's participation in the nationalist struggle against the Portuguese see John Marcum, *The Angolan Revolution*, two volumes (1969 and 1978). On the role of Savimbi and of UNITA in Angolan politics after 1975, see Arthur Jay Klinghoffer, *The Angolan War* (1980) and Michael Wolfers and Jane Bergerol, *Angola in the Front Line* (1983).

A student of the conflict in Angola will find numerous reports, many of them conflicting, in the world press. Information presented here was obtained from Internet postings by *International Peacekeeping News, Reuter Information Service, The Associated Press,* the South African *Mail & Guardian,* and Voice of America. □

Girolamo Savonarola

The Italian religious reformer Girolamo Savonarola (1452-1498) became dictator of Florence in the 1490s and instituted there, in the middle of the Renaissance, a reign of purity and asceticism.

Girolamo Savonarola was born in Ferrara on Sept. 21, 1452. He was the third of seven children of Niccolo Savonarola, a physician, and Elena Bonacossi. His father groomed Girolamo for the medical profession, but even as a youth he took more interest in the writings of the Schoolmen, particularly Thomas Aquinas. Savonarola had time for neither the comfortable, courtly life of his father's household nor youthful sports and exercises, so absorbed was he in the subtleties of the scholastics and their spiritual father, Aristotle.

Repelled by the corruption of the world around him, Savonarola withdrew ever further into solitude, meditation, and prayer. In 1475 he entered a Dominican monastery at Bologna. After living quietly there for 6 years, Savonarola transferred to the convent of S. Marco in Florence and began preaching in the church of S. Lorenzo. His style, laden with scholastic didacticism, was not appealing, and few came to hear him. In 1486, however, while preaching in Lombardy, he shed all syllogisms and circumlocutions and began to speak directly, simply, and passionately of the wrath of God. His popularity as a preacher grew immensely.

Savonarola's fame spread to Florence as he prophesied the doom of all tyrants who then prevailed in the world. In 1490, through the influence of Pico della Mirandola, he was called back to Florence and in July 1491 became prior of S. Marco. All the while he thundered against the vanity of the humanists and the viciousness of the clergy. Because he spared no one, Lorenzo de' Medici, the ruler of Florence, urged him to bridle his tongue. He would not yield, and in April 1492 Savonarola refused to grant Lorenzo absolution because the ruler would not give liberty to the Florentines.

Lorenzo's son and successor, Piero, was weak, and the 2-year period of his rule witnessed Savonarola's rise to the most powerful authority in the city. He acquired with difficulty the consent of the new pope, Alexander VI, to sever his convent from the Lombard Congregation of the Dominican order. Then, as leader of an independent monastic house, Savonarola instituted reforms that inspired respect and swelled the ranks of recruits. Admiration and wonder filled Florentine hearts when the prophecies that accompanied his fiery denunciations proved frighteningly accurate. He had predicted the deaths of Lorenzo and Pope Innocent VIII in 1492. Now Savonarola foretold the terrible fate about to descend upon Italy as punishment for the sins of its tyrants and priests. Early in 1494 he told his congregation that Charles VIII, King of France, would invade Italy and that this would be divine retribution. In September the prophecy was fulfilled.

Savonarola as Dictator

When Charles arrived in Florentine territory, Piero surrendered to the invader. When the Florentine Signory heard of this, they angrily deposed Piero and revived the republic. A delegation including Savonarola met Charles at Pisa and attempted to persuade him to moderate his demands. The King showed that he was not so disposed. After he entered Florence on Nov. 17, 1494, Charles insisted on exorbitant indemnities, yielding only to the eloquence of Savonarola, who persuaded him to reduce his demands and leave the city. Upon Charles's departure Florence's grateful citizens placed themselves in the hands of the monk.

Like the Medici before him, Savonarola held no public office, but under his guidance a new constitution was promulgated, establishing a new republic on June 10, 1495. He initiated the abrogation of arbitrary taxation and its replacement with a 10 percent tax on all real property. He undertook the immediate relief of the poor and the strict administration of justice. He also instituted a regime of austerity that seemed out of place in the Florence of the High Renaissance. Hymns supplanted profane songs, art objects and luxuries were cast aside or burned, and somber unadorned clothing was worn by all.

Fall from Power

At the height of his power, Savonarola made bitter enemies both at home and abroad. The Arrabiati, or Medicean adherents in Florence, and Pope Alexander VI were eager to rid Florence of the troublesome monk. Alexander's motives were mainly political, for he was angered by Savonarola's alliance with France. He was also displeased at the public criticism leveled by Savonarola against his scandalous pontificate. Twice in 1495 the Pope summoned Savonarola to Rome and ordered him to stop preaching, but the monk refused to obey. On May 5, 1497, encouraged by the Arrabiati, Alexander excommunicated him. Savonarola remained rebellious and continued to celebrate Mass. Alexander then warned the Signory that unless Savonarola was silenced he would place an interdict upon the city. On March 17, 1498, the Signory ordered Savonarola to stop preaching, and he obeyed.

By this time the Florentines had grown weary of puritanic life. Maddened by disappointment when an ordeal by fire to which Savonarola had been challenged did not take place because of rain, they joined the Arrabiati. With unexampled fickleness, the Florentines demanded Savonarola's arrest. A mob attacked the monastery of S. Marco, and peace was restored only when Savonarola himself begged all men to lay down their arms. Savonarola was tortured until he confessed many crimes, and on May 23, 1498, convicted falsely of heresy, he was burned at the stake in the Piazza della Signoria.

Further Reading

The definitive work on Savonarola is Pasquale Villari, *The Life and Times of Girolamo Savonarola,* translated by Linda Villari (1889). Donald Weinstein, *Savonarola and Florence: Prophesy and Patriotism in the Renaissance* (1971), emphasizes the impact of Florence on the reformer. Also useful is Ralph Roeder, *The Man of the Renaissance* (1933). Still excellent is Ludwig Pastor, *History of the Popes,* vol. 3 (1898).

Additional Sources

Erlanger, Rachel, *The unarmed prophet: Savonarola in Florence,* New York: McGraw-Hill, 1988. □

Saw Maung

Senior General Saw Maung (born 1928) was the leader of the *tatmadaw*, the Burmese armed forces, **which took power in a military coup on September 18, 1988. The new military regime renamed Burma as Myanmar, its name in the Burmese language.**

Saw Maung was born in 1928 in Mandalay, the seat of Burmese culture. He was educated at the Mandalay Central Boys (now National) High School, where he completed Standard 8. He also studied electrical engineering between 1942 and 1948.

In 1949, shortly after independence, he joined the Burmese army as an enlisted man, and soon thereafter was promoted to sergeant. He was commissioned a lieutenant in 1952. From 1962, when the Burmese army under General Ne Win instituted a coup against the civilian government of Prime Minister U Nu, he was assigned to the 29th Regiment, where he remained until 1963. He also chaired the District Security Committee during that period. He joined the Burma Socialist Programme Party in 1964, which he chaired. It was the only legal party in the state and was controlled by the Burmese military.

Saw Maung served with the 5th Regiment from 1965 to 1967, and from 1967 to 1970 was with the 29th and the 47th Regiments. After this period of regimental duty he was rotated through a variety of key regional command posts. From 1970 to 1972 he was attached to the North-West Command, in 1972 becoming deputy commander of the Eastern Command; for the next three years he served as deputy commander of the Northeast Command. He also

served as chairman of the Northern Shan State Security Committee in 1972-1973.

In 1975 Saw Maung became deputy commander of the 99th Light Infantry Division, one of the elite strike units of the Burmese armed forces, for a brief period before he became its commander, a post that he held until 1976. Saw Maung became the commander of the Northern Command in 1976 and was Kachin State Security Committee chairman until 1979. At that time, he was promoted to brigadier general and became commander of the Southwest Command in May of that year, as well as Irrawaddy Division Security Committee chairman, a post he held until 1981.

In 1981 Saw Maung was promoted to adjutant general attached to the Ministry of Defense, and in 1983 became army vice chief of staff and the following year deputy minister of defense. In 1985 he was appointed chief of staff of the Defense Services, and in November 1988 he was promoted to general. Following the coup of that year, he was promoted along with the rest of the members of the State Law and Order Restoration Council (SLORC) to the rank of senior general. With General Saw Maung as its chairman, SLORC was formed with 18 officers to restore order in a chaotic situation of nation-wide popular unrest. The SLORC functioned under a martial law regime and promised to turn the government over to civilian elected officials at some point after a new constitution was written and promulgated.

Senior General Saw Maung, who spent all his adult life in the armed forces, was said to be close to General Ne Win, former commander of the Burmese Armed Forces and former chairman of the now defunct Burma Socialist Programme Party, which ran the country until the coup of 1988. In September the armed forces, led by General Saw Maung, seized control of the government. The military moved to suppress the demonstrations, and thousands of unarmed protesters were killed. Martial law was imposed over most of the country, and constitutional government was replaced by SLORC.

The SLORC, soon after the coup, agreed that the state would move from a single-party political system to a multi-party elected government. Under the stringent rules imposed by the martial law regime, 235 separate political parties registered for a national election, and 93 participated in the polling of May 27, 1990. During that time the military declared titular neutrality, but the opposition National League for Democracy swept the election with 392 of the 485 seats, even though its top leadership was either in jail or under house arrest. The voting was generally regarded as fair.

Senior General Saw Maung and his colleagues must determine how and when the SLORC will leave power and the nature of the process to reach that end. He had already reached the normal retirement age for the military by 1990 but agreed to continue in the service for a time.

The Saw Maung regime stirred worldwide condemnation by refusing to recognize the opposition National League for Democracy's victory in the 1990 legislative elections. The league's leader, Daw Aung San Suu Kyi, was placed under house arrest, where she remained even after winning the 1991 Nobel Peace Prize. As antigovernment

protests continued, Saw Maung lost power, resigning as foreign minister in September 1991, as defense minister in March 1992, and as prime minister and council chairman in April 1992. He resigned citing health problems. "Owing to heavy responsibilities undertaken continuously by Senior Gen. Saw Maung, his health failed, necessitating a complete rest as advised by his doctors," the official Yangon Radio said.

Further Reading

Reference works on the period of Saw Maung's participation in Burma's history included David I. Steinberg, *The Future of Burma. Crisis and Choice in Myanmar,* Asian Agenda Report #14, the University Press of America and the Asia Society (1990); Bertil Lintner, *Outrage* (Hong Kong: 1989); and Mya Than and Joseph L.H. Tan, editors, *Myanmar Dilemmas and Options.* See also *The Challenge of Economic Transition in the 1990s* (Singapore: 1990) and the April 24, 1992 editions of the *LA Times* and *Chicago Tribune.* □

Comte de Saxe

Hermann Maurice, Comte de Saxe (1696-1750), was a marshal of France. His active campaigns, methods of organizing and training troops, and general principles of warfare influenced both his own and later times.

M aurice de Saxe who is known as Marshal Saxe, was born in Dresden on Oct. 28, 1696, the first of the 354 acknowledged illegitimate children of Augustus II, Elector of Saxony and King of Poland. His mother was the Countess Aurora von Konigsmark. Like his father in "his fabulous strength, the immensity of his appetites, and his limitless lust," Saxe also possessed a high intelligence.

When he was twelve years old, Saxe entered the Saxon army. He fought in the battle of Malplaquet under the Duke of Marlborough and Eugene of Savoy. By the time of the Peace of Utrecht, he had participated in four campaigns in Flanders and Pomerania and had commanded a cavalry regiment. He served under Eugene in the war against the Turks, and in 1717 he took part in the capture of Belgrade.

In 1720 Saxe went to Paris, becoming a camp marshal to the Duc d'Orléans. When his father died, he was offered the command of the Saxon army, but he preferred to remain in France. Saxe fought in the War of the Polish Succession (1733-1738) as a lieutenant general. In the War of the Austrian Succession (1740-1748), after leading his troops in a successful surprise attack on Prague in 1741, he restrained them from pillaging the city.

In 1743, made marshal of France, Saxe was placed in command of an army assembling at Dunkirk for a proposed invasion of England. When France declared war on England in 1744, he took operational command of the main army in

Flanders, led personally by Louis XV. Later Saxe took full control.

In May 1745 Saxe led his army of about 70,000 men to Tournai and invested the city, which was defended by 50,000 English troops. On May 10 he moved 52,000 troops to Fontenay to block an allied relief force, which he defeated. Then he took Tournai, Ghent, Bruges, Audenarde, Ostende, and Brussels. These battles, plus Rascoux in 1746 and the capture of Maastricht in 1748, firmly established Saxe's reputation. In gratitude for his services, Louis XV gave him life tenure of the château of Chambord.

There Saxe wrote *Mes rêveries* (*My Reveries*), his reflections on the art of war. His descriptions of how to raise and train recruits and how to establish garrison and field camps soon became standard procedure. Saxe stimulated acceptance of breech-loading muskets and cannon and invented a gun capable of accompanying the infantry. He rediscovered and initiated the practice of marching in cadence, lost since the Romans. He also modified the normal linear battle formations and tactics of his day by using an embryonic form of attack column that required less training and became the usual assault method a hundred years later.

A fearless man in battle, Saxe led a dissolute life of between campaigns. He died at Chambord on Nov. 30, 1750.

Further Reading

The standard works for information on Saxe are Leslie H. Thornton, *Campaigners Grave and Gay* (1925), and Jon Manship

White, *Marshal of France: The Life and Times of Maurice, Comte de Saxe* (1962). See also Basil Henry Liddell Hart, *Great Captains Unveiled* (1927); Edmund B. D'Auvergne, *The Prodigious Marshal* (1931); and Thomas R. Phillips, ed., *Roots of Strategy* (1940).

Additional Sources

Liddell Hart, Basil Henry, Sir, *Great captains unveiled,* London: Greenhill Books; Novato, Ca., U.S.A.: Presidio Press, 1990. □

Jean Baptiste Say

The French economist Jean Baptiste Say (1767-1832), one of the founders of the classical school, is best known for his law of markets. He was the first academic teacher of economics in France.

Jean Baptiste Say was born on Jan. 5, 1767, in Lyons of a Protestant merchant family. Though he became a deist, he retained the deep-rooted sense of moral earnestness he inherited from the martyrs of the revocation of the Edict of Nantes. His outlook was no less affected by his mercantile upbringing and education. After serving two business apprenticeships in England, he entered an insurance firm in Paris, and at the suggestion of his employer he read Adam Smith's *Wealth of Nations.* Thereupon he decided to become an economist, abandoning business to write economic articles for a republican periodical, *La Décade philosophique,* of which he was editor.

During the French Revolution, Say espoused its principles and in 1792 fought in defense of the republic. Under the Consulate, he was made a member of the Tribunate, but when he refused on principle to acquiesce to Napoleon's financial policies, he was shorn of his high official position and became a successful textile manufacturer in the north of France, where he introduced the new cotton-spinning methods copied from England. After Napoleon's fall, Say returned to Paris and instituted a series of public lectures on political economy at the Athénée. In 1819 he was appointed the first incumbent of the chair in industrial economy at the Museum of Arts and Crafts, and in 1830 he became the first professor of political economy at the Collège de France.

In his major work, *A Treatise on Political Economy* (1803), Say improved upon Smith's *Wealth of Nations* in form and content. His tripartite division of the classical doctrine into production, distribution, and consumption set a precedent which was followed in standard treatises for more than a century. He gave precision to the concept of the entrepreneur, whom Smith had failed to distinguish from the capitalist investor. Viewing the entrepreneur as buyer and coordinator of the services of land, labor, and capital, Say envisaged production essentially as a market phenomenon. This led him to his famous "law of markets," according to which production, by generating income flows without any leakage into monetary hoards, automatically assured effective demand for aggregate output. Siding with James Mill and David Ricardo, but against Thomas Malthus, he held that general gluts were impossible. Controversy over "Say's law" continues to this day, especially since it was attacked by John Maynard Keynes. Moreover, Say repudiated the labor-cost theory of value and stressed utility as the cause of value. The subsequent development of general equilibrium economics owes much to Say's contribution.

Say's introduction to economics, the ideological flavor he imparted to it, and the social purpose he hoped it would fulfill are all reflections of his life and times. In his teaching, as in his voluminous writings, which include a *Catechism of Political Economy* (1817) and *A Complete Course in Practical Political Economy* (1828-1829), his aim was to lay a new moral foundation of society by revealing economics as a science of laws of nature which cannot be violated without bad effect. Say was thus an apostle of economic liberalism, utterly opposed to government intervention in business and to all socialistic schemes. For him, moral legitimacy attaches to a social order in which individual self-interest is the only guiding rule. After his death on Nov. 15, 1832, his son Horace and his grandson Léon, who were also economists, helped propagate this ultraliberal doctrine, which dominated French economics throughout the 19th century.

Further Reading

Although there is no book in English on the life and writings of Say, useful appreciations of his contributions and historical background are in J. A. Schumpeter, *History of Economic Analysis* (1954), and Leo Rogin, *The Meaning and Validity of Economic Theory* (1956). □

Francis Bowes Sayre

Francis Bowes Sayre (1885-1972) was an American law teacher and public official. He was responsible for negotiating the treaties with European powers which ended extraterritoriality in Thailand.

Francis Sayre was born on April 30, 1885, in South Bethlehem, Pa., the son of Robert Heysham Sayre (1824-1907), a civil engineer and official of the Lehigh Valley Railroad. He graduated from Williams College in 1909 and from the Harvard Law School in 1912. Theodore Roosevelt assisted in obtaining his first job, as a deputy assistant to the district attorney of New York County. He married Jessie Woodrow Wilson, daughter of President Woodrow Wilson, in a White House ceremony in 1913.

Offered a position as instructor in government and assistant to the president of Williams College, Sayre returned there in 1914 and then went back to the Harvard Law School in 1917 to study for the doctorate in jurisprudence, which he received in 1918. He remained on the Harvard faculty until 1934, teaching international, maritime, and criminal law, and taught the first course on labor law offered in any law school.

When Eldon James, third in a series of Harvard law professors to serve as adviser in foreign affairs to the government of Siam, returned to Cambridge in 1923, Sayre was chosen to succeed him and went to Bangkok intending to serve only a year. He went at a time when decades-long negotiations to end the unequal treaties of the previous century were stalled. Sayre gave new direction to discussions with the French in Bangkok and, on suggesting that more rapid progress could be made by negotiating with the European powers directly, he took charge of treaty negotiations in Europe in 1924-1925.

Against considerable obstacles, treaties with 10 nations were concluded which ended extraterritoriality and lifted restrictions on Thai import duties. A superbly effective and principled negotiator, Sayre was entitled *Phya Kalyan Maitri* and appointed permanent minister plenipotentiary and Siam's representative on the Permanent Court of Arbitration at The Hague.

Returning to Harvard as a full professor, Sayre again entered public service as Massachusetts state commissioner of correction in 1932 and then, in 1933, as an assistant secretary of state in charge of the negotiation of trade agreements in the first Roosevelt administration. Serving also as chairman of the interdepartmental commission on the Philippines, he was appointed U.S. high commissioner to the Philippines in 1939 and was evacuated by submarine in 1942.

Sayre became diplomatic adviser to the United Nations Relief and Rehabilitation Administration (1944-1947) and then U.S. representative on the Trusteeship Council of the UN (1947-1952), of which he was the first president. In 1952-1954 he was the personal representative in Japan of the presiding bishop of the Protestant Episcopal Church, service in which his high Christian ideals were more explicitly but no less strongly expressed than in his more public appointments. Sayre died in Washington, D.C., on March 29, 1972.

Further Reading

Sayre's autobiography, *Glad Adventure* (1957), is an unusually lively and expressive self-portrait. His views on international trade are in his *The Way Forward: The American Trade Agreements Program* (1939). For background information on Sayre as assistant secretary of state see Samuel Flagg Bemis, ed., *The American Secretaries of State and Their Diplomacy*, vols. 12 and 13 by Julius W. Pratt (1964). □

Sayyid Qutb

Sayyid Qutb (1906-1966) was an Egyptian writer, educator, and religious leader. His writings about Islam, and especially his call for a revolution to establish an Islamic state and society, greatly influenced the Islamic resurgence movements of the 20th century.

Sayyid Qutb was born in 1906 in the village of Mūshā in the Asyūt province of upper Egypt. His father was Hajjī Ibrāhīm Qutb, a well-to-do farmer of the region. The family, which traces its ancestry ultimately to Central Asia via India, in addition to father and mother consisted of two brothers and three sisters, of whom Sayyid Qutb was the eldest. His brother Muhammad and two of his sisters, Amīnah and Hamīdah, were also writers active in Islamic causes; all suffered arrest for their views along with their brother in 1965.

In his writings Sayyid Qutb attributed his strong bent towards religion to the influence of his parents. His mother, Fātimah Husayn 'Uthmān, had a particular love for the Koran (Qur'ān) which she inculcated in her offspring; she was determined that her children should all become buffāz (memorizers of the holy book). It was her custom to invite professional Koran reciters to the family home during the nights of the month of fasting (Ramadān), and Sayyid Qutb later recalled listening to the chanting of the sacred verses at his mother's side. He also mentioned the care exercised by his father to impress upon the youth the significance of the coming day of judgment.

Sayyid Qutb's earliest education was in the local village school where by the age of ten he had memorized the Koran. His mother was the sympathetic ear for his recitations during this time. At age 13 he went to Cairo for further study and there entered the Dār al-'Ulūm secondary school (established 1872), which offered an essentially secular education; among its purposes was the preparation of students for employment with government. At this stage of his life he was much influenced by the Westernizing tendencies prevalent in the school and among some Egyptian intellectuals. In 1929 he gained admission to Cairo University, where he earned the B.A. degree in education in 1933. After graduation he became a professor of the college, where he taught for some time before joining the Ministry of Education as inspector of schools.

A turning point came for Sayyid Qutb in 1949 when he was sent to the United States for higher studies in educational administration. Over a two year period he worked in several different institutions including what was then Wilson Teachers' College in Washington, D.C. and Colorado State College for Education in Greeley, as well as Stanford University. He also travelled extensively visiting the major cities of the United States and spent time in Europe on the return journey to Egypt. His reaction to the Western experience was decidedly negative; he found Western society hopelessly materialistic, corrupt, morally loose, and ridden with injustice. He was especially distressed by the disrespect shown to Arabs in the United States and the overwhelming support of its people for the state of Israel, founded in 1948. One of the most popular of his books, *Social Justice in Islam* (1948), reflects his critical attitude to the West.

Even before the journey to America Sayyid Qutb had begun to manifest interest in the teachings of the Society of Muslim Brothers (al-Ikhwān al-Muslimūn), the foremost of Egypt's resurgent Islamic organizations. Founded in 1929 by Hassan Al-Banna (Hasan al-Bannā'), the society had numerous followers and sympathizers and wielded much political influence. In 1949, however, it was banned, and many of its members were arrested after the assassination of the Egyptian prime minister, al-Nuqrāshī, by one of the Brothers. The society gained a new lease on life in 1952 with the coup d'état of the Free Officers which overthrew the Egyptian monarchy. Many of the Free Officers had long had clandestine and sympathetic relations with the Muslim Brothers. The society's members were released from prison, a new leader was chosen to replace al-Bannā' (who had been murdered in the violence of 1949), and Sayyid Qutb, formerly a mere member, emerged as one of the foremost figures. He was employed in the society's Bureau of Guidance and was placed in charge of the office that bore responsibility for the propagation of the society's Islamic views. In this position he exercised the function of intellectual leader of the Brothers, expressing his opinions in books and numerous articles in a variety of journals.

In July 1954 he was made editor of the society's newspaper, *al-Ikhwān al-Muslimu*, but held the post for only two months when the newspaper was closed by Gamal Abdel Nasser ('Abd al-Nāsir) because of its opposition to the Anglo-Egyptian pact of that year. Originally, the relations between the Muslim Brothers and the Free Officers had been close, but they soured as the Brothers began to oppose government policy. There was a complete rupture in 1954 after an attempt on the life of President Nasser by a Brother. Six members of the society were executed, thousands of others were arrested, and the society was again declared illegal.

Sayyid Qutb was among those arrested and was sentenced by the People's Court to 15 years' rigorous imprisonment. The experience was extremely difficult for Sayyid Qutb, especially the first three years, for he was a generally sickly man who suffered from a number of afflictions. It is alleged also that he was made to undergo torture of various kinds. Nevertheless, during the years in jail—which lasted until mid-1964—he completed his influential commentary on the Koran (*In the Shadow of the Qur'ān*) in 30 parts (eight volumes).

Sayyid Qutb was released from prison because of an appeal by Iraq's president Abdul Salam Areb to Nasser, but he remained under surveillance. However, he continued to write and to work for the Islamic cause. After less than a year of freedom he was again arrested on a charge of attempting to overthrow the Egyptian government by force. The basis of the charge was his last book, *Milestones,* which sanctioned force as a means to bring about an Islamic revolution and to transform society. On August 19, 1966, Sayyid Qutb and two companions were sentenced to death by a military tribunal, and the sentence was carried out on the morning of August 25 following. Sayyid Qutb is, thus, known as shahīd, or martyr.

In his personal intellectual evolution Sayyid Qutb passed from a westernizing tendency in his youth to a revolutionary Islamic radicalism in the years before his death. He is a hero and one of the principal ideologues of the Islamic resurgence in the last third of the 20th century. His writings have been translated into many languages, and he is read wherever Muslims are found. His teachings concerning jihād and the Islamic revolution were major influences on 'Alī Sharī'atī' and the students who, following him, participated in the Iranian revolution.

Further Reading

There is an article on Sayyid Qutb by Yvonne Y. Haddad in *Voices of Resurgent Islam,* edited by John Esposito (1983). Detailed information on the Muslim Brothers and their history up to 1954 may be found in the work by Richard Mitchell, *The Society of the Muslim Brothers* (London, 1969). Many of Sayyid Qutb's beliefs are set forth in the paperback *Islam and Universal Peace* (1977). □

Oscar Luigi Scalfaro

Oscar Luigi Scalfaro (born 1918) was a prominent Christian Democratic leader for over forty years before becoming the president of the Italian Republic in May 1992 for a seven-year term.

Oscar Luigi Scalfaro became the president of the Italian Republic on May 25, 1992. His election took place in one of the periods of greatest political and social turmoil in the history of post-World War II Italy. Scalfaro was immediately invested with much of the responsibility for solving Italy's crisis.

Scalfaro, a native of the northwestern region of Piedmont, was known as an austere and incorruptible politician, as well as a devout Catholic attending Mass every day. This image indeed explains his election to the presidency, as the principal task at hand was to return Italian public and political life to a more moral course. Scalfaro's election was in fact prompted by harsh criticism against the government because of corruption among political leaders and ineffectiveness in several areas, especially in dealing with the seemingly all-powerful Mafia in Sicily and other parts of the country.

Votes for Scalfaro—who, according to the provisions of the Italian constitution, was elected by Italy's deputies and senators—reached the necessary majority immediately after the shockingly brutal murder of Sicilian magistrate Giovanni Falcone, along with his wife and bodyguards. Falcone had achieved national fame and popularity due to his courageous and outspoken anti-Mafia campaigns. Anger against the government erupted in the course of the Falcones' funerals, prompting many Italian members of Parliament to end political bickering over the presidential election. A 12-day stalemate was broken and conservative Scalfaro became president with the votes of the Christian Democrats as well as the Left, including the ex-Communist Democratic Party of the Left, the Greens, and the Radicals. Undoubtedly his ability to remain untainted by the widespread Italian political scandals, as well as his moral stature, were key to understanding this unusual vote of the Left for a conservative leader.

Scalfaro was born September 9, 1918, in Novara in the Piedmont. After graduating from the Catholic University Sacro Cuore in Milan and after the end of World War II, Scalfaro was continuously in public service and could indeed be considered one of the founding fathers of the Italian Republic—Italy ceased to be a monarchy in 1946. Elected to the Chamber of Deputies in 1948, he had represented the district of Turin without interruption since that time. Scalfaro was a prominent and independent-minded Christian Democratic member of Parliament for more than forty years. Over that period of time he also served as a prosecuting attorney and held several important government posts, such as minister of transportation (1966-1968), education (1972-1973), and the interior (1983-1987). Following the 1992 elections he became speaker of the Chamber of Deputies.

Despite this long and prestigious career, Oscar Luigi Scalfaro was not widely known by the public until he became president, perhaps because of his austere style. However, upon assuming the highest office in the Italian Republic, he immediately readapted the office to his own personality, creating a sharp contrast with his predecessor, Francesco Cossiga. Cossiga had distinguished himself primarily for his verbal attacks, at times quite violent, against the corrupt political practices rampant in Italy. The violence of the attacks, however, while attracting the public's attention to Italy's most fundamental leadership problems, also appeared to demean the office of the presidency. It was thus Scalfaro's task to restore a more decorous style to the presidency. That he proceeded to do quite effectively as soon as he assumed office.

He signaled immediately his support for a far more decisive struggle against the Mafia and did not hesitate to break a political deadlock that had existed since the election in April 1992, shortly before Cossiga's resignation. The voters in fact had dealt a blow to the so-called governmental parties—those centrist and moderate leftist groups that had been the Christian Democrats' cabinet partners—and it was quite unclear how a new governing majority could be formed. Scalfaro did not hesitate to appoint as prime minister a Socialist leader who, like himself, had always been considered an outsider and had remained untainted by political scandals. This man, Giuliano Amato (and later Carlo Ciampi), proceeded to restore the Italian budget, plagued by the largest deficit in the republic's history, with full support from Scalfaro. Scalfaro's choices proved wise, as the new prime minister could undertake a number of fiscal measures that, even though unpopular, began the process of budgetary restoration.

After another magistrate, Paolo Borsellino, was murdered by the Mafia, the government took decisive steps to fight the Mafia. Scalfaro, who was Interior Minister, also played a key role in cleaning up police corruption and in the prosecutions of hundreds of Cosa Nostra leaders in Sicily prompted by the defection of informant Tommaso Buscetta. He missed no opportunity to provide moral leadership to enforce the necessary sweeping and painful police operations in Sicily and other regions of Italy.

During Scalfaro's presidency other scandals broke out that threatened the very existence of the Italian Republic. Magistrates in Milan and elsewhere exposed an exceedingly extensive system of political corruption: businessmen obtained contracts from local public administrations by paying bribes to elected officials. All public projects' costs were largely inflated, at the taxpayers' expenses, so that businesses could gain sufficient funds to sustain the widespread bribe system.

If Scalfaro's task as moral leader was difficult, he generally was praised for his efforts in removing the stain of corruption from the country he was elected to represent. When in 1993 he was briefly accused in connection with one of the scandals, a thoroughly demoralized public expressed fear that their "last best hope" was also corrupt. Yet Scalfaro's nationwide televised appearance, through which he indignantly denied any wrongdoing, was so convincing that rumors about his guilt vanished quickly. The high ratings of the program and the level of national anxiety raised in those circumstances were themselves a testimony of the extent to which Italians have become accustomed to Scalfaro's moral leadership.

In the March 1994 elections a disgusted Italian electorate gave short shrift to the heretofore dominant parties of Christian Democrats and Socialists. In a whirlwind campaign, media magnate Silvio Berlusconi, under the soccer slogan Forza Italia (Go Italy), put together a loose grouping of conservatives, federalists, and neo-fascists. Calling themselves the Freedom Alliance, the new party won a clear majority in the Senate and a strong plurality in the Chamber

of Deputies. A granddaughter of former dictator Benito Mussolini was among those elected. President Scalfaro named Berlusconi prime minister, and he took office May 10, 1994, with a 25-member cabinet representing all shades of the political spectrum. Scalfaro had publicly warned Berlusconi not to choose anyone who might cause harm to Italy at home or abroad.

Scalfaro endured a very conflictual relationship with Berlusconi, who criticized the President as the spokesman and representative of the old guard, the "First Republic." Berlusconi stopped just short of calling for Scalfaro's resignation to open the way to a "Second Republic" unencumbered by the weight of the corrupt, immobilized past. Scalfaro was implicated in that past by Berlusconi because he had been elected by the scandal-ridden 1992 Parliament and because he interpreted the Constitution very strictly, thus creating obstacles for many of Berlusconi's proposed and frequently self-serving electoral reforms.

In 1996, faced with a situation in which the big parties could neither agree on a feasible governing coalition nor resolve an ongoing conflict over changes to the new predominantly-winner-take-all parliamentary electoral system, Scalfaro took the drastic step of calling for elections three years ahead of schedule. The elections were held under the existing rules in which 3/4 of the seats were winner-take-all and 1/4 were elected by proportional rules. When the secessionist Northern League of Umberto Bossi emerged from those elections with a strong showing, Scalfaro was moved to address the nation in a strongly worded speech in which he declared that Italian unity must remain non-negotiable.

Scalfaro's presidency took place during a troubled and highly transformational period for Italy. The end of the Cold War and the collapse of communism in Eastern Europe dried up U.S. aid to the ruling Center-Right, which had held power since the end of World War II and which the U.S. had nurtured as the major countervailing force to the Italian Communist Party, the largest such party in the West; the increasing economic and resulting political pressure resulting from the effort to meet European Community standards; the existence of strong secessionist and federalist attitudes within the polity; and the enormous upheaval caused by the 1992 scandal revelations—- all took place during Scalfaro's term. In this time of upheaval, Scalfaro strengthened the presidency, bringing to it an aura of personal integrity, a resolute willingness to act forcefully and decisively, and an unbending committment to national unity.

Scalfaro was a widower with one child. He lived in the presidential palace, the Palazzo del Quirinale.

Further Reading

There was not much information published in the English language about Scalfaro, owing to his relative obscurity outside Italy before becoming president. *West European Politics* provided analytic articles on the Italian political system. For the anti-Mafia campaigns in Sicily, see Alexander Stille, *Excellent Cadavers* (1995). □

Antonin Scalia

Antonin Scalia (born 1936), a conservative jurist who advocated judicial restraint, was appointed to the Supreme Court by Ronald Reagan in 1986.

American political conservatives expected to find a friend on the Supreme Court after Antonin Scalia's appointment in 1986. Instead, they found a man dedicated to enforcement of the law and to a fair and equal justice system.

Antonin Scalia was born on March 11, 1936, in Trenton, New Jersey. His father was an Italian immigrant who taught Romance Languages at New York's Brooklyn College and his mother was a schoolteacher. After receiving his undergraduate degree *summa cum laude* from Georgetown University in 1957 Scalia went on to attend Harvard Law School. There he served as an editor on the prestigious Harvard Law Review. Upon graduation from law school, Scalia stayed on at Harvard as a post-graduate fellow from 1960-1961. In 1960 he married Maureen McCarthy. They would have nine children.

His education completed, Scalia joined the private law firm of Jones, Day, Cockley and Reavis of Cleveland, Ohio and remained there for six years. During this time, Scalia decided he was best suited to teaching the art of law more than practicing it. In 1967 he joined the faculty of the University of Virginia Law School.

In 1971 Scalia left the scholar's life to serve in a variety of government posts: general counsel, Office of Telecommunications Policy, Executive Office of the President (1971 to 1972); chairman, Administrative Conference of the United States (1972 to 1974); and assistant attorney general, Office of Legal Counsel, U.S. Department of Justice (1974 to 1977). Scalia returned to teaching in 1977 as professor of law at the University of Chicago, leaving for a year to serve as a visiting professor at Stanford University (1980-1981).

During the brief period between government service and his return to the university Scalia served as scholar-in-residence at the American Enterprise Institute, a leading center of conservative thought located in Washington, D.C. His association with the institute would prove to be fruitful for Scalia, in terms of the intellectual stimulation it provided him at the time and the prominent conservative contacts it afforded. His service as an editor of *Regulation,* the institute's journal, gave him a forum to develop ideas that would later find voice in law journals and judicial opinions.

Scalia was not among the nation's leading legal scholars, but he regularly published law review articles and established a reputation in his fields of specialty; administrative law and regulated industries. In his essays, he outlined a conservative philosophy that would mark his career on the appellate bench. Scalia was an advocate of judicial restraint. Judges, he believed, should refrain from promoting their political and social convictions through their opinions. He felt judges should not make laws in the same manner as the legislature. Rather, he felt that the proper role of a judge

was to interpret the law and leave matters of legislation to the elected representatives of the people.

In 1982 Scalia was appointed to the U.S. Circuit Court of Appeals in Washington, D.C. by then President Ronald Reagan. Scalia quickly established himself as a leading conservative judge on what was generally acknowledged as the nation's most liberal appellate court. Frequently exercising his right to dissent, Scalia remained faithful to his earlier published views of the judicial role. In cases concerning libel law, sexual discrimination under the Civil Rights Act of 1964, and the Gramm-Rudman budget control measure, Scalia wrote opinions that expressed his judicial philosophy: strict interpretation of the Constitution and legislative statutes and maintenance of the power of traditional institutions and of the majority's right to make law.

These views, often noted in dissenting opinions from the court, revealed a respect for governmental authority as well as an impatience for the enforcement of minority rights.

When Chief Justice Warren Burger announced his retirement in 1986, President Reagan quickly acted to strengthen the conservative voice on the high bench by naming sitting Justice William Rehnquist as Burger's successor and by appointing Scalia to succeed Rehnquist. Confirmed unanimously by the Senate, Scalia became the first Italian-American to sit on the Supreme Court.

Predicting judicial performance on the Supreme Court has always been a tricky and imprecise business. An article in the November 5, 1990 issue of *Newsweek* noted that "Scalia sticks with his ideological cards. That tenacity, combined with a sharp pen and mind, and the personal ebullience of Willard Scott, also have made him the most provocative justice." Conservatives considered him their "savior," while liberals labeled him "The Terminator."

In 1992, in the case *R.A.V. versus City of St. Paul*, Scalia voted to strike down a St. Paul, Minnesota hate speech law as a violation of freedom of speech. Writing for the majority Scalia noted that "special hostility towards the particular biases thus singled out. . . . is precisely what the First Amendment forbids." The decision affirmed that people could not be punished for their opinions, even if they took the form of a hate crime. That same year, he dissented in the case *Lee versus Weisman*. A 5-4 majority held that it was unconstitutional to recite a non-denominational prayer at a public high school graduation. In attacking the majority, he called the decision "nothing short of ludicrous."(*New Republic* January 18, 1993).

In 1996 Scalia, labeled as angry "refused to join the rest of the court in holding that the tax-supported, men-only Virginia Military Institute violated women's right to equal protection of the laws." (*Time* July 8, 1996). The article went on to call Associate Justice Clarence Thomas "his only dependable ally."

Never one to avoid controversy or cave in to the majority, Scalia dissented in the controversial *Romer versus Evans* case. The court ruled that "a state constitutional amendment denying legal redress for discrimination based on homosexuality violated the equal-protection clause." (*Time* July 8, 1996). Scalia wrote a "withering" dissent and openly "scoffed at the majority opinion." (*Time* July 8, 1996).

In 1997 prominent Republicans mentioned Scalia as a possible presidential candidate for the year 2000, noting, "Scalia is second to none, in terms of his potential for restoring the Reagan coalition." (*Insight on the News* (February 24, 1997). He also wrote a book *A Matter of Interpretation: Federal Courts and the Law* where he discussed theories of judging and the judicial system.

Further Reading

For information on the Supreme Court and the justices, see Leon Friedman *The Justices of the United States Supreme Court: Their Lives and Major Opinions* (New York:Chelsea House Publishers, 1997); and Steven G. O'Brien *American Political Leaders* (Santa Barbara: ABC-CLIO, 1991)

See also *Chicago Tribune* August 3, 1986; *Economist* March 14, 1987; *Los Angeles Times* June 18, 1986; June 29, 1986; and July 6, 1986; *Maclean's* June 30, 1986; *New Republic* January 18, 1993; *Newsday* June 18, 1986 and August 6, 1986; *Newsweek* June 30, 1986; August 18, 1986; October 6, 1986; and November 5, 1990; *New York Times* June 18, 1986; January 24, 1987; March 4, 1987; and March 17, 1995; *Reader's Digest* July, 1991; *Time* June 30, 1986; August 18, 1986; October 13, 1986; July 6, 1987; and July 8, 1996; *U.S. News & World Report* June 30, 1986; and July 6, 1992; *Wall Street Journal* June 19, 1986.

Additional sources of information regarding Scalia's career can be found in such standard sources as *Facts on File*. Scalia's articles in *Regulation,* the magazine of the American Enterprise Institute, offered a good introduction to his judicial philosophy (see especially "Regulatory Reform—The Game

Has Changed" [January/February 1981] and "Back to Basics: Making Law Without Making Rules" [July/August 1981]). □

Arthur Scargill

Arthur Scargill (born 1938) was the militant, controversial president of the British National Union of Mineworkers who led the longest and most violent miners' strike in British history.

Arthur Scargill, the son and grandson of coal miners, was born in Worsborough, South Yorkshire, in 1938. The house in which he was born and in which he lived for his first three years had neither plumbing nor electricity. In time he and his family moved to a more comfortable, modern home in the town where he grew up.

Scargill was an only child, and his parents, Harold and Alice, doted on him. His father was a loyal member of the Communist Party, and *The Daily Worker* was read regularly in the Scargill household. As a boy Scargill read of starvation and injustice in such books as *The Ragged Trousered Philanthropists* and of the courage and nobility of the revolutionary working classes in *Twelve Months in Hell*. Spurred by the outrages he saw in capitalist society, the young Arthur vowed to work for a more equitable world.

In the Mines

After leaving Worsborough Dale School at 15, Scargill, unable to find other works, reluctantly followed his father into the pits. His first job was removing loose chunks of rock from the coal in the screening sheds of the Wooley Colliery, near Barnsley. Faced with the incredible heat and choking dust of the sheds, Scargill almost turned and ran on his first day from what he described as a scene from Dante's *Inferno*. He stayed, however, and as a self-appointed representative of the apprentices he soon began making demands for better working conditions. Experiencing first hand the plight of industrial laborers, Scargill wrote letters of complaint to a number of agencies and newspapers. The only response came from a representative of *The Daily Worker* who convinced him, at the age of 17, to join the Young Communist League of Britain. Within 18 months the energetic Scargill was sitting on the executive board of that organization.

At the age of 19 Scargill attended the 1957 world youth festival in Moscow as the representative of the Yorkshire miners. While there he met with such Russian leaders as Nikita Khrushchev and Nikolai Bulganin. Upon returning to Britain, he joined the Campaign for Nuclear Disarmament and was defeated when, in his first attempt to win political office, he stood as an independent Communist in a local council election. For reasons that remain unclear Scargill, who made no secret of his Communist beliefs, never formally joined the Communist Party and in his later years described himself as a socialist.

While working in various jobs in the mines for 17 years he continued to study economics, history, and industrial relations in day release courses. He also began to rise in the ranks of his local union and in 1964, at the age of 26, was elected representative to the Yorkshire area meetings. Scargill first gained notoriety in the strike of 1972 when, as spokesman for the Yorkshire miners, he organized the system of flying pickets who rushed to mines or plants outside of their own area to assist fellow strikers. He played a prominent role in the much-publicized "battle of Saltley Gate" that closed the huge Saltley coke depot in Birmingham. This assured his election as financial secretary of the Yorkshire area, an important victory that gave him a seat on the national executive committee of the National Union of Mineworkers (N.U.M.). A few months later, in May 1973, he was overwhelmingly elected president of the Yorkshire mineworkers.

After the miners' strike of 1974, which brought down Edward Heath's Conservative government, the militant Left under Scargill's leadership made great strides within the structure of the N.U.M. The victory of the Conservatives under Margaret Thatcher in 1979, after another wave of strikes destroyed the Labour Party's majority, was met by the N.U.M.'s election of Scargill to the presidency in 1981 with over 70 percent of the vote. The expected conflict between Scargill's union and Thatcher's government erupted in early 1984 when the National Coal Board announced the planned closure of several "uneconomic" pits across the country. In a divisive, unpopular decision the executive of the N.U.M., at Scargill's urging, declined to permit a national vote by the membership before calling local work stopages to protest the closing of the pits.

The Strike of 1984

The strike, which began on March 12, 1984, lasted for a year before ending in failure. It was one of the most violent disputes in British labor history, and both Scargill and his wife were among the hundreds of strikers arrested. Support for the walkout varied in different parts of the country, with one third of the pits remaining open, and many miners and other workers who believed the strike was unconstitutional denounced Scargill personally for its failure. The Labour Party and Trade Union Congress leaders blamed "the Scargill factor" for fragmenting the labor movement and driving moderate voters into the ranks of the opposition. The Thatcher government strategy of refusing to legitimize the union by attempts at compromise marginalized the union, and dispirited strikers broke ranks to return to work by year's end.

Despite the failure of the strike and the anxiety caused by Scargill's neo-Marxist rhetoric and confrontational tactics, he clearly remained popular with the majority of miners. To demonstrate their loyalty to him in 1985 they supported controversial changes in national procedures that permitted Scargill to remain president of the N.U.M. for life.

Picking Up the Pieces

In the years following the miners' strike, the labor battle lost on the streets returned to the newspapers and airwaves. N.U.M. supporters claimed the conservative Thatcher government, learning from Heath's mistakes, adopted strategies

to break the union even before the strike, increasing government subsidies to nuclear power and gas to undercut and weaken the nationalized coal industry. Once the government announced plans to close mines and lay off 20,000 workers, critics charged, Thatcher waged war on the union using tactics reserved for severe internal security threats. Government undercover agents infiltrated the union and wreaked havoc on public perceptions. At one juncture, a union official who later was alleged to be a Thatcher agent approached Libyan officials with great public fanfare asking for donations. That incident did much to turn public opinion against the miners' cause during the strike.

Scargill turned his attention to politics, leading disaffected members of the Labour Party to form a splinter Socialist Labour Party in 1996 after he concluded Labour leaders had betrayed the basic principles of the party constitution in a move to the right. While the first candidate backed by Scargill's new party was humiliated in polls, Scargill pressed on, despite political in-fighting which threatened to splinter the new SLP even further. Scargill personally entered the political fray for a second time in a run for parliament, but won scant support.

Scargill and his wife Anne, herself a miner's daughter and an active organizer of miners' groups, had one daughter, Margaret. They lived in the house Scargill grew up in Worsborough, South Yorkshire.

Further Reading

The best work on Scargill was Michael Crick, *Scargill and the Miners* (1985). See also V. L. Allen, *The Militancy of the British Miners* (1981); N. Hagger, *Scargill the Stalinist* (1984); and "What Drives Arthur Scargill?" *The Sunday Times* of London (July 15, 1984).
The strike of 1984 was covered in detail by the press. For more information, see *The National Review* (June 15, 1984 and April 5, 1985); *Newsweek* (July 2 1984); *Time* (October 15, 1984); *U.S. News and World Report* (November 26, 1984); and *The Nation* (Dec. 19, 1994). Accounts of the founding of the Socialist Labour party may be found in *The Guardian* (January 15, 1996 and May 2, 1996); and *The Irish Times* (February 1, 1996). A post-mortem of the 1984 strike may be obtained in *The Enemy Within* (1994), written by a *Guardian* reporter. □

Domenico Scarlatti

Domenico Scarlatti (1685-1757) was an Italian harpsichordist and composer. His harpsichord sonatas are highly distinctive and original.

Domenico Scarlatti was born in Naples on Oct. 26, 1685, the son of Alessandro Scarlatti, the most famous composer in Italy in the early 18th century. Other members of the Scarlatti family were active as professional musicians. This background may have helped Domenico, for it encouraged his musical gifts and provided contacts in the musical profession. On the other hand, it gave him the problem of developing in his own way while under the influence of his father. Alessandro was not only a composer of genius, but a man of strong personality who did not get along well with some of his pupils and colleagues.

It is natural to assume, though there is no actual proof, that Domenico studied first with his father. As early as 1701, Domenico was appointed organist in the royal chapel at Naples. The following year he went to Florence with his father and stayed there for 4 months. Domenico then returned to Naples, where several operas of his were produced in 1703 and 1704.

A more important trip for Domenico occurred in 1708, when he went to Venice. There he became acquainted with Francesco Gasparini, a leading composer and the author of an excellent treatise on thorough-bass. It has been assumed, though again not proved, that Domenico studied with Gasparini in Venice. Also while he was in Venice, Domenico met and struck up a friendship with a young man, his exact contemporary, who was to become even more celebrated a composer: George Frederick Handel. It is from this period in Venice that we have our first report of Domenico's harpsichord playing. It describes how he played at a private musical gathering and astonished his audience by his brilliant virtuoso performance.

For the next 10 years Scarlatti worked in Rome. From 1709 to 1714 he was in the service of Maria Casimira, Queen of Poland, and for her private theater he wrote a number of operas. When Maria Casimira left Rome in 1714, Scarlatti became chapelmaster of the Portuguese ambassa-

dor. Then, from 1715 to 1719, he served as chapelmaster of the Cappella Giulia in the Vatican.

In 1720, or shortly before, Scarlatti left Italy; although he later returned to his native country, it seems that he never again took up a permanent post there. Probably in 1720 he was appointed chapelmaster of the royal chapel in Lisbon. This proved to be a most consequential appointment for Scarlatti. One of his duties was to teach members of the royal Portuguese family, and one of these members, the Infanta Maria Barbara, was a gifted and enthusiastic pupil. Her devotion to music was no passing fancy: she practiced and played the harpsichord apparently all her life. She also remained devoted to her teacher.

After Maria Barbara married Fernando, Prince of Asturias, in 1729, she moved to the Spanish court at Madrid, and Scarlatti went with her. He remained in her service for the rest of his life. He was knighted in Madrid in 1738; he married a Spanish woman, after the death of his first (Italian) wife; and he died in Madrid on July 23, 1757.

Scarlatti wrote 12 operas (2 of which were written in collaboration with other composers), chamber cantatas, sacred music, and over 550 sonatas for harpsichord. He composed much of his vocal music, both sacred and secular, before he settled in Spain. Most of it is characteristic music of the period: well composed but not particularly individual. A few of his vocal works are outstanding. But by and large Scarlatti was not at his best in writing for the voice. His true genius is revealed rather in his sonatas for harpsichord.

These sonatas are so individual, so varied in their forms and styles, that it is difficult to give a general description of them. One can say that the majority of the sonatas are built of two sections: they move from the tonic to the dominant key or to the relative major or minor and then back again to the tonic key. But within this basic form there are numerous substructures. And some of the sonatas are composed in forms altogether different.

The chronology of Scarlatti's sonatas has been much discussed and is still problematic. Most of his sonatas are preserved in copies made late in his life; but this does not necessarily mean that they were composed so late. Probably Scarlatti improvised his pieces, and perhaps wrote them down partially, during the course of his life. Then, at a later date, he had them written down in fair copies.

It seems that the earliest harpsichord pieces by Scarlatti are those in dance forms, or in forms similar to the toccatas of his father. Somewhat later Scarlatti began to compose those sonatas on which his fame rests: the brilliant virtuoso pieces with striking harmonies, bold dissonances, and sudden contrasts of texture. His sonatas are remarkable for the way they exploit the resources of the harpsichord—to musical advantage. They call for a large, two-manual harpsichord and for a highly proficient harpsichordist.

But brilliance and virtuosity do not account for the greatness of Scarlatti's sonatas. The best ones are perfectly realized works of art. Each one carries through its own, distinctive musical ideas, and each one is different from the others. This individuality is a central feature of Scarlatti's sonatas.

The characteristic, unique style of the sonatas seems to be original with Scarlatti himself. Although elements of his style can be traced to earlier keyboard music in Italy, Portugal, or Spain, there is nothing quite like the total effect. On the basis of his harpsichord sonatas, Scarlatti must rank as one of the most original creative minds in the history of music.

Further Reading

The standard work on the life and works of Scarlatti is Ralph Kirkpatrick, *Domenico Scarlatti* (1953). Scarlatti's sonatas are discussed by Manfred F. Bukofzer, *Music in the Baroque Era* (1947), and William S. Newman, *The Sonata in the Classic Era* (1963).

Additional Sources

Bach, Handel, Scarlatti, tercentenary essays, Cambridge Cambridgeshire; New York: Cambridge University Press, 1985.

Kirkpatrick, Ralph, *Domenico Scarlatti,* Princeton, N.J.: Princeton University Press, 1983, 1953.

Sitwell, Sacheverell, *A background for Domenico Scarlatti, 1685-1757; written for his two hundred and fiftieth anniversar,* Freeport, N.Y., Books for Libraries Press 1970. □

Pietro Alessandro Gaspare Scarlatti

Pietro Alessandro Gaspare Scarlatti (1660-1725) was an Italian composer. Over 600 of his chamber cantatas survive; they represent the peak of the genre. The most outstanding and influential operatic writer of his day, he founded the so-called Neapolitan opera school.

The operas by Alessandro Scarlatti that primarily influenced his younger contemporaries were written during his first sojourn in Naples, when he felt obliged to cater to Neapolitan taste—one that preferred simple, immediately attractive melodies, embellished with coloratura, and that elevated the importance of the solo singer, especially the castrato, to unprecedented heights, and, as a result, severely limited the number of ensembles and the role of the orchestra. Three other important features of this period are the increasing use of the da capo form of aria, which by the turn of the century virtually ousted all other forms; the establishing of the so-called Italian overture, or sinfonia, as a tripartite form—quick, slow, quick—first introduced in the 1696 revival of Scarlatti's *Tutto il mal . . .* (1681); and the inclusion in most of the operas of two comic characters who are an integral part of the plot.

Scarlatti's greatest operas are those he wrote after he left Naples in 1702. In them the orchestra is more important and colorful, the melodies are more subtly expressive and phrased, the harmony is clearer and more varied, and the texture ranges from simple homophony to rich polyphony. It was these operas that influenced, in varying degrees and in

different ways, such composers as George Frederick Handel, Johann Adolf Hasse, and Scarlatti's son Domenico, the last two being among the most significant figures in the transition period between the baroque and the Viennese school of the late 18th century.

Scarlatti was born in Palermo on May 2, 1660, the eldest son of Pietro and Eleonora d'Amato Scarlata. Details of his early life are sketchy; he probably went to relatives in Rome in 1672 in company with his two sisters, Anna Maria and Melchiorra, and, tradition has it, became a pupil of Giacomo Carissimi. This tradition is supported by the earliest record of Scarlatti as a musician, namely, a commission, dated Jan. 27, 1679, to compose an oratorio for the Arciconfraternità del SS. Crocifisso, for which Carissimi had written several similar works.

In April of the previous year Scarlatti married Antonia Anzalone; they had 10 children, of whom by far the most distinguished was Domenico. The first of Scarlatti's operas to bring him fame, *Gli equivoci nel sembiante* (1679), also brought him an appointment, for the libretto of his next opera, *L'honestà negli amori* (1680), describes him as chapelmaster (*maestro di cappella*) to Queen Christina of Sweden, who spent most of her life in Rome after her abdication.

In 1683 Scarlatti was put in charge of the entire opera season at Naples, producing in December his first original work for the city, *Psiche*. The following year he became chapelmaster to the royal chapel in Naples, an appointment that was largely, if not wholly, due to an influential official whose mistress was Scarlatti's sister Melchiorra. In the ensuing scandal the highly esteemed second chapelmaster, Provenzale, who had expected to be promoted, resigned, the official was fired, and Melchiorra was ordered to leave the city or enter a convent!

During the next 18 years Scarlatti composed at least 38 operas, in addition to serenatas, cantatas, and church music; all but six of the operas were performed initially in Naples, and many of them received performances elsewhere. But although his fame was spreading, Scarlatti was becoming increasingly frustrated by the kind of music he was expected to produce. In 1702 he was granted 4 months' leave of absence, but once out of Naples it is clear he had no intention of returning, and for the next 7 years he looked in vain for a position that would satisfy his needs and wishes.

At first Scarlatti enjoyed the patronage of Prince Ferdinand de' Medici in Florence, for whose private theater he wrote several operas; no permanent position transpired, however, and in 1703 he accepted a very inferior post as assistant chapelmaster at the church of S. Maria Maggiore, Rome. In 1707 he became principal chapelmaster, but this did nothing to lessen his frustration, for in Rome at this time opera was virtually nonexistent, owing to strong papal disapproval. But he continued to write operas for Prince Ferdinand, most of which have not survived, and composed his first opera for Venice (1707), where he spent some months.

Although Scarlatti's operatic production had waned during this period, his reputation had not, and in 1709 he returned to his old post at Naples, with an increase in salary and free to compose as he wished. Here he remained until 1717, producing some of his best operas, notably *Tigrane* (1715), and receiving a knighthood from the Pope the following year. But Rome still held a great fascination for him, and in 1717, encouraged by a change in the papal attitude toward opera, he settled there. In the ensuing 5 years or so he composed his last works for the stage, including his one comic essay in the genre, *I trionfo dell'onore* (1718), and, according to the libretto, his 114th opera—*Griselda* (1721). (This is the last of 35 complete extant operas from a known total of 115.)

In 1722 or 1723 Scarlatti returned to Naples, where he lived in complete retirement, composing very little, and virtually ignored. In 1724 Hasse, then aged 25, became his pupil and close friend. Scarlatti died on Oct. 24, 1725.

Further Reading

An old but still useful biography of Scarlatti is Edward J. Dent, *Alessandro Scarlatti* (1905; rev. ed. 1960). He is discussed in Manfred F. Bukofzer, *Music in the Baroque Era* (1947), and Donald J. Grout, *A Short History of Opera* (1947; 2d ed. 1965). □

Hjalmar Horace Greeley Schacht

The German economist and banker Hjalmar Horace Greeley Schacht (1877-1970), widely admired and hated as Germany's "financial wizard," played a vital role in his country's economic recoveries after the inflation of 1923 and in the Hitler years.

Hjalmar Schacht was born in the small border town of Trigleff in German Schleswig on Jan. 22, 1877, shortly after his parents had returned from their emigration to America. After earning his doctorate in economics at the University of Kiel in 1900, he entered one of Germany's great Industrial "D"-banks, the Dresdener Bank, in 1903, where he remained for 13 years. During World War I he set up a new central bank in occupied Belgium to print and regulate the Occupation currency. At the end of the war—now director of the smaller National bank—Schacht participated in the founding of the new progressive liberal party, the Democratic party, to which he belonged until 1926.

Schacht first gained a national reputation when he became currency commissioner in 1923 and in that position played a vital role in the stabilization of the currency after the runaway inflation of 1922-1923 by the creation of the new Rentenmark. In December 1923 his fame as the "savior

of mark" brought him an appointment to the presidency of the Central Bank, which he held until 1930. During this time he actively fought foreign credits, and in 1929 he took part in the negotiations for a new plan of reparations, the Young Plan. On his return from the conference, however, he immediately disowned the plan in the face of opposition by fellow nationalists. After the Hague Conference of March 1930 he resigned his position and openly blamed the German Republican government for the continuation of reparations in a pamphlet entitled *End of Reparations* (1931) and other writings. In October 1931 he was instrumental in the formation of the Harzburg Front, a loose coalition of industrialists, national conservatives, and Hitler, and in November 1932 he recommended to the old president of the republic, Paul von Hindenburg, that Hitler be appointed chancellor.

After the Nazi take-over, the grateful Hitler immediately reappointed Schacht to the Central Bank. From that position and from the office of minister of economics from 1934 to 1937, Schacht presided over Germany's second interwar recovery until, by 1938, mounting armament costs began to threaten his concept of a sound, balanced economy and brought on serious disagreement with Hitler. A blunt memorandum of warning in January 1939 brought his downfall and subsequent contacts with the Resistance. After the unsuccessful coup of July 1944 he was arrested but survived the end of the war and was found not guilty at the Nuremberg Trials. After the war he lived in retirement and was called upon for economic advice by several developing nations, most prominently by Indonesia and the Philippines. He died on June 4, 1970, in Munich.

Further Reading

Schacht's autobiography was published in the United States as *Confessions of "The Old Wizard"* (trans. 1956). His self-defense against implication with Nazi crimes is set down in his *Account Settled* (trans. 1949). He wrote once more about his life experiences and his general views on finance in *The Magic of Money* (trans. 1967). The best general biography in English is Edward N. Peterson, *Hjalmar Schacht: For and against Hitler* (1954), a fair-minded, well-documented account. Norbert Mühlen, *Schact: Hitler's Magician* (trans. 1938), is a bitterly critical portrayal of Schacht as a ruthless economic dictator by a prominent journalist. The most recent biographical study in English is Earl R. Beck, *Verdict on Schacht* (1956), which deals with the question of Schacht's guilt as Hitler's chief economist.

Additional Sources

Schacht, Hjalmar Horace Greeley, *Confessions of "the Old Wizard": the autobiography of Hjalmar Horace Greeley Schacht*, Westport, Conn.: Greenwood Press, 1974, 1955. □

Philip Schaff

Philip Schaff (1819-1893) was a Swiss-born American religious scholar and a great historian of religion. His evolutionary view of Christian development led him to support ecumenical efforts in religion.

Philip Schaff (originally Schaf) was born on Jan. 1, 1819, in Chur, Switzerland. He studied in German schools. At the University of Berlin he came under the influence of the famous theologian August Neander, who impressed upon him the importance of historical insight to Christian understanding. Following his graduation in 1841, Schaff traveled in southern Europe as a private tutor, during which time he observed appreciatively the Christian heritage embodied in Roman Catholic culture.

On his return to Berlin Schaff joined the university faculty but soon accepted a post at the German Reformed Seminary in Mercersburg, Pa.; this post was apparently created to save German-Americans from religious error in the New World. He arrived in the United States in 1844. He was soon married and rapidly embarked upon an exceedingly fruitful collaboration with his brilliant Mercersburg colleague John Williamson Nevin. Schaff and Nevin, co-sponsoring the "Mercersburg theology," challenged several popular Protestant attitudes in the United States, particularly hatred of Roman Catholicism, belief that the Reformation marked a radical break from the Christian past, and fondness for revivalistic enthusiasm over organic growth. Shocked churchmen brought Schaff before the Pennsylvania Synod for heresy in 1845, but that body exonerated him.

Schaff's reputation as historian and theological critic reached a new plane with publication abroad and in the United States of his *America: A Sketch of Its Political, Social, and Religious Character* (1854). In a series of lectures given during a visit in Germany, which were the basis for the book, Schaff criticized Puritanical, antihistorical, and denominational facets of American religion. But he also told his German audiences they might well admire the religious vitality of Americans, which he attributed to the voluntarism of churchly life in the United States.

Schaff moved to New York City in 1863, and in 1869 he accepted a professorship at Union Theological Seminary. He now produced many of his most important works, among them a 25-volume *Commentary of the Holy Scriptures* (1865-1880) and a 3-volume *Religious Encyclopaedia* (1882-1884), still a major reference source. He edited a 13-volume *American Church History Series* (1893-1897), a project of the American Society of Church History, which he founded in 1888. Schaff also participated in national and international ecumenical movements. He retired in 1893, and on October 20 he died. His dedication to religious history inspired succeeding generations of scholars.

Further Reading

Probably the best book on Schaff is by his son, David Schley Schaff, *The Life of Philip Schaff* (1897). James Hastings Nichols discusses Schaff's years with Nevin in *Romanticism in American Theology: Nevin and Schaff at Mercersburg* (1961). Also revealing is Perry Miller's introduction to the edition of Schaff's *America* which Miller edited (1961).

Additional Sources

Shriver, George H., *Philip Schaff: Christian scholar and ecumenical prophet: centennial biography for the American Society of Church History*, Macon, Ga.: Mercer, 1987. □

Miriam Schapiro

Miriam Schapiro (born 1923) was one of the leaders of the Feminist Art Movement in the early 1970s. She was also one of the first artists to use the computer as a creative instrument and 14was among the founders of the "Pattern and Decoration Movement" in 1974.

Miriam Schapiro was born on November 15, 1923, in Toronto, Canada. Her artistic training began at age six when her father gave her weekly drawing assignments. She attended classes at the Museum of Modern Art and learned to draw from the nude model at age 14, when she attended Federal Art Project classes. She received both her undergraduate (1945) and graduate (1946, 1949) degrees in art from the University of Iowa, where she studied printmaking with Mauricio Lasansky.

While at the university, Schapiro met and married fellow artist Paul Brach. They moved to New York in 1951, when Abstract Expressionism was exerting a powerful influ-

ence. Schapiro's Cubist-derived style was transformed by that influence, leading her into a series of painterly, calligraphic figural and landscape works. Known as one of the "second generation" Abstract Expressionists, she began to show at the Andre Emmerich Gallery in 1958.

Beginning in 1960 Schapiro gradually eliminated the abstract expressionist brushwork from her paintings, introducing a variety of geometric forms. Rectangular window-like openings in some works were prophetic of her subsequent "Shrine" series.

Between 1963 and 1965 Schapiro painted variations on the "Shrine" motif: four framed compartments stacked vertically in a narrow strip and centered in a white rectangular field. The bottom compartment was a mirror (self-reflection); the next contained an egg (woman/creator); the third was an image fragment borrowed from the history of art; and the top frame contained the color gold (aspiration).

The "Shrine" series was pivotal in Schapiro's career and foreshadowed much of her mature work. Her use of self-referential symbols became increasingly important. Also, the motif of the centralized framed space would evolve into a womb, a house, a window, or a stage in later works.

Schapiro and Brach moved to California in 1967, where she taught at the University of California, San Diego. During the late 1960s Schapiro experimented with the window form and, aided by a computer, with strictly geometric structural compositions. In *Big Ox* (1968) a pink and orange hexagon frame surrounds a central open space, while four diagonal "arms" extend out from the hexagon. She later recognized the open central form as "vaginal iconography," a common theme in many works by women artists. In the same year, Schapiro began to use the computer to design and develop her paintings. These abstract compositions featured rectilinear forms strongly projecting into space, using multiple vanishing points.

In 1970 Schapiro met Judy Chicago. The two artists shared a feminist viewpoint and a desire to confront their own life experiences as women through the medium of art. In 1971 they founded the Feminist Art Program at the California Institute of the Arts in Valencia. They formed a program for training women artists and with their students created a major project which involved the renovation of an old mansion. By 1972 "Womanhouse," with rooms reflecting aspects of women's experiences, had become a feminist art gallery, a forum for women artists, and a stage for performance art.

Intensely involved in teaching, Schapiro stopped painting during this period. She and artist Sherry Brody created a dollhouse for "Womanhouse," a project that became an inspiration for her subsequent work. The rooms within the dollhouse were chosen to illustrate women's roles within the home: nursery, living room, kitchen, seraglio, and a studio for the woman as artist. The dollhouse was a three dimensional realization of Schapiro's earlier "Shrine" series. As a part of the project she researched the traditional types of art that women had made—usually involving stitchery and fabric.

In 1972, when she began to paint again, Schapiro moved to a completely new style. She introduced the element of fabric collage, which seemed to burst forth from the paintings, dominating the old geometric forms. Schapiro cut pieces of patterned cloth and combined them with acrylic paint to create a beautifully orchestrated symphony of pattern and color. Schapiro and Melissa Meyer coined the term "femmage" to apply to this type of collage art form that would characterize her work from this time on. Femmage utilizes arts, materials, and techniques that historically have been associated with domesticity, and therefore with women: quilts, embroidery, lace, crochet, carpets, and fabric design. In combining these art forms with her paintings, Schapiro asks that we view them in a new light and that we re-evaluate the so-called "decorative arts" in this new context.

In 1974 Schapiro and Robert Zakanitch formed the Pattern and Decoration group of New York City artists. Schapiro and Brach moved back to New York in 1975, and she increased her involvement with artists who championed the elevation of pattern/decorative arts from a secondary to a primary classification. The movement became a strong force in the art world by the late 1970s.

In Schapiro's "Collaboration" series (1975-1976) femmage patterning was employed to frame works by women artists of the past. *Anatomy of a Kimono* (1976) was a monumental ten-panel work in which she explored the beauty of pattern and color relationships in the traditional ceremonial garment. In the late 1970s she also began to incorporate actual fabric items produced by women into her canvases, such as handkerchiefs and doilies.

During the years 1979-1980 Schapiro created large shaped canvases using the archetypal images of houses, fans, and hearts. In *Homage to Goncharova* (1979) she paid tribute to the theater and costume designs created by Natalia Goncharova for the Ballet Russes in the 1920s. Her interest in theater continued in the "Presentation" series of 1982-1983, in which an abstract "figure" was enclosed by two borders resembling a proscenium arch and curtain.

The figure finally asserted itself in Schapiro's work of the mid-1980s. *I'm Dancing as Fast as I Can* (1984) and *Master of Ceremonies* (1985) each presented three dancers on a stage. The lively abstract qualities of the dancers and cut out patterns owed a debt to artists such as Matisse, Kandinsky, Sonia Delaunay. Schapiro maintained her feminist viewpoint in these works. The image of creative woman/artist was contrasted with both the male figure and woman as ballerina/vamp.

Schapiro continued to work with dancing figures in large paintings such as *Ragtime* (1988) and in her monumental public sculpture, *Anna and David,* a 35-foot outdoor piece in Rosslyn, Virginia. Her 1989 book, *Rondo,* contained a colorful accordion foldout with a string of highly animated dancing figures as well as a series of Schapiro "signature" images: the kimono, the heart, pieces of fabric, a crocheted bag.

Miriam Schapiro has been the recipient of four honorary doctoral degrees; two of the institutions to honor her were the Minneapolis College of Art and Design, Minnesota

and Miami University in Oxford, Ohio. She has received many awards including the Skowhegan Award, the John Simon Guggenheim Memorial Foundation Fellowship, the Woman's Caucus for Art honors award, the National Endowment for the Arts Fellowship and in 1996 the Rockefeller Foundation Grant for Artists Residency at the Bellagio Study and Conference Center, Italy. New York NARAL honored Schapiro on the occasion of their 25th Anniversary (fall 1996). Her published artist books included "RONDO", an accordion style art book published by Bedford Press and four "BookMobiles" for children published by Pomegranate Artbooks.

Her work can be found in numerous private and public collections. Selected Public Collections: The Museum of Modern Art and The Whitney Museum of Art, New York, New York; The Boston Museum of Fine Arts, Boston, Massachusetts; The National Gallery of Art and The Hirshhorn Museum, Washington, D.C.; The La Jolla Museum of Art, La Jolla, California; The Minneapolis Institute of Art, Minneapolis, Minnesota; The Indianapolis Museum, Indianapolis, Indiana. International Collections: The Luswig Museum, Aachen, Germany; The Australian National Gallery, Canberra, Australia; The Art Gallery of New South Wales, Australia.

Further Reading

For biographical information see *Miriam Schapiro: A Retrospective, 1953-1980,* a catalogue of her show at the College of Wooster, edited and curated by Thalia Gouma-Peterson; *American Women Artists,* by Charlotte Streifer Rubinstein (1982); and "From 'Femmage' to Figuration," by Susan Gill, *Art News* (April 1986). Her chapter in *Working it Out,* edited by Sara Ruddick and Pamela Daniels (1977), provided a personal insight into her life and philosophy as an artist. For the context of both the Feminist and Pattern and Decorative Art movements see *The Pluralist Era: American Art, 1968-1981,* by Corrine Robins (1984). Articles by Schapiro appeared in *Heresies,* a magazine she helped create. Other information was gathered from Steinbaum/Krauss and The Smithsonian Institute. □

Gerhard Johann David von Scharnhorst

The Prussian general Gerhard Johann David von Scharnhorst (1755-1813) rebuilt the Prussian army after its collapse at Jena in 1806.

On Nov. 12, 1755, G. J. D. von Scharnhorst was born in Bordenau, the son of a former sergeant. In the Prussia of Frederick the Great his origins debarred him from an officer's career, so he took service as an artillery officer in the Hanoverian army, distinguishing himself by considerable valor in the war against revolutionary France. In 1801 he was able to transfer to the Prussian army, being appointed director of the military academy in Berlin.

Two years later he was made a member of the general staff. In the campaign of 1806-1807 he served as a staff officer. He did so well in that capacity that, after the collapse, he was appointed minister of war, chief of the general staff, and head of the Military Reconstruction Commission.

Scharnhorst was convinced that only thorough reform, closely tied to the proposed reform of the civil establishment under Baron Stein and Prince Hardenberg, could restore Prussia's army. Every vestige of the brutalized peasant-soldier of Frederick the Great, living in terror of the corporal's stick, would have to go. He insisted on the introduction of universal military service to replace the practice of pressing the sons of peasants and whatever foreigners could be rounded up—and won his point. As it was not possible to keep all those liable for service under the colors at any one time, this meant organizing a reserve, the Landwehr, which consisted of men who had returned to civilian life but were subject to immediate recall and were given occasional training to keep them in trim. This enabled him to keep within the limits that Napoleon allowed the Prussian army but to have a vast reserve on hand. This new citizen army differed radically from that of the 18th century. Beatings, formerly the universal means of enforcing discipline, were abolished. There were no more automatic commissions for the sons of the Prussian nobility. Instead of tedious and endless marching drills, the infantry was schooled in the use of its weapons, techniques of rapid firing, and deployment.

As soon as his reforms had begun to take effect, Scharnhorst urged on his government a war of revenge against Napoleon. This resulted in his dismissal as minister of war

on French insistence, but he retained his other positions. In the campaign of 1813 he served as chief of Field Marshal Blücher's staff, was wounded in the battle of Grossgörschen, and died of his wounds in Prague on June 28, 1813.

Further Reading

Scharnhorst figures in a number of general works on German history: William Oswald Shanahan, *Prussian Military Reforms, 1786-1813* (1945); Koppel Shub Pinson, *Modern Germany* (1954); and Hajo Holborn, *A History of Modern Germany* (3 vols., 1959-1964).

Additional Sources

White, Charles Edward, *The enlightened soldier: Scharnhorst and the Militarische Gesellschaft in Berlin, 1801-1805,* New York: Praeger, 1989. □

Rudolf Scharping

A member of the postwar generation of German political leaders, Rudolf Scharping (born 1947) was minister-president of Rhineland-Palatinate and chairman of the German Social Democratic Party and its chancellor candidate for 1994.

Born on December 2, 1947, Rudolf Scharping grew up in the small city of Lahnstein in Rhineland-Palatinate. He was the eldest of seven children whose father, an independent furniture dealer, ran into difficult economic times after World War II. When the father found a position in the state's statistical office, the family's situation improved.

After finishing secondary education in 1966, Scharping studied political science, law, and sociology at the University of Bonn. He financed part of his studies through work, including an assistantship to a German Social Democratic Party (SPD) deputy, Wilhelm Dröscher, the party's treasurer, who became his mentor. He received an advanced degree in 1974 after completing a thesis on a regional election campaign waged by the SPD in 1969. Married in 1971, he and his wife had three daughters.

Scharping had joined the party in 1966 and swiftly rose in its ranks. Soon he was selected as state chairman, and from 1974 to 1976 he served as national deputy chairman of the Young Socialists. He became a friend of Oskar Lafontaine, an SPD leader who later became minister-president of the Saarland and chancellor candidate in the 1990 election.

In 1975, after having served on city and district councils, the 28-year-old Scharping was elected a member of the Rhineland-Palatinate legislature. In 1986 he headed its SPD parliamentary group. In the party, the ambitious politician soon became executive secretary of the SPD's state branch and, beginning in 1985, its chairman. His diligence, honesty, reliability, politeness, and unassuming and provincial manners stood him well. In successive public opinion polls

he did better in popularity ratings than the state's minister-president, a member of the conservative Christian Democratic Union (CDU).

The national SPD leader, Willy Brandt, considered Scharping as one of the most reliable young party leaders, who were colorfully labeled Brandt's "grandchildren." Brandt, before his death in 1992, advised his associates not to forget Scharping as a potential party chairman.

For some years Scharping had been consolidating his power in the state SPD. In the 1987 election he was the party's candidate for the minister-president post, but the CDU won. However, two years later the SPD became the strongest party in local and European Parliament elections held in Rhineland-Palatinate, partly because the party gained the support of middle-class voters whom Scharping had wooed.

In April 1991 the SPD mustered an unprecedented plurality of votes (nearly 45 percent) in the state election, ousting the CDU-led state government, which had been in power for 44 years. The SPD victory, much of it credited to Scharping, was partly due to his denunciation of Chancellor Helmut Kohl's failure to accurately predict the high outlays for assisting the economic recovery of eastern Germany after the 1990 unification. He convinced many voters in Rhineland-Palatinate, worried about higher taxes, to switch their votes from the CDU to the SPD.

Scharping became minister-president after forming a coalition government with the small, liberal Free Democratic Party. He also had held negotiations with the environ-mentalist Green Party, but differences on policies between them, Scharping reasoned, precluded a coalition that could govern effectively. He was pragmatically oriented and was wary of the ideological stance of the Greens.

As minister-president Scharping had to face serious economic problems in his state. He developed an expertise in economic affairs and worked closely with industrial and business leaders to encourage more private investments and to lighten the tax burden for small-and medium-sized businesses. He also sought to increase the efficiency of the state administration.

In 1990 Scharping became a member of the national executive committee of the SPD, but two years later he was unable, in a highly competitive contest, to win a seat on the party's presidium, the top policymaking organ. Nevertheless Scharping gained further national recognition when he pushed for an intraparty compromise on the political asylum issue that had pitted those who wanted Germany to provide unrestricted asylum to the politically persecuted against those who favored restrictions. As a result, the SPD was able to come to an agreement in 1993 with the other parties on changes in asylum policy. Similarly, Scharping, as a member of the Bundesrat, the upper house of Parliament, helped to arrange a compromise on unresolved questions concerning a solidarity pact to assist eastern Germany.

Scharping gained more public recognition, but he did not expect to become the SPD's national chairman. In the early 1990s the party's Old Guard decided that younger leaders needed to assume the post. In 1991 they chose Björn Engholm, minister-president of Schleswig-Holstein. However, in early 1993 Engholm unexpectedly resigned the chairmanship and his political posts as a result of an earlier scandal in his state. In an unprecedented move designed to expand grassroots democracy within the party, all SPD members were polled as to their choice of Engholm's successor as chairman. The 45-year-old Scharping won a plurality against two other contenders, a choice that a special convention in June 1993 sustained.

Scharping's selection also meant that he became the party's candidate for the post of chancellor in the October 1994 national election against CDU/CSU candidate Chancellor Kohl. Early pre-election polls had shown the SPD as likely to emerge from the federal elections as the largest party. but by September, intra-party conflicts and an attendant power struggle had lowered SPD popularity to its lowest point in 36 years. In an attempt at unity three weeks before the elections, the party agreed upon a collective leadership solution, a triumvirate shadow cabinet consisting of Scharping as chairman, Oskar Lafontaine as finance spokesman, and Scharping's chief rival, Gerhard Schroder, as economic spokesman. The CDU/CSU emerged as the winner in the elections but saw its governing coalition reduced to a thin 10-seat majority, leaving Kohl seek consensus with the opposition on important decisions.

Scharping was elected a member of the lower house of the Bundestag in the 1994 Federal elections as a member of the regional list for Rhineland-Palatinate and became deputy chairman of the federal SPD Bundestag. He became chairman of the Social Democratic Party of Europe in 1995.

Further Reading

There was no full biography of Scharping in English. Ulrich Rosenbaum's *Rudolf Scharping: Biographie* was published in Germany in 1993. For a study of the SPD and its leaders, including Scharping, see Gerard Braunthal, *The German Social Democrats Since 1969: A Party in Power and Opposition* (1994). See also Elizabeth Pond, "Rudolf Scharping: Is he Germany's Bill Clinton?" *Europe (European Economic Community)* (July-August 1994); and Joe Klein, "What's German for "Ross Perot," *Newsweek* (January 31, 1994). □

Solomon Schechter

Solomon Schechter (1849-1915), Romanian-American scholar and religious leader, laid the foundation for the development of Conservative Judaism in the United States in his capacity as president of the Jewish Theological Seminary of America.

Solomon Schechter was born into a family of Hasidic background in Focsani, Romania, in December 1849. After a traditional education in Jewish schools in Romania and Poland, Schechter studied at the rabbinical seminary of Vienna and at the universities of Vienna and Berlin. In 1882 he settled in London as a tutor. In 1887 he married Matilda Roth. In 1890 he was appointed reader in rabbinics at Cambridge University. During the next twelve years he held several academic posts, including curator of Hebrew manuscripts in the Cambridge Library and professor of Hebrew at University College in London.

During this period, in addition to numerous journal articles on Jewish history and theology—later published in book form as *Studies in Judaism* (1896, 1908, 1924) and *Some Aspects of Rabbinic Theology* (1909—Schechter published critical editions of rabbinic texts: the Talmudic tractate *Aboth de Rabbi Nathan* (1887) and two Midrashic texts, one on the "Song of Songs" (1896) and one on Genesis (1902).

Schechter's most notable achievement, however, was bringing to England much of the archive of an ancient Cairo synagogue, including thousands of fragments of manuscripts and documents shedding light on a millennium of Jewish history. Schechter's scholarly work henceforth centered on this material. His chief works were *The Wisdom of Ben Sira* (with C. Taylor, 1899), portions of the Hebrew original of the Apocryphal Book of Ecclesiasticus; *Saadyana* (1903), new material on the 9th-century Jewish scholar Saadia Gaon; and *Documents of Jewish Sectaries* (1910), dealing with the 1st-century Zadokites and the Karaites, a medieval sect.

In 1902 Schechter assumed the presidency of the Jewish Theological Seminary of America in New York and devoted the rest of his life to developing this institution and its constituency. In England, Schechter had been mainly a scholar; he now became the spiritual leader of Conservative Judaism and, to a certain extent, a leader of American Juda-

ism. He advocated the concept of the unity and solidarity of Jews throughout the world. He viewed "the collective conscience of Catholic Israel as embodied in the Universal Synagogue . . . as the sole true guide for the present and future" development of Judaism.

In 1913, attempting to unify American Jewry, he established, and served as first president of, the United Synagogue of America, an organization of Conservative Jewish congregations in America. Viewing the rebirth of Jewish nationalism as embodied in the Zionist movement as integral to the revival of Judaism, he was active in American Zionism. His other contributions included service as chairman of the committee that prepared the new English translation of the Bible later published by the Jewish Publication Society of America; editor of the department of Talmud for several volumes of the *Jewish Encyclopedia;* and coeditor of the new series of the *Jewish Quarterly Review.* He died on Nov. 20, 1915.

Further Reading

A collection of papers from Schechter's American period is in his *Seminary Addresses and Other Papers* (1915; repr. 1969). The best study of Schechter is Norman Bentwich, *Solomon Schechter* (1938). □

Karl Wilhelm Scheele

The Swedish pharmacist and chemist Karl Wilhelm Scheele (1742-1786) discovered chlorine and oxygen and isolated and characterized a variety of organic acids.

Karl Wilhelm Scheele was born on Dec. 9, 1742, at Stralsund in Swedish Pomerania. His formal education ended at age 14, when he was apprenticed to a pharmacist in Gothenburg. In this shop Scheele's scientific education began. Here was at hand a treasury of chemical materials and apparatus which excited the curiosity and latent talents of the young apprentice. In addition, he had access to his master's library, which included many of the most noteworthy chemical works of the 18th century.

Following 8 years' apprenticeship in Gothenburg, Scheele moved to Malmö as an apothecary clerk. Again he was fortunate in his master, who allowed him facilities and time for research. In Malmö, Scheele's talents received their first recognition in the person of Anders Johan Retzius, who was later to become professor of chemistry and natural history at the University of Lund. Retzius encouraged Scheele to keep a systematic record of his researches and brought his name to public attention in a paper on tartaric acid published in 1770 in the memoirs of the Royal Swedish Academy of Sciences.

Spurred by Retzius's encouragement, Scheele decided to seek employment closer to the intellectual and scientific centers of Sweden. From 1768 to 1770 he was an apothecary clerk in Stockholm and from 1770 to 1775 held a similar position in a pharmacy in Uppsala. He earned a leading position among the savants and university professors who formed the very notable elite of Swedish science at this time.

Chemical Researches

The bulk of Scheele's scientific work was published between 1770 and 1786 in the memoirs of the Swedish Academy of Sciences. He was also the author of one book, the famous *Chemical Treatise on Air and Fire* (1777). His researches cover such a broad range of topics that one can pinpoint only the highlights.

In the realm of inorganic chemistry Scheele's first important discoveries were made in 1774 in connection with a study of pyrolusite (manganese dioxide). He also discovered a new earth (baryta, or barium oxide) associated with pyrolusite. But the most important outcome of his researches on pyrolusite was his discovery of chlorine. This he prepared by heating a solution of pyrolusite in acid of salt (hydrochloric acid). He collected the greenish-yellow gas in a bladder and studied its highly reactive properties and noted its bleaching action. He thought this gas was acid of salt deprived of its phlogiston, and hence he called it dephlogisticated acid of salt.

In the realm of organic chemistry Scheele is noted for his isolation of a large number of organic acids derived from a variety of vegetables, fruits, and other sources. These included citric acid (from lemons), oxalic acid (from sorrel and rhubarb), malic acid (from apples and other fruits), gallic acid (from nut galls), lactic acid (from milk), and uric acid (from urine). These were among the first organic substances obtained in a chemically pure and well-identified form. Scheele has thus good claim to be considered the founder of modern organic chemistry.

Scheele's greatest claim to fame, however, rests on his discovery of oxygen. He performed his experiments on oxygen sometime between 1770 and 1773, but they were not published until 1777 in his *Chemical Treatise on Air and Fire,* by which time Joseph Priestley had published his independent discovery of the gas (1775). In this book Scheele first proved that common air was composed of two components: "spoiled," or "foul," air and "fire" air (oxygen). The latter was named fire air because only it will support combustion and it is therefore necessary for the production of fire. He prepared this fire air by heating a mixture of nitric and sulfuric acid in a retort and collecting the gas in a bladder attached to the neck. He also prepared the fire air by heating mercuric oxide (Priestley's method) and mixtures of manganese dioxide and sulfuric and phosphoric acids.

Later Career

In 1775 Scheele was admitted to the Royal Swedish Academy of Sciences—perhaps the only apothecary's assistant to be so honored. This same year he also achieved his lifelong ambition: his own pharmacy in the small town of

Köping. Although the time he could devote to his scientific research was reduced, he continued to work in a makeshift wooden laboratory behind the shop, and he produced some of the researches described above. By 1782 he had prospered sufficiently to build himself a new house and laboratory. He did not enjoy this newfound prosperity for long, however, for he died on May 26, 1786.

Further Reading

A selection of Scheele's works is *The Collected Papers of Carl Wilhelm Scheele,* translated by Leonard Dobbin (1931). See also J. Murray, *The Chemical Essays of Karl Wilhelm Scheele* (1901). Uno Boklund, distinguished Swedish historian of chemistry, is currently preparing a definitive biography together with editions of all Scheele's works. A very readable account of his life is in Sir Edward Thorpe, *Essays in Historical Chemistry* (1894). A well-illustrated account is in Georg Urdang, *Pictorial Life History of the Apothecary Chemist Carl Wilhelm Scheele* (1942). □

Friedrich Wilhelm Joseph von Schelling

The German idealist and romantic philosopher Friedrich Wilhelm Joseph von Schelling (1775-1854) developed a metaphysical system based on the philosophy of nature.

Born in Württemberg on Jan. 27, 1775, the son of a learned Lutheran pastor, F. W. J. von Schelling was educated at the theological seminary at Tübingen. He became friends with two older classmates, G. W. F. Hegel and Friedrich Hölderlin, and shared their ardent support of the French Revolution. Schelling read widely in the philosophies of Baruch Spinoza, Immanuel Kant, and Johann Gottlieb Fichte. His first two treatises, *Über die Möglichkeit einer Philosophie überhaupt* (1795; *On the Possibility of a Form of Philosophy in General)* and *Vom Ich als Prinzip der Philosophie . . .* (1795; *On the Ego as Principle of Philosophy),* were influenced by Fichte's philosophy of the Absolute Ego. Indeed Fichte's critics mockingly referred to Schelling as the "street peddler of the Ego."

Philosophy of Nature

In the second phase of his thought Schelling turned against Fichte's conception of nature. He then claimed that nature was not a mere obstacle to be overcome through the moral striving of the subject. Nature rather was a form of spiritual activity, an "unconscious intelligence." This organistic, vitalistic conception of nature was developed in *Ideen zu einer Philosophie der Natur* (1797; *Ideas toward a Philosophy of Nature),* in *Von der Weltseele* (1798; *On the World Soul),* and in several works on the physical sciences published between 1797 and 1803. Schelling's brilliance was quickly recognized; owing to J. W. von Goethe's influ-

ence, he gave up his position as private tutor and assumed the rank of full professor at Jena. He was only 23 years old.

Jena was the center of German romanticism. This prestigious circle included Ludwig Tieck, the folklorist; Novalis, the poet; Friedrich and August von Schlegel, the translators of Shakespeare; Caroline, August's wife; and in nearby Weimar, Goethe and Friedrich von Schiller. Schelling was briefly engaged to Caroline's daughter by her first marriage, but she died under mysterious circumstances. His affection quickly turned to Caroline, a woman of tremendous wit and intelligence. In 1803, after divorcing Schlegel, Caroline married Schelling.

In 1800 Schelling published the most systematic statement of his philosophy, *System des Transzendentalen Idealismus (System of Transcendental Idealism).* In this work and in *Darstellung meine Systems der Philosophie* (1801; *An Exposition of My System),* Schelling argued for the absolute identity of nature and mind in the form of reason. Although this third turn in Schelling's thought was probably influenced by Hegel's philosophy, it earned him only Hegel's scorn.

Munich Period

From 1803 to 1806 Schelling taught at the University of Würzburg. In 1806 he was appointed secretary to the Academy of Arts at Munich, a post that allowed him to complete his most interesting work and to lecture at Stuttgart. During this period his most important work was the *Philosophische Untersuchungen über das Wesen der Menschlichen Freiheit*

(1809; *Of Human Freedom*). Schelling's emphasis on human freedom—"the beginning and end of all philosophy is freedom"—anticipates the major concerns of contemporary existentialism.

In just 14 years Schelling's kaleidoscopic philosophy had undergone several shifts. Hegel uncharitably remarked that Schelling "carried on his philosophical education in public." Schelling was, however, a rigorous thinker, although he never constructed a complete metaphysical system. Schelling wrote eloquent and impassioned prose, liberating German philosophy from its turgid, jargonistic style.

Later Period

Schelling's wife died in 1809, and that same year marked the rising prominence of Hegel. These two events dampened Schelling's philosophical enthusiasm and self-confidence. Schelling was remarried in 1812—to Pauline Gotter, a friend of Caroline's—but did not publish another book in the remaining 42 years of his life. From 1820 to 1827 he lectured at Erlangen, and in 1827 Schelling became a professor at Munich. Extremely bitter about the success of Hegel, he accepted a post as Prussian privy councilor and member of the Berlin Academy in order to quell the popularity of Hegel's disciples, the so-called Young Hegelians.

To combat further the influence of Hegel, Schelling lectured at Berlin for 5 years. His lectures on mythology and religion signaled the last stage in his thought, the opposition of negative and positive philosophy. God cannot be known through reason (negative philosophy), but He can be experienced through myth and revelation (positive philosophy).

This relatively neglected aspect of Schelling's philosophy has aroused considerable interest among today's Protestant theologians. Never regaining his early prominence, Schelling died on Aug. 20, 1854, at Bad Ragaz, Switzerland.

Schelling was called the "prince of the romantics." With his immense charm, wit, and radiant spirit, he endeared himself to the coterie of intellectuals known as the German romantics. With them he celebrated, in both word and deed, the vision of artistic genius and the principles of organicism and vitalism in nature.

Further Reading

A short critical biography is in James Gutman's introduction to his translation of Schelling's *Of Human Freedom* (1936). Frederick Copleston, *A History of Philosophy* (7 vols., 1946; rev. ed., 7 vols. in 13, 1962), provides a thorough exposition of Schelling's thought. Other accounts of the development of Schelling's later philosophy are in the introduction to Schelling's *The Ages of the World* (a fragment of *Die Weltalter*), translated by Frederick de Wolfe Bolman (1942), and in Paul Collins Hayner, *Reason and Existence: Schelling's Philosophy of History* (1967). Recommended for the background of idealism and romanticism are Josiah Royce, *The Spirit of Modern Philosophy* (1892), and Eric D. Hirsch, *Wordsworth and Schelling* (1960).

Additional Sources

Seidel, George J. (George Joseph), *Activity and ground: Fichte, Schelling, and Hegel,* Hildesheim; New York: G. Olms, 1976.

Snow, Dale E., *Schelling and the end of idealism,* Albany: State University of New York Press, 1996.

White, Alan, *Schelling: an introduction to the system of freedom,* New Haven: Yale University Press, 1983. □